Indian Social Problems
A Sociological Perspective

Indian Social Problems
A Sociological Perspective

[For Undergraduate and Postgraduate students of all the Universities of India and candidates appearing for Competitive Examinations such as IAS, NET, SLET, etc. and various State Administrative Examinations]

C N SHANKAR RAO
Lecturer in Sociology [*Retd.*]
Canara Pre-University College
Mangalore, Karnataka

S Chand And Company Limited
(ISO 9001 Certified Company)

S Chand And Company Limited

(ISO 9001 Certified Company)

Head Office: D-92, Sector–2, Noida – 201301, U.P. (India), Ph. 91-120-4682700

Registered Office: A-27, 2nd Floor, Mohan Co-operative Industrial Estate, New Delhi – 110 044, Phone: 011-49731800

www.**schandpublishing.com;** e-mail: **info@schandpublishing.com**

Marketing Offices:

Chennai	:	Ph: 23632120; chennai@schandpublishing.com
Guwahati	:	Ph: 2738811, 2735640; guwahati@schandpublishing.com
Hyderabad	:	Ph: 40186018; hyderabad@schandpublishing.com
Jalandhar	:	Ph: 4645630; jalandhar@schandpublishing.com
Kolkata	:	Ph: 23357458, 23353914; kolkata@schandpublishing.com
Lucknow	:	Ph: 4003633; lucknow@schandpublishing.com
Mumbai	:	Ph: 25000297; mumbai@schandpublishing.com
Patna	:	Ph: 2260011; patna@schandpublishing.com

First Edition 2015
Reprints 2019, 2020, 2021, 2022

Reprint 2023

ISBN: 978-93-848-5795-0 **Product Code:** H5SIP41SOCL10ENAA15R

PRINTED IN INDIA

By Vikas Publishing House Private Limited, Plot 20/4, Site-IV, Industrial Area Sahibabad, Ghaziabad – 201 010 and Published by S Chand And Company Limited, A-27, 2nd Floor, Mohan Co-operative Industrial Estate, New Delhi – 110 044.

DEDICATED TO

My Wife Dr. Saraswathi S. Rao

My Daughters

Dr. Shruthi S. Rao

Swathi S. Rao

Deepthi S. Rao

Preface

This book entitled '*Indian Social Problems: A Sociological Perspective*' provides a glimpse of many social problems that have been haunting the Indian society since years, decades, and even centuries. I have prepared this book knowing fully well that there are already sufficient books on the topic both in English and regional languages. This book, I hope and believe, will be well received by its intended readers because of its clarity, simplicity and student-friendly approach.

Ever since I wrote a book on social problems in 1999 in Kannada with the title *Bharatadalli Samajika Samasyegalu Mattu Samajika Vighatane* [*Social Problems and Social Disorganisation in India*], which was the first of its kind in Kannada providing a wide coverage of matter, I had been nursing in my mind the idea of bringing out an English version of it. When the Kannada book went for a thorough revised edition in December 2012 with more than 1000 pages, time was actually ripe for bringing out its English version. Thus, the book is in your hands.

This book is prepared mainly to cater to the needs of the undergraduate and postgraduate students. Most of the universities in India have prescribed one paper on 'Indian Social Problems' either at the undergraduate or postgraduate level. The book also covers topics that are included in the syllabi of IAS, NET, SLET, KAS and other national- and state-level competitive examinations. It also contains lessons that form part of MBA, nursing and five-year law courses. Such students and examinees will definitely find the book highly helpful.

This book consists of 28 chapters giving useful information about more than 30 social problems of India. I have tried my best to provide the latest information and statistics about the social problems though it is a very difficult and a challenging task. The main hurdle in the task is that, systematic studies have not been made about many of the social problems and some of the studies are limited to some regions only and, hence, fail to provide an all-India picture of the same. Regular updates of the statistics pertaining to the problems are also not there. These limitations often compel authors to rely on the information and reports published in standard newspapers though they cannot be taken as authentic.

Unlike many western countries, India is very much lagging behind in the field of documentation, and this deficiency is apparently evident in the study of social problems. Being fully aware of this limitation, I submit that much of the information and descriptions given in this book are only approximations and not based on properly verified facts. As India is making fast progress in the field of information technology, I hope, at least in the years to come, we will be able to collect 'actual facts' and reliable statistics and document them properly.

Though India is fast developing, it has lots of regional, cultural, linguistic and religious diversities. These diversities are also reflected in its social problems. It is, indeed, very difficult to introduce and present almost all types of problems which are confronting different states of India in particular, and the Indian society in general, in a book of this kind. This book covers social problems which are general in nature and common to the whole nation such as population problem, poverty, unemployment, child labour, urbanization, youth unrest, problems of the aged, family disorganization, corruption, crime and delinquency, etc. The book has its limitations for it does not cover all the social problems of

India. There are many other serious problems such as criminalization of politics, problem of illegal foreign infiltration, religious conversion, brain drain, problem of mentally and physically handicapped people, commercialization of recreation, problems of drug mafia, land mafia, smuggling, etc. which have not been touched in this book. However, for the first time, I have made an attempt to throw some light on the problem of commercialization of higher education. This is not an in-depth study but only a general picturization of the problem based on some survey reports.

This book provides a lot of information, statistics, tables, charts, etc. which I have collected from various sources such as books, newspapers, magazines, periodicals, yearbooks, internet, etc. and my sincere thankfulness goes to all these sources. I have incorporated a few images here and there, selecting most of them from different websites and I convey my deep sense of gratitude to all those sources. I have profusely quoted sentences, statements and views of various sociologists and other writers to whom I am greatly indebted. As a textbook writer, I do not wish to claim originality to many of the ideas and explanations contained in this book. However, I have presented the matter in my own way to make the book user-friendly.

I am thankful to all those who have helped me directly and indirectly in preparing this book. My thanks are due to my fellow-teachers and student-readers without whose encouragement and warm support, I would not have ventured to write this book. I am grateful to all those friends and well-wishers of mine who have given valuable suggestions for preparing the book. My thanks are due to Smt. Ashalatha Kishore, Smt. Yashu Mohandas and Sri Rajesh Kumpanamajalu, who have given me able assistance in the computer-typesetting work.

I thank S. Chand and Company Pvt. Ltd, New Delhi, for having undertaken the publication work, and particularly, their Bengaluru Branch Manager, Sri Muralidhar Rao, for having shown keen interest in this book. My thanks are also due to my everloving family members Dr. Saraswathi S. Rao, my wife, and my children Shruthi, Swathi and Deepthi, who stood with me in this effort.

I earnestly believe that there is always scope for improvement in any art and enterprise, and accordingly, I shall look forward to receive suggestions for further enhancing the quality of the book.

C.N. Shankar Rao

Contents

Chapter 1

SOCIAL PROBLEMS: AN INTRODUCTION

The Concept of Social Problem-Characteristics of Social Problems as Per Weinberg's Analysis-Causes and Consequences of Social Problems - Theoretical Approaches to the Study of Social Problems - Types of Social Problems - Stages in the Development of Social Problems - Methods of Studying Social Problems - The Task of Solving social Problems- Importance and the Need for the Study of Social Problems - Social Problems and Social Disorganisation- Definition, Nature and Characteristics of Social Diorganisation- Causes of Disorganisation and Remedial Measures - Types of Disrganisation - Social Organisation V/S Social Disorganisation - Conceptual Relationship and Differences between Social Problems and Social Disorganisation.

Man's life is not always a bed of roses. It is subject to sufferings, miseries and maladies. Man's societal life is also oscillating between health and ill-health. Society is said to be in a state of disorganisation whenever it finds itself in serious ill-health. Social disorganisation creates conditions that are susceptible to social problems. These social problems are to be understood in the framework of time, place, situation and the values. Social problems are not automatic or accidental developments or happenings, but they emerge from different deep seated sources. Some problems emerge at the individual level while poverty, unemployment and such other problems are rooted in economic conditions. Specific cultural conditions may often trigger problems like widow harassment, prostitution, crime, juvenile delinquency, etc. Social problems involve human sufferings and hence their study assumes importance.

Social problems are complex and multidimensional. Even the scholars differ in their opinion about their causes, consequences and magnitude. Conditions giving rise to social problems tend to be interrelated with overlapping causes and consequences. The interrelated nature of social problems at both the institutional and individual levels play a major role in our understanding of social problems and their solutions. Social problems are difficult to solve because of lack of agreement on what problems are, their causes and possible solutions. Changes in the social structure itself will be necessary to solve most of the social problems.

India, as a fast developing nation with a vast population, has its own socio-economic problems. Finding solutions for these problems itself is a challenging task. Although we might desire a more pleasant picture of the society in which we live, we cannot avoid encountering many of these problems. These confronting social problems demand creative as well as critical thinking about potential solutions. An unprejudiced and an objective study is a sine quo non for finding out such solutions.

THE CONCEPT OF SOCIAL PROBLEM: DEFINITION AND NATURE

India Faced with a Flood of Social Problems

Anyone who reads any daily newspaper knows that Indian society is facing many problems. Newspapers publish flood of episodes and instances relating to various socio-economic problems that are haunting the Indian society. Bomb blast, naxalite violence, murder and rape occur with frightening frequency. Poverty is widespread and unemployment is rampant. The problem of overpopulation is eating the vitals of the nation while the scheduled castes, scheduled tribes and other backward classes and weaker sections are faced with innumerable hardships. Family is getting disintegrated while expolitation of and violence against women are on the increase. Gender discrimination continues unabated and incidences of divorce, desertion, rape, gang rape, domestic violence, foeticide, female infanticide, trafficking of women, etc.. do take place even now. National integration is under threat due to the prevalence of communal riots, fundamentalism, linguism, regionalism, extremism and terrorism. Illiteracy, youth unrest and commercialisation of education have made our youths relatively pessimistic and cynical. Corruption on the one hand and the flow of enormous black money on the other, have put hurdles on the path of progress of Indian economy. Alcoholism, drug addiction, prostitution, crime and juvenile delinquency, child labour, bonded labour and many such practices and problems have made the fabric of Indian society weaker. Despite India's impressive performance in the I.T, [information technology] spacecraft, engineering and medical fields, these and many other problems are posing a threat to India's progress. Let us now examine the sociological meaning and nature of the concept of *"social problem"*.

Definition of Social Problem

1. **Richard C.Fuller** and **Richard Myers :** *"When most of the members of society accept a particular condition and behaviour pattern as undesirable and objectionable, it is called social problem."*
2. **Reinhardt** defined social problem as - *"a situation confronting a group or a section of society which inflicts injurious consequences that can be handled only collectively"*.
3. **Lawrence K. Frank** in an article in the *"American Journal of Sociology"* defines a social problem as *"any difficulty or misbehaviour of fairly large number of persons which we wish to remove or correct"*.
4. **Paul B. Horton** and **Gerald R. Leslie** have defined social problem as *"a condition affecting a significant number of people considered undesirable and about which it is felt something can be done through collective social action"*.
5. **Samuel Koenig :** Social problems are *"...... situations or conditions which society regards as threats to its established ways or to its well-being and, therefore, as needing to be alleviated or eliminated."*.
6. **Walsh and Furfey** have defined social problem as a *"deviation from the social ideal remediable by group efforts"*.
7. **Robert Nisbet :** *"A social problem is a way of behaviour that is regarded by a substantial part of a social order as being in violation of one or more generally accepted or approved norms."*.

Thus, it is clear from the above definitions that social problems are undesirable conditions, situations or behaviour patterns concerning social groups or society, social institutions, social organisations, etc. Social problem is always disintegrating and disorganising for it is regarded as pathological. It is an unhealthy social condition that has to be cured.

Nature of Social Problems

Above mentioned definitions throw some light on the nature of social problems.

Let us consider the definition of **Robert Nisbet.** The definition consists of both an objective and a subjective aspect in it. ***(i) The objective aspect*** refers to the identifiable behaviour or situation itself. ***(ii) The subjective aspect*** refers to people's opinion towards it. No mode of human behaviour or a social situation can be considered a social problem, unless it is regarded as a morally objectionable deviance from some accepted norm, or norms, by a substantial number of persons in the surrounding social order.

- *"Subjective views regarding a behaviour or situation is more important than the "objective" state of affairs." - Robert Nisbet.*

According to Nisbet, people's opinions and evaluations regarding a situation or behaviour is important in considering it as a social problem or not. As he mentions, in Western civilisation, poverty as a condition affecting large number of persons, was not regarded as a social problem until perhaps a century and a half ago. *"Poverty was regarded as a built-in, inevitable, and ineffaceable part of the human condition. There are still persons in the West who appear to regard poverty in this light."*[1] However, poverty is, today, considered as a major social problem by a majority of people in the world including the poor themselves. Thus, mental disorder, alcoholism, family disorganisation have only recently become defined as social problems.

It is evident from the above, that adverse conditions that are not defined by the group as undesirable or reprehensible, are not known as social problems. *For example,* if taking bribe or gambling is not regarded as objectionable by the community, it is not considered as a social problem.

Consideration of 'Social Problems' in the Indian Context....

If we consider some of the social conditions and practices of India in the light of Nisbet's analysis, we also come to the same above mentioned conclusion. For many centuries in India, social practices and conditions such as - untouchability, casteism, *sati system*, child marriage, illiteracy, denial of freedom to women, *devadasi system*, restriction on widow remarriage, etc., were not regarded as serious social problems. These were rather accepted as part of traditional Indian social life. Such things were attributed to *'fate'*, *'bad luck'* or *one's own "karma"*. Only during the modern times, majority of Indians have started considering these as grave social problems that require immediate attention for solution.

CHARACTERISTICS OF SOCIAL PROBLEMS: AS PER WEINBERG'S ANALYSIS

Weinberg has mentioned six main characteristics[2] of social problems which may be briefly examined here.

1. **A Social Situation is Called a Social Problem Only When Considerable Number of People Define it as *"Objectionable"*.**

Accordingly, if some hopeless social conditions are not defined as *'undersirable'*, by the people of a community or society then they cannot be viewed as social problems. *For example,*

---

1. **Robert Nisbet** in *"Social Problems"* - Page :2.
2. **Weinberg**'s views as quoted by **Ram Ahuja** in *"Social Problems in India"*. [2001] Page 4-5.

MULTIFARIOUS SOCIAL PROBLEMS HAUNTING THE INDIAN SOCIETY

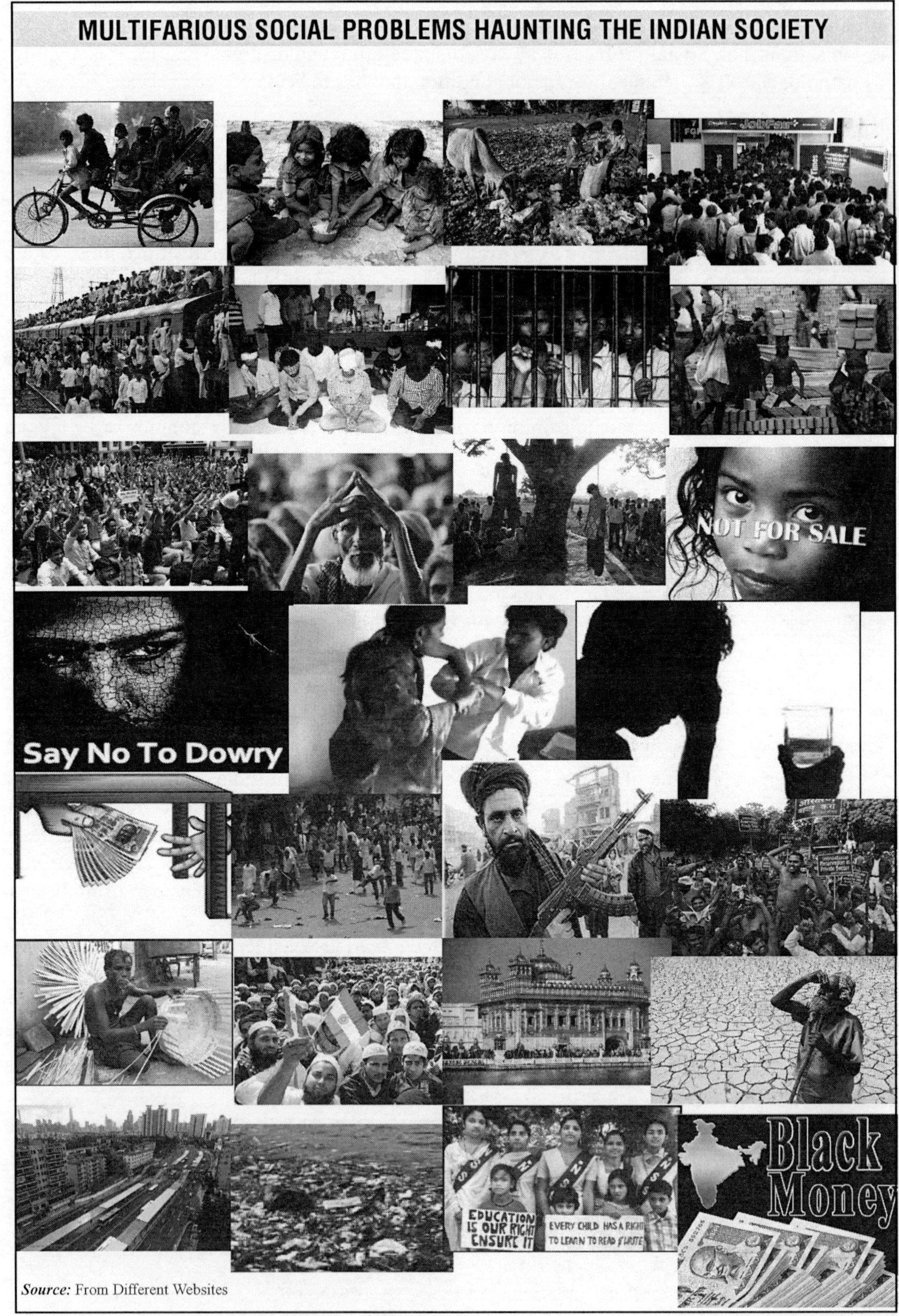

Source: From Different Websites

if brain drain or foeticide or consuming alcohol is not regarded as *'objectionable'* by the society, then, either of it is not considered a social problem.

2. Importance of Time, Environment and Social Values in Considering a Condition or Practice as Social Problem

When interpretations regarding people's behaviour patterns are changed, social problems also get changed. *For example,* intercaste marriage, widow remarriage, higher education of women, women of prestigious families going out for salaried job and such other behavioural trends were regarded in a traditional society like that of India as not only 'objectionable' but also pathological. But, the living conditions, social environment and guiding social values have changed today. Hence, the same trends are not considered as problematic. *For example,* love marriage was considered "deviant behaviour" in the past, but is no more regarded so today.

3. Mass Media Creates Awareness Regarding Social Problems

Because of the creative role of the mass media people are coming to know that some of the conditions are highly 'dangerous' and may prove to be destructive if not controlled. ***Example*** : AIDS - *[Acquired Immuno Deficiency Syndrome]* and drug addiction can be mentioned here as examples. Similarly, mass media is giving sufficient publicity to create awareness among people regarding two other modern evils of great magnitude namely; *terrorism* and *corruption.*

4. Social Problems are to be Viewed in the Context of Society's Values and Institutions

Thus, racial conflict prevalent between Whites and Negroes in South Africa and America, is different from that of the practice of untouchability found in India. People view such practices in these three nations differently. Same is true in the case of child labour which is not considered highly *"objectionable"* and *"inhuman"* in nations where it is widely practised. [***Example*** : India, Bangladesh, Pakisthan and African countries.] But the same practice is regarded as 'abhorrent' and "horrible" in the rich western nations such as America, England, Germany, etc.

5. Social Problems Vary Historically and Hence People's Reactions Towards Them Also Vary

People react to the same problem differently at different times. ***Example*** : People's reaction towards the refugees who came into India from Pakisthan at the time of partition in 1947 was different from their reaction towards the refugees who came to India from Bangladesh in 1970-71 when Indo-pak war broke out on the issue of establishing independent Bangladesh. Indians were accommodative and helpful to the refugees at that time. But their reaction towards the Bangladesh infiltrators who have started forcing their entry into India especially after 1980-81 either by hook or by crook, is full of suspicion and contempt today. There is now a public demand to drive them back.

6. Social Problems Need to be Analysed in Terms of the Influences upon them by Group Processes and Social Relationships

Sometimes, some defects or failures found at the individual, family, group or the community level often contribute to social problems. ***Example*** : If venereal disease is widespread, then we can say that it is due to the *moral lapse* on the part of a few individuals. If the disease is due to the extramarital sex relationship of a few individuals, then it may indicate *family disintegration* too. If the patients suffering from this disease spread it to all those who come in contact with them, then the *entire community* will be pushed to a dreadful condition. The problem of AIDS which is spreading at a very quick pace in some countries reminds us of such a situation.

- **Some Other Characteristics**

In addition to the six characteristics mentioned by **Weinberg**, we may also mention three other equally important aspects of social problems.

(i) Differences in the Number and Gravity of the Problems **:** Social problems are not found in the same manner and in the same number every where. Their nature, number and the magnitude are bound to be different in different nations. Underdeveloped and developing countries are definitely having greater number of serious social problems than the developed countries.

(ii) Interrelationship Between Problems **:** Problems do not emerge in vacuum. They originate because some social situations or environmental conditions are favourable to them. Further, there is no formula that one cause contributes to one problem and one effect only. Just as causation is manysided, effects are also multifarious. Further, one problem may lead to many other problems. Unemployment or poverty, for example, may lead to multiple effects.

(iii) Difference Between Social Problems and Personal Problems **:** As the famous American sociologist, **C. Wright Mills** points out *"personal troubles occur within the character of the individual and within the range of his immediate relations with others"*. They are *"felt in private and they involve only the persons in one's immediate surroundings...."* Public issues or social problems on the other hand, "*have their origins in the institutional arrangements and history of a society... Public issues transcend the local environment of the individual, though they may well affect his or her private well -being*".[3] *For example,* when a man or woman is divorced, each may experience personal troubles, but when the divorce rate rapidly rises as it is in the West, a public issue exists demanding the revision and re-evaluation of the society's policies.

Characteristics of Social Problems in a Nut Shell

On the basis of the above explanations and previously mentioned definitions, we can identify the following characteristics of social problems.

1. Social problems exist as exceptions to 'ordinary' conditions and "ideal" situations.
2. Social problems do not exist in vacuum. All problems have their own basis or origin.
3. Social problems are so interconnected that one influences the other and is influenced by others.
4. Social problems are not without injurious results or adverse consequences. They normally affect all sections of society in one way or another.
5. Social problems demand solutions. They require a collective approach for their redressal. Society has to take responsibility in this regard.
6. Social problems have different interpretations depending on time-place and values.
7. Social problem is a symbol of social disorganisation.

CAUSES OF SOCIAL PROBLEMS

Social problems are normally caused by multifarious factors. Plurality of causation in the social world is an accepted principle. An analysis of any social problem, however severe or ordinary, draws our attention towards various factors that lie at its background.

1. Social Change Leads to Social Problems

All social changes do not cause social problems. Those social changes which are ordinary in nature and do not cause any problems of adjustments for the people to carry on with their day-to-day activities rarely trigger social problems. But when problems of adjustment are created

---

3. **C. Wright Mills** as quoted by **Frank R. Scarpitti** and **M.L. Anderson** in their *"Social Problems"* [1980] Page : 13.

by social change, social problems may creep in. ***Example*** : (i) Attempts by the government to introduce educational change through a new educational policy which is basically defective, may lead to problems such as *student unrest* and *educated unemployment.* (ii) A sudden military revolt may push a nation towards *political instability* and *social insecurity.*

2. Cultural Lag Causing Social Problems

William F. Ogburn who introduced the concept of *"cultural lag"* states that changes are quick to take place in the material culture. These, in turn, stimulate changes in the non-material culture. But the non-material culture may be slow to respond giving rise to a gap or a lag between the material and non-material cultures. *This lag is called the* ***"cultural lag".***[4] This lag or cultural lag may lead to problems of adjustment and also to social problems. ***Example*** :

(i) People have changed their *methods or techniques* [that is, technology] *of cultivating soil* ; but they have not changed *the methods of owning the land* [non-material culture]. This imbalance has resulted in the *conflicts between the land owners and the tenant farmers.*

(ii) The process of deforestation is taking place faster to cater to the needs of the *growing paper industry, house construction, making furniture,* etc. [material culture]. But *the art of conservation of forest* [non-material culture] does not keep pace with these industrial developments. The result is *the problem of environmental pollution.*

3. Natural Disasters

Nature has been bountiful to man no doubt. But man often becomes a victim of its wrath. Floods, famines, cyclones, earthquakes, volcanic eruptions, tsunami, outburst of contagious diseases, etc. represent the furious faces of nature. Almost every year, lakhs of people in the world become the victims of these extremes of nature. Man's attempts to control nature and its forces has not been complete and can never become so. Somewhere at some time some people or the other will have to pay a great price in the form of facing the wrath of nature. ***Example*** : *Extreme famine that took the toll of a few lakhs in Ethiopia in 1922; earthquake which rocked India and Armania [Russia] in 1991-92, and again Bhuj of Gujarat in 2000, and a terrific cyclone that proved to be disasterous in Orissa in 1999, the gigantic "Tsunami" waves [of 26-12-2004] causing the death of more than 2.5 lakh people and damaging the property worth thousands of crores of rupees in India, Srilanka, Maldives, Indonesia, Africa,a terrific earthquake coupled with the monstrous "Tsunami waves that caused incalculable damage to Japan in 2011, the flood havocs at Uttarakhand in 2013, and in Jammu and Kashmir in 2014, etc., are only a few examples here. Natural calamities like these not only disturb the normal course of social life of the people but also create serious social problems.*

4. Political and Social Dangers

Nature is not the only source causing danger to man's life, man himself creates conditions that often prove to be not only harmful but even dangerous. ***Examples*** : Political revolutions, revolts, communal riots, racial conflicts, terrorism, ethnic clashes, mass movements, military rebellion, arson and loot, bomb explosions, etc., disturb even the society which has a well established organisation. (i) Even the rich nation like America was flabbergasted and terror -striken when its famous World Trade Centre building was destroyed by plane attack by the terrorists on Sept. 11, 2001. (ii) The unfortunate Godra incident at Gujarat that triggered after the burning alive of 58 persons [*"Ram Sevakas"*] in a railway compartment in the year 2002. (iii) Waves of political

---

4. **Ogburn's Definition of Cultural Lag :** "the strain that exists between two correlated parts of culture that change at unequal rates of speed may be interpreted as a lag in the part that is changing at the slower rate for the one lags behind the other". - **Ogburn** in his *"Social Change"*.

rebellions and mass movements that took place in the early months of 2011 against the ruling Islamic hegemony in the Muslim countries such as Egypt, Jordan, Cyria, Lybia and so on (iv) Wars that take place between any two or more nations for whatever reasons may also upset normal course of life of the people.

5. Biological and Psychological Causes

Serious ups-and downs in population, population explosion, great imbalance in the composition of population, spread of diseases, lack of supply of nutritious food and such other biological factors disturb the social balance in the society.

Man's mental tendencies, his temperament, his own inherited qualities influence his behaviour and activities. Sometimes, these aspects of man may disturb him in making adjustments with the changing times. *"Ogburn contended that many social problems are the result of the failure of the original nature of man to adjust itself to constant change in culture and its institutions."*[5] Mental qualities such as - instincts, imitation, suggestibility, hatredness, prejudice, anger, jealousy, competitiveness, aggressiveness, hysterical nature, etc. do have their own positive and negative impact on human behaviour and activities. These activities ultimately decide how efficiently or inefficiently they face social challenges or cope with the disturbing social conditions.

6. Technological Inventions

Technological development is the result of scientific progress. Modern society is fast advancing because of revolutionary scientific and technological achievements. Technological inventions have revolutionalised human life also.

Technology, has of course, its own limitations. Technology has brought both good and bad results for man. As Ogburn stated, technology widens the gap between the material and non-material parts of culture. Men are becoming more materialistic and less traditional. Men are devoted more to quantity than to quality, to measurement than to appreciation. Human beings by the use of machines have become less human, more passive and more mechanical. People have become pleasure - seekers. There has been a movement towards individualism. Extremes of individualism and hedonism [pleasure-seeking] have their own adverse effects on society.

Technological development is invariably associated with the growth of cities. These cities have given encouragement to social problems such as *slums, crimes, prostitution, environment pollution, gambling, drug addiction, etc.* Uncontrolled technological development is bound to lead towards social problems and social disorganisation.

7. Radical Changes in Social Values

Social values play a vital role in maintaining social equilibrium, but these values themselves are subject to change. There is a close affinity between social values and social relationships. Hence, when social values change social relationships also get changed. Younger generation is in a better position to adjust itself with the changing values, whereas the older generation finds it difficult to do so. This situation often leads to a gap between the generations. This *"generation gap"* gives rise to clashes and conflicts between the parents and children, students and teachers, and the old and the new.

8. Laxity of Social Control

Social organisation is possible because of the successful functioning of social control. But rigidity and failure on the part of the means of social control to adjust themselves to the changing

5. **Samuel Koenig** in *"Sociology - An Introduction to the Science of Society"* (1970) - Page : 313.

times make them to become less effective. Thus, folkways, mores, customs, religion, law, values and such other means of social control have become weak. A reduction in the effectiveness of the means of social control naturally leads to an increase in the instances of crime, violence, exploitation, terrorism, cheating, sex crimes. etc.

CONSEQUENCES OF SOCIAL PROBLEMS

Sociology which provides a knowledge of the functioning of human society also throws light on its malfunctioning, particularly when it is pressed with social problems of one type or the other. In fact, it is one of the purposes of sociology to study the origin, development, causes and consequences of social problems and to suggest effective means of tackling them. A specialised branch of sociology namely, ***"social pathology"*** is vested with the special task of studying social-problems and recommending solutions for their redressal.

The main consequences of social problems may be analysed in the following manner.

1. Social Problems - A Reflection of Social Ill-Health

An individual is said to be in a condition of disease if his health is imbalanced in one way or the other. Similarly, a society is said to be not doing well socially, economically and even politically, if it is trapped by one or more social problems. Even the politically stable and economically advanced countries also suffer problems of one kind or another. Just as diseases reduce efficiency of the individuals, social problems disturb social equilibrium and lead to confusions and sufferings.

2. Social Problems Lessen the Rate of Social Progress

Social progress is possible only in a strong and stable society which is relatively free from social ills and evils. A society sandwiched between internal troubles and external threats will have to first struggle for its own existence. African countries such as Ethiopia, Somalia, Burundi, Uganda and such other nations are not able to march ahead in the path of progress because they are already under the grip of serious socio-economic problems. India, a developing nation with great potential is also not able to achieve progress in tune with its capacity because of its pressing socio-economic problems.

3. Future Becomes Bleak due to Indefiniteness

Society which is overwhelmed by social problems is bound to be pushed towards uncertainty and indefiniteness. These problems may make the society incapable of meeting its own requirements of fulfilling the basic needs of its people and protecting its national interests from external threats. ***For example,*** (i) population is increasing at a very high rate in India [1.74% per annum as per 2011 census] and if this rate of increase continues unabated, India will definitely find itself in a precarious condition by 2020 when its population would reach a record mark of 140 crore or even more. (ii) Both corruption and terrorism have become widespread in India especially after the 1990s and the intellectuals are worried about the future of India, whether these two menaces subside or grow substantially.

4. Waste of Energy and Brain Drain

Much of time, energy and resources get wasted in any society for controlling, minimising and removing social problems. A society has to put in great efforts to counter threatening social evils such as over-population, beggary, AIDS, terrorism, corruption, crime, poverty, unemployment, etc.

• Mounting social problems sometimes bring in heavy pressure on highly talented individuals. They tend to leave their motherland in search of greener pastures. This tendency which is referred to as ***"brain drain"*** is a great loss of human resources to the countries from where the talented people emigrate to other places. Asian countries [except Japan] are mostly hard hit by this trend. India is worst affected.

5. Social Problems Lead to Political and Economic Instability and Decline

Intense social problems result in political instability and economic insecurity. If the administrative machinery does not take appropriate steps to control these problems and to improve the living conditions of the people, serious consequences would be the result. Such societies are highly susceptible to internal revolts, social upheavals and even revolution. Human history provides several examples for this. Historian **Gibbon** has stated that the glorious ancient Roman Civilisation declined mainly because of its unsolved internal socio-political problems. The French and the Russian Revolutions broke out more or less due to the serious socio-economic and political conditions that prevailed in these two countries.

Concluding Remarks

Social problems are universal for there is no country or society in the world which is totally free from social problems. Society must be able to solve them or at least control them and only then the wheels of society will be able to roll on. Depending upon the socio economic level of growth of societies, the problems that they have to face also differ. Problems of the tribals and those of the modern civilised people, are not the same. Similarly, there exists lot of differences between problems of the developed, underdeveloped and the developing countries. Society's ability to withstand these problems and to find out effective ways and means of facing them alone assures its future. It is argued that sociologists have the moral obligation of giving appropriate advices and suggestions to counter these problems.

THEORETICAL APPROACHES TO THE STUDY OF SOCIAL PROBLEMS

Social problems have been a permanent feature of human society for there is no society in the world which is absolutely free from social problems. Social scientists including sociologists have been evincing interest in studying and analysing these problems. It is unfair to say that sociologists are indifferent to moral standards of the society and in protecting its interests. They are equally interested in protecting the values and moral standards of society and hence they consider it as their responsibility to study social problems scientifically and suggest appropriate solutions to solve them.

Though many of the social problems are subjective in nature they are amenable for scientific study. Modern sociology considers it as its priority issue to study social problems systematically and scientifically. Sociologists follow different approaches to view social problems among which the following may be noted.

1. Social Disorganization Approach

Social disorganisation reflects a condition of society or community or social group in which there is a breakdown of social control, or of a social order. It is characterised by the lack of co-operation, common values, unity, discipline and predictability. It denotes a condition which involves- *a) lack of consensus, b) lack of integration of institutions, and c) inadequate means of social control.*

Elliot and **Merrill** have defined *this as a process by which relationships between members of a group are broken or dissolved.*

Social disorganisation takes place when there is a change in the equilibrium forces, a breakdown of the social structure, and the accepted forms of social control no longer function effectively. This disruptive condition of society which is witnessed in the form of normlessness, role conflict, social conflicts and demoralisation further adds to social problems. *For example*, rapid industrialisation and urbanisation have brought in disorganisation in families and communities.

Above mentioned views are not accepted by all the sociologists. According to some sociologists, the state of social disorganisation does not always create social problems. *For example,* during Hitler's regime , Germany was not a disorganised society. Similarly, during Stalin's regime, Soviet union was not in a state of disorganisation; yet there were shocking social problems in these countries. Therefore, social disorganisation theory may not explain all social problems. Despite this limitation, some scholars say that the theory may not explain all social problems, but it does explain some of the social problems.

Views of Horton and Leslie: According to Horton and Leslie, social disorganisation approach makes one to concentrate on some of the crucial questions relating to social problems. Some of these questions are as follows. *What major changes have made traditional norms and practices ineffective? What are the old rules which have broken down partially or completely? Why some of the groups have become disgruntled due to social change and what solutions they propose? What rules are likely to be accepted in the near future??*

2. Cultural Lag Approach

Cultural lag refers to a *situation in which a lag or gap between two parts of culture [namely; material culture and non material culture] that undergo change at unequal rates of speed, takes place.* This gap or lag leads to the disruption of integration and equilibrium of the culture. **Ogburn** who established this theory of cultural lag says that material culture always changes more rapidly than the non material culture. This is especially true in industrial societies through rapid advances in science and technology. This theory states that in modern societies there has been a tendency for change in the political, economic, family and religious institutions to fall behind technological changes. This tendency many a times leads to social problems. *For example*, rigid caste rules or norms prevent certain sections of Indian people to take up certain jobs or to work for industries. Some caste people refused to work along with some others on caste basis. Industrial backwardness and slow technological progress were the natural outcomes of such a cultural gap. It took more than a generation to adapt ourselves to technological development in agriculture and industry. Our social institutions lagged behind whereas global technology went ahead.

This cultural lag approach or theory, however, explains some of the social problems such as AIDS, population explosion, industrial backwardness etc.. but it does not explain all types of social problems. Therefore, it cannot be proposed as a universal explanation of all social problems.

3. Value -Conflict Approach

- *"A value is a belief that something is good and worthwhile. It defines what is worth having and worth striving for."* –**Michael Haralambos.**
- *"Values are general conceptions of the good ideas about the kinds of ends that people should pursue throughout their lives and throughout the many different activities in which they engage"* -**Peter Worsley.**

Values, thus provide the general standards of behaviour and each member of the group is expected to remain committed to the values accepted by the group. Values such as equality, justice, sacrifice, communal harmony, patriotism, mobility, collectivism, compromise, adjustment, sympathy, co-operation etc. have great influence on people's behaviour no doubt. They serve as standards for judging concrete goals or actions, and therefore they are often regarded as absolute.

One practical problem with values is that different groups have different systems of values. Incompatibility between the values of two or more groups often leads to value conflict especially in the role performance of the individuals. This state of conflict may be a short-lived one or it may continue for a longer period of time. ***For example***, conflict in values of parents and children may often lead to parent -child conflict, or to the problem of *"generation gap"*. Similarly, difference in the values of industrialists and workers may lead to *industrial unrest*.

Champions of value conflict theory such as **Fuller, Cuber, Waller, Harper** and others hold the opinion that clashes in value system are of basic importance in the origin and development of social problems.

This theoretical approach seems to be very vague. The champions of this theory have not explained their views in concrete details. It is probably true that the value conflict theory explains the problems arising in family, economies, politics but it cannot be accepted as a universal explanation.

4. Personal Deviation Approach

Deviance refers to the act of going against the group shared expectations and norms. The term refers to any failure to conform to customary social norms. In personal deviation approach, one looks to the motivation and behaviour of the deviants who are instrumental in causing the problems.

Two factors are normally emphasised in the personal deviation approach and they are as follows. Personal deviancy develops due to any one of the two factors: *a) An individual's failure to accept generally accepted norms, or b) An individual's inability to follow the generally accepted norms.*

The **first one** is caused because of person's emotional, social or biological deficiency and because of these he is incapable of adhering consistently to generally accepted standards. The incapable or the socially deficient person , does not truly violate norms, rather he manifests an inability to learn and follow the norms. The cause of emotional deficiency is bio - psychological. Such persons require medical, psychiatric and environmental or social therapies.

The **second one**, has something to do with deficiency in socialization. Although these individuals have learnt the norms and values, they cannot put them into practice. They remain disposed to telling lies, cheating, exploiting, defaming others when it suits their purposes. Their deviance does not produce any guilt feeling or shame in them. They do not bother whether social problems exist or not; or, are solved or not, as long as the situation can be used for their vested interests.

As **Horton** and **Leslie** have stated, the application of personal deviation approach gives rise to some questions such as the following: *What deviant persons/ groups are involved in social problems? Are deviants themselves the problem or they help create the problem? What deviant sub-cultures are involved? What alternatives are there for dealing with the deviants?*

5. Anomic Approach

This approach was proposed by **R.K.Merton.** According to him, anomie refers to *"a state in which socially prescribed goals and the norms governing their attainment are incompatible"*. In simple words, *anomie is a condition characterised by the relative absence or weakening or confusion of norms and values in a society or a group.*

The concept of anomie is comparable to the idea of social solidarity. Just as social solidarity is a state or condition of ideological integration, anomie, is a condition of confusion, insecurity and normlessness. According to Merton, the disjunction between goals and means and the consequent strain leads to the weakening of men's commitment to the culturally prescribed goals or institutionalised means leads to a state of anomie.

Merton maintains that people adapt themselves to this disjuction either by rejecting cultural goals or the institutionalised means, or both. Merton in this context, gives four varieties of deviant behaviour. They are; **innovation, ritualism, retreatism** and **rebellion.** *Merton, tries to locate the sources of strain not very much in the characteristics of individuals, but in the culture and or social structure.*

Merton comments, *"the social problem arises not from people failing to live upto the requirements of their social statuses but from the faulty organisation of these statuses into a reasonably coherent social system".*[6]

This theory of Merton is regarded as inadequate and incomplete. All social problems cannot be interpreted as the results of the responses to strains or mode of adaptation and adjustment.

TYPES OF SOCIAL PROBLEMS

Social problems are not uniform and they represent different varieties. Social problems can also be classified though such classifications have not assumed much prominence in sociology. However, attempts are also made by some sociologists to classify social problems in their own way.

- **Four Fold Classification of Social Problems Given by Sociologist Case**

Sociologist **Case** has made a mention of four types of social problems depending on the very basis or origin of the problems. They are listed below.

1. Problems which are rooted in some way or the other with the physical environment.
2. Problems which are inherent in the nature or distribution of the population involved.
3. Problems which result from poor social organisation, and
4. Problems which evolve from a conflict of cultural values within the society.

- **Three Fold Classification by Fuller and Meyers**

Fuller and **Meyers** have spoken of three types of social problems and they are mentioned below.

*a) **Physical Problems**:* Physical problems such as *floods, famines, earthquakes, cyclones* etc. also bring about problems for the society though their causes are not based on value conflicts.

*b) **Ameliorative Problems:*** There are some social problems and on the effects of these, there seems to be a good consensus among the social thinkers. But there are wide

6. **Merton and Nisbet**, as quoted by **Ram Ahuja** in *"Social Problem in India"* - Page: 14.

differences pertaining to their solutions. ***Example:*** *crime, poverty, AIDS, drug addiction etc..*

c) ***Moral Problems:*** There are certain social problems and sociologists differ a lot pertaining to the nature or causes of these problems. ***Example:*** *Gambling, alcoholism, drug abuse* and *divorce.*

STAGES IN THE DEVELOPMENT OF SOCIAL PROBLEMS

Most of the social problems develop over a period of time. Though problems caused by famines, floods, cyclones, volcanic eruptions, earthquakes, wars, communal riots, etc. are sudden developments, in normal situations, social problems take time to become established as social problems. It means, social problems undergo some stages before they appear to the people as social problems. **Fuller** and **Meyers** [1941] have spoken of three stages which the problems pass through in the process of being defined and solved. They are mentioned below.

1. Awareness Regarding the Problem

In the primary stage, people must be convinced that there exists a social problem. They must feel that a social development has assumed the form of a social problem and it is an undesirable condition and that something must be done about it. In the beginning, only a few people come to feel that a problem has arisen or is coming up and it is likely to pose a threat to the society, if it is not tackled well in time. But gradually, more and more people become aware of the existence of the problem. ***Example :*** In 1980s and 1990s, some student organisations along with mostly the people of Assam were expressing grave concern and anxiety over the continuous, illegal infiltration of the Bangladesh people into the Indian territories in the North - Eastern border areas. Now it is known to the whole nation that a large number of Bangladesh people [according to some estimate, around 2-3 crore people] have already entered India through illegal means. This continuous inflow of these people has changed the demographic profile, especially of the North -Eastern provinces leading to several socio-economic and political problems.

2. Determination of the Policy towards the Problem

As awareness spreads to larger segments of population or society, people start discussing the problem, its nature, gravity, dimension and possible solutions. ***Example:*** i) As we have found in the example cited above, when awareness of the dangers of illegal infiltration was created, many political parties, student and other peoples organisations have started demanding the identification of the illegal Bangla entrants and driving them back to Bangladesh. ii) Similarly, Indian people were relatively indifferent towards the various means and techniques of family planning in 1950s and 1960s; but they have now become aware of their importance. *Thus, the emphasis in the second stage shifts from what should be done to, how should it be done.*

3. An Attempt Towards Reformation

As basic solutions and policies regarding the social problem are decided upon, the stage of action is reached. ***For example,*** in the case of the *problem of slums,* not only a plan for clearing the slums is put into practice, but people living in such areas are also accommodated elsewhere. This stage is hence properly called as the stage of implementation rather than the stage of decision.

METHODS OF STUDYING SOCIAL PROBLEMS

The scientific method of studying topics, issues and problems remains more or less the same for all sciences though the scientific techniques which they prefer to adapt for their study differs significantly. Techniques are the particular ways in which scientific methods are applied to a particular problem. Each science prefers to develop its own series of techniques which fit the nature of the material it studies. Accordingly, different techniques are used in sociological research in the study of social problems. By making use of their own techniques sociologists have developed three methods of studying social problems and they are as follows:

(i) *Social Survey Method,*

(ii) *Case Study Method, and*

(iii) *Multiple Factor Method.*

(i) The Social Survey Method

The first requisite of a sociological study of any social problem is collection of data or facts. The facts that we need for the study are, sometimes not recorded or stored any where and we start collecting them by interviewing and asking questions to people. Interview and questionnaire studies, or the social survey method, thus is a valuable technique for studying social problems in contemporary society. It is possible to collect data from samples of respondents representing a cross section of a given population through a schedule or a questionnaire. This technique is frequently used in the field sociology. Studies on beggary, drug -abuse, AIDS, alcoholism, youth crime, dowry problem etc. have been made by making use of this technique. All these studies have pointed out the empirical relationship between two or more variables in creating a social problem.

Various studies have confirmed that questionnaires, schedules and interviews are the systematic ways of collecting data under scientific controls. But these methods have their own pitfalls or limitations about which the sociologists are aware of. Assuming that these techniques have a margin of error, they are still very useful, for they are more reliable than guesswork.

(ii) The Case Study Method

Fredrick Le Play [1826-1832] was the first scholar to make use of this method. Case study method is an in-depth study of an individual or a situation or an organisation or an in institution or a family or a group or a small community. It is indeed, a complete and detailed account of an event, situation or development. **Burgess** called this method *"social microscope"*.

This method involves the minute study of all the information and data collected regarding the object or case under study. This method is qualitative instead of quantitative. It analyses the social process involved in the development of a social problem as well as in the causal analysis. It focuses on the sequences of events, motivations of persons, social influences affecting persons and events, social relations, sub -cultures and so forth. It depends on both primary and secondary sources for collecting information. Depending on the nature of the social problem, the case study can be used to study a sub-culture of deviants such as that of organized criminals, smugglers, black-marketeers, drug addicts, the disorganisation of personality, or the modes of relations in an institution such as prison.

In analysing the causes of a social problem, the case study method is a qualitative procedure which seeks to formulate generalisations about the development of problem behaviour. One example of this is the analysis of the causes of drug addiction. The greatest value of the case study method, is in the suggestion of hypotheses, which can be tested with other methods. But no generalisation can be made on the basis of the study of a single case. Generalisations are based on a large mass of carefully processed data and the collection of a great many case studies is highly expensive and time consuming. Also, it is difficult to "add up" a number of case studies or compute averages.

(iii) The Multiple Factor Method

No social problem is the result of any single causal factor. Causation in the social world is pluralistic. On this assumption, this method determines the relationship between several factors and a social problem. Various factors such as the nature of associations, socio-economic status, sub-culture, marital status, residential background, intra-family relations, frustrations and inherited traits can be correlated positively or negatively with the social problem under investigation. ***For example***, the relation between crime and poverty, or between drug addiction and peer group associations and high economic status, or between wife battering and inferiority complex and alcoholism, or between suicide and feeling of isolation, marital status and religion etc., can be analysed through this method.

The multi- factor approach is used both in single, disciplinary studies[that is, for example, sociology making the study of drug addiction independently] as well as interdisciplinary studies of social problems. *For example,* in the multidisciplinary study of drug addiction, medical scientists, psychologists, sociologists and criminologists may put forth their efforts together to find out the real nature and the gravity of the problem.

THE TASK OF SOLVING SOCIAL PROBLEMS

Social problems are like social diseases and they require proper social treatment to get mitigated. No society can overlook the task of finding solutions to the social problems for a long time. Hence, social problems are to be tackled efficiently and proper solutions are to be sought at the earliest to stop their growth.

Finding out solutions or solving of a social problem depends upon finding out the causes of troublesome social conditions which create the problem. Though every social problem is caused by multiple factors, it is always possible to find out the chief factor, the co-operative factor and the minor aggravants in the origin and development of the problem.

Every problem is likely to be unique and is likely to have individualistic traits which may differentiate it from other problems. Many a time, the nature of the social problem is such, that the control becomes extremely difficult, if not impossible. This is especially so when the social problems are mostly caused by natural factors like droughts, floods, earthquakes etc.. or when revolution breaks out to change the existing socio-economic and political systems.

The society which tries to understand and judge or evaluate social problems, has to take some action in its attempts to alleviate them. The action of the society could be an organised one or a personalised one. The former is action through group effort, while the latter is action through individual life and influencing others by living a life in accordance with good principles. Gandhiji, for example, used the second method for solving the problem of untouchability by living with untouchables and treating them with sympathy and kindness. When others imitated his example and followed him, the effect became greater and greater.

Organised action, on the contrary, can be taken by the state, or a political party or by the panchayat or an official group. Sometimes the problem is solved by the combination of organised and personalised action. *Example* : Alcoholism, drug addiction, prostitution etc..

Social Attitudes Required to Solve Social Problems

Social problems can be solved with a strong social will and a determination to solve them. When the individuals in a society have a positive attitude towards countering social problems, it becomes relatively easy to tackle them. It can be said that when individuals in a society possess the following four feelings, social problems can be successfully countered.

(i) the feeling that a situation can be corrected;
(ii) the strong determination to correct the situation;
(iii) confidence in the people and a belief that there is no limit to progress, and
(iv) the use of technological and rational knowledge and skill for correcting the situation.

Three Points to be Remembered in Facing Social Problems

According to **Ram Ahuja,**[7] the following three points are to be remembered while seeking solutions to social problems.

1) ***Need to Remember the Multiple Factor Approach:*** As it is already stressed upon, each social problem is caused by a number of factors. Hence, solution to the problem must be sought from different angles. *For example,* the problem of crime cannot be contained unless it is collectively perceived in terms of poverty, unemployment, social associations, functioning of social structures, social strains and frustrations and so on.

2) ***Inter - relatedness of the Social Problems:*** No social problem can be perceived exclusively or atomistically. Each social problem is related with other social problems in some way or the other. Solutions to social problems can be effective only if these solutions are suggested in the light of the interrelatedness of the social problems.

3) ***The Factor of Relativity:*** Social problems are to be construed in the context of time and space. What is considered a problem in one society may not be considered so in the other. In the same society, what is branded as a social problem at one time may not be regarded so, in another.

IMPORTANCE AND THE NEED FOR THE STUDY OF SOCIAL PROBLEMS

1. Study of Social Problems is a Part of the Science of Sociology

Sociology is a social science which claims to study the entire social phenomena. It is the only social science which throws light on the different facets of social life. Social problems constitute an inseparable part of society or social life. It is, hence mandatory for sociology to make a scientific study of social problems Thus, sociology follows its own ways and means of studying social problems such as poverty, unemployment, over-population, crime, juvenile deliquency, family disorganisation, corruption, illiteracy, communal riots, terrorism, extremism, violence against women, and so on.

2. Study of Social Problems as the Historical Responsibility of Sociology

Study of social problems is very much associated with the origin and emergence of sociology. In fact, the serious social problems [such as poverty, unemployment, exploitation of labourers, women and children, child labour, slums, uncontrolled migration towards city, urban crowding, lack of basic amenities in cities, increasing crime rate etc.] that cropped up due to the outbreak of Industrial Revolution, disturbed the minds of social thinkers such as ***Auguste Comte. Herbert Spencer, Karl Marx,*** and others. These thinkers later on strongly advocated the need to establish a separate science of society. Comte especially believed

---

7. **Ram Ahuja** in *"Social Problems in India",* (2001) - Page: 21.

that such a science would be able to find solutions to many of the social problems of the day. Thus, historically also sociology has an obligation to study social problems for which purpose it was originally established.

3. Social Pathology as a Specialized Branch to Study Social Problems

Sociology in its attempts to study social problems systematically, scientifically, and in their entireity established a new branch known as *"Social Pathology"* It was **Ginsberg** who strongly recommended the need for establishing a separate branch of sociology and called it "*Social Pathology*". According to Durkheim, the task of social pathology is to study the abnormal or pathological conditions of society. Durkheim who founded two other branches of sociology namely; *"sociology of crime"*, and "*sociology of morals*", expressed the view that the incidences of suicide are nothing but the social consequences of the pathological conditions of society.

4. Study of Problems is Absolutely Necessary for Finding Solutions

A pathological society is like an individual with ill health. No doctor will administer treatment without examining the disease of the patient. This is equally true of society. Unless the social problems are properly studied, their causes are traced out, their nature is known, it is not possible to deal effectively with them and to find befitting solutions to them. Thus, study of social problems assumes importance in sociology. Sociologists also consider it as their social responsibility to study these problems and recommend appropriate solutions for them.

5. The very existence of social problems indicate the internal deficiency of the society on the one hand, and the failure of its social policies, on the other.

Thus, if a society is suffering from various social problems, on that basis it can be said that it has some serious internal deficiencies which need immediate correction or repair. In the Indian context, the nation has been suffering from a series of problems such as over population, poverty, unemployment, illiteracy, violence against women, corruption etc., This state of affairs reflect that many of the socio-economic plans, programmes, and policies of India have failed to bring about the expected results. It also alerts the administration to find out the mistakes and to take proper action to save the Indian society from a social collapse.

6. Social Problems Indicate that cultural Values are Changing and Getting Violated or Eroded

Cultural values normally decide or interpret what is good and what is bad, what is desirable and what is undesirable, what is sublime and what is ugly and so on. It is a sociological fact of general observation that whenever cultural values are continuously violated or eroded, social problems of some kind or the other, will crop up. This is true in the case of Indian society also.The following examples help to confirm this view.

(i) Since the cultural values of religious tolerance and *"sarva dharma samabhava*"[equal respect to all religious] are weakening; communal riots, forcible religious conversions, and religious fundamentalist activities are increasing.

(ii) Due to the decline in the value of caste harmony caste conflicts, caste competitions, caste hateredness etc.. are increasing.

(iii) Decline in the family values has led to an increase in the rates of divorce, desertion, separation and family disorganisation.

7. Social Problems Demand Quick Relief, if Progress and Development are to be Achieved

Desire for progress is found in all societies. If this desire is to be materialised, the problems that are haunting the society are to be tackled efficiently and immediately. Progress and development of India become meaningful only when poverty, unemployment, overpopulation, corruption, illiteracy and other problems are contained and all the people are provided with the basic necessities of life. Sociological studies have been of great help to those planners and administrators who are generally interested in the progress and prosperity of India.

SOCIAL PROBLEMS AND SOCIAL DISORGANISATION

Concept of Social Disorganisation

Like nature, the human society too has its own order. The orderliness of society depends on its internal strength to maintain its equilibrium. Society will be in a state of equilibrium as long as its various parts are properly adjusted and fulfil their functions. The orderliness or the equilibrium that is normally maintained in the natural world is often upset due to certain forces at work. In the same manner, the equilibrium in the social world is also often disturbed. Whenever the social equilibrium is severely disturbed 'social disorganisation' sets in. Thus 'social disorganisation' can be understood as nothing but the state of social disequilibrium, in which the smooth functioning of various parts of society gets disturbed.

The concept of *'disorganisation'* occupies a prominent place in modern sociological literature. The concept was developed by **Thomas** and **Zananiecki** in their famous book *"The Polish Peasant in Europe and America"*. According to them, the term social disorganisation' refers to *the decrease in the influence of the existing social rules of behaviour upon individual members*. As a result of this there develops individuation and lack of cohesion in society. It was explained by them as a process which will automatically and inevitably create social problems.

Definition of Social Disorganisation

1. **Emile Durkheim** considers social disorganisation as *"a state of disequilibrium and lack of social solidarity or consensus among the members of a society."*
2. **Ogburn** and **Nimkoff** have said that *"when the harmonious relationship between the various parts of culture is disturbed, social disorganisation ensues."*
3. According to **Elliot** and **Merrill**, *"Social disorganisation represents a breakdown in the equilibrium of forces, a decay in the social structure, so that old habits and forms of social control no longer function effectively."*

● Yet another sociologist states that *"social disorganisation is a disturbance in the patterns and mechanism of human relations."*

Thus, social disorganisation implies a breakdown in the bonds of relationship, coordination, team work and morale among groups of interrelated persons so as to impair the functioning of the society or smaller social organisation. *"Social disorganisation implies relative disharmony between individual attitudes and social values, when common agreement breaks down, then, consensus is partially or wholly disturbed, and when individuals view the major group interest in individual rather than in common terms, some degree of social disorganisation is present."*

CHARACTERISTICS OF SOCIAL DISORGANISATION

Just as a disease is known by its symptoms the nature of social disorganisations can be understood by means of its characteristics.

1. Conflict of Mores and Institutions: Every society has its own mores and institutions which regulate the social life of its members. With the passage of time some of these mores and institutions may become obsolete. New ideals and new institutions may arise to suit new needs. The existing mores and institutions instead of giving place to the new ones may come into conflict with them. This conflict between the old and new may destroy the social consensus. With the destruction of consensus, the organisation is disrupted. *For example*, in India, such conflicts may be found very often with regard to social practices, ideals, and institutions relating to divorce, female education, joint family, family control, widow remarriage, intercaste marriage, dowry system, untouchability, family planning, etc.

2. Transfer of Functions From One Group or Agency to Another: In an organised society, the functions of different groups are relatively well defined and almost predetermined. Due to the dynamic nature of society some of these functions either undergo radical change or get transferred to other groups or agencies. As a result of this, social disorganisation may set in even if it is for a temporary period. ***For example,*** the joint family in India is no more performing some of its traditional functions for these have been transferred to some external agencies. Hence, the joint family system is facing a crisis now. Some say, it is in a state of severe disorganisation and this may even lead to its extinction as it is happening in big cities. Similarly, the functions of caste and religious organisations have been transferred to other organisations or agencies leading to crisis.

3. Individuation: The modern age places a high premium on individualism or individualistic tendencies. Every one is more prone to think of himself and in terms of his own pleasures, wishes and expectations. Important issues such as education, occupation, marriage, recreation, morality, etc., have almost become matters of individual decisions. Individuals often fail to think in terms of the expectations and wishes of the groups or organisations of which they are a part. This tendency is, of course, caused by the changing social values. But it may shatter the social organisation and may drive it towards a state of disorganisation.

4. Inconsistency Between Expectations and Achievements: In a disorganised society, considerable inconsistency is visible between the expectations embodied in the social role and the extent to which these expectations can be realised by most persons. When a considerable number of people in the society try to achieve goals in an anti-social manner, there is a clear indication of the society being in a state of social disorganisation. *For instance,* if a large number of students take part regularly in strikes and indulge in violence and resort to malpractices in examinations, we can conclude, that the college education system has become a disorganised one.

According to **Cottrell**, *"In a disorganised society, there is a considerable discrepancy between what is given verbally and which is demonstrated in practice. An organised society has greater congruity between expectation and realisation but such is not the case in a disorganised society where the expectations do not come up to their full realisation".*

5. Inconsistency Between Status and Role: In an organised society, the statuses and roles of each individual are well defined and hence the possibility of a conflict taking place between the two is comparatively less. Changing social values and social conditions may bring about some conflicts between statuses of the individuals and their roles. Due to this, disorganisation may set in. Thus, a disorganised society is characterised by extreme uncertainity and ambiguity of social roles. ***Example*** **:** Due to the change in her status, a modern housewife in an advanced society is not sure whether she should play the role of a mother, or an employee, or a light-hearted companion, a social leader, and so on. She finds it dificult to arrange these roles imposed on her all on a sudden, in order of priority and strike a balance between them. She may even try to perform all roles assigned to her but not successfully. Her failure to perform the roles successfully may lead to personal dissatisfaction, frustration and insecurity which may disrupt her family life.

6. Other Conditions Observed in Disorganisation: It may be said that in any instance of social disorganisation, the following conditions may be present in one way or another, either individually or collectively. In most of the cases, they are found in a combined form. These conditions are : *(i) diversity of opinions; (2) heterogeneity of population; (3) mutual distrust; (4) uncertainty and insecurity; (5) individuality and variety in interests and attitudes; (6) emphasis on rights rather than on duties; (7) contradiction between status and function; (8) lack of clarity in status and roles; (9) conflict of mores and conflict between institutions; (10) absence of or decreased social control, (11) conflict between society and individual, and (12) disregard of values, norms and laws.*

CAUSES OF SOCIAL DISORGANISATION

A complex phenomenon such as social disorganisation is caused by a number of factors. These factors are so intermingled that it becomes difficult to say which of these are predominant. Different writers have highlighted the importance of different factors. ***For example,*** **Elliot** and **Merrill** have given four causes : *(1) the social processes under the three main heads : cultural, political and economic, (2) cultural lag. (3) conflicting attitudes and values,* and *(4) social crisis.*

- **Sorokin** is of the opinion that disorganisation is mainly due to cultural degeneration of values in various spheres such as art, science, philosophy, religion, law, politics, economics, family, etc. In brief, change from the *"idealistic"*, and *"ideational"* culture to *"sensate culture"* is the main cause of social disorganisation.

- **G.R. Madan** has listed a few factors that invite the problems of disorganisation. They may be briefly explained below :

1. *Psychological Factors* : Sometimes the cause of social disorganisation is to be found in the human psychology itself. Psychological factors contribute to disorganisation in two ways : *(i) Failure to maintain proper communication among fellow beings,* and *(ii) Failure to modify or change one's attitudes in tune with the demands of time*

(i) Communication is an essential psychological process among human beings. It is maintained through the social processes such as imitation, cooperation, competition, suggestion, conflict, accommodation, assimilation, etc., which are also psychological in character. Common understanding and common consciousness help the people to maintain communication. Due to lack of common consensus regarding values and due to divergent attitudes people may fail to maintain proper communication among themselves. Words, ideas, phrases and symbols that they use in their communication may sound different things to them. Thus, lack of appropriate communication or its total failure may create ill-will, prejudice and lot of psychological distance among people.

(ii) The problem of attitudes. Human tendencies and attitudes are modified very slowly whereas culture is modified with comparative rapidity. The sociocultural environment may impose much requirements on individuals which they find it difficult to fulfil. ***For example,*** the modern industrialised and urbanised society is so competitive that some find it extremely difficult to cope with. Similarly, the cultural conflict between the older and the younger generation may result in disorganisation of the adolescents, juvenile delinquency, and sometimes in family disorganisation. Conflicts of attitudes between the old and new values are always pregnant with trends of disorganisation.

2. *Cultural Lag* : 'Cultural lag', the concept used by **W.E. Ogburn,** refers to the imbalance in the rate and speed of change between the material cultural and non-material culture. Objects of material culture such as mode of housing, means of transport and communication, type of dresses, pattern of ornaments, technical and mechanical devices, instruments, etc., change very quickly. But ideas, beliefs, attitudes, tastes, philosophies, habits, ideologies, institutional structures and such other aspects of non-material culture change slowly and gradually. Hence, a *'gap'* or a *'lag'* arises between the material and non-material culture. This lag, referred to as *'cultural lag'* invites the process of disorganisation to set in. *For example,* though a good number of Indians have adopted Western technology, they have not very much changed their traditional beliefs, attitudes and customs, etc. This quality has often led to some conflicts which have opened the doors for disorganisation.

3. *Physical or Geographic Factors* : The maladjustment of man and his culture to certain extra-ordinary physical or geographic conditions or situations may cause disorganisation in society. This is especially true in the case of natural calamities such as storms, cyclones, hurricanes, famines, floods, earthquakes, volcanoes, epidemics, etc., which upset the social balance and bring in social disorganisation.

4. *Biological Factor* : Population explosion or extreme scarcity of population, instances of racial intermixture, defective hereditary traits and such other biological factors may also cause disorganising effects upon society. *For example,* if overpopulation has caused the problems of poverty and unemployment in some countries, the fact of under population has created a psychological crisis manifested in what is known as *"race extinction"*.

5. *Ecological Factor* : Social disorganisation is related to environment in terms of regions and neighbourhoods. **Professor Shaw** and his associates at the institute of ***Juvenile Research in Chicago*** found that the delinquency was unevenly distributed in the city of Chicago. They observed that the delinquents mostly concentrated in the areas of poor housing, overcrowding, and the areas in which cinema houses, hotels, night clubs, liquor shops, gambling centres were found in a large number. Some findings have revealed that per capita crime rate is relatively higher in larger cities than in smaller ones.

6. *Social Problems Leading to Social Disorganisation* : Social problems and forces such as - a revolution, a social upheaval, a class struggle, a financial or economic crisis, a war between nations, mental illness, political corruption, mounting unemployment and crime, etc., threaten the smooth working of society. The social problems are the diseases of the society and they threaten its welfare. They may bring in disorganisation.

7. *Degeneration of Values* : Social values are often regarded as the sustaining forces of society. They contribute to the strength and stability of social order. But due to rapid social change new values come up and some of the old values decline. At the same time, people are not in a position to reject the old completely and accept the new altogether. Here conflict between the old and the new is the inevitable result of which leads to the social disorganisation.

Changes in social values necessitate new social institutions and associations. These come into conflict with older existing ones. This creates disorder in society. The statuses and roles of people will have to change in accordance with the changes in social values But they take time to adjust themselves to new situations. In this way, disorganisation spreads. According to **Sorokin**, the cause of social disorganisation is nothing but degeneration of values in various spheres such as art, science, philosophy, religion, law, politics, economics, family, etc., which has led to more wars, criminality, revolution, suicide, mental diseases, etc.

8. *Disintegration and Confusion of Roles* : Members of society are expected to perform certain definite roles in accordance with their placements in society. Due to profound social changes these expectations also undergo a change. Consequently, people are confused with regard to their new roles. **Professor Faris** considers this as the most important cause of disorganisation.

According to him, it is due to the transition from pre-industrial folk society to modern complex society. ***For example,*** children are to be cared for and essential cultural education be given to them by the family members The economic order is assumed to provide for the production and distribution of goods and wealth. The religious institutions are expected to maintain the religious heritage and to pass on the same to succeeding generation. When any of these functions are not properly fulfilled, disorganisation may be the result.

9. *Political Subordination* : Political subordination of one country to another leads to social disorganisation in the former. The vanquished country is not allowed to develop its economy and institution in its own ways. It is made a means to serve the interests of the dominant country. India suffered under the British rule in the same manner. The dominant country may not even care for the basic needs such as - food, clothing, shelter, basic education, medical facility, etc., of the people of slave country. As a result, the slave country may have to face a number of socio-economic problems.

- **Other Factors**

In addition to the above, a few other factors may also cause disorganisation.

a) Conflict of goals and means : Conflict of goals and the means for achieving them may also cause disorganisation. Most of the individuals share the dominant goals of the society and act accordingly. But lacking the means for achieving the goals by legitimate means, some may resort to illegitimate and illegal means resulting in vice, crime and other expression of social disorganisation.

b) Decline of social control : The declining control of religion, morals, customs, traditions, and other institutions on the behaviour of men has also enhanced the process of disorganisation. Hence, we witness an increase in interpersonal conflicts, crimes, tensions, divorce, delinquency, mental derangement, etc. In fact, according to **Thomas** and **Znaniecki**, the very *"decrease of the influence of existing rules of behaviour upon the individual members of the group"* itself indicates social disorganisation.

c) Extreme divisions of labour : According to **Emile Durkheim,** social disorganisation is often brought about by extreme division of labour. In normal course, according to him, division of labour leads to social solidarity, but when it becomes extreme and very complex, solidarity may become disturbed.

d) Disruptive social change : Society undergoes change mainly due to the operation of physical, biological, technological and cultural factors. Sudden and radical social changes may, sometimes, disrupt the stability and the organisation of the society. The result is social disorganisation.

- **REMEDIAL MEASURES**

To face the challenges of social disorganisation it is necessary first of all to study the nature and gravity of social disorganisation. Depending on its nature steps should be taken to counteract its influence. In this connection, we may suggest the following remedial measures:

1. Able and efficient administration to fight against the disruptive forces.
2. Proper and comprehensive social and economic planning and policies.
3. Proper implementation of the plans and policies.
4. Organised social work and social welfare activities and social security measures.
5. Appropriate steps to rehabilitate and reform the beggars, criminals, juvenile delinquents, prostitutes, mentally and physically handicapped, the aged and the diseased persons.
6. Effective enforcement of land reforms and fixing a ceiling on urban property.

7. Making effective and attractive family planning and welfare programmes and projects.
8. Providing ample educational and employment opportunities especially for the talented and the aspiring youths.
9. To create a psychological atmosphere of security and confidence, assuring and providing social equality, justice, and liberty to all.
10. Taking steps to mobilise public opinion against the evil practices of bribery, corruption, casteism, communalism, racism, exploitation, etc.,
11. Instilling in the minds of people sentiments of unity, solidarity, patriotism and nationalism by making use of mass media of communication in the best possible manner.

TYPES OF SOCIAL DISORGANISATION

Elliot and **Merrill** have spoken of three types of disorganisation which are, of course, inter-related. They are as follows :

(i) ***Personal or individual disorganisation*** which includes - *crime, insanity, or mental derangement, prostitution, juvenile delinquency, alcoholism, drug addiction, gambling and suicide.* These examples of individual disorganisation indicate that some individuals find it difficult to live in harmony with the society. Their failure to cope with the changing conditions or ups and downs of the society often result in their personal disorganisation.

(ii) ***Family disorganisation*** consists of - *divorce, desertion, separation, broken home, unmarried mothers, illegitimate births and venereal diseases including AIDS, etc.* These examples indicate that family, the smallest unit of our social life is also subject to the threat of disoragnisation. When family relations become very weak, family unity or cohesion declines, harmony between the members disappears, entire family organisation may crumble leading to family disorganisation.

(iii) ***Community disorganisation*** comprises of - *poverty, beggary, unemployment, over-population, lawlessness, political corruption, crime* and so on. As these examples indicate, not only individuals and families, but the entire community may become the target of disorganisation. Community disorganisation takes place when a community is not able to maintain its hold over the behaviour and activities of the people, and fulfil and satisfy their basic needs.

It is equally important to note that all these three types of disorganisations are interrelated.

SOCIAL ORGANISATION Vs SOCIAL DISORGANISATION

The term *'Social disorganisation'* is often held in contrast with *'social organisation'*. As **Ogburn** and **Nimkoff** have pointed out, *"an organisation is an orderly relationship of parts"*. But the significance of this orderly arrangement of parts lies in what it does. ***For example,*** a factory is an organisation for the purpose of production. A factory is composed of internal suborganisations such as sales department, accounting department, supply department, etc. The factory as a social system performs yet another function. It serves to maintain a balance among its suborganisations or parts. This equilibrium of parts means a synchronisation or integration of functions. Hence, the functions of selling department, production department, buying department, etc., must be properly articulated and coordinated. *"Disorganisation is a disturbance of the balance existing in the functioning of parts. The criterion of disorganisation is function, what is done or not done"... Thus, a typewriter may write well or badly or not at all, because of an imbalance in the functioning of its parts as, for instance, in the ribbon or keys".* - **Ogburn** and **Nimkoff.**

What is true of a factory is also true of a society. Society can be said to be in a state of organisation, when all its parts such as associations and institutions are properly integrated so that they fulfil their recognised or implied functions or purposes. Social disorganisation implies some breakdown in the social organisation. Due to this breakdown, the normal functioning of the parts of the society gets disturbed leading to some or the other kind of problems. Disorganisation will lead to functional imbalance between various elements of social structure.

The terms 'social organisation' and 'social disorganisation' are relative. They represent two aspects of the whole functioning of the social system. As there may be various degrees of social organisation, so is the case with social disorganisation. No society can be in a state of either perfect organisation or disorganisation.

As **S.A. Queen, W.B. Bodenhofer** and **E.B. Harper** have said social disorganisation is a counter part, of social organisation. "Just as social organisation provides the means by which a society maintains its unity and cohesion through effective control of its members, and hence, functions smoothly, social disorganisation causes a weakening of group solidarity, loss of control over its members, and therefore, conflict and disintegration. Social organisation implies the existence of institutions, which meet the needs of the members of a society. Social disorganisation, on the other hand, means the malfunctioning of institutions, their failure to satisfy the needs of the people and the consequent frustration of their desires." Thus, *"if social organisation means the development of relationship which persons and groups find mutually satisfactory, then, disorganisation means their replacement by relationships which bring disappointment, thwarted wishes, irritation and unhappiness."*

Social Problems and Social Disorganisation :

Conceptual Relationship and Differences

The two terms "social problems" and "social disorganisation" are very often used interchangeably. They are not, however, one and the same. The thin difference that exists between the two can be stated below.

(i) Social Problem is a Symptom of Social Disorganisation **:** Social problem indicates a condition that is undesirable and harmful to the society. It also denotes a failure in social adjustments or reflects a case of social maladjustment. Social problems mirror the pathological state of society. In this sense, it can be said that it is a symtom of social disorganisation.

(ii) Existence of Social Problems Signifies a Characteristic Feature of Social Disorganisation **:** The term "social disorganisation" is very often used to mean a state of social disequilibrium, a state in which there exists no social harmony and social solidarity; and also a state in which the social rules have lost their control over people. Since social problems contribute to such state of affairs, it can be said that social problems constitute a characteristic feature of social disorganisation. Thus, society which is gripped by social problems such as revolution, revolt, war, famine, flood havoc, revolts, racial riots, ethnic clashes, caste conflicts, etc., is definitely a disorganised one.

(iii) Social Disorganisation Reveals the Presence of Not One But Many Social Problems **:** According to **G.R. Madan,**[8] there is a thin relationship between these two terms. As he states, *a number of social problems together bring about social disorganisation.* Social disorganisation is a condition in which a society is disturbed not by one or two but many social problems. *"Thus, when social problems are so many that the society cannot work smoothly or social progress is hindered, we call this a state of social disorganisation".*

●●●

8. G.R. Madan in *"Indian Social Problems"* Vol. I. [1969] Page : 8.

Chapter 2

PROBLEM OF POVERTY

Poverty As a Major Problem of India - Definition of Poverty - Absolute Poverty and Relative Poverty - Extent of Poverty in India - Distribution of Poverty and Affluence at the Level of Different Caste - Class and Religious Communities - Causes of Poverty - Remedial Measures of Poverty - Five Year Plans - Nationalisation - 20 Point Programme - Other Programmes for Employment Generation and Poverty Alleviation : JRY - PMRY - REGP - SGSY - PMGSY - PMGY - SGRY - VAMBAY - NFWP - Rural Housing Scheme. - ***Rural Poverty*** *and Its Magnitude - Causes for and Solutions to Rural Poverty* - ***Urban Poverty*** *- Indian Urban Poverty Report - 2009 - Nature and Dimensions of Poverty - Proposed Solutions to the Removal of Urban Poverty.*

1. POVERTY AS A MAJOR PROBLEM OF INDIA

Poverty is one of the most widespread socio-economic problems of India. It is, indeed, a common problem being faced by most of the underdeveloped and the developing countries of the world. It is not only socio-economic but even emotional, cultural and political in nature. The developments that have been taking place in India for the past six decades have not been able to wipe out poverty. Poverty has been the root cause of many of the problems.

The problem of poverty is very closely linked up with unemployment. Poverty and unemployment, the twin social problems are found throughout the length and breadth of this land. As **G.R. Madan** points out, *"They have been in existence since the dawn of civilization and one method or the other was devised to help the poverty - stricken, the dependent and the unemployed."*[1] These two problems are not peculiar to India for they are found in good number of Aisatic and African countries.

The study of poverty invites invariably a number of questions : *What is poverty ? What is the extent or magnitude of poverty ? What are the causes of poverty ? How to measure poverty ? What are the social effects of poverty ? What are its economic and social dimensions ? What are the effective solutions to poverty ?* etc. We shall try to analyse these questions.

Definition of Poverty

1. **Gillin** and **Gillin :** *"Poverty is that condition in which a person either because of inadequate income or unwise expenditures, does not maintain a scale of living high enough to provide for his physical and mental efficiency and to enable him and his natural dependents to function usefully according to the standards of the society of which he is a member."*
2. **Adam Smith :** A person *"... is rich or poor according to the degree in which he can afford to enjoy the necessaries, the conveniences and the amusements of life."* - Adam Smith in his *"Wealth of Nations"*.

1. **G.R. Madan** in "*Indian Social Problems*". Vol 1 [1966] Page - 251.

3. **Goddard :** *"Poverty is insufficient supply of those things which are requisite for an individual to maintain himself and those dependent upon him in his health and vigour."*

Explanation of Poverty in terms of "Poverty Line"

The first Director General of FAO *[Food and Agricultural Organization of the UNO]* was the first to explain poverty on the basis of *'starvation line'* in 1945. According to him, an intake of less than 2300 calories of food per person per day, was considered the line of starvation and this has been transformed into *"poverty line"*.

- The ***Indian Planning Commission*** defined *"poverty line"* on the basis of nutritional requirements of 2400 calories per person per day for rural areas and 2100 calories per person per day for urban areas.
- A group of Indian economists consisting of **Prof. Gadgil, Dr. V.K.R.V. Rao, Dr. Ganguli, Ashok Mitra** and **Dr. P.S. Lokanathan** worked out the poverty line in their own way. They recommended a standard of private consumption at ₹ 240 per capita per year at 1960-61 prices as the barest minimum.

2. ABSOLUTE POVERTY AND RELATIVE POVERTY

These two expressions, *'absolute poverty'* and *'relative poverty'*, are quite common in any indepth study of poverty. What do we mean by them - ?

Absolute Poverty

Right from the 19th century, some researchers are trying to fix some yardstick for measuring poverty in precise terms. Ideally speaking, such a yardstick would help us establish a fixed level of poverty, known as "poverty line" below which poverty begins and above which it ends. Such a yardstick is believed to be universal in character and would be applicable to all the societies. This concept of poverty is known as ***"absolute poverty"***.

Absolute poverty is often known as *"subsistence poverty"* for it is based on assessments of minimum subsistence requirements or basic "physical needs" such as food, clothing, shelter, health requirements etc. Some concepts of absolute poverty would even include the idea of *"basic cultural needs"*. This broadens the idea of basic human needs beyond the level of physical survival. **Drewnowski** and **Scott** include education, security, leisure and recreation in their category of *"basic cultural needs"*.

***Criticisms* :** The concept of absolute poverty has been widely criticised. It is based on the assumption that there are minimum basic needs for all people in all societies. This is a difficult argument to defend even in regard to subsistence poverty measured in terms of food, clothing and shelter. Such needs vary both between and within societies. It becomes still more difficult to defend the concept of absolute poverty when it is extended to include the idea of *"basic cultural needs"*. Such *"needs"* vary from time to time and place to place and any attempt to establish absolute fixed standards is bound to fail.

Relative Poverty

The difficulties involved in the application of the concept of *"absolute poverty"*, made some researchers to abandon the concept altogether. In place of absolute standards, they have developed the idea of *"relative standards"* that is, standards which are relative to particular time and place. In this way, the idea of absolute poverty has been replaced by the idea of relative poverty.

"Relative poverty is measured in terms of judgements by members of a particular society of what is considered as reasonable and acceptable standard of living and styles of life according to the conventions of the day. Just as conventions change from time to time, and place to

THE MULTI-FACETED PROBLEM OF POVERTY

place, so will definitions of poverty."[2] In a rapidly changing world, definitions of poverty based on relative standards will be constantly changing. Hence, **Peter Townsend** has suggested that any definition of poverty must be *"related to the needs and demands of a changing society."*

Limitations of the Usage of this Concept **:** Even the concept of relative poverty presents certain problems. It cannot be assumed that there are universally accepted standards of reasonable and acceptable life-styles. Within a particular society, ethnicity, class, religion, region, age and a variety of other factors can vary judgements of reasonable living standards.

The concept of relative poverty poses problems for the comparison of the poor in the same society over time and between societies. *For example,* it becomes difficult to make a comparison of the poor in present - day and 19th century India; or of present-day India and European countries or those of African countries.

3. EXTENT OF POVERTY IN INDIA

Though India is regarded as a developing country it is very badly facing the problem of poverty. India became independent six decades ago and still it has not become free from the stranglehold of the problems such as poverty, over-population, unemployment, illiteracy, etc. It is unfortunate that in India, appropriate and reliable data for the direct estimation of poverty are not available. The government has not made any serious attempt in this direction. However, some private individuals and agencies have made their own attempts to estimate poverty.

(i) Estimates of Dandekar and Rath **:** As per the estimates of **Dandekar** and **Rath**, as early as in 1960-61 roughly 40% of the rural population and 50% of the urban population were living below poverty line.

(ii) Estimates of S.S. Minhas **:** The study of Dr. Minhas revealed that about 65% of population in 1956-57, and 50.6% of population in 1967-68 in rural India, were living below the poverty line.

(iii) Planning Commission's Estimates **:** On the basis of a large sample survey data on consumer expenditure, conducted by the NSSO [*National Sample Survey Organization*], the Planning Commission estimated poverty in the country at the national and state level. These estimates made by the Commission at an interval of approximately five years, give us some picture about the extent of poverty in India uptil 1990-2000. ***Table - 1*** throws some light on the extent of poverty in India. As the table reveals that in 1999-2000, 26.1% of the people, that is, 260.3 million people were living below the poverty line. As per the poverty projection made for the year 2007, the figures were likely to be at 19.3% and 220 million respectively.

ESTIMATES OF INCIDENCE OF POVERTY IN INDIA — **Table 1**

Year	Poverty ratio [percent]			Number of poor [million]		
	Rural	Urban	Combined	Rural	Urban	Combined
1977-78	53.1	45.2	51.3	264.3	64.6	328.90
1983	45.7	40.8	44.5	252.0	70.9	322.90
1987-88	39.1	38.2	38.9	231.9	75.2	307.10
1993-94	37.3	32.4	36.0	244.0	76.3	320.30
1999-00	27.1	23.6	26.1	193.2	67.1	260.30
2007*	21.1	15.1	19.3	170.5	49.6	220.10

* Poverty projection for 2007, ***Source :*** Economic Survey, 2003-04.

Extent of Poverty in Different States - 1999-2000

The level of poverty is not the same in all the states. Poverty was found to be highest in Orissa [47.15%] in 1999-2000 and Bihar [46.2%] respectively. In U.P., highest number of poor

2. **M.H. Haralambos** in *"Sociology Themes and Perspectives"*, - Page : 142.

people [5.29 crore, or 31.5%] were found. The estimates reveal that in 1999-2000, about **193.2** million poor people were living below the poverty line in rural areas and **67.1** million in urban areas. In Karnataka, about 104.40 lakh [20.04%] people were living below the poverty line.

The following ***Table – 2*** reveals the number of persons living below poverty line in different states during 1999-2000.

PERCENTAGE OF POOR IN DIFFERENT STATES During 1999-2000. Table 2

States/U.T./s	No. of Persons [in lakhs]	% of Persons	States/U.T./s	No. of Persons [in lakhs]	% of Persons
Andhra Pradesh	119.01	15.77	Nagaland	5.49	32.67
Arunachal Pradesh	3.98	33.47	**Orissa**	169.09	47.15
Assam	94.55	36.09	Punjab	14.49	6.16
Bihar	425.64	46.20	Rajasthan	81.83	15.28
Goa	0.70	4.40	Sikkim	2.05	36.55
Gujarat	67.89	14.07	Tamil Nadu	130.48	21.12
Haryana	17.34	8.74	Tripura	13.02	34.44
Himachal Pradesh	5.12	7.63	**Uttar Pradesh**	529.89	31.15
Jammu & Kashmir	3.46	3.48	West Bengal	213.49	27.02
Karnataka	104.40	20.04	A & N Island	0.82	20.99
Kerala	41.04	12.72	Chandigarh	0.51	5.75
Madhya Pradesh	298.54	37.43	Dadra & Nagar Haveli	0.33	17.14
Maharashtra	227.99	25.02	Daman & Diu	0.06	4.44
Manipur	7.19	28.54	Delhi	11.49	8.23
Meghalaya	8.23	33.87	Lakshadeep	0.11	15.60
Mizoram	1.85	19.47	Pondicherry	2.41	21.67

Source : Rajya Sabha, Unstarred question 807.

Estimates of Poverty Based on NSS Data – 2004

The following ***Table - 3*** reveals yet another estimate of poverty for still later period, that is, from 1973-74 to 2004.

PERCENTAGE OF POOR AND TOTAL NUMBER OF POOR IN INDIA SINCE 1973 UPTO 2004 Table 3

Year	Percentage of Poor(%)	Number of Poor (million)	Average Annual Rate of Decline
1973-74	54.9	321	-0.59
1977-78	51.3	329	0.31
1983	44.5	323	0.31
1987-88	38.9	307	1.25
1993-94	36.0	320	-0.70
1999-00	26.1	260	3.40
2004*	23.6	250	0.82

*Based on the estimated population of 2004 and poverty ratio calculated using latest NSS data in 2004.

Source : National Institute of Rural Development [2004]; Rural Development Statistics [2002-03]

Distribution of Poverty and Affluence at the Level of

Different Caste - Class and Religious Communities, 1999-2000

Indian society consists of large number of castes and religious communities. Study of poverty reveals that it is distributed differently among these castes and communities. This holds true in the case of the distribution of affluence also. The two tables given here denote this distribution.

• *Table - 4* given below shows the percentage of the population of each caste/community that lives below the official poverty line for 1999-2000. There are two separate columns for rural and urban India.

PERCENTAGE OF POPULATION LIVING BELOW THE POVERTY LINE, 1999-2000 — **Table 4**

CASTE AND Community Groups	RURAL INDIA Spending ₹ 327 or less per person per month	URBAN INDIA Spending ₹ 454 or less per person per month
Scheduled Tribes	45.8	35.6
Scheduled Castes	35.9	38.3
OBCs	27.0	29.5
UC-Muslimm	26.8	34.2
UC-Hindu	11.7	9.9
UC-Christian	9.6	5.4
UC-Sikh	0.0	4.9
UC-Others	16.0	2.7
All Groups	27.0	23.4

Note: OBC = Other Backward Classes: UC= 'Upper Castes', i.e., not SC/ST/OBC
Source: Computed from NSSO 55th Round [1999-2000] unit level data on CD

• *Table - 5* is prepared in exactly the same way as the Table - 4, except that it shows the percentage of population living in affluence rather than in poverty. "*Affluence*" is here defined as a monthly expenditure per person of ₹ 1000/- for rural India and ₹ 2000/- for urban India. This is equivalent to a family of five persons spending ₹ 5000/- per month in rural India and ₹ 10,000/- per month in urban India.

PERCENTAGE OF POPULATION THAT IS AFFLUENT 1999-2000 — **Table 5**

CASTE AND Community Groups	RURAL INDIA Spending ₹ 1000 or more per person per month	URBAN INDIA Spending ₹ 2000or more per person per month
Scheduled Tribes	1.4	1.8
Scheduled Castes	1.7	0.8
OBCs	3.3	2.0
UC-Muslimm	2.0	1.6
UC-Hindu	8.6	8.2
UC-Christian	18.9	17.0
UC-Sikh	13.7	15.1
UC-Others	17.9	14.4
All Groups	4.3	4.5

Note: OBC = Other Backward Classes: UC= 'Upper Castes', i.e., not SC/ST/OBC
Source: Computed from NSSO 55th Round [1999-2000] unit level data on CD

Yet Another Estimate of Poverty

Report of Expert Group Headed by Prof S.D. Tendulkar 2009-10

Former Chief Economic Adviser to Prime Minister **Man Mohan Singh, Prof. S.D. Tendulkar** submitted the Report of the Expert Group to Review the Methodology for Estimation of Poverty in Novemeber 2009-10. As per the methodology suggested by Prof Tendulkar, the percentage of population below the poverty line was 45.3 in 1993-94 and it gradually came down to 37.2 in 2004-2005, and further to 29.8% in 2009-10.[3]

---

3. ***Source*** : Planning Commission Press Note March 2012. "*Press Note of Poverty Estimate 2009-10*" - as quoted by **Datt** and **Sundharam** in "*Indian Economy*"[2012] Page - 407. Publisher S.Chand and Co., New Delhi.

Final Poverty Lines and Poverty Head Count Ratio for 2009-10

As per the press note issued by the Planning Commission of India in March 2012, final poverty lines and poverty head count ratio for 2009-10 for the whole nation and for different states have been identified and the following Table reflects the same.

Final Poverty Lines and Poverty Head Count Ratio for 2009-10 Table 6

States	Poverty lines in ₹		Poverty Head Count Ratio in %		
	Rural	Urban	Rural	Urban	Total
Andhra Pradesh	693.8	926.4	22.8	17.7	21.1
Arunachal Pradesh	773.7	925.2	26.2	24.9	25.9
Assam	691.7	871	39.9	26.1	37.9
Bihar	655.6	775.3	55.3	39.4	53.5
Chatisgarh	617.0	806.7	56.1	23.8	48.7
Delhi	747.8	1040.3	7.7	14.4	14.2
Goa	931	1025.4	11.5	6.9	8.7
Gujarat	725.9	951.4	26.7	17.9	23.0
Haryana	791.6	975.4	18.6	23.0	20.1
Himachal Pradesh	708	888.3	9.1	12.6	9.5
Jammu Kashmir	722.9	845.4	8.1	12.8	9.4
Jharkhand	616.3	831.2	41.6	31.1	39.1
Karnataka	629.4	908	26.1	19.6	23.6
Kerala	775.3	830.7	12.0	12.1	12.0
Madhya Pradesh	631.9	771.7	42.0	22.9	36.7
Maharastra	743.7	961.1	29.5	18.3	24.5
Manipura	871	955	47.4	46.4	47.1
Meghalaya	686.9	989.8	15.3	24.1	17.1
Mizoram	850	939.3	31.1	11.5	21.1
Nagaland	1016.8	1147.6	19.3	25.0	20.9
Orissa	567.1	736	39.2	25.9	37.0
Pandichery	641	777.7	0.2	1.6	1.2
Punjab	830	960.8	14.6	18.1	15.9
Rajasthan	755	846	26.4	19.9	24.8
Sikkim	728.9	1035.2	15.5	5.0	13.1
Tamil Nadu	639	800.8	21.2	12.8	17.1
Tripura	663.4	782.7	19.8	10.0	17.4
Uttas Pradesh	663.7	799.9	39.4	31.7	37.7
Uttarakhand	719.5	898.6	14.9	25.2	18.0
West Bengal	643.2	830.6	28.8	22.0	26.7
All India	**672.8**	**859.6**	**33.8**	**20.9**	**29.8**

Source: Planning Commission press note March 2012: "Press Notes of Poverty Estimates, 2009-10 as quoted by "Datt and Sundharam's "Indian Economy" - (2012), Page: 407.

Estimate of Poverty in India - Rangarajan Committee Report - 2014 [Suresh Tendulkar's Report Rejected]

Estimate of poverty in India is one of the most controversial and confusing exercises for it involves political overtones. Very recently, **C. Rangarajan**, Member of Prime Minister's Economic Advisory Committee, in a press release at New Delhi, has stated that he was rejecting **Suresh Tendulkar's** Report after making a thorough study of the same.

According to **C. Rangarajan,** an urbanite in India with an average daily income of less than ₹ 47/- [₹ 1407/- per month] and a ruralite with less than ₹ 32/- [₹ 972/- per month] could be regarded as poor. His Report says that out of 10 people in India only 3 are found to be poor.

Rangarajan's Report also states that during 2009-10, the percentage of poor in India was around 38.2% and it came down to 29.5% in 2011-12.

Previously, **Suresh Tendulkar's Committee** in its Report had stated that the percentage of poor in India which was 29.8 in 2009-10 had come down to 21.9 in 2011-12. As per his Report, urban people having on an average a daily per capita income of less than ₹ 33/-, and rural people less than ₹ 27/- are considered to be poor. This Report, however, was severely criticised by the Parliamentarians, press and the public. ***Source:*** **'Hosa Diganta'**, Kannada Daily, Dated 8-7-2014.

4. CAUSES OF POVERTY

The causes of poverty are manysided. However, they may be discussed under the following heads : *(i) Individual incapacity, (ii) Economic factors, (iii) Social factors. (iv) Demographic factors, and (v) Other factors.*

(i) Individual Incapacity and Other Deficiencies

From the view point of the ideology of individualism, the individual failure itself is responsible for poverty. Success or failure in life, according to this ideology, is entirely a personal matter. Hence, it is logical to conclude that if an individual fails to achieve success in life and suffers from poverty, he himself is to be blamed for his laziness, inactivity, lack of initiative, dullness and incapacities. 'The Protestant Ethic' as described by Max Weber also emphasizes this aspect.

What factors contribute to individual incapacity ? : There are various causes for an individual's failure. Failure in life may be due to some inborn deficiencies such as physical or mental handicap, dumbness, deafness, blindness, feeblemindedness, deficient legs and hands, and so on. Some of the deficiencies might have been developed later in life. Since an individual does not have any control over many of these deficiencies, he is bound to yield to them and suffer from them. They make such an individual a parasite on society.

Some of the deficiencies which can be managed or overcome, are often neglected by some individuals and hence they fall a prey to the problem of poverty. We may include under this category, deficiencies such as illiteracy, laziness, extravagance, immorality, bad habits such as gambling, alcoholism, etc.

(ii) Economic Causes of Poverty

1. Inadequate Economic Development : Our economic development since independence has been disappointing in certain respects. The rate of growth of our economy between 1951-91 had been just 3.5% which is negligible. During the year 2004-05, though this rate of growth increased to 5%, it was not enough to fight the challenges of poverty. Our per capita income is still very less. It was around ₹ 255/- in 1950-51, and it increased to ₹ 19,649/- [at 1999-00 prices] in 2004-05. In comparison with other advanced countries, this is quite less.

2. Increasing Unemployment : Our economy has not provided enough employment opportunities for the people. Hence, unemployment is mounting. In 1952, the number of registered unemployed persons was about 4.37 lakhs and it increased to 334 lakhs in 1990. By December 1991, the figure had swelled to 36.3 millions. It further increased to 41.39 millions by the end of December, 2003.[4] But, Planning Commission itself stated that *"by the year 2000, A.D., the*

4. As per the estimates of **Bhagavathi Committee, 41.39** million people were waiting for jobs in the live registers of 945 employment exchanges scattered in different places in India.

*total number of job-seekers in India would be around **106** million"*. Fortunately, things have started improving and lot of employment opportunities are created especially for the educated youths since 2010 onwards.

3. Unmanageable Inflationary Pressures : Due to incessant inflation, the value of money has come down. It came down to 8.28 paise in 1990-91. The annual rate of inflation was estimated to be at 13.4% in 1991 and with great difficulty it was brought down to 7.3% in 1997. The value of rupee further decreased to 7.2 paise at 1960-61 prices. This uncontrolled inflation adversely affected the purchasing power of the common people.

4. Capital Deficiency : Industries require huge capital for their fast growth. But lack of enough capital has hampered the growth of our industries. The process of economic liberalization which has been let loose recently, has of course, started showing its positive results during these days. Time is not ripe to pass final judgements on its results.

5. Too much Dependence on Agriculture : Our economy is primarily an agrarian economy in the sense that more than 65% of the people are still dependent on agriculture. Agriculture has its own limitations. In India, in particular, people are following the traditional method of cultivation and hence agricultural production is comparatively very less.

(iii) Demographic Factors

Population in India is growing at an alarming rate. Within 60 years [1921-1981], it had doubled. It has reached an incredible number of 121.02 crore in 2011. Hence, the little progress that is achieved in the economic sphere is being eaten away by the growing population. Further, higher *dependency ratio* found in India is also adding to the gravity of the problem of poverty. As per 1998-99 estimate, 8% of the people [9.60 crores] are above 60 years and their capacity to contribute to economic production is limited. About 35.7% of the people are below 14 years of age and hence are incapable of earning.

The 2011 census, however, presents slightly a different picture. As per this census report, the proportion of population below 15 years is showing decline [from 34% in 2001 to 29% in 2011] whereas the proportion of elderly people in the country is increasing [from 7% in 2001 to 8% in 2011]. This means though the burden of feeding and maintaining young people is decreasing, the increase in the elderly population will impose a greater burden on the already outstretched health services in the country. A hopeful trend in this direction is that in the years to come, the dependency ratio is likely to come down further.

The size of the Indian family is relatively bigger. The average size of the Indian family is around 4.2. The growing size of the population has its adverse effects on people's health. A sizeable number of people are suffering from various diseases for which proper medical treatment is not available.

(iv) Social Causes

(a) ***Traditionalism :*** India is a land known for traditionalism, communalism, casteism, linguism, parochialism, religious and linguistic prejudices and so on. These factors have a negative effect on country's progress by making people dogmatic in their approach and narrow – minded and selfish in outlook.

(b) ***Illiteracy and Ignorance :*** Illiteracy and ignorance are supporting factors of poverty. By 2011, there were about 314.12 million illiterates in the country. Further, our defective educational system is incapable of helping to generate employment and there is no guarantee of job for the educated youths.

(c) ***Dominance of Caste and Joint Families :*** Our caste system still has its hold on the caste members. The caste system compels its members to stick on to the traditional and hereditary occupations of the caste. It does not give encouragement to the caste members to take up to jobs of their choices. In the very same manner, the joint families which are still dominant in the rural areas do not allow young members to take initiative in making new adventures in the employment and economic spheres.

(v) Other Causes

1. Long Period of Foreign Rule : India was under foreign rule for a very long period. The British who ruled India ruthlessly had systematically spoiled the basic economic structure of our land and destroyed various arts, crafts, cottage and small scale industries which we had developed previously. They exploited Indian resources for the glory of Britain and made Indians parasites in several respects.

2. Climatic Factors : Climate can also be a cause of poverty. It is said that the hot climate of India reduces the capacity of people to work, and hence, naturally, production cannot be increased in the desired quantity.

3. Wars and Threats of War : India had to spend huge amount of money on wars which she had fought with China and Pakistan. There is constant threat of war also. Hence huge amount of money is being spent on our defence industry. About 15% to 25% of national income was spent previously for defence purposes and it was reduced to 16.7% in 1989-90.

4. Defective Political System and Lack of Political Will : Indian political system is very often condemned as corrupt, inefficient and defective. Unhealthy competition among the political parties for power has many a times damaged our national interests. Our political leaders lack nationalistic fervour and the much needed will power to face the challenges that are confronting the nation. However, the present (2014) NDA Government headed by Narendra Modi as the Prime Minister, has created some new hopes for progress.

5. REMEDIAL MEASURES FOR POVERTY

The British did not bother about the poor condition of Indians as long as they ruled over India. When India became independent in 1947, it started paying more attention to the problem of poverty and undertook many measures and launched many schemes, programmes and projects for the removal of poverty. Here is a brief survey of such measures.

1. The Five Year Plans

The Indian Government set up the Planning Commission in 1950 and started the Five Year Plans with a view to develop the country in a methodical manner.

The First Five Year Plan [1951-56] had spent about ₹ 2378 crores for various developmental purposes and this amount had almost increased to 15.92 lakh crores in the 10th Five Year Plan, 2002-07. These Five Year Plans mainly aimed at – attaining self-reliance in agricultural production, removal of unemployment; achieving desirable progress in industry, increasing standard of living, and finally, at wiping out poverty.

The progress achieved through these Plans, though not satisfactory cannot be neglected. In the time span of about 40 years after Independence, India could achieve an annual economic growth of about 3% as against the world average of 4%. This annual growth rate, however, crossed 5.5% in the decade of 1980s, and the 10th Plan intended to achieve 8% growth of GDP. Between 1951-1991, the number of people living below the line of poverty has been reduced to about 28%. The 10th Plan poised to reduce it to 21% by 2007. The government is hopeful of achieving considerable progress especially in the industrial sector by means of implementation of the policy of economic liberalization.

2. Nationalisation

With a view to facilitate economic growth, 14 banks were nationalized in 1962, when Indira Gandhi was the Prime Minister of India. Afterwards in 1972, coal mines were nationalized and that was followed by government taking control of big private iron and steel company and wholesale business in food grains. Nationalisation did not provide the expected benefits. Lack of efficiency, initiative and commitment to the cause, have been the main casualities of the process of nationalization. Only in two areas, branch expansion and grant of loan to the weaker sections, the banks have achieved some progress. The overall performance of many of these banks is, far from satisfactory. Only during the recent years, these banks have started showing relatively good performances. The government now seems to have learnt that nationalization cannot be the panacea for all the problems and hence it is switching over to the opposite pole of privatization.

3. 20 Point Programme

During the period of emergency (1975-78), Indira Gandhi, the then Prime Minister of India, introduced the much publicized 20- point programme with the main intention of removing poverty (*"Garibi Hatao"*) and economic exploitation, and uplifting the weaker sections of the society.

Under this scheme ,number of programmes were included: *development of S.C., S.T., and other backward classes: distribution of surplus land to the weaker sections, providing minimum wages to the landless workers, providing irrigational facilities to the rural people and expanding their employment opportunities, family planning, extension of primary health services, welfare of women ,children and labourers, simplification of industrial policy, extension of primary education facilities, providing drinking water to all villages, etc.*

Though many of the programmes included under the 20 point programme were laudable, they could not be effectively implemented for want of honesty and commitment on the part of the government officials and political leaders. The programme could only create awareness among the weaker sections, and in various other respects, it was a failure.

4. Other Programmes for Employment Generation and Poverty Alleviation

Among other anti-poverty and employment generation programmes launched by the Government, the following ones deserve a special mention.[5]

(i) The JRY : Jawahar Rozgar Yojana 1989 : The JRY was introduced in the month of April 1989 with the intention of helping at least one member of each poorest family by providing employment for about 50 to 100 days in a year at his own work place or residential area. About 30% of the jobs under this programme are reserved for women. The expenditure of this Yojna is to be shared by the Centre and State at 80:20 ratio respectively. About 80% of the funds obtained by the Centre and State are to be utilized through the Gram Panchayats for helping the targeted beneficiaries. The rural wage employment programmes such as NREP and RLEGP were merged into the JRY.

As per the provision of this Yojna, Panchayats with a population ranging between 4000 to 5000 persons are given an annual financial assistance from ₹ **0.80** lakh to **1** lakh. But 30% of

---

5. It may be noted here that some of the schemes and programmes launched by the Government earlier were replaced by or got merged into the new ones. ***For example,*** the IRDP [*Integrated Rural Development Programme*] initiated in 1978-79 was replaced by the SGSY [*Swarna Jayanthi Gram Swarozgar Yojna*] in 1999; the NREP and RLEGP [*National Rural Employment Programme and Rural Landless Employment Guarantee Programme*] were merged into JRY that is Jawahar Rozgar Yojana in 1989; the EAS [*Employment Assurance Scheme*] got merged with the SGRY [*Sampoorna Grameena Rozgar Yojana*] and so on.

the money goes only for women. In the year 1990-91, about ₹ 500 crore was spent under this Yojna. It covers about 46% of the population.

In the 8th Plan, about ₹ 30,000 crore was allotted for rural development out of which JRY got about ₹ 18,400 crores. Apart from this Central assistance, the JRY got the state assistance of about ₹ 400 crore. In the year 1998-99, ₹ 2095 crore was allotted for the implementation of this Yojna and by the end of 1998, around 190 million mandays of employment was created for the needy people. This scheme has been implemented in 2,20,000 villages all over the country. In April 1999, in place of JRY the *Jawahar Gram Samriddhi Yojna* [JGSY] came into being.

(ii) Prime Minister's Rozgar Yojana [PMRY] – 1993 : This scheme launched in 1995, has the objective of making available self-employment opportunities to the educated unemployed youth. The PMRY is meant for educated unemployed youth with family income up to ₹ 40,000 per annum, in both urban and rural areas, for engaging in any economically viable activity.

(iii) Rural Employment Generation Programme [REGP] 1995 : With the objective of creating self-employment opportunities in the rural areas and small towns the REGP was launched in 1995. The scheme is being implemented by the KVIC, that is, *Khadi and Village Industries Commission.* The target of creating 25 lakh new jobs has been set for the REGP during the 10th Plan.

(iv) Swarnajayanthi Gram Swarozgar Yojana [SGSY] 1999 : The SGSY launched in April 1999 in place of the IRDP [Integrated Rural Development Programme], is the only self-employment programme currently being implemented. This scheme provides assistance to *'swarozgaris'* above the poverty line in the form of income-generating assets through bank credit and government subsidy. The scheme is being implemented on a 75:25 cost sharing between the Centre and the States. Since its inception, and up to April 2004, a total allocation of ₹ 6734 crore was made available for this scheme by the Centre and States.

(v) Pradhan Mantri Gramodaya Yojana [PMGY] 2000 : The PMGY was launched in 2000-2001 in all the states with the objective of achieving sustainable human development at the village level. Initially, it had five components namely; *primary health, primary education, rural shelter, rural drinking water and nutrition, and rural electrification.* The Central Assistance for this yojna amounted to ₹ 2800 crores for the period 2003-05.

(vi) Pradhan Mantri Gram Sadak Yojana [PMGSY] 2000 : Due to the initiative taken by Prime Minister **Atal Bihari Vajapayee**, this scheme came into force in December 2000 to provide connectivity to 1.6 lakh unconnected habitations with population of 500 persons or more in the rural areas by the end of the 10th plan. The scheme estimate indicated a requirement of ₹ 60,000 crores in the beginning. The present estimates reveal that it requires at least ₹ 1,30,000 crore for its achievement. It is being executed in all the States and Union Territories. The scheme is in force and about 88685 kms of rural roads have been taken up under this programme.

(vii) Sampoorna Grameen Rozgar Yojana [SGRY] – 2001 : This scheme came into force in Sept. 2001 by merging in it the on-going schemes of Jawahar Gram Samridhi Yojana [JGSY] and Employment Assurance Scheme [EAS]. This is open to all rural poor who are in need of wage employment and desire to do manual and unskilled work in and around the rural habitat. The programme is to be implemented through Panchayat Raj institutions. The cost–sharing of the scheme between the Centre and the States is in the ratio of 75:25. During the year 2003-04 alone an amount of ₹ 4,121 crore as cash component and about 50 lakh tones of food grains were released to the States / UTs.

(viii) Valmiki Ambedkar Awas Yojana [VAMBAY] 2001 : The VAMBAY, launched in December 2001, intends to find remedy to the horrible conditions of the urban slum dwellers living below the poverty line without adequate shelter. The Centre provides 50% subsidy to the states to implement this scheme. Since its inception up to December 2004, the Central Govt. has released a total subsidy of ₹ 753 crore.

(ix) National Food for Work Programme [NFWP] 2004 : This programme was launched on November 14th 2004 in 150 most backward districts of the country. Its objective was to intensify the generation of supplementary wage employment. It is open to those rural poor who are in need of wage employment and desire to do manual unskilled work. This programme is 100% centrally sponsored one and the food grains are supplied to the states freely. Rupees 2020 crore had been allocated for the programme in the year 2004-05 in addition to 20 lakh tones of food grains.

(x) Rural Housing Schemes 2004 : The Government has also launched rural housing schemes such as *Indira Awas Yojana* [IAY] which intend to provide dwelling units, free of cost, to the poor families of the Scheduled Castes, Scheduled tribes, freed bonded-labourers and also to those who are below the poverty line in the rural areas. Since its inception up to June 1st 2004, as many as 113.96 lakh houses have been constructed / upgraded by spending as much as ₹ 19,869 crore.

Conclusion

It is an indisputable fact that India still remains a poor country in spite of our various developmental projects, plans and programmes. An all-pervading problem like poverty cannot be removed all on a sudden. Governmental agencies and instruments alone cannot fix a master solution for it. People's active involvement in various developmental programmes is equally important. Above all, we require committed civil servants, dedicated bureaucrats, strong political leaders committed to the cause of nation and a 'general will' on the part of people to march ahead, facing the challenges of poverty.

RURAL POVERTY AND ITS MAGNITUDE

As per 2011 census report, about 68% of the people in India live in more than 6.40 lakh villages. Poverty, unemployment and over-population have been traditionally associated with rural India. Since majority of Indians live in villages, naturally majority of poor people are found in vilages only. All the study teams, private attempts, expert groups including the Planning Commission, have uniformly held the view that poverty is very acute in India. But the estimate of poverty and the criteria used for estimating poverty differ significantly from one study group to another.

Indian villages mainly depend upon agriculture and what it yields. As per 2005 statistics, for about 60 to 65% of the population, agriculture is the main source of livelihood but hardly around 28% of the national income is accrued out of agriculture. One main reason for this gap is the unequal distribution of agricultural land. About 10 - to - 20% of the landholders hold 70% of the total land and 50% of the landholders are marginal farmers with less than one hectare [a little less than 2.5 acres] of land. Thus, a large number of agriculturists are really poor. Any agenda for fighting poverty must address itself to the rural sector. Though our policy-makers have been stressing this point ever since we began our Five Year Planning System, we have not been able to deal with it effectively.

How to Draw the Line of Poverty?

How to decide who are poor? It is not that easy to interpret poverty and to decide the line of poverty. The concept of poverty is subjective also and hence individuals differ significantly in their view of poverty. Added to this, we do not have commonly acceptable criteria or measuring rod of poverty. Let us now consider the views of Planning Commission of India on this issue.

Magnitude or Extent of Rural Poverty:

Opinions of Minhas, Bardan, Dandekar and Rath on the Type of Rural Poverty

Unfortunately, the concepts of "*poverty*" and '*poverty line*' are not properly defined as yet. Hence, lot of controversy prevails over the estimate and extent of poverty. Economists like **Minhas, Bardan, Dandekar** and **Rath** have tried to identify the rural poor on the basis of the statistics available with the **NSS** - *National Sample Survey*. According to them, large number of the rural poor belong to the four groups mentioned below :

(i) Families of agricultural labourers which do not possess any landholdings. These people constitute 60% of the total agricultural labourers.

(ii) Families of agricultural labourers possesing or owning a very small landholding, [sometimes, less than 1/2 acre]. These families constitute 40% of the total agricultural labourer families.

(iii) Non-agricultural rural labourers including the rural artisans, and

(iv) Agriculturists who are self cultivating landholdings measuring less than 2 hectares.

The above mentioned view though gives some idea regarding rural poverty, it does not give a total picture of rural poverty as such.

Some More Views on Rural Poverty

According to **P.D. Oza**, in 1967-68, around 70% of the rural people, that is, nearly 289 million ruralites were living below the line of poverty.

- **Montek Ahluwalia** has expressed the opionion that in the decade of 1950 around 50% of the people were living below the poverty line and this percentage was decreased to 40 in 1960-61.
- **Dandekar** and **Rath** have stated that in 1960-61, around 63% of the people were living below the line of poverty.
- As per the estimate of "*Seventh Finance Commission*", around 225 million people were living below the line of poverty in the year 1970-71.
- The 6th Five Year Plan has stated that in the year 1978-79, around 260 million rural people were found to be poor.

Estimate of Poverty by Economic Survey of the Planning Commisssion (2002-03)

The report of the *Economic Survey of the Planning Commission (2002-2003)* brings to our attention that rural poverty has been consistently increasing [except in 1999 - 2000] both in terms of percentage and in number. The below mentioned Table - makes it clear that in the year 1999-2000, as many as 19.3 crore [193 million] people were living below the line of poverty. But the critics have said that the actual number of rural poor in 1990-2000 was more than 25 crore.

Extent of Poverty [Rural and Urban] : 2002 - 2003 — Table 7

Year	No. of Poor people in Millions		Percentage		Total	
	Rural	Urban	Rural	Urban	Percentage	In Millions
1973-74	261	60	56.4	49.0	54.9	321
1978	264	65	53.1	45.2	51.3	329
1983	252	71	45.7	40.8	44.5	323
1993-94	244	76	37.3	32.4	36.0	320
1999-2000	193	67	27.1	23.6	26.10	260

***Source** : Economic Survey - 2002-03 Planning Commission.*

Interpretation of the 'Poor' by the Planning Commission

• According to the Planning Commission of India, those who consume less than 2400 calories of food in the rural areas and less than 2100 calories in the urban areas could be regarded as "*poor*".

It means, those who spend [at 1984-85 prices] on an average ₹ 107/- per month for their food in the rural areas and those who spend ₹ 122/- in the urban areas for the same, can be called "*poor*".

• As per the press note issued by the Planning Commission in **March 2012**, percentage of poor living below the line of poverty has come down to 29.8% in 2009-10. According to the same press release, a ruralite spending on food per day on an average ₹ 22.42 [or ₹ 672.60 per month] and an urbanite spending ₹ 28.35 per day [or ₹ 850.50 per month] could be regarded as poor. According to this calculation or interpretation, the percentage of rural poor which was 37.2 in 2004-05 has come down to 29.9 in 2011-12, denoting almost 7.3% decrease. This interpretation of poverty came under heavy attack and criticism both inside and outside the Parliament.

CAUSES FOR AND SOLUTIONS TO RURAL POVERTY

Causes for Rural Poverty

Various factors have been contributing to rural poverty among which the following may be noted.

1. Enormous increase in rural population on the one hand and unempolyment, on the other, have caused poverty.
2. Ineffective and inadequate implementation of anti-poverty programmes.
3. Lack of skills on the part of the ruralities has made many to depend on agriculture alone but not on non-agricultural pursuits.
4. Low agricultural productivity resulting from dependence on traditional methods of cultivation and inadequate knowledge of modern skills.
5. Vagaries of monsoon and lack of irrigational facilities.
6. Defective implementation of land reforms and the continuatin of Zamindari system in many places even now.
7. Vast rural unemployment and striking diferences between the rich and poor.
8. Non-availability of electricity for agricultural as well as industrial use in most of the villages.
9. Total neglect of small scale and cotage industries, rural crafts, etc., and failure to obtain supporting side income.
10. Lack of link roads, communication facilities and markets, in brief, lack of adequate infrastructure.
11. Failure to seek women's co-operation in developmental activities and associating them with planned programmes.
12. Widespread illiteracy in the rural areas, and the total neglect of education of women.
13. Poor quality of livestock and failure to domestricate hybrid varieties of livestock.
14. Poor marketing facility and the exploitative nature of the credit market.
15. Absence of dynamic leadership in the village and widespread groupism, factionalism and casteism.
16. Intercaste conflicts and rivaliries have also damged community spirit of the rural people.
17. Wasteful spending of huge sums of money on social ceremonies like marriage, death feast, etc. and the unwillingness of the people to stop the practice of these expensive customs.

Some Suggestions for Alleviating Rural Poverty

Achieving high rate of rural development is a sine quo non for the progress of the nation. To achieve rural progress, rural poverty has to be effectively dealt with. Hence, for reducing rural poverty, the following strategies or suggestions be given serious consideration.

1. Land reforms must be properly implemented and Zamindari system in all its forms must be done away with.
2. Expansion of infrastructure facilities into the rural areas which has hither to been confined to the urban areas.
3. Development of irrigational facilities and there should be a final full stop for the total dependence of agriuclture on the monsoon.
4. Developing human resources by focussing on education, health and skill programmes.
5. Activating co-operative societies for selling products of household industries.
6. Giving encouragement to the formation and functioning of self-help groups, *stree - shakthi* groups, and strengthening the micro-finance system.
7. Making allocations in poverty alleviating programmes [PAPs] flexible and feasible, and sanctioning special allocations to districts/blocks/and villages depending on their socio-economic conditions. Due incentives and encouragements are to be given to rural units that show good performances in the PAP fronts.
8. Integrating varied PAPs in one or two major schemes and making the availability of benefits easier.
9. Regulating and controlling the growth of rural population by giving proper publicity and propaganda regarding the benefits of having small families with less number of children.
10. Creating social awareness among the people regarding the evil effects of alcoholism,. gambling, superstition, casteism, etc..
11. Activating Panchayats to focus on adult education programme, road constructions and maintaining free plantations.
12. Giving encouragement to cottage and small scale industries, rural crafts etc. and creating proper marketing facility for the products.
13. Providing cheap power supply for agricultural and industrial use.
14. Giving greater encouragement for the industries and service sector so that the greater dependence on agriculture could be lessened or minimised.
15. Strengthening credit disbursing agencies.
16. Improving animal husbandry and developing dairy and poultry farming.
17. Encouraging and persuading big industries and I-T companies to adopt specially backward villages so that vast improvement could be made in these villages.

URBAN POVERTY

Despite India's venture to achieve economic progress, poverty in general and urban poverty in particular, continue to haunt the Indian society. There is poverty in both urban and rural sectors. Scholars however, differ in their estimate and interpretation of poverty.

Indian Urban Poverty Report - 2009

Urban poverty seems to be the by product of industrialised towns and cities. Poverty and overcrowding are the two most visible features of the industrial slums. "*Ministry of Housing and Urban Poverty Alleviation, Govt of India*" [in association with the **UNDP** : (United Nation's Development Programme)] has prepared its very first report in 2009 consisting of details about the nature, dimension, dynamics and magnitude of urban poverty. This Report came to be known as ***"Indian Urban Poverty Report - 2009",*** and it consists of the views of research scholars, academicians, and representatives of civil society. Main points revealed by this Report may be stated below.

Nature, Dimensions and Dynamics of Urban Poverty - 2009 - as per the Report

The **Report-2009** identifies the problems faced by the urban poor and focuses on the systemic changes that are needed to address them. The report observed that "*the pace of urbanisation in India is set to increase, and with it, urban poverty and urban slums also, despite 62% of GDP now being generated in towns and cities*". The report examines various issues related to urban poverty such as migration, labour, the role of gender, access to basic services and the horrible condition of urban slums. It also looks at the dynamics of urban land and capital market, urban governance, and the marginalisation of the poor to the urban periphery. The Report predicts that by 2030, urbanisation in India is likely to reach 50% of its population.

Observations of the Urban Poverty Report - 2009

1. ***Increase in Urban Population is Associated with an Increase in Poverty*** : Urban population in India is consistently increasing. This means that economic reforms have not been effective in creating jobs in small and medium towns as well as rural areas. As per 2011 census, 31.16% of the total population lives in towns and cities as against 28% in 2001. With an increase in urban population, urban poverty is also increasing. More than 25% of urban population, that is nearly 80 million people [according to some other estimates it is nearly 50%] are living in poverty and most of them are concentrated in big cities.

- ***Urbanisation of Poverty*** : As per the reports given by some states, urban poverty is much higher than rural poverty. This trend has often been glorified in terms of "*urbanisation of poverty*". Though at the national level, rural poverty has greater magnitude, the gap between urban and rural poverty is lessening during the recent years.

2. ***The Apparent [Negative Externalities or] Problems of Urban Poverty*** : Unlike rural poverty, urban poverty poses different problems by imposing certain negative externalities on the urban society. Urban poverty poses distinct challenges of housing, scarcity of drinking water, sanitation, health, education, social security, livelihoods and special needs of vulnerable groups such as women, children and the aged.

3. ***Poverty Level Differs with the Size of the Town or City*** : A survey relating to urban poverty reveals that poverty is relatively greater in small towns than in the medium size towns and mega cities. Based on this reality, it is often said that the "*metro and mega cities are the sustaining mechanisms of development*". As this survey report states, in terms of the provision of basic facilities, employment opportunities, productivity, rewards obtainable for education, etc. bigger cities are difinitely better than the smaller ones.

4. ***Migrants in Cities Have Better Economic Position than the Native Urban Poor-?*** : A very recent survey has revealed an interesting fact about urban poverty. According to this report, on the basis of poverty index, it could be said that at present, the rural people who have migrated to the cities seem to have better economic position than the urban native poor people. In the light of this "*reality*", it is even suggested that it is advisable to encourage migration towards cities in order to lessen its intensity in the rural areas.

5. ***Migration and its Relationship with Urban Poverty*** : Between 1961 and 1991 the rate of migration was very less in India, but from 1991-to-2001 and onwards, it has been consistently increasing. Migration implies here, migration from small villages to cities and from small towns towards bigger cities. Economic and educational interests seem to be the motivating factors behind most of these migrations.

6. ***The Possibility of Workers in the Informal and Unorganised Sector Succumbing to Urban Poverty*** : As far as the poor workers in the informal sector are concerned, they are very much lagging behind in making use of the growing employment opportunities in the city due to their poor educational background and lack of skills. This helplessness has compelled them to embrace poverty.

7. ***Concentration of Urban Poor in the Slums*** : As it is observed in most of the cities, poor people normally concentrate in poorly equipped areas namely, slums. These slum dwellers lack access to basic services. Most slum dwellers do not have access to clean water, sanitation and healthcare facilities. They face a constant threat of eviction, removal, confiscation of goods and have virtually no social security cover.

Proposed Solutions to the Removal of Urban Poverty

Proposed solutions to urban poverty include the following:

1. ***Equity in the Provision of Basic Facilities*** : Proposed solutions to urban poverty include a greater equity in the provision of basic services avoiding all types of interstate, intercity and interdistrict inequalities or differences.

2. ***Special Assistance to Small and Medium Towns*** : Special government assistance is required to strengthen the economic bases of small and medium towns in order to prevent the migration of people towards bigger cities from smaller towns.

3. ***Strengthening the Constitutional Amendments*** : **74th** Constitutional Amendment which was brought forth to favour administrative decentralisation cannot do any magic by itself. It has to be supported and strengthened in its implementation so that better facilities are provided to the poor and vulnerable section of the city population.

4. ***Proper Organisation of Slum Communities*** : Large number of people living in slums cannot be driven out. As the survey report says, slum communities are to be organised and facilities such as provision of sewage system, electricity, public toilets, drinking water, sanitation, healthcare and security etc. are to be provided on priority basis.

5. ***Provision of Housing Facility*** : As per "*The Urban Housing and Habitat Policy - 2007*", housing is the most important need of the people next only to food and clothing. Due importance is to be given for urban housing.

6. ***Controlling Criminal Life*** : Slums are also found to be places where criminal activities take place on a large scale. Poverty and criminality often [though not always] go together. Provision of electricity facility may help to reduce criminal, immoral and anti-social activities that normally take place during night in the absence of proper lighting facility. City administration must be strong enough to suppress criminal activities.

The Report - 2009 will prove to be an important contribution to the re-evaluation of the existing urban policies and programmes to reduce urban poverty. Combining data with case studies, it will be useful for policy-makers, urban planners and researchers in the fileds of urbanisation and development studies.

SOME VITAL STATISTICS OF SPECIAL IMPORTANCE

(A) Infrastructure : Some Statistics Relating to Infrastructure in India and other Countries – 2003 — Table - 1

Country	Investment in Infrastructure as a % GDP	Access to Safe Drinking Water (%)	Access to Improved Sanitation (%)	Mobile Users/1000 People	Phone Lines/1000 People	Power Generation (kw 1000)
China	20	75	38	66	113	230
Hong Kong	4	100	100	817	560	1630
India	**5**	**84**	**28**	**4**	**33**	**107**
Korea	7	92	63	583	449	1067
Pakistan	2	90	62	2	20	109
Singapore	5	100	100	684	528	1887
Indonesia	14	76	66	18	28	97

Source: World Development Report, 2005, The World Bank Washington DC – 2004.

Note: Development of infrastructure and economic development go hand in hand. Infrastructure is the foundation of development. In this regard, India is still lagging behind. Table shows that India invests only 5% of its GDP on infrastructure whereas China [20%], Korea [7%] and Indonesia [14%] are investing more than this. India which intends to become third biggest economy in the world will have to develop its infrastructure.

Trends in Sectoral Share of Commercial Energy [Oil, Gas, Electricity, Thermal, Nuclear, Wind Power, etc.] Consumption in India in terms of Percentage — Table - 2

Sector	1953-54	1970-71	1990-91	1996-97
Household	10	12	12	12
Agriculture	01	03	08	09
Industries	40	50	45	42
Transport	44	28	22	22
Others	5	07	13	15
Total	**100**	**100**	**100**	**100**

Source: Ninth Five Year Plan, Vol. II, Chapter-6, Planning Commission, Govt. of India, New Delhi.

Note: Continued economic development and population growth demand more energy than what India is producing now. Hence, more public investment, better research and development, efforts, exploration, technological innovation and use of renewable energy sources, etc., are the needs of the hour.

Per Capita Income and Per Capita Consumption of Energy in Some Countries – A Comparison — Table - 3

Country	Per Capita Income (in US dollars) in 2003 (ppp*)	Per Capita Consumption of Energy (Kg of oil equivalent) in 2001
India	2,880	515
Indonesia	3,210	729
Egypt	3,940	737
U.K.	27,650	3982
Japan	28,620	4099
U.S.A.	37,500	7996

[Energy Consumption as an Indicator of Development]

Sources: World Development Report – 2005 and World Development Indicators – 2004.
[**PPP = Purchasing Power Parities:* The PPP is used world wide to compare the income levels in different countries and monitor the incidence of poverty and track progress towards development.]

Indicators of Health in India in Comparison with Other Countries — Table - 4

Health Indicators	India	China	USA	Sri Lanka
Infant Mortality Rate/1,000 live births	68.00	30.00	2.00	8.00
Under-5 mortality/1,000 live-births	87.00	37.00	8.00	15.00
Birth by skilled attendants	43.00	97.00	99.00	97.00
Fully immunised	67.00	84.00	93.00	99.00
Health expenditure as % of GDP	1.40	5.80	14.60	3.70
Government health spending to total government spending (%)	5.00	10.00	23.10	6.00
Per capita spending in international dollars	96.00	261.00	5274.00	131.00

Sources: World Health Report 2005 and Economic Survey – 2007-08.

Note: Explanation for Table-4 and Table-5 are given together in page: 45 under Table-5.

Public Health Infrastructure in India 1951 – 2000 — Table - 5

Item	1951	1981	2000
Hospitals	2694	6805	15888
Hospital / Dispensary beds	117000	504538	719861
Dispensaries	6600	16745	23065
PHCs	725	9115	22842
Subcentres	-	84736	137311
CHCs	-	761	3043

Sources: National Commission on Macroeconomics and Health.
Ministry of Health and Family Welfare. Government of India. New Delhi, 2005.

Note: Indicators of Health and Health Infrastructure as reflected in Table No.4 and 5 reveal that India is far behind of many other countries. Reasons are obvious. Less than 20% of the population in India utilise public health facilities. As per one study, only 38% of the PHCs have the needed number of doctors; and only 30% of them have enough stock of medicines. Only 1/5th of the hospitals are located in rural areas where 70% of the people live. Rural India has only about half the number of dispensaries that it requires. In rural areas 24% of people do not have any medical care [in 2003]. More than 50% of married women between the age group of 15 and 49 have anaemia, and this has contributed to 19% of maternal deaths. For improving the quality of life and to increase productivity and achieve development - health infrastructure has to be readically improved in India.

(B) Comparative Development Experience of Three Nations : India, China and Pakistan Select Demographic Indicators, 2000-01 — **Table – 6**

Country	Estimated Population (in millions)	Annual Growth of Population (1990-2003)	Density (per sq. km)	Sex Ratio	Fertility Rate	Urbanisation
India	1103.6	1.7	358	933	3.0	27.8
China	1303.7	1.0	138	937(*)	1.8	36.1
Pakistan	162.4	2.5	193	922	5.1	33.4

Note: (*) data exclude population of Hong Kong, Macao and Taiwan provinces.

Sectoral Share of Employment and GDP (%) — **Table – 7**

Sector	Contribution to GDP (2003)			Distribution of Workforce		
	India	China	Pakistan	India (2000)	China (1997)	Pakistan (2000)
Agriculture	23	15	23	60	54	49
Industry	26	53	23	16	27	18
Service	51	32	54	24	19	37
	100	**100**	**100**	**100**	**100**	**100**

Note: The contribution of the three sectors to India's GDP in 2009 stands approximately as follows - Agriculture - 18%, Industry - 20%, Services - 62%

Trends in Output Growth in Different Sectors, 1980-2003 — **Table – 8**

Country	1980-90			1990-2002/03		
	Agriculture	Industry	Service	Agriculture	Industry	Service
India	3.1	7.4	6.9	2.7	6.6	7.9
China	5.9	10.8	13.5	3.9	11.8	8.8
Pakistan	4.0	7.7	6.8	3.7	3.9	4.3

Growth of Gross Domestic Product (%), 1980-2003 — **Table – 9**

Country	1980-90	1990-2002/03
India	5.7	5.8
China	10.3	9.7
Pakistan	6.3	3.6

Note:

Development experience of the three countries India, China and Pakisthan [as reflected in Tables 6th to - Table 10th] reveals that till the late 1970s, all of them were maintaining the same level of low development. The last three decades have taken them to different levels.

India with democratic institutions, performed moderately; but a large number of its people still depend on agriculture. Infrastructure is lacking in many parts of the country. More than 1/4 of its people are to be lifted above the poverty line. In the recent years, it is hoping to achieve higher rate of GDP growth.

For **Pakisthan**, it was a big challenge to recover from the devastating earthquake in 2005 which took the lives of 75000 people and damaged property worth crores of rupees.

In **China**, the lack of political freedom has its own implications. Unlike, India and Pakisthan, which are attempting to privatise their public sector enterprises, China has used the market mechanism to create additional social and economic opportunities. It has maintained its high growth rate in industrial sector while it is not so in India and Pakisthan. Reforms were introduced as early as 1978 in China, whereas in Pakisthan and India, they were introduced in 1988 and 1991 respectively. In all the three countries, majority of workforce depends on agriculture. China opted to shift its developmental pattern from agriculture to manufacturing and then to services, whereas India and Pakisthan preferred to shift it directly from agriculture to service sector. China is defnitely ahead of India and Pakisthan on many human development indicators.

Some Selected Indicators of Human Development, 2003 **Table - 10**

Items	India	China	Pakistan
Human Development Index (Value)	0.602	0.755	0.527
Rank	127	85	135
Life-Expectancy at birth (Years)	63.3	71.6	63.0
Adult literacy rate (% aged 15 and above)	61.0	90.9	48.7
GDP per capita (PPP US$)	2.892	5.003	2.097
People below poverty line (%)	34.7	16.6	13.4
Infant Mortality Rate (Per 1000 live births)	63	30	81
Maternal Mortality Rate (Per 1 lakh births)	540	56	500
Population with sustainable access to improved sanitation (%)	30	44	54
Population with sustainable access to improved water souce (%)	86	77	90
Population undernourished (% of total)	21	11	20

Sources: Human Development Report 2005

●●●

Chapter 3

UNEMPLOYMENT PROBLEM

Unemployment- A Global Phenomenon - What is Unemployment ? - Magnitude of Unemployment in India - Some Estimates of Unemployment in India - Some Salient Features of Unemployment Problem in India - Types of Unemployment - Causes of Unemployment : Individual or Personal Factors of Unemployment - External Factors or Technological and Economic Factors - Effects OR Impact of Unemployment - Remedial Measures and Suggestions - Employment Prospects Under the 11th Plan : Generation of Employment Opportunities by Information Technology [IT] - Employment Guarantee Act - 2005 - Probable Cost of Employment Guarantee Programme - Critical Remarks About the Programme

Unemployment-a Global Phenomenon

Along with the problem of poverty, unemployment is also widespread in India. It is indeed, common to all the countries of the world whether they are industrially advanced or not. An international labour expert thus commented; (in September 1992) – *"About 400 million new workers are expected to enter the world's labour force this decade and prospects of finding jobs for all of them are gloomy"*. This gloomy picture of unemployment still continues though with some less intensity.

The Finnish director of the *International Labour Organization's* (ILO) employment department, **Juhani Lonnroth,** has said in one of his speeches that *"the population of the working age in the world will grow by 700 million people in the 1990s . With the conserving assumption that 55% of these people will seek employment, about 400 million jobs will have to be created to absorb the new entrants. Unfortunately, the prospects of achieving these rates of job creation are not yet very bright"*. The problem is, of course, more acute for Asian countries rather than for the African and Latin American countries because of the serious population explosion in these countries. India with its huge population, thus cannot be an exception.

What is Unemployment-?

- *"Unemployment is a state of worklessness for a man fit and willing to work, that is, it is a condition of involuntary and not voluntary idleness."*- **C.B. Mamoria.**
- Unemployment is defined as *"a condition in which an individual is not in a state of remunerative occupation despite his desire do so."* - **D'Mello.**
- Unemployment is often described as a *"condition of involuntary idleness."* – **Nava Gopal Das.**
- ***In simple words,*** it could be said that *unemployment is largely concerned with those men and women who constitute the labour force of the country, who are able-bodied and willing to work but are not gainfully employed.*

- *Unemployment is a situation characterised by the existence of those able bodied persons who are willing to work but do not get jobs which may yield them some regular income.*

MAGNITUDE OR ESTIMATES OF UNEMPLOYMENT IN INDIA

Though the problem of unemployment is growing in an unmanageable proportion we do not have authentic information regarding the exact number of unemployed persons in India. It is regrettable that institutions such as *Planning Commission; National Sample Survey*, and the *Central Statistical Organization* (or the *Indian Statistical Institute*) have not made any systematic and satisfactory attempt to collect authentic information about unemployment.

Three Sources of Information Regarding the Extent of Unemployment : We have, however, three sources to collect some statistics regarding the extent of unemployment in India. They are : *(i) The National Census* which is held once in ten years; *(ii) The National Sample Survey;* and *(iii) The Employment Exchange Registrations.* Of these, information collected through the National Sample Survey is being used widely. Neither the *Census Reports*, nor the *Directorate - General of Employment and Training* [D.G.E.T], nor the *Employment Exchanges* nor any other agency, could give any dependable quantitative estimate of the magnitude of the problem.

The statistics which we obtain through these three sources cannot be considered as highly authentic and foolproof. Many a times, they are to be treated only as approximations or rough estimates. These estimates very often take into consideration the number of persons registered in the employment exchange and these exchanges cover mainly the urban areas. Rural areas are not covered by them. Since registration with the employment exchange is voluntary, all the unemployed do not go for registration. Further, some people who are already in some ordinary jobs also go for registration for they intend to secure some good jobs. These exchanges may not supply full information about people who are "unemployed".

- **Some Estimates of Unemployment in India**

(i) The number of unemployed persons in India registered in the employment exchanges in 1952 was 4.37 lakhs and it increased to 334 lakhs in 1990.[1]

(ii) Between 1952 and 1970, that is, within the time interval of 18 years, the number of registered unemployed persons had increased about 8 times; and between 1971 and 1990 it got increased by 6.8 times . By the end of December 1991, the number of unemployed people had reached 36.3 million.[2]

(iii) Estimates of Bhagavathi Committee

As per the estimates of this Committee, there were 18.7 million unemployed persons in the country in 1971 out of which 16.1 million were in rural areas and 2.6 million in urban areas.

As per the figures for 2003, about **41.39** million individuals were waiting (for jobs) in the live registers of 945 employment exchanges scattered over the whole nation.

(iv) ***NSSO Estimates*** : As per the 55th NASSO Round of reports (1999-2000), the absolute number of unemployed increased from 20 million in 1993-94 to 27 million in 1999-2000. Out of this 27 million unemployed individuals, 7.11 million were in urban areas and 19.50 million people were in rural areas.

(v) ***Planning Commission Estimates of 8th and 9th Plan*** : *"The total number of persons requiring employment during the 8th Plan (as per the estimates of Planning Commission) would be around 65 million. It is expected that during 1995-2000, labour force would increase by 41*

---

1. ***Source***: *"India Today"*, May 31, 1991.
2. ***Source*** : Manorama Year Book-1993.

*million. **Thus, by the year 2000 A.D., the total number of job-seekers would be around 106 million.**"*[3]

- **Some Salient Features of Unemployment Problem in India**

We may identify the following as some special features of unemployment in India.

Table – 1 : PROJECTION OF UNEMPLOYMENT FOR 1990-2000	
	Millions
1. Backlog of unemployed in the beginning of 1990	- 28
2. New entrants to the labour force during 1990-95	- 37
Total unemployed for the 8th plan [1+2]	- 65
3. New entrants to the labour force during 1995-2000	- 41
4. Total unemployed for the 9th Plan (2000 AD)	**- 106**
Source : Compiled from the Planning Commission.	

1. Unemployed people are not equally distributed in all the states of India. *For example,* more than half the total unemployed persons live in three states of northern India [as per the statistics of 1990s] that is, West Bengal, Bihar, and U.P. and two states of south India, that is Kerala and Tamilnadu.
2. As per the Census report of 1991, excepting rural Kerala and urban Orissa in almost all other places, there has been an increase in the number of female employees. Of the total number of women of employable age, about 19.19% in the rural areas and about 8.63% in the urban areas were found to be full fledged employees.
3. In spite of this increase in the number of female employees, unemployment rates for women are higher than those for men.
4. The incidence of unemployment is relatively lower in rural areas and higher in urban areas and this situation is slowly getting reversed nowadays.
5. There is greater unemployment in agricultural sector than in industrial and other sectors.
6. The incidence of unemployment among the educated is much higher (about 12%) than overall unemployment that is found in the nation [that is 3.8%].
7. Finally, the growth of employment per annum is about 2 per cent.

TYPES OF UNEMPLOYMENT

We may speak of different types of unemployment such as the following : *seasonal unemployment, agricultural unemployment, frictional and technological unemployment, industrial unemployment, cyclical unemployment, educational unemployment, voluntary unemployment, involuntary unemployment or under–employment, open unemployment and disguised unemployment.*

1. Seasonal Unemployment

Seasonal unemployment is very much associated with agriculture. During the off- season, many agricultural labourers will have to spend their time idly without having any work .In some industries such as sugar, woollen and ice factories, workers get jobs only for a certain period of the year or in a particular season. When the season is over, they don't get work in the factories and they will have to wait for the next season to come to find the same work. This type of unemployment may often make the labourers to become migratory in character.

2. Agricultural Unemployment

Agricultural unemployment is caused by a number of factors such as the very seasonal nature of agricultural work, the decay of cottage industries, lack of demand for homemade products, lack of alternative work in the rural areas, sub-division of land holdings, etc. **R.K. Mukherjee** has said in his *"Rural Economy of India"* that on an average, a cultivator in north India does not remain busy for more than 200 days in a year.

---

3. **Ruddar Datt** and **K.P.M. Sundharam** in "*Indian Economy*" (2008 edition) Page : 38.7

THE UNABATED UNEMPLOYMENT PROBLEM

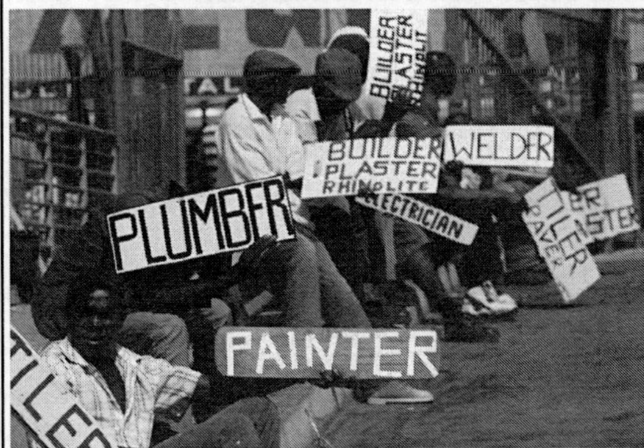

Studies have revealed that *"of the total population in the rural areas, only 29.4% people are self supporting, 59.0% are non–earning dependents, and 11.6% are earning dependents. This means that 29.4% people not only support themselves but they also support the remaining 70.6% people as well".*[4]

3. Technological and Frictional Unemployment

Sometimes, in the technological field ***'friction'*** is caused due to an imbalance between *the supply of labour and the demand for it*. This friction does not allow the potentialities of the labour to be tapped. Even though unemployed workers are there ready to work, they may not be fit for the work, or they may not have the required skill and qualification to do the work. Since the demand of the customers is constantly shifting from one product to another, it becomes difficult for workers to catch up with the tastes and choices of the workers. Such shifts in consumer demand may make certain factories to be closed down leaving behind a trail of unemployment.

Technological unemployment is caused mainly because of the introduction of labour–saving machines. It is caused due to the reduction of man power necessary to produce a finished article. The process of automation and mechanization have caused great anxieties and insecurities for workers displacing good number of them from work. Introduction of computers in the beginning stages can be cited here as an example. Every advance in technology virtually means today, displacement of human labour to some or the other extent.

4. Industrial Unemployment

Industrial unemployment is caused in another manner. Due to high pressure of people on land, a large number of rural people are moving towards urban areas in search of jobs in some factories or the other, only to get disappointment in a short time. Slow growth of industries, competition with foreign industries, unplanned industrialization, defective industrial policies, labour strikes or employer's lock-out, rationalization, etc., may also cause industrial unemployment.

5. Cyclical Unemployment

Due to the *"trade cycles"*; booms, recessions and depressions are common in the business world. Such ups-and-downs in business influence the volume of unemployment which decreases when trade is good and increases when it is bad. If depression continues for a longer period (like the *Great Depression* of 1925-30) it adversely affects the labourers by turning them out of job or by providing no fresh job opportunities.

6. Educational Unemployment

There is a close link between the job opportunities and the system of education. In fact, in one of its annual report, the UGC (University Grants Commission) itself has commented that the present system of education is *"generating much waste and stagnation"*. The ***Kothari Commission*** (1964-66) had admitted long back that there is a wide gulf between *"the contents of the present education and purposes and the concerns of national development"*. Even after 1966, thorough overhauling of our educational system to make it relevant to the needs and demands of the time, has not been made. Hence, every year we are producing thousands of degree- holders only to join the rank of the educated unemployed youths. *For example,* in 1965 there were 9 lakh unemployed graduates in the country, and the number increased to 5.6 million in 1977. The figure of educated unemployed persons in the nation was 34,66,435 as on November 30th 1991. West Bengal has the largest number of educated unemployed persons (degree holders) in the country (27.21% of the total unemployed) followed by Bihar (24.85%), Kerala (21.10%) and Karnataka (18.49%).

---

4. Ref. **Ram Ahuja in his** *"Social Problem in India"* -Page : 70.

7. Temporary Unemployment

Our young men and women who are capable of securing for themselves some jobs, do not get them soon after their education. Many of them are made to wait for some time during which they remain as unemployed. People often change their jobs, and in the interval of changing they may remain as unemployed for a short period.

8. Voluntary Unemployment

Voluntary unemployment is found when the worker voluntarily withdraws himself from the work. He may do so due to the quarrel with the employer, or he may have other sources of income. This condition is relatively rare and hence this type of unemployment is not given much importance.

9. Involuntary Unemployment or Under-employment

Lord Keynes uses the concept of involuntary unemployment for under-employment. *It refers to a condition in which the self–employed working people are not working to their full capacity.* People who are partially employed, or are doing inferior jobs while they could do better jobs are not adequately employed. It can be called a state of *"under-employment"*.

10. Open Unemployment or Structural Unemployment

Open unemployment is also called *"structural unemployment"*. It is the result of lack of complementary resources especially capital. *Open unemployment is a situation wherein a large labour force does not get work opportunities that may fetch them regular income.* Open unemployment is the result particularly when a large reserve army of labour exists which does not find any income-fetching job. Open unemployment emerges because the rate of capital accumulation lags behind the rate of population growth.

11. Disguised Unemployment

Disguised unemployment is that type of unemployment which cannot be seen or known from outside. It is concealed or hidden. *It refers to a situation in which men or women work the whole day but fail to make any contribution to the total out put.* It is a state of affair in which a person's marginal productivity or contribution is close to zero. This type of unemployment is very much acute and apparent in the rural area. *For example,* of the **10** people who have been working in a piece of land, even if **3** persons migrate to cities, the productivity of the land does not get affected. This shows that the contribution of the 3 persons to productivity is virtually zero.

CAUSES OF UNEMPLOYMENT

The problem of unemployment is becoming a colossal one. Various factors, individual as well as social, have caused this problem. Here the causation is not one-sided. *For example,* unemployment is often the cause of poverty and some other time, its consequence also. Hence, tracing the causes of unemployment is a difficult task.

C.B. Mamoria lists out the causes of unemployment in India in the following way :

(i) The policy of *"laissez-faire"* or free trade pursued by the British did not accelerate the process of industrialization in India. As a result, employment opportunities could not be generated on a large scale, during the British rule. This situation continued up to the end of their rule in India.

(ii) The unchecked growth of population from 1921 onwards posed the problems of finding job opportunities. *For example,* our population in 1921 was 251.3 millions and it increased to 361.0 millions in 1951. It has reached a record figure of 121.019 crore in 2011.

(iii) The decline of traditional skills and the decay of small scale and cottage industries led to a great pressure on land and this in turn resulted in the greater exodus of people from the rural to the urban areas. This added to urban unemployment.

(iv) The low level of investment and the neglect of industrial sector could not help the process of creating job opportunities.

G.R. Madan speaks of two main causes of unemployment : (A) *"individual or personal factors"*, and (B) *"external factors"* or *"technological and economic factors"*.

A. Individual or Personal Factors of Unemployment

(i) Age Factor : Age factor fixes limitations on the range of choice of job opportunities. Too young and too old people are not eligible for many of the jobs. Some young people due to their inexperience, and some old people due to their old age, fail to get some jobs. Young people do not get jobs soon after their studies. They will have to wait. People who are above 60 or 70 years are less adaptable and more prone to accidents. Their capacity to contribute to economic production is also relatively less.

(ii) Vocational Unfitness : Many of our young people do not have a proper understanding of their own aptitudes, abilities and interests on the one hand, and the tasks or jobs or career they want to pursue, on the other. If willingness to do some job is not followed by the required abilities and skills one cannot find a job of one's selection. Employers are always looking forward to find persons who have the ability, experience, interest and physical fitness to work. Sometimes, there may be more men trained in a particular profession than required. The demand is less than the supply, and hence, unemployment.

(iii) Illness and / or Physical Disabilities or Incapabilities : Due to the inborn or acquired disabilities or deficiencies some remain as partially employed or totally unemployed throughout their life. Illness induced by industrial conditions and the fatal accidents that often take place during the work may render a few other people as unemployed.

B. External Factors or Technological and Economic Factors

(i) Enormous Increase in Population : The population in India is growing at an alarming rate. It has already reached a record mark of **121.019** crore by 2011. Every year India adds to her population 120 to 130 lakh people afresh. More than this, every year about 5 million people become eligible for securing jobs. All these people who are eligible to work are not getting the jobs. Hence, population explosion in India is making the problem of unemployment more and more dangerous.

(ii) Trade Cycle : Business field is subject to ups and downs due to the operation of trade cycle. Economic depression which we witness in trade cycle may induce some problematic or sick industries to be closed down compelling their employees to become unemployed. Fluctuations in international markets, heavy imposition of excise duties, business strains observed in the trade cycles adversely affect the security of jobs of some men.

(iii) Technological Advance – Mechanisation – Automation : Technological advancement undoubtedly contributes to economic development. But unplanned and uncontrolled growth of technology may have an adverse effect on job opportunities. Since industrialists are more interested in maximizing production and profit they prefer to introduce labour-saving machines. They always search for ways and means of reducing the cost of production and hence go after computerization, automation, etc. The result is technological unemployment. This state of affairs is very much in evidence in the Indian context today.

(iv) Strikes and Lockouts : Strikes and lockouts had been an inseparable aspect of the Indian industrial field. Due to strikes and lockouts production used to come down and industries were incurring heavy losses. Workers used to become unemployed for a temporary period and some were being thrown out of job. This state of affairs continued almost up to 1990s, that is, till the launching of the [NEP] *New Economic Policy*. During this prolonged period of four decades our industries received severe setbacks due to labour strikes which affected adversely industrial growth and industrial potential for fetching jobs. After 1990s, things however, have been changing and labour strikes are becoming comparatively rarer.

(v) Slow Rate of Economic Growth : Job opportunities depend very much on economic growth. Since the rate of economic growth was very slow in the first 45 years after independence, the economy was not able to create enough job opportunities to the increasing number of job - seekers. *For example*, in 1980s, the rate of growth of the number of job-seekers increased by 2.2%, while the rate of growth of the number of job opportunities was only 1.5%. This difference led to an enormous increase in the number of unemployed persons.

(vi) Backwardness of Indian Agriculture : Age old mode of cultivation, too much dependence of too many people [more than 75%] on agriculture, widespread disguised unemployment, sentimental attachment towards land, etc., have adversely affected the – growth of Indian agriculture and its employment potential.

C. Other Causes of Unemployment

In addition to the two main types of the causes of unemployment as mentioned by **G. R. Madan,** we may add a few other factors causing the problem such as the following:

(i) Unpreparedness to Accept Socially Degrading Jobs : Some of our young men and women are not prepared to undertake jobs which are considered to be socially *"degrading"* or *"indecent". Example :* Autorickshaw and taxi-driving, working as salesmen or sales girls in shops, doing waiter's work and clerical work in hotels, etc., could be mentioned here as examples. Since the spirit of the dignity of labour is not properly inculcated in them, they become the victims of *"false prestige"* and face the risk of unemployment.

(ii) Defects in our Educational System : Our system of education which appears like a remnant of the British colonial administration in India, has its own irreparable defects and its contribution to the problem of unemployment can hardly be exaggerated. There is no co-ordination between our industrial growth, agricultural development and our educational system. Our education does not prepare the minds of our young men to become self-employed; on the contrary, it makes them to depend on government to find for them some jobs.

(iii) Geographic Immobility of the Workers : Occupational mobility and geographic mobility on the part of the workers lessen the gravity of the problem of unemployment. But in the Indian context, workers are not adventurous enough to move from one physical area to another in search of jobs, or to change their jobs to brighten their economic prospects. They are either clinging on to their traditional profession or occupations especially in the rural area, or concentrated in one or the other urban centre, sometimes without any job.

(iv) Improper Use of Human Resources : Lack of planning for the efficient utilization of human resources for productive purposes has been one of the causes of unemployment in India. In fact, there has been no proper co-ordination between the availability of human resources and its utilization in the productive field. As a result, in some units, there is the dearth of qualified man power and in some other units; we find its excess.

(v) Lack of Encouragement for Self-Employment : Ever since the time of British, Indians have developed a tendency to give priority for salaried jobs rather than self-employment. Our education system has also been a failure in developing the spirit of self-employment among our youths. As a result, young people tend to wait for getting some salaried jobs in offices, factories or business firms and private or public firms and concerns. They often wait for such jobs for years together as unemployed or under-employed youths.

EFFECTS OR IMPACT OF UNEMPLOYMENT

The problem of unemployment is a serious one and it leads to a number of consequences. The evil of unemployment may be discussed under four heads; *personal disorganization, family disorganization, social disorganization* and *irreparable financial losses.*

(i) Unemployment and Personal Disorganization

Unemployment is not only a social problem it is an individual problem also. An unemployed person loses self- respect and faces a discouraging and a disappointing outlook. *"Unsteady employment undermines the worker's physique, deadens his mind, weakens his ambition, destroys his capacity for continuous sustained endeavour, induces a liking for idleness and self – indulgence, saps self-respect and the sense of responsibility, impairs technical skills, weakens nerve and will power, creates a tendency to blame others for failure, saps his courage, prevents thrift, and hope of family advancement, destroys a workman's feeling that he is taking care of his family, sends him to work worried, underfed, plunges him in debt".*[5]

Young persons who finish their education, find it very painful to join the army of unemployed persons. Many of them do not get any outlet for their creative energy, and their enthusiasm and vigor dies down as days pass on.

The pitiable position of the wage- earner who has lost his job for one reason or another, is equally unfortunate. The old and retired people who are still capable of working but unable to get suitable jobs suffer from bitterness, economic insecurity and loss of self- respect.

The deplorable position of the casual workers and the underemployed persons cannot be undermined here. For them, life is full of uncertainties and insecurities. They struggle a lot to meet their minimum requirements of living.

Unemployment damages one's physical, mental and moral health also. The unemployed persons may not get sufficient food and medical assistance to maintain good physical health. Mental worries, anxieties and tensions adversely affect the mental health of the unemployed persons. The age-old saying *"an idle mind is a devil's workshop"* – speaks in volumes of the disastrous effect of unemployment on the moral health of the person.

(ii) Unemployment and Family Disorganization

Unemployment causes physical hardships and mental agony not only to the individual of the employable age, but also to his family members. If the bread-winner of the family loses the job, the entire family suffers. In the absence of regular income the family has to fall back upon its little savings; and when that is exhausted, it has to resort to borrowings. Valuable articles, golden ornaments, furniture, vessels and such other things are often sold or mortgaged to find money for immediate expenses. Families suffer starvation by resorting to unbelievable economies in food. Physical health of the family members gets damaged due to want of nutritious food and proper and timely medical care.

- ***Unemployment upsets the balance of the family life.*** Due to unemployment, entire family faces uncertainty and indefiniteness. In desperation children may be asked to stop their

5. **Mr Lescohier** in his book, *"Labour Market"* as quoted by **G .R. Madan** in his *"Social Problems"* - Page : 250.

education and join factories and such other business concerns at an early age for work. Even the wife who is not used to outside job work, may be compelled to go out of the household for work. This new role may make her to become highly irritable in temperament. Bickerings, simmerings and quarrels may become the order of the day. Since the parents are compelled to struggle a lot for the maintenance of the family, they do not get much time to give social training to their children. As a result, children may develop delinquent tendencies. This state of affairs may even lead to the breakdown of the family.

(iii) Unemployment and Social Disorganization

Unemployment, if not checked or controlled, may ultimately prepare the way for social disorganization. Due to unemployment, people fail to live up to the expectations of society. Some of them may even resort to anti-social activities. It tempts or provocates them to resort to begging, to indulge in criminal activities, to fall a prey to gambling, drug addiction, drunkenness, etc.

Unemployment is a social curse and it may even pollute the economic and political fields. It makes the non-corrupt persons to become corrupt, dishonest, the responsible and dignified to become irresponsible and indignified, the active and creative persons to become idle and lethargic, and so on. The urge to do something in life, gets dried up.

(iv) Irreparable Economic Losses

Unemployment causes incalculable economic losses. Since the unemployed persons become parasites on society they pose a big economic burden. The failure to provide jobs to all those who have the willingness and the potentiality to work, inevitably brings down economic production. Low production would cause low per capita income. People will be compelled to share among themselves country's poverty and not its affluence. Unemployment adversely affects the standard of living of the people. In the long run, this would bring down the labour-efficiency of the people.

Thus, unemployment as a socio-economic problem is capable of damaging the moral fibre of the individual and the social fabric of the society.

REMEDIAL MEASURES AND SUGGESTIONS

The problem of unemployment is growing day by day in India. It is becoming more and more complex also. Such a complex problem will have to be tackled in a planned manner. No single solution can be an effective remedy for this problem. Multi-pronged attempt is needed to face it in an effective manner. It is possible only with the combined efforts of the government and the public.

I. Population Control

The growing population in India is a major cause of many socio-economic problems. Our population as per 2011 census, is growing on an average at the rate of 1.76% per year. We are adding every year more than 120 lakh to 130 lakh people to our population. At the same time, about 5 million people attain the employable position every year. Job opportunities are not increasing at the same rate to accommodate the growing population. Hence, the population growth has to be checked. Family planning programme has to be made more popular and other suitable steps are to be taken to minimize or neutralize its growth.

II. Promoting Economic Development

The main solution for the problem lies in achieving substantial economic development. This can be materialized, only if attention is paid equally to agriculture and industry.

A. Promoting Agricultural Development

(i) ***Irrigation Projects.*** The employment opportunities in the agricultural sector may be increased through the construction of major and minor irrigation projects, expansion and development of plantation, intensive agriculture and horticulture. Unutilised land may be brought under-cultivation.

(ii) ***Development of Fisheries, Forest and Animal Husbandry.*** The development of forest and fisheries and encouragement of animal husbandry [dairy farming, poultry, piggery, etc.] is also a major step in the direction of improving agricultural production.

(iii) ***Encouragement of Cottage and Household Industries.*** In the Indian context, cottage and household industries which are often associated with agriculture play a vital role in the development of economy. Hence, they should be given due encouragement. Basket making, brick-making, toy-making, beedi rolling, agarbati making, carpentry and furniture making, leather works, carving, smithery, and such other works are to be encouraged to keep our people engaged with work that fetch economic rewards.

(iv) ***Encouragement for Growing Commercial Crops :*** Commercial crops can make agricultural tasks economically attractive. Commercial crops such as areca, coffee, tea, pepper, ginger, cardamom, cashew, tobacco, ground nut, vegetables and fruits, etc., can bring good income to the farmers. Due encouragement is to be given to the farmers to grow such commercial crops.

(v) ***Attractive Local Programmes and Projects :*** Depending upon the local needs and feasibility new agricultural programmes and projects are to be launched so that young people of the area get new opportunities to use their talents and energy for the developmental programmes. The U.P. Government, for example, introduced in 1990-91, a land army called *"Bhoomi Sena"*. *The Bhoomi Sainiks* [young men of the local area] are given funds by the state government in the form of bank loans for the aforestation of land.

B. Industrial Development

Planned development of industries is essential for creating more and more job opportunities. Development of industries may include : *(a) large-scale industries, (b) small scale industries,* and *(c) village and cottage industries including handicrafts.* Proper balance should be maintained between agricultural growth and industrial development, so that industry would not destroy handicrafts and household industries.

The *unchecked process of mechanization* and the *domination of multinational companies* are adversely affecting the creation of new job opportunities. In the name of industrial growth new labour–saving machines are installed which are taking away the jobs of men. Gandhiji had opposed the process of mechanization in this regard. Sufficient care should be taken to see no new machine takes away the jobs of existing workers.

The *process of economic liberalization* let loose by the Central Government recently has given new scope for the multinational companies to establish their domination over the indigenous industries. The governmental invitation for these companies may erode the job opportunities for millions of people. Hence, special precaution must be taken to protect the job prospects of native Indians.

III. Educational Reforms

Education has much to do with employment and unemployment. Our education is not much job-oriented, it is degree-oriented. *It caters more to urban needs rather* than to rural requirements.

It has not completely come out of the British colonial bias. Hence, it has failed to create an army of self-reliant, self-dignified young men and women. It very badly requires a thorough overhauling.

Throughout the country, primary education should be made more popular and effective. Much publicized slogan *"operation black-board"* must be transformed into reality. Our villages should become the centres of concentration in this regard. At the same time, some control has to be established over higher education. Long back in 1957, the then chairman of the UGC, **Sri C.D. Deshmukh**, had reiterated that *we shall have to restructure university education by and large to the number of university educated men and women that the country will be needing from time to time.*

Due practical training should be given to our educated youths to help them to pursue one or the other vocation, and proper guidance and information should be given to them regarding new job opportunities. Employment guidance bureaus and employment exchange agencies can play a vital role in this regard.

IV Five-Year Plans

Almost all the Five-Year Plans have given utmost importance to generate as much employment opportunities as possible. They have given priority to agricultural growth, industrial development and creation of vast employment opportunities. Expansion of employment opportunities by making use of the available man power and natural resources was indeed, the main aim of the Third Five-Year Plan.

Though the Govt. had spent about ₹ 180 crores for creating employment opportunities in the First Five – Year Plan, there were about 5.3 million unemployed people at the end of the Plan period. From the beginning of the First Plan [1951-56] till the completion of the 10th Plan in 2007, the number of unemployed people went on increasing in spite of the efforts made by the planning system to provide maximum number of jobs. It was estimated that during the Tenth Plan [2002-07], the new entrants to the labour force would be around 35 million. Adding to this, the backlog of 35 million unemployed people, the job requirements of the Tenth Plan would be around 70 million. *"Since the economy at least would be able to create 50 million jobs, the backlog of 20 million will remain at the end of the Tenth Plan. But if proper policies are pursued, the rate of unemployment which was 9.21% in 2001-02 would decline at 5.11% in 2006-07"* [6]

EMPLOYMENT PROSPECTS UNDER THE 11th PLAN

Employment Requirements During the 11th Plan : On account of the increasing participation of females, the total increase in labour force will be around 65 million during the 11th Plan [2007-2012]. To this may be added the present backlog of about 35 million. Thus, the total job requirements of the 11th Plan workout to be 100 million.

The planners intend to provide 58 - to - 65 million additional employment opportunities. Even then, the 11th Plan will not create full employment, but it will at least ensure that the unemployment rate falls somewhat.

Promotion of Employment Generation in the 11th Plan

The 11th Plan intends to generate additional employment opportunities mainly in the services and manufacturing sector. Measures would need to be taken in the Plan to boost, in particular, labour intensive manufacturing sector such as food processing, leather products, footwear, textiles and service sectors such as tourism and construction.

6. **Ruddar Datt** and **Sundharm** – Page : 411.

The planners state: *"Organised sector employment would double over the 11th Plan... but this would leave about 55 million new workers for the unorganized sector to absorb." "The 11th Plan aims to increase private organized sector employment ambitiously by at least 10 million. Along with the public sector, organized sector jobs would then expand by over 15 million, a growth rate of about 9% per annum. This would still leave nearly 50 million new workers to be absorbed in non-agricultural unorganized employment".*[7]

Generation of Employment Opportunities by Information Technology [IT]

It is heartening to note that information technology [IT] has opened enormous job opportunities for educated youths in the country. It is estimated that one segment of IT industry that is, computer system which includes – both hardware and software computer engineers and systems analysts, is having a million jobs at present. In addition to this, the IT sector provided 2.2 million jobs to computer professionals and other related personnel engaged in IT sector. It is estimated [as per *NASSOM – McKinsey Report 1999*] that by the end of the year 2008, IT enabled services will provide 11 million jobs and generate a revenue of 17 to 18 billion U.S. dollars. In this sense, IT industry has great future in expanding employment opportunities.

What is disturbing in the present economic situation is that IT education is very costly and IT jobs are being grabbed by the relatively rich section of the society. The Government here has a major role to play in expanding computer education to rural areas in the country so that the capabilities of the rural people are developed to acquire better quality jobs in the IT sector.

To conclude, it could be said that the Planning Commission has optimistic view of the economy's employment potential. As per its report, *"as against 3.9 million employment opportunities created during 1993 and 1999, additional employment generated during 1999 and 2002 averaged 8.4 million per year. There is need to increase it to 10 million per year."*

Employment Guarantee Act – 2005 *[National Rural Employment Guarantee Act]*

Under the *National Common Minimum Programme* of the UPA Government adopted in Sept 2004, and as per the advice of the National Advisory Council, the Govt. passed the *National Rural Employment Guarantee Act* [**NREGA**] in 2005. The main features of the Act are as follows :

1. Every household in rural India will have a right to at least 100 days of guaranteed employment every year for at least one adult member per family.
2. The employment will be in the form of casual manual labour at the legally fixed minimum wage that is, ₹ 60/- per day.
3. Work should be provided in the local area, that is, within the radius of 5 K.M.
4. Work should be given within 15 days of demanding it.
5. For whatever reason, if work is not given, the person shall be paid a daily unemployment allowance. This allowance will be at least 1/3 of the minimum wages.
6. For non-compliance with rules, strict penalties have been laid down.
7. The *gram sabha* will monitor the work of the *gram panchayat* by way of social audit.
8. The District Collector / Chief Executive officer will be responsible for the programme at the district level.

Probable Cost of this Employment Guarantee Programme

It is estimated that employment Guarantee Programme will cost at least 1% of the GDP [Gross Domestic Product]. The calculations reveal that the said – programme will cost ₹ 100/-

7. **Ruddar Datt** and **Sundaram** [2008] Page : 414.

per person per day at 2004-05 prices. This includes 60/-₹ as wages and ₹ 40/- for the non-labour costs [including materials and administrative costs]. Thus, the total cost for providing 100 days of employment in a year per person will be ₹ 10,000/-. As per 2001 Census, there were 20 crores of people, that is, 4 crore households, living below the poverty line. Thus, the programme per year will cost ₹ 40,000/- crores [₹ 10,000/- per person multiplied by 4 crore households]. As per this scheme, the Centre will bear 80% of the total cost [that is, 60% as wage component and 20% as share in materials component] and the State Govt. will share the remaining 20% of the total cost. The Centre, is however, conscious of the fact that once the programme gathers momentum, democratic pressures are bound to enlarge the programme to all unemployed and also to withdraw the limit of 100 days and make it a programme operative throughout the year.

Critical Remarks About the Programme

An important aspect of this *Employment Guarantee Act* is that, it gives a legal right to the people enforceable in court. This will increase the bargaining power of the people. It also makes administration accountable for if the jobs are not provided; unemployment allowance will have to be paid.

The critics have raised their own doubts about the practical benefits of this Act. The experience of Maharastra is also not encouraging. This programme has been implemented in Maharasthra for the past 30 years costing the State more than ₹ 9,000 crores and generating 370 crore mandays. But the programme has not produced adequate results either in terms of poverty reduction or reduction in unemployment. The programme still continues after 30 years without any decline in the demand for unskilled wage work under this scheme. No dramatic achievements have been made in poverty reduction or in unemployment reduction in the state. Critics also say that in fact, Maharasthra has done poorly as compared with other states.[8] Noted economist **Lord Meghanand Desai** considered this NREGA scheme as only a *"palliative"* a temporary measure and not a cure for the problem. **Dr. C.H. Hanumanth Rao** commented that the scheme was a failure in Maharasthra because it was not linked to the building up of rural infrastructure, such as rural irrigation, rural roads, etc.

MGNREGA Act From 2nd Oct - 2009: The National Rural Employment Guarantee Act came to be known as ***MGNREGA:*** *"Mahatma Gandhi National Rural Employment Guarantee Act"* and was extended to all the 625 districts of the country. Some of the deficiencies involved in the previous NREGA were rectified in this Act. In the year 2006-07, as much as ₹ 11,300/- crores were spent on this scheme to provide jobs to 2.10 crore families. This expenditure was increased to ₹ 40,100/- in the year 2010-11 and 4.10 crore families had obtained the benefit of jobs.

Though this scheme provided some financial relief to some families by providing jobs, it is highly criticised today for it involves huge amount of corruption. The Comptroller and Auditor General of India himself in his 2013 report has charged that crores of rupees earmarked for this scheme, are either diverted or abused or looted.

●●●

8. It may be noted that in view of the criticisms made against the proposed EGS Bill, the Govt made some amendments to it on 17th Aug. 2005 while getting the approval of the Parliament. For example, the scheme has been universalized to all persons living in the rural areas instead of its being available only to the families "below the poverty line". *Secondly,* there will be 1/3 preference for women in areas where the number of applicants is very large. *Thirdly,* the scheme will be introduced in 200 districts in the beginning but later on it will be extended to the whole nation in five years. *Fourthly,* the Central Govt. will provide 90% of money for the scheme. *Fifthly,* the Govt. also promised to bring a similar scheme for the urban areas. - **Ruddar Datt** and **Sundharam** – Page : 421.

Chapter 4

PROBLEM OF OVER POPULATION IN INDIA

Meaning of Demography - World Population Trends *- Growth Rate of World Population - Salient Features of World Population Growth - Demographic Trends in India - Is India Over-populated? - Population Explosion in India - Some Important Aspects of the Growth of Indian Population - Population Explosion - Tests of Over-population - Causes for the Rapid Growth of Population in India -* ***Major Demographic Trends in India :*** *1. Growth Rate of Population, 2. Uneven Distribution of Population, 3. Age Composition, 4. Sex Composition, 5. Density of Population, 6. Life Expectancy, 7. Dependency Ratio, 8. Population and Urbanisation, 9. Birth and Death Rates, 10. Literacy Structure - Occupational Distribution of Population in India - Effects of Over-population - National Population Policy 2000-* ***Family Planning and Its Achievements*** *- Difficulties Involved in the Implementation of the Family Planning - Karnataka Population Highlights-2011.*

Population of the world has been consistently increasing especially after the II world war. In demographic terms, the world is experiencing a period of population explosion. India also experienced unprecedented and accelerated growth of population. Its population has already crossed the alarming mark of one billion. Prior to 1921, the population growth in India was insignificant; between 1921 and 1951 it was rapid, and after 1951, it has become ***"explosive."***

Population, itself is not a problem, qualitatively good population with a manageable size, represents the strength of a nation. But if the size becomes unmanageable, the same population invites unwanted problems. It not only halts economic progress but also poses innumerable challenges to the social system. India is unfortunately caught in such a precarious position.

No social problem is beyond human control and solution. A serious problem like *"the problem of over-population in India"* requires an immediate solution. Though it cannot be solved by an act of legislation or by the Presidential promulgation, it can very well be handled skilfully and efficiently. The Government must be sincere and efficient in tackling this problem. But more than the Government, people must be made to realise the need for controlling the size of their population. A strong *"political will"* on the one hand, and creation of *"general social awareness"* on the other, can alone provide a lasting solution to this problem. This chapter highlights the recent demographic situation in India.

Meaning of Demography

Demography, as understood today, *is the scientific study of human population.* "*Demography is the systematic study of the growth, size, composition, distribution and movement of human populations*". [- *The Blackwell Dictionary of Sociology* (2000) Page-74]. It focuses its attention on three readily observable human phenomena : (a) *changes* in the size of population [growth or decline], (b) the *composition* of the population, and (c) the *distribution* of population in space. It deals with five *"demographic processes"*, namely *fertility, mortality, marriage, migration* and *social mobility.* These five processes are continually at work within a population determining size, composition and distribution. The main sources of demographic statistics in India are population censuses, National Sample Surveys, registration of vital events, and ad-hoc demographic studies.

1. WORLD POPULATION TRENDS

The world population is continuously increasing. Several nations of the world are gripped by the problem of overpopulation. Most of the developing countries are experiencing this problem. At the beginning of the Christian era, nearly 2,000 years ago, world population was estimated to be around 250 million. Subsequent estimates of the world population, and rates of increase are given in ***Table* 1.**

Table - 1

World Population: 1750 - to - 2010

Year	*Population (million)*	*Average Annual Growth Rate (%)*
1750	791	–
1800	978	0.4
1850	1262	0.5
1900	1650	0.6
1950	2526	1.1
1960	3037	1.79
1970	3696	1.92
1975	4066	1.89
1980	4432	1.72
1987	5000	1.63
1991	5385	1.7
1998	5884	1.6
2000	6054	1.4
2010	6893	1.15

Source : Park's *"Text-Book of Preventive and Social Medicine."* Page - 325 and other sources

It required all the human history up to the year 1800 for the world population to reach one billion. The second billion came in 130 years [around 1930], the third billion in 30 years [around 1960], the fourth billion in 15 years [in 1974], the fifth billion in 13 years [in 1987], and the sixth billion in 12 years [1999]. On October 12th, 1999 world population became 6 billion. It is expected to reach 8 billion by 2025.

Growth Rate is Faster in the Developing Countries

About three fourths of the world population lives in the developing countries. The UNO has estimated that world's population grew at an annual rate of 1.4% during 1990-2000. But China registered a much lower annual growth rate of population [that is, 1%] during 1999-2000, as compared to India [1.93%]. In fact, the growth rate of China is now very much comparable to that of USA [0.9%].

India, Indonesia and Bangladesh, the three countries of the South-East Asia Region [SEAR], are recognised among the most populous 10 countries of the world. According to UN projections,

Table - 2

Trends in Increase of Population of South East Asia Region (SEAR) Countries (In thousands)			
Country	**1985**	**2000**	**2005 *(Projected)***
India	797940	1008937	1082184
Bangladesh	99310	137439	139911
Bhutan	1451	2085	2313
DPR Korea	18942	22268	25416
Indonesia	167332	212092	226938
Maldives	184	291	355
Myanmar	37544	47749	53479
Nepal	16503	23043	27439
Sri Lanka	16060	18924	19858
Thailand	51128	62806	62612
Total	1176394	1535634	1640505

Source : WHO - World Health Report - 2001.

India's population will reach 1.53 billion by the year 2050, and that will be the highest population in the world. The trend of population increase in the SEAR countries is shown in ***Table* - 2.**

Growth Rate of World Population

The growth rate is not uniform in the world. There are many countries in the world [*Ex.* European countries] where the growth rate is less than 0.5 per cent per year. In developing countries, the growth rates are excessive - it is around 2.8 per cent in Africa, 1.5 per cent in Latin America, 0.5 in Europe and 1.9 per cent in Asia [But, China has brought it down to 0.51% in 2010]. A population growing at 0.5 per cent per year will double in about 140 years, a population growing at 3 per cent per year will double in 20-25 years. These differences in growth rates are largely the result of fertility and mortality patterns.

Salient Features of World Population Growth

The salient features of the world population growth at a glance are as follows **:**

(i) Approximately 95 per cent of this growth is occurring in developing countries.

(ii) Currently, one third of the world's population is under the age of 15 and will soon enter the reproductive bracket, giving more potential for population growth.

(iii) The UNFPA estimates that world population is most likely to nearly double to 10 billion people in 2050, peaking at 11.6 billion reaching 20.7 billion a century later.

(iv) The expected number of births per women, at current fertility rate, is : Africa 6.1; Asia, 3.2; Latin America 3.4; North America 2.0; Europe 1.6.

(v) World population is currently growing at 176 people per minute; 10,564 people per hour; 253,542 people per day; and 92,543,000 people per year.

The world population is indeed, increasing at an alarming rate. This speedy growth of population is one of the greatest obstacles to the economic and social advancement of the majority of people in the underdeveloped world.

2. DEMOGRAPHIC DIMENSIONS IN INDIA

India has a vast population, that is, **121.02** crore in 2011. With a huge population of **121** crore [April 1st 2011] India is the second most populous country in the world, next only to China,

IS NOT INDIA OVERLOADED WITH PEOPLE ?

whereas seventh in land area. With only 2.4 per cent of the world's land area, India is supporting about 17.5 per cent of the world's population. The population of India since 1901 is shown in ***Table* - 3.** In 2001, India accounted for 19.96% of the estimated population of developing countries.

Is India Overpopulated - ?

Population, if manageable and efficient, is an asset to any country. It is the index of its inner strength. It leads to a better and fuller exploitation of its natural resources. But if it becomes unmanageable, it eats into the vitals of the nation and becomes an evil. A large size of population by itself must not be confused with overpopulation. A country is over-populated or under-populated in relation to its *area, resources,* and *their utilisation.*

Table - 3

Growth of Population in India, [1901 - 2011]

Year	Total Population (in million)	Average Annual exponential growth rate (%)	Decadal increase or decrease [in crores]	Increase in Population during the decade [in percentage]
1901	238.4	-----	-----	----
1911	252.1	0.56	+ 1.6	5.7%
1921	251.3	(-) 0.03	- 0.1	0.3%
1931	279.0	1.04	+ 2.8	11.0%
1941	318.7	1.33	+ 4.0	14.2%
1951	361.1	1.25	+ 4.2	13.3%
1961	439.2	1.96	+ 7.8	21.5%
1971	548.2	2.20	+ 10.9	24.8%
1981	683.3	2.22	+ 13.5	24.8%
1991	843.9	2.14	+ 16.1	23.5%
2001	1027.0	1.93	+ 18.4	21.34%
*2011	1210.02	1.76	+18.15 (crore)	17.64

* As per the first set of data from the 2011 Census (as on March 31st)

At the present stage of her economic development, there is little doubt that India is over-populated. India's population is about *one-fifth* of the total world population. Population has become a socio-economic problem for India. The following facts would fortify this.

Population Explosion in India !

India is the 2nd most populous country in the world. Its population has been steadily increasing since 1921. Having crossed the mark of **121.02 crore** in 2011 A.D., India's population is currently increasing at the rate of **18.15 million** each year and its annual growth rate is **1.76%** as per 2011 census report. India's population is consistently increasing in all the States. State-wise break-up of India's population along with variation in sex-ratio is given in ***Table* - 4.**

Alarming growth of population has become one of the most formidable problems of India today. Massive population is seriously threatening our economic development. ***Tables* 3 - 4** make clear the abnormal growth of population which is, indeed, the population explosion.

India's population numbered 238 million in 1901, doubled in 60 years to 439 million [1961]; doubled again, this time in only 30 years to reach 846 million by 1991. India's population was projected to cross 1 billion mark on 11 May 2000, and to reach 1.53 billion by the year 2050. This will then make India the most populous country in the world, surpassing China.

Some Important Aspects of the Growth of Indian Population

- As per the 1991 census, India's population was 844 millions, and it increased to 1027 millions in 2001, and to 1070.3 million [107.3 crore] in 2004, and 121.02 crore in 2011.
- The land area of the country is only 2.4% of the total land area of the world. But its population is about 17.5% of the total population of the world as per 2011 census.
- At the present rate of growth, India is adding every 10 years a number of people more than double the total population of the U.K., or equal to the entire population of Pakistan or Brazil or more than the half the population of the USA or of the USSR.
- India is just two-fifth of the USA, but India's population is more than 2 and a half times the population of the USA and USSR put together.
- India's population is equal to the total population of 55 countries of Africa and Latin America.
- India's present population [121.02 crore] is equal to the combined population of USA, Indonesia, Japan, Brazil, Bangladesh and Pakisthan.
- In India today, 30 babies are born every minute, 55,000 babies are born everyday and about 13 million babies are born every year as per 2001 census.
- India, it is remarked, adds one Australia [that is the population of Australia] to its population every year.

The Reality of Population Explosion

It is clear from ***Table* - 3** that the population of India has increased by 21.5% during the decade 1951-1961, by 24.8% during the decade 1961-1971, by 24.8% during the decade of 1971-1981, by 23.5% during the decade of 1981-1991, by 18.5% between 1991-2001 and by 17.64 in 2011. ***Table* - 3** shows that the increase in population of India was rather slow upto 1921. The year 1921 is called *"the year of the great divide"* as the growth rate after this has been very sharp. After 1911-21, the decade between 2001-2011 is the first decade to witness a reduction in the rate of population growth. This reduction, however, is only marginal. Hence, the rate of growth of population as well as the size of the population of India is definitely very high. On the basis of the rate of growth and the size of population, one can certainly say that there is population explosion in India.

Tests of Over-Population

The following tests make it evident that India is over-populated **:**

1. The rate of population growth in India is abnormally high, that is 1.76% per annum according to 2011 census report, whereas it is only 0.51% in China.
2. The rapid increase in population is eating away the fruits of the Five-Year Plans.
3. Per capita income of India is extremely low in comparison with that of many other countries.
4. The country is not able to provide for the minimum requirements of its people for the population is too large and the production too less.
5. Population growth has created problems such as unemployment, illiteracy, poverty, beggary, housing problem, ill-health, etc., which are not met with.

3. CAUSES FOR THE RAPID GROWTH OF POPULATION IN INDIA

Various factors have contributed to the rapid growth of population in India among which the following can be noted :

(i) Peaceful Conditions: For nearly a century [1860-1960], India enjoyed comparative peace without involving herself in major inter-conflicts or wars especially after the establishment of British rule. Peaceful conditions provided an impetus for over-population.

Table - 4

Statewide Distribution of Population as per 2011 Census					
SN	**Union Territory/ State Name**	**Total Population**	**Percent(%) of Total Population**	**Males**	**Females**
1	Andaman and Nicobar	3,79,944	0.03	2,02,330	1,77,614
2	Andhra Pradesh	8,46,65,533	7.00	4,25,09,881	4,21,55,652
3	Arunachal Pradesh	13,82,611	0.11	7,20,232	6,62,379
4	Assam	3,11,69,272	2.68	1,59,54,927	1,52,14,345
5	Bihar	10,38,04,637	8.48	5,41,85,347	4,96,19,290
6	Chandigarh	10,54,686	0.09	5,80,282	4,74,404
7	Chhattisgarh	2,55,40,196	2.11	1,28,27,915	1,27,12,281
8	Dadra and Nagar Haveli	3,42,853	0.03	1,93,178	1,49,675
9	Daman and Diu	2,42,911	0.02	1,50,100	92,811
10	Delhi	1,67,53,235	1.38	89,76,410	77,76,825
11	Goa	14,57,723	0.12	7,40,711	7,17,012
12	Gujarat	6,03,83,628	4.99	3,14,82,282	2,89,01,346
13	Haryana	2,53,53,081	2.09	1,35,05,130	1,18,47,951
14	Himachal Pradesh	68,56,509	0.57	34,73,892	34,73,892
15	Jammu and Kashmir	1,25,48,926	1.04	66,65,561	58,83,365
16	Jharkhand	3,11,69,272	2.72	1,59,54,927	1,52,14,345
17	Karnataka	6,11,30,704	5.05	3,10,57,742	3,00,72,962
18	Kerala	3,33,87,677	2.76	1,60,21,290	1,73,66,387
19	Lakshadweep	64,429	0.01	33,106	31,323
20	Madhya Pradesh	7,25,97,565	6.00	3,76,12,920	3,49,84,645
21	Maharashtra	11,23,72,972	9.29	5,83,61,397	5,40,11,575
22	Manipur	27,21,756	0.22	13,69,764	13,51,992
23	Meghalaya	29,64,007	0.24	14,92,668	14,71,339
24	Mizoram	10,91,014	0.09	5,52,339	5,38,675
25	Nagaland	19,80,602	0.16	10,25,707	9,54,895
26	Orissa	4,19,47,358	3.47	2,12,01,678	2,07,45,680
27	Pondicherry	12,44,464	0.10	6,10,485	6,33,979
28	Punjab	2,77,04,236	2.29	1,46,34,819	1,30,69,417
29	Rajasthan	6,86,21,012	5.67	3,56,20,086	3,30,00,926
30	Sikkim	6,07,688	0.05	3,21,661	2,86,027
31	Tamil Nadu	7,21,38,958	5.96	3,61,58,871	3,59,80,087
32	Tripura	36,71,032	0.30	18,71,867	17,99,165
33	Uttarakhand	1,01,16,752	0.84	51,54,178	49,62,574
34	Uttar Pradesh	19,95,81,477	16.49	10,45,96,415	9,49,85,062
35	West Bengal	9,13,47,736	7.55	4,69,27,389	4,44,20,347
	TOTAL	**1,21,01,93,422**	**100**	**62,37,24,248**	**58,64,69,17**

Source: 2011 Census Report

(ii) Excess of Birth Over Death: Growth of population depends on the excess of births over deaths. Death rate has been declining rapidly in India. It was 42.6 per 1000 in 1911 and it decreased to 807 per 1000 in 2001. The birth rate is still high in India. It was 49.2 per 1000 in 1911 and it decreased to only 26.1 per 1000 in 2001. The gap between birth rate and death rate has widened leading to an increase in the population. [The average annual rate of increase of population in India is 1.76% at present [2011] whereas it is only 1.2% in U.S.A., 0.4% in U.K., .51% in China, 0.4% in France and 0.3% in Japan.]

(iii) Progress in Medical Knowledge and its application has considerably reduced the death rate. It has helped us to control the spread of diseases like Malaria, T.B., Cholera, Plague,

Influenza, Smallpox, etc., and protected the lives of people from the jaws of death. Positively, it has contributed to greater population, because, those persons saved from the death also produced children to add to the existing numbers.

(iv) Improvement in Transport Facilities has helped people to avail of medical and health facilities without much difficulty. These have saved countless lives and added to the size of the population.

(v) Improvements in the field of Agriculture and Industry also contributed to an increase in population. Uncertainties in the field of agriculture have largely been removed with the help of science and technology. Food production has considerably increased. Industries have been providing employment opportunities to thousands of persons. These developments have given people the confidence that they can afford to feed more people if they beget.

(vi) Certain Social Factors like Universal Marriage, Child Marriage, Early Marriage have also contributed to the problem. Indians consider marriage as a social obligation and almost all marriageable persons are in a married state. Life-long bachelorship is looked down upon. Particularly for women marriage is almost an inescapable obligation. Further, the number of children born per couple is also large.

(vii) Social Attitudes of Indians also favour an increase in population. Poverty, illiteracy, ignorance, absence of recreational facilities, attitudes of conservatism, orthodoxy, feeling of dependence on God, a sense of resignation towards life, looking upon children as old age pension, etc., are all responsible for the rapid growth of population.

(viii) Lack of Conscious Family Planning **:** There is the lack of conscious family planning on the part of the married people. The use of contraceptives is unknown to the illiterate masses. People feel that more children are wanted for economic purposes. Further, blind faith in fate and the existence of joint family system induce thoughtlessness in the matter of begetting children.

(ix) The Climatic Conditions of India are also very conducive to the growth of population. The tropical climate stimulates sex urge. **Montesquieu** said that people of warm land are more sex-indulgent. Further, girls become physically mature at an early age ranging from 11 to 15 years of age. Immediately after puberty they are pushed into marriage and they begin to bear children. Child-bearing capacity of women lasts in the tropical places for longer period.

(x) Added to this, during the earlier days the ***Government did not take much interest in introducing family planning*** to slow down the rapid growth of population. Though family planning programme was started under the Five Year Planning system, proper attention was not given to popularise it in the beginning. People also failed to recognise its importance. The result is the phenomenal growth of population.

(xi) Lack of Entertainment Facilities **:** It has been observed that people especially in the rural areas, have been forced to find *entertainment in the sex-play* in the absence of proper entertainment facilities. This has further aggravated the problem.

4. MAJOR DEMOGRAPHIC TRENDS IN INDIA

India, as it is made clear, is the second most populous country in the world. Its total population crossed the mark of 121.2 crore by March 2011. Its population is currently increasing at the rate of 18.15 million per year. The average annual exponential growth rate of India's population is 1.76% in 2011. The salient demographic features or trends of India's population may be noted below.

1. Growth Rate of Population

The population of India grew at a slow rate prior to 1921. But its population has started growing at a fantastic rate of speed particularly after 1931. The population growth rates in India are presented in ***Table* - 3.** The average annual growth rate of India's population was 0.56% in 1911 and it reached the record height of 2.22% in 1981. However, it has come down to 1.9% in 2001, and further to 1.76% in 2011.

2. Uneven Distribution of Population

Population of India is not equally distributed among all the states. On the contrary, we find heavy concentration of people in some states rather than in others. ***Table* - 5** shows the ten most populous states in the country by rank. As per 2011Census, the state of Uttar Pradesh comes first with about 200 million people followed by Maharashtra with 112 million, Bihar with 103 million and so on. It is significant to note that these 10 states account for about 76.34% of the total population of India.

Table - 5

Ranking of Most Populous States by Population Size in 2001 and 2011

Rank	State	Population 1-3-2001 (million)	Per cent to total population of India 1-3-2001	*Population March-2011 (Millions)	*Percent in to Total population of India
1.	Uttar Pradesh	166.05	16.17	200	16%
2.	Maharashtra	96.75	9.42	112	9%
3.	Bihar	82.87	8.07	103	9%
4.	West Bengal	80.22	7.81	91	8%
5.	Andhra Pradesh	75.72	7.37	84	7%
6.	Tamil Nadu	62.11	6.05	72.13	6%
7.	Madhya Pradesh	60.38	5.88	72.59	6%
8.	Rajasthan	56.47	5.50	68.62	6%
9.	Karnataka	52.73	5.14	61.1	5%
10.	Gujarat	50.59	4.93	60.38	5%

Source : Census of India 2001. Provisional Population Totals, Paper 1 of 2001.
* Provisional statistics Relating to 2011 censes.

3. Age Composition

As per 2011 Census, the population of children [0-to-6 years] has declined by 5 million over the 2001 Census. In general, the proportion of population below 15 years is showing decline, whereas the proportion of elderly people in the country is increasing. This trend may continue in the time to come. The increase in the elderly population will impose a greater burden on the already outstretched health services in the country.

The age composition of India's population as per Census Report 2011 is shown in ***Table* - 6.** The age composition of people in any country is very much related to components of population change like *fertility, mortality, age at marriage, migration, etc.* Its distribution also has its important socio-economic effects. A large number of people under the age group of 0.14, that is, 29% in 2011 would lead to certain effects such as – allocation of large amount of fund to provide for health, medical and educational needs for children; more dependents on working people and low productivity of labour.

• ***India - A Country with the Highest Number of Young People in the World*** : It is heartening to note that India is a country dominated by the highest number of young people. Hence, *the total dependency ratio*[1] is comparatively less in India. It means, children less than 14 years, and old

1. **Meaning of Total Dependency Ratio** : The ratio of the combined age groups 0-14 years plus 65 years and above to the 15-65 years age group - is referred to as the '*total dependency ratio*'.

people above 65 years, are considered to be dependent on the rest of the people. In the Indian context, since a large number of people are found to be in the age in between 15-65 years, the number of dependents on them is less. ***[See Table No- 6]***

• ***India Enjoying 'Demographic Dividend'***: Unlike many other countries in the world today, India is said to be benefiting from the **"*demographic dividend*"**. "*Demographic dividend refers to demographic or population advantage which is obtained due to the numerical domination of the young people in the population*". In fact, it is an advantage due to less "*dependency ratio*" as mentioned earlier.

It is estimated that by 2020, the average Indian will be only **29** years old, compared with an average age of **37** years in China and USA, **45** in Western Europe, and **48** in Japan. This implies a large and growing labour force which can deliver highest benefits in terms of growth and prosperity.

• ***Changing Age Structure by Itself Cannot Guarantee the Benefit or Dividend*** : It is to be noted that there is nothing automatic about the advange or dividend mentioned above. The changing age structure needs to be cautiously utilised through appropriate policies. India's recent experience also suggests that market forces by themselves do not ensure positive results. Unless a way forward is found, we may miss out on the potential benefits.

Table - 6

Composition of the Population of India 1911 - 2026

Year	Age Gourp		
	0-14	15-60	60 and above
1911	38.8	60.2	1.0
1921	39.2	59.6	1.2
1931	38.3	60.2	1.5
1951	37.4	57.1	5.5
1961	41.0	53.3	6
1971	41.4	53.4	5
1981	40	54.1	6
1991	38	56	7
2001	34	59	7
2011	29	63	8
2026	23	64	12

Source : IAMR, Fact Book on Manpower, and Census of India 2011.

Table - 6A

Percent Distribution of Population by Age and Sex From the NFHS - 2, India, 1998-99

Age	*Male*	*Female*
0 - 4	11.2	11.1
5 - 9	12.8	12.4
10 - 14	12.1	11.8
15 - 19	10.4	10.3
20 - 24	8.5	9.3
25 - 29	7.8	8.7
30 - 34	6.7	7.1
35 - 39	6.6	6.4
40 - 44	5.1	4.7
45 - 49	4.5	4.2
50 - 54	3.4	3.1
55 - 59	2.6	3.3
60 - 64	2.9	3.0
65 - 69	2.0	2.0
70+	3.3	2.8
Total	100.0	100.0

Source : Govt. of India [2000] Annual Report 1999-2000

4. Sex Composition - The Declining Sex Ratio in India

Sex ratio is one of the characteristics of the population. It has an important bearing upon marriage rate, death rate, birth rate and even migration rate. The sex ratio is defined as *"the number of females per 1,000 males."* In any study of population, analysis of the sex composition or sex ratio plays a vital role. The major trends in the sex ratio in the country from 1951 onwards are represented in ***Table* - 7.** According to the 2001 census figures, there are 933 females per 1000 males in India. The sex ratio recorded a slight increase from 933 in 2001 to **940** in 2011.

• ***Drastic Fall in the Child Sex Ratio*** : In addition to the wide gap between male-female sex ratio, drastic fall in the child sex ratio for the past several decades is also equally shocking.

In fact, this unhealthy trend has disturbed the minds of social demographers, policy makers, social activists, feminists and concerned citizens. The sex ratio for the 0-6 years age group is also known as "*juvenile ratio*" or "*child sex ratio*". **For example**, in 1991, the child sex ratio for the country was 945, and it decreased to 927 in 2001 and further to 914 in 2011. *[See Table No - 7]*

The Expression BIMARU V/s DEMARU Denoting High Birth Rate and Decline in Child Sex Ratio

The expressions BIMARU and DEMARU stand for the high rate of population growth and sharp decline in the child sex ratio respectively.

BIMARU stands for the States such as Bihar [**BI**], Madhyapradesh [**M**], Rajasthan [**R**] and Uttarpradesh [**U**]. These states according to 2001 census, accounted for 39% of India's population and 48% of the total illiterate population. Rate of growth of population is found to be very high here.

Yet another coinage of the 2001 census namely; **DEMARU**, stands for the sharp fall in the child sex ratio. In this expression DEMARU, **'D'** stands for daughter and **'MARU'** stands for killing. The English letter **'E'** denotes '*elimination*'. DEMARU states are thus, those states where daughters, that is, female children are killed in a large number. Punjab, Haryana, Himachalpradesh, Gujarath and Maharasthra are the **DEMARU** states known for the practice of foeticide. During 1991-2001, in Punjab, the child sex ratio declined from 875 to 793, in Himachalpradesh 951 to 845, in Gujarath 928 to 878, in Chandigarh 899 to 845, and Delhi 915 to 865. The corresponding figures for these five regions for the year 2011 are 895 [Punjab], 972 [Himachal Pradesh], 919 [Gujarath], 818 [Chandighar], 868 [Delhi] and 879 [Haryana].

- ***States With Higher Sex Ratio than the National Average*** : In states such as MP, Goa, Jammu and Kashmir, Bihar, Tamil Nadu, Karnataka and Orissa, child sex ratio is above the national average of 927 but below the 950 mark. Even in Kerala, it is only 963. The highest child sex ratio of 986 is recorded in Sikkim.

Causes of the Sharp Decline in the Child Sex Ratio

(i) Practice of foeticide through sex specific abortions to prevent girl babies from being born.

(ii) Total negligence of girl babies leading to their higher death rates

(iii) Misuse of pre-natal diagnostic test, that is, sonogram which has caused female foeticide.

There are various reasons for this imbalance in the sex ratio. Factors such as *female infanticide, neglect of female infants, early marriage, bad treatment and hardwork of women, craving for male children, practice of dowry, dominant patriarchal values, etc.* have been instrumental in reducing the number of females in India. It is also significant to note that the sex ratio is higher in the urban areas and among the educated, than in the rural areas and among

Table - 7

Age Composition of the population of India, 1961-2026

Year	0-14 years	Age groups 15-59 years	60+ Age	Total
1961	41	53	6	100
1971	42	53	5	100
1981	40	54	6	100
1991	38	56	7	100
2001	34	59	7	100
2011	29	63	8	100
2026	**23**	**64**	12	100

Source: Census Report - 2011.

the uneducated. It is also observed that there are 13 States with sex ratio above the national level, and 12 States with sex ratio lower than the national level. Kerala is the only state wherein women outnumber men.

5. Density of Population

Density is also a major factor in the study of population. In the Indian context, *density is defined as the average number of persons living per square kilometre.* The trends of the density of population in the country from 1901 onwards are shown in ***Table* - 8.** The density of population was found to be 77 in 1901 and 324 in 2001and it increased to the record mark of **382** in **2011**. Dehli with 11297 persons per sq. km in 2011 is the most densely populated state in India. Arunachal Pradesh with just 17 persons per sq. Km is the least densely populated state. Comparatively, China has a density of population of 135 persons, whereas Canada, Australia and America have 3, 2, and 31 persons respectively.

1901-2011 Table - 7

Sex Ratio in India

Year	Females per 1000 Males
1901	972
1911	964
1921	955
1931	950
1941	945
1951	946
1961	941
1971	930
1981	934
1991	927
2001	933
2011	940

Table - 8

Density of Population in India 1901-2011

Year	per sq. km.
1901	77
1911	82
1921	81
1931	90
1941	103
1951	117
1961	142
1971	177
1981	216
1991	267
2001	324
2011	382

6. Life Expectancy

Life expectancy or expectation of life at a given age is the average number of years which a person of that age may expect to live, according to the mortality pattern prevalent in that country. Demographers consider it as one of the best indicators of a country's level of development and the overall health status of its population.

***Table* - 9 & 10** present life expectancy at birth in India and those in selected countries. Japan leads in life expectancy for both males and females, 77 and 83 years respectively for the year 1998. As far as India is concerned, in the year 1901, the life expectancy of males and females at birth was found to be 23.63 years and 23.93 years, respectively. These figures have increased respectively to 62.80 years and 63.80 years in 2000.

Trends in life expectancy show that people are living longer, and they have a right to a long life in good health, rather than one of pain and disability. Health policy makers need to recognise this changing demographic pattern, and plan for prevention and control of diseases associated with old age.

7. Dependency Ratio

The proportion of persons above 65 years of age and children below 15 years of age are considered *to be dependent* on the economically productive age group [15 - 64 years]. *The ratio of the combined age groups 0 - 14 years plus 65 years and above to the 15 - 65 years age group – is referred to as the total dependency ratio.* The dependency ratio reflects the need for a society to provide for their younger and older population groups.

Table - 9

Expectation of Life at Birth – India		
Year	*Males*	*Females*
1901	23.63	23.96
1911	22.59	23.31
1921	19.42	20.91
1931	26.91	26.56
1941	32.09	31.37
1951	32.45	31.66
1961	41.89	40.55
1971	46.40	44.70
1981	50.90	50.00
1991	58.10	59.10
2000	62.80	63.80

Source : Park's *"Text-book of Preventive and Social Medicine"* [2002]. Page - 331.

Table - 9(A)

Rural and Urban Population 1901 - 2001				
Census Year	Population (m.)		Percentage of (m.)	
	Rural	Urban	Rural	Urban
1901	213	26	89.2	10.8
1911	226	26	89.7	10.3
1921	223	28	88.8	11.2
1931	246	33	88.0	12.0
1941	275	44	86.1	13.9
1951	299	62	82.7	17.3
1961	360	79	82.0	18.0
1971	439	109	80.1	19.9
1981	524	159	76.7	23.3
1991	629	218	74.3	25.7
2001	741.7	285.4	72.22	27.78

Source : Census of India, 2001

Table - 10

Expectation of Life at Birth in Selected Countries - 2000

Developing Countries	2000		*Developed Countries*	2000	
	Male	*Female*		*Male*	*Female*
Nepal	58.8	58.3	UK	75.2	80.2
Bangladesh	59.4	59.5	USA	74.1	79.9
Myanmar	53.7	58.5	Sweden	77.2	82.2
India	62.8	63.8	Switzerland	75.6	82.0
Sri Lanka	69.5	75.3	Russian Federation	61.0	73.0
Thailand	67.3	73.2	Japan	77.4	84.4

Source : Park's *"Text-book of Preventive and Social Medicine"* [2002]. Page 331.

In terms of dependency ratio, we can also speak of *young age dependency ratio* [0 - 14 years]; and *old age dependency ratio* [65 years and more]. These ratios are, however, relatively crude, since they do not take into consideration elderly or young persons who are employed or *working age persons* who are unemployed. ***Table* - 11** shows the trends of dependency ratio in India.

Table - 11

Trends in Dependency Ratio in India (per 100)

Year	*Total Dependency*	*Child Dependency*	*Old-age Dependency*
1985	71.5	64.3	7.2
1995	65.5	57.8	7.6
2005 (projected)	55.5	47.2	8.3

Source : WHO [1999] Health Situation in the South East Asia Region 1994-97.

8. Population and Urbanisation

Growth of population in most of the developing countries is closely associated with growing urbanisation. Urbanisation is taking place at a relatively greater speed in India. The proportion of urban population in India increased from 10.84% in 1901 to 17.3% in 1951, to 25.7% in 1991, and to 27.8% in 2001 and had further increased to 31.2% in the year 2011. In absolute terms, the urban population in India was 377.10 million in 2011 compared to 285 million in 2001. See ***Table* - 9(A).**

The percentage of population residing in urban areas has increased marginally. The number of urban areas and towns increased from 3,768 in 1991 to 7935 in 2011. In 2011, three major cities of India - Mumbai, Kolkota and Delhi - attained the status of **mega-cities** each with a population of more than 10 million. The pace of urbanisaion is relatively due to predominance of agriculture, slow rate of industrialisation, low rate of literacy, slow growth of towns and cities, slow rate of social and occupational mobility, shortage of capital, etc.

9. Birth and Death Rates

The birth and death rates are important components of population growth. The birth and death rates in India are shown in ***Table* - 12.** A look at ***Table* - 12** shows that whereas the death rate considerably declined from 42.6 in 1911 to 8.7 per thousand population in 2001; and the birth rate declined niggardly from 49.2 in 1911 to 26.1 per thousand in 2001.

The birth rate in India was 26.1 per thousand in 2001 and the death rate was 8.7 per thousand for the same period. This widened the gap between the birth rate and the death rate. As a result, the net rate of increase of population in the country is 1.9%. This is the most significant factor behind the population explosion in India.

India like many other developing countries is faced with the problem of a high birth rate and a declining death rate. ***The causes of high birth rate are*** – (i) universality of marriage, (ii) early marriage, (iii) early puberty, (iv) low standard of living, (v) low level of literacy, (vi) traditional customs and habits, (vii) absence of family planning habit, etc.

Table - 12

Birth and Death Rates in India

Year	*Birth Rate*	*Death Rate*
1911	49.2	42.6
1941	39.9	27.4
1951	41.7	22.8
1961	41.2	19.0
1971	37.2	14.8
1981	33.9	12.5
1991	29.5	9.8
1995	28.3	9.0
1996	27.5	9.0
1997	27.2	8.9
1998	26.4	9.0
1999	26.1	8.7
2001	26.1	8.7

Source : Govt. of India [2002], Annual Report 2001-2002, Ministry of Health & Family Welfare, New Delhi.

Table - 12 (A)

Birth and Death Rates in India

Census Year	Percentage of total Population		Urban - rural ratio
	Rural	Urban	
1901	89.0	11.0	1:8.1
1911	89.6	10.4	1:8.6
1921	88.7	11.3	1:7.8
1931	87.8	12.2	1:7.2
1941	85.9	14.1	1:6.1
1951	82.7	17.3	1:4.7
1961	82.0	18.0	1:4.5
1971	80.1	19.9	1:3.7
1981	76.7	23.3	1:2.9
1991	74.3	25.7	1:2.9
2001	72.2	27.8	1:2.6
2011	68.0	32.0	
2026	63.8	36.2	

Source : Register General, India.

Declining death rate has been attributed to – (i) mass control of diseases such as smallpox, plague, cholera, malaria, etc. (ii) better health facilities, (iii) impact of national health programmes, (iv) absence of natural checks as found in the instances of famines, floods, large scale epidemics, etc., (v) improvements in food supply, (vi) international aid in different ways, (vii) development of social consciousness among the masses. The demographers are of the opinion that in future rapid decline in India's death rate may not be continued.

10. Literacy Structure

As far as the literacy structure of the country is concerned, in 2011, on an average, around **74.04%** people are found to be literate [**82.14%** males and **65.46%** females]. Kerala is a state wherein we find the highest literacy rate, that is **93.91%** and Bihar has the lowest one, that is, **63.82%.**

Of the total literate people in India in 1991 [846.3 million], 56.7% had less than 3 years education, 23.8% 3-6 years education, 11% 7-11 years education, 6.8% 12-14 years education and 1.7% more than 14 years education. It is evident that we find a very limited number of people with college education. While the literacy rate for males rose from 75.85 to 82.14% in 2011 marking a rise of **6.29%**; it increased by **11.3%** for females to go from 54.16 to 65.46 per cent.

Table - 13 (A)

Literacy Rates in India : 1951 - 2011

Year	Total Persons	Males	Females
1951	18.33	27.16	8.86
1961	28.30	40.40	15.35
1971	34.45	45.96	21.97
1981	43.57	56.38	29.76
1991	52.21	64.13	39.29
2001	65.38	75.85	54.16
* 2011	74.04	82.14	65.46

Source : Census of India. 2001.
* Povisional Statistics, census 2011

If we look at the State-wise break-up of the literacy rate , we find that Kerala continues to occupy the top rank in the country with about 93.91% literates (2011). Ten states and union territories, including -Kerala, Lakshdveep, Mizoram, Tripura, Goa, Damun and Diu, Puduchery, Chandigarh, Delhi, Andaman and Nicobar Inlands - have attained a literacy rate of above **85%,** one target set by the planning commission to be achieved by 2011-12. **[See Table - 13B]**

Occupational Distribution of Population in India

Occupational distribution of population or occupational pattern in India refers to – *the proportion of total working population engaged in different broad sectors of the economy.* These broad sectors are – **1. *Primary sector*** which includes occupations like agriculture, mining, fishing, animal husbandry and forestry, **2. *Secondary sector*** which consists of occupations like manufacturing, construction, electricity, etc., and **3. *Tertiary sector*** which consists of occupations such as trade, transport, communications, banking, insurance, personal services, and both government and non-governmental services, etc. This sector is supposed to meet the needs of both primary and secondary sectors.

It is quite significant to note that the occupational distribution of population in the country remained almost constant over the last 90 years. ***Table* - 14** reveals the same. Even after the vigorous efforts by the Central and the State Governments to develop industries, trade, transport and communication, banking, insurance, etc. the majority of our working population are still dependent on agriculture for their livelihood. During the recent years, that is, after 1991 sizeable number of educated piople have been able to get jobs with attractive salaries in the service sector.

The occupational distribution of population in India is imbalanced. It shows that India is still backward in the field of industries and is depending too much on agriculture. Inadequate and lop sided growth of secondary and tertiary sectors is another fundamental cause for this imbalance in the occupational distribution. The performance of public sector industries is not that satisfactory, and the tertiary sector too has failed to absorb the excess population.

Literacy Rate in India - 2011 — **Table No. : 13 B**

Sl. No.	India/ State/UT	Literate Persons (%)	Males (%)	Females (%)
01	J & Kashmir	68.74	78.26	58.01
02	Himachal P.	83.78	90.83	76.60
03	Punjab	76.68	81.48	71.34
04	Chandigarh	86.43	90.54	81.38
05	Uttarakhand	79.63	88.33	70.70
06	Haryana	76.64	85.38	66.77
07	NCT of Delhi	86.34	91.03	80.93
08	Rajasthan	67.06	80.51	52.66
09	Uttar Pradesh	69.72	79.24	59.26
10	Bihar	63.82	73.39	53.33
11	Sikkim	82.20	87.29	76.43
12	Arunachal	66.95	73.69	59.57
13	Nagaland	80.11	83.29	76.69
14	Manipur	79.85	86.49	73.17
15	Mizoram	91.58	93.72	89.40
16	Tripura	87.75	92.18	83.15
17	Meghalaya	75.48	77.17	73.78
18	Assam	73.18	78.81	67.27
19	West Bengal	77.08	82.67	71.16
20	Jharkhand	67.63	78.45	56.21
21	Orissa	73.45	82.40	64.36
22	Chattisgarh	71.04	81.45	60.59
23	M. Pradesh	70.63	80.53	60.02
24	Gujarat	79.31	87.23	70.73
25	Daman & Diu	87.07	91.48	79.59
26	Dadra & Nagar Haveli	77.65	86.46	65.93
27	Maharashtra	82.91	89.82	75.48
28	Andhra Pradesh	67.66	75.56	59.74
29	Karnataka	75.60	82.85	68.13
30	Goa	87.40	92.81	81.84
31	Lakshadweep	92.28	96.11	88.25
32	Kerala	93.91	96.02	91.98
33	Tamil Nadu	80.33	86.81	73.86
34	Pondicherry	86.55	92.12	81.22
35	Andaman & Nicobar	86.27	90.11	81.84
	INDIA	**74.04**	**82.14**	**65.46**

Main Figures at a Glance

No. of States / UT 35 / 35*
No. of Districts 593 / 640*
No. of Sub-Dist. 5,463 / 5,924*
No. of Towns 5,161 / 7,935*
No. of Villages 638,588 / 640,867*
*[2001 - 2011]

Total Population - 2011

Total Persons : 1,210,193,422

	Rural	Urban
Male	427,917,052	195,807,196
Female	405,170,610	181,298,564

Total Literates - 2011

	Rural	Urban
Persons	493,020,878	285,433,242
Male	288,047,480	156,156,282
Female	204,973,398	129,276,960

Languages of India by Number of Native Speakers as per the 2001 Census

Language	Speakers	%
Hindi	422,048,642	41.03%
Bengali	83,369,769	8.11%
Telugu	74,002,856	7.19%
Marathi	71,936,894	6.99%
Tamil	60,793,814	5.91%
Urdu	51,536,111	5.01%
Gujarati	46,091,617	4.48%
Kannada	37,924,011	3.69%
Malayalam	33,066,392	3.21%
Oriya	33,017,446	3.21%
Punjabi	29,102,477	2.83%
Assamese	13,168,484	1.28%
Maithili	12,179,122	1.18%
Bhili/Bhilodi	9,582,957	0.93%
Santali	6,469,600	0.63%
Kashmiri	5,527,698	0.54%
Nepali	2,871,749	0.28%
Gondi	2,713,790	0.26%
Sindhi	2,535,485	0.25%
Konkani	2,489,015	0.24%
Dogri	2,282,589	0.22%
Khandeshi	2,075,258	0.20%
Kurukh	1,751,489	0.17%
Tulu	1,722,768	0.17%
Manipuri	1,466,705*	0.14%
Bodo	1,350,478	0.13%
Khasi - Garo	1,128,575	0.112%
Mundari	1,061,352	0.105%
Ho	1,042,724	0.103%

Note : Figures of the above for 2011 are not available

In order to forge a balance in the occupational distribution of the people, it is necessary for us to give more importance to industrial growth. Industry should be able to attract and accommodate a sizeable number of people from the rural areas to lessen their dependence upon agriculture. Further, the tertiary sector which consists of trade and commerce and service enterprises should be developed to absorb increasing number of unemployed youths.

Occupational Distribution of Working Population in India [in Percentgae] **Table - 14**

Year	*Primary Sector*	*Secondary Sector*	*Tertiary Sector*
1901	72%	12%	16%
1951	72%	11%	17%
1971	72%	11%	17%
1981	68.7%	13.5%	17.8%
1991	65%	15.0%	20.0%
1999-2000	60.4%	15.8%	23.8%
Source : Census of India, 1981 - 1991. For 1999-2000, NSSO 55th Round			

5. EFFECTS OF OVER POPULATION

If the size of population of the country reaches the optimum level, it will not pose any problem. If the growth exceeds the reasonable limits, problems will crop up and that has happened in India. It means population in excess of demand or need proves to be a great liability to the society. The unprecedented growth of population in India during the recent years, has brought about a series of serious consequences. Some of the main effects of population may be described here.

(i) Population and Poverty **:** Poverty and population very often go hand in hand. In fact, poverty is both the cause and the effect of rapid growth of population. The mass poverty of our country is due to the rapid growth of population. It is estimated that about 29.5% [2011-2012] of the people of India still live below the poverty line. They are ill fed, ill clothed and ill housed. Thus, mass poverty is mainly due to rapid and unmanageable growth of population.

(ii) Unemployment and Under Employment **:** Not only new born individuals are to be fed and sheltered but they are also to be provided with jobs. New jobs are to be created for new hands. It is not easy to create jobs. There is already unemployment coupled with under employment. Every year more than 5 million people who attain the working age join the group of job seekers. Job opportunities that are created during the course of the Five Year Plans are not enough to meet the demand. For instance, the number of the unemployed increased from 12 million at the end of the Third Plan to 16 millions at the end of the Fourth Plan, and to 21 millions at the end of the Fifth Plan. The percentage of the people who did not get employed as per 1991 census was 42.3%. As per the figures for 2003, about 41.39 million individuals were waiting [for jobs] in the live registers of 945 employment exchanges scattered over the whole nation. [Bhagavati Committee estimate]. As per the estimates of the 8th and 9th Plan, there would be 106 million job- seekers in India by 2000 A.D. Even during the 11th plan period [2007-12] also, there would be not less than 100 million job-seekers waiting for employment.

(iii) Low Per Capita Income **:** During the past 50 years of planning, the national income of the country has increased by about 3.6% per annum. But the per capita income has increased only by 1.5% per annum.[2] This low per capita income of the people in India is attributed to the rapid growth of population.

(iv) Shortage of Food **:** The rapidly growing population in India has led to the problem of shortage of food supply. In spite of the fact that more than two-third of its population engaged in agriculture, people do not get even minimum necessary amount of food. Even though we have attained self-sufficiency in food production, due to improper distribution, all the people do not get sufficient food to sustain their health. As a result one out of every four is suffering from malnutrition and two out of every four get only half of the daily required quantum of energising food.

(v) Increased Burden of Social Overheads **:** When there is rapid growth of population in the country, the government is required to provide the minimum facilities for the people for their comfortable living. Hence, it has to increase educational, housing, sanitation, public health, medical, transportation, communication and other facilities. This will increase the cost of the social overheads. Government finds it difficult to find sufficient funds to meet these *"unproductive expenses."*

(vi) Population and Labour Efficiency **:** Since an increase in population reduces per capita income, the standard of living of the people deteriorates. This affects very badly the health and efficiency of the workers. The physical and the mental efficiency of the workers naturally comes down. Labour inefficiency reduces productivity and the nation at large loses very heavily.

(vii) Population and the Standard of Living **:** The standard of living denotes the way in which people live. It reflects the quantity and the quality of the consumption of the people. Due to the rapid growth of population standard of living of the people has been adversely affected.

(viii) Population and Pressure on Land **:** Overpopulation inevitably leads to heavy pressure on land. Since land is limited and fixed in supply, an increase in population can only bring more pressure on it. Hence, the new born people will have to share the land with the existing people. With the exception of Rajasthan and Madhya Pradesh, in all the other states heavy density of the population is to be found. Further, the per head availability of the land for cultivation in the 1911 was 1.1 acres, and this has declined to 0.3 acres in 1992. On the contrary, the average size of the agricultural land that each person could get is 2.59 acres in Russia, and 2.68 acres in America.

(ix) Increased Unproductive Consumers **:** When there is a rapid growth of population in a country like India, there will be large proportion of unproductive consumers. In fact, today about 51% of the total population of India is unproductive. Rapid increase in the population contributes to an increase in the dependency ratio. [See ***Table*** - **11**].

(x) Slow Economic Development **:** Economic development is bound to be slower in a country in which the population is growing at a very fast rate. Absence of savings results in low capital formation. The shortage of capital has restricted investments and contributed to the slow economic growth of the country.

(xi) Political Unrest **:** Unmanageable population size may contribute to political instability and unrest. The failure of the government to provide the basic minimum facilities to the people contributes to agitation and unrest among the masses.

It is true that India is gripped by the problem of over-population. It has shaken the stability, integrity and the security of the nation. The progress that has been made is being eaten up by the growing population. A careful study of the adverse effects of population leads us to realise the need to control it. We cannot destroy or remove our large population so as to bring it down

---

2. Both national income and per capita income started increasing, say after 2000-01. During 2004-05 and 2011-12, we find an increase of 8.2% growth rate in the net national income and that of per capita income by 6.7% increase. This growth rate in a way, is promising, ***Source:*** **Datt** and **Sundharam**'s *'Indian Economy'* - Page: 33.

to the optimum level. We can only control it. *"If population is not checked our progress would be like writing on sand with waves of population growth washing away what we have written."*

6. NATIONAL POPULATION POLICY, 2000 [NPP-2000]

It is an undeniable fact that India is over-populated. How to face this problem of over-population ? India must make planned efforts to control the growing population for which she should have a well-thought out population policy. A more positive and more effective policy of population control is the need of the hour.

Population policy in general refers to the policy intended to *decrease the birth rate or the growth rate.* Statement of goals, objectives and targets are inherent in the population policy.

India formed its first *"National Population Policy"* in April 1976. It called for an increase in the legal minimum age of marriage from 15 to 18 for females and from 18 to 21 years for males. The policy was, however, modified in 1977. The new policy statement emphasised the importance of the small family norm without compulsion and changed the programme title to – *"Family Welfare Programme."*

***National Population Policy 2000* [NPP-2000]** – is the latest in the series. It was announced by the NDA Government headed by Atal Bihari Vajapayee on Feb - 15th 2000 A.D. It reaffirms the commitment of the government towards target free approach in administering family planning services. It has decided to encourage two-child norm [whereas in China, it is one-child norm] and aimed at stabilising the population by 2046 A.D. The NPP-2000 is not just a matter of fertility and mortality rates. *It deals with women education; empowering women for improved health and nutrition; child survival and health; the unmet needs for family welfare services; healthcare for the under-served population groups like urban slums, tribal community, hill area population and displaced and migrant population; adolescent's health and education; increased participation of men in planned parenthood; and collaboration with non-governmental organisations.*

The object of NPP-2000 is to bring the total fertility rate [TFR] to replacement levels by 2010. The long term objective is to achieve requirements of suitable economic growth, social development and environment protection. It contains the goals and the target to be achieved by 2010. They can be briefed here.

1. Giving rewards to panchayats and Zilla Parishads for promoting small family norm.
2. To reduce infant mortality rate to below 30 per 100 live births.
3. Reduce maternal mortality rate to below 100 per one lakh live births.
4. Achieve universal immunisation of children against all preventable diseases.
5. Achieve 80% institutional deliveries and 100% deliveries by trained persons.
6. Achieve 100% registration of births, deaths, marriage and pregnancy.
7. Prevent and control communicable diseases.
8. Promote vigorously the small family norm to achieve TFR.
9. Contain the spread of AIDS [Acquired Immuno Deficiency Syndrome].
10. Address the unmet needs for basic reproductive and child health services, supplies and infrastructure. Strict enforcement of *'Child Marriage Restraint Act'* and *'Pre-Natal Diagnostic Techniques Act'.*
11. Make school education up to age 14 free and compulsory, and reduce drop-outs at primary and secondary school levels to below 20% to both boys and girls.
12. Health insurance cover of ₹ 5000 per couple below the poverty line with two living children, who undergo sterilisation.
13. Achieve universal access to information / counselling and services for fertility regulation and contraception.

14. A special reward for women who marry after 21 and opt for a terminal method of contraception after the second child.
15. To take appropriate steps to make family welfare programme a people-centred programme.
16. Setting up of a National Commission on Population, headed by the Prime Minister.

The planning of the population must also include the improvement of quality of population. Further, life expectation has to be increased. If the NPP-2000 is fully implemented, it is anticipated that in the year 2010, the nation's population will be 1,107 million instead of 1,162 million projected by the Technical Group of Population Projections. Similarly, the anticipated crude birth rate will be 21 per thousand population, infant mortality rate 30 per thousand live births and total fertility rate 2.1. The NPP-2000 is to be largely implemented and managed at *panchayat* and *nagarapalika* levels in co-ordination with the concerned State / Union Territory administration.

Ninth Five Year Plan Objectives

The planning commission observed that given the present demographic situation in the country, the achievements are lagging behind the proposed goals for the year 2002. Against this background fresh targets were formulated to be achieved by the end of the Ninth Five Year Plan. The goals are revised to slightly lower levels. These are as follows:

Infant Mortality rate per 1000 live births	56-50
Crude birth rate per 1000 population	24/23
Crude death rate per 1000 population	9
Maternal mortality rate per 1000 live births	3
Life expectancy	
Male	62 [1996-2001]
Female	63 [1996-2001]
Couple protection rate (%)	51 - 60
Growth rate (%) annual	1.6 / 1.5
Total fertility rate	2.9 / 2.6
Immunization	Universal
Pregnant mothers receiving antenatal care (%)	90
Delivery by trained personnel (%)	45
Institutional deliveries (%)	35

7. MEASURES FOR CONTROLLING THE RAPID GROWTH OF POPULATION

Need For Controlling the Growth of Population

Overpopulation is, indeed, a serious socio-economic problem of India. This problem has adversely affected the progress of the economy and the standard of living of the people. The problem is an urgent one and needs immediate solution.

The problem of overpopulation is to be tackled immediately. There is an absolute need to contain the rapid growth of population. If this growth is not checked it is going to affect adversely the various aspects of our economy. It brings down per capita and national income, brings down standard of living of the people. It becomes difficult to face the challenges of poverty, unemployment and underemployment. Basic needs of the people cannot be met with, political unrest and immorality cannot be efficiently dealt with.

Overpopulation is related to *the size of the population and the utilisation of the country's resources.* The problem should be tackled from both the sides. *Firstly,* production should be increased to meet the needs of the people. *Secondly,* size of the population should be controlled and reduced.

(A) Measures to Increase Production

Growing population of the country can be supported through increased production. Agricultural and industrial productions are to be increased for this purpose.

1. *Increase in Agricultural Production* : It is necessary to resort to modern scientific cultivation in order to increase agricultural output. Use of irrigation, high yielding seeds, rotation of crops, utilisation of chemicals, fertilisers, manures and such other means are to be adopted for this purpose. *Production should keep pace with increasing population, if possible, should outstrip it.*

2. *Increase in Industrial Production* : The process of industrialisation is to be accelerated. Modern sophisticated technology must be made use of for industrial production. The industrial strategy should be such that it should be able to increase production and at the same time provide job facilities to a sizeable number of people. Industries are to be established in different places by making use of the locally available raw materials and human resources.

3. *Development of Trade and Commerce* : The development of trade and commerce will contribute to additional income and help the country to support the growing population.

(B) Measures to Control and Reduce Population

The problem of overpopulation can be effectively dealt with only if the rapid growth rate of population is contained. Various measures are to be undertaken in this regard.

1. *Family Planning Measures* : Family planning is nowadays considered an indispensable method of controlling population. The motto of family planning is – *"child by choice and not by chance"* or *"child by desire not by accident."* The size of the family must be limited voluntarily. It can be done in two ways : (*a*) *Birth control methods,* (*b*) *Other family planning methods.*

a) ***Birth control methods*** include – use of rubber contraceptives by males, use of pills by females, use of loops by females, sterilisation for both males and females [that is, vasectomy for males and tubectomy for females], abortion, *i.e.*, medical termination of pregnancy.

b) ***Other family planning methods*** include – practice of celibacy [that is, practising *brahmacharya* or self-restraint], postponement of marriage [or resorting to late marriage], observance of moral or self-restraint.

2. *Providing Education Facility to the People* : Illiteracy is one of the factors of overpopulation. It is to be countered in order to contain the population growth. Spread of education among illiterate masses is a significant step in reducing the birth rate. People must be educated regarding the benefits of small family and late marriage. Education helps to increase the earning capacity of males and females. It improves the status of women, it creates awareness regarding family planning.

3. *Rise in the Age of Marriage* : In order to reduce the child-bearing period of women [reproductive span of women], it is necessary to rise the minimum age of marriage from 18 to 20 for females and from 21 to 24 for males. Child marriages should be strictly prohibited.

4. *Improving Status of Women* : Experience in the West has shown that high status of women is closely associated with a low birth rate. The desire to rise in the social scale develops a strong feeling for a smaller family. The educated, employed urban women exhibit a desire for a small family. Efforts must be made to impress upon rural women to go in the direction of a small families.

5. ***Propaganda in Favour of Small Family*** **:** Enough publicity is to be given in a country like India regarding the benefits of small family to the general masses. Mass media of communication like the press, radio, television and movies are of great help in this regard.

6. ***Provision of Incentives*** **:** Incentives such as cash payments and promotion in jobs, free education, preference in admission to technical courses, etc. could be given to the people who accept and adopt family planning.

7. ***Increasing the Standard of Living of the Masses*** **:** People with higher standard of living normally opt for small family. Hence, it is necessary to increase the standard of living of the masses.

8. ***Providing Enough Recreational Facilities*** **:** It has been observed that lack of sufficient recreational facilities has often contributed to the problem of overpopulation. People must be provided with sufficient recreational facilities to relax and to refresh. This will prevent them from resorting to sex play whenever they feel like refreshing themselves.

9. ***Internal Migration*** **:** Unequal distribution of population in different parts of the nation can be dealt with if internal migration is allowed. It means people must be encouraged to move from the densely populated areas towards the thinly populated areas. This is not, however, easy. As **Adam Smith** observes, *"Of all sorts of luggage, man is the most difficult to be transported."*

10. ***Provision of Social Security*** **:** In the absence of comprehensive social security [especially, in old age, sickness, unemployment and accident] people have tended to depend on large families for security. The poor, in particular, consider children as their wealth. It is necessary to introduce various social insurance and social security schemes to help the poor to develop confidence to face the future.

11. ***Reduction in Infant Mortality*** **:** By resorting to suitable medical steps the rate of infant mortality is to be reduced. If it is reduced, then parents will definitely feel that their children will survive and live long.

12. ***Changes in the Tax Structure*** **: Dr. S. Chandrashekhar,** a noted Indian demographer, has suggested that by introducing a change in the taxation policy, especially that of income tax, the problem can be reduced a little. Instead of giving concessions to married people with more children, he has suggested, it is better to give such concessions to the unmarried, and also to those couples without children or with only one child.

8. FAMILY PLANNING AND ITS ACHIEVEMENTS

Family Planning and Its Meaning

Family planning basically means planning the number of children in the family. It is *"limiting the size of the family by conscious efforts."* The motto of family planning is *"child by choice, and not by chance"*. Family planning can be defined as *"an instrument of social transformation which aims at creating better parents, healtheir children and happier homes"*. It seeks to inject social responsibility into married life.

Family planning is described by an ***Expert Committee of the WHO*** in the following manner. *"Family planning refers to practices that help individuals or couples to attain certain objectives*:

(a) *to avoid unwanted births,*

(b) *to bring about wanted births,*

(c) *to regulate the intervals between pregnancies,*

(d) *to control the time at which births occur in relation to the ages of the parent; and*

(e) *to determine the number of children in the family."*

Family Planning as a Basic Human Right

The United Nations Conference on Human Rights at Tehran in 1968 recognised family planning as a basic human right. *The World Conference of the Women's Year in 1975* also declared – *"the right of women to decide freely and responsibly on the number and spacing of their children and to have access to the information and means to enable them to exercise that right."*

Scope of Family Planning Services

It is unfair to think that family planning is just equal to birth control. In fact, it is something more than mere birth control. WHO Expert Committee [1970] has stated that family planning includes in its purview the following aspects – **1.** *the proper spacing and limitation of births,* **2.** *advice on sterility,* **3.** *education for parenthood,* **4.** *sex education,* **5.** *genetic counselling,* **6.** *premarital consultation and examination,* **7.** *carrying out pregnancy tests,* **8.** *marriage counselling,* **9.** *preparation of couples for the arrival of their first child,* **10.** *providing services for unmarried mothers,* **11.** *teaching home economics and nutrition,* **12.** *providing adoption services.* These activities vary from country to country according to national objectives and policies with regard to family planning.

The Renaming of "Family Planning Programme" as "*Family Welfare Programme*"

The Government of India evinced greater interest in controlling population growth in 1976. During the emergency [1976-78] compulsory sterilisation was carried on at great speed through coercive measures in various places in North India. For example, in 1976, more than 76 lakh sterilisations were carried out against a target of 43 lakh. Coercive methods adopted for the implementation of the programme during this period resulted in people's discontentment. Hence the Janata Government, which came to power soon after emergency, wanted to follow a soft policy. It announced a comprehensive population policy in that year. Family planning programme was renamed as *"Family Welfare Programme."* This welfare programme has experienced several ups and downs in its performance over time.

Achievements

Government's efforts at controlling population through family planning / welfare programme has not yielded consistent results. The programme has experienced several ups and downs in its performance over time. *For example,* the number of sterilisations increased from around 7000 in 1956 to 1.84 million in 1970-71. This figure increased to 2.19 million during 1971-72 but it came down to 0.94 million during 1973-74. This decline was particularly due to abandonment of camp approach. During the emergency period [1975-77] sterilisation performance of sterilisations was really good [about 8.26 million sterilisation cases in 1976-77 alone]. The performance of sterilisation came down particularly after emergency. But the trend nowadays is slowly changing in favour of family welfare programme. Particularly, in the nineties the total programme seems to have greater acceptance among the public.

The Central Government has been investing more and more money for the implementation of the family welfare programmes through its five year plans. The Government, for example, spent a meagre amount of ₹65 lakhs for this purpose in the First Five Year Plan. The Government, however, started spending more and more money towards the programme in the other Plans. For example, it spent ₹27 crores in the Third Plan, ₹497 crores in the Fifth Plan, ₹1,010 crores in the Sixth Plan, ₹3,221 crores in the Seventh Plan and ₹6,792 crores in the Eighth Plan. The Ninth Plan allocated ₹ 14,194 crores for this programme.

Uneven Response of the States for the Family Welfare Programme

A state-wise break-up of the figures indicates that while some states notably Punjab, Gujarat, Maharashtra, Karnataka, Haryana and Tamil Nadu are forging ahead in the direction of family planning, some other states such as Bihar, Uttar Pradesh, Assam, Rajasthan, West Bengal, Jammu Kashmir, etc. are lagging behind.

Difficulties Involved in the Implementation of the Family Planning

(i) Birth control is associated with a high standard of living, but in India it is very low.

(ii) The available contraceptives are not safe, cheap and easily available.

(iii) Due to administrative and organisational defects, the message of family planning programme has not reached properly the remotest corners of the country where it is all the more needed.

(iv) Illiterate and ignorant people have failed to understand the significance of the programme.

(v) Traditional-minded Indians look at the programme with disfavour and suspicion. This, they feel, strikes at the very root of their belief or faith in God.

(vi) The use of contraceptives requires privacy in the houses, which is not found in some large joint families, and also in single-room houses.

(vii) Finally, the success of the programme depends upon the integrity, sincerity and honesty of the officials engaged in the programme. It is unfortunate, that these officials themselves are not much serious about it.

Karnataka Population Highlights – 2011

- ***Total population of Karnataka*** in 2001 was 52850562, and it increased in 2011 to 6,11,30,704 [Men – 3,10,57,742 as against 2,68,98,918 in 2001, and women 3,00,72,962 as against 2,69,51,644 in 2001].
- ***Sex Ratio****:* For every 1000 men, there are 968 women [as against 965 in 2001], in the case of children, sex ratio is 943 [as against 965 in 2001].
- ***In Bangalore city*****,** the state capital, there are only **908** women for every 1000 men.
- ***Rate of population growth*** has declined in Karnataka from **17.5%** during 1991-2001 to **15.7%** between 2001-2011.
- State retains its **9th** place in the total population of India as it was in 2001.
- Between 2001-2011, there was 15.46% increase in the population of men and in the case of women, the increase was 15.88%.
- The average literacy of the state in 2011is 75.60% , and it was 66.64% in 2001, and this reveals an increase of 8.96% over the previous decade.
- The State witnessed much increase in literacy over the previous decade. There were 3,04,34,962 literates in 2001 and the number increased to 4,10,29,323 [Men - 2,28,08,468 and women – 1,82,20,855] in 2011 by making 1,05,94,361 people literate.
- In 12 districts of the State, literacy rate is higher than the State average. Dakshina Kannada [D.K.] district has the highest literacy [88.62%] and it is lowest in Yadgiri district [52.36%].
- As far as ***female literacy*** is concerned, in 8 districts, it is less than 60%, in 12 districts it is between 60-70%; in 7 districts it is between 71-80%, and in 3 districts it is above 80%.
- Population growth has increased in Bangalore by **37%** over the previous decade and the share of Bangalore in the population of the state is 15.69% [95,88,910 people]. Belgaum stands second with 7.82% [47,78,439]. Mysore occupies third place with 4.90% [29,94,744]; Gulbarga [4.20%] and Bellary [4.14%] secure the fourth and fifth places respectively.

- Kodagu district has the least share in the State's population [0.91% with 5,54,762 people] and the second place in this regard is occupied by Bangalore (Rural) and its share of population is 1.61% [9,87,257 people].
- As far as ***the number of children*** between the age of 1 to 6 years is concerned, there has been a slight decrease. Their number was 71,82,100 in 2001 and it got reduced to 68,55,801, denoting a decline in the growth rate by **4.54%.** Out of these 68,55,801 children, 35,27,884 are males [that is, 1,63,114 less than what it was in 2001], and 33,27,957 are females [that is, 1,63,185 les than what it was in 2001.]
- ***Density of Population**:* There were 276 people per k.m. in 2001 and the number has increased to 319 in 2011, indicating an increase of 15.58%.
- Udupi and DK are the two districts wherein women outnumber men in 2011. For the first time in 110 years of demographic history of these two districts, there has been a slight decrease in the sex ratio of men and women. In Udupi, there were **1130** women for every 1000 men in 2001 [1107 women in 1991] and their number decreased to **1093** in 2011. In the same way, in D.K. district, there were 1029 women for every 1000 men in 2001 [and 1029 women in 1991] and their number decreased to 1022 in 2011.
- Three other districts in which women outnumber men are Kodagu [1019], Hasan [1005], and Chickmagalur [1005]. The corresponding numbers of women in these districts for 2001 are – 996, 1004 and 984 respectively.

  Source: *As per the press statement released by the Directorate of Census, Karnataka and published in "Udayavani" Kannada Daily, Dated: 07.04.2011, Udupi-Manipal, Karnataka.*

The Relative Strength of Youth Power of Some Selected Countries - 2014

Total number of youths in between the age of 10 - and - 24 years in the whole world as of 18th November, 2014 is 180 crore.

India	- 35.6 crore	America	- 6.5 crore	Bangladesh	- 4.8 crore
China	- 26.9 crore	Pakisthan	- 5.7 crore		
Indonesia	- 6.7 crore	Brazil	- 5.1 crore		

Source: UN Report released on 18-11-2014 as published in 'Udayavani', Kannada Daily, Dated: 19.11.2014

POPULATION BY RELIGION IN INDIA [1971 - 2001]

	1971		1981		1991		2001*	
Religious Group	**Number (million)**	**%age to total**	**Number (million)**	**%age to total**	**Number (million)**	**%age to total**	**Number (million)**	**%age to total**
Hindus	453.4	82.7	549.7	82.6	672.6	82.4	827.50	80.5
Muslims	61.4	11.2	75.6	11.4	95.2	11.7	138.18	13.4
Christians	14.2	2.6	16.2	2.4	18.9	2.3	24.05	2.34
Sikhs	10.4	1.9	13.1	2.0	16.3	2.0	-	-
Buddhists	3.9	0.7	4.7	0.7	6.3	0.8	-	-
Jains	2.6	0.5	3.2	0.5	3.4	0.4	-	-
Other	2.2	0.4	2.8	0.4	3.5	0.4	-	-
Total	548.2	100.0	665.3	100.0	812.3	100.0		

Source : INDIA Year Book - 1999. Page - 16, and *Census Report 2001

- As per 2011 census, the Hindu population is reduced to 78.35% and Muslim population is increased to 14.2% [0.8% over 2001 census figure of 13.4%.

  Source: *Udayavani. Dated: 25-1-2015.*

●●●

Chapter 5

CRIME AND PUNISHMENT

A. Crime and Punishment : *Concept of Crime - Definition and Characterises - Classification of Crime or Types of Crimes - Causes and Consequences of Crimes - Measures to Control Crime - Punishment as a Method of Dealing with the Criminal - Theories Relating to Punishment: Theory of Revenge, Theory of Deterrence and Theory of Reformation or Rehabilitative Theory - A Breif Assessment of the Three Theories of Punishment - Methods or Ways of Dealing with the Criminal: The Police - The Court - Probation - Parole and the Prision - A Model Prision at Lucknow-1949 - Experiment with Open Prisoners Camp - Capital Punishment - Crime in India - Two Categories of Crime: Cognizable Crimes and Non-Cognizable Crimes.*

B. Cyber Crime : *Definition of Cyber Crime - Forms of Abuse of Computer - Causes for Cyber Crime - Types of Cyber Criminals - Types of Cyber Crimes - Prevention and Control of Cyber Crimes.*

Ever since the ancient times, crime has been associated with the human society as though it is an inseparable part of it. Crimes are found in all societies and they have been there everywhere. If going against the accepted mores and such other norms of society is regarded as *"immoral behaviour"*, breaking or violating the established laws, is known as *"crime"*, and such behaviour, *"criminal behaviour"*. Crime represents a kind of 'deviant behaviour'. The term 'crime' is very commonly used by the people to refer to *'anti-social behaviour'* or *'socially harmful behaviour'*. In all societies of mankind we find people who are referred to as *'criminals'*, the term refering to those who violate the law and against whom society has got marked social disapproval. The main reason for this marked social disapproval is that the criminals are not only dangerous to the well-being of society, but to the individual liberty and property as well. In addition to that, as **Dr. Gillin** points out, *"more important is the feeling of danger to ourselves and our property that the criminal induces."*

"Crimes and criminal activities create horror in society. Most Indians are bewildered by the fact that in one hour about 187 cognisable crimes under the IPC [Indian Penal Code] and 443 crimes under the local and special laws are committed. In one day, the police grapples with 832 thefts, 258 riots, 66 robberies and 333 burglaries and 2991 other criminal offences."[1] Our bewilderment gives way to fear when we imagine our own vulnerability to crime. Repeatedly, we read or hear about the burglary of a neighbourhood home, the armed robbery of a jewellery shop or a bank, the shooting of the police and the civilians by the Naxalites, the rape of a woman in a bush, the theft of an automobile by a youth offender, etc. *"Crimes like these tend to undermine the*

1. *"Crime in India"*, 1994 : 8.9 as quoted by **Prof. Ram Ahuja** in *"Social Problems in India"* - 2001. Page : 308.

very quality of our lives by making us fearful of each other and by creating a sense of insecurity when we leave our locked homes and attempt to move freely about our communities."[2]

1. CONCEPT OF CRIME : DEFINITION AND CHARACTERISTICS

Concept of Crime

Crime has traditionally been studied as a form of deviant behaviour. Criminal and delinquent behaviours represent deviations from a very important set of social rules, namely those that have been codified in the criminal law. The dictionary meaning of the word *'crime'* refers to *"a violation of law"* or *"an act punishable by law"*.[3]

Literal Meaning of the Word "Crime"

The English word *'crime'* is derived from the Latin term *"crimen"* which means *'charge'* or *"offence"*. Thus, literally the word crime means *"an attack on norms or the law"*. It also means *"violation of norms and laws"*.

Definition of Crime

1. **Samuel Koenig :** *"Crime may be defined as any act forbidden by law which society expects its authorised officials to enforce."*
2. **F.R. Scarpitti** and **M.L. Andersen :** *"Crime can be defined in terms of the body of law that codifies a society's rules about proper and improper behaviour."*
3. **The Waverly Encyclopaedia :** *"Crime is an act forbidden by law, and for performing which the perpetrator is liable to punishment...."*

Main Characteristics of Crime

In the light of the definitions mentioned above, the following characteristics of crime can be identified.

1. *Crime is an Illegal Act* : Crime is an act forbidden by law or a legal lapse that deserves punishment. *"Where there are no written laws the forbidden acts are recognised and punished as transgressions against the traditions or mores of the community."*[4]

2. *Crime is Harmful* : Crime is normally believed to be harmful to the society. In fact, an act can be regarded as crime only when its external consequences are found to be dangerous. Criminal behaviour of the individuals is strongly disapproved by the society because it is regarded as harmful. This sociological conception of crime *"is inadequate as all acts which are socially harmful are not considered as crimes in the civilised societies unless they are in violation of the criminal code."*[5]

3. *Crimes are Linked With the Norms of Society* : An act called *'crime'* must always be interpreted in the context of *'norms'*. In fact, as **Thorsten Sellin** points out crime is a *"violation of the norms of conduct of the normative groups."*[6] The legal norms such as civil and criminal codes, for example, define certain kinds of behaviour as *"civil wrongs"* and *"offences against the state"* and such behaviours are to be penalised. An act is regarded as *"crime"* only in relation to the established norms of the society and not because of the very nature of the act. It is *'crime'* because, it is generally disapproved. Crimes and criminals, in this sense, are the creations of the society.

---

2. **Scarpitti** and **M.L. Andersen** in their *"Social Problems"*.
3. ***Source*** : *"Chambers 20th Century Dictionary"* [1964] Page : 249.
4. **Samuel Koenig** in his *"Sociology - An Introduction to the Science of Society"*, Page : 318.
5. **G.R. Madan** - Vol. I, Page : 57.
6. **Thorsten Sellin** as quoted by **Ram Ahuja** - Page : 268.

THE HORROR OF CRIME

4. *Intention Behind the Crime* : Crime is said to be an intentional act. Its intention is criminal or anti-social in nature. ***Example,*** *killing a lonely old man residing in a big mansion to rob him.* This type of intention is known as malafide intention.

Crimes may be committed with relatively good intention too. It is here sociologist **Hall** makes a distinction between *"intention"* and *"motive"*. As he opines, even though the motive behind a crime is sublime, its immediate purpose or intention may be criminal. ***Example* :** *A person who has been raping young women but escaping every time from the clutches of law might be killed by an idealistic young person, who may feel that such a rapist must be killed before he spoils many more young women.* In this example, though the *motive* of the young idealist is somewhat socially good, his immediate intention is to kill the rapist, and hence his act is a criminal act.

5. *Crime is Not Like a Vice* : Crime is anti-social and harmful no doubt, but it is not an act perpetrated against the God. It is not like prostitution, alcoholism and drug addiction. More than damaging one's own interests there is a clear attempt to destroy, weaken or damage the network of social and legal norms behind a criminal activity. Such an activity deserves to be punished though in the case of the vices stated above, one has to think of various other ways and means of stopping it.

6. *Traceable Causal Relationship* : In order to establish the fact that a crime has taken place one must be able to link the intention behind the crime and the actual act of crime. Sometimes, this *'causal relationship'* cannot be established properly and the person accused of crime cannot be branded as a *"criminal"*. ***Example* :** *If a very faithful wife dies of mental shock after being beaten up by the husband in the presence of many neighbours, the relationship between the conduct and the harm it has caused, is not clear.*

7. *Crime as a Sign of Maladjustment* : An act of crime indicates the failure of a person to adjust or cope with the prevalent norms of a community or society. Thus, we may say that due to one's maladjustment with the normative system of society, one may take recourse to criminal activity.

2. CLASSIFICATION OF CRIMES OR TYPES OF CRIMES

1. Classification Based on Criminal Behaviour and the Severity of Crime

Crime is not an activity that is appreciated in any society. Since it is regarded as *'anti-social'*, it is always condemned and disapproved. Acts that are called *"criminal"* do not always lead to the same type of consequences. Some criminal acts cause only ordinary consequences while some others result in grave consequences making the society pay a heavy price for that. *Taking the consequences into consideration,* crimes can be classified into two types namely; *(i) Ordinary Crimes,* and *(ii) Serious or Dreadful Crimes.*

***(i) Ordinary Crimes* :** Stealing, cheating, selling duplicate products in place of original ones, providing false witness, tax evasion, driving vehicles without licence or without renewing driving licence, committing crimes against one's own family members by beating them, not feeding them properly and so on, represent ordinary crimes. These are found everywhere and such crimes are regularly repeated. But these crimes do not cause any serious threat either to the existence of the society or to its social control machinery. Even in the most educated, advanced and stable societies such crimes do take place regularly.

***(ii) Serious or Dreadful Crimes* :** Murder, robbery, treason, terrorism, communal riots, ethnic clashes, genocide, bomb-explosions, selling national secrets to enemy countries, etc. constitute examples of serious or dreadful offences or crimes. Crimes like these are very dreadful in nature for they not only spoil the peace and order of a particular area/society but even pose a big challenge to the prevailing social order. They may even cause heavy loss to the lives and properties of the people.

- ***Criticism*** : This classification is severely criticised by the scholars. Since crimes are caused due to many factors, it is unfair to make a classification based mainly on external behaviour. Intention behind the criminal act is ignored in this classification for, it is possible to commit a serious crime without having a corresponding intention, or commit a crime but with a corresponding good intention The treatment of the two types must vary considerably based on the intention behind the act.

2. Classification Based on the Motive of Hatredness

Dutch criminologist **William Bonger** classified crimes into four major types depending on *the motives of hatredness behind the crimes*. They are mentioned below :

(i) *Sexual crimes* which include rape, prostitution, homosexuality, adultery, sexual harassment, etc.

(ii) *Economic crime*s which consist of offences related to financial interests.

(iii) *Political crime*s are crimes that involve unlawful attempts to get into power or to misuse power for democratic purposes.

(iv) *Ordinary miscellaneous crimes* include those crimes which are not covered by any of the above three categories.

Criticism : Bonger's classification is not universally accepted. It is not based on any scientific principle as such. It is unfair to decide that crimes are always committed with revengeful attitude or spirit. Sociologist **Sutherland** states that *"the classification of Bonger is clearly inadequate"*. ***Example*** : Let us assume that a young political leader establishes a friendly and sexual relationship with the young woman promising to marry her later, but finally cheats her and hushes up the whole episode by bribing the authorities concerned. Now, to which type of crime mentioned by Bonger does this particular criminal act gets classified ? We do not get an appropriate answer to a question of this kind.

3. Classification Based on Crime Statistics

Some scholars have classified crimes into five types on the basis of the available crime statistics. The five types are as follows :

(i) Crimes affecting persons,

(ii) Crimes affecting property,

(iii) Crimes relating to public health and sanitation,

(iv) Crimes relating to public system

(v) Crimes relating to public justice.

(i) Crimes Affecting Persons : In some types of crimes, some individuals are adversely affected or put to great loss financial or otherwise. *Example : One individual making a false allegation against another, cheating, sexual assault, giving physical or mental torture, etc.*

(ii) Crimes Affecting Property : Here, offences that are committed, adversely affect the property or economic interests of a family, group, company, business firm or community. ***Example*** : *Established merchants persecuting economically weaker retail traders, making illegal attempt to grab the property that belongs to somebody else, denial of legal rights to enjoy property, etc. belong to this category.*

(iii) Crimes Relating to Public Health and Sanitation : Offences that affect public health and sanitation, more than individual or private matter, come under this category. ***Example*** : *Behaving indecently in public, smoking in public places and in public transport vehicles, dumping garbage on the road side, conducting industrial activity in a residential area which spoils the peaceful atmosphere,* and such other offences are included under this kind.

(iv) Crimes Relating to Public Systems : Offences taking place in the public systems disturbing the day to day life activities of the people, are included here. ***Example*** : *Corrupt practices found in public transport system, electricity supply, water supply, police system, judicial system, etc.*

(v) Crimes Relating to Public Justice : Denial of fundamental rights, preventing persons from voting and from obtaining public services, police protection, legal justice and such other crimes constitute examples here.

4. Sutherland's Classification

By taking the economic status of the individuals into consideration, sociologist **Sutherland** classified criminals into two categories, namely; *(i) Economically Indigent Criminals,* and *(ii) White Collar Criminals.*

(i) Economically Indigent Criminals : Some economically poor and bankrupt people commit crimes. They commit crime under compulsion of extreme economic pressure. Most of them are driven to criminality rather than opting to become criminals. These persons are always under surveillance by the police and law enforcing authorities. Police are able to trap these people easily for they cannot defend themselves in law courts due to their poverty. They are legally and socially condemned.

(ii) White Collar Criminals : Irrespective of the type of the government, in all countries those rich people who commit crimes escape detection with the support of their money power. Outwardly, they pose themselves as decent and very dignified. But they are also criminals and such criminals are referred to as *"white collar criminals"*. The type of crimes that they commit are known as *'white collar crimes'*.[7] Big smuggling rackets, high-class prostitution, political murders, supply of cheap duplicate goods in place of original costly ones, trafficking in women and children, kidnapping business tycoons, etc. are organised by highly influential people. These persons successfully keep themselves hidden from detection with the connivance of law and detective agencies. Such persons also indulge in business malpractices, and political and social blackmail.

5. Dr. Havelock Ellis' Classification

Famous sexologist **Dr. Havelock Ellis**, has broadly classified criminals into seven major types. They are mentioned below.

(i) *Political criminals*
(ii) *Sexual criminals*
(iii) *Lunatic criminals*
(iv) *Casual criminals*
(v) *Professional criminals*
(vi) *Habitual criminals* and
(vii) *Instinctual criminals*

(i) ***Political Criminals*** : Politicians who resort to illegal and unconstitutional ways to fulfil their political purposes come under this category. ***Example*** : Politicians instigating severe caste conflicts, communal riots, supporting terrorists and anti-national organisations, taking the support of a party which is in power, etc.

---

7. *"White Collar Crime is committed by a person of respectability and high social status in the course of his occupation."* - **Sutherland**.

(ii) ***Sexual Criminals*** **:** People who resort to illegal sexual behaviour belong to this category. These sex offenders are of two types : *(i) Some persons violate the moral code due to some sudden uncontrollable impulse. (ii) Some commit sexual crimes for they are addicted to some abnormal type of sexual acts such as sodomy, incest, lesbianism, voyeurism, etc.*

(iii) ***Lunatic or Mentally Unsound Criminals*** **:** Due to mental illness or unsound mind, some commit crimes for they are not able to distinguish between the right and wrong. These lunatics have neither control over themselves before the act of the crime, nor afterwards. In this way, they are different from some normal persons who show perfect control over themselves both before and after the crime, but lose control at the moment of committing the crime.

(iv) ***Casual Criminals*** **:** Some individuals indulge in crime neither out of habit nor wilfully but out of ignorance or forgetfulness. ***Example*** **:** *Driving the vehicles without renewing driving licence.* The casual or occasional criminal is said to be the victim of social conditions, environmental factor or a very grave and sudden provocation. ***Example*** **:** *A clerk may suddenly get upset and beat his boss in the presence of the other staff members. It could be because of his inability to withstand the ugly remarks about him made by the boss.*

(v) ***Professional Criminals*** **:** For some people, crime is a source of livelihood. By experience they become skilled in the art of committing crimes. They normally belong to the condemned section of the society and the moral and legal codes of society have no meaning or relevance for them.

(vi) ***Habitual Criminals*** **:** Some who have tasted crime and enjoyed its thrill may get tempted to repeat it every now and then. ***Example*** **:** *Some have the criminal tendency of peeping into other people's bedrooms or bathrooms.*

(vii) ***Instinctual Criminals*** **:** Due to some irreparable personality defects also some individuals become criminals.

In addition to the above mentioned classifications, scholars like **Lombroso, Hayes, Lemert** and many others have also given their own classifications of crimes.

3. CAUSES OF CRIME

Crime as a universal phenomenon has been haunting all the societies and political establishments. Though it is universal, it is not uniform, and the factors causing crime are also not uniform. In the causation of crime, there is usually no single factor but a combination of factors working together mutually and supplementing. **Sutherland** and **Cressey** have said, *"crime is a product of large number of and a great variety of factors and these factors cannot now and perhaps never be organised into general propositions which have no exceptions."*[8]

Complex phenomenon like crime and the causes responsible for the same have been understood differently by the scholars of different subjects. **C.B. Mamoria** in this context writes : *"In fact, biology, sociology, medical science and psychology all have been pressed to understand the causes of crime. The biologist attributes to it the physical traits; the sociologist tends to stress environmental factors; the psychologists and psychiatrists stress on the inner conflicts and emotional insecurity and the advocates of religion find in it lack of religious and moral training; the medical experts attribute it to some mental disease like insanity, etc."*[9]

Of the various factors that influence crime, the following are more important.

---

8. As quoted by **C.B. Mamoria** in *"Social Problems and Social Disorganisation in India"* [1981] - Page : 978.
9. **C.B. Mamoria**, Page : 979.

1. Physical Factors or Environmental Factors

Physical factors or environmental fators such as - climate, seasons, natural resources, natural ups and downs, etc., influence crime, especially nature of crime and rate of crime. Social geographers like Dr. Huntington, Buckle, Le play, Lombroso and others had established the theory which is known as the *"theory of geographic determinism"* in which they stated that particular type of physical factors cause particular variety of crimes.

Lombroso believed that rape was more common in even or levelled territory than in the mountainous parts. He tried to correlate geography, climate, seasons and weather to criminality in his book *"Crime, Its Causes and Remedies"* [1918]. **Huntington**, a proponent of the *Geographic School*, asserted that a proportion of persons born in winter will have low IQ, will become criminals, or suffer from insanity. Various Italian, French and German criminologists have endeavoured to indicate correlation between different geological features and crime rate.

The arguments of social geographers relating to crime have not been totally accepted today. **Spencer, Giddings, Semple** and others have said that it is difficult to establish the theory that the physical factors exercise a determining influence on crime.

2. Biological Factors Causing Crime

Physiological factors such as bodily constitution, hereditary factor and glandular activities - are believed to be playing their role in causing crime.

Early emergence of puberty, especially in the modern civilised society, may lead to criminal behaviour. Boys and girls attain maturity much earlier and therefore, unless properly handled they fall a prey to *"passionate crimes of sexual perversities"*.

Bodily constitution is said to affect criminal tendencies. **Lombroso** argued that there was among various kinds of criminals, a *'born criminal type'* which was characterised by irregularities of body and mind. Born criminals were supposed to possess a greater measure of anamolies than ordinary criminals, occasional criminals and criminals of passion.[10]

Heredity is often regarded as a physiological factor affecting criminality. Some studies have attempted to substantiate the hereditary factor in criminality. **Dugdale**'s studies of the American Jukes family in the early 18th century, made him believe that *"pauperism, illegitimacy, intemperance and criminality were found to be rampant among the descendants of this [Jukes] family."*[11] **Dr. Adolph Lenz** of the *"School of Criminal Biology"* considers that *"hereditary predisposition is one of the outstanding factors in the causation of crime. ... The predisposition induces crime only where the pressure of the life struggle in the individual is in evidence."* [12]

Glandular factor too plays its role in crime. It is believed that the functioning of the glands is one of the basic determiners of temperament, intelligence, character and personality, as well as of physical and mental pathology. Glandular disturbances could account for many disharmonic, defective, unstable and inadequate qualities found in the suspected constitutional inferiority of criminals.

---

10. "Some of the many anatomical and mental anomalies of the born criminals were : asymmetry of skull : low retreating forehead; strongly arched brows; large outstanding ears; sparse beard; tatooing; left-handedness; relative insensibility to pain; acuteness of vision; obtuseness of the sense of smell or of taste, touch, and hearing; lack of moral sense; violent temper; extreme vanity; improvidence; and so forth." - **Lombroso** in *"Cesare, Crime, Its Causes and Remedies"* [1918], Page : 371-372 as quoted by **G.R. Madan,** Vol. 1, Page : 64.

11. **G.R. Madan**, Vol. 1, Page : 65.

12. As quoted by **C.B. Mamoria** - Page : 982.

In spite of the evidences put forward by the supporters of biological factors causing crime, it is difficult to conclude that the factors such as physiology, heredity and endocrine do play a part in the causation of crime. It is, however, equally difficult to contradict them also.

3. Mental or Psychological Factors

Mental factors such as mental deficiency, mental disorders, mental mechanisms and motivations to criminal behaviour are treated as separate factors in themselves for the causation of crime. Studies conducted by scholars like **Goring, Goddard, Dr. Lenz, Dr. Healy, Silverman, Sutherland** and others have established a causal relationship between crime and the mentality or mental conditions of the criminals.

- ***Mental deficiency*** has been regarded as one of the important causes of crime. **Goddard** had concluded that *"at least 50% of all criminals are mentally defective."*[13] He claimed that low-grade mentality was the greatest single cause of crime.

- ***Mental disorders*** constitute yet another psychological source of crime. But there is no clear indication at present that mental disorders play a very important part in the etiology of crime. **Dr. East** who studied about 2,34,000 persons imprisoned in various prisons in England in 1920s [1923 to 1926] found that the criminal insane comprised a very insignificant part of the total institutionalised insane.

- ***Mental weaknesses and abnormalities*** which include feeblemindedness, epileptic mentality, hysteria, psychosis, sensuality, hypersensitiveness, etc. are also said to influence criminal behaviour. **Goring**'s study made him believe that mental weakness of the criminal itself is the main cause of crime. **Sutherland** and **Cressy** attributed criminality to mental deficiency and epileptic mentality of the individuals.

4. Economic Factors

Economic factors such as poverty, large scale unemployment, urbanism and industrialisation, etc., often foster crime. It has been observed that crimes increase with economic depression and unemployment and decrease with good living conditions. Crimes are also committed when individuals are not satisfied with their lawful earnings and adopt unsocial conduct for the satisfaction of their desires.

Poverty is a factor which often encourages criminal behaviour. Poverty is a degrading experience. It leads to frustration, jealousy, bitterness and disappointment. When people are not able to meet their requirements of life due to utter poverty; they may think of perverse adventures. Poverty, in this way, acts as an enemy of morality and motivates a few to resort to criminal activities.

- ***Large-Scale Unemployment*** leads to social disorganisation which in turn leads to crime. Unemployment and economic distress usually bring about strain for the individual. He may find it impossible to bear it and may think of going against the expected standards of behaviour. The common saying *"an idle mind is a devil's workshop"* precisely applies to such persons who have no work to do, and thereby resort to any type of work however illegal or anti-social it might be.

- ***Phenomenal growth of cities*** and the ***spread of industrialisation*** too have their own impact on crime. Cities have been attracting large number of young people from the rural areas. Majority of people are strangers to one another. Since many of them are not accompanied by their families they are deprived of stable factors of family life. If women are also brought to urban areas, they create new problems like maladjustment and exposure to attractions of city

---

13. As quoted by **Madan** Vol.1. Page : 68.

life, its luxuries, and temptations that make young people go astray. There is absence of healthy recreation in the towns and cities. Gambling centres, indecent theatres, night clubs, pubs, clubs, brothel homes, video parlours, wine shops, shoping mals, etc. provide means of spurious recreation and this, in turn encourages crime.

Economic factors may influence criminal activities, but they do not cause them. It is incorrect to say that every man who is hungry and who is in absolute need of food and shelter, steals or commits crimes. Poverty and economic exigencies may tempt only a few to criminal activities. The question however remains why some people from poor families get involved in crime while others do not. **Healy, Burt, Morrison** and others have disproved the belief that poverty is an important causal factor of crime. Many times crimes are committed due to greed and not actually due to need.

5. Social Factors

The social circumstances of life affect one's conduct. They too constitute a factor in the total environment in which personality develops. In civilised societies, there are a number of social conditions which are unfavourable for the development of a sound social personality. The social factors surrounding the individual and exercising influence on him may be classified as follows:

(i) *The home and the family conditions,*
(ii) *Religious factors,*
(iii) *Recreational agencies,*
(iv) *Defective schooling system / education,*
(v) *Community influence, and*
(vi) *Prevailing customs, beliefs and values and declining impact of the social control machinery.*

(i) The Home and the Family Conditions **:** The home is the fundamental social institution which has enormous influence on the development of the personality especially of the children. But, adverse family conditions such as big and unmanageable size of the family, unsatisfactory parent - child relations, demoralising home conditions, lack of discipline and control over children and economic inadequacy, etc. spoil the healthy development of the children's personality and are drawn into criminal activities.

(ii) Broken Homes **:** Broken homes are those which have become the victims of unfortunate instances such as - untimely death of the father or mother, break in the family due to divorce, separation, constant quarrels between husband and wife, parents and children, and so on. Broken homes constitute an important factor in the causation of juvenile delinquency mainly because of poor mother-child relationship. *"When the home is immoral, or when there are immoral, drunken, epileptic, insane or feebleminded parents present in the family, the child is easily led astray."*[14]

(iii) Religious Factors **:** Lack of belief in God and becoming irreligious greatly affect the propensity to crime. Today the religious attitude is rapidly vanishing and because of this the moral condition is definitely deteriorating at least in the urban areas. Though true religion discourages criminal behaviour, religious perversions encourage criminal activities. Wars have been fought in the name of religion. Religions have also encouraged fanaticism, fundamentalism, and even communalism. Riots and severe violence too have taken place in the name of religion. Moreover, prison statistics show that religion does not always have the effect of curbing the anti-social potentialities of men. In some societies, people are in the grip of superstitions which make them to go to any extent in committing serious crimes.

---

14. **C.B. Mamoria**, Page : 983.

(iv) Defective Schooling / Educational System : The relationship between education to crime has been studied. The crime statistics in India reveal that very few graduates are found in our prisons and majority of the criminals are uneducated or very poorly educated. It is probable that lack of education has a definite effect upon the occupation an individual takes up. The uneducated has, usually a greater difficulty in making a living. The range of his employment is narrow. He may get a low paid job, or a part - time job and find lot of leisure time also. Thus, he may easily drift towards bad companionship especially in cities.

It is to be noted that the type of crime varies with the level of education. Crimes of violence are more frequently committed by the uneducated, while the crimes of skill like forgery, blackmailing, producing and marketing duplicate goods, indulging in modern sophisticated terrorist activities, etc., are engaged in by the educated. Children who fail to adjust to the schools also often go astray. Schools are usually meant for the average children and hence very little attention is given to the below average child. Hence, frequently children drop out of schools for lack of interest. They sometimes run away from homes and fall into the hands of anti-social elements which convert them into delinquents.

(v) Community Influence : The influences in the community have a great bearing on the conduct of the persons. Young children as well as adolescents are subject to the attitudes and opinions of the community . The child goes astray because of the bad influence in the community in which he lives. The uplift of the home is neutralised by the tide of immorality that flows out of the dance halls, gambling centres, pubs, vicious resorts, video parlours etc. especially in the urban areas. Even the good home finds it difficult to fight against such ugly influences. Many criminals who are brought to the court narrate their story, how they had a good family, came from good stock and yet had gone astray because of factors operating in the community.

(vi) Influence of Customs, Beliefs and Values and the Decline of the Social Control Machinery : Directly or indirectly, means of social control such as customs, beliefs and values often play a part in criminal acts. Customs and beliefs differ significantly from place to place and community to community. Customs and beliefs of the smaller communities are often different from and opposed to those of the larger societies. In such cases, conflicts arise between group standards and those of the larger society. Those who are not able to resolve these conflicts are likely to commit crimes. Declining influence of the social control machinery also causes a few to the community offences.

III Other Factors

(i) Political Immorality : During the recent years, political morals have declined in India. Corrupt political practices, criminalisation of politics, political leaders and police officials having illicit relationship with criminal gangs, undemocratic way of functioning, one political party instigating communal violence and caste conflicts to malign the names of other parties etc., have become rampant in India. Political developments that took place in the middle of the year 2011 in India relating to telecom license issue and the issue of illegal mining at Bellary and Andhra Pradesh, reveal that not only ordinary political leaders but even cabinet level ministers at the state and central level, state chief ministers, top government officers, high level corporate bosses are also involved in large scale corruption, that is to the extent of looting nation's wealth. All these are nothing but criminal activities.

(ii) International forces are also playing their role in instigating terrorist, naxalite, anti-national and forcible or tactful religious conversion activities in India. Continuous influx of millions of infiltrators into India from Bangladesh has become a very big menace during the recent years in maintaining law order, especially in the North-Eastern States.

(iii) Alcoholism and drug abuse are also causes of crimes. **Bacon** has said *"All the crimes on earth do not destroy so many of the human race, nor alienate so much property, as drunkenness".*[15]

(iv) Imitation too plays its role in causing crime. Children exhibit a powerful tendency to imitate the habits and practices of the parents. Children of the criminals do pick up the bad habits from their parents only.

Conclusion

Most of the conditions mentioned above, are mostly common to all the individuals in a society. It means, most of the people live in the same society being surrounded by more or less the same conditions. But only a few are affected. All those who are hard hit by these conditions do not plunge into criminal activities. Most of them suppress their criminal tendencies and wait for the things to improve. Everywhere there are millions of frustrated individuals with violent impulses suppressed inside them waiting for an opportunity to release. So, it is believed that with changes in the social environment in the right direction, criminal behaviour could be reduced to a great extent.

As **Dr. Sethna** observes, *"the causes of crime are as diverse and complex as are the crimes..."* **Dr. Burt** has also expressed more or less the same opinion. He says that *"crime is assignable to no single universal cause, nor yet to two or three. It springs from a wide variety and usually from a multiplicity of alternative and converging influences. All these problems can be grappled with a good knowledge of social pathology and criminology. What India badly needs in this direction is, therefore, a diagnostic, ameliorative, and corrective sociology so that the delinquent could be reformed, rehabilitated, and reclaimed by the society to become its useful member."*[16]

4. CONSEQUENCES OF CRIME

Crime is one of the weaknesses of man's group life. Criminal behaviour is a deviant behaviour. But this behaviour is not a phenomenon of recent emergence. The tendency to deviate from the rules or norms has started ever since the rules came to be established. All rules cannot be obeyed by all people always. No individual is able to follow or obey all the rules of the society at all times. For one reason or another, no matter how silly or serious the matter may be, people deviate some rule or rules at some time or the other. Hence, *"deviant behaviour"* is invariably and inevitably associated with our group life. These 'deviations' cause major problems for the society when they disturb the social order or the social equilibrium. If such deviations or crimes are not dealt with properly they may pose a great threat to the survival of the society or to its smooth functioning. The main consequences or problems which the crimes can cause is briefly examined here.

Consequences of Crime : A Brief Analysis

1. Crime Leads to Individual Disorganisation

No normal individual continuously and purposefully opposes the norms and laws of any society. If somebody is bent upon doing it, then it only means that he is either mentally deranged or individually disorganised. It reflects his individual deficiency. Criminal tendencies make individuals to become personally disorganised. As a result, such persons are not able to make

---

15. As quoted by **C.B. Mammoria** - Page : 986.
16. Dr. Burt as quoted by **C.B. Mamoria**, Page : 987.

use of their talents or skills for their own growth or for the benefit of the society. These persons not only cause loss to the society but they bring to themselves discredit and even danger.

2. Crime Leads to Family Disorganisation Also

Successful family life depends on the intimate and loving relationship and co-operation among the members. Family is compelled to pay a heavy penalty in terms of family peace and prestige, if any one member of the family indulges in serious crimes. If the earning members of the family are engaged in criminal activities, entire family gets stigmatised. This may influence the children of the family and they may become delinquents. Moral system of the society gets a serious setback if female members of the family are themselves involved in notorious crimes.

3. Community Disorganisation

Community's strength depends on the strong feelings of unity and community sentiment. This unity will have a negative effect on the criminal tendencies of the people. On the contrary, community organisation becomes weak where crimes are rampant and anti-societal activities are widespread. The weakened position of community organisation may finally lead to community disorganisation and related evils.

4. Crime Leads to the Decline of Morals

Committing crime is an illegal and also an immoral act. Murder, robbery, blackmailing, smuggling, cheating, giving bribes, prostitution, terrorism etc., are not only illegal, but also immoral acts. Crime is opposed to sublime values and accepted norms of life. A criminal has scant respect for the interests, satisfaction and pleasures of others. He may even have contempt for the whole society. Such persons pose serious challenges to the moral order of the society. If their criminal tendencies are not suppressed or at least controlled, the moral system of the society may become very weak.

5. Increase in Violence and Anti-Social Activities

An increase in crime rate leads to an increase in the anti-societal activities. An increase in the crimes of adults and juveniles leads to an increase in the instances of misbehaviour, misdeeds, and abuse of civilised opportunities. Values such as mutual love, co-operation, sympathy, helpfulness, etc. relegate to background, and in their place will be found mutual hatredness, contempt, non-cooperation and distrust. Loss of life, property, atrocities, violence, persecutions, harassments, loot, robbery, terrorism, blackmailing, black money, corruption, nepotism, sexual crimes, etc. represent antisocial activities and they are all the consequences or at least different faces of crime.

- ***An Increase in Crime Indicates an Increase in Violence*** : According to *"Crime Record Bureau - 1994"*, in India, due to criminal acts, every 7th minute a person loses his life, a woman is raped every 47th minute, a woman is kidnapped every 44th minute, an atrocity is committed against a woman and a robbery takes place at every 6th minute; 17 dowry - deaths are taking place every day and the statistics continue like this. These statistics confirm that crimes normally lead to greater violence in the society. Unfortunately, criminal acts have started increasing especially after the 1990s.

6. Detrimental to the Progress of Nation

Crimes have a negative influence on the progress of a nation. An individual or a group that makes use of the criminal method for fulfilling his or its selfish needs, has definitely no concern towards the societal good or national progress. Corruption, abuse of power and authority, illicit connection with underground terrorist groups and criminal gangs, selling of national secrets for money and such other criminal acts are highly dangerous and harmful to the progress of the nation. Due to a great increase in the crime rate, administration becomes weak, much of our man and money power gets wasted on the maintenance of law and order and above all, our economic system itself receives a great setback. Parallel economy created out of the flood of black money may create economic instability, inflation and financial crisis.

5. MEASURES TO CONTROL CRIME

No society free of problems ever existed, and it is doubtful that such a society will ever exist in future. As every one knows, man's social life is productive of problems. Consequently, man has always been faced with problems of various kinds, to which he was compelled to find solutions.

Throughout history, man has been employing various methods to control crime, to suppress it and to solve it. He has *not been successful in his attempts to brush aside crimes completely for they are a part and parcel* of human life. Man's efforts to control them continue unabated even today.

Two Types of Solutions to Control Crime

Man's attempts to control crime can be classified into two major types and they are : *(i) Preventive measures, and (ii) Curative or Correctional or Remedial measures.*

(i) Preventive Measures for Dealing with Crimes

Preventive measures are based on an age-old saying *"prevention is better than cure"*. This method aims at alleviating existing socio-economic evils, or at least bringing about changes in the social order that will make their occurrence unlikely. Those methods *"require the recognition of conditions that may eventually create social problems - a most difficult thing to achieve. These methods require painstaking research so that the facts underlying each problem will be fully known before preventive action is taken..."* These methods *"are undoubtedly more desirable and are bound to be more effective than the remedial approach."*[17]

"Prevention of crime aims at avoiding the occurrence of crime by mitigating its causes and then making efforts to restore the individual to a normal condition of living".[18] From the stand point of the preventive method the following measures can be suggested to prevent crimes from taking place.

1. The basic minimum requirements of the people are to be met. So that one is not compelled to commit crimes due to one's helpless economic conditions.
2. In addition to the removal of poverty, jobs are to be given to all the needy persons.
3. Family welfare measures are to be undertaken in order to prevent the family members from taking to crimes due to distressing family conditions. Families are to be encouraged to preserve *"life values"*.
4. Total ban should be imposed on the consumption of alcohol and harmful drugs.
5. Social welfare measures are to be implemented effectively so that the weak, crippled, the disabled physically and mentally, the deserted, diseased and such other persons are not forced to resort to crime.
6. Slum areas are to be made free from the hold of anti-social forces. Unwholesome conditions found in those areas and also in labour colonies, market places are to be removed so that the young people are saved from becoming the victims of criminality.
7. Effective formal education with a positive approach to life is to be given to the younger generation.

---

17. **Samuel Koenig** in *"Sociology"* - Page : 326.
18. **C.B. Mamoria**, Page : 989.

8. Social and class disparity should be reduced and social justice should be assured.
9. Political establishment should be made powerful, stable, honest, service-minded and relatively free from corruption.
10. Wholesome recreational facilities are to be provided to the people so that they are able to sublimate their feelings and sentiments.
11. People of all classes and sections of society are to be provided with enough protection and security not only to their lives but also to their material and non-material property.
12. Mass media should be encouraged to play a positive role to develop in people good tastes and interest and also to provide them proper and unperverted information.

It is easy to suggest measures like this, but it is impossible for any nation in the world to resort to these measures without compromise and with full commitment. Hence, this method has its own limitations though its importance cannot be underestimated.

(ii) Curative/ Correctional / Remedial Measures

The history of criminality reveals that crimes are bound to occur in society. All attempts made, experiments held and strategies resorted to, for removing criminality from society, have failed. At the same time, the question of tackling criminals has been an issue of debate and discussion since centuries. Some argue that due punishments be given to criminals for their crimes. While some others say that giving punishment should not be the sole purpose of the social control machinery. Most of the sociologists, social reformers, social psychologists, criminologists and liberalists are of the opinion that much importance is to be given for reforming the criminals than punishing them. They have however, conceded the point that criminals are to be punished humanistically and not revengefully.

Punishment as a Method of Dealing With the Criminal

The concepts *'crime'* and *'punishment'* normally go together. Punishment is a way of handling or treating criminals. It involves - the infliction of pain, forfeiture of property, imposing penalty and chastisement. As **Reckless** pointed out, *'punishment is the redress that the community takes against an offending member'*. The spirit behind this approach is reflected in the popular saying, *"as you sow, so you reap."*

Purpose of Giving Punishment

- As **Mamoria** points out, *"the objects of punishment are to bring about reformation of the offender ; to prevent him from committing crime again and again and to prevent other persons from committing crimes ...."*[19]
- **Jeremy Bentham** is of the opinion that *"the main ends of punishment are - scare, prevention and compensation."*[20]
- **Holmes** observes that *"prevention is the chief purpose of punishment."*[21]

Theories Relating to Punishment

The purpose of punishment has been a subject of discussion throughout history. Scholars have attributed different purposes for punishment such as - *retribution, deterrence and reformational reparation.* Let us examine, in brief, the nature of each one of these theories.

---

19. Mamoria - Page : 987.
20. As quoted by **Mamoria**, Page : 987.
21. As quoted by **Mamoria** - Page : 987.

1. Theory of Retaliation or Retribution or Revenge

This theory is supposed to be one of the oldest one. It aims at punishment exactly to fit to the crime. It is based on the fulfilment of moral justice. *"A good action deserves to be crowned with a good reward and a bad action meets its own fate."*[22] It is the punishment accorded to the accused on the same terms as *"blood for blood, tooth for tooth, eye for eye, etc."*. It is based on instinctive human reaction which may be called wrath, anger, resentment or revenge. It was very popular until 15th and 16th centuries. The punishment was aimed at the reduction of criminal tendency and the violation of law by means of creating terror and fear in the minds of the people. At a later stage, this theory was considered inhuman and slowly withdrawn.

2. The Theory of Deterrence

This theory is based on the view that punishment is meant to prevent other persons from committing similar offences. The punishment is also aimed at preventing the accused from committing the same by keeping him in jail. Confined behind the prison walls, the offender is considered unable to harm the society. As per this theory, the offender is also made to pay punitive damages to the aggrieved party in addition to spending sufficiently long period in jail. The fear of long time loss of liberty is also a real deterrent.

3. The Reformative or Rehabilitative Theory

This theory believes not in taking revenge against a criminal nor in keeping him in jail for years together. It is interested in repairing the criminal. It considers man as a helpless entity in the social environment. Society should not threaten a criminal as a big enemy but takes him as a human being and try to help him to become a good citizen of the country. The offender is taught how to go back into the law-abiding society with all proper preparations and responsibilities. In the reformatory institutions, education, recreation, and religious services, occupy very prominent position.

This theory thus believes that the offender should not only be punished by detention but also be put to *"educative and healthy influence"*.[23] The theory opines that the offender be *"re-educated, and his character traits be re-shaped and put once again in the furnace for being moulded." "Reformatory punishment may mean either that the offender is reformed while being punished, or that he is reformed by punishment itself."*

Reformative Theory is More Relevant to Modern Society

Scholars are of the opinion that the reformative theory is more suitable to modern conditions of life. In the classical theory, the purpose of punishment was to put down crime and to give the criminal his due ..But in the present day theory, the purpose of punishment is *"to prescribe treatment to one who has failed to meet the requirements of good life."*

The modern penologists look into the mental set up of the offender, that is, his good or bad heritage, environment, physical make-up, personality, etc. They hence recommend that *"it is not the physical person of the individual who is to be punished or penalised but it is his mind which needs reformation or rehabilitation. This responsibility of reforming and rehabilitation rests on the state."*[24]

A Brief Assessment of the Three Theories of Punishment

- ***Theory of retribution*** reflects the revengeful attitude of the society. It indicates the failure of the society to correct the individual and to give him an opportunity to rectify his mistakes and

22. **Mamoria** - Page : 988.
23. **C.B. Mamoria**, Page : 388.
24. **C.B. Mamoria** - Page : 989.

to prove himself to be normal and law-abiding. Retaliation cannot be the permanent solution to crime. It only means a desperate attempt on the part of the society to do away with the criminal.

- ***The theory of deterrence*** too has its own limitations. As per the requirements of this theory, even though the criminals have been given severe punishment, crimes continue to take place unhindered even today. In fact, statistics relating to criminality reveal, that instances and varieties of crimes are on the increase. The aggressive instinct hidden in man exhibits itself whenever crimes are suppressed with a heavy hand. In conclusion, it could be said that the theory of deterrence is no more accepted as an effective way of dealing with the criminals.

- ***The theory of rehabilitation or reformation*** is now being considered as preferable to the first two. The theory accepts in spirit that the society too has its role in producing criminals. Hence, the problem cannot be solved by just punishing the criminals. The attitude here is one of accepting the criminal but condemning his criminality. The criminal is given punishment with a view to reform him. There is an attempt here to make the criminal an asset of the society and not a liability. If all attempts to reform the criminal fail, only then, as an inevitable action, the criminal is given a serious punishment so that he will not pose similar challenges to the people or the law and order machinery. Severest punishment, namely, death sentence is recommended to incorrigible criminals. It means even this theory too has its own limits.

METHODS OR WAYS OF DEALING WITH THE CRIMINAL

Modern society believes more in reforming and correcting the erring individual that is, the criminal rather than taking revenge upon him. Our attempts to reform the criminals are required at three levels : (i) *police*, (ii) *prison*, and (iii) *probation*. Since the criminal is a person who breaks the law knowingly or unknowingly to fulfil his purposes, he has to be corrected or dealt with as per the provisions of law. There are some particular and clearly laid down ways of dealing with the criminal.

Methods or Ways of Dealing With the Criminal

There are some legal procedures and institutions according to which the individual who violates or breaks the laws of the society is to be dealt with. They are - *police, court, probation, parole* and *prison*.

1. The Police

The police and the other law enforcing officers are the first persons who deal with the criminal. Their chief functions are to preserve law and order and to arrest and bring to trial those who disturb peace and break or violate law. The police is comparatively a new profession originated only some 150 years ago. There were watch men in the olden days who gave only a part of their time without any payment, or at a very small remuneration, to guard the peace of the community. But with the growth of large cities and the increasing number of professional criminals, the police became prominent and they are now given special training to discharge their tasks effectively.

In the Indian context today, the special training given to the police is far from satisfactory. As we find it today, many of the police personnel are appointed through some influence from the side of the politicians. High level corruption is there in the police department and because of that merit and efficiency are ignored and appointments are made depending on the amount of bribe that one pays. If the police is to fulfil his responsibilities he must be a very much higher type of man with commonsense, niceties, civic sense and proper knowledge of law. He must be properly trained for the varied and difficult tasks of policing and hence should be selected and appointed with great care.

Nowadays, we hear about lot of criticisms being made about the police people. It is criticised that many police people, including the officials, do not know how to handle the juveniles, get along with adults, how to treat female criminals, and how to behave with those who go to police stations to lodge complaints. Since young women are also getting recruited into the police department during the recent years, it is all the more necessary for the men police personnel to behave in respectable terms with them. It is unfortunate that even within the police department complaints of sexual harassment are being lodged against men staff by the female personnel.

It is necessary for the police to understand the criminals and their ways perfectly well. Since high technology is being misused for indulging in unlawful activities, it is the responsibility of the Government to provide to the police department latest technological devices and instruments to nab the culprits. It is essential to increase the strength of the police force in proportion to an increase in the population. The police department requires expertise in order to catch the criminals who often make use of completely novel techniques to commit offences. A good law enforcement officer can do much to prevent crime as well as for its detection and punishment.

2. The Court

After a man is arrested on charge of crime he may be placed under detention to await trial or released on bail. In due course, he comes before the court for his trial. He may plead either guilty or not guilty. If he is not guilty he stands a trial for the charge made against him. The trial is a legal battle between the prosecutor and the defender. The judge is an umpire in the game. He gives judgement according to the case. In case the man is acquitted, the whole matter is ended. If he is convicted, the law provides for appeals to the higher court on the theory that every chance should be given to the man to prove himself innocent.

The courts represent the judicial institutions set up by the state to protect the citizens and to assure them justice. At the same time, they try to bring the offenders on the track of justice. They are the institutions empowered with the legal power to give punishments to the offenders depending upon the nature of crime that they have committed and which is proved.

It is again criticised that some practices of our court system create criminals, instead of preventing crime. **For example**, a poor man without efficient legal aid is likely to suffer; or at least believes, that justice is not done to him; because a rich man even though he is a party to the crime committed, escapes the criminal responsibility with the help of an expert advocate.

Furthermore, unnecessary delays that are found in many of our courts in bringing the accused to trial, allow many offenders to go unpunished. Witnesses often die or they may go away from the place, especially in cities, and this may lead to the dismissal of the case. The famous dictum, "*justice delayed is justice denied*", unfortunately becomes true in many cases.

There is yet another anomaly found in our court system. Those who cannot get bail are often made to live with the hardened criminals in the jail. People who are arrested are not necessarily criminals, and hence they must not be treated as criminals. But in our present system of justice they are often equated with the criminals.The effect of all these things upon the minds of men who very strongly feel that they have been discriminated against, may easily be imagined. Those who thus come to feel that they have not been fairly looked upon but unjustly treated, may readily develop a grudge against society and turn again to criminal behaviour by way of settling their grudge, or taking revenge. To avoid all these bad eventualities, justice should be made cheap, quick and simple. The theoretical saying that "*all men are equal before the law*" must be put into practice which will boost the credibility of our legal and the judicial system.

3. Probation

Probation is another device to mitigate the maladjustments of criminal justice to the needs of the individual. It means, that it is to the community rather than to the prison that the convicted criminal must be assigned for treatment. Probation is an alternative to prison and as a correctional method, it has been practised in India for a very long time. *In this device, an offender is put on trial under the supervision of a probation officer.* Imposition of punishment is suspended because there is less stigma attached to a suspended sentence. An offender is given time to prove that he could mend his ways. Here the supervision is of a friendly nature.

- ***Probation,*** *thus is a method by which the first offender is treated effectively outside a penal institution. Probation is not a pardon but only a conditional suspension of punishment. It is a method of bailing out the prisoners.*

Throughout the period of probation the original offence remains punishable in the case of violation of any condition of probation, or in case, the offender commits another offence. It gives the offender another chance to improve and to continue to live a life that meets with the approval of society. It averts the stigma of prison sentence. Here, the suspension is there in order to promote the offender's rehabilitation.

Probation is beneficial for the community as it helps produce well-adjusted criminals. This is beneficial especially in the case of young offenders. The individual is also put to work and his earnings are devoted to his family or saved for himself.

Probation is a kind of community treatment which permits normal social experience which is not available in the prison. Its advantages are that it does not disturb the offender's relationships with his family, with his friends, with the opposite sex and with his occupation. It saves a good deal of state and community funds.

In India, the system of probation was introduced after the successful experiments in other countries. Under sections 562, 563 and 564 of the *Criminal Procedure Code*, the court has the power to release certain convicted offenders on probation. In many states, we find special *Probation Acts* under which probation officers are appointed. The duties of these officers are to pay or to receive visits from the offenders at interval fixed in the court order. He has to report to the court on behalf of the offender. He has to assist the offender to find out suitable employment for him. However, some offenders, because of the gravity of their offences, cannot be given the benefit of this system. **The Probation of Offenders Act, 1958** is the basis of this reform. Some of the provisions of this Act are -

(i) It permits probation of all the offenders except those who are liable to be given capital punishment, and to dacoits and professional criminals.
(ii) It permits release on probation for a maximum of **3** years.
(iii) It allows social investigation by a probation officer, and
(iv) It permits revocation or premature termination of probation.

4. Parole

Parole is yet another method of treatment for offenders. *It is a form of conditional release granted after a prisoner has served a portion of his sentence in a correctional or penal institution.* He will be under the supervision of the parole official. Parole must never be confused with probation nor with pardon. It is only a permission given to the prisoner to go outside the walls of prison for some time. That is to say, parole is there along with the institutional treatment whereas as probation is an alternative to it. People are released on parole with a view to eradicate bitterness and hopelessness, particularly in the case of the poor and the accidental criminals. Parole is often looked upon as a right rather than as a privilege.

Important Characteristics of Parole

(i) Release from prison only for a short period after completing a specified portion of prison sentence.
(ii) Imposition of certain conditions of behaviour.
(iii) Persons on parole will have to remain under the control of officers or correctional institution.
(iv) After completing the parole term the criminal has to come back to the prison once again.

Limitations of this Method

(i) Parole becomes an ineffective mechanism if prisoners are released because of external pressures.
(ii) It becomes a weak method if supervision is only a farce and funds are inadequate to meet its expenses, and
(iii) This method becomes a success only if prudent selection is made to release persons or parole.

5. The Prison and Its Role in Dealing with the Criminals

- The highest penal and correctional institution is the prison. Prison has been defined as "*a place properly arranged and equipped for the reception of persons who by legal process are committed to it for safe custody while awaiting trial or for punishment..*".

As places of detention, prisons are very old institutions, as places of punishment, they are however, comparatively modern. In India also, the early prisons were only places of detention and offenders were detained under trial and judgment.

Prison is the universally accepted means of preventing crime. It is a place where every inmate is stigmatised and has to carry on tightly scheduled activities in the company of strangers. The inmates are deprived of liberty, privileges, security and heterosexual relations.

The history of prison everywhere has been a sad one. Usually, the prison is directed by officers who have no special qualification for the task either by nature or by training. From the standpoint of reforming offenders and restoring them to society as good citizens it has been a colossal failure.

No Distinction is Made Between the Inmates

It is unfortunate that we are not recognising that in the prison there are two general classes of inmates :

(i) Those who ought to be subject to custodial care as long as they live, and ought never to be permitted outside; and
(ii) Those who have seen the error of their ways and have decided to reform. This second group should be let out into the society as soon as they are fit to return.

But this is not happening. In the prison, the first type of offenders become hardened criminals due to the bad influence of others. That is why the prison is referred to as *"the school of crime"*. Criminals develop a feeling that "*once a criminal is always a criminal*".

Damaging Contacts of Inmates Inside the Prison

The contacts of different types of inmates inside the custody have great effect on the first offenders. Famous social geographer **Lombroso** found out, that "*The pick-pocket and the cut-*

throat learn in prison at the expense of the state to make fake keys, to make counterfoil money, to engrave bank notes and to commit burglaries". It is said that many a girl learn more in the first 24 hours under custody than she knew in all her life before.

Jails or Prisons Having the British Origin

The institution of jails in India is of British origin. The Indian Penal Code and Indian Criminal Procedure Code [IPC and ICPC] were enacted in 1859 and 1860 respectively. Thereafter, slowly one after another changes started taking place in the institution of prison.

The Prisons Act of 1894 : This Act led to provide some amenities to the prisoners. It also brought some changes at the level of prison officials also. Thus, as per the provisions of this Act, an Inspector General of Prisons [IGP] for each state, a superintendent, a medical officer, a medical subordinate, a jailor and other officials were appointed. This Act made provisions to have separate prison cells for male and female prisoners, convicted and unconvicted prisoners and civil prisoners and criminal prisoners. Every prisoner is visited by the medical officer at least once a day. Sick persons and prisoners desiring to see the medical officers will be allowed to do so at the earliest. As per this Act, no criminal prisoner shall be kept on work for more than 9 hours a day. The prisoner will be given leave on medical grounds. In our country today, the Social Welfare Board is taking an active part in rehabilitating the offenders whenever it is possible.

Indian Prison Reforms Committee and Its Recommendations

The conditions in Indian jails were changed especially after the recommendations of *Indian Prison Reforms Committee in1919*. Later, there were many *"prison reforms committees"* and they too have given various recommendations. Changes such as - *classification, segregation of prisoners, education, recreation, assigning productive work, providing medical facility, giving opportunities for maintaining contacts with family and society* - were introduced.Thus, over a period of time, a good deal of change has been brought about in the treatment and approach of prisoners.

Prisons In India : Some Information and Statistics

* *The Central Ministry of Home Affairs* is in charge of Prison Administration in the country.
* *Prison population for the country* as on 31-12-2007 as per National Crime Records Bureau [NCRB] was 376396, [inclusive of pre-trial detainees and remand prisoners].
* *Prison population rate* [per one lakh of national population] was **32** for 2007 [based on estimated national population of **1160.9** million at the end of 2007 -from U.N. figure].
* *Female prisoners percentage of prison population* 4.1% as on 31-12-2007.
* *Juveniles/minors and young prisoners* [all under 18 years] constitute **0.1%** of prison population on 31/12/2007.
* *Foreign prisoners percentages* of prison population 1.3% as on 31-12-2007.
* According to the Home Ministry, prisons are overcrowded by more than 135% mainly due to inmates on remand.
* About 1300 jails in India are found to contain at least double the number of prisoners they were originally built to house.
* There are 2,50,000 under trials. Seven out of every 10 persons in jail are in this situation. In some jails, as high as 300% inmates sleep in shifts.

Source: Manorama Year Book - 2012

A Model Prison at Lucknow - 1949

After independence, **Lucknow Prison** was converted into a model prison in 1949. Some specialities of this prison are as follows:-

- There is a reception centre in the Lucknow prison where detailed study of the new comer is made. Thorough enquiries are held regarding personal case history, family relationship, social and economic background, psychological and mental defects, police reports, court judgment and such other things.
- Then, he is processed through a detailed programme of educational, physical and vocational training for 6 months during which time his honesty, industry and aptitude for co-operation are judged. If he succeeds in the test and is found fit he will be admitted to the model prison where he has to work and pay to the state his cost of maintenance.
- In this model prison, there are cottage industries, vegetables and agricultural farming, etc. and an individual can choose the type of available activity that suits him, so that he can continue the same occupation after his release.The prisoners have to pay for the raw materials used. They have a canteen which is run on co-operative basis.
- From the security point of view, this model prison is a mixed institution where prisoners can be kept under maximum, moderate and minimum security depending on the individual's progress. They are gradually admitted to higher privileges and at one stage they are allowed to work outside the jail both day and night without watch and ward. The best behaved are also allowed to pay short visits to the city and other places of attraction.
- *Provision for Healthy Entertainment* : The prisoners are also entitled to dramatic performances, cinema shows, lectures, debates, religious celebrations, games, reading rooms, libraries, T.V. shows, etc. Thus, the inmates are helped to get themselves prepared to take their usual place in society after their release.

Experiment With Open Prisoners Camp

This idea was given by **Sampurnanand,** [the Home Minister in 1952] and an experiment was made in this direction by constituting semi-permanent camp of the prisoners. Under this scheme, about 2000 criminals were employed in the construction of a dam over the river Chandraprabha in Benaras district. The prisoners were housed in tents in the open without guards. Complete freedom of movement was given. They were paid wages for their work, a part of the wages was paid immediately and the balance was kept as saving to be handed over to the prisoners at the time of their release. The prisoners were given education. The teachers and the social welfare officers at the camp assisted the work of reformation and rehabilitation. The excellent work and the discipline of the pisoners at this camp gave confidence to other states to follow the Lucknow example. Later on, on the Lucknow model, two more camps were held - one in the cement factory

Number of Prison Establishments and Institutions in India (in 2011) - 1382

			Total Capaciy of the Jails	
1.	Total No. of Central Jails	123	137249	41.2%
2.	District Jails	333	124768	37.5%
3.	Sub-Jails	809	50908	15.3%
4.	Women's Jails	19	4271	1.3%
5.	Open Jails	14	3766	1.1%
6.	Special Jails	30	9279	2.8%
7.	Borstal Schools	21	2218	0.7%
8.	Other Jails	3	323	0.1%
Official Capacity of the Total Prison System in 2011			**332782**	

at Mirjapur and the other agricultural - cum industrial camp at Sitarganz. These experiments were a complete success and have shed new light on the problem of prevention of crimes.

Recent Prison Population Trend		
Year	**Prison population Total**	**Prison Population Rate**
2001	313635	30
2007	376396	32

Tihar Jail

Started in 1958, the *Tihar Jail* was a maximum security prison run by the State of Punjab. In 1966, control was transferred to the National Capital Territory of Delhi. Here, the prison status is open type and has a capacity for 6250. Right from 1984, additional facilities were constructed, and it became the Tihar Prison. After a number of prison reforms, its name has been changed to Tihar Ashram. The Integrated Counselling and Testing Centre reports that around 6% to 8% of the 11,800 Tihar inmates are HIV positive, which is considerably much higher than the general population HIV rate in India.

Achievement of Dr. Kiran Bedi as IPS Officer in Reforming the Prision Conditions

In the midst of lot of criticisms about the traditional and crude way of dealing with the criminals, some police officials have dared to experiment with novel ways of handling the criminals. The name of **Dr.Kiran Bedi** tops the list of such officials.

Dr. Kiran Bedi was the first police officer [in the Cadre of IPS] in the world to enter the police service. When she was posted as the Inspector General of Prisons at the biggest national level jail, namely, **Tihar**, at New Delhi, she resorted to some innovative ways of reforming the jail and its conditions. She sought to breakdown adversarial relations between the police and the community of prisoners. She tried *"to replace the hard hand of punishment with the soft one of correction and rehabilitation"*. In recognition of her yeomen service she was awarded in 1994 *"Ramon Magsaysay Award"* which is popularly known as the *"Asian Nobel Prize"*.

Capital Punishment or Death Punishment

Capital punishment is one of the much discussed and the most debated topic in the field of crime. It has been both opposed and defended on moral, philosophical, humanitarian and other grounds. Many people argue that death punishment is best for a criminal of too many murders and a habitual criminal. As an alternative to it, has been suggested social isolation and imprisonment for the whole span of life.

High Security Jails in India

1. Tihar Jail - New Delhi
2. Cellural Jail - Andaman Islands
3. Alipore Jail - Kolkata
4. Vellore Central Jail - Vellore
5. Arthur Road Jail - Mumbai
6. Hyderabad Jail - Hyderabad
7. Raipura Prison - Raipur
8. Chanchalguda Central Jail - Chanchalguda

As, yet another alternative, it is argued that the first obvious thing to do with a criminal is to make it clear to him that in the remaining part of his life he will have to contribute something to the family of his victim. This is a life long obligation and in the Indian context, it may not be possible to implement it. Because, most of the times crimes are committed for economic reasons.

No doubt that the argument that criminal should pay the damages is appreciated. But in practice, it is not easy because when a criminal is released from the jail he cannot get a job, because nobody wants an ex-convict on his premises.

The attitude of society towards the criminals and delinquents should be one of sympathy and genorosity rather than that of revenge, hatred, isolation and distance. We must shoulder our responsibility for the crime of our society for "*every community has the crime which it deserves*". Prevention is better than cure is true not only in the case of the health of the human body, but also in the health of the community. In a welfare state, no body who is prepared to work and earn a living should be left to starve or take up crime because of poverty.

CRIME IN INDIA

Commiting crime is not a monopoly of either men or women. Crime is not gender specific. Men and women are equal before the law, both have moral codes and both violate legal code and moral code, though not invariably and regularly, on occasions and under some circumstances which cannot be specified. Men are typically more aggressive which might make them more prone to commit crimes, but women are more likely to be psychotic. Crimes are always crimes whether committed by men or women. Violent crimes are bad because they ruin lives, ruin harmony in the society and instill fear and animosity.

Meaning of Crime Rate

Societies are often compared in terms of "*criminal rate*", which reflects the criminal trends and its intensity. *The crime rate is defined as number of crimes per* ***one lakh population*** *is universally accepted as the realistic indicator for it balances the effect of growth in population.*

Two Main Categories of Crime

People commit innumerable types of crimes. As and when new laws and legislations are made, people find out new ways of violating them. They often commit new types of crimes. But for legal and judicial purposes the Criminal Procedure Code [Cr.P.C] divides all the crimes into two categories, namely;

(i) Cognizable Crimes - Sec 2(c) Cr.P.C., and *(ii) Non-Cognizable Crimes - Sec 2(1) Cr.P.C.*

(i) Cognizable Crimes

A cognziable offence or crime is defined as the one which an officer in-charge of a police station may investigate without the order of a magistrate and affect arrest without warrant. The police has a direct responsibility to take immediate action on the receipt of a complaint, or of credible information in such crimes, visit the scene of the crime, investigate the facts, apprehend the offender and arraign or indict him before a court of law having jurisdiction over the matter. Cognizable crimes are broadly categorised as those falling either under the '*Indian Penal Code* [IPC]' or under the "*Special and Local Laws* [SLL]".

Cognizable Crimes and Crime Rate

As many as 66,75,217 cognizable crimes were reported in the country during 2009 comprising 21.21 lakh cases under the IPC and 45.53 lakh cases under the SLL. The rate of total crimes [IPC + SLL] was 570.8 in 2009 showing an increase of 25.23% over 2005 and an increase of 10.83% over 2008.

- **Crimes Under the Indian Penal Code [IPC]**
  1) *Economic Crime:* Criminal Breach of Trust, Cheating Counterfeiting.
  2) *Crimes Against Public Order:* Riots, Arson.
  3) *Crimes Against Propery:* Dacoity, its preparation & assembly, Robbery, Burglary, Theft.
  4) *Crimes Against Children :* Child Rape, Kidnapping & Abduction of Children, Procuratiuon of minor girls, Selling/Buying of girls for Prostitution, Abetment to Suicide, Exposure and Abandonment, Infanticide, Foeticide.
  5) *Crimes Against Women:* Dowry Death, Cruelty by Husband and Relatives, Molestation, Sexual Harassment and Importation of Girls.
  6) *Crimes Against Body:* Murder, Its attempt, Culpable Homicide not amounting to Murder, Kidnapping & Abduction, Hurt, Causing Death by Negligence.

(ii) Non-Cognizable Crimes or Offences

Non-cognizable crimes are defined as those which cannot be investigated by police without the order of a competent magistrate. Police does not initiate investigation in non-cognizable crimes except with magisterial permission. First schedule of the Cr.P.C. gives the classification of the offences of the IPC into cognizable & non-cognizable categories. The various crimes that are being registered and investigated by different law enforcement agencies are broadly grouped under the following categories for Statistical Information System.

Crime Incidence

[IPC + SLL] (incidence: 66,75,217) Total incidence of crime gives an absolute picture of the crime situation in the country or the State. Comparative figures over a period of time indicate an increase or decrease in the incidence of crime requiring appropriate crime control efforts by the State police. The IPC crimes reported a higher growth rate of 20.2% as compared to the fast pace of population growth of 18.5% in the decade. The crime rate in respect of IPC crimes has decreased marginally from 181.5 in 2008 to 181.4 in 2009 and that for SLL crimes has increased by 16.8% from 333.4 in 2008 to 389.4 in 2009.

- **Crimes Under the Special and Local Laws [SLL]**
  1) Relating to immoral Traffic
  2) Relating to Railways
  3) Relating to Registration of Foreigners
  4) Relating to Protection of Civil Rights
  5) Relating to Indian Passport
  6) Relating to Essential Commodities
  7) Relating to Terrorist & Disruptive Activities
  8) Relating to Explosives & Explosive Substances
  9) Relating to Prohibition
  10) Relating to Excise
  11) Relating to Gambling
  12) Relating to Narcotic Drugs & Psychotropic Substances
  13) Relating to Arms
  14) Other crimes (not specified above) under Special and Local Laws including Cyber Laws under Information Technology

15) Relating to Forest
16) Relating to SC/ST (Atrocities)
17) Relating to Sati
18) Relating to Copyright
19) Relating to Antiquities & Art Treasures
20) Relating to Dowry Prohibition
21) Relating to Child Marriage Restraint

B. CYBER CRIME

Cyber crime is one of the curses of the modern technological world.. It represents a particular type of modern crime. In fact,the very term *'cyber crime'* is a misnomer and it has not been defined any where in our statute. Virtually, the concept of cyber crime is not radically different from the concept of conventional crime. Both represent the conduct which cause or lead to breach of law.

Definition of Cyber Crime

- *Any criminal activity that uses a computer either as an instrumentality target or as a means for perpetuating further crime, comes within the ambit of cyber crime.'*
- *A generalized definition of cyber crime may be –unlawful acts wherein the computer is either a tool or a target or both*[25].

Forms of Abuse of Computer

The second definition cited above, points out at the two important forms of abuse of computer involved in the phenomenon of cyber crime.

1) ***Computer as a Tool.:*** Activities that are branded as ' cyber crimes ' are conducted by making use of computer as a tool. The following activities could be included in this category : *financial crimes,sale of illegal articles, pornography, online gambling, intellectual property crimes, forgery, cyber defamation ,cyber stalking,and e-mail spoofing, etc..*
2) ***Computer as a Target:*** The computer may also be a target for unlawful acts in the cases such as the following: *unauthorized access to computer system or computer networks, theft of information contained in the electronic form, e-mail bombing,internet time thefts, web jacking, theft of computer system, physically damaging the computer system, etc,,,*

Causes for Cyber Crimes

Social thinker **Hart** in his work *'The Concept of Law'* has pointed out that human beings are highly vulnerable to frauds and cheatings and rule of law is necessary to protect them. In the same way, computers are also vulnerable for abuse and hence require rule of law to protect and safeguard them against cyber crime.

1. ***Computer system has capacity to store data in comparatively small place :*** This gives chance for the crookedminded people either to destroy or steal the information stored in it. Crimes of this kind are increasing nowadays.

25. Source –Internet.

2. ***Easy access to information because of complex technology :***There is the problem of guarding the computer system from unauthorized access because of its complex technology. Important data, confidential reports and secrets stored in it are often stolen or meddled with,by means of secretly implanted logic bomb, key loggers, advanced voice recorders, retina imagers, etc.
3. ***Computer system is complex and hence the possibility of mistake by way of operating the system through millions of codes cannot be ruled out:*** Since human mind is falliable, there is always the possibility of lapse taking place at any stage in its operation. The cyber criminals take advantage of these lacunas and penetrate into it to fulfil their secret agenda.
4. ***Negligence in protecting the computer system :*** Negligence is a part of the human conduct. It is therefore,very much probable that while protecting the computer system there might be any negligence which in turn, provides a chance to cyber criminal to gain access and control over the computer system.
5. ***Loss of evidence :*** Since much of the data stored in the computer system are routinely destroyed, there is the possibility of the needed evidences getting lost along with them. This problem paralyses the system of crime investigation.

Types of Cyber Criminals

The cyber criminals consist of various groups or category. Depending on the object behind the criminal act,they can be grouped into the following categories.:-

1. ***Children and adolescents between the age groups of 6 to 18 years:*** The delinquent behaviour pattern often exhibited in children between the age groups of 6 to 18 ,is mostly due to the unguided inquisitiveness to know more and explore the unknown things . Sometimes,in their eagerness to prove themselves to be more outstanding and adventurous in the midst of other children,some resort to these types of crimes.
2. **Organised hackers:** Hackers are mostly organized together to fulfil their own objectives such as-catering to the needs of political bias, fundamentalism, fanaticism, etc. It is said that relatively a large number of Pakisthanis who have hateredness towards India, resort to hacking to subserve their ulterior motives. Such people are said to be targeting the Indian Government sites [websites] with the purpose of fulfilling their political objectives. It is also observed that the NASA and the Microsoft sites are always under the attack by the hackers
3. **Professional hackers :** There are some professional hackers whose work is mostly motivated by money.Such persons are mostly employed to hack the site of the rivals and get credible, reliable, and valuable secret information.
4. **Discontented Employees :** This group consists of those people who have been either sacked by their employers or, are totally disgruntled with their employers.To take revenge upon them, they often hack the system of their employers.

Types of Cyber Crimes

Cyber crimes are committed in various ways and they may broadly be classified under three broad groups:

(i) Crimes against individuals,

(ii) Crimes against organizations, and

(iii) Crimes against the whole society.

(i) Crimes against Individuals : Crimes of this kind are of two kinds : *1)crimes against persons, and 2) crimes against individual property.*

a) ***Crimes against persons*** include harassment through e-mail,defamation,indecent exposure, e-mail spoofing, dissemination of obscene material, unauthorized control over computer system,cheating and fraud, cyber-stalking etc,,

b) ***Crimes against individual property***—consist of transmitting viruses, unauthorized access over computer system, intellectual property crimes ,internet time thefts,computer vandalism,net trespass etc,,

(ii) Crimes against Organisations : Crimes that could be included under this category are as follows: Possession of unauthorised information, distribution of pirated softwares, cyber terrorism against the Government Organisation, and unauthorised access over computer system, etc.

(iii) Crimes Against the Whole Society : The following types of crimes are included under this category: Online gambling, financial crimes, sale of illegal articles, forgery, trafficking, polluting the youth through indecent exposure,pornography,(basically child pornography), and so on.

Prevention and Control of Cyber Crimes

Since cyber crimes can also occur at the international level,the U N O felt it necessary to deal with it at the legal level. The General Assembly of the U N O thus adopted *'Model Law on Electronic Commerce'* which was already adopted by the *UN Commission on Trade.* . To give effect to the UN resolution to control electronic commerce, the Indian Parliament passed the ***'Information Technology Act-2000'.*** The preamble of this Act states very clearly that its main objective is to legalise e- commerce,and as complimentary to it further *amend the Indian Penal Code1860,the Indian Evidence Act 1872,* the *Bankers Book Evidence Act, 1891,*etc,The main purpose to incorporate the changes in these Acts is to make them compatible with the Act of 2000. As a result, they may regulate and control the affairs of the cyber world in an effective manner. The *'Information Technology Act –2000'*, deals with various types of cyber crimes in its chapters 9 and 11. Important sections of the Act in this regard are-43,65,66, and 67.

Prevention of Cyber Crime

It is always better to prevent the problem of cyber crimes from taking place than to go in search of suitable remedial measures to cure it. One must take proper precaution while operating the internet. Some five principles seem to be five *mantras* for network security. They are: *precaution,prevention, protection, preservation and persevearance*. Any person who makes use of the internet facility must always keep in mind the following things:

(i) Cyber-stalking can be prevented by avoiding disclosure of any information pertaining to oneself. This is important because,disclosure of information often amounts to the disclosure of one's identity to the strangers in public place.

(ii) It is better to avoid sending of any photograph online particularly to strangers and chat friends for incidents of misuse of photographs.

(iii) It is advisable to use latest and update anti-virus software in order to guard against virus attacks.

(iv) Website owners should watch traffic and check any irregularity on the site.

(v) It is always better to keep a watch on the sites that one's children are accessing to prevent any kind of harassment or depravation in children.

(vi) One should not send one's credit card number to any site that is not secured in order to guard against frauds.

(vii) It is advisable to keep back-up volumes so that one may not suffer data loss in case of virus contamination.

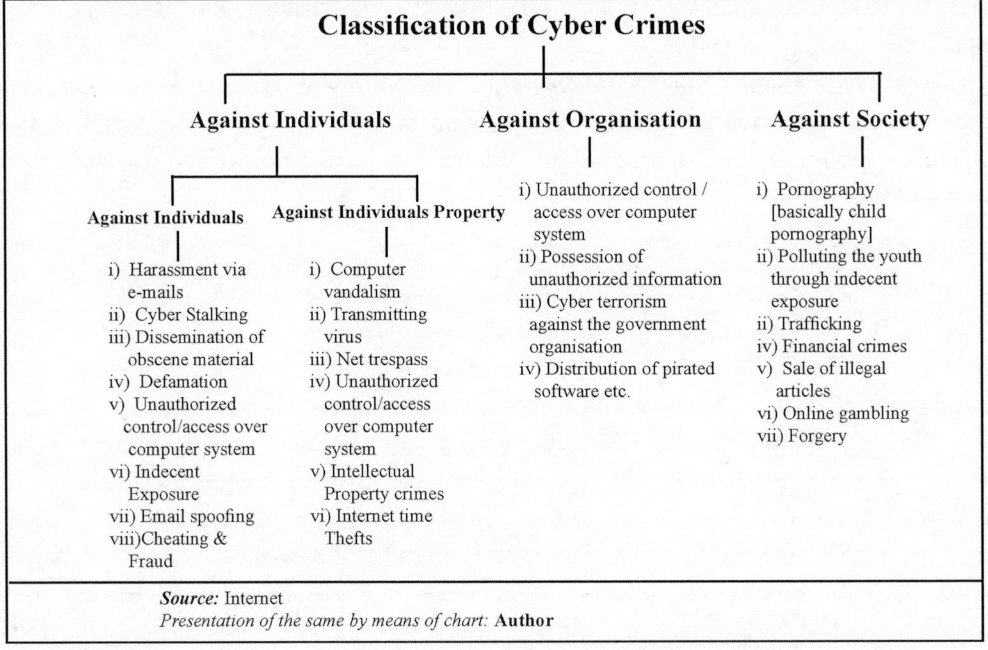

Source: Internet
Presentation of the same by means of chart: **Author**

Conclusion

As any one can understand, cyber crime is essentially connected with the human mind. The capacity of human mind is immeasurable. It is almost impossible to eliminate cyber crime from the cyber space. However, it is possible to check them. No legislation has been successful in totally eliminating crime from the globe. The only possible step is to make people aware of their rights and duties and further making the application of the laws more stringent to check crime. The Act is no doubt a historical step in the cyber world. Still there is a need to bring changes in the *'Information Technology Act' - 2000* to make it more effective to combat cyber crimes. A word of caution is necessary for the pro-legislation school. It should be kept in mind that the provisions of the cyber law should not be made so stringent so as to prevent all types of cyber crimes that retard the growth of the cyber industry as such.

Some Vital Statistics Relating to Crimes

Percentage Distribution of IPC Crimes, 2009					
Hurt	-	13.2%	Causing death by negligence	-	4.6%
Theft	-	15.3%	Cruelty by husbands and relatives	-	4.2%
Burglary	-	4.3%	Cheating	-	3.4%
Riots	-	3.0%	Molestation	-	1.8%
Murder	-	1.5%	Other IPC Crimes	-	48.6%

Percentage Distribution of SLL Crimes, 2009 [S.L.L.: Special and Local Laws]					
Immoral Traffic Act	-	0.1%	Excise Act	-	4.1%
Copyright Act	-	0.1%	Gambling Act	-	3.6%
SC/ST Atrocities Act	-	0.3%	Prohibition Act	-	8.5%
NDPS Act	-	0.6%	Other SLL Crimes	-	81.0%
Arms Act	-	1.8%			

Road Accidental Death [By Type of Vehicles for all India -2009]					
Bicycles	-	3267	2 Wheeler	-	26219
3 Wheeler	-	6616	Tempo / Van	-	7328
Jeep	-	9820	Cars	-	11682
Bus	-	12683	Truck Lorry	-	24968
Pedestrains	-	11109	**Total**	-	**126896**
Source: Manorama Year Book-2012, Page: 622-623					

●●●

Chapter 6

JUVENILE DELINQUENCY

Meaning and Definition of Juvenile Delinquency - Characteristics of Juvenile Delinquency - Types of Juvenile Delinquency - Causes of Juvenile Delinquency and Its Control - Delinquency in India: Some observations - Nature of Juvenile Delinquency as per the Data Compiled by National Crime Records Bureau-1993 - Remedies For Juvenile Delinquency : Preventive Measures and Methods of Rehabilitation - Institutions to Rehabilitate Juvenile Delinquents - Differences Between Crime and Juvenile Delinquency.

Juvenile delinquency is one of the serious problems of the modern society. It is the outcome of rapid urbanisation and industrialisation of modern age. Social conditions associated with these two processes have affected the family pattern. This has resulted in an atmosphere that is favourable to the growth of juvenile delinquency. A large number of children moving from rural areas to the cities or living in slums in cities are found to be highly vulnerable to this problem. This has almost become a universal problem in most of the industrialised countries including India. **G .C.Dutt** observes, *"Juvenile delinquency is rapidly becoming a serious menace in India and with the progressive industrialisation of many parts of the country... this problem will soon assume the same proportions as in many of the western countries"*.

1. MEANING AND DEFINITION OF JUVENILE DELINQUENCY

Delinquency is a kind of abnormality. When an individual deviates from the course of normal social life, his behaviour is called *"delinquency"*. When a juvenile, below an age specified under a statute, exhibits behaviour which may prove to be dangerous to society and/ or to himself, he may be called a *'juvenile delinquent'*. Each state has its own precise definition of the age range covered by the word *'juvenile'*.

Definitions

1. **Cyril Burt** defines delinquency as occurring in a child *"when his antisocial tendencies appear so grave that he becomes or ought to become the subject of official action"*.
2. **Friedlander** says, *"delinquency is a juvenile misconduct that might be dealt with under the law"*.
3. ***The Second United Nations Congress*** on the *Prevention of Crime and Treatment of Offenders* (1960) states, *"by juvenile delinquency should be understood the commission of an act which, if committed by an adult, would be considered a crime"*.[1]

1. The UN Congress also recommended and specified that : (1) the meaning of the term *"juvenile delinquency"* should be restricted as far as possible to the violations of criminal laws, and (2) a situation should not be created where society penalises the small irregularities or maladjusted behaviour of minors when it would not prosecute adults for the same irregularities of behaviour.

4. **C.B.Mamoria** writes, *"the phrase 'juvenile delinquency' may be loosely used to cover any kind of deviant behaviour of children which violates normative rules, understanding or expectation of social system".*
5. **K.L. Sharma:** *"A delinquent child is one who deserts his home, who is habitually disobedient or is beyond the control of his parents who violates the law of the land, or who does not abide by the rules which he is required to follow."*
6. ***In simple words,*** it can be said that *juvenile delinquency is a type of abnormal or antisocial behaviour by a juvenile who is below an age specified by statute.*

Who is a Juvenile Delinquent ?

According to ***"Juvenile Justice Act, 1986"*** juvenile delinquent is a person below the age of **18** who indulges in anti-social and or illegal activity. [The Juvenile Justice Act 1986, has been amended as ***Juvenile Care and Protection of Children***] Act in the year 2000.

Juvenile delinquents are those offenders, including boys and girls, who are normally under **18** years of age as per the *"Juvenile Justice Act, 1986"*, whereby the age of juvenile male and female is at part, that is, 18 years. A juvenile delinquent is a young person incorrigible or habitually disobedient. Acts of delinquency may include - *(1) running away from home without the permission of parents, (2) habitual truancy beyond the control of parents, (3) spending time idly beyond limits, (4) using vulgar language, (5) wandering about rail-roads, streets, market places, (6) visiting gambling centres, (7) committing sexual offences, (8) shop-lifting, (9) stealing etc.* Juveniles may do such activities singly or through a gang.

CHARACTERISTICS OF JUVENILE DELINQUENCY (JD)

Some important characteristics of J.D. are explained below. These are especially true in the Indian context and appear to be more applicable to J.D. found in India.

1. Delinquency is found more among boys than among girls : As per the available data, the delinquency rates are much less among girls than among boys. As per the figures of the year 1994, of the 17,203 juveniles apprehended under the I P C [Indian Penal Code] and other types of crimes, only 19.5% were girls. The figures suggest an overall arrest ratio of 4.5 boys for each girl.

2. J.D is more pronounced in the urban area : Big metropolitan cities are highly vulnerable to produce J.D. Crime data relating to 23 metropolitan cities in India reveal that out of 1362 juvenile crimes committed in these cities under the IPC in 1994, about 74.7% (about $3/4^{th}$) were committed in 7 cities such as Mumbai, Delhi, Bangalore, Ahmadabad, Pune, Nagpur and Hyderabad. It means, bigger the city the more it produces J.D. It is quite less frequent in small towns and rural areas.

3. Early adolescent period [12-16 yrs age group] is more prone to J.D. : Statistics reveal that, of the incidents of J.D. reported during 1989 -1994, about 2/3 delinquents [66.9%] fall in this age group. Prior to 1987, it was not so. *For example,* between 1978 and 1987, a large number of delinquents [71%] belonged to 16-18 years.

4. Low educational background is more favourable for J.D. : It was found in 1994, that about $2/5^{th}$ [43.6%] of the juveniles were educated up to primary level and less than 1/3 [29.9%] of them were found to be illiterate and about 1/5 [21%] of them were educated up to middle and secondary level.

5. Children living with parents are more susceptible to J.D. : It is a surprising fact that children living with their own parents and guardians are found to be more involved [that is, $3/4^{th}$ or 71%] in the juvenile crimes. This reveals the role of poor family environment in J.D.

6. Poor economic background is a common favourable factor for J.D. in India : Statistics reveal that about 51% of the delinquents come from homes with an income of less than Rs.500/- per month. As per 2005 statistics, out of the total number of 29,962 delinquents, 71.2% belong to poor families, and only 6.8% came from middle income groups. The upper income group delinquents were just 0.16%. Most of the studies conducted in this regard have shown that socio-economic status has a strong bearing on J.D.

7. Juvenile gangs are quite less in India : It is true that some instances of J.D. are committed in groups. But in the Indian context, juvenile delinquent gangs that have the clear support of organized adult criminals are quite less and in fact they are very rare.

8. Professional delinquency is not there in India : In most of the cases [say, 4/5th], juvenile delinquents are first time offenders. Studies revealed that only 1/10th of the delinquents are found to be past offenders.

Types of Juvenile Delinquency

Juvenile delinquency assumes various forms or types of which the following are to be considered at some length.

(i) Individual Delinquency : In this type, the cause of delinquency is located within the individual himself. Delinquent behavior pertaining to this type is mostly interpreted by the psychiatrists who feel that it is caused by the psychological problems emerging from the defective family interactive patterns. Their studies have revealed that almost 90% of the delinquents of this category have unhappy home life and felt disgusted with their life circumstances. As a result, some felt rejected by parents and others felt inferior or jealous of siblings and some others suffered from mental conflicts. They indulged in delinquency as a solution to these problems.

(ii) Group – Supported Delinquency : In this type, the cause is mostly rooted in the culture of the individual's home and neighborhood, and not in the personality of the individual. The main finding of the studies in relation to this type of delinquency is that – delinquent's association and companionship with others who are already delinquents – is the main cause of delinquency.

(iii) Organized Delinquency : This is a type in which delinquent acts are committed due to organized group efforts. As far as India is concerned, this type of delinquency is comparatively rare. American sociologists developed the concept of *"delinquent sub-culture"* to explain and analyse this type of delinquency. The concept refers to the set of values and norms that guide the behaviour of group members and encourage the commission of delinquencies'. **Albert Cohen** was the first sociologist to refer to this type of delinquency.

(iv) Situational Delinquency : The basic assumption in this type is that delinquency is not deep rooted but it is only situational. Thus, a young boy or a girl indulges in a delinquent act, say, pre-marital sexplay, without much thinking and without having any commitment to delinquency. He or she is more susceptible to do because, the individual has not developed any self-discipline to control his or her impulses, or the individual's family has less control over the behaviour of its younger members. The individual may also feel that he or she has nothing to lose, even if caught.

3. CAUSES OF JUVENILE DELINQUENCY

There is no single cause or simple explanation for the development of delinquent behaviour. According to **Healy** and **Bronner**, the causes of juvenile delinquency are : *(1) bad company, (2) adolescent instability and impulses, (3) early sex experience, (4) mental conflicts, (5) extreme social suggestibility, (6) love for adventure, (7) motion picture, (8) school dissatisfaction,*

TODAY'S JUVENILES ARE TOMORROW'S CRIMINALS - ?

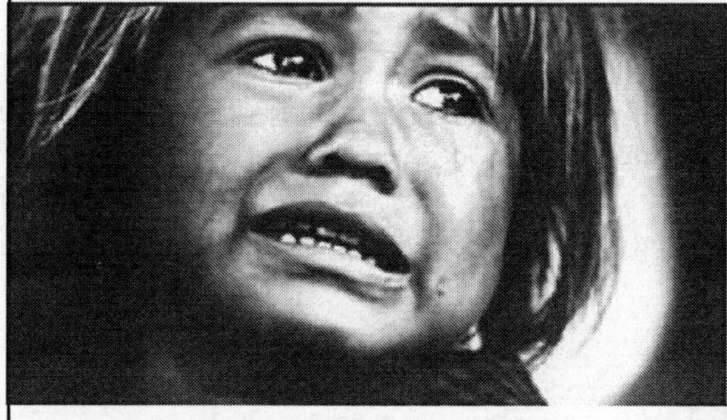

(9) poor recreation, (10) street life, (11) vocational dissatisfaction, (12) sudden impulse; and *(13) physical conditions of all sorts that are provocative of criminal acts.*

The causes of juvenile delinquency may be classified under two major factors :

(A) Social factors, and ***(B) Personality factors.***

(A) Social Factors Favouring Juvenile Delinquency

***1. Broken Homes*:** British and American investigations reveal that nearly 50% of the delinquents come from broken homes. In one of the studies conducted by **Uday Shankar** in India, only 13.3% of the 140 delinquents that he studied came from broken homes. This shows the cultural differences between Indian and the Western countries. Still it can be said that broken homes and families, lack of parental affection and security, absence of a loving mother in the childhood or an affectionate mother substitute, lack of family ties, parental irresponsibility and a steep rate in divorce, desertion and separation - are all contributory factors to delinquency.

The home may be broken up by the death of one or both of the parents, or by prolonged illness or insanity, desertion or divorce. Interaction in home is a very important means for socialising the child. The mother plays a vital role in this regard. If she divorces her husband or deserts him or dies, the growth of the child will be affected. Such a child loses not only mother's love but also parental control and becomes an easy victim to the outside anti-societal influences. It cannot, however, be said that broken home invariably leads to delinquent behaviour on the part of the children.

***2. Poverty*:** A very large proportion of delinquent children come from poor homes. It is generally, although not unanimously, accepted by professional students of juvenile delinquency that the vast majority of delinquents come from the lower class. They commit offences as members of gangs. **Uday Shankar**'s study has revealed that as many as **83%** of the children come from poor families. Still, it cannot be generalised that the children of the poor homes invariably become delinquents.

Sometimes poverty compels both the parents to be outside the home for a very long period to earn their daily bread. The children will be left uncared for. Such children may consciously or unconsciously join hands with gangsters and become delinquents. This mostly happens in slum areas and areas in which mostly working class people live.

***3. Delinquency Areas*:** It is said that some areas are highly vulnerable to delinquent trends. Long ago, **Burt** in his study showed that there are certain areas in London from which the majority of delinquent children come. Universally it is observed that the delinquents come mostly from the areas of poor housing, overcrowding and the areas in which cinema houses, hotels, night clubs, liquor shops are found in a large number. It is true that when a family is living in the heart of the town the chances are greater for the children of such families to pick up delinquent behaviour. It is to be noted that not all children living in the delinquent areas are delinquents.

***4. Companions and Gangs*:** As the child grows older he goes into the neighbourhood and becomes a member of the playgroup or peer group. If by chance he joins the group or the gang that fosters delinquent attitudes he is also likely to become a delinquent. In fact, much delinquency springs from the prevalent attitudes in the groups within which the youth has immediate contacts. **Charles Shaw** has opined that *"delinquency is a product of community forces"*.

In cities, in slum areas peculiar social groups called ***'gangs'*** are found. Generally, the gang starts as a playgroup. In the absence of playground facilities, the children will start playing in streets and finally organise themselves into gangs. The gang has all the qualities of an ingroup such as loyalty, cooperation, social solidarity and unity. These gangs are found to be associated with crime in all its aspects like delinquency, rioting, corrupt politics, and so on. Children coming from poor families and broken families easily become the victims of gangs.

Due to bad companionship also offences are committed by the adolescents. Studies have shown that delinquent acts are done in company. In his ***Illinois Crime Survey of 1928,*** **Shaw** analysed 6000 boys who were involved in crimes. He found that in 90% of the cases, two or more boys were involved in crime. But in **Uday Shankar**'s study in India, only 23% of persons had committed delinquent acts due to bad company. It cannot, however, be presumed that mere companionship by itself causes delinquency.

***5. Beggary*:** Beggary is often the cause of juvenile delinquency. Child beggars mostly come from either very poor families or broken homes. These children are deprived of the needed love and affection of the parents. They crave for the satisfaction of their inner impulses, desires and ambitions. They choose to become beggars for the same. As beggars they get annoyed to see others enjoying life. Some of them may even become rebels. They realise that only through deviant practices they can satisfy their desires and meet their needs. Thus, they become delinquents.

6. Other Social or Environmental Factors

(a) ***School Dissatisfaction*:** Some students get dissatisfied with school life. Parental irresponsibility, unmanageable student-teacher ratio, lack of entertainment and sports facilities in schools, indifference of the teachers etc. may contribute to this. Such dissatisfied students become regular absentees in schools and start wandering in streets. They may even form gangs of their own and become gamblers, eve-teasers, pickpockets, drunkards, smokers and drug addicts.

(b) ***Films and Pornographic Literature*** have also added to the magnitude of delinquency. Cinema, television and obscene literature may often provoke sexual and other impulses in adolescents. Hence, they may start their *'adventure'* in satisfying them, in the process of which they commit crimes.

(c) ***Deep-seated inner desires*** coupled with outside pressures, compulsions and temptations also contribute to juvenile delinquency. *For example,* on hearing the interesting narration of the illicit sex experiences, drug or alcoholic thrills, or such other criminal experiences from one's gangmate, one may be tempted to follow the same.

(B) Personal or Individual Factors

Personal factors such as mental deficiency and emotional disturbances may also contribute to juvenile delinquency.

***1. Mental Deficiency*:** It has been observed that good number of delinquents are mentally deficient. Studies have revealed that there is larger proportion of mentally defectives in the juvenile delinquent group than among the normal children. The relationship between intelligence and delinquent behaviour has been studied carefully. The average intelligence in a normal group of children is 100 I.Q. (Intelligence Quotient). But **Burt** in his study in London reported that the average I.Q. of delinquent children is 85, and **Uday Shankar** found it at 83. These and many other studies have revealed that the average intelligence of the juvenile delinquents is certainly lower than the average intelligence of the normal group of children of the same age.

It is quite natural to assume that the dull and mentally handicapped or defective adolescents do not have the necessary insight to make distinctions between 'right' and 'deviant' methods and behaviour. Such children are often used by the more intelligent children of the gang or the adults for their criminal purpose.

***2. Emotional Problems of the Individual*:** Mental troubles and emotional maladjustments are strong factors in delinquency. Emotional problems of inferiority, jealousy and being thwarted are very common among the delinquent children. **Healy** and **Bronner** in their study of 143 delinquents found that 92% of them revealed emotional disturbances. It is reported that in America about two-thirds of juvenile delinquents suffer from emotional problems and mental deviations. Thus, from the psychological point of view, *"Delinquency is a rebellion and an expression of aggression which is aimed at destroying, breaking down or changing the environment"*. This rebellion is mostly against the social conditions which deny the individual his basic rights and the satisfaction of his fundamental needs. Thus, delinquents are not born so, but they become so due to social circumstances and personal deficiencies. They are mostly maladjusted persons.

According to psychoanalytic view, the delinquent is an individual who is governed by the *"pleasure principle"*. He wants to get immediate pleasure and immediate satisfaction of his needs. So he becomes a victim to his own impulses. He is neither able to control his impulses nor able to imagine the consequences of his actions. It is also said that delinquent breakdown is an escape from emotional situation for some particular individuals with peculiar individual and family background. Some emotionally maladjusted children become delinquents to get the attention of their parents or as a protest against their treatment.

Thus, it may be said that juvenile delinquency is the result of both social or environmental and personal or individual factors.

Delinquency in India: Some Observations

The Children's Act of 1960 defines a *delinquent child as one who has been found to have committed an offence.*

- According to police records, in 1971, there were 103419 juvenile delinquents and most of them were male children. Violence was not much pronounced but the number of murders was quite noticeable. Drinking of alcohol, gambling and theft were found as the major deviant activities. More than 80% of these delinquents were in the lower income group and around 50% of them were illiterate.
- During 1997 to 2000, the share of the juvenile delinquency out of the total IPC [*Indian Penal Code*] crime was **0.5%,** and this percentage increased to **1** during 2003-2005.
- During 2005, the incidences of crimes were 18,939, and under the SLL [*Special Local Law*], crime incidences were 6662. Madhya Pradesh [4557], Maharashtra [4216], Chhatisghar [1557], Gujarath [1390], Rajasthan [1324] and Andhra Pradesh [1186] have reported highest incidences of juvenile crimes under the IPC. These 6 states taken together account for **74.8%** of total juvenile delinquency cases.
- Of the above mentioned delinquents, the ratio of girls to boys was **1:15**. Again, of the total number of delinquents 8660 were illiterate and 12394 had education up to primary level. Of these juveniles, 91.7% were living with their parents and only 8.3%. were homeless delinquents.

Nature of Juvenile Delinquency as per the Data Compiled by National Crime Records Bureau – 1993.

1. Juvenile delinquency is more an urban phenomenon than a rural one.
2. The delinquency rates are many times higher for boys than girls.
3. Low educational background is the main attribute of delinquency.
4. The delinquency rate tends to be highest during early adolescence [12-16 years of age group]

5. More than 4/5th of the juvenile delinquents are found to be first offenders.
6. Poor economic background is yet another important characteristic feature of juvenile delinquency in India.
7. In India, as it is mostly observed, a large number of delinquencies are committed by individuals all alone.
8. Unlike many of the Western societies, not many delinquencies are committed in groups.
9. More than the destitute or homeless children, children living with their parental home, are found to be committing greater number of crimes.
10. In comparison with the crime rate of adult criminals, the incidences of crimes among the juveniles is extremely low in the Indian context.

Crimes Against Children

In India, not only children commit crime, but lot of crimes are also committed against children like the crimes that are normally committed against women, the poor and the deprived sections. It is not uncommon in India to find children becoming victims at times of the problems of their parents, relatives and neighbours. Offences such as – murder or killing, foeticide infanticide, abetment to suicide, exposure and abandonment, kidnapping and abduction, procuration of minor girls, selling of girls, buying of girls, etc., are quite common crimes against children.

Innumerable crimes against children occur despite the legislations such as – *(a) Immoral Traffic Prevention Act – 1956; (b) Child Marriage Restraint (Amendment) Act – 1978, (c) Child Labour (Prevention and Regulation) Act – 1986 and as amended in 2006; (d) Protection of Women from Domestic Violence Act – 2005, etc.*

The following Table shows crimes against children and variations in 2005 over the year 2004.

Crimes Against Children and Variations in 2005 over 2004 — **Table No. 1**

Sl. No.	Crime Head	Years			Percentage Variation in 2005 over 2004
		2003	2004	2005	
1.	Murder	1212	1304	1327	1.8
2.	Infanticide	103	102	108	5.9
3.	Rape	2949	3542	4026	13.7
4.	Kidnapping and Abduction	2571	3196	3518	10.1
5.	Foeticide	57	86	86	0
6.	Abetment to Suicide	25	33	43	30.3
7.	Exposure and Abandonment	722	715	933	30.5
8.	Procuration of Minor Girls	171	205	145	29.3
9.	Buying of Girls for Prostitution	24	21	28	33.3
10.	Selling of Girls for Prostitution	36	19	50	163.0
11.	Child Restraint Act	63	93	122	31.2
12.	Other Crimes	3700	5107	4697	8.0
	Total	**11633**	**14423**	**14975**	

Source: **K.L. Sharma** in *"India Social Structure and change"* (2007), Page: 264-267.

4. REMEDIES FOR JUVENILE DELINQUENCY

The problem of juvenile delinquency is one that has drawn the attention of society. It is known that the delinquent child of today may turn out to be a chronic criminal tomorrow. Discussions, debates and studies have been made at the national as well as international levels by scholars to seek out effective remedy for this problem. Two methods have been suggested to deal with this problem : *(A) Preventive method,* and *(B) Rehabilitative* or *Curative method.* In the former, factors leading to delinquency are to be tackled, and in the latter, those who have already committed delinquent acts are to be helped to become normal citizens.

(A) Preventive Measures

In order to prevent juvenile delinquency the following measures may be suggested :

1. Creating and inspiring a team of workers of private and public agencies devoted to preventive work.
2. Giving proper training to the members and staff of all organisations concerned with delinquency control.
3. Establishing child guidance clinics to give appropriate treatment to the disturbed and maladjusted children.
4. Educating the family so as to help the parents realise the importance of giving proper attention to the needs of their young children.
5. Establishing wholesome recreational agencies to prevent young children from becoming the victims of illicit or unwholesome recreation.
6. Giving proper assistance to under-privileged children to build in them good character and law-abiding attitude.
7. Adopting various means of propaganda such as radio, movies, television, newspapers, magazines etc., to make children realise the importance of being law-abiding and its accompanying appreciation and rewards.
8. Improving the social environment i.e., slum areas, busy market places, gambling centres etc., to prevent children from getting polluted.
9. Spotting potential delinquents by predictive tests in schools and giving appropriate treatment to such children.
10. The problems of beggary and poverty are to be removed or atleast controlled and the general economic standards of the people must be improved to prevent children from becoming delinquents due to economic exigencies.

(B) Method of Rehabilitation

The main purpose of the method of rehabilitation is not to punish or to take revenge upon the delinquent. The intention behind this method is to help the delinquent children to get proper guidance and training so that they become normal children and never repeat delinquent acts. The measures taken for the prevention and treatment of juvenile delinquency in India after 1850 may be briefly examined here :

1. Legislative Measures

Various legislations have been made in India from time to time to deal with juvenile delinquency. Some of them may be briefed here.

(a) Apprentices Act, 1850 **:** This Act has been the earliest step taken in the direction of preventing delinquency. The Act provides for the binding of children, both boys and girls between the ages of 10 to 18, as apprentices. Orphans and poor children can also take the benefit of this Act. Employers could take such children as apprentices with the intention of training them in some trade, craft or employment by which they gain a livelihood later. The father or guardian may bind a child above 10 and under 18 upto 21 years of age for a period not exceeding 7 years. A female child may be so bound until her marriage. The Act also dealt with children who committed petty offences.

***(b) Reformatory Schools Act, 1897* :** This Act can be considered a landmark in the history of treatment of delinquency. This Act is in force in almost all the states of India. Under this Act, courts are empowered to send for detention youthful male offenders to Reformatory School for a period of not more than **3** years. It could be extended to **7** years depending on the nature of crime. No person may be detained after he attains 18 years of age. In conformity with this Act, the State Governments may establish and maintain Reformatory Schools to help the delinquents to get speedy recovery. Every school must provide sanitary arrangements, water supply, food, clothing, bedding, industrial training and medical aid to the inmates. These Reformatory Schools are reported to have done useful work.

***(c) Provision in the Criminal Procedure Code* :** Under Section 399 of the Indian Criminal Procedure Code (ICPC), convicted young offenders below the age of 15 could be sent to Reformatory Schools established by the State Government. Section 562 of the C.P.C. also permitted discharge of certain convicted offenders on probation. It also permitted their release with advice. Under Section 82 of the Indian Penal Code, children under seven cannot be held responsible for their criminal acts. Section 83 of the same Code relaxes this age upto 12 under some conditions.

***(d) Children Acts* :** Various provinces of India took interest in making some comprehensive laws in 1920 and afterwards to deal with delinquent children. Of these, Children Acts enacted by Madras in 1920 and followed by other States, are important. The main provisions of Children Acts are as follows :

(1) No child under 14 years of age can be imprisoned under any circumstance and no young person between 14-16 years of age can be imprisoned unless he is certified to be an unruly person.

(2) Except in the case of grave offences, any person arrested on a charge and is below 16, is required to be released or bailed. In any case such persons could not be kept in Jails.

(3) The child or youthful offender cannot be sentenced to death or imprisonment except under extraordinary conditions. Persons below 12 are to be sent to Junior Certified Schools and 12 to 16, to Senior Certified Schools.

(4) The court may discharge the person after due admonition, it may hand him over to his parents or guardians after taking a bond from them that they would be responsible for his good behaviour for 12 months.

(5) The state government may establish juvenile courts to hear charges against children or young persons.

(6) It is the duty of probation officer to visit, advise, befriend the youthful offender and obtain suitable employment for him.

(7) For the purpose of giving effect to the Act the state govt. may establish junior and senior certified schools and auxiliary homes.

(8) Nobody should be detained in a senior certified school after he has attained 16 years of age.

(9) For the protection of other children the Court may direct the detention of certain children less than 14 years of age in junior certified schools.

(e) Juvenile Smoking Acts : Some Acts to deal with the specific pattern of antisocial behaviour among children have also been passed. Of these, *the Juvenile Smoking Acts* are in force in most of the states. This Act prohibits the sale of tobacco to children below 16. Children below 16 are not supposed to smoke in public places according to this Act. (But these Acts were never enforced in any of the States).

(f) Suppression of Immoral Traffic Acts : These Acts are passed in order to protect young girls and to suppress prostitution. The Acts prohibit certain practices connected with prostitution such as soliciting in public places, using residential premises for running brothels, forcibly detaining young women in brothels, etc. Provisions are also made to protect girls from brothels or from moral danger.

(g) Probation of Offenders Act : Under these Acts, Juvenile Courts can place the youthful offenders under the supervision of probation officers.

(h) Borstal Schools Acts for Adolescents : These acts were passed to give special treatment for adolescent offenders, that is, offenders between 15 and 21 years of age. A Borstal School is a corrective institution and is one in which the offenders are subject to disciplinary and moral influences. These influences would help them reform.

5. INSTITUTIONS TO REHABILITATE JUVENILE DELINQUENTS

Preventive measures alone are not enough. Rehabilitative or reformative measures are also needed to solve juvenile delinquency. Some of the institutions aimed at rehabilitating the juvenile delinquents are there in India. They may be briefly examined here.

1. Juvenile Courts : Juvenile Courts are established in order to separately treat juvenile delinquents from other adult criminals. Juvenile Courts have their own building, judicial bench and other arrangements. Juvenile delinquents cannot be tried in ordinary courts. Whenever the juvenile courts are not there they could however be tried in other courts but on a separate day and at a fixed time so as to keep them away from other adult criminals. Juvenile offenders cannot be chained and they cannot be produced to the courts by the police in their uniform. No advocates are needed to plead for them. The main intention behind this special treatment is to create positive feelings in the minds of juveniles. As per the report of the Union Ministry of Education, in 1950 there were (only) 39 Juvenile Courts in India.

2. Remand Homes : When a child is arrested under the Act, he is produced before the magistrate within 24 hours and kept in Remand Home till the case is investigated. The child is kept in Remand Home until the final disposal of the case. Sometimes, persons convicted are sent to Remand Homes for a few days and released later. These homes are mostly managed by private welfare agencies with governmental assistance. The precise number of such Remand Homes in India is not known.

3. Certified Schools : Certified Schools are established mainly to give some general education and technical training to the children. Here the children are sent for a long-term treatment. They are run by voluntary bodies or local authorities with the financial assistance of the government and the public. There are two types of schools : (i) ***Junior Schools*** for boys under 12, and (ii) ***Senior Schools*** for boys under 16. The children are confined here for about 2 to 3 years. The school authorities can also make an early discharge. After their release they are put under the charge of a welfare or probation officer who observes their activities.

4. Auxiliary Home : These Auxiliary Homes are attached to Certified Schools just like remand homes. Here, the convicted delinquents are kept for some time and studied by a social worker. Later on, they are sent to certified schools depending upon the nature and attitude of the young offender.

5. Foster Homes : Foster Homes are mostly run by the voluntary agencies and the governments give grants to them. They are specially created for delinquent children under 19 who cannot be sent to approved or certified schools.

6. Reformatory Schools : In states where there are no Children Acts, Reformatory Schools are established. They are meant for the education and vocational training of delinquent children. The young convicted offenders below 15 years are detained here for 3 to 7 years. The delinquents are removed from bad environments through these schools.

7. Borstal Institutions : Under Borstal system, special treatment is provided to adolescent offenders in the age of 15 to 21 years. Borstal institutions are of two types : ***(i) open type*** and ***(ii) closed type***. *'Open'* institution is a camp in the open country with no surrounding wall. Closed institution is a converted prison building in which maximum security is given to inmates. Though it is called *'Closed'* institution, most of its activities meant for children are carried on outside the building.

Young offenders are very often sent to Borstal institution for rehabilitation rather than kept under imprisonment. The term of stay at Borstal is 2 to 3 years and in any case it should not exceed 5 years. If the offenders are found to be unruly and incorrigible, they are sent to jails. Separate arrangement is made to give training to boys and girls. The training, physical exercises and education that are given here are very tough so as to prevent the inmates from committing offences again.

8. Fit Persons Institutions and Uncared Children Institutions : These are the two non-government institutions managed by private bodies and philanthropists. These institutions give refuge and protection to the destitutes, neglected children, children in the pre-delinquent stage, and to the delinquent children. Such children and their activities are supervised by the appointed officers.

Conclusion

A grave problem such as juvenile delinquency cannot be solved by means of legislations and government efforts alone. As far as India is concerned, in many of the states Children Acts have not been effectively enforced. Some of these Acts themselves have defects. Official machinery is not effectively used for controlling this problem. Governmental as well as private agencies must work hand in hand with all sincerity and seriousness to find an effective remedy for the problem of juvenile delinquency. The public attitude towards juvenile delinquents must also change. A juvenile delinquent is a product of unwholesome environment which is not congenial for the development of his faculties in conformity with social expectations.

DIFFERENCES BETWEEN CRIME AND JUVENILE DELINQUENCY

Crime and juvenile delinquency both represent pathological phenomena and require a proper diagnosis and treatment. Both pose challenges to the law and order situation in the society and damage its moral fabric and value system. They are not, however, one and the same. Differences between the two could be stated in the following way.

1. Differences in Age

The most striking difference between a juvenile delinquent and a general criminal is one of age. From the legal point of view, that is, in the Indian context, a juvenile delinquent is a person below the age of 18 years and who indulges in antisocial and illegal activity. The word crime refers to an illegal act and the person who indulges in it is a *'criminal'*. Both the delinquent and the criminal indulge in anti-social and illegal activities. Working of both is subversive and hindering of social relationships. The difference is only that if a criminal is below a certain specified age he is designated as juvenile delinquent.

2. Difference in Action

In the type of crimes they commit, we often find a difference between the juvenile delinquents and criminals. Juvenile delinquents include vagrant, cruel, obstinate young boys who keep the company of thieves, dacoits, prostitutes who keep away from home without the permission of parents and who roam about in streets as vaga bonds aimlessly. Strictly speaking, these activities are not illegal nor do they violate any law. But these activities are socially not desirable and hence condemned. It is in this way, the juvenile delinquent who chooses to act in these ways cannot be included in the same class as ordinary criminals.

3. Difference in Characteristics

Sociologist **Cohen** has distinguished a criminal from a juvenile delinquent on the basis of the following characteristics.

(i) Normally, *a juvenile delinquent does not commit a crime on a pre-planned and well organized basis.* Whereas, a hardened criminal is more inclined to plan his moves and organizing crime with a certain show of skill.

(ii) *A juvenile mischief is lacking in utility* for he does things that do not benefit such as roaming about the streets without a cause or purpose. On the other hand, a criminal normally acts with some intention or the other to gain something.

(iii) *Sometimes, a juvenile commits a crime with only one intention, that is, to enjoy himself and to indulge in his own sense of humour or pleasure.* It finds expression in practical jokes like breaking car glasses, breaking window panes of neighbours, taking out the air of vehicle tyres; plucking out the fruits from the neighbour's gardens, etc. An adult criminal does not find this a suitable mode of manifesting his sense of humour.

As it is made clear from the above, criminals and juvenile delinquents are to be distinguished by their difference of age, kinds of actions, intention or purpose of activities and mode of working.

Different Patterns of Crime in Different States and Different Districts

Patterns of crime do not remain the same. Different states and distrcits reveal different trends. For example, there wee 698 districts in the country, 13 districts out of them have reported more than 10,000 crimes annually, while 80 districts have reported crimes between 5001 and 10,000, and a bulk of them 605 have reported less than 5000 crimes annually. The following table shows the districts which have above 10,000 crimes in 2005.

Districts that Reported 10,000 crimes or even more in the year 2005.

Name of District	No. of Criminal Incidence	Name of District	No. of Criminal Incidence
1. Mumbai	31432	8. Secundarabad	12079
2. Bengaluru	29042	9. Patna	11840
3. Jaipur	20293	10. Pune	11817
4. Chennai	20127	11. North-West District of Delhi	11019
5. Ahmedabad	17468	12. Bhopal	10850
6. Hyderabad City	17276	13. South - West District of Delhi	10529
7. Indore	16026		

Source: **K.L. Sharma**'s *"Indian Social Structure and Change"* (2007), Page: 261.

•••

Chapter 7

PROBLEM OF CHILD LABOUR

What is Child Labour ? - *Types of Child Labour - Nature of Child Labour- Different Facets of the Problem-Causes of Child Labour - Working Conditions of Child Labourers - Governmental Measures and National Policy of Amelioration - Governmental Measures - An Evalution - Some other Suggestions to Improve the Present Position of the Child Labours.*

Most of the developing countries of the world including India are facing a social tragedy found in the form of *child abuse* and *child labour*. A large number of children below the age of 12-14 are made to work as labourers in many places especially in the agricultural and industrial areas. According to one estimate, as many as **217 million** children below **14** years are working as full time child labourers at the global level. The physical, emotional, educational and medical needs of these working children are conveniently ignored. These children are made to work for long hours. They are often battered by their employers and harassed by their senior colleagues. Unlike adult labourers, these child labourers do not have a labour union of their own to fight for their rights and safeguard their interests. Hence, their exploitation continues without any protest. Neither the government nor the public is serious enough to make organised efforts to combat this problem. Even the sociologists and the psychologists had not taken much interest in highlighting this grave problem for a very long time. The nation has now become aware of the gravity of the problem. Public indignation and professional concern is yet to be translated into positive and realistic action.

The issue of child labour in India attracted public attention and debate from 1985 onwards. It has become the focus of major concern in the aftermath of globalisation in 1990s. According to **Gurupada Swamy Committee Report,** *"Child labour assumes the character of a social problem in as much as it hinders, arrests or distorts the natural growth processes and prevents the child from attaining his full-flown manhood".*

What is Child Labour ?

The term *'child labourer'* is considered equivalent to the term *"working child"* or *"employed child".*

- The term *"child labourers"* refers to *"those children who are doing paid or unpaid work in factories, workshops, establishments, mines and in the service sector such as domestic labour".*

1. According to the *Article* **24** of the **Constitution of India**, child labourer may be defined as *a person who is below the age of 14 years and is working for an earning. According to*

Article 24, "no child below 14 years of age shall be employed to work in any factory or any hazardous employment.

2. According to ***The Concerned for Working Children* [*CWC*]** of Bangalore, - a child labourer is *"a person who has not completed his/her fifteenth year of age and is working with or without wages/income on a part-time or a full-time basis".*
3. According to **Home Folks**, *"Child labour is any work by children that interferes with their full physical development, their opportunities for a desirable minimum of education or their needed recreation."*
4. ***The International Labour Organisation [ILO]*** *defines child labourers as - "children permanently leading an ardent life, working long hours under conditions bad for their physical and mental health."*
5. ***The Child Labour [Prohibition and Regulation] Act 1986,*** *states "child means a person who has not completed 14 years of age". Persons below that age are not supposed to work for monetary or non-monetary rewards, for it is prohibited as per the provisions of this Act.*

- ***Article -39[F]*** *states that "childhood and growth are to be protected against exploitation and against moral and material abondonment".*
- ***Article -45*** *declares that "the state shall endeavour to provide -free and compulsory education for all children until they complete the age of 14 years."* [It is obvious that such school going children should not be made to work like labourers.]

Types of Child Labour

Child labour, is found in different forms among which the following may be noted.

(i) ***Domestic Non-monetary Work:*** Work of domestic servants but without wages or salary, *Example*: beedi rolling at home.

(ii) ***Non-Domestic and Non-Monetary Work*** which includes the work of child labourers working in plantations, fields , mining industries and in such other places only to assist the elder members of their own family who are working as labourers.

(iii) ***Wage-Labour*** which consists of the labour of children who work in glass, slate and leather industries, fireworks, glassware industries, etc.

(iv) ***Bonded Labour:*** which includes the labour of some children who work permanently as bonded labourers and who get no salary or wages except something for their maintenance. These children have either been pledged by their parents for paltry sums of money or they are the ones who are working to pay off the inherited debts of their parents.

(v) ***Street Children:*** Children living on and off the streets, such as shoe -shine boys, ragpickers, newspaper vendors, beggars, etc. These children do not have home and are at the mercy of their employers. They live on the pavements in the bus stations and railway stations.

(vi) ***Children Used for Sexual Exploitation:*** Many thousands of young girls and boys serve the sexual appetites of men from all social and economic backgrounds. Many of them suffer from sexually transmitted diseases such as HIV, AID's etc.,

1. NATURE OF CHILD LABOUR

The problem of child labour has become a colossal one. The problem is haunting humanity at the global level. Several countries in the world, including India, are faced with this menace. India has unfortunately the largest number of child labourers in the world who are engaged in

CHILD LABOUR - THE CURSE OF CHILDHOOD

both organised and unorganised sectors. Let us now make an analysis of the nature of the problem, its causes and consequences.

Magnitude of the Problem

• ***Proportion of Children in the Total Population*** **:** As per 2001 Census report, the total population of the country is around 102.8 crores out of which 37.3% of the people **[38.8 crores]** are children below the age of 14 years with an officially estimated **12.66** million children engaged in "*hazardous occupations*". Nation-wide survey held in 2009-2010 reported that the number of child labourers had decreased to 4.98 million. India has the largest number of child labourers under the age of 14 in the world [as per Census report -2011 also]

• ***Proportion of Child Labourers*** **:** As per the well assessed statistics dated 15th June 2005, there are about **246 million** child labourers in the world. It is also learnt that out of these, the largest number of child labourers are found in India. Even though child labourers are apparently seen everywhere in the country, we do not have definite, official and reliable statistics regarding their exact number.

• As per the **I.L.O.** ***[International Labour Organisation]*** report 1995, around **15%** of the total population of children in the world, [that is, around **58.2** million] in between the age of 10 and 14, are found to be working as child labourers.

• As per the statement issued by the ***Central Labour Minister*** in Rajya Sabha on ***20th March 1995***, there were around **17** million child labourers in India out of which **9.5** million were boys and **7.5** million were girls. The number must have further increased by this time.

• Yet another private estimate of the same period, i.e. 1995, has revealed that there were as many as ***44 million*** child labourers in the country out of which majority were found in agricultural sector.

Number of Child Labourers is Increasing?

According to the Census of India 2001, out of 226 million children in India under the age group 6-14 years, 65 million were not attending any educational institution. The magnitude of

Magnitude of Child Labour in Some Selected Countries [Approximations : 2009]

- Child labour is the most rampant one in Asia with 44.6 million or 13% of its children population doing commercial work.
- Africa has the highest percentage rate of child labour, that is 23.6 million, or 26.3% of the total child population.
- In Latin America, 5.1 million or 9.8% of children are child labourers
- In India, 14.4% children between 10 and 14 years of age are employed as child labourers.
- Percentage of child labour as [in between 10-14 years] in some other countries.

Bangla Desh	30.1%	China	11.6%	Brazil	16.1%
Pakisthan	17.7%	Turkey	24%	Italy	0.4%
Egypt	11.2%	Cote D'lvorie	20.5%	Mexico	6.7%
Kenya	41.3%	Nigeria	25.8%	Portugal	1.8%
Senegal	31.4%	Argentina	4.5%		

• No reliable figures of the child workers of the above mentioned age category [10 to 14 years] or below 10 years of age are available. The above mentioned figures [relating to different countries] do not constitute official data, but they are only approximations.

Source of Data: ***Dr. G.B.Patil's 'Child Labour : A Stigma on Humanity*** - 2009 Publications KILPAR [Karnataka Institute for Law and Parliament any Reform Bangalore] pages 5-10].

child labour has increased from 11.59 million in 1991,to 12.66 million in 2001 [census 2001]. However, unofficial sources claim that the number of children engaged in labour is between 25 to 30 million since a significant number of children who are engaged in the domestic and agricultural sectors are not covered in the census of India 2001.

'Main' and 'Marginal' Child Workers: Out of 12.66 million children engaged in labour, approximately 5.78 million were identified as *"main workers"* who worked for more than 6 calendar months per year. The other 6.88 million children were identified as *"marginal workers"* who worked less than 6 month per year. Most of these are in agriculture while a few are in manufacturing.

Gender Disparity: Gender disparity among children engaged in child labour is also apparent with 25% of male children out of school in the age group of 5-14 years as against 33% of female children in the same age group.

Rural -Urban Difference: Rural children seem to be more vulnerable for the problem; 32% of rural children are out of school as against 19% of urban children in the same age of group. Rural children have greater risks of being out of school than do their urban counterparts.

Scheduled Caste Children are Worst Hit: S.C.children are more vulnerable with 25% of all male children and 37% of all female children being out of school in the age group of 6 to 14 years due to child labour. These children are traditionally entrusted with hard physical tasks.

The above mentioned figures do not give us a correct picture of the magnitude of the problem of child labourers. They, however, make it evident that the problem is a serious one affecting millions of families of India and also of the world.

DIFFERENT FACETS OF THE PROBLEM

Child labour is a social problem of far-reaching consequences. No outside observer can imagine and understand the complexity and the magnitude of the problem for it is neither entirely visible nor apparent. The problem has different facets also. Without a proper appraisal of the problem its seriousness cannot be understood. The economic, social and the legal facets of the problem may be briefly examined here.

1. Economic Face of Child Labour

In most of the underdeveloped and the developing countries, children of inappropriate age are forced to take part in productive activities due to economic distress. Parents of poor class send their children for work to increase family income while the employers of various business establishments employ children to maximise their profits. The result is economic exploitation of children. This economic exploitation continues both in the ***organised*** and ***unorganised*** sectors.

(A) Child Labour in Unorganised Sector

In the unorganised sector, child labour is mainly found in the rural areas, tea and coffee estates, mining sectors and even in urban areas.

a) Child Labour in Rural Areas

A large number of children are found to be working in rural areas. It is estimated that more than **60%** of them are below the age of **10** years. A study conducted in Western U.P. has revealed that almost **35%** of the girls in the **6-11** age-group were engaged in some economic activity. Similarly, over **52%** of the girls in the age-group **11-18** were involved in economic pursuits. In these rural areas, in addition to agricultural activities, in various economic tasks such as *beedi* *rolling, agarbatti making, cleaning hides, tanning, preparing blankets and bricks, breaking stones, assisting poultry farming, dairy farming, piggery, looking after domesticated animals such as cattle, goats, pigs and so on.*

- ***In Tea-gardens and Coffee Estates*** children below 12 years are made to work much against the law. Girls who bring food to their working mothers are often encouraged to stay back and help in the work.
- ***In the Mining Operations*** also, boys below **12** years are preferred to carry things inside the tunnels without bending their head. It is said that in the mining sector, 56% workers are children below **15** years.

b) Working Children in Urban Areas

It is difficult to estimate the number of children struggling to live in urban areas as child labourers. Sizeable number of them work in *city canteens, petty shops, restaurants, garages, work shops, etc.* ***For example,*** in Delhi alone, 60,000 children work in *dhabas,* [roadside canteens] tea-stalls, restaurants and small eating places on a daily wage of ₹ 25 to 50 . They are also found to be *picking rags, hawking goods, cleaning private cars and trucks, shoe-polishing, book-binding, looking after roadside shops, toy-making, selling fruits, vegetables, icecandy, news paper, etc., loading and unloading goods for the tempos and trucks, etc.* Some of them are working in private houses as *domestic servants*.

c) Child Labourers Working as Bonded Labourers

Child labour is also associated with bonded labour. It is said that out of the total number of bonded labourers in Karnataka, 10.3% are found to be children. The figure stands at 8.7% for Tamil Nadu and 21% for Andhra Pradesh. It is pitiable to note that there are parents who even make their 5 year old children to work as bonded labourers.

(B) Child Labour in Organised Sector

According to the UN study, about 15 million children of age group of 5 to 14 years, are working in various industries in India. Studies conducted in several mega cities have revealed some of the shocking facts about child labourers. ***For example,*** **Mumbai** has the largest number of child labourers. In **Varanasi,** more than 5000 children are found working in silk weaving industry alone. Child labourers are found to be working in many factories in several cities much against the prevailing law.

The poor economic conditions of the child labourers are such that they are found even in the so called organised sector that is, in factories and various industrial units.

- ***Working Children in Industrial Units*** **:** The most pitiable working children are those employed in hazardous industries. Some examples of such industries employing children may be cited here.

(i) In the *glass industry* of **Firozabad** in U.P., out of 2 lakh workers, 50,000 [25%] are found to be children.

(ii) In the brassware industry of **Moradabad,** [U.P.] about 40000-50000 children [27 to 30%] are working.

(iii) In the *fireworks* and *match box units* in **Sivakasi** [Tamil Nadu] 45000 children are employed for work.

(iv) In the *slate industry* in **Markapur** [Andhra Pradesh], out of 15000, around 3750 are child workers.

(v) In the *carpet-weaving industry* around **Bhadohi** [U.P.], 12500 out of 50000 employees, are children.

(vi) In and around **Surat** [Gujarat] many young boys in their teens are engaged in *diamond-cutting* operations.

(vii) Small girls are made to work in the back-breaking carpet weaving industry in **Kashmir**, and so on.

(viii) In the *stone polishing industry* at **Jaipur** [Rajasthan]; *lock-making industry* at **Alighar**, [U.P.]; *pencil and slate manufacturing industry* at **Mandsaur** [M.P.]; *cashew industries* in Tamil Nadu and Kerala, in *beedi industry* in Karnataka and Kerala - a large number of child labourers are still involved.

2. Social Face of Child Labour

The social face of child labour is a horrible one. It leads to several consequences also.

a) Parent-Child Relations Become Commercial : Child labour tends to disturb the normal family life. It spoils the emotional ties between parents and children and converts them into commercial. Parents tend to look at their children as income-fetching objects rather than as individuals with tender emotions and feelings.

b) Child Labour - An Unhealthy Social Practice : Compelling the children of inappropriate age to work for a petty amount is a very unhealthy social practice. Because, child labour adversely affects the children's balanced physical growth, spoils their education, and deprives them of their needed recreation. Child labour will have disastrous consequences on the spiritual, moral and emotional make-up of the children.

c) No Hope of a Promising Future : Child labour makes the future of the children very bleak. It disturbs their family life, hampers their socialisation and stunts their creative ability. Children caught in the vicious circle of working at such tender age can hardly lead a healthy social life in their later adult life.

3. Child Labour and Legal Face

The problem of child labour in India is such that it flourishes in spite of the constitutional provisions and legislations made against it. ***For Example***:

(i) As per ***Article 24,*** no child below the age of 14 years shall be employed to work in any factory or in any dangerous employment;

(ii) According to ***Article 39(f),*** childhood and youth are to be protected against exploitation and moral and physical vices and;

(iii) According to ***Article 45,*** the state shall endeavour to provide within a period of 10 years from the commencement of the Constitution free and compulsory education for all children until they complete the age of 14 years.

• As per the ***U.N. Declaration on the Convention of the Rights of the Child [1959],*** an individual below the age of 16 must be considered a *"child"*. It also states that any physical, mental and moral exploitation of the child is a blatant violation of the rights of the child. The U.N. Convention of the Rights of the Child [1989], however, increased this age limit to 18 years.

2. CAUSES OF CHILD LABOUR

Various factors have contributed to the problem of child labour among which the following may be noted.

1. Economic Causes

a) ***Extreme Poverty*** **:** Child labour is commonly found in all the developing countries where poverty is usually found. India is a country in which more than 29.5% of the people are living below the conditions of poverty as per 2011 estimate.[1] Many families with extreme poverty are compelled to send their children for work who contribute something for the family income. Children of poor families are forced to work particularly when the working adult members of the family become disabled due to physical and mental deformities, diseases or accidents.

b) ***Possibility of Extracting More Work for Less Wages*** **:** Employers of many enterprises search for child labourers because they can extract more work from them by giving less wages. Child labourers neither have a *"labour union"* of their own, nor the *"bargaining power"* to demand more wages. *It is observed that child labourers are employed in mining, glass-making, carpet-weaving and leather industries mainly with this intention.*

c) ***To Secure More Profit for Factories*** **:** Some industrialists [owners of fireworks, match-box units, glass and brassware industries, etc.] believe that their units are able to maximise profits because of the appointment of child labourers whose labour is very cheap. ***For example,*** the carpet industry of U.P. which employs 75000 children earns about ₹ **150/-** crore, a year in foreign exchange. In 1993, its export earnings were estimated to be about ₹ **350/-** crore. These industrialists put forward their own arguments in favour of appointing little children.

2. Familial Factors

- ***Effect of Family Disorganisation*** **:** Family disorganisation often leads to child labour. Extreme poverty and economic necessity of the family is one of the factors favouring child labour. *Divorce, desertion, rigid family relations, cruelty at home, parent child conflicts, criminal tendencies of the parents* often compel children to run away from the unpleasant family environment. Such children are often forced to work to eke out their livelihood.

- ***Street children*** **:** Those children of the rural areas who run-away from their homes due to intolerable conditions at home, normally go to cities and wander about as *"street children"*. These street children are finally compelled to get into some jobs. ***Example*** **:** According to one estimate, of the more than **4** lakh working children in Delhi; nearly **1.5** lakh children are found to be *"street children"*.

- ***Greediness of Parents*** **:** Parents without education and social consciousness rarely think in terms of the good future of their children. In expectation of some immediate returns they admit their little children for some or the other kind of work. Evil habits such as smoking, drinking liquors, drug addiction, gambling, etc., developed by parents compel them to push their children into some income-fetching petty jobs.

- ***Helplessness of the Children of Working Class*** **:** Helpless living conditions of the working class people often induce the children go astray. A large number of working children neither have families nor can rely on family support. In these circumstances, if the children do not go for work the alternative left for them is idleness, destitution, or crime.

3. Other Factors

(i) Temptation of Bad Habits **:** Children belonging to the poor families often become the victims of certain bad and costly habits such as - *smoking, gambling, purchasing lottery tickets,*

1. ***C. Rangarajan's Report*** states that during 2009-2010, the percentage of poor in India was around 38.2% and it came down to 29.5% in 2011-12. ***Source:*** *Hosa Diganta, Kannada Daily, Dated: 08/07/2014.*

seeing the movies regularly, consuming alcoholic drinks, etc. When they don't get enough pocket money from home they often resort to outside work to earn money to satisfy their bad habits.

(ii) Justification of Employers of Child Labourers **:** Some employers justify their act of employing little children for work. They argue that work keeps poor children away from starvation. They even say that they are rendering a service to the society by providing some jobs to the wandering children who would otherwise have become criminals or joined the rank of anti-social elements.

(iii) Failure of Government Machinery and Legislative System **:** Though the Government has a constitutional obligation and a moral responsibility to promote the welfare of the children, it is not serious about the problem of child labour. The half-hearted legislations undertaken in this regard, are a big failure. The government bureaucracy is also indifferent to the problems of the working children.

- ***Lack of Public Awareness*** **:** Children constitute the treasury of future wealth of any nation. But unfortunately in India, public awareness is not there regarding the social evils such as child abuse and child labour. No organisation has launched an effective movement at the all-India level to rouse the consciousness of the public regarding its responsibility towards children.

- ***Kidnapping and Blackmailing of Children*** **:** There are also anti-social forces which often kidnap children and take them to a different place for selling them to some employers who are in search of cheap human labour.

3. WORKING CONDITIONS OF CHILD LABOURERS

Not only working children are found throughout India, but even horrible working conditions exist wherever they go for work. No where in India, the working conditions of children are found to be satisfactory.

1. Horrible Working Conditions in Urban and Industrial Areas

Children who are pushed to the inevitable conditions of physical work in urban and industrial areas suffer from various hardships. They work under intolerable conditions - in private houses as domestic servants; in tea-shops and restaurants as vessel-washers and waiters; in mining and industrial units as young labourers; in garages as cleaners, in shops as salesmen, and so on.

a) Children Working in Small Industrial Units and Mining Industries are faced with hygienic problems. Some work in dangerously polluted factories while a few others toil near furnaces which burn at a temperature of 1400^0 centigrade. They handle dangerous chemicals like arsenic and potassium. Continuous inhaling of impure air adversely affects their lungs and creates diseases like tuberculosis.

b) Sad Picture of Working Children in Urban Industrial Units **:** A large number of children working in leather, glass and brassware industries, slate industries and fireworks etc., have sunken chests, and thin bone frames which give them a diseased look. As **Ram Ahuja** writes : *"There are times, when their bodies ache, minds fog, hearts cry, spirits bleed, but on orders of the employer they work for 10 to 11 hours at a stretch."*[2] Any one who visits various factories in Delhi, Andhra Pradesh, Uttar Pradesh, Tamil Nadu and Maharashtra can easily notice child labourers with these characteristics.

---

2. **Ram Ahuja** in *"Social Problems in India"*.

c) Unhygienic Shelters Provided to Working Children **:** These children not only work under insanitary conditions but also are made to stay in unhygienic shelters. A large number of child workers are huddled in small rooms under inhuman conditions. These rooms are compartments of substandard, ill-ventilated, insanitary and poorly lighted shelters. These dwelling places are virtually unfit for human habitation.

d) Children Becoming Victims of Diseases **:** Child workers who are made to toil for long hours under hazardous conditions hardly maintain good health. Many of them suffer from lung diseases, tuberculosis, chronic stomach pain, eye diseases, asthama, bronchitis, back pain, skin diseases typhoid, decentry, liver complaints, etc. Working conditions of these children are so horrible that some get injured and even disabled in fire accidents. Some of them become so much incapaciated that they are thrown out of work mercilessly to join the rank of the unemployed. Thus, many become unemployed even at the age of 20.

e) Exploitation at the Hands of the Middlemen **:** Little children are drawn from the rural areas to work as child workers by some agents on some commission basis. These children who earn on an average not more than ₹ 500/- a month have to handover almost the whole money or maximum portion of it to the so called local *"guardians"* or *"dadas"* of that area. Those children who work during night shifts are subject to several hardships.

2. Distressing Conditions of the Child Workers in the Rural Agricultural Areas

Majority of the child workers are found in the rural areas. These children are made to work hard in agriculture related works and also as domestic servants.

(i) Child Workers Mostly Belong to the Landless Families **:** The *National Sample Survey Organisation* [**NSSO**] which conducted a survey in 1971 revealed that the families to which the child workers belonged did not possess any piece of land worth mentioning. This situation has not improved much even at present.

(ii) The Supportive Rural Environment **:** Low literacy level of women, poor salary paid to adult workers, presence of large number of landless scheduled caste people, rural indebtedness and other factors in the rural areas have directly or indirectly supported the practice of child labour.

(iii) Child Workers as Domestic Servants **:** There is a greater demand for girl child workers between 10-14 years to work as maid servants at home while similar demand is there for boy child workers to work outside the family, that is, mostly in paddy fields, gardens, plantations, estates, etc. Studies have revealed that most of these domestic servants are not given reasonable salary and much work is extracted from them. Girls suffer labour exploitation to such a degree that a large nmber of girls die before they reach the age of 15. Some of them are paid a pittance as low as ₹ 20/- per day and many of them are abused physically, mentally, and sexually by their merciless masters.

4. GOVERNMENT MEASURES TO PREVENT CHILD LABOUR AND NATIONAL POLICY OF AMELIORATION

Governmental Measures

The problem of child labour has now become a colossal one. Around 15% of the child population [as per I L O estimate of 1995] is found to be child workers in India. The problem is so grave that the government believes that it is not possible to remove the problem completely at a stretch. Hence, it has decided to improve their working conditions, reduce the hours of work, ensure minimum wages and provide facilities for health and education.

1. Legal Measures Against Child Labour

(a) In the very ***Constitution of India,*** provisions are made to protect the interests of children. **Article 24** of the Constitution states that children below 14 years shall not be employed in any factory or in any hazardous unit.

(b) Directive Principles of the State Policy also declare their commitment to safeguard children's interests. Though some legislations were undertaken during the British rule,[3] they were not properly enforced. The fate of a few more legislations undertaken soon after independence was also no better.[4]

(c) Legislation at the National Level - The Child Labour [Prohibition and Regulation] Act, 1986 **:** The first national level and universally applicable legislation undertaken by the Govt. of India to prevent the appointment of children below 14 years is *"The Child Labour [Prohibition and Regulation] Act, 1986."* This Act insists on providing minimum necessary facilities to the child workers. Other than this national level legislation, different states have their own state-level legislations to control and regulate child labour. ***Example*** **:** States such as Assam, Andhra Pradesh, Bihar, Kerala, Maharashtra, M.P. Punjab, Tamil Nadu, U.P. and West Bengal, have such legislations.

2. Creation of a National Authority to Eliminate and to Regulate Child Labour in Hazardous Industries - 1993

With the intention of removing the practice of child labour in total especially in the hazardous industries by the end of the 20th century, the Central Govt. constituted a ***"National Authority"*** on 2nd Oct. 1993. The Govt. decided to spend nearly ₹ **850** crores for the benefit of at least **2** million children out of a total of 17 million child workers. This institute intended to rehabilitate the child workers in at least **15,000** schools spread over the whole nation. The institution had plans to give compensation to the families whose children are taken away for hazardous works. [Though this institute was established with high hopes nothing worth mentioning has been achieved so far].

3. Supreme Court's Order for Setting up Child Labour Rehabilitation Welfare Fund [CLRWF], 1996.

In its judgement to a public interest litigation, the Supreme Court ordered the setting up of *a Child Labour Rehabilitation Welfare Fund* [on 10th December 1996] to prevent the exploitation of children and to safeguard their economic interest and humanitarian rights. The Court in its judgement also banned child labour in hazardous industries.[5] Any employer deviating from this order will have to deposit ₹ 20.000/- as compensation for each child in the Fund which could be used for the continuation of his education.

---

3. *Examples of the Legislations Undertaken During British Rule Affecting Children* :
   1. **The Factories Act, 1881,** which forbids the appointment of children below 7 years.
   2. **Indian Merchant Shipping Act, 1923** which prevents appointing children below 14 in ships,
   3. **The Children Pledging of Labour Act, 1933** according to which no children can be pledged for the purpose of getting loan nor for repaying loan.
4. *Examples of the Legislations Undertaken After Independence* :
   1. **The Indian Factories Act, 1948** which forbids appointing children below **14** years for work and fixes the duration of work at $\mathbf{4^1/_2}$ hrs per day;
   2. **The Plantations Labour Act, 1951** which forbids appointment of children below **12** years for plantation work;
   3. **The Mines Act, 1952** which prevents the appointment of children below 15 years from working in deep mines.
5. The Court identified 9 industries as the most hazardous ones. They are 1. Match Industry in Shivakashi, TamilNadu; 2. Diamond Polishing Industry in Surath, Gujarath; 3. Precious Stone Polishing Industry Jaipur, Rajastan; 4. Glass Industry in Firozabad, U.P.; 5. Brassware Industry, Moradabad, UP; 7. Lock-Making Industry, Aligarh, UP; 8. Slate-Industry, Markapur, AP; 9. Slate Industry in Mandsaur, MP.

As far as the non-hazardous jobs are concerned, the Court directed the State Govts to establish an appropriate authority to ensure not more than **6 hours** of work a day, and at least **2 hours** of time for the child's education. The Court also directed that the entire cost of education is to be borne by the employer.

National Policy Towards Child Labourers

The Government of India decided to face the problem of child labour through a national policy and accordingly it was framed in August 1987. As per the *National Policy on Child Labour* [NPCL], the Government started its schemes in 1988 to rehabilitate child labourers. Since total eradiation of the problem at one stroke is not possible, the Govt. has only tried to improve their working conditions, minimise their exploitation and promote their welfare.

The Indian government's approach towards tackling the issue of child labour consists of the following three steps.

(i) ***Resorting to legal actions focusing on the general welfare of the child labourers*** - such as reducing hours of work, ensuring minimum wages, assuring hygienic and sanitary conditions of work, providing for minimum necessary civic facilities. These facilities include - toilets, resting rooms, canteens, reading rooms, periodic medical check-up, entertainment facility, etc.

(ii) ***Undertaking developmental programmes for child workers*** and their families so as to cover their education, health, job prospects, and so on. Much stress is laid on providing educational facilities to the child labourers. Programme of free and compulsory education upto the age of 16, must be extended to these children also. It is believed that only education would fetch them salvation from their present state of affairs.

(iii) ***Launching project-based action plan*** in order to achieve the first two purposes.

In the beginning, it was suggested to take up ***ten projects*** to cover areas where child labour was found to be widely prevalent. These projects included - *match works in Shivakashi, diamond cutting industry in Surat and Jaipur, carpet-weaving in Mirzapur, brassware industry in Moradabad, glass industry in Ferozabad*, and so on. Of these ten projects, only three were taken up for implementation.

5. GOVERNMENTAL MEASURES : AN EVALUATION

Failure of Legislation : The problem of child labour continues to exist in spite of the measures of the government to contain it. Legislaions undertaken to cover certain specific areas [***Example*** : *The Indian Factories Act, 1948; The Plantations Labour Act, 1951;* and *The Mines Act, 1952.*] have also not been successful. The much expected and an all-comprehensive national-level legislation such as *the Child Labour [Prohibition and Regulation]* ***Act, 1986*** has also not inspired the governmental machinery to take serious steps to remove and to regulate the practice of child labour.

- ***Half - Hearted Welfare Projects Regarding Child Labour*** : Though the Central Labour Ministry made an announcement in Aug. 1987 that it would launch the *project based action plan* as an essential component of the national policy on child labour, it failed to keep up the promise. The Govt. hoped to start 10 projects simultaneously covering vulnerable areas such as glass industry, brassware industry, match-works, diamond-polishing industry, etc. But considering the magnitude of the problem, it decided to take up only the match industry on an experimental basis. Even with regard to this project which would have benefited 30,000 working children, nothing concrete has been done except defining the responsibilities of the States and the Centre in such projects.

● ***Indifferent and Corrupt Enforcement Machinery*** : The 1986 legislation permits the employment of children below 14 years in some selected areas of the *non-hazardous organised sector*. It, however, insists on some safeguards against their exploitation and provides for educational and recreational facilities. A grave defect of this legislation is that it has to rely on the corrupt and inefficient enforcement machinery. This indifferent and corrupt machinery which is bribed by the industrialists keeps its eyes closed even when the provisions of the legislation are openly violated.

● ***Lack of Clarity in the 1986 Legislation*** : The 1986 Act fails to define properly *"what constitutes hazardous jobs"*. A committee which was set up to identify the permissible jobs for working children has also not made much progress.

Some Suggestions to Improve the Present Position of the Child Labourers

It is a matter of disgrace for the society to make the children work as full-fledged employees. Enforcing them to work in conditions dangerous to their health and safety is a crime. Under no circumstances, they be compelled to work before they become matured enough to work.

1. ***Existing Legislations be Made More Effective*** : The government instead of thinking in terms of introducing new legislations must take necessary steps to implement effectively and strictly the already existing legislations.
2. ***Punishments for Violators*** : To ensure compliance with the 1986 Act, stringent punishments should be given to those who violate its provisions.
3. ***Promotion of the General Welfare of the Child Workers be Insisted Upon*** : It must be made compulsory for all the employers to take proper steps to promote the vocational, educational, medical and intellectual well-being of the child workers whether they are working as domestic servants, factory workers or hotel-workers.
4. ***Law Enforcement Machinery be Instituted*** : Laws and regulations relating to child labour must be backed by effective enforcement machinery with statutory powers to take necessary action. This helps the strengthening of labour inspection and related services.
5. ***Maintenance of Registers be Made Compulsory*** : It should be made mandatory for employers to maintain registers and documents indicating the names and age of all the employed children.
6. ***Exploitation of Children be Stopped in the Unorganised Sector Also*** : It is necessary for the government to make proper arrangements and take appropriate precautions to prevent unhealthy and exploitative child labour not only in the organised field but also in *the unorganised sector.*
7. International agencies such as the ***World Health Organisation*** *[WHO]*, the ***United Nations' International Children's Emergency Fund*** *[UNICEF]* and the ***International Union for Child Welfare*** *[IUCW]* are also working for promoting child welfare. Due co-operation must be provided to these agencies to obtain their best help.
8. ***Need to Protect the Rights of Children, the U.N.O. Appeal :*** *The UN Declaration on the Conventions of the Rights of the Child, 1959 and 1989,* has stressed that every member nation must make honest attempts to protect the following rights of children.

● ***Rights of Children As Per the UN Declaration***

1. Every child has an inherent right to life.
2. No discrimination be made against the child.
3. State must stop the abuse and neglect of child.

4. Child has the right to reasonable standard of health and medical care
5. Child has the right to seek protection against labour which is detrimental to its health and personality.
6. Child has the right to get good education and it is the duty of the state to ensure free primary education.
7. Child has the right to a reasonable standard of living.
8. Child has the right to expect from the parents its protection and nourishment.
9. Child has the right to freedom of thought, expression and religion,
10. Child has the right to obtain relevant information and privacy.

Some other Suggestions

a) Creating Social Awareness: Systematic and serious attempts must be made to create a social atmosphere against the practice of child labour. People must be made to know about its evil consequences. The need to protect children against forced work at a tender age should be stressed among employers, trade unionists, bureaucrats, parents and administrators. Voluntary organisations must be encouraged to create this social awareness in society. Mass media including print media and electronic media should play an important role in this regard. It should educate the public about the importance of protecting children and at the same time, expose those individuals, companies or bussiness units which exploit child labourers and damage their future life.

b) Making Primary Education Compulsory: Mere declaration of giving free education to all children is not enough. Free and quality oriented primary education must be made compulsory. Both governmental and non-governmental agencies and machineries must work sincerely in this direction to make this declaration a reality. Providing education to children will definitely reduce this problem and help its eradication.

c) Giving Economic Assistance to Poor Families: Poor families must be given due economic assistance through various schemes of the Government so that no family is compelled to send its children for wage - based work. Economic assistance given by the government must help such poor families to become economically independent and not permanent parasites on the government.

d) Child Labour is to be Replaced by Adult Labour: Strict instructions are to be given by the government to all employers to replace child labour with adult labour so that children can be made to join schools and continue education.

e) Role of N.G.O.s - Non-Governmental Organisations: A complex and at the same time, a serious social problem such as child labour cannot be solved by governmental efforts alone. Voluntary organisations and private agencies with a strong commitment to social service must also play a vital role in identifying the child labourers and in liberating them from their helpless situation and bondage. **Kailash Satyarthi**'s ***"Bachpan Bachavo Andolan"*** [*"Save Childhood Campaign"*] has done a commendable work in this regard by liberating more than 80,000 child labourers from 1983 uptil now. In recognition of this great service, he has been awarded the ***"Nobel Prize for Peace"*** [which involves ₹ 6.6 crore cash amount] in the year 2014 [October 2014] which he has shared with 17 year old **Miss Malala Yusaph** of Pakisthan, who raised her voice against the fundamentalist Pakisthani Talibanese [even at the gun point] in favour of the education of Muslim girls. [See Page: 143 for more details]

Conclusion

Children are the future custodians of all the present philosophies, including sovereignty, rule of law, justice, liberty, fraternity and international peace and security. They have the right to joyful childhood. Every child has the right to grow up in a safe and nurturing environment with protection and guidance from their guardians. Whether in the cities or in the villages at home or in schools, a child is always a child and deserves a childhood free from exploitation and abuse. Yet millions of children are being robbed of their childhoods everyday. It is a crime on humanity and must be stopped as immediately as possible.

Children are the potential embodiment of our ideals, aspirations, ambitions and future expectations. They are the only messengers of our ideologies, philosophies, knowledge and cultural heritage. They are, indeed, future shoulders in the form of great scientists, rulers, administrators, philosophers, legislators, teachers, judges, engineers, technologists, industrialists, planners, workers and politicians on whom the nation rests. Children are an important asset not only for their country but also for the whole mankind. Welfare and development of a society largely depends upon them. They are not merely future adults, they are tiny apostles of peace, prosperity and contentment. Protecting the health and education of today's children is the first and foremost right of these children, but it is also the most basic and wiser of all investments and thus, for social and economic development of society. Thus, we must have proper national plans for the development of human resources, so that our children grow up to become robust citizens physically fit, mentally alert and morally healthy, endowed with the skill and motivations needed by the society.

In conclusion, it could be said that the Government in co-operation with the public should take such appropriate steps with the help of which the child of the 21st century will find himself into the *"heaven of freedom."*

KAILASH SATYARTHI WINS NOBEL PRIZE FOR PEACE FOR THE YEAR 2014

Deserving Award for the Noble Cause of Liberating the Bondage of 80,000 Children

It is really paradoxical that in the present world when people are running after globalisation, liberalisation, digitalisation, etc. there are about **one crore** children who are dragging on their life as bonded labourers, while another nearly **21 crore** children are burdened with the druggery of child labour. These children are deprived of the tenderness of their childhood, the pleasure of playing and the rightful opportunity of reading and writing to equip themselves as civilised people.

In the midst of this scene, **Kailash Satyarthi**, a 60 year old social worker of Vidisha place of Madhya Pradesh, floated his *"Bachapan Bachavo Andolan"* [*'Save Childhood Campaign'*] almost 31 years ago, that is, in 1983 at the age of 26, has been working silently since then, for the release of the bondage of thousands of children who have been forced by the circumstances to work either as bonded labourers or as child labourers.

Most of the Indians came to know about Sri Satyarthi only when he was awarded the prestigious Nobel Peace Award for his yeomen service in saving the invaluable childlife of more than 80 thousand children through his persistent *"save childhood campain"*.

Shri Sayarthi played an important role in persuading the Central Government in bringing an amendment to the child labour Act to make it more stringent. He worked a lot to bring about *"The Right to Education Act, 2009"*. He also built-up pressure at the international level to declare child labour as illegal. He carried on a campaign at the international level against the sale of the commodities [such as rug, carpet, chocolate, sports materials, etc.] by the companies which practice child labour. He and his followers appealed to the customers not to purchase goods or articles which are prepared by making use of child labour. Responses which he obtained for his appeal were really encouraging.

Kailash Satyarthi believes that this problem of child labour will have to be faced by three types of activities. They are...

- ***Taking all the precaution*** to see that child labour is not practised any where;
- When once an incident of its practice is found ***strict economic, legal and police action should be taken*** to stop it immediately giving no scope for it to rise its head at any time in future.
- ***The liberated child labourers must be properly rehabilitated*** so that they are made able to find out a suitable avenue to lead an independent, dignified and satisfactory life.

Sri Kailash Sathyarthi who is honoured by the Nobel Prize Award for his service, is magnanimous enough to dedicate this coveted award for the cause of child labourers.

●●●

Chapter 8

YOUTH UNREST AND AGITATIONS

Youth Unrest - A World Phenomenon - Youth Unrest in India - Concepts of Youth Unrest, Youth Protest, Youth Agitation and Youth Movement - Causes of Youth Unrest - Growth of Youth Unrest in India before Independence - Student Unrest After Independence - Types of Youth Unrest - As per Myron Weiner - Types of Youth Agitations : Ram Ahuja's Classification - Nature of Youth Agitation - Some Examples of Major Youth Agitations in India - Limitations of Youth Agitations - Remedies for Youth Unrest and Agitations.- Student Activism After the 1999s.

YOUTH UNREST

'Youth unrest' which is often described as *'student revolt'*, *'student power'* and *'student activism'*– has become today an established fact, a reality. The three decades, that is, between 1960 and 1990, have witnessed innumerable outbursts of student power in many nations of the world.[1]

Youth Unrest – A World Phenomenon

The phenomenon of *'youth unrest'* which also normally implies *"student unrest"* has become worldwide. As **Gareth Stedman Jonse** has rightly observed: "*From Berlin to Peking, from Tokyo to New York, in Paris and in Prague, the rise of these movements (student movements) has altered the nature of politics. Virtually, every government has some reason to fear its students, with good reason. From Cuba in 1958 to Czechoslovakia and France in 1968, students have played a crucial role in political change again and again helping to discredit, transform or topple governments. Students have erupted in the world of politics with a suddenness no one could have foretold*". The students are today a new social force of incalculable significance.

The student power seems to have an anti-establishment and a revolutionary tone. In **Germany**, *the Socialist Student Union* (S.D.S.) declared the students' lack of confidence in political parties and parliament and justified their "*taking democracy into the streets*". In **Italy**, student strikes accompanied by an *'anti-university'* stance marked the happening at Turia and other universities including those of Rome, Naples, Bologna, etc. In Feb. 1968, the disturbances in the Belgian University of Louviah contributed directly to the fall of the Belgian Government. In **Czechoslovakia**, in the movement towards liberalism the students and the youth union's joined hands with workers in "*heralding the democratic revolution*". In **America**, the anti-Vietnam and civil rights issues brought about confrontation between students and the authorities. The students were led by the S.D.C "*Students for Democratic Society*". In May-June 1968, **France**

1. This chapter provides a glimpse of the nature of student unrest/ activism of the 1960s and 1990s [1960 to 2000] and it is significant to note that it has taken a different turn especially after the onset of globalisation in the 1990s -Author.

saw battles between demonstrators and police and violent attack of students and workers. Students boycotted examinations in Sorbonne and occupied the administrative buildings. When the crisis was over, the Minister of Education was no longer in the Government for he had to resign. It is said that this event accelerated the downfall of De Gaulle. In **England**, the London School of Economics was the scene of confrontation between the radicals and the authorities. In **Indonesia**, the partnership of the students and the army militated against Communism and brought about the fall of the Sukarno regime. **Japan** has witnessed the most massive demonstrations by students. In **Bangladesh**, the students played a key role in its liberation movement in 1970s joining hands with the Mukti Bahini.

Youth Unrest in India

In **India,** the student activism has erupted in different forms and for totally unconnected reasons in different parts of the country. A quarrel between the staff of the bus transport and a group of students in Jabalpur led to massive demonstrations and strikes in the whole of M.P. and U.P. sometime ago. A change in the method of payment of examination fees resulted in total strikes in Lucknow University. A demand for a steel plant brought the Andhra students on the street. Vietnam has always provided an early opportunity to the Calcutta students to agitate. Demand for an Agricultural University gave rise to a massive agitation in the Vidarbha regions of Maharashtra. A demand for reforms in the Agricultural University was the reason behind agitation in Jammu and Kashmir. A few rusticated student leaders aided by the 'disgruntled politicians' brought the closure of the Banaras Hindu University. A rivalry between student factions, one supporting the Vice-Chancellor and the other Chief Minister of Andhra Pradesh in the Osmania University, was said to be the real beginning of the Telengana agitation. Anti-Hindi agitation and the Expo- 70 agitation resulted in the closure of all the colleges in Karnataka. Semester system was the target of attack for the students of the Mysore University some years back that is in, 1970s. The '*Nav Nirman Andolan*' of Gujarat (which toppled down Chimanbhai Patel's Government) ultimately gave birth to the *Chhatra Sangharsha Samities* guided, inspired and led by Late Sri Jayaprakash Narayan, and the Assam agitation spearheaded by the All Assam Students Union (AASU,being supported by the Gana Sangrama Parishad) -have been the recent examples [of 1970s and 1980s] of student agitation of semi-political nature. Barring a few successful agitations the student solidarity has failed to be peaceful in its agitations.

The Concepts of *"Youth Unrest"*- *"Youth Protest"* - *'Youth Agitation'* and *'Youth Movement'*

The concepts such as *youth unrest, youth protest, youth agitation and youth movement* are very often used in our daily talks many a times interchangeably. Even in sociological literature, these terms are used most of the times to convey more or less the same meaning. For the sake of conceptual clarity the thin differences that exist between them may be noted here.

Concept of 'Youth Unrest'

- The word '**unrest**' refers to a '*disturbed condition*'. It is a "*state of disillusionment and dissatisfaction.*" The term '*youth unrest*' thus, simply means general dissatisfaction found amongst youths.
- The concept of ***'youth unrest'*** can be defined in simple words as - *"the manifestation of collective disillusionment or dissatisfaction or discontentment and frustration found among the youth of a community or society"*- **Ram Ahuja**

- In brief, youth unrest may be defined as *"the manifestation of collective frustration of the youths in the society"*.

It should be noted that the term "*youth unrest*" or "*student unrest*" does not just refer to the discontent or unrest found for some reason or the other in a particular college or university. The term however, is applicable only when the students or youths as a community all over the country or society feel frustrated on common issues like educational policy, admission policy, syllabus pattern, examination system, fee structure, representation for students in the university academic bodies etc., Just as the terms '*industrial unrest*', '*tribal unrest*', ' '*peasant unrest*', etc. are made use of to refer to the unrest or discontent found in the entire community of workers, tribals and peasants respectively ; *the term 'youth unrest' refers to the unrest found among the youths in a society as such.*

Meaning of 'Youth Protest'

"***Youth Protest***" *is a form of social protest. Youth protest is a mode of communicating discontentment. It is, indeed, an expression of outrage against injustice.* The youth protestors may indulge in looting, cause damage to public or private property, shout slogans against a person/s who are in power, stage '*dharanas*', picketing and so on. It must be remembered, that all these methods are resorted to not with the purpose of acquiring property, nor to take revenge upon any person. They are resorted to by the youth only to express their dissatisfaction towards the indifference and irresponsible response shown by the people in power towards their grievances.

Youth protest is normally temporary in nature. But, it may also get transformed into 'youth agitation and "youth movement".

Concepts of "Youth Agitation" and "Youth Movement"

Youth protest may sometimes lead to *'youth agitation'* and *"youth movement'*. ***Youth agitation*** *represents a form of collective behaviour found in the community of youths.* Its main purpose is to bring grievance and injustice to the notice of the people in power. In it, there is an attempt to shake up, or to stir up the power holders and to cause tension and anxiety in them.

*The term **'youth movement'** denotes a form of social movement.* As we find in any social movement, *youth movement is a collective effort to promote or resist change. Youth movement denotes a sustained and organised effort to bring some change based on some ideology.*

The difference between the two terms '*youth agitation*' and '*youth movement'* is that youth movement may often take the form of youth agitation but every movement does not do so. 'Agitation' is normally not be based on any ideology and it is more temporary than a movement.

CAUSES OF YOUTH UNREST

Student unrest in this country has earned a peculiar connotation because of the unprecedented social dimension achieved by the student leadership at least in some instances. The unrest is there no doubt but the student movement is not in sight anywhere. The leftist slogan of the sixties, '*Students today and workers tomorrow*' seems to have become hollow. The students are no more visualized as '*Vanguards in a revolution led by and controlled under the hegemony of the working class*'. The students do not constitute a '*revolutionary class*' as such. *'The promise held out by the activism in the sixties was, however, belied by the apathy in the seventies'*. The American student activism has slowly evaporated. The Japanese student enthusiasm has gone dormant. The

YOUTH AND STUDENTS' POWER - NATION'S POWER

student energy in India is dissipated. Lack of proper leadership, absence of clear national goal, lack of guidance and inspiring model have all made the youth power in India to become idle.

Youth Unrest – A Reflection of Society !

It is true that *social situation breeds frustration.* It is also true that there is no national goal beckoning the spirit of the youth. It is a fact that the present education has failed to give any direction or purpose to the life of the student. The student is always asked to behave without any guidance as to how he should behave. He has tremendous energy but there is no consciousness as to his rights and responsibilities. By and large, he is apathetic, drawn in struggle only when mass frenzy grips his mind. There is no connection between his struggle for survival and the education which is supposed to help him in the matter. He is not interested in knowledge in the abstract. He goes to the college because he has no alternative. He must get a degree if he has to 'make it'. He has no option. '*Therefore, his only aim is to get in, get out and get on with it*'. The university is no more an isolated community of scholars but is more a community of young people. The reality of the world today involves serious problems and the universities just are not doing much about it.

Causes of Youth Unrest

Various factors have contributed to the problem of youth unrest of 1960-1990s. Some of them may be noted here.

1. Improper Socialisation and Family Problems: The failure on the part of parents to bring up their children in accordance with the cultural expectations of the society has made the youth to go astray. Evil habits and bad qualities of the parents also have a harmful effect on the personality growth of children. Family problems spoil the mental peace and emotionality of the growing children.

2. Political, Social and Economic Inequalities: The young people are more sensitive to the political, economic and social inequalities and exploitations. They have contempt for the existing corrupt 'system'. They are disillusioned with what they are having and are pessimistic about the future.

3. Defective Educational System: Students do not have any respect for the present defective educational system. The outdated, uninspiring, unintegrated, and irrelevant educational system cannot make the students to become disciplined and responsible.

4. Unemployment: Unemployment of the educated youths is on the increase. Education that they receive does not enable them to become economically self-reliant. On the other hand, the government is not in a position to provide employment to all the educated youths. As a result, the youths are losing confidence in themselves and are becoming more and more restless.

5. Corrupt and Discredited Authority: Youths are disappointed with the corrupt and discredited authority. Corruption, craziness for power, moral lapses, opportunism, nepotism, discrimination, etc., found among the political and social leaders have made the youths to have nothing but contempt for them. Political or social leadership has failed to set a good model for the students to emulate.

6. Misuse of Student Power by the Politicians: The corrupt and unscrupulous politicians, who are making use of student power to further their partisan political interests, are also contributing to the problem. Students are becoming puppets in the hands of some disgruntled politicians to serve their selfish ends.

7. Administrative Failures: Youth unrest is often caused by administrative errors and miscalculations. Indifference and lack of sympathy for the student demands on the part of the administrations (of the university as well as the government) many times force the students to resort to strikes.

8. Communication Gap: Lack of understanding and lack of proper communication between the students and teachers on the one hand, parents and children on the other, also cause youth unrest. Failure on the part of the parents to understand the aspirations of their young children also adds to the problem.

9. Value Differences and Conflict of Value: Value differences in society, changes and conflicts of values also contribute to youth unrest.

(i) Some of the old values are at conflict now. The traditional beliefs, practices, ideas and values appear to be outmoded, unscientific, irrelevant and irrational for the modern youths.

(ii) Youths are becoming more and more rationalistic. They are impressed by the modern values based on science and rationalism. Still, they are not in a position to give up the traditional values completely. They are in a state of confusion. They can neither accept the new completely nor do away with the old once and for all. This has made them to become restless.

(iii) Youths are influenced by values of individualism and democracy. Hence, they are revolting against the old traditional order.

(iv) Youths feel they are also matured, responsible and sensible. They resent their elders treating them as *'immature' and 'irresponsible lot'*. They feel annoyed and embarrassed to find themselves in a helpless situation. They do not want to remain dumb witnesses to all the unfortunate and unwanted events that happen in society.

(v) Some of the youths are carried away by the hedonistic values or pleasure philosophy. They want to take maximum benefit out of the disturbed social situations. They have no respect for any values for they have lost faith in them.

10. Lack of Opportunities: Youths do not get proper opportunities to express their talents, cultivate their interests and develop their personality. This has contributed to their dissatisfaction.

11. Gap between the Aspirations and Achievement: Youths are likely to have their own aspirations and ambitions. They will be dreaming about it all the while. But the reality of life makes them to become disgusted. The youths with unfulfilled desires and aspirations can hardly be at rest.

12. Lack of Determination and Self-Responsibility: Some of the youths lack will power and self-determination. They depend more on others rather than on their intrinsic abilities and talents. They apishly imitate others and fail to develop the spirit of self-reliance. They are hesitant to assume responsibilities. Such youths are highly vulnerable for any kind of use or abuse.

13. Influence of Movies: The modern movies which mostly portray violence, arson, loot, rape, murder, immorality, crimes, etc. have a great demoralizing effect on the modern youths. Students and youths very often imitate their pet film actors and actresses considering them as their models. Scant respect for cultural values and the apish imitation of the western tendencies on the part of youths have further contributed to the problem.

GROWTH OF YOUTH UNREST IN INDIA BEFORE INDEPENDENCE

Youth unrest in India started in the beginning of the 20th century. Unorganized youth movements were taking place here and there. Most of them were directed against the British rule in India. Youths joined hands with the people in launching protest movements against the British. They played an important role in the freedom struggle.

Role of Students in Indian National Movement

Students took part in the Indian freedom struggle on a very wide scale for the first time when Lord Curzon partitioned Bengal in 1905. Since then, students have been taking part in all the major national struggles. The youths were mainly behind the Indian National Congress at that time. When Congress was split into two groups of *extremists* and *moderates* in its Lahore Session in 1907, students also distributed themselves between these groups. They rallied round the leadership of *Bal Gangadhar Tilak* and later on, *Subhaschandra Bose* and *Mahatma Gandhiji*. Under the leadership and guidance of Gandhiji, students became a formidable force in India.

Role of Gandhiji in Student Unrest

After his return from South Africa, Gandhiji entered politics, i.e., the freedom struggle in 1919 on the advice of his "*political guru*" *Gopalakrishna Gokhale*. Gandhiji launched his campaign against " *The Rowlatt* Act (1919), the *Jallianwalla Bagh* atrocities in 1919 in which students had taken part in a big number. Gandhiji called the nation to wage a passive resistance movement against the government; to boycott all things British, break links with the government, resign from posts and govt jobs, surrender titles and offices, and withdraw from schools and colleges. The nation responded promptly and the students in a very big number boycotted schools and colleges. For the first time, the student force was organized and mobilized against the British rule.

In 1920, the First '*All-India Students' Conference* was held in Nagpur under the presidentship of *Lala Lajpat Rai*. Students could now get the support and guidance of leaders like *Pandit Nehru, Subhas Chandra Bose* and others. Students took an active role in various campaigns launched by Gandhiji against the British such as – the *'No Tax' Campaign 1921, the Civil Disobedience Movement, the Dandi Satyagraha of 1930*, etc. They also took interest in Gandhiji's constructive programmes such as – removal of untouchability and casteism, adult education, popularizing '*Swadeshi*' articles and the use of '*Khadi*', cleaning of villages, promotion of communal harmony, and so on.

Birth of the First Student Organisation in India and its Split : In 1936, *All-India Students' Federation*, the first student organization of India, was born in order to support the Indian National Congress in its struggles. The followers of Gandhiji and also the communists supported this organization in the beginning. Due to the clash of personalities and differences of opinion regarding its principles, the Students' Federation was divided into two factions (in 1938) such as – (i) the *All-India Youth Congress* and (ii) *All-India Students' Federation* (AISF). Socialists within the Congress and the Gandhians supported the former, while the Communists who wanted to follow violent methods took into their hands the latter. Since then, the AISF is in the hands of the Communists.

Role of Students in the Quit India Movement of 1942

The '*Quit India*' Movement launched by the Indian National Congress under the leadership of Gandhiji was an important event in the Indian Freedom Struggle. The students' participation in the freedom struggle took a new dimension in this movement. It was almost the climax of the youth movement. Students in the nook and corner of India took part in it. They came out of schools and colleges and universities and boycotted the educational institutions. They organized mass processions and rallies in towns and cities. They educated the illiterate and ignorant masses to fight for the cause of the nation.

Students took to some violent actions to paralyze the British administration : They resorted to such methods as cutting telephone wires, blocking transport routes, destroying public property, disturbing postal, police, banking and other services. They ransacked government offices, burnt official documents and gheraoed police stations. They brought the government machinery to a stand-still. They also kept in touch with the underground leaders and carried on the tempo of agitation. The British Government resorted to suppressive measures. The police lathi charged on student gatherings, arrested and imprisoned a number of them and gave physical harassment to many of them. Some of them were killed in police firings also. Students made considerable sacrifice in this movement and demonstrated that the youths of India never lagged behind in the national struggle. They continued their struggle with the same spirit even up to 1947, that is, till India got the Independence.

Two Political Functions of Student Organisations

It is true that student movement in India was very much associated with politics before independence. But the *student energy was spent for a national cause*. From the political point of view, the youth movement in India before independence performed two important *political functions: **Firstly**, the youths supported national freedom struggle and joined hands particularly with the Congress to disrupt the British institutions and paralyze the government. **Secondly**, youth organizations and movements served as recruitment centers for the political parties*. The then existing political parties (such as the Congress, Muslim League, Hindu Mahasabha) were looking forward with eagerness to catch young and dynamic persons for their parties from these movements and organizations.

STUDENT UNREST AFTER INDEPENDENCE

After the Independence, student unrest, student organizations and youth movements assumed different roles and different proportions. Before Independence, the students had before them one common national goal, and that was to secure for India, freedom. The student energy or power was mobilized and directed for the fulfilment of that goal. They had good leadership and obtained noble guidance. But the national scene had changed after Independence. The Congress which was a national movement then, became the ruling party and a number of political parties were also born. In the beginning, political parties seemed to have neglected the student force. They were more busy with their power politics. But after 1960s, the student force gained strength. The incidence of student unrest rose to unimaginable proportions between 1960s and 1970's.

Philip G. Altabch observes: *"Student unrest has been one of the India's most serious educational and political problems. Student agitation in India has caused State Governments to fall and it has forced the Central Government to revise its language policies. Students have paralyzed colleges and universities and have caused serious damage to public properties as well as to educational institutions".*

Social Composition of the Students after Independence

Soon after Independence, the Government started giving more importance to education and hence vast educational opportunities were created for all the sections of the people, without any discrimination. Those sections of the people which had ignored education or were deprived of educational facilities during the British rule, started availing of the same after Independence. This resulted in a change in the social composition of the students. Students belonging to almost all the *castes, classes, religious groups, tribal groups, linguistic, ethnic* and *racial groups* are found studying in schools, colleges and universities. Education is no more the monopoly of upper classes and the upper castes. The *Harijans* and *Girijans*, *Hindus* and *Muslims*, *Christians* and *Anglo-Indians*, the rich and the poor, the so-called '*forward communities*' and '*backward communities*' go to the same educational institutions. Education has become completely secular today. The depressed classes and communities are provided with special facilities to avail of educational opportunities. The student mass is mostly *heterogeneous*, especially in the cities. This heterogeneity has also contributed to the growing unrest among the students.

Student Unrest and Political Parties

Student unrest has been closely associated with politics in India. It cannot be completely divorced from the political movements and manoeuvrings. After the Independence, no attempt has been made by any political party, including the ruling party, to depoliticalise the youths and to disaffiliate them from political activities. There has been no attempt to make the students feel that Independence has been achieved and there is no need for political activities by the youths. On the contrary, political parties have found that student force constitutes one of the most powerful instruments to achieve their political ends.

Most of The Political Parties Have their Own Student Wings

Indian political parties have started taking more interest in student activism for their political gains. Political parties have started their own youth wings. Almost all the political parties have their own youth organizations now. *For example,* Congress Party has its *National Students' Union of India* (NSUI), the Bharatiya Janata Party, has its *Janata Yuva Morcha*, the Communist Party of India (CPI) has its *All-India Students Federation* (AISF), the Communist Party of India, Marxist (CPM) has its *Student Federation of India* (SFI), the Janata Party has its *Yuva Janatha*, the Indian Union Muslim League (IUML) has its *Muslim Students Union of India* and so on. Even the regional parties also have their own youth wings.

In addition to these, the *Rashtreeya Swayam Sevak Sangna* (R.S.S.), which was started in 1925 and the *Akhil Bharatiya Vidyarthi Parishad* which was founded in 1949 – the two other prominent organizations also have been attracting good number of youths. Of the non-political student organizations, the *Akhil Bhartiya Vidyarthi Parishad (*ABVP) seems to be the largest one. It claims to have more than 20 lakh members belonging to more than 3000 branches spread over almost all the major States of India and its activities are found in more than 300 universities. The ABVP claims itself to be a non-political nationalist student organization committed to the cause of the unity and welfare of the educational community of India. The ABVP which has a soft corner towards BJP, seems to have a great appeal for teachers also. It has gained ground in a number of universities.The R.S.S, on the other hand, is a cultural organisation committed to the Hindutva ideology also has a strong influence over a substantial chunk of student and youth community. The R.S.S. however, does not indulge directly in organisational activities in college campuses but supports ABVP in its work.

Student Unrest Due to Political Games

Student unrest in India has been in many instances an expression of political unrest. The politicians very often use students for their political ends and cause student unrest. Hostilities between political leaders and parties and similarly political conflicts, rivalries and differences of opinion have often been expressed through student agitations. Political parties with ulterior motives often fabricate student problems and champion such causes. Educational and student problems are often taken in hand by the political parties to serve their political interests. Some instances may be cited here.

(i) The DMK and ADMK (the two prominent parties of Tamil Nadu) had been supporting the anti-Hindi agitation to stabilize themselves and to win students to their sides.

(ii) Devraj Urs when he was alive, himself and his group supported the *Expo-70 agitation* in 1970's to topple *Virendra Patil's ministry* in Karnataka.

(iii) Opposition parties supported *Nav-Nirmana Kranti* a protest movement of the students to topple *Chimanbhai Patel's ministry in* Gujarat in 1974.

(iv) Similarly, students with the help of the opposition parties brought down *Abdul Gaffor's ministry* in Bihar in 1974.

(v) Students took an active role in the *J.P. movement* [1974-75] which was supported by all the democratic parties to topple Mrs. Gandhi's Government just before the emergency.

• ***Students are highly vulnerable to political influences.*** They are prepared to defy authority and to wage battles against the established order. As ***Peter Worsely*** has pointed out that students have few family or financial responsibilities. They risk less than other social groups in espousing causes hostile to the established interests of their society. "*Students have the time and the intellectual inclination to attend to the politics of their country. They are one of the few social groups available for political action*". Peter Worsely further writes: *"that in most of the countries of the world, students regard themselves as the vanguard of political action, with a special responsibility for advocating the interests of social groups who are unable to protest. The growth of students protest movements is thus closely related to the emergence of political problems and cleavages within the existing economic order of society".*

TYPES OF YOUTH UNREST

Youth unrest has assumed different forms. In no country, youth unrest takes place for the same reason and assumes the same form all the time. The nature of youth unrest is that it is unsteady, irregular and sometimes happens spontaneously. ***Myron Weiner*** has classified student unrest into four types.

Myron Weiner's Classification of Youth Unrest

According to *Myron Weiner*, youth OR the so called student unrest assumes four forms. They are as follows:

1. Student Unrest Associated with Political Activities and Movements : In some instances, youth unrest is associated with the larger political movements. Students often take up political issues and join hands with other non-youth organizations and political parties and fight for them. Students have participated in various political movements launched for issues such as – border disputes, steel plant location, price rise, water dispute, anti-Hindi and anti-English agitations, protest against emergency, postponement of elections, dismissal of ministers, ministries, etc. They have taken out processions, staged demonstrations, *gheraoed* ministers, resorted to violence and conflicted with police authorities.

2. Student Agitations for Educational Causes : Students have agitated for educational causes also. Students have agitated demanding the appointment of lecturers, adequate supply of laboratory equipments and library books, cancellation of donations and capitation fees, reforms in examination system and type of question papers, postponement of examinations, retainment of carry over system, recognition of the students union, participation of students in University administrative bodies such as senate, syndicate, academic councils, etc.

3. Agitations Against Non – University Authorities : Students have agitated for non-educational and non-political causes also. *For example,* they have agitated demanding special concessions for travelling in buses and trains, concessions in commercial recreational centers like cinema theatres, etc.,

4. Spontaneous Student Agitations **:** Sometimes, students do agitate suddenly in an unexpected manner. They may quarrel with bus conductors, auto-rickshaw drivers, hotel-owners, police and public servants, and may even go on strike against them. These agitations can be treated as spontaneous outbursts of youth force. If these agitations are not handled carefully they may be intensified and prolonged in still worse a way.

Ram Ahuja's Classification

Prof. Ram Ahuja has classified youth agitations into three important categories; *1) Persuasive agitations, 2) Resistance agitations.* and *3) Revolutionary agitations.*

1. Persuasive Agitations

Students and youths often resort to agitations in which their *main intention is to change the attitude of those in power* and accept their viewpoint or demands by discussing their problems with them. Such agitations are *persuasive in character.* These agitations are staged, for example, to demand the postponement of examinations, to extend the date of admission, to increase student strength in a class room so as to accommodate greater number of students in a college, to introduce a new subject of study and so on. The agitators may also hold demonstrations, shout slogans, stage *dharanas* persuading power-holders to understand and accept their viewpoint. The anger and discontent expressed through this method may serve to arouse and mobilise popular support of even passive students and youths. At the same time, it provides an outlet for expressing the discontentment in a relatively harmless way.

2. Resistance Agitations

In these types of agitations, the main object is to register protest of the agitators against the power-holders. The changes and policies intended to be introduced by the authorities may appear to be highly disturbing; and inconvenient to the students / youths. *For example,* university's decision to introduce semester scheme, or internal assessment scheme, or to introduce compulsory papers such as Indian Constitution, Environmental Studies etc., without making proper preparation; or to withdraw the *"carry over system"* etc.. may be resisted by the students. By protesting such measures or decisions the students want to express their deep disappointment at the direction in which the university is moving.

3. Revolutionary Agitations

Revolutionary agitations demand not hotch potch changes but sweeping or revolutionary changes in the educational or the social systems as such. Revolutionary leaders very often believe that basic or revolutionary changes can be brought about only if the existing system is overthrown or removed. *For example,* students may demand that all students be admitted to the courses of their choice irrespective of the marks scored by them. At the political level, for example, they may demand the total removal of the caste system and establishment of social equality. *Some examples* :

1) The Chinese students resorted to a revolutionary agitation in 1989 in China demanding the establishment of democracy and the overthrow of communism.
2) In 1984, the AASU (All Assam Students' Union) staged a statewide agitation against the illegal infiltration of the Bangladesh people and insisting on the wholesale driving away of all those who had already infiltrated.
3) *The Uttarakhand Agitation* in Uttara Pradesh in 1994 demanding the establishment of a separate state called Uttaranchal, and the Bodo Agitation for the creation of a separate Bodoland—represent two other examples. *The Bodo Agitation,* for example, had even resorted to militant and extremist activities such as – smuggling into Assam weapons from abroad, creating a reign of terror, and resorting to violence, etc.

NATURE OF YOUTH AGITATION

- Youth agitation is a type of collective behaviour and its main goal is social protest.It is not an instinctive behaviour but a learnt one.
- Youth agitation assumes various types such as - *demonstrations, slogan-shouting, strikes, hunger strikes, road-blocks, boycott of examinations, etc..*

Youth agitations perform some functions such as the following : - (i) creating collective consciousness and group unity, (ii) organising the youth for some programmes and plans, (iii) giving opportunities for the youths to manifest their strong feelings, and (iv) providing opportunities for the development of youth leadership.

Youth agitations could assume violent or non-violent forms. *For example*, of the total incidents of youth agitations that took place in India in the year 1986, nearly 43% of them were violent as against only 18% in 1988. Youth agitations may be related to *academic issues* (say 19% in 1988), or *non-academic issues* (56%) or even *social issues* (25%).

Categories of Youth Agitations : Youth or student agitations could be categorised into (i) *student - oriented agitations* and (ii) *society - oriented agitations*. The first category is associated with mostly educational issues whereas the second one revolves round the social issues.

SOME EXAMPLES OF MAJOR YOUTH AGITATIONS IN INDIA

In independent India, in the time span of 60 years, many student or youth agitations have taken place. Their number even runs to a few thousands. While majority of such agitations were, from the point of view of consequences very insignificant, a few of them led to some important changes. A few examples are worth mentioning here.

(i) Gujarath Agitation 1973 - 74

Students and youths belonging to different organisations joined together and formed '*Navnirnama Samiti*' and fought against the corrupt state Government of Gujarat, headed by Chimanbhai Patel of the Congress party for months together. This agitation which took the form of a people's movement ultimately led to the downfall of the ministry and the dissolution of the State Assembly on March 15, 1974.

(ii) Bihar Agitation 1974 - 1975

The Gujarath agitation inspired the youths of Bihar who had already started an agitation to bring down the corrupt State Government headed by Abdul Gafoor of the Congress, to further intensify it. The slogan *"The Gujarath victory is ours, it is now Bihar's turn"* became very popular among the students and youths. On March 19th 1974, the great freedom fighter **Lokmanya Jayaprakash Narayan** (J.P.) consented to give his leadership for this agitation. Under the guidance and leadership of J.P. the agitation took the form of a statewide movement in which politicians, legislators, students, women, children and common citizens had taken part in a large number. J.P. called this movement the beginning of his concept of a mass struggle known as "*total revolution*" or "*Samagra Kranti*". This peaceful struggle which was often called "**J.P. Movement**", went on for 15 months and caused the dissolution of the State Assembly. When the movement was about to take an all-India pattern, the then Prime Minister of India, Indira Gandhi declared **emergency** in the nation on 26th June 1976 and brought the democratic machinery to a stand still. J.P. movement later on took the form of "*Lok Abhiyan*" and decided to fight for the restoration of democracy.

(iii) Assam Agitation 1983 - 84

In 1983 - 84, the youths of Assam started an agitation on the issue of refugees from East Bengal (Bangladesh), and ultimately, majority of the people of Assam joined this agitation and made it a state wide movement. The decision of the Central Government to permit refugees from the neighbouring country to enter Assam precipitated the situation and the youths revolted against it and this led to the birth of "**All Assam Students Union Movement**". The agitation became so popular that when elections were held in 1985 for the State Assembly, the student leaders of this movement won the Elections and formed the Government for the first time in the history of the nation.

When the State Government failed to deliver the good, some of the youths felt agitated and formed an extremist organisation known as ***ULFA - United Liberation Front of Assam.*** The ULFA, born out of "*anti-foreigner sentiments*", now started indulging in selective violent activities. When its violent activities went beyond control, the State Govt was dismissed from power (Nov. 1990) and the President rule was imposed. Very soon the army was called into action and it conducted *"Operation Bajarang" (1991)* and finally suppressed the movement. Though the militant activities of the ULFA did not subside till 1997, it started losing ground especially after the year 2000.

(iv) Anti - Mandal Agitation 1990 - 1992

Anti Mandal Agitation represents yet another student agitation staged in 1990s against the new reservation policy of the Govt. The Janata Coalition Govt. headed by Prime Minister V.P. Singh at the centre, all of a sudden announced on 7th Aug 1990 the Govt's acceptance and the implementation of Mandal Commission's recommendation of reserving 27% Govt. jobs for OBC (Other Backward Classes) candidates. This politically motivated announcement sparked of a youth agitation in Delhi and it soon spread to various other states of North India.

The student agitation against the Mandal Report became very violent and some young students immolated themselves as a protest against it and many attempted the same. The Govt however tried to diffuse the crisis with some new proposals. The B.J.P. (Bharatiya Janata Party) which had given its support to the coalition Government, withdrew its support on this issue and the Govt. fell immediately. However, states like Bihar, U.P. and almost all states in the South accepted the new reservation policy. The new revised reservation policy announced by the Congress Govt in 1991 and then again in 1993 contributed to calm down the agitation. The anti-reservation agitation of the students and youths in the hilly regions of U.P. in sep. 1994 finally led to the demand of establishing a separate state called **Uttarakhand**.

Limitations of Youth Agitations

However silly or serious a youth agitation may be, it has its own limitations among which the following may be noted :

(i) number of students / youths participating in the agitation.

(ii) the nature of youth leadership,

(iii) the feelings and attitudes of the agitators, and

(iv) the external controls over the agitation.

(i) Number of Persons Participating in the Agitation: The agitation may not last long if it has only a meagre strength. Only if the number of agitators is large and adequate enough to attract the attention of the power-holders it may get strong grounding and last longer. The agitation will be able to muster strength only if its cause is attractive, leadership is able and efficient and method of agitating is found to be convincing and appealing.

(ii) Feelings, Sentiments and Attitudes of the Agitators also provide sufficient stimulus to the agitation. If a large number of members of the aggressive group share common feelings, the agitating group is likely to move forward.

Youths who are volatile normally do not hesitate to express their hostility without much hesitation, whereas those who are more passive usually refrain from expressing their emotions and impulses. In general, youths who are extroverts are more vulnerable to the influence of agitations rather than introverts.

(iii) Youth Leadership : Youth agitations continue to gain strength if it has a good leadership. The youth leader affects the intensity and the direction of agitation. A skillful leader can convert a group of frustrated and discontented and resentful young people and direct their aggression at an enemy which they are already hating. Most of the youth agitations are unstructured with no designated leaders. Hence, any one with some leadership quality may become a leader and give directions to it in an authoritative manner.

(iv) Limitations Due to External Controls : External forces and powers sometimes impose limitations on the youth agitations. One or two thousands of students agitating against the authoritarian attitudes and policies of the college principal, may not care for the the presence of 5 - 10 police constables posted in the campus. But three - four vans of police force deployed in the campus with lathis, tear gas shells and guns in their hands, may bring heavy pressure on the students to wind up their agitation soon. Cold weather, heavy rains, unsympathetic onlookers - may also exercise constraints on the agitations.

REMEDIES FOR YOUTH UNREST

The problems of the youths must be understood in connection with the relationships of the students with parents, teachers, politicians, police authorities, student union leaders, university authorities, and the values, traditions, needs, motivations and aspirations of the students. Patterns of these variables are found to be associated with the tension in the college-going youths A few suggestions may be made here to minimise the youth unrest.

1. Restructuring of our System of Education. A thorough overhauling of our education system is necessary to help students to face the problems and challenges of life. No hotch-potch change in education suffices. But education requires a comprehensive planning and an integral approach. This would bridge the gap between what the students actually experience and what is taught to them in schools and colleges. Colleges and universities should make proper provisions for (*a*) *adequate boarding and lodging facilities, (b) better libraries and reading rooms and laboratories, (c) enough facilities for recreation and extra-curricular activities (d) seminar and tutorial, system.*

2. Extending Useful and Adequate Employment Opportunities **:** Efforts should be made to provide opportunities for the students to offer courses in agriculture, engineering, business managements, commerce, medicine, etc. The spirit of self – reliance must be created and the students should be encouraged to set up business and cottage industries of their own.

3. *Provision for Leisure – time Activities* **:** Students should not be allowed to idle their time. Hobby clubs and workshops catering to painting, music, photography, stamp collection, swimming, etc. may be established in the colleges. Indoor games, dramatic performances, excursions and picnics, functions catering to the interest of fine arts, literature, sports, etc., must be encouraged among them.

4. Economic Help to Meet Difficulties : Poor and the needy students should be given financial help through scholarships, freeships, loan scholarships, free hostel facilities stipends, etc. So that they do not drop out of schools and colleges. The programme of '*earn while you learn*' needs to be well organized and encouraged.

5. Due Attention to Develop Self Discipline: Students should be assisted in developing self-discipline for it is long lasting than the imposed discipline. Acts of indiscipline should be dealt with sternly, but of course, humanistically. The teachers must play an important role in this respect.

6. Encouragement and Training for Developing Able Leadership: Students very badly need able and efficient leadership. In any democratic set up, leadership is very important. Leadership training programmes under supervision should be introduced in colleges. Politicians must not be allowed to misguide the students.

7. Responsible Role of Political Parties: Political parties should be kept out of the college campuses. Students should have political awareness, but their active participation in politics would spoil the peaceful atmosphere of the campus. Student leaders, teachers and university authorities must make joint venture to save education and campus from power politics.

8. Students' Participation in the University Administrative Bodies: As Dr.V.K.R.V.Rao, Ex-Union Minister for Education, has suggested (in his address to the Commonwealth Inter-University Conference in New Delhi, Jan. 1970) *'Students the world over have become restless and are demanding a voice in the affairs of universities and a fair share in running the machine and in decision-taking. This demand cannot be evaded for long except at great peril'.* In brief, the students should be given ample opportunities to take part in the administrative bodies of the university so that students voice is properly heard and their grievances are given due attention.

9. Proper Communication between Students and Teachers: The communication gap between the students and teachers should be bridged. The teacher must not look at the students with suspicion. He must have confidence in them. He must act as their friend, guide and philosopher. The teacher-student ratio must be reduced. Every student must get due attention of the teacher. More than this, basically the teacher must change his attitude towards the students and the profession.

10. Developing Better Emotional Understanding between Parents and Children. An average modern youth is said to be individualistic, imaginative and competitive. He expects good guidance from his elders so that his enthusiasm and wisdom could be channelised. Parents should guide their children to vent their difficulties and discomforts in a proper manner.. To speak in terms of psychiatry, one's accumulated aggressive energy, needs a release. Parents have to encourage their children's release of emotional tension in various kinds of activities. This is possible only when there exists a good emotional understanding between parents and children.

11. Youth Problems Cannot be Solved for Them but Only with Them. The youths should understand that their problems could be solved only with their co-operation. Therefore, co-operation of the students and youths need to .be sought by parent's, teachers, and administrators in dealing with their problems and issues. In handling the sensitive issues of the youths, parents, teachers, administrators, policemen, policy-makers, politicians, political parties and managements of educational institutions must be prepared to co-operate with one another and with the students.

12. Special norms be framed for police intervention in educational institutions: The police force should not be called in for handling youth conflicts unless it is very much necessary. In fact, definite rules and norms be framed regarding police interventions in college campuses. It is advisable to make use of specially trained police personnel for dealing with student problems.

Conclusion

It is true that there is youth unrest. But it is a part of the national malady. The student as a class can play a vital role to change the national scene. Student activism is positively anti-establishment. As *Peter Worsley* says, it is quite obvious. *If the establishment, by the same logic tends to be anti-student it will create an extremely unfortunate situation.* Asking the students to behave, without the authorities doing anything to solve their problems, is not only unjust to the students but will further alienate them from the authorities. *The student is a force. He is not a citizen of tomorrow, but he is very much a citizen of today.* He has a participatory role to play in the task of nation-building. What he wants is not a dose of advice but he wants to see the models to be emulated by him. Events, crises and challenges of constructive activity have shown that he can rise to the occasion and meet the challenges of reconstruction. In the changing society where the authority stands discredited, the youth shall triumph and usher in an era of social change. The student power has shown that it is a potential factor that can bring about vast socio-political changes.

STUDENT ACTIVISM AFTER THE 1990s

It is interesting to note that *'student unrest'* or *'student revolt'* has taken a new turn especially after the 1990s. The processes of globalisation, liberalisation and privatisation have added new dimensions to student unrest. The very nature and character of the student movement has changed today. On the basis of careful examination of the present day student behaviour, the following observations could be made.

(i) Due to the realisation of the importance of higher education students today are behaving responsibly. Except on some educationally crucial and socially important issues, they are not prepared to boycott classes nor ready to conduct strikes.

(ii) Most of the student agitations and strikes which have taken place in the recent years have been highly peaceful. They seem to have given up violent way of agitating. There is much maturity in their behaviour. Fear of losing public sympathy and support has also compelled them to eschew violence.

(iii) Students seem to take more serious interest in their academic activities for they have become more career-conscious. Due to the wide-opened job opportunities for higher educated people, even the parents are also taking interest in the education of their children.

(iv) There is less political interference in the college campuses and hence student community is not divided into several conflicting factions as it was the case two decades ago. As a result, academic activities of the college, conduct of examinations and celebration of college programmes are not very much disturbed nowadays.

(v) There is a change in the social composition of the students. A large number of students belonging to scheduled castes, scheduled tribes, backward classes and minority communities are found learning at the graduate and postgraduate levels. In most of the urban areas, higher educational institutions seem to be numerically dominated by girl students whose academic performances are consistently found to be better than those of boys. This new development has brought astonishing control over the unruly behaviour of those students who used to vitiate the academic atmosphere within the campus and inside the classrooms.

(vi) Introduction of the semester system in most of the universities of India both at the graduate and post-graduate level, has kept the students busy throughout the academic year with their entrance tests, admission process, periodic internal examinations and the two final examinations. In this academic schedule of activities, they do not find much time to spare for unwanted agitations and strikes.

• The above observations should not lead anyone to conclude that students of today are only career-conscious and are indifferent towards the socio-political developments that take place in the society. On several occasions they have shown their concern towards important social and national issues. *For example,* they have conducted huge protest demonstrations throughout India against the Pak provoked terrorist activities. They have urged the Central Govt, by staging mammoth rallies in various cities to drive out all the illegal immigrants who have infiltrated into India from Bangaladesh. They supported Anna Hazare-led Civil Society's movement against corruption by taking out huge processions in various places of India and so on.

Looking Ahead : Youth Activism / Movement in the Coming Years

The youths of India who constitute nearly 40% of India's population represent a powerful social force. In the present politically corrupt, socially discredited and economically imbalanced Indian social system, the youths still remain as a ray of hope for the bright future. Thinkers and national visionaries like Dr. A.P.J. Abdul Kalam, ex-President of India, feel that *"ignited minds of the youth is the most powerful resource on earth". Dr. Abdul Kalam writes : "I am convinced that the youth power, if properly directed and led, could bring about transformational changes in humanity for its progress, meeting its challenges and bringing peace and prosperity".*[2] Dr. Kalam is of the opinion that *"ignited minds of the youth contribute not just to a society that is prosperous, but also to prosperous nation and world."*

The youths have the power to change the society and the nation and what is required of them is the strong determination. The youths can make a difference in the Indian society where they are living in the areas of literacy, environment, social justice, minimising urban-rural divide and work towards national development, while working towards an individual goal. The youth development has multiple dimensions. The youth working hard on improving his knowledge with a career goal, can serve the family, can serve society, can serve the nation to which he or she belongs and can serve the humanity as a whole. All are complementary. It is in this regard, the youths can aim at higher things and are capable of doing so. The youths aiming small is a crime "says Dr. Kalam. The youths must shake themselves *"out of a mindset of limited achievements".* High hopes are heaped on the youths of the nation in building a strong and vibrant India. **Dr. Kalam** writes : *"In transforming India into an economically developed nation, the youth setting a high aim is the key, followed by hard work and perseverance."*

Oath for the Global Youth as Suggested by Dr. APJ Abdul Kalam - Former President of India

1. I will have a goal and work hard to achieve that goal. I realize that aiming small is a crime.
2. I will always be righteous in the heart which leads to beauty in character; beauty in character brings harmony in the home, harmony in the home leads to order in the nation and order in the nation leads to peace in the world.
3. I will work with integrity and succeed with integrity.
4. I will be a good citizen, a good member of my family, a good member of the society, a good member of the nation and a good member of the world.
5. I will always try to save or better someone's life. Wherever I am, a thought will always come to my mind. That is "What can I give?"
6. I will always protect and enhance the dignity of every human life.
7. I will always remember that, "Let not my winged days be spent in vain".
8. I will always work for Clean Green Energy and Clean planet Earth.
9. As a youth of the Globe, I will work and work with courage to achieve success in all my tasks and enjoy the success of others.

May God bless you

Source: **Dr. Abdul Kalam** *in his article "Ignited Minds : The Power of the Youth", in Manorama Year Book - 2012. page - 34.*

•••

2. **Dr. Abdul Kalam** *in his article "Ignited Minds : The Power of the Youth", in Manorama Year Book - 2012. page - 29.*

Chapter 9

PROBLEMS OF THE AGED IN INDIA

The Social Constitution of Aging OR the Nature of the Problem of the Aged: The Concept of Aging and the Three Dimensions of Old Age – The Changing Role of the Aged in Family and Community – Population of the Aged: The Demographic Position of the Aged in India – Problems of the Aged: Economic, Health, Familial and Social Problems of the Aged – Some Socio-cultural Factors of the Problem – Remedial Measures for the Problem of the Aged: Providing Economic Assistance to the Aged – National Level Welfare Programmes and Projects for Promoting the Welfare of the Aged – Welfare Programmes of the Aged: Old Age Home Scheme – Day Care Centres for the Aged, Mobile Medical Care Service, Adoption Services for the Aged – Some Special Concessions and Facilities Given to the Aged – Voluntary Organisations for the Services of the Aged: Help Age India – 1978, Age Care India-1980 – Some other Voluntary Organisations – Looking Ahead: Aging in the Second Half of the 21st Century

Though India is regarded as the *"grand land of children"* especially after the 2011 census, the number of aged people is also increasing. Aging is associated with couple of problems and the problem of aging has a special significance in the contemporary societies. Understanding the *"sociology of aging"* reveals that age matters, not just to individuals, but also to the structure of society. The age composition of a society makes a difference in the social issues that society faces.

Society differentiates people on the basis of age. Thus, different age groups experience different life situations – situations that are further shaped by people's race, class, and gender. The way in which people of different age groups are looked upon also differs with time. In the past, old age was not a problem at all. Elderly people were respected, and they were the chief patrons of the family, they held authoritarian position in the family and community and played a significant role in the decision making process. This was mostly true of most of the Eastern societies. In the Indian context, the stable joint family system ensured the old people protection and security during their later life. Despite their old age, they exercised power because they owned and controlled property and had freedom to dispose it. At the community level also, the elders used to be the leaders in such affairs as political, religious, and legal activities. Even in the beginning of the 21st century, the tradition of respecting the aged continues in India though much of their other power and responsibilities are comparatively lessened.

Things are fast changing in India, especially after the onset of globalization. With the fast spreading of industrialization, urbanization and globalization, changes began to take place in the family system, community administration, property relations, occupational structure, and so on. Increase in the size of population, migrations of youth from rural to urban areas, increase in the size of elderly population, disintegration of joint families and the employment of women, etc., denote some of the important factors that not only brought about a significant change in the role of elderly people in society but also the so called problems of the aged.

A man's life is normally divided into five main stages namely; infancy, childhood, adolescence, adulthood and old age. In each of these stages, an individual has to find himself in different situations and face different problems. Infancy and childhood are periods of dependence. One is normally at the mercy of one's parents. In the later stage of childhood and during the period of adolescence, how circumstances make a few of them to become delinquents, we have already examined. It is during the adulthood that an individual has to bear the main brunt of life. Old age is not free from problems. Though from the point of view of wider society, the problems of old age are comparatively less, but from the standpoint of the individual, the problems are not less significant. In old age, physical strength deteriorates, mental stability diminishes, money power becomes bleak and eye-sight suffers a setback. It is only for a blessed few old age may prove to be a stage of contentment and satisfaction. But, for a large number of people, it may actually become a period of disappointment, dejection, disease, repentance, and loneliness. In order to find some solace for their distressed mind, good number of people turn towards religion. They become more and more other-worldly in their attitude. Some seek to get satisfaction through the achievements of their children or grandchildren. Some old people cut off their relations with the external world and prefer to live in solitude. Only a few make compromises and try to equip themselves to sail along with the currents of life. Old age, thus, has its psychological and socio-cultural sides. An insight into these may help us to understand the problem better.

The Social Construction of Aging OR Nature of the Problem of the Aged

Aging is a biological fact and is a natural process of becoming older and older. It is a universal reality. The final phase or stage in the life of a person is ordinarily referred to as the "old age". In some countries, persons who have crossed the age of 60, are regarded as old or aged people or senior citizens and in a nation like America the cut off year is 65. In India, the cut off year varies between 55 - to - 65 in different states and departments.

The Concept of Aging

1. According to **Becker**, in the broadest sense, aging represents, *"... those changes occurring in an individual as a result of the passage of time."*
2. **Hess** is of the opinion that ageing is *"an inevitable and irreversible biological process of life."*
3. As per the views of **Stieglitz**, *"Aging is a part of living. Age begins with conception and terminates with death."*
4. **Halder** says that *"- aging is the deterioration of a mature organism resulting from time, dependence, especially irreversible changes, intrinsic to all members of the species, such that, with the passage of time, they become increasingly unable to cope with the stresses of environment, thereby increasing the probability of death."*

Three Dimensions of Old Aage

As it is made clear from the above explanations, aging has three important facets or dimensions, namely; *(i) physiological aging, (ii) psychological aging,* and *(iii) social aging.*

1. Physiological or Biological Dimension of Aging

Biological aging is the product of biological process. It is a process by which physical and mental changes occur through growth and decline. In the early years of life, *"growth"*

THE UNHEARD PROBLEMS OF OLD AGE

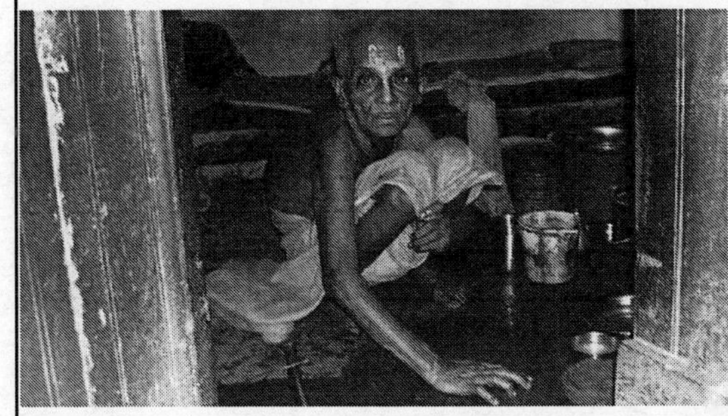

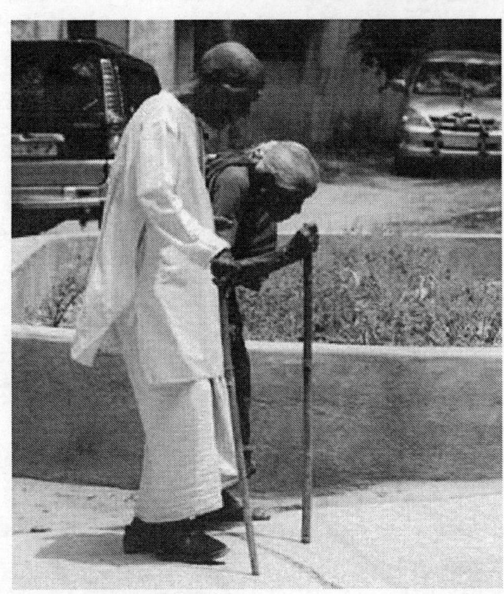

predominates and in the later years *"decline"*, dominates. Physiological aging is invariably associated with some of the fast fading physical conditions. Physiological changes that take place in the individual due to aging cannot be stopped. Thus, desperate attempts to hide gray hair, eliminate wrinkles and reduce middle aged bulge, aging is inevitable. The skin creases and sags, the hair thins, metabolism slows, and one's bones become less dense and more brittle by losing bone mass. Older persons have slower psychomotor responses and reflexes. Apart from the external changes, some other changes also take place inside the body such as deterioration of cardiovascular system, reproductive system, endocrine system, digestive system, skeletal system and nervous system. Their short-term memory becomes less accurate, although they can usually remember events in the distant past with great accuracy.

2. Psychological Dimension or Facet of Aging

The aging process has also psychological effects, which are linked to physical changes. *For example,* the hearing loss that accompanies advancing age can have psychological consequences. As a person grows old, changes take place in his mental conditions and emotional stability. However, the stereotyped belief that old people become highly forgetful, dumb and their intelligence also fades, is not entirely true. Although some measures of intelligence may decline slightly with age, such as speed in solving mathematical problems and speed in overall problem solving, other dimensions of intelligence may actually increase with age. Some artistic abilities such as painting have been shown to develop and flourish in later life. Thus, **Wechsler** states that *"the psychological capacities may show decline with age, but traits like interpretations and imagination may decline very little over the years"*. However, loss of memory, inability to withstand traumatic experience and sleep disorders occur in old age.

3. Social Dimension of Old Age

Social definition of 'old age' is more important than the physiological and psychological interpretation of old age. *Social aging is a process by which the society defines a person as old and thereby sets him aside from adult roles and responsibilities.* Every society has its own conception of aging and age groupings. Social aging, as distinct from biological and psychological aging, thus refers to the stage in the life span of the individual that is regarded as old age by the group. It is difficult to define social aging, but however, it is administratively determined for the purpose of social security, retirement from job, for demographic classifications and for assignment of social responsibilities.

The Changing Role of the Aged in Family and Community

Due to the changing socio-cultural conditions of society, the social role of the aged people too has changed considerably. The changing role of the aged people in the family and community has created problems of adjustment for them. Their failure to adjust with the changing conditions and roles has often given rise to some serious personal problems.

1. The Fading Away of the Authoritarian Role

For generations together in the past, the elderly people in the family possessed position of authority and decision making. In the joint families which used to consist of members of three or four generations, the eldest members of the family used to enjoy much respect and authority. They played crucial role in decision-making in matters connected with family affairs. The *'Karta'* or *'Karnavan'* of the joint families were usually the eldest members of the family. They used to remain in the family as authority figures.

Today, things have changed. Joint families have been disintegrated and there is a liking for only nuclear families. Accordingly, the role of the eldest members as heads of family has changed. They have just become the dependent members of the family like the young children. They have lost their decision-making powers and authority over other members.

There are also some cultures in which adults who no longer contribute to the society because of old age or illness may become perceived as extreme burdens. Among the *Comanche Indians*, for example, mourning was reserved only for those who died in their prime because they were seen as a greater loss to the well-being of the community. There are many such tribal communities wherein the aged people neither command authority nor respect. They are just treated as insignificant dependent members.

2. Inability of the Aged to Perform the Role of Grand Parents to Their Satisfaction

In the traditional families, elderly people used to play the role of grand parents by taking care of grand children, telling them stories, playing with them, protecting them when their parents become angry with them, and so on. That role was very much satisfying for them. In the modern days, where most of the families are nuclear families, there is virtually no place for the grand parents. Even when they find place to live with the grand children, they find it difficult to play their *"grand parenting role"* at home. Because, the role played by the grand parents are now taken over by the schools, kindergartens, baby sitting centers, *anganawadis,* and other child care centers.

3. No More Opportunity to Play the Role of Repository of Knowledge and Experience

For a very time, elder members of the family and society were revered and respected for their vast knowledge and experience. Especially in agricultural communities, their knowledge and experience in agricultural processes, domestic affairs, in the conduct of religious programmes and marriage ceremonies and other kind of activities were very much relied upon and well appreciated. They were consulted and their opinion was taken into consideration while taking important decisions. But in the recent times, due to the completely changed social scenario, the younger generations consider the knowledge; experience and opinion of the elders in many issues and matters, as outdated and useless. This attitude of the younger people is not only paining them, but also has made them to think whether they are becoming useless entities. Thus, there is a great *"generation gap"* between the older generation and the younger generation.

4. Decreasing Importance of the Role of the Aged as Leaders of the Community and Caste Members

As in most of the Eastern societies, in India also, traditionally, elderly people in the society played an important role as community leaders and village panchayat members. In the *caste councils* or *Jati Panchayats* in India, the eldest members of the caste used to exercise authority in giving judgements on caste disputes and controversies that were referred to them. In the village councils also the elderly people enjoyed enormous influence and power. They were given power to take decisions on the political affairs of the community. But during the recent times, drastic changes have taken place as a result of which the elderly members have lost most of their power and influence as family and community leaders. In fact, they are no more accepted as leaders just because of their age. With the advent of democracy and constitutional form of governance, the rule of gerontocracy has disappeared.

5. Difficulty in Accepting the Inevitability of Change

There is a continuous interplay between age and social change. Social change is taking place with enormous rapidity for which there is no parallel in history. This is the hard reality of the modern times. Though many elderly people have come to accept this reality, many find it difficult to accept it, make compromises and finally adjust with it. They actually face both social and psychological problems. This is virtually due to the erosion of social institutions which provided social security to them in the traditional social environments.

POPULATION OF THE AGED

The Phenomenon of 'Population Ageing'

Never before in the history of a large number of Western countries have so many people lived so long. It means, in all these countries today, any one can find a large number of old people. This fact, in itself, has a number of implications. As to how society is to be organized and the issues to be faced in the years to come. The increasing number of elderly people in the

Table – 1

Nations Having the Highest Number of the Aged - 2004
Percentage in the Population of the Aged 65+ in 26 Nations

Sl. No.	Nations	Continents	% of the Aged 65+ in the Population
1.	Italy	Europe	18
2.	Greece	Europe	17
3.	Sweeden	Europe	17
4.	Belgium	Europe	17
5.	Spain	Europe	17
6.	Japan	Asia	17
7.	Bulgeria	Europe	16
8.	Germany	Europe	16
9.	England	Europe	16
10.	France	Europe	16
11.	San Merino	Europe	16
12.	Portugal	Europe	15
13.	Denmark	Europe	15
14.	Lativa	Europe	15
15.	Lethunia	Europe	15
16.	Yugoslovia	Europe	15
17.	Austria	Europe	15
18.	Norway	Europe	15
19.	Hungery	Europe	15
20.	Switzerland	Europe	15
21.	Finland	Europe	15
22.	Zec Republic	Europe	15
23.	Lurenberg	Europe	14
24.	Estonia	Europe	14
25.	Netherlands	Europe	14
26.	America	Europe	13

Source: From Different Sources

total population leads to the demographic phenomenon called *"population aging"*. Increase in the size of elderly population implies increased dependency and burden on the adult population, as well as greater need for social security for the elderly people. The deteriorating condition of the elderly people implies declining health status, poor quality of life and greater suffering by the elders in society. In fact, there is a branch of knowledge called ***"gerontology"*** which deals with the problems and issues of old people or old age.

Enormous Increase in the Population of the Aged in the World

As per 1985 statistics, the world consisted of 427 million old people, that is, those who crossed **60** years of age, and they constituted 8.8% of the total world population. In the year 2000, the total population of those who crossed **65 years** of age, was around 420 millions. With the exception of India and some other Eastern countries, in most of the Western countries, the population of the aged has been continuously increasing during the recent years and that is why some have called the 21st century as *"the era of aging"*. [See Table No. -1] Even in the developing nations also the number of the aged people is consistently increasing.

The Demographic Position of the Aged in India

The demographic profile of India's population reveals the fact that the size and proportion of the aged population is steadily increasing over the years. In the beginning of the 20th century, the population of the aged 60+ was 12.1 million, and in the time span of 100 years it increased to 76.39 million in 2001. The increase in the population of the aged obtained a special speed especially after 1961. [See Table No. 2.]

Table - 2

Increase in the No. of Aged 60+ People in India - 1961 to 2011				
Year	**% in Total Population**	**No. of men in Millions**	**No. of women in Millions**	**No. of 60+ Poeople in Millions**
1961	5.58	12.36	12.35	24.71
1971	5.97	16.87	15.83	32.70
1981	6.49	22.49	21.49	43.16
1991	6.70	28.93	27.77	56.70
2001	7.42	38.22	37.71	76.39
2011	8.00			96.08
Sources: Census Report, Govt of India				

As per 2011 census, in general, the proportion of population below 15 years is showing decline, [from 34% in 2001 to 29% in 2011] whereas the proportion of elderly people in the country is increasing. [from 7% in 2001 to 8% in 2011]. This trend may continue in the time to come. The increase in the elderly population will impose a greater burden on the already outstretched health services in the country.[1]

Increasing Population of the Aged in Karnataka

In Karnataka also population of the aged 60+ is increasing almost in proportion to the increase at the all-India level. In 2001, the percentage of population of the aged in the total population was 7.66 [See Table – 4.]

1. **Projected Age Structure in 2026:** It is estimated that the 0-14 age group will reduce its share by about 11% that is, from 34% in 2011 to 23% in 2026 while the 60+ age group will increase its share by about 5%, that is, from 7% in 2001 to 12% in 2026.

India is one Among the Nations having the Highest Number of the Aged

Predictions made about the increasing number of the aged people in India have almost come true. *For example,* on the basis of the existing statistics about Indian population, it was predicted in 1989, that the population of the aged would be increased to 75.6 million by 2000 [i.e., around 7.8%], and it has come true. It is again predicted in 2001, that the population of the aged in India would be around 137 million in 2021 and their number is very fast increasing in this direction.

Table - 3

Composition of the Population of India 1911 - 2026

Year	Age Gourp: Percentage		
	0-14	15-60	60 and above
1911	38.8	60.2	1.0
1921	39.2	59.6	1.2
1931	38.3	60.2	1.5
1951	37.4	57.1	5.5
1961	41.0	53.3	6
1971	41.4	53.4	5
1981	40	54.1	6
1991	38	56	7
2001	34	59	7
2011	29	63	8
2026	23	64	12

Source : IAMR, Fact Book on Manpower, and Census of India 2011.

Table - 4

Number of the Aged in Karnataka - 1961 to 2011

Census Year	Total Population in Crores	Population of the Aged in Millions	Percentage of the Aged Population
1961	2.35	1.35	5.72
1971	2.92	1.78	6.09
1981	3.71	2.32	6.02
1991	4.49	30.4	6.76
2001	5.25	4.05	7.66
2011			

Total Population of Bangalore City in 2001 - 60 lakhs.
Percentage of the Aged - 15%

PROBLEMS OF THE AGED

The journey of human life is not always free from hurdles nor is it the bed of roses. Man has to face different types of situations and problems in different stages of his life. Old age is almost the final stage of his life. In a way, we find the climax of problems at this stage. At the same time, it is very difficult to make generalizations about the problems of the aged. Because, the socio-cultural, familial and economic backgrounds of the old people do not always remain the same. *For example,* the problems of the old people in cities and villages, in nuclear families and joint families, organized sector and unorganized sector, in upper classes, lower classes and middle classes, etc. are not always the same. Similarly, the problems of those who have just stepped into the old age and those who have crossed their 80s, are not the same. Despite these variations, there seems to be a few problems which are common to most of the old people. These varied problems of the aged can be grouped under the following heads: *(i) Economic Problems, (ii) Health Problems (iii) Familial Problems, and (iv) Social Problems.*

1. Economic Problems Haunting the Aged

In a developing country like India where a large number of old people belong to the poor classes and unorganized sector, loss of employment and the consequent economic dependency seems to be a major problem haunting them. Its intensity differs in the organized and the unorganized sectors.

(a) ***Economic Problem of the Aged in the Unorganised Sector:*** People working as ordinary farmers, agricultural labourers, casual labourers, industrial labourers working on the basis

of daily wages, domestic servants, workers, engaged in self-employments face intense economic problems during their old age. These who could not save anything throughout their working career, face severe economic crisis when they reach old age. Since they do not get any pension, they are forced to depend on the earnings of their children for purchasing petty things like soap, tooth powder, some cheap tablets, tobacco, snuff, clothes, footwear, umbrella, etc.

(b) ***Old People in the Organised Sector*** seem to be comparatively better economically for the retirees here earn some pension from their former employment. But even here, retirement and reduced income may create a feeling that one's usefulness is essentially over and the economically productive activities are almost over. In the case of large number of retirees there is a feeling that the pension they are getting is not at all enough to make their both ends meet for the cost of living is going up with rapid speed and the prices of essential commodities are consistently soaring. This situation may compel a few retirees to take up to some work to compensate their expenses.

As it is made clear, poverty, rising health expenditure, lack of financial resources and compulsion to work even at old age, dependence on the earnings of the younger members of the family constituted a few of the economic problems of the elderly people. Due to poverty, the elders find it difficult to get nutritious food, comfortable shelter and clothing, much needed medical assistance, etc. Poverty makes them dependents on the younger generations and hence they lose their authority and hold over the family. Deterioration of their physical health on the one hand and the rising cost of medicines on the other, further add to their helplessness. Poverty thus pushes the older people to work for wages even during their old age. Many elderly people of the lower and middle classes are compelled to work even after retirement or at old age for their own survival.

2. Health Problem of the Aged

(i) Problems Related with Bodily Health: Old age brings with it several health related problems and age related changes in an individual. Several age related changes occur as an individual is approaching old age, such as graying hair, wrinkles in the skin, bones becoming more porous, hearing impairment or even deafness, weakening eye sight, inability to walk sometimes even short distance, urinary problem, arthritis, nervousness, insomnia or sleeplessness and so on. Many of these deficiencies could be identified even from outside.

- ***Attack of Diseases:*** Some old people have become the victims of some diseases such as – high blood pressure, diabetes, arthritis, paralysis, loss of sight and hearing, asthama, osteoporosis, parkinson's disease, Alzheimer etc. The phenomenon of several diseases simultaneously attacking the individual is often known as *"multiple disease syndrome"*. This situation virtually makes the life of old people very much sorrowful and miserable. Women with delicate health who reach the stage of menopause also face several physical problems. If proper medical treatment is available for them, they can somehow pull on, otherwise, their remaining life will be very much horrible.

(ii) Problems Related with the Mental Health: The growing incidence of mental disorders is much associated with old age. Even the ancient classical Roman writer **Juvenal** was quite aware of the mental problems associated with old age. Hence he wrote: *"But worse than any loss of limb is the failing mind, which forgets the names of slaves, and cannot recognise the face of the old friend who dined with him the last night, nor those of children whom he has forgotten and brought up."*

More than the physical disability, mental disability and disorders make the old people to suffer. Long-standing neurotic, alcoholic, or drug-dependent patterns may continue into old age, or may make their appearance during this life period for the the first time. Older people are very much susceptible to psychotic depressions. The two major psychotic disorders of older people are - *"senile dementia* (associated with cerebral atrophy and degeneration) and psychosis with **cerebral arteriosclerosis** (associated with either blocking or ruptures in the cerebral arteries)". It has been observed that these two disorders account for approximately 80% of the psychotic disorders among older people in the civilised societies.

1. Senile Dementia. Older people who suffer from senile dementia develop some symptoms such as the following - poor memory, intolerance of change, disorientation, restlessness, insomnia, failure of judgement, a gradual formation of delusions and hallucinations, extreme mental depression and agitatedness, severe mental clouding in which the individual becomes restless, combative, resistive and incoherent. In extreme cases, patients eventually become oblivious of their surroundings, bedridden, and reduced to a vegetative existence. Resistance to disease is lowered and death usually results.

2. Psychosis with Cerebral Arteriosclerosis. This is accompanied by physiological symptoms such as acute indigestion, unsteadiness in gait, small strokes resulting in cumulative brain damage and gradual personality change, convulsive seizures are also relatively common. Some patients suffering from this will be in confusional state and may even die without being cleared of from that state. This is also associated with symptoms such as weakness, fatigue, dizziness, head-ache, depression, memory defect, periods of confusion, lowered efficiency in work, heightened irritability accompanied by suspiciousness.

(a) ***Worry about reduction in physical attractiveness:*** This is especially more stressful for persons whose feeling of femininity or masculinity depends on their attractiveness to the opposite sex.

(b) ***Functional deficiency and decline:*** Old age is associated with loss of functions. As one moves from his early old age to late old age, he begins to lose his physical functions and activities due to the deteriorating physical and mental conditions. It becomes difficult for some of the old people even to do their daily activities such as getting up from bed, going to toilets, dressing, bathing, etc.

(c) ***Cruelty of Solitude:*** Old people also suffer from isolation and loveliness caused by the loss of contemporaries and loved ones. Negligence and indifference of others also impair the feelings of the aged people.

(d) ***Inevitability of others' support:*** Due to extreme old age, ill health and diseases, the old people are obliged to take the support of others to carry on their activities. Sometimes, they require the artificial support systems such as walking sticks, wheel chairs, hearing aides, etc.

3. Familial Problems

As a result of changes in the traditional value systems and norms, the gap between the old people and the younger members of the family is increasing. Even though the old people become weaker physically they want to tighten their grip over the younger ones in the family. Hence, the younger members instead of developing a sympathetic attitude towards the old, start asserting their rights and power. This may create tension in the family and conflict between the young and the old. Neither one is prepared to understand or cope with the other. This does happen due to what is known as *'generation gap'*, and *'communication gap'*.

Elderly people in the family suffer from various problems such as – abuse of elders by the younger members of the family, ill-treatment and neglection at home. Sometimes, the elders are also made to work hard. They are given the work of washing clothes and cleaning, fetching firewood, and so on and their physical disabilities are never taken into consideration. Quarrels between the elder people and their in-laws are the common cause of problems of elders in the family.

4. Social Problems of the Aged

Old age has become highly problematic in many societies today. In the olden days, old age was regarded as honourable and the wisdom, experience and suggestions of the elderly people were highly respected and appreciated. Not only inside the family even outside also they were treated in respectable terms. This situation has changed today. With the onset of industrialization, urbanization, mechanization and the recent phenomenon of globalization, vast social changes have taken place in the society. Many of these changes have affected the conditions of the old people and brought about problems for them also. *For example,* the old people today suffer from social discrimination, ill-treatment, social and physical abuse, lack of security, etc.

Old people face social problems not only inside the family but also outside. They are often discriminated in their community and subjected to ill-treatment, insult and negligence in public places such as railway stations, bus stops, hospitals, market places, public transports, etc. They often suffer from the fear of death especially when they hear the news of death of their friends, colleagues and agemates. Loss of meaningful social role, power and authority has a disheartening effect on the senior citizens. The feeling of worthlessness often haunt them powerfully and in the case of some, when it reaches its peak, the tendency to commit suicide suddenly develops.

Lack of social security measures, deficiencies and failures of old age homes and elder care institutions make the lives of a few other elderly people, still more miserable.

Some Socio-Cultural Factors of the Problem

Sociocultural factors relating to the problems of the aged are equally significant. Cultural peculiarities and rural or urban background of the old people, for example, have a close bearing on this problem. In one interesting study, psychologist **Carothers** (1947) found a high rate of senile psychoses among natives in Kenya and Africa. It is also observed especially in United States that the senile psychotic cases reported and hospitalized in the urban set up were almost twice the number of cases reported in rural set up. It can only be generalized that the urban set up is more favourable to the development of mental disorders than the rural set up. In the rural areas, the older person enjoys higher social status and is generally able to work productively for a longer period. He is much cared for and respected at home.

But in the urban industrial society the problems of the old age have gripped the people for they are unprepared to face them. Proper opportunities and suitable conditions are not created for utilizing the experience and wisdom of our older people. We have not provided conditions necessary for them to live in reasonably respected and useful positions. On the contrary, they are treated as though they are persons who have outlived their usefulness. This attitude of modern urban society may contribute to the incidence of old age psychoses.

It is true that the experience of an older person seems to have little relevance to the problems of younger generations. He is deprived of active participation and decision making in both occupational and family settings. As **J.C. Coleman** and **W.E. Broen Jr.** have remarked, *"Not infrequently children assume a patronizing and protective attitude toward the aging parent, and in other ways tend to deprive him of dignity, responsibility, and a feeling of importance. Many parents are treated as unwanted burdens and their children may secretly wish that they would die to relieve them of financial and other responsibilities."*

"In a study of older people in France, **De beauviour** *(1970) has pointed out that when the French go away for vacations, they sometimes 'deposit' their aged parents in rest homes. Then, on their return home, they "forget" to pick them up, abandoning them like dogs in a Kennel"* – (**Coleman**). Most of the civilized societies have *"youth-oriented cultures".* In the nuclear families in such cultures generally, there is no place for the grandparents unless they are self-sufficient.

Even in the U.S.A. many older people are *"deposited"* in rest or nursing homes to die even though they may be in relatively good health. The older people who have already developed some physiological problems feel extremely bad to know that they are cast aside simply for *"being old"*. Such a treatment would have devastating effects upon them.

Reactions to aging and reaching the status of *"senior citizen"* – are quite subjective. How people react to aging depends heavily on their personality make up and on the challenges and frustrations of their life situations. A sense of status, self-identity and meaning are very important in old age for they are most threatened at this stage.

REMEDIAL MEASURES FOR THE PROBLEM OF THE AGED

The problem of the old has become more pronounced now than before. The advent of industrial revolution, advancement of science and technology and development of medical science have added new dimension to this problem. Prior to the industrial revolution, the average *'life expectancy'* of man all over the world was very low. Now it has increased tremendously. In most of the European nations the average life span of people has crossed the mark of 65 years. In India, at the time of Independence, i.e., around 1950's, the life span of an average Indian was about 28 years and now it has increased to 50 years. As a result of this, the number of old people has increased in almost all the countries. The presence of a large number of old people has affected the composition of population especially in countries such as Russia, Britain, Norway, Sweden, Switzerland, France and so on.

Measures that are Helpful in Solving the Problems

During the recent years, an awareness has arisen at the global level regarding the problematic life of the senior citizens. This awareness has made many national governments, including India, to take some proper steps to mitigate their problems and provide them enough social security. Some of the measures that are highly useful and helpful in handling the problems of the aged and provide them much needed security are stated below:

1. *Providing suitable economic assistance to the aged.*
2. *National level welfare programmes and projects for promoting the welfare of the aged.*
3. *Welfare programmes of the aged,*
4. *Some special concessions and facilities given to the aged,*
5. *Voluntary organizations for the service of the aged,*
6. *International level measures for the aged.*

In fact, these are the days in which almost all the developed and the developing countries undertake several social, legislative, reformative and welfare measures to protect the interests of the senior citizens. Governments as well as non-governmental organizations undertake diverse activities for the benefit of old people.

1. Providing Financial Assistance to the Aged

There are many schemes in the world to provide financial security to the aged people so that they do not suffer from economic insecurity at the fag end of their life. In our nation also, number of such schemes are there. *For example:*

***(a) Retirement Pension*:** Those who put in some minimum years of service are provided with old age pension after their retirement. This pension is assured to all government employees who have eligibility to it, and also to employees in some private companies and industrial units.

***(b) Other Financial Benefits to the Retired*:** Government servants who have completed their full time service are also entitled for certain types of financial benefits such as – gratuity commutation, family provident fund, personal provident fund, [PPF], group insurance, leave encashment, general provident fund [GPF]; some higher percentage of interest over the fixed deposits kept in the name of senior citizens, and so on.

(c) Old Age Pension Scheme for the Poor and Needy**:** *"Old Age Pension Scheme"* – is in force in states such as U.P., Rajasthan, Tamil Nadu, Kerala, Punjab, West Bengal, Karnataka and so on. It came into force in 1964. As per this scheme, some amount is given every month as old age pension to those who have crossed 60, and those who do not have sufficient economic support to fall back upon.

(d) Providing Employment even to the Aged**:** Those who are retired, but still are interested in and capable of working are also given work in nations like Britain, America, Australia, Canada and such other countries. This will not only fetch income to the needy people but also keep them engaged in their retired life. There are also separate universities or colleges for the aged people offering different courses for study in nations like Australia. **Dr. S.D. Gokhale** (*President (India) International Federation on Ageing*] had stated sometimes earlier that more than 10,000 aged people had registered their names for higher studies in such institutions in Australia. Even in India, in many educational institutions and private and public limited companies, the services of retired people are hired on contract basis.

2. National Level Welfare Programmes and Projects for Promoting the Welfare of the Aged

National Policy for the Aged – 1999**:** In order to safeguard the interests of the aged, the Government of India has formed a national level policy in 1999 known as *"The National Policy for the Aged"*. In order to implement this policy, an action plan was also getting ready. The government is also trying to implement its action plan by establishing proper co-ordination with *the Social Justice and Empowerment Ministry.*

National Council for Old Persons (NCOP) – 1999**:** As per the National Policy for the Aged, the government has also given birth to yet another institution namely *"National Council for Older Persons"* on May 14th 1999. Its main task is to provide information to the Government about the way of implementation and effectiveness of various programmes and schemes undertaken for the benefit of the aged and to prepare a detailed report of the same. This institution has the responsibility of looking into the grievances of the old and also complaints lodged by the agencies and institutions working for the services of the aged, and to make arrangements for providing justice.

3. Welfare Programmes of the Aged

The Ministry of Social Justice and Empowerment has been implementing many programmes ever since 1992 for the benefit of the aged and for protecting their interests. Some of them are mentioned below.

(i) ***Old Age Home Scheme:*** *'Old age homes'* are to be found in all the nations including India to give physical protection, medical aid, and economic security to the old. Those poor old people who are often deserted by their own children, normally take shelter in these homes. The destitute and helpless aged persons belonging to lower middle class groups are covered under this scheme. The inmates of old age homes are kept in familial environment and social workers and counsellors take utmost care. Their physical and psychological well-being is also taken care of by the trained medical practitioners. Private agencies can also run such homes with government aid. But even in these homes old people often suffer from emotional problems.

(ii) ***Day-care Centres for the Aged:*** Day-care centre is the scheme to keep the aged integrated in their respective families and to supplement their activities at the family. The aim of this scheme is to benefit all the old people irrespective of their social class. Some non-governmental organizations also maintain day-care centres.

(iii) ***Mobile Medical Care Service Units for the Aged:*** Mobile medical services are provided to the old people residing in rural and urban slums. Medical consultations and treatment are provided to the old people for their age-based disease through mobile health camps.

(iv) ***Foster Care OR Adoption Services for the Aged:*** Under this programme, various services are provided to the homeless and lonely old people who lead a pitiable life because of utter poverty and helplessness. Arrangement is made to place such old persons with the willing families considering the culture and social values of them.

(v) ***National Social Assistance Programme [NSAP]:*** The NSAP has been functioning in India since 1995. It consists of the schemes like *National Old-Age Pension Scheme [NOAPS], National Family Benefit Scheme [NFBS],* and *National Maternity Benefit Scheme [NMBS].*

(vi) ***Minimum of one Old Age Home for the District:*** As per the 1996-97 project, Government can give assistance to the Panchayat Raj or to N.G.O.s to establish Old Age Homes. Wherever such homes are not there, the Government gives due assistance to the tune of 30 lakh rupees to establish at least one Old Age Home per district.

As per the available statistics, upto 2005, under the auspices of the Ministry of Social Justice and Empowerment, there were 298 old age homes, 425 day-care centres, 58 mobile medical service units activity functioning in various places of the country.

4. Some Special Concessions and Facilities Given to the Aged

The Central and the State Governments have been giving some special concessions and facilities to the aged people among which the following may be noted.

(i) National Old Age Pension Scheme [NOAPS]: As a part of NSAP, the National Old Age Pension Scheme has been in force from 15th Aug. 1995. This scheme intends to give financial assistance to the aged persons who do not have any other financial source to support themselves. A committee under the charge of the district collector, looks after the implementation of this scheme. As per this scheme, such identified aged persons are given monthly pension of ₹ 75. This pension amount has been increased during the recent years.

(ii) Income Tax Concessions for the Senior Citizens: As per Section 88 B of Income Tax, senior citizens above 60 years of age with a total annual income of ₹ 2.5 lakhs need not pay any tax. The NDA Government headed by Narendra Modi has increased this income level to ₹ 3 lakhs in its budget for the year 2014-15.

(iii) Concession in Train and Bus Journey: Aged men above 60 and women above 58 years are provided with 1/3 concession on their ticket rates if they are travelling in trains. Similarly, some state governments have given concession for aged passengers travelling in state transport buses. *For example,* the Government of Karnataka has started giving 1/4 rebate on the ticket rate of all those passengers who have crossed 60 years of age from December 2011. [However, this is not applicable to those who travel in the super luxury Volvo buses].

(iv) Annapoorna Yojana: As per this scheme, the aged people (above 65) who are helpless and therefore in need, are given free of cost 10 kilos of rice every month as food security. This assistance, however, is given only to those who are not the recipients of *National Old Age Pension Scheme*. Grama Panchayats and Town Panchayats have the responsibility of preparing the list of those people who are eligible to receive the benefit of this scheme.

5. International Level Measures for the Aged

The international community including the U.N.O has expressed great concern about the problems of the aged people who are distributed throughout the world. The U.N.O. with the due assistance of its units such as the W.H.O. and the UNESCO [*World Health Organisation*, and *United Nations Educational Scientific and Cultural Organisation*] has been spending huge sums of money on various schemes and programmes undertaken for promoting the welfare of the aged people. These institutions have already spent more than 850,000 pounds on more than 30 welfare programmes arranged in the Asia-pacific region for the benefit of the aged people.

In order to draw the attention of the world regarding the increasing number of the aged and their problems, the UNO has called upon the nations of the world to observe some practices and programmes in the name of the aged. Some examples of these programmes are mentioned below.

(a) International Year of the Aged Persons, 1999

(b) International Day of the Old Persons (October 1st)

(c) International Pensioners' Day (17th December)

6. Voluntary Organisations for the Service of the Aged

In addition to governmental institutions, several voluntary organizations also undertake various measures to protect the interests of the old people in India. Even before independence, attempts were made to safeguard the interests of the aged by some voluntary organizations. *For example,-*

(i) The Friend in Need Society – 1840, (Bangalore) was making attempts to give protection to the aged, the infirm and the orphans.

(ii) The David Sasson Infirm Asylum – 1865, (Poona) was another attempt made in Poona to provide accommodation and other needed help to the deserted, handicapped and helpless aged persons.

(iii) Little Sisters of the Poor – 1882 (Calcutta) was yet another organization providing more or less the same type of service and help to the aged and the infirm, and the orphans.

In the beginning of the 20th century, a few more such organizations came into being among which mention may be made of

(i) Ashakth Ashram – 1912, Surath,

(ii) Grant Govan Memorial Home Society – 1940, New Delhi, and

(iii) Seva Sadan – 1940, Lucknow.

The speciality of these organizations is that they were not only giving protection to the aged and the orphans, but also giving training in some crafts, skills and home industries in addition to entertainment and medical aid.

(iv) Yet another organization by name *"Aram Ghar" (1910)* though in the beginning was run by the government in Hyderbad, it was later on handed over to the Andhra Pradesh Unit of *"Indian Conference of Social Work"* in 1957. Such type of *'Aram Ghars'* also came to be established in other places such as Punjab, Kerala and Secundarabad.

Voluntary Organisations in the Service of the Aged After Independence

After independence, the number of institutions and agencies providing protection to the aged people has considerably increased. As per 1986-87 report, these institutions at that time were catering to the needs of hardly 0.4% of the total number of the aged in the country.

There are some voluntary agencies which are established specifically for the sake of old people in India. Of these agencies, *Help Age India (1948), Age Care India (1980)* are very famous.

1. Help Age India - 1978

Help Age India is a nationwide organization having its headquarters in New Delhi. It is devoted to promote the welfare of the aged people irrespective of caste, religion, tribe or region. Its activities include creation of awareness among younger generations about the needs of the aged, conduct of competitions, debates, meetings, etc. and making provision for homes for the aged, day centres, and mobile medical services. This institution makes arrangement to collect donations from the public through its own permanent employees and hand over the collections to different welfare organizations of the aged.

The officials of Help Age India often visit schools and through little children they try to send the message to their parents to look after the elderly people at home with great concern, care and affection. The Help Age unit of India has established link with the International Help Age and with its advice and guidance has started a scheme by name *"Adopt a Granny"* through which it tries to adopt poor and helpless aged destitutes.

The Help Age India has its own schemes to give training to those people who are running old age homes on charity basis. This organization has so far given assistance to more than 1300 welfare programmes conducted by more than 700 voluntary social organizations spread over India helping the cause of the Poor and helpless aged people.

2. Age Care India – 1980

Age Care India is a voluntary organization which was founded in 1980 has its head quarters in New Delhi. Its major aims and purposes are as follows:

(i) It intends to help aged persons above 50 years of age through domiciliary, residential and institutional services and provide them education, recreation and social, cultural and spiritual services.
(ii) It arranges for the aged medical service, part time employment to supplement their income and organizes tours trips, pilgrimages, etc.
(iii) It seeks to arrange for professional consulting services for taxes, duties property, pension and other economic and financial requirements of the aged,
(iv) It intends to conduct research and studies on the problem of the aged.
(v) It aims to create a suitable climate for better understanding and social integration between younger and older generation.

Various Programmes of the Age Care India

Age Care India organisation which is committed to the service of the aged people also conducts some socio-cultural programmes among which the following may be noted.

(i) Organising library, reading room, resort houses and various recreational programmes.
(ii) Adopting a village to take care of all the aged people of the village.
(iii) Building low cost houses for the aged widows, widowers, isolated individuals and to make provision for their food, and clothing free of cost.
(iv) Arranging mobile medical service and free medical treatment camps for the benefit of the old and especially the diseased.
(v) Creating awareness among the public regarding old age problems and the actual problems of the aged ones through public debates, discussions, speeches, T.V. discussions, etc.

Some Other Voluntary Organisations

(i) ***'Little Sisters of the Poor'***, a French based organization opened its first branch in Calcutta in 1882, which later on established 12 more units in the country including the 4 which are found in Karnataka. All these four branches are at the service of the aged.

(ii) ***Nightingales Medical Trust:*** This organization which was founded in Bangalore in 1998 intends to provide medical help at the doors of the aged. The trust functions through the following two units or branches.

(a) ***Nightingales Elders Enrichment Centre*** **– [NEEC]:** This branch is in Malleshwarm area of the Bangalore city and it functions like a Day Care Centre for the Aged. Its main purpose is to provide medical service to the aged, that is, to protect their physical as well as mental health.

(b) ***Elders Helpline 1090:*** This has the main purpose of providing immediate assistance to those aged persons who find themselves in sudden distress, with the co-operation of the police department. It runs to rescue those elderly people who contact the organization through *"Elders' Helpline – 1090"*.

The Nightingales Medical Trust is also conducting service activities through its other service projects such as – *'Nightingales Life Saving Services'*, *Nightingales Life Savers Club, Nightingales Project for the Urban Poor,* and so on.

Looking Ahead: Aging in the Second Half of the 21st Century

Throughout the world, in almost all the countries, the average life expectancy of the people has been consistently increasing for the past 2-3 decades. By 2001 itself in more than 20 – to – 25 nations of the world the elderly people constituted more than 15% of their total population. If the same trend continues by 2050, in more than at least 50 nations, the elderly people will constitute almost 25% of their population. Gerontology, a branch of knowledge that deals with the old people, is bound to become one of the important branches of study.

Some Characteristics of the Societies in which Old People Become Numerically Powerful

1. In such societies special arrangements may have to be made for providing medical service and treatment to a large number of aged people.
2. *The aged people of tomorrow are likely to have comparatively better health.* Due to the greater awareness that is created regarding health and advancement in the field of medical science, people will be able to maintain relatively good health even in their old age. They are not likely to become a burden on their younger ones at least in the early years of their old age.
3. *The financial position of the old people has improved tremendously.* Today's middle aged people earn good income and hence they will definitely save a substantial amount to face the problems of their old age without depending much on others.
4. There is a need for today's youth and adults to learn the art of looking after the needs of elderly people so that they can expect at least the same kind of treatment at the hands of their younger ones when they become old.
5. In many of the Western and a few of the Eastern countries, the percentage of the aged constitute more than 15% of their total population. Hence, the aged may become politically also somewhat influential for they constitute a powerful *'vote-bank'*.

Percentage of Different Age Groups in the Total Population of India as of 2013-14					
0-14 Years	-	28.5%	65+ =	Total No. of Men : 34133175	5.8%
15-24 Years	-	18.1%		Total No. Women: 37810599	
25-54 Years	-	40.6%		Total 71943774	
55-64 Years	-	7.0%			
65+	-	5.8%		***Source:*** www.indexmundi.com	

•••

Chapter 10

PROBLEMS OF WOMEN IN MODERN INDIA

***A. Some Major Problems of Indian Women** : (1) **Discrimination Against Girl Child :** The concept of Gender Discrimination - Areas of Severe Discrimination : Female Foeticide, Female Infanticide, Selling of Girl Children, Girl Child Prostitution and Sexual Abuse of Girl Children. (2) **Violence Against Women :** Increasing Crimes Against Women - Violence in the life of Women - Incidences of Crimes Against Women, Violence Against Women within and outside Family or Domestic Violence: Forms of Domestic Violence - Rape as a Heinous crime Against Women : (3) **Problems of Health and Nutrition :** Causes for Women's Poor Health-Problem of Nutrition and Consequences of Nutritional Deprivation. (4) **Problem of Women's Education and Gender Bias in Education :** Problems Relating to Women Education in India - Gender Disparity in Education - A Global Perspective - Gender Bias in Education - (5) **Trafficking in Women :** Problem of Run-Away Cases-Causes of Human Trafficking Including Traffficking in Women-Trafficking in Women and Love-Zihad - (6) **Differential Treatment Given to Women :** Decline in the Female Population - Discrimination in the Distribution of Power and Work-Gender Discrimination in Occupation and Public Life. (7) **Problems Relating to Employment and Unemployment of Women :** (8) **Harassment of Women at Work Place :** Sexual Harassment of Women-Sexual Harassment as a Common Issue - Helpless and Confused State of Female Employees and Fear of Losing Job (9) Exploitation of Women in the Media : Advertisements and Women-Media and Women Movements. (10) **Hardships Due to Divorce, Desertion and Dowry :** The Hardship of Desertion and the Agony of Divorce. (11) **Decline in the Political Participation of Women :** Minimum Representation of Women in the Lok Sabha - Poor Participation of Women in the Indian Parliamentary System and in Party Politics (12) **Globalisation and Its Impact on Women :** Positive and Negative Effects of Globalisation :*

B. Empowerment of Women-Strategies for Women's Development - Towards Equality Report - 1974 : Formation of National Commission to study the Status of Women - *Factors Facilitating Empowerment of Women - Human Rights and Women-Rights and Protection Given to Women in the Indian Constitution - Strategies for the Protection of Women's Rights and Rehabilitation of Women - **Strategies of Economic Empowerment of Women** : Self - Help Groups and Micro-Finance - Some successful **Examples** : Stree Shakthi Groups of Karnataka, Shri Mahila Griha Udyog Lijjat Pappad and Self-Employed Women's Association [SEWA] The Position and Problems of Indian Women - Future Prospects.*

Sixty five years of Indian independence has witnessed many changes in many fields of our national life. From the women's point of view also these changes are significant. Many of the issues and problems which were bothering our women 65 years ago have either disappeared or given place to new ones. Hence, issues relating to the practices of *'sati', 'devadasi', purdah, imposition of inhuman restrictions on women, child marriage, etc.,* have either become insignificant or drastically reduced or not found at all. It does not mean that Indian women in the beginning of the 21st century have become totally free from all these unwanted problems and inhuman practices.

Women of India today are faced with new situations, trapped by new problems and encountered with many challenges. Girl children are put to various disadvantages and in many fields they experience bitter discrimination. Women have become victims of violence both inside the family and outside. Women's health is never considered seriously and is often neglected. Women are denied nutritious food for most of them are not regarded as *'bread winners'*. Women's education never assumed priority for it is considered as *"wasteful"* by a large number of ruralites and urban illiterates. Male prejudice towards female education, particularly higher education, still continues to hold its sway. Women are often treated as *"sex commodities"*, and trafficking in women assumes ugly forms. There are national and international level networks and organisations engaged in the profitable business of the sale of women. Added to all these things, the process of *"globalisation"*, let loose at the fag end of the 20th century, has brought for women new opportunities and at the same time, created new anxieties, fears and challenges. Unless women are 'determined to fight back with all the power at their command against these forces, and unless society itself makes a determined effort to find effective solutions to women's problems, and unless society itself makes a determined effort to find effective solutions to women's problems, they cannot become free from these anxieties and fears.

A) SOME MAJOR PROBLEMS OF INDIAN WOMEN

The traditional male-dominant Indian society has posed some problems to women which are really challenging for them to achieve equality. These problems are very much interlinked and hence overcoming all of these is equally a tough task. Here is a glimpse of some of these problems :

1. **Discrimination against girl child.**
2. **Increasing violence against women.**
3. **Problems of health and nutrition.**
4. **Problem of women's education and gender bias in education.**
5. **Trafficking in women,**
6. **Differential treatment given to women,**
7. **Problems relating to employment and unemployment of women,**
8. **Harassment of women at work place,**
9. **Exploitation of women in the media.**
10. **Hardships due to divorce, desertion and dowry**
11. **Decline in the political participation of women**
12. **Globalisation and its impact on women.**

1. DISCRIMINATION AGAINST GIRL CHILD

The Concept of Gender Discrimination

Gender discrimination is one of the manifestations of gender inequality. It is nothing but discrimination against people based on their gender. Like many other societies, in the Indian society also men and women are never treated on par. Women are always discriminated against. This is due to the traditional practice of gender discrimination.

- *Gender discrimination refers to "the practice whereby one sex is given preferential treatment over the others."*[1]

1. **David Jary** and **July Jary** in *"Collins Dictionary of Sociology"* - Page : 588.

The above simple definition of '*gender discrimination*' implies three subtly different beliefs or attitudes:

- It implies the belief that one sex is superior to the other.
- It also implies the belief that men and women are very different and this should be strongly reflected in society, language, law and the right to have sex.
- It may denote some type of hatredness towards men or towards women [misogyny].

The practice of giving social importance to the biological differences between men and women is there everywhere. In some societies, these differences are very much pronounced while in others, they are given less importance. Even the Indian society is not an exception to this.

Different Faces of the Practice of "Gender Discrimination"

Discrimination against girl child reflects *the practice of giving preferential treatment and importance to male child over female child.* This is also a case of *'gender discrimination'*. In comparison with some other social problems, *"gender discrimination"* does not "appear" to be a serious problem in India for many people even now. It is so because, it has not been made a very big social issue so far. But in reality, it has weakened not only the strength of the female community of India but also of Indian society in general. Though constitutionally men and women are equal, socially men are given priority and importance sometimes to the disadvantage of women. This disadvantage or discrimination is to be faced by women right from their childhood. In fact, there are many areas in which discrimination against the girl child, in particular, is practised.

Some Major Areas of Discrimination Against Girl Child

The practices of - female foeticide, female infanticide, child marriage, child labour, pushing girl children into bonded labour; sale or trafficking in young girls, abduction of girl children; sexual exploitation and sexual abuse of girl children, girl child prostitution, neglect in respect of providing educational and health facilities, and opportunities of decent life, etc. reflect the discriminatory practices against the girl child.

Discrimination in Socialisation

In our socialisation process, female children are becoming victims of discrimination. In the Indian social context, even today male children are preferred to female children. Male preference and female negligence has almost become a working policy especially in the rural areas. Discrimination between male and female children is made in *matters relating to food, dress, healthcare, education, domestic work, etc.* The policy of male preference and female negligence has led to what are known as *"female disadvantages"*.

Continued Craving for Male Child

In India, due to the predominance of patriarchic values, mothers show preferences for male children. They give them importance because - *males are wanted during their old age to offer protection, males have greater scope than women and occupational avenues are also wider for males than for females.* Woman especially in North India is made to feel that her image would go down in the circle of relatives if she fails to fetch to her husband's family a male child. Women with only female children are often humiliated and illtreated. Hence, the craving for male children continues even now. This male preference has led to the abuse of advanced technology. The sophisticated scanning and supersonographic equipments are being misused to find out the sex of the child; that is to go for abortion if the child is found to be an "unwanted female child". These medical tests which would cost between ₹ 200/-to 800/- are within the reach of the lower

THE UNMITIGATED VIOLENCE AGAINST WOMEN

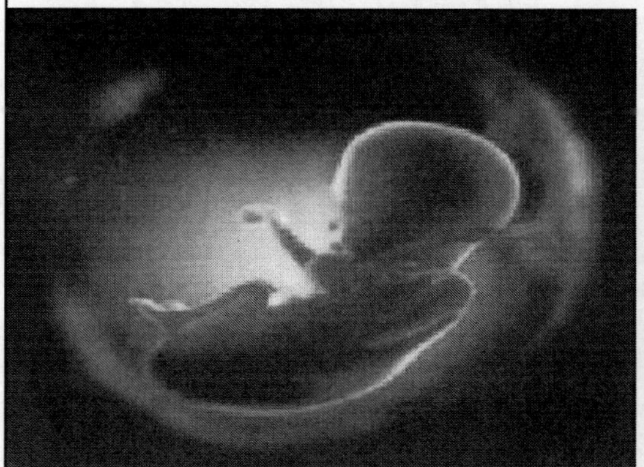

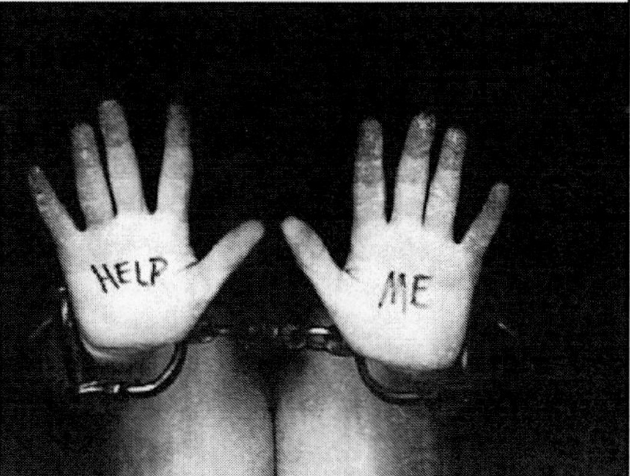

middle class and even the middle-lower class resulting in the killing of the female foetuses in a large number. Between 1978 and 1982, more than 78,000 known cases of foetuses were killed mainly because of these medical tests.[2] Since foeticide is done illegally and secretly, for there is a legislation against it, it is very difficult to have an exact estimate of such cases today.

Areas of Severe Discrimination

According to **Vir Bala Agarwal,**[3] there are five major areas of severe discrimination against the girl child. They are -

(i) Female Foeticide **(ii) Female Infanticide** **(iii) Selling of Girl Children** **(iv) Girl Child Prostitution,** and **(v) Sexual Abuse of Girl Children.**

(i) FEMALE FOETICIDE

This refers to an atrocity against a girl even before she is born. Female foeticide is forced abortion of unwanted pregnancies and it has been present in all societies in one or the other form since ages. Female foeticide is a sex-selective abortion and is a feature of modern consumerist and sex-biased societies. This is the most unfortunate sophisticated way of getting rid of daughters through sex determination tests in which greedy doctors are involved. Though the latest legislation namely, ***Prenatal Diagnostic Techniques Regulation and Prevention of Misuse Act, 1994,*** prohibits such an act, it is carried on secretly. The unfortunate trend is that this is far stronger in urban areas and among literate women than in the rural areas among illiterate women..

Causes of Foeticide

1. Absence of Rights of Women Over Reproduction : Female foeticide has been on the increase inspite of the presence of different laws for protecting the right of the unborn child. This is because, women's right to control over her own body and her rights to decide whether or not to have a child, have not received due attention in India. Unlike in the West, the concept of *Reproduction Rights of Women* has not been recognised in India. There are instances in which the urban girl child is finished of before it is born, without taking the consent of the mother.

2. Continued Predominance of Patriarchy : Since India socially continues to be a male-dominated society birth of male children is welcomed and female ones is despised with. Many parents, including well-educated, are hankering after male children and are ready to resort to foeticide when they come to know that they will get only a female child. Some scholars consider the phenomenon of "*son worship*" as the greatest single cause contributing to foeticide.

3. Fear of Heavy Dowry : In communities where dowry is compulsorily practised, poor families shudder to think of getting female children one after another repeatedly. No wonder if such families decide to opt for foeticide.

4. Poverty and Economic Crisis : Many Indian families consider the birth of female children as a great economic burden. Till the girl is given in marriage to some other family, parents will have to invest and spend a lot on them. Speaking in monetary terms, it is an "*unproductive investment*" for the parental family for she will be joining her husband's family after marriage. Hence, such poor families think that their economic position becomes still more precarious if they get female children, that too, repeatedly.

5. Role of Greedy Doctors : Too much greediness for money on the part of some modern doctors is also playing havoc in this notorious practice. By abusing the provisions of "*The Medical Termination of Pregnancy Act, 1971*", and also of another Act namely; "*Pre-Natal Diagnostic*

2. ***Source*** : *Times of India,* Editorial June 1982.
3. **Vir Bala Aggarwal** in *"Status of Women in Modern India"* - Edited by **S.B. Verma** [2005] Page : 4-8.

Techniques [Regulation and Prevention] Act, 1994"; many doctors help the parents to remove the unwanted embryo of their female child by receiving huge sum of money.

6. Women Suffering from Several Problems Often Themselves Decide not to Give Birth to Female Children : Social situations and circumstances often make women to become stone-hearted and insist on the removal of the unwanted female child growing in their womb.

7. Weakness in the Enforcement of Law : Though foeticide is declared as illegal, instances of foeticide are still continued. Those responssible for foeticide escape from the clutches of the law giving scope for the practice to continue.

Consequences of Foeticide

(i) Leads to Continuous Decrease in the Child Sex Ratio : The inevitale consequence of the practice of foeticide is the sharp fall in the child sex ratio. To indicate this, some states are known as DEMARU states. In this expression DEMARU, '**D**' stands for daughter and '**MARU**' stands for killing. The English letter '**E**' denotes '*elimination*'. DEMARU states are thus, those states where daughters, that is, female children are killed in a large number. Punjab, Haryana, Himachalpradesh, Gujarath and Maharasthra are the **DEMARU** states known for the practice of foeticide. During 1991-2001, in Punjab, the child sex ratio declined from 875 to 793, in Himachalpradesh 951 to 845, in Gujarath 928 to 878, in Chandigarh 899 to 845, and Delhi 915 to 865.

(ii) A Problem that Haunts Even the Educated and the Urban People : The recent demographic statistics reveal that the rate of foeticide is comparatively higher in urban areas and among the educated than in the rural areas and among the illiterate. As per 2011 census report, there are only 926 women per 1000 men in the urban areas whereas this number is 947 in the rural areas.

(iii) Possibility of Drastic Change in the Sexual Behaviour : Significant decline in the number of women as we find in Punjab, Haryana, Maharasthra, Gujarath and Himachala Pradesh may lead to serious changes in the marriage patterns, fertility rate, male- female relationships and more importantly, in the sexual behaviour of the people. Shortage of women in the society may create problems for men to find marital life-partners. This situation may also lead to an increasing number of sexual atrocities on women.

(iv) Foeticide in a Way, Reflects Atrocity Against Two Women Simultaneously : Foeticide is abhorrent for it causes great harm to two victims of gender violence namely, the female foetus, and *its mother* who has little or no control over her own body and hence is often forced unwillingly to abort the unborn girl-child.

(ii) Female Infanticide

This refers to the practice of killing female babies as soon as they are born. It is reported to be currently in existence in parts of Haryana, Rajasthan, Bihar, U.P., W.Bengal and Tamil Nadu. A few districts of Tamil Nadu have been notorious for this practice. The practice continues to exist even though its magnitude is reduced a little.

India and China are perhaps, the only countries in Asia where there has been the practice of female infanticide, that is, killing a female child before she completes one year. The British banned this practice in India in 1900, but the practice continued even afterwards. In the povertyridden **Kallar** community of **Usilampatti** in Tamil Nadu, it is widely practised. Hospital records at Usilampatti reveal that out of 80% births of girl children more than 75% become victims of infanticide. It is shocking to note that it is openly practiced. Mothers, who mercilessly killed their own babies openly and strongly defended their action.

Some Observations Regarding Female Infanticide

1. Studies reveal instances of female infanticide are higher in number in North India than in South India.
2. Illiteracy, superstitious beliefs, anti-women attitude, predominant patriarchical values or the so called pratice of "*son worship*", coupled with poverty and the burden of dowry are found to be the causes of female infanticide.
3. Soon after birth, unwanted female children are throttled to death, or given water or milk mixed with poison to drink, or made to eat poisonous worms, or exposed to unbearable chill, or extreme heat till their death. These are some of the cruel ways in which the unwanted female children are killed before they properly see the world.
4. During the 19th century, among the Jats, Ahirs, Khatris and Gujjars of North India, female infanticide was in practice. It is said that some remnants of it could be found here and there even now.
5. **Dr. R. Indira** in her articles and studies has stated that the practice of female infanticide is not a secret issue but is quite known to the people in the areas where it takes place and those in authority are also quite aware of it. The police and other people with authority are either not interested in taking strict action against such practices or do not have the will to take action.
6. **Dr. L.S. Vishwanath** who has made a sociological study of this practice writes at the end of his article :- *"However, the data from the historical records and other studies indicate that the actual killing and deliberate neglect of female infants was caste specific and related to a complex set of factors..... Besides dowry and status, ideology of the caste, its cultural traits, and the rural milieu in which the caste lived and interplay of these and other factors seem to determine whether a caste practised female infanticide or not"*.[4]
7. The practice of female infanticide sometimes assumes a serious form posing great problems to the communities which practice it. *For example,* there are a few villages in Rajasthan wherein one very rarely finds female children moving about in public for they are not there, or, in an insignificant number. There is a report of a village in Rajasthan which has 1000 total population out of which hardly 50 female children are there. There are instances of giving severe punishments to those women who refuse to allow their female children to be killed. Some mothers who refused to kill their female children have even deserted the village to seek shelter somewhere outside.
8. This practice is also found in some places of China. As per a recent newspaper report, one village in China has 38 unmarried men and no young women are available to marry them.[5]

It is a pity that wherever female infanticide is a common practice, cases relating to it are rarely reported to the police. It is difficult to prosecute and convict any one when the people of the entire village or community are involved in it. In a society where women have in actuality limited rights, the problem can be solved through awareness building, education and removal of poverty. Due to poverty, traditional belief and pressure from the male members of family, women of some tribal communities practice infanticide.

(iii) Selling of Girl Children

This is the practice of selling girl children for money just as any one sells commodities. There are organisations and agencies doing this work in a secret manner with the co-operation of

4. **L.S. Vishwanath** in *"Female Infaticide and the Position of Women in India"* Page 203.
5. **Source** : *"Gender Equity"*, M'lore University Publication [2007] Page No. - 44

corrupt government officers, police, border security forces, etc. Girls from our nation are being sold mainly to Arab countries and the trade continues even today secretly.

(iv) Girl Child Prostitution

The girl child is highly vulnerable to sexual exploitation at home and outside the home. Among the *Jogins* of Andhra, *Basavis* or *Devadasis* of Karnataka; *Bedias*, *Nats* and *Gandharvas* of North India, there is the practice of forcing young girls to resort to prostitution. These child prostitutes are found to be suffering from skin diseases, venereal diseases, T.B., anaemia, AIDS, etc.

(v) Sexual Abuse of Girl Children

Girl children often become the victims of sexual abuse. ***Sexual abuse*** *refers to the forced involvement of children in sexual activities who are immatured to understand or enjoy sex.* Most of them become the victims of it at about 14 years of age or a little above that age. Around 20% of the girls suffer from it in one way or another. Girl children are abused at home, neighbourhood, school, hospital and such other places. In more than 65% of the cases, they become the victims at the hands of employers, co-workers, tenants, neighbours and acquaintances.

2. INCREASING VIOLENCE AGAINST WOMEN

Most societies exhibit violence in one way or another. Violence against men or women is a social problem because, a large number of people are affected by it almost everyday. Each of us is affected in countless ways by the climate of violence. Violence disrupts society. Every society creates institutions designed to achieve certain ends. Violence cuts short normal institutional functions. Every act of violence, from assault to armed revolution, detracts to some degree from the authority normally vested in society.

• ***Women as Easy Victims of Violence*** : Who is most likely to be victimised by violent crime? Women are less likely to be victimised by violent crime than men, though for some crimes and among some groups of women, victimisation is higher among women than men. Compartively, women become easy victims of crimes. Violence against women includes those damages which are caused by physical and psychological roughness against women of any age, caste, class, region or religion. Violence against women is not a new phenomenon in India. *"Women in Indian society have been victims of ill-treatment, humiliation, torture, and exploitation as far as the written records of social organisation and family life are available. These records are replete with incidents of abduction, rape, murder, and torture of women. But, regretfully, female victims of violence have not been given much attention in the literature on social problems or in the literature on criminal violence."*[6]

• ***Violence in the Life-Cycle of Women :*** Violence against women has become an integral part of their whole life span. Even in the civilised world, it is found throughout the world. Violence against women is the most shameful violation of human rights. **Table-1** gives a glimpse of the types of violence that are committed against women at different stages of their life cycle.

• ***Increasing Crimes Against Women*** : Crime against women is an ever-increasing problem. This problem has been growing more and more acute in India during the recent years. Crimes against women include *violence against women, rape, molestation, dowry harassment, wife-battering, kidnapping female children to be sold into brothel homes, forcible embracement, forcible religious conversion, cheating young women with a promise to marry them or fetch them a job, and various types of sexual harassments and abuse of women including eve teasing.*

6. **Prof. Ram Ahuja** in *"Violence Against Women"* [1998]. Page - 11.

Table -1

Incidences of Crimes that Took Place Every Year Between 1990-1994					
Eve Teasing	-	10,000	Cases of Dowry Death	-	5,000
Rape Cases	-	11,000	Cases of Torture of Women	-	20,000
Kidnapping of Women	-	12,000	Molestation of Women	-	21,000
Statistics for the Year 1994 **: In the Year 1994 Itself the Following Different Cases were Recorded**					
Eve Teasing	-	10,496	Dowry Deaths	-	4,935
Rape Cases	-	12,351	Cases of Torture of Women	-	25,946
Kidnapping / Abduction of Women	-	12,998	Molestation of Women	-	24,117

Incidences of Crimes Against Women

As per the report [1994] of the *"Crime Record Bureau"* of the Central Home Ministry,[7] incidences of crimes against women increased to a great extent in the year 1993-94. As per this report, in India on an average,

(i) every day for every 6 minutes one atrocity is committed against women;
(ii) for every 44 minutes a woman is kidnapped;[8]
(iii) for every 47 minutes a woman is raped;[9]
(iv) every day 17 dowry deaths take place.

- **The same report says that :**

(i) crimes against women increased ***two times*** in the last 10 years [1984-1994];
(ii) instances of rape by 400% in the last two decades [1972-1994];
(iii) instances of kidnapping and blackmailing women by 30% between 1974 and 1993.
(iv) In 1993 alone, about 82,818 instances of crimes against women were registered. Many cases were not registered. It is said that only 10% of the rape cases are usually reported.

Some More Facts About Violence Against Women

The details of the reported cases of criminal violence against women can be obtained from the records of three important agencies, namely : *(i) Ministry of Home Affairs, (ii) Police Research Bureau, and (iii) National Institute of Social Defence.* Crime figures pertaining to 6 types of crimes against women in India in the 5 years between 1990 and 1994 as per the report of these agencies, are constantly increasing every year. During this period, incidences of crimes that took place every year, are mentioned below.

Violence Against Women Within and Outside Family

In a male dominated society like India, violences against women are unfortunately increasing at an alarming rate. Such violences can be grouped into two types : *(a) violence against women within the family, and (b) violence against women outside the family including the criminal violence.*

7. ***Source*** : Report in *"Udayavani"* Kannada daily dated 27th Feb - 1994.
8. ***Kidnapping*** refers to the illegal act of taking away of a minor without the consent of the lawful guardian.
9. ***Rape*** refers to the act of forceful or illicit sex with a woman against her will.

Table - 2

Select IPC Crimes Against Women, NCRB and RGI 2003-2012					
Sl. No.	Crime Head	Incidence 2003	Rate	Incidence 2012	Rate
1	Rape [Sec. 376 IPC]	15847	3.07	24923	4.25
2	Kidnapping and abduction [Sec. 363 to 373 IPC]	13296	2.57	38262	6.53
3	Cruelty by Husband and Relatives [498A IPC]	50703	9.81	106527	18.17
4	Assault on women with intent to outrage her modesty [Sec. 354 IPC]	32939	6.37	45351	7.73
5	Insult to the modesty of women [Sec: 509 IPC]				
	Total IPC	**131364**	**25.42**	**232528**	**39.66**

Source: *Manorama Year Book - 2014, Page: 810*

(a) Violence Against Women Within the Family or Domestic Violence

Women are often subject to violence within the family, a place which is expected to protect their dignity and assure their safety. Violence taking place inside the family which is also known as ***"domestic violence"*** refers to a pattern of violent abusive and coercive behaviour through which one member tries to gain power and control over another person inside the family. This type of violence includes crimes such as --- *dowry related harassments including death, wife-battering, marital rape, sexual abuse of female children and women of one's own family, deprivation of sufficient food to female members, committing incestuous offences, inducing female members of the family to resort to sex-trade, female genital mutilation, abusing female servants of the family, and so on.*

Forms of Domestic Violence

Domestic violence may assume four different forms which are mentioned below.

(i) **Physical Assaults :** Physical assaults on women include beating, wife battering, pushing, kicking, burning, causing injury, confining one's movements to four walls of the house only, etc. Physical assaults may take place frequently or infrequently.

(ii) **Psychological Assaults :** These include isolation from family and friends, verbal and emotional abuse, forced financial dependence, threats of intimidation, control on women's movements, etc.

(iii) **Sexual Assaults :** Enforcing the partner for sexual acts especially when such acts are unwanted or declined by the other partner.

(iv) **Attacks on Property and Pets :** These include destruction of property belonging to the victim, and killing or abusing pets of the victim.

The quality of life of the people and the values of the group to which the family members belong mostly decide the nature and magnitude of domestic violence. Offences of this kind were not properly dealt with the Indian civil law. The recent legislation namely, ***"The Protection of Women from Domestic Violence Act, 2005"***, however gives some protection to women against domestic violence cited above.

(b) Violence Against Women Outside the Family or Social Violence

Kidnapping, raping and murdering women are very serious offences. The society at large itself is to be blamed for many types of violences that are committed against women especially outside the family. Such violences include — *compelling women for abortion and to undergo tubectomy operation, eve-teasing, kidnapping girls of pre-matured age and forcing them to marry, sexual harassment of women employees in workplace, immoral trafficking in women and girls, forced prostitution, kidnapping and mutilating the organs [such as hands, legs, ears, nose, etc.] of female children to use them for the purpose of begging, resorting to forcible religious conversion of young women, female genital mutilation,*[10] *blackmailing of women, throwing acid at the faces of girls who refuse to marry, the police and the jail personnel committing sexual crimes against female prisoners, the police, armed forces and the border security forces committing sex crimes against the female citizens in the border areas, and so on.*

Rape as a Heinous Crime Against Women

Rape is considered as a heinous form of crime against women in almost all the countries of the world. However, statistically, that is, in terms of magnitude, it is not as serious in India as it is in the Western societies. For example, in the U.S. the annual rate of rape offences per **one lakh** population is about **26**, in Canada it is about **8**, in the U.K. it is about **55**, whereas in India, it is **0.5**. As per the reported rape cases in our country between 1990 and 1994, it may be said that there are **30** reported rape cases per day.

Increasing Instances of Rape and Murder in India – U.N.O. Report – 2012

- As per U.N.O. report, in 2010 as many as **22,172** rape incidents have taken place in India. India, unfortunately stands third in this regard the first place is occupied by America with **85593** rape incidents in 2010, and the second place by Brazil with **41180** incidents.
- Looking at the rape incidents from the demographic perspective, in America, for every one lakh people, **27.3** rape incidents are taking place and the corresponding figures for Brazil and India are – **21.09** and **1.8**.
- As per 2012 statistics, in murder cases relating to that year, India stands **second** at the global level with **43,435** murders; and Brazil and Nigeria occupy the first and the third places respectively with **50,108** and **26,037** murder cases.

Source: Written reply given to Rajya Sabha by the Central Home Minister for States **Sri Kiran Rijiju.** ***Quoted*** by Kannada Daily *"Udayavani"* Date: 24.07.2014, Page: 1.

What does the Section 375 of the IPC say About Rape ?

Though women have been idolised in India they have been exploited and denied justice. Increasing instances of rape in India clearly reveal that women continue to be the objects of sexual exploitation here. Section 375 of the ***Indian Penal Code*** says that rape is committed when a man has sexual intercourse with a woman -

(i) against her will, or

(ii) without her consent, or

(iii) with her consent, when her consent has been obtained by putting, or any person in whom she is interested in, to fear of death or hurt, or

(iv) with her consent when he by deception makes her believe that he is her lawful husband;

(v) with her consent, given on account of her unsoundness of mind or intoxication when she is incapable of understanding the consequences of her consent, or

(v) with or without her consent when she is under 16 years of age.

---

10. ***Female Genital Mutilation*** or ***Female Circumcision***, is known to be performed in more than forty countries around the world, particularly in Africa. The practice is common and affects a majority of girls in the eastern African nations of Sudan, Ethiopia, and Somalia. It is said that at the world level at least 100 million women are affected by this cruelty. ***Source*** **: J.J. Macionis** *"Sociology"* - Page : 340.

Rape as a Cruel Expression of Male Dominance

Rape is the cruelest form of violence against women for it damages the dignity of all women. It is one of the manifestations of women's oppression and an expression of male chauvinism. The very incidents of rape reveal that women and girl children are still being treated as sex objects for satisfying the lust of men. Even in the rural and tribal world cases of rape and sexual offences are common.

Rape cases are not always reported to the police : Very few women report the crime of rape to the police because of the fear that such a report would damage theior social reputation. The police attitude is also not very much sympathetic towards the rape victims in the Indian context. Most women are also not aware of the laws relating to rape and other sexual offences and the legal means available to them to punish the guilty. Their ignorance is exploited by police, lawyers and their opponents.

Women of various walks of social life are vulnerable to rape : Agewise, the percentage of victims of rape is highest in the age - group of 16 to 30 years [about 64%]. Women in some fields of social life are more susceptible to rape crimes. *For example*, it is found that women inmates in jail are raped by the jail superintendents, women patients by the hospital personnel, maid-servants by their masters, women daily wage-earners by contractors and middlemen, women crime suspects by the police officers and so on. Even deaf and dumb, lunatic and blind, and women beggars are not spared. Women who come from the lower-middle class and who are the main bread-winners of their families bear sexual abuse quietly and without protest. Rape does not always take place between total strangers. Surprisingly, it takes place in most of the cases within the circle of known persons. Normally young women, that is, between the age group of 23-30 become the main targets of rape crimes.

Rape is no doubt a great social evil. A stringent law against rape is necessary to prevent it. More than that, honesty and commitment to profession on the part of the law enforcing authority, play a major role in preventing it. A well organised women's organisation, civil and human rights groups, and social activists and enlightened public also play an important role in preventing rape cases.

3. PROBLEMS OF HEALTH AND NUTRITION

Most of the studies conducted in India have revealed that healthcare of women is neglected and both nutrition and health services are not adopted. Due to gender prejudice, proper attention is not given to the needs of women at all stages of the life-cycle. This is one of the reasons for their low status in society.

Problem of Health

Poor Supply of Water and Sanitary Facilities

Millions of houses in India, Africa and many Asian countries are not provided with enough water and sanitary facilities. As revealed by **C.Chandramouli,** the Commissioner of Census-2011, has revealed in his report that out of **24.66** Crore houses, only 46.9% of the people living in such houses have toilets and 49.8% of them use open space for toileting while the remaining 3.3% of them use public toilets. One can imagine the plight of women living in such houses without toilets. Provision of good water and sanitation facilities at home helps women more than men in performing routine works at home. Non-availability of proper sanitary facilities would cause serious gynaecological problems such as urinary infections and white discharge among women.

Daily Struggle to Get Drinking Water **:** There are lakhs of families for which good drinking water facility is also not provided and women are the worst sufferers in these families for they are often made to walk a few kilometers every day to fetch drinking water. This irritable exercise makes them neglect their health and also of their children for it is believed that more than 30-40% of the ordinary diseases are caused by infected water.

Lack of drinking water facility disturbs the schooling of young girls for they are normally given the daily task of fetching water from a distant place. In fact, school attendance by girls has risen since the introduction of water points in four communities in **Arappalipatti** and **Panjappatti** in Tamil Nadu.

Female Child is Given Less Health Care

Indian women's craving for male children is quite well-known. This craving for male children makes them give less attention to female children and even to neglect their health. "The practice of breast-feeding female children for shorter periods of time reflects the strong desire for sons. If women are particularly anxious to have a male child, they may deliberately try to become pregnant again as soon as possible after a female is born. Conversely, women may consciously seek to avoid another pregnancy after the birth of a male child in order to give maximum attention to the newly born son."

Women's Health is Ignored

Women suffer from some distinctive health problems from which men are free. Women have to undergo the distinctive biological processes of pregnancy or child-bearing, delivering, nursing, feeding, child-caring or rearing etc. These are their maternal functions. But the insistence on the family planning has posed many health hazards. The use of contraceptives, copper-T, sterilisation, abortion and hormonal drugs has an adverse effect on health. Those who make use of them suffer from problems such as *bodily weakness, bloodlessness, high bleeding, fatness, problems in uterus, discomfort in breast, chronic back pain,* etc. As **Neera Desai** and **Vibhuti Patel** have criticised, the advocates of family planning do not seem to bother much about these problems.

Women Neglecting their Own Health

Studies have revealed that our women are neglecting their own health. Normally Indian women consume less food [that is, on an average 1000 calories a day] and spend more energy on work. Women toil for the good of the family and children even at the cost of neglecting their own health. Women very rarely complain about their ill-health because of their virtue of *"self-denial".* The records in the health centres reveal that women are lagging behind men [that is, 1:3, meaning only one woman is taking medical help for every 3 men] even in matters of availing of medical help.

- **Causes for Women's Poor Health**

Following factors contribute to the neglect of women's health.

(i) Women who are made to discharge heavy domestic work rarely find time to go to health centres to seek medical assistance.

(ii) A large number of women especially in the rural areas are illiterate and hence fail to understand the beginning symptoms of some big diseases. Men - folk at home never bother to take them to seek medical advice well in time but pay a big price for it later when it is too late to get an easy cure.

(iii) Impact of pollution, industrial wastes and smoke emanating from household biomass [made-up of wood, dung, crop residues] stoves and also kerosene stoves on the health of women who work in a poorly ventilated house has been found to be serious. Such women suffer from eye problems, respiratory problems, chronic bronchitis, and lung cancer.

(iv) Inability on the part of women to walk a long distance to reach a well equipped health centre in the absence of required transportation facility.

(v) Non-availability of female doctors in the nearby health centres and reluctance of many women to seek medical check-up by male doctors.

(vi) Parents often discriminate against their girl children by neglecting their sickness. When sick, little girls are not taken to the doctor as frequently as are their brothers. A study in Punjab shows that medical expenditure for boys are 2 to 3 times higher than for girls. As adults also women get less healthcare than men.

Problem of Nutrition

Women are Denied Nutritious Food : Studies have revealed that gender disparities are evident from infancy to adulthood. Girls are breast-fed less frequently and for shorter durations in infancy and childhood. Girl children and women do not consume much nutritious food like milk, curds, ghee, butter, fruits, eggs, etc., for they spare the same for the menfolk as a matter of family practice. According to one estimate from Punjab, adult women consume approximately 1000 or even less calories of food per day than men. Further, men are fed first and better than women. Nutritional equity between males and females is lower in northern than in southern states. It is observed that parents discriminate against their girl children by neglecting them during illness.

Consequences of Nutritional Deprivation

Nutritional deprivation has two major consequences on women : *(i) they never reach full growth potential, and (ii) they suffer from anaemia.* Both are risk factors in pregnancy. More than 40-50% of women in urban areas and 50-70% in rural areas are said to be suffering from anaemia. This condition complicates child-bearing and results in maternal and infant deaths and low birth weight infants.

One study has revealed that even in big cities like Calcutta [95%], New Delhi [73%], Hyderbad [67%], Chennai [18%] large number of girls aged between **6** and **14** suffer from anaemia. The prevalence of anaemia among women with age between **15** and **44** poses not only risks during pregnancy but also reduces their energy to carry on daily activities. Severe anaemic persons find it difficult even to walk at an ordinary pace.

4. WOMEN'S EDUCATION AND GENDER BIAS IN EDUCATION

Social reformers and social thinkers believe that in a nation like India giving education to women in as large a number as possible can prove to be a panacea for many of the problems of women. Accordingly, much attention has been paid to the education of women after independence. The female literacy level has increased steadily. It has increased from 18.7% in 1971 to 39.42% in 1991, to 54.16% in 2001, and to **65.5%** in 2011. In spite of this change in the trend towards higher literacy, some problems have cropped up. We find glaring differences between the level of education of men and women.

Problems of Women Education in India

• It is found ***that girls are being discouraged*** to go for higher education that is, college and university level education and also for professional and technical education.

• ***There are regional imbalances also.*** In states like Kerala, Tamil Nadu, Gujarath, Punjab and Maharashtra, female education is encouraged and given almost equal importance. Whereas in states like Bihar, Uttar Pradesh, Rajasthana, etc. education of girls is neglected even today.

In 2001, ***female literacy was highest in Kerala [88%]*** whereas it was ***lowest [35%] in Bihar,*** while the average female literacy stood at **54.16%.** However, female literacy has increased radically in Bihar between 2001 and 2011 from 35% to 53% registering an increase of 18% in the time span of a decade. In Kerala, it has crossed the mark of 91.78%.The percentage of female literacy level, however, varies with different states. ***[See Table No. 2]***.

Table - 2

MALE - FEMALE LITERACY RATES IN MAJOR STATES OF INDIA IN 2001 AND 2011

	2001			2011		
State	Male Literacy	Female Literacy	Total Literacy	Male Literacy	Female Literacy	Total Literacy
U.P. & Uttaranchal	71	44	58	83.78	64.98	74.67
Bihar & Jharkhand	62	35	49	75.92	54.77	65.72
Rajasthan	76	44	61	80.51	52.66	67.06
M.P. & Chhattisgarh	77	51	64	80.99	60.30	70.83
Haryana	79	56	69	85.38	66.78	76.64
Assam	72	56	64	78.81	67.27	73.18
Gujarat	80	59	70	87.23	70.73	79.31
Orissa	76	51	64	82.40	64.36	73.45
Maharashtra	86	68	77	89.82	75.48	82.91
Punjab	76	64	70	81.48	71.34	68.00
West Bengal	78	60	69	82.67	71.16	77.08
Karnataka	76	56	67	82.85	68.13	75.60
Andhra Pradesh	71	51	61	75.56	59.74	67.66
Tamil Nadu	82	65	73	86.81	73.86	80.33
Kerala	94	88	91	96.62	91.98	93.91

Source : Govt. of India [2001] Census of India 2001. Provisional Population Totals, Paper 1 of 2001. India - 2011 - Census and Yojana, July 2011.

• ***Rural - Urban Difference*** **:** It is observed that literacy level in general is higher in the urban areas than in the rural areas. Some difference is observed at the level of women also. ***For example,*** in 2001, female literacy was found to be **65.66%** in urban areas, whereas it was only **30.58%** in the rural areas.

• ***Increasing drop-out of female children*** from schools is another problem. Though female children are getting admitted to primary, middle and high schools in a substantial number, many of them drop out of the schools in the middle without completing the course. *For example,* as per the data furnished by the Ministry of Education [New Delhi], in 1984-85 the number of female children enrolled at primary school crossed the figure of 34.2 million, and at middle school level the enrolment crossed 9.2 million. More than 74% of these female children, between the age-groups of 6 and 14 years, quit schools and lapsed into ignorance.

• ***Less Number of Girls' Admission to Schools*** **:** Even in the matter of admitting children to school at elementary level, female children are discriminated against male children. *For example,* in 1984-85, the admission of male children to school was around 90%, the percentage of female children was only 66.2. It means complete awareness is not there among people regarding female education.

• ***Low Level of Literacy Among Lower Classes*** **:** In spite of the increasing awareness of the people towards the importance of education, a larger number of people, especially in the rural areas and many low classes and low castes, still believe that education for girls is not as important as that of boys. The rate of literacy is also very low in these communities.

• ***Educational Gap Between Boys and Girls*** **:** According to one estimate, in India, in spite of the growing literacy rate among women in the recent years, there exists a gap of about **20%** between the enrolment of girls and boys at all levels of education, that is, primary, secondary and higher level. Census reports also confirm the same. **[See Table - 3]**

Table - 3

LITERACY RATES BY SEX IN INDIA [1961 - 2011] [In percentage]

Census Year	Females	Males	Persons	Male-Female gap in literacy rate
1961	12.95	34.44	24.02	21.49
1971	18.70	39.45	29.45	20.75
1981	20.76	56.38	43.57	26.62
1991	39.29	64.13	52.21	24.84
2001	54.16	75.85	65.38	21.69
2011	65.46	82.00	74.00	16.54

Note : 1. Literacy rates for 1951, 1961 and 1971 Censuses relate to population aged five years and above. The rates for the 1981, 1991 and 2001 Census relate to the population aged seven years and above.

Source : Census of India, 2001, "Provisional Population Totals".
* Yojana, Magazine July - 2011

Gender Disparity in Education - A Global Perspective

- The rate of drop-out of female children from schools is higher than those of boys. It was reported in the year 2000, that in a nation like **Mali**, **84%** of girls have never attended schools; of those who attend, **60%** dropout in the primary grades. In India, **50%** of the girls dropout before completing the **5th** std.
- Of the nearly **one billion** illiterate adults in the world, **2/3** are women living in South Africa, sub-Saharan Africa, the Middle East and India.

  In more than **29** countries, less than **30%** of women are literate. The female literacy rate as a percentage of male literacy rate, is only **28%** in Sudan, **39%** in Somalia, **46%** in Cambodia and **75%** in Guatemala.

Education - A key to Women Empowerment **:** Studies have revealed that education of girl children has its positive impact on infant mortality, maternal mortality, health and hygiene, productivity, etc. Education is a key to women empowerment which in turn is key to achieve various other developmental goals.

Gender Bias in Education

Indian Education Commission had cautioned in ***1966*** itself that in educational programmes, syllabus etc., no attempt should be made to distribute responsibilities and roles on the basis of sex, and to inculcate the concepts of 'masculinity' and 'femininity', gender disparity, etc. It stressed that such attitudes should be kept outside the educational system. ***National Education Policy*** which came to be implemented in ***1986*** also made it clear that all impediments to popularise female education must be removed immediately. In spite of such official pronouncements gender disparities and bias in education have not come to an end.

Gender Bias in the School Curriculum

Our syllabus system, textbooks, classroom teaching, co-curricular activities are still not free from gender bias. Examples of textbook lessons at primary level education may be considered here. *"Father is the head of the family", "Mother cooks food", "Daughter helps mother in the kitchen work", "Son goes to town along with the father for marketing", "Father and the son are sitting in the hall discussing politics, mother and daughter are spreading washed clothes for drying", etc.* Lessons, examples and photos depicting examples like these are bound to add to the existing gender bias. Our educational system has failed to project the image of a family in which men and women share among themselves all types of domestic work [including kitchen work, washing, cleaning and other work] and co-operate with each other for the smooth functioning of the family.

Women's Achievements are Ignored

It is observed that in the school lessons, references relating to the achievements of women are almost nil. No attempts are made in them to present an impressive image of *"empowered women".* In providing teaching opportunities also women candidates are preferred at primary and kindergarten levels, whereas men candidates are given priority at the higher - level. Even while selecting courses and subjects for study, gender bias is observed. Some courses are regarded as *"more suitable for men"* while some others are considered as *"preferable to women".* In matters such as - treatment of male and female students, rules relating to dress, selection of candidates for sports events, distribution of responsibilities, etc., gender prejudice is experienced.

5. TRAFFICKING IN WOMEN

Trafficking in women, which is known as commercial sexual exploitation of women and girl children is an all pervasive and a global problem. It is a flourishing trade associated with one of the oldest professions of the world namely; prositution. It is a blatant violation of human rights and an inhuman practice wherein females are treated as commodites.

- ***Trafficking in women'*** *- refers to the heinous trade of luring, kidnapping and selling young girls and women for sexual purposes.*
- *It is also known as sex trade in which women are attracted, kidnapped or purchased by some secretly organised criminal agencies and compelled to offer sex services to the paying customers.*

Two Dimensions of Trafficking in Women

Trafficking in women consists of two main dimensaions - that is, (i) *trafficking for domestic labour*, and (ii) *trafficking for prostitution.*

The first case refers to the "*virtual sale*" of destitute women or girls for purposes of domestic work. This is particularly widespread in backward or famine/drought prone areas of the country. This type of trafficking has been exposed several times by the media. It continues even now. **The Second Aspect of trafficking**, that of prostitution is based on the commercialisation of women's bodies, and also on double standards of sexuality for the male and female.Young girls are often unknowingly lured into the traps of trafficking. Numerous young Muslim girls from poor families in Hyderabad and also from coastal Karnataka and Kerala are being married to rich old Arabs [who visit India for a month] and then being subjected to triple '*talaq*' [divorce]. Such divorced young women are pushed to prostitution.[11]

The trafficking of women for sexual exploitation has unfortunately become a well organised criminal phenomenon. It is a phenomenon that violates basic human rights, and leads to total destruction of the victims' lives. Trafficking of women is the extreme manifestation of dehumanising and objectification of humans, especially women. Though it is illegal all over the world, it is estimated that any where from **7 lakhs** to **40 lakh** persons are trafficked annually world wide. Of these persons, women constitute the biggest number. This trafficking trade is considered the third largest source of profit in organised crime next only to drugs trade and arms trade. It is estimated that on an average, 12,000 cases of kidnapping and trafficking are reported every year in India. In the year 1993 itself, as many as 12,426 cases of this crime were recorded.[12] On an average, in India, about 33 girls/women are kidnapped or abducted in a day. The extent of abduction in India is 2 per one lakh population.[13]

III Problem of Run Away Cases

Yet another shocking trend which is being observed during the recent years is the phenomenon of run-away cases of women. It is witnessed in several states of India. Young unmarried girls and sometimes even married women run-away from their families for reasons not properly known. **C. Manjula,** President of Karnataka State Women's Commission has recently said [March 2012] that in 70% of the run-away cases of young girls, love affairs is the main reason. Cases of kidnapping of girls under the pretext of love also cannot be ruled out. The ***Table no. 4*** given below reveals that in Karnataka alone, between 2007-2011, as many as 22447 such cases in relation to women and 12,703 cases in relation to unmarried girls are reported. Bangalore city is leading in this unwanted trend. The following ***Table -5*** shows how sporadic it is in Bangalore. In most of these run-away cases in Karnataka, young girls between the age of 16 to 30 are involved. C. Manjula has pointed out that modern technological means such as movies, T.V, mobiles etc. have been misused in these cases. Though police have been able to trace out some of these cases many still remain as a mystery. Further, sizeable number of such cases are not reported to the police at all - due to ignorance, helplessness, family prestige, lack of faith in police and so on. It is also assumed that all major cosmpolitan cities of India are facing this problem.

Table No. 4

Run-Away Cases of Young Girls/Women in Karnataka Between 2007 and 2011.

Year	Young Girls	Women
2007	1898	2757
2008	2563	3354
2009	3047	4720
2010	2791	6005
2011	2404	5611
Total	**12703**	**22447**

Source : Karnataka Women's Commission President C.Manjula in her Press Statement in "Hosa Digenta", Kannada Daily Dated: 08.03.2012.

11. ***Source :*** "*Gender Equity*"- A Mangalore University Publication, (2007) - Page - 52-53.
12. ***Source*** : **Ram Ahuja** in *"Social Problems in India"* - Page : 245.
13. ***Source*** : *Crime in India - 1993.*

Table - 5

Run-Away Cases of Girls/Women as Reported in Bangalore City - 2010 and 2011				
Year	Young Girls		Women	
	Cases Reported	Cases Traced out by police	Cases Reported	Cases Traced out by police
2010	1352	823	3524	2044
2011	681	427	2426	1168
BANGALORE Rural District				
2010	123	60	159	54
2011	133	64	250	115
Source: As per the Statement of State Women's Commission on 8-3-2012				

Legislation is Ineffective

Of the total victims abducted / kidnapped every year, 87% are females and 13% are males. On the issue of kidnappings, generally males are arrested [96%] and sometimes women are also taken to custody [only 4%]. The Act, namely, ***Immoral Traffic in Persons [Prevention] Act, 1986*** passed in this regard to protect women, has not been a success. Not only India, various other countries are affected by this problem in different ways. Some countries lose their women who are lured to desert their home countries permanently, only to end up in the *sex industry* abroad. Some other countries play their role mainly as transit countries. But many countries are *"profited"* by this *'trade'* for they receive women who become the victims of sexual exploitation.

Unwanted Girls are Often Sold

India is also a victim of the criminal phenomenon of women trafficking. It is said that there are areas in India where female children are so unwanted that *"if they are not killed, they are sold."* In the tribal areas of **Nalgonda** [Andhra Pradesh], the girl child is a curse and female infanticide is common. An NGO [Non-Governmental Organisation] discovered that some people in this area found it easier to get rid of the unwanted child by way of selling it to some agency which exports the same to some foreign country. It is also reported that girls from India are being sold to Arab countries.[14]

Causes of Human Trafficking including Trafficking in Women

The causes of human/female trafficiking are many :- Poverty, illiteracy, run-away from family, unemployment, polygynry, divorce, separation, enforced widowhood, failure in love, victims due to natural disasters, favourable religious beliefs, or social taboos, ethnic or racial minorities, victim of communal violence and ethnic clashes, migration in search of livelihood or desire for glamourous jobs in cities, sexual exploitation, abuse and rape by lusty villagers, gangsters, or even relatives, political refugees due to war or border clashes, etc...

---

14. ***The Centre of Concern for Child Labour***, in its report says that export of children gets a boost during the ***Haj*** season every year. The children are sent to ***Mecca*** and ***Medina*** for begging as the pilgrims make generous donations, not only in the form of money but also in the form gold ornaments. Some children are brought back but those with good looks and good health are held back. But where they disappear no one finds out." - **Vir Bala Agarwal** in *"Status of Women in Modern India" [2005]* - Page : 6, Edited by **S.B.Verma**.

Trafficking in Women a Flourishing Trade

Exporting girl children to foreign countries is a well organised flourishing trade. It has direct or indirect link with police, border forces, bureaucrats, hotel owners, long distance bus drivers and conductors and even the village level workers. One group locates and collects the girls while the other one provides the funds for shelter and spends money to silence the law enforcing authorities. Another group manages the export promotions. Some of these operators have their offices in **Saudi Arabia** and **Oman**. [V.B. Agarwal]

Trafficking in Women and "Love Zihad"

During the recent years, the States of Kerala and Karnataka have been experiencing yet another ugly development in the field of trafficking in women. In both these states, large number of young and educated girls belonging to Hindu and Christian Communities are disappearing from their place of living. According to one estimate, in Karnataka during the year 2010-2011, around 5000 girls left their families unauthorisedly and disappeared from their place of living. A big commotion was created in Kerala in the year 2010 when news papers reported the missing of nearly 4400 young girls out of which 2400 girls belonged to Christianity and 2000 to various Hindu Castes. News papers reported this as constituting instances of *"love-Zihad",* that is, a deliberately hatched out strategy to love young girls belonging to Christian Community and Hindu Castes and tempt and pressurise them to get converted into Islam so that they could marry Muslim boys with whom they are already in love. It is said that huge amount of money is spent on these boys to woo young girls so that they fall a prey to the already hatched conspiracy. The Kerala High Court had taken exception to the inability of the police authorities to curb and control this anti-social trend which has been fast developing in the college campuses especially in Kerala. Almost everyday, Kannada and Malayalam papers flash news about the instances of missing women.

6. DIFFERENTIAL TREATMENT GIVEN TO WOMEN

In the Indian family, women and men are never treated on par. Women are always discriminated against. This is due to the traditional practice of gender discrimination. As we know, in *gender discrimination one sex is given preferential treatment over the others."* The practice of giving social importance to the biological differences between men and women is there everywhere. In some societies, these differences are very much pronounced while in others, they are given less importance. The Indian society is not an exception to this.

Secondary Place for Women in Social Life

At every stage in their social life women in India come to feel that they are given only secondary place in society. In social gatherings, programmes and functions men are given importance. Most of the times, men are invited as speakers and chief guests and they only dominate the stage performances. In religious functions and public programmes, men play more important role than women. Even at home, differential treatment is given to men and women when they make family visits. It is only during the recent years, some changes are taking place in the direction of giving equal treatment to men and women.

Preference to Male Children and Negligence of Female Children

The practice of gender discrimination is very much visible in almost all fields of our social life. Male child preference and neglect of female child has been associated with most of our families. This is slowly giving rise to an imbalance in the sex ratio of the population.

Decline in the Female Population

Normally, in the population of any country, male-female ratio remains more or less the same, that is, 50:50. In India, as the census reports reveal, female population has been steadily declining ever since 1901. It is for this reason, **Neera Desai** and **Vibhuti Patel** raised the point whether the womenfolk in India represent a *"declining sex"*. According to 2001 Census, there is a deficit of **35** million women as compared to **3** million in 1901. For every 1000 men, we have only **940** women at present [2011] as against **972** women in 1901. The male preference has led to the abuse of technology. Thousands of "unwanted female" children are killed at the stage of foetus itself. It is said that in India, out of **12** million female children born every year, around 25% of them die before they attain the age of 15. Of the children which die every year, about **3** lakh female children, that is, more than the number of male children, die for one or the other reason. Of the children which die every year in India, the **6**th child dies due to gender discrimination.[15]

Discrimination in the Distribution of Power and Work **:** Most of the Indian families are patriarchal. Hence, the philosophy of equality of sex is not acceptable to them. Domestic works such as - cooking, looking after the children, washing clothes and vessels, keeping the house neat and clean, looking after the domesticated animals, serving family members like a nurse on all days and especially when they fall sick, etc., are branded as *"women's work"*. Very rarely men do these works.

But when the question of exercising power comes, it is always the man who dominates. His decisions are final and his orders are ultimate. The female voice is always suppressed.

Gender Discrimination in Occupations and Public Life **:** Women workers are paid less than the male workers for the same type of work. Much labour is extracted from women by giving them very minimum wages. In matters of giving treatment, promotion, increment, facilities, etc., discrimination is normally made. In *pubic life* also men are given priority. Excepting the glamorous film actresses and politicians, in all other fields, women are not given importance on par with men. Government officials also practise this discriminatory treatment in dealing with the people. It is only during the recent years, things have started changing slowly.

7. PROBLEMS RELATING TO EMPLOYMENT AND UNEMPLOYMENT OF WOMEN

In the economic field, the situation is such that majority of women who are ready to work are not finding suitable work to their satisfaction. Those who are in the employment sector are becoming the objects of exploitation and harassment. Though an increase in the female literacy level and extensions of employment opportunities for women in the non-agricultural sector, have added to the trend in favour of female employment, these two problems continue to exist.

- ***Large Number of Employed Women are Illiterate*** **:** Of every 100 women employed, 52.59% of them are illiterate and 28.56% of them have studied only up to elementary level. Of every 100 women working in the rural areas, 88.11% are illiterate. These illiterate women in the unorganised sector are totally exploited by their employers. Women working in factories, mining industries, building construction process, in dams, bridges and road repair or construction work are not only paid less but also made to work in unhealthy surroundings.

- ***Decreasing economic participation of women :*** Technological development seems to have a negative effect on the employment opportunities of women. Studies conducted between 1975-85 have revealed this fact. Application of new technology in agrarian sector, textiles, mines, jute, pharmaceuticals, small scale industries like coir, handloom, weaving, spinning, cashew, fisheries, tobacco, animal husbandry, fruits and vegetable processing etc.

15. *Source of Statistics* **: Dr. R. Indira** in her *"Mahile - Samaja Mattu Samskriti"* - Page : 93.

rendered many women jobless. Computerisation has also adversely affected the job prospects of women as clerks, typists and accountants.

8. HARASSMENT OF WOMEN AT WORK PLACE

Women constitute an important labour force in all the countries. During the recent years there is an increasing number of women especially in the Indian context, who are working outside the family to get more income for the family. In fact, *"the term working woman" refers to one who works outside the home for a wage or salary"*.[16]

Nearly **1/3** of our labour force [32%] consists of women. Working women constitute 16.43% of the female population of the country. As per 1991 Census, the number of working women was around **278.35** million, representing a growth rate of 26.12% over the previous decade. The percentage increase of working women during the last decade was double that of male workers. The main problem with these female workers, is that they are harassed in work place in different ways. *"Harassment" refers to the basic violation of an individual's rights*. Not only the rights of working women are violated, they are often sexually harassed also.

• ***Economic Exploitation*** : Women workers are given much work but are paid less wages or salary especially in the unorganised sector. *"Equal pay for equal work"* remains only a slogan. ***"Equal Remuneration Act, 1976*** has proved to be a dead letter in this regard. There are also sufficient instances of such exploitation even in the organised sector.

• ***Threat of Removal from Job*** : In the Indian context, majority of women go for work not for fun but out of necessity. Some are compelled to work because of poor family conditions. Employers who are aware of the helplessness of these female employees exploit them in all the possible ways. They do not tolerate any type of opposition or protest from the side of the female workers. Due to the fear of losing the job, women bear all the exploitations, and do not protest.

• ***Women are Given More Work*** : Women normally work with devotion, seriousness and sincerity. This commitment to work is proving to be a big disadvantage for them. Hence, every time they are given more and more work which is not duly rewarded.

• ***Discrimination in Giving Opportunities*** : In spite of the hard work which women do, many employers consider these working women as *"non-serious workers"*. They are also regarded as *"non-permanent employees"* especially in the case of unmarried female workers. They are discriminated with regard to recruitment, promotion, increment, training, over-time allowance, facilities at work place, and so on. Male workers are given preference in these matters.

Sexual Harassment of Women at Workplace

Sexual harassment of women at workplace refers to giving indecent treatment to women workers by violating all the norms of modesty. Many female workers have complained of such harassments during the recent years. This harassment by men includes - continuous staring at women, making women the targets of lewd remarks, dirty jokes, repeated invitation to meals and outings, offers to drop them home, making unwanted comments about dressings, making "accidental" touches and dashes, making them stay back in the work spot even after the working hours, male bosses calling smart female employees to their chambers and making unwanted "advances" towards them, molesting women workers and so on.[17]

---

16. **Anjana Maitra Sinha** in *"Women in a Changing Society"* - (1993) - Page : 105.
17. In 1998, the *"National Commission for Women"* conducted a survey in five States consisting of 1211 female workers in order to assess the extent of harassment of female workers in the work spot. The survey reported that 68% of women were mentally harassed by men, 26% of them physically tortured, and 38% of them had become the victims of gender discrimination. ***Source* : *"Out look"*** (English Weekly) dated : 19/4/1999 - Page : 66.

Sexual Harassment As a Common Issue

Sexual harassment is a complex as well as a common issue found in almost all the modern civilised societies. However, sexual harassment of working women has been the most pervasive but carefully ignored feature of our modern societies including India. All working women, regardless of their age, physical appearance, social status and job security may encounter sexual harassment in one way or another. But the main difference is that women working at the bottom of economic scale are subject to more gross expression of sexual harassment. They very often face crude, vulgaric comments and even physical assaults. Professional and managerial women, on the other hand, receive more subtle treatment. Instead of direct physical abuse, they are subject to psychological intimidation. Men co-employees or their bosses may often give them offers such as - afterwork - drinks, expensive lunches or dinners, business trips, birth day gifts, financial helps etc., with an implicit message that sexual favours are expected.

Helpless and Confused State of Female Employees

Women employees faced with unwanted and unexpected sexual advances may feel confused and often frustrated. They may get angry also but they find it difficult to protest. Some such harassed women are not always sure whether real injustice is done to them. They are not certain that they have become objects of sexual exploitation. They are only confused. In addition to that, harassment has been a hidden problem, sometimes treated as a joke. Since the public has been silent on this issue for a very long time, women feel embarrassed or, are uncomfortable to speak about their personal experience of harassment even with their own friends and nearest relatives.

Fear of losing Job : Sexual harassment is very often tolerated by women because of their fear of losing the job, if reported to higher authorities. They also feel that such complaints would tarnish their image and reduce job prospects.

Sexual harassment deprives women of opportunities that are available to male employees. In the modern context, work is essential and critical to women's survival, independence and empowerment.

Sexual harassment degrades women and makes them object of sex. Such harassment at work reduces women's potential for social equality. In the present context of globalistaion, things are changing fast. Women are asserting themselves through united efforts and hence the instances of harassment are comparatively diminishing. In many offices, both private and Govt., women have shown that they have a right to work with dignity.

9. EXPLOITATION OF WOMEN IN THE MEDIA

The mass media such as the radio, television, news papers and the cinema play a vital role in social change and social development especially in the modern societies. But unfortunately, the media has not been playing a positive role in the case of women. The media is even condemned of exploiting and misrepresenting women.

(i) Journalism as Print Media and Women

Newspapers, weeklies, monthlies or other types of magazines seem to be interested in increasing their circulation by rousing the cheap emotions of the people. *"They target the woman's body to get their things done."* Papers no doubt give due publicity to some unfortunate events under the captions such as *"Atrocity Against Women"*, *"Dowry Costs A Woman's Life"*, *'Mass Rape of a Woman'*, *'Sexual Harassment of Women'*, etc. But in doing so, they give the least information about the culprit of the crime. On the contrary, they take more interest in weaving stories about the victim of the event which often amounts to character assassination.

(ii) Visual Media and Women

Since about 25% of the people in our society are illiterate, [as per 2011 census], visual media such as television and the cinema have a greater impact on people. The Indian visual media is a failure in playing a positive role in educating people and enriching their knowledge. Like the newspapers, they also exhibit the female body and make it their main capital to mint money. Modern movies believe in achieving success by portraying more and more sex, violence and murder. Women are shown as targets of attack, sex, rape and such other exploitations.

Unfortunately, our T.V. is also following the example of the movies. With the invasion of our skies with a number of T.V. channels, the choice of T.V. viewers has greatly expanded. T.V. channels such as the Star Plus, MTV, Asian TV Network, Zee TV, and other Cable channels, are promoting a lifestyle which is totally alien to us. As usual, women are presented in these channels in an indecent manner. Indian movies and T.V. serials are often criticised for damaging the modesty and dignity of women.

(iii) Advertisements and Women

Advertisements whether in newspapers or T.V. play no less an important role in debasing women. Advertisement firms also make use of female body in a cheap manner to get publicity for things which they want to promote.

(iv) Media and Women Movements

Media has an important role to play in strengthening women's position. While pronouncing women's weaknesses, it must also emphasise their strength. It must awaken women from the slumber of centuries, inform them, mobilise them and motivate them whenever required. It must give due publicity to women's struggle for justice, equality and fairplay. This will help them in regenerating power. The present role of the media in this regard is not that encouraging, but disappointing.

Legislation to Regulate the Media

The Government had passed as early as in 1986 a legislation namely; ***"The Indecent Representation of Women [Prohibition] Act, (1986)*** in order to prevent the media from misrepresenting the women. Any attempt to degrade and discredit women, insult and humiliate them, assassinate the character of women, and present them in an indecent manner, is declared punishable. The provisions of this Act are applicable to all the means of the mass media and also to advertisements, books, handbills, posters, etc. Violation of this Act is liable for punishment, which amounts to 2000 ₹ fine and 2 years imprisonment.

10. HARDSHIPS DUE TO DIVORCE, DESERTION AND DOWRY

During the recent years, instances of desertion and divorce are increasing making the lives of many women very miserable.

The Hardship of Desertion

Desertion is defined as *"deliberate abandonment of conjugal relationships."* As a matter of fact, desertion may take place at the behest of any one of the two, or both together. In actuality, in the Indian context, it is mostly the husband who goes away from the family leaving the wife and children at home to fend for themselves.

Desertion causes lot of hardships especially for women. It immediately drives a woman to a state of uncertainty and helplessness. Deserted women belonging to poor families all of a sudden become orphans especially when they are disowned by their own parents. Some of them may resort to immoral activity, some others fall prey into the hands of anti-social elements, while a few of them may commit suicide.

The Agony of Divorce

Divorce is *"...an institutional arrangement for terminating marital relationship..."*[18] It has now become a serious problem haunting thousands of Indian women.

Causes of divorce are many. Sociologists like **Damle, Fonseca** and **Chaudhary** together conducted a study in India which revealed the following causes of divorce : *marital disharmony, sexual conflicts, maladjustments between husband and wife, marital desertion, husband's cruelty, prostitution on the part of wife, sexual impotency, severe and unmanageable clashes with the in-laws, mother-in-law's harassment, including dowry harassment, illicit sex relationship on the part of either the husband or the wife, irreparable health hazards, mutual distrust, total irresponsibility of the husband or wife towards the family matters and so on.*

Divorce causes lot of hardships especially for the women

Divorce damages the social image of the wife. It becomes a permanent stigma in her life. Many sensitive women find it difficult to come out of the shock of divorce. The impact of divorce on children is also very severe. The burden of protecting and rearing of children also lies on the wife. Jobless and resourceless divorced women find themselves in a big economic crisis. Young and beautiful divorced women find it difficult to suppress their sex urge. They are often forced to resort to illicit ways of satisfying it. It usually leads to family disintegration.

The Problem of Dowry

Dowry is both a practice and a problem associated with the Indian marriage. Though it was more in practice among the Hindus, it has now spread to almost all the religious communities of India.

- Dowry refers to *".... the property, money, ornaments or any other form of wealth which a man or his family receives from his wife or her family at the time of marriage."*

The age-old practice of dowry has now assumed the form of a social evil because the bride's family is compelled to give some dowry *as a 'price for marriage'*. It has become a social bane and a kind of bargain. It has caused unhappiness, misery and ruin of the bride's family. Huge amount of money is demanded at the time of marriage and the failure to give the promised amount would make the bride to suffer the consequences at the hands of her in-laws and also the husband.

Dowry harassments are many

Women are ill-treated, disrespected, man-handled, tortured and subject to all sorts of cruelties in the name of dowry. Very often, our daily papers flash news about the tragic results of the dowry system, in which the newly married girls are always the victims of harassment, violence, murder and suicide. Dowry is demanded as though it is a fundamental right of the bridegroom. Violence against women who bring less dowry or no dowry include – *wife battering, emotional neglect / torture, verbal abuse, refusal of sufficient food, imposition of heavy physical work, severe physical harassments to the extent of killing the victim, and so on.*

In spite of the legislation against the practice of dowry, it persists. Demands for dowry have even caused dowry deaths. According to an estimate, as many as 4148 dowry deaths were

---

18 W.P. Scott in *"Dictionary of Sociology"*

reported in the year 1990 and it increased to 4366 in the year 1993, and to 6205 in the year 1994, that is, at the rate of one dowry death for every 17 minutes.

Dowry leads to the degradation of women

Prevalence of the practice of dowry reflects the inferior status of women in society. It makes a girl a great liability on her family's resources. Some unscrupulous and money-minded young men contract more than one marriage just for money. It disturbs the normal relationship between the married women and her in-laws in the husband's family. Some poor parents who cannot pay a huge amount as dowry, are often compelled to arrange the marriage of their daughters with old men, or physically or mentally handicapped persons. Such marriages prove to be miserable for women.

As early as in **1961** itself, ***The Dowry Prohibition Act*** was passed in order to prevent the practice of dowry. It was amended in 1986 to make its provisions more severe and stringent. In spite of this Act, the practice continues to be in vogue.

11. DECLINE IN THE POLITICAL PARTICIPATION OF WOMEN

Participation of women who constitute around 50% of our total population, in politics and public life is very much negligible in India. We find only a negligible number of women in prestigious political positions like those of Central and State cabinet ministers, governors, secretaries and legal advisers to the governments, ambassadors to other countries, IPS, IAS, IFS officers, judges in courts, mayors of big cities, office bearers of all-India parties, etc. No political party in India has given position to women in accordance with their number in the total population. In some areas, seats are reserved for women as we find in Gram Panchayat, Jilla Panchayat, University Senate, etc. Even in these areas women have not constituted themselves into a powerful *"pressure group"*. Thus, in our political life, we have caste lobbies, linguistic lobbies, capitalist lobbies, minority lobby, etc. but we do not have *"women's lobby"* to bring pressure on the government.

- ***Increasing Violence and Terrorism in Politics:*** Political corruption, criminalisation of politics, erosion of political values, disappearance of political decency, instability, lawlessness, terrorism and confusion have been increasing in our public life since 1980s. This state of confused political situation has discouraged women from taking active role in politics.
- ***Minimum Representation of Women in Lok Sabha:*** The representation of women in Lok Sabha has been very poor since 1962 elections. **For ex:** there were only 33 elected women members in the third Lok Sabha [out of 494 members] after the 1962 elections. In the 6th Lok Sabha out of 544 elected members, there were only 19 women members and their percentage was only 3.4. In the 10th Lok Sabha [1991 Elections], there were 39 elected women members and their percentage was 7.4.
- ***In the 1996 Elections for the 11th Lok Sabha*** though the total number of women voters increased to 28.24 crores [47%], only 477 women candidates as against 14,250 men candidates contested for 543 seats. [In the 1991 Elections for the 10th Lok Sabha 325 women candidates contested as against 8,374 men candidates for 521 seats]. These figures reveal that only a small number of women are interested in political life.
- ***In the 1999 General Elections for the 13th Lok Sabha*** also women's participation was the poorest one. Though political parties were speaking vociferously in terms of 33% reservation for women in legislative bodies including the Parliament, no political party had given more than **10%** tickets to women. In some parties, the percentage of women candidates was not even **2** to **3.**

• ***Poor Participation of Women in the Party Politics*** : Not only in the legislative bodies but even within the framework of the political parties also the participation of women is very poor. Political parties are still male-dominated and unwilling to give sufficient representation to women. ***For example,*** in 2001, the Congress Party had only 3 women in its 20-member Working Committee. During the same period, in the BJP Working Committee, out of **75** members there were only 8 women, and in its **650** member National Council, there were only **150** women. The Communist Party [Marxists] had only **12** women in its **150** member National Council, and **3** women in its **21** member National Executive. Though theoretically, equal representation for women in politics is regarded as the first step towards women empowerment, the socio-political atmosphere has not yet become condusive for that.

Poor Participation of Women in the Indian Parliamentary System

Though amongst the democratic nations of the world, India is in the forefront due to its huge size, the number of women participants in its parliamentary system is quite less. On the contrary, in the smaller democratic systems such as Pakistan, Bangladesh and Nepal, the participation of women is comparatively better.

In the 15th Lok Sabha [2009-13], the participation of women was just 11% [that is, 60 women members out of 543 members, and in the Rajya Sabha, it was 10% [that is, 24 women members out of the total of 240 members]. [It must be noted that in March -2012, two Lok Sabha seats and five Rajya Sabha seats were vacant]. In the **16th Lok Sabha Elections** which were concluded in May - 2014, for the first time, **61** women candidates got elected to the Parliament.

India is lagging behind Nepal and Pakistan as far as women's participation in the parliamentary democracy is concerned. The position of China and Bangladesh is better than India in this regard. However, the position of Sri Lanka and Mayanmar is worse than that of India. At the world level, India occupies 105th position in this regard whereas the positions of Sri Lanka and Mayanmar are 129 and 134, respectively.[19]

12. GLOBALISATION AND ITS IMPACT ON WOMEN

"Globalisation" represents one of the aspects of the new economic policy launched in the decades of 1980s and 1990s. The new economic policy has also made the economy outwardly oriented such that, its activities are now to be governed both by the domestic market and the world market. This will mean *unification or integration of the domestic economy with the world economy*. The measures taken by the Government of India added momentum to this progress.

The process of *"globalisation"* has today become one of the important issues of politico-economic discussions. In the media and also in the press, this issue is getting lot of propaganda and publicity. In the first half of the 20th century, *the process of industrialisation, urbanisation and modernisation* were considered to be significant while at the fag end of the same century, *the processes of computerisation, liberalisation, privatisation and globalisation* became the most important processes. Since 1990s, the issue of globalisation has become the most crucial one and almost every nation is directly or indirectly involved in it and influenced by it.

- ***"Globalization** means*, in simple words, *integrating the economy of a country with the world economy"*.[20]

19. ***Source*** : *'Udayavani'*, Page - 4, *Kannada Daily, 9-3-12.*
20. **S.K. Misra** and **V.K. Pure** in *"Indian Economy"* [2000] - Page : 738.

• The ***main purpose of globalisation*** *is to integrate international market across the geographic and political boundary, so that goods, commodities, services, capital, labour and human population can move freely without any barrier and restriction from one corner to any other corner of the world.*

Impact of Globalisation on Women

Globalisation has led to some positive and many negative consequences. Globalisation has also affected womenfolk of the world in various ways. In fact, globalisation has led to some contradictory effects on women's life and status. In some respects, it is beneficial to them while in some others, it has brought them great disadvantages.

- **Some Positive Effects of Globalisation on Women**

1. Greater Freedom to Women : Globalisation has brought greater freedom and exposure to women, especially in traditional and conservative countries like Indonesia, Ireland, Thailand, India, etc.

2. It has given women economic independence. By bringing women into workforce, globalisation has given women the economic power which they lacked in the past.

3. Widened Better Employment Opportunities for Women : Majority of women who entered workforce as a result of globalisation, are in the service sector-jobs which used to be well-paid and mostly occupied by men. *For example,* women who are in services today like banking, insurance companies, computer software companies, have virtually displaced large number of men from their jobs.

4. Globalisation has led to a radical improvement in the standard of living of the families in which women are earning outside the home. Working women have started using labour - saving devices like cookers, washing machines, water pumps, dish washers, vacuum cleaners, mixer-grinders, microwave ovens, etc., and these instruments have radically transformed women's lives in countries where they are easily afforded.

5. It has hastened the emergence of child-care facilities on a very wide scale. As a result, number of baby-sitting centres, kindergartens, creches, *'anganawadis'*, *'balawadis'*, etc., have come in. This provided lakhs of women jobs outside the family.

6. It has led to the rise of fast food chains in society. Since many women, especially those working in "white-collared" jobs in urban areas, are no longer at home for cooking food during the day time, the fast food producing industry received a great fillip. In fact, the fast food industry has also provided some job opportunities to women to prepare and supply food on contract basis.

- **Some Negative Impacts on Women**

1. Increased Gender Disparity : Since the benefits of the growing global economy have been unevenly distributed, wide economic gap is created between people leading to disparities. It has even increased gender inequality by providing unsafe working environment and unhygienic working conditions. Women are at a disadvantage in entering some jobs thrown open by globalisation. Married women with small children find it difficult to manage with those jobs which involve 'shift system', night work, late night work, more than 10 hours of work a day, regular touring, vast field work, etc.

2. Globalisation has led to feminisation of labour. As more and more women are forced to look for employment, an overwhelming majority of this labour is being concentrated in low-wage industries like textiles, leather works, readymade dresses, footwear production, food processing, etc. These industries are notorious for exploiting their workers by denying them job security, their right to organise, etc. Women employees in these industries are subject to long working hours without even being provided with basic amenities.

3. *Problem of Security and Protection for Working Women* : Globalisation opens up vast job opportunities for women especially in the developing countries like India. In big cities, *'call centres'* associated with business houses and industries are opened and these provide jobs with attractive salaries to both men and women and make them work on shift system. The temptation of handsome salary has made many women take the risk of working in places where adequate security arrangements are not made for them. Such a situation has often led to sexual harassment and exploitation of women. The tragic episodes that took place in the "call centres" at Bangalore, are an example in this regard.

4. *Double Burden for Women* : Women are made to bear the brunt of *"double burden"*, that is, one at office [or at workplace] and another at home. After their toil at the workplace, women are made to undertake *"second shift"* at home, cooking, cleaning, washing clothes, vessels, serving food and caring for children and such other routine household works. Thus, women's growing participation in the paid labour force is not bringing them greater freedom and power as it was expected.

5. *Continuation of Family Traditions Disturbed* : Pre-occupation of women with jobs outside the family has its *adverse consequences on the maintenance and continuation of the family traditions and religious customs.* Employed parents, are no longer able to give cultural training to their children in family traditions and religious practices.

6. *Socialisation of Children Affected* : Employment of women outside the family has adversely affected the socialisation of children. The inability of employed women to spare enough time for their children has often resulted in emotional and psychic problems.

B) EMPOWERMENT OF WOMEN AS A MAIN STRATEGY TO FACE THE PROBLEMS OF WOMEN

Towards Equality Report - 1974

Formation of National Commission to Study the Status of Women in India

Just as the Indian community neglected its own women folk for centuries together, the independent Indian Government also had a negligent attitude towards women in the beginning. Though India attained independence in 1947 itself, for more than 25 years, that is almost upto 1974, no proper attention was paid either to study the actual position and problems of women or to seek measures to counter them. For the first time, a *National Commission* was formed to examine the status and problems of Indian women. The report submitted by this Commission in 1974 came to be known as. "*Towards Equality Report-1974*". As **Maithreyi Krishnaraj** has pointed out, research made by this Commission relating to the status of women represents a milestone in the field of women studies in India.

Main Objectives Kept Before the National Commission

1. To examine whether the constitutional, legal and administrative provisions have any impact on the social status of women, their education and employment.
2. To evaluate the impact of these provisions on the status of women in the country during the last two decades especially in the rural sector and to suggest more effective programmes.
3. To estimate the development of education among women and find out the factors responsible for the slow progress in some areas and suggest remedial measures.
4. To study the problems of working women including discrimination in employment and remuneration.
5. To assess the status of women as housewives and mothers in the changing social pattern and their problems in the sphere of further education and employment.

6. To make case studies on the implications of the population policies and family planning programmes on the status of women.
7. Finally, to suggest suitable measures which would enable women to play their roles to the fullest possible extent in contributing to the development of nation.

Importance of - "Towards Equality Report - 1974"

"*Towards Equality Report - 1974*" is of great social, sociological and administrative importance. The Report reflects that for the first time in the history of India an attempt was made to collect vast information or data relating to women's life, living conditions and problems with an academic approach. Main highlights of the Report could be enlisted as follows.

1. ***Main Areas Covered Under the Study*** : Data collected by the study team mainly included statistics relating to declining sex ratio, life expectancy of women, extent of women's participation in the productive economic activities. Main trends in these areas were observed.

2. ***Very Poor Participation of Majority of Women in Educational, Economic and Other Fields*** : The study revealed that in the fields of education and employment women belonging to middle class had achieved some moderate success. In almost all the other fields, the percentage of participation by women was found to be extremely low.

The study pointed out that large number of women worked longer hours for very low wages. Most of the women actively participated in the economic activities of their families without any financial benefit. They were busily engaged in collecting firewood, carrying drinking water, taking care of the aged and the diseased, looking after the children and so on.

3. ***Exposed the Hard Realities of Women*** : The study report revealed that the equality principle adopted by our Constitution remained only in theory in the case of majority of women. Only the middle class women were able to achieve some amount of progress in the fields of education and employment.

• ***Has Thrown Some Light on the Problems of Women*** : The study team came to know that majority of Indian women were still the victims of violence, dowry, gender discrimination, etc. The commission was shocked to observe among women, lower rates of life expectancy, declining sex ratio, high death rates, low participation in economic activities etc. These trends belied the hopes and expectations created by the accepted goals of the Constitution.

4. ***Pointed Out the Failures of Political Parties and Leaders in Realising the Role of Women in Nation Building*** : During the 19th century, women were seen as *the victims of certain social evils* and in the post-independence period, they were seen *as beneficiaries of development projects*. There was a failure to realise that women could be as active participants in the development projects as men are.Their role in the national movement, labour movements and peasant movements is ignored.

• ***Reluctant Acceptance of the Role of Women in Development Works by Political Parties*** : Scholars in the field of women studies have observed that political parties, of late, have accepted the role of women in nation building, but rather reluctantly.

5. ***Influence of the Report on Government Policies*** : Report of the National Commission is of great importance because, it influenced the policies of the government while formulating developmental projects and programmes. It made the government to recognise the existing wrong concepts and opinions pertaining to the role of women in society. As per the Report, two factors were mainly responsible for the low status of women, namely; *ignorance* and *attitudes of individuals*.

6. ***Inspiration to Series of Women's Studies*** : The Commission's work was a starting point in the field of women's studies and it provided a strong inspiration for many more future studies of women with a new perspective.

Though the Report has some merits, it has its own demerits also. Feminists of India have pointed out various deficiencies involved in the commission's study and report.

As it is wellknown, women are traditionally regarded as belonging to weaker sex. Many of the problems with which women are suffering today are due to the fact that most of them are physically, psychologically and even economically dependent on men. This weakness of women is often taken undue advantage by men and in several ways they are exploited. It is in this context, many right thinking people have felt that the hands of women are to be strengthened so that they will be able to face the challenges that come across their way. This idea has given rise to the concept of *"empowerment of women"*.

The Concept of "Empowerment of Women"

The term *'empowerment of women'* has become popular especially after 1980s. It refers to the process of strengthening the hands of women who have been suffering from various disabilities, inequalities and gender discrimination.

- *The term "empowerment of women" refers to the process of providing power to woman to become free from the control of others, that is, to assume power to control her own life and to determine her own conditions.*
- *The term of "empowerment of women" could also be understood as the process of providing equal rights, opportunities, responsibilities and power positions to women so that they are able to play a role on par with men in society.*

The Background of the Emergence of the Concept

Historically, women have been regarded as constituting a weaker section. They have often been treated as *"second grade citizens"*. They have been pictured and presented as *"home - makers"* who are good in household chores. This image of women has been changing every where. Extension of the voting right to women in Britain and America in the beginning of the 20th century brought about a series of changes in the status of women especially in the western world. Many of their disabilities and inequalities came to an end in due course. The quest for equality was pursued consistently by the western women.

On the contrary, women of Asia and Africa were not able to secure equal status and opportunities even after 1950s. Women continued to suffer from one or the other kind of disability. Their exploitation was also continued. They were given unequal treatment on the basis of sex. This development was termed as *"gender discrimination"*. The United Nations also through its various meetings and pronouncements was giving call to its member-nations to remove as early as possible, the ugly practice of *"gender discrimination"*.

Shift in the Emphasis From Women's *"Welfare"* to *"Development"*

Due to the efforts of the UNO, the issue of empowerment of women became an international issue. The UN declared the **Year *1975 as the International Women's Year.*** Further, the U.N. Declaration of 1975 compelled the national governments *to shift their emphasis on women's programmes from welfare to development.* The Declaration prescribed for the all-round development of women.

Women's World Congress Insistence on Empowerment of Women

In continuation of the UN Declaration of 1975, the ***"Third Women's World Congress"*** [or Conference] was held at **Nairobi** [Kenya] in 1985. A document released on this occasion recommended efforts towards empowerment of women. *"In this document, the question of women's political participation was highlighted and it was recommended that 35% of the total seats should be reserved for women. It was also recommended that some posts should be reserved for women at the block and village level bureaucracy. On the economic front, a number of income generating schemes were introduced for women. In addition to that, provisions were also made to certain proportion of women as beneficiaries in all the developmental schemes like the IRDP, JRY, TRYCEM, and so on."*[21]

The Fourth World Conference on Women was held in **Beijing** [China] in 1995 in which representatives from 189 nations including India had taken part. The Conference recognised some 12 serious areas such as - *women and poverty, health, economic position, media and rights, environment, girl child, human rights and women, institutional arrangement for women's development, women in decision - taking process, education and training for job,* etc. in order to strengthen women. The Conference unanimously passed a resolution on *"gender equality"*.

• ***Special Session of the United Nations General Assembly*** was also convened in the year 2000 in New York to assess the progress of the programmes held in the direction of establishing gender equality. The topic of the conference was *"Women 2000 : Equality, Development and Peace for the 21st Century."* Only the NGOs, [Non-Governmental Organisations] had to take part in it. The basic purpose of the conference was to convince the member nations regarding the need for empowering women and to take appropriate steps in that direction.

The Indian Response Towards the Conference Issue

On the basis of the proceedings of the world conference on women, the Government of India prepared a *National Document* concerning the development of women. The document lays down various strategies for women's development. The Government also declared the year ***2001 as the "Year of Women's Empowerment".***

STRATEGIES FOR WOMEN'S DEVELOPMENT

The *national document* which the Government of India had prepared with the intention of promoting women's development, highlights the importance of three strategies which are mentioned below.

(i) Obtaining Greater Political Participation of Women **:** The document recommends that 33% of the seats should be reserved for women in order to get the effective participation of women in politics. It was also recommended that some power positions [posts] should be reserved for women at the block and village level bureaucracy.

(ii) Income Generating Schemes for Women **:** On the economic front, a number of income-generating schemes were to be introduced to women as per the provisions of this document. It was insisted that sufficient provisions were to be made in all the rural developmental programmes [such as, for example, IRDP: *Integrated Rural Developmental Programme;* JRY : *Jawahar Rozgar Yojana;* TRYSEM : *Training of Rural Youth and Self-Employment,* etc.] enabling a certain proportion of women to become their beneficiaries.

(iii) Increasing Female Literacy Level **:** On the social front, it was recommended to obtain proper co-ordination between government and non-governmental institutions to increase

21. **S.L. Doshi** and **P.C. Jain** in *"Rural Sociology."* Page - 341.

considerably the literacy level of women. It was hoped that with the help of literacy, women would be able to lead a life of self-reliance.

Empowerment of Women and "The 73 Constitution Amendment Act, 1993"

'The 73 Constitution Amendment Act 1993' was undertaken mainly to give constitutional status to the *"The Panchayat Raj System"* and to introduce it in India on a uniform basis. Another purpose behind the Act was *to assure the empowerment of women.*

The framers of the *73rd Constitution Amendment Act believed that "social and economic status of women could not be improved much without political power. The females in the village need to be given some political power. They should have their share in the decisions made about the development of their villages. The new Panchayat Raj is a part of the effort to empower women at least at the village level"*[22]

One-Third Reservation of Seats For Women

The 73rd Constitution Amendment Act has made an effort to give some special powers to women in all the three tiers of *Panchayat Raj*. As per this Act, 1/3 of the seats are reserved for women in addition to the reservation for SCs and STs. It was, indeed, a very bold step towards the empowerment of women. Rural women who have been working as farm labourers, cleaning the utensils, washing clothes, sweeping the court-yard, fetching drinking water from a distance, cooking food and serving the same to all, labouring in the fields, etc., are now able to exercise some amount of political power on par with men. They now have the role to play in matters of decision making that affect village affairs. *"The provisions of Act for the women are in no way less than a revolution."* [**Doshi** and **Jain**]

A Brief Assessment of 73rd Constitution Amendment Act

The 73rd Constitution Amendment Act came into force in April 1993. The Act, however, has not brought about miraculous changes as expected. Though it has created some awareness among women it suffers from many drawbacks. Some of them may be noted as below.

1. ***Illiteracy*** **:** Since female literacy rate is very poor in our villages, female members at different tiers of *Panchayat Raj* are not able to assert themselves. On the contrary, they are forced to work according to the wishes of the male members.
2. ***Non-Availability of Women*** **:** It is very difficult to find out adequate number of females to work as members of the *Panchayat Raj* Committee. Either we will have to make a compromise with less qualified and totally ignorant women or be content with inadequate number of women.
3. ***Corrupt Leadership and Bureaucracy*** **:** Our leadership is highly selfish and our bureaucracy is totally corrupt. In this situation, it is very difficult for the women to work and to achieve progress.
4. ***Bias Towards Elites and Middle Class*** **:** The Act focuses its attention on women and weaker sections of the society no doubt. Women who are better off in one way or another alone can take the proper benefit of this Act. It means the creamy layer of the disadvantaged groups would corner most of the benefits of the Act. As a result, the weakest of the weak, the poorest of the poor would continue to suffer in the pattern of the *Panchayat Raj* also.

---

22. **S.L. Doshi** and **P.O. Jain** in their *"Rural Sociology"*, - Page : 338.

Factors Facilitating Empowerment of Women

A big nation like India which consists of more than 50 crores women cannot afford to ignore the role of women in the national development. It is in this demographic context also, the process of empowerment of women has assumed importance.

Women cannot be empowered in a magical manner. It is not an automatic or a spontaneous process but requires deliberate and consistent efforts. It is through the combined and co-ordinated efforts of the Government, people and the women, the task can be fulfilled. Women cannot be effectively empowered by statutory provisions or governmental efforts alone. *"Women are empowered through -- women emancipation movement, education, communication, media, political parties and general awakening."* - [**Doshi** and **Jain**]

Various socio-economic and political factors facilitate the empowerment of women. Among them the following may be noted.

1. ***Acknowledging Women's Rights*** : Society should recognise that like men, women are also entitled to equal rights.
2. ***Freedom to Take Decisions and Make Choices*** : Women should have freedom to decide whether to marry or not to marry; and after marriage, the freedom to decide as to how many children that they should have, and so on.
3. ***Access to Education and Employment*** : Women can become stronger only with educational and economic power. Mere expectations cannot help. Conditions must be created in such a way that women get easy access to education and later on become employed. Sufficient economic freedom is a must for women to lessen their dependence on men.
4. ***Opportunities for Political Participation*** : If women's voice is to carry more weight they must be given political power. They must be free to take part in the administrative process.

The process of empowerment of women belonging to weaker sections will definitely have multiplying effects on society. ***For example,*** when a woman in the village gets elected as member of the Gram Panchayat Samithi, she becomes automatically powerful in the family, kin group and village. She is listened to by the people for she has the power to take a decision and she can do and undo certain things in the village, and so on. ***For example,*** she can expand the facilities of the village school including toilet rooms for school children, and raise it to higher standard; she can get a borewell and a water tank for the village, she may fetch for the village a community hall, a reading room, and so on. She is not, of course, everything. But by becoming the member of the *Gram Samithi,* she can definitely influence the decisions of the *Samithi.*

REASONS BEHIND THE NEED FOR EMPOWERMENT

In a nation like India, the need for the empowerment of women is justified on account of the factors like the following.

1. Education or Literacy

Among other countries of the world, India has the highest number of illiterate people. As per the 2011 Census report, 82.14% men are literate while only 65.46% women are found to be so. In the rural areas, the level of illiteracy is still higher. [*For example,* the female literacy rate in rural Rajasthan was only 12%, while it stood at still a lower level, that is 10%, in rural Bihar in 1991.] As per 2011 cemsus, out of the total rural female population of about 405.17 million, only 204.97 million [around 50%] women are literate and the remaining 200.19 million women are still found to be illiterate. At the same time, in the urban area, out of the female population of 181.29 million, only 52.02 million are found to be illitrate. Illiteracy is the biggest weakness of women. *Giving them education means empowering them to enjoy the benefits of development* which in turn enables them to contribute further to the national progress.

2. Health Problem of Women

Poor health on the part of women has also added to their weakness. Women consume less food and work more. They are shy of complaining about their ill health. They prefer to suffer silently than to approach a medical practitioner for obtaining medical assistance. This is mostly true in the case of a large majority of rural women. Surveys and studies have revealed that traditional importance shown towards the male children is also one of the reasons for neglecting the health of female children. Women are found to be maintaining relatively good health in the regions wherever the rate of female literacy is higher. Kerala provides here the best example. *Thus, from the health point of view also, womenfolk who are found to be weaker, are to be made stronger.*

3. Economic Exigencies of Women

Indian women are economically weak in two respects : (i) The per capita income of the Indians is quite low and a large number of families are under the tight grip of poverty. This economic distress naturally affects women who are a part and parcel of the family; (ii) Since property laws in this country were not in favour of women for hundreds of years, women do not seem to be possessing any property of their own. Even the working women who get some income give it to the custody of their menfolk who take decisions to spend it. Economic dependence of women on men still continues. This dependence weakens them economically. *Thus, women require economic power to stand on their own legs on par with men.*

4. Atrocities Against Women

Women constitute the weaker sex. This fact is also borne by the number of crimes and atrocities committed against them. There are cases of rape, kidnapping of girls, dowry harassments, molestation, sexual harassments, abuse of women, incestuous sex relations and so on. Women in all walks of life are discriminated against by men. They become the victims of atrocities in a number of ways. *They require empowerment of all kinds in order to protect themselves against all types of atrocities and to preserve their purity and dignity.*

HUMAN RIGHTS AND WOMEN

The Concept of Human Rights

The concept of "human rights" did not exist the way it does, until recently. The *"human rights"* refer to all those rights which are common to all human beings. These rights were slowly incorporated into society, in different parts of the world. In the West, the British political thinker **John Locke** gave birth to the concept of *"human rights"* in the 17th century in his book *"The Second Treatise of the Government"*. But the idea of human rights assumed the form of an international movement only in the second half of the 20th century. The *'human rights movement'* gained momentum in the decades of 1950, 1960 and 1970. It was during this period that human rights became a major political issue. The UNO took the issue of *"human rights"* as an article of faith and insisted on all its member countries to make provision for human rights in their respective territories. The UN General Assembly adopted the *Universal Declaration of Human Rights* [UDHR] a statement of universal goals concerning human rights and freedom. Although it is not legally binding, its content has been incorporated into many national constitutions including ours. People are slowly becoming aware of the human rights. Hence, they have increasingly refused to accept regimes that do not provide for the free exercise of human rights.

Meaning and Definition of Human Rights

The concept of 'human rights' does not have one single explanation or definition for it includes a multiplicity of factors that are interlinked. For the purpose of our study, we may consider a few of the simple definitions of the concept.

- *"Human rights are literally the rights that one has simply because one is a human being".* - **Jack Donnelly**, *a leading human rights activist.*
- *"Human rights are those basic rights which everyone inherits the moment one is conceived in the mother's womb."*
- In simple words, it could be said that *"human rights are those basic standards without which men cannot live in dignity".*

The Main Human Rights

The above definitions or explanations make it clear that human rights are a part and parcel of human life. People, thus, cannot lose their human rights, no matter what they do. These rights constitute the basic requirements of dignified life. Hence, they form a basic framework for the administration of society and political organisation. All civilised societies are expected to protect and ensure these human rights.

- ***Human rights include the following rights -***
  - the right to life
  - the right to food
  - the right to shelter and necessities
  - the right to health
  - the right to education
  - the right to dignity and liberty, and
  - the right to be free.

Main Characteristics of the 'Human Rights'

The 'human rights' mentioned above reveal certain characteristics which may be mentioned below :

1. Human rights are **natural** rights that all human beings possess simply by virtue of being human.
2. Human rights are held by all persons **equally** and **universally.**
3. Human rights are **irrevocable** - they cannot be revoked or suspended for political expediency.
4. Human rights are **inalienable** - one cannot lose these rights any more than one can cease being a human being.
5. Human rights are **indivisible** - one cannot be denied a right because it is *'less important'* or *'non-essential'.*
6. Human rights are **interdependent** - all human rights are part of a complementary framework. ***For example,*** the ability to participate in government is directly affected by the right to express, to get some education, and even to obtain the necessities of life.

Human Rights and Women

"Human rights" - as the very term indicates represent the rights of all human beings of both the sex, men and women. Individuals of both the sex are born with these rights. Human rights are God-given or Nature-given rights. Both men and women have equal access to these rights. No discrimination is allowed or imposed in the exercise of these rights.

It is a fact of history that women have been denied equal rights for centuries. The *"philosophy of human rights"* became popular only during the second half of the 20th century and the issue of *"gender equality"* and *"equal rights"* for women assumed importance only after 1970's.[23]

Women's Rights and the Declaration of Human Rights

The *"Universal Declaration of Human Rights"* by the UNO on 10th December 1948 both directly and indirectly influenced its member nations to extend these rights to women also. India which joined the UNO after its independence paid sufficient importance to the human rights by incorporating many of these in its constitution. India which adopted a Constitution of its own in 1949 contains several Articles mandating equality and non-discrimination on the ground of sex.

RIGHTS AND PROTECTION GIVEN TO WOMEN BY THE CONSTITUTION OF INDIA

The Constitution of India in its attempts to provide equal rights and opportunities to women, and to ensure protection and justice has made the following provisions.

1. ***Article - 14:*** Constitution assures equality to all its citizens including women.
2. ***Article - 15(1):*** Ensures that no discrimination be made against its citizens on the basis of caste, class, creed, race, sex, place of birth or region.
3. ***Article 15 (2):*** Does not deny or impose sanctions or conditions on its citizens to make use of any public place or institutions on the basis of sex, race, caste, religion, etc.
4. ***Article - 15(3):*** Recommends the State to make certain special arrangements in order to provide protection to women and children and to promote their welfare.
5. ***Article - 16:*** No discrimination be made by the State against its citizens including women while providing jobs.
6. ***Article 39(a):*** To pursue a policy of providing the minimum necessities of life to the citizen without discriminating between men and women.
7. Fixing "equal remuneration for equal work" without discriminating between men and women.
8. ***Article - 42:*** To provide human conditions for the citizens to fulfil their occupational obligations. The state shall take it as its responsibility to provide maternity benefits for its women employees.
9. ***Article 51 (A) and (e):*** Promoting harmony and fraternity among people and doing away with all the humiliating customs in respect of women.
10. ***Article - 243 D (3) 1/3 Reservation For Women in the Panchayats*** **:** Reserving not less than 1/3 of the total number of seats for women in the Panchayats [including the women belonging to the SCs and STs] for which direct elections are held. These reserved seats in the range of the Panchayats are to be kept on rotation basis.
11. ***Article 243 D (4) 1/3 of Reservation for women in the Presidential Posts of the Panchayats*** **:** Reserving not less than 1/3 of the total number of the presidential posts at all the levels of the Panchayat [Gram Panchayat, Thaluk Panchayat and Zilla Panchayat] systems.
12. ***Article 243 (T) 3 1/3 of the Reservation for Women in the Municipalities*** **:** Reserving not less than 1/3 of the total number of seats for women in the town municipalities [including the women belonging to the SCs and STs] for which direct elections are held. These reserved seats in the range of the town municipalities are to be kept on rotation basis.

23. However, the *"Women's Suffrage Movement"* demanding the right to vote during the first phase of the 20th century, proved to be the beginning of women's rights as "human rights".

13. ***Reservation for Women in the Presidential Posts of the Town Municipalities*** **:** While reserving the presidential posts of the town municipalities for women and also for the SCs and the STs, the relevant law framed by the state legislative body is to be followed.

STRATEGIES FOR THE PROTECTION OF WOMEN'S RIGHTS AND REHABILITATION OF WOMEN

1. Laws Pertaining to Women OR Legislative Measures Safe -guarding Women's Interests

Independent Indian Government has undertaken a number of legislative measures with a view to promote the welfare of women and to safeguard their interests. In tune with various provisions of the Constitution, the State has enacted various legislations to protect women against social discrimination, violence and atrocities and also to prevent social evils like child marriages, dowry, rape, practice of *sati*, etc. Some such Acts or legislations are mentioned below.

Some of the legislations which were undertaken with more or less the same intentions during the British period, were also retained, and they are still in force. A list of both the types of these legislations is given below.

- **Social Legislations Introduced During the British Rule**

1. The Hindu Widow Remarriage Act, 1856 **:** This legislation was complementary to the previous social legislation, the first of its kind, i.e, ***'The Prevention of Sati Act of 1829'***. Though widows were saved from the jaws of death they were subject to exploitation and humiliation. To remove the deplorable condition of the Hindu widows, a leading social reformer of the day, **Pandit Ishwara Chandra Vidya Sagar,** brought pressure on the British Govt. to make legal provision for widow marriages. T*he Hindu Widow Remarriage Act of 1856* was hence passed. It removes restrictions imposed on the remarriage of widows.

2. The Indian Divorce Act, 1869 lays down the conditions under which Christians can obtain or seek divorce through the court. It also deals with the dissolution of the marriage declaring the marriage as null and void on the specific grounds. It provides for judicial separation, protection to the spouses and restitution of conjugal rights.

3. The Indian Christian Marriage Act 1872 **:** This legislation [including its Amendments up to 1928] covers various aspects of Christian marriage. *The legislation strictly prohibits the practice of polygamy and polyandry among them and prescribes strict monogamy.* Several aspects such as – who should perform marriage, the place where it is to be performed [in which church], the time of performance, the relative age of the boy and the girl concerned, etc., are all dealt with by this legislation.

4. The Child Marriage Restraint Act 1929 **:** This Act came into force on April 1, 1930. The Act prohibited the marriage of a child. According to this Act, marriage of boys under 18 and girls under 14 years of age was an offence. In its amended version, the age at marriage was fixed at **21** for boys and **18** for girls.

5. The Parsi Marriage and Divorce Act, 1936 **:** This is an Act which governs the marriage and divorce that take place among the Parsis. It was amended and expanded in 1988 and it is now almost equal to the Hindu Marriage Act, 1955.

6. The Dissolution of Muslim Marriage Act, 1939 entitles a married Muslim woman to seek dissolution of her marriage on some specific grounds. [*For example,* whereabouts of husband not known for 4 years, husband's imprisonment for 7 years; husband's impotency, cruelty on the part of the husband, husband's insanity for at least 2 years, failure to provide for maintenance for more than 2 years, in case the marriage is thrusted on her before she attained the 15th year; etc.] Prior to this Act, giving divorce was only the privilege of the husband.

- **Legislations Undertaken After Independence**

1. ***The Special Marriage Act, 1954*** which provides rights to women on par with men for inter-caste marriage, love marriage and registered marriage. The Act has also fixed the minimum age of marriage at **21** for males and **18** for females.
2. ***The Hindu Marriage Act, 1955*** which prohibits polygyny, polyandry and child marriage also concedes equal rights to women to divorce and to remarry. The main provisions of this Act are mentioned below.

   (i) This Act gives permission for intercaste and inter-religious marriages; (ii) It provides for equality of sex; (iii) It provides equal rights for men and women in marriage, divorce or separation; (iv) Its 1986 amendment permits divorce on the ground of incompatibility and mutual consent; (v) During judicial separation and after divorce, both husband and wife have the right to claim maintenance allowance.
3. ***The Hindu Succession Act, 1956*** according to which not only a daughter is given a right in her father's property equal to her brothers, but a widow also gets a share in her deceased husband's property equal to her sons and daughters.
4. ***The Hindu Adoption and Maintenance Act, 1956*** which gives a childless woman the right to adopt a child and to claim maintenance from the husband if she is divorced by him.
5. ***The Suppression of Immoral Traffic of Women and Girls Act, [SITA] 1956*** which gives protection to women from being kidnapped and or compelled to become prostitutes.

- The above Act was amended and changed into the ***"Prevention of Immoral Traffic in Persons Act"*** [PITA] in 1986. The main purpose of the Act was to broaden the definition of immoral trafficking to include any person, i.e., male children and men in addition to women and girls, offering sexual services. The other main thrust of the amendment is to enhance punishments for prostitutes and brothel keepers and others connected with the trade except the male clients and create new categories of offences.[24]

6. ***The Maternity Benefit Act, 1961*** which gives maternity benefits such as two months leave with salary to the married women workers in the organised sector.
7. ***The Dowry Prohibition Act, 1961*** which declares the taking of dowry an unlawful activity and thereby prevents the exploitation of women.[25]

   The above Act was amended in 1984 and also again in 1986 and it now reads as - ***Dowry Prohibition Amendment Act, 1984.***
8. ***The Medical Termination of Pregnancy Act, 1971*** which legalises abortion conceding the right of a woman to go for abortion on the ground of physical and mental health.

---

24. ***This amended version of the Act includes three important things*** : (i) Police raids [without warrants] can take place to any brothel home or place of prostitution only with the assistance of at least two female police officers. (ii) Interrogation can be done only by women police officers or in the presence of a female member of a recognised welfare institution. These two clauses are added to maintain the dignity of the prostitute as a woman. (iii) The Act also incorporates a new clause concerning rehabilitation of prostitutes.
25. The focus of the amendments in the Dowry Prohibition Act, 1961 was three fold : (i) Its main focus was to make punishments for both givers and takers of dowry, more stringent, (ii) It intended to widen the definition of dowry, so as to include 'costly gifts' demanded at the time of marriage and such other things, (iii) The third focus is to extend woman's control over dowry items - This Act is, however, regarded as the one which has lot of inherent contradictions.

9. ***Prenatal Diagnostic Techniques Regulation and Prevention of Misuse Act, 1994*** **:** This Act was specially designed to prevent selective foeticide [that is, removing unwanted girl child] under the pretext of saving health.
10. ***The Equal Remuneration Act, 1976,*** which removes wage discrimination between male and female workers.
11. ***The Factories Amendment Act, 1976*** which includes provisions dealing with working laws, weekly rest, standards of cleanliness, ventilation, temperature, first-aid facilities, rest rooms etc. The legislation also provides for establishing of creches for children [if the factory employs 30 or more women]; separate toilets for females and lays down a maximum of 9 hours of work a day for women and no employment of women during night, that is, between 10-00 P.M. and 5-00 A.M.
12. ***The Criminal Law Amendment Act, 1983*** which seeks to stop various types of crimes against women.
13. ***The Family Court Act, 1984,*** which seeks to provide justice to women who get involved in family disputes.
14. ***The Indecent Representation of Women [Prohibition] Act, 1986*** prevents the media from misrepresenting the women. Any attempt to degrade and discredit women, insult and humiliate them, assassinate the character of women, and present them in an indecent manner is declared punishable. The provisions of this Act are applicable to all the means of the mass media and also to advertisements, books, handbills, posters, etc. Violation of this Act is liable for punishment, which amounts to 2000 ₹ fine and 2 years imprisonment.[26]
15. ***Commission of Sati [Prevention] Act, 1987*** **:** During the British rule itself this inhuman practice was declared unlawful as per ***The Sati Prevention Act, 1829.*** Some reported instances of the practice of *'Sati'* that took place after independence [i.e., in 1986] compelled the Central Government to make the Act more stringent by giving a new shape to it in the form of ***Commission of Sati [Prevention] Act, 1987.***[27]
16. ***Muslim Women's Protection of Rights on Divorce Act 1986 and Iddat*** **:** Provides the right for a divorced Muslim wife to demand from her husband her maintenance during the Iddat [that is, the waiting period of three months.]
17. ***The National Commission for Women Act, 1990*** **:** As per the provisions of this Act, *"The National Commission for Women"* was set up on 31st Jan 1992 to ensure better legal protection for women.

---

26. Though the law on obscenity already existed in the *Indian Penal Code*, a need was felt to specifically prohibit obscene representation of women as sexual objects for commercial gain in advertisements, posters and in other media. Indecent representation of women has been defined to mean *"the depiction in any manner of the figure of a woman, her form or body or any part thereof, in such a way as to have the effect of being indecent or derogatory to, or denigrating women, or is likely to deprave, corrupt or injure the morality or morals."* - as quoted by **Sadhana Arya** in *"Women Gender Equality and the State"* - 2000, Page : 237. - ***Publisher*** : Deep and Deep Publications Pvt. Ltd., New Delhi.

27. The public burning of **Roopa Kanwar** on Sept 4, 1987, termed as *"sati"* and state-response to the incidence opened up this issue of the practice of 'sati' for further discussion. The state of Rajasthan quickly responded to the incident. In October 1987, *The Rajasthan Sati [Prevention] Ordinance* was passed which was followed by a Central legislation in Jan. 1988. *The Commission of Sati [Prevention] Act, 1988* was passed through both the houses of the Parliament in a hurried manner. The Act states that - *"Sati or the burning or burying alive of widows is revolting to the feelings of human nature and is nowhere enjoined by any of the religions of India as an imperative duty."* - **Sadhana Arya** in *"Women, Gender, Equality and the State"*. Page : 240. The state's hesitation in calling 'sati' an act of murder, because of the supposed religious sanction behind it, - has been criticised by the radicals.

III Legal Protection to Women Through THE INDIAN PENAL CODE [IPC]

Indian Penal Code [IPC] also gives protection to women especially when crimes are committed against them.

- ***The seven crimes under the IPC are** : rape, kidnapping and abduction, homicide for dowry, torture, [physical and mental], molestation, eve-teasing; and importation of girls up to 21 years of age.*
- ***Four crimes under the local and special laws are** : commission of sati, dowry prohibition, immoral traffic, and indecent representation of women.*

Reported cases of crimes identified under the IPC are taken up for giving justice to women. It is said that as many as 80,000 cases of crimes against women under the IPC, are being recorded every year. Some sections of the IPC deal with such specific cases of crimes against women. ***Examples*:**

1. ***Kidnapping and Abduction of Women*** : Cases of this kind are tackled according to ***Sections 363 - 373 IPC***
2. ***Rape*** : Instances of rape are dealt with under ***Section - 376, IPC.***
3. ***Molestation*** attempts are handled as per ***IPC Section - 354.***
4. **Torture, Both Mental and Physical** : Complaints of this nature are dealt with under ***Section - 498 - A IPC.***
5. ***Sexual Harassment*** of women of any sort is taken up as per ***Section - 509 IPC***.
6. ***Homicide for Dowry, Dowry Deaths or Their Attempts*** : Complaints of this kind are taken up seriously as per ***IPC Sections 302/304 B.***[28]

2. National Commission for Women [NCW]

The Central Government established as per the provisions of the National Commission for Women Act, 1990 statutory body, namely; *"National Commission for Women"* [NCW] in 1992. Its main purpose is to protect the rights and interests of women and to deal with matters relating to the constitutional and legal safeguards provided for women. In fact, the *Committee on the Status of Women in India* [C.S.W.I.] had recommended nearly two decades prior to that the necessity of setting up such a commission to supervise the functions of the Government aimed at the redressal of the grievances of women. The committee also felt that such a Commission would help to accelerate the socio-economic and educational development of women.

- **The Structure of the Commission**

The Commission for women has a woman Chairman, **5** members, and a Member Secretary of IAS cadre, all nominated by the Central Government. It is mandatory that out of these 5 nominated members one should be from the S.C. and the OBC communities. The tenure of office of all these nominated members is **3** years. **Smt. Jayanthi Patnayak** had functioned as its first president [1992 - 1995] and **Smt. Lalitha Kumaramangalam** is its present (2014) national level president.

- **State Level Women's Commissions**

In addition to the NCW, several states of India also established ***State Women's Commission*** [SWC]. By 2001, as many as **17** states had their own SWCs. The Karnataka

28. ***Amendment made to IPC Section 304 B in 1986*** : It now reads as - ***Section 304B - Dowry Death*** : Where the death of a woman is caused by any burns or bodily injury or occurs otherwise under normal circumstances within seven years of her marriage and it is shown that soon before her death she was subjected to cruelty or harassment by her husband for or in connection with any demand for dowry, such death shall be called "dowry death" and such husband or relative shall be deemed to have caused her death.

The offence is punishable with a minimum of seven years and a maximum of life-imprisonment. The presumption of guilt is on the accused and he would have to prove that he is innocent.

Government established its first *"State Level Women's Commission"* in Aug 1996 and **Smt. M. Prabhavathi** became its first president and **Smt. Manjula Manasa** is its present (2014) president.

Functions of the Women's Commission

(i) The basic task of this Commission is to protect the rights of women and to promote their interests.

(ii) Commission continues to pursue its mandatory activities, namely, review of legislations, interventions in specific individual complaints of atrocities and remedial action to safeguard the interests of women.

(iii) The Commission has accorded highest priority to securing speedy justice to women.

(iv) Another main function of these Commissions [State as well as National level commission] is to inquire into the *"unfair practices"* meted out to women which includes *"mental and physical torture"*.

(v) Its other functions include studying inadequacies in laws, monitoring enforcement of laws, inspecting prisons, police stations, lock-ups, refuges for women victims of violence, etc.

(vi) It makes recommendations for prosecution in individual cases.

(vii) It probes into the alleged cases of gender disparity and if required, provides financial help to fight out litigations on behalf of women.

(viii) It submits reports regularly to the government regarding the conditions of women in general, and their problems and grievances in particular. These reports are placed before both the houses of the parliament along with the recommendations.

NCW in the Action Front

• ***The Commission Receives Complaints about Various Issues Affecting Women*** **:** The NCW has been receiving complaints relating to issues such as - domestic violence, harassment, dowry torture, desertion, bigamy, rape, refusal to register FIR, cruelty by husband, deprivation, gender discrimination and sexual harassment at workplace, etc. It takes necessary steps in these matters to protect women's interests and provide justice to them.

• ***Expediting Investigations*** **:** NCW tackles the problems by ensuring that investigations by the police are expedited and monitored

• ***Providing Counselling Service*** **:** Due to the Commission's mediatory role, family disputes are resolved or compromised through counselling.

• ***Institutes Inquiry Committees*** **:** For various crimes of serious nature, the Commission constitutes Inquiry Committee which makes spot enquiries, examines various witnesses, collects evidence, and submits the report with recommendations. The implementation of the report is monitored by the NCW.

• ***Conducts Seminars, Workshops, etc.*** **:** The Commission conducts seminars, workshops and conferences and also sponsors such events by providing financial assistance to research organisations and the NGOs. The seminar and workshop topics already covered include - violence against women, sexual harassment at workplace, women in agriculture and *Panchayat Raj* sector, educational, health and employment aspects of women, women in detention, custodial justice to women, etc.

• ***The Commission Institutes Studies Relating to Various Issues*** **:** NCW has conducted special studies on issues related to women. ***Examples*** **:** Women labour under contract, divorced women, gender bias in judicial decisions and family courts, gender component in various commissions' reports on women, *Panchayat Raj* in action, women's access to health and education in slums, violence against women, mentally disabled women, credit needs of women, socio-economic development of SC women, women of weaker section, and so on. These studies are of great help in the formulation of NCW's policies for recommendations.

• ***Library, Books and Publications*** : The NCW has started its own library in 1994 which has a collection of nearly 2300 books covering different issues relating to women's advancement. The library has a good number of reference books also. The NCW makes its own publications from time to time and sponsors research studies on various aspects concerning women issues. The NCW has so far brought out nearly 100 publications both in English and Hindi.

• ***Visiting States*** : The Commission visits different states to evaluate the progress of development of women. It has already visited and evaluated the position of women in states such as Tamil Nadu, A.P., U.P., M.P., Orissa, Rajasthan, Sikkim, Assam, Tripura and Manipura.

• ***Interaction With the Media*** : The Commission interacts with the NGOs and the State Commissions for ensuring gender equality and empowerment of women. The Commission also maintains interaction with the media, social activists and university level professors and scholars to suggest ways of protecting women's interests and ensuring proper means of representation to women in all spheres.

3. Legal Assistance to Assure Justice to Women

The government established a special ***'Cell'*** [attached to labour department] in 1976 with a view to provide due assistance to women in distress. The responsibility of this cell is entrusted to the *'Commissioner of Police'*. The Central Government has also established a separate ministry with a cabinet rank to deal with the issues and problems concerned with women. To assist judiciary in its task of ensuring judicial protection to women *"social vigilance groups"* are established. Family Courts established according to *"the Family Court Act, 1984"*, are giving legal protection to women. The Social Welfare Department has established *"Women's Bureau"* in order to look into the problems of women and to find solutions for the same.

4. Relief and Rehabilitation to SC and ST Women Subjected to Atrocities

As per ***The Scheduled Castes and Scheduled Tribes [Prevention of Atrocities] Rules, 1989,*** compensation is to be paid to members of those communities who have suffered abuses. This compensation includes ₹ 50,000, to a woman who has had her modesty "outraged" or been sexually exploited, and ₹ **2 lakh** to a woman who has been raped. But it has been observed that proper economic and social rehabilitative facilities are not provided to the victims though such legal provisions are there.

5. Government's Concern for Women Through the Observance of Women's Day Programmes

The Government's concern for women has been expressed by means of its observance of *"Women's Day Programmes". For Example* : -

(i) The *year 1975* was observed as ***"International Year of Women"*** as per the call of the UNO. From 1975 onwards, the *8th Day of March* is being observed as *"International Women's Day"*.

(ii) The year ***1990*** was observed as ***"SAARC year of the Girl Child".***

(iii) The Decade between ***1991-2000*** AD was observed as ***"The SAARC Decade of the Girl Child".***

(iv) The year ***2001*** was observed as the ***"Year of Women's Empowerment".***

6. Social and Economic Programmes For the Benefit of Women

In order to protect the social and economic interests of women, the Government has undertaken a variety of programmes among which the following may be mentioned.

a) ***Educational Development Plan for Women*** - through women study Centres, Human Resources Department, the UNICEF, NCERT, Ford Foundations, and so on.

b) ***Programmes for Improving Women's Health*** - through Indian Council of Medical Research, Ministry of Health and Family Welfare, Central Govt. Health Services Scheme, and so on.

c) ***Economic Development Programmes For Women*** - Through various schemes such as - Institute for providing vocational training for women, Women's National Training Institute, Working Women's Hostels, the National Committee for Women Welfare, Social Assistance Schemes, The Scheme of Training, - Employment Cum Production Centres, Rastriya Mahila Kosh (1992); Mahila Samriddhi Yojana, Indira Mahila Yojana (1995), Women's Development Corporation [WDC - 1986-87], Welfare and Support Services, and so on.

a) Educational Development Plan for Women

The University Grants Commission had stressed as early as in 1948 the essential need for the education of women. *The Central Education Department,* the [NCERT] *National Council of Educational Research and Training,* the [NAEP] *National Adult Education Programme* and other institutions have evinced greater interest in providing educational facilities for women.

• ***Women Study Centres*** have been established with the assistance of [UGC] University Grants Commission to study the status of women and problems and issues concerned with women.

• ***Other Institutions:*** Institutions such as - (i) **UNICEF:** *United Nations' International Children's Educational Fund;* (ii) **ICSSR:** *Indian Council of Social Science Research;* (iii) **UNESCO:** *United Nations Educational Scientific and Cultural Organisation;* (iv) **CSIR:** *Council of Scientific and Industrial Research;* (v) *Ford Foundation,* etc. have shown a special interest in studying women's problems.

b) Programmes for Improving Women's Health

Various organisations, independent surveys and studies conducted by prominent individuals and private institutions brought to the notice of the Central Government at different times between 1975-85 the urgent need for improving women's health. Various governmental agencies such as *"Indian Council of Medical Research, Ministry of Health and Family Welfare, Central Government Health Services Scheme [CGHS]* etc. have been paying much attention to promote women's health.

• ***In rural areas,*** institutional systems such as rural *Primary Health Centres* and *Family Welfare Centres* are trying to promote women's health. *World Health Organisation, World Bank* and *Ford Foundation* are also showing concern in providing medical protection to women and children.

c) Economic Development Programme for Women

The Five Year Plans launched by the Government have paid due attention to enable women to attain greater economic participation. In some of the areas such as *factories, offices, mining, clerical posts, teaching, nursing, banking, tea and coffee plantations,* etc. women employees are found in a large number. To protect the economic interests of the employed women various legislations such as *Minimum Wages Act, 1948; Equal Wages Act, 1976; the Factories Amendment Act, 1976;* etc. have been undertaken. The Karnataka and Andhra Governments have reserved some jobs for women in government sector.

• ***Employment and Training of Women*** : The *Programme of Support to Training-cum-Employment for Women* [STEP] was launched in 1987 to strengthen and improve the skills for employment opportunities for women below poverty line in traditional sectors of agriculture, small scale industries, animal husbandry, handlooms, handicrafts, cottage and village industries, sericulture, etc. where women are employed on a large scale.

The scheme of *Condensed Courses of Education and Vocational Training* [CCE&VT] for adult women started in 1958, is implemented by the ***Central Social Welfare Board.*** It aims at providing new vistas of employment through continuing education and vocational training to women and girls, particularly to school drop-outs. During the years 1997-1999, as many as 2,000 courses were sanctioned to benefit about 50,000 women and girls.

• ***Institutes for Providing Vocational Training for Women*** have been established at various places and in 1984 there were about 125 such institutes throughout the nation.

• ***Women's National Training Institute*** was started in 1977 and its regional units in places such as Bombay, Bangalore, Thiruvananthapuram, Hissar, Calcutta were also opened. *The Regional Training Institute* at Bangalore gives *"basic"* and also modern training to about 1,426 girls and part-time training to about 141 girls every year.

• ***Socio-Economic Programme*** : Under this programme, the Central Social Welfare Board gives financial assistance to the voluntary organisations for undertaking a wide variety of income-generating activities, which include the production of central components in ancillary units, handlooms, handicrafts, agro based activities such as animal husbandry, sericulture, and fisheries, and self employment ventures like vegetables or fish-vending, etc.

• ***The Dairy Scheme*** focuses exclusively on women's organisations having at least 20 women members, including *Mahila Mandals, Indira Mahila Kendras, Self Help Groups*[29] and organisations already assisted under STEP scheme. The benefits of the scheme are meant for women whose families are below the poverty line.

• ***Mahila Samriddhi Yojana*** : This scheme was launched on 2nd Oct. 1993, through a network of 1.32 lakh rural Post Offices to promote thrift among rural women and to empower them with greater control over their household sources. After the completion of 2 years of implementation of this *Yojana* it was decided to launch a new scheme which would cover approximately 885 blocks in which about 20 lakh women would be benefited.

• ***Rashtriya Mahila Kosh* [RMK]** : The national credit fund for women called *The Rashtriya Mahila Kosh* was set up in 1992-93 with a corpus fund of ₹31 crores with a major objective of meeting the credit needs of poor women, particularly in the informal sector. The Minister of State for Women and Child Development is the Chairperson of this *Kosh*. The RMK has sanctioned up to 31st March 1998, loans of ₹47.85 crores to benefit 2.50 lakh women through 256 NGOs.

• ***Working Women's Hostels*** have been established in towns and cities mainly to provide board and lodging facilities to rural women who move on to urban centres to obtain jobs. Governmental and private agencies are taking initiative in opening such hostels.

---

29. ***Stree Shakti Scheme [Self-Help Groups - SGHs] to Empower Women Economically : Karnataka Model*** : In order to empower rural women economically, the Karntaka Government [under the Chief Ministership of S.M. Krishna] launched the *'Stree Shakti Scheme'* to forge *"Self-help Groups"* among women. ***Purposes*** : (i) To strengthen the process of economic development of women. (ii) To establish at least **one lakh** SHGs during 2000-2001. (iii) To enhance financial stability in rural women by involving them in income generating activities such as producing - detergent powder, cleaning powder, bleaching powder, candle making, coirs, mat-making, toy-making, agarbatti making, etc. This scheme was intended to empower at least two million rural women in Karnataka by the end of the year 2002. These SGHs seem to be functioning comparatively well in many of the rural areas of Karnataka at present.

In some hostels, day-care centres for children of these women are also attached. During 1992-93, as many as 23 additional hostels were sanctioned to provide accommodation to 2,269 working women. This brought the total number of hostels to over 811 [by 1999] benefiting over 56,974 working women.

• ***The National Committee For Women Welfare*** is instituted for framing appropriate policies for women welfare to suit to the changing needs of time.

• ***Indira Mahila Yojana*** **[IMY] :** The *Indira Mahila Yojana* that aims at organising women at the grass root level to facilitate their participation in decision-making and empowerment, was launched on 20th August 1995, in 200 *Integrated Child Development Services* [ICDS] blocks. The strength of the scheme lies in the strength of group dynamics. The objectives of the scheme are – *awareness generation among the women from rural areas and urban slums and economic empowerment of women.*

7. The Central Social Welfare Board

The Central Social Welfare Board **[CSWB]** was set up in 1953 with the objective of promoting social welfare activities and implementing welfare programmes for women, children and the handicapped through voluntary organisations. The CSWB is unique in the sense that it was the first organisation in post independent era to achieve people's participation for implementation of welfare programmes for women and children through the Non-Government Organisations [NGOs].

The CSWB established by the *Planning Commission,* has its own women welfare programmes such as *providing housing protection to weak and helpless women, fallen women, helpless widows; creating centres of social education for women and adult education centres, condensed courses of education and vocational training courses for women and girls, awareness generation projects for rural and poor women, family counselling centres, holiday camps for children, welfare extension projects in border areas, opening centres for giving healthy entertainment to the women, giving assistance to creches and hostels for working women,* etc. The Board gives financial subsidy of ₹ 50,000/- annually to those private agencies [NGOs] which provide good service to the women. Presently, more than 18,000 NGOs are receiving financial assistance and guidance from the Board.

8. Department of Women and Child Development (1985)

The Ministry of Human Resources Development opened [in 1985] a new department under its purview namely Department of Women and Child Development with the sole purpose of assisting women and children to develop into their full potentials. This department also intends to bring proper co-ordination between the government and the NGO's which are striving to promote the development of women. This department prepared a "National Policy of the Empowerment of Women in the year 2001. The goal of this policy is to bring about the advancement, development and empowerment of women.

The major programmes of this department are -

(i) promotion and capacity building of women's Self-Help Groups,

(ii) management of institutions for *Destitute Women Crisis Centres*, [*Santhwana*], Shelter Homes, Helplines and other programmes for women who are victims of violence.

(iii) management of childcare centres.

(iv) providing scholarships for girl-students from economically and socially backward communities.

(v) Other programmes for the welfare of women and children.

9. Family Laws or Personal Laws

In India, in personal matters like marriage, divorce, inheritance and adoption, each religious community has its own laws. They are known as personal laws or family laws. They are recognized by the state. These laws are derived from the scriptures, customs, traditions and statutory codification. Thus Hindus, Muslims, Christians and Parsis have separate personal laws. In some places, the Government has set up separate family courts to deal with litigations concerning family matters. Women belonging to Hindu, Muslim, Christian, Parsis or any other community can seek justice under the provision of these laws in case of a need or in case of injustice done to them.

10. Recognition of Women's Right to Property

Owning property is very crucial to women's empowerment and hence all family laws provide property rights to women. They can buy, sell and inherit movable and immovable property just like men but the proportion of the share of property inherited depends on her religion and on her relationship with the property owner.

11. Compulsory Registration of Marriages

Karnataka state has brought in a legislation making registration of marriages compulsory. According to this law, all marriages performed by any religious community or caste has to be registered. There are registrars appointed at the taluk level to register a marriage. A simple procedure of filling a form with a photograph or proof of marriage has to be followed with payment of a small fee. This is very important as it will protect women and enable them to fight for rights within marriage.

12. Safeguards Available to Women in Criminal Law

The Indian Penal Code and other Acts, however, consider certain specific acts against women as offences punishable by law.

(a) Offences Against Marriage: A man who deceives a woman into a belief that a certain ceremony which he causes to be performed by some accomplice constitutes a valid marriage and thus entices a woman to co-habit with him will be punished under Section 493 of IPC. Maximum punishment of 10 years imprisonment can be imposed for that offence.

If a man or a woman marries a second time when his or her spouse is alive, he/she is committing an offence of bigamy. The punishment for this offence is imprisonment up to 7 years and fine. The second wife has no status in the eyes of law. She cannot claim maintenance and has no right in the husband's property. Concealing a former marriage from the person with whom a subsequent marriage is contracted is a crime under this section (Section 495). This offence is punishable for a term which may extend up to 10 years and is also liable to fine. Adultery by a married man is also a punishable offence under Section 498 IPC. The punishment for the offence is imprisonment upto a period of 2 years of fine or both.

(b) Outraging a woman's modesty (Section 354): Many girls experience sexual harassment by fellow travellers in the bus like pinching, touching her private parts, etc. This behaviour does not amount to rape. A woman need not tolerate such behaviour as this is an offence under Section 354.

Using any physical force upon a person (in this case, a woman) with the intention of causing or knowing that it will cause injury or fear, is punishable with imprisonment upto two years or fine or both. What is meant by modesty of a woman will depend upon the national, social and cultural values and customary norms. This offence is punishable.

• ***Voluntary organisation in the service of women:*** (i) *Mobile Creches* for working mother's children aged upto 12 years; (ii) *"Annapoorna"* Women's Co-operative Society to provide mid-day meal to working women; (iii) *Self-Employed Women Association,* a registered trade union to organise women rag-pickers, head-loaders, junksmith, fish vendors, bamboo-workers, beedi workers, block-printers, used garment dealers and such other women workers, has come into being to get a fair deal for women workers.

Conclusion

It is true that the Central and the State governments have undertaken various legislative and other measures for promoting the welfare of women. We cannot, however, say that the intended purpose of the Governments is fulfilled and the targeted persons have received all the benefits. The educated, middle class and upper caste women of towns and cities have taken relatively greater advantage of these measures, whereas the vast mass of uneducated, lower class and lower caste women of the rural areas are not even aware of most of these welfare measures. The deficiencies involved in these measures and the inefficient implementation of the developmental programmes by the indifferent bureaucrats have come in the way of the success of these measures. In spite of these shortcomings, the awareness of women regarding these measures is slowly growing. After the lapse of a few centuries, the society is becoming slowly aware of the historic necessity of providing women a respectable position in society and paying special attention to the problems haunting them.

Strategies of Economic Empowerment of Women : SELF-HELP GROUPS [SHGS] AND MICRO FINANCE

(A) Self-Help Groups [SHGs] and Their Role

Self-Help Groups [SHGs]

In the Indian context, self-help groups represent one of the forms of micro-finance enterprise. It is now almost universally acknowledged that self-help groups are the most effective and successful means of making the economically weaker sections of the rural society to become free from poverty and to move in the direction of self-reliance with utmost self-confidence. The successful experiments with SHGs in Bangladesh and Kenya have given wide publicity to them throughout the globe. It is for this reason, the State and the Central Governments have stressed the importance of active participation of SHGs in different developmental programmes. What then do we mean by SHGs?

Meaning of Self-Help Groups [SHGs]

- *Self-Help Group is a small local group consisting of 12-to-20 self-conscious and self-motivated members who have mutual trust among themselves decide to work together by making self-efforts for the fulfilment of their socio-economic needs on a co-operative basis.*
- A self-help group comprises of a group of micro entrepreneurs having homogeneous social and economic backgrounds coming together voluntarily to save small sums of money regularly, and mutually agreeing to contribute to a common fund and to meet their emergency needs on the basis of mutual help.

Objectives of SHGs

The main objective of SHGs is to achieve economic development in the circle of rural poor. Its aims, however can be stated in the following words.

1. Promoting economic progress of members by enabling the members to engage in income generating activities.
2. Encouraging the members to engage in economically productive activities that would fetch income and increase production.
3. Giving encouragement to members to avoid extravagance and develop the habit of saving.
4. Helping the members to become relieved of poverty.
5. To give motivation and encouragement to the members to establish small enterprises.
6. Enhancing the general knowledge and business approach of the members.
7. **Other Objectives** :
   (i) Helping members to develop self-confidence.
   (ii) To encourage members to develop collective leadership.
   (iii) To give suggestion to the members to settle misunderstandings, if arise, through mutual talks.
   (iv) To inspire members to develop community sentiment and collective spirit.
   (v) To encourage members to develop the quality of taking collective decision.
   (vi) To motivate members, especially female members, to shoulder collective responsibility in getting the things done.

Structure of the Self-Help Group

The structure of the SHG whether it is formed in the rural area or urban area remains the same. The most important aspects of the structure of the SHG are mentioned below.

1. Membership: Membership of the SHG is normally limited to 12-to-20 members. It is insisted that members must have more or less the same socio-economic background and there should be no discrimination among them based on caste, religion or political affiliations, etc. Individuals between the age of 18-to-60 are normally taken as members.

2. Bye-laws: SHG is a group formed without any formal registration but on the ground of mutual understanding. The group, however, should have a set of written byelaws indicating rules and regulations for its functioning and also regarding roles and responsibilities of members. These rules are framed with the mutual consensus of the members.

- **Bye-laws cover such matters as** - group meeting, normal time of meeting, attendance, venue, roles and responsibilities of leader, nomination and rotation of leaders, savings, credit, penalty for not attending meeting or non-payment of loan, service charges, other charges and addressing communication, etc. At the time of framing bye-laws, all the members must be present and each one be given opportunity to express his or her opinion. Selection of the leader of the group is very crucial for the success of the group actually depends much on the efficiency of leadership.

3. Group Meetings : SHG normally conducts its meeting once in a week and regular attendance of the members is insisted upon.

4. Savings and Credit : The group gives encouragemet to its members to save money. Once a SHG has accumulated sizeable amount in the form of savings for a period of about 3-6 months, the members may be allowed to avail loans against their savings for emergency.

5. Transparency in Functioning : The group is expected to function in a transparent manner. Free and frank communication helps such a transparency. The financial and non-financial transactions are to be carried on in a transparent manner so that members develop mutual trust, faith and confidence. Maintenance of books of accounts as also other records like the minutes books, attendance register, etc. are important.

6. Other Important Activities of the Group: The SHG must establish linkage with the lead bank of the area after six months of operation. Training to the members on financial mangement, book keeping, vocational training to the members on selected economic activity, exposure visits to the members for building marketing network, organising Mahila Mela for interaction of various SHGs among themselves, repayment of SHG/bank loan - are some of the important activities expected to be carried out by the groups. SHG accounts must be audited at least once in a year, and twice is more advisable.

7. Operations of SHGs : As soon as SHG is formed and a couple of group meetings are held in a systematic manner, a SHG can open a Savings Bank Account with the nearest commercial, or Regional Rural Bank or a Co-operative Bank.

Achievement and Progess of Self-Help Groups

Within the time span of 10-15 years, the SHGs have achieved tremendous success as an effective means of micro-finance enterprise. All the 563 districts in all the States and Union Territories came under this programme. As many as 560 banks including 48 commercial Banks, 196 Regional Rural Banks, 316 Co-operative Banks, and 3024 non-governmental organisations [NGOs] have joined hands in this great venture. By December 30th 2004, total number of bank-linked SHG members was 12.76 lakhs. In the same period, total amount of money given as bank loan to SHGs was ₹5038 crores.[30]

According to yet another estimate, the total number of SHGs has increased to 3.47 millions covering as many as 45.1 million houses by 2010. The most striking aspect of the development of the SHGs is, at the national level, around 90% of these are operated by women. The same trend is found in Karnataka where around 85% of these SHGs are run by women. Women-operated SHGs have been able to achieve 95% success in bank-loan repayment. Yet another achievement is found in savings. By 2010, 4.16 million SHGs, saved around 35.12 billion ₹ in banks and this amounts to, on an average, ₹ 8443/- per SHG.

By registering such an impressive success, the SHGs have proved themselves as effective means of achieving rural economic development and progress.

MICRO FINANCE

The Concept of Micro Finance

India consists of millions of poor people who are spread over the entire land. Economic development of the nation can be assured only when these poor people are given due financial support to come out of the clutches of moneylenders, to become free from all kinds of financial deathtraps, and are encouraged to develop the habit of saving and investment. "*Micro credit*" or "*micro finance*" is one of the time tested means of helping the poor to avail of the banking service.

Meaning of Micro Finance

- *Micro finance is defined as financial services such as savings account, insurance fund, and credit given to poor and low income clients so as to help them to rise their income and improve their standard of living.*
- "*Micro credit or micro finance is a novel approach to banking with the poor*".[31]
- *In simple words, it can be said that micro finance is an attempt to help the poor to make use of banking facilities or services.*

30. **Source of Statistics** : H.R.K's "*Bharatada Arthika Vyavasthe*" (2007) Page-504.
31. **Gaurav Datt** and **Ashwani Mahajan** in "*Datt and Sundharam Indian Economy*" (2012 Edition) - Page - 642.

Micro finance is a way to promote economic development, employment and growth through the support of micro-entrepreneurs and small business. Micro finance is a broad category of services which includes micro credit. Micro credit is provision of credit services to poor clients.

Speciality of Micro Finance Approach

Micro finance is a novel approach which was very successfully tried in Bangla Desh and in this bank credit is extended to the poor through *Self-Help Groups* [SHGs], *Non-Government Organisations* [NGOs], *Credit Unions,* etc. It attempts to combine lower transaction costs and high degree of repayments. This is essentially because of the involvement of potential beneficiaries of rural credit in the credit delivery system. Many of those who promote micro finance generally believe that such access will help poor people to come out of poverty. This is also a source of financial services for individual entrepreneurs and small businesses lacking access to banking and related services.

The Beginning of the Micro Finance System

Muhammad Yunus of Bangladesh, a Nobel Prize winner, introduced the concept of Micro Finance in Bangladesh in the form of **Grameena Bank.** More than **7 million** poor Bangladeshi women are enjoying the benefits of his new venture. This success has inspired the whole world. Yet another pioneer in this sector is **Akthar Hameed Khan**. One of the major rural financial institutions of India, namely; **NABARD [National Bank for Agricultural and Rural Development]** picked up this idea from Bangla Desh experiment and started the concept of micro finance in India. In this concept, there exists a link between SHGs, NGOs and Banks. The SHGs are formed and nurtured by NGOs and only after accomplishing a certain level of maturity in terms of their internal thrift and credit operations, they are entitled to seek credit from the banks. There is an involvement of the concerned NGO before and even after the SHG-Bank linkage.

The SHG-Bank linkage programme which was undertaken since 1992 in India, had financed about 22.4 lakh SHGs by 2006. It involved commercial banks, Regional Rural Banks [RRBs] and co-operative banks in its operations.

The SHG-bank linkage programme, introduced and encouraged by NABARD, is now being implemented vigorously by more than 30000 branches of commercial banks, RRBs and Co-operative Banks in over 520 districts in 30 States and Union Territories.

Main Features of Micro Finance

1. In the micro finance system, loans are given without demanding for security.
2. Loans are mainly given to those people who live *below the line of poverty* [BPL].
3. Members of Self-Help Groups are also entitled to avail of micro finance benefits.
4. Maximum limit of loan under micro finance is ₹ 25000/-.
5. The terms and conditions given to people are decided by the NGOs.

What is important here is that micro finance is a source of financial services for entrepreneurs and small businesses lacking access to banking and related services. Two types of clients are entitled to take financial services from micro finance : (i) *individual entrepreneurs and small businesses*; and (ii) *several entrepreneurs come together to apply for loans and other sevices as a group and not as individuals.*

- **Types of Needs that Compel People to go in Search of Financial Help or Loans**

Stuart Rutherford in his book "*The Poor and Their Money*" makes a reference to **4** main types of needs which are mentioned below :[32]

32. **'Life-Cycle' OR 'Life Course'** : The term '*life-cycle*' refers to the orderly progression of individuals through a series of different stages in life from birth to death - *Encyclopaedia of Anthropology* Page - 247.

(i) ***Life-Cycle Needs*** : These refer to certain life needs in which some expenses are incurred in observing certain customary practices associated with some personal events of the individual. **Example** : *Child-birth, education, marriage, homebuilding, widowhood, old age, death and funerals.*

(ii) ***Personal Emergencies*** : Some unpredictable and unforeseen events that happen in the personal life of an individual may often compel one to seek economic assistance. **Example** : *sickness, injury, unemployment. theft, accident harassment or death.*

(iii) ***Disasters*** caused by nature in the form of floods, famines, cyclones, earthquakes, forest fires, attack by wild animals, etc., and man-made events such as-wars, bulldozing of dwellings, confiscation of land by the government, or road-widening authority, etc. force individuals to seek economic help.

(iv) ***Investment Opportunities*** are positive avenues through which one can come up in life but initially require financial support. **Example** : *Expanding business, buying land or house or costly equipments including machineries, improving house, securing a job, etc.*

Types of Micro Finances

There are three major types of micro finances and they may be briefly examined here.

1. Informal Financial Service Providers

These include moneylenders, pawn brokers, savings collectors and input supply shops. Since people who live in the same locality seek to avail of the services of these people, they know each other well and understand each other's financial positions and can offer very flexible, convenient and fast services. But the problem is, they are normally costly and the choice of financial products are limited and very short-term. Informal servcies that involve savings are also risky, and many people lose their money.

2. Members - Owned Organisations

These include self-help groups, credit unions and a variety of "*financial service associations*". They are generally small and local, which means they have access to good knowledge about each other's financial positions and can offer convenience and flexibility. **Grameena Bank**, *for example*, is a member-owned organisation. They have proven very innovative, pioneering banking techniques like village banking and mobile banking that have overcome barriers to serving poor populations.

3. Formal Financial Institutions

In addition to commercial banks, these include state banks, agricultural development banks, savings banks and non-bank financial institutions.They are regulated, supervised and offer a wide range of financial sevices. The problem with these institutions is that, they have been proved to be reluctant to adopt social missions, and their costs of operation are also very high. Often,they do not deliver services to poor and remote populations.

It is possible for each of these institutional types to find solutions to micro finance problems by making appropriate regulations and supervisions. **For example**, efforts are being made to link self-help groups of commercial banks, to network member-owned organisations together to achieve economies.

PRINCIPLES OF MICRO-FINANCE

Some principles of micro-finance identified, endorsed and declared in 2004 by the institute namely **CGAP [Consultative Groups to Assist the Poor]** are mentioned below.

1. Poor people need not only loans but also savings insurance and money transfer services.
2. Micro-finance must be useful to poor households helping them to raise income, build up assets and perparing them to face external shocks.
3. Micro-finance can pay for itself.
4. Micro-finance means building permanent local institutions.
5. Micro-finance also means integrating the financial needs of poor people into a country's mainstream financial system.
6. The job or the task of government is to enable financial services and not to provide them.
7. Donor funds should complement private capital, not compete with it.
8 Micro-finance institutions should measure and disclose their performances both financially and socially.
9. There is the shortage of strong institutions and managers. Donors should focus on capacity building.

• ***Micro-Finance is not Charity*** : Micro-finance is considered as a tool or means for socio-economic development. Hence, it should be clearly distinguished from charity. Families which are resourceless or very poor, are unlikely to be able to generate the cash flow required to repay a loan. Hence, they should be the receipients of charity and not micro-finance. Others are best served by financial institutions.

- **Obstacles or Challenges to Micro-Finance Industry**

There are obstacles or challenges for building a sound commercial micro-finance industry among which the following may be noted.

1. Poor regulation and supervision of deposit-taking Micro-Finance Institutions [MFIs].
2. Limited management capacity in MFIs.
3. There are virtually limited or no MFIs that meet the needs for savings, remittances or insurance.
4. Institutional inefficiencies that lead to malfunctioning of the MFIs.
5. Inappropriate donour subsidies, and
6. Need for more dissemination or diffusion and adoption of rural, agricultural micro-finance methodologies.

- **Two Main Weaknesses of Micro-Finance**

Despite significant progress of micro-finance or micro-credit programmes in the country, its two main weaknesses seem to put hurdles on its path towards rapid growth.

a) Rate of Growth of SHG-bank Linkage is not upto Requirement : Out of an estimated 56 million poor families at the end of March 2004, only 17 million poor families [or 85 million poor or 30% of the poor families] have been covered by micro-finance schemes. Nearly 70% of poor families are yet to be covered. In other words, the SHG-banking is gaining momentum, but it has to grow still faster.

b) Lack of Interest on the Part of State Governments : At present, Andhra Pradesh accounts for **40**% of SHGs linked to the banks. The next three states namely;Tamil Nadu, Karnataka and Uttara Pradesh together account for only 30% of SHGs linked to bank credit. Thus, only **4** states in the country account for 70% of SHGs linked to bank credit and 80% of bank loans. Most of the states have not encouraged the organisation of micro-finance and promotion of SHG bank-credit link.

In fact, the **RBI** [Reserve Bank of India] has been making efforts to give encouragement to micro-finance initiatives through creating a favourable environment. Observations by economic experts have revealed that the success of SHGs in both urban and rural areas will have a positive effect on poverty alleviation.

Progress of Micro-Finance Programme

At the end of March 2007, as many as 209 million SHGs are linked with banks and 7000 NGOs are associated with the scheme. The reports revealed that by the end of March 2007.....

(a) 20 million very poor families were brought within the hold of formal banking services.
(b) More than 90% of the groups linked with banks were exclusively women groups.
(c) There was strong repayment performance at more than 95% of the loans disbursed.
(d) Disbursement of bank loans to SHGs was ₹18,040 crores in 2006-07 [whereas it was ₹ 11400 crores in the previous year].
(e) Average loan per SHG came to nearly ₹30,000/-, and
(f) Average loan per family came to ₹1770/-.

Micro-finance has been hailed as the best method of creating additional employment and removing poverty.[33]

SOME SUCCESSFUL EXAMPLES OF ECONOMIC EMPOWERMENT OF WOMEN

(a) Stree Shakthi Groups of Karnataka

Stree Shakthi Groups are formed in Karnataka at the behest of the former Chief Minister **S.M. Krishna**, at the village level to inculcate the savings habit in the women members empowering them economically.

The programme was launched during 2000-01 to establish Stree Shakthi Groups througout the state to empower rural women and make them self-reliant.

About 15 to 20 women members who are from below povertyline families, landless agricultural labourers join together to form Stree Shakthi Groups. Such groups are also formed through Anganawadi workers.

At present, there are about 1.40 lakh Stree Shakthi Groups functioning in the state and approximately 21 lakh women members are organised in this way.

Aims and Objectives of Stree Shakthi Groups

1. To strenghten the process of economic development of rural women and create a favourable environment for social change.
2. To establish self-help group based on thrift and credit principles which develops self-reliance and enable women to have greater access and control over resources.
3. To increase the income levels of rural women by engaging them in income-generating activities and creating financial stability.
4. To provide opportunities to the members of the groups to avail the benefits of other departmental schemes by converging the services of various departments and lending institutions to ensure women's access to credit financing.

Achievements in Savings and Internal Loaning

Stree Shakthi Group members have saved a huge amount of ₹1118.05 crores since their inception (2001). About 1,20,155 groups have availed bank loans to the extent of ₹ 1305.97 crores and have done internal lending of ₹3215.88 crores to take up various income generating activities.

---

33. **Source of Statistics**: "*Datt and Sundharam Indian Economy*" by Datt and Mahajan, pub. S. Chand, Delhi. (2012) Page No. -642.

(b) Shri Mahila Griha Udyog Lijjat Pappad [SMGULP]

SMGULP - popularly known as "**Lijjat**", is yet another successful story of women's venture in the direction of their economic empowerment.

Lijjat is an Indian women's co-operative enterprise involved in manufacturing of various fast moving consumer goods. The organisation's main objective is empowerment of women by providing employment opportunities.

Started in the year 1959 with an initial capital of only ₹ 80/- **Lijjat** has an annual turnover of around 6.50 billion ₹ in 2010, with ₹290 millions in exports. It provides employment to around 42,000 people. It has its headquarters at Mumbai and has 67 branches and 35 divisions all over India.

Lijjat is primarily a cottage industry and is urban by its origin; but now it has spread to rural areas also. It stands out as one of the most remarkable entrepreneurial initiatives by women contributing to female empowerment.

(c) Ela Bhatt's Dream Child - "SEWA"[Self- Employed Women's Association SEWA : Ahmedabad - 1972]

SEWA - *Self-Employed Women's Association* - signifies a good example of a women's group that has made a great contribution to the empowerment of women. It has made a successful attempt to integrate self-employed poor women with the mainstream economy through the twin strategies of *struggle* and *development*.

Self-employed women of Ahmedabad, organised and established the SEWA, that is, Self-Employed Women's Association in the year 1972, under the leadership and guidance of **Ela Bhatt**. The successful adventure of SEWA later on fetched her the famous honour of **Ramon Magasaysay Award**.

SEWA strived to create conditions of full employment and self-reliance for all its members. The concept of full employment is related to the employmnet for every single family so as to ensure food security, income security and societal security [health care, child care and shelter]. The notion self-reliance envisaged economic independence of members while simultaneously encouraging them for making their own decisions.

The SEWA has been able to secure financial support for its members in the form of micro-finance to self-employed women. In order to provide finance facility without involving any delay, ***"The Shri Mahila SEWA Sahakari Bank Ltd"*** was registered in 1974. Though in the beginning, the SEWA Bank started functioning in urban areas, it later on extended its operations to rural areas also. SEWA began its activities in rural areas in 1975.

The successful functioning of SEWA has clearly revealed that the poor women are not a burden on society. The root causes of women's plight have been - *unemployment, lack of income and economic dependency on family and community at large.* Creation of income generating opportunities is found to be an effective means of empowering women and improving their socio-economic condition in society. Their self-employed activities have tremendous potential to generate economic surplus in society. If the poor are provided with motivation and guidance and committed leadership, and are made to participate and manage a voluntary enterprise, they may be able to produce maximum surpluses.

THE POSITION AND THE PROBLEMS OF INDIAN WOMEN : FUTURE PROSPECTS

The discussion regarding the position and problems of Indian women has been there since decades. It is an acknowledged fact that though the Indian women are given importance in our modern society, their status is not equal to that of men and they are not completely free from problems with which they suffered for centuries. Indian women are not able to lead a free and independent life as their counterpart do in the West. Still it is heartening to observe that Indian women who suffered from various problems and setbacks for more than 2000 years, have been trying to come out of their traditional shells and getting themselves ready to make the best use of the opportunities offered to them.

Future Prospects

What will happen to the status and position of Indian women in the near future? Will they become free from the problems with which they suffered for centuries? Can we expect better status and brighter prospects for our women in the years to come? Will they be able to lead a free and independent life as their counterparts do in the West? Or, whether their status is going to deteriorate further in future? Will they attain equality with their menfolk? These are some of the questions currently being discussed in connection with the position and problems of Indian women. On the basis of the existing state of affairs some observations and broad generalisations could be made regarding this issue.

1. New Problems in Place of Old Ones **:** It is true that age-old problems of Indian women such as *child marriage, sati system, prohibition on widow remarriage, purdah system, devadasi system* etc. have almost disappeared or, they are on the verge of disappearance. If at all these problems have disappeared, they have done so only to give room for some other problems of modern times such as *atrocities against women, rape, dowry harassments and deaths, immoral traffic of women, oppression and exploitation of 'dalit' and minority women, torture and harassment of women undertrials, sexual harassment of employed women* etc. These problems have made it difficult for women to lead a life on par with men.

2. Continued Dominance of Male Supremacy **:** The Indian society continues to be a male dominated society. Though equality of sex has been achieved by law, it is difficult to practise socially. The belief that the biological and cultural roles of men and women are different, is very strong in India. As long as this belief persists, and the value of male dominance prevails, so long male-female equality cannot be achieved in the Indian context.

3. Regional, Caste and Class Differences **:** As **Andre Beteille** has observed that there is a close link between the problems of women on the one hand and the region, religion, caste and class to which they belong, on the other. These differences may continue in the coming years also. These differences are putting some hurdles on the way of Indian women developing some *"common interests"*.

4. Traditional Control Over Women **:** As **S.C. Dube** has pointed out there are three principal areas in which controls are traditionally exercised on Indian women:[34] (i) *Women's sexuality is controlled much more strictly than men's;* Implicit in the control of sexuality is the control over reproduction; i.e, giving birth to progeny. (ii) *There are restrictions on women's movements and contacts;* This is to prevent women from yielding to temptation and transgressing sexual norms; and to protect their resources - property, cash, jewels, labour and skills - from exploitation. (iii) *Women's resources [labour and skills] are under regulation and control.* This is to exercise control over the earnings and spendings of women.

On these three issues, modern Indian women are comparatively more free, no doubt; but they are not equal to men. Most of them do not bother about attaining equality with men in these areas.

5. Women Exploiting Women **:** In the Indian context, we also find social situations in which women themselves are exploiting women in one way or another. *Examples:*

---

34. S.C. Dube in his *"Indian Society"* - Page: 107-108.

'Gharwalis' or *'lady bosses'* in the brothel homes exploiting prostitutes, mothers-in-law harassing and torturing daughters-in-law, lady manager or officer harassing her female subordinates, etc. This situation is improving today for the educated women are becoming quite conscious of their rights.

6. Lack of Powerful Women Organisations and Movements **:** Indian women are forging ahead in the fields of education and employment. But they have not developed powerful women organisations nor movements to safeguard their interests. Neither at the national level nor at the state level, is found such a strong women's organisation. Absence of such an organisation or movement has further added to the exploitation of women.

7. Is There Not a Need for Women's Liberation Movement in India?**:** On the basis of the existing social conditions, it can be said that there is no possibility of a ***feminist movement*** or a ***women's liberation movement*** emerging out in India to assert the rights of women. Since Indian women give due importance to motherhood, rearing of children and household work which they consider as *"women's tasks";* they do not appreciate *"women's liberation movement"* of the western type which fights for equality with men in all respects. As **Romila Thapar** has observed, *"women's liberation does not have any immediate relevance to the Indian social situation."*[35]

8. No Protection to the Interests of Lower Class and Lower Caste Women **:** In all discussions and debates relating to the position and problems of Indian women, much is said about middle and upper class and upper caste educated women. The statuses and problems of lower class and lower caste women who constitute the majority of womenfolk, are not given due importance. A large number of rural Indian women [i.e. around 50%] who are illiterate and ignorant are not capable of changing their life-styles, beliefs and values overnight. They take time to change themselves. Hence, no revolutionary change can be witnessed in the overall social position of Indian women at least in the immediate future.

9. Indifferent Attitude of the Governments and Political Leaders **:** The measures taken and the programmes implemented by the Central and State governments so far in the direction of solving the problems and raising the status of Indian women and protecting their interests, are neither promising nor adequate. Laws and legislations alone cannot bring about desired changes in the society. Consistent and honest efforts on the part of people's representatives and social leaders are required to persuade people to accept new situations and challenges. Such efforts are conspicuously absent in India.

Conclusion

Women in India are not yet equal to men. But there is no legal or constitutional barrier to equality. There is only the social barrier. Women in India want to have a *"respectable"* and *"meaningful"* social status which is free from all sorts of exploitation. There is no urge in them to outsmart men. They want their interests to be protected and problems solved. As long as the problems of women remain as *"women's problems"* and not as *"societal problems",* so long, attempts at the solution of these problems do not get the required speed.

No doubt, Indian women cherish equality with men. But, more than that, they expect a change in the attitude of men towards them and their position and problems. *They expect greater freedom, better education, self-dependence, decent jobs, a proper and respectable treatment by menfolk, and a socio-economic environment free from all types of exploitation.* Our attempts to create such a type of socio-economic environment to women will definitely influence their social position and socio-economic conditions in the days to come.

---

35. Romila Thapar in her article *"Looking Back in History"* in *"Indian Women"* - Page: 5-6.

Women's Rights - A Ready Reference

The following Table gives a ready reference regarding the rights of Indian Women as guaranteed in the Constitution, Law and Legislation and IPC [Indian Penal Code]

Rights of Women	Reference in Constitution / Law
1. Right to Equality	1. Article 14 of the Constitution / CEDAW
2. Prohibition of any discrimination on the basis of sex (in home or in the society)	2. Article 15 of the Constitution
3. Special provision for the benefit of women like reservation in education, employment or special facilities available in criminal law to working women.	3. Article 16 of the Constitution
4. Right against exploitation [Forced labour, Child marriage, prostitution]	4. Article 23, 24 of the Constitution
5. Righ to be born as a girl child (Right to Life and Liberty)	5. Article 21 of the Constitution PNDT Act Indian Penal Code.
6. Right for love and parental care and protection	6. Article 21 of the Constitution
7. Right to Education.	7. Article 21 A of the Constitution
8. Freedom (Right) to work or have an occupation. Right to an adequate means of livelihood	8. Article 19 (g) of the Constitution Article 21 of the Constitution This is also a directive principle of state policy.
9. Equal pay for equal work for men and women	9. Article 39 (b) of the Constitution and Equal Remuneration Act.
10. Right to renounce practices derogatory to the dignity of women like forced widowhood, untouchability, devadasi system, sati system, dowry, etc.	10. Article 51 A (e) of the Constitution, Article 17 of the Constitution Laws against devadasi, sati and dowry systems
11. Right to marry or not to marry	11. Article 21 of the Constitution/CEDAW
12. Right to choose a life partner	12. Article 21 of the Constitution/CEDAW
13. Righ to plan the family size (Right to use or not use contraceptives).	13. Article 21 of the Constitution/CEDAW
14. Right to have a name (not to force to change one's name on marriage)	14. CEDAW*
15. Right to move freely anywhere inside India	15. Section 498A of IPC, Law on Dowry and Law for protection of women againts domestic violence.
	16. Article 19 (d) of the Constitution
17. Right to a nationality	17. Article 21 of the Constitution/CEDAW
18. Right to inherit property and also buy or sell property	18. Article 14 of the Constitution and recent amendment to the Hindu law of inheritance. Also, property laws of different religions.
19. Right to form associations or unions.	19. Article 19 (e) of the Constitution

* CEDAW is an international instrument addressing the equality of men and women. It was adopted by the U.N. General Assembly in 1979. CEDAW spells out the rights of women that they should enjoy in order to realize complete equality in the society. CEDAW further places responsiblity on the member states that ratify the convention to ensure that their laws and policies are consistent with its provisions. So far 179 countries are party to this convention. India has ratified CEDAW. It therefore has international obligation to eliminate discrimination against women in all spheres. India has to adopt all necessary measures at the national level aimed at acieving full realization of the rights recognized under CEDAW.

Source : **Mrs. Merlyn Martis**, advocate and director DEEDS, in "*Gender Equity*" - A Mangalore University Publication (2007), Pages - 88-90. [page-42]

INDIAN WOMEN ON THE PATH OF EXCELLENCE.....

- During the recent years, Indian women have been forging ahead as a powerful force of social change. This fact is borne out by their exceptionally impressive achievements in certain fields. Some examples:
- So far 4 Indian women have secured "Bharata Ratna", the highest national award. The recipients of the award are : (i) **Indira Gandhi** [1917-1984] awarded in 1971; (ii) **Mother Teresa** [Mary Teresa Bojaxhiu [1910-1997] awarded in 1980; (iii) **Aruna Asaf Ali** [1909-1996] awarded posthumously in 1997; and (iv) **Lata Mangeshkar** [Sushri Lata Dinanatha Mangeshkar - [1929 ...] awarded in 2001.
- Indira Gandhi could rise to the level of Prime Minister and rule India for 10-11 years, while more than 11 other women could excel themselves as state Chief Ministers.
- ***Women as IAS, IFS and IPS Officers*** **:** In 1948, there was not a single woman in these posts. In 1951, one woman was recruited to the post of I.A.S., it increased to 18 between 1951 and 1960, and then to 339 in 1987 [By then, women IAS officials constituted 7.45% of the total 4548 posts]. By 1993, 17 women IAS officers were working as Deputy Commissioners and around 87 women officers were working in different departments of the Central Government.
- ***Women in IFS and IPS*** **:** Up to 1993, around 409 people were selected IFS officers out of whom 40 were women. Of these 40 officers, only 6 were selected as Indian ambassadors in foreign countries.
- **Dr. Kiran Bedi** and **Kanchan C. Bhattacharya** have made name as IPS officers. [***Achievement of Dr. Kiran Bedi as IPS Officer*** **:** Dr. Kiran Bedi was the first police officer [in the Cadre of IPS] in the world to enter the police service. When she was posted as the Inspector General of Prisons at the biggest national level jail, namely, **Tihar**, at New Delhi, she resorted to some innovative ways of reforming the jail and its conditions. She sought to breakdown adversarial relations between the police and the community of prisoners. She tried *"to replace the hard hand of punishment with the soft one of correction and rehabilitation"*. In recognition of her yeomen service she was awarded in 1994 *"Ramon Magsaysay Award"* which is popularly known as the *"Asian Nobel Prize"*. **Kanchan C. Bhattacharya** has been the first to become the woman DGP [Deputy General of Police] and was serving [2005] the State of Uttaranchal.
- ***Women in the Field of Judiciary*** **:** In 2005, there were about 19 women judges out of a sanctioned strength of 647 judges in 21 high courts. **Fathima Bibi** of Kerala became the first woman judge in the Supreme Court.
- ***Women in the Educational Field*** **:** The literacy level of women has risen from 39.29% in 1991 to 54% in 2001 and to 65.46% in 2011. As per 2005 report, 1.25 lakh women graduate as doctors in India every year. This is 50% of the total number. Further, 21% of India's software professionals and 25% of science and engineering graduates are women. More than 50% of the students who pass out every year with a bachelor's degree in humanities are girls. Women are also not lagging behind in the fields such as art, literature and sports. Some have reached great heights in these fields.

[***Source of these Vital Statistics*** **:** *"India Today"*, April 4, 2005, Page : 32.]

●●●

Chapter 11

DOWRY AS A SOCIAL PROBLEM

Meaning and Definition of Dowry - Dowry As a Social Evil - Causes or Motivations for Dowry - Arguments in Favour of Dowry - Arguments Against Dowry or Advantages and Disadvantages of Dowry - Measures Towards the Abolition of Dowry : Legal and Non-Legal Measures.

Dowry is both a practice and a problem associated mainly with the Hindu marriage. Its practice is also found among almost all the religious communities of India. Dowry is generally understood as money, goods, estate, ornaments or any other kind of wealth that a woman brings to her husband at the time of marriage. The practice of giving dowry in any of the forms mentioned here, is very common among all the people of the world. It exists in all communities and nations of the world in one form or the other. Among Hindus, the girls used to get at the time of their marriage from their parents as a kind of gift [if not as dowry as it is understood today], all domestic utensils that are necessary to set up a new family. But, since a few centuries, this ancient practice of dowry has been developed into a social evil. Let us look to the sociological meaning and the legal definition of dowry.

Meaning of Dowry

1. The dowry refers to *"....... the property which a man receives from his wife or her family at the time of his marriage"* - **Max Radin**[1]
2. Dowry is *".......... the property that is given to a woman at the time of her marriage"* - ***Encyclopaedia Britannica.***
3. Dowry may be broadly defined as *"gifts and valuables received in marriage by the bride, the bridegroom and his relatives"* - **Ram Ahuja.**
4. Dowry is defined as *"the money, goods or estate, which a woman brings to her husband in marriage"* - ***The Webster's New International Dictionary.***

Legal Definition of Dowry

The Dowry Prohibition Act, 1961, defines dowry in the following words : *"Dowry means any property or valuable security given or agreed to be given either directly or indirectly -*

(a) by one party in marriage to the other party in marriage; or

(b) by the parents of either party to a marriage or by any other person to either party to the marriage or to any other person;

1. **Max Radin** in *"Encyclopaedia of Social Sciences."* Vol.5. Page - 240.

at or before or after the marriage as consideration for the marriage of the said parties, but does not include dower or mahr in the case of persons to whom the Muslim Personal Law [Shariat] applies."

DOWRY AS A SOCIAL EVIL

Dowry as a Social Bane or Evil

As it is mentioned earlier, the practice of dowry is almost universal. If the social practice of dowry were to be limited to its social meanings and the legal definitions as mentioned above, it would not have emerged as a social problem. It is unfortunate that the age-old practice of dowry has now assumed the form of a social evil because *the bride's family is compelled to give some dowry as a price for marriage*. The custom has now taken an acute form and has assumed scandalous proportion. It has become a social bane and a kind of bargain. It has caused unhappiness, misery and ruin of the bride's family. Huge amount of money is demanded from the bridegroom's side at the time of marriage and the failure to give the promised amount would make the bride to suffer the consequences at the hands of her in-laws and also the husband. The practice of dowry has become so horrible that it has lost its original meaning and its pronouncement tantamounts to its condemnation. It has assumed several dimensions and reached undesirable proportions for it has now become a serious social evil.

Spread of Education has not Decreased the Intensity of the problem

It was expected that the problem of dowry would diminish with the spread of education. Much against this expectation, dowry is at its heights at the level of the educated people. We have today relatively a larger number of engineers, advocates, doctors, college / university professors, bank / LIC officers, chartered accountants, government officers, and so on at the level of whom dowry is still in practice and often thriving. The extent of dowry depends on the socio-economic status of the bridegroom and differs in different regions and in different caste groups. There are more or less well-defined grades of dowry for men in different professions. For example, men in the IAS, IFS, IPS, and such high cadres belonging to well-to-do families usually expect minimum of 20 to 25 lakh rupees in cash in addition to many other items in kind. Business executives and industrialists expect lakhs of rupees of dowry at the time of their marriage. Engineers and doctors are also in high demand in the marriage market. Their "dowry price" is also relatively high. **Kapadia** thus remarks that *"the amount of the dowry is generally regulated by the social and economic status of the bridegroom's father, the social prestige of the bridegroom's family, and the educational qualification of the bridegroom. A girl's physical beauty or educational qualification may reduce this amount at times, but often this reduction is very meagre."*[2]

Damand for Dowry both in Terms of Cash and Kind

Young persons with high qualifications are demanding huge amount of dowry as prospective grooms. Since their price in the marriage market has gone up, the parents who have to give their daughters to such young men, are now faced with difficulties in finding money. In addition to money, these boys also demand jewellery, scooter / motor bike / car, gadgetry, refrigerator, T.V. sets, furniture, clothes, utensils, etc. from the girls' side. In addition to this burden, the girls' family has to spend a huge amount on marriage ceremony. The burden of hospitality is generally heavier on the bride's kinsmen than on the groom's. Marriage decorations, and wedding dinner expenses which run to thousands and lakhs of rupees are also to be borne by the bride's parents.

2. **K.M. Kapadia** in *"Marriage and Family in India"* [1966 edition]. Page - 137.

THE PANGS AND AGONIES OF DOWRY

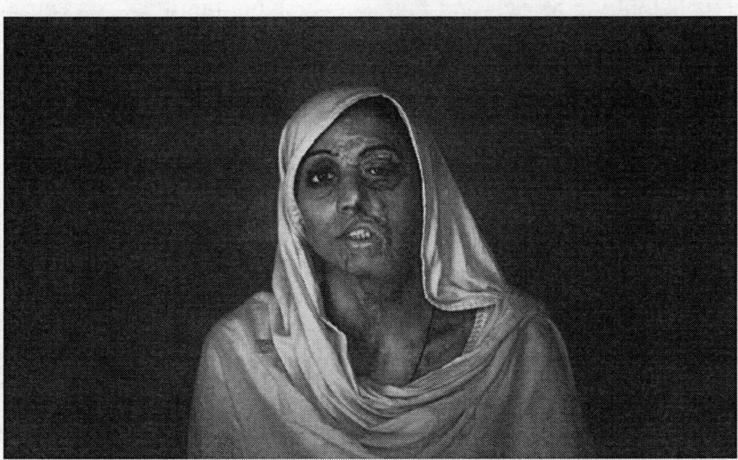

Continued Shadow of Dowry Even after Marriage

The burden of giving money and other gifts to the groom and to his family does not stop when once marriage is over. On the contrary, the girl's parents have to give gifts to her, her husband and her in-laws long after the marriage on festivals and on varied minor or major occasions. In some castes, [for example, Brahmins of Karnataka] expenses incurred on the married daughter's first pregnancy, delivery and childcare for a couple of months, are to be borne by the girl's parents. Gifts, gold ornaments and clothes are also to be given to the new born infant by its grandparents from the mother's side. Hence, **Altekar** has rightly said, *"it is now high time for the Hindu society to put an end to this evil custom, which has driven many an innocent maid to commit suicide."* ***The Crime Record Bureau of the Central Home Ministry*** has also reported in 1994 that on an average everyday 17 dowry deaths [6205 deaths in a year] take place.

CAUSES FOR DOWRY OR MOTIVATIONS FOR DOWRY

The problem of dowry is a longstanding and a deep rooted one. It has its roots in our socio-religious system itself. It has long back spread its tentacles in to our institutional network. Hence, it cannot be attributed to the opertion of any single facotr. Various factors have contributed to the problem of dowry among which the following may be noted.

1. Pressure of the Caste System

Practice of dowry is supported by the caste system, sometimes directly and some other times indirectly. Caste is endogamous and even sub-castes are also endogamous. Since marriage has to take place within the boundary of sub-caste, the range of selection of life-partners becomes extremely limited. In each caste or sub-caste, there is a paucity of young boys who are highly educated, who have high salaried jobs or promising careers in the profession. They become *"scarce goods"* for whom their parents demand high amount as dowry. Girl's parents who seek a good boy as their son-in-law, are now compelled to pay that amount for they have only a limited range of selection.

2. Aspiration to Establish Marital Relation with Rich Family

Girls' parents are always interested in giving their daughters in marriage to well-to-do families. Many of them do not want to take a risk in arranging the marriage of their daughter with a boy who belongs to a poor family just because the boy is good. They look in to the future prospects of their daughter, her comforts, her pleasures, her satisfaction, and so on. High market value of the boys belonging to rich and high social status families, has caused the amount of dowry to go up.

3. False Conceptions of Social Status

Many a time girl's parents themselves offer huge amount of money as *"dowry gift"* just to exhibit their high social status and parade their economic capacity. Jains and Rajputs, for example, spend lakhs of rupees in this way on marriage. Bunts of Dakshina Kannada district [Karnataka], Catholic Christians of Kerala, also spend too much of money on marriage ceremony either to keep up their prestige or to make a show of their status.

4. Hypergamous Marriage System Favouring Dowry

Hypergamous or *Anuloma* system of marriage which is permitted by the caste system has also contributed to the practice of dowry. *As per the rule of hypergamy, a girl of a higher caste cannot marry a boy of a lower caste. But a lower caste girl marrying an upper caste boy is permitted.* Such marriages often prove to be costlier. Particularly when boys belonging to higher castes marry girls of lower castes, they demand high dowry. Thus, a person often pays a huge amount of dowry to get a son-in-law from a higher caste. Girls' parents also find prestige in arranging their daughter's marriage with a man of higher and prestigious caste.

It is in the context of the practice of dowry on the one hand, and hypergamy on the other, **K.M. Kapadia** [Page - 108] commented, *"the practice of hypergamy has brought in its train problems of no mean significance. Every parent desired his daughter to be married into the highest social group to keep up or to add to his prestige, and this made him acquiesce these abuses. When a number of offers were made to a single person, he naturally insisted on his terms and the bridegroom price would go on swelling."* **Kapadia** further writes, *"Legislation against dowry will have little effect until it is visualised in this perspective."*

5. Practice of Dowry As a Long Standing Social Custom

Giving dowry and receiving the same has become a matter of *"social custom"* in the Indian social system which consists of innumerable castes and sub-castes. Many of the caste norms and practices have also strengthened this social evil. Practice of dowry has a longstanding role of its own like that of *"the devadasi system"* and *"child marriage"*. All these had obtained social recognition at one time or the other. Sometimes, a religious touch was also given to the practice of dowry and it was regarded as a *"dakshina"* or fees, in addition to being called as *"Kanyadana"* or the gift of the girl. The daughter's right to inheritance also helped to make the dowry system rigid among the propertied class of the people. It means many parents felt that it was obligatory for them to give the girl's share of ancestral property in the form of dowry at the time of her marriage. Further, many people give and take dowry only because their parents and ancestors had been practising it. Those who stick to this practice and those who pressurise for the same, are getting financial profit and hence they do not want to do away with it.

6. Impact of the Vicious Circle Which Dowry Has Created

The practice of dowry has become very dominant because many parents demand dowry on behalf of their sons just to compensate the dowry they have given while celebrating the marriage of their daughters. Sometimes, individuals who are against this system are also compelled to accept a few thousands or lakhs of rupees in cash as dowry only because they have to spend an equal amount or even more on their sisters' or daughters' marriage. Thus, the vicious circle of dowry starts operating and individuals get entangled with it, whether they desire it or oppose it.

7. Practice of Child Marriage Favouring Dowry

In early times, girls were permitted to marry in their teens, that is, soon after their puberty. Advanced maidenhood was also tolerated. But when pre-puberty marriages came into existence, the father of the girl became anxious to get her married. being afraid of social ostracism for keeping the girl unmarried. Thus, the girl's parents desired to dispose her of within the limited time by paying huge amount of money, which the father of the bridegroom demanded. Practice of taking dowry continued even after the gradual disappearance of child marriages.

ARGUMENTS FOR AND AGAINST DOWRY OR ADVANTAGES AND DISADVANGES OF DOWRY

- **Advantages or Arguments In Favour of Dowry**

Though the practice of dowry is publicly condemned, legally banned and morally despised of, in actuality, it persists. Many people are practising it as though it is a matter of their family tradition. Some people support the practice by citing its advantages. Some of the arguments which the supporters of dowry put forward in defence of it, may be mentioned here.

1. ***Dowry Helps Newly Married Couple to Establish Their Family*** **:** The advocates of the practice of dowry say that the dowry money and the utensils and other household articles that are given along with, or in the form of dowry help the newly married couple to establish their new home and to furnish it with necessary accessories.

2. ***Provides Hopes of Marriage for Ugly Looking Girls*** **:** Practice of dowry helps to increase the possibility of marriage of ugly-looking, uneducated and aged girls. It is normally difficult to get a match for such girls. But if their parents are willing to spend a huge amount in marriage, by way of dowry, it becomes comparatively easier for them to find bridegrooms. In our society it is not difficult to find poor young unmarried men who are waiting for such financial offers as a remedy for the economic problems of their family.

3. ***Supports the Higher Education of Poor Boys*** **:** Meritorious boys of poor classes often find dowry as supportive of their higher education. Girl's parents, if they are rich, often make such proposals to prospective bridegrooms. They show their inclination to spend money on higher education of the grooms, if they are ready to marry their daughters.

4. ***Increases the Status of Women in Family*** **? :** It becomes possible for a lower class / caste woman to marry an upper class / caste boy through which she can increase her status. Further, a woman who brings rich dowry is given greater attention and importance than the woman who belongs to a poor family and brings nothing in cash or in terms of adequate ornaments.

5. ***Promotes Intercaste Marriages*** **:** Many a time when parents are not able to get suitable boys for their daughters in their own caste, they seek alliances with other castes. They may take a bold step to violate the caste rule with the sole intention of finding the most suitable match for their daughter.

6. ***Other Factors Favouring Dowry*** **:**

(a) It is argued that dowry money can help to reduce the intensity of housing problem by encouraging the new married couple to establish their separate household.

(b) It is said that dowry helps to reduce the difference between sons and daughters in the family. Just as parents spend a huge amount on the education of their sons, they spend almost an equal amount on the marriage of their daughters and also on dowry.

(c) Some people who practise dowry defend it as a kind of future protection assured to the girl at the time of marriage. Girl's parents who put forward this argument also look at the dowry money that they are giving as a kind of *"provident fund"* guaranteed to the girl to face financial hazards.

- **Disdvantages or Evil Effects of Dowry OR Arguments Against Dowry**

Practice of dowry which assumed the form of an institution over the years has caused lot of hardships to a large number of people in the Indian society. At one time, dowry was being given willingly by the bride's parents, and it was being "accepted" by the groom's party as a kind of voluntary gift. But today, dowry has come to be *"demanded"*. In marriage negotiations, very often dowry considerations become primary ones, and all other considerations become only secondary. Dowry is demanded by the groom's party without taking into consideration the paying capacity of the bride's party. Hence, in many poor families the birth of a female child is very much despised. From the day of the birth of the girl, the problem of dowry haunts the minds of the parents. Dowry has virtually become a menace in the Indian society. Its practice leads to various evil consequences among which the following may be noted.

1. Dowry Causes Great Economic Burden on the Bride's Family

Dowry has become a great economic burden to the middle and lower-middle class families. People belonging to these classes spend on maintaining the family standard, in providing the necessities of life, educating children, and meeting various social obligations. These people who live from hand to mouth rarely save money. Hence, to arrange the marriage of their daughters they have to borrow money or sell a piece of their property and mortgage valuable articles of the family. The debt thus incurred, is passed on from generation to generation which ultimately leads to the total economic collapse of the family.

2. Dowry Lowers the Status of Woman and Damages Her Dignity

Prevalence of the custom of dowry reflects upon the inferior status of woman in the society. In her own natal home, a girl is considered a liability on the family's resources. This has its effect on the socialisation of children. In respect of food, dresses, medical care, education, etc., in middle class families boy is given more importance than the girl. Particularly, when the family income is very less, boy is likely to obtain preference to girls in the matter of education. Dowry is thus a great impediment in the progress of education of girls. Without higher education, girls can hardly get into high positions which help them to increase their status. As it is already noted, even the education of girls has in no way led to its disappearance.

Dowry lowers the status of woman in another way. As every marriage brings a substantial amount of money and or property, one would naturally be tempted to contract a second and a third marriage just for its monetary benefit. Though such marriages have not become the order of the day, here and there we do hear of such marriages taking place. This naturally affects the status of the wives.

The boy who receives huge amount of dowry may think of himself as more dignified as having a higher status, greater prestige and more respectful than the girl. This may make the married woman to develop a sense of inferiority. It wounds the self-respect of the woman.

3. Dowry Causing Child Marriages

Dowry system is one of the very strong factors leading to the practice of child marriage. Many people arrange the marriage of their daughters in childhood, that is, prior to puberty, in order to escape from dowry. When the boys become mature they often find it difficult to adjust with their wives. Even today child marriages are not completely eradicated.

4. Dowry Harassment and Murders

Women are ill-treated, disrespected, man-handled, tortured and subject to all sorts of cruelties in the name of dowry. Very often, our daily papers flash news about the tragic results of the dowry system, in which the newly married girls are always the victims of harassment, violence, murder and suicide. Dowry is demanded as though it is a fundamental right of the bridegroom. Violence against women who bring less dowry or no dowry include – physical battering, emotional neglect / torture, verbal abuse, refusal of sufficient food, imposition of heavy physical work, and so on.

In spite of the legislation against the practice of dowry, it persists. Demands for dowry have even caused dowry deaths. According to an estimate, as many as 4148 dowry deaths were reported in the year 1990 and it increased to 4366 in the year 1993, and to 6205 in the year 1994, that is, at the rate of one dowry death for every 17 minutes.

5. Dowry Leading to Immorality

Practice of dowry is not only regarded as unlawful but even immoral. Gandhiji, Jayaprakash Narayan and other national leaders condemned it in very strong words. According to **Gandhiji,** one who makes dowry a pre-condition for his marriage, not only shows disrespect to a woman but also humiliates his own nation, education and womanhood. He even said that such young persons should be socially boycotted. Practice of dowry leads to some immoral practices.

Example **:** (i) In order to escape from the menace of dowry some unmarried young girls take up some petty jobs to earn money in order to reduce the financial burden of their parents / brothers. These young innocent girls are often sexually cheated by young boys who make false promises to marry them. These girls who become pregnant are socially defamed and sometimes forced to commit suicide.

(ii) Some parents who cannot pay substantial dowry to a boy of their selection helplessly decide to give their daughter in marriage to an aged man or physically disabled man or diseased man or to a divorcee. This may make many a girl to become unhappy throughout their lives.

(iii) Further, failure on the part of the parents to arrange the marriage of their daughters because of dowry, sometimes makes the girls to carry on illegal sex relations which may even lead to prostitution.

(iv) Dowry system enhances the importance of male children at home. Due to this, female children are neglected and put to all sorts of hardships. More than that, unwanted female children are often killed with the help of modern medical equipments when they are at the stage of foetus in their mother's womb. These killings have led to an imbalance in the sex ratio.

6. Psychological Crises and Emotional Disturbances in the Family

Practice of dowry may cause emotional upsets within the family. Some such situations may be cited here.

(i) Girls with strong character and self-dignity may refuse to marry a boy who demands dowry. Some of them may be forced to remain spinsters throughout their lives. Forcible suppression of sex urge may make them to become irritable, frustrated, disgusted and pessimistic. *They may even develop neurotic diseases and get involved in emotional problems.*

(ii) Some courageous women resist the way in which they are treated at the house of their husbands even after the payment of dowry. *This type of resistance may spoil their mental peace and cause continuous irritation.*

(iii) Even when the boy and girl who love each other are agreeable for marriage, the groom's parents often forcibly arrange the marriage of their son with some other girl with the expectation of high dowry. Marriages arranged in this way against the wishes of the marriage partners on account of dowry rarely bring happiness in the family.

(iv) Practice of dowry creates an unwanted and an unhealthy competition among the brides' parents which ultimately destroys peace and happiness in the family.

(v) Practice of dowry creates misunderstandings, quarrels and conflicts between mother-in-law and daughter-in-law, husband and wife, daughter-in-law and other in-laws at home. These things may become a permanent feature of such families.

MEASURES TOWARDS THE ABOLITION OF DOWRY

Legislative Measures : *Dowry Prohibition Act, 1961:*

Dowry system and its practices are highly criticised. Social reformers and right thinking persons recommended strong legal measures to remove its practice. Some of the State Governments such as Andhra Pradesh, Kerala, Punjab and Bihar Governments have passed anti-dowry legislations.

The Dowry Prohibition Act, 1961: At the all - India level, *Dowry Prohibition Act* was introduced in the Parliament on 27th April 1959 and was ultimately passed on 20th May 1961. Main provisions of this Act are mentioned below :

1. The Act defines in clear cut terms the meaning of dowry.[3]
2. ***Penalty for Giving or Taking Dowry*** **:** If any person, after the commencement of this Act, gives or takes or abets the giving or taking of dowry, he shall be punishable with imprisonment which may extend to six months, or with fine which may extend to five thousand rupees, or with both.
3. ***Penalty for Demanding Dowry*** **:** If any person, after the commencement of this Act, demands, directly or indirectly, from the parents or guardian of a bride or bridegroom, as the case may be, any dowry, he shall be punishable with imprisonment which may extend to six months, or with fine which may extend to ₹5,000/- or with both.
4. ***Dowry, if paid, should be for the Benefit of the Wife or Her Heirs*** **:** Where any dowry is received by any person other than the woman in connection with whose marriage it is given that person shall transfer it to the woman —
   (a) if the dowry was received before marriage, within one year after the date of marriage; or
   (b) if the dowry was received at the time of or after the marriage, within one year after the date of its receipts; or
   (c) if the dowry was received when the woman was a minor, within one year after she has attained the age of eighteen years; and pending such transfer, shall hold it in trust for the benefit of the woman.
5. ***Dowry to the Tune of ₹2,000/- only Permitted*** **:** The Act permits gifts in the form of ornaments, clothes and other articles not exceeding ₹2,000/- in value. The Act thus legalises dowry only to the tune of ₹2,000/-.
6. ***Cognisance of Offences*** **:** As per the provisions of this Act, no court shall take cognisance of any such offence except on a complaint made within one year from the date of the offence.

This Act which was amended in June 1986, was made more rigorous and stringent.

Poor Enforcement of This Legislation

As anticipated, this legislation failed to produce the desired results. ***"The Committee on the Status of Women"*** in India [1974] reported that *The Dowry Prohibition Act,* 1961 has failed to curb the evils of dowry. In spite of the rapid growth of this evil practice, there are very limited number of cases reported under this Act. No law can be enforced without the whole-hearted co-operation of the people. Social reformers were successful in getting the legislation passed to abolish the practice of dowry. But they were not successful in persuading the people to accept the legislation in principle and abide by it with the spirit of committment. No one can eradicate this evil unless the people carry the philosophy behind the law much further. Proper efforts are not made to convince people regarding the evils of dowry. As a result, legislation as such prevails, but its violations take place uninterruptedly. Number of cases taken up under this Act have been awfully insignificant. In fact, **P.N. Sapru,** a former Judge of Allahabad High Court and the then member of Parliament [1960s], had described the Bill as *"ridiculous"* and even went to the extent of suggesting its withdrawal. What he meant was that - it would be meaningless to pass legislations which cannot be enforced. Effective enforcement of legislations such as this obviously demand the willing co-operation of people.[4]

---

3. *Note* :Legal definition of dowry as per this Act is given in the beginning of this chaapter.
4. It is curious to note that the Supreme Court has given instructions very recently [in 2014] to the legal authorities to take proper precaution before arresting individuals under the charge of practising dowry, because several instances of abusing the legal provisions of this Act by a few unscrupulous women, has come to its notice. - Author.

Non-Legislative Measures Towards the Abolition of Dowry

Mere legislations cannot do any magic. They are to be accepted and adopted by the people as their own. Sometimes, special efforts are required to persuade them to accept and comply with the legislations. Hence, non-legislative measures are also required to face the social menaces like dowry system. Some such measures are worth mentioning here.

1. Propaganda and Publicity Against Dowry

Modern media of propaganda including the electronic media such as radio, T.V., movies, dramas, newspapers, internet, and social networking system [SNS]etc. must be effectively made use of to convince people that the practice of dowry is not only illegal but also unethical and it is against the familial and the social harmony of the society. It is essential to make use of the media in diverse ways and not in a uniform manner taking into consideration the level of education of the people, their rural and the urban background.

2. Creating Public Opinion and Rousing Social Conscience

In marriage negotiations, material considerations such as wealth, ornaments, money, jobs and professional opportunities, etc., have always formed an important incentive. What is deplored in the case of dowry is its compulsive character and material transactions in actual consideration for marriage. Proper measures are to be taken to do away with this. The attack on dowry has to be a multi-pronged. Social legislation alone cannot help in this regard.

(i) A social understanding must be created in the public by bringing to their notice the evils of dowry.

(ii) Social consciousness needs to be aroused, particularly amongst women. They must be properly educated and told that their encouragement of dowry will perpetuate the inequality of the sexes.

(iii) Since practice of dowry is at its heights among the higher educated people, formal education alone cannot mitigate this problem. Greater stress is to be laid on moral education and value education. Education that is given to the youths must help to broaden their minds and widen their outlook.

3. Encouraging Inter-Caste Marriages

It is quite known that the endogamous nature of caste and sub-caste restricts the range of selection of life-partners. Hence, it is suggested that intercaste marriages must be encouraged among the youths so that they would get a wide range of selection in finding a suitable mate for marriage. This "self-choice" opportunity given to the youths will help them to get out of the vicious circle of dowry. Though this suggestion sounds alright we must not be over-enthusiastic about the outcome of this. Because, the hold of the tradition and the influence of the caste are still powerful in the Indian society.

4. An Appeal to Idealism of the Youth

Youths are the only ray of hope to combat effectively against the dowry. Youths must be given education and inspired to take initiative towards its actual abolition. Youths are basically idealistic. The gospels and sermons of the charismatic leaders like Vivekananda, Gandhiji, Jayaprakash Narayan and others could appeal to the idealism of the youth and make them committed to the non-acceptance or total rejection of the dowry. In fact, Gandhiji had given a call to the social boycott of the supporters of dowry. It may be recalled that **Jayaprakash Narayan** [J.P.] who for sometime spearheaded a movement known as *"Samagra Kranti"* [or "Total Revolution"] had made an appeal to the young men and women of the day to take an oath *"that they would never ask for dowry, and reject and boycott those who ask for it."*

5. Role of Voluntary Associations

It is suggested that voluntary associations should take initiative in this regard and make propaganda against the evils of dowry. It is also advocated that such associations should take up the cases of victims of dowry harassment and get them justice with due publicity. This will definitely create a social wave against the practice of dowry. In fact, organisations such as *"Saheli"* in Delhi, *"Women's Centre"* in Mumbai, *"Shakhi Kendra"* in Khanpur, *"Stree Adhar Kendra"* in Poona, and others are already in the field doing some work in this direction.

Conclusion

It is clear from the above analysis, that the dowry system in our country has become a kind of business deal, a big bargain in matrimony. It is unspiritual and is devoid of ethical values. It is a stigma associated with the Indian marital system. It is no more the problem of the Hindu community alone . It has become equally rampant in other religious communities of India such as Christians and Muslims. It has made a few young women to remain as spinsters throughout their lives. It is high time that it is stopped.

The successful abolition of the practice of dowry would be a landmark towards social reform. But it is not an easy task. Some of the highly educated and professionally well-placed individuals including the foreign-returned young men are still cherishing and supporting it. Determined efforts should be made on an all-India basis to combat this problem. Rousing the social and moral consciousness of the people, spreding education and economic independence of women, inter-caste marriages, effective enforcement of legislation against dowry system, establishment of voluntary associations to discourage dowry, enouranging civil marriage, arrangement of *"samuhika vivaha"* or community weddings, launching of the youth movements against the dowry system – are some of the means of countering this practice. The sooner it disappears the better it will be for the progress of this society.

●●●

Chapter 12

FAMILY DISORGANISATION: DIVORCE AND DESERTION IN INDIA

*(A) **Family Disorganisation in India:** Meaning of Family Disorganisation – W.J. Goode's Classification of Types of Family Disorganisation – The Nature of Family Organisation – Causes of Family Disorganisation – Personal and Impersonal or Socio-cultural Factors – Effects of Family Disorganisation:*

*(B) **Desertion, Separation and Divorce:** Desertion, Separation and Divorce as Reflections of Family Disorganisation – Separation – Desertion: Types of Desertion – Divorce in India – Meaning and Definition of Divorce – Divorce Among the Hindus – Some Provisions for Divorce in Ancient India – Divorce Among the Hindus in Modern India – Legislation to Legalise Divorce – Provisions for Divorce in the Hindu Marriage Act-1955 – Causes of Divorce – Types of Divorce as per Wikipedia Encyclopaedia – Factors that Affect the Rate of Divorce and its Intensity – Individual and Social Consequences of Divorce – Remedial Measures for Divorce : Avoidance of Family Tensions and Divorce – Family Welfare Services and Its Functions – Divorce Among the Muslims: Three Ways of Obtaining Divorce – Importance of Iddat in the Muslims' Divorce – Divorce Among the Christians – Legislations Relating to Christians' Marriage and Divorce.*

The human family has a prolonged history of its own. When, where and how precisely it was founded, and how exactly it underwent different stages of development to attain the present position – is very difficult to say. But there is nothing to dispute about the fact that it constituted the most basic of all social groupings. The family is the most important primary group in society. It is the simplest and the most elementary form of society. It is the first and the most immediate social environment to which a child is exposed. It is an outstanding primary group, because, it is in the family that the child develops its basic attitudes.

Further, of all the groups that affect the lives of individuals in society none touches them so intimately or so continuously as does the family. From the moment of birth to the moment of death the family exerts a constant influence. The family is the first group in which we find ourselves. It provides for the most enduring relationship in one form or the other. Every one of us grows up in a family and every one of us too will be a member of one family or other.

"The family, almost without question, is the most important of any of the groups that human experience offers. Other groups we join, for longer or shorter periods of time, for the satisfaction of this interest or that. The family, on the contrary, is with us always. Or rather more precisely, we are with it." - ***Robert Bierstedt.***

The family, as an institution is *universal.* It is the most permanent and the most pervasive of all the social institutions. All societies both large and small, primitive and civilised, ancient and modern, have some form of family or the other. No one knows, or can know, how or when the family began. It is safe to surmise that the family in some form will always be with us. With regard to the future, as the mind can imagine, the family will continue to be a central and indeed a nuclear component of society. *"There may be no families in utopia, and none in paradise, but the planet we know best will probably always contain them."* - ***Robert Bierstedt.***

Like all other social institutions, the family is also subject to change and it is changing. Its structure and functions are changing. During the recent years, family is undergoing very fast changes. Though some of these changes are beneficial to the effectiveness of the role of family, some others are highly challenging. A few of them create problems of adjustment while a few others threaten its very existence. Various developments that are taking place within the family such as – family clashes, husband and wife conflicts, parental clash with children, desertion, isolation, divorce, domestic violence, cruelty to children – and many such events have started weakening the organization of the family and pushing it towards *"disorganization".*

Meaning of 'Family Disorganisation

The term family disorganization refers to *the failure of the organisational structure of the family*. It denotes a state of non-harmonious functioning within the family. It points out a family where in we find the breakdown of interpersonal relations of the members. Thus, it may include bickering and simmering and open clashes between husband and wife, tensioned relationship between parents and children, mutual aversion between mother-in-law and daughter-in-law and so on. In most of the cases, the family disorganization is mainly related to the disorganization of the marital relationships.

Family disorganization indicates the failure of the family to conduct its activities in a smooth manner. It also reflects the failure on the part of the members to fulfil their roles towards the family and other members of the family.

William J. Goode, a well known sociologist of family, defined *'family disorganization'* in the following way –

- Family disorganization refers to the *"break-up of a family unit when one or more members are unwilling or unable to perform their role obligations adequately, as these are viewed by other members".*

Family Disorganisation Reflects Maladjustment, Disharmony and Lack of Understanding

Family disorganization normally indicates lot of tension and misunderstanding on the relationship between husband and wife. It is not just that. Modern studies indicate that lack of understanding between parents and children and lack of communication between parents and children are the two important aspects of the problem of family disorganization.

A family is said to be disorganized when it is subject to desertion, separation, divorce, physical violence and the use of very abusive language in the interpersonal relations of the members. A few more things may aggravate family disorganization. Sexual maladjustment and misunderstanding regarding the way of spending family income are the two other reasons for conflict between husband and wife, especially in the Western context. But in the Indian context, many couples, men and women make fairly satisfactory adjustment for the reason of social pressure, family prestige, religious pressure and social prestige.

Family tensions are found not only due to the lack of understanding between husband and wife but also because of quarrels between parents and children. However, in the Indian context, children's conflict with parents does not usually threaten the family organization to such an extent as the conflict between husband and wife over fundamental values. Therefore, the family disorganization is mostly related to the disorganization of the marriage relationships.

W.J. Goode's Classification of Types of Family Disorganisation

Family units break up for various reasons. Sometimes, as a result of external problems such as war, economic depression, death, imprisonment, floods, famines, forcible religious conversions, etc. family units get dissolved. Failure to fulfil role obligations has always been the internal factor causing family disintegration. In fact, **William J. Goode** has also spoken of different forms of family disorganization which are mentioned below.

1. ***Illegitimacy OR the Uncompleted Family Unit*:** In this type of disorganization, role of father-husband or mother –wife is missing. It is reflected in terms of illegitimacy or unwed parenthood. Here, the source of illegitimacy is to be found in the failure of family members, say father and mother, to carry out their role obligation.
2. ***Voluntary Departure of one or Both the Parents or Spouses OR Annulment Due to Separation, Desertion and Divorce:*** In this type of disorganization, one of the couple decides to leave the other, carrying dissolution without discharging the role obligation.
3. ***Changes in the Role Definitions:*** These changes may result from the differential impact of cultural changes. *Example*: Social movements like women's liberation movement may affect relations between husband and wife.
4. ***Vacuum Family OR the Empty Shell Family:*** This is the type of family disorganization in which individuals live together but have minimal communication and contact with one another. They fail in the obligation to give emotional support to one another.
5. ***Unwilled Absence of One of the Partners OR Family Crisis Due to External Events:*** This type of disorganization results because of the temporary or permanent involuntary absence of one of the spouses because of imprisonment, conversion or death or due to catastrophes as flood, war, riots, severe economic depression, earthquake, cyclones, etc.
6. ***Unwilled Major Role Failure Or Family Disorganisation Due to Internal Catastrophes:*** This type is the result of catastrophes taking place within the family. Catastrophes include mental, emotional or physical pathologies, severe mental retardation, psychosis, chronic or incurable physical conditions of any member in the family.

Every family witnesses or experiences one or the other type of the above mentioned forms of disorganization to some extent or the other. *For example,* misunderstanding between husband and wife, quarrels between parents and children etc. are normally found to some extent in all families. But when these unhealthy trends reach their extremity, then problem arises. Society also cares to provide or seek solutions but not for all types of family disturbances. *For example,* the society is normally unconcerned with vacuum family and in ordinary circumstances, it does not want to interfere much with strained relationship between parents and children or husband and wife. But as far as illegitimacy is concerned, it tries to provide social agencies to give professional help to meet role expectations.

All Forms of Family Disorganisation Must be Given Proper Attention and Importance – W.J. Goode

Whenever we hear of the instances of family disorganization, we normally take it to be the cases of divorce or desertion, and we tend to ignore the other forms and concentrate our attempts

INCREASING DIVORCES AND DWINDLING FAMILIES !!

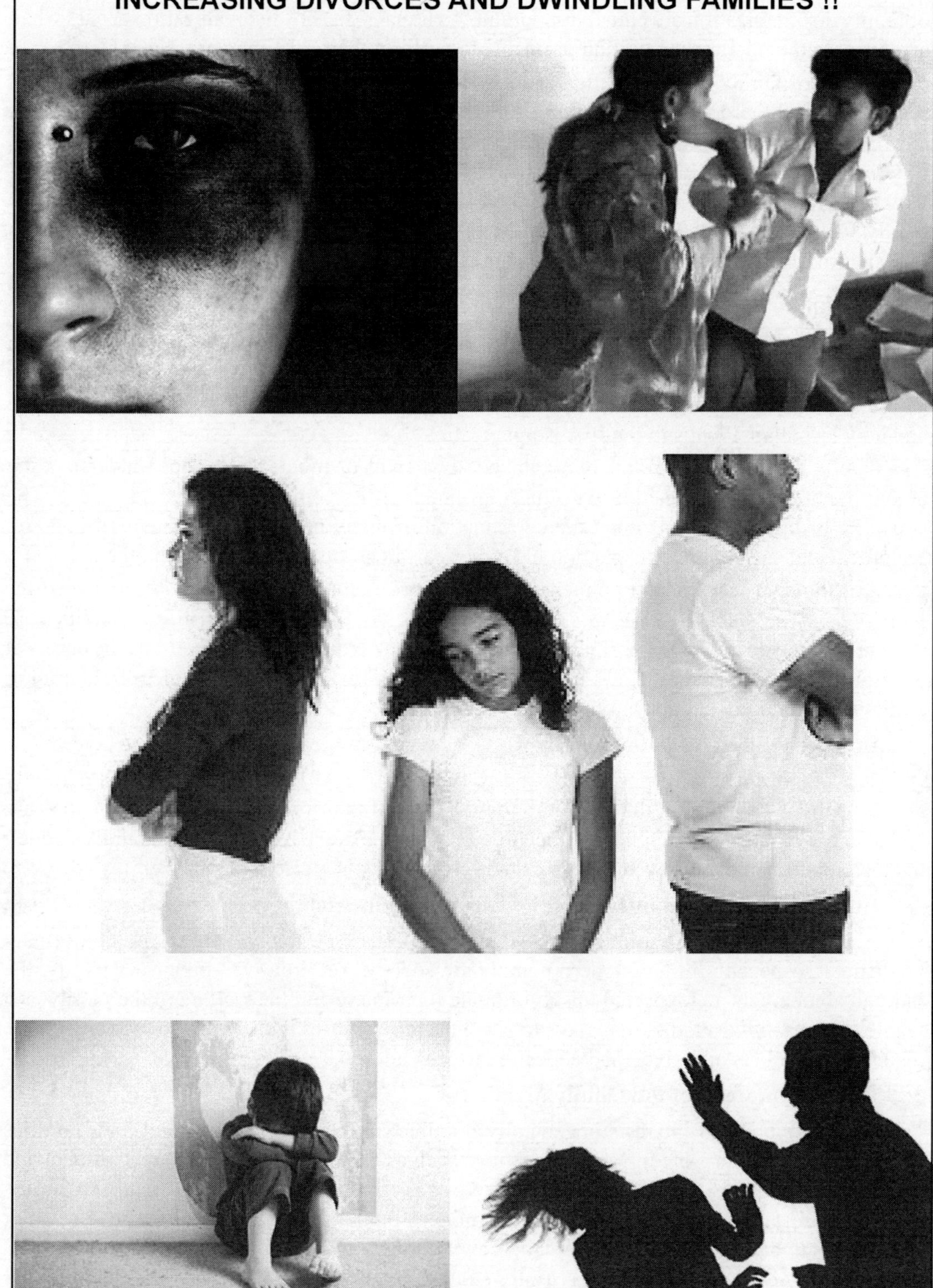

to address the issue of divorce only. According to **Goode**, this is not proper for the other forms of family disorganization are equally important. As he says, family disorganization occurs when one or more members are unwilling or unable to perform their role obligations adequately.

Trends of family disorganization are found everywhere, in the eastern as well as western societies. But the process of disruption of the family may be slow or rapid. It is tangible and clearly visible when the ties of relationships are severed, the individual family is dissolved. External manifestations like separation, divorce, desertion, failure to support the family, physical violence, etc, are the main symptoms of a breakdown in the intimate relationships within the family. Only a few limited number of families may have the pride of being completely free from the types of disorganization which we have mentioned above.

The Nature of Family Organisation

The terms *'organisation'* and *'disorganisation'* are interrelated. 'Disorganisation' as a term indicates the absence of, or collapse of the state of organization. Thus, in order to understand the nature of family disorganization, it is essential for us to know the nature of family organization and how its collapse leads to family disorganization.

Family is said to be in a state of organization when its members have proper understanding among themselves and function with unity to maintain its common culture and values. The existence of family depends upon the continuation of many personal relationships which are reciprocal and each member is playing his or her part in co-operation with each other.

As **Elliot** and **Merrill** have pointed out, organization is characterized by – *unity of objectives, unity of personal ambitions, and unity of interests*. Each of these characteristics or qualities are present in some degree in the normal and unified primary group. Family represents the classical example of the primary group and let us examine as to how these characteristics are helpful to family to maintain its organization.

1. Unity of Objectives in the Family

The organized family possesses a unity of objectives. The members of such a family possess similar attitudes on the most important aspect of their joint activities, such as the care and discipline of the children, their education, allocation of various items on the family budget, the location of home and several other matters which may be personal in nature.

2. Unity of Personal Ambitions on the Part of Family Members

Achieving complete harmony of personal ambitions with the welfare of the family may be difficult, especially in the modern democratic society. Yet, in a well-organised family, the individual members are expected to sub-ordinate their interest to the welfare of the family as a whole. *For example,* a father may have to cut short his expenses with a view to feed and clothe his family members and give good education to his children.

3. Unity of Interests of the Family Members

Complete unity of interests is generally possible in traditional agricultural joint families where members participate in various activities such as religious, educational, recreational and economic activities as a unit. Similarity of interests is more favourable for an organized family. On the contrary, this is rather difficult in the modern family where the members develop their own interests due to the influence of the developments that have taken place in the socio-cultural environment. Moreover, it requires subordinating the individual aspirations to family interests for its harmonious functioning.

Due to the changes in the patterns of life, family has undergone a number of changes both in its structure and in its functions. Thus, unity that was expected of a family in the past, is difficult to be found in modern society where the members of the family develop different interests by virtue of their roles in various secondary groups.

Further, it is difficult to find two extremes of family organization – *a perfectly organized family and a completely disorganized family.* They are only *"ideal types"*. In relation to actual family unity, all families are subject to infinite gradations. Majority of families continue to function on a fairly acceptable plane in spite of the bickerings, simmerings and tensions that are found within the families. There are also many exceptions to this. For some members, tensions become so great that they fail to continue their relations. These tensions may be gradual developments growing out of cultural dissimilarities or disparities in age, religious differences, economic difficulties or differences over fundamental values. When these tensions are accumulated, they precipitate crisis within the family. The crisis may have a disorganizing effect upon the individual, and it may, in course of time, lead to family disorganization also.

CAUSES OF FAMILY DISORGANISATION

Family disorganization is a complex phenomenon. According to an Indian social thinker **Kumarappa,** *"crisis in a family is created by a variety of factors such as lack of money, illness, existence of physically or mentally handicapped member, or an unhealthy emotional situation which creates problems of human relationships. Often these factors are so intermingled that it becomes difficult to identify the real cause of the family trouble."* Thus, many factors conspire to bring about family disorganization. These factors that lead to family disorganization first of all, create severe tensions in the family. These tensions which arise in modern families may be grouped into two types namely; *(i) primary tensions,* and *(ii) secondary tensions.*

(i) Primary tensions mainly arise out of personality structures of the mates and make them more or less incompatible at the outset. These include all the sources of friction like temperament, philosophy of life, personal behaviour patterns [including sexual incompatibility], psycho-pathic personality [including mental instability] among the mates and inhuman treatment.

(ii) The secondary tensions are those which arise out of circumstances or situations – economic or occupational. These include cultural differences, educational differences, differences in social status, matters of ill-health, parent-child relationship, interference of in-laws [sister-in-law, brother-in-law and others], disparity in the age of husband and wife, economic factors like poverty, business reverses, the economic dependency of the wife and finally the unstable occupation in which the husband is engaged.

The factors mentioned above, are both personal and impersonal in nature. But the family conflict and the find disintegration often results by a combination of several factors rather than any one specific factor.

The Causes

The causes or factors that are responsible for family disorganization may be classified into two types namely; *(A) Personal Factors,* and *(B) Impersonal Factors.*

(A) Personal Factors Causing Family Disorganisation

Personal factors or causes are normally understood as the subjective factors that are basically in the nature of individual thinking, feeling, ideology, physical or bodily characteristics and physical appearance, exposure, orientation towards life / job and such other things, and so on. To some extent, individuals themselves are responsible for these factors. Hence, they may be corrected by proper orientation and guidance. Some of the personal factors causing family disorganization may be analysed here.

1. Romantic Fallacy: In the present condition in the society, due to lessened parental role and control in the choice of mates young people commit the romantic fallacy. A marriage which is based exclusively upon the dreaming on romantic idealism without consideration of money, social position, cultural dissimilarities and parental objections, faces a tremendous handicap. To many persons, romantic love is the essence of all affectional functions of the family. These persons enter into marriage with ideas derived from many romantic sources, the movies, popular magazines and the like. Gradually, the romantic ecstasy will be decreased and they begin to question the validity of their marriage. Thus, the romantic fallacy is the cause of many family tensions for newly married young couples. In the beginning, they fail to realize it, after sometime, they will recognize the disparities in their temperament, attitudes, habits or emotional nature.

2. Clashing Temperament: In the initial stages of marriage, when each partner is bent on making a good impression on the other, the real personality and temperament are not brought to light. Later, however, clashes in temperament may take a violent turn. Highly individualized temperament takes on a characteristic pattern of behavior which the other resents and dislikes despite a certain bond of affection. *For example,* the over-critical, pessimistic nagging wife may make life wretched for a happy carefree youth who may spend the evening with his friends. On the other hand, one person may be hot tempered and the other quiet and slow to anger. Therefore, one's personality make-up may be the cause for disruptions in the interpersonal relationships.

3. Philosophy of Life: More important than temperament is the role of individual's philosophy of life in the marital relationships. If both husband and wife possess some identity of important values as expressed in the social attitudes, their marriage problems will tend to be adjusted successfully. On the other hand, if they differ on fundamental values, the relations are likely to be strained easily. *For example,* it is very difficult for an individual with secular ideas to get adjusted with someone who is highly religious, or sometimes a fanatic.

4. Personal Behaviour Patterns: This may include both habits and manners of conduct. Initially, petty habits though they seem to be insignificant, they may bring high marital friction. No doubt there will be irritating little habits and many times the partners may lead a most successful life neglecting such things in a spirit of tolerant give-and-take, but this cannot be found always. Small habits or mannerisms like smoking, way of dressing, and even walking or talking may trigger out to be an issue to quarrel. *For example*, a woman who is fun-loving and mixing freely with many friends at social gatherings may find it difficult to adjust with a man who is tradition-bound, reserved and highly pius.

5. Psychopathic Personalities: Psychopathic personality of one partner or the other may affect marital relationships. Such persons have mental instability and are often charged with cruel and inhuman treatment, mental cruelty or physical violence. Such patterns exhibit the symptoms of psychoses or neuroses. Neurotic cases like obsession, compulsive behaviour, perfectionism, possessiveness, etc., will find hard to make adjustments in marriage.

6. Sexual Maladjustment: Sex drive is one of the strongest drives in organisms and human beings are also not an exception to it. Making proper provision for the satisfaction of sex is one of the main functions of both marriage and family. Sex need is common to all no doubt but its intensity is not the same in all. While some are more enthusiastic about it, others are not. Unless there is proper understanding between husband and wife in obtaining sexual satisfaction, they cannot have a happy married life. Hence, as far as sexual matters are concerned, one has to understand the need of the other and make mutual efforts to obtain satisfaction. The failure to this effect may create sexual maladjustment and for various reasons may create dislikeness between each other. Wide gap between husband and wife on this matter may lead to infidelity and extra-marital relationships. This has been an important factor that has brought about family disorganization.

7. Problem of Double Standards of Morality: In the male dominated patriarchal society, moral lapse on the part of the husband in sex matters is overlooked and strict chastity in unmarried women and fidelity in married women, is insisted upon. Though the family norms and values have changed today, this typical patriarchal thinking has not much changed in the Indian society. But the modern educated, learned, well-informed and progressive minded women have started questioning this philosophy. According to them, men and women are equal in all respects and it holds true even with respect to sex morals. They have questioned the sex related double standards of morality and argued that fidelity is a value that both husband and wife must respect and practice. Wide differences between the views of husband and wife on this issue may, in the long run, lead to the breakdown of the marriage and also family.

B. Impersonal Factors or Socio-Cultural Factors Causing Family Disorganisation

Impersonal factors are also known as external factors or socio-cultural factors and they are to be located in the society, culture and in the social milieu. Some of the main impersonal factors that cause family disorganization may be examined here.

1. Economic Tensions or Factors: Economic factors include a wide range of factors among which the important ones are – *poverty, business reverses,* and *economic independence of wife.*

(a) Sheer Poverty: Poverty is one of the reasons in family tension. Despite romantic ideal of love, long continued worry over financial matters is not conducive to the healthy marital relations. A person whose income is not sufficient to meet the necessities of life in a particular position may affect his temper. His wife may be sympathetic but she is equally worried. She may lose temper or her husband may leave the house. Most cases of desertion among the lower working classes are related to poverty and lack of steady income. The family members always look upto man for the satisfaction of economic needs. Poverty, thus is always a threat to a poor man in his happy family life.

(b) Business Reverses: Business reverses may cause troubles in the family. This happens particularly when the wife comes from an upper class family and is of aristocratic nature and she is not able to adjust with the existing lower income of the husband. Conflicts between husband and wife, separation and even divorce are common in such cases.

(c) Economic Independence of Wife: Economic independence of wife has a major share in family tensions. The girl who has had special training and tasted the success in her job may find it difficult to leave the job and husband may resent her taking a job. This condition though not very common, is often found in India. The woman may find it difficult to adjust her expenses to fit the scale of her husband's purse in case she leaves the job. As a result, she my become dissatisfied with the whole relationship. Sometimes, the economic independence of the wife may give rise to professional rivalry or jealousy in a male dominated and tradition-oriented family.

2. Occupational Tensions: Closely related to economic tensions are those developing out of the peculiar nature of the day's work. The mobility, that is, going out of family reach for purposes of job for weeks and even months together, though necessary to a particular line of work [as we find in army and shipping business] is often a source of family tension. Sometimes, they become so accustomed to living apart that they get on each other's nerves when they are together for a long time. The unstable occupations may also lead to tensions in the family. As

Burgess and **Cottrell** have pointed out low scores in marriage adjustments are correlated with frequent changes made in occupations.

Occupational misfits may be another cause of marital discord. *For example,* a young man of literary and academic taste fails to appreciate the income that the business brings for him. Besides these things, occupational stresses and problems of the work place may affect the cordial relationships between husband and wife. This will result in conflict and may easily become a source of friction in the family.

3. Differences in Cultural Background: Husband and wife come from different cultural backgrounds. Hence, there may be difficulties for both to adjust each other. If they are brought up in approximately the same cultural background, the difficulty will not be much. This factor is an important one affecting family adjustment.

4. Disparity in Age: Regarding the age at the time of marriage, there can be no absolute rule as to the ideal age for marriage. Yet both of them at the time of marriage will be successful if both of them are fairly matured. Wider disparity in age is likely to mean divergence in attitudes and interests among the marriage partners. Wide disparity in age creates problems of understanding each other and dissimilarity in interests and likeness.

5. Ill-health: A sick wife or husband may disturb the family relationship. Long continued ill-health procures unhealthy conditions in the family leading to frustration and finally to disorganization. Ill-health will be a long continuous drain on the family budget. The lack of stimulating contact, monotonous aspects of housework, coupled with the husband's indifferent expression of affection may lead to wife's nervous breakdown. This may become a source of many difficulties of family. There are instances of individuals with chronic illness and incurable diseases, leaving the family, absconding or running away, not to burden the family with the expenses due to illness. Thus, good health is an accepted condition for satisfactory marriage.

6. Parent – Child Relationship: Although childless marriages on the whole are admittedly less successful than those with children, the children themselves may be the centre of family tension and family conflict. Spouses may differ from each other in matters of child's education, type of training, discipline, social activities, etc. The husband may even become jealous of his wife who gives more importance and attention to children, particularly to the son, and he may even feel deceived of his wife's affection. The reverse may be the feeling in the case of the wife. She resents the favourtism which the father displays for his daughter.

7. Interference of In-Laws: Parents are often imbued with ambition and the desire for their children's happiness and consequently they often insist upon imposing their decisions upon the reluctant children. The parents – in – law interfere in these matters. In India, due to the system of joint family, the interference from the in –laws is too much. Too much interference of in – laws leads the daughter – in – law to revolt and breakdown her relations with joint family or traditional family. It is a well-known fact that many of the married couples [in most of the cases, the wife] end up even committing suicide due to conflict with their in-laws.

8. Deterioration of Religious Control: The deterioration of religious control in matters of life and activities which has been accompanied by a widespread acceptance of the individual's right to happiness and to an expressive and creative existence, has, to some extent, resulted in the disorganization of family in India.

CONSEQUENCES OR EFFECTS OF FAMILY DISORGANISATION

One of the most alarming and disturbing social trends of the modern society is the increasing rate of family disorganization. Since family occupies the central position in the social structure its disorganization is bound to have multifarious effects on different faces of our social life. Disorganisation of a family unit, however, is a gradual process, and it usually starts with one casual factor, but later gets linked to many other related factors and forces.

Family as an institution is still strong and does not breakdown so easily. Individual families also make enough efforts to survive despite the breaking trends. Family continues to offer to the majority of people lovable companionship, sympathetic attitude, and conjugal affection. If there are loved children, the parents find much of their happiness in providing a suitable environment for them and in accepting their role as parents. They come to realize the fertility and hollowness of romantic raptures of motion pictures in their daily life. They make sincere efforts to adjust to each other's temperament, interests, attitudes, etc. They find pleasure in companionship and mutual dependence in the petty details of their daily life. Majority of men and women make fairly satisfactory adjustments, whether from force of habit, social pressure or for inescapable destiny.

Thus, many families stay united despite the tensions and the breaking of relationships and interpersonal communication. They make temporary adjustments to save the face in social life. However, when all efforts fail, the external manifestation of family disorganization may take the forms of desertion, legal separation or divorce. They become the obvious criteria for family disorganization.

B. DESERTION, SEPERATION AND DIVORCE

Desertion, Separation and Divorce as Reflections of Family Disorganisation

Family having the firm social support tries to withstand all ordinary social shocks. All silly incidents that take place in a family are not taking it to a collapse. Many disorganized families maintain over legal solidarity for reasons of religion, prestige or social pressure, while others severe such bond. *Separation, desertion* and *divorce* are the final stages of family disorganization.

1. SEPARATION

Separation refers to an informal preliminary step towards divorce for the couple may live separately for a temporary period to lessen the immediate conflict. Separation could also be a legally recognised decision to live separately without divorcing. In any instance of marital separation, the mates are deprived of normal marital association, affecting their health, security and happiness. As far as the children are concerned, there is the loss of daily love and counsel of one parent. *The Hindu Marriage Act,* 1955 also makes provision for judicial separation.

Legal Interpretation of 'Separation'

From the legal point of view, separation is the time bound legal breakage of the co-habitation. The legal proceedings order the partners for temporary separation from the marital relations. The duration of separation is specified and during this period the parties involved are not supposed to cohabit or resume conjugal relations. Separation is the time and option provided for the partners to take stock of the situation once again and to have an understanding of the issues that may find the help of the counsellors for proper guidance. At the end of the specified period, it is the choice of the partners to revoke their claim for total separation or resume their relationship as husband and wife. Even outside the legal proceedings also, that is, at the level of the concerned community, religious group, or community of relations, and elders, separation may be agreed upon. In fact, many marriages are saved from this kind of provision.

2. DESERTION

Desertion denotes an unofficial dissolution of marriage bond. It implies disintegration of family and not disorganization, though it may ultimately lead to disorganization. It also indicates a failure on the part of the husband and wife to live together with proper understanding. In this, either the husband or wife simply moves out of the family and may not return for considerable length of time.

Definition of Desertion: Desertion according to **C.B. Mamoria**, is defined as *"deliberate abandonment of conjugal society."* Desertion is an evasion of marital responsibilities and hence, we have no way of ascertaining its true nature. According to **Mamoria**, desertion, as the term is ordinarily employed, means *"the irresponsible departure from the home on the part of either husband or wife, leaving the family to fend for itself."*

Types of Desertion

Desertion may assume five forms or types. **Eubank** speaks of five types of deserters –

1 ***The Spurious Deserter:*** He who leaves his family in order to escape from financial responsibility or to secure charitable relief is called the *spurious deserter*.

2 ***The Gradual Deserter:*** The gradual deserter is one who is forced to stay away from home by reason of his occupation or because he is an immigrant away from his family and native land.

3 ***The Intermittent Husband:*** This type represents a chronic periodic desertion. Intermittent husband is one who leaves home at somewhat regular intervals due to some domestic difficulties and returns home when he is free from difficulties.

4 ***The Ill-advised Marriage Type:*** This is the type in which the individual deserts the wife as he finds the relationship between him and his wife is quite unsatisfactory because of hastily arranged or ill-suited marriage.

5 ***The Last Resort Deserter:*** The last resort deserter is one who makes a complete break with his family only when he finds it difficult to make any more adjustments with his wife.

Though instances of desertions are found here and there, they are not always officially recorded. It means, a large share of desertions are never broughtout before any public agency. Many wives do not prefer to report about their husbands for they do not want to suffer from the stigma of being abandoned from their husbands. Since divorces are costly and also time-consuming processes, many deserted women do not take the matter to the court to get a permanent relief.

Desertion may be temporary or permanent. Temporary desertion may be due to low family income and is considered *"poor man's vacation"*. He may come back once the problem is solved. On the other hand, permanent desertion is complete abandonment of the responsibility towards the family. This has been done after having made successive attempts for readjustment. Therefore, it is a final termination of unsatisfactory relationship. Further, some of the consequences of desertion are similar to those of divorce, for the family may be permanently dissolved.

DIVORCE IN INDIA

Marriage is one of the universal social institutions of mankind. In almost all the societies of the world, both uncivilised and civilised, majority of the people enter into marital relationship at an appropriate age in their own way. Though majority of the people enter into wedlock there is no guarantee that their marriage would ultimately end in success. Many marriages end in failures and wind up with divorce. The rate of divorce is fast increasing in many of the Western countries posing a serious social problem.

Meaning of the Word *"Divorce"*

The English word *"divorce"* is derived from the Latin word *divortium* which again is derived from *dis* which means *"apart"* and *vertere* which means *"to turn."* Divorce is the dissolution of the tie of marriage.[1] So, *divorce is the turning away of partners from each other. It truly is a complete turn from the way of life the couple had so far.* [**S. Pothen.** Page - 2.]

It is clear from the above description, the term *"divorce"* refers to the complete rupture of the marital bond. The persons thus divorced go back to the original position of being free to marry again. *"Divorce" is the word which is normally given to the legal ending of marriage.* In the legal language, it might appear as a simple phenomenon, but in practical life its implications are massive and many-faceted. Divorce represents the end of hopes that husband and wife had for each other; it is the certificate that their relationship failed.

Definition of Divorce

1. ***Ian Robertson*** **:** *"Divorce constitutes official social recognition that a marriage has failed, and it can be a traumatic experience for all concerned".*
2. ***Wallace*** *and* ***Wallace*** **:** *"When a marriage does not have a sufficient base upon which to survive, it may end in divorce".*
3. ***W.P. Scott*** in *'Dictionary of Sociology'* **:** Divorce is *"an institutionalised arrangement for terminating the marriage relationship and allowing each partner the right to remarry".*
4. ***The Hindu Marriage Act,*** **1955** gives the following explanation. According to this Act, *"any marriage solemnised, whether before or after the commencement of this Act, may, on a petition presented by either the husband or the wife, be dissolved by a decree of divorce"* on the grounds mentioned therein.

DIVORCE AMONG THE HINDUS

Divorce is not unfamiliar to modern India. In modern India, divorce rate is found to be higher than what it was a few decades ago. In the absence of the reliable statistics it is very difficult to estimate the actual rate of divorce in India. It could however be generalised that the rate of divorce is higher in the cities and nuclear families than in the villages and undivided families.

Hindus, in general, still believe that *"marriages are arranged in heaven."* Hindus consider their marriage irrevocable and indissoluble. According to the traditional Hindu belief, marital bond is said to be inseparable and irrevocable. The parties to the marriage cannot dissolve it at will. They are bound to each other until the death of either of them. The belief states that the wife is supposed to be bound to her husband even after his death.

This concept of marriage that it is indissoluble, is itself a sublime one which makes husband and wife to adjust their tastes, tempers, ideals, interests, choices and preferences. It thus involves sacrifices on the part of both husband and wife for each is called upon to bear with the other. Each individual is here called upon to make marriage a success by means of compromise and adjustment.

Divorce was almost unknown in the ancient period in India. In spite of having divergent and opposite views, wife and husband were made to live together. There is no reference to divorce in the whole of Vedic literature. According to ***Manu Smriti,*** Dharma is based on the life long mutual respect for each other by wife and husband. The Puranic writers who popularised the ideal of *"Pativratya"* also expected the Hindu wife to be devoted to her husband and husband alone. Fidelity and modest service to the husband were regarded as the sole duty and main purpose in her life. The ideal of *"pativratya"* gave rise to and glorified the practice of *"sati"* or *"self-immolation"* during the later days.

---

1 *Encyclopedia Britannica,* Vol.III, Cambridge, 1910. Page - 334.

Some Provisions For *"Divorce"* Even in the Ancient World ?

Though the Hindu thinkers, in general, were against divorce, some of them had made some provisions for divorce. Even **Manu** had recognised the husband's right to divorce the wife particularly when the bride's basic and irreparable physical and mental defects such as epilepsy, leprosy, adulterous relations with other men, etc., were concealed by the parents prior to marriage.

Kautilya's *"Arthashastra"* also provides some ground for divorce. Accoding to Kautilya, if there is mutual envy or jealousy between the wife and husband, then they can leave each other. However, consent of both is necessary for this. Kautilya mentions four kinds of marriages, such as *Brahma, Prajapatya, Arsha* and *Daiva* in which the question of divorce does not arise at all, because these marriages are subject to the approval and blessings of the father.

Narada and **Parashara,** two other *Shastrakaras* had conferred on the Hindu wife the right to divorce her husband on certain specific grounds such as the following : (i) *the death of first husband;* (ii) *whereabouts of the husband not known for months together;* (iii) *impotency of husband;* (iv) *husband becoming a "sanyasi";* (v) *husband's failure to honour and obey the requirements of Varna Dharma resulting in his outcaste;* (vi) *mutual enmity.*

According to **Valvalkar,** *"divorce is not known to the Hindu institution of marriage."*[2] A married partner, particularly a woman, was expected to undergo any hardship in order to salvage her marriage. The Hindu writers seem to be partial and lenient towards men right from the beginning. Strict fidelity and devotion was demanded from a woman, whereas a man could marry again even in the life-time of a wife. In fact, writers during the later days even debased womanhood. Women were pictured as lesser human beings, with only low desires and goals. A woman is depicted as a temptress, who contempts and seduces any man, even the most learned one. Through centuries, Hindu women were suppressed, fettered and ill treated for no fault of theirs. Hindu womanhood was derided and looked down upon. Hence, any attempt to change the nature of Hindu marriage was violently opposed by traditionalists. Vast majority of Indian men were thus not prepared to risk a change even mentally.

Even though some provisions were made by the ancient *Smritikars* for giving divorce, people, on the whole were not in favour of divorce. **Fonseca,** who made a research on the subject under the guidance of eminent sociologist, **Prof. G.S. Ghurye,** came to the conclusion that *"it can be safely asserted that separation, desertion and divorce as they represent various degrees of dissolution of the family are generally not favoured in Indian society."* This is possibly due to the adverse effects of divorce.[3]

Divorce Among the Hindus in Modern India

Though some ancient *Shastrakaras* did make some provision for divorce under some extra-ordinary circumstances the main stress was on the irrevocability of marital bond. During the second half of the ancient period, and medieval and early modern period, even those provisions disappeared. Thus Hindu marriage which was regarded as *dharmic* [religious] in the traditional Hindu society did not permit divorce.

Hindu marriage is gradually becoming secularised in the modern period. In spite of the pressure and influence of modernism, the Hindu Law did not permit divorce till 1950s, though some castes did sanction the dissolution of marriage on some grounds.

Legislation to Legalise Divorce

The first legislation in respect of the dissolution of marriage in India was enacted for **Christians** in 1869 called the *"Indian Divorce Act",* for **Parsis** in 1936 called *"Parsi Marriage*

2. **P.A. Valvalkar** in *"Hindu Social Institutions"* [1939]. Page - 145.
3. **S. Pothen** in *"Divorce - Its Causes and Consequences in Hindu Society"* [1996]. Page - 7.

Divorce Act"; and for **Hindus** in **Kolhapur** State in 1920. When the Bombay state passed the *"Bombay Hindu Divorce Act"* permitting divorce on the grounds such as – impotency, lunacy for more than 7 years, leprosy for 7 years, desertion for 4 years, and bigamy, etc. – *as many as 5,500 petitions for divorce were filed within the time span of five years* [1947-52]. This made our legal experts to introduce legislations on an all-India basis permitting the Hindus to avail of the facility of divorce if required.

On an all-India level, *the Special Marriage Act* was passed in 1954, and *the Hindu Marriage Act,* in 1955 which legally permitted divorce to Hindus. The latter one was amended in 1976 and also in 1981 and it provides for judicial separation, divorce, nullity of marriage and annulment of marriage.

Provisions for Divorce in *"The Hindu Marriage Act, 1955"*

This Act which came into force from May 18, 1955 brought about revolutionary changes not only in the marital relations but also in various other social aspects. This Act applies to the whole of India, except Jammu and Kashmir. The word **"Hindu"** in the Act includes Jains, Sikhs, Buddhists and the Scheduled Castes.

Conditions for valid marriage as provided in this Act **:** (1) neither party has a spouse living; (2) neither party [bridegroom or bride] is an idiot or a lunatic; (3) the groom must have completed 21 years and the bride 18 years of age as per the 1978 Amendement brought to this Act; (4) the parties should not be 'sapindas' of each other unless the custom permits such a marriage.

"The Hindu Marriage Act - 1995", amended in 1976 and 1981, lays down various grounds for divorce, judicial separation, nullity of marriage and annulment of marriage such as the following [applicable to both the spouses] :

(i) Impotency at the time of marriage until the institution of the proceedings.

(ii) Voluntary sexual intercourse with any person other than his or her spouse;

(iii) Cruel treatment which includes physical and mental cruelty;

(iv) Desertion for two years;

(v) If the marriage has taken place because of force or fraud.

(vi) Ceasing to be a Hindu by conversion to another religion;

(vii) Of incurably unsound mind / mental disorder; lunacy at the time of marriage,

(viii) Suffering from veneral disease in a communicable form;

(ix) Renouncing the world by entering any religious order;

(x) Suffering from a virulent and incurable form of leprosy;

(xi) Has not been heard of as being alive for a period of seven years or more;

(xii) No resumption of cohabitation as between the parties to the marriage for a period of one year or upwards after the passing of a decree for judicial separation;

(xiii) No restitution of conjugal rights as between the parties to the marriage for a period of one year or upwards after the passing of a decree for restitution of conjugal rights;

(xiv) Mutual consent, [as per 1976 amendment] on the ground that they have been living separately for a period of one year or more, that they have not been able to live together, and that they have mutually agreed that the marriage should be dissolved, on the motion of both the parties made not earlier than six months after the date of the presentation of the petition, and not later than 18 months after the said date.

CAUSES OF DIVORCE

The phenomenon of divorce is caused by many factors some of which are very general in nature. They may be discussed as below.

1. Stresses and Strains on the Nuclear Family

The nuclear family has many dysfunctions in modern society. It is highly vulnerable to break up if the bread winner is for any reason unwilling or unable to meet economic obligations. The spouses in a nuclear family have a very strong mutual dependency, especially after the children have left home. They may make extremely heavy demands on one another for emotional support. The failure of one partner to meet the expectations of the other endangers the marriage. But such dangers are not usually seen in the case of the extended family system.

2. The Fading of Romantic Love

The western people are socialised in such a way that they are made to believe that romantic love would make their marriage happy and successful. But the hard realities of life make them understand that the joys of romantic love are usually short-lived. As a result, the excitement of the earlier relationship gets diminished or lost in the daily routines of job and housework. This does not mean that the partners no longer love one another, but their love is likely to be of a different kind. This could be mature, companionable, and deeply fulfilling, but many people fail to appreciate it. Hence, they consider the fading of their romance as a symptom of marital failure. They lose faith in their marriage and may start looking for romance elsewhere.

3. Changing Role of Women

In the past, *"the role of the wife was assumed to be that of housekeeper, child-rearer and nurturant supporter of a husband who was active in the world beyond the home"*. The modern women are rejecting this role, and in doing so, are challenging the established structure of the nuclear family. Women are no longer confined to the home for much of their lives through pregnancy and the care of infants. Woman in the modern family is becoming more and more independent. Most of the modern families do not have appropriate norms for the woman who wants an independent career; and for the wife who earns more than the husband and becomes the primary bread winner. This situation often develops complexes in men. The growing economic independence of women makes it much easier for them to divorce their mates.

4. Sexual Permissiveness

The widespread availability of contraceptives has separated two different functions of sexual relations - *procreation and recreation.* The use of sex by the marital partners for the purpose of procreation is understandable. But the use of sex for recreational purpose creates problem. Due to the introduction of contraceptives, the danger of pregnancy is removed and hence people feel free to engage in premarital and extramarital sexual intercourse. The nuclear family is built on an assumption of monogamous fidelity, but the growing permissiveness encourages people to search for sexual satisfaction outside their marriage. Sexual permissiveness, thus makes husband and wife develop mutual distrust, dislike and even contempt. The emotional relationship between them collapses making any one of the two take the earlier opportunity to go away from the other.

Causes of Divorce in the Indian Context

In addition to the general causes of divorce cited above, various other factors have also added to the phenomenon of divorce especially in the Indian context. **Dr. S. Pothen** in her book *"Divorce - Its Causes and Consequences in Hindu Society"* points out at some of the causes, which may be noted below :

1. *Cruelty* : Cruelty is one of the most important factors responsible for starting serious conflicts between husband and wife. The complaint of cruelty has been found to be maximum in the lower class than in the middle and upper classes. Physical cruelty like, assaulting and not giving food is more common in the lower classes, but is also found to be present to a certain extent in the middle class. Cruelty may be physical or mental; it may be by words, gestures, or by mere silence.

2. *Interference by in-laws* : An important problem of the married Hindu women is adjustment with the in-laws, more so in large joint families. In Indian families, a son's loyalty is divided among his parents, his spouse and in the authoritarian joint family, the greater share of his loyalty goes to his kin and not to the spouse. The female spouse finds herself in the midst of strangers, many of whom are hostile. She cannot expect any kind of sympathy, support and understanding from her in-laws, such as – the mother-in-law, father-in-law, sister-in-law, brother-in-law, uncle or aunt-in-law, grand-in-laws, and so on. Pothen's study has revealed that 41.5% of the female spouses have reported that they have had problems with their in-laws.

3. *Mental Problems* : Modern life brings on us lot of stress and strain. **Reimer** has pointed out that *"neurotic as well as psychotic ailments have been attributed to stresses inherent in the urban way of life."*[4] Various pressures such as economic, familial, social and cultural act directly or indirectly on the minds of people. With reference to the changing societies like India, cultural lag and cultural conflict often add to the mental stresses and strains. Dr. Pothen's study has revealed that mental breakdown is one of the causes of marital breakdown in some instances. Both men and women suffer from this problem, though the sufferings of women are comparatively more.

4. *Unplanned and Unthought of Marriage* : It is observed that marital relationship is established without sufficient forethought. In case of arranged marriages, many people do not care to make rational enquiries about the other party. Most of the information given may be only to impress the person at first sight, and unless carefully scrutinised, there can be a lot of discrepancies between the real conditions and the information given. This type of hurried marriages are arranged more in the case of girls than boys. Such hasty marriages can also lead to unpleasant or even shocking discoveries later, which will ultimately shatter the chances of happiness in marriage.

5. *Economic Hardship* : Family life and problems are closely associated with economic hardships and problems. With increasing cost of living, economic problems are soaring high. Such economic problems are more experienced, when the husband is partially or poorly employed or when he is forced to spend his income on certain unwanted things. In such cases, food, clothing, housing and education of the members of the family, particularly the children, are adversely affected. In such a situation, frustrations arise, creating conflicts and tensions in the family. Such state of affairs will also result in desertions and divorce.

6. *Education and Economic Independence of Women* : Emancipation and economic independence of women have been important causes of rapid rise in divorce rate throughout the world. **Fonseca's** study has also showed that *"women today no longer occupy a subordinate position in the family."* Enlightened women are inclined to take advantages of the legal provisions of divorce wherever it is badly and necessarily required. The available data and information are sufficient to conclude that education, employment, emancipation and enlightenment of the Hindu women are causing more and more divorces.

7. *Sexual Maladjustment* : Sexual relationship is considered to be one of the strong bases of any marriage, more so, in the initial stages. Whenever, the spouses are unable to establish

---

4. **Reimer** in *"The Modern City"* as quoted by **Dr. S. Pothen.** Page - 134.

satisfying sexual relationship between themselves, marriage is in danger. Physical causes like, impotency of the male and structural malformation of the female sexual organs, may incapacitate the couple to enter into healthy sexual relationships. Further, sexual relationship in human beings is not a mere physical activity. Several physical, psychological and emotional aspects come into play in sexual life. When the favourable circumstances do not prevail in these fields, sex life may be unsatisfying. Sexual maladjustments, thus, can cause divorce.

8. *Other Factors* :

Dr. S. Pothen in her book has also mentioned various other factors contributing to divorce, which may be briefed as follows :

1. Child marriage, which is still in practice in India, especially among lower castes and classes, contributes to divorce.
2. Marriages, which are arranged against the wishes of the spouses often end in unwanted divorce.
3. Incompatibility of the spouses has been an important cause of divorce in the Indian context. [Sizeable number of individuals (39 husbands and 32 wives) complained of the incompatibility between their temperaments and those of their spouses].
4. Quarrlesome nature of the spouses is another common complaint of men and women of all economic classes. In some cases, the allegation is both ways, and in some others, it is the onesided allegation.
5. Unhealthy habits like alcoholism, gambling, immorality, often contribute to family tensions, conflicts between husband and wife, and eventually to divorce.
6. Barrenness is considered a curse in the Indian society. A wife, who is found to be barren or infertile, or a husband, who is found to be impotent, often contributes to marital unhappiness and failure. The desire for progeny tempts either one of them to go for divorce.
7. Many a time in our society, there is a tendency to hide physical defects of the parties to marriage before its solemnisation. When the defects are disclosed after the marriage, they get disillusioned.
8. Dowry has become an inseparable part of our marriage system. The husband or his parents would like to extract as much dowry as possible. Unhappiness that is caused because of dowry makes the parties to the marriage go apart.
9. A few women have complained of their husbands forcing them to lead an immoral life in order to earn money. These women who belonged mostly to the middle and lower classes were disappointed with their marriage because of this some have sought divorce on account of this.
10. Lack of affection on the part of spouses towards each other has been found to be one of the causes of divorce. In **Dr. S. Pothen**'s study, around 19.5% of the husbands and 27% wives have complained of lack of affection.

Causes of Divorce : Views of Dr. Damle, Fonseca and Choudhry

The empirical studies undertaken by **Dr. Damle, Fonseca** and **Choudhry** have revealed the following factors contributing to the phenomenon of divorce in the Indian context.[5]

1. Divorce is *not always the result of marital disharmony* especially in the Indian context.

5. **Prof. Ram Ahuja** in *"Indian Social System."* Page - 182.

2. Some wives tolerate the alleged neglect, callousness, and even cruelty at the hands of their husbands *but cannot tolerate the trouble, irritation and insult caused by their in-laws.* Such women often seek divorce.
3. Some husbands apply for divorce either because they *doubt the sincerity and single-minded devotion of their wives* towards them or because they find wide intellectual and educational gap between them and their wives.
4. The *failure on the part of the wives coming from the highly orthodox families to keep up with their husbands' social life* - is often the cause. The opposite also sometimes holds good [though less often] where the wife finds life with husband of quiet habits, colourless and dull.
5. In the arranged marriages, where the reason for entering into matrimony is not mutual attraction but a variety of other factors [for example, respect for parents, good dowry, high family connections, etc.] there is less chance for give and take and a low desire for mutual adjustment. People of such *unsatisfying marriage* may often resort to divorce.

Types of Divorce as Per Wikipedia

The Wikipedia free encyclopedia mentions different types of divorce in terms of causal factors and they are stated below.

1. No-Fault Divorce: In this type of dissolution of marriage, it is not necessary to find a proof of fault to make an allegation against either party. Common reasons contributing to no-fault-divorce include – incompatibility, irreconcilable differences and irremediable breakdown of the marriage. In fact, the divorce application can be made by both parties jointly.

2. Uncontested Divorce: When the parties to the marriage can agree and present the court with a fair and equitable agreement, approval of divorce is almost guaranteed. When the parties cannot come to an agreement they may ask the court to decide to deal with the property, children and so on.

3. At Fault Divorce: If the marriage has taken place by fault, then at-fault divorces are the only way to break marriage; and people who had severe differences have only the option to separate and are prevented from legally re-marrying. At - Fault divorce can affect the distribution of property depending on the law of the land.

4. Collaborative Divorce: This type of divorce helps the couples to come to agreement on divorce issues. The parties negotiate an agreed resolution with the help and guidance of the attorneys who are trained in collaborate divorce process. The parties are permitted to make their own decisions based on their own needs and interests, but with complete information and full professional support.

5. Summary Divorce: A summary divorce is available in some jurisdiction and used when spouses meet certain eligibility requirements, or can agree on key issues before hand. ***Example:*** Parties having no children.

6. Mediated Divorce: Here, divorce takes place through mediation and not through litigation. In a divorce mediation session, a mediator facilitates the discussion between the husband and wife by assisting with communication and providing information and suggestions to help resolve differences. Divorce mediation can be significantly less expensive than litigation.

Factors that Affect the Rate of Divorce and Its Intensity

Sociological studies pertaining to the various instances of divorce have revealed that certain factors influence and affect the rate of divorce and its intensity. Among those factors the following may be noted.

1. How old the Marriage is-? OR Number of Years Married: It has been observed, if the couples are able to live together for a number of years after the marriage, then the possibility of these people going for a divorce becomes very bleak, for they have already learnt the art of adjusting and co-operating with each other. The common divorces are likely to occur in the early years in the case of mismatched marriages.

2. Occupational Factor: In comparison with the general tendencies towards divorces, it is observed that certain occupations show high rate of divorces. It is found that occupations as commercial travellers, artists, occupations requiring long separation or dislocation from the family and that demands round the clock duty - are more prone to divorce. Recent statistics have also revealed that people working in the I.T. [Information Technology] field are also more inclined to go for early divorces.

3. Families with and Without Children: It is a general observation that holds true in almost all places that divorces are common between couples without children than between those with children. People with children are less willing to allow the home to be broken up. Selfishness thrives in the childless home, and the ties between the partners get weakened in the absence of children.

4. Divorce and the Sex of the Petitioner: Who actually appeals for or initiate divorce, husband or wife? This factor varies culturally. In many Western countries, husband and wife make appeals for divorce almost in an equal number. But in the Indian context; many women prefer to suffer the tragedy quietly than face the shame of divorce. During the recent years, at the level of educated and employed women this shyness or cultural inhibition is not there and hence they are also equally ready to appeal for divorce if they are disillusioned with their marriage.

5. Divorce and Cultural Differences: Rate of divorce differs from society to society depending upon the cultural peculiarities or differences. It is generally observed that the rate of divorce is higher in the Western countries than in the Eastern countries. In countries such as India, China and Japan the rate of divorce was found to be very less for a very long time due to the influence of well established family system.

INDIVIDUAL AND SOCIAL CONSEQUENCES OF DIVORCE

The doubling of the divorce rate since 1950s has meant that many more couples and their children experience the disturbances that frequently accompany divorce. Some of the main consequences or the after-effects of divorce could be listed below.

1. Emotional Upsets, Anguish and Anxiety: Studies have revealed that divorced men and women experience intermittent *longing for their husbands or wives,* with an accompanying anxiety, even if they themselves had initiated divorce.

2. The immediate impact of divorce on children is very severe. Preschool children experience fright, and bewilderment and tend to blame themselves for separation, while the older children express their anger more directly.

3. The high divorce rate has created large number of non-traditional single-parent homes. This is particularly true in the Western context. For example, in 1985, 23.4% of America's 62.5 million children under the age 18, lived with only one of their parents [**N.J. Smelser.** Page : 260].

4. Divorce affects economic position also. Economic adjustment after the divorce becomes a greater problem if the party is dependent or the legal proceeding orders to maintain the aggrieved party. The unemployed partner is forced to hunt a job and sometimes has to be contented with a menial job with meager salary. If the husband is to pay for the maintenance of the divorced wife, then it becomes an additional burden. Sometimes, even wives are forced to take up employment.

5. Divorce very badly damages the personality development of children. In fact, adverse effect upon the children of a dissolved marriage is one of the most forceful arguments against divorce. In the cases where children's parents with whom they are living, decide to remarry, children face the problem of step-parent. Children also face the social criticism when they are teased and taunted by their playmates. In this way, children face personal disorganisation. Children in a broken home, have often resorted to juvenile delinquency, adolescent crimes, sex offences or become vagrants. A sense of guilt is often developed by these children which will hinder their normal personality growth.

6. Divorcees often suffer from emotional problems such as indecision, frustration, disappointment, sleeplessness, mental ambivalence, guilt-consciousness, self-contempt, etc. The divorced person faces greater hardships after the separation. His prestige, future economic standing and social status may be very badly affected. The future may appear to be so frightening that the entire family may attempt suicide. The divorced man or woman who faces hardships may select suicide as the best way out of the problem.

7. Divorcees face the problem of sex adjustment. Strong sexual urge on the part of the divorced husband and wife often push them to seek satisfaction in an immoral way.

8. Divorce affects the divorcees' habits and regular life. Due to the marital breakdown, the routinised habits struggle to find their customary expression, but their failure to do so brings unrest, irritation and dissatisfaction. When the marriage is broken some habits find their usual expression. Drinking, addiction to drugs, gambling, prostitution, etc. are some of the reported habits.

9. Divorce affects the network of social relationships of husband and wife. It introduces complications into the relations of both husband and wife after separation. Especially in the Indian context, both the individuals become the victims of gossip and irritating comments. Even the close friend of the divorced person becomes suspicious and avoids company.

10. Refusal to Marry due to Fear of Divorce: Due to the fear of divorce many young men and women in the western countries remain unmarried. While some of them, knowingly or unknowingly, delay it for a long time.

11. Divorce injures the ego of the persons involved. Both in desertion and divorce, there is a sense of rejection which is humiliating to the person who feels that he or she is lacking something to fill in the life of the other. Injured ego might lead these people to commit acts of revenge on others.

12. Effects on society as a whole: Disruption in family relations affects the entire society. The insecurity caused by divorce and desertion may give rise to a number of anti-social tendencies among those affected. Socialisation will suffer while prostitution and extra marital relations may ruin many more families.

REMEDIAL MEASURES FOR DIVORCE : AVOIDANCE OF FAMILY TENSIONS AND DIVORCE

Various factors discussed above have been causing family tensions, desertions and even divorces. The rate of divorce is slowly increasing in the Indian context. Therefore, steps must be taken to lessen such tensions in the early stages by various means to save marriage and family. Some of the remedial measures can be suggested in this regard.

1. Education About Proper Selection of Mates

Modern young men and women who are very much influenced by movies, T.V. shows, literature, and other media, are more prone to be romantic especially in marital matters. While selecting their life partners, they give more importance to romantic matters rather than to hard reality. Young people must be made aware of the consequences of romantic marriages and need to be advised to become more realistic and to have faith in their parents, who can choose a better companion for them according to their own cultural settings.

Landis P.H. points out, *"many divorces arise because the romantic expectations with which young people often enter marriage, are frustrated by the unromantic realities of the marital situation. If these expectations could be modified in the direction of greater realism, large number of marriages might conceivably be saved."*[6]

The caution given by **Eliot** and **Merrill** in this regard is worth considering – *"Men and women are demanding greater personal satisfaction from the estate of matrimony. But then one has to work harder at making marriage a success. Also greater emphasis upon personal happiness in marriage deserves analysis as to its essential validity. Life exacts difficulties as well as pleasures and is full of petty annoyances, disappointments and disillusionments, both in and out of marriage. Probably no married person is completely happy before marriage, nor he can expect to be completely happy after marriage. Many young men nourished in the romantic tradition, may blame their marriage, if they feel unhappy whereas the difficulty may be either within themselves or in situations external to marriage."*[7]

2. Family Counselling Agencies

Family tensions are often due to differences in temperaments, attitudes and social values, economic difficulties, ill health, conflict on child's training, etc. These differences arise due to the lack of understanding between the spouses. Family counselling agencies with trained social workers in family matters can be of great help in mitigating these differences and helping the spouses to develop mutual understanding. Family counselling agencies are commonly found in industrially advanced countries, such as America, Britain, France, Canada, etc. Only recently such agencies have started functioning in India that too in cosmopolitan cities.

Family counselling agencies should be established at all district and taluk centres. They must act as welfare agencies. These welfare agencies which add to the welfare of the family, and ease tensions. Agencies rendering financial assistance to economically backward families or family planning clinics should be assisted and encouraged by the state.

3. Family Counselling Courts

When matters relating to family disputes, conflicts, etc. come to the court for divorce, attempt should be made by the concerned authorities to gather facts relating to the cases through the social workers and analyse them properly before giving a decision. The courts should not act just on the basis of statistics, evidences, facts, figures, etc. in a mechanical manner. Its main intention should be to save the marriage and to help the spouses to live together with better understanding and mutual support. *The Family Court Act, 1984* makes provision for that.

4. Help After Divorce

In spite of all the best possible efforts to save a marriage, some cases ultimately end in divorce only. In some cases, that is, constant tension in the family not only affects the life organisation of husband and wife, but also their children. In such cases, efforts should be made to provide financial assistance to the forsaken wife and to the maintenance of children. Divorced women should not be compelled to resort to prostitution if they are not able to secure employment. No

6. **Landis Paul H.** in his article *"Control of the Romantic Impulse Through Education"* as quoted by **G.R. Madan** in his *"Indian Social Problems"* Vol.I. [1966]. Page - 386.
7. **Eliot** and **Merrill** quoted by **G.R. Madan.** Page - 386.

other environment has proved so favourable for the upbringing of children as the home, which the parents create. If the home is utterly inharmonious or positively harmful, the state must seek to protect the children in some way or the other.

5. Family Welfare Services [Agencies]

Whenever serious social, economic and emotional problems arise in the family, it often finds it difficult to settle or solve these problems satisfactorily. In the olden days, the joint family system, caste system with its caste panchayat and the community of close relatives used to provide guidance and the needed help in facing such crises or disturbing situations. Today, all these are not available for the family members to seek timely help and support. Social security protection formerly provided by the joint family is not found in the modern family. Hence, some alternative is the need of the hour. ***Social Welfare Agencies*** have been founded especially to face such grave situations.

- ***Objectives of Family Welfare Agencies***: According to *"Encyclopaedia of Social Work in India"*, the purpose of social and family welfare agencies is – *"to contribute to harmonious family interrelationships to strengthen the positive values of life, to promote healthy personality development and to ensure satisfactory social functioning of various members of the family."*

Functions of Family Welfare Agencies

In general, the family welfare agencies function with the following objectives:

1. To help individuals to overcome problems of adjustment in intra-family relationships.
2. To ensure life of mutual love and affection in the family which will provide security to all its members.
3. To impart family education so as to make family living a happy and wholesome experience for all.
4. To organize courses in family life education so that members realize their rights, duties, obligations and adjust themselves through understanding.
5. To foster healthy development of the family to keep it strong and stable.
6. To provide shelter and counsel for women in distress.
7. To provide family counseling, medical aid, financial assistance, legal aid and case work service in adolescent problems, mental problems and parental problems.
8. To arrange for marriage counseling and pre-marriage counseling and to help families experiencing difficulties.
9. To understand, to face, and to resolve their problems through competent guidance.

As the above points make it clear, the family welfare services help to clarify family relationships, deal with problems confronting the family and its members, and give emotional support and general help to overcome family tensions. These agencies have given lot of help in areas such as – *adoption, family adjustment, placement of women and children in institutions and pre-marriage, marriage and family counseling and reference to child guidance clinics, vocational guidance, and other social welfare agencies.*

6. Uniform Divorce Laws

It is often suggested that there should be uniform divorce laws, and uniform family norms in the state applicable to people of all the castes, classes and religious groups. This would help the partners to adjust to the new set up after the marriage and to reduce contemplation on separation by all means. If there is diversity regarding rules of divorce [as we find in India today in the form of separate rules for Hindus, Muslims and Christians], then people take more chances to justify divorce. Such a situation makes the position of women all the more precarious and insecure. This is, however, possible only when *'Common Civil Code'* is introduced in the country, and the time is ripe for it.

7. Stricter Regulation of Marriage

We find lot of laxity in family norms and relation in rules guiding the marriage. Marriages are being contracted casually and without responsibility. Greediness for dowry and craziness for sex have been the driving force in the case of a few individuals for contracting series of marriages. A case of a psychopath who successively contracted more than 21 marriages after collecting relatively huge sums of money from each one of the girls who married him, has been reported recently [2012] in the Dakshina Kannada District of Karnataka. [A primary school teacher who has been found to be the culprit has been arrested and several criminal cases are going on against him for he has killed more than 20 women soon after marrying them and fulfilling his purposes]. Although dissolution of marriage is a social problem of grave concern, it has become a business for many legal advisors.

8. Eugenic Marriage Law - ?

These days, relatively a large number of marriages are ending in failures mainly because of chronic and serious ill-health of either one of the partners in marriage the fact of which was kept secret before the marriage. If eugenic marriage laws are implemented, then it becomes mandatory for one to provide a certificate of sound health and freedom from disease, especially from venereal diseases and dangerous diseases like AIDS, to the other party prior to the contracting of the marriage. Marriage between mental defectives and insane should also be avoided. Similarly, the physically challenged; no matter their human rights are respected; however there should not be any social compulsion to marry them.

Conclusion

Modern family is in problems everywhere. No society is equipped with ways and means to provide readymade solutions to these problems. Since the modern society gives primacy to individualism and upholds individual interests, marital and family values are relegated to the place of secondary importance. Unless the partners are ready to make necessary adjustments and sacrifices, they will not be able to build a healthy and united family unit. Some of the problems of family can be solved with the help of the specialists, a few more can be settled with the help of social welfare agencies. Counselling courts and counselling agencies can also play their role to a certain extent in saving the family from being crumbled down. All these external agencies can only provide temporary relief or a short-run solution to the problems of the family. But the permanent solution lies with the individuals themselves who are a party to the marriage and the pillars of family. It is necessary for these partners of marriage to change their mindset and make voluntary mental preparation to make marriage a success and family a place of happy living. It is possible only when the social ideals of marriage are raised to a higher level.

Marital Success is Necessary for the Prevention of Divorce

Divorce can be defeated, only when marriage becomes a success. Families continue to thrive only if they are not threatened with desertions and divorces. Though marriage is being eulogised on various grounds, we have not been able to stop divorce from taking place. Divorce rate is increasing in the West. The trend towards higher rate of divorce is seen in India too. The main reason for divorce is marital failure. Hence, finding out the secrets of marital success is the best solution for divorce. A great gynaecologist **Th.H. Van de Velde** in his book *"Ideal Marriage - Its Physiology and Technique"* [Page : 4] has suggested four important points for attaining happiness in marriage.

They are mentioned below:

1. A right choice of marriage partner.
2. A good psychological attitude of partners, both to the world in general and to each other.
3. A solution of the problem of parentage which meets the wishes of both partners, and
4. A vigorous and harmonious sex life.

DIVORCE AMONG THE MUSLIMS

Prophet Mohammed was, in the initial stages, against any inconsiderate haste in divorcing a wife as well as any harsh treatment to her. But later on, he gave his consent for divorce. In fact, the Muslim husband has been given the greatest freedom in regard to divorce. But nothing is mentioned about the grounds on which divorce may be obtained.

Three Main Ways of Obtaining Divorce

With the passage of time, Muslims, however, have found out three main ways of obtaining divorce. In other words, the Muslim marriage which is treated as a contract can be dissolved as per the following three important ways:

1. *Divorce as per the Muslim law but without the intervention of the court;*
2. *Divorce as per the Shariah Act, 1937;*
3. *Divorce as per the Muslim Marriage Dissolution Act, 1959, that is, as per the court's intervention.*

1. Divorce According to Muslim Law: *Khula / Mubarat* and *Talaq*

According to the traditional Muslim law, divorce can be obtained directly in two ways without the intervention of the civil court. They are: (A) *Khula / Mubarat* and (B) *Talaq*

(A) Khula or Kohl and Mubarat: Husband and wife can obtain divorce by mutual consent either by *'Khula'* or by *'Mubarat'*. Difference between *Khula* and *Mubarat* is simple: In *Khula,* divorce is initiated at the instance of the wife. In *Mubarat,* since both the parties desire separation, the initiative may come either from the wife or from the husband.

(B) Talaq: *Talaq* represents one of the ways according to which a Muslim husband can give divorce to his wife as per the Muslim law without the intervention of the court. In *talaq,* the husband has the right to dismiss his wife by repeating the dismissal formula thrice. The *talaq* may be affected either orally by making some pronouncements or in writing by presenting *'talaqnama'*. *Talaq* may be given in any one of the following three ways.

(i) Talaq-e-Ahasan: This involves *a single pronouncement of talaq* followed by a period of conjugal abstinence till the completion of *'iddat'*.

(ii) Talaq-e-Hasan: This consists of three pronouncements of 'Talaq' made during three successive menstrual periods and no sexual contact be taken place between the spouses during these months.

(iii) Talaq-e-ul-Bidat: Here, *talaq* pronouncement takes place in any one of the following ways. (a) in a single sentence, for example, *"I divorce thee thrice"* or in three separate sentences: *"I divorce thee, I divorce thee, I divorce thee"* (b) in a single but clear pronouncement such as, *"I divorce thee irrevocably"*.

In the first two types cited above, there is a chance for re-establishing the marital ties but not in the third form.

2. Divorce as Recognised by *The Shariah Act, 1937*

The Shariah Act, 1937 provides for three forms of divorce. They are mentioned below.

(i) ***Illa:*** If the husband swears by God to abstain from sexual relations with his wife for a period of four months or more, or for a specified period, he is said to make *illa*. If he sticks on to his words, then marriage gets dissolved.

(ii) ***Zihar:*** In this type, the husband of sound mind declares in the presence of two witnesses that his wife looks like his mother to him. Though marriage is not dissolved with this, it gives scope for the wife to go to court on this ground.

(iii) ***Lian:*** In this type the husband accuses his wife of being guilty of adultery. This, however, gives an opportunity for the wife to go to court insisting on her husband either to withdraw such an allegation or prove the same.

3. Provisions for Divorce as per *The Dissolution of Muslim Marriage Act, 1939*

The Dissolution of Muslim Marriage Act, 1939 passed during the British period entitles a Muslim woman to seek the dissolution of her marriage on the following grounds.

(i) whereabouts of husband not known for **4** years.
(ii) failure of husband to provide for her maintenance for **2** years.
(iii) imprisonment of husband for **7** years or more.
(iv) impotency of husband since the time of marriage.
(v) failure of husband to fulfil marital obligations for **3** years.
(vi) insanity of husband for a period of **2** years and husband's incurable diseases like leprosy, venereal diseases, etc.
(vii) husband's physical and mental cruelty.
(viii) marriage being thursted upon her before she attained **15** years, [but in this, the wife has to seek divorce before she completes **18**th year].
(ix) any other valid ground which the Muslim law permits.

Importance of *"Iddat"* in Muslims' Divorce

"Iddat" plays an important role in Muslims' divorce cases. *"Iddat" denotes a period of awaiting.*

- ***Iddat*** refers to a period of seclusion for three menstrual periods for a woman after the death of or divorce by her husband to ascertain whether she was pregnant at the time of divorce.
- *"Iddat" ".....implies the period of waiting incumbent on a woman between dissolution of one marriage and the contracting of another."*[8] It is important to note that in this period of waiting [for three consecutive menstrual periods] husband and wife are not supposed to have sexual contact.

Legal and Social Effects of Iddat

- ***Legal Effects:*** (i) In a divorce case the wife involved is bound to wait for *"iddat"* period. (ii) During the period of *"iddat"* the husband is obliged to provide for her maintenance. (iii) The wife is not supposed to give her consent for another marriage till the *iddat* period is completed. (iv) On the completion of *'iddat'* period, the wife can legitimately demand the *"deferred mahr"*.
- ***Social Effects:*** (i) *'Iddat'* serves as a restraining influence on inconsiderate haste on the part of the husband and on the tempo of divorce. It gives time for the husband to think and act.

8 As quoted by **C.B. Mamoria** in his *"Social Problems and Social Disorganisation in India."* Page 224.

The husband may simply take back the wife during the period of *iddat* and suspend the divorce. (ii) *Iddat* makes it clear whether the wife is pregnant or not. The fact of pregnancy sometimes brings reconciliation between them. (iii) If it becomes apparent during *'Iddat'* that the divorced wife is pregnant, the husband is recommended to take her back and treat her with consideration till the child is born. The child belongs to the husband if it is not born out of adultery. The wife also cannot marry any one else until her delivery. (iv) The *iddat* period is normally **three** months. In the case of a widow the duration is *4* months *10* days.

It may be noted that according to the **Muslim Women's Protection of Rights on Divorce Act 1986 and Iddat,** a wife can demand from her husband her maintenance during the Iddat.

DIVORCE AMONG THE CHRISTIANS

The ***Christian community*** has got two major sects or divisions within itself, namely the *Protestants* and the *Catholics.* The Catholics are further subdivided into *Latin Catholics* and *Syrian Catholics.* Each sect and each subgroup is endogamous. Catholics marry amongst themselves and do not normally marry Protestants. Further, the Latin Catholics and the Syrian Catholics do not normally intermarry. Marriage as a social institution is common to all the sects and subgroups in the Christian community. As it has been in the case of the Hindus and Muslims, marriage is quite popular among the Christians of India.

Legislations Relating to Christian Marriage and Divorce

The Indian Christian Marriage Act, **1872** [including its Amendments upto 1928] covers various aspects of Christian marriage. *The legislation strictly prohibits the practice of polygamy and polyandry among them and prescribes strict monogamy.* Several aspects such as – who should perform marriage, the place where it is to be performed [in which church], the time of performance, the relative age of the boy and the girl concerned, etc., are all dealt with by this legislation.

Provision for Divorce

The Indian Divorce Act, 1869 lays down the conditions under which Christians can obtain or seek divorce through the court. It also deals with the dissolution of the marriage declaring the marriage as null and void on the specific grounds. It provides for judicial separation, protection to the spouses and restitution of conjugal rights.

Section 10 of the Indian Divorce Act, 1869 gives right to the husband to divorce his wife on the ground of debauchery. The wife can also give or demand divorce from her husband on some conditions as –

(i) Leaving of religion by the husband and adoption of another religion or to marry another wife.
(ii) Debauchery of the husband.
(iii) His marrying a second wife.
(iv) Rape, sodomy or bestiality.
(v) Cruelty.
(vi) Besides being accused of debauchery if the husband has been living away for two years.

Section 18 of the legislation provides the right to husband and wife to submit an application for the declaration of marriage as null and void. A marriage can be declared so, on the grounds mentioned below.

(i) The respondent had been impotent at the time of marriage.

(ii) The respondent is a blood relation of the prohibited degrees.
(iii) Either of the party to a marriage was insane or an idiot at the time of marriage.
(iv) Wife and husband or either of the party is living and has re-married.
(v) Some property has been acquired by coercion or fraud by either of the party to a marriage.

Section 22 of this Act provides judicial separation. Besides this, the *Act* also provides for the protection of the wife and her rights.

Law Commission in its report submitted in 1998 recommended certain changes in the Christian marriage especially relating to some of the provisions of the *Indian Divorce Act, 1869.* It recommended the omission of certain irrelevant things and inclusion of the new ones that suit the modern conditions. Discussions are still going on between the leaders of the Christian communities and the Church authorities on the one hand, and the Central Government on the other, to bring about a comprehensive amendment to the Indian Divorce Act, 1869 to make it more relevant to the modern conditions.

It is clear from the above, that unlike the Hindus, the Christians do not consider marital bond as an indissoluble bond. Further, remarriage of the widows is not only possible but also accepted and encouraged among the Christians. Marriage is treated as a covenant between a man and a woman in which more stress is laid on love, mutual help and friendship or companionship.

●●●

Chapter 13

PROSTITUTION AND AIDS

(A) Prostitution: Definition – Nature and Characteristics of Prostitution – Types of Prostitutes: The Professionals and the Unconventional Types – Causes of Prostitution – Consequences of Prostitution – Prevention and Control of Prostitution: Legal Measures and Other Measures for Rehabilitation and Protection of Prostitutes – Some Proposals and Suggestions for the Rehabilitation of Prostitutes\

(B) HIV and AIDS: Meaning, Nature and Magnitude of AIDS: What is AIDS? AIDS at the World Level - AIDS in the Indian Context - Causes of HIV AIDS – Categories of Persons Likely to Get and Spread HIV – Early Symptoms of HIV Infection – HIV – AIDS is Not Spread the Following Ways – Consequences or Implications of HIV AIDS – Measures to Deal with HIV –AIDS: The Preventive Method and Curative Method or Method of Treatment – Major Information Centers of AIDS.

(A) PROSTITUTION

"Prostitution as a commercialised device and as a profession has existed in the world from times immemorial. As the world's oldest profession prostitution has undoubtedly existed in some form or the other as long as society has attempted to regulate and control sex relationships through the institutions of marriage and family."[1] This institution has existed in all the civilised socieities from the earliest times.

"In pre-industrial societies, where a woman's means of finding a legitimate occupation outside of marriage or of engaging in social or intellectual activities were limited, it was possible for wealthy courtesans to enjoy relatively high social status. The harlots of ancient Athens were among the best-educated women of Greece. They maintained saloons distinguished for the wit and intellectual inquiry to which philosophers and statesmen flocked. The mistresses of Louis XIV and Louis XV held official positions at the French Court, counselled their lovers in affairs of state, and were fawned over by courtiers eager for political advancement."[2]

In India also prostitution has a long and an ancient history. There are references in the Vedas of organised prostitution. During the Vedic period, the *"Ganika"* [the courtesan] had her prescribed place and functions in society. It existed in a well established form during the time of **Manu** and **Kautilya**. In *Vishnu Samhita, Matsya Purana* and in Vatsayana's *"Kama Sutra"*, we have vast references to prostitution. In Ramayana, Mahabharatha and in Puranas we find references to courtesan women like Rambha, Urvashi, Menaka, Tilothama who used to exhibit their skills and artistic excellence in dance, music, etc., in order to please Gods and the king of Gods, Indra.

The profession of prostitution was so widespread in the ancient period that the Hindu *'shastrakaras'* like **Manu, Gautama** and **Brihaspati** recommended for suppression of prostitution.

1. **G.R. Madan** in *"Indian Social Problems"*, Vol. I - Page : 200.
2. **Scarpitti** and **Andersen** in *"Social Problems"* - Page : 119.

During Mohammadan period also, prostitution was much in vogue and many Mohammadan kings had their harem. However, the rapid urbanization and industrialization during the British period increased this evil, and certain legislative measures were taken to stop it.

The ***Devadasi system*** has a significant place in the annals of prostitution in India. *Devadasis* are girls dedicated to temples by persons seeking merit. The persons so dedicated were assigned certain duties to be performed at the temples, their major function being singing and dancing before the deity. In course of time, however, the Devadasis were found to be deviating from their original function and indulging in deviant moral behaviour. Thus, Devadasi has now come to mean a woman prostituting in the name of religion. We get the survivals of this practice in *'Muralis'* of Maharasthra, *"Basavis"* and *"jogathis"* of Karnataka, *"Goumantak Maharatias"* of Goa, *"Basavi"* and *"Koyi"* of Andhra, *"Kudikas"* of Kerala and so on.

The problem of prostitution is becoming more and more acute in the country as the country is getting more and more industrialised. The problem of prostituion as we understand it today, is mostly urban and more particularly metropolitan. Unsatisfactory housing conditions and imperfect family patterns in cities have led to an increase of prostitution in the cities and metropolitan areas.

1. DEFINITION AND CHARACTERISTICS OF PROSTITUTION

Definition of Prostitution

1. **Havlock Ellis :** *"A prostitute is a person who makes it a profession to gratify the lust of various persons of the other sex or of the same sex."*
2. **Elliott** and **Merill :** *"Prostitution is an illicit sex union on a promiscuous and mercenary basis with emotional indifference".*
3. **Geoffry :** Prostitution may be defined as *"the practice of habitual or intermittent sexual union more or less promiscuous for mercenary inducement".*
4. **May G.** in **"Encyclopaedia of Social Sciences" Vol. 12:** Prostitution is *"an act of sexual intercourse characterised by barter, promiscuity and emotional indifference."*
5. **G.R. Scott :** *"A prostitute is an individual who for some kind of reward or for some other form of personal satisfaction engages in normal or abnormal sexual intercourse with various persons who may be of the same sex or the opposite sex."*
6. **The Suppression of Immoral Traffic in Women and Girls Act - 1956 :** defines prostitution as *"an act of a female who offers her body for promiscuous sexual intercourse for hire whether in money or in kind".*
7. **In Simple words,** we may define....

- *Prostitution as a sexual union by a woman with a person who is not her husband, for some consideration in cash or kind.*
- *Prostitute is a woman who sells her sexual favours indiscriminately and takes money or other valuables for each act of intercourse; and who has no psychic involvement.*

Main Characteristics of Prostitution

1. *Prostitution - An Immoral Act* : Prostitution denotes an immoral sex relationship between individuals though it cannot be categorically branded as "illegal relationship". In no society, it is justified universally as a moral act. However, there are licensed prostitutes also.

2. *Acceptance to use the Body Against Money / Material Things* : The harlot or female prostitute offers the use of her body to various men whosoever approach her in exchange for money / material things.

THE MISERIES AND SUFFERINGS OF SEX TRADE

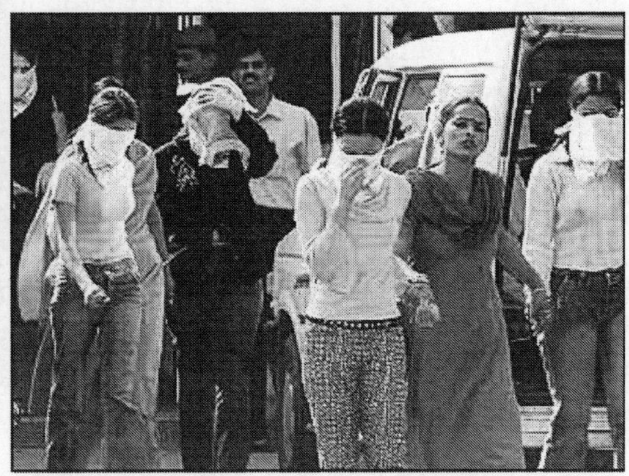

3. ***Involves Emotional Indifference of the Prostitute in her Act*** **:** Prostitution involves a sexual intercourse characterised by barter, promiscuity and emotional indifference. The woman never goes through the sexual act devoid of any pleasurable feeling. There is no scope for the expression of real love and affection.

4. ***Not a "Volcano of Lust"*** **:** A prostitute cannot be regarded as a person having uncontrollable sexual desire. She is not a "volcano of lust"? for all the men she attracts. Hence, she cannot be branded as nymphomaniac in characters, she cannot attract all types of persons in spite of her expertise in the art of her profession.

5. ***Involves Normal and Abnormal Sex Relationship Also*** **:** A prostitute engages in sexual intercourse - which may be normal or abnormal - with persons of the same or the opposite sex.

6. ***May involve Artificial Demonstration of Love*** **:** A prostitute is a professional "love-maker". She has the skill or the attribute of demonstrating her love outwardly. She performs her part in the transaction completely and passionately not out of sensuality or lust, but sheer expertise in the field.

7. ***Part-time or a Full Time Job*** **:** Depending upon her objective which she wants to achieve, a prostitute may carry on her profession on a part-time or full-time basis. Her objectives could be monetary gain, mere sexual thrill, or satisfaction of excessive sex lust, etc. In most of the cases, the objective or purpose is found to be nothing other than monetary reward or gain.

8. ***Different from Illegitimacy*** **:** According to **Weaver**, prostitution is different from illegitimacy, which invariably involves an *"illicit sex relationship"* which refers particularly to the production of a child outside the socially approved reproduction.

- **Weaver** also says that prostitution is *"different from the broader concept of sexual immorality due to the commercial nature of the relationship."*

Relationship Between the Prostitute and Her Clients

On the basis of the definitions mentioned earlier, the relationship between the prostitute and her clients can be analysed in the following manner.

1. ***Commercial or Money based Relationship*** **:** The sexual relationship which a prostitute maintains with her male customers is based on money or material considerations. She takes money or other valuables for every act of her intercourse with the customers.

2. ***Temporary Relationship*** **:** Relationship between a prostitute and her customers is not a permanent one like the relationship between husband and wife. It is purely temporary and its tenure depends on the quantity of monetary or material reward which the customer gives to her and the way in which it is given.

3. ***Impersonal Relationship*** **:** The relationship found between the prostitute and her customers is purely commercial, artificial and impersonal in nature. Most of the times they remain as anonymous persons. It is thus, an example of the secondary type of relationship.

4. ***Predetermined Type of Relationship*** **:** The type of relationship that exists between the prostitute and her customer is a predetermined one. Hence, qualities such as love and affection, friendliness, mutual respect, admiration etc. are rarely found in this relationship.

It must be noted that though in most of the cases, the relationship between the prostitute and her clients exhibits the qualities mentioned above, there are also exceptional cases in which very friendly, respectful and permanent type of relationship prevails between the two.

TYPES OF PROSTITUTES

G.R. Madan [Page : 206] and **C.B. Mamoria** [Page : 755-756] have mentioned about two general types of prostitutes. They are :

1. ***the overt** or **the professional prostitutes,*** and
2. ***the clandestine** or **unconventional type of prostitutes***

1. The Overt or Professional Prostitutes

The overt or professional prostitutes include both registered and unregistered prostitutes. In practice, these include two kinds of prostitutes :

(i) those who operate independently without agents like pimps, and

(ii) those who operate through the agents.

(i) Some prostitutes operate independently without the support of the pimps, brothel-keepers, etc. They are referred to as *"singly operating prostitutes."* It is said that these prostitutes normally get less income and their 'business" is also not prosperous. Their number is rather limited and they carry on their *"trade"* in a secret manner so that *"respectable men"* can visit them without any hindrance. Some of these prostitutes are normally employed at other type of work, notably in personal service or as entertainers like dancers, musicians, etc. Such girls are accustomed to practice prostitution as a more or less regular supplement to their legitimate earnings.

Some of the prostitutes that belong to this category are mostly seen roaming about the cinema houses, restaurants, hotels, public parks and other places of gathering, always looking for customers who may either go to their house or take them to their house or to a hired house.

(ii) Those who operate through the agents such as pimps, brothel-keepers are found to be having good *"business"* taking as many as 10 to 12 men for sex-act. They usually live in *"houses of ill-fame"*, that is cheap brothels attracting customers through agents. It is said that in West Bengal, there are **5695** brothels and more than **45000** prostitutes, in Patna and Mirzapur [Bihar] there are **100** brothels, in the cities of Orissa there are more than **200** brothels, and in Mumbai the number of prostitutes exceed **one lakh** and that of the brothels exceed 10,000.[3] Some women themselves attract customers sitting outside their doors or through the windows, settling bargains with the passer by. In big cities like Mumbai, Kolkatta, Lucknow, Kanpur, Nagapur, Hyderbad, Chennai, Delhi, Bangalore, etc. there are thousands of such prostitutes carrying on their business.

2. The Clandestine or the Unconventional Type of Prostitutes

The clandestine prostitutes include a variety of women who carry on their sex trade for monetary considerations. Some such type of women may be identified as follows :

(i) There are ***occasional prostitutes*** who include large number of women belonging to sophisticated class of educated strata and from well-to-do families.

(ii) There are the ***incidental prostitutes*** who want to increase a scanty legitimate income by the sale of sex favour. Girl clerks earning a meagre salary, cast-off mistresses who often enter this profession as a last resort - constitute examples of this kind.

(iii) ***Married women*** on occasions resort to mercenary and adulterous practices and serve a restricted number of clientele.

(iv) ***Concubinage system*** under which the mistress or her guardians enter into an agreement with a male member for a stipulated period. Here the sex relationship is restricted to only two parties and not indiscriminate. *"In India, the mistress mostly belongs to the*

3. ***Source*** **:** **R.K. Sharma**'s *"Urban Sociology"*, Page : 221 and other sources.

class of professional singers or temple dancers who performed at the temple ceremonies in the olden days."[4]

2. CAUSES OF PROSTITUTION

Prostitution as a grave social evil has been haunting many of the civilised countries of the world including India. The problem is becoming more and more rampant in India especially in the urban area. There are many factors and forces causing this problem for it is not an isolated unit. It is indeed, a product of economic, social, psychological, pathological and other factors. Here is a brief analysis of the factors contributing to the problem of prostitution.

1. Economic Factors

There is no doubt that poverty or economic necessity is the most important factor behind prostitution. **M. Londres** is of the opinion that *"the foundation of prostitution is hunger."*[5] Studies made by the *League of Nations* in different countries have revealed that *"poverty, overcrowding and low wages are clearly contributory causes of prostitution"*.[6]

It is observed that many women having no other visible means of support in order to eke out a livelihood often resort to prostitution. Most of the prostitutes come from under privileged economic groups. Surveys conducted in 1960s revealed that poverty and lack of employment opportunities are the biggest factors causing prostitution. Over **55.4%** of the prostitutes said that they took up this profession due to poverty. In a sample survey conducted by **Shri Kanga** in the 1990s itself, it was found that **41%** took up this profession because of poverty. **Miss Kamala Rao** and **Dr. Punekar** in their survey held in Bombay found that **71%** of the women took up this profession due to poverty.[7]

In addition to poverty, other economic factors such as - *unemployment, under-age employment, unhealthy working conditions, corruption in industrial centres, sexual exploitation in workplace, immoral trafficking in women and children, etc. have also contributed to this problem in no small measure.*

2. Social Factors

Various social factors such as broken home, unsatisfactory marital life, [conflicts between the in-laws], lack of love and affection in the family, cruelty of dowry, evil effects of double standard of morality, polygyny, disintegration of joint family and several others have indirectly instigated a few women to resort to prostitution.

(i) Disintegration of Joint Families and Unhealthy Home Conditions **:** Family itself is often the starting point of prostitution. Unsatisfactory home conditions. disintegration of joint families, broken homes due to divorce or desertion of the parents, immoral character of either parents or both, also breed prostitution. **G.R. Scott** writes, *"In many cases, the mother is a prostitute herself, the father is a pimp and they send their daughters in the streets with the slightest compunction often themselves initiating her in sexual intercourse"*.[8] Lack of understanding, sympathy and affection from the parents during childhood and adolescence, and lack of discipline, marital conflicts and maladjustments, loose habits of the husband all play no small role in the commission of prostitution.

(ii) Double Standard of Morality **:** We find double standard of sex morals for men and women in the Indian society. It requires a woman to be chaste and pure but gives free latitude

4. **G.R. Madan** - Page : 206.
5. **M. Londres** as quoted by **C.B. Mamoria**, Page : 761.
6. As quoted by **C.B. Mamoria** - Page : 762.
7. ***Source of statistics*** **: C.B. Mamoria**, Page : 762.
8. **G.R. Scott** as quoted by **R.K. Sharma** in his *"Urban Sociology"* [2007] - Page : 221.

to man for his sexual satisfaction. This is also responsible for lowering the position of women. The erring woman has no other way but to commit suicide or join the rank of the fallen women. Further, a girl who has illicit sex experience because of any reason is often made to feel that she has nothing left to lose for she has already lost all.

(iii) Unhappy Marital Relations **:** Unhappy marital relationship with the husband, sexual impotency and physical weakness or chronic diseases on the part of the husband, sexual incompatibility between husband and wife, loose sex habits of the husband etc., are also factors driving a woman to such an action.

(iv) Inordinate Sex Desire and Craving for New Sex Experience **:** Some girls have inordinate sex desire and craving for sex stimulation for its own sake. They do not bother much about sex morals, observing restraints on sex behaviour, etc.

- ***Desire for thrilling sex adventure*** pushes a few girls to this field. It is also possible that when a girl is under the influence of alcohol she may undergo her first sex relationship. Her continued use of immoderate alcohol may further affect her sexual promiscuity. Childhood assaults also initiate many into this profession.

(v) Restrictions on Widow Remarriages and Ill-treatment of Daughters-in-law **:** In spite of the legislation that is passed permitting widow remarriage, majority of the Hindu widows in India, do not opt for remarriage because of the social disfavour. Young widows who are not ready to re-marry but at the same time, find it difficult to live a life of chastity may fall a prey to seduction. The first instance of seduction may show her a new way of living.

Dowry harassment, ill-treatment of the daughter-in-law either at the hands of the mother-in-law, sisters-in-law or by the husband himself are also factors responsible in driving the woman to lead a life of prostitution.

(vi) Social Customs and Practices Favouring Prostitution **:** Hindu social customs and practices are also contributory factors. The practice of dowry system makes it almost obligatory for many girls to remain as spinsters, till old age. Child marriage practice still continues, and young widows when forced to live a life of chastity, find it hard to do so, and often fall a prey to seduction. Old maidenhood and enforced widowhood is a rich ground for recruitment to the field of prostitution.

The difference made between sons and daughters in many Hindu homes, the general subjugation of women are also factors conducive to prostitution. Social customs like the *Devadasi* system prevailing among castes in many places, provide excellent opportunities for traffickers to kidnap women.

(vii) Kidnapping and Seducing Women **:** Kidnapping or seducing young girls under the promise of marriage, employment, etc. also contribute to the problem. Procurers, indecent employers, bogus lovers, characterless co-workers, stranger - friends with suspected morals all play their own conspiracy to trap young, innocent and helpless women to lead finally the life of a prostitute.

(viii) Unhealthy Recreation **:** Dangerous forms of recreation such as drinking, gambling, cabaret dances, dubious clubs, video parlours, amusement parks, sexy films, bad company, etc. may also lead to breakdown of women.

(ix) Hazards of Industrialization and Urbanisation **:** Rapid industrialisation and urbanisation have brought about the problem of housing in big cities. In Mumbai, for example, it is said that 89% of the people in the city especially in the slum areas live in one room tenements. In Khanpur, Nagpur, Chennai, Ahmedabad, Jabbalpur, Kolkatta, etc. more than 50% of the people live in single room tenements especially in the labour areas. Privacy is badly affected in these areas and healthy sex relationship becomes a casualty.

In all industrial and commercial centres we find an inequality of sexes. This enforced separation of the sexes creates a need for *"red light areas"*. Thus, prostitution flourishes in industrial areas, *busties* and mining areas. They help fill up a *"sexual void"*. Large cities are the *"hunting grounds"* of prostitutes for customers. It is here, "primarily due to shortage of housing, slum-living, bad and inadequate lighting, lack of healthy outlets and continued deprivation of normal family living", balanced sex life is damaged. As **Dr. Mukherjee** writes *"in thousands of slums of Indian industrial centres manhood is brutalised, womanhood dishonoured and childhood poisoned at its very source."*[9] Prostitution in such areas leads to an increase in the spread of venereal diseases.

3. Religious Causes

Some of the religious factors are also favourable for prostitution. The prevalence of the practice of *devadasi system* in states like Karnataka, Andhra Pradesh, Kerala, Tamil Nadu, Maharasthra itself reveals that prostitution has been carried on in these areas with the stamp of religion. *Devadasi* has now come to mean a woman prostituting in the name of religion. Under this system, women who are dedicated as *'devadasis'* to Hindu deities at temples are considered unfit to marry later on and this leads them to a life of prostitution.

Some of the socio-religious customs found among the Naiks in U.P., Nambudiris of Malabar, the Kulina system of Bengal were supportive of prostitution. Among the Muslims of Hyderabad a custom known as *"parwardah"* prevailed in which poor families gave their female children to the wealthy families for a consideration, relinquishing all rights over them. These children after their maturity were obliged to serve the needs of the young men of the family.[10]

4. Physiological and Psychological Causes

Physiological, biological and personal factors also play an important part in causing sex delinquency. Physical deformities, feeblemindedness, adolescent disturbances and unsatisfied sexual desires, desire for enjoying sex varieties, lack of control over sexual impulses and such deficiencies also cause prostitution.

Mental deficiency is yet another cause. A large number of young sex offenders and the common prostitutes show certain deficiency in mental constitution. *'The League of Nations' Advisory Committee on Social Questions* found that **1/3** of the women prostitutes studied were found to be either mentally abnormal or subnormal.

5. Demand and Supply Theory

It is often said that the real cause for the problem is the demand for supply. So long as there is demand, there is bound to be supply. The supply is assured by a prostitute, who absorbs the cosmic passion of man. The demand solely arises because sexual desire is a part of the very nature of man. As it is pointed out by many; *"without demand there would be no prostitution...."* It is said that man's *"passion has to be channelised, controlled and guided properly; and this is not possible by eliminating the institution of prostitutes, call-girls, brothels or red light areas."*[11]

9. **Dr. Mukherjee** as quoted by **Mamoria**, Page : 765.
10. Source : C.B. Mamoria, Page : 764.
11. "Report of The Advisory Committee of League of Nations" - as quoted by **Mamoria** - Page : 768.

Why men visit prostitutes ? is a question which is probed into by a few studies.[12]

- **Men frequently visit prostitutes for the reasons stated below :**

  (i) less effort is enough to secure a sexual partner.

  (ii) insufficient and unsatisfactory marital relations.

  (iii) end of responsibility on pecuniary payment.

  (iv) teenagers in the experimental stage.

  (v) sexually isolated.

  (vi) less expensive than non-prostitutes.

  (vii) due to physical deformity and can get only prostitutes to have relations with them.

  (viii) married men with frigid wives,

  (ix) to satisfy desire for sexual deviation,

  (x) refusal from married partner to engage in sexual relation,

  (xi) bad company, and

  (xii) the existence of pimps, and procurers who arrange for the contact with the prostitutes.[13]

6. Other Factors

The above causes by no means exhaust all the causes of prostitution. There are many "other factors" such as the following :

a) ***Lucrative Business*** **:** In big cities, prostitution is thriving because it has become a very profitable business.

b) ***An accepted practice among some tribals*** **:** Some tribals have made it their profession for it is not condemned or prohibited among them.

c) ***Society is tolerant towards it*** **:** Prostitution has been in existence in many places because society has not only tolerated it but also indirectly given support for it.

d) ***Sophisticated medical devices*** have given substantial support for this practice for it can be resorted to without the risk of pregnancy. Effective contraceptive devices have rendered virginity "obsolete" and chastity "outmoded".

e) ***Instigation through pornographic literature, electronic media, etc.*** **:** Sex hunger in the modern youth of both the sexes hass increased due to these means.

f) ***Favourable modern processes*** **:** Modern processes such as urbanisation, industrialisation, westernisation, globalisation, cultural invasion - have given impetus to prostitution.

In conclusion, it could be said that prostitution is almost universal. It is observed that different causes work in three different groups of persons to resort to prostitution; *(i) the male and the female unmarried; (ii) the married persons, and (iii) the widows and widowers.* **C.B. Mamoria** [Page : 771] thus concludes : *"the fact is that wherever restless men and money congregate, there are women seeking to sell a "moment of pleasure" for the highest possible price, where there is easy money, women are drawn to the demi-monde[14] of prostitution."*

---

12. Some Justifications for the Prevalence of Prostitutes

- "... It would be better that man should sin with a prostitute for his partner than rape a respectable woman." - **Saint Augustine** [1700 AD]
- "Solon sanctioned the purchase of female slaves to be used to prevent the raping of respectable women." - **Ahenaeus**
- "... society was indebted to the prostitutes for the safety of female morals." - **Mandeville**.
- "prostitutes were "human sacrifices on the altar of monogamy" - **Schopenhauer**.
- that the harlot was "the most efficient guardian of virtue and chastity of the woman" - **Lacky**.

Source **: C.B. Mamoria** - Page : 769.

13. Hatata, Mohd, Niazi in "English Prostitution Offences", 1961, Page : 329. as quoted by **C.B. Mamoria** - Page : 769.

14. demi-monde = group considered on the fringe of respectable society / a class of women in an equivocal moral and social position.

3. CONSEQUENCES OF PROSTITUTION

Prostitution as a social evil exists in all the countries of the world. The problem has become more intense and widespread in highly industrialised and urbanised countries. It is often treated as a challenge to family norms and values and a stigma attached to the modern civilised society. Problem of prostitution has its own consequences on the society among which the following may be noted.

1. Prostitution - A Disgraceful Profession

Prostitution, as it is already stated, is a black spot on the body politic of the modern civilised society. Though prostitution is found everywhere, in no society of the world today, prostitution as a profession is held in high esteem, nor prostitutes are highly respected. It is branded as a disgraceful profession. Prostitution is a sex-specific crime that punishes women not men, for their behaviour. An increase in the number of prostitutes in any society only reveals that it is a society suffering seriously from family disorganisation and sexual deviance. Life also becomes miserable for many women especially during their old age. Studies have revealed that many such women die of exposure, general physical debilitation or weakness and infections. Many end their career as drug addicts or alcoholics.

2. Reflects Personal Disorganisation

Prostitution is a symbol of personal disorganisation and the person involved receives condemnation at the hands of men and women and is excluded from the society. Women suffer great personal deterioration than men due to the double standard of morality. Prostitute's life is very often associated with mental conflict, physical strain and irremediable loss of status. It is also found to be associated with smoking, drug addiction, alcoholism and such other evils.

3. Denotes Family Disorgainsation

Prostitution adversely affects not only the concerned man or woman, but his or her family also. The married person may get some venereal disease from the prostitute which may affect his wife and children. A married person who resorts to prostitution secretly may get the disease from her other clients. Studies have revealed that more than *"half of those suffering from venereal diseases have acquired it through promiscuous sex relationships. The other half are innocent victims - the wives and children of men who acquired the disease in premarital or extra-marital contacts."*[15] Illegitimate sex relations of the wife or husband may also be the cause of friction in the family, and divorce may even be the ultimate result.

4. Prostitution Leads to Community Disorganisation

Prostitution brings widespread disorganisation of community in which it operates. In two ways it brings harm to the community at large. They are, its commercial aspect and its health aspect.

- ***Its commercial aspect*** makes it commercially exploitative and to become institutionalised. When it becomes institutionalised, it gets deeply rooted and assumes a permanent pattern. In its permanent position especially in towns and cities, it becomes more accessible to the public and as a result many more people get attracted by it and finally become its victims. This situation in turn strengthens the hands of those who are engaged in this business.

- ***Its health aspect*** is still more dangerous. Not only those who are engaged in it suffer from health problems especially venereal diseases, but also, they spread them to all those who come in contact with them.

---

15. **Elliot** and **Merrill** as quoted by **G.R. Madan**, Page : 209.

5. Results in the Degradation and Exploitation of Women

Inequality generally found between men and women is reflected in the profession of prostitution too. It reveals that man makes use of woman like an instrument to satisfy his lust. Woman's helplessness, weaknesses and misfortunes are taken undue advantage of by men.

- ***Exploitation in the Brothel Homes*** **:** Elderly prostitutes, or *'Gharwalis', 'madams',* or *'mothers',* who are managing and running the brothels, exploit the new young recruits to the profession. The new recruits are provided with very minimum physical comforts, and only a paltry sum is given as remuneration for their service and a major portion is retained for themselves.

- ***Prostitution is often associated with threats, violence, cruelty, coercion*** **:** It is especially so in organised prostitution where it is carried on in brothel homes. Rowdies are appointed to keep an eye on the movement of the prostitutes. Those who refuse to give *"satisfactory service"* to the clients are given punishments such as whipping, physical torture, mental torture with abusive and vulgar language, not giving food, locking them in rooms, and so on.

- ***Threat of prisons, hospitals and underground world*** **:** Wherever it is regarded as illegal, prostitution means for many women frequent jail terms. For some others, it means venereal infections from time to time. Some women are even connected with the underworld, and their association with it, tends to lead them to alcoholic and narcotic addiction. In some cases, a large portion of girl's earnings is paid out in advocate's fees. Much of what is left may be squandered on a succession of pimps and other exploiters. For the poor prostitutes, prisons and hospitals may alternate. With every arrest and conviction, they are likely to emerge with a much more hardened and resentful personality. These frustrations and miseries are also conducive to alcoholism and drug addiction.

6. Prostitution Leads to the Spread of Dreadful Venereal Diseases Including AIDS

Prostitution that is carried on in an uncontrolled manner, especially in the big cities is leading to the spread of venereal diseases which brings in train many other social problems. As **Elliot** and **Merrill** observe, *"the venereal diseases - syphilis, chancroid and gonorrhoea - are of vital social concern not only because they are epidemic and devastating diseases but also because they are factors in so many other social problems. Venereal disease produces a large share of insanity. Its victims are particularly likely to commit violent crimes. Children of syphilitic parents are apt to be maimed for life. Many are born blind. The result of syphilitic and gonorrheal infections are so appalling that they rank as the major public health problems in the western world."*[16]

4. PREVENTION AND CONTROL OF PROSTITUTION

The problem of prostitution is not just a problem confronting the prostitutes and their families, but has become a big menace to the public morality and social health. It is necessary to handle this problem in two respects. Two types of measures to deal with the problem are as follows:

A) *Legal measures to control prostitution, and*

B) *Rehabilitative and protective measures to reform them and to help them lead a normal social life.*

A) Legal Measures

Attempts were made even during the ancient period to control and to remove prostitution. Early *Dharmashastrakaras* like **Manu, Narada, Gautama, Parashara** and others condemned this practice in their treatises and recommended measures to suppress it. During the medieval

16. **Elliott** and **Merrill** as quoted by **G.R. Madan**, Page : 210.

period, the Muslim rulers made no attempt to curb it, for they were not against the practice. The British made some half-hearted attempts to control it.

Legal Measures taken Before Independence

• The British included in the ***Indian Penal Code*** [IPC] some sections such as 354, 373, 375 and 495 which made the practice of illicit sex relations a "punishable offence". Purchasing of young women below 18 years for prostitution and selling them to national and foreign agencies were declared as punishable offences.

• ***The Bombay Prevention of Prostitution Act, 1923*** was indeed, the first legislation to be undertaken in this regard to prevent prostitution, and to keep women away from taking up this profession.

• Following the example of Mumbai State, the other States such as Madras [1930] Uttar Pradesh [1935] and Punjab [1935] also enacted the same type of legislation. After independence, Bihar [1948], Travancore [1952], and Mysore States also followed the same direction.

• ***Association for Moral and Social Hygiene,*** a non-governmental organisation [N.G.O.] strongly recommended to the Government to take legal steps to stop women's sex trade in order to protect public morality and social health. In fact, on its recommendations, the Bengal State passed the *Bengal Suppression of Immoral Traffic Act, 1933.*

Governmental Measures After Independence

After the attainment of freedom, the *Association for Moral and Social Hygiene* intensified its campaign for checking this evil. In 1953, at its third All - India Conference, the Association strongly recommended that the individual as well as commercial prostitution should be abolished.

• ***Appointment of Social and Moral Hygiene Advisory Committee*** **:** In pursuance of the International convention signed at Geneva in 1950, the Central Social Welfare Board [of the Central Govt.] appointed an *Advisory Committee on Social and Moral Hygiene* in 1954. The Committee headed by **Smt. Dhanawanti Rama Rao** was entrusted the responsibility of investigating the problem in all its aspects throughout India.

• ***Recommendations of the Committee headed by Dhanawanti Rama Rao*** **:** The committee recommended measures for the suppression of immoral traffic, among which the following may be noted.

(i) It pressed the need for a comprehensive legislation on all - India basis to check prostitution.

(ii) There should be an Inter-state Police Organisation in order to have a strict control over this illicit trade.

(iii) No institution be given permission to take care of and protect such women and girls' unless its bonafides and ability are tested.

(iv) There should be a special police squad for the enforcement of this Act with the squad having a fair proportion of women police.

(v) Special courts should be constituted, consisting of a few trained women to look after the social and human aspects of the problem.

(vi) Those who make use of any brothel or other public or private place for the purpose of prostitution must be severely punished.

(vii) Those women protected from brothel homes or other places of prostitution must be sent to remand homes where they can be contacted by service-minded social workers.

The Suppression of Immoral Traffic in Women and Girls Act, 1956

On the recommendation of the Advisory Committee on Social and Moral Hygiene, the Parliament passed the *Suppression of Immoral Traffic in Women and Girls' Act in 1956*. This Act came into force from Ist May 1958. The main provisions of this Act are mentioned below.

- **Main Provisions of the Act**

(i) The Act prescribes punishments for keeping and managing a brothel home. [Section - 3]

(ii) It prohibits persons from living on the earnings of the prostitutes. [Section - 4 and 5].

(iii) It detains women or girls in premises where prostitution is carried on. [Section - 7].

(iv) It prohibits soliciting in public places [Section -8].

(v) It provides prostitutes right to seek protection in a protective home [Section - 19].

(vi) Provides authority to magistrates to remove any girl or woman carrying on prostitution at any place from there to any other place which they consider proper [Section - 20].

• The Act also envisages setting up of an adequate number of protective homes for the rehabilitation and the educational and vocational training of women and girls recovered and detained under this Act.

B) Measures for Rehabilitation and Protection of Prostitutes

A big social evil like prostitution cannot be completely solved just by legislative measures. In no country of the world legislative measures alone have brought success in solving the problem. Hence, rehabilitative and protective measures are equally needed to deal effectively with the problem.

- **Some Institutional Attempts to Rehabilitate the Prostitutes**

Institutions like *(1) The Association for Moral and Social Hygiene,* and, *(2) The Central Social Welfare Board* have rendered yeoman service in the task of the rehabilitation of the prostitutes.

1. *Association for Moral and Social Hygiene* : This non-governmental Organisation has been working actively throughout the country in its task of rehabilitating the prostitutes. It has its branches in 128 districts of 18 states. Its membership exceeds 10,000. Main objectives of this association are mentioned below :

(i) Mobilising public opinion against those who exploit women for sexual purposes;

(ii) Assisting the authorities in effectively implementing *the Suppression of Immoral Traffic in Women and Girls Act,*

(iii) Protecting those women who are already trapped in the trade and rehabilitating them in safe places;

(iv) Helping the prostitutes to get medical aid to get cured of the venereal diseases; and

(v) Conducting surveys and researchers on this issue.

The Association has set up two *"Rescue Homes"*, one at Mumbai, and another at Hyderbad to give protection to prostitutes and is running hospitals to provide treatment to prostitutes suffering from venereal diseases in places such as Delhi, Meerut, Nagpur and Patna. The Association is giving training on issues such as *"family welfare education", "sex education", etc.*

Rescue Homes and Shelters

On the recommendations of the Advisory Committee of the Central Social Welfare Board, the Government decided to launch two centrally sponsored programmes under the head : *"Social and Moral Hygiene and the Aftercare Programmes"*. Under the scheme it was proposed to establish in all, 80 *State Rescue Homes* and 324 *District Rescue Shelters* in different parts of the country to enable the stray women and prostitutes to find a place where they can receive preliminary training for rehabilitation in society.

Rescue Homes and *Protection Centres* established under the *Aftercare* Programme can also be utilised as Protective Homes. There are about 100 Protective Homes which include Government as well as private ones and they have a total capacity to accommodate around 4420 inmates. In addition to these, there are also other agencies which are active in helping and reforming prostitutes and finding them useful work. ***Examples*** : *The Women Home,* Madras; *Shradhanand Ananth Ashram,* Bombay, *The Good Shepherd Home,* Madras, *Christians Home,* Poona; *The Salvation Army Home,* Bengal; *The Feudal Home,* Bengal; *All Bengal's Women's Union Home,* Bengal; *Khushal Bagh Mission Orphange,* Gorakhpur; *Mahila Anathalaya,* Varanasi are some of the important centres for rehabilitation of fallen women.

Central Social Welfare Board

The Central Social Welfare Board which is a Central Government established institution has been paying sufficient attention towards the problem of prostitutes also. It conducted a *"National Workshop on Prostitutes and Their Children"* in May 1990 at New Delhi in which social work activists, educationists, doctors, journalists and judges had taken part. The Conference passed a resolution recommending the Government to undertake a comprehensive programme to rehabilitate the prostitutes on a permanent basis.

5. REHABILITATION OF PROSTITUTES : SOME PROPOSALS AND SUGGESTIONS

Legislative measures and governmental efforts are necessary and unavoidable for the control of prostitution. These measures by themselves are not sufficient. Some other measures as mentioned below are also needed to root out the evil.

1. ***Economic Measures*** : Sufficient economic provisions must be made, and suitable employment opportunities be created so that young girls and women are not compelled to take to prostitution under the heavy heels of poverty and unemployment. Even the rescued women must also be provided with some decent job, or a remunerative economic task, so that they are not forced to plunge into the same life once again.

2. ***Removal of Inhuman Socio-religious Customs that Favour Prostitution*** : Various outmoded traditional practices such as *devaadasi* system, *jogathi* system, *kulina* system, child marriage, *nagnika vivaha*, polygyny, bigamy, *"nude service to the God"* [*"bettale seve"* as practiced in a few places in Karnataka], dowry system, restrictions on widow remarriage, etc. have been forcibly pushing many women into this unwanted profession. All these practices should be stopped, and customs outlawed and public opinion must be mobilised against them. Remarriage of young widows be encouraged and dowry system should be suppressed with a heavy hand.

3. ***Double Standard of Morality Should be Discouraged*** : Men and women should be treated in equal terms in sex matters and there should be no double standards. As **Smt. Ranganayaki** observes; *"It is in reality impossible to have a double standard morality in matters of sex for without male chastity, female chastity is impossible ....* "[17] As long as the double standard continues, so long the *"tolerated vice"* continues to stay.

4. ***Sex Education*** : To prevent young girls from entering into prostitution, education and character strong enough to resist demoralisation, are to be developed. Instructions in religious education will help them to think in the right direction and to reject the immoral behaviour.

---

17. **Smt. Ranganayaki** in her article on *"Can We Prevent Prostitution"* in *"Social Welfare"* April 1958 as quoted by **Madan**.

Men and women should be educated as to the dangers of venereal diseases and its effects on marriage relations in case of married persons. There is need for educating the public on the seriousness of the consequences of the evils of prostitution both to the individual and to the society as a whole. There should be sex education and some training for family life to young people in schools and colleges.

5. *Severe Action Against those who Kidnap and Sell Women* : All attempts be made to suppress the anti-social activities of those who kidnap the helpless women and children and sell them to anti-social agencies. Those involved in this trade of supplying women for prostitution must be very strictly punished.

6. *Effective Propaganda and Publicity* : The print media and the electronic media must be made use of in an effective manner to give proper information and knowledge to the people about the problems and dangers of prostitution, illicit sexual behaviour, venereal diseases and their horrible consequences, and so on.

The public should be enlightened about the law and to report any such nuisance in their surrounding area to the law enforcing authorities. Blue films be banned, video parlours must be brought under vigilance, and strict censorship be imposed on electronic media so that, it would not tempt young people to go on sex adventure.

7. *Other Suggestions*

(i) Special care should be taken to prevent the children of the prostitutes from taking up the same profession,

(ii) Young men must be encouraged to marry the rescued young girls from the prostitute homes.

(iii) Efforts must be made to assess the implications of providing conditional licenses to prostitutes to run their trade as it has been done in big cities like Bombay, Chennai, Kolkotta and New Delhi.

(iv) Suitable jobs may be offered to prostitutes, their children, the pimps and such other people depending on that profession, so that they may be persuaded to leave that ugly profession once and for all.

(B) HIV - AIDs [HIV - Human Immunodeficiency Virus] [AIDS : Acquired Immune Deficiency Syndrome]

6. MEANING, NATURE AND MAGNITUDE OF AIDS

What is HIV - AIDS ?

AIDS [Acquired Immuno - Deficiency Syndrome] seems to be the most dreadful disease of the 21st century. It started taking roots in the last phase of the 20th century and is now spreading at a very fast rate in many countries of the world. It is a fatal disease which is haunting the modern civilised society.

AIDS is a very serious and almost a deadly disease which is caused by a virus called HIV or Human Immunodeficiency Virus. AIDS is said to be the last stage of infection with the HIV. This virus, known as HIV is fatal and dangerous because it destroys the immune system of the body, that is, the capacity of the human body to resist diseases. It remains in the body for years together without any visible symptoms. In fact, after getting infected with the HIV, it may take 8 to 10 years of time to develop into AIDS. This virus is said to be even smaller than bacteria and is not traceable even with the microscope. Its danger lies in the fact that it can be transmitted to other persons in a number of ways and make others its victims. No effective medicine has been invented till today as a cure for AIDS or for protecting people from the HIV.

AIDS is a viral infection got chiefly by sex with strangers. HIV is the virus which causes the infection. *HIV is transmitted through semen and vaginal fluids, infected blood and blood products, infected mother to her baby before birth, during birth or through breast milk.* It can be called our modern pandemic affecting both industrialised and developing countries.

AIDS – At The World Level

The phenomenon of AIDS was traced out in 1980s and soon after that it rapidly spread to various nations of the world. In fact, it evolved from a mysterious illness to a global pandemic which has infected tens of millions in less than 20 years.

Promising developments have been seen in recent years in global efforts to address the AIDS epidemic, including increased access to effective treatment and prevention programmes. However, the number of people living with HIV continues to grow, as does the number of deaths due to AIDS. A total of 39.5 million [34.1 million to 47.1 million estimated] people were living with HIV in 2006, about 2.6 million more than in 2004. This figure includes the estimated 4.3 million [3.6 million to 6.6 million] adults and children who were newly infected with HIV in 2006. The global epidemic of HIV / AIDS by the end of 2006 is summarized in *Table - 1.*

HIV / AIDS Affected at the Global Level **Table - 1**

Global HIV / AIDS Epidemic as of December 2006	
Number of people living with HIV in 2006	**[Range]**
Total	39.5 million [34.1 - 47.1 million]
Adults	37.2 million [32.1 - 44.5 million]
Women	17.7 million [15.1-20.9 million]
Children under 15 years	2.3 million [1.7 - 3.5 million]
People newly infected with HIV in 2006	**[Range]**
Total	4.3 million [3.6 - 6.6 million]
Adults	3.8 million [3.2-5.7 million]
Children under 15 years	530,000 [410,000 - 660,000]
AIDS deaths in 2006	**[Range]**
Total	2.9 million [2.5-3.5million]
Adults	2.6 million [2.2-3.0 million]
Children under 15 years	380,000 [290,000 - 500,000]
The ranges around the estimates in this table define the boundaries within which the actual numbers lie, based on the best available information.	
Source : UNAIDS, WHO [2006] AIDS epidemic update, December 2006 as quoted by K. Park in *"Park's Textbook of Preventive and Community Medicine"* - 2007 [19th Eidtion], Page : 285.	

Young People Becoming the Victims : In many regions of the world, new HIV infections are concentrated among young people [15-24 years of age]. They accounted for 40 percent of new HIV infections in 2006.

AIDS Dominating the Sub-Saharan Africa : Sub-Saharan Africa continues to reel under the stranglehold of this disease. Two-thirds [63 percent] of all adults and children with HIV globally, live in this region, and almost 72 percent of all adults and child death due to AIDS in 2006 occurred in this region with its epicentre in Southern Africa. About 32 percent of all people with HIV globally live in southern Africa and 34 percent of all deaths due to AIDS in 2006 occurred there. Overall, Sub-Saharan Africa is home to an estimated 24.7 million [21.8 million - to - 27.7 million] adults and children infected with HIV in 2006 (2).

Globally More Adult Women are Getting Infected **:** Globally, in every region, more adult women than ever before are now infected with HIV. 17.7 million [15.1 million - 20.9 million] women were living with HIV in Subsaharan Africa in 2006. In the Caribbean, the Middle East and North Africa and Oceania, close to fifty percent adults infected with HIV are women. Meanwhile, in many countries of Asia, Eastern Europe and Latin America, the proportion of women living with HIV continues to grow.

Globally, unprotected heterosexual route is the predominant route of transmission of the virus. Other modes of transmission include unprotected penetrative sex between men, injecting drug use, and unsafe blood transfusions or injections.

Increasing Trends of AIDS in the South East Asia Region [SEAR] Countries **:** Rate of increase of AIDS continues to be high in the SEAR countries. As of December 2006, an estimated 7.2 million people are living with HIV/AIDS in this region. The potential for continued spread of HIV / AIDS in Asia and Western Pacific is real, and requires determined and sustained prevention efforts. Several countries have already experienced intense epidemic in certain population e.g., of all HIV positive cases in SEAR about 49 percent are commercial sex workers and their clients, injectable drug users about 5 percent, is in men who have sex with men (2). In these countries, including Cambodia, India, Myanmar, and Thailand, AIDS has imposed new demands on health care systems. The WHO estimates for SEAR countries are as shown in *Table 2.*

Table - 2

Reported AIDS Cases and Estimated HIV Infections in the SEAR Countries, as on of December 2005

Country	Estimated AIDS Cases	Estimated HIV Infections	Adult HIV Prevalence
Bangladesh	1300	7500	< 0.2
Bhutan	< 100	< 100	< 0.1
India	970,000	5,200,000*	0.9
Indonesia	18,500	110,000	0.1
Maldives	n/a	< 100	< 0.1
Myanmar [Burma]	67,000	373,000	1.3
Nepal	11,000	61,000	0.55
Sri Lanka	< 500	3,500	0.1
Thailand	100,000	541,000	1.4

* age 15 - 49 years

Source : Internet [2006], Facts and Figures about HIV/AIDS in South East Asia Region.

● ***The Speed of Spreading*** **:** AIDS as a disease caused by the HIV is spreading at a very fast rate. By the end of the 20th century, HIV was spreading in the world at the rate of one new infection for every 50 seconds. HIV/AIDS spares no class or community. It is spreading in all communities, social classes, racial and ethnic groups, religious and professional groups, age and sex-groups. As per *Indian Health Organisation* [IHO] report, women and children are believed to be more prone to AIDS than others.

AIDs – in the Indian Context

The first case of AIDS in India was reported in 1986 from Chennai. Since then there has been an increase in the number of HIV infections over the years. By March 2002, as many as 29,007 cases of AIDS, and an estimated 38,60,000 cases of HIV infections were reported in India.

HIV / AIDS is spreading rapidly in India. During the year 2005, the number of HIV cases rose to 5.2 million. The estimates from the year 1981 to 2005 are shown in *Fig. 1.*

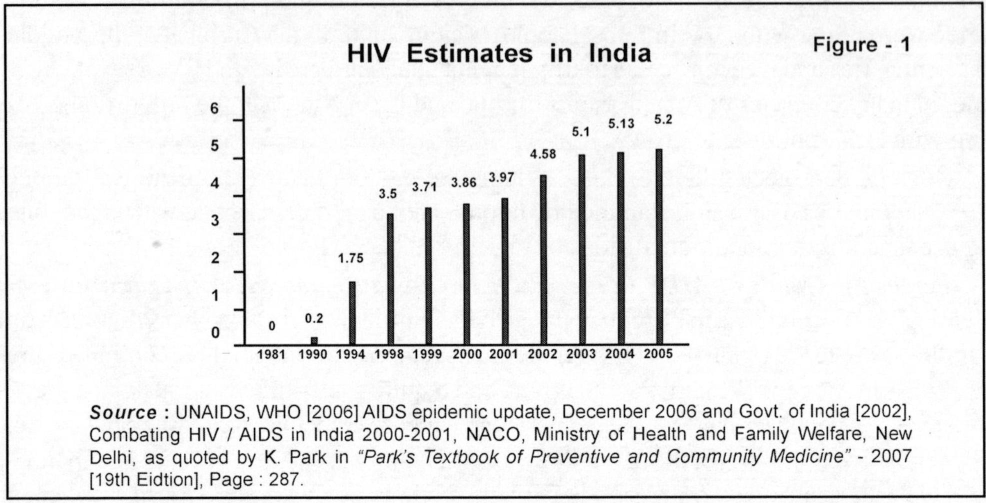

Source : UNAIDS, WHO [2006] AIDS epidemic update, December 2006 and Govt. of India [2002], Combating HIV / AIDS in India 2000-2001, NACO, Ministry of Health and Family Welfare, New Delhi, as quoted by K. Park in *"Park's Textbook of Preventive and Community Medicine"* - 2007 [19th Eidtion], Page : 287.

In India, the early cases of HIV / AIDS were concentrated primarily in Chennai and Mumbai. The disease soon spread to other parts of the country, often following the path of major highways and labour migrants. By mid - 2003, Tamil Nadu had nearly half of the reported AIDS cases. Mumbai and rest of Maharashtra now share about 19.74 percent of the AIDS reported cases. *Fig. 2* shows the distribution of reported AIDs cases by states upto August 2006.

Figure - 2

Distribution of Reported AIDS Cases by States Upto Aug - 2006

State		Percentage
TamilNadu	-	41.63%
Andhra Pradesh	-	12%
Maharashtra less Mumbai	-	11.46%
Mumbai	-	8.28%
Gujarat	-	5.49%
Karnataka	-	3.47%
Manipur	-	2.35%
Delhi	-	2.2%
West Bengal	-	1.97%
Madhya Pradesh	-	1.38%
Nagaland	-	0.58%
Others	-	9.19%

[*Source* : NACO [2006], Monthly Update on AIDS, 31 Aug. 2006, Internet.]

In India, the cumulative number of AIDS cases in the country has risen to 1,24,995 by August 31st 2006. This includes 88,245 males and 36,750 females, 126 new cases of AIDS were detected in the month of August 2006 [90 males and 36 females]. The distribution of likely source or route of infection and the percentage is as shown in *Table 3.* More than 85% of all new infections are through sexual transmission, 3.80% through perinatal transmission, 2.34% through injecting drug among users, 2.05% through blood transfusion.

Table - 3

THE ROUTE OF INFECTION IN INDIA, AUG. 2006		
Risk / Transmission categories	**No. of Cases**	**Percentage**
Sexual	106669	85.34
Perinatal Transmission	4755	3.80
Blood and blood products	2563	2.05
Injecting drug users	2930	2.34
Others [not specified]	8078	6.46
Total	**124995**	**100.00**

Source : **NACO [2006], Monthly Update on AIDS, 31 Aug. 2006, Internet.**

In India too Young People are Getting Trapped by the AIDS

The prevalence of HIV in all parts of the country by 2000 itself highlights the spread of the infection from urban to rural areas. AIDS is affecting mainly the young people in sexually active age group. Majority of the HIV infections [88.55 per cent] are in the age group of 15-49 years, out of which 31.8 percent is in the age group of 15-29 years. The majority are infected through unprotected sex. Impoverished, unemployed, under employed, mobile and migrant youth, and street children are also particularly vulnerable to HIV, as they are less likely to have information about HIV or access to preventive measures, and they may face repeated risks of HIV infection. As of 31st Aug. 2006, males account for 70.59 per cent of AIDS cases and females 29.40 percent, the ratio being 2.41.

Various factors contribute to the speedy spread of this disease. *Migration of labour, low literacy levels leading to low awareness, gender disparities, sexually transmitted infections and reproductive tract infections among the population* – are some of the factors attributed to the spread of HIV and AIDS in India.

7. CAUSES OF HIV / AIDS

Though HIV/AIDS is spreading at a fast rate, it is not a contagious one. It is not like cholera, plague, tuberculosis, small pox, chicken pox or even measles. It mainly spreads through a sexual route and blood to blood contact. The main causes are :

(i) Infected blood, that is, transfusion of blood and blood products infected with the HIV,

(ii) Infected needles, that is, through injecting drugs with infected syringes or needles,

(iii) Multiple sex partners, that is, by having sex with an infected partner - heterosexual as well as homosexual, and

(iv) Infected mother to her baby before its birth and around 30 to 50% chance of transmission of the disease with each delivery has been observed.

- **Multiple Sex Partners or Sexual Contact With the Already Infected Person - A Major Cause of the Spread of Disease**

Intimate sexual contact with the infected person seems to be the major cause of this disease because HIV virus is generally transmitted through such contacts. HIV is passed on by infected people because the virus is present in the sexual fluids, saliva and blood. If infected blood or sexual fluid of the first person gets into the blood of the second person, then the second person becomes infected. If a man or woman with HIV has sex without a condom, infected fluid could pass into their bloodstream through a tiny cut or sore inside the body. This can be so small that the partners can hardly identify or understand it. Other sexual practices are equally at risk of infection. If there is any contact with blood during sex, this increases the risk of infection. Recent researches have found that deep kissing, where saliva is exchanged, can infect the partner.

Main Sources of Transmission of HIV Virus

It can be inferred from the above analysis that some type of persons play an important role in passing on this disease to a large number of people. Among them could be included prostitutes, homosexuals, drug addicts, professional blood donors, pathological laboratory technicians and women with HIV infection giving birth to children.

***1. Prostitutes of all Types and Call Girls* :** Female sex workers are normally involved in selling sex. These sex workers called prostitutes and call-girls who are infected with HIV pass on the infection to their customers. According to one estimate, there are more than 20 lakh prostitutes distributed over 817 red-light areas having the potentiality of spreading the disease through their infections.[18]

2. Homosexuals are comparatively in lesser number in India than in U.S.A., U.K. and other Western nations. They are mostly found in prisons, correctional reformatories, rescue homes, etc. Even outside these institutions they are found but their number is very difficult to estimate. Surveys and studies have revealed that the risk of HIV infection through homosexuality cannot be ruled out.

3. Drug Addicts, especially those who take drugs through injections carry the possibility of spreading the HIV infection through infected needles. A large number of students, auto-rickshaw drivers, slum-dwellers, industrial workers, truck-drivers and garage workers, are becoming the victims of drug addiction. Many of these people become so addicted to drugs, they develop the habit of taking drugs through self-injection. Sometimes, the same syringes are used by many drug - addicts and this definitely increases the possibility of spreading HIV infection.

***4. Professional Blood Donors* :** There are, in India, both government run blood banks and privately managed blood banks. These supply lakhs of bottles of blood every year. Among the blood donors there are some professional donors also whose blood sometimes contains the HIV. If their blood is transfused without proper testing, then along with the blood, even HIV gets transmitted. Pathological laboratories and irresponsible technicians also sometimes add to this kind of dangerous and careless HIV transmission.

***5. Pregnant Women* :** The most unfortunate case of HIV transmission is the one in which the pregnant woman who is HIV positive transmits the virus to her own new-born child. Anaemic pregnant women also get infected with the HIV when they undergo blood transfusion. Indian prostitutes are said to be giving birth to about 50 lakh children a year and the chances of these women transmitting the HIV to their children, are definitely not negligible.

Categories of Persons Likely to Get and Spread HIV

On the basis of the above explanation, it can be generalised that the following varieties of people act as the agents of spreading the HIV

1. Homosexual men
2. Bisexual men and women having a large number of sex partners,
3. Prostitutes and their male counterparts,
4. Drug addicts who use a common needle and syringe for injecting drugs,
5. Patients of Sexually Transmitted Diseases [STDs],
6. Professional blood donors,

---

18. HIV is fast spreading among the prostitutes in big cities. It is said that in Mumbai alone, between years 1989 to 1991, HIV infection increased by 30%. [*Source* : **Ram Ahuja** in *"Social Problems in India"* - [2001] Page : 41.

7. Patients who need repeated blood transfusion, and
8. Children of HIV (positive) mothers.

Early Signs and Symptoms of HIV Infection

AIDS does not attack any person like heart attack or paralytic stroke. It is a disease caused in a slow and gradual manner. Early signs and symptoms experienced or exhibited by its victim may be enlisted here.

1. Significant and unexplained loss of body weight by about 10%,
2. Intermittent low-grade fever,
3. Swollen Iymphatic glands,
4. Persistent watery diarrhoea,
5. Night sweating,
6. Pain all over the body,
7. Formation of white patches or ulcers in the mouth as well as in the food pipe,
8. Itchy skin rashes that appear on many parts of the body,
9. Excessive fatigue after normal daily activities. It may be noted that signs and symptoms of AIDS may appear at any time after 6 months of the entry of HIV virus.

Table - 4

AIDS INFECTED PERSONS IN KARNATAKA : 2002

- By the end of March 2002 there were 1,442 AIDS afflicted persons in Karnataka.
- Number of persons who died due to the disease is 146.
- Number of persons newly infected with HIV by the end of March 2002 is 11,583.
- Of the newly traced cases of infection by the end of March 2002, as many as 2.14% of the cases were found among children.
- In a selected persons survey conducted in **Bijapur,** blood test was held for about 400 pregnant women and of these, 13 persons were found to be infected with HIV.

Source : *Statement issued by the Additional Director [Planning]* ***Dr. D.Thimmaiah,*** *Karnataka State AIDS Prevention Society, and reported in "Udayavani" Kannada daily dated 4-6-2002.*

HIV / AIDS is Not Spread by the Following Ways

There is a lot of misconception about AIDS and the HIV and the way in which they are spread. It should be remembered that ***HIV or AIDS is not spread by the following ways or means or persons*** –

1. Drinking water or eating food from the same utensils - cups, glasses, plates, etc. used by infected persons,
2. Sharing toilets,
3. Shaking hands,
4. Hugging or facial kissing,
5. Donating blood,
6. Working with people who are HIV infected,

7. Massage and rubbing each others bodies,
8. Swimming in pools used by people with HIV / AIDS.
9. Through mosquito bite,
10. Socialising or casually living with people with HIV / AIDS,
11. HIV is not spread by sitting next to some one who is infected, coughing or sneezing,
12. It is also not spread by travelling with some body in public transportation [bus, train, air, etc.] or taking food with someone in a hotel or using a public telephone, etc.

8. CONSEQUENCES OR IMPLICATIONS OF HIV-AIDs

Some of the serious consequences of the problem of HIV-AIDS may be mentioned below.

1. HIV-AIDS - A Deadly Disease **:** The devastating effect of HIV-AIDS is very difficult to estimate. Nobody could imagine that an illness initially causing irritation, uneasiness, excessive fatigue, etc., to a few homosexuals could affect millions of men, children and women all over the world within the time span of a decade or two. This haunting disease has threatened the public health security measures of many nations of the world. The disease is not only dreadful but also is spreading at an alarming rate.

2. AIDS is a Societal Problem and a Social Stigma **:** It is not just a health problem it is rather a societal problem. *It is associated with social stigma,* AIDS is a disease with a difference. It is not like other contagious diseases. AIDS affected persons are subject to prejudice and discrimination. Those who are the victims of the disease are treated as *"untouchables"*. They are branded as people with immoral character. The disease creates lot of social distance between the people who are afflicted by it and those who are not. Even the family members of the diseased person look down upon him / her.

3. Victims of Prejudice and Discrimination **:** There has been a significant increase in the number of medical personnel [doctors and dentists] and institutions such as nursing homes, hospitals, etc., which decline medical services to AIDS affected persons.

4. Victims of AIDS Facing Social Disapproval **:** AIDS as a social problem has cultural, psychological and economic dimensions also. It threatens the basic social institutions at the individual, family and community levels. HIV - AIDS infected *person may face dismissal from work, refusal of work,* refusal of admission to medical and educational establishments, refusal of service at board and lodging establishments, and so on.

5. A Costly Disease **:** The economic consequences of the disease are very serious. The economic and social *costs of maintaining and treating the AIDS affected persons are also very high.* No man of average income can afford to pay for the medicine that is required to cure AIDS. If the bread-winner of the family is affected by AIDS, then the entire family collapses economically.

9. MEASURES TO DEAL WITH HIV - AIDS

AIDS as a socio-physiological problem has posed a serious threat to the safety and security of the entire humanity. If it is not tackled well and in time, we may have to pay a heavy price for that later. Hence, medical scientists, administrators and social reformers are seriously finding out ways and means of dealing with it.

Scholars have suggested two methods to deal with it. They are -

1. Preventive method, and

2. Curative method

1. The Preventive Method

The main purpose of this method is to create awareness among people about the dangerous consequences of AIDS and to persuade them to keep themselves away from it. The popular saying *"prevention is better than cure"*, holds especially true in the case of the horrible disease like AIDS. Until an effective medicine or cure for AIDS is found, the only means at present available is health education to create awareness among people to keep themselves away from the reach of the tentacles of AIDS. Certain precautions are necessary in this regard.

The horrible and the deadly disease of AIDS can be effectively prevented by observing the following practices and methods.

The Ways of Keeping AIDS At a Distance

1. Avoiding sex relations with many partners [multiple partners],
2. Keeping away from unknown sexual partners,
3. Keeping away from persons suffering from sexually transmitted diseases [STD],
4. Making it a policy to have sex with one's own spouse, and if this cannot be followed strictly, using good quality condom [nirodh] of ISI standard, whenever the occasion arises,
5. Avoiding kisses with tongue [especially with unknown sex partners],
6. Avoiding sharing of the needles used to inject narcotic drugs,
7. Avoiding homosexual relationship,
8. Avoiding the consumption of marijuana [intoxicating oral drug], alcohol and tobacco,
9. Women suffering from AIDS should decide not to conceive.
10. Reported rates of HIV infection among STD cases are very high [infact, it increased three times in between 1986 and 1996]. Hence, programmes for the prevention and control of STDs should be given top priority.
11. Proper precaution must be taken before approaching the blood banks to request for blood. Blood or blood products must be tested for HIV before transfusion.
12. Doctors should ensure that injecting equipment is properly sterilised. The use of disposable syringes should be encouraged.
13. Good quality condoms should be freely distributed or supplied at cheap rates in red-light areas to prostitutes.
14. Drug-users should be persuaded to stay away from intravenous drug use.
15. The NGOs should help spread knowledge on AIDS to different vulnerable groups.

It is necessary that educational material and guidelines for prevention should be made widely available. All mass media channels should be involved in educating the people on AIDS, its nature, transmission and prevention, this includes international travellers also.

For the first time, there is a clear sign of reduction in HIV infection rate in a number of developing countries. In USA, about 40,000 new HIV infections were reported in 1996 as against 1,00,000 per year a few years ago. In Thailand, there has been a six fold increase in condom usage, and 90% of the sex workers demand the use of condom. The number of men visiting sex workers has gone down and the use of condom has gone up. Ugandan cities have also seen a reduction in HIV infection rate. [It should however be noted that there is no guarantee that the use of condoms gives full protection.] In Kolkota [India], the *"Sonagachi health care and education project among sex workers"* has become a model of successful peer education. The latest data shows that HIV prevalence continues to be low [around 1.4%] and STDs [Sexually Transmitted Diseases] are declining. Community-based treatment approach has been effective in bringing about behavioural changes among injecting drug users in Mynmar and Nepal. This has led to a reduction in HIV infection rates.

2. Curative Method or Treatment Method

At present, there is no effective vaccine or cure as treatment for HIV infection / AIDS. However, the development drugs, helps the suppression of HIV infection. Though the drugs do not promise a permanent cure, they have proved to be useful in prolonging the life of the severely affected patients. Though medicines such as AZT [Zidovudine] and the PROTEASE - INHIBITOR have been discovered, they are very costly and no person of average income can afford to avail of them. Hence, much stress is laid on preventive method. Still search is on to discover other drugs to control and cure HIV infections / AIDS.

Some Curative Measures

- ***Attempts to Detect AIDS Cases* :** Government of India had identified 13 medical colleges all over the country in the decade of 1990s itself where the facilities for the effective clinical management of AIDS could be set up. More than 100 surveillance centres have been established for detecting AIDS infection.

Under the *National AIDS Control Programme*, the Government intended to train one specialist from each hospital in metropolitan areas for the early detection of AIDS cases. These specialists inturn, [called **PRADS :** *Physicians Responsible for AIDS Diagnosis*] were expected to give training to atleast one doctor in each district so that suspected cases of AIDS could be referred to for further medical check-up and treatment.

- ***Counselling Centres for the AIDS Patients* :** Counselling centres are very much needed to interact with the patients [HIV carriers as well as AIDS] and to give them proper advice and psycho-social support to face it. Since effective training and skill is necessary, only doctors, nurses, psychologists, social workers and para-medical staff could be given training to give counselling.

- ***Role of Voluntary Organisations [N.G.O.s]* :** The Government alone cannot be expected to take up the total 'control programme'. Voluntary organisations must be involved in "behaviour change" programme. The W.H.O. [World Health Organisation] has also stressed the participation of the N.G.O.s in this regard. These N.G.O.s can focus on the social factors influencing the vulnerability of people to HIV infection and provide information regarding services, medical assistance and other social support system to people in danger of catching the disease.

- ***Major Informationn Centres of AIDS***

There are several institutions in India which provide proper information regarding AIDS. The below mentioned are some such centres.

- National Aids Control Organisation [NACO], New Delhi.
- TATA Institute of Social Sciences, Mumbai.
- Indian Health Organisation, Mumbai.
- Voluntary Health Association of India.
- Aids Research Foundation of India, Chennai.
- South India Aids Action Programme, Chennai.
- Child In Need Institute, Calcutta.
- Parivar Seva Samsthan, New Delhi.

- Women and Aids Cell, New Delhi.
- All India Institute of Medical Sciences [AIIMS].
- Human Service Centre, Varanasi.
- Community Medicine Centre [AIDS Section].

No. of HIV Infected People in Some Selected Countries - 2013					
India	-	21,00,000	Brazil	-	7,30,000
Indonesia	-	6,40,000	Zimbabwe	-	14,00,000
Myanmar	-	1,90,000	South Africa	-	63,00,000
Source: UNAIDS as quoted by "The Hindu," English Daily, 17-7-2014					

AIDS - Hit People in Karnataka - 2014

Health Minister **U. T. Khader** in his written reply to a member in the Karnataka Assembly said on 12th July, 2014 that there are 2.45 lakh AIDS-hit people in Karnataka, and so far 45000 people have died because of AIDS. Of the HIV contaminated people 1,20,818 are found to be women, 1,25,806 are men, and 518 are sex workers [or prostitutes]. Of the people who died because of AIDS, 16552 were women, 28315 were men and 75 were sex workers. ***Source:*** 'Udayavani' Kannada Daily, Page: 1, Dated: 13/07/2014]

●●●

Chapter 14

ALCOHOLISM AND DRUG ADDICTION

A. Alcoholism : *Defintion and Characteristics of Alcoholism and Types of Alcoholics - Causes of Alcoholism - Effects of Alcoholism - Measures to Control Alcoholism - Myths and Misconceptions About Alcoholism.*

B. Drug Addiction : *Meaning, and Characteristics of Drug Addiction - Some Basic Concepts : Drug, Drug Abuse and Drug Dependence - Signs of Drug Dependence and Signs of Established Drug Addict - Types of Drugs OR Nature and Impact of Abusable Drugs : Alcohol, Sedatives or Depressants, Stimulants, Narcotics, Hallucinations, Nicotine or Tobacco - Causes of Drug Addiction OR Motivations in Drug Usage - Effects of Drug Addiction - Control of Drug Abuse / Addiction.*

Man, like every other living beings on this earth, seeks pleasure in living his life. Seeking pleasure also implies escaping from and reducing pains and sufferings.

Nature has provided means of achieving this goal to all of us. Apart from the pursuits of food and shelter, which help the organism to maintain itself, nature seeks to ensure continuity of life through procreation. Human being, who at present is on the top most step of the evolutionary ladder, is essentially a social animal. Hence, apart from the pleasurable pursuits of food, shelter and sex, he also seeks social security. His social pursuits include interacting with other members of the society, helping other members of the group in achieving their goals, earning a respectable status in the society, maintaining peace and harmony among the members of the group and also between the groups etc. All these biological and social activities are essentially pleasurable and gratifying. But, unlike the other living beings, man has easy access to unnatural means of seeking pleasure and escaping from or reducing physical as well as psychological sufferings. It is this tendency of resorting to easy and artificial means, which has given rise to the phenomenon of dependence on certain substances like *alcohol* and *drugs*. Being unnatural methods, the use of such substances is bound to have adverse effects on one's physical and psychological health as well as social life.

(A) ALCOHOLISM

Alcoholism is a form of individual as well social disorganisation created by the individual's maladjustments with the complex conditions of the modern society. Alcoholism which is basically a human weakness has been widespread in India as a social evil. As per one estimate, three decades ago, there was one alcoholic for every 300 people, and today, we find 10 alcoholics for the same number of people. What is more disturbing and distressing is, an increasing number of youths, women and even school going children are becoming its victims.

1. DEFINITION OF ALCOHOLISM AND ITS NATURE AND TYPES

It was the Sweedish doctor **Magnus Huss** who used the term *"Alcoholism"* in the year **1849** for the first time to denote a disease which is the result of excessive consumption of alcohol. Since then the concept of *"alcoholism"* has become a popular expression to signify the cases of excessive drinking.

Definition of Alcoholism

1. **Johnson :** *"Alcoholism is a condition in which the individual has lost control over his alcohol intake in that he is constantly unable to refrain from drinking once he begins."*
2. **Keller and Efron :** *"Alcoholism is characterised by the repeated drinking of alcoholic beverages to an extent that exceeds customary use or compliance with the social customs of the community and that interferes with the drinker's health or his social or economic functioning."*
3. **Clinebell :** *"An alcoholic is one whose drinking interferes frequently or continuously with any of his important life adjustments and interpersonal relationships."*[1]
4. **Collins Dictionary of Sociology :** Alcoholism refers *"to the consumption of alcohol to excess; leading to psychological and physical dependency and addiction."*[2]
5. **Seldon Bacon** defines alcoholism as *"a disease characterised by a compulsion to drink in order to face the ordinary life problems."*

Characteristics of Alcoholism

Alcoholism as a social evil is associated with characteristics which are mentioned below.

(i) An alcoholic is overwhelmed by an intense desire or need or compulsion to drink and to continue drinking, and to obtain it by any means.

(ii) The alcoholic normally exhibits a tendency to increase the dose of drinking.

(iii) The alcoholic has a psychic or psychological and sometimes a physical dependence on the effects of the drinks.

(iv) The alcoholic is comparatively worried about his weakness to drink.

(v) In spite of his worry about his weakness of drinking, the alcoholic has no control over his drinking habit.

(vi) Due to his practice of excessive drinking the alcoholic is made to face many problems in the discharge of his social responsibilities.

Types of Drinkers or Alcoholics

Different writers have given different classifications of the types of drinkers. We may mention here three such classifications.

(A) According to **G.R. Madan** and **C.B. Mamoria**, there are two types of drinkers.[3] They are as follows :

(i) ***Moderate Drinkers*** **:** These are the drinkers who take liquor in quantity they can tolerate. These drinkers are not *"drunkards"* for they have some control over their habit.

(ii) ***Problem Drinkers*** **:** These are the drinkers who take liquor in quantity they cannot tolerate or withstand. For them, drinking has become their routine. As **Dr. Durfee** points

1. Two -fold classification as referred to by **G.R. Madan** and **C.B. Mamoria** in their books, pages 154 and 730 respectively.
2. *Ref:* **Ram Ahuja**'s *"Social Problems in India"* - Page: 332.
3. **David Jarry** and **Julia Jary** in *"Collins Dictionary of Sociology"*, Page : 12.

out, problem drinker is one whose *"health is endangered, peace of mind affected, home life made unhappy, business jeopardised and reputation clouded, drinking becomes a routine matter".*[4]

(B) Don Cahalan has spoken of a five-fold classification of alcohol drinkers on the basis of the frequency of drinking and not the quantity of alcohol consumed.[5] It is mentioned below.

1. ***Rare Users*** : Those who desire alcoholic drink very rarely, say, once or twice a year.
2. ***Infrequent Users*** : Those who drink infrequently are called *"infrequent users"*. Such persons drink once or twice in 2-3 months, that is, less than once a month.
3. ***Light Drinkers*** : Those who drink relatively frequently in comparison with the drinkers of previous category. Such persons drink once or twice a month.
4. ***Moderate Drinkers*** : Those who have control over drinking, but slowly becoming habituated to it for they consume alcohol three or four times in a month.
5. ***Heavy Drinkers*** : Those who drink every day or consume alcohol several times a day. They are actually the alcoholics. They can even be called *"had-core"* drinkers.

(C) Marshall B. Clinard in his *"Sociology of Deviant Behaviour"*[6] has mentioned about four types of drinkers taking into consideration the type of drinking and the quantity of drinking.

1. Moderate Drinkers: Those who are not drunkards nor or they habituated to it. They drink occasionally in parties, sometimes due to the pressure of the companions or to the special social circumstances. Drinking of these people cannot be considered a problem nor a great weakness from the point of view of modern norms.

2. Excessive Drinkers: Some are habituated to drinking. These people drink excessively and experience the compulsion of drinking again and again. Though they have not become the slaves of drinking, they often lose control over their drinking. Even at this stage, these people have sufficient mental stamina to take a firm decision to have control over their drinking.

3. Morbid Drinkers: These are the people who drink excessively and also frequently for they have become the slaves of drinking. They drink for various purposes say, to forget family problems, to run away mentally from the personal economic crises, to overcome physical inabilities and so on. Their excessive drinking may even make them to become diseased.

4. Alcoholics or Continuous Drinkers: Drinking habit reaches its climax in these persons. They consider drinking as their great ideal in life. They believe that they cannot live or survive without drinking. Day in and day-out they think of only drinking. Drinking habit overrules them and in the real sense of the word they become alcoholics or drunkards. They lose their physical, mental and moral health and finally become the victims of drinking.

2. CAUSES OF ALCOHOLISM

A grave social evil like alcoholism is not due to any one single factor. It is the result of the operation of multifarious factors. Further, while analysing the causes of alcoholism one must always bear in mind that *all those who take alcohol or not alcoholics.*

The key to alcoholism is to be found in the motive for continuously drinking. Hence, psychological aspects involved in the habit of excessive drinking must be given due recognition.

Writers like **Catlin, Starling, Bonger, Janet** and others have attributed several reasons for alcoholism. Their views may be summarised in the following manner.[7]

4. **Charle's Durfee**, in *"To Drink or Not to Drink"* [1937], Page : 11, as quoted by **G.R. Madan**, Vol. I - Page : 154.
5. ***Ref*** **: Ram Ahuja** in his *"Social Problems in India"* [2001], Page : 368-369.
6. **Marshall B. Clinard** in *"Sociology of Deviant Behaviour"* 3rd Edition, Page : 412-415.
7. ***Ref*** **: G.R. Madan**'s *"Indian Social Problems"* - 1969 (Vol. 1) - Page : 154-157.

THE DEADLY HABITS OF INTOXICATION AND DRUG ADDICTION

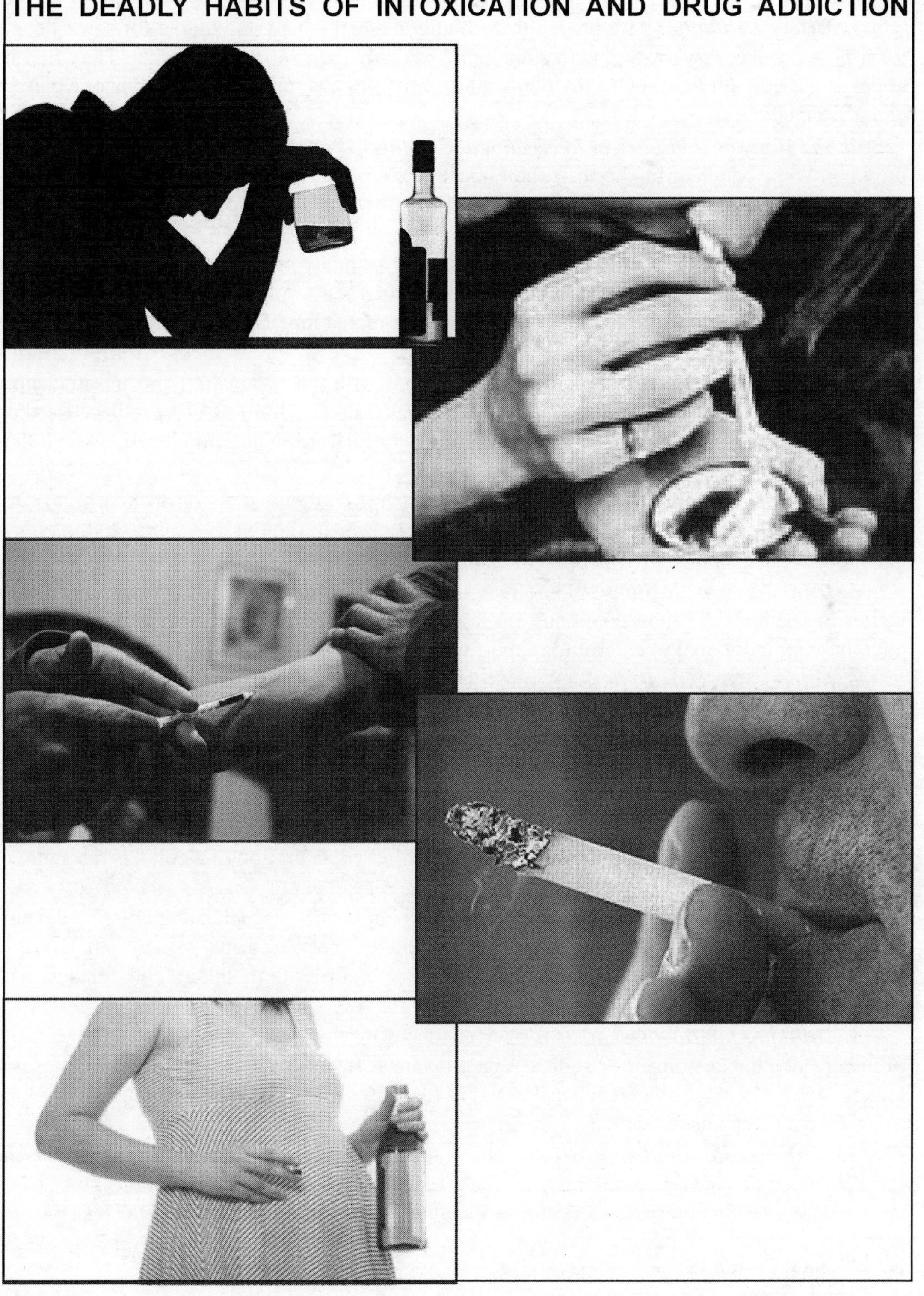

CAUSES OF ALCOHOLISM

1. Misery Drinking : Life proves to be highly miserable and intolerable for some people for it provides them no joy and no contentment, but only hardship and suffering. They find no hopes of fruitful future. In such a life of unending struggles and toils, they find drink as a blessed palliative medicine.

2. Bad Housing and Lack of Recreational Facilities : Poor housing conditions often induce drinking. Some people drink because their houses are so cold, dark, dismal and sordid that they do not feel like staying there for a long time. The house does not provide them mental peace and contentment.

Not only the physical conditions of the house of so many people are poor and distressing even the emotional atmosphere in which they are living is also unfavourable for a safe living. The community fails to provide them soul-elevating recreation. These conditions push a few individuals to become alcoholic addicts.

3. Occupational Factor : Total dissolutionment with the occupation and unsatisfactory conditions of work make a few to become habitual drinkers. Men also drink because their occupation has completely exhausted them. They look forward to get more energy which they believe they would get through drinking.

4. For Companionship and Fun : A large number of young people resort to drinking due to the pressure of the company. Some consume alcohol for fun in the beginning, and in course of time, the fun becomes their permanent habit.

5. Drinking as a Fashion : Some pick up the habit of drinking for they consider it as a matter of fashion and an accepted custom in some circles. Drinking also reflects the pathetic attempt of an individual to enter into rapport with his fellows.

6. Inherent Nervous Defects : Some drunkards are often referred to as born drunkards for they have some inherent neurological defects due to which they are unable to face the reality. In their desperate attempts to run away from the real world these unhappy persons become hopeless and helpless alcoholics.

7. Ignorance : Some people who involve themselves in heavy physical work are under the wrong belief that alcohol furnishes them added strength and vigour with which they can pursue their labour. This illusory feeling of vitality after consumption of alcohol is the cause of drunkenness.

8. Sudden Success in Business : When some people become rich suddenly they develop the habit of spending more in arranging parties where alcoholic drink is the main centre of attraction. They too develop the habit of taking drinks in order to maintain their contacts with people of business magnets.

9. Drinking for Business Reasons : Men also drink for business reasons in the capacity of either potential customers or sellers. When business reverses happen, or uncertainities and tensions involved in business reach their heights, then also some people take recourse to drinking as an escape mechanism.

10. Urbanisation and Industrialisation : Increasing urbanisation, industrialisation, and mechanisation that have been taking place have added additional motivation for drinking. These are the processes that increase worldliness and at the same time increase the weakness towards worldly enjoyments including drinking. When once a person is introduced to that type of material culture, he finds it difficult to come out of it.

11. Social Inadequacy : Human life is subject to joys and sorrows, ups - and downs, pains and pleasures. One must have proper balance of mind to face these realities of life. But there are some persons who are unable to face the hard realities of life and start drinking to overcome their social inadequacy temporarily which later on takes the form of habitual drinking.

It is clear from the above, that drinking alcohol is due to the operation of so many factors. Still the question persists why do certain persons choose drinking as a remedy to environmental pressures and problems while others do not ? Why some who develop the habit of drinking do not get lost in it while a few others make a total surrender to it ? Questions like these throw light on both personality and cultural factors that act as the major conditioning elements in the individual experience. Environmental pressures, cultural norms, individual tendencies, family atmosphere etc. together compel a man to become alcoholic. Thus, one many conclude from this that alcoholism can be explained only on the basis of a holistic approach rather than as a single factor approach.

3. EFFECTS OF ALCOHOLISM

Alcoholism as a social evil is causing lot of damage to the individuals concerned, their families and to the community at large. It brings individual misery, family discord and community disorganisation.

1. Drinking and Individual Disorganisation

(i) Dangerous Effects on the Physical Health : The effects of alcohol upon the human organism are many and varied. The effects depend much on the quantity of alcohol and the frequency with which it is consumed. Taken in moderation in the form of wine, or beer, etc., it does not cause serious or harmful effects on the health of the person. Nor even a periodic dose is permanently injurious to the physical mechanism. It is only acute drinking which carries a train of ill effects. It leads to nervous degeneration, liver cirrhosis, chronic gastritis, high blood pressure and a host of other diseases. The drinker habitually has a shaky hand, and unsteady gait, dull-eyes, pale face, haggard look and black expression. He loses memory, becomes rash and violent towards others and becomes a menace to the society. He dies a lingering death or sometimes even a quick death due to heart trouble. Besides these specific diseases, the general resistance to all diseases is considerably reduced by heavy and frequent consumption of alcohol.

(ii) Disturbance in the Mental Health : Alcoholism lowers the efficiency of the person who becomes its victim. When the bodily health is damaged and mental ability affected, the fall in efficiency is inevitable. The alcoholic person is whimsical in nature and incapable of sustained attention and concentration. Thus, he cannot pursue any work seriously.

(iii) Damages Family and Social Connections : Excessive drinking makes the person to become indifferent in his approach towards others. Drinking makes him to forsake his home, his family and his business. His conversation may seem vulgar to the sober observer. When he is under the grip of alcohol he behaves like a liar, a scoundrel and is prepared to commit any type of crime including murder. A person with such a weakness grows careless, irresponsible, indifferent and even immoral. He fails to make out any difference between morality and immorality. All these individual trends produce personality disorganisation.

2. Drinking and Family Disorganisation

Alcoholism and family disorganisation are very closely linked. More homes are broken due to drinking than any other single cause. Alcoholics directly affect four or five other persons such as *wife, parents, children, siblings, close friends and co-workers.* An alcoholic shows little or no respect to his wife or children. This often leads to divorce and constant family tension. Family violence and family unrest is also caused by alcoholism.

***(i) Alcohol makes domestic relations miserable* :** Liquor has been a traditional enemy of love and marriage, because it often leads to promiscuity and breach of moral standards of the spouses. Domestic unhappiness, moral degradation, divorce and family disorganisation and juvenile delinquency are the resultant consequences.

***(ii) Negligence towards wife and children* :** Happy family life depends on the harmonious relationship between husband and wife. It is generally said that habitual drinkers feel uneasy in the presence of women. Chronic alcoholics often become completely disinterested in the opposite sex. Hence, even wives, and their basic emotional needs are neglected by the alcoholics.

***(iii) May lead to divorce* :** A strong prejudice against drink on the part of the husband or wife of one who drinks is a constant source of friction in the family and leads to divorce later on. Wives who are fed up with the excessive drinking habit of their husbands often decide to take divorce to save the good future of the children. In lower class families where people have neither the knowledge of law nor the resources to seek divorce, drunkenness often causes untold misery..

3. Drinking and Community Disorganisation

***(i) Economic loss* :** The effects of alcoholism are far reaching. It disturbs the normal course of community life. Drinking affects the business, the office efficiency and factory productiveness also. Absenteeism, low output and poor judgement leading to work related accidents cost the government crores of rupees.

***(ii) Damages the moral health of the society* :** Drinking is associated with cabaret dances, prostitution and gambling especially in public places such as clubs, pubs, hotels, public halls, etc. The increased presence of women in such places both as patrons and entertainers, will have the most devastating effect on the public morality. Prostitutes openly solicit in many such places. *"Young girls are often engaged to act as "hostesses" in order to stimulate the consumption of liquor. Such a combination of alcoholic indulgence and sexual licence have disorganising effect both upon the hostess and the patron."*[8]

***(iii) Increase in Crimes* :** It has been found that there is a close relationship between drinking and crime. *"Partial or complete intoxication is an important element in many types of crimes including arson, stabbing, manslaughter, assaults and sex offences. Drink has a close kinship with cruelty, heinousness and depravity. It is associated with debauchery and prostitution."*[9]

***(iv) Increases accident proneness* :** Studies have revealed that *"drink is closely related with increasing accidents which take a heavy toll of human life and maim those who survive."*[10] There is a direct ratio between alcohol and increase in accident proneness.

(v) Drink addiction lowers industrial production. Drunkards are often inefficient due to physical weakness. *The Royal Commission on Labour* in India stated: *"Alcohol offers its dangerous relief to a fatigued body and that a reduction in the consumption of liquor would increase the welfare and efficiency of industrial labour."*[11]

It is clear from the above description, that drinkers are a blot upon the society, a stigma upon the community, a shame to their parents and a disgrace to themselves. Hence, judged from any angle - social, economic, moral, spiritual, and even legal - public opinion is to be created and developed against alcoholism and in favour of prohibition.

Enlisting the deadly and disastrous effects of alcoholism **Evangeline Booth**, one time *Head of the Salvation Army,* observed : *"Drink has drained more blood, hung more crape, sold more*

8. **G.R. Madan** [Vol. 7] Page : 161.
9. **C.B. Mamoria** in *"Social Problems and Social Disorganisation"* - 733.
10. **C.B. Mamoria** - 733.
11. As quoted by **C.B. Mamoria** - Page : 734.

homes, plunged more people into bankruptcy, armed more villains, stained more children, snapped more wedding-rings, defiled more innocence, blinded more eyes, twisted more limbs, dethroned more reason, wrecked more womanhood, dishonoured more womanhood, broken more hearts, blasted more lives, driven more to suicide, and dug more graves than any other poison scourge that sent its death-dealing waves across the world."[12]

Sri Bharatan Kumarappa, a reknowned Gandhian, has summed up the evil consequences of alcoholism in the following words : Drinking leads to *".... besides the money loss and food loss, great as they are, we must add to the debit side of drink immorality, murder, theft, family squabbles, broken homes, hungry children, and ruined earners - in short, a general lowering of moral sense, judgement and intelligence."*[13]

4. MEASURES TO CONTROL ALCOHOLISM

Alcoholism has been one of the earliest habits of man. Attempts have also been made from the times immemorial to control it. Over the years this habit has grown into a social evil posing a big challenge to public health. It has become necessary for the people vested with authority to introduce various measures to control its practice in some way or the other. Let us now discuss the ways and means of controlling alcoholism.

1. Not the Removal, but Control of Alcoholic Drinks **:** The practice of alcoholism which has been associated with the human life since centuries, cannot be removed immediately. No country has been successful in this regard so far. **Kautilya**, the author of *"Arthashastra"*, had recognised this fact long ago and hence suggested that provision should be made to establish "liquor houses" [*"panagrihas"*] on the outskirts of the towns. He was also of the opinion that men's weakness towards alcohol could never be completely suppressed, but only controlled. Since all drinkers are not alcoholics, it is more appropriate to make provision for drinking under vigilance and control, than to make a futile attempt to remove it once and for all.

2. Drinking as a Habit of Physical Labourers and Workers **:** 'Liquor shops' are often regarded as *"poor men's clubs"*. It has been observed that labourers who are engaged in tight hard work want to have some relaxation after their toil. To forget the boredom of work and to relax and refresh, they want to consume alcohol which they believe will be of great help. Thus, it is necessary to provide for good entertainment facilities at affordable cost for the labour class to discourage them to resort to alcohol.

3. Welfare of People is more Important than Increasing Revenue through the Sale of Alcohol**:** The Government should take appropriate legal and administrative steps to introduce prohibition on the sale of liquor. If the supply is not there, one can expect the demand to die down at least gradually. In the Indian context, many state governments are not prepared to introduce prohibition for the simple reason that they get lot of income for the state treasury by way of tax imposed on the sale of liquor. It is difficult to have control over the consumption of alcohol in a nation like India if the state governments are not taking initiative in imposing prohibition. They must understand that promoting people's welfare is the primary duty of the Government. They must make alternative arrangements to collect revenue for the state to make good the loss which they are said to incur due to the introduction of prohibition.

4. Making Campaign Against Alcoholic Drinks and Creating Awareness About its Evil Effects**:** It is necessary to launch a campaign against the evil of alcoholism to make the people

---

12. As quoted by **C.B. Mamorial**, Page : 735.
13. As quoted by **C.B. Mamoria**, Page : 735.

know about its harmful effects. Government alone cannot do it effectively. Government, non-governmental organisations, private individuals of great repute, religious, political and social leaders should launch a combined campaign against alcoholism.

Modern means of mass media such as radio, television, advertisements, news papers, cinema, etc., can also play an effective role in impressing upon the people about the disastrous effects of the ugly practice of alcoholism.

5. Introduction of Prohibition Act : Several nations have tried to stop the practice of taking alcohol by introducing prohibition acts. But the experience of these nations have revealed that legislation alone cannot do any magic here. America, Russia and France, for example, have tried with legislative enactments to stop the practice of taking drinks. Different states in India also have experimented with such legislations. Neither in India nor elsewhere, these legislations have been a total success. This does not mean that legislation in this regard is useless and ineffective. It only means that the legislations have not been implemented honestly and effectively.

In a nation like India where millions of poor people have become the victims of the ugly practice of alcoholism, introduction of legislation against it, is a must. Educated public and non-governmental organisations must give their full co-operation to the Government to implement the legislation.

6. Need for the Widespread Campaign Against Drinking : Educated and well informed people who have a strong public concern must take initiative in launching campaigns against the practice of drinking. Some such efforts made by some individuals with strong determination have fetched positive results. ***Examples*** : Women of Nellur District of Andhra Pradesh launched such a campaign in their district in 1990s which later on was spread to the whole of Andhra Pradesh. The Telugu Desham Party which supported this campaign was voted to power in 1994 and the party introduced prohibition soon after assuming power.

On the model of the Nellur campaign, if peaceful agitations are organised against alcoholism throughout India, the so-called "liquor kings" are bound to step down. In Karnataka also such campaigns are going on peacefully here and there. *For example,* under the leadership of Sri Veerendra Heggade, [Dharmadhikari, Dharmasthala] a campaign against alcoholism is silently doing its work in Belthangady thaluk of Dakshina Kannada District [Karnataka]. It has been able to persuade successfully as many as 2115 alcoholics to give up the deadly habit of drinking in the beginning years of 21st century. The campaign has set its target to make Belthangady Thaluk, totally free from the stranglehold of alcoholism.

MYTHS AND MISCONCEPTIONS ABOUT ALCOHOL

There are many myths and misconceptions in the minds of people regarding alcohol and its use. Some of these have been clarified and discussed below.

1. Alcohol a Nutrient ? : No, alcohol is not nutritious. Modern technology which is applied in the production of alcohol completely destroys every dietary property in alcohol except for providing calories. The calories in most alcoholic beverages are known as "empty" calories since they do not provide any nutritional benefits.

2. Alcohol A Sex Stimulant ? : Alcohol is not sex stimulating. It is a sedative and in sufficient quantities an anesthetic. People mistake it for an aphrodisiac because of its inhibition lowering effect. A large quantity of alcohol acts as a sex inhibitor and can render a man [who is addicted to it] temporarily impotent.

3. Alcohol a Stimulant and An Energising Drink ? : Alcohol is neither stimulating nor energising. It is a depressant, especially of the central nervous system.

4. Is Drinking Essential in Certain Occupations ? : It is a created myth that drinking is very much needed to carry on some occupations which inovlve physically strenuous and tough work. Drinking is never essential. Any occupation can be carried on and very well too by a non-drinker if he has the occupational abilities and skills needed for that job.

5. Ability to Drink More than Other People, a Sign of Virility ? : Ability to drink more and virility or masculinity need not go together. On the contrary, the ability to drink more is likely to be an early symptom of alcoholism. Most alcoholics have the capacity to drink more than their friends when they start drinking.

6. Drinking Helps Creativity ? : No, it is only an illusion. Alcohol releases inhibition, and small amounts may help some people overcome certain blocks caused by inhibition. However, since even a small amount affects judgement, the results are not as good as the drinker believes.

7. Anybody can Become an Alcoholic ? : Alcoholism makes no discrimination among people. Any type of person can and does develop alcoholism. There is no immunity conferred by background, position in life, money, profession or occupation. Many people think that alcoholics are only found in slums and they are jobless, without family and home. It is not true. Alcoholics may also be married, employed, living with their family, just like those around us.

8. Beer Drinkers Never Become Alcoholics ? : There is no such guarantee. There have been alcoholics who were almost exclusively beer drinkers.

9. Alcoholism is a Disease ? : It is definitely a disease. The American Medical Society has classified alcoholism as a disease and through the years this has proved to be a helpful concept in the treatment of alcoholism. Once an alcoholic starts drinking he may not be able to control his compulsion to continue drinking just as T.B. patients cannot voluntarily control their coughing.

10. Alcoholics Can Go Back to Social Drinking ? : Never, it is not safe for an alcoholic to imbibe alcohol in any form including wine, beer, certain cough medicines / tonics, or anything else that contains alcohol even in small quantities. Even the smallest amount of alcohol can and sometimes does trigger the disease into becoming active again.

11. Switching Drinks from One Type to Another Keeps One Away from Getting Drunk? No. It is the alcohol content that causes drunkenness irrespective of whether it is wine, beer, whisky, gin, brandy or rum.

12. Something Wrong With People Who Do Not Drink ? : Actually, the converse is true. One who does not drink is absolutely a normal person, and the one who is addicted to it, is an abnormal person. Drinking or abstaining from alcohol is purely a personal choice. Apart from religious and health reasons, a total abstainer may dislike the taste or the effect of alcohol on him. Even on moral grounds, he may exhibit his aversion towards it. He may also be aware of the long-term effects of alcohol.

(B) DRUG ADDICTION

Drug addiction is a state of indiscriminate use of herbs and herbal preparations, which enslaves the user to them. This is not something new in human society, what is now alarming is the indiscriminate use of drugs on an unimaginably large scale, which may be attributed to breakdown of spiritual and religious value systems that kept man integrated as person and with his family and society.

Drug abuse, instead of leading man towards peace of mind and state of equilibrium, throws him into oblivion and causes decay at almost all planes – physical, emotional, psychological, societal and spiritual.

MEANING AND NATURE OF DRUG ADDICTION

Drug abuse, drug addiction, drug trafficking, becoming victims of drug addiction - etc., have been the tragedies of the 20th century. They have been passed on with no less vigour to the 21st century. Intoxicating drugs such as *brown sugar, opium, heroin, alcohol, marijuana, ganja, bhang, cocaine, charas, morphine, L.S.D* and such other things are even known to the street children in big cities. Some of them take a chance to taste them. Each year we are adding to more and more such harmful compounds to the already existing ones. What is more distressing today is the abuse of drugs. The abuse of drugs affect adversely the user's mind and body. The victims of the abuse of drugs are also increasing in number.[14] The phenomenon of drug addiction has become a colossal one in a developing nation like India.

Meaning of Drug Addiction

Man has been using or consuming for the past several thousands of years some substances or the other to intoxicate himself for various reasons. More commonly, these substances are used for personal reasons, either to induce states of elevated mood or relieve inner feelings of anxiety, misery and despair. What we presently call *'drugs'* belong to that category of such substances.

Definition of Drug Addiction

- **W.H.O.** *[World Health Organisation]* defines drug addiction as – *"a state of periodic or chronic intoxication detrimental to the individual and to society produced by the repeated consumption of drug, natural or synthetic..."*

The word *"addiction"* implies physical dependence. *'Drug addiction'* obviously means *the physical dependence of a person/s on the use of some drugs.* The drugs could be any one of the intoxicants such as *heroin, brown sugar, cocaine, bhang, ganja, marijuana, etc.* Addiction involves totally a drug-centred lifestyle. This lifestyle takes an individual to *"a state whereby the body requires continued administration of the drug in order to function."* The functioning of the body is so attuned to the drug, if it is withdrawn the person becomes totally uncomfortable and the *"withdrawal symptoms"* appear. Thus the person helplessly depends on the use of drugs.

Characteristics of Drug Addiction

The W.H.O. in its enlarged definition of drug addiction points out the following important characteristics of drug addiction.

1. An Uncontrollable Desire for Drugs **:** Drug addiction includes an overpowering desire or need [compulsion] to continue taking the drug or to obtain it by any means. The desire for drug is so strong and powerful in the individual that he is prepared to do anything and everything, even if it is immoral and illegal, just for getting and using it.

2. A Tendency to Increase the Doze **:** It involves a tendency to increase the doze. The *"thrill"* that the consumption of drug creates in the person actually overpowers him and he wants to have it again and again and to increase its doze. In fact, the chronic drug – user develops a feeling that he must constantly increase the doze in order to produce the same effect as that from the initial doze. This phenomenon is called *"tolerance". Tolerance represents body's ability to adapt itself to the presence of a foreign substance.* This "tolerance" level of the individuals who use drugs, and the tolerance development to the use of different drugs, vary significantly.

3. Physical and Psychological Dependence on Drugs **:** It includes a psychic or psychological; sometimes a physical dependence on the effects of the drug. It means that the body of the drug-user gets conditioned to such an extent he feels that he just cannot do anything without it.

---

14. A survey report states that in 1990 in America, there were **1.45** crore cocaine addicts and 10 lakh heroin addicts. In the same year, in Pakisthan, the number of registered heroin addicts had reached a mark of 7 lakhs. ***Ref*** **:** *'Uthana'* Kannada Monthly, Page : 81-85, Sept. 1990.

4. Harmful Effects on the Individual and the Society **:** It unavoidably includes an effect that is detrimental to the individual and to the society. Sales and consumption of most of the narcotic drugs are legally banned in most of the countries for they have disastrous effects on the individuals and the society. Drug addiction ultimately destroys the individual, his family relations and social connections. Drug addicts virtually become parasites on society contributing nothing to its effective functioning.

6. SOME BASIC CONCEPTS : DRUG – DRUG ABUSE, DRUG DEPENDENCE

Concepts such as *"drug", "drug abuse", "drug dependence"* etc. are very commonly used in our discussion of the problem of "drug addiction". Hence, it is necessary to clarify the difference in the meanings of these terms.

1. "Drug" and its Meaning

What is Drug ? **:** It is necessary for us to know the meaning of the word "drug" before we make an attempt to understand *"drug addiction"*.

In an ordinary sense, the word *"drug"* denotes any medicine, solid or liquid prescribed by a physician for the cure of a disease. It is in this sense, equated with medicine. But when used in a specific sense, the word "drug" connotes a different meaning; it represents various narcotic drugs. It is with this meaning the word is analysed here.

- ***"Drug"*** *is a chemical substance associated with distinct physical and / or psychological effects. It alters a person's normal bodily processes or functions.*
- The **WHO** [World Health Organisations] Expert Committee defines drug as – *any substance that, when taken into the living organism, may modify one or more of its functions.*
- **Joseph Julian** states that drug is *"any chemical substance which affects bodily function, mood, perception or consciousness which has potential for misuse and which may be harmful to the individual or the society."*[15]

Joseph Julian's definition signifies that the frequent use of drug is considered very dangerous and even immoral and anti-social for it arouses a variety of indignant and hostile sentiments on the part of the general public. The use of illegal drugs such as *heroin, brown sugar, cocaine, L.S.D.* – belongs to that category.

2. Drug Abuse

The word *"abuse"* refers to improper or wrong use of a thing. Obviously, *"drug abuse"* means improper and even illegal use of drugs. It could be more appropriately defined in the following manner.

- **Paul Fuqua** refers to 'drug abuse' as – *"the use of a substance in such a way that it leads to such personal and / or social consequences as impaired physical or mental health, impaired maturation, loss of productivity, and involvement in socially disruptive or illegal activities."*
- **Ram Ahuja** states that *"drug abuse is the use of illicit drug or misuse of legitimate drug resulting in physical or psychological harm."*
- **Drug abuse is defined as** – *"self administration of drug for non-medical reasons, in quantities and frequencies which may impair an individual's ability to function effectively, and which may result in social, physical or emotional harm."*[16]
- ***In simple words,*** *drug abuse is using natural / and or synthetic chemical substances like alcohol, tobacco, ganja, opium, cocaine, etc., for non-medical purposes to experience pleasure.*

---

15. As quoted by **Ram Ahuja** in *"Social Problems in India"* – Page : 387.

16. As quoted by **C.B. Mammoria,** Page : 719.

Drug abuse includes, for example, *smoking ganja or hashish, taking heroin, cocaine or L.S.D., injecting morphine, drinking alcohol, licking brown sugar,* and so on. All these drugs are narcotic in the sense; they give a *'kick'* and psychic ecstasy.

Characteristics of Drug Abuse

As per the above definitions, drug abuse implies the following characteristic features.

1. The use of drugs in any form or style is considered as 'illegal'.
2. The drug is used without proper medical advice and supervision;
3. It is used in excess of accepted standards of self-medication, and
4. The use of drugs in this context leads to loss of control over the user's behaviour.

3. "Drug Dependence"

"Drug dependence" is yet another concept associated with the analysis of drug addiction. The term denotes habitual or frequent use of a drug. The use is so frequent that the individual virtually becomes dependent on it. This dependence is of two types : *(i) Physical dependence,* and *(ii) Psychological dependence.*

(i) ***Physical dependence*** refers to the bodily dependence of a person on the use of the drug. Due to the continuous use of the drug, the body becomes so adjusted to the presence of the drug that it will suffer pain, severe discomfort or even illness if the use of the drug is not continued. In a state of drug-addiction of a person, physical dependence reflects the bodily position of a person which requires continued administration of the drug in order to function.

(ii) ***Psychological dependence*** refers to the strong craving for the drug. The craving is so strong that the individual feels that his well-being depends only on its use. Sometimes, the word ***"habituation"*** is used to refer to psychic or psychological dependence.

- **Drug Habituation and Drug Addiction**

These two terms are not one and the same though often used interchangeably. Both involve repeated consumption of a natural or synthetic drug.

In the case of ***'drug habituation'***, there is a desire but not a compulsion to continue taking the drug. There is also a little tendency to increase the dosage and there is some psychological dependence but not a physiological one. Drugs associated with habituation are cocaine derived from the *coca shrub*; derivatives of *hump* [hashish, marijuana] and the *tranquillising drugs*.

Addiction to a drug means that the body becomes so dependent on the toxic effects of the drug that one just cannot do without it. Most commonly used drugs which lead to addiction are the opium derivatives such as *morphine, heroin*, etc.

Signs of Drug Dependence

As pointed out by **C.B. Mamoria,** drug dependence on the part of the drug addicts reveals certain signs among which the following may be noted.[17]

1. Persons experiencing a static panic and exhibiting anxiety reactions.
2. Impaired judgement and distorted perceptions of space or time.
3. Excessive suspicion of others [or attitudes of paranoia]
4. Occasional convulsions
5. Mental confusion, loss of contact with reality and lapses of memory.
6. Unhealthy physical appearance because of poor diet and personal neglect.

17. C.B. Mamoria in *"Social Problems and Social Disorganisation in India"* – Page : 719.

7. Severe drousiness and finding oneself in sleepy mood.
8. Indifferent, apathetic and sometimes compulsive behaviour.
9. Dilated pupils, a flushed face, and a feeling of being chilly.
10. A deterioration of values.

What is to be borne in mind is that all individuals who suffer from drug dependence need not necessarily exhibit all the above mentioned symptoms. Symptoms also vary with the stage of addiction and the type of the drug used, as well as with the experience of the drug user.

Signs of Established Drug Addict

Continuous use of drugs makes a person to become a drug addict. When once he becomes addicted to its use, he finds it difficult to come out of its clutches. An established drug addict normally exhibits the following signs or features.

- Poor personal appearance
- Absenting from college / work
- Poor performance in college / work
- Poor and odd eating habits, loss of weight
- Prefers to be alone or with few others who also have the addiction.
- Erratic sleeping pattern; often found sleeping during the day and awake in the night.
- Telling lies to get money – for procuring the drug
- Stealing, selling personal and others' articles to get money.
- Needle marks on arms and legs and attempts to conceal them by wearing clothes with long sleeves.
- "Doped" appearance : appear dreamy, have slurred speech, swaying gait tremors of hands.
- Frequent clashes with law, involvement in accidents and in criminal acts.
- Moral deterioration
- Sickly appearance : disheveled hair, muddy eyes, dark and dry lips, skin and bones, skin infections.

Who is Likely to Become a Drug Addict ?

Studies of have revealed that the following types of persons are more vulnerable to drug addiction.

- Young people and adolescents [teenagers]
- Persons from broken family [divorced / separated parents]
- Having history of alcohol / drug abuse, suicide among the near relatives, especially in parent[s]
- Having had difficult childhood, being treated with cruelty in childhood
- Persons with excessive shyness, poor social abilities, poor self-esteem [i.e. inferiority complex]
- Persons with easy access to money as well as drugs.
- Persons associating closely with drug peddlers, drug users
- Persons with emotional disorders like depression, severe tension/ anxiety due to whatever reasons.
- Persons with antisocial behaviour patterns.
- Persons in certain occupations are prone to develop addiction. ***Eg*** **:** *Doctors, nurses, jobs involving frequent travels, actors, bar attenders, etc.*

- Persons with constant source of stress, having problems which are difficult to solve.
- Persons with rebellious attitude, scant respect for social norms and authority.

7. TYPES OF DRUGS OR NATURE AND IMPACT OF ABUSABLE DRUGS

The conditions of modern society often give scope for drug abuse. These drugs which cause serious health problems to the individuals who use it also lead to some sort of dependence. Hence they are also called *"dependence – producing drugs"*. Though legal restrictions and prohibitions are imposed on these drugs, many individuals are found to be using them escaping the notice of the law enforcement authorities.

The abusable drugs or *"dependence producing drugs"* belong to the following six main categories. They are *(1) alcohol, (2) sedatives, (3) stimulants, (4) narcotics, (5) hallucinogens, and (6) nicotine.* The impact of these drugs on the individual users is not the same, but different.

1. Alcohol

By pharmacological definition, alcohol is a drug and may be classified as a sedative, tranquillizer, hypnotic or anesthetic, depending upon the quantity that is consumed. It relieves tension and lessens aggressive inhibitions. It includes intoxication. Of all the drugs, alcohol is the only drug whose self-induced intoxication is considered as somewhat socially acceptable.

Over the 30-40 years, increasing percentage of young people have started to drink alcoholic beverages. Their alcohol consumption has increased in quantity and frequency and the age at which drinking starts has declined. This situation is socially disturbing.

Alcohol has a marked effect on the central nervous system. It is not a "stimulant" as it was previously believed, but a primary and continuous depressant. Alcohol produces psychic dependence of varying degrees from mild to strong. Physical dependence develops slowly.

2. Sedatives OR Depressants

Barbiturates, bromides and *tranquillizers* belong to this category. These drugs are also called *"drowners"*. They act to relax the central nervous system and induce sleep and provide a soothing effect. Medically, these are used in high blood pressure, insomnia, epilepsy and to relax patients before and during surgery.

When these depressants are taken in small quantities, they slow down breathing and heart-beating. Taken in higher doses, their effects resemble alcohol intoxication. Higher doze of its consumption impairs person's ability to think, concentrate and work. His emotional control is also weakened.

3. Stimulants

The most widely known stimulants are *amphetamines* [popularly known as '*pep-pills*']. When administered by a medical practitioner, moderate dose of *amphetamine* can check fatigue and produce feelings of alertness and self-confidence. But the heavy dose of the same may cause extreme nervousness, irritability, head ache, sweating, diarrhoea and unclear speech.

These drugs, however, do not cause physical dependence, though they are psychologically addicting. It is not advisable to take a heavy doze of it for a long time. In such cases, it may cause varying degrees of intellectual, emotional, economic and social deterioration. Sudden stopping of the same is also harmful for it may result in mental illness and a deep suicidal depression.

4. Narcotics

Narcotic drugs are many for they include *opium, marijuana, heroin, morphine, cocaine, codeine, methadone, pithindine and cannabis* such as *charas, ganja, bhang, etc.*

Continued taking of these is regarded as the worst type of addiction because it produces craving and psychic dependence. Narcotic drugs are taken to produce the feelings of pleasure, strength and superiority. They reduce hunger, increase suggestibility and lessen inhibitions.

5. Hallucinogens

These include *mescaline, DMT, STP, MDA* and *LSD* [Lysergic acid diethylamides]. These drugs are called *"psychedelics"*. Their use is not advised by medical practitioners. The well-known drug in this group is LSD which is a man-made chemical. LSD is taken orally and it may also be injected. It is a powerful drug and its effect on the individual lasts for 8 to 10 hours. Any attempt to withdraw from its use leads to panic, depression and permanent severe mental derangement on the part of its addict.

6. Nicotine or Tobacco

This includes *beedi, cigarettes, cigars, snuffs* and *beeda* [which includes tobacco]. This leads to relaxation, stimulates the central nervous system, increases wakefulness, and removes boredom. The frequent and heavy use of nicotine may cause heart attack, lung cancer, and bronchitis. From the legal point of view, this is not a drug.

"Tobacco is in legal use everywhere in the world, yet it causes far more deaths than all other psychoactive substances[18] combined. About 3 million premature deaths a year [6% of the world total] are already attributed to tobacco smoking. Tobacco is responsible for about 30% of all cancer deaths in developed countries. More people die from tobacco related diseases other than cancer such as stroke, myocardial infarction, ... peptic ulcer .... There is evidence that earlier a person begins to smoke, the greater is the risk of life-threatening diseases such as – chronic bronchitis, cardiovascular diseases and lung cancer."[19]

8. CAUSES OF DRUG ADDICTION OR MOTIVATIONS IN DRUG USAGE

Every one knows that drug abuse or addiction has become one of the grave problems of the modern society. The socio-economic conditions of the modern society seem to be favourable for the growth of drug abuse. The questions such as – *why people become drug addicts ? or why drug abuse is found ? what motivations provoke people to become addicts ?* – seem to be tantalising. These questions are to be addressed in order to have a clear picture of the way in which people become the victims of drug abuse.

According to **Ram Ahuja**, the causes of drug abuse may be classified under the following four main heads :

1. ***Psychological Causes*** **:** Psychological factors such as – getting *'kicks'* and *'thrills'*, relieving tension, removing inhibitions, avoiding boredom, easing depression, satisfying curiosity, feeling high and confident and intensifying perception, etc. may motivate individuals for drug abuse.

2. ***Physiological Factors*** like removing pain, getting sleep, heightening sexual experiences, staying awake, getting more physical strength, etc. also induce people to become drug addicts.

3. ***Social Causes*** that favour drug abuse are -- to become acceptable to friends, the desire to join *"high society"*, facilitating social experiences, challenging social values, to set new social trends, etc.

---

18. ***Psychoactive substances*** or ***drugs*** include stimulants, depressants, narcotics and hallucinogens.

19. ***Ref*** **:** **Park**'s *"Textbook of Preventive and Social Medicine"*. [17th Edition, 2007.] – Page : 688.

THE FOLLOWING CHART WILL HELP US TO HAVE A CLEAR IDEA ABOUT THE VARIOUS DRUGS ABUSED, THE METHOD OF ABUSE, THE EFFECTS PRODUCED AND THE NATURE OF THE WITHDRAWAL SYMPTOMS.

Name of the Drug	Method of Abuse	Short-Term Effects	Long-Term Effects	Withdrawal Symptoms
I. **Stimulants** Amphetamines	Pills Capsules Injected	Sense of well-being, Increased alertness, Loss of appetite, Increased pulse rate and blood pressure, Increased physical activity and speech, Inability to sleep	Weight loss, Acute anxiety, Irritability, Hyperactivity, Skin rash, Mental illness, (amphetamine psychosis)	Long periods of very disturbed sleep, Depression, Extreme fatigue, Increased appetite
II. **Depressants** Sedative Hypnotics Alcohol	Tablets, Capsules Injected, Taken only in liquid form,	Drowsiness, Relaxed feeling, Relief from anxiety and tension, Slurred speech, Poor co-ordination	Clumsy movement, Slurred speech, Unclear vision, Anaemia, Impairment of liver	Anxiety, Sleeplessness, Tremors, Fits, Delirium tremens
III. **Hallucinogens** L.S.D.	Tablets	Sensory experience gets heightened, Distortions in the way one feels, sees and hears, Mixing up of senses (seeing music, hearing vision etc.)	Mental illness (L.S.D. psychosis), De-pression, Flashbacks occur, (pleasant and unpleasant experience of the past occur even after drug use is stopped)	Not reported
IV. **Cannabis** Ganja/Marijuana	Smoked	Feeling high, Non-stop talking and laughing, Heightened sensory perception, Craving for sweets, Rapid heart beat	Loss of interest in everything around, Fear (paranoia), Mental illness (psychosis), Impaired memory and concentration	Anxiety, Nervousness, Sleeplessness, Loss of appetite
Hashish/Charas	Smoked or Eaten after cooking with food			
Bhang	Taken after boiling with milk			
V. **Narcotic Analgesics** Brown Sugar	Kept in spoon and heated. The smoke is inhaled (chasing)	State of well-being in which hunger and pain are not felt, Pleasurable drowsiness	Damage to respiratory system, Severe constipation, Contracted pupils, Severe mood swings, Infection at injected sites	Watering of eyes and nose, Uncontrollable sweating and yawning, Vomiting and diarrhoea, Feeling chill (cold turkey), Stomach cramps
Opium Morphine Codine Pethadine Heroin	Injected			

4. ***Miscellaneous Causes*** backing the ugly practice of drug abuse include – sharpening religious insight or to get new spiritual light, improving study, solving personal problems, deepening self-understanding, increasing efficiency, to refresh the mind, and so on.

Some Specific Causes

In addition to four broad categories of factors causing drug abuse, as mentioned above, some specific causes may also contribute to it. Among such causes, the following ones deserve a special mention.

1. Using Drugs for 'Kicks' or 'Thrills' **:** Sizeable number of street children, educated and uneducated youths become drug addicts because of their intense eagerness to taste it once. They get initiated to its use in the beginning only for *'fun'*, or for a *'thrill'* or *'kich'*. When such experiences are repeated they find it impossible to come out of the drug trap to which they have already fallen.

2. Peer Group Influence **:** Peer group influence seems to be very powerful in initiating a new person to drug-taking habit. To get recognition in the company, to satisfy other members of the peer group, to feel superior in the presence of a boy friend or girl friend, to avoid ridicule at the hands of fellow-members – and due to such other factors, young people become victims of drug abuse.

3. Feeling of Alienation and Lack of Motivation **:** The conditions of modern society are such that they may push some mentally weak or delicate persons towards loneliness. Such persons though live in the midst of people tend to feel that they are alone in the world for they do not have any companions. They are devoid of love, affection, companionship and fellowship. Life becomes monotonous and boring for them. Some of them become introverts by turning increasingly inwards. In order to find a fuller meaning in life some of them resort to drugs.

● ***Lack of motivation*** is another important factor. Many young people fail to get good guidance for setting their aims and missions in life. They find no one to inspire them, correct them, pat them at their back and provide them a model to emulate. They very often experience frustration, disgust and disappointment. To avoid such discouraging things of life, some resort to drugs.

4. To Escape from the Pressures and Conflicts of Life **:** Our living conditions also impose various pressures, conflicts, tensions and dangers in our life. One requires courage and a realistic approach to face such challenges of life. All are not mentally equipped to face successfully such realities of life. Mentally timid, intellectually average and physically weak individuals may harbour in their mind all negative thinking particularly when they feel that they are incapable of meeting the immediate challenges before them. Some such persons become mentally depressed while a few others exhibit suicidal tendencies. There are also persons of that nature resorting to drugs.

Why Do People Seek Drugs ?

At first, many young people experiment with drugs for which the reasons include ....

- Peer pressure i.e. pressure from friends.
- To feel one with the group in which they live.
- To feel "grown –up"
- To rebel against parents, teachers bosses, and other authority.
- Curiosity to have the experience, i.e. for "kicks".
- To kill boredom
- To escape or reduce unpleasant experiences of life
- As an adventure
- Easy availability of money as well as the "drug"
- Adult examples, i.e., emulating others.

The danger with experimenting is that drugs can become an important part of their daily life. They can also become a means of trying to cope with or avoid problems.

Later, some people may decide to continue using drugs either occasionally or as a regular part of their life. They do so ....

- To relieve boredom
- To get more energy

- To feel "great" or "high"
- To feel more "creative"
- To reduce guilt feelings
- To feel good about oneself, i.e. to boost one's self-esteem
- To "solve" or to escape from problems
- To cope up with certain social situations, to improve social interaction
- To facilitate adventures
- To stay awake
- To reduce pain
- To "enjoy" week ends or to "celebrate" success.

Finally, some people come to need drugs. These hardcore drug users need to continue the drugs because ....

They become physically and / or psychologically dependent on them. i.e. they suffer from the withdrawal effects of the drug even if they miss a single dose of it.

9. EFFECTS OF DRUG ADDICTION

Drug addiction is one of the grave social evils of the modern complex society. Unfortunately, it is becoming more and more widespread in the economically and educationally advanced societies. It is indeed becoming a growing threat to humanity. Some of the disastrous effects of drug abuse may be noted here.

1. Physical and Mental Decline **:** Individuals who become the victims of drug addiction soon deteriorate mentally and physically. Though the consumption of drug gives them *'thrill'* or *'kick'* in the beginning, its continuous use makes them to become its slave and they get emaciated soon.

2. The Tragic Dependence on Drugs **:** Frequent use of drug makes a person to become *'dependent'* on it. In the beginning, he will be intensely aspiring and craving to get it. This is a stage of *"psychological dependence"*. Consistent use of a drug at this stage slowly pushes him to the next worst stage of *"physical dependence"*. At this stage, the individual's body gets so adjusted to the drug that without the drug the body suffers pain, illness, shivering and total discomfort. This is the stage of addiction, a stage in which the drug habit makes the person to dance according to its tune.

3. Great Damage to Health **:** Drug habit at its height is dangerous for health. If the habit becomes a permanent habit then it makes the person to become the victim of many types of diseases and health upsets such as – nervous weakness, bodily weakness, loss of body weight, indigestion, peptic ulcer, liver complaint, sleepiness, higher B.P., and so on.

4. Moral Degradation **:** Drug addiction leads to moral degeneration also. The drug addict gives no respect to moral values and ideals. He does not obey the rules. He is interested in only one thing in life and that is drug. For obtaining it, he is prepared to do anything including the criminal acts such as cheating, stealing, killing, and so on.

5. Blackmailing the Drug Addicts for Criminal Purposes **:** Drug addicts are increasing in number. Huge amount of money is wasted by these drug addicts for purchasing drugs worth more than ₹ **100** billion dollars every year for their consumption.

Further, anti-social elements and criminals make use of the drug addicts for their criminal activities. They exploit the weakness of the drug addicts and even blackmail them to get their things done.

6. ***Other Harmful Effects of Drug Addiction*** :

(i) Drug addiction causes waste of huge amount of money on drugs.

(ii) It damages family relations, leads to an increase in divorce, desertion and family disorganisation.

(iii) It spoils human potentiality and prevents a large number of people from utilizing their talents and abilities for their own betterment and for the betterment of the society.

CONTROL OF DRUG ABUSE / ADDICTION

Problem of drug addiction has become one of the serious and pressing social problems of the civilized societies. The problem has to be tackled effectively and the drug addicts are to be persuaded to give up their deadly habits. The programme of prevention of drug abuse / addiction should have realistic aims. Over ambitious hopes of eradicating the drug problem in a short time are likely to lead to policies that are unrealistic and self-discrediting. Changes in cultural attitudes and alteration in relevant aspects of the environment can be brought about only slowly.

1. Educational Approach : Imparting education about drugs and the evil effects of their consumption is of great importance. Common approaches here include educational programmes for school children / college and university students and public information campaigns on electronic media. Students and youths who are living away from their parents particularly in hostels/ hotels / private rooms are to be given special attention. People living in slums, industrial workers, street children, truck drivers and autorikshaw pullers must be taken proper care.

• ***All Misleading Knowledge to be Removed*** : General principles of communication can be applied to increase the effectiveness of educational approach. The method of education should be such people involve themselves actively and there is a free exchange of valuable information. The type of education must be such that all inaccurate information and misleading knowledge that people have about the physical and psychological effects of taking drugs must be removed.

• ***Clear Message to be Given*** : The message should be clear and unambiguous to the intended audience of the specially conducted programme and come from credible source of information. The message should also provide specifice advice, rather than general; and as far as possible the information should be new to the audience and should be capable of provoking discussion or action. Educational approach should not be planned and carried out as an isolated activity. To be effective, such approaches should be regarded as a part of integrated plan of action involving other strategies.

2. Community Approach : The rapid changes taking place at present time in the relations between individuals, groups and nations are also reflected in a rapidly changing pattern of drug use in many parts of the world. There should be a strong emphasis on action at the community level to prevent drug abuse. Primary health care centers should be strengthened so as to initiate preventive action that will influence people's every day lives and actions. Action at the community level is also important since communities often bear the brunt of dealing with the harmful use of drugs and drug related problems.

3. Legal Approach: The legal control on the distribution of drugs, when effectively applied has been and remains an important approach in the prevention of drug abuse. Controls may be designed to impose partial restrictions or to make a drug completely unavailable. *"Legislation may be directed at controlling the manufacture, distribution, prescription, price, time of sale, or consumption of a substance."*[20]

Legislation restricting or prohibiting advertisements that directly or indirectly promote the use of tobacco and alcohol has been increasingly common in recent years. The minimum age at

---

20. K. Park in *"Park's Textbook of Preventive and Social Medicine"* [2007] – Page : 690.

which minors may legally have access to alcoholic beverages, has been raised in some countries. There is also legislation controlling the distribution of alcohol in some countries. In India, in Andhra Pradesh, for example, sale of alcohol is prohibited.

• ***The Narcotic Drugs and Psychotropic Substances Act – 1985*** : The Central Government introduced this Act in the year 1985 to combat trafficking in drugs. It was amended in 1987 to make the legislation still more stringent. The Act provides for a minimum punishment of 10 years rigorous imprisonment for its violation, and it could be extended to 20 years with a fine of **1** to **2** lakh rupees. The courts are also empowered to impose still heavier amount of fines. The Act also lays down imprisonment of one year or fine or both for the illegal possession of any narcotic drug or psychotropic substance in small quantity for personal consumption. The Act makes provision for the establishment of as many centers as the government thinks fit for identification, treatment, education, after care, rehabilitation and social reintegration of addicts.

4. Punishment to Corrupt Enforcement Agencies Including Police : No law or legislation is effective by itself. It gets strength only if it is effectively enforced. Police and the enforcement agency play an important role in enforcing the law. When law enforcers are found working in collusion with drug-peddlers, they deserve severe punishment. Corrupt police officials do a great damage in this regard.

5. Changing the Attitudes of Doctors : The practising doctors will have to change their approach in prescribing too many and too costly drugs. They have to be careful about the side effects of the drugs which they are prescribing. Though drugs help many, yet there are dangers of over-dependence. Once a patient gets a prescription from a doctor that cures his ailment, he ceases to consult the doctor and continues to use the drugs indiscriminately or excessively whenever he suffers from the same ailment. It is in this way, people often come to depend more on medication than on physician which is a dangerous practice.

6. Follow-up Study of Drug Addicts Under Treatment : It is necessary to make follow-up study of drug addicts treated under detoxification programmes. This helps the doctors and the consultants to know the effectiveness of the treatment.

7. Role of Teachers : Teachers can play a vital role in the prevention of drug abuse. They can talk openly and freely with the students and can discuss the dangers of drug abuse. They can come to know about their students' interests and activities. They can talk about the problem of adolescence and guide students how to solve them. They can encourage their students to talk freely about their personal problems [in relation to parents, peer groups, money, etc.] and give proper suggestion and advice. Teachers can help the students in selecting career options and setting goals.

8. Role of Parents : Parents' role is no less significant, Drug abuse, at times, may have its roots in parental neglect, over-hostility, rejection, marital disharmony, etc. It is thus necessary that parents have to take more care in keeping the family environment congenial and harmonious. No one becomes an addict overnight. It involves a process of evolution of losing interest in studies, activities and hobbies, indulging in irresponsible behaviour, irritability, impulsive conduct, etc. If the parents are alert and responsible, they can locate these early signs and take proper precaution in protecting their children.

• ***Parents can do a lot in the prevention of drug abuse.*** They could talk to their children openly and affectionately, listen to their problems patiently and suggest them how to handle the problems effectively. Parents need to spare much time to know the activities of their children, their circle of friends, their hobbies, etc. Parents themselves must set a good model for the children by not taking drugs or alcohol. Parents must keep themselves informed about the modern drugs, the drug lobbies, their style of operation, etc. – in order to keep their children away from such influences.

9. Providing Alternative Activities : A popular approach to the prevention of drug abuse is providing for alternative activities which may help to prevent drug abuse. Youth centers and teen centers could provide activities attractive to the adolescents and youths who might otherwise drift in to drug taking subculture. Such activities include the establishment of groups or organizations interested in athletics, sports, music, public policy, religion, artistic activities of various kinds. Non-governmental organizations play a crucial role in the development of such activities and are likely to become important.

- **Giving Special Attention to the Teenagers to Prevent Drug Abuse**

Choosing the most vulnerable persons i.e., the teenagers, as the target group and giving them proper education regarding the ill effects of alcohol and drug use - is yet another step.

1. Teaching teenagers to chanalise their curiosity and energy in socially acceptable, constructive and healthy pursuits like sports, music, painting, social service, trekking, mountaineering, good reading etc.
2. Encouraging youngsters to shed off shyness and inhibitions to realise their potentials and talents.
3. Setting clear goals in life and constant persuasion of the goals.
4. Elders in the family and teachers can do a lot in this direction to effect a positive outlook about life in these youngsters.
5. Warding off tension and depression among youngsters by encouraging frank discussion. on topics which they find otherwise embarrassing.
6. Respecting the honest views expressed by the teenagers and not snubbing them unnecessarily.

Conclusion

Drug abuse today has become a big menace, a threat to humanity. Law enforcement authorities alone cannot do any magic in preventing it. Corrupt police authorities and politicians, mafia gangs, drug lobbies, international terrorist organizations all have added much strength to this menace. Entire society has to take this as a challenge and create awareness among the public. To create awareness among the people, ***"International Day Against Drug Abuse and Illicit Trafficking"*** has been in observance every year on **June 26** ever since 1991. Persuasion, motivation coercion, compulsion and punishment are the measures all of which have to be used so that drug-abusers can be made to live a wholesome drug-free life. Prevention, treatment and rehabilitation all require a positive and life-affirming campaign.

Thus, families and voluntary organizations, local agencies, youth forums, women's organizations, religious associations, all must work together not only to prevent people from becoming victims of this problem, but also to bring back the recovered addicts into the mainstream of social life.

•••

Chapter 15

CORRUPTION IN PUBLIC LIFE AND NEPOTISM

A. Corruption in Public Life : *Corruption, Meaning and Nature – Causes of Corruption – Conditions and Practices Favouring Corruption – Corruption in the Private Sector – Corruption in Public Services – Some Notorious Instances of Political Corruption and Scandals – Impact of Corruption or Harmful Effects of Corruption – Measures to Control Corruption : Legislative Measures and Other Types of Measures – Santhanam Committee and its Recommendations – The Lokayukta and the Lokpal – The Lokayukta at the State Level : Functioning of The Lokayukta in Karnataka – The Lokpal at the National Level – Other Suggestions to Contain Corruption – Empowering people is the Most Powerful Remedy For Corruption – Corruption is Growing in India – Anti-Corruption Movement Led by Civil Society – The Lokpal Bill Movement – Anna Hazare Staged Fast Unto Death Protest – Main Differences between the Govt. Bill and the Jan Lok Pal Bill Proposed by civil society.*

B. Nepotism : *Meaning of Nepotism - Instances of Nepotism and its Evil Effects - Suggestions to Control Nepotism.*

A. CORRUPTION IN PUBLIC LIFE

Corruption as a phenomenon is both universal and historical. It is a fact of history that there existed no society in the past in which corruption was totally absent. At the same time, corruption is practised in one way or another in all the existing societies of the world. Its content and character, its forms and intensity, of course, may differ from society to society.

Corruption as a Social Evil

Corruption is one of the social evils found in all the societies of the world. It is more rampant in some societies, than in some others. Unfortunately, India is regarded as one of the countries where corruption has become very much widespread during the recent years. Corruption is one of the factors that has contributed to the degradation of the Indian politics and public life. Rajiv Gandhi, when he was the Prime Minister of India, himself had acknowledged in a public statement in 1988 that *"out of one rupee that is spent by the Government for developmental works, hardly 15 paise reaches the common man"*. Things have been worsened since then. Corruption in India has become deep-rooted and its growth is unchecked and unhindered. All those leaders who declared war against corruption have either shamelessly succumbed to corruption or miserably lost the battle. Tall claims made by political leaders to fight out corruption have proved to be shallow.[1]

1. **Sri K.R. Narayanan,** one time President of India too had stated in his address to the Lok Sabha in 1997; *"Sheer opportunism and valueless power politics have taken over the place of principles and idealism, relationship between people, groups and parties.... and corruption is corroding the vitals of politics and our society."* - as quoted by **Ruddar Datt** and **K.P.M. Sundharam** in *"Indian Economy"* - 2005, Page: 393.

Corruption is widespread no doubt but it is condemned everywhere. At the political and administrative levels in the state, it is still more dangerous. As pointed out long back by the ancient Roman author **Cicero**, *"it is not so great an evil that a prince should go astray, though that is indeed a big evil in itself as that he corrupts others and brings it about that as his own life is changed so are the morals of his people."*[2]

- ***"Power corrupts and absolute power corrupts absolutely."*** That is what the events at the Indian national political scene seem to suggest, at least during the last couple of years. Practice of corruption at lower levels by some clerks, peons and attenders for some petty amount, is understandable and tolerable. They may practice it due to tough financial conditions, excessive demands from family, friends or society, health hazards, or some other kinds of pressures. What is more disturbing and dangerous is the corruption at higher levels, that is, at the level of higher officials.[3] Corruption in various forms has become the mainstay of our national polity in the recent past. It is needless to say that the evil of corruption meaning bribery and graft, is not conducive to social stability and equilibrium. It invariably involves negation or betrayal of normative values of society which are essential for its functioning.

Corruption is Ancient as Well as Modern

Corruption is not only a global phenomenon at present, it also existed in the ancient world. Corrupt practices as existed in the ancient world have been reported in the historical documents. Corruption in one form or the other, was there in all the leading civilisations of the ancient world. **Kautilya** also mentioned **40** types of corrupt practices which were adopted by the government servants during his time. During the British rule also corruption continued. After independence, particularly after 1970s, it has assumed new proportions. The decade between 2004-2013 can be regarded as the *"decade of corruption"* in the post independent era since during the period the practice of corruption broke all its previous records.

1. CORRUPTION : MEANING AND NATURE

Definition of the Concept of Corruption

The meaning of the concept of corruption can be made clear by means of some definitions.

1. The **English dictionary** defines corruption as *"an inducement to wrong by bribery or other unlawful means : a departure from what is pure and correct."*
2. **D.H. Bailey** says corruption can be understood as the *"misuse of authority as a result of consideration of personal gain which need not necessarily be monetary."*
3. **Andriski** considers it to be *"the use of public power for private advantage in ways which transgress some formal rule or law."*
4. ***In simple words,*** corruption refers to *"an act of bribery." It is abuse of political power or public office for personal or private gain brushing aside all formal rules.*

Nature of Corruption in Public Life

Corruption has become a widespread practice today. It has percolated through almost all the fields of our social life. No part of our public life is spared from it. A large number of public servants are guilty of either practising or supporting corruption. According to one estimate, the total

2. **P. Krishna Gopinath** : *"Corruption in Political and Public Offices : Causes and Cure"* [quoted in] : Indian Journal of Public Administration, Vol. XXVIII, No. 4, Oct-Dec. 1992, Page : 897.
3. It is estimated that by way of corruption, in India, on an average every year a sum of ₹ **26,768** crores is extracted by officials at various levels in India from citizens in the following sectors -education, health, power, telephone, railways, land and building administration, judiciary and the public distribution system. ***Source*** : *Transparency International, Berlin* - as quoted by **Ruddar Datt** and **Sundharam**, Page : 393. -2005.

amount being collected every year by the so called public servants by way of bribe money exceeds ₹ 21,068 crores.[4] ***Transparency International*** [Berlin] an international organisation, estimates it at ₹ 26,768 crores per year. But developments that took place especially after 2010 in the field of political corruption give us an impression that the figure relating to bribe money must have been doubled. The term *"corruption"* has a very wide meaning, and from the legal point of view, the following behaviour patterns can be dubbed as corrupt practices, according to **Malhotra.**

1. ***Receiving Bribe / Reward for Doing One's Duty*** **:** Receiving some reward on the part of a public servant, for the work done by him in his official capacity. ***Example***: *A doctor in a Government hospital receiving monetary reward from a patient for having treated him.*
2. ***Show of Official Power to Obtain Reward*** **:** Public servants obtaining any object or pecuniary advantage illegally by means of exhibiting their official power, is also corruption. ***Example***: *Police officers receiving "mamul"*[5] *at the hands of small vendors found in footpaths of busy areas of a city.*
3. ***Misuse of Public Property*** **:** This refers to misappropriation of public property. ***Example***: *Government officers using their departmental vehicles for their personal tours, marketing, family outings and other purposes, etc.*
4. ***Ownership of Undeclared Wealth*** **:** Possessing property or financial resources disproportionate to one's declared sources of income. ***Example***: *Clerks and officers in R.T.O. [Regional Transport Office] and Commercial Tax Department, high level police officials, owning film theatres, hotels, couple of acres of high yielding agricultural lands, house sites in cities, palacial buildings, etc.*
5. ***Abuse or Misuse of Official Position*** **:** ***Example***: Police officers misusing their position to get free supply of fruits, vegetables and daily required things from the petty businessmen.
6. ***Tax Evasions*** **:** Disregard of rules purposefully to help citizens in avoiding dues / taxes that are to be paid to the government. ***Example***: *Income tax, sales tax, commercial tax, and other tax officers favouring some people either in reducing tax dues or in waiving of the same after obtaining some financial benefits from them.*
7. ***Helping Law-breakers*** **:** Refusal to discharge one's official duty on some plea which may benefit the other party. ***Example***: Police officer not registering a case to protect a criminal for having received some bribes from him.
8. ***Receiving Gifts for Doing Favours*** **:** Accepting gifts [such as car, gold chain, fridge, colour T.V., etc.] by *"persons of positions"* that is, from persons with whom they have official dealings. ***Example***: *Building contractors giving gifts to the corporation commissioner, businessmen giving gifts to commercial tax officers with the expectation of getting some favours which would cause loss to the government.*
9. ***Unfair Acceptance of Financial Help*** **:** Borrowing money for purchasing a costly thing from a person with whom one has official dealings. ***Example:*** *Income tax officer borrowing money from a businessman to purchase a house, the act of which compels him to do some official favours to the lender of money.*

Corruption is so rampant that it is found in all the ministries and departments of the central and the state governments. In some ministries in the union government such as defence, petroleum, power and communication, chances for "making money" through corrupt practices, are more. In the same way, certain departments such as police, transport, income tax, sales tax, commercial

4. *"Hosadiganta"* Kannada Daily, Dt. 21-11-07.
5. ***"Mamul"*** - is an indigineous term which refers to the practice of giving or taking of some money regularly for an illegal purpose, or for a legal purpose illegally.

CORRUPTION IS EATING THE VITALS OF INDIAN SOCIETY

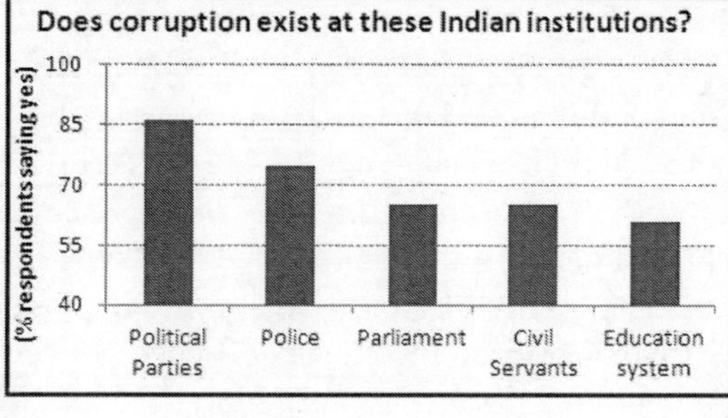

tax, revenue department, etc., provide lot of opportunities for the public servants working in them to make money in an illegal way.

Corruption is so widespread today that people have come to accept it as a commonly approved practice. No wonder, if it becomes institutionalised in the days to come.

Main Characteristics of Corruption

The above cited definitions and descriptions point out the following characteristics of corruption.

1. Corruption, as it is understood today refers to an irregular, illegal and immoral practice associated with our public life.
2. An act of corruption involves dereliction of duty, moral and legal lapses.
3. Persons party to corruption tend to neglect their prescribed duty deliberately.
4. Individuals who are charged of corruption are those who deviate from their fixed official duty in order to obtain some economic gains or to provide some physical comfort or convenience to his family members.
5. Corruption involves the practice of receiving bribe not only for getting wrong things done, but also getting right things done at the right time.
6. Corruption involves the abuse of power associated with a public office or public life.

2. CAUSES OF CORRUPTION

Corruption is like blood cancer. It has taken deep roots in the country. It has spread its tentacles to almost all fields. Corruption in Indian public life is *"all pervasive"* and that businessmen, bureaucrats, contractors, industrialists, entrepreneurs, journalists, vice-chancellors, teachers, doctors, nurses and the politicians all come under suspicion. As the time passes, more and more people come under its sway.

Corruption is a complex phenomenon and various factors and forces have conspired to cause it and spread it everywhere. The causes responsible for corruption as enlisted by **C.B. Mamoria**[6], may be discussed here.

1. *Scarcity of Goods and Services :* Corruption raises its head wherever there is a scarcity of goods and services. The scarce goods are made available to the needy at the price which includes an illegal premium. ***Example*** : *Collecting extra money than what is fixed for selling cinema tickets, music party tickets, etc.*

2. *Economic Insecurity* : This is regarded as the most important cause of corruption. The poor people become corrupt in the hope of becoming rich. The rich indulge in it for fear of losing what they have. The rich have a craving for luxurious goods and imported commodities such as - dresses, telephone receivers, mobile sets, cameras, furnitures, golden ornaments, cosmetics, air conditioners, T.V.s, wrist watches, big houses, sites, etc. A strong temptation to possess these desired things, encourages people to resort to corrupt practices on a massive scale.

3. *High Rate of Income Tax* : Since tax rates are comparatively high in India even the honest people are often tempted to escape from it by making false returns of their property and income. Many of the officers in the income tax department are also equally corrupt and they thrive on bribery. Income tax officers, policemen, sales tax officers, excise inspectors and others are minting money not only from the black marketeers and tax evaders, but also from innocent people who give bribes in order to avoid suffering and humiliation at the hands of these officials.

---

6. *C.B Mamoria in his "Social Problems and Social Disorganisation in India"*, Page : 844.

4. *Meagre Salary Being Paid to the Government Servants* : Employees in some of the government departments are paid comparatively very less salary. This situation is said to be the cause of corruption in administration. Clerks in the court, peons and attenders in all government departments, police constables and such other employees draw comparatively poor salary. They expect tips and bribes even for doing their regular or routine duties. It has been estimated that 60% to 70% of the officers in India are corrupt in one form or the other.[7]

5. *Emergence of New Sources of Wealth and Power* : The modern political and economic set up provides a chance for the politicians in power to make money through illegal means. As **Lincoln Steffens** has said, *"the politicians took bribes because businessmen gave them and businessmen gave them because they had to."* This unholy understanding between the businessmen and the politicians always encourage corruption. The recent episodes of corruption as mentioned earlier, reveal that the unscrupulous politicians can stoop to any level in looting the wealth of the country by corrupt means.

6. *Complex Laws and Procedures* which are prescribed by the state in most of its departments provide enough scope for dishonest bureaucracy to harass the public and collect from them illegal money.

7. *Regularisation of Illegal Use of Civic Facilities* : Sometimes, leaders in power give political protection to slum dwellers, and people belonging to poor classes to use water and electricity, to cut trees in state forests, to construct houses in government land, etc., without any charge, and this is also a source of corruption.

8. *The System of Democracy and High Costs of Elections* : The present style of functioning of democracy in India also contributes to corruption. All parties, especially the ruling party spends crores of rupees on each election. Elections have become so costly affairs in India today that no ordinary man with average income can think of even fighting thaluk panchayath or municipal corporation election. Both votes and voters are purchased in elections. Both the opposition and the ruling parties spend wrecklessly in elections. This money comes from the big businessmen, industrialists and such other rich men who have their own vested interests in financing the elections. They supply money to the party elections in the form of *"black money."* This in turn, gives them licence or a 'moral' justification for accumulating *"number - two"* money [unaccounted money] in different forms.

9. *The Very Presence of Black Money* : Existence of large amount of unaccounted black money is one of the main sources of corruption. ***Black money is nothing but unaccounted and undisclosed money collected through illegal means and tax evasions.*** *"This money is obtained through various ways, namely, tax evasion, smuggling, speculation in immovable property and shares and stocks, receiving fees and remuneration partly or wholly in cash without showing them in the accounts, trading in licences and permits, ..., etc."*[8]

10. *"Get - Rich - Quick" Attitude* : It is said that modernisation breeds corruption in industrial society, which *"offers prizes such as money, position, power for doing evil, etc"*. It brings about attitudinal changes in the system. Time tested ideals and values lose their meaning and new loyalties and new identifications emerge among individuals and groups. More than any other thing, *"the get-rich quick"* motivation inspires a large number of people both at the top and bottom of the society to become corrupt.

11. *Social and Economic Modernisation* : It is said that modernisation breeds corruption in industrial society, which *"offers prizes for doing evil; money, position, power"*, besides

---

7. **C.B. Mamoria** - Page: 845
8. **C.B. Mamoria** - Page : 847.

bringing about attitudinal changes in the system. New loyalties and new identifications emerge among individuals and groups. This contributes to an increase in the incidence of corruption. As **Huntington** has said, *"Corruption in a modernising society is in part not so much the result of deviance of behaviour of norms from the established patterns of behaviour."* More than any other thing, *"the get-rich quick"* motivation inspires a large number of people both at the top and bottom of the society to become corrupt.

Other Important Causes

In addition to the list of causes of corruption mentioned by **C.B. Mamoria**, there are also other factors contributing to it. Some of them are mentioned here.

(i) ***Lack of Severe Punishment for the Offenders*** **:** Though corruption is ripe, corrupt people are rarely caught legally and given punishment. Virtually, there is no fear of punishment for those who practice it.

(ii) ***Weakened Public Opinion and Protest*** **:** Everyone grumbles about corruption, but no body dares to protest against it. Movement against corruption launched long ago by the great leaders like **G.L. Nanda** and **Jayaprakash Narayan** and such other persons, have become totally dormant. Almost upto 2011, not a single serious protest movement was launched in India to root out corruption in public life.[9]

(iii) ***Deception Through Advertisements*** **:** Modern age is an 'age of advertisements'. Attractive offers that are announced through advertisements very often prove to be a big fraud. Gullible people still succumb to the glamour of advertisements and get cheated.

(iv) ***Cut-Throat Competition in the Business World*** **:** This is a world of competitions. The "open-market system" encourages competition which often proves to be disastrous and cut-throat. People struggle to win over it by hook or crook. This tendency naturally favours corruption.

(v) ***Ineffective Court System*** **:** Indian judicial and court systems also encourage corruption indirectly. Our judiciary system is known for its delay. Even if cases are filed against corrupt persons, for years and decades, the cases are not going to be settled. Till then, the accused are free to carry on their usual trade. There is no fear of punishment as such.[10]

All the factors mentioned above, have generated a favourable atmosphere for corruption.

CONDITIONS AND PRACTICES FAVOURING CORRUPTION

Dr. Sammuel Paul is of the opinion that certain conditions and traditional practices prevailing in India are very much favourable for corruption.[11] They are mentioned below.

(a) Practice of Paying Bribes : Indians have developed over the years certain practices s of paying bribes to public officials which may have created a tolerance of corruption in our society. For example, in many government offices such as registrar's offices, it was a normal practice to pay bribes. Giving bribes to police officials is taken as an accepted practice throughout India. Political parties continue to distribute openly cash and goods to voters during election time. Once such practices are widespread, it is difficult to root them out.

---

9. But for the first time in the history of independent India, a strong people's movement against corruption seems to be in the offing under the leadership of Sri Anna Hajare of Maharasthra a Gandhian who is ably assisted by Sri Aravinda Kejrival, Right to Information Act activist, Smt Kiran Bedi, retired police official, and a few others.

10. ***Pending Cases in Court*** **:** Upto Feb. 27th, 2006, as many 33635 cases in the Supreme Court, 33.4 lakh cases in the High Courts and 2.53 crores of cases in the lower courts were found to be pending and waiting for settlement. ***Source*** **:** *Hosa Diganta*, Kannada Daily, Dt : 21-11-07.

11. **Dr. Sammuel Paul**, former Director I.I.M, Ahmedabad, founder of *"Public Affairs Centre"*, Bangalore and a former World Bank and UN Adviser, in his article *"Corruption in India"*, in Manorama Year Book – 2012, Page: 899-900.

(b) **Monopolistic Government Services :** Since many government services are monopolistic in nature [only government supplies them], it becomes easy for corrupt officials to extract money or favours from those who seek the services.

(c) **Lack of Transparency in the Decisions :** At the official level that is relating to public offices, decisions are made without transparency. It becomes easier for public officials to favour those who are willing to give them bribes.

(d) **No Monitoring of the Work in Public Offices :** When those in authority are unwilling or unable to monitor the actions and performances of those working under them, corruption becomes a low risk activity. In many of our offices, doing one's duty honestly and responsibly is never appreciated and remunerated, and at the same time, not discharging one's responsibility and work, is neither condemned nor punished but only tolerated.

(e) **Unaccounted Collections for Electioneering :** Political parties need large funds for fighting elections. But there is little or virtually no accountability and transparency in the collection and use of those funds, creating in the process enormous scope for corruption.

Corruption in the Private Sector

Corruption is also there in the private sector. *For example,* to avoid paying tax, many persons and businesmen and firms engage in real estate and other transactions in cash creating unaccounted money in the process. Many firms generate black money in order to make political donations or to win contracts. It encourages them to divert some of their funds away from business thus evading taxation and deceiving their shareholders. We have here a vicious circle that is difficult to break and that perpetuates corruption and abuse of power all around.

Corruption in Public Service

According to **Dr. Sammuel Paul**, there are four major gaps in the public service that breed corruption and hence need to be rectified.

(i) **Lack of Information :** There is a lack of information that makes it difficult for citizens to know what they should do to get access to services, and what they are entitled to, once they gain access to services.

(ii) **Onesided Agreement of the Citizens with the Service-Provider :** In the public service sector, there is only onesided agreement a citizen must enter into with the service provider. The service provider will insist on the citizen paying the fee, providing the needed documents and other terms, but does not promise to deliver the expected service or benefit. The citizen cannot hold the provider accountable for time deadlines, quality and standards of service, or penalty in case of failure. This helplessness on the part of the citizen often compels him to give bribe to get the service.

(iii) **Lack of Grievance Redressal Machinery :** There is the lack of grievance redressal machinery especially when problems arise. Government can terminate a service provider or penalize the citizen if he fails to comply with the rules. But the government does not provide the citizen with a reliable grievance redressal machinery to respond to his/her complaints.

(iv) **Indifferent Attitude of the Public Officials towards the People :** The public officials are reluctant to listen to the voice of the people, especially, the poor. Though the govt. has control over its services and makes the laws and rules, it rarely monitors the actual delivery of its services.

Under the above mentioned conditions, corruption is bound to thrive. Influential citizens may make their voice heard. Some others pay bribes and get what they need from the government. But the vast majority of the people do not get their entitlement in full.

SOME NOTORIOUS INSTANCES OF POLITICAL CORRUPTION AND SCANDALS

Corruption is ubiquitous. It is found in almost all the major fields of our life such as - political, administrative, legal, judicial, literary, educational, religious, economic, occupational, etc. It is also found in the fields of art, filmland and journalism. Of all these fields, corruption in the political field has been the most notorious one for it is capable of bringing about great sensation in the whole society. Innumerable instances of political corruption have been reported ever since the days of independence. A few such notorious instances of political corruption and scandals may be mentioned here.

1. ***V.K. Krishna Menon and the Zeep Episode - 1947*** appears to be first major episode of political corruption soon after independence. In this episode, Nehru's friend and Cabinet colleague V.K. Menon cheated the country to the tune of ₹ 216 crores in the zeep episode.

2. ***The Bofors Guns Scandal - 1986*** in which Rajiv Gandhi, the then Prime Minister, [Congress party] was said to be involved. It was a case of purchasing bofors guns from a Swedish firm for the military in which the nation was said to be cheated to the tune of ₹ 200 crore.

3. ***The Animal Husbandry Scam [1990-1995]*** took place in Bihar in which the then Chief Minister of Bihar, Laloo Prasad Yadav was said to be involved. In this episode, the State Treasury was said to be cheated to the tune of ₹ 950 crore. It was a case of large-scale misappropriation and fradulent transaction in dealing with public funds. Laloo Prasad Yadav had to step down on this count.

4. ***J.M.M. Scam - 1993*** in which the then Prime Minister, P.V. Narasimha Rao [Congress Party] was said to be involved in giving money to purchase votes from the members of the Jharkhand Mukthi Morcha in favour of his Congress party in the Parliament to form the ministiry.

5. ***Indian Bank Scam - [1996]*** in which several politicians, bureaucrats and the general manager of the bank were said to be directly involved in indulging in financial irregularities. More than ₹ 2300 crores were involved in this.

> **Ram Ahuja**'s observations in this regard present the most horrible picture of political corruption taking place in this land... ***Ram Ahuja writes*** **:** *"If we consider only the mega scams in a period of ten years between 1986 and 1996, the country lost about ₹ 15,000 crore or ₹ 1500 crore a year. If we take various other 'questionable deals' in which colossal sums of money were lost, India has been losing about ₹ 20 crore every single day. This is surely a big threat to the very survival of democracy in our country." Some of the recent scams and scandals reveal that every year India's losses due to corruption amount to a few lakh crores especially after the year 2000-01. Common people remain dumb witness to all these scandals.* **Ram Ahuja** in *"Indian Social Problems"* 2nd Edition, (2003) Page : 462.

Some of the Recent Scandals and Scams

(i) **2G. Spectrum – Scam of Scams 2010-11 :** The 2G Spectrum Scam involving a group of top politicians and bureaucrats has been labeled the biggest scam in independent India's history. Some say, it is one of the biggest scams of the world also. It involved allegations regarding the under-pricing of the 2G Spectrum of the Dept. of Telecommunications which resulted in a heavy loss to the Govt treasury. The loss to the national exchequer was assessed by the Govt auditor at an astonishing amount of **₹1.76 lakh crores.**

This episode has already witnessed a cabinet minister [A.Raja of Tamil Nadu, D.M.K. M.P.] an M.P. [Smt. Kannimozhi,[D.M.K]. daughter of M. Karunanidhi], corporate big bosses – some of the biggest names in the telecom industry going to jail.

(ii) **Common Wealth Episode- 2010-11 :** Common Wealth Games were held in Delhi in 2010 for which initially the Govt had allotted a budget of ₹1899 crore. But the actual expenses exceeded ₹ 87000 crore.

The CBI arrested **Suresh Kalmadi** congress M.P. and former Chairman of the organising committee for the Delhi Common Wealth Games, in connection with the alleged corruption and financial malpractice regarding the event held in October 2010. Mr. Kalmadi and his team allegedly received *kick backs* from a Swiss time keeping company that provided equipment and services at exorbitant rates causing a loss of crores of Rupees to the govt.

(iii) Hasan Ali Episode : Hassan Ali a scrap dealer and an alleged friend of Ahmad Patel, an alleged close associate of Congress Supremo Sonia Gandhi, amassed wealth worth a few lakh crores within 5-10 years. The Central Govt imposed ₹ 50000 crores of tax which he never paid. He was arrested and later on the let free. In 2005-06 alone, his business transaction exceeded 1.02 lakh crores.

(iv) I.P.L. 20-20 Cricket Match Episode Involving ₹ 7520 Crores : In the IPL 20:20 Cricket Match held in 2010 there took place a financial scandal amounting to ₹ 7520/- crores and it ultimately led to the resignation of the Central Minister for State [Foreign Affairs], Shashi Taroor {M.P. from Tiruvanantapura, Kerala].

(v) L.I.C. Housing Loan Scam : Salaried employees in the public and private sector can avail of loan from the L.I.C. [Life Insurance Corporation of India] for building their houses. Recently, instead of helping ordinary employees in their house construction venture, the L.I.C. diverted its fund towards big builders for developing their real estate business. It is said that this episode involved a financial scandal and amounting to ₹ 20,000/- crores.

(vi) Illegal Mining and Public Land Denotification Episode [2010-11]: Illegal mining is going on in Karnataka, Andhra, Goa and some other States in which politicians, govt bureaucrats and big industrialists are involved. Karnataka State has become notorious with the illegal land denotification episode. In both of these scams, government is losing crores of rupees of revenue and also precious natural resources. The then Chief Minister of Karnataka, B.S.Yadiyurappa [BJP] had to step down from his post on this issue. His cabinet colleague B.Janaradhan Reddy had to go to jail, and he is still there [2014].

(vii) Commercialisation of Education : In many States, private professional educational institutions have started minting money by collecting huge sums of money as capitation fee or donation; many a times against the established State rules. They have converted education into a salable commodity. These institutiions are collecting crores of rupees in this way.

The above mentioned episodes are only a few examples. Innumerable such instances[12] of corruption have taken place in the political and other fields at the national as well as state levels causing heavy losses to the nation.

3. IMPACT OF CORRUPTION *OR* HARMFUL EFFECTS OF CORRUPTION

Corruption is dangerous and spreads speedily in all fields of social life. If its growth is not checked in the initial stages, it eats into the vitals of society. As **Ronal Segal** points out, *"Corruption, like sacrifice starts at the top and percolating down, colours the whole society."*[13] The disastrous effects of corruption can be enlisted like the following

---

12. ***Some Other Instances of Corruption:*** (1) *The Cement Scandal of 1982,* [Maharashtra], (2) *The Securities Scandal 1992* [Maharashtra] - This is the Notorious Harshad Mehta Episode, - Amount involved ₹ 4024 crore. Loss to the Country ₹ 8383 crore], (3) *The Sugar Scandal - 1994* - Loss to the Country. ₹ 650 crore, (4) *The Treasure Fraud Scandal* - [Assam] *1995*. Amount involved ₹ 200 Crore, (5) *The Hawala Scandal [1991]* Involvement of the Jain Group - Amount Involved ₹ 68.8 crore, (6) *The Urea Scam [1995]* Amount involved ₹ 133 crore, (7) *The Telecommunication Department Scam [1996]*, (8) **Kareem Lal Telagi**'s *Stamp Papers Scandal* [Karnataka] Amount involved more than ₹ 5000 crore, (9) *Terrorist Veerappan's* case was also an episode of political corruption. ***Main Source :*** **Ram Ahuja**'s *"Indian Social Problesm"* - Page : 457 - 463.

13. **Ronal Segal** in *"The Crisis of India"* as quoted by **C.B. Mamoria** in *"Social Problems and Social Disorganisation in India"* - Page : 850.

1. ***Corruption Undermines Morality and Weakens One's Loyalty Towards the Nation and the Society.*** It encourages parochial loyalties, fosters narrowmindedness and contributes to the growth of casteism, linguism, communalism, regionalism and political opportunism.

2. ***Corruption Retards Economic Development*** **:** Corruption disturbs the processes of socio-economic planning. It leads to certain weaknesses such as - inactivity, inefficiency, irresponsibility, delaying attitude, deliberate derailment of administrative machinery, negligence towards socially significant issues, etc. These tendencies disturb the processes of socio-economic development. As the ***Santhanam Committee*** has stated in its report the *"speed money"* [which is referred to as *'bribe money'*] *can only protect some private interests and not the public cause.*

3. ***Rules and Regulations Become Farce*** **:** As long as corruption reigns supreme, so long morals and rules remain as a farce. As a result, the weaker sections lose their morale, and hence their faith in the establishment becomes shaky. Corruption leads to violence and lawlessness in the society since the corrupt man has the money power to purchase protective service.

4. ***Corruption Weakens the Social Organisation and Encourages Anti-Social Elements*** **:** Corruption narrows down the gap between right and wrong, justice and injustice and "moral and immoral". In a corrupt system, the will of the lazy people, public cheats, blackmailers, smugglers and tax evaders is imposed on the law-abiding and right thinking people. Corruption lowers the general morality and destroys the individual character.

5. ***Corruption Increases the Misery of Common Man*** **:** Where corruption is rampant, common people become subject to frustration, disappointment and insecurity. It adds to inefficiency, nepotism, lethargy, and creates indiscipline in all fields of administration making the life of common men most miserable. They fail to get even their ordinary things done without paying bribe and hence get frustrated.

6. ***Corruption Leads to Waste of Money and Waste of Time*** **:** Since corrupt officials stick on to delaying policy, much of the public time and money get wasted. Official delay causes more and more cost for developmental plans and projects. Corruption reduces the credibility of the officials in the eyes of the public.

7. ***Corruption Gives Scope For Vested Interests*** **:** When corruption enters public life, it starts taking strong roots in politics, administration, education, social welfare, economy, employment, judicial system, and service sectors, and so on, particularly when it is not contained effectively.

In all these fields, vested interests are developed. In addition to the influence of "speed money", the influence of very important persons [VIPs] also increases. In such a situation, common people who become helpless are 'pulled' and 'pushed' in various directions.

8. ***Corruption Leads to Regression*** **:** Unchecked corruption drives society towards disaster. Spread of corruption in fields such as - health, manufacture of medical drugs, higher education, military and defence establishments, higher level research in scientific, technological, nuclear and other fields, judiciary, vigilance etc. - is sure to take society towards a great downfall. It leads to adulteration of eatables, spurious drugs and shortage of many consumer items.

9. ***Hindrance for the Inflow of Foreign Money*** **:** Some of the studies have revealed that foreign investors are hesitant to invest their capital in a country where corruption is too much rampant. These investors have come to believe that they will have to spend at least 20- to 25% extra money which will go away as *"speed money"*.

- ***Outflow of Indian Currency*** **:** It is said that in India, higher level corrupt political leaders have made it a practice to keep their unaccounted money in foreign banks especially in Swiss

Banks, to save themselves from being caught. According to one estimate, the total amount of such money exceeds 410 billion dollars.[14]

10. ***Future Becomes Bleak*** **:** A society where corruption is at its height cannot be hopeful about a bright future. The prophecy of a corrupt society can only be a prophecy of doom, despair and despondency. In such a society, the young cannot cherish promising dreams for the future appears to them gloomy, indefinite and bleak. Corruption destabilises the government and demoralises the public. It is bound to take society towards a great fall.

11. ***Corruption Breeds Other Evils*** **:** Corruption has led to some other social evils such as casteism, nepotism, linguism and communalism. These evils do not allow the ideals such as "fraternity" [or the universal brotherhood of man] and "social justice" to become an actuality. Ethical norms are thrown away which weakens democratic ideals.

4. MEASURES TO CONTROL CORRUPTION

Corruption which has become widespread in the Indian society, has to be contained in some way or the other. Legislative measures are very much necessary for this. Though not satisfactory, the Government has taken some measures in this regard which can be grouped into two categories namely; (A) *Legislative Measures*, and (B) *Other Types of Measures.*

(A) Legislative Measures to Contain Corruption

1. Prevention of Corruption Act, 1947

Certain sections of the IPC [Indian Penal Code] could be used for punishing those who are guilty of taking bribe. The Central Government introduced in 1947 ***"The Prevention of Corruption Act"*** for the more effective prevention of bribery and corruption. The Act, of course, has been a miserable failure in reaching its target. We know that corruption has increased out of all proportions.

2. Prevention of Corruption Act, 1988

In order to bring together all relevant legal provisions relating to the practice of corruption, the Central Government introduced the *Prevention of Corruption Act, 1988.* The Act consolidated the provisions of the *Prevention of Corruption Act, 1947,* some sections of the *Indian Penal Code,* the *Criminal Procedure Code,* and the *Criminal Law Act, 1952.*

This [1988] ***Act*** enlarged the scope of the term *"public servant."* The Act is now applicable to all the employees of the Central and the Union Territories. The employees of nationalised banks, public undertakings, University Grants Commission [UGC], Vice-chancellors, professors, scientists, and others receiving financial aid from the Central and State governments or even local authorities, office-bearers of the co-operative societies of the central and the state governments, also come under the provisions of this Act. Offences committed by the public servants, if proved in a court of law, are effectively dealt with as per the provisions of this Act. However, M.P.s, M.L.A.s, and M.L.C.s, are kept out of the purview of this Act.

(B) Other Types of Measures

1. The Santhanam Committee and Its Recommendations

Corruption which has gone deep into our social life cannot be removed very easily. In fact, it can only be reduced or minimised. Even for minimising this problem, both preventive and punitive measures will have to be taken. Thus, the Central Government appointed in 1960,

---

14. Raghupathi Tantri in his article in *"Hosa Diganta"*, Kannada Daily, Dt : 21-11-07.

a Committee on *"Prevention of Corruption"* under the chairmanship of **K. Santhanam.** The Committee gave its report in 1962 in which it recommended various steps to be taken to contain corruption. The Committee observes..... *"corruption cannot be eliminated or even satisfactorily reduced unless preventive measures are planned and implemented in a sustained and effective manner. Preventive action must include administrative, legal, social, economic and educative measures".*[15]

Santhanam Committee Recommended following Measures

1. A thorough study of the extent possible, scope and modes of corruption, should be undertaken regarding each department, public undertaking or ministry. The study must also suggest preventive remedial measures for the same.
2. Administrative delays should be reduced to the minimum to avoid corrupt practices. For this purpose -
   (a) existing procedures and practices should be reviewed to avoid delays;
   (b) time-limits should be prescribed for dealing with receipts and should be strictly enforced; and
3. Attempts should be made to educate citizens with regard to their rights, responsibilities and the procedures of the government.
4. Improvement must be made to increase the salary of the employees besides making necessary provisions for housing, medical facilities for the government employees, etc.
5. Informal codes of conduct for different categories of employees particularly belonging to the departments dealing with economic affairs must be evolved insisting on them not to avail themselves of entertainment and other facilities provided to them by those with whom they have official dealings.
6. Officials should not have any dealings with a person claiming to act on behalf of an industrial house unless he is properly authorised to do so.
7. Companies and businessmen should be obliged to keep detailed accounts of expenditure.
8. Officers for the administrative posts should be selected with great care. Only those whose integrity is tested to the fullest satisfaction must be appointed for the key posts.
9. There should be a complete ban on government servants accepting private, commercial or industrial employment for two years after retirement.

• The Central Government established the ***Central Vigilance Commission [CVC]*** in 1964 itself as per the recommendations of this Committee.

2. Creation of Four Departments to Contain Corruption

To prevent corruption in public life, the Central Government established four departments as anti-corruption measures :

(a) Administrative Vigilance Division [AVD] in the Department of Personnel and Training.

(b) Central Bureau of Investigation [CBI].

(c) Domestic Vigilance Units in the Ministries / Departments / Public Undertakings / Nationalised Banks, and

(d) Central Vigilance Commission [CVC].

3. Central Vigilance Commission and its Functions

The *Central Vigilance Commission* which was set up in 1964 itself as per the recommendations of the Santhanam Committee, is the main legal body at present for dealing with the cases of

15. **K. Santhanam Committee** as quoted by **C.B. Mamoria** - Page : 865.

corruption. This commission is independent of government and works as an autonomous body like the union public service commission. It is an one man commission headed by the Central Vigilance Commissioner assisted by a secretary, **5** branch officers and **11** Commissioners for Departmental Inquiries [CDIs]. Its role is only advisory and it does not have independent executive power. It has the following main functions.

Functions of Central Vigilance Commission [The C.V.C.]

(i) to make an inquiry into any complaint of corruption against a public servant;

(ii) to advise appropriate type of proceedings to be initiated against the accused person involved in corruption.

(iii) to give directions to the CBI to register a regular case against the corrupt persons, and

(iv) to exercise general check and supervision over the vigilance and anti-corruption work in ministries / departments / banks / public undertakings, etc.

- The Central Vigilance Commission and the C.B.I. together arrested around **13265** individuals and subjected them to inquiries under the charge of corruption. Between 1998-2001, as many as 2256 cases of corruption were officially recorded and inquired into by these institutions.

4. Commissions Instituted to Probe Charges of Corruption Against the Politicians and Public Companies With Some Examples

From 1955 to 1999, various commissions were appointed by the Central Government to probe into the charges of corruption made against the politicians. ***Examples*** **:**

(1) *Das Commission* against Sardar Pratap Singh Kairon;

(2) Iyengar Commission [1965] against Jammu - Kashmir Chief Minister Bakshi Gulam Mohammed.

(3) Kapoor Commission [1968] against Goa Chief Minister Dayananda Bandodkar.

(4) Mudhokar Commission [1968] against Assam Chief Minister V.K. Mahtab.

(5) *Sarkaria Commission* against Karunanidhi, Chief Minister of Tamil Nadu [1976];

(6) *Grover Commission* against Devraj Urs, Chief Minister of Karnataka [1977].

(7) Vimadalal Commission [1977] against Andhra Pradesh Chief Minister Vengal Rao.

(8) *Kapur Commission* against Biju Patnaik, Chief Minister of Orissa [1987];

Dozens of such Commissions were instituted either by the Central Government or the State Governments to probe into the charges of corruption levelled against politicians, including ministers. It is a pity that none of these Commissions has been able to hold the enquiry successfully and find out the truth and punish the real offenders.

5. The Vohra Committee and Its Report

The Government had set up in July 1993, ***The Vohra Committee*** to find out the links between Government functionaries and political personalities, and crime syndicates and mafia organisations. The Committee which submitted its report in october 1993, strongly recommended the setting up of an independent agency to probe into corruption cases.

6. Establishment of "Lokayukta" and "Lokpal" to Contain Corruption

Many states in India have set up Lokayukta for investigating charges of corruption against Ministers, Members of Legislative Assemblies [MLAs] and other public functionaries. During the last few years, attempts have been made to introduce Lokpal Bills in the Parliament in 1968, 1971, 1977, 1985, 1989 and 1996. The Lokpal Bill was intended to probe into the charges of corruption levelled against those holding high offices at the national level including the Prime Minister.

LOKAYUKTA AND LOKPAL

Corruption is at its heights at the level of the politicians and top level government officers who are known as civil servants. This is due to one peculiar feature of the democratic practice in India. It is a matter of fact that all people are not equal before the law in India. *"India is probably the democracy where prosecution of public servants is deliberately designed to be a cumbersome process."*

In all Western democracies, governors, prime ministers, presidents, and members of parliament are routinely investigated by law enforcement agencies, to find out whether there is a suspicion of wrong-doing about them. Since no one is above the law, no permission is required from the boss to hold an enquiry or conduct an investigation. But in India, we cannot prosecute even an ex-minister without the permission of the cabinet and the governor or the president. The procedure often means that you end up getting permission from the accused or his party colleague. During the colonial rule, the British had such a rule to protect British Officers and their minions from the Indian legal system.[16] If the legal procedure itself permits such type of special privileges to the leaders, there is all the possibility of abusing it. Hundreds of our politicians have done the same.

In the above context, experts have suggested that unless all people are not treated equally, corruption cannot be contained. Hence, they have recommended the establishment of two institutions namely, Lokayukta at the State level and Lokpal at the national level in order to investigate the charges of corruption against all level government officials, ministers, M.LAs, M.LCs, M.Ps, Chief Ministers and even ex-prime minister.

Lokayukta at the State Level

What is Lokayukta ? : *Lokayukta at the state level refers to one-man or two-man committee established to investigate charges of corruption against ministers, M.L.A.s, M.L.C.s, and other public functionaries such as medical officers, PWD engineers, regional transport officers, and so on.*

Orissa is the first state to enact the Lokayukta Act and Maharashtra was the first state to appoint Lokayukta. Rajasthan enacted the Act in 1973. Bihar, Uttar Pradesh, Madhya Pradesh and Andhra Pradesh also followed the example of Rajasthan. Karnataka promulgated the ordinance in 1983 and made it an Act in 1985. In Kerala, there is the *Publicmen [Prevention of Corruption] Act, 1983* and in Nagaland there is the *Vigilance Commission* to contain corruption. Thus, many states in India made an attempt to introduce and implement this act to combat corruption.

- ***Lokayukta in Delhi*** : *"The Delhi Lokayukta Act"* was passed in 1996 which empowers the Lokayukta with huge powers. It not only investigates the complaints received by him but also empowers him to award punishment to those found guilty of corruption. Any citizen who has a complaint of corruption against a bureaucrat, government employee, legislator, municipal councillor or a cabinet minister or Chief Minister of Delhi can submit the complaint directly with the Lokayukta. He has powers equivalent to the High Court which means that an appeal against his judgement could be made only to the Supreme Court.

Lokayukta in Karnataka

In Karnataka, *Lokayukta and Upa Lokayukta Bills* were initiated by the Janata Government under the Chief Ministership of Sri Rama Krishna Hegde. Lokayukta and Upa Lokayukta are two different and independent functionaries created to investigate the actions and decisions of public

16. **M.F. Abraham** in *"Contemporary Sociology"* [2000 Page No.178].

servants. Retired judge of Supreme Court or Chief Justice of the High Court may be appointed to the position of Lokayukta, and a retired judge of the High Court for Upa Lokayukta. They are appointed by the Governor with the aid and advice of the Chief Minister in consultation with the Chief Justice of the High Court, Speaker, of the Assembly, Chairman and opposition party leaders. Both of them enjoy a term of **5** years. They are to be removed only through the orders of Governor passed after an address to both the houses of the legislature. To ensure their independence, they are not supposed to become members of the Parliament or state legislature and cannot hold any office of profit.

Jurisdiction of Lokayukta

Both these can investigate into any allegation like corruption, nepotism, favourtism, injustice and grievances arising out of bad administration. It is also vested with enormous powers to investigate into actions and decisions of public servants. The definition of 'public servant' includes the chief minister, ministers, legislators and salaried officials, secretaries. The Upa Lokayukta covers other government servants not covered by the Lokayukta.

However, judges, the Speaker of Lok Sabha, Chairman of the Legislative Council, the Accountant General, Chief Election Commissioner and his Commissioners, the Chairman and members of the Karnataka State Public Service Commission and officers of civil and criminal courts do not come under the purview of Lokayukta and Upa Lokayukta.

Functions of Lokayukta

Lokayukta is in charge of probing into the corruption charges made against higher level public servants, whereas the Upa Lokayukta is responsible for the lower levels. They are supported by enquiry, investigation *(police),* investigation *(technical)* and administrative. *The District Grievance Cell* and *Lokayukta Police Stations* are also performing functions similar to the Lokayukta.

The District Grievance Cell headed by the Deputy Commissioner is responsible for citizens and their grievances, whereas the ***'Lokayukta Police Stations'*** manned by the police personnel are directly under the control of the Lokayukta and receive allegations and corruption charges against the public servants.

Lokayuktas are not given statutory power anywhere. In eleven states, Lokayukta have been suffering from numerous limitations and disabilities which make the institution impotent and ineffective.

Functioning of the Lokayukta in Karnataka

The institution of Lokayukta in Karnataka has created big news during the recent years in its attempts to expose the corruption of top-level government officials. The previous "JDS-BJP Combine Government" [2006-07] had appointed Justice Santhosh Hegde [Ex-Justice of the Supreme Court] as the Lokayukta of the state. He had been taking keen interest in his work and showing courage in conducting surprise raids to the houses of various top-level police officers and officials of the revenue, P.W.D., transport, sales tax and commercial tax and other departments who had amassed crores of rupees by corrupt means. Justice Hegde's style of functioning was well appreciated in the media and in the public. Santhosh Hegde'strict and honest investigations led even to the resignation and arrest of Chief Minister B.S. Yadiyurappa and two of his cabinet level ministers in 2011 under the serious charges of corruption and fradulent practices. Though Yediyurappa was released very shortly from the jail, charges of corruption are still there against him and the inquiry is still going on. The two other ministers were in jail for several months; and one is still there (2014).

Lokayukta's Report Led to the Resignation and Arrest of Karnataka Chief Minister

The fact that Lokayukta could be a powerful instrument in exposing the corruption of top people at the State level has been proved in the case of Karnataka Lokayukta. Karnataka Chief Minister B.S. Yediurappa, for example, was forced to resign following his indictment in an illegal mining scam by the Lokayukta. The Lokayukta report stated that there is sufficient evidence to indict him of granting illegal mining licenses to mining companies and benefitting through them. He and his family members are also alleged to have received bribe from mining companies.

Yediurappa was also alleged to have used his position as Chief Minister to unfairly favour his sons in the allotment of prime land in Bangalore. The Lokayukta investigated this case and submitted its report on 27-7-11 to the State government and the Supreme Court. The Governor recommended his prosecution under the provisions of corruption Act. The Lokayukta Report caused demands from within his party for his registration. Following the submission of the Lokayukta report, he resigned on 31st July 2011. During the course of the investigation of this case, he was arrested at one stage and kept behind bars for a couple of weeks. He is indeed, the first Chief Minister to be arrested and kept behind bars on corruption charges when in power.

LOKPAL AT THE NATIONAL LEVEL

It is suggested that in order to look into the charges of corruption at the level of those holding the highest offices such as Prime minister, deputy Prime minister and cabinet level ministers, special bodies such as the ***Lokpals*** be instituted. The Central Governemnt previously tried to introduce the *Lokpal Bill* in the Lok Sabha several times in the time span of about 29-30 years [1968, 1971, 1977, 1985 and 1989] but was not able to pass the Bill for want of consensus. The BJP-led NDA [National Democratic Alliance] Government under the Prime Ministership of Sri Atal Bihari Vajpayee, had also shown great interest in introducing this Bill in the Parliament. However, it could not proceed further with it for want of support from the political parties. It was only in the year 2012-13, it became an Act.

What is Lokpal ?

Lokpal at the national level is a machinery headed by one-man committee, meant for the redressal of citizen's grievances and to check corruption and misuse of power by the highest public authorities which include the offices of Prime Minister, deputy prime minister and cabinet level ministers.

The Lokpal has been empowered to inquire into complaints about a public functionary who has committed an offence which is punishable under the *Prevention of Corruption Act 1947* or under chapter IX of the Indian Penal Code

Offences Dealt with Under Chapter IX of the IPC : Under this code, are included offences such as - *taking gratification in respect of an official act, adoption of corrupt and illegal means to influence a public servant, obtaining in an official capacity a valuable thing from a person concerned with a business transaction, disobeying the law or framing an incorrect document to cause injury to any person, unlawfully engaging in trade, or buying or bidding for property and abetment of offences.*

Coverage : Under the Lokpal, a public functionary includes Cabinet ministers, ministers of state, deputy ministers and parliamentary secretaries of the Union Government.

Organisation of Lokpal

The Lokpal shall be appointed by the President in consultation with the Chief Justice of the Supreme Court of India for a fixed term of five years. He could be a sitting or retired judge of the Supreme Court. Such a judge should be selected by a Committee of four persons consisting of the Prime Minister, Chief Justice of India, Speaker of the Lok Sabha and the Leader of the Opposition. The Lokpal needs to submit the report to the Prime Minister who, in turn, will inform him of the action taken against the offender. The Lokpal cannot hold any office of profit nor can he be a member of Parliament or of the state legislature. This is to ensure his independence. He can be removed only by an order made by the President on the ground of proved misbehavior or incapacity.

Functions of Lokpal

The main function of the Lokpal is to investigate and not to adjudicate. After investigation, he is empowered to make a report with his recommendation to the competent authority concerned. That authority should remedy the case within certain time. He is to submit annually, a report to the President who is required to place it before each House of Parliament.

Suggestions to Make Lokpal More Effective

The above are the provisions of the Lokpal Bill placed in the Lok Sabha in 1985. In 1996, one more new Bill was presented to Parliament. It became an Act only in the year 2012-13 with several modifications. Following suggestions have been made to make Lokpal more effective that is, to serve as a remedy for corruption.

1. Lokpal should have a chairman and members.
2. It should bring under its purview all cases of corruption with powers of investigation.
3. It should have a constitutional status
4. It should also have the power to review and revise.
5. It should be provided with the power to summon service at the central and state levels.
6. The report of the Lokpal should be made public.
7. A uniform pattern of Lokayuktas should be formed at the level of regional states.
8. It should help to evolve a co-ordinating mechanism to ensure good governance.

Conclusion

The creation of these two institutions, that is, Lokayuktas and Lokpal as a remedy to corruption, has increased the hostility of the politicians towards it. Besides, the delay involved in clearing the cases, absence of independent agency to inquire into complaints and the problem of the jurisdiction of the Lokayuktas have been the weaknesses of this institution. But the very fact that these are the institutions meant to deal with corruption cases, they are likely to create a sense of fear and that sense of fear will check corruption to some extent. What is required today is the co-operation of the politicians and administrators towards these institutions.

Other Suggestions to Contain Corruption

It is to be noted that legal measures alone are not sufficient to contain corruption. As complementary to them, various other measures are to be undertaken to control the practice of corruption. The following suggestions may be considered with a view to eradicate or minimise corruption:

(a) The taxation laws must be modified, licenses and permit system must be thoroughly reviewed.
(b) The law enforcing authorities must see that the laws are rigorously enforced without any fear or favour.
(c) Since elections promote corruption, expenses in elections will have to be strictly controlled.

(d) Mass communication media must play a more positive role in encouraging honesty and discouraging and condemning dishonesty and corruption.

(e) The salaries of government officials and the ministers and legislators must be increased in tune with the price index.

- Artificial shortages and scarcities which facilitate illegal practices must be controlled.

(f) Vigilance must be increased in all departments. Bureaucratic corruption must be reduced by stringent enforcement of punitive measures against bribe-taking.

- For important and very sensitive posts, only honest officials and men of integrity must be appointed. Reservation, minority quota and such other considerations should be overlooked in such cases.

(g) Corruption trials should be given the widest possible publicity.

(h) For successfully containing corruption, the co-operation of people must be obtained.

Corruption is a serious evil which is eating the vitals of the Indian society. It seems that corruption as such cannot be completely wiped out. At least, it can be minimised and held under control. Time is ripe for controlling it at the earliest. More than the legal measures, the public opinion is to be moulded and mobilised against the practice of corruption. That is the need of the hour. Indian citizens should be encouraged to honour and respect honest and dedicated public servants including political leaders. People, instead of making compromises with corruption must make up their mind to fight it. Only then, the evil practice of corruption could be contained.

Empowering People is the Main Remedy for Corruption

Dr. Samuel Paul is of the very strong opinion that empowering people in various ways is the most important remedy for corruption.

(i) ***Empowering People with Information :*** People must be provided with maximum information about their legitimate claims, rights and entitlements. This would reduce the exploitation of the poor at the hands of the officials. If the people are informed about their rights and entitlements, they get more courage to demand for them instead of resorting to pay bribes.

(ii) ***Establishing a more balanced and transparent contract between citizens and service providers*** is another important step in this direction.

(iii) ***Effective Grievance Redressal Mechanism:*** Establishing effective grievance redressal mechanism, using new technologies wherever it is appropriate, is yet another requirement in this regard. Several experiments are under way in this area.

(iv) ***Systematic Feedback from Citizens :*** All governments and their service providers must periodically gather systematic feedback from citizens on their services and programmes. They must make sincere efforts to use the findings of the feedback to continuously improve their quality and reduce corruption.

(v) ***Penalties for the Guilty :*** There should be quick and severe penalties for those found guilty of corruption. Today, corruption is a low risk activity. Our judicial system is very slow and very few are caught and punished and it has no deterrent effect on others. A strong Lokpal/ Lakayukta institution could make a difference in this regard. It remains to be seen whether the proposed Lokpal Bill, in fact, live up to the expectations of the people.

ANTI-CORRUPTION MOVEMENT BY THE CIVIL SOCIETY

Corruption has been growing consistently in India during the recent years. It is reaching new heights with different dimensions. In fact, India's corruption stories made headlines in 2011. As some analysts pointed out, the year 2011 will be known in future as the *"year of scams"*.

The Adarsh Housing Scam in Mumbai, The Commonwealth Games Scam, the Telecom 2G Spectrum Scam, Illegal Mining Scam, Land Denotification Scam, etc. - made media headlines for months. The fall of corrupt chief ministers such as Yediyurappa, the arrest of telecom-minister Raja and his business accomplices, jailing of Parliament members such as Suresh Kalmadi, Kanni Moli; detention of state cabinet level ministers such as Katta Subramanya Naidu and Janardhan Reddy in Karnataka – and such other incidents signaled the deep inroads that corruption has made in our political and governmental machinery both at the State and at the Central level. At the same time, public anger against corruption reached an all time high. These developments have definitely damaged India's international image as a fast emerging economic power.

Anti-Corruption Movement Led by "Civil Society"

Delayed actions by the Governments to deal with scams, coupled with the harassment of the public at the hands of officials, lack of integrity and duty consciousness on the part of the bureaucrats propelled anti-corruption movements led by civil society in 2011.

Anna Hazare – The Main Leader of Civil Society

Kisan Baburao Hazare, popularly known as Anna Hazare of Maharastra, a 75 years old popular social worker and reformer launched a movement against corruption known as- *"The Bhrasthachar Virodhi Jan Andolan"* [*People's Movement Against Corruption*] to create awareness among people against corruption and also to fight against it by means of forming a Civil Society. The Civil Society consists of intellectuals such as retired IPS officer Kiran Bedi, Justice Santosh Hegde [former Supreme Court Judge and former Lokayukta of Karnataka], Prashant Bhushan [Supreme Court Advocate], Aravind Kejriwal [RTI activist and a few others.

JAN LOKPAL BILL MOVEMENT

Anna Hazare and his associates consisting of the members of the Civil Society launched the *"Jan Lokpal Bill Movement"* [*Citizens Ombudsman Bill*] and advocated the appointment of a Jan Lokpal, an independent body that would investigate corruption cases of the top people. Justice Santosh Hegde, Prashant Bhushan, Aravind Kejriwal and others have drafted this Jan Lokpal Bill as a powerful alternative to the proposed Lokpal Bill of the Govt, and urged the government to incorporate in its Bill, the important aspects of the Jan Lokpal.

The Jan Lokpal is intended as a more effective improvement over the original "Lokpal Bill" that is being proposed by the government. The prefix *"Jan"* which signifies *"citizens"* has been added to highlight the fact that the Bill is having strong public support.

The argument made in favour of Jan Lokpal Bill is that, if made into a law, it will create an independent ombudsman body outside the government to probe into corruption cases. It will have

Civil Society -As a People's Movement

The earliest usages of the term civil society in political and social philosophy were to contrast both civil society and civil government with natural society or the state of nature. Hegel and Marx used the term civil society to distinguish life under capitalism from the medieval world.

More recently, **Antonio Gramsci** has argued that the core of civil society is not only the individual and individualism but also private organisations such as corporations. He has also argued that the state and civil society overlap and merge with each other to such a degree that it is hard to tell where one leaves off and the other begins. From this perspective, it is important to understand the mutually reinforcing relationship between the two.

Source: *The Blackwell Dictionary of Sociology* page 36.

A Brief Profile Of Anna Hazare [1937...]

Anna Hazare's name came to limelight mainly because of his wide spread campaign against corruption under the auspices of the "Civil Society" formed in his leadership in the year 2011. He and his team mates strongly opposed the Government's efforts to introduce an ineffective and a defective Lokpal Bill in the Parliament in Aug 2011. Even at his seventies, Anna Hazare has the enthusiasm and the spirit to fight against the weak and ineffective Lokpal Bill which the Govt intends to pass in the Parliament. Here is a brief profile of Anna Hazare the main architect of the Civil Society, and the campaign against corruption.

Anna Hazare was born on 15th June 1937, in Bhingar Village in Ahmadnagar district of Maharasthra to the couple Baburao Hazare and Laxmi Bai. His actual name is **Kisan Baburao Hazare**. He is well known for his organisation - the *"Bhrashtachar Virodhi Jan Andolan" (People's Movement Against Corruption)*. He began his career as a driver in the Indian Army in 1963. During the mid-1970s, he was involved in a road accident while driving. He was, however, honourably discharged from army in 1975 after completing 12 years of service. During his 12 year tenure as a soldier, he was posted to several places like Skkim, Bhutan, Jammu-Kashmir, Assam, Mizoram, Leh and Ladak.

Anna Hazare gained wide acclaim for transforming his once drought-prone, improverished village to a prosperous model village by encouraging sustainable farming and rural life as envisioned by Mahatma Gandhi. He was awarded the *Padma Shri* (1990) and *Padma Bhushan* (1992), the nation's fourth and third highest civilian awards respectively, for his social work. Hazare lives on his pension from army service in his village. His campaigns are financed by voluntary donations by his supporters. He is always seen in white clothes with a traditional Indian cap (Gandhi Topi).

Though Hazare is not an intellectual, the modern youths of India have found in him the *"Gandhi of the freedom movement"*. They have a great admiration for him for his honest and uncompromising commitment to campaign against corruption. He stands out as a living ideal for Gandhian approach to public cause.

the power to register and investigate complaints against politicians and public servants without the need of a prior approval from the government. The proponents of Jan Lokpal believe that it will effectively reduce citizen's grievances and deter corruption.

The Jan Lokpal supporters claimed that their draft bill envisages a system where a corrupt person found guilty would go to jail within two years of the complaint being made and his ill-gotten wealth being confiscated. It also seeks power to the Jan Lokpal to prosecute politicians and bureaucrats without government permission.

Hazare Staged "Fast-Unto-Death" Protest

Anna Hazare, the anti-corruption crusader went on "*fast-unto-death satyagraha*" in April 2011, demanding that the Bill drafted by the Civil Society be adopted. After 4 days of fast, the Govt agreed to set up a joint committee with an equal number of members from both the sides, the side of Civil Society and that of the Govt. The two sides met several times and could not agree on fundamental elements. Eventually, both sides drafted their own versions of the Bill.

The Govt introduced its own version in the Parliament and Team Hazare being upset with this protested its introduction and dubbed the govt. version as the "**Joke Pal Bill**". Hazare threatened to begin another fast in Delhi on Aug-16 . Even before he was to begin his hunger strike, the Delhi police detained and arrested him.

The arrest of Anna Hazare resulted in huge public outcry and under heavy pressure the govt. released him in the evening of 15th Aug. However, Anna refused to come out of Jail and started his indefinite hunger strike from the Tihar Jail itself. Finally, the police had to yield to pressure and Anna and his team were permitted to use Ramlila Maidan for the proposed fast agitation. Anna's fast began and went on for around 288 hours [12 days from 16th Aug to 28th Aug. 2011]. Anna ended his 12 days strike after the Parliament broadly agreed for three key demands of his

Civil Society. The battle against corruption started by Anna and his team though is dormant at present [2014], it is not totally dissolved.

Main Differences between the Government Bill and the Jan Lokpal Bill Proposed by the Civil Society

Anna Hazare and other spokesmen of the Civil Society have been publicly arguing that the Govt proposed Lokpal Bill is highly defective and in order to make it effective and strong it has to incorporate many of the salient features of the Jan Lokpal Bill which they have been campaigning for. It is in this context the main differences between the Govt Bill and the Jan Lokpal Bill, are highlighted here.

Main Defects of the Govt Lokpal Bill [as Criticised by the Civil Society]

1. ***Not Independent but only a Subservient Body :*** The Lokpal here does not have the power to receive complaints from the general public. They can lodge complaints with the speaker of the Lok Sabha or Rajya Sabha and only with their consent enquiry could be instituted. Thus, it gives oppoprtunity for the ruling party to protect its members.
2. ***Delay in Investigations :*** Cases against corrupt people could linger on for years for there is no time restriction to complete the investigations. Naturally, delay is involved in its functioning.
3. ***No Power to Dismiss the Corrupt Official :*** Because, the Lokpal's task is only to suggest and recommend, it does not have statutory power to dismiss from service the guilty and the corrupt.
4. ***Complaints are Not Easily Accepted :*** Even if corruption is exposed by the public, no complaints could be lodged easily against the corrupt persons. Because, it is not supposed to receive complaints directly from the public.
5. ***Corrupt Judges cannot be Tackled :*** Even if rcorruption charges are made against the sitting judges, Lokpal/Lokayukta cannot hold an inquiry against them for it has to take the permission of chief justice.
6. ***No Transparency :*** There is no transparency in the investigations of the CBI and the CVC [Central Bureau of Investigation and the Central Vigilance Commission]. Their agenda and working styles are highly confidential and secret.
7. ***Incompetent and Inefficient Persons are also often selected as Chiefs :*** The power to select officers to head the institutions lies with the politicians. They may sabotage the purpose of the bodies by selecting incompetent and corrupt officials to these bodies.
8. ***No Legal Provision to collect back the Looted Wealth :*** Under the present law, there is no provision to recover from the convicted, already looted property of the public.
9. ***No Salvation for the public from the Corrupt Officials :*** Hence, people are obliged to give bribes to get their things done. Even if one complains with the higher officials, it is of no use for they are also often party to the corruption.
10. ***Minimum Punishment :*** At present, in this system there is minimum punishment of 6 months imprisonment and or maximum punishment of 7 years imprisonment. This is quite less for serious offences.

Salient Features of the Jan Lokpal Bill Advocated by the "Civil Society"

1. ***Autonomy in Functioning :*** As per the provisions of the Jan Lokpal Bill, an institution called ***"Lokpal"*** at the Centre and ***"Lokayukta"*** in each State will be set up. Like the Supreme Court and Election Commission, they will be completely independent of the governments. No minister or M.P. or bureaucrat will be able to influence their investigations.
2. ***Time Bound Investigation :*** All cases referred to must be investigated within one year and the related enquiry and trial must be over within another year, and by the end of the second year, the convicted corrupt officials must be sent to jail.
3. ***Statutory Power to Dismiss the Corrupt :*** The Central Vigilance Commission's power must be merged with the Lokpal, so that it gets Statutory power to dismiss the guilty and the corrupt officials.
4. ***Power to Receive Complaints :*** The Lokpal and the Lokayukta must have the power to receive complaints from the public and conduct inquiry on their own without seeking any one's permission.

5. ***Corrupt Judges could be Handled :*** Complaints against the judges could also be received and investigations be held if found necessary.
6. ***Fully Transparent :*** The entire functioning of the Lokpal and the Lokayukta will be completely transparent. Any complaint against any officer of Lokpal shall be investigated and the officer dismissed within two months.
7. ***Competent Persons are Selected :*** Members of these institutions will be selected by judges, citizens and constitutional authorities through a completely transparent and participatory process, and not by politicians,
8. ***Provision for Recovery :*** The loss that a corrupt person has caused to the government will be recovered by him at the time of his conviction.
9. ***Public Grievance is Heard and Properly Compensated :*** If any work of any citizen is not done in prescribed time in any Govt office, Lokpal will impose financial penalty minimum of ₹ 250/- per day on guilty officers, which will be given as compensation to be complainant.
10. ***Increased Punishment :*** In the Jan Lokpal, the minimum punishment is 5 years where as life imprisonment is the maximum punishment. This will definitely create fear in the minds of the officials and may deter them from becoming corrupt.

The Jan Lokpal Bill has a few More Advantages

There is no protection in the Govt Bill for those who lodge complaints against officials. Whereas it will be the duty of the Jan Lokpal to provide protection to those who may become victimised for raising their voice against corruption.

The Govt Lokpal Bill Has kept the Prime Minister and the judiciary as well as the conduct of MPs in Parliament out of the ambit of the anti-corruption watchdog. The P.M, however, will come under the purview of Lokpal after he demits office.

The Jan Lokpal Bill gives permission to Lokpal to probe any Union minister or officials of "Group A" and above rank without any sanction.

According to the govt draft, the body will have a Chairperson and 8 members, including 4 judicial members who will be former or sitting judges of the Supreme Court or chief justices of the high court. The Civil Society spokespersons have commented that too many judicial members in the body might create a vested interest among the judges, especially retired judges to seek the favour of the Govt to get selected to the body. It is difficult to expect impartial functioning on the part of those judges who got selected to the body through influence or favour.

However, the Lokayuktas in the states do not come under the purview of this Bill as the Centre cannot interfere in the powers of the state.

Finally, the Lokpal will have its own prosecution and investigation wing with officers and staff necessary to carry out its functions. The Civil Society is of the firm opinion that corruption can be wiped out only if we have a public will to establish a corruption-free system. The Governmental effort to introduce the Jan Lokpal Bill and implement the same when it becomes an Act, is only one important step in this direction.

B. NEPOTISM

Meaning of Nepotism

Nepotism is a practice associated with the social evil of corruption. Nepotism means *favouritism shown towards one's own relatives.* According to the dictionary meaning, nepotism refers to *"giving undue patronage to one's own relations."*[17]

17. **Chambers 20th Century Dictionary** [1964]. Page - 715.

Nepotism As A Social Evil

Like corruption, nepotism is also a social evil. It is an evil practice in which persons in some public offices bestow patronage on their own relatives in consideration of the family relations and in disregard to merit. In this practice, something is done or undone under the influence of the family relations and in disregard to the accepted norms.

Nepotism Due to the New Trend in One's Loyalty ?

Favouring one's own relatives or showing favours to one's own kith and kin is not an uncommon practice. It is not a new trend. It represents one of the oldest forms of corruption. Sociological analysis reveals that social bonds and kinship play an important role in corruption. There seems to be a change in the individual's primary commitments or loyalty. Today, family considerations, kinship ties, friendship obligations, caste, religious and parochial loyalties get precedence in public servant's mind. One's commitment to rules, regulations, laws, values, ideals, morals and societal and national interests become secondary. *"The first obligation of a modern administrator is to his family members, followed by close kin, lineage, or ethnic group. Such ties are more compelling than administrative rules and procedures."*[18] The person in the public office who shows favours to his own kith and kin, does not consider his act as a *"corrupt practice"*, nor as a *"deviation from rules"*, but as *"family obligation."* It appears that nepotism has become widespread today because of this new trend in one's loyalty.

This tendency of nepotism is very much rampant among our administrators, bureaucrats and political leaders. In fact, it is connected with power and authority and originates when it is misused. It has become a common thing for our people to expect favours from their relatives who happen to assume public offices. This explains corrupt actions of many a public servant both at the lower and higher levels. Hence, men in high and low positions have often indulged in nepotism. Politicians in office, the high-ups in the bureaucracy or officers at lower levels have often been found to be guilty of nepotism.

Some Instances of Nepotism

Recent history of Indian politics and public life gives ample instances of corruption which could be listed under the heading of "nepotism." There are chief ministers and ex-chief ministers who have openly shown unfair and unjstifiable favours to their own sons, daughters, and wives. Political leaders including ministers at both state and national level have, on several occasions, unfairly favoured their own children and kith and kin in getting them coveted political positions at the cost of merit, efficiency and political seniority. There are innumerable examples in this regard and only a few of them are cited below.

1. In the Congress party, the supreme political position or leadership has been flowing down from Pandit Nehru to his daughter Indira Gandhi, from Indira Gandhi to her son Rajiv Gandhi, from Rajiv Gandhi to his wife Sonia Gandhi who has been trying to project the leadership of her son Rahul Gandhi.
2. In Bihar, at one stage its ex-chief minister Laloo Prasad Yadav, who was forced to quit his Chief Ministership, made his own politically inexperienced wife as the chief minister of Bihar.
3. In U.P., Mulayam Singh Yadav has used his political influence to make his son, a political junior , to become the chief minister of U.P.
4. In Tamil Nadu, the D.M.K. supremo Karunanidhi is trying to make his son Stalin his successor.

---

18. Prof. Ram Ahuja in *"Society in India"* [199]. Page - 403.

5. In Karnataka, K. Bangarappa (one time chief minister of the state) used his political office to bring both of his sons Kumara Bangarappa and Madhu Bangarappa to political limelight. Both had become M.L.A.s also.

- Similarly, B.S. Yediyurappa, exchief minister of Karnataka, went out of the way to get ticket for his son Raghavendra to contest for parliamentary elections in the 15th Lok Sabha Elections.

6. In Orissa, Biju Patnaik's political position had helped his Western educated son, Naveen Patnaik to become the chief minister of Orissa.
7. In Punjab, Prakash Singh Badal has been successful in getting chief ministership to his son.
8. In Kashmir, Sheik Abdulla became successful in fetching political leadership to his son Umar Abdullha and to make him its chief minister.

The list runs for pages if we include in it all instances of unfair political favours distributed by the political leaders of India to their kith and kin or other kinds of relatives.

There are any number of ministers who are protecting their kith and kin who have indulged in immoral and illegal activities, by bestowing on them special favours. There are vice-chancellors who have abused their power and position in giving appointments to their own children and relatives by denying the same opportunity to the more qualified and meritorious persons. At the bureaucratic level, nepotism is not uncommon. Ministers, judges, police inspectors, company directors, deputy commissioners, college principals, vice chancellors, and such other persons occupying responsible public offices, are often found to be guilty of nepotism.

Nepotism As a Common Practice

Nepotism today has become a common practice. *"Nepotism has come to be accepted as a form of prerogative or a privilege inherent in office, and the man in office feels himself free to exploit it to his maximum advantage. Like corruption, if not checked at top, it percolates to the lower levels with sanctity."*[19]

Evil Effects of Nepotism

(i) Nepotism negates talents, abilities, merits, efficiency, commitment to rules and norms and committment to rules and norms.

(ii) Practice of nepotism abrogates rules, neglects laws and brushes aside morality.

(iii) It damages the activism and enthusiasm of the really talented people who are discriminated against to favour somebody.

(iv) It spoils the morale of the people, makes them to give up idealism and commitment to values and induces them to become opportunists.

(v) Nepotism adversely affects the general credibility of the public servants and makes the general masses to become cynics. The nation's future will be doomed, if nepotism becomes rampant.

(vi) Due to nepotism unqualified, ineligible and inefficient people occupy important public offices and as a result performance and productivity are very badly affected.

Suggestions to Control Nepotism

Nepotism as a social evil leads to serious consequences. It is necessary to contain it. Since nepotism is associated with human weakness, it cannot be completely eliminated but only contained or controlled. In no period of history, human society any where in the world was

19. **Kachroo** and **Kachroo** in *"Society in India."* Page - 415.

free from the hold of nepotism. Human history also cautions that a society strongly gripped with the menace of nepotism is doomed to decline.

Some Solutions

- ***Moulding Public Opinion Against Nepotism :*** The public opinion should be strong enough to make the people practising nepotism either to do away with it or to step down from their office which they have occupied immorally and often illegally.
- ***Proper Inculcation of Values through Socialisation :*** The family and the school should play a major role in imbibing proper values in the children through socialisation, so that they develop dislike and aversion towards nepotism and its practice in any kind.
- ***Efficient Legal Machinery :*** Indian legal and judicial machinery is not only slow but also inefficient. Undue delay involved in our judicial system has made people to lose faith in it. Proper steps should be taken immediately to streamline the legal as well as judicial systems so as to make them vigilant, efficient, fast and honest.
- ***Due Recognition to Honest, Non-Corrupt and Efficient Public Servants :*** All honest and efficient officials must be publicly praised and honoured so that others also get influenced to be honest.

●●●

Chapter 16

CHALLENGES FOR NATIONAL INTEGRATION

NATIONAL INTEGRATION: Meaning and Its Essentials - Need for National Integration- Challenges for National Integration : Communalism - Fundamentalism - Nepotism - Regionalism - Linguism and Casteism. Efforts to promote National Integration - The Challenges of Communalism, Fundamentalism and Casteiesm.

1. COMMUNALISM : Meaning and Definition - Background of the Growth of Communalism - Characteristics and Causes for Communalism in India- Communalism as a Challenge to Secularism -Communal Riots- Some Features of Communal Riots Taking Place in India - Suggestions to Control and Eradicate Communalism - Immediate and Long Term Remedial Measures.

2. FUNDAMENTALISM : Religious Fundamentalism - The Concept of Fundamentalism - Its Origin and Features - Religious Fundamentalism in the Indian Context.

3. CASTEISM : Meaning and the Origin of Casteism - Causes of Casteism - Consequences of Casteism - Solutions to the Problem of Casteism.

1. NATIONAL INTEGRATION : MEANING - AND ITS ESSENTIALS

Meaning of National Integration

'National Integration' refers to national unity and a sense of belonging to the nation. It is an essential aspect in the making of a nation. Promotion of national integration is regarded as a part and parcel of the policy of any country. In the Indian context, it is a much talked phenomenon for almost all national level leaders who give to it utmost importance. When the nation became independent, they felt the necessity of suppressing the divisive forces and encouraging the unifying factors. They wanted to create conditions which would help people to forget their differences and unite together. It is in this context, the concept of *"national integration"* has assumed importance.

Definition of National Integration

1. **Benjamin :** National integration refers to the *"assimilation of the entire people of a country to a common identity."*
2. **Myron Weiner-** in *his book "Politics of Scarcity : Public Pressure and Political Response in India"*writes - *"National integration implies ..... the presence of attitudes throughout the society that give preference to national and public interest as distinct from parochial interests."*

3. **H.A. Gani-** National integration refers to *"A socio-psychological and educational process through which a feeling of unity, solidarity and cohesion develops in the hearts of the people and a .... feeling of loyalty to the nation is fostered among them."*
4. ***In simple words,*** national integration refers *to the process wherein a feeling of togetherness, a sense of national unity and above all, a - sense of national belongingness are developed among people.*

Essential Elements of National Integration

A nation is not just a group of people living over a piece of land. Apart from the territorial bond, there are many other ties that bind them together to make them a nation. *A common language, common historic tradition, common cultural heritage, common national values and ideologies* - all play their role in welding people into a unity. The main requirements or elements of national integration may be mentioned below.

1. ***National Attitude :*** National integration is basically an attitude and a kind of broad but self-less feeling. It is a concern with a feeling of national unity and national consciousness. One important aspect of the term *"national integration"* is that people belonging to a society share common ideas, aspirations, emotional bonds and values.[1]
2. ***Accommodative Spirit:*** National integration is not just political consolidation. "It is a state of accommodation among different groups - caste, ethnic, religious, linguistic, etc.., It is a state of affairs in which the *"communal identity goes along with the national identity"*.[2]Pluralism with cohesiveness is certainly an indication of national integration.
3. ***Unity in Diversity :*** It implies an attempt to achieve the unity of hearts irrespective of religion, race, creed, language and sex. The purpose here is not just to bring about uniformity but "*to achieve unity in diversity*". This is especially true in the case of India. National integration is dependent upon structural, cultural and ideological congruity and harmony among different sections of Indian society.
4. ***Supreme National Loyalty :*** It upholds the supremacy of national loyalties and supersedes all other types of affiliations and commitments.
5. ***All-Embrasive :*** National integration is all-inclusive in the sense it covers the wide range of political, economic, social, cultural, emotional and other aspects of life.
6. ***Suppression of Anti-National Forces*** : National integration in order to achieve its purpose, suppresses the divisive forces, disruptive elements and disintegrating tendencies.
7. ***Attainment of National Goals :*** The ultimate purpose of national integration is to achieve undisturbed national progress and national glory. In this regard, it struggles for the attainment of ideological goals such as social justice, fraternity, equality, nationalism, secularism, democracy, etc. These values and many other norms stated in the constitution of India provide the basis for national integration.

Need For National Integration

The unity of a nation depends upon the extent of feeling of national unity on the part of its citizens. National unity does not automatically develop just because its citizens live within the same geographic boundaries. *National integration is basically an emotional integration.*

---

1. *In the context of the newly independent nations,* ***Gunnar Myrdal*** *[1968] writes. "People must have a conception of the nation as a whole and attach positive valuations to this idea [nationalism] before they can feel national independence and national consolidation as goals worth striving for and that all the other "modernization ideals" can only be realized in the setting of an independent and consolidated nation- state."-* ***Gunnar Myrdal*** *as quoted by* ***K.L.Sharma*** *is his "Indian Social Structure and Change" [2007] Rawat publications, New Delhi –page357*
2. **K.L. Sharma** in his *"Indian Social Structure and Change"* page 361.

COSTLY CHALLENGES FOR INDIAN UNITY AND SOLIDARITY

Just like emotional integration keeps members of a family united, national integration helps the citizens of a nation to get organised to achieve national purposes.

National integration does not emerge on its own automatically. It is only when conditions are created in which people seem to forget their differences and unite together, that national integration emerges. But absolute integration is a myth especially in a country like India which is characterised by widespread heterogeneity. Such heterogeneity tends to reduce the chances of national integration to some extent.

India is a wonderland known for wide diversities. One finds here marked differences in the living standards, food habits, dress styles, spoken languages, customary practices, religious beliefs, cultural elements of the various people living in different parts of the country. We find extreme poverty on one side, and on the other, we find a small section of the populace rolling in prosperity. There are believers and non-believers in religion; there are highly educated people and also the most illiterate masses, there are the most modernised people and at the same time, there are people away from the world of civilization and so on. *These apparent differences imply that we are facing enormous challenges.* These challenges have emanated from various historical, political, cultural, as well as socio-economic factors. *These challenges also emphasise the need for the promotion of national integration.*

CHALLENGES FOR NATIONAL INTEGRATION

Among the various factors that pose serious challenges to the promotion of national integration in India, the following may be noted.

CHALLENGES BEFORE NATIONAL INTEGRATION

Comm-unalism	Caste-ism	Regio-nalism	Linguistic Factionalism	Regional Parties	Extremism Terrorism	Class Cleavages

1. Rise of Communalism

• *"The antagonism practised by the members of one community against the people of other community and religion can be called communalism".*[3]

Communalism is responsible for the hatred which one religious group fosters for another. It is a kind of antagonism which is found between religious communities. *Communalism and communal riots normally arise when religious matters are politicalised.* It fails to separate religion from politics. It leads to the abuse of power. Because of communalism communal interests always superimpose themselves on national interests. *Communalism rests on religious prejudices.*

The effects of communalism are disastrous. Communalism causes rivalry and violence among masses. It strikes at the root of secularism and national integration. It leads to mutual distrust, illwill and hatred between the communities. The fire of communalism between different religious groups [mainly between Hindus and Muslims, Hindus and Christians] was kindled by the British. The British policy of *"divide and rule"* caused lot of damage to our national interests. Even after independence we have not been able to deal successfully with the challenge of communalism.

2. Challenge of Casteism

Casteism is understood as *a partial or one-sided loyalty in favour of any particular caste.* As **D.N. Prasad** points out, *"Casteism is loyalty to the caste translated into action."*[4]

3. **Ram Ahuja** in *"Society in India" (1992)*, Page : 25.
4. **D.N. Prasad** in *"The Myth of Caste System"* - Page : 124.

Casteism is due to multiplicity of causes. (i) The feeling of superiority and inferiority, high and low, sacred and unsacred associated with caste is the main cause of casteism. (ii) It is also due to the practice of caste endogamy which unduly restricts one's marital relations. (iii) Caste is a strong cohesive group. It has a powerful hold over its members. Hence, its members are hesitant to deal freely with the members of other castes. (iv) The practice of untouchability on the one hand, and (v) the rise of SCs and the OBCs due to reservation facilities, on the other, have further widened the gap between the castes.

Consequences of Casteism are many. Casteism hinders the development of national feeling. It is dangerous to democracy for it supports inequality. It is contrary to the spirit of our constitution. It leads to moral degeneration by encouraging nepotism. It ignores the human values and social welfare. It may contribute to the neglect of talents and efficiency. Brain-drain is often the result of casteism. Casteism plays an ugly role in elections. Rise in casteism leads to the weakening of national unity.

3. Challenge of Regionalism

- ***Regionalism*** refers to *an extreme loyalty or love to a particular region which may undermine the interest of the nation.*

India is a nation with wide regional differences also. When a person goes from one part of the country to another, he often finds himself as a foreigner there. Our imbalanced economic plans also have widened the gap between states. Some states have been greatly benefited by the fruits of industrialisation and mechanisation of agriculture, while on the other hand, some states have miserably lagged behind. It is said that rich states are getting richer, and poor, poorer. People are slowly becoming aware of these disparities. It has now assumed the form of regionalism.

Regionalism is expressed in the desire of people of one region to promote their own regional interest at the expense of the interests of other regions. It has often led to separatism and instigated separatist activities and violent movements. [***Ex.*** : *Kahalisthan Movement in Punjab, Bodoland Movement in Assam.*] It has gained tremendous momentum during the recent years because it is exploited by the selfish politicians. Its linkage with linguism has worsened the situation. Regionalism challenges the primacy of the nationalistic interests and undermines national unity.

4. The Menace of Linguism

- *Linguism implies an one-sided love and admiration towards one's languages and a prejudice and hatred towards others' languages. It is the prejudice of the speakers of a particular language to develop their language to the detriment of all other languages.*

India is a land of many dialects and has been called a *"museum of languages"* and also as a *"linguistic madhouse"*. According to 1961 Census report, there were 1018 different languages including the 18 constitutionally approved languages. This linguistic diversity has led to linguism. It has often been manifested into violent movements posing a threat to national integration. Linguistic tensions are often manifested in the borders which are bilingual. ***Ex*** : *(i) In Karnataka, there is a tug of war between Marathi and Kannada speaking people in Belgaum. (ii) The Goans are divided on the basis of Marathi and Konkani languages. (iii) Assam is confronted with Bengali and Assamese, and so on.*

Consequences of linguism are many. (i) Linguism leads to the persecution of linguistic minorities. (ii) Linguism begets regionalism and parochialism. (iii) It undermines the importance of national issues and makes people to become narrow-minded. (iv) It provides fertile ground for regional political parties. (v) It causes permanent river-water sharing disputes, border disputes between states, and so on. (vi) In its extreme form, it leads to the demand for separate states. In brief, it erodes national feelings and damages national integration.

5. Regional Political Parties

Strong regional feelings, interest in intra-state politics and regional aspirations have given birth to regional political parties. Linguism also encourages the formation and development of regional political parties. Regional political parties confine their interests only to their regions and fail to understand and appreciate things in a larger national perspective. They are narrow-minded and their way of approach may endanger the national interests.

In India, there are some regional parties which are demanding more and more autonomy in their function. ***Examples*** **:** *Telugu Desham in Andhra Pradesh, D.M.K. and A.D.M.K. in Tamil Nadu, Akalidal in Punjab, and Shiv Sena in Maharashtra* and so on. The *Akali Dal and* the *D.M.K. at one time had even demanded not only total autonomy but also the status of independent nations.* Such approaches towards politics can never strengthen national feelings or unity.

6. Extremism and Terrorism

Political extremism and inhuman terrorism have emerged during the recent years as the most formidable challenges to national integration.

- ***Extremism*** refers to the *readiness on the part of an individual or group to go to any extreme even to resort to undemocratic, violent and harmful means- to fulfil one's objectives.*
- ***Terrorism*** is *a method whereby an organised group or party seeks to achieve its aims by generating fear and horror in the community and through the systematic use of violence.*

In fact, terrorism is also a kind of extremism. Extremist and terrorist crimes are taking place in the form of kidnapping and killing of political leaders and government officials, blackmailing the rich and the industrialists, attacking police stations, urban bombings, blasting bridges, T.V. centres, telephone exchanges, microwave stations, looting banks, setting fire to government buses and private vehicles, etc. Various terrorist organisations such as - (i) JKLF - *Jammu and Kashmir Liberation Front,* (ii) the LTTE - *Liberation of Tamil Tigers Elam,* (iii). *All Qaida,* etc. are resorting to very harmful terrorist activities endangering national integration. (iv) *Naxalite terrorism* is also causing new anxieties, tensions, fears and monetary losses and even extreme violence including bloodshed and mass killings.

Consequences of Extremism and Terrorism

1. Extremism and terrorism prove to be a big threat to democracy. They destroy the democratic fabric of society and induce insecurity and rebellion everywhere.
2. Terrorism creates serious law and order problem from local level to global level.
3. It leads to uncertainity and an atmosphere of fear and panic all around.
4. It causes heavy loss of life and property both public and private.
5. It encourages smuggling as we find it in the case of international drug mafia.
6. All economic and developmental activities get disturbed.
7. It erodes authority of the state and leads to the alienation of the helpless people.
8. It may even cause demograhic ups and downs due to migration. Mass exodus of the Hindus from the Kashmir region is an example in this regard.

7. Class Cleavages

Though the Indian Constitution assures in its very preamble to all its citizens fundamental rights, liberties and justice, the Government in reality, has not been able to translate these ideals into actuality. Poverty and illiteracy are the big hurdles on the way.

• ***Illiteracy:*** There exists in India a gap between the literates and illiterates. Even today more than 43 crores [431,739,294 persons] of people are illiterate as per 2011 census report. Among the literates, only an insignificant minority is able to avail of higher education. Naturally, the benefits of education are grabbed by this small minority. Rural-urban divide exists in matters of literacy and illiteracy.

• ***Poverty:*** Economic extremes are very common in India. Wide disparity between the rich and poor exists in both urban and rural areas. Even after 65 years of independent rule, poverty is not wiped out. Around 29.5% of the people live below the line of poverty as per 2011-12 estimate made by *C. Rangarajan Committee Report* [2014]. Economic processes such as liberalisation, privatisation and globalisation let loose by the government have only added to rural poverty and unemployment.

EFFORTS TO PROMOTE NATIONAL INTEGRATION

Dr. Sampurnananda Committee's Recommendation

The importance of the issue of national integration made the Central Government to do something in this regard. The Central Education Ministry organised a *'Committee for National Integration'* in 1961 under the chairmanship of **Dr. Sampurnananda**. The Integration Committee gave some suggestions to promote national integration. Some of these suggestions are stated below.

1. Reorganisation of syllabi at various levels of education - primary, secondary, college and university level - to promote national integration.

(i) At the ***primary stage,*** stress should be laid upon nationalistic stories, heroism, gallarntry and sacrifice of national heroes, patriotic dramas, poems and songs etc.,

(ii) At the ***secondary stage,*** in addition to the other subjects being taught, special attention should be given to the study of national literature, social studies, moral and religious guidance, and extra-curricular activities.

(iii) At the ***college and university level,*** the syllabi should include various social sciences, languages, literatures, cultures and arts. Students and teachers should be given facilities to tour various parts of the country to see places and things of great historical importance.

2. Giving due encouragement to extra- curricular activities besides imparting formal knowledge to the students with the intention of promoting national unity. Extracurricular activities taking the form of cultural and other type of programmes must also represent the entire nation. Such programmes help in the development of "we- feeling", a feeling of unity and sympathy. Inter - university cultural festivals in which students and teachers participate from all parts of the nation, for example, represent one such programme.

3. Improvement of textbooks helps a great deal in giving a true national perspective to the students. They can be made to understand their rich cultural heritage and feel proud of their nation. The textbooks should be designed to encourage a sense of emotional unity with people living in different parts of the country. Special precaution must be taken while preparing history textbooks. Such a precautionary step helps to check the growth of communal feelings. It should also be remembered that such modifications should not be done at the cost of historical truth, because such a clandestine repudiation of truth is counterproductive. Neither communal harmony, nor national integration could be achieved by concocted stories and fabricated incidents or events.

4. Conducting community prayers, mass meetings, speeches by respected leaders, etc., help to bring the people together.

Other Suggestions

In addition to what the National Integration Committee suggested for promoting national integration, we may also consider the following for the same purpose.

1. ***At the all-India level, one language should be developed as a link language to help proper communication among people.*** Hindi seems to be the main language capable of performing this role. Hence, people living in different parts [especially in the non-Hindi speaking area] must be encouraged and motivated to learn Hindi. Precaution should also be taken to see that the people living in the non-Hindi belt do not feel that Hindi is forcibly imposed upon them and that would damage the growth of regional languages.
2. ***An all-India level educational policy is to be evolved with a view to bring about uniformity and to achieve unity.*** Education is the most effective instrument for spreading emotional and national integration. A well thoughtout educational plan will definitely help the students to develop a national perspective. Textbooks that are prepared must be of great help for the students to develop the nationalistic fervour. All India organizations such as NCC, Scouts, Girl Guides, etc.. should be given proper encouragement.
3. ***Special social , cultural and entertainment programmes must be chalked out to promote national unity.*** Cinema, television, radio, drama, dance, art exhibitions, musical concerts and such other media instruments could be made use of in this regard. Radio and television can also be used effectively in this regard. All India competitions and meetings can be organised in various parts of the country to increase national unity. Tour and travel facilities should be made more common among the students, national level seminars, symposiums, cultural meets and delegations etc., help to promote national integration
4. ***Role of teachers teaching at all levels and in different fields must be properly made use of in promoting emotional integration.*** Teachers themselves must rise above their petty narrow-mindedness and create ideals. By becoming members of all India teachers organizations the teachers can develop broadmindedness. Teachers with commitment and nationalistic approach can wield tremendous influence on the students.
5. ***Due importance is to be given to develop inter-cultural understandings*** [that is, understanding between different religious, linguistic, regional, tribal, caste and other groups] to promote unity. A healthy and a harmonitus atmosphere should be created in the society so that all these diverse social groups come closer and engage in activities that help to promote national welfare and unity.
6. ***Governmental efforts are also necessary in this regard.*** The Government must have sincere dedication towards achieving the goal of national unity. Hence, Government officials should invariably be above all pressures and expressions of linguism, communalism, regionalism, casteism, nepotism, untouchability and so on. It is essential to have necessary control over political parties that damage and destroy national integration. Any individual or collective efforts to give expression to linguism, communalism, regionalism, casteism, untouchability etc.., should be suppressed and stringent actions be taken as per the provisions of law. Finally, it can be stated that national integration becomes successful only if political, economic, social and cultural integrations are attained prior to it.

1. COMMUNALISM

Communalism has become one of the biggest menaces of modern India. Problem that arises between the socio-religious relations of the people who belong to various minority communities on the one hand and the majority community on the other, can be referred to as *"communalism"* or *"communal problem."* Communalism and communal riots normally arise when religious matters are politicalised. *Communalism is often understood as an ideology which states that the society is divided into religious communities whose interests differ and are, at times, even opposed to each other.* It is a kind of antagonism which is found between the religious communities.

Definition of *"Communalism"*

1. **D.E. Smith :** *"Communalism is generally associated with a narrow, selfish, divisive and aggressive attitude on the part of a religious group".*
2. **Rasheeduddhin Khan :** *"Exploitation of religion is communalism."*
3. **Prabha Dixit :** Communalism is *"a political doctrine which makes use of religio-cultural differences to achieve political ends."*
4. **Bipin Chandra :** *".......... the concept of communalism is based on the belief that the religious distinction is the most important and fundamental distinction and this distinction overrides all other distinctions."* .... He further adds *"since Hindus, Muslims and Sikhs are different religious entities, their social, economic, cultural and political interests are also dissimilar and divergent. As such the loss of one religious group is the gain of another group and vice versa. If a particular community seeks to better its social and economic situation, it is doing at the expense of the other."*[5]
5. **Ram Ahuja :** *"The antagonism practised by the members of one community against the people of other community and religion can be termed as communalism."*
6. **Robert Melson** and **Howard Wolpe :** *"Communalism is the political assertiveness of a community to maintain its identity in a plural society undergoing modernisation."*[6]

Communalism denotes antagonism between different religious groups. This antagonism goes to *"the extent of falsely accusing, harming, and deliberately insulting a particular community and extends to looting, burning down the homes and shops of the helpless and the weak, dishonouring women, and even killing persons."*[7]

- **Different Dimensions of the Term Communalism**

1. Communalism implies an attitude of exclusiveness and separatism whereby the members of one community look towards others with a sense of hatred and enmity.
2. Communalism in India has two dimensions- broader and narrower. In the broader sense, it covers the major religious groups and organisations whereas in the narrower sense, it covers the regional, local, religious and caste organisations that exhibit the same tendency.
3. Communalism is exploitation of religion for political ends.
4. Communalism is a highly complex and a multi-dimensional phenomenon.
5. It regards communal interests as equivalent to national interests or above national interests.

---

5. **Bipin Chandra** in *"Communalism in Modern India."* Page - 2.
6. **Robert Melson** and **Howard Wolpe** in their article in *"American Political Science Review."* Vol. 64, as quoted by **A.P. Avasthi** in *"Indian Government and Politics"* [2001]. Page - 578.
7. **Ram Ahuja.** Page - 245

Background of the Growth of *"Communalism"* in India

The origin and growth of communalism has its own history in India. In fact, communalism was part and parcel of the British policy of *"divide and rule."* The beginning of communalism can be traced to the pre-independence days. In the first war of independence [1857], the Hindus as well as the Muslims had united to throw the British imperialism out of India. The British suppressed the movement and later on started making use of the policy of *"divide and rule"* to instigate the Muslims against the Hindus and vice versa.

The British Government, for quite a long time, looked upon the Muslims as untrustworthy and disloyal. In fact, it interpreted the 1857 movement as an attempt by the Muslims to revive the Mughal rule in India. The Muslims were purposefully kept out of the government jobs for the British had continued to nurse a prejudice against them. The Muslims too had their bitter resentment against the British. Later, Lord Minto further contributed to widen the gap between the Hindus and the Muslims. He introduced communal electorate for Muslims but its outcome was disastrous. Muslims were elected to the legislature. The encouragement given by the British made the Muslims to become more and more communal and hence the Muslim League started demanding partition of India on religious grounds. In spite of Indian National Congress' opposition to communal politics of the Muslim League, the partition of the country was effected..

Main Characteristics of Communalism

Communalism as a socio-political problem is becoming more and more complex today. Unless we know the real nature of communalism it becomes difficult for us to differentiate between what communalism is, and what is not. It is important to note that adherence to a religion or attachment to a religious community is by itself not communalism. The religiosity of a community is also not communalism. But *using one religious community against other communities and against the whole nation is communalism.* Let us now discuss the main characteristics of communalism especially in the Indian context.[8]

1. ***Communalism is Narrow and Selfish*** **:** In a positive sense, communalism implies a person's attachment with the good of his 'community'. However, it is closely associated with politics and indicates the fact that it *"is generally associated with a narrow, selfish, divisive and aggressive attitude on the part of a religious group."*
2. ***Communalism is Opposed to Secularism*** **:** If by secularism, we understand the separation of the state from religion, neutrality of the state towards religions and equality of treatment towards all religions; then communalism is the opposite of it. Many times, people regard secularism as the answer or solution to the problem of communalism.
3. Communalism considers a particular religious community as separate from the rest of the communities.
4. It believes that not only religious but also secular interests of that community are separate from similar interests of other communities.
5. Communalism believes that the specific interests of the community can be promoted by maintaining its separate identity and organising it separately for the promotion of those interests.
6. *Communal interests always superimpose themselves* on the national interests.
7. Communalism *breeds mutual distrust and disharmony among the communities.* It adopts an attitude of hostility towards other religious communities.
8. Communalism treats some citizens not as citizens *but as members of some specific religious community.*

---

8. ***Source*** **: A.P. Avasthi** in *"Indian Government and Politics."* Page - 579.

9. Communalism makes a particular religious community to impose its religious views and *social norms on the members of other religious communities also.* It denies freedom to the members of other religious communities and the right to have their own religious views and social norms. The freedom in religious and social matters is also denied to them.
10. *Communalism fails to separate religion from politics.* It tries to conduct government on the basis of religious dogmas.
11. ***Communalism is a Political Ideology*** : Communalism is an ideology which is employed to attain political ends. Thus, communalism involves the pursuit of political goals through appeal to religious sentiments. It is a political strategy to attain political ends. **Prabha Dixit** says that communalism is *"a political doctrine which makes use of religio-cultural differences to achieve political end."*[9] Many consider that communalism is not religiously inspired but politically motivated.
12. ***Communalism leads to the abuse of power.*** It seeks to impose the social and religious norms of the community on other communities by several means including force, fraud, economic and other allurements and even assistance from foreign powers.
13. In its extreme form, *communalism claims nationhood for the community concerned* and seeks to raise it to a status of sovereign state.
14. ***Communalism is a Colonial Construction*** : Communalism in India is said to be the creation of the British rule. Many believe that there was amity between Hindus and Muslims prior to the British rule. British policy of *'divide and rule'* led to the emergence of communal organisations which in turn reinforced communal politics. In **Gyanendra Pandey**'s phrase, *'Communalism was a colonial construction'.*[10]
15. ***Varieties of Communalism*** : Communalism is unfortunately practised by all religious groups. Hence, we may speak of Muslim communalism, Christian communalism, Sikh communalism, Hindu communalism, and so on. It is said that the communalism of one community feeds on the other. In India, the tension among communities runs in the spectrum of majority - minority distinctions. Earlier, communalism referred primarily to the antagonism between Hindus and Muslims but now it has been extended to cover Hindu, Christian and Hindu - Sikh communities as well.

Causes for the Growth of Communalism in India

The main factors and forces which have encouraged the growth of communalism in India as listed by **A.P. Avasthi** [Page - 580], can be mentioned below.

1. *Communal political parties and organisations* have been fanning the fire of separatism.
2. *Minority appeasement policy* which the *Congress Party[I], Samajavadi Party, DMK, Janatha dal* and some other political parties have been nursing since decades.
3. The elections which make the political parties and organisations to make a *communal appeal to the voters* and to keep alive the communal feelings.
4. *The media, literature and textbooks that have communal slant* and that give support to communal forces.
5. *Separation and isolationism* found among the Muslims.
6. The economic and educational backwardness found amongst the big minority group , that is, the Muslims.
7. The *aggressive Hindu chauvinism* championed by a few forces.

9. **Prabha Dixit**, *'Communalism - A Struggle For Power'*, New Delhi, Orient Longman, 1974, Page : 1.
10. See **Gyanendra Pandey**, *'The Construction of Communalism in Colonial North India'*, Delhi, OUP, 1990.

8. *Political opportunism* which is found in almost all the political parties in India which makes the political leaders to give priority to their partisan political interests rather than to the national interests.
9. *"Divide and rule"* policy which the British had followed, caused lot of damage to our national interest. The same type of policy is continued in a surreptitious manner even now.

- **Other Factors :** In addition to the above factors mentioned by **Prof. Avasthi,** we can also list a few other factors which are contributing to the phenomenon of communalism.

10. *Role of foreign forces* which have been instigating communal activities and communal riots in India. The role of these forces in giving training to the communal extremists and in supplying sophisticated technical equipments for fanning the fire of communalism, can hardly be exaggarated.
11. *Large scale conversion activities taking place in India* are also contributing to communalism. Both the Christian and the Muslim minority forces are indulging in these kinds of conversion activities. These conversions are often made in a forcible manner and sometimes by means of temptations and so on.
12. *The subversion of secularism by the political parties* is also a factor encouraging communalism. Political parties which speak of secularism pay only lip sympathy to secularism but in practice support communalism.
13. *The growing disappointment among the Hindus* who constitute the majority community is also a factor in favour of communalism. The Hindus believe that due to the *"vote bank politics"* pursued by many political parties, the larger national interests are sacrificed.
14. *The Hindu militancy* too has added to the problem of communalism. In their attempt to defend Hindu interests and hit back attacks on it, some Hindu organisations have resorted to militant activities. These activities have caused communal frictions and conflicts.

COMMUNALISM - AS A CHALLENGE TO SECULARISM

The concept of secularism requires the state to be neutral and equidistant from all religious communities. The state cannot have its religion. Secularism was adopted at the time of independence because even though 85% of the total population were Hindus, there were about fortyfive million Muslims, ten million Christians and five million Sikhs. There were also many Parsees, Jains, Buddhists and Jews. This kind of scattering of different religious communities is quite common in many nations today. But in India, communalism has led to communal riots. According to one monograph [1977], about 8000 riots occurred after India's gaining of independence. Let us analyse as to how communalism poses a big challenge to the effective functioning of secularism.[11]

1. Violence and Bloodshed

Communalism is often a challenge to secularism as it culminates in communal riots involving violence and bloodshed. Secularism believes in peaceful co-existence of different communities and resolving any dispute through peaceful means. Secularism is an integral part of a democratic polity but communalism breeds intolerance resulting in communal riots causing death and human injury. Appeal to communal sentiments brings about communal tension and violence. Provocative speeches often result in the creation of a communal atmosphere leading to the outbreak of communal riots. These riots have taken place frequently in India leading to lot of destruction, death and hatredness. India cannot be described as a peaceful secular nation due to these communal riots which are often engineered by political parties and have acquired a communal character.

---

11. Source: **Dr.Parvathy Appaiah**'s "political Process in India" [2007] Jai Bharath Prakashan M'lore page 158/-161.

2. Creation of Hatredness

Communalism results in the creation of hatredness between one religious community and the other and also between one caste and the other. Many leaders are involved in this process for whom the end justifies the means. Democratic secular means allows them little chance of winning. So, one caste is set against another and one religion against another which results in hatredness. This process is carried on in such a way that the entire society gets divided on the basis of religion or caste. As a result, it is very difficult to practice secularism in the society and the state. The prevalence and the practice of communalism is a threat to secularism. Secularism preaches love of all communities and is based on the principle of equality. Whereas, communalism preaches hatredness, separatism and inequality.

3. Feeling of Separation

Secularism as an ideology desires the creation of unity and integration of all communities. But communalism tends to create a feeling of separatism and this in turn prevents them from integrating with the others. Identities become more strong with the communalist identity. Naturally, the communalist does not believe in integration or assimilation but instead wants to maintain separate and distinct identity.

4. Hostility Towards Minorities

Communalism is a challenge to secularism as it tends to develop hostility towards minorities. Majority-minority consciousness becomes stronger due to communalism. Pre-conceived ideas about a certain community creates a general 'bias' towards that entire community for generations to come. This hostility indirectly leads to a condition of tension ultimately manifesting in a communal riot. Sustained communal propaganda leads to the riots. Each community is projected in a particular way leading to antagonism. With such feelings, even an ordinary incident or trivial incidents trigger chain reactions ending in violence.

5. Communal Movements are a Threat to Secularism

Many communal organisations either through their definition of nationhood or culture or writings bring about a communal atmosphere which is a challenge to secularism. The existence of many communal organisations fomenting communal trouble has been established by various commissions of enquiry. Communal organisations of all communities create an atmosphere of distrust through their movement. There are militant communal organisations which promote communal ideology and politics. In fact, these organisations are responsible for the desecularization of civil society and the state. Communal movements are organised in a powerful way which poses a threat to secularism.

6. Communalism Leads to Partisanship of State Apparatus

Many times, the communal forces engaged in communal activities collaborate themselves with the police and administration. This is a threat to secularism which seeks to separate the state and religion. Usually, police force plays a crucial role in any communal riot. Sometimes, the state apparatus itself is responsible for such incidents. Politicisation of the police force often makes communal riots, state sponsored.The concept of secularism requires the state to be neutral and equidistant from all religious communities. But communal state is a challenge to secularism.

7. Majoritarianism

Communalism is often regarded as the opposite of secularism. It seeks to attain the domination of the majority community and subordination of the minorities to the majority.

Thus, it seeks to exercise control over the social, economic, political and cultural spheres. In other words, communalism advocates complete control of the whole system by a community which is strong, dominant and enjoys numerical superiority. Supremacy of one religion and majoritarianism are a challenge to the concept of secularism which is based on the principle of equality of religions and freedom of religion.

8. Minoritism

In a liberal democratic system, often the concept of minorities and their separate rights could pose a challenge to secularism. The communal identity of minorities creates a feeling of alienation and the majority community tends to view them suspiciously since they do not like to integrate into the entire society and the state. The special rights given to them along with the appeasement policy of the government creates disharmony and enmity between the majority community and the minorities. Aggressiveness on the part of minorities when combined with terrorism poses a challenge to secularism. India is very badly facing such a situation.

9. Communalism Suppresses Freedom of Religion

In a communalised society, many religious issues are politicised which makes one to doubt as to whether there is really the freedom of religion. By criticising each and every act of religious community as communal, there is a danger of suppression of certain religions and their practice which is not good for the secular society and the state.

Conclusion

Due to all the reasons mentioned above, communalism may be regarded as a problem unique to India alone, which is also a hindrance to the progress of the nation and the secular democratic system which we have adopted.

However, the Indian secularism tends to keep religion and politics separate through various constitutional provisions. The constitution combats communalism at every plane whether it is religion, caste, race, etc. **Dr. Ambedkar** made it explicit in the Constituent Assembly the dynamic and progressive implications of our secularism that it *"is quite impossible for anybody to conceive that the personal law shall be excluded from the jurisdiction of the state".*[12] He also said, *"let no community be in a state of mind that they are immune from the sovereign authority of this Parliament."*[13] Therefore, in the provisions of the constitution with regard to secularism, there *"is a determined attempt in them all to avoid an alliance of religion and politics, which often leads to dangerous consequences, to the stability of a state ... This is as it should be in a progressive modern democracy".*[14]

COMMUNAL TENSIONS OR RIOTS

The biggest outcome of the communalism is communal tensions or riots. When religious matters are politicalised it leads not only to communalism but also to the communal riots. *The riots that take place due to clashes of communal interests of two or more communities are regarded as **communal riots.***

The concept of communal violence or riot can be defined in the words of **Prof. Ram Ahuja** as follows : *"Communal violence involves people belonging to two different religious communities mobilised against each other and carrying the feelings of hostility, emotional fury, exploitation, social discrimination and social neglect. The high degree of cohesion in one community against*

12. *Constituent Assembly Debates, Vol. VII,* Page : 781.

13. *Parliamentary Debates, 1951, Vol. VIII,* 2950.

14. **Bannerjee D.N.** : *'Our Fundamental Rights'*, Page : 273.

another is built around tension and polarisation. The target of attack are the members of the 'enemy' community.......... It could thus be said that communal violence is based mainly on hatred, enmity and revenge."[15]

The incidences of communal riots are steadily increasing in India. Ever since politics came to be communalised, communal violence has increased quantitatively. According to a study conducted in India in 1966-67, as many as 310 instances of communal riots were reported and the figure increased to 1300 in 1985-86.

All the provinces and all the places are not equally sensitive to communal riots. *For example,* 61 districts out of 350 districts in India were identified as sensitive districts in 1961, whereas 216 districts were identified so in 1979, and 186 were regarded so in 1989. It is reported that property worth ₹14 crore was damaged in communal riots between 1983 and 1986 [*Times of India* - July 25, 1986]. In the incidences of communal riots in 3 years between 1986 and 1988, both the years inclusive, 1024 persons were killed and 12352 injured. It is observed that some states are found to be regularly suffering from the problem of recurring communal riots.

Some Features of Communal Riots Taking Place in India

Various studies have been conducted in order to collect enough information about the phenomena of communalism and communal riots. A study instituted to go into the major communal riots that took place in the country for the last five decades has revealed some special features of the communal riots.[16] They can be stated below.

1. Studies of communalism and communal riots have stated that in most of the instances, the communal riots are found to be politically motivated and not instigated by religious factors. Even the **Madan Commission** instituted to look into the communal disturbances in Maharashtra in May 1970 emphasised that *"the architects and builders of communal tension are the communalists and a certain class of politicians.........."*
2. In addition to the political interests, economic interests also play a vital role in augmenting communal clashes.
3. Statistics have revealed that communal riots seem to be more common in north India than in south India.
4. The possibility of recurrence of communal riots in a town where communal riots have already taken place once or twice is greater than in a town in which riots have never occurred.
5. It is observed that most of the communal riots take place on the occasions of religious festivals.
6. It is also observed that communal riots are found in a larger number in urban areas rather than in rural areas. The concentration of people of the minority communities in urban areas is a factor favourable for communal riots.
7. Normally, on the occasion of the communal riots deadly weapons are used by people involved in the communal riots.

SUGGESTIONS TO CONTROL AND ERADICATE COMMUNALISM

Communalism has been increasing in this country for the past 5 decades. It has impeded the process of development and also has hurt the scientific temper and the secular spirit. *"Communalism emerges in India as the most dangerous threat to the cultural modernisation.*

15. **Prof. Ram Ahuja** in *"Society in India"* [1999]. Page : 251 - 252.
16. **Ram Ahuja** in *"Society in India."* Page : 252 - 253.

It is a complex process but its causes generally subsist in the contradictions generated by the forces of social restructuration."[17]

A study [conducted by *Mainstream*, Feb. 9, 1988] has revealed that in the time span of 37 years after independence as many as 10,000 communal riots had taken place due to which more than 1,000 people lost their lives and property worth a few crores was damaged. The Ayodhya incident excelled the previous records and a few hundreds lost their lives in 1990s. The communal riot which took place in Gujarat very recently [February - May 2002] costed the lives of more than 800 people and property worth crores of rupees was destroyed.

Communalism is a creeping paralysis which demands solution. Communal riots pose a permanent threat to the religious harmony in this land. They must be effectively dealt with and minimised. A few of the suggestions in this regard may be noted. It is true that giving suggestions is an easy task but putting them into practice is itself a big challenge. **Prof. Ram Ahuja** suggests that the problem of communal riots must be tackled in 2 ways :

(A) *undertaking immediate remedial measures,* and

(B) *resorting to long term remedial measur*es.

(A) Immediate Remedial Measures

1. Setting up Peace Committees: In the riot-torn places, *"peace committees"* consisting of the respected leaders of different religious communities are to be formed immediately after the outbreak of communal violence. These leaders must exercise their goodwill on the respective communities and persuade them to maintain peace and harmony.

2. Use of New Strategies and Plans by the State: Since rioters are making use of modern sophisticated equipments and weapons to spread communal riots everywhere, it is necessary for the State to resort to new strategies and plans to hook and book those rioters and instill confidence in the minds of riot-hit individuals and innocent people.

3. Supervision of the Media: The role of the media is very important in the course of communal riots. The media must exercise great restraint in spreading rumours and reports of communal riots. The State must have strict vigilance over the media.

4. Suppressing the Extremists: The Government in power must use its authority and power in an impartial manner in suppressing the communal riots. It should not hesitate to impose ban on communal organisations directly or indirectly indulging in communal riots. All dangerous and extremist communal leaders must be arrested during the course of communal riots preventing them from fanning the fire of communal riots.

5. Other Measures:

(i) In the riot-torn areas, efficient and secular-minded police officials must be posted.

(ii) Special Courts should be established to deal with the cases of communal riots. Speedy disposal of the cases is an essential step in this direction.

(iii) The riot affected people must be given protection immediately and sufficient care should be taken to make arrangements for their rehabilitation, if needed.

(iv) Immediate legal action should be instituted against those who instigate communal riots.

(B) Long Term Remedial Measures

1. To Make the People Free From Communal Frenzies and Passions: It is necessary to educate the people to become free from communal prejudices, feelings, etc. Steps should be taken to expose the communalist tendencies of the leaders who normally instigate riots.

---

17. Views of **Prof. Yogender Sing** as quoted by **J.L. Kachroo** and **Vijaya Kachroo.** *"Society in India"* [1997]. Page - 282.

2. Preventing Communalisation of the State and the Political Elites in Power: Communal riots often reach new heights due to the support given to it by the political parties, leaders and some bureaucrats. Hence, it is necessary to see that the political elites in power become free from communal attitude. All communal forces to be tackled and treated equally.

3. Protecting the Civil Society from Being Communalised: Communal riots grow into new proportions when supported by people. Sometimes, ordinary people are also drawn into communal carnage. Hence, it is necessary to see that common people do not become the victims of communal strategies of the leaders. It is in this regard that the intellectuals, writers, journalists, voluntary organisations, freedom fighters and non-controversial political leaders should take a lead in building up public opinion against communalism and communal riots.

4. Educational System should be Free from Communal Ideas and Ideologies: It is necessary to see that importance is given to the development of communal harmony at all levels of education. The young minds should not be polluted with the narrow communal ideas. Hence, patriotic feelings and sentiments must be strongly encouraged. Extra care should be taken in writing and teaching lessons in history. Distorting historical facts to glorify communal harmony is also equally unfair.

5. Role of the Media: This is an era of publicity and propaganda. The electronic media such as television, radio, newspaper, etc. must play a very responsible role. They must not be allowed to contribute to communal feelings or riots. Communal press must be banned and legal actions must be instituted against communal writers.

6. Ideology that Economic Development by Itself Brings Down Communalism is Not Correct: Some argue that economic development, industrialisation, growth of capitalism, and the growth of working class would automatically weaken communalism. But our experience has proved to be contrary. Unless special care is taken, communal riots cannot be suppressed even in times of economic prosperity. Economic development alone cannot contain communalism. In fact, communal violence is more prevalent in developed states like Maharashtra, Gujarat and also in developed cities like Mumbai, Ahmedabad, Jamshedpur and Kanpur. Hence, separate and well planned efforts are needed to curb the growing disease of communalism.

7. Legislation Against Forcible Conversions: Since forcible conversion of persons from one religion to another, particularly from Hinduism to Christianity and Islam, is one of the major causes of communal riots; it is necessary that all conversion activities be banned and declared illegal. In fact, a legislation could be introduced in this regard at the all-India level. At the States level, Arunachal Pradesh, Madhya Pradesh, Orissa and Tamil Nadu governments have already made legislations prohibiting conversion activities.

• **Mahatma Gandhiji** was also very much against religious conversions. Long back he wrote : *".......Every nation considers its own faith to be as good as that of any other. Certainly, the great faiths held by the people of India are adequate for her people. India stands in no need of conversion from one faith to another."*[18]

As early as in 19th Jan. 1928, Gandhiji wrote in *"Young India"* that we should not even secretly pray that anyone should be converted, *"but our utmost prayer should be that a Hindu should be a better Hindu, a Mussalman a better Mussalman and a Christian a better Christian. This is the fundamental truth of fellowship."*[19]Gandhiji was totally against the proselytising activities of the missionaries. In his reply to Mahadev Desai's question, **Gandhiji** had once replied : *"If I had power and I could legislate, I should certainly stop all proselytising. It is*

18. As quoted by **Prof. K.N. Vaswani** in *"Gandhiji on Conversion"*, Page - 25.
19. As quoted by **Prof. K.N. Vaswani** in *"Gandhiji on Conversion"*, Page - 10.

the cause of much avoidable conflict between classes and unnecessary heart-burning among missionaries."[20] On various occasions, Gandhiji had expressed his views very strongly against forcible religious conversion.[21]

2. FUNDAMENTALISM

Religious Fundamentalism

"Religious fundamentalism" belongs to the same series of social evils such as communalism, regionalism, casteism, racism, sexism, ethnicism, and so on. Communalism often assumes the form of *religious fundamentalism*. It has both national and international dimensions. Religious fundamentalism is posing a new threat to the secular character of the Indian society. Especially after 1980s, it has become a more serious socio-political evil. It is necessary here to know the concepts of *"fundamentalism"* and *"religious fundamentalism"* and their nature.

Concept of *"Fundamentalism"*

1. *"Fundamentalism refers to a firm dogmatic belief in certain principles that are held to be basic or fundamental."*[22]
2. Fundamentalism refers to *"A religious movement that emphasises Biblical literalism and the final authority of the Bible. The term is sometimes applied to all those who have accepted the literal truth of the Bible even in past centuries.........."*[23]
3. *"Fundamentalism is a religious movement that emphasises the absolute truth of essential or "fundamental aspects" of faith, especially those rooted in sacred texts such as the Christian Bible or the Islamic Koran."*[24]
4. **Macionis** defines fundamentalism as *"a conservative religious doctrine that opposes intellectualism and worldly accommodation in favouring of restoring traditional other worldly spirituality".*
5. **M.F. Abraham** says *"....fundamentalism denotes the unconditional acceptance of the literal truth of the faith and there is no scope for debate."*

As it is made clear from the first definition, fundamentalism represents a strong dogmatic belief or an uncompromising belief in some religious, racial, linguistic and other matters. Depending upon the fundamentalist approach, then, we may speak in terms of different types of fundamentalism such as *religious fundamentalism, racial fundamentalism, ethnic fundamentalism, linguistic fundamentalism,* and so on.

Origin of the Concept of Fundamentalism

The origin of the concept of *"fundamentalism"* is to be found in the history of the development of Christianity. Fundamentalism originated in America in the form of a conservative movement in the 19th century emphasising as fundamental to Christianity the literal interpretation of the Bible. *"Christian fundamentalists believe the Bible to be the word of God."*[25] They believe in the explanation given in the Bible regarding the – *"physical second coming of Jesus Christ, the Virgin Birth; Resurrection, and Attainment. Fundamentalism came into its own in the early*

20. **Gandhiji** in *Harijan* dated 11-5-1935 as quoted by **Prof. K.N. Vaswani.** Page - 21.
21. For example, **Gandhiji** wrote in ***"Young India"*** [23-3-1931] : "I hold that proselytising under the cloak of humanitarianism work is, to, say the least unhealthy..... Conversion now a days has become a matter of business like any other. I remember having read a missionary report saying how much it cost per head to convert and then presenting a budget for "the next harvest"." – Quoted by **Prof. K.N. Vaswani.** Page - 24.
22. **David E. Hunter** and **Phillip Whitten** in their *"Encyclopaedia of Anthropology."* Page - 182.
23. **W.P. Scott** in his *"Dictionary of Sociology."* Page - 167.
24. **Allan G. Johnson** in *"The Blackwell Dictionary of Sociology."*
25. *The Blackwell Dictionary of Sociology.* Page - 118.

20th century in opposition to the Modernist tendencies in both the religious and secular life of America. In the late 20th century, the movement was represented by numerous church bodies, educational institutions, and special interest organisations."[26] However, most of the conservative or orthodox Christians today resent being referred to as *"fundamentalists." The term should be reserved today for those groups and fractions that stress the literal truth of the Bible in its entirety.*

The term *"fundamentalism"* is now being used in a loose manner with a wide variety of meanings. Sociologically also fundamentalism is important not only because of its unique place among religions, but because it easily extends itself into the political realm. In the Middle East, [in Iran, for example] and in Pakistan, Afghanistan and such other countries, fundamentalism plays an important role in the conservative political movements and nationalism. But even in India, especially after 1980s, religious fundamentalist trends are slowly spreading.

Features of "Religious Fundamentalism"

The main characteristics of religious fundamentalism can be mentioned below.

1. *Dogmatic Belief* : *Fundamentalism is basically a dogmatic belief* in certain principles. Those who justify religious fundamentalism are generally those individuals who are of the very strong opinion that the religious principles, values and ideologies in which they believe are beyond question.

2. *Total Surrender to a Sacred Book and a Religious Leader*: Religious fundamentalists implicitly believe that what is stated in a *"sacred book"* is *unchangeable, unquestionable and unalterable*. In the same dogmatic manner, they submit themselves completely to a religious leader.

3. *Fundamentalism is Opposed to Liberalism* : Liberalism depends upon mutual tolerance of divergent views, opinions and beliefs. But in fundamentalism, there is indifference and even intolerance towards the views of others. It does not accept the stand that differences are probable and are bound to be there. It goes to the extent of suppressing the difference and the opposition. Such tendencies are commonly found in the theocratic states. Some of the Muslim countries such as Pakistan, Iran, Iraq, etc. have become such theocratic states. Pakistan Government's intolerance towards its religious minorities is quite known. Because of its fundamentalist attitude, it has been persecuting and torturing its religious minorities [particularly the Hindus and Christians] right from its very inception.

4. *Religious Fundamentalists Oppose Any Change in What is Stated in the Sacred Book or the Tradition They Believe* : This tendency is opposed to science and modernity. *For example*, the orthodox Muslims believe that the Islamic law called *"Shariat"* is not created by man, but emerged from God through Mohammad. They also believe that it contains the will of the God; and the terms of law are fixed and unchangeable. It is for this reason, Shariat law became rigid and static. The Talibanese who ruled over Afghanistan for about 10 years, had such an uncompromising belief in the divine law for which they were branded as *"fundamentalists."*

5. *Religious Fundamentalism is Opposed to Secularism* : Secularism states that religion should not be mixed up with the governance of the state. Since it gives equal importance to all religions, it does not recommend a state religion. On the contrary, fundamentalism does not separate state and religion. It always upholds the supremacy of a particular religious philosophy, principle or tradition.

6. *Religious Fundamentalism May Have Its Own World View*: Fundamentalism may have a world-view of religion to which all other aspects such as political, cultural, economic,

---

26. *The New Encyclopaedia Britannica* - Vol.5. Page - 51.

educational, etc. are sub-ordinated. It is for this reason, fundamentalism is opposed to a scientific, rationalist and secular world-view.

7. *Fundamentalism May Assume the Extreme Form of Terrorism* **:** Fundamentalists may resort to any type of extreme activity in order to spread their religious views and to suppress the opposition. ***Example*:** Muslim fundamentalist organisations such as *Hijbul Mujahiddin, Jaishe Mohammad, Al Kaida, Lashkare Toiba, Huriat, I.S.I.* [*Inter Services Intelligence*], etc. have been committing lot of atrocities against the Hindu minorities especially in Kashmir. It is said that in a time span of about 15-20 years, [that is, since 1980s] these fundamentalists have killed more than 65,000 civilians, police, soldiers, politicians, Government officials with a view to separate Kashmir from India and to establish a separate Muslim State like that of Pakistan.

8. *Fundamentalism Breeds Separatism* **:** Fundamentalism of any type promotes belief in a particular ideology and is unwilling to consider other ideologies or viewpoints. The fundamentalists keep themselves separated from others. ***Example*:** Those *racial fundamentalists,* who believe in the supremacy of the white race normally do not want to have links with the people of the Black Race especially in South Africa and America. Similarly, the ethnic fundamentalists have contributed to separatism in Sri Lanka. Muslim fundamentalists have posed a similar problem in Kashmir because of their encouragement of separatism.

9. *Fundamentalism is a Type of Extreme Ethnocentrism* **? :** Religious fundamentalism gives rise to a feeling among its adherents whatever the things or views they have, are supreme and sacred. Once this feeling enters the mind, it draws a black curtain against rationalism and free thinking. Such individuals fail to develop an independent thinking. They try to develop friendship with those who support their views. They tend to develop disrespect and intolerance towards others. They may even go to the extent of attacking their opponents as an attempt to unify all those who share the same views and ideologies.

Characteristics of Fundamentalism - Views of Macionis

According to **Macionis**, religious fundamentalism is distinctive in five ways.[27]

1. ***Fundamentalists interpret the scriptures literally.*** *Example:* Christians believe that God created the world precisely as described in the Genesis.
2. ***They do not accept religious pluralism.*** They thus believe that their religious beliefs are true and other beliefs are not.
3. ***They pursue the personal experience of god's presence.*** Fundamentalism seeks to return to *"good old time religion"* and spirtiual revival.
4. ***Fundamentalism opposes secular humanism.*** It opposes the secular tendency to turn to scientific experts rather than god for answers.
5. ***Fundamentalists endorse conservative political goals:*** Some fundamentalist leaders have entered politics to oppose *"liberal agenda"* that includes, for example, feminism, right to abortion, gay marriages, etc. They are unhappy with the mass media for it colours the news with liberal sentiments.

Religious Fundamentalism in the Indian Context

It should be reckoned here that India as a nation was divided into two / three separate political units [India, Pakistan and the present Bangladesh] because of the fundamentalist approach pursued by some of the political leaders on the eve of independence. The same fundamentalist trends are making their re-appearance today. Pakistan which is known for its fundamentalist

27. **J.J. Macionis** in his "Sociology", 10th Low Priced Edition - (2006), Page: 510-511.

approach is trying to give its support to the Muslim fundamentalists found in India. Pakistan which wanted to grab Kashmir politically but failed to do so, is now making fresh attempts in this direction by giving secret support to the pro-Pakistan Muslim fundamentalists in India to let loose communalism, terrorism, violence, etc. wherever possible. Series of bomb explosions, planned kidnappings, merciless killings of minorities, frequent attacks on military headquarters, etc. that are taking place, especially in the Kashmir region make it evident that religious fundamentalists and fundamentalism pose a serious threat to the integrity and the secular character of our nation. Government alone cannot fightout this problem. People with nationalist fervour and commitment to real and not pseudo-secularism must take an active role in creating an awareness among the people about the dangers of fundamentalism. The Government must also deal stubbornly with these anti-national fundamentalist forces and suppress them with a heavy hand. Those who support fundamentalist forces secretly must also be nabbed and punished.

3. CASTEISM

Casteism is a social problem associated with the caste system. Just as caste system is exercising its influence in all the fields of social life casteism too has become all pervasive. It makes one to like, love and admire one's own caste and as a result, one develops a blind loyalty to one's own caste group.

What is Casteism ? / Meaning of Casteism

Casteism is understood as a partial or one-sided loyalty in favour of any particular caste. It makes members of the caste to become conscious of their membership of the caste and look at everything from the standpoint of the caste.

1. According to **D.N. Prasad**, *"Casteism is loyalty to the caste translated into politics."*[28]
2. **R.K.Sharma**: *"Casteism is a blind group loyalty towards a caste which does not care for the interest of other castes and seeks to realize the social economic, political and other interests of its own group"*
3. According to **Kaka Kalelkar**, *"Casteism............. is an over-riding, blind and supreme group loyalty that ignores the healthy social standards of justice, fairplay, equity and universal brotherhood."*[29]

It is clear from the above, that *casteism is a blind group loyalty towards one's own caste or sub-caste which does not care for the interests of other castes and their members.*

Origin of Casteism

In the closeness and rigidity of the four ranks of the Indian social order, the beginnings of casteism is found. Devotion and loyalty to one's primary group was a value of paramount importance for centuries. With the change of time, the virtue of old has assumed the form of deviation of the worst order of today. But unlike today, the loyalty to primary group such as one's family or caste, in the early days, resulted in the noblest voluntary social agencies in the service of mankind.

According to **Kalelkar,** the caste system has produced a peculiarly strong and almost indissoluable loyalty of the members of the caste to each other, both for maintaining a standard of life and looking after each other's self-interest. Many times, caste loyalty is proved stronger than loyalty to the whole nation and to humanity. Caste loyalty frequently drives a man to subordinate his sense of justice, fairplay and humanity to the interest of casteism.

---

28. **D.N. Prasad** in his *"The Myth of Caste System."* Page - 124.
29. **Kaka Kalelkar** - as quoted by **R.N. Sharma** in his *"Indian Social Problems."* Page - 47.

Casteism thus makes a man to become blind to the virtues of justice, fairplay, equity and universal brotherhood. Casteism is not only peculiar to the Hindu society, but Muslims and Christians in India have also fallen a prey to this form of social deviation. Since most of Christians and Muslims in India are converted Christians and Muslims, they too have nursed this deviant trend along with the rest of the Hindus. Surprisingly, casteism instead of becoming weaker and weaker, is becoming stronger and stronger day–by–day by assuming different forms. Its worst manifestation we find in the field of politics and administration. It has percolated into the educational institutions also.

Causes of Casteism

Casteism which exercises a negative influence on the network of social relations is caused by several factors of which the following may be noted.

1. *Endogamous Nature of the Caste* : Casteism is often the result of restrictions imposed on the marriage that takes place in the Hindu society. Each caste and sub-caste is endogamous in nature. It means that member of a caste or sub-caste has to marry within his or her own caste or sub-caste. Because of this rule of endogamy, marital relations are confined to a small circle / section of the people. Individuals are more prone to develop their loyalties and admirations to their own caste or sub-caste people. This practice of endogamy makes the people to become somewhat narrow-minded.

2. *Strong Desire to Enhance Caste Prestige* : People belonging to a particular caste or subcaste have the tendency of developing loyalty to their caste or subcaste and to become more conscious of its relative prestige in society. Every member thus tries his level best to see that his caste prestige is safeguarded and enhanced. This type of loyalty towards the caste makes the members of the caste to favour their own members of the caste wherever they get the opportunity. Excessive caste loyalty tends to keep other caste people at a distance.

3. *Improvement in the Means of Transport and Communication Leading to a Better Organisation of Caste* : Advancement that has taken place in the field of transport and communication has helped the members of the caste to be in touch with one another regularly. It has also helped them to strengthen their caste organisation and conduct activities on caste lines. Caste organisations and caste-get-togethers are on the increase now.

4. Urbanisation Indirectly Favouring Casteism : Industrialisation and urbanisation have been attracting people in a large number towards the cities. When the rural people go to the cities they naturally search for their nearer and dearer ones on the basis of caste. They consider their own caste people as their potential friends and well-wishers. Hence, the city atmosphere has also contributed to the strengthening of caste feelings and caste-mindedness. Further, city provides lot of opportunities for casteminded people to rally round the caste issues.

5. Powerful Hold of the Caste Over the Members : Caste is a strong cohesive group. It has a powerful hold over its members. Members of the caste also look to the caste to obtain the needed help and assistance in times of crises, difficulties and emergencies. Dependence of the members on the caste in this way has further added to the solidarity of the caste and also to the problem of casteism.

Consequences of Casteism

Casteism though has certain benefits to the members of the caste on the individual basis, it has several harmful effects on the society as a whole. Some of the major harmful consequences of casteism can be noted here.

1. ***Hinderance to the Development of National Feeling*** : Members of the caste imbued with the spirit of casteism are more prone to show their loyalty to the caste rather than to the community at large. Casteism divides people in the name of caste and encourages intolerance, jealousy, rivalry and conflicts among members of the caste. Caste clashes and tensions that arise in society for one reason or another wrecks the unity of society and damages social harmony.

2. ***Dangerous to Democracy*** : Strictly speaking, caste and democracy cannot go together. Caste is based on inequality, whereas democracy assures equality and equal opportunities to one and all. Since democracy and caste system are co-existing in India clashes between them are inevitable. Indian politics has become very much complicated because of the caste interference. Caste plays its role in the processes of selection of candidates to the elections, electioneering, formation of cabinet, distribution of portfolios, and so on. It means at every stage in politics caste creates tensions, misunderstandings, infights, rivalries, etc. It is in this way, national interests are undermined and national unity is underscored.

3. ***Encourages Moral Degeneration*** : Casteism contributes to the moral fall. It encourages nepotism. It makes one go out of the way to help and favour people of one's own caste. People of the same caste also look to the caste leaders to favour them in all situations. This kind of favour damages the moral values and encourages corruption.

4. ***Casteism Leads to the Negligence of Talents and Efficiency*** : If candidates are selected and appointments are made on the basis of caste, it definitely damages talents, abilities and efficiencies of the people. When unwanted and inefficient people are selected for high offices in the name of caste, honesty, efficiency and duty consciousness become the first casualty.

5. ***Casteism May Even Lead to Brain-Drain :*** It has been observed that some of the most efficient and talented persons have left India and gone abroad for the simple reason that their merits and talents are not properly recognised. Casteism which comes in the way of the recognition of merit and efficiency indirectly promotes brain-drain.

It is clear from the above, that casteism has dangerous effects on the society. Though people know that casteism is bad they have become its victims . Even those who condemn it in public are practising it privately. **Prof. M.N. Srinivas** has rightly said that the caste *"is so tacitly and so completely accepted by all, including most vocal elements in condemning it, that it is everywhere the unit of social action."*[30]

More than the common people, politicians seem to be contributing much to the survival of casteism. *"Political leaders belonging to different castes seem to secure political and other advantages for themselves at the expenses of others, and to this end they utilise the caste sentiment. Caste consciousness and caste prejudices which exist among the masses are thus turned by politicians into caste passions."*[31]

One of the seasoned politicians of India by name **Namboodiripad** himself had once stated that *"The existence of caste consciousness, caste prejudices, discontent on the basis of caste inequalities – all these are impediments in the way of the development of the country as a whole, and therefore, of the development of "lower" and "backward" castes themselves. Caste separatism, therefore, hinders rather than helps, the advancement of the "lower" castes themselves."*[32]

Solutions to the Problem of Casteism

Casteism is no doubt a social evil that has to be counteracted and removed. As a solution to casteism, some scholars have gone to the extent of telling that the entire caste system is to be

30. **M.N. Srinivas** in his *"Caste in Modern India."* Page - 225.
31. **A.P. Avasthi** in *"Indian Government and Politics"* [2001]. Page - 576.
32. **A.P. Avasthi** in his *"Indian Government and Politics."* Page - 577.

wiped out. But removal of caste and casteism is not an easy thing. Caste has very strong roots in our social set up and hence it cannot be uprooted from our society. It is not the need of the hour; but only the ugly face of the caste, that is, casteism, is to be wiped out. We can suggest some solutions in this regard to counteract the problem of casteism.

1. Education : Education seems to be the most ideal solution to the problem of casteism. People must be properly educated about the dangers of practicing casteism. Parents, teachers, elderly people, political leaders should take precautions against contaminating the young minds with casteism. The educational institutions should be able to provide an atmosphere in which caste distinctions are not encouraged while at the same time the children are allowed to develop distaste towards discrimination. Education should help them to think above caste and caste considerations.

2. Encouragement to Intercaste Marriages : Marital relations represent the most intimate relations between men and women. Encouragement and promotion of intercaste marriages will help young men and women of different castes to come closer and to develop healthy relations among them. Children born out of such intercaste marriages are believed to possess broadmindedness and hence the hold of caste over members, become weaker and weaker in course of time.

3. Minimum Use of the term "Caste" : Necessary precautions must be taken to see that the word "caste" is used only in limited context. The young generations must be encouraged to give the least importance for it. This is possible only when we make lesser and lesser use of the term "caste." It we are able to do so, then there would be no traces of castesim left in the minds of the children of impressionable age.

4. Promotion of Economic Equality : Wide economic gap is found between the upper caste people and the lower caste people. This economic gap widens the social distance and contributes to the development of caste prejudices. Hence, efforts must be made to provide equal economic opportunities for the lower caste people to attain economic prosperity. It is thus suggested that the restoration of cultural and economic equality of various castes is an important step towards the abolition of casteism from the society.

●●●

Chapter 17

THE MENACE OF TERRORISM

Concept of Terrorism and its Definition - Nature and Characteristics of Terrorism - Differences between Terrorism and othe Forms of Violence - Causes of Terrorism - Terrorism in India: Naxalite Terrorism, Terrorism in Punjab - ULFA Terrorism in Assam - Terrorism in Kashmir - The Effects or Impact of Terrorism on Indian society - Combating Terrorism: The Israeli Model, American Model and the Indian model - Remedial Measures for Terrorism or Other Ways of Combating Terrorism: The Enactment of POTA: Prevention of Terrorism Act, 2002 and Non-Legal Measures to prevent and Control Terrorism - Sociology of Terrorism.

Terrorism is one of the types of grave violences of the present world. Crossing the national boundaries terrorism has become a global menace. In the recent times, it has affected both the developed and the developing countries. Everywhere, the phenomenon of terrorism is understood as a problem capable of affecting not only national but also international politics. The 11th Sept. 2001 plane attack on the twin towers of the *World Trade Centre* [WTC], New York, U.S.A. stands out as a powerful evidence to this fact. Bomb explosions that took place in Taj Hotel International, at Mumbai on 12th March 1993 and the merciless killing of innocent people on the same day at different places in Mumbai by Pakisthan sponsored terrorists reveal, that terrorism continues to be a major threat to India's security and integrity. Progress achieved in the fields of science and technology and particularly in information technology has helped in making terrorism a global phenomenon.

Terrorism which is closely associated with violence, destruction and death has become a major concern of international relations in the contemporary period. It is a serious problem capable of destabilising a nation since it is often driven by transnational ideology. Its cadres are drawn from multinational sources, its funding and weapon sources are international and its operations are also international. Thus, terrorism is a global phenomenon which is easy to recognize but difficult to define.

Terrorism is neither a political philosophy nor a movement, nor can it be identified with political violence in general. It is a process which is employed by a large number of groups in order to realize their objectives. Thus, there are a variety of interpretations of the term. Unfortunately, terrorism has assumed catastrophic proportions. It has endangered the world environment of peace and security. Terrorism is totally opposed to democracy and humanity and causes bloodshed, destruction and anarchy all round.

Concept of Terrorism - Its Definition

Terrorism which is a product of the Western civilisation has entered almost all nations including India. Various words such as *insurgency, civil war*, etc. - are often used to mean terrorism. But it is actually different from all these. Terrorist activity is basically a violent activity. It includes - exploding of bombs, kidnapping, setting fire to houses, organising mass murders, blackmailing, highjacking, intimidation, and such other dangerous and extremely violent activities.

Definition of Terrorism

1. According to **Encyclopaedia of Social Sciences,** terrorism is *"a method whereby an organised group or party seeks to achieve its avowed aims chiefly through the systematic use of violence."*
2. **F.R. Scarpitti** and **M.L. Andersen :** Terrorism refers to *"The collective mode of politically oriented violence".*
3. **Ram Ahuja :** Terrorism can be broadly defined as *"violent behaviour designed to generate fear in the community, or substantial segment of it for political purposes."*
4. **Yonah Alexander :** *"Terrorism is the use of violence against random civilian targets in order to intimidate or to create generalized pervasive fear for the purpose of achieving political goals."*
5. **Brian Jenkins :** *"The threat of violence, individual acts of violence or a campaign of violence designed primarily to install fear is terrorism."*
6. **In simple words,** terrorism can be understood as *a forceful and unlawful method to achieve the desired goal.*

NATURE AND CHARACTERISTICS OF TERRORISM

Terrorism is characterised by a deliberate use of violence against civilians, armed personnel, and the state by some group of misguided persons to bring about the desired political intimidation, coercion, or destruction of human lives and property to obtain realistic or illusory goals.

Terrorist activities are carried on in such a way that it is difficult to give an appropriate definition of terrorism. However, its main characteristics can be summed up as follows :

Characteristics

1. ***The Usual Forms or Manifestations of Terrorism :*** Terrorism is basically a type of violence and is manifested in the form of blatant criminal acts such as kidnapping, kidnapping government officials, political leaders, and even passangers, mass murders, attacks, intimidations, bomb blasting, plane hijacking, exploding bridges, dams, industrial units, hospitals and such other public utility places.
2. ***People who Constitute Targets of Attack :*** It is directed against civilians, armed personnel, a linguistic, religious, racial, or ethnic or other kind of community, government or state.
3. ***It is Normally Organised :*** It is not a sudden outburst or a spontaneous manifestation of wrath. On the contrary, it is an organised, planned and deliberate act of selective violence carried out only by a handful of people. However, all organised violences are not terroristic in nature. In organized crimes also, violence is often used profusely and even dacoits, loots and murders are committed. But these instances do not represent terrorism. However, a Naxalite group which is committed to its own socio-political philosophy resorts to the same means

THE MENACE OF TERRORISM

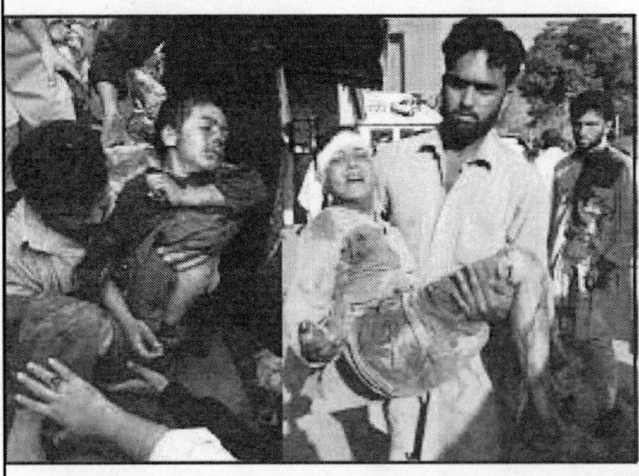

for collecting money to meet its expenses, then only such instances can be called 'terrorist' activities. Many terrorist groups thrive around a dense network and hierarchical structures which are similar to the modern army but their mode of operation remains unconventional. Most of these groups operate with flexibility while protecting the security of the organization. Modern day terrorists are so well organized that it becomes difficult to dismantle the entire organizational structure of modern terrorism.

4. ***Terrorism of any Type is Unlawful, Illegal, Inhuman and Anti-democratic :*** Terrorism has no faith in the democratic means and has utter disregard for human values. The eternal values of Indian culture such as love, truthfulness and nonviolence are disregarded by the gospel of terrorism.
5. ***Terrorism is Mainly Politically Motivated Violence:*** Terrorism is very often resorted to and terrorist activities are held with the sole motive to overthrow or challenge the existing order. Though terrorist type of violence is documented in various civilisations throughout recorded history, it is popularly believed that political terrorism is of recent origin and unique to contemporary society.
6. ***It is a weapon of blackmail coercion and imposition of minority will against and upon a majority decision [Wilkinson].*** Terrorism is not just intimidation nor insurgency. It is not a fight between individuals but a struggle between social groups and political forces. The terrorists normally punish those individuals whom their organisation considers guilty of interfering with their agenda of socio-political activities.
7. ***Terrorism to Create Fear in the Minds of the Public :*** It uses violence to create a psychological impact for making their demand accepted. It aims at creating an impact of fear and panic not only for the victim but also for the people at large. It aims at demoralising people, governmental authority or an institutional establishment. Sometimes, terrorism may also use mob violence as its method of achieving its goal.
8. ***It Clouds Rational Thinking :*** Violent activities branded as "terrorism", are devoid of rational thinking. Such activities are normally indulged in due to emotional outbursts. It is because of lack of thinking and high emotional outbursts that some terrorists go to the extent of playing the role of 'human bomb' and get killed when the bomb tied to their body explodes.
9. ***Terrorism Contains Arbitrariness in Violence :*** In selecting its victims and in perpetrating violence against them, it does not follow any definite policy and is normally indiscriminate in doing so. It does not take into consideration whether innocent people become its victims and unnecessarily undergo limitless sufferings. In many acts of its violence its real opponents or enemies are not targeted but only ordinary innocent people become the victims.
10. ***Terrorism is Frightening :*** Terrorism is normally accompanied by a feeling of helplessness on the part of the general masses. In fact, it is the purpose of terrorists to create chaos, confusion and fear in the minds of the people. It wants to weaken the morale of the people and also its opponents.

- ***Terrorism, however, is not always reactionless.*** Sometimes, people react strongly to it and fight back. But when it is sudden and strong enough to overpower the masses, they resort to flight.

11. ***Terrosists Have a Great Technological Capacity :*** Many terrorist groups operate with sophistication as they have access to many chemical, biological and nuclear weapons which act as a strong base to their activities which are conducted with confidence. Thus, the modern day terrorism has increased the real danger of rising the scale of destructiveness to new

heights. Modern terrorism uses modern technology like fax, internet, etc. in order to carry on its operation. The technical skill of the terrorists was well evident in the 11th September [2001] attack on WTC. There is today the threat of new cyber terrorism.

12. ***Terrorists Obtain Financial Strength by Carrying on Illegal Activities :*** Many terrorists carry on illegal activities such as drug trafficking which provide them with large amount of money. For instance, under Taliban, out of 31 provinces, 18 were under illicit cultivation of opium. So, such illegal activities provide financial strength to the terrorist networks.

Differences between Terrorism and Other Forms of Violence

It is important to differentiate terrorism from other forms of violence and force. As noted in the definitions cited above, terrorism is a premeditated violence unleashed for the purpose of creating extreme anxiety or terror among the target group. This has a political objective and often there is the acceptance of responsibility for the acts perpetrated by these terrorist groups. Political terrorism is resorted to by groups or even by states to further their viewpoint. Thus, terrorism is the violent act which is symbolic of the larger message or challenge. *For instance,* the attack on World Trade Centre is seen as a symbolic attack on American might. The attack on Indian defence structure is considered as an attack on defence structure and the attack on our Indian Parliament is regarded as an attack on Indian democracy and so on. Other forms of violence do not have these objectives.

• ***There are different varieties of terrorism.*** It may be revolutionary, religio-political or state sponsored. Terrorists create panic, undermine confidence in the government and weaken the enemy. Thus, terrorism does not make a difference between the population and the state in its target. So, it is entirely different from other forms of violence. The process of globalization has also helped terrorism to operate everywhere easily and the legitimacy of the nation-state is declining.

- ***Terrorism is different from other kinds of violence in the following ways.***

1. Terrorism creates the reign of terror and the kind of terror may have different faces.
2. Terrorists create lawlessness in the society by dictating terms to the people who may gradually lose confidence in the political system. *For instance,* many Naxalite areas of Andhra Pradesh and Bihar, run parallel courts to settle disputes among the village.
3. Terrorists do not respect the law of the land and kill innocent people. They do not have belief in the Constitution and want their demands to be met unconditionally.
4. Terrorism does not value democracy and try to disrupt the institutions.
5. Terrorists are nameless and placeless and so it is difficult to monitor terrorist activities.
6. Terrorists target the heads of the state to create distrust in the government.

Other forms of violence do not have the above characteristics of terrorism which are exclusive to only terrorism and not any other kind of violence.

CAUSES OF TERRORISM

It is very difficult to specify the definite causes for terrorist activities. Various factors are at its background. Writers like **Alexander** and **Finger** have expressed the opinion that the causes for terrorism lie in the very nature of modern civilisation and the present complex industrial system.They have enlisted some five major causes contributing to the origin and development of terrorism.

1. Availability of the Most Modern and Destructive Type of Weapons: Deadly and devastative weapons such as time bombs, hand bombs, gillentin sticks, R.D.X, grenades, automatic rifles, missiles and remote controls and such other most sophisticated weapons are being used by the terrorists for their terrorist activities. It seems as though in the years to come the terrorist groups will probably have access even to chemical and nuclear weapons and such other instruments. The possibility of getting such deadly weapons through smuggling has added to the strength and courage of terrorists.

2. Areas or Fields of Modern Technology that Cannot be Protected: Ours is a complex technological society consisting of a large number of multistoreyed buildings, corporate houses, big business establishments, sophisticated hospitals, banks, transportation systems, attractive malls and the like which cannot always be protected. At the same time, they are highly vulnerable to unsuspected and ruthless attacks by the terrorists who normally prefer to make them their targets of attack.

3. Availability of Modern Communication and Transportation Facilities have Made Possible International Terrorism: Rapid development that has taken place in the fields of transport and communication has given scope for the terrorit organisations to have their centralised base in one particular country and carry on their terrorist operations in some selected countries. It has helped them to have collaboration among ideologically linked groups. Extremists who are committed to the Marxist ideology though are scattered over a number of countries, modern network of communication has helped them to have a network of co-operation.

4. Availability of War Weapons Transforming the Terrorists Group into "Sub-national" Groups: The terrorist groups have assumed new strength due to the availability of modern warfare capabilities. Hence, the earlier powerless terrorist groups have been transformed into subnational groups with substantial strength and power. They are even capable of creating states within states, thereby undermining the ability of the legitimate governments to rule or to survive. **Example** : *The L.T.T.E of Srilanka, the BODOS of Assam, the Naga Commandos of Nagaland and the Mizo Extremists represent such sub-national groups.*

5. Terrorists Resorting to Violence not only Against their Immediate Victms but also Aganist General Public: The terrorists today create mental fear and anxiety make money through blackmailing people and resort to violence wherever necessary without any hesitation. They use violence not only against their immediate victims but intend to create terror and horror in the minds of general public.

6. Other Factors that Favour Terrorism

(i) ***Terrorism is Often used as a Technique by One Country to Weaken its Enemy Countries :*** Pakisthan, for example, has been using this technique to weaken India by supporting Naxalite extremists and terrorists who are engaged in subvertive and sabotaging activities in India. During the decade 1980-90, Pakisthan supported extremists of Punjab known as Khalisthanists who were fighting for the establisment of a separate nation for Sikhs under the leadership of Bindranwale.

(ii) ***Assistance to Terrorists from Non-Residential Citizens:*** There are many instances in which the rich non-residential citizens have extended their financial support to terrorist groups on religious and cultural basis. **For example**, it is wellknown that **Dawud Ibrahim**, notoriously known in India as the *"king of the underworld"*, who has escaped from India and currently staying either in Pakisthan or gulf countries, has been continuously supporting Muslim terrorist groups working against the interests of India, finacially and otherwise.

(iii) ***Smuggling and Drug Trafficking Methods*** are also resorted to by the terrorist groups for getting sufficient money for purchasing modern sophisticated weapons.

(iv) ***Ideological Clashes:*** Deep ideological conflicts that are found between the East and the West, the Leftists and the Rightists, the rise in religious, ethnic, linguistic, racial and national consciousness of groups throughout the world, often trigger terrorism.

(v) ***Sharp Opposition to Repression :*** People often resort to terrorist methods to register their opposition to the repressive and suppressive type of administration of the dictators.

(vi) ***Feelings of Deprivation and Frustration :*** It is said that strong feelings of deprivation and frustration among the minorities struggling for their liberation [as we witnessed in the case of the Tamil minorities of Sri Lanka] may also give rise to terrorism.

THE IMPACT OR EFFECTS OF TERRORISM ON INDIAN SOCIETY

Terrorism which has grown to international level has assumed unimaginable proportions especially in the 21st century. It is indeed, a very serious and a dangerous problem haunting many countries of the world. It has not spared world's most powerful country, that is, America. Unfortunately, India is also one of its worst hit countries. Terrorism of any kind disturbs peace, threatens security, weakens law and order system, damages economic development and causes incalculable material and non-material losses. The major impact or effects terrorism on society can be analysed here.

TERRORISM IN INDIA

India has been witnessing terrorist activities since a long time. Though they are found in various places they can be grouped into four main types. They are as follows.

a) ***Naxalite Terrorism found in Bengal, Bihar and Andhra;***

b) ***Khalistan - Oriented Terrorism in Punjab;***

c) ***ULFA - Terrorism in Assam; and***

d) ***Terrorism in Kashmir.***

a) Naxalite Terrorism

The Naxalite terrorism which took inspiration from the Chinese Revolution under the leadership of Mao-Tse Tung, first appeared in West Bengal in 1967. This ideology based terrorism later on spread to Andhra Pradesh, Kerala, Orissa, Tripura, and very recently to Karnataka. One of the initial Naxalite leaders by name Charu Mazumdar[1] had declared that *"China's chairman is our chairman, and China's way is our way."* Inspired by the communist thoughts, the Naxalite movement was highly charged by the ideology of violence. Its leaders had given call for the total annihilation of the big farmers, landlords and *jagirdars.*

Though the initial *Naxalbari Movement* [1967 movement] was not successful in reaching its objectives, it was able to create serious law and order problem. It made many idealistic young Naxalite men and women kill landlords, moneylenders and police officers. As many as **2000** persons were killed in between 1969 and 1972. More than **700** cases of looting, and **9000** acts of serious violence by the Naxalites were reported. The police also killed about **400** and arrested more than **6000** terrorists. The movement lost its idealistic flavour when professional criminals also joined it. When the main leaders of the movement [like Charu Majumdar, Kanu Sanyal, Punjab Rao, Panchanana Sarkar, Jungle Santal, and others] were arrested, it slowly switched over from west Bengal to other states such as Bihar, A.P., Tamil Nadu, Kerala, Orissa, Tripura, and so on.

1. **Charu Majumdar** [1918-1972] was a communist revolutionary and the leader of the Naxalbari uprising. He participated in the Tebhaga farmers movement before independence. He left the CPI and founded the Communist Party of India [Marxist-Leminist]. He very strongly believed in the Maoist path of peasant rebellion and defended the revolutionary violence. He was arrested during the Naxalbari uprising and finally died in police custody.

Naxalites believe in violent way of settling problems. They organise killings, blasts, extortions and kidnappings. At present two important left-wing militant organisations namely; (i) *People's War Group [PWG]* and (ii) *Maoists Communist Centre [MCC]* are having their network in different parts of the country. The PWG activists are concentrated in Andhra Pradesh, Chhttisgarh and Orissa, while the MCC is mostly active in Jharkhand and Bihar. Currently, more than 75 districts in nine states are very badly affected by Naxalite violence. Most of these are very backward areas inhabited by the Adivasis. Their exploitation and atrocities committed on them have led to the growth of Naxalite movement in these areas. The secret support of China is also there. Some Governments have often taken stern measures against the movement. But human Rights activists have criticised these measures. Some pseudo-intellectuals have also joined them in doing so. The previous UPA Government's [2004-2014] liberal attitude towards these extremists had given them a new lease of life to spread their tentacles in various parts of the nation. Thus, of all the types of terrorists, the Naxalites seem to be in a bigger number operating in a wide network of areas.

b) Terrorism in Punjab

Terrorism in Punjab is also known as *"Sikh - terrorism"*. This made its appearance in 1980s when some militant groups of Punjab demanded the establishment of an independent sovereign state known as *"Khalistan"*. These militants wanted to make Punjab a *"theocratic state"*. In order to draw the attention of the government and to bring pressure on it to fulfil their demands, these militants resorted to large scale violence. Between 1982 and 1983, its violence continued unabated. The main strategies of the pro-Khalistan militants were as follows:

(i) The militants intended to demonstrate that they were more powerful than the political administration,

(ii) Claiming themselves to be the champions of Sikhs and Sikh religion.

(iii) Killing innocent people, looting banks, and shops and creating a general atmosphere of horror and terror.

(iv) Developing their own connections with the smugglers who were made to supply funds for the militant activities inside Punjab.

(v) Persecuting the Hindus of Punjab and enforcing them to migrate to other states so that the Sikhs alone could live there.

Militants supporting Khalistan turned places of worship into places of hideouts and anti-national activities. When the violence reached its peak the army conducted what is known as *"Operation Blue Star"* on June 6th 1984 to remove the terrorists from the Golden Temple at Amritsar. During this army operation", leader of the terrorists called **Bhindranwala** was killed and thereafter terrorism in the state slowly subsided.[2] It almost came to an end due to the strict action taken by **K.P.S. Gill** when he was made the Director General of Police, Punjab.

c) ULFA Terrorism in Assam

Insurgency in the North-East **:** Since the days of independence insurgency has been a permanent problem for the nation especially in the North-east. Various ethnic factors, forest cover, hilly terrain, networking among militant groups, involvement of foreign agencies, prevalence of international border especially with Bhutan, Bangladesh, China, have further complicated the situation in this area. The north-eastern states such as Nagaland, Tripura, Manipur, Mizoram,

2. **Punjab terrorism,** however, costed the life of Prime Minister Indira Gandhi who was assassinated in the year 1984 by the terrorist instigation. Her assassination immediately led to anti-Sikh riots in Delhi which resulted in the killing of more than **3000** Sikhs. This riot itself gave further inspiration for the terrorists to muster mass support.

Arunachal Pradesh, Meghalaya and Assam all have been experiencing the problem of insurgency as well as terrorism in one way or the other. Let us now have a glance of ULFA [United Liberation Front of Assam] terrorism in Assam.

ULFA Terrorism in Assam

In the North-eastern region, Assam has been the worst sufferer due to various ethnic movements. Its territorial area has been reduced considerably with the creation of the states such as Mizoram, Nagaland, Meghalaya and Arunachal Pradesh. Still Assam has been experiencing terrorism almost since 1980s.

More than any other thing, *"anti-foreigner"* sentiments led to the militant and terrorist activities in Assam. Assamese demand for removing *'foreigners'* [mainly the infiltrators from Bangladesh] and deleting their names from the electoral rolls was turned down by the Congress government. When the elections were declared in the midst of agitation in 1983, more than 5,000 persons lost their lives due to the violence that sparked of there on account of that. After a prolonged *"student - cum peoples' movement"*, fresh elections were held in 1986 in which *Assam Gana Parishad* [AGP] which had the support of the students led by the *All Assam Students' Union* [AASU] came to power. The AGP was, however, a failure and factions in it led to its split. Two militant organisations namely, ***United Liberation Front of Assam*** [ULFA] and the ***United Minorities Front*** [UMF] emerged. Of these, the ULFA became more dominant.

The **ULFA**, born out of *"anti-foreigner sentiments"* indulged in selective violent activities. It resorted to campaign of murder, loot and kidnapping. It brought the law and order machinery to a grinding halt and disturbed the state's economy. The army which was called into service conducted *"Operation Bajrang"* (1991) in order to suppress the secessionist and militant activities in Assam. The army was successful in its task and the June 1991 Elections took place without much disturbance.

The Bodo Movement

At the time of the split in the AGP in 1986, yet another student organisation, namely; *All Bodo Students' Union [ABSU]* also took its birth. It demanded a separate state of Bodoland and indulged in violence. The Bodo movement gave birth to two militant organisations, namely : ***(1) National Democratic Front of Bodoland*** **[NDFB]**, and ***(2) Bodoland Liberation Tiger Force*** **[BLTF]** which have caused considerable violence. They continue to indulge in arson, loot, attacks, killings, kidnappings, etc., The Assam problem is not yet solved.

d) Terrorism in Kashmir

Ever since the days of partition, Kashmir has been a trouble spot in India. Though Jammu and Kashmir is an integral part of India, Pakistan has illegally occupied a part of it and intends to swallow the whole of it. Pakistan waged thrice war with India on the issue of Kashmir and both the times, received humiliating defeats. Therefore, Pakistan adopted a new strategy of terrorising the people of Jammu and Kashmir. Its intention is to gain what it has lost in the two battles. Terrorism assumed new proportions in Kashmir especially after 1988. Thousands of people [mostly the Hindus who constitute the minority in this region] have been forced to flee from their homes and they are living the life of refugees in their own homeland in several places. *"It is claimed in one report that nearly 2 lakh Hindus fled Jammu and Kashmir between 1988 and 1991."*[3] Thousands of people including security personnel have been killed. The militants resort to extortion, kidnapping and killing of innocent people to meet their ends.

3. **Ram Ahuja** in *"Social Problems in India"* - Page: 433.

Innocent Hindus who have been driven away from their original homeland are of the opinion that the Muslim fundamentalists and militants have infilfitrated every sphere of the government in the Kashmir valley. They have also alleged that the government is under the mercy of the militants and the life of the loyalists has been made miserable. According to them, pro-Pakistan forces have overtaken especially the Kashmir valley and there is virtually a total collapse of the administration.

On the contrary, the ordinary civilian Muslims are of the opinion that they are ignorant of what is happening in the valley. They also complain that they are unnecessarily harassed both by the militants and by the security forces. They further claim that they too have become the target of attack of the fundamentalist terrorists.

• ***Various Terrorist Organisations*** : Terrorist organisations such as *(i) Hizab - Ul - Mujahedeen, (ii) Jammu and Kashmir Liberation Front [JKLF], (iii) Muslim Janapaez Force, (iv) Iqwan - e - Musalmeen, (v) Allah Tigers, (vi) Lashkar - e - Toiba, (vii) Jaish - e - Mohammad, (Viii) I.S.I. - sponsored terrorists, 'Al.Qaida' etc.,* with thousands of their activist militants are posing a permanent challenge to the security forces on the one hand, and national integrity on the other. The first three of these aim at independent state of Kashmir, some others want the merger of Kashmir with Pakistan.

• ***Role of Muslim Countries in Kashmir Terrorism*** : According to some sources,[4] a large number of terrorists consisting of foreign mercenaries coming from Muslim countries such as Pakistan, Bangladesh, Sudan, Turkey, Libya, Lebanon, Afghanistan are indulged in acts of terrorism in Kashmir. Militants are given training in the camps across the border located in Pakistan and Pakistan Occupied Kashmir [POK].

Main Purpose of Terrorism is to Destabilise India : It is said that the ISI [*Inter Services Intelligence*] of Pakistan is the master brain behind all the terrorist activities going on in Kashmir. The main purpose behind all the militant and terrorist activities has been to destabilise the Indian Union and the state of Jammu and Kashmir. The most dangerous attack of 13th December, 2001 on the Indian Parliament by these terrorists, is an example in this regard. Yet another major terrorist attack that took place on 5th July 2005 on the disputed place at Ayodhya [*Ram Janmasthan*] has also been suspected to be the monstrous handiwork of I.S.I.

IMPACT OF TERRORISM ON SOCIETY

1. Terrorism Creates Serious Law and Order Problems: Terrorism has grown into global level and it poses a threat to world peace and order. It creates a serious law and order problem and if unchecked, leads to the disintegration of society. Its immediate aim is to challenge the existing law and order system and it gets its things done by exercising terroristic power. It intends to create fear even in the minds of the rulers. Yielding to terrorism or making compromises with the terrorists only mean the total collapse of the morale of the people and the socio-moral order of the society.

2. Leads to Uncertainty: Life becomes uncertain and it reels under the mercy of terrorists. The horror and terror let loose by the terrorists create an atmosphere of fear and panic all around. In order to spread terror and fear everywhere the terrorists even kill unarmed civilians including women and children. Organised crime and violence of this kind cause social disharmony and may make a large number of people hopeless and helpless. Failure to effectively combat terrorism, further intensifies this uncertainity.

---

4. **India Today,** May 15 , 1994.

3. Causes Heavy Loss of Life and Property: Terrorists kill people indiscriminately and damage public as well as private property wrecklessly. Conflicts between terrorists and security forces result in enormous loss of life and property. Terrorists have no concern for human lives and hence they do not bother about the loss of human lives caused by their deadly activities.

Some Examples :

(i) During the *"Reign-of-terror"* let loose at one stage of the Frech Revolution, [1789][5], in the time span of 6 weeks, more than 1300 men and women including the king and queen were guillotined to death.

(ii) Between 1984 and 1992, due to the terrorist activities of the Khalisthan terroritss of Punjab, more than 11543 ordinary people and 1667 policemen were believed to have been killed.

(iii) Due to the Pakisthan sponsored terrorism, between 1988 and 1999 alone more than 17000 policemen and border security force personnel, were stated to have been killed.

(iv) Due to Naxalite terrorism, in Andhra Pradesh alone, between 1968 and 2004 more than 2722 civilians and 518 policemen, were reported to have been killed. The story of devastation and mass killings runs like this.

4. Encourages Smuggling: Since terrorism has become a global phenomenon, the terrorists of one country may establish their linkage with other terrorists in a foreign country. Various insurgent groups which have secret connection bring illegal money and encourage smuggling. Terrorism has become almost synonymous with illegal drug trade. Most of the sophisticated weapons which the terrorists are making use of, especially in India are obtained by them through smuggling. There seems to be an illicit understanding between smugglers on the one hand and terrorists on the other. The drug mafia also takes the support of terrorists to carry on its illicit drug trade.

5. Retards Economic Development: In an atmosphere of insurgency, uncertainty and terrorism, neither business nor industry flourishes. Terrorists and insurgent groups often collect certain percentage of money from the employees and businessmen on regular basis besides collection through loot, and ransom. People who invest in business or public sectors start withdrawing from the area for safer places. Terrorism, thus demobilises capital and hampers the process of economic development. In India, both the public and private sectors have been spending every year crores of rupees to offer proper protection to their establishments. The Central and the State Governments are also spending crores of rupees every year just to offer protection to the VIPs.

6. All Developmental Activities are Disturbed: Terrorists very often target their attacks on Government installations like radio and T.V. stations, bus stands, railway stations, aerodromes and harbours, big factories, research centres, I.T. companies, defence establishments, etc. Disruptions in these only add to the problems of the common man. Condition of the poor becomes pathetic. Governments in power are forced to spend huge amount of money to meet the challenges of terrorism and ensure protection to the people which otherwise could have been spent for developmental works. In brief, because of the menace of terrorism, all developmental activities of the society come to a stand still or get disturbed.

A rich country like America, had to spend heavily to curb terrorism. Small and economically weaker countries like Afghanistan find it difficult to use its resources to fight terrorism but it is compelled to do so. As a result, all developmental activities have been

5. The political terrorism which we find everywhere today is believed to have originated during the time of French Revolution.

stopped there. Pakisthan which has been breeding terrorism, has also been affected by its own terrorists. Developing nation like India is also forced to spend a huge amount of money to curb terrorist activities.

7. Terrorism Causing Demographic Ups and Downs and Leads to Migration: Terrorists are not found in all the countries, and in the countries where they are found, they are not equally distributed. They are selective in concentrating in a few places from where they can carry on their terrorist activities. Ordinary people living in the vicinity of the terrorist centres get frightened at these activities. When terrorist explosions do take place every now and then, the regular victims of such activities, become hopeless, helpless and terror-striken. Failure of the Government authorities to give them adequate protection and security, ultimately force them to leave their place of birth and migrate to other safer places. **Examples** : Hindus, especially Kashmir Pandits, who were there in a relatively large number in Kashmir area, were forced by the Muslim fundametalists and Pakisthan supported terrorists to desert their original places and move towards Delhi, U.P., and other States.

8. Terrorim is Haunting Democracy as a Big Threat: Terrorism is a nightmare of democratic system. Democracy is a type of government which believes in healthy discussions, debates even peaceful conflicts. It does not believe in violence nor in the exercise of unlimited power. It is confident of solving and settling all disputes amicably and through peaceful methods without resorting to force. Terrorism is just the negation of it. The terrorist group always tries to impose its will on others through violent means. It believes in its ideology which it considers as ultimate and final. Hence, it is uncompromising on its aims and purposes and is not ready for any discussion or debate. Thus terrorism destroys the fabric of democratic society as it induces insecurity and rebellion apart from hampering the smooth democratic process.

9. Leads to the Alienation of People: It is common for the states affected by terrorism to make laws which tend to deprive the civil liberties and human rights of ordinary people. Illegal detention, house to house searches, denial of privacy, encounter deaths, harassment and punishments are the ways through which the state displays its power to deal with terrorists. As a result, many innocent citizens are affected which alienates them in general against the state which is the usual effect of terrorism in many states.

10. Erodes the Authority of State: Majority of the terrorists have transnational linkages and they carry on their operations in such a way that it appears worse than the conventional war. Sometimes, the states affected by terrorism carry on their own counter-terrorist activities through their defence forces or army in some areas which become vulnerable to terrorist attacks. Despite all efforts, the state fails to control terrorism and thus there is the erosion of the authority of state.

COMBATING TERRORISM

Terrorism has grown into a problem of serious consequences. Politicians alone cannot find a lasting solution for it. *Creating a general awareness among the masses and building up strong public pressures to combat terrorism* seem to be the only solutions.

The menace of terrorism has been tackled in different ways in different countries. It is not out of place to make a mention of three models or modes of combating terrorism. They are as follows: ***(i) the Israeli Model; (ii) the American Model,*** and ***(iii) the Indian Model.*** Let us now consider, in brief, each one of these models for the purpose of better understanding of the ways and means of combating terrorism.

1. The Israeli Model : *Counter-Terror and Anti-Terror Model*

Israel has been successfully meeting the challenges of terrorism for the past 60 years. The Palestinian guerillas and terrorists [i.e., the **P.L.O.**: *Palestinian Liberation Organisation* and its supporters] had been causing lot of irritations to Israel, right from 1950s. The Israel Government decided to suppress them with a heavy hand. The Israelis sharply reacted to the challenges of the P.L.O. by carrying out air attacks on the P.L.O. camps. They never hesitated to bombard the P.L.O. centres in the neighbouring territory of Jordan. They used tanks, war planes and sophisticated war weapons to destroy the enemy camps. These attacks caused heavy damage to Jordanian army and property. As a result, the public opinion in Jordan turned against supporting the P.L.O. When the P.L.O. shifted its base towards Lebanon, another neighbouring country, the Israelese turned their attention towards Lebanon. They invaded Lebanon and totally removed the PLO bases in its soil. Israel did the same thing to Arab countries when they intended to protect the terrorists.

The Palestinians later resorted to the tactics of highjacking Israeli civilian aircraft and also kidnapping the Israel civilians. This they did in order to demand the release of their leaders kept in Israeli jails. Israel government instead of yielding to their pressures intensified its attacks on Palestinian camps. It never budged to the criticisms hurled at its policy. It was finally, successful in humbling the Palestinian terrorists through its *"counter-terror"* and *"anti-terror model"* of combating terrorism.

- **Main Elements of Israeli Strategy**

1. No negotiations be held with the terrorists. If one yields to the pressures and demands of the terrorists they would multiply manifold.
2. Weakening the terrorists by organising calculated raids on their organisational bases.
3. Introducing tight and uncompromising security measures
4. Resorting to open violence against the terrorists and their sympathisers.

2. The American Model : *The Counter - Terror Campaign*

America which has its economic supremacy over the world, is highly vulnerable to terrorism. It has its economic hold over many nations of the world. Whenever the American economic interests are attacked or endangered, it first resorts to its economic weapon of immediately stopping its trade, technology export and all economic aids to its targeted nation.

When the economic weapon becomes unsuccessful America resorts to bombarding the enemy country and its supporting terrorists. ***Examples*:**

(i) America resorted to this method for Cuba in 1962 and for Libya in 1986 when its leader **Col. Gaddafi** supported terrorist movements like those of the PLO.

(ii) Very recently also America adopted the same method for humbling Afghanisthan which gave shelter for Bin Laden who was instrumental in organising a plane attack on the twin towers of the World Trade Centre [WTC], New York, U.S.A. on 11th Sept. 2001. America carried on for years its determined "hunting operation" against the terrorist **Osama Bin Laden** and his terrorist organisation Al Qaida. Finally, on May 1st 2011, Bin Ladan was shot dead in his secret hiding place at Pakistan by the American forces.[6]

---

6. ***Glimpse of the American Approach to Terrorism in the words of US. President Barack Obama:*** On december 1, 2009, speaking on Afghanisthan policy at west point, Obama had said : "Our over-reaching goal (in Afghanistan] remains the same : to disrupt, dismantle, and defeat Alqaeda in Afghanistan and Pakistan, and to prevent its capacity to threaten American and our allies in the feature." On May 2, 2011, Obama announced to the world : "... I can report to the American people and to the world that the United States has conducted an operation that killed Osama bin Laden, The Leader of Alqaeda, and a terrorist who is responsible for the murder of thousands of innocent men, women, and children". - ***Source*** : *Manorama Year Book* - 2012 Pg. 903.

(iii) Against **Saddam Hussein** - led Iraq also, U.S.A. resorted to the same strategy.

As it is made clear from the above, the American model of combating terrorism is basically *"counter terror campaign" and invasion.*

3. The Indian Model : *'Anti - Terror Model'*

Terrorism is not a new phenomenon to India. Ever since 1960s, India has been facing the challenges of violence and terrorism. As early as in 1960s and 1970s, the Government had tackled the problem of insurgency and violence in the North-east region and also in Jammu Kashmir through political methods. These methods however, were not successful.

The Indian Government organised a semi-military operation known as ***"Operation Blue Star"*** on June 6th 1984 against the Punjab terrorists. Similarly, it conducted ***"Operation Black Thunder"*** in Assam to counter terrorism. These measures were mainly ***"anti-terrorist measures"*** and not *"counter -terrorist measures"* in which police and military forces had taken part. Unfortunately, both the measures were not successful in either containing or removing terrorism. The Indian model of combating terrorism [as evidenced in the above mentioned measures] consists of the following aspects:

(i) Introducing frequent road checks; that is, checking the moving vehicles and individuals in strategic places;

(ii) Keeping police, military or para-military forces on temporary or permanent basis in sensitive or highly vulnerable areas; and

(iii) Providing elaborate security for the VIPs.

Unlike America, India is not able to show its physical power, or at least give a serious warning to those countries which supply the bulk of arms, or give shelter to terrorists or finance terrorism. On the contrary, the government on several occasions exhibited its weakness in succumbing to the illegal and disastrous demands of the terrorists as happened in Kashmir, Andhra Pradesh and Bihar. The Central UPA Government's failure to implement immediately the Supreme Court verdict of the death sentence given to the terrorist Afjalguru who was the main architect of the conspiracy to explode the Parliamentary House with a bomb blast) when the session was going on; and to another culprit and equally an inhuman terrorist Kasab who had taken a direct part in a barbarous attack on the famous star Hotel Taj, killing several innocent people and damaging crores of rupees worth property; has been widely criticised by the public, media and the political parties.[7]

The Israeli Model - More Suitable to India - ?

Of the three models of combating terrorism, the Israeli model seems to be better suited to the Indian conditions. The Israeli model is a combination of *"counter-terror"* and *"anti-terrorist"* measures. Wherever terrorism is found, its support bases are to be destroyed, even if they are found in the neighbouring countries. It is suggested that all those who directly or indirectly support terrorism of any kind must be mercilessly sacked. If the government in power resorts to "vote-bank politics", and shows softness towards the supporters of terrorists and ignores to take stern action against them, the final result will be suicidal to the country.

Mere police and military operations alone are not sufficient. As revealed in the Israeli model, people's active co-operation is very much needed in effectively dealing with the problem of terrorism.

---

7. Both the convicts had been in Indian jails since years under the most expensive protection of the Government, making a mockery of the Court Verdict. It was only after lapse of several years of the Court Judgement, that both of them were hanged to death in the beginning of the year 2013, that too after Pranab Mukherji became the President of India.

SOCIOLOGY OF TERRORISM

Terrorism as a global phenomenon, has several dimensions. It is both a problem and a challenge for the present world. Since it is spreading its tentacles to the nook and corner of the world, all right thinking people have reasons to be very much concerned about it. Of late, sociologists too have started making their own observations and studies of terrorism. They have now realised the need for developing a new branch of sociology called ***"sociology of terrorism"***. This new field of specialised study is expected to throw more light on the nature and dynamics of terrorism.

Basic Questions Confronting "Sociology of Terrorism"

"Sociology of Terrorism" as a specialised field of study has to address itself to some basic questions such as the following,

(i) How exactly "terrorism" or "political terrorism" or "terroristic violence" - originated?

(ii) In what way terrorism disrupt the political as well the social organisation ?

(iii) Is terrorism being used as a means or method for bringing about rapid social change?

(iv) How does terrorism explain the nature of the social relationship prevailing between a frustrated minority which has resorted to violence and insurgency and the ruling political elite which has the monopoly on the use of force ?

Basic Sociological Observations of Sociology of Terrorism

Though sociologists have not yet made any in-depth study of the phenomenon of terrorism they have made some interesting sociological observations about the same. Some such observations are worth mentioning here.

1. Terrorism is Not a Special Method for Initiating Historical Changes in Society: Though terrorism creates serious law and order problem by resorting to killing, attacking, blasting, kidnapping, blackmailing, and such other violent means, it does not proclaim to change the social system as such. Terrorism is not a special method to destroy the existing social order in order to bring a new one. *"No terrorist movement has ever succeeded in achieving its goals. Terrorists, therefore do not shape the course of historical events."*[8]

2. Terrorism Sometimes Helps to Unite People: It is true that terrorism demoralises and demobilises people and disintegrates societies. It is equally true that terrorism in some instances helps to unite people to fight against common enemy. ***Example*** : (i) On many occasions, Indians have expressed their solidarity and unity as one national community particularly against Pakistan sponsored insurgent and terrorist activities. (ii) Similarly, the Americans very strongly stood with their national leadership headed by President George Bush in suppressing the terrorist activities supported by Bin Laden of Afghanisthan.

3. 'Sociology of Terrorism' suggests that Both the Quantitative and Qualitative Aspects of Violence are to be given Importance in our Study: The *quantitative aspect* of violence refers to the amount of violence engaged in by the terrorists, the quantum of force utilised by the security forces, number of persons killed or seriously injured on both the sides etc. It may also include the amount of loss incurred due to terrorist activities and so on. The *qualitative aspect* refers to the effect of terrorist violence on the social order and particularly on people's faith or trust in the existing social order.

Example : In the Indian context, a relatively large number of people were killed due to terrorism in Punjab and Kashmir; Naxalite terrorism and ULFA terrorism. Two prime ministars of India namely Indira Gandhi and Rajiv Gandhi were assassinated by the terrorists. In spite of

8. **Ram Ahuja** in *"Social Problems in India"* - 2001, Page: 446.

these killings, people's faith in the democratic social order continues to exist. Does it mean that the terrorist activities were unsuccessful . ? We cannot, however, consider them as "unsuccessful" because, the terrorists have been able to shake and loosen the existing order. They have weakened the legitimating capacities of administrative officials and the pioneer elite. They have added much to the seriousness of the security measures and made the government to spend a huge amount on it. These measures have lessened and complicated the opportunities of the ordinary people to approach the leaders. Sociological approach towards terrorism makes us to give more weightage to the social impact of terrorism than to its "success" or "failure".

4. Sociology of Terrorism Warns that Terrorism Has to be Contained: Terrorism and political violence have become the bane of Indian society as they are so in many other countries. Both contribute to anarchy and chaos. Unfortunately, the disappointed and frustrated young people are falling a prey to the temptations of terrorists. It is high time that such deprivation and frustration spreading among the youths be checked. Simultaneously, the government has to take all precautionary steps to suppress terroristic tendencies. Sociology of terrorism suggests that nations of the world must make united efforts to face the challenges of terrorism.

As **R. Prasannan** has stated[9] the American success in killing the world's most notorious terrorist **Bin Laden** on May 1st 2011 could only reveal that its goal of defeating Al Quaida was achieved; but definitely not of terrorism. *"Terrorism never began with Al Quaida and Bin Laden"* and hence it never ends with them. It was there even before, and it continues even after the killing of Bin Ladan. [The attacks in Mumbai in July 2011 weeks after the killing of Osama Bin Ladan, are a case in point. Though they were low-key attacks they too killed people. Such attacks may be continued by the terrorist groups in one form or the other.] As Prasannan writes, *"Osama is gone but terrorism will continue to haunt the world because the issue has several other faces".* It is not enough if the world makes united attempts to suppress terrorism, it is equally important to isolate those countries which give direct or indirect support to terrorists and terrorist groups and exercise stringent economic and other sanctions against them in order to humble them. Only then, the world can witness a terrorism - free global atmosphere.

III Remedial Measures for Terrorism / Other Ways of Combating Terrorism

Terrorism which has grown into global level has posed the greatest threat to international peace and order. More than any other country in the world, India is hard hit by this problem due to the incessant support extended to terrorist groups by Pakisthan. Our newspapers and the media have been continuously highlighting the dangers of this problems and warning about its consequences.

Terrorism is basically a political problem which requires a political solution. Once a terrorist, is forever a terrorist, is the normal attitude towards terrorists. It is a fact that the terrorist is a product of society. The primary causes of ordinary people taking to terrorism are many and the basic causes are — *poverty, unemployment, illiteracy, low standard of living, religious indoctrination, etc.* A terrorist is born out of a combination of these factors or out of any one particular cause. A terrorist is a misguided and a mis-directed person and the political system becomes incapable of meeting his demands and also of the terrorist group to which he belongs. Counter-terrorism is strategically adopted by the state to deal with terrorism. *However, the state ends up eliminating some terrorists but not terrorism.* Thus, it is essential that the state facilitates democratic political negotiation, bargain and compromise between different interests so that it can initiate measures to weaken the foundation of terrorism. Ultimately, eliminating terrorism is not the sole responsibility of the state alone but of every individual, community and the society. No terrorist with such a destructive

9. **R. Prasannan** *[Chief of Bureau "The Week", New Delhi]* in his article *"Terrorism post -Osama" [in Manorama Year Book - 2012] - page - 903.*

approach can claim to be a freedom fighter. Terrorism undermines the authority of the state and so every effort must be made to fight against terrorism.

Though the Indian Government has not been able to contain it completely, it has taken some measures to control it. There seems to be two important ways in which problem can be tackled. They are mentioned below.

(a) Legal and Legislative Measures, and

(b) Non-legal and Non-Legislative Measures.

(a) Legal and Legislative Measures

The Indian Law Commission considered terrorism as organised crime and hence it had taken some legal measures to control it as early as in 1971. Right from that year to this day, the Government of India had taken some important legal measures to assure national security in the wake of terrorism. Of those legal measures the following ones may be noted.

(i) **MISA** : ***Maintenance of Internal Security Act - 1971***

(ii) **NSA** : ***National Security Act, 1980***

As per the provisions of these Acts, the Government had the power to arrest and keep under detention without any trial, those individuals and organisational heads whom the Govt considered as instigators of violence and chaos.

(iii) TADA : Terrorists and Disruptive Activities Prevention Act - 1985

The TADA was the first major legal measure that had been undertaken by the Government to tackle terrorism. TADA did not give scope for bail and those who were arrested under it were at the mercy of men in power [police and magistrates] for a period of at least one year. TADA was renewed in 1987, 1989 and 1993.

TADA was not found to be effective to fight against terrorism and by 1994, *National Human Rights Commission* [NHRC] and other human rights activists strongly demanded for its repeal. Strong criticisms were hurled against it. It was criticised as being misused by the police to harass people. Hence, it was allowed to have expired on May 23rd 1995.

From 1995 onwards, for a couple of years there was no special law to deal with terrorism. This situation never brought down the intances of terrorism. On the contrary, violence by terrorists only increased. The Government was again forced to think in the direction of a new legislation to curb violence. The Sept 11 (2001) incident at U.S., once again made the Govt of India to introduce a new legislation to counter terrorism.

The Enactment of POTA : Prevention of Terrorism Act, 2002

As mentioned earlier, it was only after the Sept. 11, 2001 terrorist attack on the U.S., the Government of India thought of once again enacting a law against terrorism in India. The terrorist attack on Parliament on Dec 13, 2001 further strengthened the resolve to carry forward the fight against terrorism. The President of India, hence, promulgated an ordinance called POTO [*Prevention of Terrorism Ordinance*]. This ordinance was later on approved and enacted in the joint session of the two houses as POTA [*Prevention of Terrorism Act*]. **Arun Jaitley**, the then Law Minister, described this act as follows *"An effective law to blunt the edge of the terrorist campaign which had claimed more lives than the four full-scale wars the country had fought since independence."*[10]

---

10. The Times of India, March 14, 2002 (Law Minister in Lok Sabha) The Bill was passed in the Lok Sabha after a long debate with 264 members supporting and 148 opposing it.

Following are the Provisions of the Act.

1. This Act defines terrorist activity as the one which has the intention of threatening the unity and integrity of India or striking terror in any section of the people. Possession of unlicensed fire arms also constitute terrorism.
2. A person is said to have committed an offence if he organises, arranges, manages or assists in arranging or managing a meeting with a terrorist organisation. The penalty is up to 10 years imprisonment.
3. An individual should also provide information to police about terrorist offence. If he fails to do so it can lead to three years of imprisonment.
4. It conferred legislative powers to an executive officer to make orders to cope with terrorist activities.
5. The police can hold or arrest anyone for six months without trial on suspicion of being a terrorist.
6. Life of the new bill is for 3 years.

Merits of the Act

1. ***Prevents Terrorist and Secessionist Activity* :** Terrorism is a violation of human rights. This Act is a big deterrent and a major instrument in dealing with terrorists and secessionist elements.
2. ***Prevents Destruction of the State* :** Cross border terrorism has become a deadly menace in the Kashmir valley. This Act is useful to isolate terrorist groups. Otherwise, terrorism may destroy the nation.
3. ***Protects Innocent Lives*:** Terrorism destroys the right to lead a life of security. This Act seeks to protect the civilians from unnecessarily becoming the victims of ruthless terrorists.
4. ***Helps the Nation to Prosper* :** Effective and strong laws help the nations to prosper economically as they need not show softness towards terrorists. Terrorists shed the blood of innocent victims which tends to demoralise the state. Acts like POTA allow the state to take up firm action towards the terrorists and proceed towards progress in the future.
5. ***Democracy Thrives* :** Democracy thrives in a peaceful and happy atmosphere. When the law and order situation is under the control of the state, it leads to a kind of confidence in the functioning of the state. This confidence is absolutely essential for the democratic system to thrive.

Criticisms

1. ***Unnecessary Detention Due to Suspicion*:** Terrorism is a very difficult problem. This Act provides easy solution of detention on suspicion. Difficult problems do not have easy solutions. POTA if misused may result in the whole prison filled with "suspected terrorist" citizens.
2. ***Misuse for Political Reasons* :** *"Peoples' Union for Democratic Rights"* conducted a study in which it found that out of 53,000 detainees under TADA, only 1% were actually convicted by the court. Of these, 30,000 cases have been pending for the past five years. In Jammu and Kashmir 20,000 TADA cases were filed but none convicted. In the light of this experience, it is contended that POTA may also be similarly misused for political reasons.
3. ***Innocent Citizen Likely to Become a Terrorist* :** As per the POTA, mere possession of unlicensed firearms constitutes terrorism. Anybody can plant unlicensed firearms on an innocent citizen and get him arrested on suspicion of being a terrorist.

4. ***Rights Not Protected*** **:** In a democratic society, right to life and liberty are very important but this Act seeks to take them away during certain circumstances.
5. ***Financial Terrorists Left Free*** **:** It is required, in the light of these criticisms that the scope of terrorism should include not only political terrorism but financial and social as well. *For instance,* there are many people who loot the savings of thousands of people. Such people should also be treated like the terrorists.

The UPA government [2010-2014] almost immediately after assuming power removed POTA including its provisions in another Act. The fear of POTA was mainly due to the bitter experience from similar legislation.

III (b) Non-Legal Measures to Prevent and Control Terrorism

For a complex problem like terrorism, legal or legislative measure alone cannot be the total solution. Since terrorism is caused due to economic, political, social, religious, ethnic, linguistic and other causes, its solution must take into consideration all these factors. In this regard, following non-legal measures may be suggested to contain and curb terrorism.

(1) Assuring Social Justice and Fulfilling Basic Economic Needs: Any strategy for preventing terrorism should have a short term method which is effective to deal with poverty and disease, suffering and injustice, social atrocity and exploitation. Poverty, hunger, disease and exploitations are the conditions that provide a fertile breeding ground for unrest and violence. It is said that many Indian youths have taken recourse to terrorism due to these reasons. What is required today is a reconstruction plan and such a plan for socio-economic development is an effective remedy against terrorist activity.

(2) Solution through Negotiations and Peaceful Talks: Terrorism is like a poisonous snake. The state should take strong action to crush the head of the snake when it is still small. For this, one should know the cause of terrorism and a motivating factor for a person to become a terrorist. Terrorists are not born. They are created by society. *"Nothing rankles more in the human heart than a brooding sense of injustice."* Observed **Justice Brannan** of the U.S. Supreme court. *".....injustice makes you want to pull things down"* says an Algerian terrorist **Frantz Fanon**. Violence allows a terrorist to overcome his inferiority complex, despair and inaction. It makes him fearless and restores his self-respect. Hate represents the first emotional step towards terrorism.[11] Hateredness breeds hateredness. It is only sympathetic and humanistic approach that wins the hearts of many misguied and misled youths. An appeal made with such an approach by Loknayak **Jayaprakash Narayan** won the hearts of many dacoits of Chambal Valley in Madhya Pradesh who surrendered their weapons and agreed to follow normal peaceful social life.

(3) Conducting Enquiry and Providing Justice without Delay: Legal appeals made by the exploited people must be looked into at the earliest and proper enquiries be held and justice be given. This will make the people to repose confidence in our legal and judicial system. They may not turn towards terrorism for *"obtaining justice"*.

Secondly, judicial enquiries must also be held immediately regarding the cases of individuals who are arrested as terrorists or their supporters. The process of judicial trial and judgement must be quickened and should not be dragged for years and decades. Real culprits must be punished and the innocent people must be let free. Justice delayed is often considered as justice denied. No individual should be forced to become a terrorist because of the failure of our legal and judicial system.

(4) Toning up of Police and Armed Forces: Terrorists throughout the world are making use of the most modern weapons and the most sophisticated technology for their destructive activities. Unless our armed forces and the police forces are given proper training and equipped

---

11. The anatomy of terrorism : Mahmood Bein Muhammad, The Hindu, Dec. 4, 2001. OB - 1.

with the modern sophisticated instruments they cannot do their best in tracing out and trapping the bases of terrorists.

(5) Role of Intellectuals and the Media in Mobilising Public Opinion Against Terrorism: Eliminating terrorism is not the sole responsibility of the state alone but of every individual, community and the society. One man's terrorist cannot be another man's freedom fighter. Terrorism undermines the authority of the state and so every effort must be made to fight it out.

The intellectuals of the society and the enlightened media must play a very positive role in creating awareness among the people to co-operate with the state authority in its task of suppressing the terrorists. Those who support terrorists and their terrorism in any form, may be under the pretext of ideological cause, are doing a great disservice to the society. It is very surprising that in India there are a few intellectuals, leftist writers, and university level professors who often directly or indirectly support Naxalite terrorists, fundamentalist terrorists, and terrorists committed to regionalism. Unless their connection with the terrorists is exposed the intellectual background and the support for the terrorism cannot be properly understood.

Some Instances of Pakisthan Sponsored Bomb Explosions that Took Place in India

Pakisthan which is in the neighbourhood of India is known to the world as the great breeding ground of terrorism. Pakisthan has been giving protection and shelter to world's most notorious Muslim fundamentalist and terrorist organisations such as - *Lushker-e-Toiba, Jaishe-a-Mohammed, Hijab-ul Mujahiddeen, Iquan-a-Musalmeen, Muslim Janapaze Force, Al Qaida* - and so on. It is also said that crores of petro-dollars from the Gulf countries flow to Pakisthan every year to meet the expenses and to support the cause of these terrorists.

As everyone knows, Kashmir is the bone of contention between India and Pakisthan. Pakisthan had waged three wars against India on the issue of Kashmir, that is to occupy it, and all the times Pakisthan was given a crushing defeat at the hands of Indian armed forces. What Pakisthan could not do through the direct wars it wants to achieve indirectly by encouraging terrorists to resort to terrorism in India and to create horror-and-terror in the minds of Indians particularly in Kashmir, and throughout India in general. Right from 1993, till today these terrorists have caused series of bomb explosions in different places of India causing untold miseries and incalculable human and material losses. Here is a list of some such major explosions and the losses caused by these terrorists.

- **12-3-1993** : In the **Mumbai** explosions that took place on this day, 257 people were killed and more than 700 were wounded.
- **29-10-2005** : In the series of bomb explosions that took place on this day in **New Delhi**, 70 were killed and more than 100 people were injured.
- **30-10-2008** : In more than 18 places bomb explosions took place on this day in Guahati [capital of Assam] killing 81 people and seriously injuring 450 people.
- **13-5-2008** : In the **Jaipur** series of bomb explosions, 63 were killed and 200 were wounded.
- **26-7-2008** : In the **Ahmedabad** series of bomb explosions, 56 were killed and 200 were wounded.
- **21-2-2013** : In the **Dilsukh** area of **Hyderabad** [Andhra Pradesh], that is near the public bus stand, there took place twin explosions in which 12 were killed on the spot and 84 were injured. There were rumours that the explosions were deliberately caused by the terrorists in relation to the hanging of **Afjalguru** [a notorious terorist who attempted to blast the Indian Parliament House when it was in session]on 13th Feb 2013.

In addition to the above mentioned major bomb explosions, the terrorists have attempted at various times and places in India to cause explosions to take place. Many such attempts were detected well in advance and a few of them were suppressed.

•••

Chapter 18

THE SCHEDULED CASTES THEIR PROBLEMS, AND WELFARE MEASURES FOR THEIR UPLIFTMENT

The Scheduled Castes [SCs] - Emergence of the Term Scheduled Castes - No Precise Definition of the Term SCs - Numerical Strength and Distribution of the SCs - Problem of Untouchability: Who are the Untouchables ? - Some Ancient References to Untouchable Castes - Criteria of Untouchability - Untouchability Within Untouchable Castes - Gradations Among the Untouchables- Origin of Untouchability : Traditional Theory - Racial Theory - Theory of Ceremonial / Occupational Purity and Occupational Theory - Problems of Untouchable Castes : Social, Economic and political Disabilities of Untouchable Castes - Harmful effects of the Practice of Untouchability - Removal of Untouchability : Early Attempts - Role of Dr. Ambedkar in the Upliftment of Untouchables : A Brief Biographic Sketch of Dr. Ambedkar - Role of Gandhiji : A Brief Biographic Sketch of Gandhiji - Measures for the Welfare of Scheduled Castes: Constitutional and Legislative Measures - Other Welfare Measures - A Brief Evaluation of Welfare Schemes - Increasing Dalit Consciousness and Its Effects.

All permanently organised societies are stratified. Most societies of the world have had their type of what **Ward** calls *"the lowly"*. The Romans had their *plebeians,* the Spartans their *'helots',* the British their *villains*, the Egyptians their *slaves*, the Americans their *Negroes* and the Germans their *Jews.* Likewise, the Hindus have the ***"untouchables."*** Slavery, serfdom, villeinage have all vanished. But untouchability still exists. The practice of untouchability from which the Scheduled Caste people have been suffering is the reflection of the state of affairs of more than 1/6 of the population of this country. For no sins of theirs a large section of the population is suffering from a number of disabilities arising out of untouchability.

All sane people say that there is no rationale behind untouchability and it must go. As **Gandhiji** said, *it must become a thing of the past.* Dr. Ambedkar and Gandhiji did their best to condemn the practice and to campaign against it. The Constitution of independent India declares in an unequivocal voice that *untouchability is abolished and its practice in any manner is punishable.* Various welfare measures are also launched by the Central and the State Governments to uplift the Scheduled Castes and the Scheduled Tribes.

For ages certain groups of people in India's hilly areas and villages have suffered isolation and disability. Geographic and social factors have added to their isolation. They have lived in a state of social and economic stagnation. These people belong to certain castes and tribes listed by the President of India in pursuance of the relevant provisions of the Constitution. These castes and tribes are known as ***"Scheduled Castes"*** and ***"Scheduled Tribes."*** Together they constitute about 25% of the total population of India. These two groups along with the so called *"denotified tribes"* and *"other economically backward groups"* are sometimes referred to as ***"backward classes."***

THE SCHEDULED CASTES [SCs]

Definition of the Term "S.C." – Numerical Strength and Distribution of SCs

The Scheduled Castes occupy the bottom most rung of the Indian social ladder. They form the majority of the *"backward"* or *"depressed"* classes. The term *"Scheduled Castes"* signifies those groups of people who were out of the caste system or the Varna hierarchy in the past. They comprise the bulk of *"untouchables"* or *"untouchable castes"*. These groups or castes have been discriminated against by the superior castes through the ages and they never had any kind of social acceptance from the majority of the people who belonged to the upper castes. They are distributed throughout India. Nowhere in India the Scheduled Castes occupy the top most position in the social, political or economic field, as a group. Their low social position continues even now though lot of measures have been taken to make them equal with others.

Emergence of the Term "Scheduled Castes"

The term *"Scheduled Castes"* is a politico-legal one. It was introduced by the British. It was first coined by the ***"Simon Commission"*** in 1928 and then incorporated into the ***"Government of India Act, 1935".*** The word *"schedule"* refers to a *"list"* or *"table"*. *The Govt. of India Act, 1935 "listed"* out or *scheduled* a few of the castes as the most inferior ones which required some special attention. This schedule or list of castes was designated as *"Scheduled Castes"*.[1] When India became independent, this term was adopted by the Constitution for the purpose of providing them some special facilities and constitutional guarantees.

No Precise Definition for the Term "Scheduled Castes"

The term "Scheduled Castes" is nowhere defined in the Constitution. Article 341 and 342 of the Constitution empowers the President of India in consultation with State governments to notify by an order, the castes, races and tribes which can be deemed as "Scheduled Castes".

Attempts Towards A Definition

Sociologists have tried to define the term in their own way. We may consider here the definitions of *Dr. D.N. Majumdar* and *Dr. Ghurye.*

1. **Dr. D.N. Majumdar** uses the term *"Scheduled Castes* to refer mainly to the untouchable castes. He defines: *"The untouchable castes are those who suffer from various social and political disabilities many of which are traditionally prescribed and socially enforced by higher castes."*
2. **Dr. G.S. Ghurye:** *Scheduled castes are those groups which are named in the Scheduled Caste Order in force from time to time.*
3. ***In simple words,*** the term can be defined this way: *The term Scheduled Castes which comprises of the bulk of the "untouchable castes", includes all those groups which are subject to some disabilities in major fields of life - social, religious, educational, economic and political.*

---

1 It may be noted that these castes were referred to as ***"exterior castes"*** in 1931 Census. The British described them as ***"depressed classes"***. **Dr. Ambedkar** also referred to the economically, socially and religiously exploited group of lower castes suffering from "untouchability" as *"depressed classes"*.

UNTOUCHABILITY - A LEPER WOUND IN THE INDIAN SOCIETY

• ***Examples for SCs:*** C.B. Mamoria has listed the following castes as the most important castes that come under the category of *"untouchables"* – Chamar, Khatik, Regar, Pasi, Kori, Dom, Dhobi, Dusadh, Balai, Mochi, Meghwal, Od, Bagdi, Bhuiya.[2]

• ***Some Scheduled Caste Groups of Karnataka:*** *Adi-Karnataka, Adi-Dravida, Holeya, Holer, Korama, Moger, Mundala, Madiga, Bhovi,* etc.

All the SCs Are Not Untouchables

It should be noted that all the Scheduled Castes are not untouchables. The list of Scheduled Castes also includes some *"touchable"* castes. Almost about 80% of the Scheduled Castes are *"untouchables"* suffering from various kinds of disabilities. However, people in general use the terms *"Scheduled Castes", "Untouchables", "Harijans", "Dalits",*[3] *"depressed classes"* in more or less the same way without making any difference between them. In this book also these terms are used synonymously.

Numerical Strength and Distribution of the SCs

The population of the Scheduled Castes has been steadily increasing. According to 1941 Census report, their population was about 48 million and it increased to 140 millions as per 1991 census report. This would constitute 16.48% of the total population of India. As per 2011 census report, the SCs constitue **16.6%** of the total population of India. Its share in the total population; almost remains the same for two decades [1991-2011]. The Scheduled Caste people are not to be seen in Nagaland, Andaman Nicobar and Lakshadweep. Their number is almost insignificant in Meghalaya, Arunachal Pradesh, Mizoram, Dadra and Nagar Haveli. In the remaining states, there is not a single thaluk in which Scheduled Caste people are not found.

As per 1981 and 1991 Census report, about **2/3** of the Scheduled Castes live in six states only. The highest number of Scheduled Castes is found in Uttar Pradesh [22.3%] of the total SC population in the country followed by West Bengal [11.4%], Bihar [9.6%], Tamil Nadu [8.5%], Andhra Pradesh [7.6%] and Madhya Pradesh [7.0%]. As per the 1991 Census report, in Karnataka there are 73,69,279 SCs [**5.3%** of State's total population] and majority of them live in rural areas.

Faster Growth of the Scheduled Caste Population

The number of people belonging to the Scheduled Castes has grown much faster during 1981-1991 than other people in the country put together. While the overall growth of population during the decade was 23.79%, it was much higher in the case of Scheduled Castes, that is, 30%.[4]

Concentration of the Scheduled Castes in Rural Areas

About 84 to 85% of the SC people live in rural areas and about 80% of them depend on agriculture. According to a survey report, almost 50% of the SC people are agricultural workers and they would constitute about **1/3** of the total number of agricultural workers in the country. Majority of them do not own any land. Of those who possess land, **68.8%** of them own land which is less than one hectare in size. About **2/3** of the bonded labourers are from the Scheduled Castes. Their literacy level is extremely low. It was 21.4% in 1981 as against the all India average of 41.3% [exclusive of SC and ST groups].[5]

The SC people who belong to the rural areas virtually live as agricultural labourers, tenants, and marginal farmers. Almost all persons engaged in jobs like *sweeping, scavenging* and *tanning*

---

2 **C.B. Mamoria** in his *"Social Problems and Social Disorganisation"* - 307.

3 *Dalit*: The term "*dalit*" can be used in a very broad sense to include all those people who are the victims of social, educational, economic and cultural exploitation. - Opinion of **Prof. Rao Saheb Kasabe,** Maharasthra.

4 *Ref:* **Ram Ahuja** in his *"Social System"* - Page: 365.

5 ***Source of Statistics:*** **Ram Ahuja's** *"Indian Social Problems"* Page: 143.

belong to the Scheduled Castes. In addition to the majority of agricultural labourers, we also find among them good number of *leather workers, weavers, fishermen, toddy-tappers, basket/rope - makers, washermen, scavengers, artisans, fruit-vegetable sellers, shoe-makers, liquor manufacturers, drummers, carpenters, iron-smiths and some others following petty occupations.*

PROBLEM OF UNTOUCHABILITY

Who Are the Untouchables ?

People who constitute the bottom most place in the Indian social stratification system are often regarded as *"untouchables"*. All of them come under the category of what our Constitution calls the *"Scheduled Castes"*. The word *"untouchable"* applies to the despised and degraded section of the Hindu population.

• According to **Dr. D.N. Majumdar,** *"the untouchable castes are those who suffer from various social and political disabilities many of which are traditionally prescribed and socially enforced by higher castes." In fact, he uses the term Scheduled Castes to refer mainly to the untouchable castes.*

• **In simple words,** *"untouchables" are those who occupy the bottom most place in the society and have been subjected to various social, cultural and other kinds of disabilities and exploitation for their very touch is regarded as contaminating or polluting the higher caste people.*

Meaning of Untouchability

Untouchability is a mass phenomenon of group prejudices and discrimination affecting about 140 million people. It is an ignoble practice associated with the Indian caste system.

- ***Untouchablity** is a practice in which some lower caste people are kept at a distance, denied of social equality and made to suffer from some disabilities for their touch is considered to be contaminating or polluting the higher caste people.*

The practice of untouchability is a stigma attached to the Indian society. It is an age-old practice and has its roots deep down in our social and religious system. **Gandhiji** regarded this practice as *"a leper wound in the whole body of Hindu politic"*. He even considered it *"the hatefullest expression of caste"*. He carried on a campaign against it throughout his life. Though the practice of untouchability in one form or another has been there in many other countries of the world, it has taken its ugliest shape in India. Millions of people have suffered from it and the suffering still continues though with less intensity.

Some Ancient References to "Untouchable" Castes

The untouchable castes were called by different names such as *chandalas, panchamas, svapachas, antyajas, atishudras,* etc. during the early days.

• **Vedic literature** also makes a mention of some *"impure"* groups which were there as early as in 800 B.C. People born of the prohibited *"pratiloma"* marriage belonged to that category and were called *"Chandalas", "Svapacha"* and so on.

• *Shastrakara* **Manu** was of the opinion that the *progeny of the most hated pratiloma union would become chandalas* or *untouchables*. In the vedic literature, we find the mention of *chandalas* as an ethnic group originating from inter-breeding of a higher caste or varna female [mostly Brahmin] and lower caste or varna male [mostly Shudra]. In simple words, *the chandalas who were regarded as "untouchables" were the children of the most hated union of a Brahmin female with a Shudra male.*

Table - 1

Total Population and Percentage of Scheduled Caste and Scheduled Tribe -1991

Sl.No	India / State or Union Territory	Total Popu- -lation ('000)	Scheduled Caste		Scheduled Tribe	
			Population ('000)	Percentage of total population	Population ('000)	Percentage of total population
	INDIA	**8,38,584**	**1,38,223**	**16.48**	**67,758**	**8.08**
	STATES					
1.	Andhra Pradesh	66,508	10,592	15.93	4,200	6.31
2.	Arunachal Pradesh	865	4	0.47	550	63.66
3.	Assam	22,414	1,659	7.40	2,874	12.82
4.	Bihar	86,374	12,572	14.56	6,617	7.66
5.	Goa	1,170	24	2.08	---	0.03
6.	Gujarat	41,310	3,060	7.41	6,162	14.92
7.	Haryana	16,464	3,251	19.75	---	---
8.	Himachal Pradesh	5,171	1,310	25.34	218	4.22
9.	Karnataka	44,977	7,369	16.38	1,916	4.26
10.	Kerala	29,099	2,887	9.92	321	1.10
11.	Madhya Pradesh	66,181	9,627	14.54	15,399	23.27
12.	Maharashtra	78,937	8,758	11.10	7,318	9.27
13.	Manipur	1,837	37	2.02	632	34.41
14.	Meghalaya	1,775	9	0.51	1,518	85.53
15.	Mizoram	690	1	0.10	654	94.75
16.	Nagaland	1,210	---	---	1,061	87.70
17.	Orissa	31,660	5,129	16.20	7,032	22.21
18.	Punjab	20,282	5,743	28.31	---	---
19.	Rajasthan	44,006	7,608	17.29	5,475	12.44
20.	Sikkim	406	24	5.93	91	22.36
21.	Tamil Nadu	55,859	10,712	19.18	574	1.03
22.	Tripura	2,757	451	16.36	853	30.95
23.	Uttar Pradesh	139,112	29,276	21.05	288	0.21
24.	West Bengal	68,078	16,081	23.62	3,809	5.59
	UNION TERRITORIES					
1.	Andaman and Nicobar Islands	281	---	---	27	9.54
2.	Chandigarh	642	106	16.51	---	---
3.	Dadra & Nagar Haveli	138	3	1.97	109	78.99
4.	Daman and Diu	102	4	3.83	12	11.54
5.	Delhi	9,421	1,795	19.05	---	---
6.	Lakshadweep	52	---	---	48	93.15
7.	Pondicherry	808	131	16.25	---	---

Note **:** Excludes figures of Jammu & Kashmir where 1991 census was not taken.
Source **:** Census of India 1991, Series 1, Paper 2 of 1992, Final Population Totals.

Ref. : **"INDIA - 1999"** - Page-13.

Table - 2

Increase in the Scheduled Caste Population in Decades			
Year of Census	Total Population of SCs in Millions	Percentage of the SC Population out of the Total Population	Increase in Percentage from Decade to Decade
1941	48 Millions	–	–
1951	55.3 "	–	–
1961	64.5 "	–	–
1971	89.5 "	15.50%	–
1981	104.75 "	15.75%	0.25%
1991	140.00 "	16.48%	0.73%
Ref. : "INDIA YEAR BOOK - 2001".			

- **Patanjali,** yet another *dharmashastrakara* considered *chandalas* as a variety of *shudras.*
- Most of the *dharmashastrakaras* considered the *chandalas* as forming a fifth category [that is outside the four varnas] and called them ***Panchamas.*** The Panchamas were *'untouchables'*. Since they were outside the varna system they came to be known as ***"Avarnas".***
- **Alberuni** referred to these *"untouchables"* as a social group called ***"Anthyaja"*** constituting the last and the lowest position in the society. Their socio-economic life was worse than that of the Shudras [of the Varna category] and hence they were called ***"Atishudras".***

Criteria of Untouchability

Untouchability in the Indian context has become hereditary. If a person is regarded or branded as *'untouchable'* for some reason or the other, not only he would remain throughout his life as *"untouchable"* but his children also would become *"untouchables"*. Still it should be remembered that untouchability did not and does not arise by birth alone. Persons become *"outcastes"* and *"untouchables"* by being guilty of certain acts that amount to grave sins. Untouchability indicates not only a low place in the caste hierarchy together with the existence of social and religious disabilities but also a low economic position as well. Most of the scheduled castes [about 80%] are considered to be untouchables.

As **C.B. Mamoria** has cited,[6] according to ***1931 Census report***, if a caste suffers from the following restrictions, it may be termed as an *"untouchable"* caste.

(i) Inability to be served by twice born or clean Brahmins.

(ii) Inability to be served by barbers, water carriers, tailors, hoteliers, etc. who serve caste Hindus.

(iii) Inability to serve water to the caste Hindus.

(iv) Inability to enter Hindu temples.

(v) Inability to use public conveniences such as wells, schools.

(vi) Inability to dissociate oneself from a despised occupation.

6 **C.B. Mamoria** in *"Social Problems and Social Disorganisation."* Page 306.

Untouchability within Untouchable Castes

Certain anomalies are found among the so called *"untouchable"* castes.[7] **D.N. Majumdar** [1948] summarised the position of the depressed [untouchable] castes in 1940s in the following way.

- These castes are not depressed in all states; the same caste may be *"depressed"* in one but may not suffer from any social or political disability in another. In Madhya Pradesh the same caste has different social rights and disabilities even in adjacent districts.
- The disabilities are more rigid where the depressed castes are numerically small and fewer or on the decline, than where they are numerically strong.
- Where the castes are of the same ethnic stock or are largely so, social disabilities are not numerous and are usually confined to those whose function is considered degrading.
- Where the higher castes are in a minority and the depressed castes constitute the majority, the degree of ceremonial pollution observed is quite less and often we find few disabilities attached to the inferior castes.
- Individual members of the depressed castes who have succeeded in life and who are wealthy and own property have been admitted to a higher social status.

Gradations Among Untouchables

"It is not to be imagined that within the circle of untouchability, for instance, there are no sub-gradations and all untouchables are equal among themselves".(1) **Mahatma Gandhiji** himself wrote: *"All the various grades of untouchables are untouchable among themselves, each superior grade considering the inferior grade as polluting as the highest class of the caste-Hindus regard the worst grade of untouchables."*(2)[8] ***Example:*** A *Chamar* thinks that he would be polluted by coming into physical contact with a Dom or a Bhangi. Untouchable castes such as Bhuyar, Byar, Khatik and Majhwar are very particular in keeping the castes they consider *"untouchables"* at a distance.

According to **Sir Blunt,** *"Eleven castes will not touch a Bhangi, seventeen will not touch a Chamar, ten will not touch a Dhakar, six will not touch a Dhobi or a Dom."* It is said that in Tamil Nadu alone there are not less than 80 sub-divisions, those at the top considering the less fortunate of their own brothers as *untouchables.* [**C.B. Mamoria** – 307]

Origin of Untouchability

It is difficult to estimate the exact period in which the practice of untouchability originated. Still it can be said that it existed in India even 2000 years ago. Thus untouchables have been in existence for the past 2000 years. There are different theories of the origin of untouchability. We shall consider briefly some of these theories.

(i) Traditional Theory

According to ***Manu,*** the *prohibited pratiloma marriage was the cause of the origin of untouchability.* Children born out of such a marriage were kept out of the Varna fold and were branded as *chandalas* who constituted an untouchable group. In the ***Chandukya Upanishad*** also there is reference to *chandalas.* In the ***Buddhist Jatakas,*** there is a mention of *chandalas* as the lowest caste people who were following the most degraded professions.

7. **C.B. Mamoria** has also cited some such anomalies. [Page: 306]. ***For example:*** *(i) There are untouchable castes with touchable sections. (ii) A caste may be regarded as untouchable by some of the "twice-born", and not by others. (iii) There are castes that are touchable to a Rajput but untouchable to a Brahmin. (iv) While in South India, the untouchables are supposed to pollute a Brahmin from a distance of as much as 32 yards, in North India, their untouchability is not so apparent.*
8. *Ref:* (1) and (2) quoted by **C.B. Mamoria** - Page: 306.

(ii) Racial Theory

Sir Herbert Risley and **Dr. Majumdar** are in favour of the racial explanation of the origin of untouchability. They say that the Indo-Aryans regarded the aborigines of India as a kind of inferior human beings and addressed them as *"dasas"* or *"dasyus"*, meaning *slaves* or *servants.* They also placed them in the lowest strata of the society and deprived them of all social and religious ceremonies. Dr. Majumdar argues that *the disabilities of the so called "depressed castes are not ceremonial, but are founded on racial and cultural differences."*

(iii) The Theory of Ceremonial/Occupational Purity

J.H. Hutton and **Prof. G.S. Ghurye** are in support of this theory. While analysing the origin of caste [also of untouchability] **Hutton** suggests that ideas of ceremonial purity were first applied to aboriginals in connection with sacrificial, ritual and certain occupational activities. According to **Dr. Ghurye,** *"Ideas of purity, whether occupational or ceremonial, which are found to have been a factor in the genesis of the caste are the very soul of the idea and practice of untouchability." Scholars* like **Laxman Shastri Joshi** have also supported it.[9]

(iv) Occupational Theory

According to **Nesfield,** association with dirty and impure occupations gave rise to the feeling of untouchability. It means low social status attached to certain occupations is the cause of untouchability. It relates to impure occupations such as removal of human waste and carcass, leather works, spinning, tanning, scavenging etc.

There are also other explanations for the origin of untouchability. It is evident from all these theories that the caste system, to a very great extent, is responsible for the development of the practice of untouchability. Conservation of the caste always supported the feeling of untouchability. The caste system also gave rise to the practice that *"untouchables" are born into untouchable castes and remain so till their death.* This feeling perpetuated untouchability. The practice of untouchablity assumed different forms and proportions in its prolonged history of more than 2000 years.

PROBLEMS OF UNTOUCHABLE CASTES

Majority of the castes that come under the category of *"scheduled castes"* are regarded as *"untouchables"*. These untouchable castes have been suffering from various disabilities throughout the history. After independence, the practice of untouchability was declared unconstitutional, but the fact is that it still exists. The sufferings of the untouchables have not come to an end. This problem cannot be solved by an act of legislation.

According to **Dr. Majumdar,** *"the untouchable castes are those who suffer from various social and political disabilities, many of which are traditionally prescribed and socially enforced by the higher castes. Thus, if the whole bases of untouchability are not destroyed, a simple provision for its legal status will bear scanty fruits."*

The "untouchable" castes have been suffering from various social, religious, legal, political, educational, economic and other disabilities. For centuries, they were denied political representation, legal rights, civic facilities, educational privileges and economic opportunities. During the British rule also, no proper attention was paid to uplift the untouchables to relieve them from their bondages. Even today they are not completely free from the problem which

9 "..... The entire system of caste gradation depends on the insistence on ceremonial purity, a counter part of pollution which is the main source of untouchability in various forms. The spirit of caste exclusiveness is inculcated by exaggerated notions of purity and pollution..." - **Laxman Shastri Joshi,** Chairman, Maharasthra Board of Culture - as quoted by **C.B. Mamoria.** Page 303.

made them to suffer for centuries. These problems can be grouped into three main categories. (i) *social problems* (ii) *economic problems* and (iii) *political problems.*

1. Social Problems and Disabilities

The untouchable castes have suffered for centuries from a number of social problems and disabilities among which the following may be noted.

(i) Lowest Status in the Social Hierarchy: In the caste hierarchy, the untouchable castes are ascribed the lowest status. They are considered to be *'unholy', 'inferior'* and *'low'* and are looked down upon by the other castes. They have been suffering from the stigma of *'untouchability'.* Their very touch is considered to be polluting by the higher caste people. Hence, they have been subjected to exploitation and humiliation. They have been treated as the servants of the other caste people. The untouchable castes have always served the other castes, but the attitude of other castes is of total indifference and contempt. They were kept at a distance from other caste people. In some instances (in South India), even the exact distance which an upper caste man was expected to keep between himself and the "untouchables" was specified. During the early times, they were branded as *"Panchamas, Antyajas, Svapachas, Atishudras, Chandalas, Avarnas"* etc. and were given the bottom most place in society. The distinction that arose between ***Aryans*** and ***Anaryas*** centuries ago, culminated in the practice of untouchability. *Anaryas* were branded as *"dasas"* or servants and kept at a distance. They were not given any good position in the army, politics and public life, but made to follow *"unclean"* occupations such as scavenging, removing human waste and dead animals, tanning, shoe-making, spinning, washing clothes, barbering, supplying water and so on. The physical touch of these people following "unclean" occupations was considered enough to pollute the so called upper caste [varna] people. Thus, the so called 'untouchables' were not only kept at a distance but also denied various civic facilities. Several disabilities were attributed to them.

(ii) Civic Disabilities: For a long time the untouchable castes were not allowed to use public places and avail of civic facilities such as - village wells, ponds, temples, hostels, hotels, schools, hospitals, lecture halls, dharmashalas, choultries, etc. They were forced to live on the outskirts of the towns and villages during the early days. Even today they are segregated from others spatially. They were not allowed to enter the houses of the higher castes. They were allowed to work as labourers during the construction of houses or repair, storing grains, etc. But later, the houses were purified by sprinkling cow urine or cow dung. In South India, restrictions were imposed on the mode of construction of their houses, types of dresses and patterns of their ornamentation. Some lower caste people were not allowed to carry umbrellas, to wear shoes or golden ornaments and to milk cows. They were prohibited from covering the upper part of their body. The services of barbers, washermen and tailors were refused to them. In the court of justice also, they had to shout from the pointed distance and take their chance of being heard.

(iii) Educational Disabilities: The untouchables were forbidden from taking up to education during the early days. Sanskrit education was denied to them. Public schools and other educational institutions were closed for them. Even today majority of them are illiterate and ignorant.

The literacy level of scheduled castes is extremely poor [21.4% in 1981]. It is less than half of the national average. In some places of the states like Bihar, Rajasthan, Madhya Pradesh and Uttar Pradesh, their literacy level is less than 1/4 of the national average. The literacy percentage among the SCs, however, had increased to 37.41% in 1991 [SC males 49.9% and SC females 23.76%] and the corresponding national average figures were 52.21% [64.13% and 39.29%]. Female literacy is still poorer among them. In 1991, only 23.76% of SC women were literate while in Bihar, SC women's literacy level stood at the lowest minimum. At college level and university level and in professional courses, comparatively a very limited number of S.C. students are studying even after more than six decades of independence.

• ***Poor Educational Performance:*** The performance of Scheduled Caste students in the educational field is also relatively poor. The pass percentage of the SCs at the high school level is 53, at the graduate level 35, and at the post-graduate level 60. The corresponding general pass percentage figures are : 65, 57 and 76 respectively. In professional courses, their pass percentage is 60.[10] Even in the entrance tests for professional courses, the poor quality of their education is very much evident. The enrolment of SCs at primary, secondary and high school levels is also far less than the national average.

(iv) Religious Disabilities: The untouchables also suffer from religious disabilities even today. They are not allowed to enter temples in many places. Even after the successful campaign of **Dr. Ambedkar** demanding the untouchables right to enter the **Kalaram** temple at **Nasik** in 1930, things have not improved much. The Brahmins who offer their priestly services to some lower castes, are not prepared to officiate the ceremonies of the 'untouchable' castes. They do not even bow down to the deities of these 'untouchable' castes. The *Vedic mantras* which are considered to be more pure, could not be listened to and chanted by the untouchables because of the taboos. They were only permitted to make use of the *upanishadic mantras* which are considered to be less pure and more secular. Burial grounds were also denied to them in many places. However, things have started improving radically in these matters especially after 1990s.

2. Economic Problems and Disabilities

The untouchables are economically backward and have been suffering from various economic disabilities.

(i) Right of Landed Property Ownership Denied for Centuries: For centuries the untouchables were not allowed to have land and business of their own. It is only recently their ownership to the property has become recognised. The propertied people are comparatively less among them. Majority of them depend upon agriculture but only a few of them [hardly 28%] own land.

(ii) Selection of Occupations Limited: The caste system imposes restrictions on the occupational choice of the members. The occupational choice was very much limited for the untouchables. They were not allowed to take up to occupations which were reserved for the upper caste people. They were forced to stick on to the traditional inferior occupations such as curing hides, removing the human wastes, sweeping, scavenging, oil grinding, spinning, tanning, shoe-making, leather works, carrying the dead animals, etc. These occupations were regarded as *"degraded"* and *"inferior"*.

(iii) Failure to Fill in the Full Quota of Reserved Posts: The SCs have not been able to take full advantage of the reserved seats allotted to them in government jobs. The data collected from the Reports of the Commissioner for SCs and STs reveal that the representation in Central Government departments, public sector undertakings, and the nationalised banks in 1993 was **7%** to **10%** in **"A"** group posts, **9%** to **14%** in **"B"** group posts, **13%** to **19%** in **"C"** group posts, and **21%** to **23%** in **"D"** group posts. It is known that their [SCs] full quota positions in **"A"** and **"B"** groups is not filled in because eligible candidates are not available. The poor educational performance of the SC candidates has been the major obstacle in this regard.

---

10 ***Source*:** **Prasad L.M.** in the article *"Educational Policy for SCs and STs and its Implementation"* in *"The Indian Journal of Public Administration"*, New Delhi, October-December, 1996 : 908-932.

(iv) Landless Labourers: Majority of untouchables are today working as landless labourers. More than 90% of the agricultural labourers in India belong to the depressed classes which include the Scheduled Caste and Scheduled Tribes. According to 1981 census, more than 52% of the Scheduled Caste workers in rural areas are agricultural labourers. A large number of SC families are in debts. Their indebtedness is increasing day by day. The SCs are economically exploited by the upper caste people. Even today they are the lowest paid workers. Some of them continue to suffer as *bonded labourers* at the hands of the other higher caste people. The untouchables constituted 90% of the total number of the bonded labourers found in India, according to a recent survey report. It is also observed that a large number of atrocities are committed against the untouchables because of economic reasons. **For example,** In 1977, as many as 10879 atrocities were committed against them and the figure increased to 15,053 in 1978 and then to 32,990 in 1995. Though jobs are reserved for them in government department due to lack of eligibility they are not able to get into them.

3. Political Disabilities

The untouchables hardly participated in the political matters for centuries. They were not given any place in politics, administration and the general governance of the country. They were not allowed to hold any public post. Political rights and representation were denied to them. Under the British rule, they were given the right to vote for the first time. After independence, equal political opportunities and rights have been provided for the SCs also. Politically, the SCs are yet to become a decisive force.

The untouchables or the SCs living in the city are trying to organise themselves in the form of *"Dalit Sangharsha Samithi"* and such other organisations to fight for their rights. But the vast mass of rural SCs are totally unorganised. Political parties such as *"The Republican Party of India"*, started by **Dr. Ambedkar,** *"Dalit Panthers' Party"* [of 1970s], *"Bahujana Samajavadi Party"* [BSP of 1980s] are no doubt mobilising the SCs but so far they have not been able to form a *"dalit lobby"* at the national level except in some pockets. Their political influence is mostly localised. Their total influence in the Indian politics is, so far, not very much impressive.

4. Problem of Atrocities Against Untouchables [SCs]

Another problem confronting the untouchables is that lot of atrocities are being committed against them. In fact, such atrocities are on the increase now. According to the report of ***"Crime in India"*** [1995], *"Every 2 hours, 1 dalit is assaulted, every day, 3 dalit women are raped, 2 dalits are murdered and 2 dalit houses burnt."* Further, as per the same report, in 1955, about 180 cases of atrocities committed against the SCs were registered with the police, and this number increased to 32,990 in 1995.

In some states, severe caste conflicts are taking place and in many instances the targets of attack are the SCs. Bihar is notorious for caste conflicts. Bihar has sheltered several ***"jati senas"*** which take a leading role in caste conflicts. For example, *Bhoomi Sena* of Kurmis, *Lorik Sena* of Yadavs, *Brahmarshi* and *Ranvir Sena* of the Bhumihars, *Ganga Sena* of the Brahmins, and the *Kunwar Sena* of the Rajputs, represent such *jati senas.* Further, there are also the Naxal groups of *Maoist Communist Centre* [MCC] which normally consist of people who belong to communities of the Yadavs, Koeris, and the Paswans. These jati senas and Naxal groups organised mass murders in the past. The reason for these murders was a long standing conflict between upper caste landowners and landless *dalit* farmers. The National Commission of the SCs and STs have also been regularly reporting an increase in the number of atrocities against the SCs. The Central and the State governments are also seriously concerned with these crimes.

Harmful Effects of the Practice of Untouchability

The practice of untouchability gave rise not only to various kinds of disabilities but also caused damage to the Indian society. A few of such evil effects are mentioned below.

1. Untouchability *divided the Hindu society into the 'touchable'* and *'untouchable'* groups and served to develop mutual dislike, contempt and sometimes even enmity between the two. It damaged social harmony and created wide social distance between the two groups.
2. Since more than 1/6 of the total population of this land was labelled as *"untouchable"*, its *socio-economic and educational progress was unwarrantedly halted for centuries.*
3. *Untouchability perpetuates inequality.* Hence it cannot support the development of healthy democratic traditions. It has affected our democratic system very badly.
4. *Untouchability provided scope for religious conversions.* Those untouchables who got disillusioned with the Hindu society got converted to other religions such as Christianity or Islam. Dr. Ambedkar himself had joined Buddhism at the fag end of his life in protest against the caste-controlled Hinduism.[11]
5. Untouchability led to *perennial conflicts between the upper castes and lower castes* for generations, sometimes resulting in loot, arson, murder, rape, molestation, burning of houses and crops and so on.
6. *Untouchability has damaged the self-image of the SCs.* It has developed in them a sense of inferiority and lack of confidence which damaged their personality development.
7. Due to the practice of untouchability, the nation was *deprived of the opportunity for making use of the talents, abilities and creative capacities* of a sizeable number of people for hundreds of years.
8. *The practice of untouchability is a black spot on the Hindu society.* It is an insult to the Hindu society. It has brought down the image of the Indians in the eyes of the foreigners.
9. Social reform movements and developmental activities could not take place in the Hindu society smoothly and effectively for it was divided vertically into *"touchable"* and *"untouchable"* castes. Even the great reformers like the Buddha, Mahaveera, Basavanna, Shankaracharya, Vivekananda, Dayananda Saraswathi, Gandhiji, Ambedkar and a host of others could not attain complete success in their attempts to remove untouchability.

Untouchability has done enough damage to the Hindu society. As **Gandhiji** said *it should become the thing of the past.* It is slowly disappearing. The earlier it goes the better it will be for the nation.

REMOVAL OF UNTOUCHABILITY

Early Attempts of Eradication of Untouchability

Ever since the time of the Buddha and Mahavira attempts have been made to remove the social disabilities of the degraded castes including untouchability. The Buddha and Mahavira said that caste is no bar to communion with God. In fact, the Buddhism and Jainism rose as a challenge to the rigid caste system with all its evils. Thinkers and reformers like Basavanna, Kabirdas, Santa Tukaram, Guru Nanak, Tulsidas, Ramdas, Namadeva, Santa Jnaneshwar and a host of others have advocated the removal of caste distinctions, including untouchability for the good of humanity. The ***Bhakti* Cult** popularised by Purandara Das, Kanaka Das, Vadiraj and others, and the ***Veerashaivism*** established and propagated by Basavanna contributed a great deal to the removal of untouchability.

11 Such conversion of religion was reported in Meenakshipuram in Tamil Nadu in February 1981 in which about 1000 Harijans were converted into Islam.

During the British rule in the 19th and 20th centuries, a number of social reformers tried to eradicate untouchability. They launched movements against untouchability and built organisations to reform the Hindu society. Swami Vivekananda's *'Sri Ramakrishna Mission'*, Raja Ram Mohan Roy's *'Brahma Samaj'*, Swami Dayananda Saraswati's *'Arya Samaj'*, Atmaram Panduranga's *'Prarthana Samaj'*, Dr. Anni Besant's *'Theosophical Society'*, Thakkar Bapa's *'Harijan Sevak Sangha'*, Dr. Keshav Baliram Hedgewar's *'Rashtreeya Swayam Sevak Sangha'*, the Indian National Congress under the leadership of Mahatma Gandhiji, Dr. B.R. Ambedkar's All-India Scheduled Caste Federation, Sri Narayana Guru and S.N.D.P. Yogam in Kerala, the Vishwa Hindu Parishad and other organisations have played an important role in the removal of untouchability.

Intellectuals like Keshabchandra Sen, Iswara Chandra Vidya Sagar, Justice Ranade, Jyoti Rao Phule, Sri Narayana Guru, Gandhiji, Sri Guruji Golwalkar [of the R.S.S.] and others also tried to rouse the conscience of the people against the practice of untouchability. *The Harijan Sevak Sangha, Depressed Class Union, the Social Service League, Depressed Class League, the Scheduled Classes Federation* etc. also tried to remove the caste disabilities.

Role of Dr. Ambedkar and Gandhiji in the Removal of Untouchability and Upliftment of Scheduled Castes

ROLE OF DR. AMBEDKAR

Dr. Bhim Rao Ambedkar [1891-1956] was a great modern social thinker, a born fighter, a famous advocate and a humanist. Dr. Ambedkar who was born in an *"untouchable"* or *"dalit"* community called **"Mahar"** in Maharashtra took a leading role in promoting the welfare of the untouchable castes and in elevating their status. Being the most highly educated untouchable in India, Dr. Ambedkar became the undisputed spokesman of the untouchables. He took many steps to reform the ways of the untouchables. He fought against many of the injustices done to the untouchables by establishing a political party and a couple of organisations for the upliftment of the untouchables. **Pandit Nehru** rightly described him as the *"symbol of the great revolt against all the oppressive features of the Hindu society"*.

1. Dr. Ambedkar was the first man to make a scientific study of "untouchability" **:** Even though Gandhiji had thought of the ways of removal of untouchability before the birth of Dr. Ambedkar, it was Ambedkar who drew the attention of the Congress Organisation and also of the entire nation towards the grave problems of the untouchables and their deplorable conditions. Ambedkar had made a detailed study of the problem of untouchability, its origin, development etc.

2. Self-Respect Movement **:** Dr. Ambedkar had made it clear that his main aim in life was to remove the practice of untouchability and to take the so called *"untouchable community"* towards socio-economic equality and justice. Through his social-movement he wanted to instill in the minds of the untouchables the ideas of *self-dignity, self-confidence* and *self-respect*. Thus his movement is often called *"self-respect movement."* Ambedkar established an institution called *"Bahishkrita Hitakarini Sabha"* which added momentum to this movement.

3. Five-Principles or "Pancha-Sutras" for the Progress of the 'Dalits': Dr. Ambedkar wanted the untouchables or *'dalits'* to follow some principles in life so that they could attain a respectable status by their own efforts as a community. He recommended *"Pancha-sutras"* for them. They are :

(i) Self-Improvement: Making one's own efforts for one's improvement without expecting much from others;

(ii) Self-Progress: Making self-efforts for achieving progress in life;

(iii) ***Self-Dependence:*** Learning to lessen one's dependence on others and attaining finally self-reliance;

(iv) ***Self-Respect:*** Maintaining self-dignity and never sacrificing it for any reason.

(v) ***Self-Confidence:*** Developing confidence in oneself, in one's capacities and in one's efforts.

4. Call to Reform the Style of Life **:** Ambedkar made an appeal to his community people to change their style of life to suit to the needs of time. *"He urged them to stop the dragging of dead cattle out of the village. He wanted them to give up eating carrion, alcoholic drinks and begging. He wanted them to become literates and send their children to schools. Finally, he wanted them to dress well and have self-respect for themselves. Thus, one of his chief aims was to bring about a revolution in the way of life of the untouchables and in their aspirations for themselves and for their children."*[12]

5. Three Principles of Dalit Movement: "Education, Agitation and Organisation" **:** Dr. Ambedkar suggested three principles to govern the *"dalit movement"*. These principles are: *"education, agitation* and *organisation"* **:**

(i) ***Education*** is essential for helping the *dalits* to take out their mask of ignorance;

(ii) ***Agitation*** becomes inevitable to fight against all the exploiters and cheats;

(iii) ***Organisation*** is necessary to thrash out individual differences, to realise community interests and to fight for a common cause collectively.

After the ***All-India Depressed Class Conference in Nagpur*** in 1942 Ambedkar declared, *"My final word of advice is to educate, agitate, organise and have faith in yourself. It is a battle for the reclamation of human personality."*

Personal efforts to put the three principles into practice **:** Ambedkar himself worked to put these three principles into practice. Ambedkar encouraged the ***education*** of *dalits* through the organisations he established namely, *"Bahishkrita Hitakarini Sabha", "Independent Labour Party" and "Depressed Classes' Education Society".*

Ambedkar organised ***agitations*** in the direction of reaching his goals. His own words reveal his faith in agitations. *"The direct action in respect of Chowder Tank in Mahad [of Kolaba District, Maharashtra], the Kalaram Temple at Nasik and the Guruvayur temple in Malabar have done in a few days what milllion days of preaching by reformers would never have done".* He personally led the temple entry agitation at Nasik. In 1930, just 10 days before Gandhiji's *"Dandi March"*, Ambedkar launched a big temple entry movement at Nasik before the Kalaram Temple in which more than 15000 volunteers including 500 women, had taken part. *The programme of temple entry was more for creating social consciousness than for asserting religious rights.*

Dr. Ambedkar realised the importance of **"Organisation"** and worked to build a few of them. ***Examples:*** *"Bahishkrita Hitakarini Sabha"* [1924], *Mahad Conference or Dasgaon Dalit Conference* [1927], *"Independent Labour Party".* As early as in 1920 he had made attempts to organise all the untouchable castes and bring them under one banner. He had organised the first *All-India Conference of Untouchables* in May 1920 at Nagpur.

6. Call to Destroy the Caste System **:** Ambedkar in his efforts to raise the status of untouchables considered the caste system one of the great obstacles. He expressed his great disappointment with the caste as well as varna system. He even gave a call to destroy the caste system in his famous book namely ***"Annihilation of Caste"*** [1936]. He wrote in **"Harijan"** in 1933 - *"The Outcaste is a byproduct of the caste system". "Nothing can emancipate the outcaste except the destruction of caste system."* As an expression of his disillusionment with Hinduism,

12 ***Ref:*** **B. Kuppu Swamy** in his *"Social Change in India"* - Page: 207.

A Brief Biographic Sketch of
DR. B.R. AMBEDKAR [1893 – 1956]

Dr. B.R. Ambedkar is well known as a great thinker, a social reformer, a fearless fighter, a famous advocate and a great humanist. As a contemporary of Gandhiji, he rendered a yeoman service to the nation by way of his relentless fight against untouchability, inequality, injustice and casteism. He is ever remembered for his great contribution to the drafting of the Constitution of India.

☞ Ambedkar was born in an untouchable Mahar family on 14th April 1893 in the Ratnagiri district of Maharasthra. His father was Ramji an officer in the Indian Army and mother, Bhima Bai. Since he was born of an untouchable family he was humiliated by his high-caste school-mates. Ambedkar made determined efforts to continue his education undeterred by such humiliations. Awarded a scholarship by the Gaekwar [the ruler of Baroda], he studied at the universities in the United States, Britain and Germany. He entered the Baroda Public Service at the Gaekwar's request, but again ill-treated by his high-caste colleagues, he turned to legal practice and teaching. He soon established his leadership among *dalits* and became the chief spokesman of the untouchables.

☞ Ambedkar carried on his battle against untouchability throughout his life. Since he himself had suffered in his life as an *"untouchable"* at the hands of the Caste-Hindus, he had the strong urge to do away with it. He wanted to organise his community and to create awareness among his own people. He started a paper called *"Mooka Nayaka"* and organised *"Bahishkrita Hitakarini Sabha",* a depressed classes union. He endeavoured to convene an all-India conference to bring all the untouchable castes under one banner, *All-India Depressed Classes Conference.* He was not able to achieve it due to the non-cooperation of his own community people. He however continued his campaign against untouchability, both before and after independence.

☞ In 1947, Ambedkar became a law minister of the government of India. He took a leading part in the framing of the Indian Constitution, outlawing discrimination against untouchables. "He resigned in 1951, disappointed at his lack of influence in the government."

☞ Dr. Ambedkar's thoughts, ideas and philosophy are reflected in his books. His writings such as *"Origin and Mechanism of Caste", "Annihilation of Caste", "Who Were The Shudras?", "Who Were the Untouchables?"* etc. reveal his scholarship and the clarity of his thought. He was a legal luminary and is rightly rememberd as *"Abhinava Manu"*. He was awarded the *"Bharata Ratna"* title posthumously.

☞ Ambedkar's disappointment was growing because of the perpetuation of untouchability in the Hindu society. Finally, in great despair he renounced Hinduism and became a Buddhist in October 1956, together with his fellow untouchables at a ceremony in Nagpur in Maharasthra. He never got converted into Islam though he was tempted to do so by the Nizam of Hyderabad who was ready to offer him a huge amoung of money. He, however, died in the very same year.

☞ Dr. Ambedkar's thoughts and ideas are getting greater currency now. The number of his followers is also increasing. The struggle he carried on against inequality is also getting revived and reinforced.

he rejected Hinduism and embraced Buddhism with his followers in 1956. [He, however, died in the very same year, that is on 6th December 1956].

*7. **Political Role of Ambedkar*** : Ambedkar made use of political instruments to achieve the purpose of protecting *dalit* interests.

Demand for Separate Electorate for Dalits : In the *First Round Table Conference* convened in London in November 1930, Dr. Ambedkar who attended it on behalf of the depressed classes, spoke about the loathsome condition of the untouchables in India. He prepared a declaration of the fundamental rights of the depressed classes and submitted it to the minorities sub-committee. He demanded the abolition of untouchability and the establishment of equal citizenship. *He vehemently demanded a separate electorate for the depressed classes.* Gandhiji who boycotted the First Conference and participated in the Second Round Table Conference at London along with Ambedkar, opposed the proposal. He said *"the political separation of the untouchables and the Hindus would be suicidal to the nation."* He even said that he would resist such a proposal with his life. He declared his resolution of *"fast-unto-death"*. The conflict between the two leaders was, however, settled by the famous *"Poona Pact"* [1932][13] Ambedkar, thus, was able to get some reasonable representation for the untouchables.

Ambedkar who met Gandhiji in 1931 insisted on making the removal of untouchability a pre-condition for a person to become a member of the Congress. He supported the ***Anti-Untouchability League*** which launched a campaign all over the country to secure for the depressed classes enjoyment of their civil rights such as taking water from the village wells, admission of the children in village schools etc.

8. Ambedkar as the "Abhinava Manu" : Ambedkar was invited by the Prime Minister Nehru to be the Law Minister in the First Cabinet of Independent India. Ambedkar accepted the offer. He was made the *Chairman* of the *Drafting Committee* to draft the Indian Constitution. Article 17 of the Constitution abolished untouchability. Ambedkar had once declared that he would burn *"Manu Smriti"* for its failure to provide justice to the *dalits*. The same Ambedkar now could get the opportunity and the honour of giving to the people of India their Constitution. He is rightly called the *"Abhinava Manu"* [or *"Modern Manu"*]. He was awarded the *"Bharata Ratna"* title posthumously. Ambedkar's ideas, views and thoughts continue to influence and inspire a number of his followers who are spread over the entire nation.

ROLE OF MAHATMA GANDHIJI

Mahatma Gandhiji played a memorable role in uplifting the untouchables. Gandhiji popularised the word ***"Harijan"***[14] meaning *"the people of God"* - a word which was first coined and used by a Gujarathi Brahmin saint by name **Narasinha Mehta.** According to Gandhiji, the practice of untouchability is *"a leper wound in the whole-body of Hindu politic"*. He even regarded it as *"the hatefullest expression of caste"*. He made it his life mission to wipe out untouchability and to uplift the depressed and the downtrodden people. As a servant of mankind, he preached that all human beings are equal and hence the *Harijans too* have a right to social life along with other caste groups.

13 Through the **"Poona Pact"** [1932] Gandhi ensured that the election of the SC and ST representatives would be by all the voters in territorial constituencies allotted for the purposes. As there is no constituency in which SCs are in a majority, the Pact makes sure that the elected SC candidates are in practice acceptable to the other castes and communities in the area.

14 **Harijan** - "was a word used by the great saint **Narasinha Mehta,** who belonged to the Nagar Brahmana Community and who defied the whole community by claiming the *"untouchables"* as his own. I am delighted to adopt the word which is sanctified by having been used by such a great saint, but it has for me a deeper meaning than you may imagine. The *"untouchable"*, to me, is compared to us, really, a Harijan - a man of God, and we are "Dhurjan" [men of evil].

Source: **M.K. Gandhi** in ***"The Removal of Untouchability"*** - 1954 Page No: 14. Compiled and edited by **Bharatan Kumarappa** - Published by **"Navajivan Publishing House"**, Ahmedabad.

Gandhiji's Appeal to the Conscience of the People

Gandhiji believed in the fourfold division of the Hindu society into four *varnas.* He regarded untouchables as Shudras and *not as the Panchamas* or *fifth Varna* or *Avarna.* Hence, he sincerely felt the need for bringing about a basic change in the caste structure by uplifting the untouchables and *not by abolishing the caste as such.* He appealed to the conscience of the people to realise the historical necessity of accommodating the *"Harijans"* by providing them a rightful place in the society.

Gandhiji's Compassion for the Harijans : Gandhiji had much compassion for the *Harijans.* He said: *"I do not want to be reborn. But if I am to be born, I would like to be born an untouchable, so that I may share their sorrows and sufferings." He was of the opinion that the practice of untouchability was a moral crime. He said that "if untouchability is not wrong, then nothing in the world is wrong."* He believed that *a change of heart on the part of the Hindus was essential to enable the social and cultural assimilation of Harijans.* He was very much moved by their social distress and started a nationwide movement to remove their disabilities.

Gandhiji's Campaign Against Untouchability

Gandhiji who regarded untouchability as a blot on Hinduism wanted to do away with it completely. He wrote in 1920 *"... Without the removal of the taint [of untouchability], "swaraj" is a meaningless term."* He even felt that the foreign domination of our country was the result of our exploitation of almost one-sixth of our own people in the name of religion.

Gandhiji decided to stage a campaign against untouchability and was unprepared to make any compromise with it. He advocated positive means for the uplift of *Harijans.* He addressed various public meetings reposing doctrines of *Harijan* welfare. He led several processions of *Harijans* with other upper caste people and made them participate in *"poojas, bhajans, keerthans* and *puranas*". He believed that opportunities of *education* and *temple entry* would reduce social inequalities between *Harijans* and caste Hindus. He launched movements for cleaning *Harijan* residential areas, for digging wells for them and for similar other beneficial things.

Gandhiji wrote in *"Young India"* in April 1925. *"Temples, public wells and public schools must be open to the untouchables equally with caste Hindus."* He started two journals, *'Harijan'* and *'Young India'* through which he advocated his ideas. He started an *ashrama* where people of all castes and creeds could come and stay without any differences.

Gandhiji served the *"Harijan Sevak Sangha"* started by the social reformer **Takkar Bapa** in the year 1932 in order to promote the religious and social welfare of the Harijans. This organisation opened schools and dispensaries in various places and arranged for free educational facilities and scholarships for *Harijan* children.

Political Role of Gandhiji

As a much respected political leader of the masses, Gandhiji could never ignore the tasks of the removal of untouchability and upliftment of *Harijans.* Gandhiji entered the Indian freedom struggle in 1919. From 1920 onwards, under the leadership of Gandhiji the Indian National Congress committed itself to get the independence on the one hand, and the removal of untouchability, on the other. In 1920 itself, he declared that *"Untouchability cannot be given a secondary place in the programme"* of the Congress.

Gandhiji's Protest Against the Proposal of Separate Electorate for Harijans: Gandhiji was very much against the British policy of *"divide and rule".* He condemned the British policy of *separating the Harijans from the rest of the Hindus.* Hence he protested against the proposal of creating separate electorate for the *Harijans.* He said to Ambedkar who was in favour of the

A Brief Biographic Sketch of
MAHATMA GANDHI [1869 – 1948]

Mahatma Gandhiji acclaimed as the architect of Indian Independence, the *"Father of the Nation"* and the great *"messenger of peace"*, is known to the entire world. He was not just an individual but a great living force, a silent revolutionary, a man of courage, self-confidence and conviction. As **Dr. Radhakrishnan** points out, *his message is not just for the present generation but for the generations to come.* He ranks among the greatest leaders of the world of all times.

☞ ***Mohandas Karam Chand Gandhi*** was born in Porbander in Gujarath on October 2, 1869. Mohandas Gandhi, the son of Karam Chand Gandhi and Puthali Bai, did his early education in India and went to England, studied law and started practising as a lawyer in South Africa. He came under the great influence of **Leo Tolstoy** and **John Ruskin.** It was there he started his new career as an uncompromising fighter for human cause. He developed *Satyagraha* a new method of fighting against oppression. With this new instrument of *Satyagraha* he gave a severe blow to the British policy of colour discrimination.

☞ Gandhiji came to India and plunged himself into the freedom struggle in 1920s. Afterwards upto 1947 his battle against the British continued. He stood as a guiding force for the Congress Movement which had taken up the cause of freedom struggle. The nation stood as one man under his leadership. The British had to bow down and finally had to quit the land. Gandhiji could have become the Prime Minister at that stage. But he was not after power. He preferred to serve the people in his usual style without resorting to political instruments or power. Gandhiji did not have the fortune of living long to see the progress of independent India. He was treacherously assassinated on 30th Jan. 1948. Though he died, his thoughts, principles and ideals are still alive inspiring millions both within and outside India.

☞ The Gandhian views have a great value in the realm of human thought. His *"Satyagraha"*, a unique type of non-violent movement created history. It inspired leaders at the world level. **Martin Luther King, Nelson Mandela, Yaser Araafat** and a host of others derived inspiration from him.

☞ Gandhiji was an ardent believer in truth and non-violence. Search for truth was his life-mission. Where there is no truth there is no knowledge. This was not just a matter of his belief, it was his life-view. He was a strong advocate of *"Swadeshi* and *Self-dependence"*. *Khadhi* and *Charaka* which he introduced are only symbolic. He had the ambition of establishing a *"Sarvodaya Samaja"*. His concept of *"Rama Rajya"* is only complementary to it.

☞ Gandhiji took up the cause of the removal of untouchability as his another great life-mission. But he believed in the method of persuasion and not conflict. He carried on a relentless fight against alcoholism, exploitation, casteism and religious fanaticism. He really remained a great messenger of peace.

☞ The Gandhian views, thoughts and ideals are now facing an ordeal. Has the Gandhian way become irrelevant today? Is Gandhian achievement getting defeated in his own land? These are the haunting questions. No one need spend much energy to find an answer for these questions. Our own life-style and our own practice are themselves the answer.

proposal, that *"the political separation of the untouchables from the Hindus would be suicidal to the nation."*

Gandhiji declared at the *Minorities Committee* of *the Second Round Table Conference* in London [1932] that *"we do not want the untouchables to be classified as a separate class. Sikhs may remain such in perpetuity, so may Muslims and Christians. Will the untouchables remain untouchables in perpetuity? I would rather feel that Hinduism died than that untouchability lived. I will resist it with my life."*[15]

Impact of Gandhiji's "Fast-Unto-Death Satyagraha: In spite of Gandhiji's protest, the British Prime Minister decided to grant separate seats for the depressed classes and the right of double vote in which they could elect their own representatives and also vote in general elections. In protest against this *"communal award"* Gandhiji decided to stage the *fast unto death satyagraha.* This declaration of Gandhiji opened the eyes of the whole country towards the problem of untouchables.

In 1932, the *Harijan Sevak Sangh* was formed and its Conference at Bombay pledged that the right to use the public roads, wells etc. would be given statutory recognition when the Swaraj Parliament met. This pledge was stressed by Gandhiji in 1932 when he said, *"There could be no rest... until untouchability becomes a thing of the past."* The *Harijan* movement gained strength throughout the country. Gandhi went on an all-India tour to collect huge sums of money for the programmes of the Harijan Sevak Sangh.

Gandhiji Commits Congress for the Removal of Untouchability: At the behest of Gandhiji and the Congress, all the Congress candidates who contested elections in 1937 had pledged themselves to the removal of untouchability. As early as in 1931 itself, in the *Karachi Session of the Congress* and at the behest of Gandhiji, a resolution was adopted. It declared, *"All the citizens are equal before law irrespective of caste, creed or sex."* In 1938, the *Removal of the Civil Disabilities Act* was passed by the Madras Legislature which provided that no *Harijan* shall be disabled from any social or public amenity. In the same year, it also passed the *Malabar Temple Entry Act* which threw open the temples in Malabar region for all the castes. In 1939, the temple of Madurai was opened to the *Harijans.* Thus, Gandhiji's fast and his *Harijan* movement released tremendous forces throughout the country, which led to the removal of some of the disabilities of the *Harijans.*

- ***Gandhiji's personal involvement in the Harijan welfare activities:*** Gandhiji was not just a preacher. He practised what he preached. He could win the hearts of millions of *Harijans* because of his sincere approach to solve their problems. Gandhiji lived with the *Harijans* and shared their distress by inculcating in them the ideas of better social adjustment with the rest of the Indian community. He advocated equal opportunities of education and intermingling of *Harijan* students with those of the upper castes. He fought for various legal protections against several kinds of injustices done to them. He adopted a *Harijan* child and set an example for others to emulate. As a result of his sincere efforts and strong recommendations, untouchability was declared illegal under the Indian Constitution. At his behest, an opportunity was given to **Dr. B.R. Ambedkar,** leader of the depressed classes, to join the Central Cabinet and to be the chief architect of the Indian Constitution.

Gandhiji's Proposals for Harijan Welfare

Gandhiji's proposals for *Harijan* welfare include the following:

1. Those who claim themselves to be the servants of *Harijan* must serve the *Harijans* with all the dedication.

15 As quoted by **B. Kuppu Swamy** in *"Social Change in India"* Page: 211.

2. Awareness must be created among the *Harijans* regarding cleanliness, sanitation and health.
3. The practice of carrying human waste on head must be stopped.
4. They should be persuaded to drop their habit of eating carrion and dead animals.
5. Practice of untouchability must be immediately stopped by all.
6. *Harijans* must be provided with drinking water facility.
7. Good houses at low cost but with enough provision for lighting and ventilation must be built for *Harijans.*
8. *Harijan* children must be made to go to school and even adult education programme should be introduced.
9. Harijans must be persuaded to drop their habit of drinking alcohol.
10. Harijans must be allowed to enter all the public places and to draw water from the wells.
11. There should be no bar for the entry of *Harijans* to temples.
12. *"Harijan Day"* should be observed by all at least one day in a year.

Ambedkar and Gandhiji who fought against the problem of untouchability and served to promote the welfare of "untouchables" are not alive today. Their followers are, however, continuing their work. Untouchability has not yet become *"the thing of the past"*. The removal of untouchability requires a basic transformation in the general attitude towards it. Gandhiji was right when he wrote in his letter to Thakkar Bapa: "*The salvation of the depressed class will come only when the caste Hindu is made to think and is forced to feel that he must alter his ways. I want a revolution in the mentality of the caste Hindus.*" The country is awaiting such a revolution.

MEASURES FOR THE WELFARE OF SCHEDULED CASTES

The Government of independent India has been trying to uplift the Scheduled Castes and Scheduled Tribes right from its very inception. The Governmental attempts to promote the welfare of the SCs and STs can be classified into two group. (A) *Constitutional and legislative measures* and (B) *Other welfare measures and programmes.*

A. The Constitutional and Legislative Measures

The Government of India has incorporated some special provisions in its Constitution for the removal of untouchability and to promote the welfare of SCs and STs. The constitution ensures the protection and assures the promotion of interests of SCs, STs and other weaker sections of the population in the fields such as (1) *political representation,* (2) *representation in services,* (3) *economic development,* (4) *socio-cultural safeguards* and (5) *legal support.*

1. The Preamble of the Constitution of India declares that it assures equality, promotes fraternity, guarantees liberty and ensures justice to one and all.
2. Articles 15, 16, 17, 38 and 46 guarantee that the state shall not discriminate between persons on account of their religion or region and caste or class.
3. Article 15 prohibits discrimination on grounds of religion, caste, race, sex or place of birth.
4. ***Article 17 abolishes untouchability.*** It is further provided that the enforcement of any disability arising out of untouchability shall be an offence punishable in accordance with law.
5. Article 46 promotes educational and economic interests of Scheduled Castes, Scheduled Tribes and other weaker sections.

6. Article 330 reserves representation for Scheduled Castes and Scheduled Tribes in the Houses of the People.
7. Article 334 relates to reservation of seats and special representation to cease after fifty years [Originally reservation was made for ten years and it was extended five times].
8. Article 335 mentions the claims of Scheduled Castes and Scheduled Tribes to services and posts.
9. Article 338 empowers the Central Govt. to appoint a National Commission for Scheduled Castes and Scheduled Tribes.
10. Article 339 empowers the President to appoint a Commission to report on the administration of the Scheduled Areas and the welfare of Scheduled Tribes in the States.
11. Article 341 empowers the President to specify the castes, races or tribes deemed as Scheduled Castes in a particular State or Union territory.
12. Article 342 empowers the President to specify the tribes or tribal communities deemed to be Scheduled Tribes in a particular State or Union Territory.

Legislative Measures For the Removal of Untouchability

The Government has been taking up the required legislative measures for the removal of untouchability. In pursuance of the provision of the Article **17** of the Constitution which declares the practice of untouchability a punishable offence, the Parliament passed the ***Untouchability Offences Act, 1955.*** It was later substituted by ***the Protection of Civil Rights Act, 1976.*** According to this Act the offences of untouchability include the following.

- **Offences of Untouchability as per the *"Protection of Civil Rights Act, 1976"***

  (i) Committing any kind of social injustice, such as denying access to any shop, restaurant, public hospital, educational institution or any place of public entertainment.

  (ii) Preventing a person, on the grounds of untouchability, from entering a place of worship and offering prayers, or from drinking water from a public well or spring.

  (iii) Refusal to sell goods or render services to a person on the grounds of untouchability is an offence punishable with imprisonment for six months or a fine upto ₹ 500 or both.

  (iv) Enforcing occupational, professional, trade disabilities in the matter of enjoyment of any benefit under a charitable trust, etc.

Measures to Check Atrocities Against SCs and STs

Scheduled Castes and Scheduled Tribes [Prevention of Atrocities] Act, 1989, which came into force on 30th January 1990, specifies offences, which are considered as atrocities and provides for deterrent punishments for commission of the same. Comprehensive rules were also framed under this Act in 1995 to provide relief and rehabilitation of the affected persons. All the States and UTs [except Arunachal Pradesh and Nagaland] have specified Special Courts for trial of offences under this Act. Under the centrally sponsored scheme for implementation of the Act, State Governments are funded on 50 : 50 basis and UTs are given cent per cent assistance.

• ***Scheduled Castes and Scheduled Tribes [Prevention of Atrocities] Act, 1989*** describes the following acts as punishable crimes:

1. Forcibly occupying and cultivating the land of SC / ST man.
2. Confiscating the land / property of any SC / ST person.

3. Forcing an SC / ST person to eat or drink some disgraceful substance.
4. Throwing into the house or the neighbourhood of SC / ST person any rubbish or dead animal, etc. to humiliate him.
5. Forcibly snatching away the clothes from the body of SC / ST person and making him naked.
6. Insulting a SC / ST person in some way or the other.
7. Sexual harassment of an SC / ST woman.
8. Molesting or raping an SC / ST woman.
9. Polluting the drinking water source of any SC / ST person.
10. Forcibly evacuating an SC / ST person from his house, neighbourhood or village.
11. Preventing an SC / ST person from voting or forcing him to vote for a particular person.
12. Compelling an SC / ST person for forced labour or using him as a bonded labourer.

- **Special Measures Undertaken by Some States to Give Protection to SCs / STs Against Atrocities**

In order to assure security and give more protection to the SCs and STs some states have resorted to some special measures among which the following may be noted.

1. Assisting the SCs in obtaining the possession of lands belonging or allotted to them;
2. Helping the SCs agricultural labourers in getting statutory minimum wages;
3. Setting up state-level communities to look after various aspects concerning the welfare of the SCs.
4. Establishing special SC cells under the DIG Police to ensure that crimes against the SCs are properly registered, investigated and quickly prosecuted.
5. To ensure quick disposal of cases pertaining to the SCs special courts are set up in some states.
6. The bureaucratic machinery is properly dealt with for solving disputes of low wages, etc., concerning the SCs.
7. Specially instructing the police authorities to treat cases of crimes against the SCs as special cases and arrange for quick trial and prosecution.

B. Other Welfare Measures and Programmes for the Upliftment of SCs

1. Appointment of a National Commission for the Welfare of Scheduled Castes

A *National Commission for the Scheduled Castes and Scheduled Tribes* has been set up by the Central Government to safeguard the interests of the SCs and STs. It functions as an advisory body on issues and policies related to the development of the SCs and STs. The State Governments have separate departments to look after the welfare of the SCs and STs. Their administrative set up varies from state to state.

2. Educational Opportunities

Due attention is paid to extend the educational opportunities of SCs and STs and hence special provisions have been made in this regard. Free education, free distribution of books, stationery, uniform etc. giving scholarships, banking loan facilities, providing mid-day meal, arranging for free boarding and lodging facilities, reserving seats for SCs and STs in all the government and government aided institutions, etc. are some of the concrete steps which the Government has taken in this regard.

Centrally Sponsored Schemes: In addition to the above, there are some centrally sponsored schemes also for the educational benefit of both SCs and STs.

(i) ***Free Coaching and Training*** for various competitive examinations [IAS, IPS, IFS, etc.] to increase their representation in various services. Some of the coaching centres have made considerable contribution enabling SC / ST candidates to get into IAS and allied services, medical, engineering and banking services. During the year 1999-2000, ₹2.30 crore were released for this purpose.

(ii) ***Book Bank Scheme*** : Book bank scheme is intended to provide text books required for the students belonging to SC / STs pursuing medical and engineering degree courses. From 1991-92, agricultural, veterinary and polytechnic courses have also been included under this scheme. During 1999-2000, ₹2.43 crore were released for this.

(iii) ***Post-matric scholarships for providing financial assistance for higher education.*** Govt. spent 66.5 crore rupees for this purpose in the year 1993-94. The *University Grants Commission* [U.G.C.] and the *Ministry of Education* had earmarked 15% of their budget for this purpose during the 6th Plan - 1980-85. Beginning with mere 114 students in 1994-95, the scheme is presently covering nearly 20 lakh students. During 1999-2000, Central assistance of ₹160.89 crore was released for this scheme.

(iv) ***Construction of hostels*** for providing residential facilities to SCs and STs studying at college and university level.

(v) ***Financial assistance*** to those SC and ST students going to reputed research institutes for research work.

(vi) ***Providing Text-books*** to those studying in medical and engineering courses.

(vii) ***National Overseas Scholarships and Passage Grants for Higher Education*** : This scheme provides financial assistance to selected meritorious students for pursuing higher studies abroad in specified fields of Masters level course, Ph.D. and Post Doctoral research programmes in Engineering, Technology and Science only. The modified scheme would provide maintenance allowance of US Dollars 7700 per annum, or Pounds Sterling 5000 per annum per candidate in U.K. for courses covered under the scheme. From the very inception of the scheme in 1954-55, a total of 732 scholarships have been offered, out of which 532 scholarships have been availed of till 1998.

3. Expansion of Economic Opportunities

Government has taken up economic programmes also for the benefit of SCs and STs. **Examples:** Landless SC labourers are allotted land. Land reforms have been undertaken to bring benefits of land ownership for them. Poor SC farmers are supplied with seeds, agriculture implements, fertilizers, pesticides, interest-free loans, pair of bullocks for ploughing, subsidy for developing dairy farming, poultry farming, piggery, animal husbandry, handicrafts, spinning and weaving. The *"loan-mela"* programme of Rajiv Gandhi Govt. [1984-89] also provided small loans for the poorer section to help them to earn money through some secondary sources such as toy-making, basket-making, agarbatti and beedi-rolling, tailoring, shoe-making, etc.

4. Expansion of Employment Opportunities and Reservation

In order to enhance the economic position of the SCs and STs, the Constitution has provided for the *reservation in services.* Reservation of jobs operates in the All-India Services, Central Government, State Governments, and Government owned and managed public sector units and institutions. Reservation exists in all these for the SCs and STs to the tune of 15% and 7.5%

respectively. Several State Governments have introduced reservation for OBC's [Other Backward Classes] also.

In government services, special quotas are also allotted to them. The reservations are also extended to promotions[16] to higher positions to facilitate their adequate representation. Concessions such as relaxation of age limit, *relaxation in the standards of suitability, relaxation of the qualification and experience,* have also been provided to them.

5. Upliftment of Scheduled Castes through Five Year Plans

The welfare of the Scheduled Castes [and STs] has been given special attention in the **Five Year Plans.** The size of investment on the special programmes has been increasing from plan to plan. The expenditure of ₹ **30.04** crore in the First Plan [1951-56] increased to ₹**79.41** crore in the Second Plan [1956-61], ₹**100.40** crore in the Third Plan [1961-66], ₹**172.70** crore in the Fourth Plan [1969-74], ₹**296.19** crore in the Fifth Plan [1974-79], ₹**1337.21** crores in the Sixth Plan [1980-85], and ₹**1521.42** crore in the Seventh Plan [1985-90].[17] The State Governments have also been spending a sizeable amount on the welfare of these people.

- **Development Strategies in the Five Year Plans**

The Central Government sponsored a comprehensive three-pronged strategy for the development of the SCs during the 6th Five Year Plan [1980-85]. This consisted of three schemes: (i) *Special Component Plan* [SCPs] of the central ministries and State governments. (ii) *Special Central Assistance* [SCA] to SCPs for the Scheduled Castes of the States and (iii) *Scheduled Caste Development Corporation* [SCDCs] in the States.

***(i) Special Component Plan [SCP]*:** The main objective of this plan is to assist the SC families to substantially improve their income. This plan envisages identification of schemes of development which would benefit SCs, quantification of funds from all programmes and determination of specific targets as to the number of families to be benefited from these programmes. During the 6th Plan [1980-85] ₹ 4,481 crore were earmarked for the SCPs. Till the year 1990, only eight central ministries had formulated the SCPs for the SCs.

***(ii) Special Central Assistance [SCA]*:** The main purpose of this scheme is to provide additional assistance to the States from the Centre to help the economic advancement of the maximum possible number of Schedule Caste families living below the poverty line. This assistance is given through the SCPs. During the 6th plan, ₹ 600 crore was earmarked for this purpose. Later, in 1993, in one year, about ₹ 273 crore was provided as SCA.

***(iii) Scheduled Caste Development Corporation [SCDC]*:** The SCDCs have been set up in 18 states and 3 union territories. These SCDCs provide money and loan assistance to these families, thereby helping to increase the flow of funds from financial institutions to SC families. These Corporations established in the States are expected to interface between the SC families and financial institutions including banks. Both the Central and the State Governments are contributing grants to these SCDCs. For example, the State Governments' contribution in 1989-90 was ₹ 19 crore and the Central Government's ₹15 crore.

At present [2001], SCDCs are functioning in 25 States / UTs. The Centre contributes 49% to the Authorised Share Capital of the SCDC against the 51% contributed by State Governments. In 1999-2000, an amount of ₹20 crore was released as the Government of India's contribution. From 2007-08 to 31-12-09, Govt released ₹ 51.17 crore for the SCDCs.

---

16 "The Supreme Court in its recent judgement on the reservation issue on Nov. 15th, 1992 adjudicated that there can be no reservations in promotions but the Central Government decided to continue them for some time. The Supreme Court also declared that reservation in certain technical posts like *scientific departments, super-specialities in medicine, engineering and defence research, professors in education, pilots in Indian Airlines/Air India,* etc. is **not advisable.**"

17 ***Source of Statistics:*** **Ram Ahuja's** *"Indian Social System"* - Page: 370.

The Corporation also provides loan to the SC families upto ₹ 12,000. They not only arrange to provide financial assistance for occupations like agriculture, animal husbandry and household industry but also for small shops, industries, auto-rickshaws and many other trades and professions. Some corporations also arrange for irrigation facilities like digging wells and tubewells.

6. Other Welfare Programmes

(i) Drinking Water Facility: In SCs colonies and in the areas where they are found in large number, drinking water facility is provided through the construction of wells and borewells.

(ii) Medical Facility: Free medical check-up facility is provided for the SCs. Those who undergo family planning operations are given financial assistance for purchasing required medicine and energising tonic.

(iii) Janata Houses: In various States, the SCs are given financial assistance to have their own houses. In States like Karnataka and Tamil Nadu, low caste houses having all minimum required facilities, known as *"janata"* houses are built for them at State expenses.

(iv) Liberation of Bonded Labourers: A large number of bonded labourers particularly belonging to the SCs have been liberated. As per the report of the Labour Department of the Central government in 1983 about 1.13 lakh bonded labourers [out of a total of 1.61 lakh] were liberated from their bondage with the Governmental assistance.

***(v) Sulab Sauchalaya Scheme* for the Liberation and Rehabilitation of Scavengers :** This has been launched in several States for converting dry latrines into water-borne latrines in order to liberate SC scavengers and rehabilitate them in alternative occupations. During 1999-2000, ₹70 crore was released to the States for the implementation of this Scheme.

***(vi) Baba Saheb Dr. Ambedkar Foundation* :** The Foundation was set up on 24 March 1992 as a registered society initially to implement / administer four schemes, viz., (i) *Dr. Ambedkar National Public Library;* (ii) *Dr. Ambedkar National Award;* (iii) *Dr. Ambedkar Overseas Fellowships;* and (iv) *Dr. Ambedkar Chairs in Universities.* The Foundation has been reconstituted to include eminent persons in the fields of education, social work and development of scheduled castes. The scope of the Foundation has been enlarged to include more activities connected with the life and mission of Dr. Ambedkar. These, among others, include publication of books, foster academic contract, promote research, instituting awards, etc.

7. Voluntary Organisations

In addition to the Governmental schemes and instruments, some of the voluntary organisations are also playing an important role in promoting the welfare of the SCs. **Examples:** (i) *Harijan Sevak Sangh* [New Delhi], (ii) *Indian Depressed Classes League* [New Delhi], (iii) *Hind Sweepers Sevak Sangh* [Delhi], (iv) *Servants of India Society* [Poona], (v) *Indian Red Cross Society* [New Delhi], *"Ishwara Sharana Ashrama"* - Alahabad, (vi) *Sri Ramakrishna Mission* [Narendrapura, Purulia, Silchar, Puri], (vii) *Bharatiya Adimajati Sevak Sangh* [New Delhi], (viii) *Bharatiya Samaja Unnati Mandala* [Bhivandi, Maharashtra]. The Central Government has been giving financial assistance to these organisations for their Harijan Welfare activities. In 1994, the Govt. spent about ₹ 6.5 crore for giving such an assistance.

The Government also provides grants in aid to voluntary organisations of local character working among Scheduled Castes. During 1999-2000, 376 voluntary organisations were given grant in aid to the tune of ₹26 crore.

Some other organisations which are not getting any financial help from the Government are also rendering yeomen service to the Scheduled Castes. **Example:** *"Hindu Seva Prathisthana", "Vishwa Hindu Parishad", the service units of Rashtreeya Swayam Sevak Sangha, "Dalit Organisations"* and some of the *Christian Missionary Organisations.*

A Brief Evaluation of Welfare Measures

Have the above mentioned welfare measures really contributed to the upliftment of the SCs? The answer is somewhat disappointing.

- The Scheduled Castes spend their social energy in *sanskritising* themselves on the model of the locally dominant castes. They do not gain much out of this. Their *social mobility is very much limited.* They continue to remain weak in the local power structure for asserting their rights. They still are economically insecure.
- Majority of the SCs are still illiterate and ignorant and hence they are *not able to make use of the constitutional provisions guaranteed to them.*
- The reports of the National Commission on Scheduled Castes and Scheduled Tribes reveal that *the crimes against SCs are increasing.* **Example:** The number of crimes against SCs recorded by the police in 1955 was 180; it increased to 13,884 in 1979 and to 19,342 in 1987 and further to 32990 in 1995.
- There has been a quality of *ritualistic formalism* about many welfare and development schemes formulated for the benefit of these people. *Lack of enthusiasm* and *sincerity* on the part of the Government officials and agencies have also been the cause of failure of many of the welfare schemes.
- The benefits of the SC welfare programmes have been availed of by *a few people belonging to Scheduled Castes.* This small minority has developed *vested interests* and contributes nothing for the benefit of the majority.
- The Scheduled Castes are largely concentrated in rural areas and 90% of them [including 35% agricultural labourers] derive their sustenance from agriculture. In most of the villages, they continue to suffer from residential segregation. Hence, many of their disabilities still persist.
- It is unfortunate that in spite of 60 years of consistent efforts to elevate the position of the SCs, expected success has not been achieved. Socially, economically and politically, their status has improved very little. Socially, they have not changed many of their evil customs and their status remains the same; economically, more than 30 per cent of the SCs live below the poverty line and their occupational mobility does not lead them to social mobility; educationally, they are very backward; politically, they are not organised and remain weak in the local power structure for asserting their rights.
- The *"dalits"* are also not satisfied with their present position. Hence, they launched a nationwide campaign for the *dalit human rights* on 10th December 1998 [that is, on the *World Human Rights Day*] which focused on three important issues : (i) *right to touch and be touched;* (ii) *"no" to untouchability in the 21st century,* and (iii) *cast out caste.*
- The *dalits* demand for the effective implementation of the *SC / ST [Prevention of Atrocities] Act and Rules,* and to provide full protection to all *dalits* who participate in Panchayat Raj and other institutions – only reveals that they still suffer from a sense of insecurity.

• The SCs are still *tradition-bound.* They suffer from *a sense of inferiority* and this takes away their *'push'* to develop further. They are not well-organised. Only in cities some *"dalit organisations"* are trying to fight for their rights. Politically also they are not a single homogeneous entity. Hence, their political bargaining power is comparatively less. However, their political consciousness is growing. The younger generation among them is becoming more assertive. There is a positive change in the attitude of the caste-Hindus towards the SCs. Hence the social distance between the two is gradually getting narrowed. The social position of the SCs is comparatively better in South India than in North India. In Kerala, for example, the SCs do not suffer from the traditional type of disabilities. Greater changes are expected in their living styles in the years to come.

Increasing *Dalit* Consciousness and Its Effects

The untouchables or Scheduled Caste people are also generally referred to as *"dalits."* The term ***"dalit"*** has been interpreted in different ways.

1. According to the ***Marxists,*** *"dalits"* are those who are the victims of socio-economic and political explanation.
2. According to the ***Ambedkar School of Thought,*** *dalits* are those who are branded as *"untouchables"* on caste basis.
3. According to the ***Lohiya School of Thought,*** *dalits* are those poor caste people including the so called untouchables, who have been the victims of exploitation.

Of the three views cited above, the second one is more popular and widely prevalent. Thus, *"dalits"* are normally understood as *"untouchables."*

Increasing Awareness Among the *Dalits*

"Dalits" are becoming more and more aware of their position in the society. Various constitutional provisions that safeguard their interests, on the one hand, and the continuous exploitation of the *"dalits"* on the other, have led to an increase in what is known as *"dalit consciousness."* The continuous exploitation has made the SCs to become conscious of their separate identity. They have become more self-conscious. This growing awareness in them has led to the emergence of various SC movements and activated the process of Sanskritisation which M.N. Srinivas had spoken of. This awareness and movements have led to certain consequences.

Consequences of *Dalit* Consciousness

1. *Dalit consciousness has enabled the SCs in different parts of the country to form political groups.* **Example** : *The Republican Party of India, The Dalit Panthers Party* [Maharashtra]; and the *Bahujan Samaj Party* [U.P., M.P. and Punjab] could be cited here as examples.

2. *Dalits are becoming increasingly aware of the fact that they have a great political potentiality.* They have decided to take advantage of their numerical strength by converting it into votes. Where they cannot form their own political parties, they extend their support to the national-level political parties and demand attractive *"price"* for their support. However, in this process of political bargain only the educated and the organised *dalits* are taking an active role, but not the uneducated masses in the rural areas.

3. *The dalits are now putting pressure on the national leadership* for taking measures to remove the social disabilities of the *dalits*.

4. *They have been demanding the effective implementation of the constitutional safeguards* to protect their interests.

5. The *dalits have launched various "alienative movements"* which Dr. Ambedkar had advocated, and also a few *"integrative movements"* strongly recommended by Gandhiji. The alienative movements led to the caste consolidation of the SCs by fusion of a number of sub-castes into one caste group. ***Example***: *In Maharashtra, more than 52 sub-castes of Mahars got fused to forge one community.*

6. Apart from these movements, the *dalits*, especially the educated ones, are becoming **individually conscious of achieving social mobility.**

An analysis of *dalit* consciousness and its effects invites lot of questions : *Will the dalits ever be integrated into the main stream of the Hindu society ? Will they insist on reservation for all times to come ? Will this consciousness help them to forge ahead economically and educationally? Or Will this lead to ever deeper conflicts with the other caste groups in the society ? Will this consciousness help them to tred the path of peace, co-operation and harmony, or the path of conflict and confrontation with the other groups ? What will be the impact of dalit consciousness on the larger Hindu society ? Will they wind up the practice of untouchability ?* Many questions like these crop up in our mind demanding an answer.

It is difficult to find a satisfactory answer for each one of these. On the whole, the discussion could be summed up by quoting the views of **Sachidananda** [1976] : He holds that *"the combination of factors like ameliorative efforts of the government, the growing consciousness of the dalits and the liberal attitudes of caste Hindus will diminish the disabilities and discriminations with the passage of time."*[18]

About the Population of Scheduled Castes : As per Census - 2011

Primary Census Abstract

- The SCs constitute 16.6% of the total population.
- Between 2001-2011, the SCs grew by 20.8%, whereas the total population has witnessed a decadal increase of 17.7% to touch 1.21 billion.
- The highest S.C. population, 31.9% of the state's total number is in Punjab.

Source: *Manorama Year Book - 2014.* Page: 672.

●●●

18 Views of **Sachidananda** as quoted by **Ram Ahuja** in *"Society in India."* Page - 86.

Chapter 19

PROBLEMS OF SCHEDULED TRIBES

Definition and Characteristics of Tribe - Problems Due to the Contact With the Outside World - Problems of the Scheduled Tribes - Tribal Movements : Causes of Tribal Unrest and Discontent - Measures for the Upliftment of Scheduled Tribes - Three Views to Solve Tribal Problems : Policy of Isolation, Policy of Assimilation, Policy of Integration - The Tribal Panchasheela- Tribal Welfare Programmes and Projects- Brief Assessment of the Welfare Programmes : Their Deficiencies and Failures.

The tribal communities represent an important social category of Indian social structure. The tribals are said to be the original inhabitants of India. India is a country of multiracial stock. Different types of groups occupy different parts of India, having their own cultural characteristics and levels of development. A number of groups are still in primitive stage and they are very often referred to as *"tribals", "primitives", "adivasis"* and so on. The tribal population in India, according to the 1991 census, was **67.76** million. This was almost equal to the population of Britain. At present, India has the second largest tribal population in the world next only to Africa and their number must have crossed the mark of 10 crore. Tribals in India are spread over the length and breadth of the country.

"Tribes" in the Indian context today are normally referred to in the language of the Constitution as ***"Scheduled Tribes."*** It was **Dr. B.R. Ambedkar,** the chairman of the drafting committee of the constitution, who preferred the concept of Scheduled Tribe to *"Adivasis"* for it enumerates the tribes and hence has a specific meaning. The *"Scheduled Tribes"* constitute the second largest group of the backward classes that come under what is known as the *"unprivileged section"* of the populace. The scheduled tribes, generally known as *"tribes",* constitue **8.6%** of the total population [*2011 census report*] of India. The tribal people who are regarded as the earliest among the present inhabitants of India have survived here with their unchanging ways of life for centuries. Many of them are still in a primitive stage and are far from the impact of modern civilization.

The term ***"scheduled tribe"*** or ***"tribe"*** has been explained variously. For example, *Scheduled Area* and *Scheduled Tribes Commissioner,* in this regard observes – *"The term "tribe" is nowhere defined in the Constitution and, in fact, there is no satisfactory definition anywhere. To the ordinary man the word suggests simple folk living in hills and forests; to people who are a little better informed, it signifies a colourful people famous for their dance and song; to an* *administrator it means a group of citizens who are the special responsibilities of the President of India; to an anthropologist it indicates a special field for study of a social phenomenon. In their own way, all these impressions are correct. No standard term has been accepted to denominate the people who are classified as of tribal origin."*[1] **S.C. Dube** has also commented that *"the term tribe is used indiscriminately."* A few examples of the use of the term "tribe" can be cited in this regard. The tribals are referred to by various terms such as - *Adivasis, Adi Praja, Aranyavasis, Vanavasis, Vanya Jatis, Girijans, aboriginals, hill tribes, primitive tribes, indigenous people, etc.* **G.S. Ghurye** called them *"backward Hindus"*; whereas the Constitution of India prefers to use the term *"the scheduled tribes"* to refer to these people.

The *"Backward Classes Commission"* which was asked to revise the list of the scheduled tribes, states that *"the scheduled tribes lead a separate excluded existence and are not fully assimilated in the main body of the people. Scheduled Tribes may belong to any religion. They are listed as scheduled tribes because of the kind of life led by them."* At another place it said that *"the scheduled tribes could be recognised by their way of living, the way of their living being peculiar."* [**C.B. Mamoria.** Page - 170.] This definition puts emphasis on the peculiarity of the mode of life of the tribals.

There is no Definition but Reference only in the Constitution for the Term "Scheduled Tribe": The term *"tribe"* is nowhere defined in the Constitution. Though the Indian Constitution has not defined clearly the term *'tribe'*. Article 366 (25) of the Constitution says that *Scheduled Tribes are the tribes or tribal communities or parts of or groups within such tribes or tribal communities which the Indian President may specify by public notification under Article 342(1).*

It is relevant here to know the sociological meaning, definition and characteristics of the word *'tribe'* before studying the problems of the Scheduled Tribes and finding solutions for the same.

DEFINITION AND CHARACTERISTICS OF TRIBE

Definition of Tribe

There is no agreement among the sociologists and anthropologists regarding the definition of the term *"tribe."* Some of the definitions may be examined here:

1. **D.N. Majumdar:** A tribe is *"a collection of families bearing a common name, members of which occupy the same territory, speak the same language and observe certain taboos regarding marriage, profession or occupation and have developed a well assessed system of reciprocity and mutuality of obligation."*
2. **Imperial Gazetteer of India:** *A tribe is a collection of families bearing a common name, speaking a common dialect, occupying or professing to occupy a common territory and is not usually endogamous, though originally it might have been so."*
3. **Gillin** and **Gillin:** *"A tribe is a group of local communities, which lives in a common area, speaks a common dialect and follows a common culture."*

CHARACTERISTICS OF TRIBE

Definitions of tribe cited above point out some of the characteristics of tribe. Tribal community including the tribals of India generally reveals some of the characteristics of which the following may be noted.

1. *Common Territory* : A tribe is a territorial community. It means the tribe has a definite territory in which its members reside. **For example,** the *Naga, Rengma Naga, Sema Naga* and

1. **C.B. Mamoria** in his *"Social Problems and Social Disorganisation."* Page - 170.

other tribals reside in Nagaland; *Garos, Khasis, Khasas* live in Assam; *Bhils* in Madhyapradesh; *Soligas* in Mysore; *Thodas* in Niligiri Hills of Tamil Nadu, and so on. In the absence of a common locality or territory a tribe would lose its uniqueness.

2. *Collection of Families* : As the definitions of tribe cited above clarify, tribals constitute a collection of families. This collection may have various sizes. These families which normally have blood relationships among themselves could be matriarchal or patriarchal in nature.

3. *Common Name* : Every tribe has its own name. Each tribe is known to other tribes by its distinctive name. ***Examples of some Indian Tribes***: *Garo, Khasi, Khasa, Naga, Rengma Naga, Sema Naga, Limbu, Santal, Munda, Gond, Kota, Badaga, Urali, Thodas,* etc.

4. *Common Language* : The members of a tribe speak a particular language. Different tribes speak different languages. These languages are not only different from the language of the civilised people, but they themselves differ from one another. Common language contributes much to the development of community feeling. Since these languages do not have a script of their own, education of the tribals has become problematic.

5. *Common Ancestor* : The tribals claim that they have a common ancestor. A major cause of the sense of communal unity in the tribe is *"the tie of blood relationships"* between its members arising out of common ancestry. The tribals are bound by kinship bonds.

6. *Common Religion* : Religion plays an important role in the tribal organisation. The members of a tribe usually worship a common ancestor. Also, nature worship is common among them. In addition to the ***ancestral worship*** and ***nature worship,*** the tribals practise other types of faith such as - ***fetishism, animism*** and ***totemism.***[2] Magic is also widespread among them. The tribal social and political organisations are based on this religion. Participation in common religious ceremonies, functions and festivals contributes to the unity of the group. A sizeable proportion of Nagas, Mizos, Santhals, Oraons and Munda, etc., have embraced Christianity while some tribals such as *Butia, Lepcha Chakma* have largely identified with Buddhism.

7. *Common Culture* : Each tribe has a way of life of its own. Each tribe has its own way of behaving, thinking, feeling and acting. Each has its own customs, traditions, morals, values, its own peculiar institutions in brief, its own culture. The very peculiarities of a tribe reveal that it has a distinctive culture of its own.

8. *Common Political Organisation* : Each tribe has its own political system. The tribal chief normally exercises authority over all the other members. The chieftainship is normally hereditary. He occupies an important position in the tribal society. The tribals do not possess a government in the modern sense of the term. But they do have their own tribal government, tribal council and tribal court or judicial system. *Santhal,* for example, an advanced tribe, has a village council the members of which are democratically elected. Nagaland emerged on the first of December 1963 as the 16th State of the Republic of India and Meghalaya in the month of April 1970.

9. *Feeling of Unity* : The members of a tribe always feel that they are united. This sense of

---

2. **Fetishism** is nothing but the adoration of material things because of their mysterious power. It is an attempt to find divine power or mysterious power in the fetishes or inanimate things such as a leaf, a feather, a horn, a stone or any such thing.
   - **Animism or Animatism:** According to **Tylor,** animism is essentially a belief in the spirit of the dead. It is a belief in the existence of some supra-physical being within the body of every living or non-living being.
   - **Totemism:** This is an extension of fetishism. "A totem is a species of animal or plant; or part of an animal or plant, or a natural object or the phenomenon of the symbol of any of these which signifies distinguishing features of a human group as against other groups similarly represented, in the same society." - **H.D. Munro** in *"Dictionary of Sociology"*. Totemism is associated with the tribal organisation. The relation that exists between the totem and the people is sometimes taken to be one of blood relationship. Hence totemism has to be crossed in marriage. The totem may be *wolf, bear, turtle, hawk, fox,* etc.

SCHEDULED TRIBES - STILL FAR AWAY FROM CIVILIZED AMENITIES

unity is essential for them to retain their identity. Tribals are normally cohesive and they fight against common enemies as one man. They are ever ready to avenge the injustice done to the group or the individuals.

10. *Common Economic Organisation* : More than 90% of the tribal workers are engaged in agriculture. About **3%** of tribals are engaged in manufacturing against the national average of **11%;** and **5%** in tertiary servicing [against the national average of **16%.**] Just **1%** tribals are engaged in forestry and food gathering. Their economic position is very poor. Though they are poor, nearly **57%** of tribals are economically active. In spite of that, they get very poor returns for their efforts.

11. *Organisation of Clans* : The Clan or sib is an important part of tribal-organisation. *The **clan** includes all the relatives of mothers or fathers and the children of one ancestor.* People belonging to a clan trace their origin to one ancestor. The descendants of a clan are of either matrilineal or partilineal lineage. The tribal society may include in itself many clans. There exists mutual helpfulness among the members of different clans.

12. *Prevalence of Dormitories* : Tribal community has a peculiar feature which is evident in the form of *common sleeping chambers* or dormitories. Such organisations train the youth in the tribal ways of life. These are the centres which preserve tribal legends, music, dance, paintings, etc. Young boys and girls spend much of their time in the night in these dormitories and often they are vested with the responsibility of giving protection to the community people. Till they get married they continue to become the members of the dormitories and are supposed to maintain secrecy relating to their activities. After their marriage their membership of the dormitories get cancelled. Members of the dormitories are expected to follow the rules and regulations strictly.

13. *Simplicity and Self-Sufficiency* : A tribal society is not complex but simple in character. Hunting, fishing and collection of roots, fruits, nuts, berries, honey and forest products are their main means of subsistence. Some have taken to cultivation also. They do not possess, neither do they enjoy the facilities of civilised people. There was a time when the tribals were self-sufficient. Due to the increase in their population and changed economic conditions, their self-sufficiency has gone. They are becoming more and more dependent on the civilised community and also the government help. They are simple, honest, frugal and some of them very hospitable also. Majority of them are not educated, neither are they interested in it.

14. *The Need for Protection* : The tribals always experience the need for protection. Hence they are a *cohesive group.* The tribe is a *homogeneous* group also. There is less diversity and more unity and uniformity. Ethnic, political, religious and other kinds of prejudices and mutual distrust between the civilised and the tribal people have made the tribals feel insecure. Hence they experience the need for protection. Their political organisation is established mainly to protect themselves.

15. *Endogamous Group ?* : Though not always, the members of a tribe generally marry among themselves. *Marrying within one's own group is called endogamy.* Each tribe has many clans within itself and these are *exogamous in nature.* The tribals practise endogamy probably to maintain the purity of blood and cultural peculiarities and to preserve the property within the group. But today, due to the influence of the civilised people and increased contacts, *exogamy* is also practised. The tribe is not necessarily an endogamous group, though originally it might have been so says *Imperial Gazetteer of India.* All known tribal societies have laid stress on the rule of exogamy. An individual is not allowed to marry inside a definite set of his own kin-group, that is, clan. In conclusion, it can be said that taken together as a unit, each tribe is largely endogamous, but various sub-groups that it consists, namely clans, are mostly exogamous.

Problems Involved in the Contact of the Tribals with the Outside World

Contact of the Tribals With the Civilisation

Tribals live away from the civilised life and are mostly found in remote areas such as forest areas, hilly areas, mountainous regions, deep forests, dense valleys and so on. There was a time when no one could travel over vast areas of the world exclusively inhabited by savage and semi-savage peoples who had never come into contact with the civilised races. In the case of India, there were many tribes who lived in secure asylums in hills and forests, lived on fruits, nuts, berries, etc. and wore leaves or rags round their loins. Today, most of these tribes have come into contact with the advanced community and have learnt cultural traits of their neighbours. They have borrowed the patterns of their dress and developed an intricate material economy. Some of these tribes have progressed at a tremendous speed, effecting in a few years, changes which have taken centuries to achieve in other areas.

The Ways of Contact of the Tribals With the Civilised People

The tribals came in contact with the civilised people in a number of ways. **D.N. Majumdar** points out at some of these ways[3] **:**

1. Existence of mineral resources in and around the primitive tracts helped the immigration of the outsiders who influenced the culture, the way of life of the tribals in a number of ways.
2. The administrative officers introduced significant changes in the cultural life of the primitive tribes everywhere. They introduced to the tribals various aspects of the civilisational amenities.
3. The Christian missionaries who entered these places to spread the religion and convert the tribals into Christianity also influenced the tribals. Due to the continuous interaction with the officers of the government and the Christian missionaries the tribal people in many areas have learnt to imitate the ways of these foreign elements in the population.
4. The itinerant vendors of imported toys and trinkets, the shawl merchants and travelling agents who tour with modern medicines, imported textiles and brass and other metal utensils have gone into the most inaccessible parts of hills and jungles.
5. In due course, the tremendous development of transport and communication has led to the infiltration of foreign traits of culture.
6. The displacement of the tribal people in many areas from their hereditary possession of *jhums* lands has led to a change of occupation. Some tribals used to go out of their place to the far away tea gardens and plantations to work for small cash earnings which do not even supply their primary material needs. Yet they bring back with them traits of culture which are passed on and accepted by the community on account of the prestige they possess.

- ***Adivasis* Under the Influence of Caste ?**

Most of the primitive tribes have come under the influence of the caste system and have increased the number of "depressed" communities; while others have been converted to Christianity and have escaped the tyranny of caste rules. *"Where the tribals have lived for long in association with the lower castes and where the tribes do not suffer from much discomfort*

3 *Source* : **D.N. Majumdar** in his *"Races and Cultures of India"* published in 1944 Reprinted 1973. Page - 371.

or exploitation at the hands of the alien groups, the tribes have gradually entered into the social economy of the caste system." [**Majumdar.** Page - 372]. However, the line of demarcation between popular Hinduism and tribal religions is thin and it is difficult to know when a tribe crosses into Hinduism. As **Majumdar** has pointed out, where there is a clash of interest between the tribal people and the Hindu landlords the tribals have been subjected to hardships or have been dispossessed of their rights to land or have been reduced to servitude, and where the middlemen have forced them into the grip of moneylenders, Christianity has proved a great friend of the tribes. Majumdar cites the example of the rapid spread of Christianity in Chota Nagpur where 98% of the Indian Christians have been recruited from the tribal population. *This conversion is due more to the secular benefits, the Christian converts enjoy, than to the spiritual side of the new religion.*

The Effects and Problems Due to the Contact With Civilisation

The contact with civilisation has brought about a series of changes in the tribal areas and also in the tribal way of life. At the same time, this contact has been responsible for some of the tribal discomforts and disadvantages. **Majumdar** [Pages : 372 - 374] makes a mention of some of the effects and problems of this contact.

1. The excise laws of the government in the primitive areas are hitting them hard. This policy has led to an increase of drunkenness and immorality in the tribal areas. The government is accused of making money by these means. Liquor has become cheap and the tribals who had been preparing it in their own way find it now highly uneconomic to do so. This has led to their economic downfall and misery.
2. The displacement of the tribal officers by those who are nominated by the state for administrative efficiency has disorganised the tribal life in various ways. These young officers from outside show scant respect to the tribal way of life, values, morals and culture. Tribal people have found it extremely difficult to accept these young officers as their own.
3. The tribal land used for *jhumming* is held to be *"unclassed state forest"* and the possessors of these lands could be ousted without giving any compensation. This annoyed the tribals very badly.
4. Quarrying stone, gravel and ores for private use is forbidden to the owner of the *jhum* land where there may lie. The licence fee demanded for quarrying has further complicated the issue.
5. *Jhumming* or *Dahiya* cultivation has been prohibited by the State. This has forced the primitive tribes to a kind of agriculture which is unsuited for them.
6. *"Marriage by capture"* practised amongst the primitive tribes is often treated as abduction and the offenders are punished under the provisions of *The Indian Penal Code.* The primitives have been prevented from practising this type of marriage which used to help them to escape from the clutches of the practice of the heavy bride price.
7. Tribal ceremonies, festivals and dances have been replaced or superseded by fairs and weekly markets which attract the people by their novelty, but ultimately bring about financial ruin.
8. The system of education which has been introduced in the tribal areas, either through the missionary efforts or by the local governments, is mostly unsuited to their life and ideals. The tribals have not completely realised the relevance and the importance of these new types of education.

9. Tribal customs and practices are often at variance with the complicated system of law and legal procedure. Hence, the tribals had to suffer and endure discomforts due to the fact that the judges and magistrates who never knew the languages, customs and mentality of the tribals, are to give judgements many a time against the tribal spirit.
10. Missionary influence has not been all the while good as far as the tribals are concerned. The new converts to Christianity who started despising the tribal way of life have disturbed the traditionalists.
11. Finally, the occurrence of the diseases, through the contact of especially the foreigners, has invaded the security of the tribal life. The medical aid available is too insignificant to cope with the situation.

Thus, the contact of the tribals with the civilisation has brought them some good things, it has also led to the new problems, anxieties and challenges.

3. PROBLEMS OF THE SCHEDULED TRIBES

The tribals who constitute 8.6% of the total population of India as per 2011 census, are distributed in various states of the country and are facing many problems. Some of these problems are peculiar to some areas while some others are common to tribals of all the areas. Many of these problems are the direct outcome of the changes that are taking place in the tribal community. These changes are also not uniform. Hence, it is not easy to understand the tribal problems in their true perspective.

Tribals in India, in general, are facing some common problems such as *problem of geographic separation, economic problem, cultural problem, social problem, educational problem and health problem.* These problems are briefly discussed below.

1. Problem of Geographic Separation

Most of the tribals of India are in a way geographically separated from the rest of population. Some of them are living in the unapproachable physical areas such as deep valleys, dense forests, hills, mountains, etc. It is difficult for them to establish regular relations with others, and hence, socially they are away from the civilised world. This kind of physical as well as social isolation or seclusion has retarded the tribal development. The welfare programmes and developmental projects undertaken by the government many a time do not reach the tribals because of this geographic isolation. Hence, the tribals need to be protected from leading an isolated life away from villages, towns and cities. Regular contact should be maintained with them through the network of roads and communication system.

2. Cultural Problem

The tribal culture is entirely different from the way of life of the civilized people. The tribals fail to understand the civilised people, their customs and practices, beliefs and attitudes and so on. They are suspicious of the civilised people. They are clinging tenacioulsy to their customs and traditions. During the British rule, some foreign Christian missionaries made an attempt to propagate their religion in some of the tribal areas, particularly in the North-Eastern provinces. They even tried to impose their culture on them. Even today such an attempt is going on.

"In several tribal areas, mass conversion to Christianity had taken place during the British period. While the missionaries have been the pioneers in education and opened hospitals in

tribal areas, they have also been responsible for alienating the tribals from their culture. Christian missionaries have many a time instigated the tribals to revolt against the Indian government."[4]

On the other hand, the Ramakrishna Mission, R.S.S. [Rasthreeya Swayamsevak Sangh] the Vishwa Hindu Parishad and other organisations are spreading Hinduism in some of these areas. Further, some of the tribal leaders have now started popularising their tribal religion. These different propagandas have created a great confusion and conflict for them. The cultural gap between the civilised and the tribal people is coming in the way of the harmonious assimilation and integration of the tribal people into the mainstream of the national life of India.

3. Social Problems

The tribals have their own social problems. They are traditional and custom-bound. They have become the victims of superstitious beliefs, outmoded and meaningless practices and harmful habits. *Child marriage, infanticide, homicide, animal sacrifice, exchange of wives, black magic* and some other harmful socio-religious practices are still found among them.

Hinduisation of tribals has led to problems such as dowry, divorce, untouchability, child marriage, etc. Various studies on tribal communities in India have provided information about the impact of Hinduisation. Studies on the *Konds* of Orissa, *Kotas* of the Neelagiris, *Bhumji* in West Bengal, *Bhotias* of Uttar Pradesh and *Santhals* of Bihar indicate the general trend of change owing to cultural contact with the neighbouring Hindus. ***Example*** : "A recent study of *Botia* women of **Pithoragarh** district of U.P. by **Dharmaveer** and **Manral** [1990] reveals that the status of *Botia* women has changed for the worse. Traditionally, they had a fairly high status and enjoyed considerable freedom in different spheres of life. But their status has declined significantly due to Hinduisation, Sanskritisation and modernisation."[5]

Christianisation of tribals has led to problems of separatism, alienation, religious conflict and cultural confusion. Christianity has been an important factor of tribal change in India. "Many tribals have become Christians during the last 100 years. Thus, there are a large number of Christians among the *Khasis* and *Garos* of Meghalaya, *Oraons* of Chota Nagpur, *Bhils* of Madhya Pradesh, *Mizos, Nagas* and many other tribals of North East. *According to one estimate, the tribal Christians constitute about 1/6th of the total Christian population of India.* The traditional tribal cultures and institutions have been adversely affected under the impact of new ideas, ethical values and a new style of life......... **Vidhyarthi** [1977 : 460] is of the opinion that Christianity has provided the first model of Westernisation to the tribals in the shape of "Church Organisation", western education, and above all, western values and morals."[6]

Many tribals still believe in ghosts and spirits. They have a keen desire to maintain their own practices, beliefs, etc. Hence, it is said that *"the tribals are tribesmen first, the tribesmen last and the tribesmen all the time."*

4. Economic Problems

The tribal people are economically the poorest people of India. Majority of them live below the poverty line. The tribal economy is based on agriculture of the crudest type. The main economic problems of the tribals are explained below.

(i) Exploitation: The innocence, illiteracy and helplessness of the tribals are exploited by the outsiders. The British policy, in particular, had led to ruthless exploitation of the tribals in

4 *Ref:* **Prof. Ram Ahuja** in his *"Social Problems in India"* - Page: 137.

5 **Dr. Y. Ravindranath Rao** in his article on *"Tribal Social Transformation"* published in *"Samaja Shodhana"* Vol.1, No.2., Oct. 1992. [Page - 62.] Journal of the Mangalore University Sociology Teachers Association.

6 *ibid.* Page - 63.

various ways as it favoured the zamindars, landlords, money-lenders, forest contractors and excise, revenue and police officials.

(ii) Unprofitable Agriculture: About 90% of the tribals are engaged in cultivation and most of them are landless and practise *"shifting cultivation."* They need to be helped in adopting new methods of cultivation. The tribals possess uneconomic holdings because of which their crop yield is very less. A very small percentage of the population participates in occupational activities in the secondary and tertiary sectors.

(iii) Problems of Land Ownership: A good portion of the land in the tribal areas has been legally transferred to non-tribals. Tribals demand that this land should be returned to them. In fact, the tribals had earlier enjoyed much freedom to use the forest and hunt the forest animals. They are emotionally attached to the forests for they believe that their gods, spirits live in forests. The tribals who are *"deprived"* of their rights to the land and forest have reacted sharply to the restrictions imposed by the government on their traditional rights.

(iv) Unemployment and Underemployment: A large number of tribal young men and women are either unemployed or underemployed. They are unhappy for they are not able to get jobs that can keep them occupied throughout the year. They need to be helped in finding secondary source of income by developing animal husbandry, poultry farming, handicrafts, handloom weaving, etc.

(v) Non-Availability of Banking Facilities: Banking facilities in the tribal areas are so inadequate that the tribals have mainly to depend on the money-lenders. The tribals, therefore, demand that *"Agricultural Indebtedness Relief Acts"* should be enacted so that they may get back their mortgaged land.

5. Educational Problems

Illiteracy is a major problem of the tribals. More than 70% of them are illiterate. Literacy among them has increased from 0.7% in 1931 to 11.30% in 1970 and to 16.35% in 1981 to 29.60% in 1991. Compared to general literacy rate of 52.21% [in 1991] in the country, this is very low. Even now millions of tribals are illiterate. Further, the growth of literacy rate in the past three decades in the country as a whole was 28.21%, but among the STs, it was only 11.7% [*The Hindustan Times,* July 11, 1955]. Even though tribal literacy rate in Mizoram is 82.71%, and between 57 and 61% in Nagaland, Sikkim and Kerala; there are regions [example, Orissa, U.P., Bihar] wherein the literacy level is extremely poor.

Tribals, who are far away from the contact of the civilised world have no faith in formal educational organisation. Many of them do not know any thing about education, schools, colleges, universities, degrees, etc. They feel no urge to educate their children. Since most of the tribals are poor, education appears to be a luxury for them. Tribal people who are engaged in agriculture want their little children to work along with them either in the fields or at home. The illiterate parents do not consider it as their primary responsibility to give education to their children.

The Problem of Language: The medium of instruction is another hindrance to the promotion of education among the tribes. Most of the tribal languages do not have a script of their own. Hence the children are obliged to learn things in a language which is foreign to them. Even in tribal areas the number of tribal teachers is very less and hence communication problem always arises between the students and the teachers.

The Curriculum of Education is Another Main Problem : The existing curriculum, as experts rightly have pointed out, is not suited to their needs and has little relevance for the tribal life.

6. Problem of Health and Sanitation

Due to illiteracy and ignorance, the tribals are not able to appreciate modern concept of health and sanitation. They do not take much care pertaining to their own health. They believe that diseases are caused by hostile spirits and ghosts. They have their own traditional means of diagnosis and cure. Good number of them fall a prey to the diseases such as skin disease, forest fever, typhoid, T.B., leprosy, malaria, venereal diseases, small pox, etc. Contact with outsiders further added to a few more diseases in the tribal areas. **Example:** *It is observed that the Thodas of Niligiri Hills have been suffering from some modern diseases like venereal diseases, diabetes, blood pressure, etc. after coming into touch with the British who made Niligiri Hills one of their summer resorts.* These diseases take a heavy toll of tribal life. Their suspicion and lack of faith in modern doctors have made them not to avail themselves of the modern medical facilities.

7. Problem of Separatism

The *"divide and rule"* policy adopted by the British did a lot of damage to the tribal community of India. The British had superimposed their own administrative patterns in tribal areas and deprived the tribals of their traditional methods of interacting with people. The *"Criminal Tribes Act"* which the British had introduced gave an impression that the tribals were either *"criminals"* or *"anti-social beings"*. The tribal groups such as *Kolis, Mundas, Khasis, Santals, Nagas,* etc, who fought against the British were branded as *"dactoits"* and *"robbers"*. The British government which wanted to humble these tribals and *"correct"* them gave direct encouragement to the foreign Christian missionary activities especially in the Central and the North-Eastern Zone. These activities which went on for more than 200 years, alienated many of the tribals and developed in them separatist tendencies.

Relations between tribals and non-tribals have started worsening. In states like Mizoram, Nagaland, Meghalaya, Bihar, Manipur, Tripura, and Arunachal Pradesh, demand for separate state for tribals took the shape of insurgency, revolt, terrorism and so on. Neighbouring countries which are unfriendly to India, have instigated the tribals to rebel against the establishment. They have exploited the anti-Indian sentiments of the tribals to their advantage.

8. Tribal Revolts and Uprisings

Numerous revolts and uprisings of the tribals have taken place beginning with the one in Bihar in 1772, followed by many other revolts in Andhra Pradesh, Arunachal Pradesh, Assam, Mizoram and Nagaland. During the recent tribal uprisings the *Nagas,* the *Mizos* and the *Bodos* took part in them in a large number and created serious law and order problem.

Smuggling, Infiltration and Drug Addiction: The foreign infiltrators especially from Bangla Desh, Pakisthan, Burma and China are entering the borders of India through what are known as *"tribal belts"*. Some of them take undue advantage of the tribals' innocence and ignorance for their *smuggling activities.* Prohibited drugs and unlicensed weapons are smuggled inside the land and beyond the borders of India through the tribal areas. Some of the tribals have been made the victims of drug addiction also. Hence, tribal areas in the borders have become extremely sensitive areas.

CAUSES OF TRIBAL UNREST AND DISCONTENT

Tribals in India led a comparatively contented and peaceful life prior to the coming of the British. Along with the British rule there came in series of social changes. Some of these changes affected tribal life also. Exposure of the tribals to the modern civilisation also resulted in their exploitation at the hands of the non-tribals. Conversion activities of the Christian missionaries encouraged by the British, especially in the tribal areas, further added confusion to the tribals. Tribals reacted very strongly when their religious beliefs were mocked at, when their rights over the forests were removed and when their very way of life was disturbed.

Even now, tribals in India are not happy and are agitated over several things. Ever since the days of the British rule they have been revolting against the establishment, for various reasons. The important tribes involved in revolt in the 19th century were *Mizos* [1810], *Kols* [1795 and 1831], *Mundas* [1889], *Daflas* [1875], *Khasi* and *Garo* [1829], *Kacharis* [1839], *Santhals* [1853], *Muria Gonds* [1886], *Nagas* [1844 and 1879], *Bhuiyas* [1868] and *Kondhs* [1817]. After independence also many tribal revolts took place. The continued state of discontent among the tribals is revealed through the contemporary tribal movements. Some of the contemporary movements are – ***the Jharkhand movement, Gond movement, Naga movement, Mizo movement, Bodoland movement,*** etc.

Some Major Types of Tribal Movements

It is possible to identify some of the major types of tribal movements.

1. *Religious and social reform movements.*
2. *Movements for statehood within the Indian Union, or for autonomy for tribal areas.*
3. *Insurgent movements for independence from the Indian Union,* and
4. *Movements for asserting cultural rights.*

It is significant to note that there are lots of variations in tribal movements from region to region. In the North East, the tribals are in an overwhelming majority in some of the states. ***Example*** : Meghalaya, Mizoram, Nagaland. Their tribal economy and social systems are relatively stable. The tribal movements in these areas are essentially ***political in nature.*** Here, some of the tribal groups [***Ex.*** Nagas in Nagaland, Mizos in Mizoram] demanded autonomy and for that sake carried on continuous agitations some times back.

The situation in Middle India is far more complex. The tribals have been reduced to a minority in many areas in which they were dominant numerically at one time. Further, they have been exposed to the process of rapid social change. The tribal movements in this region have essentially an ***agrarian character*** and are often related to the exploitation of forest resources.

In some regions, the tribal movements have a ***cultural dimension*** in the sense that they are related to language, tribal art and religion. Tensions have often prevailed in these regions on account of religious conversions and linguistic tussles.

Tribals in South India are either too backward or too few in number or widely dispersed over a large area to organise any movement in spite of their exploitation and discontent. *"However,* **Mishra** [1982] *says that there is evidence of incipient political mobilisation among the tribals in South India. In fact, political consciousness among the tribals of Kerala may be the highest in the country."*[7]

The study of the tribal movements is relatively recent in the field of social anthropology. Tribal movements may be seen as an aspect of social change. *The policy of the colonial administration regarding forest and land, later on alienation of the tribal land, the immigration and settlement of an increasing number of non-tribals, the slow pace of industrialisation and modern developments* – have been some of the reasons for the emergence of various tribal movements in the North Eastern states of Manipur, Mizoram, Meghalaya, Arunachal Pradesh and Assam.

---

7 **Dr. Y. Ravindranath Rao** in his article on *"Tribal Social Transformation."* Page - 63 published in *Samaja Shodhana.*

According to **A.R. Desai,** the fundamental problems of the tribal population are economico-political such as the security of a job, a decent standard of living, easy accessibility to the resources of civilised life, the acquiring of education, which can enable them to decide what customs, what rituals, and what aesthetic and cultural elements they should retain, or eliminate or absorb from their culture and various other cultures. He is of the opinion that the violent and militant struggles which are being launched by the tribal populations are revolts against various inhuman conditions to which they have been subjected and which are being perpetuated even after independence. He points out : *"The tribal problem is a problem which raises the fundamental issue – the issue of the establishment of a social order founded on equality of opportunities and the elimination of exploitation."*

THE CAUSES OF TRIBAL UNREST

Tribal unrest and discontent are a cumulative effect of a number of factors. The factors or causes that led to the tribal revolt, unrest and discontent may be listed here.

1. *Governmental Failures* : The failure of the Government to take appropriate measures to rehabilitate the tribal population both before and after independence had disappointed the tribals. Independent India's Constitution envisages a comprehensive and well designed scheme of action for the tribal protection and development. The State Governments are vested with the responsibility of implementing the Constitutional provisions. Unfortunately, these Constitutional provisions have remained non-operational. Land continues to pass out of the tribals to non-tribals. Money lenders continue to exploit them. There has been a heavy influx of outsiders into the tribal areas and they have grabbed most of the opportunities.

2. *Irresponsibility and Lack of Accountability of the Agencies of Tribal Development* : Indifference, irresponsibility, lethargy and lack of sympathy on the part of the administrators and bureaucrats in dealing with the tribal problems and grievances have been very much evident. There are a number of agencies to look after and supervise the implementation of the tribal welfare programmes and schemes. At the level of the Central Government, for example, there are five major agencies namely; (i) *the Welfare Ministry,* (ii) *Commissioner for Scheduled Tribes and Scheduled Castes,* (iii) *National Commission for Scheduled Castes and Scheduled Tribes,* (iv) *Secretary in Cabinet Secretariat,* and (v) *the Planning Commission.* In addition to these, the development and administration of the tribal affairs is spread over a number of ministries and departments. Such multiplicity of agencies divides the responsibility and leads to irresponsibility and unaccountability.

3. *Unjust Forest Policy* : Inconsiderate and unsympathetic forest laws and regulations damaged the tribal emotionality. Lands traditionally owned and cultivated by the tribals have been branded as *"forest lands"* under the new Forest Policy. As a result, the tribals have become strangers and encroachers in their own land. This has annoyed them very badly.

4. *Alienation of Tribal Land to the Non-Tribals* : Lack of legislation to prevent the passing of the tribal land into the hands of non-tribals has added to tribal unrest. Due to some loopholes in the existing system of law the tribal land continues to be alienated to non-tribals for their own exclusive uses. The state governments have also acquired tribal land for industrial, irrigation, power, mining, and other projects. As a result, the tribals have been deprived of their rights over the land.

5. *Political Indifference* : Lack of interest and dynamism among the political elite to solve the tribal problems made them to become disgusted. National level political parties have not paid due attention to the genuine problems of the tribals. They have been speaking of the tribal development and the tribal welfare only for the name sake. Tribals are remembered only at the time of elections. The political indifference has made the tribals to organise their own political parties at local level. Because of their groupism they have not been able to forge a unity to fight for their own cause.

6. *Absence of Efficient Tribal Leadership* : Tribals should be able to develop their own leadership to fight against exploitation and to secure justice. But unfortunately, various vested interests have prevented the emergence of powerful tribal leadership. There is virtually a vacuum of tribal leadership. This has very badly affected their development.

7. *Forceful Cultural Impositions* : Tribals are trying to come in touch with civilised people. Leaders of various religious communities such as the Hindu, Christian and the Muslim, are trying to approach them and influence their way of life. Tribals who want to retain their original culture are bewildered at this. The Hinduisation, Christianisation and also the Islamisation of the tribals have caused lot of anxiety and a sense of insecurity for them.

It is clear from the above, that various social, political, economic and legal factors have contributed to the problem of tribal unrest.

MEASURES FOR THE UPLIFTMENT OF SCHEDULED TRIBES

Independent India has been paying some attention to the problems of the scheduled tribes and attempts are being made to deal effectively with those problems. Before the independence, the British Government was only discussing the issues and problems of tribal development and practically did nothing either to face them or to solve them. The only thing the British did was that, they kept the tribals away from the contact of the civilized people. Through their *"policy of indirect rule"* they wanted to "protect" them from the neighbouring dominant communities.

The British followed their so called *"policy of giving special protection"* to the tribals till the *Government of India Act, 1935* came into force. Afterwards, though the elected provincial legislative bodies were established, some tribal areas known as *"the excluded areas"* were brought under the direct control of the British Governor.

The British policy of separating the tribals from the rest of the people created suspicion in the minds of the nationalists. They severely criticised the British policy and charged the British with preventing a large section of our countrymen from joining the mainstream of national life. *"In practice what happened was that the tribes were isolated and then left to stagnate, halting the evolving process of cultural fusion."* - [S.C. Dube][8]

This brings us to the questions *whether the tribals should be assimilated into the mainstream or whether they should be kept separately from the rest of the communities and protected? And in what way they will benefit from the developments taking place in the country?* Let us consider the different approaches or view-points which the scholars have developed regarding the solution of tribal problems and tribal development.

Three Views or Approaches to Solve Tribal Problems

Various solutions have been presented for dealing effectively with the tribal problems. The tribal problems have been approached from three viewpoints. They are as follows: *(i) policy of isolation, (ii) policy of assimilation* and *(iii) policy of integration.*

---

8 *Ref:* **S.C. Dube** in *"Encyclopaedia of Social Work in India"* - Vol. III.

1. Policy of Isolation

Hutton, who was a Commissioner for Census of 1931 and **V. Elwin** have suggested that the tribals must be kept at a distance from the rest of the society. **Hutton** and others condemned too much of isolation as also of complete assimilation of tribals. **V. Elwin** wanted a revivalist policy to be adopted. He proposed a scheme of *"National Parks"* for the tribals and pleaded for the complete non-interference of the British forces and their withdrawal from the tribal areas. Keeping the tribals in isolation in some *"National Parks"* or *"reserved areas"* would solve two problems: (a) *the tribals would be in a position to maintain their independent identity,* (b) *they would be free from the exploitation of outsiders.* The champions of this approach are of the view that sufficient time must be given to the tribals to assimilate themselves with the rest of the community.

- The ***limitation of this approach*** is that when once the tribals are kept in isolation, they are likely to develop vested interests and keep themselves permanently away from others. **G.S. Ghurye** and others criticised this approach and advocated complete assimilation of the tribals.

2. Policy of Assimilation

*"Assimilation is the process whereby individuals or groups once dissimilar become similar and identified in their interests and outlook" [**Ogburn** and **Nimkoff**].* Assimilation is one of the ways of dealing with the tribal problems. Assimilation or the *"missionary solution"* has been advocated by Christian missionaries, Hindu social reformers and voluntary organisations. According to this solution, assisting and encouraging the tribals to assimilate themselves with the mainstream of national life, can alone permanently solve the tribal problems. Thus, according to this approach, we cannot deal with tribal problems on the basis of tribal culture and life but by changing them into the frame of new community. **Prof. G.S. Ghurye**, a senior sociologist made a case for the complete assimilation of tribals with the rest of the people in India. He said that it was misleading to call the tribes *"aborigines"* as they were actually only *"backward Hindus"* and the solution of all their problems cultural as well as economic and social lay in their complete assimilation into the Hindu society. The Christian missionaries on the one hand, and the Hindu social reformers like **Thakkar Bapa** on the other, have been trying to assimilate them into Christian and Hindu community respectively.

- ***This approach has its own limitations.*** Complete assimilation is a difficult task. The tribals are not prepared to give up all their traditional tribal beliefs, practices and ideas. Any attempt to impose the external cultural practices on them, creates in them guilt feelings, confusions and mental conflicts. This solution may even create economic, religious and moral degradation among them. Tribal culture has many happy and useful aspects and the same must be preserved. **D.N. Majumdar** opines that the best policy about tribes would be for their controlled [planned] and limited assimilation. By limited assimilation he implied the need and desirability of preserving their useful institutions, customs, practices, etc. though these are tribal in origin and character.

3. Policy of Integration

The third view, which is actively followed in the recent years, is that of *integration.* The policy of isolation is neither possible nor desirable and that of assimilation would mean imposition. Hence, integration alone can make available to the tribes the benefits of modern society and yet retain their separate identity. *This view recommends the rehabilitation of the tribals on the plains along with the civilised people, but away from their native places such as hills, mountains, forests, etc.*

This suggestion has also been criticised. It is said that this suggestion has been advocated in order to further the interests of the industrialists and capitalists. This solution is not appreciated on the ground that it may create economic and moral decadence to those who are separated from their beloved land to plains. Still, the policy of integration which aims at developing a creative adjustment between tribes and non-tribes has been supported by thinkers and writers like **Pandit Jawaharlal Nehru.**

Conclusion

The solutions to the tribal problems mentioned above, have their own merits and demerits. Tribal problems are simple but very delicate to handle. No solution can be experimented with before winning the confidence of the tribals. The modern culture must not be imposed on them. It is essential to establish a harmonious compatibility between the tribal mode of living and the material advancement of culture. The integration of the tribal society into the Indian society takes time and it has to be promoted while retaining the good points of the tribal culture. Only those elements of new culture which may vitalise them for material advancement must be infused in them. **Pandit Nehru** observes that, *"Tribal people possess a variety of culture and they are in many ways certainly not backward. There is no point in trying to make them a second rate copy of ourselves".*[9]

With regard to the tribal development and welfare, Pandit Nehru observes that our duty which comes *"First is to preserve, strengthen, and develop all that is best in tribal society, culture, art and language. The second is to protect the tribal economic rights. The third is to unite and integrate the tribes in a true heart unity with India as a whole, so that they may play a full part in their life. And the last is to develop welfare and educational facilities so that every tribesman may have an equal opportunity with the rest of the fellow citizens who work in the fields, factories, and workshops in the open country and the plains".*

- **The Tribal *'Panchasheela'***

Pandit Jawaharlal Nehru in 1957 in his foreword to **Verrier Elwin's** *"The Philosophy for NEFA"*, laid down five principles known as *"Panchasheela"*, as a part of the policy of integration. The tribal *"Panchasheela"* as has been enunciated by him are as follows.

(i) *Nothing should be imposed on the tribal people. They must be allowed to develop along the lines of their own genius. We should try to encourage in every way their own traditional art and culture.*

(ii) *Tribals' right on land in which they are living and also on the forests must be respected.*

(iii) *Attempt must be made to train and build up a team of their own people to the work of administration and development. Some technical personnel from outside will be of great help for them in the beginning. But too many outsiders must not be sent to the tribal territory.*

(iv) *Over-administering the tribal areas or overwhelming them with too many schemes must be avoided. We should not work in rivalry to their own social and cultural institutions.*

(v) *The results of the work must be adjudged by the quality of the human character that is evolved and not by statistics or the amount of money spent.*

The Ministry of Home Affairs and the Ministry of Community Development (under the Article 46 of the Constitution), set up 43 sub-multipurpose tribal blocks in the various States of India to promote the welfare and the integration of the tribals. Two committees were set up, one

9 ***Ref:*** Quoted by **C.B. Mamoria** in his *"Social Problems and Social Disorganisation"* - Page: 203.

in May 1959 under the chairmanship of the anthropologist **Verrier Elwin** and the other in April 1960 under the presidentship of **U.N. Dhebar**, to examine the programmes and projects of these blocks. Both the committees submitted their reports in 1960 and 1961 respectively. The reports have emphasised and amplified the five fundamental principles enunciated by Nehru in 1957.

WELFARE PROGRAMMES AND PROJECTS FOR SCHEDULED TRIBES

The tribals constitute a sizeable proportion [8.6% in 2011] of the total population of India. The tribals are also the citizens of India and hence promotion of their welfare is of equal importance. Not only the Central and the State Governments have undertaken various steps in this regard, but also various voluntary organisations have evinced interest in this task. Organisations such as the *Bharatiya Adim Jati Sevak Sangh, the Bhil Seva Mandal, Kasturba Gandhi National Memorial Trust, the Indian Red Cross Society, the Vishwa Hindu Parishad, the Vanavasi Kalyanashrama, The Ramakrishna Mission, The Rastreeya Swayam Sevak Sangh and several Christian organisations* carry on welfare activities among the tribals. The Government through its *Department of Tribal Welfare* and through its Five Year Plans has been trying to elevate the tribals from the state of ignorance, illiteracy and poverty. Some of the tribal welfare measures of the Government may be examined here.

1. Constitutional Safeguards

The Constitution of India has made various provisions to safeguard the interests of the tribals.

1. *Article 15* of the Constitution provides equal rights and opportunities to all the citizens of India (including the tribals) without any discrimination.
2. Reservation in employment is made for the tribals under *Article* 16(4), 320(4) and 335.
3. Seats have been reserved for them in the legislatures (in Lok Sabha and State Vidhana Sabhas) under *Articles* 330, 332 and 334.
4. Under *Article* 19(5) the tribals can own property and enjoy it in any part of the country.
5. According to the *Article* 275 a large amount of money can be taken from the *Consolidated Fund of India* to be spent on tribal welfare activities.
6. *Article* 338 empowers the President of India to appoint a Commissioner to look after the tribal welfare activities.
7. Under *Article* 339(2) the Central Government can give directions to the States in the formulation and execution of tribal welfare plans, projects and programmes.
8. Under *Article* 275(i) the Centre is required to give grants-in-aid to the States for approved schemes of tribal welfare.
9. *Article* 164 empowers the State Governments to appoint a separate minister to look into the welfare of the tribals.
10. *Article* 46 consists of provisions that protect the economic and educational interests of the tribals.
11. *Article* 224 gives instructions to the administration to take special care to protect tribal interests in *"Scheduled Tracts"* or *"areas"*.
12. *Article* 342 gives power to the President of India to declare on the recommendation of the Governor some groups or communities as *"scheduled tribes"*. It also gives details on the basis of which new groups could be recommended as *"scheduled tribes"* entitling them for all the constitutional benefits.

Committees and Commissions

In addition to the constitutional provisions mentioned above, the government appoints committees, commissions and study teams from time to time to look into the way in which the target groups are making use of the constitutional provisions, the problems faced by them and to suggest measures for further improvement. ***Examples of Some Commissions and Study Teams:*** *(i) Backward Classes Commission [1953-55], headed by* **Kaka Kalelkar**; *(ii) The Study Team of Social Welfare and Welfare of Backward Classes [1958-59] headed by* **Renuka Ray**; *(iii) The Scheduled Areas and Scheduled Tribes Commission - 1960-61 under the chairmanship of* **U.N. Dhebar**; *(iv) The Second Backward Classes Commission [1979-80] under the chairmanship of* **B.P. Mandal,** *etc.]*

2. Special Central Assistance [SCA]

Special Central Assistance is given to States and Union Territories to supplement their efforts in tribal development. This assistance is basically meant for family oriented income generating schemes in the sectors of agriculture, horticulture, minor irrigation, soil conservation, animal husbandry, forests, education, co-operatives, fisheries, village and small scale industries and for minimum needs programme. During 1999-2000, an amount of ₹400 crore was released to the States / Union Territories [UTs]. Grants are given to States / UTs to meet the costs of the projects for tribal development [as per the provisions of Article 275(1)]. An amount of ₹100 crore was provided as grants to States / UTs during 1999-2000.

3. Economic Programmes and Facilities

Majority of the tribals are extremely poor and economically backward. Various economic programmes and projects have been undertaken to improve their economic position.

(i) Development Through Five Year Plans: The Government spent ₹ 30 crores, ₹ 80 crores, ₹ 101 crores, ₹ 172 crores and ₹ 257 crores on tribal welfare activities during the 1st, 2nd, 3rd, 4th and 5th Five Year Plans respectively. ***Integrated Tribal Development Projects*** [**ITDP**s] evolved for the tribal development during the 5th plan [1974-79] cover today 19 States / Union Territories and 374 lakh tribal population.

The amount allocated for the tribal sub-plans in the **5th plan** was ₹ 1100 crores, in the **6th plan** [1980-85] it was ₹ 5,535 crore and in the **7th Plan** [1985-90] it was ₹ 10,500 crore.

• ***Tribal Sub-Plan [TSP] Strategy:*** TSP is a part of the overall plan of a State / UT or a Central Ministry / Department and hence is called a Sub Plan. It seeks to ensure adequate flow of funds for tribal development from every state plan as well as Central Plan funds. It tries to promote development activities through legal and administrative support. The TSP strategy is being implemented through legal and administrative support. The TSP strategy is being implemented through 195 *ITDPS'* and *Integrated Development Agencies* [TDAs], 259 modified Area Development Approach [MADA] and 82 clusters.

Specific objectives set forth under the tribal sub-plan strategy were: *(i) raising production in the field of agriculture, small industries, horticulture and animal husbandry; (ii) elimination of exploitation of tribals in money lending, bondage, forest, liquor vending, etc; (iii) development of education and training programmes; (iv) development of tribal areas; (v) upgradation of environment of tribal areas.*

(ii) Establishment of "LAMPS": Large-sized Multi-Purpose Co-operative Societies: These co-operative societies are established in the tribal areas for giving productive and unproductive loans, for sale of surplus produce and purchase of necessities of life to the tribal people. Through these societies the tribals are supplied with improved seeds, modern agricultural equipments, chemicals and fertilizers, pesticides, etc. These societies are striving to relieve the tribals from the exploitation of middlemen, contractors and money-lenders.

***(iii) Tribal Co-operative Marketing Development Federation of India* [TRIFED] :** The *Tribal Co-operative Marketing Development Federation of India* was set up by the Govertment of India in 1987 with a prime objective of providing marketing assistance to ST communities. The TRIFED also provides remunerative prices for the minor forest produce and surplus and agricultural produces of the tribal communities so as to protect them from the hands of the exploitative private traders and middlemen. The authorised share capital of TRIFED is ₹100 crore and its paid-up capital has gone upto ₹99.98 crore in 1999-2000. The Govt. of India's contribution is ₹99.75 crore in that.

(iv) The 20 Point Programme focussed its attention on the development of the scheduled tribes, including assisting the tribal families economically to enable them to cross the poverty line.

***(v) Vocational Training in Tribal Areas* :** This scheme under the Central Sector introduced in 1992-93 aims at developing skills of the tribal youth in order to gain employment / self-employment opportunities. The scheme envisages setting up of *Vocational Training Centres* [VTCs]. During 1999-2000, an amount of ₹375 lakh has been released for 19 VTCs.

(vi) Encouragement to Crafts and Home Industries: Encouragement is given to the existing crafts and home industries among the tribals and such new endeavours are also encouraged. **Example:** (i) In West Bengal, tribals are encouraged to develop silk industry. A training institute is established in Darjeeling to give proper training to those engaged in sericulture. (ii) In **Bihar, M.P., Orissa** and **West Bengal,** wax industry is encouraged among the tribals of these provinces. (iii) **Madhya Pradesh** Government is helping its tribals to prosper in their economic pursuit of collecting beedi leaves. (iv) **Bihar** Government has established a Woman's Co-operative Society for its tribal women to give encouragement to them to pursue their handicrafts.

(vii) Agriculture Made Stable: The tribals are persuaded to give up their system of *"shifting cultivation"* and to settle permanently in a place of their selection by making agriculture their occupation. Thousands of tribals in Assam, Bihar, M.P., Orissa and Tripura, have been made to settle down permanently for agriculture. *Thodas* of Niligiri Hills and *Soligas* of Biligiri Rangana Hills in Mysore provide two other examples in this regard.

(viii) Promotion of Labour Interests of Tribals Engaged in Mining Industry and Tea Plantations: Attempts have been made to protect the labour interests of the tribals in Bihar, West Bengal, Mandhya Pradesh and Orissa who are engaged in mining industry and of the tribals such as Santals, Gonds, Khondas and others who are working in tea plantations of Assam.

(ix) National Scheduled Tribes Finance and Development Corporation [NSTFDC]: With a view to pay focused attention and accelerate the pace of economic development of STs the Govt established the ***NSTFDC*** in April 2001 under the Ministry of Tribal Affairs. This Corporation is promoting Self-Help Groups and Co-operative Societies among the STs, and is giving marketing support assistance also.

4. Educational Facilities

Measures to provide educational facilities to the S.T. have been taken by the Government. Schools are established in some tribal areas. In the First Five Year Plan itself about 4000 schools were opened in the tribal areas. Education upto 10th standard has been made completely free for them. The students belonging to S.T. are getting various concessions such as free tuition, stipends, scholarships, free supply of text books, stationery and other equipments. In some places mid-day meals are also supplied. Free boarding and lodging facilities are provided for them. For the S.T. and S.C. candidates, 20% of the seats are reserved in technical education and relaxation is made in respect of age limit and qualifying marks.

• ***Education of ST Girls in Low Literacy Pockets*** **:** This scheme launched in 1993-94 aims at raising the literacy level of tribal females in 48 identified tribal districts in 8 states with female literacy below 2%. This scheme was revised in July 1998. This scheme envisages residential educational complex from 1st to 5th standards. The scheme is to be implemented through the voluntary organisations and State Governments / UTs. During 1999-2000, an amount of ₹183.76 lakh was released for 75 complexes.

• There are ***Ashrama Schools*** for providing basic education and vocational training for S.T. In these schools, education and training is given in areas such as agriculture, forestry, animal husbandry, poultry farming, bee-keeping, handicrafts, etc. There are 600 Ashrama Schools of residential character situated in Andhra Pradesh, Gujarat, Himachal Pradesh, Madras, Karnataka, Orissa, Rajasthan and Tripura.

• ***Ashrama Schools in Tribal Sub-Plan Area*** **:** This centrally sponsored scheme was started in 1990-91 to provide assistance to the states and Union Territories on 50 per cent and 100 per cent basis, respectively. During 1999-2000, ₹532.28 lakh have been released for the construction of 36 Ashrama Schools.

• ***Pre-Examination Training Centres for S.C.s and S.T.s*** are established in some places to help them to appear for UPSC Examinations and for I.A.S. and I.P.S. Examinations. The 1971 Census Report indicates that literacy has gone down in some tribal areas, while it has registered a slight progress in some other areas. Even in 1981 the literacy campaign could reach only 16.35% of the tribals.. In some cases 100% of the expenses of the students may have to be met by the Government.

• ***Post-Matric Scholarships for ST Students:*** The objective of the scheme is to provide financial assistance to students belonging to STs pursuing post-matriculation recognised courses in recognised institutions. The scheme covers professional, technical, non-professional and non-technical courses at various levels.

• ***Girls / Boys Hostels for STs*** **:** Girls hostel scheme was started in the Third Five-Year Plan with the aim of providing residential facilities to tribal girls in pursuit of education. For this scheme, the central assistance [till 2007-08] is about 50% of the cost of construction of the hostels. During 1999-2000, an amount of ₹393 lakh has been released for 29 hostels. ***Boys hostel scheme*** was started in 1989-90 under the same pattern of the scheme. During 1999-2000, an amount of ₹698.43 lakh has been released for the construction of 77 hostels.

5. Medical Facilities

Various medical facilities have been provided for the tribals in the tribal areas. In some places, hospitals are established and in many places mobile hospital facilities have been provided. Many preventive and curative measures to combat the diseases like malaria, leprosy, forest fever, monkey fever, typhoid, small pox, skin diseases etc. are undertaken. Medical camps are organised in the tribal areas to enable the tribals to realise the importance of modern medical facilities.

6. Research Work into the Problems of the Tribals

Tribal Research Institutes, which undertake intensive studies of tribal art, culture and customs and problems have been set up in Bihar, Madhya Pradesh, Orissa, Gujarat, Kerala, Maharashtra, Tamil Nadu, Andhra Pradesh, U.P., Rajasthan and West Bengal. The research work done in this field has thrown light on the tribal life and problems.

The research institutes are engaged in providing planning inputs to the State Governments, conducting research and evaluation studies, collection of data, conduct of training, seminars and workshops. Some of these institutes are also having museums exhibiting tribal artefacts. During 1999-2000, a sum of ₹105.53 lakh was released to the State Governments for this purpose.

7. Special Schemes

(i) Adivasi Mahila Sashaktikarna Yojana [AMSY] is an exclusive scheme for the economic development of ST women, at a highly concessional rate of interest. Under the scheme, NSTFDC provides term loan for schemes and projects costing upto 50,000/- per individual unit / profit centre.

(ii) Micro-credit Scheme - Launch of a New Scheme: This scheme is meant to provide financial assistance for undertaking small self-employement ventures / activities by the eligible STs through existing profit - making SHGs. In case of need, NSTFDC may provide 100% of the funds required as term loan subject to maximum of ₹ 15000/- per member.

8. Role of Voluntary Organisations

The tribal welfare is not the concern of the government alone. Private organisations and individuals interested in the task of tribal upliftment must also be given due encouragement in this regard. **Takkar Bapa** and **Gandhiji** have shown that individuals and voluntary organisations with social commitment can do a lot for the welfare of tribals. Organisations such as – *Sri Ramakrishna Mission, Vanavasi Kalyanashrama, the Rastreeya Swayam Sevaka Sangha and a number of Christian Missionary Organisations* are already working in the field. Such organisations can help the tribals to develop better interaction with the neighbouring people.

- ***Aid to Voluntary Organisations Working for the Welfare of the STs*** **:** The ministry gives grant in aid to voluntary organisations working for the welfare of the scheduled tribes for projects like residential schools, hostels, medical units, computer training units, short-hand and typing training units, balawadis / creches, libraries and audio - visual units. The grant is generally restricted to 90% of approved total cost of the project and the balance 10% is borne by the grantee organisations. During 1999-2000, an amount of ₹14.74 crore was released to 137 NGOs [Non-Governmental Organisations]. During the 10th Five Year Plan period, ₹ 146.16 crores were released under this scheme. An amount of ₹ 27.80 crore was released during 2009-10.

9. Recognition of Forest Rights of STs:

The Scheduled Tribes and other Traditional Forest Dwellers [Recognition of Forest Rights] Act 2006, seeks to recognise and vest the forest rights and occupation in forest land in forest dwelling of the Scheduled Tribes and other traditional forest dwellers who have been residing in such forests for generations. The Act has been notified for operation with effect from 31 December 2007.

Brief Assessment of the Welfare Programmes : Their Deficiencies and Failures

The Government of India which claims itself as a welfare state has no doubt made several constitutional and legislative provisions for the development and the welfare of the tribals. In almost all the Five Year Plans, crores of rupees had been earmarked for undertaking tribal developmental activities. All the Ministries in the Central Cabinet had their own wings to look into the needs of the tribals and to promote their welfare. Various committees and commissions were constituted from time to time to recommend new programmes and schemes for the tribals. State Governments are also being encouraged to take initiative in help solving the problems of the tribals.

In spite of all these attempts to improve the living conditions of the tribals and promote their welfare, tribals of India have not been benefited much. They continue to suffer from the same age-old problems though their intensity is somewhat reduced now. Governmental efforts to promote tribal welfare have not been attained the expected success. On the contrary, many of these programmes and projects have proved to be a failure. **S.C. Dube** in his article in *Encyclopaedia of Social Work in India* Vol.3 points out various defects and deficiencies involved in the tribal development and welfare programmes. The views expressed by S.C. Dube in this connection can be briefly mentioned here.

1. The planners of the Tribal Developmental Projects have *failed to understand the diversities that exist between different tribal groups.* On the contrary, they treated the tribal community as *"a monolithic and undifferentiated entity."* Hence most of them ended in failures.
2. The planners *never took into account the relative numerical strength of different tribal groups.* There are tribal groups which have lakhs of members, while there are certain others which have only a couple of hundreds which are struggling for their existence. This difference is ignored by the planners.
3. The planners resorted to the *"omnibus planning, with a generalised conception of tribal problems"* and this led to *"misdirection of efforts."* When the tribals have got so much of cultural and physical diversities no single plan or project could be deemed as all comprehensive or all inclusive.
4. Most of the projects and schemes that were launched by the government *never took into account the felt-needs of the people.* Priorities were never fixed taking into account the immediate needs of the tribals. On the contrary, what the planners considered important was imposed on the tribals. Needless to say, they met cold reception.
5. A major portion of the money allotted for developmental programmes was *spent on the establishment of the plans and projects.* The amount of money that was really spent on the tribals was the least one. Much of it was spent on the salaries of the planners, the bureaucrats, employees of different cadres, on buildings, offices, employees' quarters, vehicles and their maintenance, roads and bridges, and so on.
6. The type of the services such as educational, medical, etc. that is being given to the tribals in the name of "tribal welfare" is found to be of very *poor standard.* This has annoyed the feelings of the tribals.
7. *Tribals are not supplied with enough foodgrains.* There are many tribal groups residing in the distant corners of the forests who are not even supplied with pure drinking water. In some areas, tribal women and children are made to walk miles of distance eveyday to fetch drinking water. This picture has not changed yet.
8. There are tribals who *do not have proper and enough dresses to wear, and good houses to live in.* Some of the tribals are so poor that they do not have even a second pair of clothes to wear when the first one is kept for drying after wash.
9. The new economic system has posed new problems and challenges for the tribals. It has neither provided them *a job for the entire year nor enough salary to make their both ends meet.* Unemployment and under-employment coupled with poverty have made them borrow money at the hands of money lenders. Their economic helplessness compel them to get trapped in this vicious circle.
10. Education has been considered a panacea for all social problems including the tribal problems. *But educational programmes launched by the governments are found to be disappointing. Ashrama* schools which posed themselves to be attractive in the beginning have failed to get enough children. Teachers who are appointed in the schools in the tribal areas are also found to be insincere having no concern for the tribal children.

11. It appears as though the central and the state governments are treating the tribals as things that could be "paraded" or "exhibited" to the dignitaries who visit national or state headquarters. Tribals are slowly becoming aware of the fact that they are being paraded to the so called dignified visitors as "show-pieces" of indigenous culture. This has hurt their self-respect.
12. It has also been found that several state governments have miserably failed in making effective use of the central financial assistance given for promoting the welfare of the tribals. There are also instances in which the funds that were allotted for the tribal welfare were diverted to other departments. In some other cases, the unutilised funds came back to the centre.
13. Indifference, irresponsibility, and lethargy on the part of the government employees have made many plans to meet with miserable failures. Hence, **Dube** cautions that one should *"....... not have an illusion that good plan necessarily produces good results."*

Conclusion

Though the Central and the State Governments have taken much interest in the tribal welfare programmes, projects and schemes, much remains to be done. The progress achieved in this field is far from satisfactory. The Sixth Plan document notes with concern that *"three decades of development have not had the desired impact on the socially, economically and educationally handicapped section"*. The Welfare programmes have not been effective due to the *"inadequacies in the administrative machinery, lack of sensitive trained management, lack of general preparedness for large investments, deficiency in accounting systems, procedural delays and lack of proper monitoring and evaluation...."* The plan document admits [in its clause 26-10] that *"no positive steps were taken to ensure that S.C. and S.T. obtained their share of the benefits of public distribution."* Even after the completion of the 9th Plan things have not radically improved. It is necessary that in the years to come due attention is to be paid for the over all improvement of the tribals.

S.C. Dube is of the opinion that in the absence of *"strong political will"* and *"bureaucratic commitment"* all our plans and projects are bound to become failures. He bitterly criticises the manner in which the list of the Scheduled Tribes is prepared. The process of preparing the list has become a matter of *"political policy"*, and hence cultural, economic, sociological and ethnic criteria are conveniently ignored. In order to provide the real benefit of the welfare programmes to the needy persons *"an economic criteria will have to be introduced"* in the process of the preparation of the list of Scheduled Tribes. Dube has warned about the political interference in the implementation of welfare programmes. He was also aware of the difficulties involved in de-politicalising the developmental programmes. Hence he suggests *"It is not possible to de-politicise the development process, but institutions will have to be built to take over the responsibility of this programme ultimately."*[10]

Dube has also recognised the need to harmonise the national and tribal interests. He states : "........ let it be understood that the tribal problem cannot be isolated from the broader national problems. Its solution will have to form part of the overall strategy for the regeneration of Indian society and polity........" **Dube** has stated that there are certain problems which are uniquely tribal. These problems are to be studied in detail sympathetically and scientifically. The studies must help us to find out a long lasting solution for these problems. He concludes : *"The tribes have to find themselves a place in Indian society consistent with their conception of honour, but this must be done without detriment to the integrity or strength of India as a nation."* At the same time, it is also necessary to appreciate and retain the distinct cultural ethos of the tribal communities.

10 **S.C. Dube** in his article on the *"Welfare of Scheduled Tribes"* in *Encyclopaedia of Social Work in India.* Vol.III.

The Major Tribal Groups Which Inhabit India	
1. Abors - Arunachal Pradesh and Assam	25. Khinds - Orissa
2. Adi, Apatami - Arunachal Pradesh	26. Kol - M.P
3. Angami, Ao - Nagaland	27. Kotas - Tamil Nadu
4. Badagas - Tamil Nadu	28. Kuki - Manipura
5. Baigas - M.P, Rajasthan, Gujarath	29. Lepchas or Rongpa - Sikkim
6. Bhils - M.P, Rajasthan, Gujarath	30. Lushias - Tripura
7. Bhotias - U.P [Garhwal and Kumao]	31. Meiteis - Manipura, Nagaland
8. Bhutias - Sikkim	32. Mina - Rajasthan
9. Birhor - Bihar	33. Miri - Arunachal Pradesh
10. Bodos - Assam	34. Mikirs - Assam
11. Chenchus - A.P and Orissa	35. Mundas - Bihar
12. Chutia - Assam	36. Oarons - Bihar, Orissa
13. Dangs - Gujarath	37. Onges - Little Andmans
14. Gaddis - H.P [Himachal Pradesh]	38. Rabhas - Assam
15. Garos - Meghalaya	39. Rengma - Nagaland
16. Gonds : M.P, Bihar, Orissa, A.P	40. Santhals - West Bengal, Bihar
17. Great Andamanese - Andaman Island	41. Sema - Nagaland
18. Irulas - Tamil Nadu	42. Sentinelesse - Andman and Nicobar Island
19. Jaintias - Meghalaya	43. Shompens - Great Nicobar Island
20. Jarawas - Little Andamans	44. Tagin - Arunachal Pradesh
21. Kanis - Kerala	45. Todas - Tamil Nadu
22. Kacharis, Karbi - Assam	46. Uralis - Kerala
23. Khampti - Arunachal Pradesh	47. Zeliang - Nagaland
24. Khasis - Meghalaya, Assam	

Source : *Manoram Year Book 2014*, Page No. 574.

No. of Tribes Notified Under Article 342 of the Constitution of India and Some Other Information About the Indian Tribals

As notified under Article -342 of the Constitution, there are **700** tribes [with many of them overlapping in more than one State] spreadover different States and Union Territories of the country.

It is worth noting that no community has been specified as a Scheduled Tribe in relation to States of Haryana and Punjab and the Union Territories of Chandigarh, Delhi and Puduchery.

- According to the 2001 Census, the population of STs in the country was **8.43** crores, i.e., constituting **8.2%** of the total population of the country. It increased to 8.6% in 2011.
- The tribal communities live in about **15%** of the country's area in varying ecological and geo-climatic conditions, plains, forests, hills and inaccessible areas.
- More than **50%** of the total ST population of the country is concentrated in 6 States : Madhya Pradesh, Chhatishgarh, Maharasthra, Orissa, Jharkand and Gujarath.
- The largest number of tribes that is **62**, are in the State of Orissa and the next major concentration is in the North - Eastern States.
- **Sex Ratio** : Sex ratio for the over all population was only 933 females [for one thousand males] whereas for the STs. It was 978 in 2001.
- There are about **2474** forest villages in 12 States which are managed by State Forest Departments and in these villages there are about **2.5** lakh tribal families still managing to pull on.

Source : *India Year Book* - 2011. Page - 987-1002, **Govt of India Publication**.

Scheduled Tribes: As per Census 2011

Primary Census Abstract

- The STs constitute 8.6% of the total population.
- Between 2001-2011, the STs grew by 23.7% and the all India percentage for the same period is 17.7 [Between 1991-2001, this growth rate of tribes was 24.45%]
- The highest proportion of the S.T. population is to found in Lakshadweep, and that is 94.8%.
- More than half the STs population is concentrated in the States of Madhya Pradesh, Chhattishgarh, Maharatra, Odisha, Jharkhand and Gujarat.
- There are about 75 tribals who are known as primitive tribal groups [PTGSs]. They are characterized by – (a) pre-agricultural level of technology, (b) declining population, and (c) subsistence level of economy. They are the poorest tribals.

Source: *Manorama Year Book - 2014*. Page: 672.

●●●

Chapter 20

BACKWARD CASTES / CLASSES [OBCs] THEIR PROBLEMS AND WELFARE

Who Form the Backward Classes ? - Definition of Backward Classes - Description of Backward Classes - Indian Constitution Does Not Define OBCs - Appointment of Backward Classes Commission : First Backward Classes Commission 1953 : Kalelkar Commission - Observations Made by the Kalelkar's Commission- Policy of the Central Government - Negotiations With the States- Decision of the Central Government - Second Backward Classes Commission 1979 : Mandal Commission - Acceptance of Its Recommendations - Reservation Policy as per Mandal Commission - Criteria of Backwardness - Weightage Given to Each Category of Criteria - Reservation for the OBCs Among the Non-Hindus ? - Four Channels for Collecting Data to Identify the OBCs - Main Recommendations of Mandal Commission - Some Other Special Recommendations - Historic Judgement of the Supreme Court and Its Impact - Arguments For and Against Reservation - Conclusion - Problems of Backward Castes / Classes and Mainly OBCs - Various Schemes and Measures for the Welfare of the Backward Castes, Particularly the OBCs.

India is a country where a large number of people are found to be illiterate, ignorant, poor and backward. India is a classical land of caste in which caste is the main form of social stratification. The backwardness of Indian people is closely connected with the type of the stratification system that it has, that is, the caste. The main disadvantage here is that the people's status is ascribed to them by birth in certain castes and tribal groups. Thus the problem of majority of the Indians can be understood, as **Prof. B. Kuppuswamy** has pointed out, *"....... only in terms of the basic character of Indian society which consists of a multitude of closed status groups with unequal ranks, each with its own privileges and disabilities supported by traditional sanctions. Thus it must be recognized at the outset that the term class is not appropriate since that term is associated with an economic category and indicates an open status group. By contrast, the backward classes in India form an aggregate of closed status groups; they belong to these groups by birth, not because of their individual economic characteristics."*[1]

---

1 **B. Kuppuswamy** in his *"Social Change in India"* 2nd Edition [1975]. Page - 192.

Hence, it is clear from the above, that the concept of caste is more helpful in understanding the Indian stratification system rather than the concept of class. The British people too had made use of the concept of *"backward classes"* to refer to the most *"backward castes"* of India. In fact, the British Government had used the concept of *"backward classes"* as early as in 1885 in its **"Port Saint George Gazette"** dated 5th November 1885. **M.N. Srinivas** has also stated that the term *"backward classes"* represents in the Indian context, lower castes including the scheduled castes. Thus, according to him, the term *"backward classes movement"* must be understood in the Indian context, as *"backward castes movement."*

WHO FORM THE "BACKWARD CLASSES" ?

The term *"backward classes"* has not been defined properly either by the sociologists or by the constitution-makers. The backward classes are a large mixed category of persons with boundaries that are both unclear and elastic. They seem to comprise roughly one-third of the total population of the country. They consist of three main categories – ***the scheduled castes [SCs], the scheduled tribes [STs]*** and *the* ***"other backward classes"[OBCs].*** The scheduled castes and scheduled tribes are comparatively better defined and they form roughly 22% of the total population according to the 1971 Census. The "other backward classes" is a *residual category.* Their position is highly ambiguous and it is not possible to give an exact statement of their numbers.

Definition of Backward Classes

Though the term *"Backward Classes"* is popularly used by sociologists it is not defined properly. Still for our purpose of study we may define it in the following way:

1. **Justice K. Subba Rao,** former Chief Justice of India, defined *"backward classes"* as – *"an ascertainable and identifiable group of persons based on caste, religion, race, language, occupation and such others, with definite characteristics of backwardness in various aspects of human existence – social, cultural, economic, political and such others."*
2. We can generally define *"backward classes" as those social groups or classes or castes which are characterised by low literacy and lack of education, poverty, exploitation of labour, non-representation in services and untouchability.*
3. In simple words, the term *"backward classes"* can be defined as *a social category which consists of all the socially, educationally, economically and politically backward groups, castes and tribes.*

Description of the Backward Classes

The *Backward Classes Commission* in its Report [1956] described the Backward Classes as consisting of the following groups:

1. *Those who suffer from the stigma of untouchability or near untouchability.* These groups are classified as ***Scheduled Castes [SC].***
2. *Those tribes who are not yet sufficiently assimilated into the mainstream of the national life.* These groups are classified as ***Scheduled Tribes [ST].***
3. *Those tribes who, due to long neglect, have been forced to commit crime.* These tribes were previously known as criminal tribes [before 1953] and are presently called ***Denotified Tribes*** *or* ***Ex-Criminal Tribes.***
4. ***"Other Backward Classes"*** **[OBCs]** consist of the following groups or communities:
   (a) Those nomads who have no occupation of a fixed habitation and are given to mimicry, begging, jugglery, dancing, etc.

(b) Communities consisting largely of agricultural or landless labourers,

(c) Communities consisting largely of tenants without occupancy rights and those with insecure land tenure,

(d) Communities consisting of a large percentage of small land owners with uneconomic holdings,

(e) Communities engaged in cattle breeding, sheep breeding or fishing on small scale,

(f) Artisan and occupational classes without security of employment and whose traditional occupations have ceased to be remunerative,

(g) Communities, the majority of whose people do not have sufficient education and therefore have not secured adequate representation in Government services,

(h) Social groups from among Muslims, Christians and Sikhs who are still backward socially and educationally, and

(i) Communities not occupying positions in social hierarchy.

Of the four major groups that constitute the **"backward classes",** the third category or group [denotified tribes] is normally included in the 2nd category of STs. Hence, for all practical purposes, the *"backward classes"* normally consist of the following three major category of groups : (i) **SCs,** (ii) **STs,** and (iii) **OBCs.** About the SCs and STs, we have already dealt with in two separate chapters. The third category of OBCs may thus be analysed here.

- **Indian Constitution Does Not Define But Makes Reference to the Concept of OBCs**

The third major category of *"backward classes"* consists of a large number of educationally and economically backward people. Though the term *"backward classes"* has not been defined by the Indian Constitution, the characteristics of backwardness are described here and there and also sometimes the categories are mentioned.

- *Article 15(4)* speaks of the socially and educationally backward.
- *Article 16(4)* uses the term *"backward class"* and speaks of inadequate representation in services.
- *Article 45* mentions free and compulsory education.
- *Article 46* mentions the weaker sections of the people and includes the expression "the Scheduled Castes and Scheduled Tribes."
- *Article 340* empowers the State to investigate the condition of the Backward Classes and to help them by grants, etc.

Thus the Constitution has accepted the following elements of backwardness; *illiteracy and lack of education, poverty, exploitation of labour, non-representation in services and untouchability.*

APPOINTMENT OF BACKWARD CLASSES COMMISSIONS

First Backward Classes Commission - 1953

Kalelkar Commission

As it is made clear, the term *"backward classes"* is vague in the sense that it includes a wide variety of lower classes as well as castes consisting of millions of people. *Article* 340 of the Constitution provides for the appointment of a commission to investigate the conditions of backward classes. Accordingly, the President [that is, the Union Government] appointed on Jan. 29, 1953, **The Backward Classes Commission** under the chairmanship of **Kakasaheb**

PROBLEMS OF THE CHALLENGING BACKWARDNESS

Kalelkar. The Commission prepared a list containing as many as 2,399 communities which were treated as socially and educationally backward. Out of these, 913 communities alone had an estimated population of 115 million. The Commission adopted the following criteria for determining backwardness:

1. *Low Social position in the traditional caste hierarchy of Hindu Society.*
2. *Lack of general advancement among the major section of a caste or community.*
3. *Inadequate or no representation in Government services.*
4. *Inadequate representation in the field of trade, commerce and industry.*

Observations Made by Kalelkar Commission

Some of the major observations and recommendations made by the Kalelkar Commission and as referred to by **Prof. B. Kuppuswamy**[2] can be mentioned here.

1. One of the first recommendations of the Commission was that the 1961 census should provide caste-wise figures so that *"before the disease of caste is destroyed all facts about it have to be noted and classified in a certain manner as in a clinical record."* [Page - 11 of the Report of the Commission].

2. The Commission also pointed out the anomaly which arose when some Scheduled Caste persons called themselves *"Harijans"* but found that they were not eligible for scholarships, etc. since the term *"Harijan"* is not in the authorised list.

3. The Commission also recommended that certain sections of the Muslims, Christians, Sikhs should be included among the "Other Backward Classes" [Page : 27 - 29 of the Report].

4. The Commission prepared a list of about 2,400 castes on the basis of the position of the caste in social hierarchy, percentage of literacy and its representation in government service and in industries, etc. The Commission also revised the lists of Scheduled Castes and Scheduled Tribes on the basis of the new information available.

5. "The Commission noted that the great majority of the backward classes are ignorant, illiterate, and poor. They are easily exploited by several classes of persons like the traders, the moneylenders."

6. The Commission also noted that the administration system itself, which has to implement the Constitutional provisions, is tainted by casteism; this is one of the reasons why the backward classes have no confidence in securing a fair deal even from the administration. The Commission warns that unless this is immediately remedied there would be class conflicts which would affect national solidarity. [Page - 101].

7. The Commission also draws pointed attention to the contradiction between the theory and the practice of Hinduism. While in theory Hinduism recognises the concept of universality in practice it follows the Laws of Manu which perpetuate the four-fold divisions of the social order and the superiority of the Brahmin class.

8. The Commission notes *"A complete revolution in the social outlook of the people is necessary for rendering social justice to all the backward people."* [Page - 104].

9. Dealing with the problems of educational backwardness, the Commission noted that the only general figures available are the literary rates which show a very slow progress. *"The problem of education in most of the States is chiefly the problem of the backward classes, for it is they who are extremely backward in education."* [Page - 109]. Even when special scholarships and other facilities are provided the children of these classes do not study. The Commission recommends liberal budget provision to give scholarships to the students of the backward classes.

2 **B. Kuppuswamy** in *"Social Change in India."* Page : 227 - 231.

The Commission recommends that 70% of the seats in professional colleges should be reserved for them; and in making selections, preference should be given to those coming from *the most backward classes* which are indicated in the lists drawn up. [Page - 125].

10. With respect to representation in government and local body services, the Commission recommended the reservation of 25% of the Class I vacancies, one-third of the Class II vacancies, and 40% of the Class III and Class IV for the Other Backward Classes. [Page - 142]. This percentage has to be over and above that which has already been conceded to the SCs and STs.

11. As regards reservation in services, the Chairman of the Commission laid down : *"In this matter one clear principle must be accepted and observed. Reservations, if contemplated, must not exceed 49% whatever the total population of all the Reserved Communities be, as far as Classes III and IV are concerned. In the case of Classes I and II he recommended that "the backward classes will stand to gain both morally and materially, if they do not demand a reservation percentage in vacancies...... They should demand greatest facilities for training and education in order to fit themselves for the highest jobs, as speedily as possible"."* [Page - IX].

Policy of the Central Government

Kalelkar Commission's report was not accepted by the Central Government due to lot of criticisms and objections against it. The Government decided to find out highly objective, realistic and workable criteria to identify the real backward groups and communities of India. The Deputy Registrar General of Census was also consulted to collect through his department information regarding the jobs in which the so called socially and educationally backward people are found in a large number. Even that did not yield any fruitful results.

Negotiations with the States

The Central Government initiated talks with at least 8 State Governments to identify the castes / groups / communities which could be included in the list of backward classes. In these negotiations with the States, various views came to limelight. Some of the opinions expressed are given below :

1. Some States expressed the view that it is better to identify "backward areas" rather than backward castes / classes.

2. More than the caste, economic factor should be the main criterion.

3. Some States insisted that no change should be made in the existing caste-based list of "backward classes."

4. Central Government has no legal or constitutional obligation to prepare such a list of "backward classes." Even if the Central Government proposes such a kind of list the State Governments must have freedom to prepare their own list of backward classes.

5. Some states expressed their fear that the attempts to classify people either in the name of caste or class would not only damage the unity of the nation but also encourage divisive forces such as caste.

6. Some expressed the view that the attempts to prepare such a list of backward classes is against the principles of a secular, classless democratic socialist society. Hence, it must be dropped once and for all.

Decision of the Central Government

In the light of the expressed views as mentioned above, the Central Government decided to go forward very cautiously. It decided not to prepare a separate list of backward classes /

castes other than the SCs and STs. However, it accepted in principle the right of the State Governments to find out their own criteria in order to prepare a list of backward classes. The Central Government also suggested to the State Governments that it would be better for them to find out economic criteria rather than caste for this purpose.

Preparation of a list of backward classes has become more complicated nowadays because the recent censuses do not contain statistical information about the castes. [The First Backward Classes Commission, however, had taken into consideration caste-wise statistics available in the reports of censuses held in 1911, 1921, and 1931, and also taken into account their approximate increase by 1951.] The existence of certain castes which were never taken into account in the census held prior to independence, have further complicated the process of preparing the list of backward classes. In fact, some such castes also figured in the list of backward classes prepared by the First Commission, and this led to further confusion. Hence, even though the report of the First Backward Classes Commission was published in 1955, it was not accepted by the Government. It decided to provide an opportunity for a nation-wide discussion on the issue. Finally, it instituted the Second Backward Classes Commission in 1979 under the Chairmanship of **B.P. Mandal,** an ex-judge, and a member belonging to the backward caste. The Commission submitted its report in 1980.

Second Backward Classes Commission - 1979 : Mandal Commission

The Government considered seriously the objectives of Articles 15 and 16 of the Constitution and accordingly the *'Second Backward Classes Commission'* [*'Mandal Commission'*] was appointed in 1979. The terms of reference of the Commission included -- *(i) determination of the criteria for defining the socially and educationally backward classes, (ii) steps to be taken for the advancement of socially and educationally backward classes, (iii) desirability or otherwise of making provision for the reservation of appointments in favour of backward classes which are not adequately represented in public service and (iv) presenting a report setting out the facts as found by the Commission for making such recommendations.* - The Commission submitted its Report on 31 December 1980.

Acceptance of the Recommendations of Mandal Commission

After long deliberations on the recommendations of the Mandal Commission, it was decided by the then Government to implement the same. The Mandal Commission in its report [1980] has listed 3743 castes and communities in the Central List whose population is estimated to be 52% of the total population of India. The Commission has recommended 27% reservation for such a large segment of the Indian population. Several Writ Petitions were filed in the Supreme Court questioning the said Reservation. All the Writ petitions were disposed off by the Honourable Supreme Court by its judgement dated 16th Nov. 1992. The Court also directed the Government and each of the State Governments to set up a permanent body for reflecting upon the request for inclusion and complaints regarding inclusions in the list of OBCs. Accordingly, a **National Commission for Backward Classes** [NCBC] was set up on 14th Aug. 1993, which had been reconstituted on 28th Feb. 1997.

As per the directions of the Supreme Court, the Govt. of India has notified the Central List of OBCs comprising in first phase, the castes / communities which are common both in the list prepared by the Mandal Commission and State Backward Classes List for 21 states and 5 Union Territories. Recently, three notifications on inclusion / amendment in the Central List of OBCs have been issued by the Government.

Reservation Policy As Per Mandal Commission

Criteria of Backwardness

Reservation facility has been provided for people who are considered to be backward. But how is the backwardness of a community decided ? At present, as we are discussing the issue of reservation in the context of Mandal Commission's recommendations, it is relevant here to mention 11 criteria for determining social and educational backwardness as used by the Commission. In the social and economic indicators, there were four criteria each, while in the educational indicators, there were three criteria. Thus, in total there were 11 indicators. These 11 indicators or criteria which fall into three categories are mentioned below :

A. Social Criteria

1. Social backwardness as considered by others.
2. Dependence mainly on manual labour for livelihood.
3. Marriage of 25% girls and 10% boys in rural areas, and of 10% girls and 5% boys in urban area below 17 years.
4. Female work Participation 25% above the State average.

B. Educational Criteria

5. Children between 5 and 15 years never attending school 25% above the State average.
6. Student drop-out rate 25% above the State average.
7. Matriculation rate 25% below the State average.

C. Economic Criteria

8. Average value of family assets 25% below the State average.
9. Families living in *Kachcha* houses 25% above the State average.
10. Sources of drinking water beyond 500 metres for more than 50% of the families.
11. Consumption loans by households 25% above the State average.

Weightage Given to Each Category of Criteria

The above mentioned 11 criteria were differently weighted. Social criteria were given a weightage of **3** points each, educational criteria **2** points each, and the economic criteria one point each. Thus the total value was 22 [4X3+3X2+4x1=22] points. Any caste getting more than 50% of the points, that is, 11 points, was counted as backward.

Reservation for the OBCs Among the Non-Hindus ?

Mandal Commission extended the reservation facility to the OBCs among the non-Hindus. The above mentioned 11 criteria are mostly applied to the case of Hindu communities, including the tribes, to decide their backwardness. Some other criteria are adopted for determining the OBCs among the non-Hindus. All untouchables converted to non-Hindu religions are considered as OBCs. If a non-Hindu community continued its traditional occupation, and if that occupation qualified a Hindu community to be treated as backward, then the non-Hindu community would be included among the OBCs.

Four Channels For Collecting Data to Identify the OBCs

The Mandal Commission found out four channels to collect data to identify castes, communities and groups that could be included among the OBCs. These four channels were :

1. Detailed questionnaires for the public advertised extensively in English and vernacular dailies;
2. Evidence from 97 MPs;
3. Extensive tours of States and Union Territories for meeting elected representatives, leaders of social and caste associations, and representatives from the public.
4. Survey of 405 of the 406 Districts of the country.

Main Recommendations of Mandal Commission

1. The Commission recommended 27% reservation of the jobs for the OBCs. It enlisted 3743 castes and communities which are entitled for this reservation. As per the Article 15(4) and 16(4) of the Constitution, total quota of reservation should not exceed 50%. Hence, the Commission recommended only 27% reservation for the OBCs though their share in the total population exceed 52%.
2. The Commission recommended that those candidates from the OBCs who were selected through open competition should not be adjusted against the reservation quota.
3. The system of reservation should apply to all levels of promotions.
4. Unfilled reservation quota should be carried on over for **3** years and de-reserved only thereafter.
5. Relaxation of upper age limit for direct recruitment from the SCs and STs should be extended to the OBCs.
6. A roster system for each category of posts should be adopted as in the case of the SCs and STs.
7. The 27% reservation to OBCs is applicable to the jobs in central government services and public sector units including the banking sector, LIC, etc.
8. This reservation is also applicable to the private sector undertakings such as educational institutions which receive financial grants from the central or state governments.
9. All the universities and colleges that receive financial assistance from the government are expected to implement this reservation.
10. Due modifications in the existing system of law, if necessary should be undertaken in order to enforce this reservation.

Some Other Special Recommendations

1. In order to improve the backward community students' cultural environment especially in the places in which OBCs reside in a large number, *special efforts must be made to give them additional coaching, vocational training and other educational facilities.* OBC students studying in professional courses may require such an assistance in order to keep pace with the other community students.

2. In all the States *rural people belonging to the OBCs must be given financial assistance* either through subsidy or cheap rate loans in order to encourage them to take more and more interest in industrial and commercial activities. If needed, the rural semi-skilled and skilled persons of these communities must be provided facilities to improve their expertise in their respective fields.

3. All the State governments are *advised to implement land reforms in a strict manner* in order to remove the dependence of the tenants, landless labourers, rural professions and the owners of small land holdings on the money-lenders and the rich farmers.

4. The *Central Government must provide financial assistance to the State governments* if they are not able to mobilise sufficient funds in order to take up the various welfare activities mentioned above, for the benefit of the OBCs. This assistance the Central Govt. must provide just as in the manner in which it is providing such an assistance to the States for the welfare activities of the SCs and STs.

Historic Judgement of the Supreme Court [15-11-1992] : Its Impact

After the fall of V.P. Singh's and Chandrashekar's ministries at the Centre, 10th Parliamentary Elections took place in 1991 in which Congress came back to power and P.V. Narasimha Rao became the Prime Minister. His Government announced in Sept. 1991 that within the 27% of the Union Govt.'s civilian jobs reserved for socially and educationally backward classes [SEBC], preference would be given to the poorer sections of such classes. He went a step further, and declared *10% reservation for the other economically backward sections of the people who were not covered by any of the existing schemes of reservation.*

The controversial issue of the implementation of Mandal Commission's Report was taken to the Supreme Court which gave a historic judgement on it on 15th Nov. 1992. The Court upheld 27% reservation recommended by the Mandal Commission but struck down the Narasimha Rao Govt.'s decision to reserve 10% jobs for other economically backward sections.

Important aspects of this judgement as enlisted by **Prof. Ram Ahuja** are : [3]

1. Caste has been accepted as a basis for identifying the beneficiaries of reservations.
2. The upper limit of reservations has been fixed at 50 per cent.
3. *"Creamy layer"* has to be excluded from reservations.
4. Reservation in certain technical posts is not advisable.
5. There can be no reservations in promotions.
6. The Union Government shall specify the socio-economic criteria to exclude socially advanced persons among the backward classes.
7. Permanent commissions should be set up by the union and state governments to examine complaints of over-inclusion and under-inclusion and requests for inclusion in the list of backward classes.

In the light of these developments which are at the background of the Mandal Commission's Report and its implementation, it is relevant here to discuss the pros and cons of the present reservation policy.

ARGUMENTS *FOR* AND *AGAINST* RESERVATION

The National Front Government's [1989-90] sudden announcement of accepting the recommendations of Mandal Commission's Report in August 1990 evoked widespread resentments and supports throughout the nation. This announcement of Prime Minister V.P. Singh was described as a political decision. The student community in particular protested against it very sharply in North India. Spontaneous agitations took place in several places of the nation. During mid-September and mid-October 1990 more than 160 young people attempted to commit suicide as a mark of their protest against the unjustifiable reservation policy. However, not a single political party openly protested the government's reservation policy.

Mandal Commission's recommendations which formed the primary bases of the reservation policy, have both positive and negative aspects. The recommendations were warmly welcomed in some circles while they were strongly opposed in some other circles. Arguments both *in*

3 **Prof. Ram Ahuja** in his *"Indian Social Systems"* [1993]. Page - 381.

favour of the recommendations and *against* them have been advanced. Let us now consider these arguments.[4]

Merits of Reservation OR Arguments In Favour of It

1. Providing Justice to All: Reservation policy is likely to satisfy and uplift all those weaker sections of the society which were discontented and had suffered injustice and insults for decades. If fundamental rights are to be guaranteed to all, then, they are to be guaranteed to the weaker sections also. Reservation is one of the *means* of guaranteeing such an equality. *Competition becomes just only when participants are equal.*

2. Reservations Are Not Made On Caste Basis Alone: It is wrong to say that reservations are made *only* on the caste basis and hence such a policy is likely to perpetuate casteism. **For example,** Rajputs in Bihar are not included in the list of backward classes whereas Rajputs in Gujarat are included; similarly, the Yadavs of Bihar and U.P. are included but not the Yadavs of Haryana; Patels of Gujarat are not included but Patels of Bihar are in the list. Reservations are made on the basis of educational and economic backwardness also.

Further, **to remove inequalities of caste, actions on casteline are necessary.** Upper castes monopolised the privileges and high income occupations for centuries. To remedy this situation, jobs must be preferentially allotted to the backwards and admissions for them in educational institutions must be provided, until parity is restored.

3. Economic Factor As a Criterion Will Help Only the Poor Among the Forwards: A poor member of a forward community will definitely fare better than the poor among the SCs, STs and OBCs. This is quite natural because the forwards are mostly literate and are in touch with the latest developments. Further, they are in regular social contact with the other forwards who have already progressed. Possessing upper caste culture helps them to be at ease with the ways of those who judge merit.

4. Merit Will Not Become a Casuality: The argument that reservation policy damages the principle of merit is untenable. If merit were to be the sole factor for providing opportunities to the people, then the country should have progressed a lot with the leadership of the "so called merited" people. Administration by the *"meritorious"* for the last 45 years has been unable to implement land reforms and programmes to remove untouchability and backwardness among the masses of India. They have no right to speak about merit.

5. Influence of Caste is Present in the Current Product: Reservation is sought not to compensate for the past wrongs, but for removing the injustice in the present dispensation, where the forward castes continue to grab all the privileges. The handicaps experienced by the SCs, STs and OBCs are nothing but the accumulated effect of exploitation at the hands of the upper caste people who reserved all the privileges for themselves.

6. Lower Castes Do Not Have Benefits of Connections Which the Upper Castes Have: Proper socio-economic and political connections are an important asset among the forward castes. Because of such connections, even the poorest among the upper castes are able to get benefits without much difficulty. Whereas the lower caste people are always at a disadvantage in establishing such useful socio-economic connections.

7. Reservation Is To Be Made Meaningful Through Other Efforts: It is unscientific to believe that reservation alone can bring about widespread changes among all the members of the backward classes. On the contrary, various other measures such as the spread of education,

4. *Main Source* : **Prof. Antony P. Palatty's** article on *"Reservation and Its Implications"* published in *"Samaja Shodhana"*, Journal of the Mangalore University Sociology Teachers' Association, Vol.I, No.2, Oct. 1992. Pages : 79 - 82.

increase in infrastructural facilities in the areas where the SCs, STs and OBCs live, are very much necessary. Reservation facility is to be supplemented through other efforts.

8. Social Benefits of Reservation Do Spread Very Rapidly: Various studies and observations have revealed that even though only a few families are going to be benefited directly out of reservation, the social benefits of the reservation are going to spread very rapidly. It means reservation facility can create a new awareness, self confidence, courageousness, adventurous spirit and self respect among the backward castes / classes.

Demerits of Reservation OR Arguments Against It

1. Gross Neglect of Merit: One of the most widely criticised aspects of reservation policy is that it affects very badly the merit. Candidates are to be recruited for jobs and admission is to be made to the educational institutions on merit basis. This is required in the interest of the concerned agencies, disciplines, individuals and also in the larger interest of the nation. Neglect of the principle of merit will bring down efficiency and lower the morale of the meritorious. This double effect is dangerous for national growth and development. As **Guha** [1990] has pointed out reservation *"mortgages the future of India."*

2. Provision of Reservation is an Insult to the Fundamental Rights and Equality of Opportunities: The Constitution should treat the people of India on equal terms. But reservation provides some special treatment for some sections of the society which is unfair. As the fundamental rights have an overriding power, reservation should not be allowed to stand in their way.

3. Providing Compensation for the Past Injustice is Meaningless: It is true that some sections of the Indian society were treated very inhumanly and were exploited in various ways. But those exploited are dead and gone. Causing injustice to the forward castes in the present generation will not restore the losses of the past generations of the backward castes.

4. Reservation Causes Great Injustice to the Forward Castes and Classes: It is very unfair to do injustice to one section of the society in order to assure justice to another section. Reservation thus does great injustice to the forward castes. The forward castes have given their own contribution to the march of society. Their members are also prepared to put forth efforts to help the nation to take a big leap towards progress. Denying them an equal opportunity is not only injustice but also unfair.

5. Poverty and Economic Criteria Should be the Basis of Reservation: Reservation is required for the people who are genuinely poor. Irrespective of the caste, class, region or religion or sex to which they belong, must be assured of help through reservation. If reservation is given in this way it can be regarded as just and appropriate. But the present reservation policy benefits only a small elite fringe among the lower castes.

6. Reservation Contributes to the Perpetuation of Caste: Modern independent India visualises a casteless society. Attempts to provide reservation on the basis of caste will only enhance the importance of caste and increase the caste mindedness and *"caste patriotism."* Reservation policy will only lead to the reversal of historical cycle by enlivening the caste. In other words, reservation will create a backward moving society.

7. Removal of Corruption Should Be Our First Priority, But Not Reservation: From the point of view of national development what is more important is an honest administration, and not an administration by the inefficient and meritless people. Reservation will only add to the corruption because people try their level best through all possible means to reap the benefits of reservation.

8. There are Other Better Solutions to the Progress of Backward Classes: It is wrong to think that reservation alone is the master-fixer of solutions to the problems of backward classes. Social and educational backwardness is mostly due to the habits and attitudes of the people. These could be changed through the spread of education including what can be called a *"cultural revolution."*

9. Reservation is Only a Political Game and Nothing Else: The haste with which the reservation policy came to be introduced during V.P. Singh's administration itself makes it evident that it is more a political gimmick than a considered scheme for the amelioration of the problems of the backward classes. Political parties and their leaders wanted to create a permanent *"vote-bank"* through the implementation of the reservation policy.

10. Fear Experienced by the SCs and STs: Reservation policy has vertically divided the Hindu population into *"forward communities"* and *"backward communities."* It has fanned the fire of animosity, ill-will, jealousy, contempt and hatred between these two communities. Instances of clashes and conflicts between the two have been on the increase ever since the policy of reservation came into force. Hence, it has created terror and horror in the minds of the poor SCs, STs and OBCs. Further, clashes between the backward castes on the one hand, and SCs on the other, have also increased. Continuous attacks on some sections of SCs by the backward caste communities in Bihar, can be cited here as examples.

Conclusion

The policy of reservation has a great implication for the Indian society. It has *"........ set in motion processes that are capable of transforming a hierarchical society into an egalitarian one. The caste system effectively restricted privileges for a few upper castes and enforced difficult menial labour on the lowest castes."*[5]

Reservation and other aspects of positive discrimination have virtually put a limitation on the actual monopoly of the forward castes on legislation, government, administration and education. The SCs, STs and OBCs have now greater fortunes to occupy positions in the legislature, posts in the administration, and seats in educational institutions.

Reservation is an attempt to provide enough opportunities to the neglected sections of the Indian society to take part in the national development processes. It is believed that *"........ native intelligence has a tendency to be normally distributed and evenly shared by all human groups. Therefore, for the development of the nation's economy, society, and polity, the best from all sections of the population, including the SCs, STs, and OBCs, should be encouraged to participate in national life."* [**A.P. Palatty.** Page - 83.]

We are now living in an age of growing liberalisation and globalisation. In the growing liberalisation of the economy, the role of the government, including regulation, is decreasing. More liberty is given to the people and to the men of talents. In this age, *"more and more talent of all sections, forward, backward and others, can be more usefully marketed in the private sector – producing more, by more and for more."*

Certain precautions are however necessary to see that reservations do not create a permanent vested interest in small sections of the group for whom reservations are provided. The present reservation system is not a fool-proof system. It has its own limitations no doubt. In spite of its limitations the policy of reservation continues to stay. It is inadmissible and practically impossible at this stage to scrap the policy altogether. According **Roy Burman**, the policy of reservation has to be made more rational and scientific. In the given economic and political structure, caste should not determine one's life chances.

---

5 **Antony P.Palatty** in his article on *"Reservation and Its Implications."* Page - 82.

B.S. Bhargava and **Avinash Samal** [1998] have given some suggestions to improve the policy of reservation.[6] According to them, – 1. Income should be given more importance in determining the backwardness of the individual and not the caste to which he belongs. 2. The concept of *"creamy layer"* should be applied to SCs and STs also. It means rich people who belong to the category of SCs and STs should not be given reservation facility. 3. Reservation should be restricted *only to the first generation beneficiaries.* Children belonging to those who have availed of the reservation facility should not be given the same facility once again. 4. Concession of scholarship may be provided to SC, ST and OBC students securing more than a prescribed percentage of marks [say, 50% and above].

If the above mentioned suggestions are implemented then the benefits of reservation will be spread more evenly and widely within the targeted growth. This will also help to reduce opposition for the reservation by the forward castes. Nation building or national prosperity is not the responsibility of any particular section alone. On the contrary, it is a collective process in which all sections of the society should play an equally important role. The purpose of reservation is to provide a chance for those sections of the society which have been neglected so far, to play their role in this collective process.

Problems of Backward Castes / Classes and Mainly "OTHER BACKWARD CLASSES" [OBCS]

The underprivileged sections of the Indian society to which normally the SCs, STs and OBCs belong have been suffering from a number of problems since a long time. Some of the problems are commonly shared by these people with the lower sections of all the communities of India, while some others are unshared, and specifically faced by them only. Some of the socio-economic and political problems with which the *"Other Backward Classes"* / Castes are confronted, are analysed here.

1. Backward Castes [Classes] As Constituting An Indefinite, Abstract and Unorganised Category

What are the backward castes, which are the castes that come under this category – and for such other questions as these, there is no common satisfactory answer. Consensus is not formed yet. In fact, the Union Government had appointed the Backward Classes Commission under the chairmanship of **Kakasaheb Kalelkar** [on Jan. 29, 1953] to prepare a list of communities that would come under this category. Since the recommendations of this commission failed to obtain the consensus, from many sections of the society and also some of the political parties, the Government appointed the *Second Commission* under the chairmanship of **B.P. Mandal** in 1979 and it submitted its report in 1980.

The Mandal Commission listed 3743 castes and communities as belonging to the category of *"Other Backward Classes"* [These castes and communities are different from those already recognised as SCs and STs]. Some of the sections of the people belonging to the category of minorities also come under this category if they satisfy the conditions of backwardness.

The main problem here is that most of the communities, which belong to the category of OBCs are themselves strangers to one another. *The differences that exist among them are such that they do not have any common awareness regarding their own problems* and hence, uniformity in opinions about the problems is rarely formed. Conflicts do arise among themselves regarding the very issue of *"backwardness."* No single all-India level organisation has been established as

6 ***Source*** : **Prof. Ram Ahuja** in *"Society in India"* [1999]. Pages : 91- 92.

yet to unify these communities. These groups are scattered over almost all the States and exhibit lot of diversities making the task of unifying them almost an impossibility.

2. Economic Backwardness

"Backward Classes" / "Castes" – as the very term indicates are economically backward. Though most of these communities are comparatively better than those of SCs and STs in economic matters, they are not self-reliant. Most of these communities are poorer than the other general populace. A large number of poor, unemployed, under-employed and only seasonally employed are found in this category. Negligible number of these people are self-employed, but majority of them are working for poor wages. Sizeable number of economically exploited people belong to this category.

3. Educational and Social Backwardness

Other Backward Classes are educationally and socially backward also. Illiterates are found in a large number in this category. Those who are interested in education are not able to continue higher levels of education for obvious financial reasons. Only during the recent years, some of these have pursued their education at higher levels due to the reservation facilities provided for them.

Socially, the OBCs are not only backward but also innocent and ignorant. This is especially true in the case of rural people belonging to lower castes. The poorer sections belonging to the upper castes but get included in this category – are also suffering from inferiority complex, self complacency, lack of courage to march forward and such other weaknesses. Even though people who belong to this category of OBCs are not directly the victims of untouchability, lot of social distance prevails between these and the so called forward castes.

4. Politically Unorganised

The Other Backward Classes, in comparison with other major castes, are not very much organised. No single backward caste is numerically dominant in any province. Hence, they are politically ineffective for they cannot impose their will on the other castes or communities. They are not able to work as powerful *"pressure groups"* at the all-India level. However, in some States, they have been able to assert their existence especially after the implementation of 27% reservation. After 1990s, however, some attempts have been made in some States to unite these backward castes politically. For example, the political parties such as *"Samajwadi Party"* under the leadership of Mulayam Singh Yadav in U.P., and *"Rastreeya Janata Dal"* under the leadership of Sri Laloo Prasad Yadav in Bihar, are trying to consolidate the strength of OBCs. These parties have attained some promising success in their attempts.

5. Problem of Ever Increasing Number of Backward Castes and Communities

One of the peculiar problems found in India is that the number of castes and communities belonging to the category of OBCs, is continuously increasing. Some of the lower castes, who have an eye on the attractive benefits of reservation are building up *"lobbies"* to bring pressure on the Government and also on the **Permanent Backward Classes Commission,** to include their castes into the official list of the OBCs. *For example,* due to such pressure, the Government of Karnataka [as per the recommendations of the Permanent Backward Classes Commission] in its notification dated 10th April 2002, included 11 castes into the State list of OBCs. These castes are : *Jangama, Namadhari Gowda, Kodagu Hegde, Nayiri, Rajabhori, Usthama, Pakanathi, Jangala, Kumbari Marathi, Baggaru,* and *Kodagu Kapala.* This kind of effort is being made in every State and hence the number of OBCs is incessantly increasing.

6. Abuse of the Facility of Reservation

Some of the castes want to claim themselves to be *"backward castes"*, because they want to enjoy the benefits of reservation. Members of the backward castes, who have been enjoying the benefits of reservation and attained richness, want to enjoy the same permanently, and hence are not ready to give up these benefits voluntarily. Political parties, which have been successful in creating a *"vote-bank"* of the backward castes are also putting up resistance against any attempt to withdraw the facilities to those members and families of the backward castes, who have become economically forward over the years.

Backward castes and classes are engaged in a kind of extreme political rivalry and violence particularly because of reservation. Clashes between the Scheduled Castes and Tribes on the one hand and the newly declared Other Backward Classes, on the other, are on the increase especially in States like Bihar and U.P. Scheduled Castes are now inevitably drawn into permanent rivalry and violence in these States.[7] The Scheduled Castes are afraid that their interests would be endangered with the upsurge of these OBCs. The current political developments make it evident that these castes have reasons to fear about such things.

Reservation facility which has been provided for the backward castes has done more harm than good in certain areas, particularly in the area of fanning the fire of caste politics. Hence, it is argued that *as long as this facility continues so long caste consciousness, caste rivalry, caste politics, caste hatred and caste conflict will continue.* In order to grab the benefits of reservation, some of the sub-castes belonging to the upper castes are also bringing pressure on the Government and the Backward Classes Commission to declare their sub-castes as *"backward castes."* There is an impression among the people belonging to the lower castes and backward castes that they could come up in life and achieve social progress only through reservation, governmental programmes, schemes, concessions, facilities, etc. This kind of an attitude is damaging the self-confidence and attempts at self-dependence of these people and putting hurdles in the path towards social development.

Various Schemes and Measures For the Welfare of the Backward Castes Particularly the Other Backward Classes [OBCs]

The Central Government has launched various schemes and undertaken several measures, such as the following, for the welfare of the OBCs.

1. National Backward Classes Finance and Development Corporation

The National Backward Classes Finance and Development Corporation [NBCFDC] was set up by the Govt. of India under the then Ministry of Welfare on 13th Jan. 1992 as a company [not for Profit]. The objective of this Corporation is to provide concessional finance to the members of the backward classes living below the poverty line for their socio-economic development. The Corporation extends them loans for income generating schemes.

The Corporation provides financial assistance in terms of loans/ grants to the eligible beneficiaries in the following sectors : agriculture and allied; artisans and traditional occupations; technical trades; small business, small scale industries and transport services. Upto 1999-2000, the total cumulative disbursement by the Corporation has gone upto ₹424.83 crores covering 3,09, 597 beneficiaries.

---

7 Clashes and rivalry between the Samajwadi Party, which has been banking on the support of mostly the OBCs and Muslims and led by leaders like Mulayam Singh Yadav and Akhilesh Yadav, on the one hand; and the Bahujan Samaja Party, which is embanking the support of the Scheduled Castes and led by leaders such as Mayavathi, on the other, in the State of U.P., could be cited here as an example.

2. Permanent Statutory Body: National Commission for Backward Classes [1993]

In pursuance of the Supreme Court Judgement popularly known as 'Mandal Judgement' [1992], the National Commission for Backward Classes was set up in 1993 as a permanent body for entertaining any matter or dispute connected with reservation for the OBCs. *For example*, requests for new inclusions, complaints of over-inclusions or under-inclusions in the list of the OBCs are considered by this Commission is binding on the Government in ordinary cases.

3. Various Schemes Launched

The following schemes were launched in 1998-99 for the welfare of the OBCs by the Govt. of India.

(i) Pre-Examination Coaching: The objective of the scheme is to coach candidates belonging to OBCs to enable them to compete in various competitive / entrance examinations. Candidates whose parents' / guardians' total annual income is below Rupees **one** lakh are eligible for this. ₹23 lakhs was released to 8 organisations under this scheme in 1999-2000.

(ii) Hostels for OBC Boys and Girls: The hostels under the schemes will be constructed in States / UTs having a large OBC population but inadequate hostel facilities. The hostels will be constructed for middle, secondary, college and university level students. At least 1/3 of the hostels to be set up will be for girls. Central assistance for construction will be 50% and the remaining cost will be borne by the State Govt. An amount of ₹4.30 crore was released under this Scheme to Bihar, Madhya Pradesh, Karnataka, Andhra Pradesh and Sikkim in 1999-2000. During 2009-10, an amount of ₹ 35 crore was released to 11 states and UTs for construction of 17 hostels and for covering 1050 seats.

(iii) Pre-Matric Scholarship for OBCs: Scholarship award will be sanctioned to students, whose parents' annual income does not exceed ₹44,500/=. The scholarships will terminate at the end of Class X. The scholarship will be paid for 10 months in a year. The scholarship will be applicable to the institutions recognised by the concerned State Govts. / UTs. The central assistance will be 50%. An amount of ₹5.75 crore was released under the Scheme to A.P., Bihar, M.P. and Tripura in 1999-2000. An amount of ₹30 crores was released under the scheme to 12 states during 2009-10, for covering 900 beneficiaries.

(iv) Post-Matric Scholarships to the OBCs: The scheme provides financial assistance to the OBC students at post-matriculation / post secondary stage to enable them to complete their education. Hundred percent central assistance will be given for this. Indian nationals belonging to OBCs studying in recognised institutions and whose parents' annual income does not exceed ₹44,500/- will be entitled for this. An amount of ₹961.86 crore was released under this scheme to A.P., Bihar, Karnataka, M.P. and Tripura in 1999-2000. An amount of ₹ 135 crores was released under this scheme to 16 States / UTs during 2009-10 for covering nearly 800 beneficiaries.

(v) Assistance to Voluntary Organisation for Welfare of OBCs: The scheme involves voluntary sector to improve educational and socio-economic conditions of the OBCs, that is, to get them gainfully employed. Assistance will be given to establish centres and develop services which equip the OBCs to start income generating activities. The quantum of assistance is determined on merit by the Govt. of India, which may be upto 90% of the approved expenditure. An amount of ₹1.73 crore was released under the scheme to 119 non-governmental organisations in 1999-2000.[8] This amount was increased to ₹ 5 crore in 2009-2010.

3. Reservation Facility to the Backward Classes

Reservation is a part of our Constitution which is intended to create equal in opportunities

---

8 *Note*: Information and Statistics provided here relating to the welfare of Backward Classes, are obtained from *"India Year Book* - 2001*"*. Page : 237 - 240, and also *"India Year Book - 2011"*, Pages: 1002-1008.

among Indians belonging to groups unequally placed in the social hierarchy. This Reservation has three principal components :

(i) Reservation of seats in legislative houses.

(ii) Reservation in jobs in Govt. and Public Sector Units.

(iii) Reservation in admission to courses in professional colleges and other institutions of higher learning.

(i) Reservation of Seats in Legislative Houses : Reservation of seats in the legislative houses on the basis of social backwardness is provided only for the SCs and STs. Explicit constitutional provision is made for seats in the Lok Sabha, Rajya Sabha, Vidhana Sabha and Vidhana Parishads. Laws relating to local bodies have incorporated it as a normal legislative practice.

(ii) Reservation of Jobs in Govt. and Public Sector Units : This Reservation operates in All India Services, Central Govt., State Govts. and Govt. owned and managed Public Sector Units and Institutions. Reservation exists in all these for the SCs, STs and the OBCs to the tune of 15%, 7.5% and 27% respectively. In direct recruitment on all- India basis, otherwise than by open competition, reservation is 16.66% for the SCs, 7.5% for the STs and 25.84% for the OBCs. Several State Governments have introduced reservation for the OBCs much before the introduction of the Central Government.[9] In case of promotion, SCs and STs get reservation at the rate of 15% and 7.5% respectively. .There is no reservation for OBCs in case of promotion. In fact, some have demanded reservation in the private sector also.

(iii) Reservation for Admission to Courses in Professional Colleges and Other Institutions of Higher Learning : Reservation of admission is found in the Govt. owned and aided educational institutions of professional and higher learning, such as engineering colleges, medical colleges. Reservation for SCs and STs exists in all such institutions. Several State Governments such as Karnataka, Kerala, Tamil Nadu, for instance, have also provided reservation for the OBCs.

• ***Relaxation in Rules and Provision of Concessions*:** To ensure that reserved vacancies are filled by candidates belonging to appropriate category, certain relaxations and concessions like relaxation in upper age-limit, etc., are provided. Liasion officers have been appointed for SCs, STs and OBCs in each ministry / Dept. to ensure proper implementation of reservation policy for them.

Reservation Strictly Followed: The scheme of reservation is being followed by public sector undertakings including nationalised public sector banks. State governments have also provided for reservation of posts for SCs, STs and OBCs, etc., and have taken steps to increase their representation in State services. Reservation in State Government services, however, is under the exclusive jurisdiction of respective State Governments.

Representation of SCs, STs and OBCs in Central Govt Services as on 01-01-2005

Group	Total	SCs	%	STs	%	OBCs	%
A	80589	9551	11.9	3448	4.3	3791	4.7
B	139958	19194	13.7	6230	4.5	3252	2.3
C	2036103	333708	16.4	131678	6.5	119968	5.9
D	767224	140469	18.3	55032	6.9	32973	4.3
Total	**3023874**	**502922**	**16.63**	**194388**	**6.43**	**159984**	**5.29**
Sweepers	81174	48067	59.2	4012	4.9	1834	2.3
Toal [Including Sweepers]	**3105048**	**550989**	**17.74**	**198400**	**6.39**	**161818**	**5.21**

Note: This does not include information in respect of two ministries.

Source: **India Year Book - 2011**, Page: 1005.

•••

9 For example, since 1990 itself reservation for OBCs exists in 13 out of 22 states. In 6 states, the total reservation exceeds 50%.

Chapter 21

PROBLEMS OF THE RELIGIOUS MINORITIES

& PROBLEMS OF THE PRACTICE OF SECULARISM

A. Religious Minorities in India and their Problems : *Concept of Minority - Religious Minorities in India - Problems of Religious Minorities - Some Common Problems of Minorities in India - Some Specific Problems of Muslim and Christian Minorities- Welfare of the Minorities. Protection Against Communal Riots - National Commission for Minorities.*
B. Secularism and Problems of Its Practice : *Meaning of Secularism and Its Definition - Meaning of Secularisation - Articles in the Indian Constitution Promoting Secularism- Three Types of Secular States - General Characteristics of Secularism and Secularism in Practice- Problems of or Impediments in the Practice of Secularism.- Importance of Secularism.*

A. RELIGIOUS MINORITIES AND THEIR PROBLEMS

India is a multi-lingual and a multi-religious country. Indian society is pluralistic in character from the religious and other points of view. Since a very long time people belonging to various religious communities have been living together in this nation. Though majority of the people living in this land are **Hindus** [80.44%], people belonging to other religious communities such as **Muslims** [13.42%], **Christians** [2.33%], **Sikhs** [1.84%], **Buddhists** [0.68%], **Jains** [0.38%] and **others** [0.65%] are also living along with the Hindus by enjoying on par similar rights and opportunities. By virtue of their numerical strength Hindus constitute the majority while the rest of the religious communities come under what is known as *"religious minorities." [See Table No - 1]*

Concept of *"Minority"* : Some Definitions

1. The dictionary meaning of the word *minority* is that it signifies *"a smaller number" in opposition to the other party that is, the majority group or party.*[1]
2. *"A minority is a category of people singled out for unequal and inferior treatment simply because they are identified as belonging to that category."*[2]
3. Minority group refers to *"any recognisable racial, religious, or ethnic group in a community that suffers from some disadvantage due to prejudice or discrimination."*[3]

1 **Mamoria C.B.** in *"Social Problems and Social Disorganisation."* Page 140
2 ***The Blackwell Dictionary of Sociology.*** Page - 179.
3 **W.P. Scott** in *"Dictionary of Sociology."* Page - 258.

4. *"The most common general description of a minority group used, is of - an aggregate of people who are distinct in religion, language, or nationality from other members of the society in which they live and who think of themselves, and are thought of by others, as being separate and distinct."*[4]
5. **Louis Worth** defined minority collectivity *"as a group of people who, because of their physical or cultural characteristics, are singled out from others in the society in which they live for differential and unequal treatment, and who therefore, regard themselves as objects of collective discrimination."*
6. According to the **UNO**, minority is a *"group numerically inferior to the rest of the population of the state, in a non-dominant position, whose members - being nationals of the state - possess ethnic, religious or linguistic characteristics differing from those of the rest of the population and show, if only implicitly, a sense of solidarity, directed towards preserving their culture, traditions, religion or language."*
7. According to the **Random House Dictionary,** minority is *"a group differing, especially in races, religion or ethnic background from the majority of population, especially when the difference is obvious and causes, or is likely to cause members to be treated unfairly."*

No Proper Definition of the Minority in the Constitution

Speaking about the concept of *"minority"* in the Indian context, it can be said that the term has not been properly defined anywhere in the Indian Constitution. But *"minority status"* has been conferred on many groups.

- According to the ***Article 29*** of the Constitution, *any group living within the jurisdiction of India is entitled to preserve and promote its own language, script or literature, and culture.*
- ***Article 30*** states that a minority group *"whether based on religion or language shall have the right to establish and administer educational institution of their choice."*
- ***The preamble of the Indian Constitution*** guarantees for all of its citizens *justice, liberty, equality* and *fraternity.* There is no discrimination against the minorities on any ground whatsoever.

A Brief Mention of Characteristics of Minorities

There are certain central features of minority groups which are as follows.

1. The members of a minority group suffer various disadvantages at the hands of another group. Normally, minority group suffers from unequal treatment.
2. A minority group is identified by group characteristics that are physically socially visible.
3. A minority is a self-conscious group with a strong sense of "oneness".
4. People usually do not become members of a minority group voluntarily, they are born into it.
5. Minority status does not always depend upon numerical strength.
6. By choice or necessity, members of a minority group tend to marry within the group.

PROBLEMS OF RELIGIOUS MINORITIES IN GENERAL

Minority groups of ethnic, religious, racial or linguistic character are found in several countries of the world. The recent history of these minority groups reveals that most of these groups are faced with two main types of problems: (i) *the problem of prejudice and discrimination,* and (ii) *the problem of preserving the distinct social and cultural life.*

4 ***The New Encyclopaedia Britannica*** Vol. 27. Page: 356.

1. Prejudice and Discrimination

Prejudice and discrimination are found in any situation of hostility between racial and ethnic groups and divergent religious communities. The two terms are often used interchangeably in ordinary speech, but in fact, they refer to two different, but related phenomena :

a) ***Prejudice*** refers to a *"pre-judged" attitude towards members of another group.* These groups are regarded with hostility simply because they belong to a particular group, and they are assumed to have the undesirable qualities that are supposed to be characteristic of the group as a whole.

b) ***Discrimination,*** on the other hand, *refers to action against other people on the grounds of their group membership.* It involves the refusal to grant members of another group the opportunities that would be granted to similarly qualified members of one's own group.

Speaking about the Indian context, ***discrimination*** *especially in providing opportunities to people of different religious communities,* ***is not at all in practice.*** The Preamble of the Constitution itself declares that all people irrespective of their caste, class, colour, creed, sex, region or religion will be provided with equal rights and opportunities. *Article 15(1) and 15(2)* prohibit discrimination on grounds of religion. *Article 25* promises the right to profess, propagate and practice religion. It is clear that there is no legal bar for any religious community in India to make use of the opportunities [educational, economic, etc.] extended to the people. It is true that some religious communities [for example, Muslims] have not been able to avail themselves of the opportunities on par with other communities. This situation does not reflect any discrimination. It only reveals that such communities are lagging behind in the competitive race.

As far as ***prejudices*** are concerned, prejudices and stereotyped[5] thinking are common features of a complex society. India is not an exception to this. For example, commonly used statements such as – *"Hindus are cowards and Muslims are rowdies; Sikhs are dullards and Christians are converters",* etc. – reflect the prevalent religious prejudices. Common people who are gullible in nature never bother to find out the truth behind these statements, but are simply carried away by them. Such prejudices further widen the social distance among the religious communities. This problem still persists in India.

2. Problem of Preserving Distinct Social and Cultural Life

India is one among the very few nations which have given equal freedom to all the religious communities to pursue and practice their religion. *Article 25 of the Constitution* provides for such a right. Added to this, *Article 3D(1) states all minorities whether based on religion or language shall have the right to establish and administer educational institutions of their choice.* They are given the right to preserve their socio-cultural characteristics. It has set up a *"Minorities Commission"* to help the minorities in seeking justice. No minority community can have a grievance against any government particularly in this matter.

RELIGIOUS MINORITIES IN INDIA

According to the 1931 census, there were 10 religious groups in India. These included; *Hindus , Jains, Buddhists, Zoroastrians, Muslims, Sikhs, Christians, Jews and other tribal* and *non tribal religious groups.* The 1961 census listed only 7 religious groups namely, Hindus, Jains, Buddhists, Muslims, Christians and other religions and persuasions.

5 ***Stereotypes*** **:** "Prejudiced thought always involves the use of a rigid mental image that summarises whatever is believed to be typical about a group. This kind of image is called a ***stereotype.***" - **Ian Robertson** in his book *"Sociology."* Page - 275.

DIVERGENT MINORITIES ADDING TO THE DIVERSITIES OF INDIA

- ***Religious minorities in India, may be grouped into three categories.*** They are,
  a) *The protest religions of India*, e.g. Jainism, Buddhism and Sikhism.
  b) *Migrant religions*, e.g. Judaism, Zoroastrianism.
  c) Religions which are perceived to be the *products of conquest and colonialism*, e.g. Islam and Christianity. India is thus, a multilingual country with different communities.

POPULATION BY RELIGION IN INDIA [1971 - 2001] Table No - 1

Religious Group	1971 Number (million)	1971 %age to total	1981 Number (million)	1981 %age to total	1991 Number (million)	1991 %age to total	2001* Number (million)	2001* %age to total
Hindus	453.4	82.7	549.7	82.6	672.6	82.4	827.50	80.44
Muslims	61.4	11.2	75.6	11.4	95.2	11.7	138.18	13.42
Christians	14.2	2.6	16.2	2.4	18.9	2.3	24.05	2.33
Sikhs	10.4	1.9	13.1	2.0	16.3	2.0	-	1.84
Buddhists	3.9	0.7	4.7	0.7	6.3	0.8	-	0.68
Jains	2.6	0.5	3.2	0.5	3.4	0.4	-	0.38
Other	2.2	0.4	2.8	0.4	3.5	0.4	-	0.65
Total	548.2	100.0	665.3	100.0	812.3	100.0		

Source : INDIA Year Book - 1999, Page - 16 *Census Report 2001 and other sources.

Some of the Common Problems of Minorities in India

In spite of the provisions of the constitutional equality, religious minorities in India often experience some problems among which the following may be noted.

1. Problem of Providing Protection

Need for security and protection is very often felt by the minorities. Especially in times of communal violence, caste conflicts, observance of festivals and religious functions on a mass scale, minority groups often seek police protection. Government in power also finds it difficult to provide such a protection to all the members of the minorities. It is highly expensive also. State governments which fail to provide such protection are always criticised. ***For example,*** (i) the Rajiv Gandhi Government was severely criticised for its failure to give protection to the Sikh community in the Union Territory of Delhi on the eve of the communal violence that broke out there soon after the assassination of Indira Gandhi in 1984. (ii) The Gujarat state government was criticised for its inability to provide protection to the Muslim minorities during the [Feb. Mar. - 2002] communal violence that burst out. (iii) Similarly, the Government of Kashmir's inefficiency in providing adequate security to the Hindu and Sikh minorities in that state against the atrocities of Muslim extremists, is also widely condemned.

2. Problem of Communal Tensions and Riots

Communal tensions and riots have been incessantly taking place since independence. However, there are ups and downs in the incidents of communal riots. [Please see **Table - 2**] Whenever the communal tensions and riots take place for whatever reason, minority interests get threatened; fears and anxieties become widespread. It becomes a tough task for the government in power to restore the confidence in them. The Delhi [1984] and the Gujarath [2002] episodes of communal riots as stated above clearly reveal this situation.

Communal Riots in India 1992-96			Table - 2
Years	No. of Communal Incidents / Riots	No. of Persons Killed	No. of Persons Injured
1992	1601	1681	10417
1993	2292	952	2989
1994	179	78	794
1995	203	73	1050
1996	161	39	612
Source : **Organiser,** 272 April 1997, as quoted by **Dr. Parvathy Appaiah** in her *"Hindutva Ideology and Politics"* [2003]. Page - 238.			

3. Problem of Lack of Representation in Civil Service and Politics

Though the Constitution provides for equality and equal opportunities to all its citizens including the religious minorities, the biggest minority community, that is, Muslims in particular, have not availed themselves of these facilities. There is a feeling among them that they are neglected. However, such a feeling does not seem to exist among the other religious communities such as the Christians, Sikhs, Jains and Buddhists, for these are economically and educationally better than the majority community.

4. Problem of Separatism

Some of the demands put forward by some of the religious communities in some areas are not acceptable to others. This has widened the gap between them and others. ***Examples*:** The separatist tendency present among some Muslim extremists in Kashmir and their demand for the establishment of Independent Kashmir is not acceptable to others. Such a demand is regarded as anti-national. Similarly, some of the Christian extremists in Nagaland and Mizoram are demanding separate and independent statehood for their provinces. Both these demands are supportive of *"separatism"* and hence cannot be accepted.

Some fanatic Sikhs also staged the "**Khalisthan Movement**" in Punjab during 1980s under the leadership of Bindranwala and others demanding the establishment of a separate, autonomous State for the Sikh Community. They wanted to make Punjab a theocratic state though majority of the Sikhs were totally against it. They had resorted to large scale violence and terriorist activities. The Government had to bring in the army which conducted what is known as "*Operation Blue Star*" on 6th June 1984 to pull out the terrorists who had taken shelter in the Golden Temple at Amritsar. Supporters of such demands in other states have been causing lot of disturbances and creating law and order problems in the respective states.

5. Failure to Stick on Strictly to Secularism

India has declared itself as a *"secular"* country. The very spirit of our Constitution is secular. Almost all political parties including the Muslim League claim themselves to be secular. But in actual practice, no party is honest in its commitment to secularism. There is not a single political party in India which is committed to the principles of secularism in the strict sense of the term. All political parties look to their party interests whenever politico-religious controversies crop up. Purely religious issues are often politicised by these parties. Similarly, secular issues and purely law and order problems are given religious colours. These parties are always waiting for an opportunity to politicalise communal issues and take political advantage out of it. Hence the credibility of these parties in their commitment to secularism is lost. This has created suspicion and feeling of insecurity in the minds of minorities.

6. Problem Relating to the Introduction of Common Civil Code

Another major hurdle that we find in between the majority and minority relations is relating to the failure of Governments which have assumed power so far, *in the introduction of a common civil code.* It is argued that social equality is possible only when a common civil code is enforced throughout the nation. Some communities, particularly the Muslims oppose it. Even though some progressive Muslims are in favour of the Common Civil Code, the orthodox Muslims have been opposing it very strongly.Pressure is mounting on the Government to introduce such a uniform code. The Supreme Court itself had issued directives to the Government to take necessary steps to introduce such a Uniform Civil Code. Some intellectuals have, for example, cautioned that the Government must be very careful in introducing it. **Prof. M. Mujeeb** has stated : *"A uniform Civil Code is a good idea, but the necessary integration of different communities should be achieved first through judicial decisions and practical government measures."*[6]

The traditional Muslims who are not in favour of this proposal argue that the imposition of common civil code will take away their religious freedom for it is opposed to the *"Shariat."* The Governments which ruled over the country so far have not dared to take the risk of introducing it for fear of losing Muslim votes. Intellectuals like **Justice Krishna Iyer** too have cautioned the Government to be very careful in taking steps in this direction. Sri Iyer had stated in one context: *"Hurried remedies, enthusiasts and Chauvinists, will aggravate the malady; for in the socio-political field one wrong step forward is two regrettable steps backward and a policy of principal compromise, not of doctrinaire as sectarian rigidity, moving up in zigzags, may be, is the right approach."*[7] The very issue of Common Civil Code has become controversial today. It has further widened the gap between the religious communities.[8]

It is important to note that though the major political parties, except *one or two,* politicians are hesitant to take up the issue of Uniform Civil Code and legislate on it though majority of the people seem to be supporting it. Some of the survey reports also confirm this. [See **Table - 3.]**

---

6 **Prof. M. Mujeeb's** views as quoted in *"Encyclopaedia of Social Work in India"* Vol.II.

7 **Justice Krishna Iyer** as quoted in *"Encyclopaedia of Social Work in India"* Vol. II. Editor **S.C. Dube.**

8 ***Supreme Court's Support Towards the Common Civil Code*** : It is significant to note that though the major political parties are not ready to take the *risk* of initiating and supporting a Bill on the politically controversial issue of the Common Civil Code, the Supreme Court in the context of giving a judgement [dated 23rd July 2003] on a case relating to Section 118 of *the Indian Succession Act,* has observed that the Common Civil Code *"would help the cause of national integration."* The **Chief Justice S.N. Khare** has said in his Judgement that *"It is a matter of regret that Article 44 of the Constitution has not been given effect to. Parliament is still to step in for framing a Common Civil Code in the country. A Common Civil Code will help the cause of national integration by removing the contradictions based on ideologies."* **Mr. Justice S.N. Sinha** and **Mr. Justice A.R. Lakshmana** who concurred through their separate judgements also said : *"We would like to state that Article 44 provides that the State shall endeavour to secure for the citizens a uniform Civil Code throughout the territory of India.* The aforesaid provision is based on the premise that there is no necessary connection between religious and personal law in a civilised society." It is **Mr. Justice Khare** who discussed the need for a common civil code. This topic was not discussed by the other two judges who gave separate judgements concurring with the Chief Justice on the constitutionality of the Succession Law provision. – ***Source*** : *"Deccan Herald"* English Daily [Bangalore] dated 24-7-2003.

Previous Judgements of the Supreme Court : As early as in 1985 itself, [that is during Congress rule headed by Rajiv Gandhi], in the much controversial ***Shabano Case,*** the Supreme Court Bench headed by Chief Justice **Chandrachud**, in its judgement had clearly stated that the absence of Common Civil Code would be dangerous for the national integration, security and protection. It also stated that it would be unfair to discriminate among the citizens of a country. It stressed the need for introducing the Common Civil Code.

Court's Reiteration of the Need for the Uniform Code in 1995 : Further, in 1995, the divisional bench of the Supreme Court had taken the Congress Government headed by Narasimha Rao into task for not having taken any step towards the introduction of the said Civil Code. It even issued directive to the Government to inform the court about the steps taken by the Government in that direction within one and a half year and also to appraise the court frequently about the Government's attempts to fulfil the requirements. It is a pity, that Narasimha Rao's Govt. lost its power within that specified period. The Governments which came later also failed to take any measures in this direction.

Of the people surveyed in 1996, around **77%** expressed their support in favour of the Common Civil Code. Of the men took part in the survey 53%, and of the women 46% were in favour of a Common Civil Code.

It is true that communal disturbances, religious conflicts, group clashes are taking place frequently. In spite of these disturbances, the nation has maintained its secular character for the past 64 years. Further, the government has been making special efforts to safeguard the interests of the religious minorities. Some of the governmental efforts in promoting the welfare of the minorities are mentioned below.

Survey Topic : Do You Support a Uniform Civil Code - ?	Table - 3
Yes	77%
No	12%
Can't say	11%

Source : *"India Today"*, 28-12-1996. Page - 26, as quoted by **Dr. Parvathy Appaiah** in her *"Hindutva Ideology and Politics"* [2003]. Page - 249.

Some Specific Problems of the Muslim and Christian Minorities in India

A) Problems of muslim Minorities in india

Muslims constitute the biggest religious minority group in India and their numerical strength exceeds 16 crores. In addition to the problems of the minorities mentioned above, the Muslims in India, in particular, are faced with a few other problems among which the following are important.

1. Poverty Among the Muslims: Approximately 29.5% of the total population in India [as per **C. Rangarajan's Report** for the year 2011-12] are to pay found to be extremely poor. Of the various minorities, the Muslims are the poorest in India. As per 1999-2000 report, more than 26.8% of the Muslims [Indian average for the same period 27.0%] in the rural area and 34.2% in the urban area [Indian average 23.45] live below the poverty line. The poverty condition of the urban Muslims is worse than that of the OBCs. Collapse of the handloom industry and the introduction of synthetic yarn adversely affected lakhs of Muslims who were mainly dependent on the industry. Due to their poor education, they could not get into other jobs easily and remained poor.

2. Widespread Illiteracy: As per 2011 census report, 74.04% of the Indians are literate and Muslim's literary position is definitely less than that. Added to this, only a very small number of Muslims have received higher level of education.Hence, employability of the Muslims in the modern economic scenario is comparatively less. Muslim women's educational position is still worse.

3. No Proper Leadership: There is no proper guidance for the Muslim masses. Those who receive good education are joining the mainstream of India by securing important positions in administration, judiciary , etc. Yet another section of the highly educated Muslims are tending to migrate to the Western countries, and a small number even to Pakisthan. This factor has deprived the Muslim masses of the good leadership of their educated brothern. In the absence of good leaders, they often fall a prey into the hands of some fanatic leaders.

4. Absence of Entrepreneurship: Entrepreneurship demands leadership, taking bold decisions and accepting challenges. It requires courageous initiatives also. It presumes hope, self confidence and trust. It often needs good financial backing also. The religious education which they receive in the *madrasas* or elsewhere is of not much help in this direction. The social environment is thus not favourable for the Muslims to develop entrepreneurial capacities.

5. Religious Mentors Hindering the Progress of the Community: Most of the Muslims cling on tenaciously to their religious beliefs and practices. Their religious leaders time and again overemphasise this aspect. The religious oriented Muslims do not accept the priority of poverty alleviation, removal of illiteracy or of any economic programme. The traditional mindset of the Muslim scholars as well as activists is not encouraging.

6. Discrimination in Recruitment in Government Services: There is no special consideration from the side of either the Central Govt or the State Govt to recruit the personnel belonging to the minority communities. Hence, in the army, railways, postal services, banking, and police forces, the percentage of their recruitment is far from satisfactory. Poor educational position of the Muslims is a big hurdle in this direction.

7. Absence of Reservation: Under the Constitution, Muslims are not provided with reservation in political office, employment and education as is the case with other weaker sections like the scheduled tribes. There is a feeling among them that due to their extra backwardness, they require reservation to cope with other communities in job, education, services etc..,

- ***Sachar Committee Report:*** A high level committee headed by justice [Rtd] **Rajinder Sachar** has given its report as per which Muslims across India are under-represented in Government employment including Union Public Servces. In education, health, transport, or home, the share of Muslims employed is below their share in the population. If Muslims are worse off than SCs, when it comes to education, they trail behind other backward classes in many areas such as education, employment, poverty levels and land holdings.

Regarding the impact of the Sachar Committee Report, **Prof. K.L.Sharma** writes: *"Certainly, the report of the Sachar Committee would embolden the Muslim Community in general, and the "underdog" from amongst them in particular. In due course of time, the Muslim community may demand "reservation" on the pattern of SCs, STs and OBCs. Many political parties have appreciated the report, however, The Bharatiya Janata Party [BJP] considers the report as " a launching pad for religion based reservations" in the country..."*[9] As predicted by **Prof. Sharma**, the Muslim community has started demanding *"reservation"* for them. The right wing political parties including the BJP, have very strongly opposed this demand. This issue has further widened the gap between the Hindu and the Muslim Communities.

8. Increase in Communalism: Communal riots and tensions are on the increase in the nation. These riots make the minorities to live in fear and insecurity. Number of attacks on the lives and properties of minorities cause deep sorrow. After the Godra incident in Gujrath in 2002, the gap between the Hindus and Muslims is further widened. Very recently, Muslims suffered a great deal because of communal riots in Mujafurpur [U.P.] in 2013 in which more than 60 people lost their lives and thousands of Muslims became refugees and hundreds lost their houses and properties. A few people belonging to both the communities, Hindu and Muslim, received severe injuries, and were even killed.

9. Suspicious Attitude towards Muslims: During the recent years, especially after 1990s, Muslim fundamentalist attitudes and terrorist activities are increasing througout the world. India is also hard hit by the Pakisthan sponsored terrorist activities in which some Indian native Muslims are also found to be involved. Series of bomb explosions that have taken place due to these terrorist activities in places such as Mumbai on 12th march 1993, New Delhi on 29th October 2005; Jaipur on 13th May 2008, Ahmedabad on 26th July 2008; Hyderabad on 21st Feb 2013, have further widened the mutual trust gap between the Muslims and the rest of the people in India . Naturally, it is a painful experience for the vast majority of the Muslims to face the suspicious look of the rest of the people.

9 **K.L.Sharma** in *"Indian Social Structure and Change"* [2007] *Rawat Publications,* page 363.

10. Problem of Discrimination: Wherever Muslims live as minorities, they increasingly face problems of discrimination. These are partly due to historical and political factors and the media which has depicted them as violent, unreliable and prone to anarchy. There are a few things that the Muslims are sensitive about. The most important one is religion. Moreover, they like to live as Muslims and by Muslim traditions. These include family laws, inheritance, religious holidays and religious festivals. When these are threatened, Muslims also feel threatened which builds up hostility and anger in them. In the modern state, this is seen as a desire for separation and secession which causes problems for the minorities. Moreover, some Islamic ideas place Muslims and the non-Muslim majority on a confrontation. *Example: The Islamic ideas or notions which transcend national borders, like the idea of jihad, struggle to fight for a just and correct world order,* and so on.

11. Failure to Cope with the Demands of Globalisation: We are today living in an era of globalisation. Globalisation is being adopted by the entire global humanity in the wake of the revolution in information technolgy and communication. Cultures and images from four corners of the globe are brought into common man's living rooms. It is possible today to live a free and culturally satisfying life. The role of the state in taking care of the people has decreased and those who need care will have to do more and more for themselves, both individually and collectively. So, the Muslims need to develop their own resources to meet the demands of globalisation. Their unpreparedness to cope with the global trends has created a few more problems for them.

12. Other Factors

Apart from the specific causes mentioned above that contribute to communal tensions between the Muslims and the rest of the communities in India, there are some other factors that are at the root of communal clashes.

(i) ***Selfish politicians*** are found to be doing a great disservice to the communal harmony by further widening the gap between the minority and majority relations.

(ii) ***The presence of anti- social elements*** in society always does another damage. They are ever ready to exploit every opportunity that comes in their way, be it communal or otherwise.

(iii) ***Bitter memories of the past*** is yet another factor that leads to tension. The very fact that communal disturbances occur very often in the northern belt, reveals that the bitter memories of the partition days still rankle their minds.

(iv) ***Hindu revivalist organisations*** are also active in the society trying to refresh the bitter memories of history for the majority people. This kind of attempt often damages the mutual trust between the majority and the minority communities.

Conclusion

Muslims constitute the biggest weaker section, next only to the scheduled castes. Problems relating to Muslim minorities are genuine and require urgent solution. However, without the full participation of Muslims and other minority groups in all aspects of national life it is not possible to promote the cause of national integration. Underlying the communal disturbances between Hindus and Muslims is the hard truth that a minority community anywhere tends to be very sensitive and it also happens to be the first community to react whenever any suspicion is aroused. The psychology of the minority, too, cannot be helped. But it is necessary in the Indian context for the minority communities to have enormous patience before reacting to any untoward incident that might provoke communal clash. They must also be aware of the role being played by the selfish politicians who are always looking to protect their *"vote banks"* and not national interests.

B) PROBLEMS OF CHRISTIAN MINORITIES IN INDIA

Though Christianity is the biggest religion of the mankind judged in terms of its followers, it is comparatively a small religious minority group in India. Two Christian saints namely, **St. Thomas** and **St. Bartholomew** [both around 50 A.D.] are believed to have introduced Christianity to India. British Raj that ruled India for almost two centuries provided lot of encouragement and support for the Christian missionaries to spread their religion in India.

Unlike many of the Muslim rulers, the British rulers never imposed forcibly their religion on the Indians. They were more interested in ruling India taking all the economic advantages rather than spreading Christianity at the cost of losing their political hold. They never believed in mass conversions at the gun point. Hence, much allegations were not there against the British rulers and their religious highhandedness. This aspect is borne out by the fact that during the British rule the Christian population of India never exceeded 3% of the total population.

Numerical Strength and Geographic Distribution

According to the 2001 census report, there are about **24** million Christians in India consisting **2.34%** of the total population. They are widely scattered over. Various Christian sects include the Syrian, Roman Catholic and the Protestant.

Speaking about the geographic distribution of the Christians, about 2/3rd of the total Christians are concentrated in South India. The southern states of A.P., Tamil Nadu and Kerala together account for nearly 60% of the Christian population in India. In **Meghalaya** [67%], **Nagaland** [67%] and **Mizoram**, they constitute the majority community. The numerical strength of the Christians is also increasing due to conversions as in the case of Islam. Most of the converts are from the low castes. But caste distinctions continue even after conversions.[10] The Christian community has rendered a yeomen service to the Indian society in the fields such as - *education, medicine, social work, social welfare,* and so on.

PROBLEMS OF THE CHRISTIAN MINORITIES

In comparison with the Muslim minorities, the problems of Christian minorities are quite less. It is not only because they are less in number but also because, they are economically well of and educationally forward and politically shrewd and alert. Their relations with the majority community, that is Hindus and other communities are quite normal. Even then , they too have some problems among which the following may be noted.

1. Small Minority though not Insignificant

On many occasions Christians feel that their problems and demands are not properly looked into by the Governments because of their small size. The reality faced by Christians in modern India is that they are a small minority and not noticeably present in public life. They are dwarfed by the majority as well as by the substantial number of Muslim minorities. Even though, the Christian population had grown from 2.53% of the total population, to 2.61% before 1971; between 1981-1991, Christians declined from 2.45% to 2.32% of the entire population. Moreover, while the population of India increased by 23.79% between 1981 and 1991, the Christian population grew by only 16.89% in the same period. However, the total population of the Christians in India increased from 18.9 million in 1991 to 24.05 million in 2001. In comparison with the Muslim population of 138.18 million in 2001, the numerical strength of the Christians is

---

10 *"The Indian Church now realises that approximately 60% of the 19 million IndianChristians are subjected to discriminatory practices and treatedas second -class Christians or worse"* - **S.C.Dube** in *"Indian Society"* page 48.

quite less. Hence, they cannot constitute a powerful lobby to influence the government. Because of their meagre strength, they feel, that they are not given proper attention.

2. Instances of Anti-Christian Violence

Many incidents of violence have taken place against Christians in India. From 1964 to 1996, **38** incidents of violence against Christians were registered in the country. In 1997, **24** incidents were noted by the United Christian Forum for Human Rights. In 1998, the number had gone up to 90. Most of the violence has taken place in the North, Central and Western India. Anti-Christian violence in India has been widely noted which makes them feel insecure.

3. Charges of Large Scale Conversion

The main criticism raised against the Christians is regarding the large scale religious conversion carried on by them to convert the lower castes to Christianity. The Christians claim this as a constitutional right given to them under the right to freedom of religion according to which the people have the "*right to propagate religion*". It is alleged that the Christian missionaries are trying to convert Hindu-Indian society to the Western cult of individualism.

Champions of Hindutva consider the conversion activity of the Christians as a major threat to the unity of the Hindu society. They have been publicly opposing it right from the days of **V.D.Savarkar** who was also a leader of the Hindu Mahasabha. He openly said that "*Indian converts to Christianity tend to be disloyal to India*". "V.D. Savarkar *of the Hindu Mahasabha advised Hindus to resist conversion on the ground that a change of religion amounted to a change of nationality*" – [*"Times of India"*, dated 2-1-1954]

Opposition of the Christians to the "Orissa Freedom of Religion Act 1967"

When the Orissa Government passed the **Orissa Freedom of Religion Act 1967,** prohibiting all kinds of forcible religious conversions and conversion by temptations and deceit, the Christians opposed it for they considered it as a blatant violation of Article 25 of the constitution which guarantees to all the citizens the right to profess, practice and propagate religion:. Despite the opposition of the Christians, the governments of Madhya Pradesh and Arunachal Pradesh also passed similar Acts on the model of the Orissa Act preventing and prohibiting conversions by "*force, fraud and allurement*". The Acts made a clear distinction between ***"propagation of religion"*** *and* ***"conversion"*** though the Christian community expressed its dissatisfaction with that interpretation. In fact, **O.P. Tyagi** of the undivided Janata Party under the leadership of Prime Minister Morarji Desai, wanted the Central Govt. to introduce in 1978 itself such a kind of an Act at the all India level. However, such a proposal was opposed by a large number of parliamentarians.

4. Integration Without Syncretism?

According to **D.E.Smith,** yet another problem is found in the relationship between the Hindu and the Christian communities. This problem, according to him, is mainly due to the paradoxical attitude or relationship which the Christians have towards the Hindu culture. Christians have been very much eager to emulate many of the aspects, practices and customs of the Hindus. At the same time, they oppose any attempt to equalize Indian culture with the Hindu culture. They argue that Indian culture is a *"composite culture"* which includes in itself Hindu, Jain, Buddhist, Sikh, Islamic, Christians and even European cultural traditions and that it cannot be considered equal to Hindu culture which comparatively has a limited range. D.E.Smith criticizes this attitude of the Christians when he says " *Indian church is fearful of the all embracing religious syncretism* *of neo-Hinduism, which would all too readily accept Christ on its own terms.. Indian Christians are unhappy about attempts to define "The Indian view of religion as the belief that all religions are equally true. The logical inference is that Indian Christians possess Un – Indian beliefs"*[11]

The problem that arises here is that Christians accept the integrity of India and the composite character of its culture; but they are not ready to accept the syncretism or the syncretic character of Indian culture. This has been referred to by **D.E.Smith** as *"integration without syncretism"*.

Apart from the above, a number of serious problems involving the Indian Christian community such as - *the right to propagate religion by following different techniques of their own; the missionary controvessy, giving reservation to Christian converted Harijans; state control of educational institutions run by them, imposition of restrictions on foreign aid coming to India as charity for conducting social welfare and service activities*, and so on, have also arisen over the years.

WELFARE OF THE MINORITIES

Government of India has notified **5** communities, viz. *Muslims, Sikhs, Buddhists, Christians* and *Zoroastrians* as religious minorities at the national level. As per the Census of 1991, population of the minority groups constitutes 17.17% of the total population of the country. The Constitution of India protects the interests of the minority and recognises their rights to conserve their languages, scripts or culture and establish and administer educational institutions of their choice.

1. Constitutional Provisions For the protection of Minorities

Constitutional provisions that are made for protecting the interests of the minorities can be classified into two groups: (a) *General provisions*, and (b) *Specific provisions.*

a) *General Provisions* : The Constitution of India treats the minorities on par with the other people.

- ***Article 14*** of the Constitution assures them equality before law, *Article 15* prohibits discriminatory treatment,
- ***Article 16*** provides for equal employment opportunities in the public sector,
- ***Article 29(2)*** provides for equality of educational opportunities,
- ***Article 325*** and ***326*** provide for right to universal adult franchise to all, including the minorities, and
- ***Article 44*** makes provision for *"common civil code"*.

b) *Specific Provisions*

There are certain specific provisions in the constitution to protect the minorities.

- ***Articles 29 and 30*** of the Constitution provide protection to the linguistic, educational and cultural rights of the minorities.
- ***Article 29*** states that any community in India is entitled to have and preserve its own specific language, script or culture.
- ***Article 30*** declares (a) that all minorities in India are having constitutional right to establish and run their own educational institutions. (b) it also states that the State, while giving grants shall not discriminate against any institution just because it belongs to a linguistic or religious minority.

---

11 **Donald Eugene Smith** *in his book "India as a Secular State".*

(c) *Articles 331* and *333* also make provisions to give protection to the interests of the Anglo-Indian communities.

2. Fifteen Point Programme For the Welfare of the Minorities

In 1985, the then Government of India, under the directions of the Prime Minister Rajeev Gandhi, framed a 15 point programme to promote the welfare of the minorities. The programme consists of the following recommendations and activities.

a) Protection Against Communal Riots

1. In areas identified as sensitive from the religious point of view, very efficient, honest and strict police officers known for their secular outlook should be appointed so that better protection could be given to the minorities.
2. Police officers and district collectors who render an impartial and an efficient service in controlling communal riots must be felicitated.
3. Stringent legal action must be taken against those who instigate communal riots and violence.
4. Separate courts to be established to investigate into the criminal cases connected with communal riots.
5. Immediate legal steps to be taken to give reliefs to those affected by communal riots, they must also be rehabilitated at the earliest.
6. Mass media such as radio and T.V. etc., must assist the establishment in reviving communal harmony, peace and mutual understanding in the riot-hit areas.
7. Newspapers and periodicals are specifically requested not to disturb the communal harmony of an area through their prejudiced articles.

b) Appointment in State and Central Services

8. The States are to be instructed to take extra care regarding the minorities in making appointments for the police department.
9. The Central Govt. must also have the same stand while making appointments to Central Reserve Police-force.
10. The railways, nationalised banks and industries in the public sector do provide employment opportunities to a large number of people. These establishments should pay proper attention to the employment needs of the minorities.
11. Special training classes should be held in the minority institutions to the candidates belonging to the minority communities, so that they improve their qualities in competing for competitive examinations. Such a training may help them to become successful in getting jobs.[12]
12. Special encouragement must be given to open technical institutions such as ITI, polytechnics and engineering colleges in the areas in which the minorities are found in a large number.

c) Other Programmes

13. In the various developmental programmes and projects of the Government including the 20 point programme, care should be taken to see that the minority people are also able to obtain their due share in these programmes.

---

12 For improving the employability of minorities in public employment and increasing their intake in professional courses, a pre-examination coaching scheme is being implemented by the **Ministry of Social Justice and Empowerment** since 1992-93. During the Eighth Five Year Plan period (1992-93 to 1996-97) ₹ 3.65 crore has been sanctioned for training 9,480 candidates of the weaker sections among minorities and SEBCs. [that is, socially and economically backward communities During the year (1997-98), an amount of ₹ 82 crore has been released benefiting 1,360 candidates. The overall success rate under the scheme is 21.7 percent. **Source:** *India Year Book - 1999*, Page: 201.

14. In addition to the above mentioned general matters, many local issues such as Wakfs properties, cremation ground encroachment disputes, conversion cases, etc. may create lot of tensions. If these are not settled immediately and amicably they may turn out to be big problems tomorrow. Local administrations must pay proper attention to these.
15. Problems confronting the minority groups must be frequently dealt with and settled to their satisfaction. This may help them to develop confidence in the establishment. A separate wing in the Home Department could be created to look into the grievances of the minority groups.

The Central and the State Governments frequently meet to discuss the various aspects of the above mentioned 15 point programme. They also take suitable decisions to assure better protection to the minorities. The Central Cabinet Committee which met on Jan. 30th 1990 decided to take some short-term measures to promote the welfare of the minorities. Some of these decisions are as follows.

- **Special Recommendations of the Central Cabinet Committe for the Protection of Minority Interests.**

a) The Cabinet Committee decided to establish special courts in the areas which are susceptible to frequent communal riots, to look into criminal cases and settle them at the earliest. It also decided to establish such courts in Delhi and Meerut.
b) The Committee decided to increase the compensation amount payable to the victims of communal riots from ₹ 20,000 to 50,000 in case of death or permanent disability.
c) It was also decided to pay a monthly allowance of ₹ 500/- to the riot-hit widows with the lowest income.

3. National Commission for Minorities

The Govt. of India, that is, the first non-Congress Government had set up a *"Minorities Commission for Minorities"* in January 1978 to evaluate the working of the various safeguards in the Constitution for the protection of religious minorities and to make recommendations to ensure effective implementation of enforcement of all the safeguards and laws. It appointed **M.R. Masani** as its president and justice M.R.A. Ansari and Prof. V.N. John as its members.

The Commission was Assigned the Following Tasks.

1. The commission was expected to assess the implementation of the various laws, policies and programmes of the Union and the State Governments towards minority. It was also asked to report on the working of the various provisions of the Constitution towards the welfare of the minorities.
2. It was asked to give suggestions regarding the effective implementation of the protective measures.
3. The Commission was assigned the task of reviewing the Central and State Governments' policies towards the minorities.
4. To review the complaints lodged with it relating to the abridgement of the rights and protection of the minorities.
5. To conduct studies, and make analysis and researches relating to the issues of discrimination against the minorities.
6. To give regular reports to the Government on the working of the Commission.

The National Commission for minorities was not having any statutory status. It came into being only because of the Governmental decision. Due to its weak legal position, the Government was also not serious about its reports and recommendations. Hence, the Commission itself had requested the Govt. in its 3rd annual report that it should be provided with a statutory status with greater power and authority. The Govt. accordingly introduced the *National Commission for Minorities Act. in 1992.*

Provisions Made in the National Commission for Minorities Act, 1992.

The National Commission for Minorities Act, 1992 was passed by the Parliament with the main intention of providing protection to the minority community. Under this Act, the National Commission for Minorities was constituted on 17th May 1993, with a statutory status replacing the previous Commission. The Commission has a Chairperson, a Vice Chairperson and five members to be nominated by the Central Government. The National Commission was reconstituted with effect from 21st January 2000.

Appointment of Commissioner for Linguistic Minorities

The Commissioner for Linguistic Minorities appointed under the *Article 350-B* of the Constitution investigates all matters relating to the safeguards provided for the linguistic minorities. He looks into representations and complaints received from various associations and individuals belonging to the linguistic minorities. The Commissioner has his headquarters at Allahabad, with regional offices at Calcutta, Belgaum and Chennai. So far [upto 2001], 35 reports have been laid before the Parliament.

Pre-Examination Coaching Scheme for Minorities

For improving the employability of the minorities in the public employment and increasing their intake in the professional courses, a pre-examination coaching scheme is being implemented by the *Ministry of Social Justice and Empowerment,* since 1992-93. During the Ninth Plan, provision of ₹12 crore was made of which ₹5.51 crores was released for training 13,150 candidates of the weaker sections among minorities upto March 2000. The Government has approved area-based approach for socio-economic development of the minority concentration areas. In the first phase, 41 districts identified on the basis of 1971 census would be taken up.

4. National Minorities Development and Finance Corporation

The Government has set up a *National Minorities Development and Finance Corporation* with an authorised share capital of ₹500 crores. The Corporation would provide economic and developmental activities for the benefit of the backward sections among the minorities. Preference is given to the occupational groups and women among minorities. The Govt. of India has raised the level of contribution from ₹125 crore to 300 crore subject to pro-rata contribution from the State Governments and Unon Territories towards the share capital of the Corporation. During 1999-2000, Corporation disbursed ₹60.78 crore as loan covering 22,510 beneficiaries. The cumulative assistance provided by the Corporation since 1994-95 amounts to ₹224.34 crore for 66,891 beneficiaries.[13]

5. Administration of Wakfs to Promote Muslim Interests

The Ministry of Welfare of the Central Government takes upon itself the responsibility of administering the Wakfs, the institutions meant for the protection and promotion of the Muslim interest. *"Wakfs are permanent dedication of movable or immovable properties for purposes recognised by the Muslim Law as religious, pious or charitable. Better management of these institutions and fuller realisation of their objectives contribute to development and progress of the society."*[14]

13 *Note* : Source of the statistics **India – Year Book 1999** and **2000.**

14 *"India Year Book - 1999"* - Page: 202.

The Wakfs Act, 1995 **:** Provisions in order to further strengthen administration of Wakfs a legislation known as *"The Wakfs Act 1995*" was passed in 1995. This legislation came to be enforced from Ist Jan. 1996. This Act which repeals the previous ones [of 1954 and 1984] extends to the whole of the country except the State of Jammu and Kashmir. It envisages a decentralised set up and also provides for democratisation of Wakfs Boards. As per this Act, the manager of each individual Wakf who is known as *"Mutawali"*, retains his autonomy in the discharge of his responsibilities. This Act, however, states that the general superintendence of all 'wakfs in a State vests in the Wakf Board, set up by each State Government. The Board has to ensure that the Wakfs are properly maintained and administered and that their income is duly spent on objectives for which such Wakfs were created. The Board has its own office and staff. The overall supervision of the Wakfs Boards rests in the State Government concerned which appoints the Chief Executive Officer or the Secretary of the Board and audits its accounts. The Central Government has the power to co-ordinate the functions of the Central Wakfs Council and the State Wakfs Boards. The Central Wakfs Council was reconstituted on 26th June 1997 under the provisions of the Wakfs Act, 1995.

6. Maulana Azad Education Foundation

The Maulana Azad Education Foundation was established by the Central Wakf Council to promote education amongst minorities and backward classes in particular. It has now been delinked from the Council. The foundation was registered as a Society under the *Societies Registration Act, on 6th July 1989.* The Govt. of India provides grants-in-aid to the Foundation to achieve its aims and objectives. During 1994-95, a sum of ₹ 25.01 crore was released and it was increased to ₹ 40.00 crore during 1997-98.

7. National Foundation For Communal Harmony

The Central Govt. recently established the *"National Foundation For Communal Harmony"* as an autonomous body under the purview of the Home Department, to work for the rehabilitation of children who become victims of communal riots and terrorist violence. Children and women normally become the suferers of the group riots. The above mentioned *'Foundation'* is established especially to make proper provision for the future of the riots hit children.

The U.N.O also has stressed the importance of providing protection and promoting the welfare of all types of minorities. The U.N.O. states in one of its documents that *".... The promotion and protection of the rights of persons belonging to national, ethnic, religious and linguistic minorities contribute to the political and social stability of states in which they live".*

B. SECULARISM AND PROBLEMS OF ITS PRACTICE

The concepts of ***"secularism"*** and ***"secularisation"*** which are closely related to contemporary Indian politics are subject to lot of criticism. Heated discussions and debates are still going on throughout the nation about these concepts. These discussions are still inconclusive.

The spirit of our Constitution is *"secular"* though originally the word "secular" did not occur in our constitution. ***The Constitution [42nd Amendment] Act, 1976*** added the term *"secular"* to the Preamble of our Constitution. Accordingly, now India is a *"Sovereign, Socialist, Secular Democratic Republic."* As per the provisions of the Constitution, the Indian State cannot establish, recognise or patronise any particular religion. It does not discriminate against its own people in the name of religion. Hence, India is called a *"secular state."* It is surprising that endless discussions are going on even today about the very secular nature of the Indian polity. These discussions however, point out two important things :

(i) The concept of *"secularism"* still continues to be a controversial one for it has not been properly and unambiguously explained;

(ii) Though India has been declared as a *"secular state"* constitutionally, the governments which have ruled over the country have failed to develop or to shape India as a *"secular state"* in the real sense of the term.

Concept of Secularism

It is generally felt that the growth of modernism and modern civilisation has affected religion, its functions and the religiosity of the people. Developments in the fields of science, technology and education have also adversely affected religion and its traditional functions. There is a growing trend towards secularism and secularisation today.

The term secularism is given a variety of meanings as it implies different aspects to different people. The English word *"secular"* is derived from the Latin word *"saeculum"* which basically means "*the age, the world*", or "*this age or this world*". Hence, literally the word *"secular"* means *pertaining to this world or the present life, or dissociation from religion and religious teachings.*

Meaning and Definition of "Secularism"

Meaning of Secularism

The word *"secularism"* can mean different things to different nations, society and people.

(i) *It means generally the separation of religion from the state.*

(ii) *But it also means equal treatment of all religious communities* or *equal distance from all religions* and particularly the religious freedom that is granted to many communities.

(iii) In communist states, it may mean even *the absence of religion in the functioning of the state* and concentration on economic or material welfare of citizens.[15]

Definition of Secularism

1. *"Secularism is a system of social or political philosophy that rejects all forms of religious faiths"* – ***Random House Dictionary.***
2. *"Secularism........ means liberation of politics from the hegemony of religion"* – **Sri Asghar Ali Engineer,** [*Indian Express* dated 30-4-1991.]
3. ***Secularism*** **:** *"Belief that morality, education, etc. should not be based on religion"* – ***Oxford Advanced Learner's Dictionary.***
4. **Dr. S. Radhakrishnan :** *"Secularism does not mean irreligion or atheism, or even stress on material comforts. It proclaims that it lays stress on universality of spiritual values which may be attained by variety of ways."*[16]
5. **A.P. Avasthi :** *"Secularism is a way of life and conduct guided by material considerations devoid of religion and spirituality."*
6. **Mahatma Gandhiji** *stressed upon the "Sarva Dharma Samabhava" when he said "my veneration for other faiths is the same as for my own".*
7. **Raja Gopalachari** *referring to India as a secular state said "..... if it is to be a true democracy and not a superimposed western institution staged in Indian dress, religion must have an important and recognised place in it, with impartiality and equal reverence for all creeds and denominations prevailing in India".*

---

15 **Dr. Parvathy A.A.** in her article on *"Secularism Vs Communalism"* in the Journal *"Third Concept"* – July 2003. Page - 28.

16 **Dr. S. Radhakrishnan** as quoted by **Prof. Parvathy A.A.** in her *"Secularism and Hindutva – A Discursive Study"* [1994]. Page - 15.

8. ***Webster's Dictionary:*** a) Secularism is "*Wordly spirit, a system of doctrines and practices that disregards or rejects any form of religious faith or worship.*"

b) Secularism refers to "*the belief that religion and ecclesiastical affairs should not enter into the function of the state.*"

• According to **Pandit Lakshmi Kant Maitra,** "*by secular state, as I understand it, is meant that the state is not going to make any discrimination whatsoever on the ground of religion or community against any person professing any particular form of religious faith...... The state is not going to establish, patronise or endow any particular religion to the exclusion of, or in preference to, others that no citizen in the state will have any preferential treatment or will be discriminated against simply on the ground that he professes a particular form of religion. In other words, in the affairs of the state, the professing of any particular religion will not be taken into consideration. This I consider to be the essence of a secular state.*"

Meaning and Definition of "*Secularisation*"

1. **M.N. Srinivas :** "*The term 'secularisation' implies that what was previously regarded as religious is now ceasing to be such, and it also implies a process of differentiation which results in the various aspects of society, economic, political, legal and moral, becoming increasingly discrete in relation to each other.*"[17]
2. **Ian Robertson :** "*Secularisation is the process by which traditional religious beliefs and institutions lose their influence in society.*"[18]
3. ***In simple words,*** "*secularisation means separation of matter ecclesiastical from matters temporal.*"

III Articles in the Indian Constitution Promoting Secularism

The principle and the ideology of secularism are strongly upheld by the Indian Constitution. Various Articles of the Constitution including its very preamble declare their commitment to secularism. Following is the summary of Articles in the constitution promoting secularism.

1. **The Preamble** of the Indian Constitution declares India as a secular state and speaks of promoting the liberty of faith, belief and worship.
2. **Article 14** says that the state shall not deny to any person equality before law or equal protection of law within the territory of India.
3. **Article 15 (1)** and **(2)** says that the state shall not discriminate against any citizen on various grounds like religion, race and caste, place of birth with regard to access to shops, public restaurant, hotels and places of public entertainment and the use of wells, tanks, bathing ghats, roads and places of public resort wholly or partly maintained by the state funds.
4. **Article 16 (1)** and **(2)** says that no citizen on several grounds like those of religion, race or caste among others shall be ineligible for, or discriminated against in matters of public employment nor shall he be denied admission into any educational institution wholly or partly maintained by the state.
5. **Article 17** says that untouchability is abolished and its practice in any form is forbidden. The enforcement of any disability arising out of untouchability shall be an offence punishable under the law.
6. **Article 25 (1)** says that all persons are equally entitled to freedom of conscience and have the right to profess, practice or propagate any religion.

17 **M.N. Srinivas** in "*Social Change in Modern India.*"
18 **Ian Robertson** in "*Sociology.*" Page - 384.

7. **Article 26** provides that every religious denomination or any section thereof shall have the right to establish and maintain institutions for religious and charitable purposes, to manage its own affairs in matters of religion, to own and acquire movable and immovable property, and to administer such property in accordance with law.
8. **Article 27** says that no person shall be compelled to pay any taxes, the proceeds of which are specifically appropriated in payment of expenses for the promotion or maintenance of any particular religious denomination.
9. **Article 28** provides that no religious instruction shall be provided compulsorily in any educational institution, wholly or partly maintained by the state.
10. **Articles 29** and **30** provide that the state shall not impose upon it any culture other than community's own culture and that every community shall have the right to establish and administer an educational institution of its choice and the state shall not, in granting aid to educational institutions discriminate against such an educational institution maintained by a minority community on the ground that it is under the management of a religious community.

The inclusion of all these provisions in the Indian constitution makes India a truly secular state. In the words of **Basu**, *"the sum total of the above provisions makes our state more secular than even the United States of America."*

Three Types of Secular States

It can be said in a general manner that there are three kinds of secular states :

(a) ***Secular States of the Western Type*** in which the governments remain completely neutral in religious matters. They do not discriminate among people and treat people of all the religions as equal. In such states, politics is free from the hold of religion. Religion is not supposed to interfere in the affairs of the government in any manner.

(b) ***Communist States*** claim themselves to be *"secular states."* They are religionless states. **Karl Marx,** the father of communism, called religion *"the opium of the masses."* He spoke in terms of materialism. According to communists, materialism is another name for secularism. It means that matter is the ultimate reality. There is no life beyond or after the world. Hence, there is no scope for believing in spiritual things.

(c) ***Secularism in a Multi-religious States like India*** **:** India is trying to imitate the Western model of secularism by making certain modifications. *For example,* secularism in the Indian context is expected to establish harmony between religious communities and forge national integration. Whereas Western secularism does not have such commitments.

General Characteristics of Secularism

Secularism of whatever model is, in general, expected to possess the following characteristics.

1. ***Religious Neutrality*** **:** Whatever that is secular should not meddle with religion. It is supposed to show equal respect and treatment to all.

2. ***No Proposal of Religion*** **:** It does not establish, recognise or endow any religion.

3. ***Religious Freedom to All*** **:** It assures full religious freedom to all of its citizens. Citizens are allowed to follow their religion, build and maintain places of worship and other institutions. It treats alike adherents of all religions.

4. ***No Proposal to Promote the Welfare of Any Particular Religion*****:** In what it does for the welfare of its citizens, it is guided by worldly reason and considerations of worldly happiness. It is not guided by the dogmas of any particular religion or consideration of other worldly happiness.

It does not take responsibility for the promotion of religious or spiritual welfare of its citizens. For all practical purposes, religion is not considered as the domain of the State.

5. *Secularism is Founded on Scientific Knowledge* : Secularism connotes secular knowledge which is considered as scientific. This knowledge is founded upon experience of this life and can be tested by reason and experience. Secularism always deals with the known world whereas theology interprets the unknown world. *"It is the province of this worldly endeavour and neither subscribes to nor denies a transcendental sphere."*

6. *Secularism Promotes Humanitarian Values* : Secularism is based on humanitarian values and *not on the spiritual beliefs or values of any particular religion.* It looks at citizens as *"human beings"* and not as adherents of any particular religion. "Secularism" is not just the ideology of the state, it is the ideology of the individual also. Secularism in this way aims at universal humanism.

7. *Secularism is Not Against Religion, Nor Morality* : It is wrong to believe that secularism strikes at the very root of religion and questions its existence. In fact, *"Secularism does not subscribe to irreligion or atheism. It does not deny spiritual quest. What it subscribes to is that there are different paths of such quest."*[19] *"It only denies the rationale and appropriateness of religious way of life."*

It is equally significant to note that *secularism is not against morality.* It does not deny ethical and moral values. In fact, they are reasserted. However, man is capable of arriving at or devising the same.

8. *Secularism Does Not Recommend State Religion* : A secular state does not have an official religion of its own. It gives equal importance to all religions. Government officials and those who rule the country in the capacity of ministers, legislators, etc., *are not supposed to take part in the religious activities of any particular religion as a matter of official programme.* Secular state is not supposed to sponsor or prevent any religious programme.

9. *Secularism As An Aspect of Modernisation* : Progress of modernism can be assessed by means of secularism also. Modernisation gives importance to individual freedom and as a result of that religion becomes more a matter of individual belief and practice than a collective endeavour. In fact, modernisation undermines the importance of religious organisations and collective participation in religious practices.

10. *Secularism Purports to be a Cultural Environment* : Secularism as an ideology can exist only when it becomes a practising ideology. It can succeed only when the cultural environment is favourable to it, and only when it becomes a part and parcel of people's life.

True Nature of Secularism is Still Debated

At the global level, India has a recognition as a *"secular nation"*. Even after putting the principles of secularism into practice for more than 66 years, the term is debated and discussed in different platforms in India. It has evoked a huge controversy also. There are supporters of this doctrine as well as those who are highly critical of it.

India has no established Church as we find it in Great Britain, and all religions are placed on a footing of equality *[Sarva Dharma Samabhava]*. Nehru and many leading men in the country described India as a "*secular state*". But Nehru himself stated as early as in 1954, that the use of the term 'secular' to describe the nature of Indian state was *"perhaps.... not a very happy one."* and that the term, was being used *"for want of a better word"*. **Dr. S. Radhakrishnan** observed that *"the religious impartiality of the Indian state is not to be confused with secularism or atheism. Secularism as defined here is in accordance with the ancient religious traditions*

19 **Prof. Parvathy A.A.** Page - 17.

of India". Even in the Constituent Assembly, two attempts were made to introduce the word 'secular' in the constitution but failed.

India is a Secular State as it is a Democracy: The question as to whether India is a secular state has been answered by **D.E. Smith** as follows *"my answer is a qualified. Yes'... India is a secular state in the same sense in which one can say that India is a democracy. Despite various undemocratic features of Indian politics and government, parliamentary democracy is functioning and with considerable vigour. Similarly, the secular state; the ideal is clearly embodied in the constitution, and it is being implemented in substantial measure. The question must be answered in terns of a dynamic state which has inherited some difficult problems and is struggling to overcome them along general sound lines".*

SECULARISM IN PRACTICE

Secularism is our Constitutional commitment. The spirit of our Constitution is secular. The Preamble declares that India is a ***"Sovereign Socialist Secular Democratic Republic."*** The Indian State does not establish, recognise or endow any religion. It gives special protection to the minorities.

- *Article 15 (1) and 15 (2)* prohibits discrimination on grounds of religion.
- *Article 25 (1)* guarantees freedom of conscience and the right to profess, propagate and practice religion.[Here, the word '*propagate*' applies to the Christians whose religion professes to propagate religion. Moreover, in the same Article it is said that the wearing and carrying of kirpans [bayoncts] shall be deemed to be included in the profession of the Sikh religion.
- *Article 27* bars compelling anybody to pay any taxes for the task of promoting or maintaining any particular religion or its denomination.
- *Article 30 (1)* lays down that all minorities whether based on religion or language shall have the right to establish and administer educational institutions of their choice.

Interference of the State in the Practice of Secularism in the Name of Social Welfare

However, Indian secularism allows the state to interfere in the sphere of religion in the name of social welfare. Indian secularism also seeks to reserve some seats in public institutions, employment and also elections to uplift the weaker sections of the society. It also has specifically provided for the ban on untouchability which shows its concern to bring about equality which is an integral part of secularism. Though the spirit of Indian Constitution is secular, secularism in its practice, is very much distorted. The idea that Indian society has become secular is easy to grasp but complex to demonstrate. Though the *framers of the Constitution had their own differences relating to the very meaning and definition of secularism*[20] *they had consensus regarding India remaining as a secular state.* It is significant to note that no political party which ruled the

20 ***Some of the Divergent Opinions which the Framers of Our Constitution had:***

(i) **Prof. K.T. Shaw :** "The State in India being secular shall have no concern with any religion, creed or profession of faith."

(ii) **Tejamual Hussain :** "........... that this is a secular state [it] should not have anything to do with religion........"

(iii) **K.M. Munshi :** "A secular state is not a Godless state. It is not a state which is pledged to eradicate or ignore religion.......... Any state that seeks to outlaw God will very soon come to an end."

(iv) **Shri Loknath Mishra :** "..... that the secular state of partitioned India was the maximum generosity of a Hindu dominated territory for its non-Hindu population..... that our secular state is a slippery phrase, a device to by-pass the ancient faith and culture of the land....... Justice demands that the ancient faith and culture of the land should be given a fair deal if not restored to its legitimate place after a thousand years of suppression......"

(v) **Shri Damodar Swarup Seth :** "Recognition of minorities based on religion or community is the very negation of secularism."

country could escape from the criticisms levelled against it by the opposition parties in its task of implementing the principles of secularism. Parties which have accepted secularism as one of their basic political ideologies too have not remained sincere to its philosophy. Hence, secularism still continues to be one of the topics of heated discussions. The most controversial Ayodhya issue has further complicated the theory of *"secularism"* especially in the Indian context. Several impediments come in the way of effectively implementing the principles of secularism.

Conclusion

Despite criticisms from different circles, India continues to practice secularism and in India, democracy and secularism go together. Indian secularism was thus designed to be an ideal to suit the dynamics of a progressive nation. Our model of secularism is unique and has its own characteristics. It is not only liberal but dynamic and flexible. However, our present day political leaders are following policies which are bound to undermine the principle of secularism. Today, the concept is politicised to such a great extent that it remains volatile.

The practice of secularism in India made Chester Bowles, the American Ambassador to India to remark that the greatest achievement of Nehru is the creation of a secular state *"in which the forty million Muslims, who chose not to go to Pakisthan, may live peacefully and worship as they please."*

PROBLEMS OF OR IMPEDIMENTS IN THE PRACTICE OF SECULARISM

The practice of secularism has been encountering many problems in India. Some of the main impediments in the implementation of secularism may be briefly discussed here.

1. Problem of Communalism

The greatest hurdle for practising secularism in India is communalism. Communalism is virtually the negation of secularism. Communalism has bedevilled India for long both before and after independence. It is regarded as the most serious challenge facing the secular nature of the state.

Communalism as a term has several interpretations. Generally, as a term, *"communal"* is referred to as something pertaining to a community as a whole or relating to a "commune." In the current English usage, it does not have any adverse connotation. But in the Indian usage, it has acquired a negative meaning. In the Indian usage, communalism usually implies a conflict ascribed to religious communities. This conflict or antagonism or tension usually leads to and often anticipates a sense of fear, superstition and hostility. As **C. Subramanyam** pointed out, *"Religion when used for political purposes degenerates itself into communalism."* Extreme loyalty which people show towards their caste and religious community often negates the basic purposes of secularism. As a result of that, religious loyalty often turns out to be religious rivalry and religious conflict. In a multi-religious country like India, religious conflicts in the form of communal riots have been taking place between two or more religious communities or castes. These communal riots have caused lot of damage in terms of human lives and property. Neither the Central Government nor the State Governments have been successful in handling these riots in an impartial manner. Hence the trust in secularism has been shaky.

2. Communal Based Parties

"The greater danger to secularism in our country is that communal political parties are allowed to exist and openly participate in the political processes........."[21] Indian Muslim League,

21 **A.P. Avasthi** in *"Indian Government and Politics."* Page - 603.

the Hindu Mahasabha, and Akali Dal, for example, are existing and functioning on the basis of the support given to them by religious communities such as Muslims , Hindus, and Sikhs respectively. It is quite natural that these parties have a greater commitment to their religious communities than to secularism. Christians too have their own political parties drawing support mostly and mainly from the Christians. Similarly, some political parties are banking on the support of some particular caste communities. In a situation like this, the State claims to follow secularism on the one hand, and on the other, enters into agreements and makes compromises with communal parties.

3. Religious Bigotry

Religion plays a significant role in Indian elections. Parties select their candidates taking into consideration with an eye on the religious composition of various constituencies. The leaders of all political parties keep aside their commitment to secularism and seek the support of religious leaders to mobilise the votes of common people who belong to their respective religious communities.

Even at the time of forming the ministries, both at the Centre and at the State level it is regarded as almost obligatory to give adequate representation to every powerful community. Political experience and administrative ability are thought to be secondary considerations. Secularism has become a mockery at the hands of these political leaders.

4. Problem of *"Vote-Bank"* Politics

What is very commonly observed in the Indian politics is that even those political parties and their leaders who claim themselves to be *"secular"*, conveniently sacrifice the principles of secularism for the sake of obtaining votes at the time of elections. The practice of such type of secularism is often branded as *pseudo-secularism.*[22] Even those political leaders who are known to be *"honest"* also extensively practice casteism and communalism and accuse political leaders of opposite parties for being communal. **Ram Ahuja** thus observes : *"It may, thus, be said that secularism for political parties has implied the creation of a vote bank comprising Muslims, the Scheduled Castes, the Scheduled Tribes and OBCs."*[23]

The communal - secular card is now being played for political motives only. Sincere commitment to secularism is found nowhere and in no political party. The bogey of communalism is being kept alive not for checking national disintegration but with a view that *"minority vote bank"* does not dissipate itself into the larger Indian ethos. The power-seekers in India are using secularism as a shield to hide their sins thereby ensuring that people remain polarised on the basis of religion and India remains communalised.

5. Disharmony Caused Due to the Inability to Introduce a *"Common Civil Code"*

Failure to introduce a common civil code throughout the nation has posed a big challenge to secularism. Though the adherents of Hinduism, Islam and Christianity are considered citizens of this nation with equal rights and opportunities, they are governed by different inheritance laws, marriage laws, etc. Though the Directive Principles of the State Policy of the Constitution has stressed the need to have a Common Civil Code as applicable to all the citizens of India; so far

---

22 "In India, with the rise of Hindutva forces in the 1990s, there is a new interpretation of secularism, i.e., pseudo-secularism which is considered to be fake-secularism as practised by the Congress party. Usually when such a reference is made it implies that the party in power speaks of equal distance from all communities but practices appeasement of certain communities just to ensure their votes in the elections. It is referred to as *"vote-bank politics."* Such a secularism is regarded as unnecessary for any state, therefore, such a pseudo-secularism is culled out to be communalism." – **Dr. Parvathy A.A.** Page - 28.

23 **Prof. Ram Ahuja.** Page - 270.

we have not been able to have such a code, for want of support from the minorities, especially from the Muslims. Muslims who give importance to the provisions of Muslim Personal Law called *"Shariat"* are not prepared to accept the introduction of Common Civil Code. As long as it is not introduced, so long the differential treatment of people on the ground of religion would continue and so long achievement of national integration becomes impossible. This will only add to the mutual prejudices between the religious communities.

6. Interference of the Government in the Hindu Religious Institutions

Hindus though constitute the majority community, have neither an all-acceptable leadership nor an all-commanding single organisation to obtain the obedience of all. In the absence of these things, as **Donald Eugene Smith** has pointed out, the Government claims that it has the right to intervene in the Hindu religious matters in order to bring about suitable reforms in them. It has established the *"Hindu Religious Endowment Department"* through which it is trying to regulate the administration of the Hindu temples. **C.P. Ramaswamy Iyer Commission** also reported long back that there is the *"danger"* of the government officials getting more and more involved in the reformative activities of the Hindu religious institutions including the temples. Not only at the provincial level, but also through the central legislations, the interference of the Government officials in the internal administration and management of the Hindu religious institutions is likely to be increased. This tendency of the government is very much against the spirit of secularism.

This tendency of the government and many other practices have made a few to consider the principle of secularism as an unwanted Western concept "which is unnecessarily leading to communal riots." *"Many claim that secularism is natural for India and need not be imposed by the state machinery since the basic term itself is misunderstood by many. Tolerance, freedom, pluralism are all values which are inherent in the Hindu history and heritage. Therefore, ... that special efforts need not be made to incorporate the secularism of the Western kind which is not suitable to India."*[24]

Conclusion

The theory of secularism has become highly controversial today. It is under heavy attacks from all sides. Political parties openly proclaim themselves to be *"secular"*; but in practice prove to be highly *communal.* No single party is sincerely committed to this ideology in its actual practice. Hence people's faith in it is slowly dwindling.

Theoretically, *"secularism in the Indian context has tried to enhance the power of the state by making it a protector of all religious communities and an arbiter in their conflicts. It checks patronising any particular religion by the state."*[25]

When we take into consideration the present day Indian politics especially in the light of Ayodhya dispute, it becomes clear that we have given undue importance to secularism. *"Nirbhai Singh has maintained* [1994 : 111] *that the present crisis in India is partially due to over-emphasis on secularisation and politicisation of religion by the fundamentalists and politicians."*[26]

Secularism does not mean atheism. The process of secularism should not lead to the devolution of religious values. At the same time, it should not pose a challenge to the religious plurality of India. What is needed today is new insights and openness of mind towards other religious faiths – to appreciate other faiths is to guarantee freedom to them. As **John F. Kennedy** once remarked – *when one's loyalty towards one's religion comes into conflict with one's loyalty*

---

24 **Dr. Parvathy A.A.** Page : 28.

25 **Ram Ahuja** - 269.

26 Views of **Nirbhai Singh** as quoted by **Prof. Ram Ahuja.** Page: 271.

towards one's nation, one should lean towards one's nation and not otherwise. It is with this spirit secularism is to be understood and religion is to be practised.

IMPORTANCE OF SECULARISM

The problems or impediments in the practice of secularism do not by any means under estimate its importance. In fact, the importance of secularism as an ideology in multicultural states like India cannot be overemphasised. It brings about not only better understanding between people and among communities but it also leads to peace and happiness. Following are the reasons as to why secularism is important.

1. ***Secularism neither glorifies nor condemns any religion:*** The concept of secularism neither favours nor disfavours any religion. All the religions are given equal treatment and all the persons professing any religion are given similar opportunities. Thus, the practice of secularism brings about equality within a state.
2. ***Assures equal opportunities to all :*** In a state practicing secularism, all the people enjoy equal opportunities to make progress which leads to happiness and stability. As a result, nationalism gets strengthened and the country makes all-round progress in all fields.
3. ***Reduces religious conflicts:*** The concept of secularism tends to reduce religious conflicts since the people enjoy the freedom to practice any religion of their choice. As a result, secularism brings about a peaceful atmosphere in the state creating a sense of tolerance among the people. This kind of tolerance is necessary to promote national integration and national unity within a state.
4. ***No scope for feelings of insecurity :***The concept of secularism does not allow the members of any religious community to feel insecure. So, they tend to develop positive feelings and attitudes towards the members of other communities which promote the feeling of fraternity. This feeling is absolutely essential to prevent violent conflicts based on intolerance of religion.
5. ***Promotes individualism :*** Freedom of religion given to individuals in secularism tends to promote individualism. Every man takes independent decisions in relation to religion which tends to sharpen his thinking and rationality.
6. ***Makes unity in diversity possible:*** Unity in diversity is possible only with the adoption of secularism. For countries like India, secularism is most suitable due to its vast diversity. Religious sentiments are not hurt as the state has no religion in India.
7. ***Secularism softens the expression of religious passion:*** The need for secularism is not because it will eliminate religious passion from human affairs, but it may, to some extent, neutralise and soften its expression in public life. *"However, ardently one may desire the separation of religion and politics, it is impossible in a democracy to prevent political leaders from exploiting religious sentiments or religious leaders from seeking political alliances".*
8. ***Secularism ensures different religious identities:*** India is both culturally and demographically different from the Western countries such as Britain, America or France. India's religious minorities may comprise only a small proportion of the total population, but in absolute numbers, they are very large. *For example,* today [2014] there are not less than 16 crore Muslims, 3 crore Christians and 2.5 crore Sikhs living in India along with 100 crore Hindus. There is no question of obliterating the different religious identity of any group either by peaceful assimilation or through forcible conversion, either in the long run or short run. Secularism ensures that no religious doctrine or community exercises its unwarranted domination over the other.

9. ***Secularism is a philosophy of moderation:*** Secularism makes it particularly compatible with democratic politics. Secularism either in the sense of equal respect for all religions or in the sense of indifference to religion in selected spheres of social life, is a philosophy of moderation. It is undermined only when political parties heighten or exploit religious differences for the mobilisation of political support. Secularism as such is neither pro-religion nor anti -religion.

10. ***Political turmoils make secularism still stronger:*** There is a growing skepticism among the intellectuals about the use of secularism in India, whether it is good for India particularly in the wake of social and political upheavels witnessed in the past few years. **Andre Beteille**, noted sociologist writes in this context, "*... The social and Political turmoil in the country does not make the case for secularism weaker, it makes it stronger*".[27]

Numerical Strength of Major Religious Groups - At the Global Level - 2010

SIZE OF MAJOR RELIGIOUS GROUPS

Religion	Percentage of the Global Population[%]
Christians	31.5
Muslims	23.2
Unaffiliated	16.3
Hindus	15
Buddhists	7.1
Folk Religionists	5.9
Other Religions	0.8
Jews	0.2

Includes followers of African traditional religions, Chinese folk religions, Native American religions and Australian aboriginal religions.

Majority or Minority

Percentage of each religious group that lives in countries where its adherents are a majority or a minority

	Living as Majority	Living as Minority
Hindus	97%	3%
Christians	87	13%
Muslims	73	27
Unaffiliated	71	29
Jews	41	59
Buddhists	28	72
Folk Religionists	1	99
Other Religions	0	100

Religious Population in Some Selected Countries - 2010

10 Countries with the Largest Number of Christians

Country	Estimated 2010 Christian Population	% of Population that is Christian	% of world Christian population
United states	243,060,000	78.3%	11.2%
Brazil	173,300,000	88.9	8.0
Mexico	107,910,000	95.1	5.0
Russia	104,750,000	73.3	4.8
Philippines	86,370,000	92.6	4.0
Nigeria	78,050,000	49.3	3.6
China	68,410,000	5.1	3.1
Democratic Rep. of the Congo	63,210,000	95.8	2.9
Germany	56,540,000	68.7	2.6
Ethiopia	52,070,000	62.8	2.4
Subtotal for the 10 countries	1,033,670,000	40.0	47.6
Subtotal for Rest of World	1,139,500,000	26.4	52.4
World Total	**2,173,180,000**	**31.5**	**100.0**

27 **Andre Beteille's** views as quoted in *"Indian Society Structure and Change"*, Page 295, Edited by **J.K. Chopra.**

10 Countreis with the largest Number of Muslims – 2010			
Country	**Estimated Muslims Population**	**% of Population that is Muslims**	**% of world Muslims population**
Indonesia	209,120,000	87.2%	13.1%
India	176,190,000	14.4	11.0
Pakistan	167,410,000	96.4	10.5
Bangladesh	133,540,000	89.8	8.4
Nigeria	77,300,000	48.8	4.8
Egypt	76,990,000	94.9	4.8
Iran	73,570,000	99.5	4.6
Turkey	71,330,000	98.0	4.5
Algeria	34,730,000	97.9	2.2
Morocco	31,940,000	99.9	2.0
Subtotal for the 10 Coutries	1,052,120,000	47.0	65.8
Subtotal for Rest of world	546,400,000	11.7	34.2
World Total	**1,598,510,000**	**23.2**	**100.0**

10 Countreis with the largest Number of HINDUS – 2010			
Country	**Estimated Hindus Population**	**% of Population that is Hindus**	**% of world Hindus population**
India	973,750,000	79.5%	94.3%
Nepal	24,170,000	80.7	2.3
Bangladesh	13,520,000	9.1	1.3
Indonesia\	4,050,000	1.7	0.4
Pakistan	3,330,000	1.9	0.3
Sri Lanka	2,830,000	13.6	0.3
United States	1,790,000	0.6	0.2
Malaysia	1,720,000	6.0	0.2
Burma [Myanmar]	820,000	1.7	0.1
United Kingdom	800,000	1.3	0.1
Subtotal for the 10 countries	1,026,780,000	44.9	99.4
Subtotal for Rest of world	6,290,000	0.1	0.6
World total	**1,033,080,000**	**15.0**	**100.0**

Population estimates are rounded to the ten thousands. percentages are calculated from unrounded numbers. Figures may not add exactly due to rounding.

Source: Pew Research Centres Forum on Religion & Public life Global Religious landscape December 2012 - as quoted in **Manorama Year Book - 2014**, Page: 447-448.

Some Vital Facts Regarding the Religions of the World: 2012 Report

[Statistics as per the PEW 2012 survey report released on 19th December 2012 as quoted by Manorama Year Book 2014. page 676. These are based on the demographic analysis of more than 22500 censuses, surveys and population registers].

- As per the above report, there are 2.2.billion Christians constituting 32% of the world's population; and
- There are 1.6 billion Muslims [23%], 1 billion Hindus [15%] nearly 500 million Buddhists [7%] and 14 million Jews [0.2%] around the world.
- An estimated 58 million people [a little less than 1%] belong to other religions including the Bahai faith, Jainism, Sikhism, Shintoism, Taoism, Tevnikyo wicca, Zoroastrianism and others.
- 97% of the Hindus live in world's **3** Hindu majority countries, namely India, Nepal and Mauritius; and nearly 87% of the Christians [9 out of 10 Christians] are living in the world's 157 Christian majority countries.
- Hinduism is the most geographically concentrated of the 8 religious groups analysed in this report. Less than 1% of the Hindus live outside Asia and the Pacific.
- India is home to 11% of the world Muslim population, the second largest after Indonesia.
- India has the largest share [47%] of the members of the world's other religions including millions of Jains, Sikhs, etc.
- Outside India, the largest shares of people who belong to the faiths in the category of *'other religions'* are in China [16%], Japan [10%], Taiwan [7%] , North Korea [5%] and the U.S.A.[3%]
- The 10 Muslim countries with the largest number of Muslims are home to fully 2/3s [66%] of all Muslims largest share lives in Indonesia [13%] followed by India [11%], Pakistan [11%], Bangladesh [8%] , Nigeria [5%], Egypt [5%], Iran [5%] , Turkey [5.1], Algeria [2%] and Morocco [2%]
- Muslims constitute the majority of the population in 49 countries. Nearly, three quarters of all Muslims [73%] live in these countries. Although Muslims are a minority in India [with 14%] share in the total population] India nonetheless has one of the largest Muslim populations in the world.
- The median age of two major groups Muslims [23 years] and Hindus [26 years] is younger than the median age of the world's overall population [28%].
- Christians have a median age of 30 followed by the members of other religions [32] the adherents of folk religions [33] the religiously unaffiliated [34] and the Buddhists [34]. Jews have the highest median age [36] more than a dozen years older than the youngest group, the Muslims,

Source: *Manorama Year Book 2014,* Page No.: 676.

●●●

Chapter 22

PROBLEMS OF INDIAN VILLAGES

Types of the Problems of Indian Villages – Economic Problems of the Villages: Agriculture Related Economic Problems and Other Economic Problems – Social Problems and Political Problems of the Villages – Agrarian Crisis and Farmers' Suicide – Causes and Solutions for Agrarian Crisis – Farmers' Suicide in Karnataka and Its Causes – Causes of Suicide: As Per Deshpande and Saroja Arora's Analysis - Measures Taken by the Government of Karnataka to Face the Problem of Farmers' Suicide - Problems Created by the Special Economic Zones [SEZs] – Is SEZ Proving to be Harmful to Indian Agriculture? – Criticisms Against the SEZ's.

The global importance of the villages continues unabated even in the beginning of the 21st century when many countries have become highly urbanized. About half of the world population still lives in villages. The Indian scenario continues to be rural dominated, because India is basically a land of villages. In spite of the increasing trend towards urbanisation, around **68.8%** of the population of India resides in more than **6.38** lakh villages. The study of the Indian society becomes meaningful and fruitful only if its villages, their problems are studied carefully.

Villages existed in India during the Vedic period and even prior to that. Some scholars like **Charles Metcalf** even described these villages as *"self-contained little republics"*. Indian villages have been undergoing a fast change especially after the end of the British rule. These changes have not always brought the positive results in all the spheres of village life. There are a large number of villages which suffer from major problems such as *poverty, unemployment, illiteracy, indebtedness, superstition* and the like. Progress of the nation can be ensured only if these rural problems are dealt with carefully and efficiently. Sociologists have time and again emphasised this point.

Problems of Indian villages are multifarious and many faceted. They include -- *child marriage, indebtedness, malnutrition, factionalism, groupism, illiteracy, alcoholism, untouchability, conservatism, narrow-mindedness, casteism, nepotism, etc.* There are aged people and helpless women who lead a very pitiable life. Despite their poverty, people waste their money in practising age old social customs and in entertaining unwanted and unnecessary litigations. Their hard-earned money is not only wasted, they even borrow loan to fulfil their "obligations". Added to this, their income is very meager and the method of cultivation remains mostly the old fashioned one. The whole process of land reforms is very slow in many states [mostly in the North] and the poor people are ruthlessly being exploited by big landlords and money-lenders. People are orthodox and are not prepared to accept radical changes which can transform their life. But they have tremendous patience and have learnt to live with problems. Sizeable number of ruralites neither understand the nature and causes of their problems nor their gravity and magnitude.

This is not to say that changes are not taking place in the rural society and it still remains as a rigid and unchanging entity. Though slowly, change is taking place in the rural society and the younger generation is not only able to adjust with it, but also eager to welcome it. The problem is mostly with the older generation. They are looking towards the Government for help especially to face the challenges of poverty. Independent Indian Government has launched many programmes and projects for the benefit of the villages. Introduction of the *Panchayat Raj* system is believed to add new dimension to the rural progress. The magnitude of rural problems is such, that no radical progress could be witnessed in the rural areas within a short span of time.

TYPES OF THE PROBLEMS OF INDIAN VILLAGES

Indian villages are in the midst of crises and changes. Though India is known as the classical land of the villages her villages are not free from problems. Ever since the beginning of the Muslim rule, the Indian villages have been receiving one or the other setbacks. The Muslim rule and later the British rule brought enough hardships to the villages. The villages could no longer preserve their self-sufficiency and autonomy. The centralised administration of the British and their industrial economy including the factory system of production brought untold miseries to the Indian villages. The villages gradually became the centres of problems. The problems of the villages continued even after independence. Some of the major problems with which the Indian villages are confronted even today can be grouped into three major types :

(i) Economic Problems,
***(ii) Social Problems,* and**
(iii) Political Problems.

1. ECONOMIC PROBLEMS OF THE VILLAGES

One can find lot of disparities of region and class in relation to the economic growth in contemporary India. Agricultural sector seems to be neglected and its importance in country's economic growth is undermined. Economist **Amarthya Sen**, Nobel – Prize winner of international reputation, comments that *"... as these inequalities intensify, one half of India will come to look and live like California, the other half like sub-Saharan Africa".* Here we find prosperity co-existing with misery, and technological sophistication with human degradation. Such miserable conditions of human degradation we find in the rural areas giving rise to various economic and other problems.

The economic problems of the Indian villages can be sub-divided into two types : (A) *Agriculture - Related Economic Problems,* and (B) *Other Economic Problems.*

(A) Agriculture Related Economic Problems

In India, today more than 60% to 65% of the people are depending on agriculture and allied occupations. Due to the poor economic conditions of the villages, Indian agriculture is faced with many problems among which the following may be noted.

(i) Traditional and Unscientific System of Cultivation: Even today [i.e., in 2014] more than 60% to 65% of our people are depending on agriculture and what it produces. Agriculture is the largest industry that provides employment to the biggest number of people. Since most of the farmers are uneducated and custom-bound they follow traditional methods of agriculture.

PROBLEMS OF INDIAN VILLAGES

Agricultural operations such as ploughing, planting, putting chemicals and fertilizers, taking out grains, cutting crops, separting grains from the plants, cleaning the grains - are carried on through human or animal power. The farmers are not able to follow the modern scientific mode of cultivation and this is reflected in the relatively poor agricultural production.

(ii) Lack of Irrigational Facilities and Dependence on Nature: A large number of Indian farmers still depend on monsoon. In many places dams and tanks are built and canal water facility is provided. But this is not in tune with the demand. *For example,* before Independence about **18%** of the land was irrigated. In spite of all our efforts to provide better irrigation facilities, the ratio of irrigated land to total cultivated land is [in 2000] about 33% per cent. Majority of the villages thus continue to suffer on the one side, by the onslaughts of famine, and on the other, by the floods. Vast land lies unutilised due to lack of water facility.

Lack of irrigational facilities, has yet another dimension. Despite the demand for irrigational facilities for cultivation, the actual area under canal and tank irrigation has been on the decline since the 1990s. At the same, there has been an increasing dependency on the ground water resources through the wells and borewells. It is also observed that uncontrolled growth of the borewells coupled with monsoon failure, has led to drying up of borewells due to inadequate recharge.

***(iii) Sub-Division and Fragmentation of Land-Holdings*:** The size of the land-holdings in the Indian context, is very small. As per the *Agricultural Census Report - 1975,* more than 51% of the total land holdings [that is about 35.7 million land-holdings] in the country are smaller than one hectare. The average size of land holdings in India is very low, less than **2** hectares or **5** acres. As and when partition takes place in the family, land gets further partitioned and fragmented. Small-sized holdings lead to waste of time, labour and cattle power, and also to difficulty in the proper utilisation of irrigation facilities, loss of crops in the absence of proper fencing, etc. Thus, the small land holdings have their own practical difficulty and hence are not amenable for scientific farming.

Official data about land distribution indicate that **61** per cent of the rural households either own no land or small fragments of land or marginal uneconomic holdings of less than **1** hectare. Taken together, **61** per cent of households own barely **8** per cent of cultivated area. Out of them, **22** per cent households own no land at all; another **25** per cent own less than half a hectare [1.2 acre]. Since these landless labourers subsist at the border of the poverty line, they have been gradually slipping below poverty line.

Increase in the cost of cultivation on the one hand, and *environmental degradation* on the other, have made the small farmers hopelessly vulnerable. The growing predominance of small and marginal farmers itself has led to the marginalisation of the peasantry. Small farmers who do not have much bargaining power are forced to face high transaction costs. Due to low prices for their output or agricultural products, they get very poor returns which damages their enthusiasm in cultivation work.

- ***Environmental degradation is also causing anxiety for the farmers.*** The ecological crisis in the rural region manifests itself in the declining water tables, loss of agricultural bio-diversity and the onset of a variety of plant diseases

(B) Other Economic Problems

(i) Burden of Loans or Rural Indebtedness: It is often said that *"the Indian farmer is born in debt, lives in debt and finally dies in debts."* Village economy gives little scope for saving. The poor position of the Indian farmer compels him to borrow money from the local money lenders who charge exorbitant interests and squeeze their clients to the maximum. It is a kind of vicious circle. When once a person gets into that he finds no way of coming out of it. They become ultimately the bonded labourers of these money-lenders who are, in many instances, big land-lords. Absence of banking facility, and the procedural delay involved in the sanctioning of the loan also make many to go to money-lenders for immediate financial help.

It is true that due to the operation of institutional financial agencies especially after independence, the rural money-lenders are losing ground. For instance, according to the ***"All India Rural Credit Survey"*** undertaken in 1951, the money-lenders accounted for nearly 70% of all rural credit. In 1991, they accounted for only **17.6%** of rural credit. Further, as it is made clear in the **Table 1,** given below, that for all rural groups the average debt per household has risen steadily from ₹500 to ₹1906 between 1971 and 1991. [However, this increase is partly due to the process of inflation that has been taking place consistently.] This only shows that rural indebtedness is still having its hold on the rural people.

Table - 1

Average Debt of Rural Households			*In Rupees*
Year	***Cultivators***	***Non-Cultivators***	***All***
1971	605/-	223/-	500/-
1981	803/-	205/-	661/-
1991	2,294/-	1,151/-	1,906/-

Source : *Reserve Bank of India Bulletin,* May 1999.

There is yet another way in which the farmers get trapped into indebtedness. Despite heavy fluctuations in agricultural production, prices of agricultural production do not increase. At the same time, cost of cultivation goes on increasing resulting in the stagnation of the net income flow to the farmers households. The farmer is now forced to borrow to meet the increased cost of cultivation, or for an irrigation well and pump sets, or a pair of oxen, but the decreasing net income will not allow him to make payment of debt. As a result, the farmer household's indebtedness gets increased.

(ii) Helplessness of Small Farmers: As it is made clear large number of our farmers are small farmers. Their land can fetch them limited income. Unless they earn something more than that through one or the other means, they cannot survive. For centuries together, such small farmers were depending on handicrafts, and home industries such as pottery, basket-making, mat-making, toy-making, brick-making, etc. The factory-made goods have destroyed their market. Hence, they struggle a lot for finding out alternate source of income and finally fall a prey into the hands of local money-lenders.

(iii) Problem of Landless Labourers: All those who live in the villages are not the owners of the land. Only a few own the land but many work as landless labourers in the field. In many instances, the upper caste people own the land and the low caste people toil in their land as agricultural labourers.

According to the *"Second Agricultural Labour Enquiry"* published in 1960, agricultural labour families constituted nearly **25** per cent of all rural families. According to this, more than **85** per cent of the rural workers are casual, serving any farmer who is willing to engage them and only **15** per cent of agricultural labourers are attached to specific landlords. More than half of the workers do not possess any land, and rest of them own only very little of land. Agricultural labourers predominantly belong to the Scheduled Castes, Scheduled Tribes and Other Backward Classes. According to one estimate, between **75** and **80** per cent of all agricultural labourers belong to the Scheduled Castes. According to the data provided by *The Census of India* [1991], the number of agricultural labourers increased from **27.5** million in 1951 to **74.6** million in 1991.

- ***Bonded Labourers*** : It is well known that the landless labourers who live in the rural areas depend upon agriculture and majority of them are found to be Scheduled Caste people. Many of these people have become *bonded labourers.* Bonded labourers are - *"persons who are forced to work for the creditors for the loan incurred, either without wage or on nominal wage."* [*Commission for Scheduled Castes and Scheduled Tribes*]. Surveys held in the year 1978-79 by the *Gandhi Peace Foundation* [GPF] and *National Labour Institute* [NLI] have revealed that more than **87%** of the labourers belonged to Scheduled Castes and Tribes. *It is also said that around **5.7%** of the total agricultural labourers working in India, constituted bonded labourers.* Many of them have become bonded labourers due to their inability to pay back the loan borrowed from the land-owning money-lenders. Of the existing bonded labourers, around 90% of them are found to be Scheduled Caste and Tribe people who are exploited in several ways. Some of these labourers do not get an annual income of ₹1,000/-.

(iv) Defective Marketing System: Small farmers can lead a comfortable life only when good marketing facility is provided and minimum rate for their produce is assured. This cannot be expected in the Indian rural context. Lack of transport and storage facility and absence of systematic marketing facility have damaged the economic strength of the people. *For example,* the storage facilities which are available in the village at present are so poor that **10** to **20** per cent of the produce is eaten away by rats. In the absence of good storage facility, the farmers cannot store their produce and wait till they get a good price. The small farmers have the feeling that they are not getting the right value for their produce. Due to the lack of the marketting facility the agricultural surplus reaches the intermediaries or middlemen which results in exploitation of villagers. At the time of purchasing the agricultural produces the illiterate farmers are cheated in weights and measures. Only recently the government has taken serious steps to improve this marketing condition. Co-operative Marketing and Regulated Market facilities are only the recent developments. It is stated in the First Five Year Plan document that *"the purchase of the agriculturist's requirements and the sale of his produce are key activities in the business of farming and their importance is likely to be even more crucial in a socially regulated economy....... Due to his inability to secure a fair deal at these two stages, the average agriculturist is denied the full fruits of his industry."*[1]

(v) Lack of Transport and Communication Facilities: Transport and communication systems in society are like the circulatory system in human body. Unfortunately, these facilities are not available to a sizeable number of our villages. There are villages which are almost like islands. There are villages with no proper roads, bridges and transport facilities. Hence, the farmers find it extremely difficult to take their produce to a market where the prices are comparatively attractive. They are made to walk miles together to reach a town to obtain newspapers, and to get postal, banking, medical and telephone services.

(vi) Poverty and Unemployment: Poverty has become an inseparable part of our rural life. More than **27%** of our farmers are living below the poverty line even today [2002-2003]. The following Table gives us a glimpse of the estimate of poverty in Inida.

Though more than 60% to 65% of our people depend upon agriculture, as per 2010-11 report, agricultural output accounts for less than 23% of our national income. Our land distribution system is one of the reasons for this. About 10 to 20% of landholders hold 70% of the total land, and 50% of the landholders are marginal farmers with less than one hectare of land. This disparity has added to rural poverty. There are poor householders in the rural areas who are called *"destitutes"* [by the *Ministry of Rural Development*] with an annual income of less than ₹4000/- [at 1991-92 price-level]. The decline of the traditional skills and handicrafts, slow disappearance of home

---

1 As quoted by **Ruddar Datt** and **K.P.M. Sundharam.** Page - 584.

industries and the increasing industrialisation have deteriorated the economic conditions of our farmers. Poverty has adversely affected the standard of living of the ruralites.

Table - 2

Number and Percentage of Population Below Poverty Line
[*Modified Expert Group Methodology*]

	Rural Number of Persons [In Laksh]	*%*	*Urban Number of Persons [In Laksh]*	*%*	*Combined Number of Persons [In Laksh]*	*%*
ALL INDIA						
1973-74	2,613	56.4	600	49.0	3,213	54.9
1977-78	2,642	53.1	647	45.2	3,289	51.3
1983	2,520	45.7	709	40.8	3,229	44.5
1987-88	2,319	39.1	752	38.2	3,071	38.9
1993-94	2,440	37.3	763	32.4	3,203	36.0

Source : Planning Commission, *Ninth Five Year Plan* [1997-2002]. Vol.1, p. 29.

Unemployment is another serious problem of the Indian villages. For example, open unemployment was around 1.91% in the rural areas in 1983 and this increased to 3.07% in 1987-88. Destruction of village crafts, and cottage industries have virtually thrown lakhs of farmers out of job. Due to their illiteracy, and lack of experience in other fields these unemployed people are not able to find alternative job. The only job that is known to them is snatched away making them unemployed. Rural youths are also not able to get any job opportunities in the villages. Self-employment opportunities are also not being availed of by many youths due to lack of education, confidence and proper guidance. We find total unemployment, seasonal unemployment, under-employment also in the villages. For example, ***"Committee of Experts on Unemployment"*** [1973] has estimated that 8.5 million persons were working less than 14 hours per week; and 23.50 million persons [15.9% of the rural labour force] were working less than 28 hours per week. They were all severely underemployed. This problem of underemployment continues even today though with some what less intensity.

1. Discriminatory Effect of the State Policies: The farmers are under the impression the state policies always tend to favour the urbanites at the cost of the villages. They feel the discrimination particularly when the state spends more money for providing better infrastructure facilities [good roads, public health and sanitary facilities, educational institutions, etc.] to the towns and cities than for the villages. This is not to say, that the state is virtually discriminating against the villagers as a group; but its policies and some of the practices are sufficient to widen the gap between the villages and towns. This feeling has become more and more aggravated especially after the introduction of the New Economic Policy, that is, after 1990s. Since the contribution of the agricultural sector to the national income has become less than 25%, the governmental approach towards agriculture has also changed.

2. Withdrawal of Welfare Programmes From the State: During these days, the state has deliberately withdrawn its role of promoting the welfare of farmers and agricultural labourers. The capitalist agriculture in India, however could thrive because of the proactive role of the state in providing infrastructure, irrigation and credit through institutional agencies. The state investment in agriculture is also getting gradually reduced and its effect is witnessed in the decline in agricultural productivity.

3. Villages Becoming Victims of Exploitation at the Hands of Big Corporates: National and international economies are under the tight grip of the process of globalization. This has been proved to be fatalistic for the Indian farmers the fact of which could be witnessed in the spate of farmers 'suicides'. Our agrarian sector is in crisis and this is also due to the adoption of World Trade Organisation model of agriculture. [also known as Mckinsy Model of Development]. Much against the traditional pattern of agriculture, it created spaces for industry – driven agriculture which ultimately resulted in agri-business development including information technology. This model of development has not only aggravated the crisis leading to environmental catastrophe but also destroyed millions of rural livelihoods.

4. Non-Availability of Loans from Institutional Sources Due to the Strict Traditional Banking Practices: For agricultural purposes, normally two types of institutional finance are available as for instance we find in Karnataka, such as (i) *commercial banks*, and (ii) *the regional rural banks* [or *'pradeshika grameena banks'*]. These are the professional banking institutions and hence their transactions always depend upon lot of paper work and documentation. It is not easy for the farmer to satisfy the bank officers regarding his eligibility to obtain the loans. Hence, credit from these institutions gets delayed due to the tedious process of documentation.

The co-operative credit structure also provides credit with comparatively little ease. But the availability of the credit is very much limited due to various impediments in the co-operative sector.

NABARD [National Bank for Agricultural and Rural Development] is yet another source of rural finance. The NABARD which refinances the co-operative banking institutions always imposes certain conditions for delivery and recovery of credit. "Eligibility" is probably the most important concept in dictating the performance of the sector. Eligibility or non-eligibility of the branch of a co-operative bank is based on its repayment performance. Naturally, the Primary Credit Co-operative Societies in the underdeveloped regions have lower repayment performance. As a consequence, over the years, these societies do not get adequate supply of credit and therefore, farmers from these regions have to depend upon the informal sources of credit which are invariably costlier.

5. Failure of the Co-operative Sector to Save the Farmers from the Trap of Indebtedness: What the commercial banks and the NABARD could not do, the co-operative institutions could have done, had they been a little more active and dynamic. As far as Karnataka is concerned, the Government was neither able to control the growth of money - lenders nor to make the co-operative movement a success. For example, in Karnataka, there are about 32,382 co-operative societies at the village level and almost 40% of them are running under heavy losses while another 20% of them are either defunct or liquidated.

2. SOCIAL PROBLEMS

(i) Illiteracy: Indian villagers are mostly illiterate. As per the 2001 Census report, about 64.8% of the people in the total population are literate. Though this rate of literacy increased to 74% in 2011, illiterates are found in a bigger number in villages i.e., 341 millions. There are villages wherein not even 10% of the people are literate. Lack of reading and writing ability has made our farmers to turn their back to the progress in modern science and technology. Illiterate parents who do not know the value of education are unfortunately denying education to their own children. Those children who join the school also drop out in the middle. As far as female children are concerned, no one is bothered about their education. Though the village people of the present generation give relatively more importance to education, the performance of the rural children is not that impressive.

(ii) Traditionalism, Conservatism and Superstitions: Indian ruralites are known to be conservative, traditional, dogmatic and superstitious. Rural people are under the grip of caste, customs, traditions and superstition. They are unprepared to change their way of life and outlook. They are slow to change and very often resist changes. They are in a way status quoists. New things and novel ideas are looked with suspicion by them. They lack initiative, and the urge to prosper. Their fatalistic attitude does not allow them to take risk and experiment with new things.

(iii) Casteism and Untouchability: Indian villages are in a way controlled by the caste system. It is the dominant factor that decides almost all aspects of rural life. During the early times, there were caste councils which used to rule or govern the social life of the caste members. Even today in remote villages such *'caste panchayats'* are still alive and powerful. Since caste constitutes the social base and the source of individual's identity, no one is able to ignore it in the village. Caste identification leads to casteism also. Strong identification with the caste and the increase in the horizontal solidarity of the caste lead to caste conflicts damaging the unity of the village.

Untouchability and ***casteism*** often go together in the village. The practice of untouchability is more alive in the village than in the town. The difference between the *"touchable"* and the *"untouchable"* is more apparent here. The untouchables who are mostly working as landless labourers are exploited to the maximum and put to various hardships. Their literacy level is also very low. Crimes and different types of atrocities are committed against them by the upper-caste people. The *dalit* farmers who own small size of land are always harassed and put to inconveniences by the large-farmers belonging to the upper-caste. ***Ex.***: By 1978, about 15 lakh crimes were registered in the country out of which about 3 lakhs were connected with land disputes. In these disputes, in many instances the upper-castes were found to be guilty of harassing and exploiting the lowest caste people, that is, Scheduled Castes. Since the *dalits* are unorganised they are not able to put up resistance. *"Crimes in India"* [1995] reports that there is an increase in the number of crimes against SCs which is evident from the fact that as against 180 cases registered with the police in 1955, the number of cases increased to 18,336 in 1991 and to 32,990 in 1995.

(iv) Low Status of Rural Women: Women in the Indian villages have a very low social status. They are confined to kitchen work and to look after the children. They are treated as non-entities and also as the servants of menfolk. Their education is neglected. They are subject to early marriages. They are not consulted in taking any major decision regarding family matters and all the decisions are enforced on them. They do not have any individuality. Due to their illiteracy they are not able to give proper social training to their children.

(v) Lack of Civic Facilities: Many of our villages are deprived of the basic required civic facilities such as - medical facilities, schooling facility, banking facility, postal services, bus and other transport facility, and so on. While the villages that exist near the towns and big cities have access to all these facilities, those that exist in the remotest corners are deprived of them. Lack of these facilities has halted their progress.

(vi) Rural Ill-health: Rural people are facing the problem of ill-health. The rate of birth and also rate of death are relatively higher in the village. Due to their illiteracy the rural people neglect their health and do not take proper medical advice when required. Rural women very rarely complain of diseases and prefer to suffer than to go for medical check-up and advice. The ill-equipped primary health centres are also not able to give medical assistance whenever it is required. Though the government has spent huge amount of money for improving rural health, the progress achieved in this field is far from satisfaction.

(vii) Problem of Rural Insanitation: The problem of rural health and sanitation was neglected for more than 4 decades that is, after independence. It was only after 1991, both the Central and the State Governments started giving attention to this problem. As a result, by 1991 not even 1/10 of the houses in the villages had toilet facilities. 2011 census report says that around **50%** of the ruralites are still depending on the nearby open ground for toileting. This inevitability has affected adversely their individual health and also the sanitation of the neighbouring area.

(viii) Problem of Alcoholism: Excessive drinking of intoxicating liquor has been a social problem for both the rural and urban communities. Alcoholism in the rural area has become a disease characterized by a compulsion to drink in order to face the ordinary life problems. Ruralites have several reasons to cultivate and to become the victims of this habit. Drinking alcohol has become a habit with many ruralites. Many lower caste people do not consider drinking as a stigma for it is like any other type of drink such as tea or coffee. Due to the liberal governmental policy, liquor shops are opened in remote villages and government itself has given permission to private agencies to supply alcohol at relatively cheap rate in plastic packets. There are some lower castes which have been used to drinking since centuries because preparing alcohol is the traditional occupation of their community. There are also people who drink because of their illiteracy and ignorance.

Alcoholism or addiction to alcohol in the rural areas has been causing lot of damages not only to the individuals who are addicted to it but also to their families and dependents. Alcoholic addict is branded as a *'drunkard'*, himself and his family members are always looked down upon because of his habit. Many families suffer from poverty due to the alcoholic addiction of the breadwinner. Alcoholism also leads to group clashes, communal and caste riots, sexual assaults against women, etc. Future of the family and its young children become very bleak because of this habit. Village unity and its peaceful atmosphere will become casualties due to this ugly practice of sizeable number of rural people.

(ix) Problem of Child Labour in the Rural Area: Labourers below the age of 14 are considered to be child labourers and in the Indian context, out of nearly 15 to 20 million child labourers, majority are found to be working in the rural areas. Most of these children in the rural areas belong to the landless families. There is also a greater demand for girl child workers between 10 to 14 years to work as maid servants at home while similar demand is there for boy child workers to work outside the family, that is, mostly in the paddy fields, gardens, plantations, estates, etc. Most of these domestic servants are not given proper salary and much work is extracted from them.

Low literacy level of women, poor salary paid to workers, presence of large number of landless scheduled caste people, rural indebtedness – and other factors in the rural areas have directly or indirectly supported the practice of child labour. The very existence of child labour clouds the future of millions of young children both in the urban and rural sectors.

(x) Problem of Farmers' Suicide: Yet another rural problem of grave concern is that of farmers' suicide which was not there previously and is becoming serious nowadays, that is, especially after 1990s. As per the **NCRB** [*National Crime Record Bureau*], between 1997 and 2008 as many as **2 lakh** farmers had committed suicide. Most of the studies have revealed that due to the - *burden of loans, failure of crops, lack of alternative source of income, feeling of economic and social insecurity, exploitation of money-lenders and middlemen, natural havocs caused by floods and famines* -- and such other causes these farmers are committing suicide. Lack of protective measures on the part of the government has further added to their disappointment and frustration.

3. POLITICAL PROBLEMS OF THE VILLAGES

For centuries, national and state level politics did not affect our villages much. Villages could continue their normal life unhindered by the political developments taking place at a higher level. The introduction of the democratic political system provided a new opportunity for our villagers to show some interest in politics. Villagers' active participation in the democratic system, is of course, a good sign of a healthy development in our politics. But unfortunately, it has led to some problems.

(i) Decline in the Standard of Politics **:** Illiteracy is a nightmare of democracy. Many people with very poor educational background are entering politics. It is more so in the case of the rural areas. The tendency of the uneducated poor people to *"sell their votes"* for money, the control of politics by the dominant castes, the inability to elect competent representatives - have led to further degradation of politics. Even though 1/3 of the seats are reserved for women in the local bodies as per the provisions of *Panchayat Raj system*, they are still under the control of their menfolk.

(ii) Politics Proving to be Harmful for Rural Unity **:** The present political system has been successful to a great extent in establishing relative equality, in providing for distribution of power, in ensuring political participation for the rural poor and so on. But it is a failure in safeguarding the unity of the villages which they have been able to maintain for centuries. Due to caste politics and party politics each village is divided into several conflicting factions. The *Panchayat Raj system* has further complicated the issue by converting villages into political battlegrounds.

(iii) Politicalisation of Rural Life **:** Villages too have become hot-bed of local politics today. All local issues, disputes and problems are looked at from political angle. This tendency has made people to become too much dependent on the politicians and the government. Even for ordinary things such as cleaning village tank or well, repairing village mud road, levelling school playground, etc. - people expect village political leaders to get governmental help. This attitude of the villagers is proving to be harmful for the progress of the village.

Conclusion

It is evident from the above that the Indian villages are faced with a number of problems. The problems are not, however, equally found in all the villages. There are also villages quite advanced. In such villages many of the problems mentioned above are not found. But villages in the remote corners are full of problems. It is necessary to study these problems in a scientific manner to find suitable solutions for them. Study of the Indian villages is a need of the hour especially for the rural sociologists and rural economists. It is a matter of regret that no systematic and comprehensive study of the problems of the Indian villages on an all-India basis has been made so far.

AGRARIAN CRISIS AND FARMERS' SUICIDE

The Indian agricultural sector is facing a crisis today inspite of the continued dominance of agriculture in the Indian economy. India is still an agrarian country with around **60**-to-**65%** of its people depending directly or indirectly on agriculture. Agriculture in India has been facing problems ever since independence and the problems assumed the nature of serious crisis especially after 1990's when newspapers started reporting series of incidents of farmers' suicides.

Shocking News of Farmers' Suicide !

P. Sainath, '*Rural Affairs*' Editor of the English daily "*The Hindu*", highligted for the first time that large number of suicides were taking place among the farmers. His news report published in 1990's made Indians to wake up to a spate of farmer's suicides. Though official reports initially denied the incidents of such suicides, the Government had to concede the reality when more and more information regarding suicides came to limelight. The reports virutally shocked the nation.

Thousands of Farmers Committted Suicides in Different States Including Karnataka - Between 2002-09

Newspapers reported that on an average more than 17500 farmers killed themselves a year between 2002 and 2006. **The National Crime Record Bureau** [NCRB] itself stated that at least 17,368 farmers committed suicide in the year 2009 alone. In 2006, the State of Maharashtra alone accounted for more than 25% of the all-India total of 17060 incidents. The States of Andhra Pradesh, Karnataka, Kerala and even Punjab were hard hit by the problem.

A large number of cotton growers especially from Vidarbha [Maharashtra] committed suicide in the beginning.The government appointed a number inquiries to look into the causes of farmer's suicide and farm related distress in general. Subsequently, Prime Minister **Man Mohan Singh** visited Vidarbha and promised a package of ₹ 110 billion to be spent by the Government in Vidarbha.

Package Solutions Could Not Stop the Tragedy

It is a matter of regret that neither the packages announced nor the assistance schemes declared by the Governments could put a total stop to these incidents. We still hear of such reports now and then in one or the other part of the nation. Unless our farmers are equipped to face the challenges of globalisation, agricultural crises with which the farmers are confronted, cannot be resolved.

Agrarian Crisis Due to the Policy of Globalisation -?

Though globalisation provided several opportunities for the growth of Indian economy in general, it proved to be a big challenge for Indian agriculture. In fact, it created crisis for agricultural sector. People's protest against the creation of Special Economic Zones [SEZs] in various parts of the country [including at Nandigram in West Bengal], stagnation in agriculture, large scale mobility of rural youths towards big cities, import of foodgrains, fall in prices of agricultural products, widespread suicide of farmers and such other developments only reflect the simmering discontent in the agricultural sector.

The policy of globalisation introduced in India in 1991 further worsened the situation. Indian economy had to undergo changes as per the requirements of World Bank, International Monetary Fund and World Trade Organisation. Export-import policy was liberalised, customs duties were lowered on imported goods, private sector was encouraged, public distribution system was altered, subsidies being given to farmers were drastically reduced or cancelled and many such changes were witnessed. These changes associated with globalisation affected Indian agriculture seriously.

Immediate Consequences of Globalisation on Agriculture

Fifteen years of economic liberalisation has very badly affected Indian agriculture. Three major consequences of this process are stated below.

1. *Drastic Decline in the Growth Rate of Foodgrains :* From 1950 to 1990, the rate of growth of agricultural output was gradually increasing at least by 4% per annum. After the start of liberalisation, the rate of growth declined to 2% and between 2002 and 2005 it was just 1%. As a result, the per capita availability of foodgrains decreased. Whereas the growth rate of population was higher than that of foodgrains. India helplessly started importing foodgrains at a much higher price than that in the domestic market.

2. *Unemployment in the Agricultural Sector Increased :* Agriculture became no more profitable due to the fall in the price of farm products. According to National Sample Survey, the annual rate of growth of employment in the rural areas was 2.07% between 1987 and 1994. It further declined to mere 0.66% between 1993-2000. Not only the farmers, even *dalits* and tribals, who heavily depend on agriculture became unemployed.

3. *Farmers' Suicide Due to Heavy Loans and Stagnation in Agriculture :* When agriculture failed to be remunerative and profitable, the life of farmers became desperate and many resorted to suicide. The then Union Agricultural Minister **Sharad Pawar** stated in the Lok Sabha in 2004 that as many as **one lakh** farmers committed suicide in India after the economic reforms started. According to **National Crime Record Bureau** [NCRB], 17,060 farmers committed suicide in the country in 2006. The tragic stories of farmers suicides point to the acute nature of the agricultural problem. But unfortunately, the Government and the general masses of India failed to grasp the seriousness of this crisis.

CAUSES FOR AGRARIAN CRISIS

1. *Liberal Import of Agricultural Products* : Due to liberalisation policy, all restrictions to import agricultural products especially of cash crops were removed. **For example**, when the Govt.of India reduced the import duty on tea and coffee from Sri Lanka and Malaysia, their prices in the domestic market got reduced drastically. Thus, cultivaion of such products became unprofitable and so their production was partly stopped or considerably reduced.

2. *Cutback in Agricultural Subsidies* : In the post-reform period, the govt reduced different types of subsidies to agriculture and this led to an increase in the cost of production of cultivation. Cutback in subsidy and control of fertilisers over the last few years has adversely affected the agricultural sector.

3. *Lack of Easy and Low Cost Loan to Agriculture* : After 1991, the commercial banks changed their pattern of lending loans to agriculture and tightened their rules. As a result, loan was not easily available and the interest was not affordable. This made the farmers to depend on money lenders and finally get into their trap. Studies reveal that most of the farmers' suicides were due to debt trap.

4. *Decline in Government Investment in the Agricultural Sector* : Due to the pressure of the policy of globalisation, the government's expenditrue and investment on agriculture got reduced drastically. Expenditure of the governemnt in rural development, agriculture, organisation, flood control, village industry, energy and transport, declined from an average of 14.5% in 1986-1990 to 6% in 1995-2000. This led to several consequences. Rate of capital formation in agriculture came down, agricultural growth rate was reduced, purchasing power of the rural people was adversely affected and standard of living deteriorated.

5. *Restructuring of the Public Distribution System [PDS]* : The Government restructured the PDS by creating two groups. Below Poverty Line [**BPL**] and Above Poverty Line [**APL**] and continuously increased the prices of foodgrains distributed through ration shops. As a result, even the poor people did not buy the subsidised foodgrains and it got accumulated in godowns to be spoiled or sold in the open market. This situation very badly affected the market and farmers.

6. *Special Economic Zones [SEZs]* : As part of the economic reforms, the system of taking over land in the name of SEZ by the government for commercial and industrial purposes was introduced in the country. As per the ***Special Economic Zones Act, 2005,*** the government has so far notified about 400 such zones in the country. Very often, it is fertile land which has been acquired. Experience of the farmers with the SEZ is that, it deprives them of their land and livelihood and is proving to be harmful to agriculture.

SOME SOLUTIONS TOWARDS AGRARIAN CRISIS

Agrarian crisis is getting deepened year by year. The crisis is affecting millions of Indians, both farmers and non-farmers. Farmers who produce food materials are in serious crisis. The weaker sections of the country like the Dalits and Tribals, who depend on agriculture are becoming unemployed. They are virtually struggling for their livelihood. The poor have lost their food security. The crisis in agriculture has become a crisis of the country as a whole. Hence, it demands urgent attention and some suggestions may be recommened in this regard.

1. *The government should increase its investment and expenditure in the agriculutal sector* especially in areas such as -irrigation, transport, communication and farm research, etc.. The *National Rural Employment Guarantee Scheme [MGNAREGA]* should be completely rationalised and made useful and effective.

2. *Implementation of land reforms in all the states is a must*. Feudal structures and landlordism based on large holdings of land by high castes and classes must go. There is a need for conscious efforts and positive steps from the government to implement land reforms. Surplus land acquired must be distributed to the *dalits* and *adivasi* farmers.

3. *The government's policy towards Special Economic Zones [SEZs] should be revised*. No fertile agricultural land be acquired for SEZs. When it does take land for essential public utilites, farmers' consent should be obtained and due compensation at market rate be given to them. Further, there is a need to implement honestly the policy of relief and rehabilitation of people displaced due to SEZs and other developmental projects.

4. *Quantitative restrictions be imposed on import of agricultural products*. Necessary import duty and quantitative restrictions should be imposed on imported goods to protect Indian farmers.

5. *Bank loans should be made easily available for the farmers.* "*M.S. Swaminathan Commission for Agriculture*" has recommended a low rate of 4% interest for the farmers, and the government must seriously think of implementing this.

6. *Subsidy and concessions given to agriculture but removed during the post-reform period, be restored*. This step will make agriculture somewhat remunerative and attractive. It may be recalled that the U.S. and the European Union had given high subsidies to their farmers despite the WTO regulations.

7. *There should be periodic revision of the procurement prices for farm produces*. This will make agriculture remunerative. In fact, **Swaminathan Commission** has suggested 50% more of the total production cost as supportive price for foodgrains. The Commission clearly stated that unless agriculture is made a profitable enterprise, the present crisis cannot be solved.

8. *The rural economy including agriculture will be greatly benefited* if programmes meant for economically backward people including *Integrated Child Development Schemes, Mid-Day Meals for School Children, The National Rural Employment Guarantee Scheme, etc.* are effectively implemented. Food security of the poor be ensured by making public distribution system more efficient. All these programmes will ultimately help to increase the purchasing power of the rural people.

Conclusion

There is no dispute about the fact that agricultural factor is facing a crisis today. Announcement of a few "*packages*" as a form of political gimmick is not going to solve the crisis. The government should be ready to take bold steps. Farmers, agricultural labourers and people's organisations in civil society should work collectively to assist the government. India cannot think of becoming economically strong unless the vast majority of the rural people especially the real farmers become prosperous and duly empowered. To quote **Dr. Swaminathan**'s words; "*In a country where 60% of the people depend on agriculture for their livelihood, it is better to become an agricultural force based on food security rather than a nuclear force*".

FARMERS' SUICIDE IN KARNATAKA

As it has already been referred to, the problem of farmers' suicide has drawn the attention of the whole nation towards agricultural crisis. The problem is so serious that it cannot be neglected. As per one estimate, between 1997 and 2005, on an average, for every 32 minutes a farmer has committed suicide in India. During the same period, as many as **1.5 lakh** farmers have killed themselves due to unbearable agricultural conditions. The NCRB [National Crime Records Bureau] referred to five big states of India namely; Maharasthra, Andhra, Karnataka, Madhya Pradesh and Chhatishghar as constituting a "*suicide belt*". Because, in these states, as many as 10,797 farmers committed suicide during the year 2008 which constituted 66.6% of the total suicide instances of the country for that year.

Unfortunately, Karnataka is also a state where farmers'suicides are on the higher side. Between 2003 and 2010, as many as 2597 farmers had committed suicide in Karnataka and in the year 2010 alone, around 140 farmers had killed themselves due to agricultural hazards.[2]

Farmers Suicide in Karnataka: Study by Deshpande and Saroja Arora

On the basis of their field study, **R.S. Deshpande** and **Saroja Arora** in their work *"Agrarian Crisis and Farmer Suicides – 2007"*[3] have tried to analyse the agrarian crisis and the related farmers suicide in Karnataka. Their views can be summarized in the following way.

Farmers' Suicides Not Confined to Karnataka Alone: According to Deshpande and Saroja Arora, the problem of farmers suicide is not peculiar to Karnataka, because between 1993 and 2003 as many as 100,248 farmers committed suicide in India as such. It has been reported among the sugarcane growers of U.P., cotton growers of Andhra Pradesh, and spice / coffee growers of Kerala. There are reports of the same from Orissa and West Bengal.

Deshpande and Arora have stated that Karnataka had no history of farmers committing suicide even during the worst situations of agrarian crisis. The trend, however, started only after 2003. As per the Agricultural Department, Government of Karnataka, between 2003 and 2007, [up to 1st Jan 2007] as many as 1193 farmers committed suicide in Karnataka. But the Central Govt's report estimated it to be around 8600 between 2000-01 and 2005-06. However, *'Veeresh Committee Report'*, and some other press reports estimated the number of suicides to be more than 5000 for the same period. As per the *Crime Branch of Karnataka*, the number of suicides under the heading *"farming and agricultural activity"*, comes to 15804 between 1998 and 2002. In this way, different estimates are there regarding the magnitude of farmers suicide. However, the recent report says that as many as 1,50,000 Indian farmers committed suicide in 9 years from

---

2 **Source of Statistics** : **K.Nagaraj's** article "*Farm Suicides Rising*", in "*The Hindu*", Dated 12-11-2007, and Prajavani Dt. 12-1-2011.

3 This field work study was conducted by *Centre for Rural Studies, Lal Bahudur Shastri National Academy and Administration Mussoori* in 2007.

1997 to 2005. Nearly, 2/3 of these deaths have taken place in only five states of India namely; Maharastra, Andhra, Madhya Pradesh, Karnataka and Kerala.

Table No.: 1

Farmers' Suicides in India From 1997 - to - 2005

Year	Total Suicides		Farmers' Suicides		Suicides by Pesticides	
	Number	Rate of Suicide per 10,000 people	Number	% in the Total No. of Suicides	Number	% in the Total No. of Suicides
1997	95829	10.0	13622	14.2	8311	19.1
1998	104713	10.8	16015	15.3	19075	15.3
1999	110587	11.2	16082	14.5	20251	18.3
2000	108593	10.6	16603	15.3	21801	20.1
2001	108506	10.6	16415	15.1	21530	19.8
2002	110417	10.5	17971	16.3	21414	19.4
2003	110851	10.4	17164	15.5	23001	20.8
2004	113697	10.5	18241	16.0	23311	20.5
2005	113914	10.3	17131	15.0	22316	19.6
Total Suicides	**977107**		**149244**		**191010**	

Source: P.Sainath, *"Farm Suicides rising, most intense in 4 States"* The Hindu, 12-11-2007 p.11

Table No.: 2

Farmers' Suicides in Four Important States: 1997 - 2005

Year	Maharashtra	Andhra Pradesh	Karnataka	Madhya Pradesh	Total No. of Suicides in Four States a Year
1997	1917	1097	1832	2390	7236
1998	409	1813	1883	2278	8383
1999	2423	1974	2379	2654	9430
2000	3022	31525	2630	2660	9837
2001	3556	1509	2505	2824	10374
2002	3050	1896	2340	2578	10509
2003	3836	1800	2678	2511	10825
2004	4147	2666	1963	3033	11809
2005	3926	2490	1883	2660	10959
Total	28911	**16770**	**20093**	**23588**	**89362**

Source: P.Sainath, one Farmer Suicides every 30 miniutes, The Hindu 15-11-2007

Observations of the National Social Watch Coalition [NSWC]

As per NSWC, at least 11387 farmers must have committed suicide between 2001 and 2006 in Karnataka. Relatively higher instances of suicide were reported from the Old Mysore areas, followed by the Old Bombay Presidency area, and the Old Hyderabad Region. But such instances were relatively less in the Madras Presidency area as well as Coorg. In fact, Old Mysore and Old Bombay Presidency areas are better known for canal irrigation. Here, the suicides reflect the failure of the state to distribute water judiciously. It is observed that most of those who committed suicide lived near the tail end of the canal.

Speaking about the beginning of the unfortunate incidences of suicide, it was in the year 1998, when turdal, a market oriented agricultural crop failed, some farmers in Bidar who were involved in cultivating it, committed suicide. In the two more years, such instances were largely confined to the drought–prone districts of north–Karnataka, or say, to the backward districts such as Gulbarga and Bidar. From the year 2000 onwards, this phenomenon was shifted to relatively progressive agricultural regions, particularly Mandya, Hassan, Shimoga, Davangere, Koppal, and even Chickmagalur and Kodagu.

Recent [Nov-2013] Instance that Created Sensation

Very recently, that is, in the month of November 2013, a sugarcane grower by name **Vittal Arabhavi** (aged 60) of **Kankanwadi** village in Raibhag Thaluk of Belgaum District, committed suicide. While participating in a protest outside the Suvarna Vidhana Soudha in Belgaum, demanding remunerative price for sugarcanes and payment of dues, he consumed pesticide and later died at the K.L.E. Hospital. This incident triggered tension in the city of Belgaum and shocked the whole State of Karnataka. This recent episode points out that agrarian crisis is still simmering in the State.

CAUSES FOR FARMERS' SUICIDE IN KARNATAKA

1. ***Burden of Loans*** **:** Most of the poor farmers borrow money from one or the other source and later find it difficult to make repayment especially due to failure of monsoon and /or failure of crops. They feel helpless and think of committing suicide when they come under heavy pressure to make repayment.

2. ***Floods, Famines and Extreme Variations in Weather*****:** Indian agriculture in many places depends on the vagaries of monsoon. Many districts of Northen part of Karnataka are not properly provided with irrigation facility. Irregularity in the monsoon is a big hazard for the farmers in these regions. In some years there will be scant rainfall and in some others there will be floods. **For example**, in the year 2013, these districts experienced heaviest rainfall which destroyed crops in many places.

3. ***Unprofitable Land Holdings*****:** Most of the farmers in India as well as in Karnataka, are small scale farmers. Their land holdings are smaller than 2 to 3 acres. Subdivision and fragmentation of land holdings has made cultivation totally unattractive, expensive and less profitable. Many stick on to these holdings for they do not have any other alternative. Farmers with these small holdings will get very meagre income which is not even sufficient for their maintenance. Many of them are compelled to borrow money or to take loans, whcih will only increase their hardship.

4. ***Price Rise and Non-Availability of Sowing Seeds, Fertilisers and Pesticides*** especially at the time of cultivation, cause lot of hardship for the farmers.There were also instances in which the farmers due to their helplessness took to violence by attacking shops, go-downs and company show-rooms that deal with sowings seeds, chemicals, fertilisers and pesticides.

5. ***Alienation Haunting the Farmers*****:** Disappearance of joint families, decline of caste panchayats, frozened community sentiment, money and market-centred economic life, lack of understanding and co-operation among the farmers due to caste or political prejudices, etc. have created a sense of alienation among the poor farmers. These cruelties of social life, sometimes drive them to take the drastic step of ending their life.

Causes of Farmers' Suicides: As Per Deshpande and Arora's Analysis

Deshpande and Arora have tried to interpret the causes of this unfortunate incident in terms of four important factors namely; *(i) events, (ii) stressors, (iii actors,* and *(iv) triggers.*

(i) ***Events:*** Events that caused suicides include – crop loss, price crash, failure of a borewell, death of oxen, daughter's marriage, family problems, property disputes, etc.

(ii) ***Stressors:*** These refer to stress creators. Heavy stresses are created when two or more such 'events' combine together. Pointing out specifically, when illness of any of the family members or of the individual himself, heavy borrowings, continued disputes in the family or land related problems, etc. are combined; heavy *"stresses"* are created for the farmer. They virtually become fatal but the final ignition comes through the *'actors'* or *'catalysts'* and what are called *'trigger'* incidences.

(iii) ***Actors:*** As Deshpande says, the actors or catalysts create a sense of 'insecurity' or 'insult' to the potential victim. These catalysts include – *the moneylender, banker, spouse, relatives* and *close friends.*

(iv) ***Triggers:*** When the potential victim is already having the background of the *"events"* and *"stressors"*, at any weak moment or time, the actors or catalysts can perpetrate the final act of igniting the fire for the unfortunate incident.

As Deshpande comments, with this complex nature of the phenomenon, it is really difficult to pinpoint any one particular reason for the suicide. In the Durkheimian language, it can be said that *growing alienation of the individual from the family, society and religion, pushes him in the direction of taking off his own life.* As Durkheim says, large instances of suicide reflect nothing but social disintegration. Various studies have indicated that farmers' suicides are invariably associated with more than one factor.

It is important to note from the studies, that suicides are occurring in the high and medium growth states and are comparatively very low or even absent in the backward [BIMARU] states like Bihar, Rajasthan, and Uttar Pradesh [Madhya Pradesh, seems to be an exception to this observation where farmers' suicides are found to be on the higher side]. Scholars are of the opinion, that *'high aspirations'* or a strong *'urge for upward mobility'* in the absence of public policy support, must have been a major cause for the suicides in the backward areas of medium growth states.

Measures Taken by the Government of Karnataka to Face the Problem of Farmers' Suicide

When the farmers were committing suicide in a large number due to helpless situations, the Government of Karnataka was forced to take some serious steps to face this problem. Some of the measures taken by the government in this regard may be mentioned here.

(A) Committees to Study the Agrarian Crises

(a) Dwarakanath Committee – 2000: Of the various commissions and committees appointed by the Government of Karnataka to study the problem of agrarian issues, the committee headed by an agricultural scientist Dwaraknath is worth mentioning here. This commission stated categorically that *"Indian agriculture is irrevocably integrated with the larger economy"*, and hence ups and downs – in the Indian economy are found to affect Indian agriculture. It had even encouraged field trials of BT Cotton and thereby supported Bio-technology in Karnataka.

(b) G.K. Veeresh Committee – 2002: This committee which was given the responsibility of studying the agricultural crisis, tried to link farmers' suicides with their psychological or personal factors. These factors include – alcohol, gambling, extravagance [20.35%], failure of crop [16.81%], chit funds [15.4%], family problems [13.27%], chronic illness [9.73%], burden of marriage of daughters [5.31%], political affiliations [4.42%], property disputes [2.65%], debt burden [2.65%], price crash [2.65%], borrowing beyond paying capacity, house construction and other factors [2.65%], loss in non-agricultural activities [1.77%] and finally failure of borewells [0.88%]. Veeresh Committee's Report was however, severely criticized mainly for its type of approach to the problem.

(B) Policy Initiatives to Face the Problem

The Government of Karnataka tried to counter the problem by means of some recent policies and initiating relevant activities.

*1. **Financial Relief by Waiving of the Loans:*** The Government took a decision in 2007-08 to waive of the principal amount of outstanding loan to all farmers up to ₹ 25,000 and also waived the interest to those who have borrowed above ₹ 25,000/- if they pay the principal amount before 31st March 2008.

*2. **Legislative Measure: Exorbitant Interest Rate Act, 2004:*** In order to check levying exorbitant rates of interest by private money lenders, the Govt introduced the Exorbitant Interest Rate Act in the year 2004. This Act imposes strict action against the money lenders who violate it, which includes 3 years imprisonment or a fine of ₹ 30,000/- or both.

*3. **Responding to the Problems of the Farmers:*** Realising the gravity of the problem of farmers' crisis, the Government appointed a committee under the chairmanship of **G.K. Veeresh** to give appropriate suggestions to the govt to handle the situation. The Committee made several recommendations such as – *(i) Creation of farmers' welfare fund; (ii) establishment of nodal department [consisting of mediators] for the welfare of farmers' welfare, (iii) providing social security to the farmers,* and so on. On the basis of the recommendations of this committee and with the due guidance and advice of its members, the Government of Karnataka took series of measures to face the crisis.

Measures Taken By the Govt to Face the Agricultural Crisis

1. ***Reduction in Bank Rates of Interest:*** The rate of interests on loans from co-operative banks were reduced to 6% per annum, and further to 4% in the year 2007-08.
2. ***Giving Compensation to the Family of Victims:*** The Govt reviewed its policy of giving compensation and decided to give it only in the case where suicide was directly related to farming activities.
3. ***A New Scheme of Seed Subsidy*** was implemented and farmers were given seeds with a subsidy upto 50%.
4. ***Crop Insurance*** was taken up to Hobli level and compensation provided to the farmers on the Hobli level data.
5. ***Raita Samparka Kendras*** were equipped with internet and telephone facilities so that the initial signals of crisis could be communicated directly to the state headquarters.
6. ***Investment on Watershed Development Programmes*** was increased 10 fold and this created lot of employment opportunities for the people in the rain-fed areas.
7. ***Health Insurance Scheme*** 2000, namely; *'Yashaswini'* was launched to provide for the farmers the best medical facilities available in the state-run hospitals. A farmer's family needs to pay a premium payment of ₹ 120/- per year and the scheme covers all surgical

interventions and outpatient services at any of the designated network hospitals. The scheme became very popular among the farmers today.

8. ***Agricultural Universities*** were directed to focus on research and development in tune with the necessities and demands of the time.

III (C) Measures to Face the Challenges of Crisis on Long –Term Basis

The problem of farmers' crisis including suicide, has to be tackled on a long-term basis also. This could be done in two ways: *(i) increasing the income of farmers,* and *(ii) increasing the provision of infrastructural facilities to the farmers.* These measures, in general, include the following steps.

(1) Bringing a Social Reform in Villages: A social reform is necessary in the rural areas to improve the standard of living of the villagers. This includes creating a general awareness against alcoholism, drug addiction, gambling, smoking and other bad habits, and also regarding the need for cutting down unwanted and unnecessary expenditure on festivities, marriages, feastings, religious and social ceremonies and other non-productive activities.

(2) Encouraging Community – Oriented Development: This type of development helps provision of local goods, basic services and the management of natural resources. Participation in such community–driven or community–oriented development includes – information dissemination, consultation and collaboration to support empowerment or the control of community groups over decisions and resources.

(3) Short-Term Credit Measures: These include the following:

(a) ***Provision for short-term agricultural credit:*** The NABARD has ensured that the banks would provide short–term credit for farmers to continue their farming operations.

(b) ***Grameen Tatkal Scheme [GTS]:*** This scheme functions under a *"family centric approach",* and as a part of the banking system it provides flexible, cost-effective and easy credit facility to rural households. It will aim at merger of all the schemes in the rural areas such as *Kisan Credit Cards* [KCC], *General Credit Cards* [GCC], and *Swarojgar Credit Cards* [SCC] and so on. This scheme is believed to act as an effective means in planning all rural economic activities at reduced cost and achieve significant rural development. This is already being implemented [on a pilot basis] in states like Andhra Pradesh, Karnataka, Maharastra, Punjab, Haryana, Tamil Nadu, Uttar Pradesh and West Bengal.

(4) Non-Credit Relief Measures: A few more measures are taken up under *"the PM's relief package"* to face the crisis among which the following are to be noted.

(a) ***Rainwater Harvesting:*** To create rainwater harvesting structures covering at least 1000 beneficiaries per district per year.

(b) ***Construction of Check Dams:*** To construct 500 check dams per district per year.

(c) ***Watershed Development:*** As part of the package relief measures to the affected districts, the NABARD has launched a *National Holistic Watershed Development Programme* [NHWDP] combined with livelihood support activities such as animal husbandry, micro-finance activities, etc.

(d) ***Promotion of Need-based Localised Schemes:*** The state governments [that is, Govts of suicide-hit states] have introduced need-based localized schemes to strengthen the farming activities.

(e) ***Assurance of a Minimum Support Price for Agricultural and Horticultural Commodities:*** To protect the farmers from being compelled to sell their agricultural

/ horticultural products at a throw-away price, the state govt has created a revolving fund of ₹ 2.60 billion. The fund is created to offer a minimum support price to the farmers in case of the worst market situation.

THE SPECIAL ECONOMIC ZONES [SEZ]

PROBLEMS CREATED BY THE SPECIAL ECONOMIC ZONES [SEZ]

Along with the processes of globalization, liberalization and privatization, and the GATT [General Agreement on Trade and Tariffs] agreement came in yet another phenomenon known as Special Economic Zone [SEZ]. All these are the creations of the Western people, fashioned and designed mainly to serve their capitalist interests. In the Indian rural context, these SEZs have also posed some serious challenges and problems.

What is Special Economic Zone [SEZ]-?

- *Special Economic Zone, or briefly called as SEZ, is basically an economic plan designed to promote development in an economically backward area by making use of the opportunities provided by globalisation.*

SEZ is also defined as an earmarked geographic area meant for production of goods and services mainly meant for the purpose of export where economic laws are different from other areas and various facilities and concessions are given.

Different Names of SEZ

SEZ is called in different ways in different places. **Examples** : It is called in some places **FTZ** [*Free Trade Zone*] and in some others as **EPZ** *[Export Processing Zone]*. It is also called **IPZ** *[Industrial Pre-Zone]* in some more places. In China, it is called **SEZ** *[Special Economic Zone]* and the same name is in currency in India.

The supporters of globalization have put forward the proposal of SEZ which appears to be very attractive from outside. As per this proposal, certain geographic area is given to some private companies with the consent of the Government for making it economically strong and wealthy. These SEZs are established for augmenting export, attracting foreign investment, improving infrastructure on par with global standards and creating enough employment opportunities especially for localities.

The Beginning of SEZ in India

India was one of the first countries in Asia to recognise the effectiveness of the EPZ [Export Processing Zone] model in promoting exports, with Asia's first EPZ set up in Kandla, in 1965. With a view to attract larger foreign investments in India, the Special Economic Zone policy was announced in April -2000. SEZs in India functioned from 1-11-2000 to 9-2-2006. Under the provisions of the Foreign Trade Policy.

The Special Economic Zones Act- 2005, was passed by the Parliament in May 2005 and obtained presidential assent on 23-6-2005. The main objectives of the SEZ Act are mentioned below.

Main Objectives of SEZ

SEZ Act 2005, specifies the objectives of SEZ in the following way.

(i) generation of additional economic activity;

(ii) promotion of exports of goods and services

(iii) promotion of investment from domestic and foreign sources;
(iv) creation of employment opportunities, and
(v) development of infrastructure facilities.

It is expected that this will trigger a large flow of foreign and domestic investment in SEZs in infrastructure and productive capacity, leading to generation of additional economic acivities.

Enormous Liberal Concessions for the SEZs

Enormous facilities are provided to the firms or industrial units operating in the SEZs among which the following may be noted.

1. Industrial units under SEZ are license free to import and no customs duties be livied on them.
2. They have neither sales tax nor service tax, and are exempted from the State Taxes.
3. Water and electricity be provided to these areas at reduced rates.
4. Areas identified under SEZ, need not obtain permission from Pollution Control Board.
5. Amendments are made to Forest Acts to give forest areas also to SEZs if needed.
6. A special transportation facility in the form of corridor be given to SEZ areas.
7. Employees working in SEZ, must be provided with accommodations inside the SEZ and their management be given to the administration.
8. No elected representatives interfere in the SEZ areas.
9. There should be separate VISA and Passport to get inside the SEZ.
10. Governing laws and rules, administration, control and maintenance of the SEZ area are the responsibility of SEZ themselves.
11. There is no relationship between the elected local bodies and the SEZ.
12. SEZs will have their own police and the security arrangement and the government cannot interfere in it.

The Position of SEZs in 2008

- By 2008, as many as 439 SEZs obtained legal consent and permission.
- Around 138 SEZs after securing legal consent, have been waiting for the governmental acceptance.
- About 195 SEZs have obtained the legal consent at the final round.

Total No. of SEZs Ready to Function - 762.

As per the 2005 Act, SEZs could be set up in public sector, private sector or joint sector or even by the State Governments in collaboration with any corporate houses.

Is SEZ Proving to be Harmful to Indian Agriculture - ?

In spite of the attractive benefits of the SEZ, its initial implementation has been proving to be against the agricultural interests of the people. In the very first stage of its implementation in 19 states, around 34861 hectares of fertile agricultural land has already been captured for nearly 237 SEZs [out of which 135 SEZs [57%] belong to I.T. sector, while 89 [38%] belong to other sectors and B [5%] belong to productive sectors. In Karnataka, 29 SEZs have already obtained permission to start their business out of which 21 [72%] belong to I.T. sector.[4]

4 ***Source*: Prof. B.M. Kumara Swamy,** noted Swadeshi Economist, Karnataka, in his article in "Utthana" special Issue (2008).

The initial experience of the people with the SEZs has been very bitter and disappointing. Much against their promises they have started acquiring fertile agricultural land of our farmers rather than the barren lands. In many places, they have made use of physical force to capture the land. Hence, lot of criticisms have been levelled against the SEZs among which the following may be noted.

Criticisms Against the SEZs

1. *Forceful Capture of Agricultural Land* : As it is stated above, a major objection raised against the SEZs is that, in the name of development fertile and highly valuable agricultural land is being forcefully acquired and converted into SEZs at subsidised rates. The land is acquired at a subsidised rate and the compensation given to the land owner is far less than the market price. Every where the State Governments are acquiring lands under *The Land Acquisition Act* for industrialists and corporate agencies. The marginal and small farmers are rendered landless in all instances of establishing SEZs.

2. *Add to the Disparity Between the Rich and Poor* : Another criticism is that, creation of SEZs is going to increase the income disparity between the rich and poor.

3. *Expolitation of Labour* : The SEZs are found to be exploiting the labour and displacing the livelihoods in the agrarian economy. SEZs are being criticised as sacrificing the interests of the poor for the sake of capitalists. There are also instances of small farmers having lost lives in their fight against capitalists.

4. *SEZs Keep Silent Regarding the Betterment of the Poor* : In a nation like India, large number of people are poor, illiterate, unemployed and unskilled. SEZs which take lot of special concessions from the government, do not bother about the well being of the poor and the downtrodden.

5. *Common People Have Lost all the Faith in SEZs* : It is for this reason, farmers of Nandigrama Village [West Bengal] fought vehemently against the acquision of fertile land for the SEZ proposal of starting TaTa "Nano" car project in their village. There is not a single incident of a place wherein people have voluntarily and willingly handed over their land for the SEZ.

Conclusion

The above mentioned criticisms drive any one to the inevitable conclusion that the SEZs are harmful to the Indian agriculture. Really speaking, it need not necessarily be so. The fundamental idea behind SEZ is to improve a backward area by making use of its barren land and extending employment opportunities to the local people. If its main purposes are honestly and meticulously implemented, definitely it will prove to be beneficial to the Indian farmers. But the sad part of it is that, the hither to experience of the people with the SEZ has been highly discouraging.

•••

Chapter 23

PROBLEMS OF URBANISATION

Concepts of Urban, Urbanisation and Urbanism - Charactristics of Urban Community or Urban / System or Urbanism - Advantages and Disadvantages of the City - Urbanisation in India - Some Trends of Urbanisation in India - Some Demographic Dimensions of Urbanisation in India - Factors or Causes of Urbanisation in India - Urban Influence on the Rural Community - Cleavages and Conflicts between Rural and Urban Sectors - Rural Migration towards Urban Centres - Rural - Urban Convergence - The Rural-Urban Continuum - Problems of Urban Society or Urbanisation - Some Suggestions to Face and to Solve Urban Problems.

Urbanisation, that is, unprecedented growth of cities, is one of the most significant trends in the modern world. Human beings have inhabited the planet for over a million years, yet our ancestors lived in small primary groups for about 5 to 6 thousand years of that time. The growth of large cities that contain the bulk of a society's population is a very recent development. But this growth of cities is taking place all over the world at an astonishing speed. Our new and highly urbanised social environment offers opportunities and challenges that are without precedents in the history of humanity.

Urbanisation is a part of the development process. In backward and stagnant societies, the process of urbanisation, that is, growth of cities, is rather slow, because cities fail to offer employment opportunities to the people living in the countryside. But urbanisation process is faster in rapidly growing economies where newly established industries and other commercial establishments provide jobs to the people. The economic attractions of the cities in this phase of development become particularly strong if industrial growth is fast. The process of urbanisation slows down only when the proportion of urban population to total population in a country becomes very high. This stage has been reached in some 30-odd countries which are regarded as *developed and highly industrialised countries.* India is definitely not in this list for it is regarded as a *developing nation.*

Though India is traditionally regarded as the land of villages, towns and cities are not strange things to India. India has a long standing tradition of urban living and has been a land of cities from pre-historic times of the Indus Valley, going back to nearly 6000 years. The two cities of Harappa and Mohen-jo-daro of Indus Valley are known for high standards of town planning and architecture. The process of industrialisation and urbanisation obtained new speed especially after Independence. By 2011, there were about **37.71** crores of urban dwellers living in **7935** towns and cities in India. It means around 31.16% of the people are living in towns and cities according to 2011 Census report. Some of the economic reform measures such as liberalisation, privatisation and globalisation initiated by the Government have further added to the process of urbanisation and made it more complex. The already existing big cities are getting overcrowded and becoming centres of congestion, confusion, indefiniteness and insecurity. There is a brief attempt here in this chapter to take a glimpse of the city life in India including its major problems.

CONCEPTS OF 'URBAN' OR 'CITY', 'URBANISATION' AND 'URBANISM'

The Concept of 'Urban' or 'City'

The terms such as *"city", "urban area", "city community", 'urban system'* etc. are all often used interchangeably in sociological literature. By *"urban system",* we mean urban community. Urban community life represents the city-life. Though the term *"urban"* is popularly used, it is not properly defined. There is no single all-inclusive definition of a city or urban community.

Definition of 'City' or 'Urban' Community

1. The urban sociologist **Howard Woolston,** in his *"Metropolis"*, defines the city as a *"limited geographic area, inhabited by a largely and closely settled population, having many common interests and institutions, under a local government authorised by the State."*
2. **James A. Quinn** in his *"Urban Sociology",* views the city as a *"phenomenon of specialisation",* as a population aggregate whose occupations are non-agricultural.
3. **Louis Wirth** in his essay *"Urbanisation as a Way of Life",* writes : *"For sociological purposes a city may be defined as a relatively large, dense and permanent settlement of socially heterogeneous individuals........"*

- *The term "city" is defined as a small community characterised by a large heterogeneous population, large scale division of labour, a high degree of specialisation, predominance of non-agricultural occupations, wide opportunities for social mobility, heavy dependence on formal social control, and a formalised system of local government.*

Determinants of City as Prescribed by 1991 Census

The 1991 Census has defined a city or urban place on the basis of certain determinants which are mentioned below.

1. An urban area to be called so, must have a minimum of 5000 people.
2. At least 75% of its male workers' population is engaged in non-agricultural pursuits.
3. A density of population of atleast 400 persons per square Km [or 1000 persons per square mile].
4. All places with a municipality, corporation, cantonment board or notified town area, are also regarded as *"urban."*

As far as the *"determinants of city"* are concerned, 1961 basis was adopted in 1971, 1981 and 1991 censuses also for defining an urban area or town. This definition of the *"urban area"* is still not comparable with the definition of urban area provided in other countries. For instance, in **Japan,** a place having 30,000 or more inhabitants, is classified as *"urban."* This number is fixed at 3500 in **U.S.A.,** 20,000 in **Netherlands** and **Holland,** and just 2000 in **Austria, Germany** and **France.** Sociologist **Mark Jefferson** fixed this at 10,000. Sociologists, however, do not attach much importance to the size of the population in the definition of city. They give importance to the characteristics of the city such as - *heterogeneity of population, complex division of labour, prevalence of impersonal secondary relations, dependence on formal social controls, predominance of non-agricultural occupations,* and so on.

Concept of *"Urbanisation"*

The concept of *"urbanisation"* generally refers to the concentration of people in towns and cities. This has become a continuous and almost a universal process in all the modern societies. The term indicates the movement of people from the less concentrated areas to the more concentrated ones. As urban sociologists have noted, this process need not take place in the very same manner, but can take place in diverse ways in different places. Sociologist **Munro** is of the opinion, that *the process of urbanisation or unprecedented growth of cities stands out as one of the greatest developments of the recent one hundred years.*

Definition of *"Urbanisation"*

1. **C.B. Mamoria :** *"Urbanisation refers to a process by which the urban values get diffused, behaviour patterns are transformed and movement from villages to cities occur."*
2. **Wallace** and **Wallace :** Urbanisation refers to *"the movement of people from rural areas to city."*
3. **Anderson** is of the opinion that *"urbanisation involves not only movement of population to cities but also change in the migrants' attitudes, values, and behaviour patterns."*
4. **Ram Ahuja :** *"Urbanisation is the movement of population from rural to urban areas."*
5. **Thompson Warren :** *"Urbanisation is the movement of people from communities concerned chiefly or solely with agriculture to other communities generally larger whose activities are primarily centred in government, trade, manufacture, or allied interests."*

Importance of the Study of Urbanisation

The study of urbanisation has its own importance and **C.B. Mamoria** mentions four important factors in this regard.

1. The cities, once established, tend to develop into centres of political, economic, industrial and other activities.
2. The cities have proved themselves to be not only centres of heavy concentration of people, but also as places of intellectual, scientific, artistic, educational, political and other achievements.
3. The development of cities has been a recent trend in human history and it has contributed to changes in various other fields.
4. Urbanisation has been a product of economic and technological development. Once it sets in, it goes on influencing the rural people, their lives and activities.

Concept of "Urbanism"

The concept of *"urbanism"* represents a way of life. The term generally denotes the diffusion of urban culture and the evolution of urban society. The term urbanism can be defined in the following way :

- **C.B. Mamoria** is of the opinion that *"Urbanism is a cultural - social - economic phenomenon which traces interaction between the social and technological processes."*[1]
- **Louis Wirth** has mentioned four characteristics of urban system or urbanism : *heterogeneity of population, specialisation of function, anonymity and impersonality, and standardisation of behaviour.*

---

1 **C.B. Mamoria.** Page - 459.

IS URBANISATION GAINING MOMENTUM IN INDIA - ?

- **Prof. Ram Ahuja** says that *urbanism is a way of life which is characterised by certain elements such as transiency [short-term relations], superficiality, anonymity and individualism.*

As a result of urbanism, a market economy grows, innovations that take place come to conflict with traditions, complicated type of division of labour is introduced and more than any other thing, a new way of living gets evolved. Urban way of living may even spread to villages.

CHARACTERISTICS OF URBANISM OR URBAN COMMUNITY OR URBAN SYSTEM

Urbanism is a way of life. It denotes how the city people are living a life of their own. It mirrors the characteristic style of city life. Different scholars have highlighted different aspects of the city style of life or urbanism. **For example :**

- **Ruth Glass** has mentioned following characteristics of urbanism : *anonymity, individualism, impersonal relations, social differentiation, transience and organic type of solidarity.*
- **Louis Wirth** has given five characteristics of urbanism - *heterogeneity of population, specialisation of function, anonymity, impersonality and standardisation of life and behaviour.*
- **Kingsley Davis** has spoken of 8 characteristics of urban system - *social heterogeneity, secondary association, social mobility, individualism, spatial segregation, social tolerance, secondary control, and voluntary associations.*

Though the characteristics mentioned above present an exaggerated picture of the city man and city life, they give us a glimpse of the city way of life. Here is a brief analysis of these characteristics.

1. ***Social Heterogeneity*** **:** An urban system or society is heterogeneous. The city is complex and manysided. Wide difference is found in the ways of living of the people. Uniformity and similarity are rarely found, here. It is more characterised by diversity. As **Louis Wirth** in his *"Urbanism as a way of life"*, points out "*the greater the number of individuals participating in a process of interaction, the greater the potential differentiation between them ....*" Louis Wirth further says that "*the city has been the melting-pot of races, peoples and cultures, and a most favourable breeding ground of new biological and cultural hybrids.*" He also says that the city "has brought together people from the ends of the earth *because* they are different and thus useful to one another, rather than because they are homogeneous and likeminded." The ways of thinking, behaving, acting, the habits, morals, religious beliefs and practices, food and dress habits, occupations, etc., of the people differ significantly. Differentiation is potent in urban life.

2. ***Secondary Relations*** **:** The urban community is characterised by secondary relations. A city by virtue of its size cannot be a primary group. It is a secondary group. People are indifferent towards one another. Face-to-face, friendly or intimate relations may not be observed among people. Mass media of communication such as telephone, radio, press, post and telegraph, etc. are often resorted to by the urbanites for contacts. In cities, people rarely take personal interests in others' concerns. Superficial form of politeness and manners are commonly found. Physical contact rarely results in intimacy and closeness. Even the neighbours are often found to be strangers. Private interests prevail over the common interests.

3. ***Anonymity of City Life*** **:** The city is an ocean of strangers. Heavy concentration of people in a limited space makes it impossible for people to know one another. Every one appears to be a stranger for every other person. There prevails a state of namelessness in which the individual identities remain unknown. This kind of namelessness that is found in the city is often referred to as *the anonymity of city life.* The anonymity of city life makes the problem of social control more complex.

4. *Secondary Control* : Control of social behaviour is more difficult in a city. Predominance of secondary relations makes it more complex, the social control. The social behaviour of the people is no more regulated by customs, traditions, religion and group standards. Instances of social deviation are commonly found in a city. As the city is the ocean of strangers, violations of standards of behaviour may pass unnoticed and unchecked. In this way, informal means of social control are not very effective. Regulation of social behaviour is largely done through the specialised agencies like law, legislation, police, court, etc. The larger the city, the greater it becomes the problem of control and more complex the agencies of secondary regulation.

5. *Large-scale Division of Labour and Specialisation* : An urban community is known for its large-scale division of labour and specialisation. Specialisation is visible in every walk of life. The larger the city, the greater is the specialisation. Hence we find different people in society engaging themselves in different kinds of activities like mechanical, commercial, educational, political, recreational, artistic, literary, scientific and so on. There are skilled, unskilled and semi-skilled workers, the artisans, the technicians, the *"paper expert"*, the *"white-collar"* employees, the financiers, the businessmen, administrators, the politicians, the artists and others in society specialising themselves in some particular kind of activity or the other. City depends on large-scale division of labour. Work is divided among people on the basis of interests, talents, efficiency, opportunities, age, sex and so on. Division of labour and specialisation are possible because of co-operation.

6. *Large-scale Social Mobility* : An urban community is characterised by intense social mobility. *"Social Mobility" refers to the movement of people from one social status to another, from lower status to higher status or from poor position to rich position.* An individual's position in an urban community is determined more by his achievements than by his birth. *The status is not predetermined.* High stress is laid on accomplishments. Urban life in this way is highly competitive. The city with its elaborate division of labour, its competitiveness, its impersonality, has a tendency to emphasise the achievements of people. A city judges status according to what the individual does and how he speaks and what he accomplishes.

An urban society provides for social mobility in countless ways. It provides for *occupational mobility and geographic mobility* on the one hand, and *horizontal social mobility and vertical social mobility,* on the other. Individuals are busily engaged in improving their *"career."* An element of chance is always present in city. **MacIver** and **Page** write - *"An accident, a lucky contract, a sudden opportunity seized or missed, a change of style or fad, a happy or unhappy forecast of some event far beyond his control, may revolutionise his prospects in a day."*

7. *Individuation* : In an urban community, people are more individualistic in their attitudes. As **Kingsley Davis** points out, *"the secondary and voluntary character of urban association, the multiplicity of opportunities and the social mobility all force the individual to make his own decisions and to plan his life as a career."*

The concentration of people in a limited space has the effect of emphasising individuality. The city dweller takes his independent decisions on such matters as education, marriage, occupation, enterprise, adventure, and so on. *He is more selective in his choice and more individualistic in his preferences.* He is guided by his own whims and fancies. *He is detached except for the attachment of his own choice.* He is not tied to any particular relationship or any particular cause. As **Davis** points out, *"the individual stands over against the whole city, never completely absorbed by any one social group."* The city provides wide opportunities for the adventurous spirit of the individuals. **Simmel** observes, *"the city person is free in behaviour, less restrained, more individualistic, more formal and less sympathetic, and less of a conformist than the country person."*

8. *Voluntary Association* : An urban community is the breeding centre of a number of voluntary associations. The size of the urban population, its close proximity, diversity, and easy contact, make it the proper ground for voluntary associations. *"No matter what a person's hobby or vocation, national background or religion, age or colour, he can always find others with a similar basis of interest."* As a result, new kinds of groups arise based on extremely specialised interests. The group must organise or its cause will perish. People normally become members of a number of associations which may be called *"secondary groups"* in order to fulfil their varied interests.

9. *Social Tolerance* : Social tolerance characterises city life. Diversity of population, impersonality of contacts and heterogeneity in living style make it almost inevitable for the city people to develop the spirit of tolerance. *"People rub elbows with and become indifferent to extremes of all kinds - extremes of opinion and interest, extremes of poverty and wealth, extremes of education and background."* The spirit of tolerance gives the strength of unity in diversity to the life in a city. *"Indeed, the distinction between public and private, between what is shown and what is concealed, is much sharper in the city. It is the public behaviour that the city regulates, the private behaviour that it ignores. Its control is impersonal and general, that of the country, personal and particular" - Kingsley Davis.*

10. *Spatial Segregation* : Due to its very nature, the city is bound to be overcrowded. It attracts a large number of people from the village areas. It is found that various types of business tend to concentrate in different spots of the city. Occupational groups of people also prefer to live together in distinct zones of a city. That is to say, some kind of *functional segregation* is found there. Commercial activities in the form of big departmental stores, showrooms, fancy stores, legitimate theatres, fine hotels, jewellery stores, etc. are located in the centre. The same is true of high-priced professional services - *e.g.* clinics, law offices, accounting firms, government offices, etc. Retail grocery establishments, filling stations, cleaning and pressing shops, shoe repair shops, garages, drug stores, etc., may be found at the cross-roads of the entire city. In the city, land is so costly that the buildings expand vertically, filling the centre of the city with skyscrapers.

11. *Unstable Family* : It is said that the urban family is not firmly organised. Many of the traditional functions of the family are transferred to the external agencies. Family is no longer the economic, educational, protective, recreational and affectional unit. Family has lost much of its control over its individual members. Individualism is developing inside the family. Nowadays women are getting employed outside the family. Relations between the husband and wife, parents and children are strained to some extent. Some sociologists have even remarked that the urban family is much more disorganised.

Advantages and Disadvantages of the City

ADVANTAGES OR MERITS

*1. **The city offers opportunities and facilities*** for making full use of one's abilities and talents. City is a centre ever ready to welcome talents from any corner. It is a laboratory for experimenting various plans, projects and schemes.

*2. **It can make life joyful and comfortable**.* Major *service agencies are centralised* in the city to satisfy various interests of the people such as work, education, health, recreation, religion and politics.

3. It encourages new ideas and inventions. People of the city are said to be broad-minded and ready to welcome divergent ideas, views, plans and projects. It is even ready to accommodate conflicting ideas, attitudes and philosophies.

4. It quickens social movements and enlarges social contacts. Social mobility is relatively easier in a city. People move up and down the status scale relatively with greater speed. Consolidating public opinion and mobilising people either in favour of or against something, is not very problematic due to the availability of modern means of communication.

5. There is less social distance being kept among people of different castes, races and religions. Hence there is *more tolerance* towards others.

6. The city is dynamic. This dynamism contributes to social changes. Life is not static but dynamic here. Things are always in flux and flow. Accepting the new and rejecting the old, embracing modernity and keeping tradition at a distance is not a big problem here.

7. The city has liberated women from the exclusiveness of domesticity. It has made women to stand on an equal footing with men. City has made women to become aware of the multifarious facilities which the modern society has offered them. It has boosted the status of women in various respects. City has contributed to the emancipation of women from the bondage of the tradition.

8. The city provides various means of recreation. In a city, there is *scope for personal advancement.* The multifarious associations of the city cater to the multiple needs, interests and tastes of the people. By providing various avenues the city can add to the intellectual delight, artistic ecstacy and scientific urge of the educated people.

9. That is why, as **Quinn** says, *"the great civilisations of antiquity - Mesopotamian, Egyptian, Greek, Roman, - were cradled in cities, that urban communities typically have led in the creation of art, the advancement of science, and the dissemination of learning." The Indus Valley civilisation was also basically urban in character.*

10. The city functions as a laboratory for human genius. It is in the city that man tries to explore the different dimensions and horizons of knowledge. City poses a permanent challenge to human genius and at the same time provides ample opportunities for developing it.

DISADVANTAGES OR DEMERITS

The city has its dark or the ugly side too.

1. The city makes life materialistic and mechanical. It takes away from man his human aspect. In a city everything becomes a means to means and for no values beyond. City encourages the hedonistic outlook which makes man to think in terms of obtaining maximum advantage for minimum efforts.

2. Secondary relations are dominant in the city. People are *indifferent* to one another. Superficial forms of politeness and manners are commonly found. There is lack of *intimacy* and *privacy* in the city. Individuals are always interested in themselves, in their interests, aspirations, ambitions and achievements. Individual interests prevail enormously over the collective interests and the community spirit.

3. The city makes the people to become individualistic, selfish, rationalistic and calculative. Human relations are commercialised here. All relations are means to means and to no final ends. Individuals are so much occupied with themselves and their aggrandisement that they have scant respect for others and for their interests. Often, family and community interests are sacrificed at the altar of personal glorification, and individual achievement.

4. The city poses a challenge to family. The urban family is said to be in doldrums. It is less balanced and more unstable. Individualism is ripening within it. We find clashes of interests of husband and wife, brothers and sisters, and parents and children. The rate of *divorce, desertion* and *separation* is increasing. Joint family has disappeared in the Western cities and is on the verge of total collapse in the Indian cities. Urban family is cut to size.

5. Social control is complex and less effective in the city. Informal means of social control such as family, neighbourhood, morality, religion, education, etc. have become less effective in exerting a restraining influence on the behaviour of the individual members. Further, agents of socialisation are also not able to exercise the required moral influence on the behaviour of the children. Hence, instances of *social deviance* are more in the city.

6. City makes human life to become uncertain, insecure and competitive. It is true that city provides ample opportunities for the adventurous spirit of the individuals. For the very same reason he feels unrestrained. New adventures, new inventions, new experiments, new plans and projects may yield materialistic benefits, but at the same time they may bring lot of pressure on our nerves. Rate of speed of social change is so fast in the city that it may rise the status of the individuals and at the same time reduce it to nothing.

7. City is said to be the centre of problems of economic, social, political, psychological and religious nature. Problems of the city such as economic insecurity, mental illness, gambling, prostitution, drunkenness, drug addiction, corruption, nepotism, environmental pollution, crime, juvenile delinquency, dowry, violence against women, ect., often make city life miserable and disappointing.

8. Concentration of people in the city gives rise to the problem of providing basic civic amenities to the people. The city administration, especially in a densely populated nation like India, fails miserably to cater to the fundamental needs of civilised living. Cities are normally faced with the problems such as acute shortage of housing, lack of water supply, failure of power supply, poor drainage facility, overcrowdedness, insanitation, ill health, etc.

Cities are thus condemned as *"abnormal seed-beds of sin, scepticism, greed, crime, misery, filth and congestion."* city is branded as the centre of *crime, vice and misery.*

URBANISATION IN INDIA

Towns and cities are not new things for India. In fact, India has a tradition of urban living and has been a land of cities from pre-historic times of the Indus Valley Civilisation. The famous cities of **Harappa** and **Mohen-jo-daro** existed in the Indus Valley more than 6000 years ago. These two represent the earliest examples of the well planned and best maintained cities of the ancient world. *"These cities were centres of rich and varied urban culture and a progressing order of social life. They were well laid out with wide streets, market places, public offices, religious halls, community baths and drainage and sewage systems."*[2] The people in these cities had attained high standards of town planning and architecture.

After independence, some of the old cities became enlarged and some new cities also emerged. Some cities came to be known as *industrial cities. Examples* : Rourkela, Durgapur, Bhilai, Chittranjan, Roopnarayan Nagar, Sindri, Nangal, Neyveli, Vishakpatnam, etc. Cities such as Faridabad, Rajpur, Nilokheri, Ulhasnagar, Kalyani and others were developed to rehabilitate the refugees who came from Pakistan during partition. Some cities evolved into *port cities. Examples* : Kandla, Haldia, Paradeep, New Mangalore, Tuticorin, etc. Some cities were developed as *capital cities. Examples* : Chandigarh, Bhuvaneshwar, Bhopal, Hyderabad, etc. Some cities

2. C.B.Mamoria page 459 These figures exclude population of Assam and Jammu & Kashmir. - *Manpower Profile, India,* 1998 - 23-24.

became centres of attraction due to the vast employment opportunities available in them. *Example*: Mumbai, Chennai, Kolkota, Kanpur, Ahmedabad, Pune, Dhanbad, Bangalore, etc.

Table - 1

Relative Growth of Urban and Rural Population: *1901-2011*

	Population in millions			*Percentage of total population*		*Percentage increase in urban population during the decade*	*Urban-Rural Ratio*
	Total	*Rural*	*Urban*	*Rural*	*Urban*		
1901	232.9	207.3	25.6	89.0	11.0	-.-	1 : 8.1
1911	246.0	220.4	25.6	89.6	10.4	0.0	1 : 8.6
1921	244.3	216.6	27.7	88.7	11.3	+8.25	1 : 7.8
1931	270.8	237.8	33.0	87.8	12.2	+19.1	1 : 7.2
1941	309.0	265.5	43.5	85.9	14.1	+32.1	1 : 6.1
1951	361.1	298.7	62.4	82.7	17.3	+43.2	1 : 4.7
1961	439.2	360.3	78.9	82.0	18.0	+25.3	1 : 4.5
1971	548.2	439.1	109.1	80.1	19.9	+38.0	1 : 3.7
1981*	685.2	525.7	159.5	76.7	23.3	+46.8	1 : 3.3
1991**	844.3	627.1	217.2	74.3	25.7	+35.6	1 : 2.9
2001	1028.73	742.05	286.1	72.22	27.78	-.-	-.-
2011	1210.2	833.1	377.1	68.8	31.2		

*Includes projected population of Assam.

**Includes population projection for Jammu & Kashmir.

Source : Registrar General, India., Census 2011, Provisional population totals

SOME TRENDS OF URBANISATION IN INDIA

1. There is a Growing Trend Towards Urbanisation

Urban population is slowly but steadily increasing in India. It increased from about 26 million in 1901 to 62 million in 1951 and then to 218 million in 1991. During the decade 2001-2011 alone urban population increased by 91.7 million which indicates a growing trend towards urbanisation. It means urban population increased to 285.4 million in 2001 and to 377.10 million in 2011. Around 31.16% of the people are urbanites in India in 2011 as against 27.78% in 2001.

2. There is a Trend Towards Concentration of People in Big Cities

A glance of ***Table* - 2** shows that the proportion of urban population in Class I [with a population of over one lakh] has increased from 26.0% in 1901 to 68.67% in 2001. It only confirms that there is a greater trend towards concentration of people in bigger towns. The Table also shows that the relative proportion of urban population in Class II and Class III towns taken together, has remained practically constant, that is around 21 - 27% from 1901 to 1990-91. In contrast to this, relative proportion of population in Class IV, Class V and Class VI towns taken together, has come down sharply from 47.2% in 1901 to barely 9.93% in 2001.

3. Degree of Urbanisation in India - A Comparison

In comparison with the developed countries of the world, the level of urbanisation in India is far behind the high income countries. The proportion of urban population to total population in India was 31.16% in 2011, whereas it was 74% in Russia [in 1972], 76% in U.S.A., 77% in Japan, 85% in Australia and 89% in U.K. The experience of other countries would reveal that creation of employment opportunities can bring about the much desired change towards urbanisation.

Table - 2

Trends of Urbanisation in India: *1951-2001*

	Towns with different population size-classes						
	Class I 1,00,000 *& above*	*Class II* (50,000 to 99,999)	*Class III* (20,000 to 49,999)	*Class IV* (10,000 to 19,999)	*Class V* (5,000 to 9,999)	*Class VI* (*Less than* 5,000)	*All Classes Total*
Number of Urban Agglomerations / Towns							
1951	76	91	327	608	1,124	569	2,795
1961	102	129	437	719	711	172	2,270
1971	148	173	558	827	623	147	2,476
1981	216	270	738	1,053	739	229	3,245
1991	296	341	927	1,135	725	185	3,609
2001	393	401	1151	1344	888	191	4368
Urban Population (Lakhs)							
1951	275	61	97	84	80	19	616
1961	399	87	132	99	53	6	776
1971	612	117	171	117	48	5	1,070
1981	945	182	224	149	56	8	1,564
1991	1,388	233	281	165	55	6	2,128
Percentage Distribution of Urban Population							
1901	26.0	11.3	15.8	20.9	20.1	6.2	100.0
1951	44.6	10.0	15.7	13.6	13.0	3.1	100.0
1961	51.4	11.2	16.9	12.8	6.9	0.8	100.0
1971	57.2	10.9	16.0	10.9	4.5	0.4	100.0
1981	60.4	11.6	14.3	9.5	3.6	0.5	100.0
1991	65.2	10.9	13.2	7.8	2.6	0.3	100.0
2001	68.67	9.67	12.3	6.84	2.86	0.23	100.0

Note : *Excludes Assam and Jammu & Kashmir.*

Source : *Registrar General of India.*

Note : *With the inclusion of these two states, total no cities is 5161*

4. Population of Large Cities with 10 Lakh or more Population

According to 2001 Census, there are now 35 large cities [mega cities] accounting for 107.88 million people. The population of these 35 cities was about 38% of total urban population. Greater Bombay ranked first with a population of 16.36 million, followed by Calcutta with a population of 13.21 million. The population of Delhi was only 8.4 million in 1991, it has jumped to 12.79 million by 2001. The overall decadal increase in population in 35 mega cities was about 68% during 1991-2001. Between 1991 and 2001, Jaipur witnessed the highest rate of population growth [55.0%], followed by Delhi [52%]; Pune [50%]; Lucknow [41%] and Bangalore [39%]. [*Note* : See ***Table* 3**]

5. Regional Pattern of Urbanisation

Urbanisation has not taken place uniformly in all the states. It reveals regional variations. The rate of growth of population in various states in 2001 reveals that some states like Himachal Pradesh [9.79%], Bihar [10.47%], Assam [12.72%], Orissa [14.97%], Sikkim [11.11%], Meghalaya [19.63%] have urbanised more slowly than the old industrialised states like West Bengal, Gujarat, and Tamil Nadu. In the states such as Delhi 93.01% Maharashtra 42.4% Goa 49.77%, Chandighar 89.78%, Pandicheri 66.57%, Tamil Nadu 43.86% the growth rate of urban population is very high. In other poor states like U.P., A.P. and Rajasthan, the growth rates have risen over the period very marginally. Urbanisation was faster in old industrially advanced states than in some poorer states during the fifties, but the process in the former did not get accelerate over the years as it happened in the latter.

Table - 3

Population of Large Cities with a Population of 1 Million and Above From 1981 to 2011

Metropolitan Cities in 1991	*Population in* 2011 *(in millions)*	*Population in* 2001 *(in millions)*	*Population in* 1991 *(in millions)*	*Population in* 1981 *(in millions)*
Greater Bombay	18.41	16.36	12.6	8.2
Calcutta	14.11	13.21	10.9	9.2
Delhi	16.31	12.79	8.4	5.7
Chennai	8.69	6.42	5.4	4.3
Hyderabad	7.74	5.53	4.3	2.9
Bangalore	8.49	5.66	4.1	2.5
Ahmedabad	6.24	4.51	3.3	2.5
Pune	5.04	3.75	2.5	1.7
Kanpur	2.92	2.69	2.1	1.7
Nagpur	2.49	2.12	1.7	1.3
Lucknow	2.90	2.26	1.6	1.0
Jaipur	3.07	2.32	1.5	1.0
Surat	4.58	2.81	-	-

Source: **Ruddar Datt** and **K.P.M. Sundharam's** *"Indian Economy."* Page - 58 and other sources.

6. Relatively High Stability of Urban Settlements

It has been observed that the urbanisation process in India is very closely associated with the relatively high stability of urban settlements. Since the very beginning of the 20th century, the urban population of the country has grown upto 2001 almost **11** fold [i.e, from 26 million in 1901 to 285.4 million in 2001] and the number of towns has also increased significantly [from 1814 in 1901 to only 5161 in 2001] and thus they have grown in size. The total number of towns and cities in 2011 was 7935 The number of villages developing into town status over the period is **not** very large. The stability in the structure of urban settlements reveals built-in-resistance to change in the socio-economic structure of the country.

7. Migration of Rural Population to Urban Areas

It is observed that the urban population is steadily increasing in India. One of the main reasons for this is the migration of rural population towards the urban areas. It has been estimated that *around 45% of the annual increase in urban population is due to migration.* ***Example***: The population of Bangalore increased by 75.6% during 1971-81. Similarly, population of Asansol in West Bengal increased by 108.7%, of Faridabad in Haryana by 85.5%, of Guwahati in Assam by 188.3%, of Thane in Maharashtra by 105.9%, of Vishakapatnam in A.P. by 75% and of Bhuvaneshwar in Orissa by 87.7% during 1981-91. Because of this shift in population Class I cities with a population of 1,00,000 and above accounted for 65.2% of the total urban population in 1991 as against 44.6% in 1951.

At present, as per 2011 census, India's urban population [37.71 crores] is larger than the urban population of any other country in the world except China. In absolute terms, India's urban population is quite large and its significance must be properly understood for the future development planning in this country.

UNO Report 2014

The UNO in its Report 2014 has stated that the population of Delhi has doubled between 1990 and 2014. The report has given the second place for Delhi in the list of world's most populous cities. The report has predicted that between 2014 and 2050 , urban population of India , China and Nigeria is going to be tremendously increased and together they will be adding almost 37% to the existing urban population of the world.

Source: *Udayavani leading kannada Daily, Karnataka,* Dated 12th July 2014.

SOME DEMOGRAPHIC DIMENSIONS OF URBANISATION IN INDIA

1. As it is already made clear, though India is regarded as a classical land of villages, it occupies the second place in terms of possessing the highest number of urban dwellers. The first place is occupied by China in this regard.

2. As per the 2001 census, there were about 28.54 crores of urban residents, who constituted 27.78% of the total population and it increased to 31.16% [377.10 million] in 2011.

3. Between 1901 and 2011 India's rural population had increased by more than 3.9times whereas during the same period, the urban population had increased by **14.5** times.

4. Between 1971 and 1981 the population of urban area increased at the rate of 3.4% per annum. As per the records of 1991 census, the growth rate of population of the cities with an average population of one lakh or over, was found to be 4.68% per annum.

5. As per 2011 census report, around 377.10 million people are living in 7935 towns and cities.

6. *Urbanisation in India is taking place relatively in a slow manner.* For example, in 1901, there were around 1916 cities and this number was increased to 7935 in 2011. It means in the time span of 110 years the number of towns / cities in India increased almost by **4** times whereas the urban population increased by more than 14.5 times. The urban population, during the same period, increased from 26 million to 377.10 million. This only shows the increasing concentration of people in the existing cities.

7. In 1981, there were 12 large cities in India, each with a population of more than one million. The combined population of these cities was around 42.1 million then. In 2001, both of these that is, the number and the population of the cities, had increased more than 2.5 times. The number of large cities had increased to 35 and their combined population to 107.8 million or 10.78 crores in 2001.

8. As far as the mobility is concerned, it is greater in the cities than in the villages. In 1991, of the 225 million migrants in the country, 17.7% had migrated from rural to urban areas, 11.8% from urban to urban areas, 64.5% from rural to rural areas, and 6% from urban to rural areas [*Manpower Profile, India,* 1998 : 26]. *This reveals that mobility in urban areas is more from one city to another city than from villages to the cities.*

Population of World's Biggest Cities 2014	
Tokiyo	3.8 crore
Greater New Delhi	2.5 crore
Shanghai	2.3 crore
Mexico	2.1 crore
Savopolo	2.1 crore
Greater Mumbai	2.1 crore
Source: *"Udayavani"*, Daily, 12-07-2014	

11. According to 1991 census report, of the 74.27% population living in villages, 36.57% villages have population of less than 2,000, 21.37% between 2,000 and 5,000, and 13.33% more than 5,000.

On the other hand, of the 25.73% population in urban areas, 0.72% urban areas have less than 10,000 population, 5.27% between 10,000 and 50,000, 2.75% between 50,000 and 1,00,000, and 16.4% above 1 lakh.

12. As per 2011 census report, the population of four major cities of India is as follows : Mumbai - 184.14 lakhs, Kolkota - 141.12 lakhs, Delhi - 163.14 lakhs, and Chennai - 86.96 lakhs.

13. In 1950, Kolkota was the only city to be included in the 15 largest agglomerations in the world. In 1995, Mumbai and Delhi were added to the list. The U.N.O. defines **mega-city** as the one with a population of 10 million or more. In 1950, only New York was classified as a mega-city. By 1995, the number rose to 14 mega-cities and Mumbai, Calcutta and Delhi were included in the list.

FACTORS OR CAUSES OF URBANISATION IN INDIA

Urbanisation has been taking place incessantly in India. The process assumed greater momentum soon after independence. As reflected by the figures, the old cities are growing and new cities are coming up. In 1901, only 10.8% of the total population of the country lived in towns and cities and this percentage has increased to 31.16 in 2011. In the time gap between 1901 and 2011 the rural population in India increased by 3.9 times whereas urban population increased by 14.5 times. By 2011, there were as many as 7935 cities and towns with a combined population of more than 377.10 million. Though the rate of growth of cities is said to be comparatively very slow, the growth is witnessed consistently for the past five decades.

Various factors have contributed to the rapid growth of cities in India. **A.N. Agarwal**[3] in this regard, speaks of the role of a few factors which are mentioned below :

1. *Natural increase in population.*
2. *Continuous migration of people towards cities due to:*
   (a) the "push" factors, and
   (b) the "pull" factors which include :
      (i) the "pull" of the job opportunities, and
      (ii) the "pull" of city attractions.
3. *Changes in city-boundaries.*

1. Natural Increase in Population

Population is consistently increasing in the country. Naturally, the urban population is also increasing. The natural cause for the increase in urban population is that, in the urban areas always the number of birth exceeds the number of death. ***Example*** **:** The birth-rate in the urban areas in 1971 was estimated at 30.1 [per thousand] with death-rate at 9.7 [per thousand]. In 1978, the birth-rate declined to 27.8. The death-rate fell slightly to 9.4. This caused the growth rate to be high because of large differences between the two rates. Availability of better medical and health services, good drinking water supply and sanitation, higher rate of literacy, etc., must have been the reasons for the relatively low level of death rate in the urban areas.

2. Continuous Migration of People Towards the Cities

Both economists and non-economists are of the opinion that the economic and non-economic forces have been playing their role in driving the people from the rural hinterland to the urban areas. Of the total rise in urban population, while a major contributory factor is the natural growth, a part is also contributed by immigrations from rural areas. Their exact number at the moment is not properly known. It can only be guessed. The factors that induce people of the rural areas to shift towards the cities are of two types, namely : (a) the ***"push"*** factors, and (b) the ***"pull"*** factors.

3. **A.N. Agarwal** in his *"Indian Economy - Problems of Development and Planning."* 22nd Edition - 1996. Page - 83.

(a) Role of *"Push"* Factors

People from the rural areas are moving towards the cities for economic reasons also. A large number of agricultural workers, small and marginal farmers depend upon agriculture for their subsistence. Many of these people who possess small holdings are not able to ensure productive employment to all the adult members of the family. Added to this, there is also the disguised unemployment. These people all the time feel pressure to migrate to towns / cities. Most agricultural workers find only seasonal work and the wages they earn from this work are not sufficient to maintain them throughout the year. Hence they look forward to some other work in their own village or nearby villages. If they are not able to get any one, then the economic forces *"push"* them out of the village, mostly towards towns and cities in search of better opportunities.

(b) Role of the *"Pull"* Factors

If certain factors are forcibly *"pushing"* the villagers towards the cities, certain attractions of the cities are also *"pulling"* or drawing the ruralites towards them. These ***"pull"*** factors are of two types : (i) *The "pull" of the better job opportunities,* and (ii) *the pull of city attractions.*

(i) The "Pull" of Better Job Opportunities : The comparatively better job opportunities that are available in some cities, are attracting people towards them. All cities do not have such attractions. Cities or towns where heavy public investments in industry and mining and other establishments are made as we find in Ranchi, Dhanbad, Bokaro [of Southern Bihar], Durgapur, Bhilai, Raipur [of M.P.], people tend to concentrate. In the same manner, industrially advanced cities such as Bangalore, Mumbai, Khanpur, Ahmedabad that belong to the industrially developed states of Karnataka, Maharashtra, U.P. and Gujarat respectively are attracting ruralites towards them with the promise of better wages and salaries. Urban wages are generally higher as compared to rural wages. Therefore, the *"pull"* of relatively high urban wages is quite strong and a large number of people, particularly the young men and women, keep on migrating to the cities.

(ii) The "Pull" of City Attractions : The city is a centre of attraction. From the beginning the city has been attracting a large number of people especially from the village areas. The city is pulling people from various corners towards its nucleus. The rural people who are faced with various economic problems, burdened with a large number of children, bored with the monotony of the routine life, and attracted by the glamour of the city, have started moving towards the cities. The city is tempting rural people with its employment opportunities, educational facilities, medical facilities, recreational facilities, such as movies, dramas, night clubs, cabarets, gambling centres, horse race, library, public parks, museums, orchestra, zoo, circus shows, etc.

In comparison with the village, the city provides ample opportunities for personal advancement. The city is a centre of brisk economic, commercial, artistic, literary, political, educational, technological, scientific and other activities. The rural people who come in contact with the city for a brief spell of time get themselves impressed by its appearance, glamour, comfort and luxuries. They are likely to develop rosy imaginations of the luxuries of the city life. They come to believe that money-making is easier in the city. The city men and women, their dresses, fashions, habits, styles, tastes, interests, intelligence, talents, comforts, luxuries, etc., have great impact on the rural people. As a result, they have started flocking towards the cities in a big number. This has contributed to the process of urbanisation. Urbanisation resulted in urban concentration on the one hand and rural depopulation, on the other.

3. The Changing Boundaries of Cities

For various reasons and at different times, the boundaries of the towns have been extended. As cities get expanded, the semi-urban or entirely rural areas that are found in the outskirts of the cities also get included in the urban areas. It is not that these rural areas suddenly become urban areas. They may even continue to retain some of the characteristics of villages. But their inclusion in the expanding cities put them under the areas classified as "towns". The people living in these areas start acquiring the features of urban life. The rural population that gets included in these areas increase the number of urban population.

It is clear from the above explanation that the process of urbanisation continues to take place even today. It has acquired new momentum at the fag end of the 20th and in the beginning of the 21st centuries. Expansion of educational facilities, technological and industrial development, availability of employment opportunities, and such other factors continue to play their role in accelerating the process of urbanisation.

URBAN INFLUENCE ON THE RURAL COMMUNITY

In the recent years, it has been evident everywhere that the city is growing in population at the expense of the village. It has also been observed that urban culture is spreading to the rural areas. As **Kingsley Davis** says that *"The city effects are wider than the city itself."* **McKenzie** has proved conclusively that *"the influence of a city varies with its size and that it tends to wane with distance outward."* The growing transport and communications, the increased urban newspaper circulation in rural areas, advancement in science and technology, etc., have gone a long way in diffusing a wide variety of urban attitudes, ideas and habits from the city to the village.

The rural - urban interaction is very widely recognised today. In fact, it is an important aspect of urbanisation. It is quite understandable that urbanisation and urban growth do have their impact on the rural areas and activities. Similarly, rural areas do have their effect on the nearby towns and cities. A few studies have been made on this rural - urban interaction. These studies have highlighted three important aspects:

(i) *Urbanisation has impact on the economy of the surrounding villages.* ***Ex.*** There is an increase in farm productivity due to the availability and utilisation of fertilisers, better seeds, pesticides, modern agricultural implements, tillers, tractors, and so on. These things could be purchased from the nearby towns.

(ii) *Level and pattern of migration has been affected.* There has been a continuous migration of the people from rural to the urban areas.

(iii) *Villagers have imbibed several urban characteristics.* City culture is spreading to the villages. People in the villages look to urban models in various fields.

1. Extension of Urban Facilities to the Rural Areas

Some of the *facilities and comforts* of the city like electricity, radio, newspapers, hotels, libraries, post offices, community halls for conducting programmes, schools and even colleges, games and sports facilities and various electrical appliances are now diffused to the rural areas. The newspapers carry the stories and editorial comments about politics, sports, prominent persons and a host of ideas about religious, civic, economic, artistic and other interests and events. As readers of these newspapers the people in the rural area share these interests.

2. Urban Impact on the Rural Family

Urbanism or the urban way of life, has affected the size and character of the rural family. The *size of the family* in the village is decreasing. Joint families are slowly disappearing. The family is losing its control over its members. The younger generation wants to enjoy more freedom like its counterpart in the city. The present day rural youths are also becoming career-conscious and many look to nearby towns and cities for continuing their education and to get into jobs so that they can settle permanently in the urban centres.

3. Extension of Modern Means of Transport and Communication Facilities

The *modern means of transport and communications* are introduced in many villages. Cycles, scooters, motor cycles, taxies, cars, vans, trucks are also found in many villages which are equipped with post and telegraph services. Radios and transistors are commonly found in villages. Many villages have even phone connections. The recent invention of mobile phones has becomes so common that almost all villages have access to them. Further, rural occupations and agricultural operations are slowly being *mechanised in some places.* The blacksmiths, goldsmiths, silversmiths, coppersmiths, barbers, carpenters and others are now using modern tools in their work. The city as a market for rural products, and as a centre of trade and financial control over the rural regions, provides for the increasing dominance over the village.

4. City Affecting the Character of Rural Recreation

The *mode of rural recreation* has changed due to the urban influence. Radios and gramophones and tape recorders have changed the tastes of rural people. Football, volleyball, cards, chess and such other plays also becoming popular. The cricket is equally interesting for the rural youth. The fashions of the ruralites have changed.There are also villages with modern computers, laptops and internet conections.

5. Urban Community Serving as a *"Reference Group"* for the Village

City normally serves as a model for the villages. Changes are quick to take place in the cities. Villagers, particularly the rural youths are always looking to the city for novelty. The rural youths are slowly becoming *conscious of personality development.* Education is becoming popular among them. The rural people also take interest in political and cultural activities. They look to the city for guidance and imitation.

6. Migration of Ruralites Towards the Cities

Throughout the world the cities are proving to be the centres of multifarious activities. Hence, the tendency of the rural people to move towards cities continues unabated. The *"push"* [mostly economic pressures] factors and the *"pull"* [the attractions of the city] factors have made the rural people to rush to the cities. This has resulted in *urban concentration* and *rural depopulation* in many places. The city has continued to absorb the people from the hinterland. The process will be faster, the more the city is linked with its rural hinterland.

7. Ugly Impact of the City on the Village Life

The *rural people have also acquired some of the evil habits of the people of the cities.* Drunkenness, gambling, prostitution, smoking, crimes, etc. have made inroads into the villages. Rural morality has fallen, costly fashions and expensive habits of the city people, are acquired. Life in the country is slowly becoming more city oriented, and more individualistic, materialistic, rationalistic, commercial and calculative.

8. Interdependence of Urban and Rural Communities

In spite of the rural - urban contrast, there is an inevitable interdependence of rural and urban communities. The ruralites are dependent on the urbanites for their banking and credit needs, for the purchase of agricultural equipments and other supplies, for marketing of farm products, and even for commercial recreation. In the very same manner, urban communities are also dependent on the rural sector for their food supply, for cheap labour, and for vast market of their manufactured goods. Further, urban professionals like advocates, doctors, mechanics, repairers, electricians and others, draw a large number of their clients, patients, customers from the rural masses. A good harvest in the village side leads to an increase in marketing activities whereas a bad harvest leads to a dull and discouraging market.

9. Dominance of the City Continues Unabated

It is true that the city continues to dominate the country. Even with respect to birth rate, death rate, age at marriage, infant mortality, divorce, suicide, church affiliation, etc., rural indices are moving nearer to urban indices. The dominance of the city over the country is regarded by some sociologists as a dangerous trend. **Oswald Spengler** in his *"Decline of the West"* points out that *"the city destroys the solidarity of the kin, the family, the "blood", the nation and with its competitive stress fosters the disintegrating attitudes of individualism, socialism, rationalism and cosmopolitanism."* However, sociologists like **MacIver,** are of the opinion that there is no need to be pessimistic about the city as such. Man is gradually making the urban environment more suited to his needs. In spite of the widespread urbanisation, about 50% of the population of the world is rural in character.

Cleavages and Conflicts Between Rural and Urban Sectors ?

The above description makes it evident that there exists co-operative relationship and functional interdependence between rural and urban communities. However, possibilities of rural - urban conflicts cannot be ruled out. Such conflicts often do erupt open violence. **Nagpaul** in his study identified three factors which promote cleavages and conflicts among the rural people for the urban people. They are – (i) *contrasting environmental subcultures,* (ii) *modernisation,* and (iii) *urban bias.*[4]

(i) Contrasting Environmental Subcultures **:** Rural and urban environments are not the same. If the former is more natural the latter is more artificial. Rural work is mostly decided by seasons and weather factors, and most of it is done outside the dwelling place. On the contrary, urban work is carried on under predictable conditions mostly within the building structures. Though rural people are bigger in number they are not able to dominate or boss over the urban people. In economic matters, in political issues, in educational fields, in employment sectors and in various other areas, urban people ride over the rural people and their views and opinions are simply brushed aside. This has created a kind of ill -will towards the city, city life and city dwellers.

(ii) Modernisation **:** Modernisation is said to be another major factor that fosters conflict. Four important consequences of modernisation programmes undertaken by the government for the benefit of the rural people have been – "(a) *increasing pace of urbanisation and concentration of power in the urban sector,* (b) *political democratisation,* (c) *weakening of traditional institutional structure based upon caste and religion,* and (d) *widespread emergence of revolution of rising expectations.*" [**Nagpaul.** Page : 160 - 161].

Modernisation has made rural people to move toward the cities in a large number particularly draining off young males from the rural sector. Rural people feel jealous of the material comforts enjoyed by the city people. Increasing contacts between city and village promote more and more cleavages and conflicts between the villagers and the city dwellers. Political democratisation has

4. **Nagpaul** [1996] : 158 - 160 as quoted by **Prof. Ram Ahuja** in *"Society in India"* [1999]. Page: 348.

brought new tensions and anxieties. Increasing involvement of women in the newly introduced democratic processes has produced some conflicts and strains. The introduction of modernisation programmes has weakened traditional institutions such as caste, family, religion, etc. Agitations and movements which were unheard of in the past have become almost common today in the rural areas.

(iii) Urban Bias : Urban bias also acts as a source of conflict between rural urban sectors though the government has been giving much importance to rural development, rural reconstruction and poverty alleviation programmes. In actuality, very less has been done to improve the lot of the rural people. Rural people very strongly feel that rural income and funds are diverted toward the cities to develop urban infrastructure such as education, health, housing, road, transport, communication, sanitation, etc. Partial attitude of political leaders and bureaucrats towards the cities and city dwellers has been very much criticised by the rural people.

However, scholars like **B.R. Chauhan, N.R. Seth,** and others have highlighted the intimate relationship between urban and the rural sectors. Conflicts and cleavages between the sectors should not be exaggerated to the extent of undermining the co-operation between the two. *"A town and a city, by and large, act as service centres for their surrounding village communities. L.K. Sen [1971] has shown that like a town and a city, a large village also performs central-place functions for the city as well as surrounding smaller villages."*

Rural Migration Towards Urban Centres

One of the most obvious and apparent changes taking place in the rural areas in India, in general, is migration of rural people towards the cities. This migration is also referred to as migration from farming sector to non-farming sector. Both economists and non-economists are of the opinion that the economic and non-economic forces have been playing their role in driving the people from the rural hinterland to the urban areas. Of the total rise in urban population, while a major contributory factor is the natural growth, a part is also contributed by immigrations from rural areas. Their exact number at the moment is not properly known. It can only be guessed. The factors that induce people of the rural areas to shift towards the cities are of two types, namely : (a) the ***"push"*** factors, and (b) the ***"pull"*** factors.

Migration Towards the Cities :

There has been a continuous migration of people from rural to the urban areas. Most rural migrants who move to urban areas are young males who take up unskilled and semi-skilled occupations. Those ruralites who obtain higher education prefer to settle in cities for they do not get the required opportunities in the village. This migration from rural to urban areas leads to heavy pressure on urban public services. This continuous pressure creates problems of disorganisation for the city, particularly shortage of essential services and facilities. [***Ex*** : *Housing problem, over crowdedness, traffic problem, sanitary and health problem, shortage of drinking water, power shortage, environmental pollution, etc.*]

- ***Migration is not of the Same Type*** :

Migration of rural people assumes three different patterns. These patterns or types of migration are referred to respectively as

(i) *"translocatory migration"*, Some individuals decide to settle down permanently in the urban areas of their choice. [*"translocatory migration"*.]

(ii) *"circulatory-migration"* some others hang on to their rural base but migrate repeatedly for different durations either to the same city or to different ones. [*"circulatory migration"*.]

(iii) *"step-migration"*. A few more migrate from village to small town, and then towards big cities in different stages. [*"step-migration"*.]

It is also observed that relatively a larger number of people from higher occupations consider their stay in the city as permanent, than the migrants from lower-prestige occupations.

Some Observations Regarding Farm-to-Non-Farm Migration

Mary Chatterjec's study of rural-urban migration has revealed some socially important points.

- The stability of migration depends on the distance from the native place and also occupational status.
- The longer the distance from the native place, the greater the number of migrants who regard their stay in the city as temporary.
- More migrants from lower-prestige occupations [than those from higher occupations] consider their stay in the city as temporary.
- Migration from rural to urban areas mostly depends upon the "*pull*" factors at the urban end, and "*push*" factors at the rural end.
- As a result of this type of migration, urban and rural sectors are likely to develop somewhat distinctive sub-cultures of their own which further shape their social institutions and personalities.
- Although ruralites outnumber urbanites numerically, urbanities usually come to dominate in most facets of life.
- Since, urbanites enjoy a better living standard, they dominate rural people both economically and politically.

Rural - Urban Convergence

Though the communities are normally divided into *"rural"* and *"urban"*, the line of demarcation is not always clear as **MacIver** has remarked, between these two types of communities *"There is no sharp demarcation to decide where the city ends and country begins."* Every village possesses some elements of the city and every city carries some features of the village. The concept of *"rural-urban convergence"* refers to the striking similarities between the village and the town in some aspects of community life.

Cities are growing in number and size everywhere. It is true that the urban culture is diffusing at a very fast rate in the rural areas. As **Kingsley Davis** has said, *"the city effects are wider than the city itself."* The influence of the city varies with its size also. The urban way of life can be carried far beyond the city boundaries and can thus characterise people who do not actually live in cities.

With the diffusion of urban culture to the rural areas, the extreme differences between rural and urban cultures have diminished. The growing transport and communications, the radio, press, television, telephone, etc., growing circulation of urban newspapers in the rural areas have changed the attitudes and outlook of the ruralites. Medical, educational, commercial, recreational and other facilities are also being enjoyed by the rural people. The automobile has played an important role in the rural areas. It has ended the secluded life of the ruralites. People prefer to reside near the highways now. Villages in a way are closely linked with the cities. Buses, trains, taxies and motor cycles, etc., have helped the city people to go out and stay in the fringes of the city.

Everywhere big cities are characterised by sub-centres or sub-urban areas. In structure and function, they are like cities. Too much concentration in the city contributes to an opposite process of decentralisation. The sub-centres or sub-urban areas resemble the city in several respects. A single city may have a number of small *sub-urban* areas. These sub-urban areas may retain in them some of the features of the city. They are like *satellite cities* built around a major city. *Sub-urban areas represent the rough amalgam of rural and urban ways of living.* Here, we may find the urban way of life being mixed with the rural way of life. In these areas we find the ***"rural-urban convergence."***

The Rural-Urban Continuum

Some sociologists have used the concept of *"rural-urban continuum"* to stress the idea that there are no sharp breaking points to be found in the degree or quantity of rural urban differences. The impact of urban life over rural life is evident in many ways. With regard to birth rate, age at marriage, infant mortality, church affiliation, divorce, suicide, etc., rural indices are moving nearer to urban indices. In this way, rural areas can become highly urbanised.

As the contacts of the city become closer, as transportation and communication become more rapid, the rural community tends to assume more closely the urban social structure. We may even speak of different degrees of *"urbanness"* or *"ruralness."* One country can be demographically more urban and yet socially more rural than another. ***Example*** **:** Chile has a greater percentage of its population living in cities than does Canada, but its people, by almost all sets of indices, are less urban.

PROBLEMS OF URBAN SOCIETY OR URBANISATION

The process of urbanisation has been taking place continuously in India. Migration of rural people towards the cities continues unabated. Once the rural people move towards the cities either in search of job or better prospects, they rarely go back to the villages. They become permanent residents of the city. Thus, urban concentration is taking place consistently. This uncontrolled and limitless concentration of people in the city areas has led to several problems. Some of them are : *problem of overcrowdedness, problem of urban housing, problem of drinking water, problem of drainage, transport and traffic problem, problem of power shortage, problem of environmental pollution, problem of slums, and problem of social evils such as drug addiction, alcoholism, crime, juvenile delinquency, gambling, commercialised recreation, beggary, and so on.* Let us now analyse in brief the gravity of some of these problems of urban society.

1. Problem of Overcrowdedness

Heavy concentration of people in a limited place has led to the problem of overcrowdedness. Due to the attractions of city life [*pull factors*] men have started flocking towards the cities. Lack of educational and employment and other opportunities in the rural areas [*push factors*] also forced people to desert villages and start moving towards the cities. This has led to urban concentration which has added to overcrowdedness in the city. People are forced to live in large number in small residential houses. Some houses are so overcrowded that **5** to **6** persons live in one single room. Urban neighbourhoods are also heavily crowded.

Overcrowding has its own adverse effects. It damages privacy, disturbs intimacy, spoils mental peace and moral health and encourages deviance. It also leads to the spread of diseases and creation of conditions that are favourable for developing bad habits such as drinking and drug addiction.

2. Problem of Urban Housing

Growth of population in cities is so fast that it has become impossible to provide adequate residential accommodation to all. Hence housing problem or what is known as *"houselessness"* has become one of the serious problems of the city. The pressure on space in cities is so tremendous that large number of people are forced to live on roads, bus stands, railway stations, slums, and in poorly equipped houses. It is said that around 50% of the city people, are either ill-housed or pay more than 20% of their income on rent. According to 1991 census report, around 27.4% of the city houses are *kachcha* houses, 30.9% of the houses are *semi-pakka* houses and only 41.7% of the houses are *pakka* houses. According to one estimate [as reported in *The Hindustan Times* dated 9-5-1988], around 50% to 75% of the people living in urban areas are either residing in temporary houses or slums. The rate of overcrowding is so high that in a city like Delhi, the population has increased from 2 millions in 1957 to 9 million in 1990, and then to 1.63 crore in 2011. Hence, every year Delhi is forced to provide accommodation for more than 60,000 people. According to paper reports, more than 70% of the people in Delhi are not residing in *"safe houses"*.

Mega cities like Mumbai, Kolkota, Delhi and Chennai are suffering from acute housing problem. In a heavily concentrated city of Mumbai, more than 77% of the houses are found to be single room houses wherein on an average, more than 5.3 persons are living. A survey conducted in 53 cities in addition to the four mega cities revealed that more than 44% of the people are living in single-room houses in the urban areas.

Not only good houses are not available for living but also exorbitant rent is charged. Housing boards such as the *Housing and Urban Development Corporation [HUDCO], the Housing Development Finance Corporation Ltd. [HDFC], the Apex Housing Financing Co-operative Societies, the State Housing Boards,* and various co-operative housing boards and nationalised banks are helping people to go for their own independent houses, the problem of housing is not solved yet.

Table - 4

Households Having Drinking Water, Electricity & Toilet Facility (Percentage)

	1991*	1981*
Households with Safe Drinking Water	62.72	37.91
Rural	55.92	26.34
Urban	81.59	74.13
Households with Electricity	42.98	25.74
Rural	31.10	14.29
Urban	75.93	61.60
Households with Toilet Facility	23.55	*n.a.*
Rural	8.84	*n.a.*
Urban	63.58	57.44

* Excluding Jammu & Kashmir in 1991 & Assam in 1981.

Source : Statistical Outline of India - 1995-96. ***Pub.*** : Tata Services Ltd., Department of Economics and Statistics.

3. Problem of Slums

Increasing industrialisation and urbanisation have created slums in the city. Slums consist of substandard, ill-ventilated, insanitary and poorly lighted houses. They consist of houses which are unfit for human habitation. Slum dwellers live in the most unhygenic areas. Their living conditions are really horrible. The low-paid workers normally live in these slum areas. The facilities that are generally found in the cities are not found in these slums. The *Ahatas* of Kanpur, *Bastis* of Delhi, *Chawls* of Mumbai, *Cheries* of Chennai, and *Kolegeri* of Bangalore are stigmas on the face of India. According to **Dr. Radhakamal Mukherji,** *"In the thousand slums of India's industrial centres manhood is unquestionably brutalised, women dishonoured and childhood is poisoned at its very source."* **Pandit Nehru** was so moved emotionally on seeing slums that he wanted them to be burnt down and the persons responsible for them to be hanged.

Slums are a black spots on our cities but their number and the number of people living in them are cosistently increasing. According to 1991 report, the country's slum population stood at nearly 40 million. Slum dwellers form 44% of the population in Delhi, 45% in Mumbai, 42% in Kolkota and 39% in Chennai. All the other major cities such as Bangalore, Hyderabad, Ahmedabad, Pune, Nagpur, Kanpur, Lucknow, Jaipur are faced with the problem of slums. Slums which are often called *"living dustbins"* have also become centres of filth, immorality, alcoholism, gambling, crime, beggary, prostitution, juvenile delinquency and so on. They have also become the breeding centres of various diseases such as cholera, T.B., typhoid, AIDS, venereal diseases, etc.

4. Problem of Drinking Water

Water is an essential requirement for living beings. But it has become a scarcity in various cities. In the whole nation there is no big city in which water supply is assured all the 24 hours a day. Cities like Chennai, Hyderabad, Rajkot, Ajmer and Udaipur get water from municipal sources for less than an hour a day. Most towns and cities which normally get good rain every year, have been undergoing the agony of acute water shortage in the last 90 years. Unfortunately, we do not have a well planned and an efficiently workable national water policy. States like Tamil Nadu and Karnataka, for example, quarrel between themselves almost every year on the water issue. It has been estimated that atleast 30% of the people living in cities are consuming *"unsafe"* water. However, the 1991 census report says that only 18.59% of the people living in cities are not supplied with "safe" drinking water.

5. Problem of Drainage

Water problem is closely associated with the drainage problem. Continuous water supply is necessary to maintain cleanliness. Continuous flow of water in the drainage pipes helps the maintenance of drainage system. But in the Indian context, shortage of water supply has added to the drainage problem. Efficient sewage or drainage system is essential for the maintenance of cleanliness in any city. But unfortunately, drainage system is deplorably bad in India. There is not a single city in India which is completely sewered. Even the so called planned city of Chandigarh is not an exception to this. Due to the inefficient or non-existent drainage system, stink water gets collected everywhere, spoiling cleanliness and spreading diseases. In fact, we need to have a national and also a provincial drainage policy.

6. Problem of Transportation and Traffic System

Continuous increase in population in cities puts heavy pressure on a good transportation and traffic system. Such a system is very unsatisfactory in the Indian cities. Vast majority of people use buses, mini buses, tempos, while a few use train as transit system. Large number of middle class people and a few upper class people use scooters, motor cycles, mopeds, cars, vans, jeeps, which make the traffic system very worse. ***For example,*** in Mumbai, automobiles have trebled [from 3.1 lakh to 8.73 lakh] between 1986 and 1996 [*The Hindustan Times,* 29-11-1996]. These vehicles also add to pollution. In Mumbai alone, daily pollutants let out into the air amount to about 3,000 tonnes, of which 52% come from automobiles, 2% from domestic fuels, and the remaining 46% from industries.

City bus services, metro train service and other private service systems are also not able to meet the transportation requirement of the people. Hence, even in vehicles we find heavy load and overcrowdedness. Road accidents are also found to be very high in the Indian cities. In addition to the regular residents of the city, people who shuttle between cities and their nearby native places also add to the overcrowdedness in the city traffic. It is also observed that most of the vehicles that are being used for meeting the city traffic requirements are found to be very old and hence they also add to the pollution problem.

7. Problem of Power Shortage

Power shortage is becoming a major crisis in the urban areas today. Use of electricity and electrical gadgets has become a part and parcel of city life. Hence, city people want 24 hours power supply. Even after 65 years of independence we have not been able to provide adequate power supply to the people though they are ready to pay the charges for the same. Slums and poor people's houses are not completely connected with electricity. According to 1991 census report, only 75.93% of urban houses are supplied with electricity. [See ***Table*** **4**]. The demand for electricity is consistently increasing in spite of the attempts that are being made to supply power. ***For example,*** the difference that was there between electricity supply and demand increased from 6.1% in 1993-94 to 13% in 1994-95. It means the demand for electricity is increasing at a greater speed than the attempts at supplying it.

8. Problem of Environmental Pollution

The city atmosphere is highly polluting. As **Margaret Mead** pointed out long back, environmental pollution is the worst problem which the modern industrial and city-centred civilisation has created. This is often highlighted as a *"rape on environment."* Most of the Indian cities have become the victims of environmental pollution. The cities themselves are polluting the environment. Several cities discharge 40 - 60% of their entire sewage and industrial effluents untreated into the nearby rivers. These rivers get polluted. Urban industry pollutes the atmosphere with smoke and toxic gases from its chimneys. The city of Delhi is branded as the 4th most polluted city in the world. The vehicular emissions in Delhi account for 64% of Delhi's air pollution load, power plants are responsible for 16% and industries account for 12%. The poison we put in to the environment [by way of carbon monoxide, smoke, garbage, solid wastes, etc.] comes right back to us through our air, water and food, slowly seeping into our bodies and showing up as cancer, immune disorders or as hormonal system disorders. Doctors are of the opinion that the chances of getting caught by cancer by the residents of the cities of Delhi, Mumbai, Bangalore and Chennai are as high as 7 - 11% during their life time. More than the rich, the poor people always suffer most from the polluted atmosphere of the city.

9. Other Social Problems

Problem of Privacy : Lack of privacy and intimacy are the natural outcome of the city life. Due to the indirect and impersonal relationships, closeness and intimacy will not develop. Life becomes mechanical, competitive and charmless.

Problem of Individuation : The urban community encourages *individuation.* Individuals are moved by their own aspirations, ambitions, aims, and interest. They have become more and more *career-conscious.* They are invariably caught in the competitive race for a successful career. The competitiveness of the city, places one over against everyone else. The materialistic outlook that a city-dweller develops may often result in what is known as the *"loss of community."* An individual may become *"alienated"* from his own community, his own people, his own profession. This state of affair, when it reaches the extreme, may drive a depressed and an *"alienated"* man to commit suicide.

Problem of Vices : The city is a centre of economic insecurity, mental illness, gambling, prostitution, drunkenness, crimes, juvenile delinquency, alcoholism, environmental pollution and such other vices. There is poverty in the midst of plenty. The city life endangers the physical, mental and moral health of the people.

Adverse Effects on the Rural Areas : Cities often provide a wrong model to the villages. Villagers who are in touch with the cities get influenced by the extremes of hedonism, individualism, self-centredness and such other ugly aspects of the city life. The tendency of the rural people to move towards the cities often leads to rural depopulation. Western countries are faced with such a situation. Further, the rivers that pass through the industrial cities often spread diseases in the rural areas also for the river water contains lot of industrial wastes and effluents which are poisonous in character.

Heavy Pressure on Municipal Administration : Most of the Indian towns and cities are heavily crowded. Hence, it has become a big challenge for the city municipal authorities and administration to provide the basic civic facilities to all the urban residents. City budget is not sufficient to meet with such requirements. Hence, most of the cities are known for ill-administration.

Encouragement to Beggary : It is a known fact that the city atmosphere is conducive for begging. We find a large number of beggars in cities rather than in village areas. It is easier for the lazy people, unemployed persons, work-evaders and public cheats to eke out their livelihood by means of begging. City environment also tempts social parasites and public cheats to plan what is known as *"organised beggary."*

It is clear from the above, that Indian cities are suffering from various problems. Though cities have their own positive aspects they have their ugly side also. Life is not a bed of roses in a city. It poses problems, challenges, breeds diseases, encourages ill-will in spite of all the attractions that it has at its command. The quicker these problems are solved the better it will be for the cities and for the city dwellers.

Some Suggestions to Face and to Solve Urban Problems

There is no city in the world which is free from problems. Indian cities are not an exception. It does not mean that these problems are beyond solutions. Efficient urban planning and effective implementation of the same can bring about positive results. A few suggestions to face and to solve the urban problems can be mentioned here :

1. ***Efficient and Integral City Planning*** : Lack of proper planning is one of the major causes of urban problems. Hence, city administration has to take sufficient care in making a comprehensive planning for the improvement of the city. The city planners must have far-sightedness and must take into account the probable growth of the city in atleast another 50 years. There should be co-ordination among the city administration, the state administration and also the central administration. While drafting a plan for the improvement of the city, advices and suggestions of the experts must be sought. It is equally important to make use of the latest technological know - how in preparing the plan for the future. Political interference should not be there in the implementation of the plan.

2. ***City Administration to Become Financially Independent*** **:** It is essential that the municipal administration must have sufficient financial resources to undertake developmental programmes for the benefit of the city dwellers. City administration cannot always depend upon the state and the centre for finance. It has to find its own financial resources to meet its requirements. By revising property, water and electricity taxes, money can be collected and more money per head per annum can be made available for providing necessary facilities. City administration is to be toned up and bureaucrats must be made to commit themselves to the service of the people.

3. ***Creation of More Job Opportunities*** **:** We have been concentrating on the rural areas to provide more job opportunities for rural people through IRDP, NREP, JRY and such other programmes to hold back people in rural areas. It is time now to do something for creating better job opportunities for the urban people. This will not only help jobless urbanites but also add to the urban income. By spreading out various economic activities and by increasing income in the city it is possible to pay more attention to the requirements of the people.

4. ***Providing Better Transportation Facility*** **:** Most of the cosmopolitan cities of India are overcrowded and are not able to provide the necessary transportation facility to the people. Hence, it is necessary to make proper arrangements to face this problem. Private transport system can be encouraged along with the existing public transportation system. Healthy competition between the two systems can help solve the problem to a great extent.

5. ***Adopting An Efficient and a Workable Housing Policy*** **:** People who migrate to the city face the housing problem. Existing residents of the cities are also not having satisfactory housing accommodation. Hence, city administration must make it a policy to encourage housing industry. It can give encouragement to the private builders, relax the rigid rules for the construction of houses and the private, public and the co-operative housing boards may be given all the necessary help to construct as many houses as possible. Employees, government servants and private individuals who want to construct houses for self-occupation must be helped in getting loans from the nationalised banks, housing boards, co-operative societies, etc. The *National Housing Policy* which the central government presented in 1988 to the Parliament should be made more workable. The existing Rent Control Act must further be amended so as to give courage to the owners of houses to give houses on reasonable rent to the needy people.

6. ***Environmental Pollution to be Checked*** **:** Environmental pollution is becoming a major problem in the mega cities. Sufficient care is to be taken to control this pollution. New industries should not be given permission to start their establishments near the residential areas. On the other hand, industries should be established far away from the cities. Scientific arrangement is to be made to dispose of the solid waste including the garbage . People should be educated properly in order to maintain cleanliness in the city. Voluntary organisations and the media can play a vital role in this regard. The ***"Swachhta Abhiyan"*** [*Cleaning Campaign*] which the Indian Prime Minister **Narendra Modi** introduced on 02-10-2014, and its message must be honestly taken to the nook and corner of the nation, basically covering all the towns and cities of India

To conclude, it may be said that urbanisation wherever it takes place, is bound to create socio-economic problems. These problems are to be countered in a planned and in a scientific manner though they cannot be completely solved. However, we can keep them under control and find effective solutions for some of them. City administration or government alone cannot do that. City dwellers themselves should take an active role and must be prepared to co-operate with the administration in the removal of these problems.

STRIKING RURAL-URBAN CONTRAST IN THE INDIAN CONTEXT

Sl.No.	Main Areas of Noticeable Differences (2011)	Village	City
1.	Total Number of villages and cities in India – (2011)	640867	7935
2.	Total population of villages and cities – (2011)	833.08 ml	377.10 ml
3.	Percentage in the total population of India – (2011)	68.14	31.16
4.	Total Number of men in villages / cities (2011)	427.91 ml	195.80 ml
5.	Total Number of women in villages / cities (2011)	405.17 ml	181.29 ml
6.	Sex Ratio – Number of women per 1000 men (2011)	947	926
7.	% of Decadal difference in the growth of population (2001-11)	12.18	31.80
8.	% of the total usage of the nation's total income	48	52
9.	% of women's literacy rate in villages and cities (2011)	59	80
10.	% of men's literacy rate in villages and cities (2011)	64	81
11.	% of total literacy rate in villages and cities (2011)	59	75
12.	% of families living in building houses (2011)	25.5	74.1
13.	% of the houses having toilet facility (2011)	25.9	83.1
14.	% of the houses that make use of electricity (2011)	55.7	93.1
15.	% of houses that make use of pipe water (2011)	27.9	71.0
16.	% of houses that make use of L.P.G. for cooking (2011)	5.7	48.0
17.	No. of clinics for every one lakh people	1.49	102.90
18.	No. of hospital beds available for every one lakh people	3.60	15.05
19.	% of families making use of T.V.	19	64
20.	% of families that make use of radio	31	44
21.	% of families that make use of cycles	43	46
22.	% of families that make use of motor cycle/scooter	6	24
23.	% of families that make use of cars/ zeeps / vans etc.	1	5
24.	% of families that make use of banking facilities	30	50
25.	% of families that make use of telephone	2	N.A.
26.	Number of illiterate persons in millions (2011)	340.8	91.7
27.	Number of literate persons in millions (2011)	493.0	285.4

Source: Census Report - 2011 and Other Sources

●●●

Chapter 24

ENVIRONMENTAL POLLUTION

(A) Environmental Pollution: Meaning of Environment and Environmental Pollution – Environment Management – Causes of Environmental Pollution – Types of Environmental Pollution: ***Air Pollution:*** Meaning and Causes of Air Pollution – Effects of Air Pollution – Air Pollution Control Measures – ***Water Pollution:*** Meaning and Causes of Water Pollution – Effects of Water Pollution and Measures to Control Water Pollution – ***Sound Pollution:*** Meaning and Sources of Sound Pollution – Effects of Sound Pollution and Control of Noise Pollution - ***Soil Pollution:*** Meaning and Causes of Noise Pollution – Effects of Soil Pollution and its Prevention – ***Pollution of Solid Wastes:*** Meaning of Solid Wastes – Causes of Solid Wastes – Adverse Effects and Strategy for its Management – ***Other Sources of Pollution*** – Nuclear Radioactive Pollution – Pollution by Pesticides – Thermal Pollution – Marine or Sea Pollution and its Causes and Effects – Prevention of Environmental Pollution – Governmental Efforts: Legislative Measures – Salient Features of Some of the Major Legislative Measures – Problems Involved in the Enforcement of Legislative Measures – Some Suggestions for the Prevention of Environmental Pollution – Environmental Movements in India – The Example of Chipko Movement – Role of the Individual in the Prevention of Pollution.

(B) Some Environmental Issues and Problems: Environmental Pollution – the Curse of Man-made Progress –Some Environmental Issues of Serious Concern – Global Warming or Greenhouse Effect: Meaning of Global Warming and its Causes – Effects of Global Warming – The Challenge of Preserving Rain Forests – Loss of or Declining Biodiversity: Meaning of Biodiversity and Its Loss – Importance of or the Need for Protecting Biodiversity – Water Conservation and its Methods – Ozone Hole or Ozone Layer Depletion: Meaning – Causes – Effects and Protection – Acid Rain: Meaning – Causes and Adverse Effects of Acid Rain – Towards a Sustainable Development: Meaning and Characteristics of Sustainable Development – Strategies of Sustainable Development.

(A) ENVIRONMENTAL POLLUTION

"Environmental Pollution" has become today one of the biggest menaces of the modern civilised world. Due to ever increasing human population the pressure on the environment is continuously mounting. The developed countries are engaged in abusing the limited natural resources for their pomp, splendours and luxury, while the underdeveloped countries are tapping these resources for their existence and to achieve some development. In both the cases, the natural environment is the target of attack. Preserving the natural resources for the future generations has become a big challenge.

Our vital and fragile eco-system is today increasingly threatened by commercial exploitation, growing population demands and industrial pollution. Our mother Earth's rivers and oceans, forests and plain lands, grasslands and wet lands are fighting for survival. Great efforts are necessary to protect the natural environment threatened by over-population and misguided technology. Though the problem of pollution is as old as Industrial revolution, it has attained new proportions today.

Pollution has invaded all the three states of matter we are familiar with - solid, liquid and gas. Nay, there are new forms of pollution also. There is *"noise pollution"* and *"nuclear pollution."* Pollution is causing a great danger to human existence. Not only human beings but even plants, trees and animals are affected by pollution. Petrol or diesel fumes from lorries, buses and cars contain certain chemicals which on coming in contact with sunlight, are transformed into poisonous substances. These poisonous substances can affect sensitive plants like tobacco, tomato and potato, some varieties of beans and spinach, some cereal crops and certain flowers. Smoke from factories manufacturing plastic produce chemicals which injure cotton and rose plants. Factories processing metal ore produce silver dioxide which has destroyed tens of thousands of hectares of timber plantations.

The problem of pollution is spreading its tentacles in different fields. The *land* in which we live, the *air* that we inhale, the *water* we drink and the *sound* that we hear – are all polluted. Economists, sociologists and presently the environmental scientists and administrators are very much worried about this menace and are seeking to find a solution for the same.

The key to man's ill-health lies largely in his environment. In fact, much of man's ill-health can be traced to adverse environmental factors such as water pollution, soil pollution, air pollution, poor housing conditions, presence of animal reservoirs and insect vectors of diseases which pose a constant threat to man's health. Often man is responsible for the pollution of his environment through urbanization, industrialization and other human activities. In 1972, the *UN Conference on the Human Environment* focussed world-wide attention on the environmental hazards that threaten human beings. To facilitate work in this area, the *World Health Organisation* [WHO] has compiled a wide-ranging survey of environmental hazards to human health.

In the past, sanitation was centred on the sanitary disposal of human excreta. Even now, to many people, "sanitation" still means the construction of latrines. In actual fact, the term sanitation covers the whole field of controlling the environment with a view to prevent disease and promote health. Man has already controlled a number of factors in his environment, ***e.g.,*** food, water, housing, clothing, sanitation. These controllable factors are those included in the *"standard or living."* It is the control of these factors that has been responsible for considerable improvement in the health of the people during the past century in the developed countries.

As old problems are being solved, new problems are arising. Air pollution is of growing concern in many urban centres. Industrial growth has given rise to the problem of environmental pollution by industrial wastes. Advances in nuclear technology have produced the problem of radio-active pollution of the environment. The demographic growth and fast urbanisation all over the world are bringing profound social and environmental changes. Therefore, the attainment of a healthy environment is becoming more and more complex. The term *environmental sanitation* is now being replaced by *environmental health.* Proper environmental health now requires the services of the public health qualified doctor, the epidemiologist, the public health engineer, the town planner, the sociologist, the economist, and the health inspector. A purely medical or engineering approach by itself is no longer sufficient; a combined multi-disciplinary programme of action is needed to achieve a healthy environment.

POLLUTION OF THE ENVIRONMENT PERVADING THE SOCIETY

MEANING OF "ENVIRONMENT" AND "ENVIRONMENTAL POLLUTION"

Meaning of Environment

The term ***environment*** implies *all the external factors – living and non-living, material and non-material – which surround man.* In its modern concept, environment includes not only the water, air and soil that form our environment but also the social and economic conditions under which we live.

The term ***"environment"*** etymologically means *"surroundings"* which comprise of air, water and land. Environment creates favourable conditions for the existence and development of living organisms. The term environment can be defined in various ways. *For example –*

1. *The term environment refers to anything that immediately surrounds an object and exerts a direct influence on it.*
2. *Environment is the sum of all social, economic, biological, physical or chemical factors which constitute the surroundings of man, who is both creator and moulder of his environment.*
3. **C.C. Park** defines the term in the following way **:** *"Environment refers to the sum total of conditions which surround man at a given point in space and time."*

For descriptive purpose, environment has been divided into three components, all closely related:

(i) *Physical* : Water, air, soil, housing, wastes, radiation, etc.

(ii) *Biological* : Plant and animal life including bacteria, and

(iii) *Social* : Customs, culture, habits, income, occupation, religion, etc.

Environment Management

Environmentalism is a fairly new movement in the world in the recent years. It is getting a top priority in the national policies among the developed and developing countries. The environmental experts, during project planning give due consideration to social, cultural and environmental impacts. It is in this context, the Govt. of India, in the Sixth Five-Year Plan [1980-85] had formed the following policy : – *"It is imperative that we use our renewable resources of water, soil, and vegetation to sustain our economic development. Over exploitation of these is visible in soil erosion, floods, deforestation, siltation, floral and wild-life resources. The depletion of these resources tends to be irreversible and since the whole population depends on these natural resources to meet their basic needs i.e., fuel, fodder and land, it has meant a deterioration in their standard of life."*

Objectives of *"Environment Management"*

Environment management has become an important aspect of the modern economic planning. It has got its own aims and objectives. The main objectives of environment management are stated here.

1. Maintenance of environmental quality.
2. Balancing the ecosystem.
3. Restrict and regulate the exploitation of natural resources.
4. To protect the environment from degradation.
5. To renew natural resources and reduce natural disasters.
6. To adopt engineered technology without creating adverse effects on the environment.
7. To formulate laws and regulations to control pollution.

Meaning of "Environmental Pollution"

The environment we live in is a complex and dynamic one in which all forms of life are interdependent on each other. But in his quest to improve the quality of his life man has changed this balance in nature by adding some of the essential components. *This very human act of spoiling or contaminating the environment and disturbing the ecological balance can be called* ***"environmental pollution".*** The concept can be better be defined in the following ways.

- *Contamination of the environment by the addition of undesirable substances produced by human activities which cause damage to the living organisms is called "environmental pollution."*

The undesirable substance that is added is called ***"pollutant"***. ***Ex.*** Carbon monoxide is an air pollutant, sewage is a water pollutant, and so on.

1. *Pollution is the contamination, unfavourable alteration or desecration of any part of the environment by products produced by human activities.*
2. *Pollution is an undesirable change in the physical, chemical or biological characteristics of air, water and land that may harmfully affect living organisms, industrial processes or raw materials.*
3. *"Pollution is the release of harmful substances or energy into the environment by man in quantities that damage health and resources"* [**Edwards** - 1972].
4. Pollution is viewed as – *"the release of substances and energy as waste products of harmful activities which result in harmful changes within the natural environment".* [**National Environmental Research Council,** 1976].

CAUSES OF ENVIRONMENTAL POLLUTION

Pollution of the environment is one of the most horrible ecological crises to which we are subjected today. We know that three basic amenities for living organisms are ***air, land*** or ***soil*** and ***water.*** The earth is the only object known in the entire universe capable of supporting life. The amenities of life such as air, land and water are found in our mother earth. Unfortunately, all these amenities are polluted and this pollution has posed a very serious threat. Pollution is caused by so many factors among which the following may be noted.

1. According to **Write** [1970], *human greed and ignorance* have allowed our culture to develop an ecological crisis like pollution.

2. According to **Southwick** [1976], *human population explosion is the main cause of pollution.* He pointed out that with more people, there is more sewage, more solid wastes, more fuel being burnt, more fertilisers and insecticides being used to produce more food for hungry mouths.

3. The root cause of environmental pollution has been *man's misbehaviour with the nature under the false ego that he is the master of the nature.* This undesirable situation created by man has threatened the survival of man himself and other living beings on the earth.

4. Modern ecologists have pointed out some important factors of environmental pollution. They can be stated here. Factors such as – *human population explosion, rapid industrialisation, deforestation, unplanned urbanisation, scientific and technological advancement, etc.* are mainly responsible for the pollution crisis on earth.

Industrialisation is the Greatest Menace of Pollution. Man is forced to set up more factories to provide the clothes we wear. We have to use more insecticides and fertilizers, and to make a large number of tractors to cultivate the land to supply food for ever increasing number of people. Hence, more factories are built and more oil and coal are burnt. Burning of both adds to pollution.

Coal is called the *"Black Diamond"* and oil *"Liquid Gold"* since both are valuable fuels in producing energy that is required to run factories. *"Unfortunately, these valuable fuels are among the world offenders in the pollution of air. Over the past 50 years, nearly **half** the known reserves of coal and oil in the world have been burnt. Industrialisation is taking place so rapidly that it won't be surprising if the **remaining half** is exhausted within the next twenty-five years."*[1] One can imagine how much more pollution will be caused by that time.

5. ***Industrialised countries are mainly responsible for the environmental pollution.*** For example, the United States with its vast infrastructure of industries is one of the leading polluters of the world. The worst pollution occurs in countries where there have been the greatest scientific, technological and industrial advances. Developing countries such as India, Thailand, Philippines and others have been caught in the spiral of industrial growth. But they are not aware of the dangerous consequences of pollution. ***For example,*** pollution in the textile city of Kanpur in Uttar Pradesh is six times more than that of the famous cotton city of Manchester in England in the latter half of the nineteenth century. In Kanpur, the factories alone contribute as much pollution as that from all the inhabitants. Bombay is another case in point. Within the next twenty years, the number of factories in and around Bombay will have increased threefold. But even today, more than 1,000 tonnes of poisonous chemicals, soot and dirt are emitted into the atmosphere over Bombay.

6. ***Thoughtless burning of agricultural wastes and destruction of forests can cause pollution.*** Rich industrialised countries are not the only culprits in causing pollution. Recent investigations indicate that tropical grassland fires and the burning of agricultural wastes contribute almost as much pollution as do factories all over the world. There are 2,000 million hectares of burnable land in the world in the form of cultivated land, permanent meadows and pastures. These areas are often subjected to seasonal burning. It is estimated that more than 6,000 million tonnes of agricultural wastes and other vegetation are burnt every year, and dust and soot is being continuously injected into the atmosphere. [**N. Sheshagiri.** Page - 39].

6. ***Rapid population growth combined with modern technology has caused a serious environmental crisis.*** This is because of the fact that in well developed countries, citizens consume more food, use more fertilisers and pesticides, fuel, minerals, automobiles [cars, scooters, vans, trucks, etc.] and other manufactured products of all kinds. Almost all of these products are manufactured in one or the other kinds of the industries. These industries are responsible for adding pollutants to our environment [land, soil, water and air] and hence cause pollution.

7. ***Both the developed and the developing countries are contributing to pollution:*** The environmental pollution seems to be the necessary evil of all man-made progress. It is not only the industrialised countries which are threatened with the environmental pollution, *but the developed countries are also contributing to it and at the same time struggling to face it.* The developed countries dump lot of affluents into the environment polluting the whole globe. The newly developing countries are also adding to it. *For example,* New York in U.S.A. is the most polluted city of the world and New Delhi is the fourth most polluted city. India occupies **7th** place among the industrialised developing countries of the world. Hence, its contribution to environmental pollution is not insignificant.

TYPES OF ENVIRONMENTAL POLLUTION

The environment in which we are living is being polluted in various ways. Many a times man himself is responsible for this pollution and consequently suffers from his own misdeeds. Environmental pollution assumes different forms : ***air pollution, water pollution, sound pollution,***

1. **N. Sheshagiri** in *"Pollution."* Page - 24.

land pollution, marine pollution, thermal pollution, *and* ***pollution by radioactivity or nuclear pollution.***

1. AIR POLLUTION: CAUSES - EFFECTS - SOLUTIONS

Meaning of Air Pollution

The phenomenon called *"pollution"* is an inescapable consequence of the presence of man and his activities. The term *"air pollution"* signifies the presence in the surrounding atmosphere of substances [***e.g.,*** gases, mixtures of gases and particulated matter] generated by the activities of man that interfere with human health, safety and comfort. In the past, air pollution was mostly understood as 'pollution by smoke'. Today, air pollution has become more subtle and it recognizes no geographical or political boundaries. Air pollution is one of the present day health problems throughout the world.

- *Air or atmospheric pollution* refers to *the contamination of the air by the addition of unwanted solid wastes or gases produced by human activities.*
- *"Excessive release of air pollutants in the atmosphere by anthropogenic activities disturb the dynamic equilibrium in the atmosphere and thereby affect man and his environment."*[2]

Sources or Causes of Air Pollution

(i) Air Pollution Caused by Industries : Air pollution is caused mainly by harmful gases released by industrial plants. The most important air pollutants are gases like carbon monoxide, carbon dioxide, sulphur dioxide, oxides of nitrogen, hydrogen sulphide and particulates like dust, smoke and lead particles.

(ii) Air Pollution by Automobiles: *Air pollution is the greatest threat to our health in the future.* Factories with chimneys throwing out smoke into the air are not the only sources of this air pollution; a major offender is the automobile - cars, vans, lorries, and buses. The smoke belching from the exhausts of lorries and buses is a familiar sight everywhere in big cities. *For example,* the five big cities - Mumbai, Kolkota, Delhi, Chennai and Bangalore - spew daily into the air we breathe more than *one crore* kilograms of smoke.[3] It is said that every moment Mumbaiyites breathe air containing so many poisonous chemicals that 10% more of them suffer from *asthama, bronchitis, coughs, colds and headaches* than citizens of almost any other city or town in India.[4]

(iii) Air Pollution by Sources of Fuel and Energy: Air pollution is normally caused whenever different sources of energy such as atomic energy, coal, petrol, kerosene, etc.., are used for serving human needs. Coal, iron ore, manganese and such other types of mining also cause air pollution.

Some Vivid Examples of Air Pollution

The **National Environmental and Engineering Research Institute** [NEERI] has also pointed out that many monuments in India are being affected by the fumes emitted by industries. *For example,* the Government-owned Oil Refinery which is 4 kms. away from Taj Mahal, spews out 24 tonnes of sulphur dioxide daily.

---

2. As quoted by **S.S. Dara** in *"A Text Book of Environmental Chemistry and Pollution Control"* [1998]. *Pub.* S. Chand & Co. Ltd., New Delhi. Page - 23.

3. ***An illustration of the smoke emitting out of vehicles*** **:** If hundred diesel lorries throw out smoke for five minutes continuously, together they would produce one kilogram of smoke.

4. **An Example of Air Pollution : Badarpur** and **Indraprastha** Thermal Electric Plants [both in the State of Delhi] produce on an average per day 180 tonnes of fly-ash and 70 tonnes of sulphur dioxide which contaminate the atmosphere. A number of monuments close to Rajghat and Indraprastha Power Stations in Delhi are turning black due to the fumes and smoke.

In **Bhatinda** of Punjab, the *Thermal Electric Plant* produces on an average per day 1200 tonnes of fly-ash which pollutes the nearby atmosphere.

The Dangerous Air Pollution

Air quality in Latin America's most major cities threatens human health. In Sao Paulo and Rio de Janeiro, air pollution is estimated to cause 4000 pre-mature deaths a year. The region, nearly 75% of whose population is already urbanised, is responsible for 4.3% of the world's total carbon dioxide emissions from industrial processes and 48.3% from land-use changes.

The NEERI which has conducted a study in **Kolkota** has stated that in the city on an average, 1299 tonnes of polluted things join the atmosphere everyday. It is because of this atmospheric pollution, 60% of the citizens are suffering from disease connected with lungs. Further, the marbles of *Albert and Victoria Memorial* in Kolkota are attacked by stone cancer.

Toxic air pollutants may also do immediate damage to human health and life. The accidental leak of deadly gas at the Union Carbide Plant in **Bhopal** [M.P.], in 1984 cost 4,000 lives and an estimated 4,00,000 people were injured or affected to this day. Similar accidents have happened in United States and also in the then U.S.S.R. causing lot of damage to a large number of people. More frightening is the deliberate pollution of the air with toxic chemicals because it is the part of the manufacturing process of many industries.

Adverse Effects of Air Pollution

About **1.3** billion urban residents worldwide are exposed to air pollution level above recommended limits. Air quality in the developed countries has generally improved in the past two decades, but in many developing countries air quality has deteriorated because of rising industrial activity, increasing power generation, and the congestion of streets with poorly maintained motor vehicles that use leaded fuel. Air pollution can affect us by several ways.

(i) ***Air pollution affects the health of the human beings adversely.*** It causes diseases like heart disease, lung disease, high blood pressure, nervous debility, eye sore, paralysis, throat irritation, chronic bronchitis, lung cancer, bronchial asthama, emphysema, respiratory allergies, etc. It may even cause death. Epidemiological studies have shown that a sudden increase in the air pollution has often been associated with immediate increase in morbidity and mortality.

- ***Heavy release of carbon monoxide alone causes*** – headache, decrease in usual perception and paralysis. It affects the cardio-vascular system. It reacts with haemoglobin of blood and thereby reduces oxygen carrying capacity of haemoglobin.
- ***Lead itself poisons many systems in the body*** and is particularly dangerous to children's developing brain and nervous system. Elevated lead levels in children have been associated with impaired neuropsychological development as measured by loss of I.Q. [Intelligence Quotient], poor school performance and behavioural difficulties. ***Table* - 1** shows the major air pollutants, their source and adverse effects on health.

(ii) ***It affects the growth of plants and trees.*** It causes corrosion of metals, damages buildings, leads to high cost of cleaning and maintenance. It also causes repairs and aesthetic nuisance.

(iii) ***It results in the formation of smoky atmosphere*** which is dangerous to vehicular traffic. Air pollution reduces visibility in towns. It can spoil and damage clothings.

(iv) ***It affects the weather adversely,*** raises the temperature, reduces the humidity and adversely affects the rainfall.

(v) ***It causes corrosion of metals, damages buildings*** and leads to high cost of cleaning and maintenance.

Table - 1

Major Air Pollutants, Their Sources and Adverse Effects		
Noxious Agent	***Sources***	***Adverse Effects***
Oxides of nitrogen	Automobile exhaust, gas stoves and heaters, wood-burning stoves, kerosene space heaters	Respiratory tract irritation, bronchial hyperactivity, impaired lung defences, bronchialitis obliterans
Hydrocarbons	Automobile exhaust, cigarette smoke	Lung cancer
Ozone	Automobile exhaust, high altitude aircraft cabins	Cough, substernal discomfort, bronchoconstriction, decreased exercise performance, respiratory tract irritation
Sulphur dioxide	Power plants, Smelters, oil refineries, kerosene space heaters	Exacerbation of asthma and COPD, respiratory tract irritation, hospitalization may be necessary, and death may occur in severe exposure
Lead	Automobile exhaust using leaded gasoline	Impaired neuropsychological development in children
Source : As quoted by **K. Park** in *"Park's Text Book of Preventive and Social Medicine"* [2002]. Page 515.		

Air Pollution Control Measures OR Solutions to Air Pollution

1. Air pollution can be prevented by controlling the emission of particulate matter by using *Electro Static Precipitators (ESP), fabric filters, wet scrubbers and cyclone separators.*
2. By using the fuel free of lead, automobile emissions can be reduced. Catalytic converters, efficient four stroke engines and use of liquified petroleum gas can go a long way in preventing the pollution of air by automobiles.
3. Using coal with low sulphur content will reduce the sulphur dioxide contamination of air. Use of smoke filters and increasing the height of smoke chimneys can reduce the industrial contamination of air.
4. Developing forestry and spreading green atmosphere wherever possible. Plants and trees are to be protected everywhere.
5. Cancelling the licences of industries that cause air pollution.
6. Enforcing the vehicle owners to equip their vehicles with proper pollution control devices.
7. Keeping away industries from the residential areas.
8. Proper awareness is to be created among the people regarding the dangerous effects of air pollution. This awareness is to be created among children at their primary school level education itself.
9. In India, both State and Central Governments have passed several legislative measures to prevent and control different types of air pollution. These are to be implemented strictly.

   1. Bengal Smoke and Nuisance Act, 1905;

   2. The Motor Vehicle Act, 1938;

   3. The Gujarat Smoke Nuisance Act, 1953;

   4. The Air (Prevention and Control of Pollution Act), 1981;

   5. The Environmental (Protection) Act, 1986 ;

   6. The Motor Vehicles Act, 1988 [This Act came into force from 1.7.1989.]

2. WATER POLLUTION

Water is essential for the survival of any form of life. On an average, a human being consumes about 2 litres of water everyday. Water accounts for about 70% of the weight of a human body. About 80% of the earth's surface [that is, 80% of the total 50,000 million hectares of area] is covered by water. Thus, a great quantity of water exists on the earth, but only a fraction of it is usable, and that fraction is shrinking due to pollution. As usual, the combined pressures of the population growth and industrial development have imperilled the world's water supply. Thus, unscrupulous industrial growth, and uncontrolled increase in human population are the root causes for water scracity and also water pollution.

Meaning of *"Water Pollution"*

- The term *water pollution* refers to *the contamination of water by toxic pollutants*[5] *that may either eliminate some living organisms or all forms of life.*
- *"Any human activity that impairs the use of water as a resource may be called water pollution.*
- *Water is polluted when it is contaminated by sewage, chemicals, affluents of water given out by factories, automobiles, etc. When all these substances flow into the river water, or lake water, or well water, or sea water, pollution of water takes place.*

Causes or Sources of Water Pollution

Water can purify itself of a certain amount of pollution. But if pollution becomes too great, it cannot purify itself. Water pollution comes from three major sources – (i) *Domestic Sewage,* (ii) *Industrial waste,* and (iii) *Agricultural waste.* Today, industry contributes more to water pollution than do household users.

(i) Due to Industrial Wastes, Rivers and Lakes are Polluted: The nation's rivers and lakes have long been the dumping grounds for many industries. The rivers such as Ganga and Cauvery, the lakes such as the Dal and Nagin [Srinagar], Loktak [Manipur], Chilka [Orissa] and many others are becoming the dumping grounds for poisonous chemicals, factories, agricultural wastes, insecticides and even acids. *"Major industries – paper, steel, automobile, cotton textile, leather industry, etc. depend on water in their production processes. They take water from the rivers and return it polluted and heated, thus doubly affecting aquatic life. Pollutants that industries discharge into rivers and oceans are many and various : solid wastes, sewage, non-degradable byproducts, synthetic materials, toxic chemicals, and even radioactive substances. Added to this are the polluting effects of sewage systems of towns and large cities, detergents, oil spills and also pesticide run-off from agricultural areas.*

(ii) Domestic Sewage: Waste water containing human and animal excreta, food residues, organic waste from tannaries & canning industry and discharges from commercial establishments connected to public sewage system is called *domestic sewage*.

(iii) Agricultural Waste: In agriculture, chemicals are used as fertilizers and as pesticides. Many of the pesticides are non biodegradable, i.e. they persist in environment harming organisms and affecting human health.

(iv) Other Causes of Water Pollution:

Water pollution can take place due to our defective arrangement of water supply. Hence, even if the source of water supply and its treatment are of a high standard, water pollution may

5. **Pollutants :** Pollutants are by-products or waste products, which when released into the environment cause pollution.

still occur as it often happens, due to corrosion of pipe lines, leaky joints and cross connections between water supply pipes and sewage drainage pipes. Surveillance has to be exercised at every point in the distribution system to ensure supply of safe water to the consumer.

"***Even oceans have been polluted :*** More than half the oil produced in the world is transported across oceans by ships and oil-tankers. One part in a thousand of this is lost by spillage and leakage. In fact, into the oceans encircling India alone is spilt more than 1 million tonnes of oil annually. Much of this oil will not leave the ocean because unlike water it does not evaporate easily and year after year it accumulates."[6]

Damage Caused by the Industries and Sewage Systems in India : Most of the rivers in India are polluted either by industries or by sewage systems. *For example,* the **Hoogly** river flowing through **Kolkota** is polluted because 350 factories are spread over on both the banks of this river within a distance of about 100 Kms. The river **Damodar** supplies water to all the families and industries in the two major industrial cities of **Durgapur** and **Asansol.** In between these two cities there are about 70 big factories and 250 coal mines. These factories and mines have made the Damodar water almost poisonous. The river **Vrashabhavathi** that flows near the city of **Bangalore** is so polluted that its colour has completely gone black.

Damage to other forms of living beings : Polluted water can cause damage not only to the human beings but also to the cattle, fish, plants, trees and other forms of living beings. Experiment of **Malappadu** villagers of Guntur district of A.P. reveals that polluted water can create a serious problem for the people.[7]

Most of the Available water in India is polluted - ? India receives about 1,400 - 1,800 mm of rainfall annually. It is estimated that 96% of this water is used for agriculture, 3% for domestic use and 1% for industrial activity. A study conducted in 1982 revealed that about 70% of all the available water in our country is polluted. [**S.S. Dara.** Page - 65.]

No Arrangement for Purifying Polluted Water : A study conducted in 1989-90 has revealed that out of 3119 big cities in India, only in 8 cities there is arrangement for purifying the polluted water; there is partial arrangement in 209 cities. But virtually there is no arrangement to purify the polluted water in any manner in the remaining 2902 cities. The polluted water in these cities directly flows down and joins various rivers thereby polluting them. The extent of water pollution is such that around **60%** of the diseases in India are caused due to the consumption of the polluted water.

- As per the report given by the ***"Central Pollution and Control Board",*** of the nearly 8000 cities and towns, in India, only 160 towns are having arrangement for purifiying waste water uptill 2011-12. The report also points out that 80% of the waste water that joins drinking water sources such as rivers, lakes, tanks, etc. is never purified.[8]

Adverse Effects of Water Pollution

(i) ***Water pollution causes number of diseases*** like cholera, typhoid, dysentery, jaundice, and viral diseases. Typhoid and cholera are very big killers. It is estimated that during

6. **N. Sheshagiri** in *"Pollution"* [1994]. Page : 4 - 5.
7. ***The Case of Malappadu Village*** : Malappadu village is in Guntur district of A.P. "This village is situated on the banks of the river-stream Chappadibagu. Less than 1,000 people known as Lambadas live here with their cattle. The cattle drink water from this stream. Around 1977, this peaceful village became the victim of a strange disease. The cattle developed diarrhoea and within a few days suffered paralytic strokes. This was followed by more complications and ultimately death. Scientists who investigated the disease found that the stream was polluted with lead-based chemicals and the cattle had died of lead poisoning. The Government of Andhra Pradesh immediately ordered a nearby factory to stop poisoning the stream." [**N. Sheshagiri.** Page - 13].
8. **M.V. Kamath** in his article in ***'Udayavani'***, Kannada Daily, dated 29.06.2014.

a nine-year period in India [1898 and 1907] about 3,70,000 people died of cholera alone. In 1947, in a widespread epidemic of cholera an estimated 10,000 people died in Egypt. ***Table* - 2** shows that a large number of people in many of the South-East Asian countries do not have access to safe water and adequate sanitation.

Table - 2

Population with access to safe water and adequate sanitation in South-East Asia countries 2000

Countries	***Safe Water* (%)**	***Adequate Sanitation* (%)**
India	88	31
Bhutan	62	69
Bangladesh	97	53
Indonesia	76	66
Maldives	100	56
Mynmar	68	46
Nepal	81	27
Sri Lanka	83	83
Thailand	80	96

***Source* :** *"Science Today"* Oct. 1970 as quoted by **K. Park.** Page 489

(ii) ***It adversely affects the growth of plants and trees and also animal life.*** The industrial effluents are toxic to animals. The death of marine and fresh water fishes is largely due to industrial pollution. Presence of chemicals released by industries into water makes it unfit for consumption.

(iii) ***It takes away the lives of fish and other animals that live in water.*** The occurrence of a crippling disease, *"Minamata disease"* in Japan was due to the consumption of mercury poisoned fish/animal. It is a classical example of industrial effluents on organisms.

(iv) ***It also affects the marine transport and inland waterways.***

(v) Water is absolutely essential for *maintaining cleanliness*. When water itself is polluted, the question of maintaining cleanliness is to be dropped once and for all.

(vi) ***Water pollution can cause damage to the nervous system*** and can cripple people, especially children. It may even affect adversely the unborn children in their mother's wombs.[9]

(vii) ***Usage of polluted water lessens agricultural yields*** at least by 17% to 30%.

While pollution seems to be an inevitable consequence of modern industrial technology, the problem now, is to determine the level of pollution that permits economic and social development without presenting hazards to health. The evaluation of the health effects of environmental pollutants is currently being carried out as part of the WHO Environmental Health Criteria Programme.

---

9. ***Polluted Water Adversely Affects Even the Unborn*** **:** Example of Japan is worth citing here. "A chemical factory in Japan was pouring its mercury into Minamata Bay. All those who ate fish from this bay got a terrible illness now popularly known as the "Minamata disease." This is a strange ailment of the nervous system. It killed many and crippled numerous others. Children were the worst affected. Even unborn children in their mother's wombs were afflicted. The worst of it was that this particular factory had been throwing out this poison into the water for fifty years without anyone being aware of the hazard. The danger is, therefore, our ignorance of the poisonous materials around us." ***Source* : N. Sheshagiri** in *"Pollution."* Pages : 58 - 59.

Control Measures for Water Pollution

1. The sewage should be treated in oxidation ponds or waste stabilization ponds. The processed sewage is non toxic and can be used for agricultural purposes.
2. Use of non-biodegradable pesticides should be discontinued. Naturally occurring or available herbal products should be used as pesticides.
3. Discharge of untreated industrial effluents should not be allowed.
4. Waste water from large cities and factories should be purified before letting it to river or lake or sea.
5. Dead bodies of any type of animals including human beings, should not be thrown into river water.
6. Governmental policies and legislations pertaining to pollution [***Ex:*** *The Water Prevention and Control of Pollution Act, 1971* and *Environmental Protection Act, 1986]* should be effectively implemented.
7. People must be made aware of, through proper means, the dangerous consequences of water pollution.

3. SOUND (NOISE) POLLUTION

Noise is often defined as *"unwanted sound."* This definition is subjective because of the fact that one man's sound may be another man's noise. Perhaps a better definition of noise could be stated in the following words:

Meaning of Noise Pollution

- Noise is *"wrong sound, in the wrong place, at the wrong time."*
- *"The term **noise** may also be defined as an unwanted sound at a wrong time and at a wrong place."*
- *Intrusion of unwanted sounds into our life is noise pollution.*

Man is living in an increasingly noisy environment. The previous 20th century has been described as the *"Century of Noise."* Noise has become a very important *"stress factor"* in the environment of man. The term *"Noise Pollution"* has been recently coined to signify the vast cacophony of sounds that are being produced in the modern life, leading to health hazards.

Although noise is undesirable, it could be meaningful or meaningless. An irresponsible or meaningless noise is disturbing and annoying. Prolonged and loud sound is generally considered as noise which is mostly caused because of industries, vehicles, trains, loudspeakers, aeroplanes, etc. Since such a noise is found to cause some kind of physical, physiological or psychological harm or stress to human beings, it is also considered as a pollutant. Noise is a byproduct of human activity. Excessive noise can result in loss of hearing, increase in accidents, and decrease in productivity. Hence, it is essential to take suitable precautions to reduce noise pollution particularly in urban and industrial areas.

Causes or Sources of Noise Pollution

The sources of noise are many and varied. These are *automobiles, factories*, industries, air-craft, etc.

(i) ***Road, air and railway traffic contributing to sound pollution :*** Noise levels are particularly acute near railway junctions, traffic roundabouts, bus terminuses and airports. Use of pressure horns, recreational noise of loudspeakers with full volume during festivities particularly at night are other sources of noise pollution.

(ii) ***Pollution due to the use of domestic consumer products :*** The domestic noises form the radios, transistors, T.V. sets – all add to the quantum of noise in daily life. Industrial activities is leading to noise pollution.

(iii) ***Pollution due to the use of domestic consumer products:*** Household consumer products like refrigerators, mixies, radios, transistors, T.V. sets, vacuum cleaners, air conditioners, etc. are also responsible for noise pollution for they generate lot of sound.

(iv) ***Other Varieties of Sound:*** Various types of music systems playing loud music, sirens of ambulances, police vehicles, generators, crackers, loud speakers in public functions etc. are other sources of noise pollution. Noice generated by humans and barking dogs also contribute to the noise pollution.

People located near the industrial plants are subjected to noise originating from the industrial activities. People working in such industries are specially affected by severe noise pollution.

Noise has two important properties: loudness **or** ***intensity;*** **and** ***frequency.*** The loudness of noise is measured in decibels [dB]. ***For example,*** normal conversation produces a noise of 60-65 dB; whispering, 20 db; heavy street traffic, 60-80 dB; and boiler factories, about 120 dB. A daily exposure upto 85 dB is about the limit people can tolerate without substantial damage to their hearing.

Table - 3

Acceptable Noise Levels (dBA)		
Residential :	Bed room	25
	Living room	40
Commercial :	Office	35 - 45
	Conference	40 - 45
	Restaurants	40 - 60
Industrial :	Workshop	40 - 60
	Laboratory	40 - 50
Educational :	Class Room	30 - 40
	Library	35 - 40
Hospitals :	Wards	20 - 35

Table - 4

Sound Levels of Some Noises

Sources of Noise	*Sound Level* (dB)
Wishper	10
Speech, 2 - 3 people	73
Speech on radio	80
Music on radio	85
Children shouting	79
Children crying	80
Vacuum cleaner	76
Piano	86
Jet take off	150

Noise pollution or environmental noise is one of the new killers of our society. If we live near a busy airport or big industry we come to know what noise pollution is. As civilisation grows noise pollution also grows. It is said that Julius Caeser banned chariots from the Cobblestone streets during evening hours because of the noise they made. Noise pollution has become the subject of study for our scientists very recently. They have cautioned about the undesirable consequences of noise pollution. The scientists at the Indian Science Congress in 1991 also discussed at length the consequences of sound pollution and the ways and means of reducing it.

Effects of Sound Pollution

(i) Sound pollution has adverse effects on a human life. *It damages man's hearing,* reduces his age, causes loss of mental peace and results in emotional upsets.

(ii) *It has also an adverse effect on animal life.* It retards their growth and affects their working ability.

(iii) It increases rate of heart beat, B.P. and heart related problems.

(iv) Sound pollution offen causes loss of memory.

Control of Noise Pollution

To control noise pollution, three methods can be adopted

a) Reduction of noise at source

b) Interruption of path of transmission, and

c) Measures to protect the receiver

Different measures used to control noise pollution are ;

- Lubrication of the machines, tightening of loose nuts, reducing the vibration of the machines etc. can reduce the noise at the source.
- Construction of silence zones around hospitals and educational institutions will lessen noise pollution.
- Covering the noise producing machines by sound insulating materials or use of sound proof chamber can reduce the noise at source.
- Growing trees around all noise producing regions reduces noise as trees and shrubs act as *Green Muffler* i.e. act as sound insulators.
- Ear muffs / cotton plugs should be used to reduce the effect of noise in case of occupational exposure to noise.

4. SOIL POLLUTION

Earth's uppermost surface is covered by a thin layer of organic and inorganic material called *"soil"*. The organic part is called top soil. This is obtained by the decaying process of remains of plants and animals. This layer supplies the necessary nutrients essential for the growth of plants. The biological system exists because this soil has been feeding the plants.

Introduction of man-made substances, biological organisms or energy into the soil altering its physical, chemical and biological characteristics is known as ***"soil pollution"***.

Meaning of Soil Pollution

- ***Soil pollution*** *is desecration of soil by man-made substances that alter its physical, chemical and biological characteristics.*
- *The decrease in the quality of soil and changes in it due to various human activities is called "soil pollution".*

Causes or Sources of Soil Pollution

1. ***Industrial wastes*** thrown out by paper, chemical, rubber, cement, sugar, fertiliser, textile, and other industries, the fly-ash thrown out by furnaces pollute not only the soil but also air and water.
2. ***Agricultural wastes*** include artificial fertilisers, pesticides, farm wastes, etc. Some of these are biodegradable.
3. ***Radioactive wastes*** are those released during nuclear explosions, and those released from nuclear power plants, and by institutions using radioactive substances.

Adverse Effects of Soil Pollution

(i) Soil or land pollution reduces fertility of the soil. This results in the reduction in crop yield.

(ii) Due to excessive use of chemicals and fertilisers our land is losing its natural capacity to support growth of plants and trees.

(iii) Soil pollution also leads to water pollution.

(iv) Food obtained by the contaminated soil spoils human health.

(v) Soil pollution is causing water scarcity in some regions.

Prevention of Soil Pollution

(i) Industrial waste and agricultural wastes etc. must be properly processed before they get mixed up with soil.

(ii) Usage of organic manures must be made popular in place of chemicals and fertilisers.

(iii) Using of harmful and deadly pesticides and insecticides must be stopped, and if possible, legally banned.

(iv) Decay of forest be stopped and afforestation including social forestry be encouraged.

(v) Soil erosion be stopped and soil fertility to be increased by resorting to the organic strategies such as rotation of crops, etc..

(vi) *Soil Pollution Control Board* established in India must be made powerful and effective.

5. POLLUTION BY SOLID WASTES

All solid waste things thrown out by human beings themselves contribute to pollution. It means increasing solid wastes on earth itself is contributing to a form of land pollution. This is becoming a serious problem in all the highly advanced countries of the world.

- *"Any unwanted or discarded material from residential, commercial, industrial, mining and agricultural activities that cause environmental problems may be termed as pollution by solid wastes.* [**S.S.Dara.** Page 100]
- *Solid wastes can be broadly defined as those wastes which have been rejected for further use and which can neither be transported by water into streams nor can readily escape into the atmosphere. They include all the discarded solid materials from municipal, agricultural and industrial activities.*

Mounting Garbage - World's Most Serious Environmental Problem !

Among the world's most serious environmental problems is, how to dispose of its wastes. From Kashmir to Kanyakumari, tonnes of garbage are produced everyday, including paper, yard wastes, glass, metals, food, plastic and wood.[10] This garbage which is termed as *"solid wastes"* includes – food wastes, rubbish things consisting of metal, plastic and glass, demolition products such as bricks, masonry and pipes, sewage treatment residues, dead animals, manure and other discarded material. The output of daily waste depends upon the dietary habits, life styles, living standards and the degree of urbanisation and industrialisation. The per capita [that is, per head] daily solid waste produced, ranges between 0.25 to 2.5 K.G. in different countries.

Each family is adding everyday to this Garbage Mountain : Not only the processes of urbanisation and industrialisation are causing land pollution, but each family is contributing to it in one way or another. ***For example,*** *"In India, there are more than 100 million families. They account for as much as 50 million buckets of solid waste every day. In a year, nearly 20,000 million buckets of these wastes find their way to garbage yards. If such garbage yards are not provided, people throw garbage wherever it is convenient for them."*[11] In the absence of proper

---

10. "The quantity of domestic and municipal solid wastes generated in some major cities of India is 300 - 600 grams per person per day. Since the quantity of waste generated depends on the affluence of the society, the per capita waste produced in India is naturally lesser as compared to that produced in affluent western countries. The amount being spent in municipalities in India for solid waste management is estimated to be 805 to 1200 million rupees annually which accounts for about 10% of their total budgetary provisions" **S.S. Dara.** Page 102

11. **N. Sheshagiri** in *"Pollution."* Page - 8.

arrangement for the disposal of solid wastes, each family is adding to land pollution in one way or another.

Solid waste, if allowed to accumulate, is a health hazard : Because it decomposes and favours fly breeding, it attracts rodents and vermin. The deadly bacterias present in the solid waste may be brought back to man's food through flies and dust. Heaps of refuse here and there present an ugly scene and a nuisance, and contribute to intolerable bad odours. Studies have revealed that there is a correlation between improper disposal of solid wastes and incidence of vector-born diseases. Therefore, in all civilised countries, there is an efficient system for the periodic collection, removal and final disposal of solid wastes without risk to health.

Irresponsible disposal of wastes leads to pollution of all kinds : The solid waste is typically disposed of by burying it in landfills, burning it, and sometimes even recycling it. In some cases, it is dumped into the ocean. Except for recycling, all of the traditional disposal methods create problems of air, land or water pollution. They also create potential public health risks and spoil the beauty of the land and seascape.

The Challenge of Waste Management is Now being Faced at the Global Level

The industrialised nations, with their higher standards of living, consumption and disposal face increasingly serious problems of waste management and control. All over the world, people throw away 1,000 crore tonnes of solid wastes every year. According to one estimate, *"All over the world, every year we throw away 15,000 crore cans and 8 crore tonnes of bottles and 15 crore tonnes of paper and plastic, creating larger and larger mountains of garbage whose disposal we are leaving to the future."*[12] What to do with this, and where to deposit this and how to get away from their evil effects ?? – These questions are haunting the environmentalists.

Causes or Sources of Solid Wastes

1. ***Domestic Waste or refuse*** which consists of ash [residue from cooking and heating], rubbish [including paper, clothing, bits of wood, metal, glass, dust, etc.] and garbage [consisting of waste food, vegetable peelings and other organic substances] also add to solid waste.
2. ***Street Refuse*** consisting of leaves, straws, paper and plastic pieces, animal droppings, and heaps of all kinds collected by the street cleansing agency, especially in the towns and cities.
3. ***Market Refuse*** that is collected from markets, consists of a large proportion of rotten vegetables, packing materials and animal matter.

Adverse Effects of Solid Wastes

(i) ***Solid wastes adversely affect animal and human life.*** The accumulation of the pesticides in the soil on the one hand, and the accumulation of tonnes of garbage on the other, pose a serious threat to our health. Such accumulations contaminate the plants and animals that are consumed by human beings. Human health is also endangered due to the diseases caused by heaps of the garbage.

(ii) ***Solid waste breeds diseases :*** Solid waste is posing a serious problem. Every cubic meter of garbage can foster about 750,000 flies, not to mention rats, mice, mosquitoes, cockroaches, etc. It becomes the breeding ground for disease-bearing bacteria. It spoils the landscape and devours our living space. Every passing day brings in more solid waste which cannot be destroyed easily. Today's industry is greatly contributing to this menace.

---

12. Whole or part of any captive wild animal preserved by natural or artificial means is called trophy. Rugs, skins, antler, horn hair, feather, nail, tooth musk, eggs and nests would also be called trophy.

(iii) An Unbearable Nuisance: Solid wastes, if not cleared regularly and properly, creates a big nuisance for the civilised people. Uncleared heaps of garbages in every corner of the city, in market places, near bus stands, railway stations, in narrow streets, near living houses, etc., not only spoil the beauty of any city but also invites plenty of health problems.

Strategy for the Management of OR Measures to Deal with Solid Waste

Management of solid waste would include the following four main strategy : (i) *Source reduction* (ii) *Recycling* (iii) *Treating or Composting* and (iv) *Disposal of Waste*

(i) Source Reduction: One of the successful methods of reducing waste generation is '*source reduction*'. Several practices such as two- sided copying of paper, back yard compositing etc. will result in the reduction of waste generation.

(ii) Recyling: Paper, glass, plastic & metals are sorted, collected and processed to manufacture new products. This *recycling* reduces water pollution, supplies raw material for industries and conserves resources for future.

(iii) ***Composting*** is the biological decomposition of organic wastes by microorganisms under controlled conditions. In the process of composting *a soil like material* is obtained which is highly fertile. Thus, organic solid wastes could be used for preparing manure. Composting reduces the amount of waste that ends up in land fills or incinerators.

(iv) ***Disposal of the waste*** is done either by *incineration - burning the waste at high temperature* or by *land fills* - the *treated wastes are filled into land.*

6. OTHER SOURCES OF POLLUTION

In addition to the above mentioned sources, there are also other sources among which the following may be noted: ***(i) pollution by pesticides, (ii) nuclear radioactive pollution, (iii) thermal pollution, and (iv) sea pollution.***

(A) NUCLEAR RADIOACTIVE POLLUTION

Radioactive pollution *results out of atomic radiation during which there is a spontaneous emission of particles [electrons] and rays [electromagnetic].* These radiations are invisible and penetrate living tissues.

Nuclear power plants are becoming one of the biggest sources of radioactive environmental pollution. The reason is that they produce a large quantity of nuclear waste. It remains radioactive for thousands of years. It cannot be stored without the risk of leakage. Developed nations dump the waste in the oceans in closed containers. Radioactive particles can get into the food chain and can create an extremely alarming situation.

Adverse Effects of Nuclear Radioactive Pollution

(i) High doses of *radiation can cause death.*

(ii) In lower doses *it can cause serious effects,* impairing the functioning of organic systems.

(iii) Repeated and long exposure can cause cancer.

(iv) Embryos of man and animals are highly sensitive to radiation. It has been observed that handicapped children were born to persons exposed to atomic radiation.

(v) The deadly and the disastrous effects of radioactive pollution could be found in atomic explosions. During the second world war, when America exploded the first nuclear device by dropping a bomb on **Hiroshima** [Japan] on 6th August 1945, more than 1,47,000 people were killed. The second bomb that was exploded on **Nagasaki** on 9th Aug. 1945 killed more than 67,000 people. In 1986, the leakage of nuclear reactor plant at Chernobyl [USSR] also caused the death of large number of people.

(B) POLLUTION BY PESTICIDES

Pollution is also caused by the use of pesticides in agriculture and also in our houses to destroy harmful bacteries, pests, insects etc.. Realisation of this fact has made many western countries including America to ban many types of pesticides like D.D.T., Endosulphan and so on. Awareness is slowly increasing among people to minimise the use of pesticides.

(C) THERMAL POLLUTION

- *Thermal pollution can be defined as the pollution of water bodies by the addition of hot water discharges.*
- *Industries and power plants use water to cool the machinery. After cooling, the hot waste water is discharged into the stream, river, lakes etc. threatening the acquatic life.*

Adverse Effects

(i) Increased temperature in stream or river water due to the addition of hot waste water, dissolved oxygen level of the water gets reduced. This leads to suffocation and even death of acquatic life.

(ii) Increased metabolic activities of animals such as fish decrease the life expectancy of animals leading to early death.

(D) MARINE OR SEA POLLUTION

Sea or marine pollution can be defined as the pollution of marine environment due to the direct or indirect introduction of substances arising out of human activities.

Main sources of marine pollution are - *(i) industrial effluents, (ii) sewage and domestic wastes* and *(iii) oil discharges*

Causes of Sea Pollution

(i) Untreated sewage and industrial effluents along with detergents are let off directly into the sea polluting sea water.

(ii) Untreated sewage and domestic wastes that are let off to the sea also damage the usual quality of sea water.

(iii) Accidential oil spills due to accidents of tankers and pipeline breakage also contribute to sea pollution.

Effects of Sea Pollution

(i) Poisonous chemical elements present in the sewage lead to the death of marine life.This causes depletion of marine biodiversity.

(ii) Pathogens found in industrial effluents and sewage, contaminate sea food, cause public health problems on consumption.

(iii) Oil spills in the sea prove to be deadly for the birds that feed on acquatic animals.

Preventive Measures

(i) Industrial effluents should be treated and processed and only then discharged.

(ii) The sewage should be treated in waste stabilisation ponds before being discharged to the sea.

(iii) Dumping of unwanted substances into oceans is to be regulated.

(iv) Ships and oil tankers are to be fitted with modern equipments so as to prevent oil spillage.

PREVENTION OF ENVIRONMENTAL POLLUTION

Environmental purification is the need of the hour today. Environmental purification means purifying the environment which has been polluted in various ways. Therefore, it refers to the prevention and control of environmental pollution through various measures. Like all other developing countries, India entered the area of environmental protection in the 1970s itself. It has taken some measures in the direction of stopping or reducing environmental pollution. Some of the legislative measures taken by the Government are worth mentioning here.

Constitutional Provisions to Protect Environment

The constitution insists that the protection of environment is the primary duty of the nation. **Article 21** of the constitution speaks of the *"Right to Life"*, and the Supreme Court in one of its judgements has stated that it applies to each and every living being.

- **Article 48(A)** of the constitution, gives direction to the states to protect environment. The states must safeguard their forests and animals.
- **Article 51(A) and 51(B)** say that state shall protect and preserve natural resources like forests, reservoirs, rivers and forest animals.

Governmental Efforts : Legistative Measures

1. In 1974, the *Water [Prevention and Control of Pollution] Act* was passed by the Central Government in order to prevent water pollution.
2. The *Air [Prevention and Control of Pollution] Act* was passed in 1981 with the intention of controlling air pollution.
3. At the state levels, the State Governments have also enacted water and air protection Acts and set up *State Pollution Control Boards.* These are strengthened by the formation of *Central Pollution Control Board* [CPCB] at the national level.
4. The CPCBs made a study of polluting industries and evolved guidelines to reduce pollution by introducing *Minimum National Effluent Standards* [MINAS] in respect of selected industries.
5. The Central Government has established the ***Department of Environment* - DOE** - in order to co-ordinate and integrate various schemes and projects which have been undertaken with an intention of preventing environmental pollution.
6. The Central Government has realised that the environmental protection and economic development of the country are closely related. Hence, it has started working in this direction as per the advices and suggestions given by the environmental scientists.

Major Legislative Measures Undertaken Since 1972

1972 The Indian Forest Act
1972 The Wildlife (Protection) Act
1974 The Water (Prevention and Control of Pollution) Act
1980 The Forests (Conservation) Act
1981 The Air (Prevention and Control of Pollution) Act
1986 The Environment (Protection) Act
1991 The Public Liability Insurance Act
1995 The National Environmental Tribunal Act
1997 The National Environment Appellate Authority Act Policies
1988 National Forest Policy
1992 National Conservation Strategy and Policy Statement on Environmental Development
1992 Policy Statement on Abatement of Pollution

Salient Features of Some of the Major Legislative Measures

1. The Wildlife Protection Act, 1972

The Wild Life Protection Act, 1972 emphasizes protection of wild and other animals within a broad ecological perspective. *Some salient features of this Act are;*

a) According to the provisions of the Wild Life Protection Act, every State Government shall constitute a *Wild Life Advisory Board.*
b) The Board provides for establishment of sanctuaries and national parks.
c) Formulates policies for protection and conservation of wild life.
d) Takes measures for hormonizing the need of tribals and other dwellers of forest with the protection and conservation of wild life.
e) Hunting of any wild animal is prohibited under Schedules I, II, III and IV.
f) Under Schedule IV, it is prohibited to pick, collect, damage or uproot specified plants.
g) Trade or commerce in trophies,[13] animal articles, etc. in Schedule I, part II of Schedule II are prohibited by law.
h) Dealing with trophy, ivory, captive animals or their meat are prohibited.

2. The Water [Prevention and Control of Pollution] Act, 1974

In 1974, the Central Government passed *The Water [Prevention and Control of Pollution] Act* in order to prevent water pollution and to maintain and restore wholesomeness of water. *Some salient features of this Act are as follows;*

a) Under the Act, the assessing authority levies and collects cess based on the amount of water consumed by the industries. The rate is determined by the purpose for which water is consumed.
b) Standard water meters are to be installed by industries in required places so that the concerned authority can measure and record the quantity of water consumed by industry.
c) The Act provides for 25% rebate on the cess payable to those industries which consume water within the quantity prescribed for that category of industries.
d) The industries have to comply with the effluents standards prescribed under *The Water Act or the Environment [Protection] Act.*
e) Aggrieved person may appeal against the assessment to the Apellate Authority.
f) Based on the cess returns furnished by industries every month, the amount of cess is assessed by the assessing authorities.

3. The Forest Conservation Act, 1980

The Forest Conservation Act came into existence with effect from October 25, 1980. *Salient features of the Forest Conservation Act are as follows:*

a) Prior approval of Central Government is essential for diversion of forest land for the non-forestry purposes.
b) Compensatory afforestation is implemented when forest land is allowed to meet the developmental projects such as power projects, defence related projects, railway lines, roads, mining, etc.
c) An authority named as *"Compensatory Afforestation Management and Planning Authority"* [CAMPA] is constituted to monitor the effective implementation of the compensatory afforestation.

---

13. Whole or part of any captive wild animal preserved by natural or artificial means is called *"trophy"*. Rugs, skins, antler, horn, hair, feather, nail, tooth musk, eggs and nests would also be called trophy.

d) *'The Ministry of Environment and Forests'* has set up a monitoring cell to look into the movement of proposals at various stages and the compliance of conditions stipulated for the forestry clearance by the user agencies.

4. The Air [Prevention and Control of Pollution Act, 1981

In line with the decisions taken at the ***United Nations Conference on the Human - Environment*** held in **Stockholm** in June, 1972, in which India participated, India enacted *The Air [Prevention and Control of Pollution] Act in 1981* with the intention of preventing, controlling and reducing the air pollution. According to the provisions of the Air Act, Central and State Pollution Control Boards are established.

Objectives of the Air Act - 1981

a) To prevent, control and reduce air pollution including noise pollution.
b) Setting up of *Central and State Pollution Control Boards* to monitor/ control the air pollution.
c) The person desirous of establishing / operating any industrial plant should get the permission from State Pollution Control Board in the prescribed form accompanied by the prescribed fees.
d) The specifications of pollution control equipment are to be installed by the industries as a prerequisite to obtain the consent from the board.

5. The Environment [Protection] Act, 1986

The Government of India enacted *The Environment [Protection] Act, 1986 [EPA]* under article 253 of the Constitution after the Bhopal gas tragedy.

The **EPA** is designed to provide a framework for Central Government to co-ordinate the activities of various Central and State Control Boards established under Water and Air Act. *Some salient features of this Act are;*

a) The Central Government may also put restrictions on an area in which any industry, operation or process shall not be carried out. If they are to be carried out, they may be permitted with certain safeguards.
b) Emission and effluent standards in respect of 61 industries have been evolved and is notified.
c) Industries identified as highly polluting, should achieve standard in respect of pollutants within a period of one year from the date of notification.
d) Environmental audit report is to be submitted to the concerned State Pollution Control Board on or before 30th September every year by those industries which require consent under Water Act, Air Act or both.

- **Other Major Legislative Measures Undertaken Since 1972**

1972 The Indian Forest Act
1988 National Forest Policy
1991 The Public Liability Insurance Act
1992 National Conservation Strategy and Policy Statement on Environmental Development
1992 Policy Statement on Abatement of Pollution
1995 The National Environmental Tribunal Act
1997 The National Environment Appellate Authority Act Policies

Issues or Problems Involved in the Enforcement of Environmental Legislation

The mere enacting of legislations is not sufficient for protection and conservation of environment. Only when these legislations are properly used, the environmental conservation is made possible.

Despite various environmental legislations being present, we are unable to achieve the desired results. This is because of some problems associated with the enforcement of environmental legislations. Some of them are:

a) ***Lack of Public Information:*** The general public is unaware of various rules and regulations of environmental protection. This is rendering the laws ineffective as people don't know what is to be done when they are observing environmental pollution.

b) ***Lack of Environmental Awareness:*** The general public is unaware of the various consequences of the pollution they are observing. This lack of environmental awareness is rendering the general public ineffective to protest against the environmental destruction.

c) ***Lack of Will for the Implementation of Environmental Laws:*** Among the administration and political leadership, lack of will for implementation of laws is observed. This is due to the political and money power used by the industrialists running polluting industries.

d) ***Lack of Environmental Sensitivity:*** Utter lack of environmental sensitivity is observed when the question of development v/s environment arises. Usually, the administration and political leaders choose development. This is hampering the implementation of environment protection laws.

PREVENTION OF ENVIRONMENTAL POLLUTION : *SOME SUGGESTIONS*

Pollution of our environment is increasingly posing problems for man's survival on earth. This has not happened in a day or two. Continuously we have been contaminating and damaging our environment. Man has been continuously ignoring *"the laws of nature"* and disturbing the ecological balance. Scientists and environmentalists have already warned about the impending tragedy of the continuous contamination of the environment **Dr. Einstein** said, *"All our technological progress – our very civilisation – is like the axe in the hand of the pathological criminal. So like pathological criminals we have mercilessly destroyed the forest and converted fertile land into desert."*[14] There should be a final stop for this creeping paralysis. We must think in terms of protecting our environment which protects us in turn. Some suggestions could be given in this regard.

Suggestions to Protect Environment

1. It is necessary to undertake an appropriate National Industrial Policy so as to protect our national interests including the environmental interests. It is a known fact that unregulated industrialisation has been causing environmental pollution. Hence, it is necessary to implement very strictly the National Industrial Policy.

2. Uncontrolled urbanisation is to be stopped. Urbanisation has been taking place in an unprecedented manner. Existing cities are growing and new cities are coming up. There is no regulation nor any control over the growth of the existing cities. These cities are spoiling the nearby environment. Only through proper regulations and control the unwanted effects of urbanisation on the environment could be stopped.

---

14. **Dr. Einstein** as quoted by **Biswanath Ghosh** in *"Contemporary Social Problems of India"* [1988]. Page - 95.

3. Owners of motor vehicles are to be instructed strictly to use pollution control gadgets. The use of these instruments can help to reduce pollution caused by vehicles.

4. The sewage system of the cities is to be revised. Sewage wastes let into streams, rivers, lakes and coastal waters are causing several problems. Hence, sewage water is to be purified before it is allowed to join rivers, lakes or coastal waters.

5. A separate arrangement is to be made to collect and transport the inorganic and non-degradable garbage wastes to a distant place. The unwanted inorganic substances like tins, plastic bags, boxes, bottles, etc. are to be deposited separately in the dustbins so as to help the municipal administration to collect and take it to a distant place. People should also learn to minimise the use of such things. The Government can also think of banning the use of plastic bags at least in some specified fields and areas.

Recycling Non-Degradable Materials **:** It is necessary to minimise the use of non-degradable materials. We must also make necessary arrangements to recycle and reuse discarded materials. People must extend their co-operation to organisations which recycle such materials.

6. Regular removal of the garbages. The municipal and city administrations must take steps to remove regularly the garbage, dust and other thrown away articles deposited in the dustbins. Only a few muncipalities are prompt in this task. People also should learn the art of depositing the garbage only in the dustbins and not throwing it everywhere.

7. Encouragement to conservation of forests **:** It is necessary to awaken the people about the importance of forests in preserving the purity of our environment. Appropriate steps should be taken to conserve the existing forests. Special efforts should also be made to develop gardens, parks, within the premises of hospitals, educational institutions, industries, government offices, etc. *"Vanamahotsava"* should not become a governmental ritual. There should be active participation of the people in it. *"Plant a tree before cutting one"* should become a meaningful and a practical slogan.[15]

8. Launching of "save environment campaigns and movements". Since sizeable number of Indians are still illiterate, it is necessary to educate them to keep the environment neat and clean. They must also be educated regarding the adverse consequences of pollution. A national level campaign or movement such as *"save environment"* could be launched with the active participation of political leaders, labour leaders, peasant leaders, student leaders, and leaders of various religious and cultural organisations. Whenever and wherever the safety of environment is threatened, the enlightened people of the affected area must make it a point to launch a *"save environment movement"* in order to arouse public awareness and to bring pressure on the government to take immediate steps to protect the environment.

9. A Special Care is to be Taken to Protect the Ozone Layer **:** Between heights of twenty and thirty kilometres from the ground the earth's atmosphere is covered by what is called the *"ozone layer."* A few kilometres thick, this layer is spread over the entire globe and shields all

---

15. ***Our Forest Area :*** As far as forests are concerned, they now comprise of about 64 million hectares, or about 19% of land area of the country. Roughly 33% of it represents primary forest. About 10 million hectares are managed as *"Protection Forests"* for ecological stability, 15 million for production of timber, and 25 million as social forest to meet the demand for the fuel wood and fodder. About 14 million hectares lie within national parks and wildlife sanctuaries. This forest area is to be preserved and expanded.

There are schemes to protect wildlife and its habitat : A wide network of 83 National Parks, 447 Wildlife Sanctuaries, 25 (+6) Project Tiger areas, 200 zoos and 8 Biosphere reserves have contributed towards conservation of these species. As per the Tiger Census carried out in the Tiger Reserves, the total number of tigers recorded was 3750. There are about 1500 to 2000 elephants settled in more than 15 states' isolated forest areas. They are under severe ecological stress. Because, more than 250 elephants have been killed in the past 3 years. The National Wildlife Action Plan adopted in 1983 provides the framework of strategy as well as programme for conservation of wildlife. ***Source*** : *Manorama Year Book* - 2002. Page - 592.

living things below from ninety-nine per cent of the sun's ultra-violet rays. Destruction of this layer could create a suicidal effect. It is, therefore, absolutely essential to protect the thin, sensitive ozone layer. Hence, it is necessary to ban S.S.T. flights,[16] stop atmospheric nuclear explosions [at present only France and China have stopped this], and ban aerosol containers [such as aerosol cans like hair-dye or perfume-spray containers].

10. Special Financial Assistance for Protecting the Environment. In our national budget there should be a provision for a special fund to give financial assistance to the local bodies to safeguard the environmental interests.

***11. Creating Environmental Awareness Among the Children*:** Special arrangements must be made to create environmental awareness among the children and the young people. Training given to the children in this direction at an early age especially in schools and colleges go a long way in creating awareness to protect the environment.

***12. Launching of Environmental Education Programmes* :** It is necessary to educate the people to take proper precaution to save our environment. A specialised body of the U.N.O. namely UNEP [*United Nations Education Programme*] has stressed the importance of such a kind of education long back in 1977.

• ***The Environmental Education Programmes should include the following* :** The print and electronic media can play a major role in spreading environmental awareness. Newspapers and televisions by highlighting environmental problems can create awareness among the general public. The environmental education programmes should include the following.

(i) ***Environmental education and training*** at school, college, and university level.

(ii) ***Environmental sciences,*** which deal with advanced science and its effect on air, water, and soil degradation.

(iii) ***Environmental engineering,*** which includes the study to assess the impact of engineering science on environment.

Some Examples of Environmental Movements in India

1. Silent Valley Movement represents a successful environmental movement that took place in Kerala in 1976 against the installation of a 240 Mega Watt Hydro-electric project on **Kuthipuzha** [a tributary of Periyar river] on the dense ever green forest region of Western Ghats. The Silent Valley of the Palghat area where the Hydo-electricity project was to be installed is a home to many rare species of plants and fauna which would otherwise have been destroyed by inundation. Due to the strong protest of the people, it was finally cancelled and people have celebrated the Silver Jubilee of their successful struggle in 2009-2010.

2. Narmada Bachao Andolan was another major environmental movement that took place in Gujarath demanding the proper rehabilitation of over 100,000 people being evicted for building ₹1,000 crore multipurpose project over Narmada river. The movement was led by **Baba Amte** and **Medha Patkar**. The Oct. 19th, 2001 decision by the Supreme Court allowing the Gujarat Govt. to proceed with the construction was a heavy blow. But the movement is still simmering.

***3. Successful Protest Against Cogentrix Company* :** Villagers, students, particularly Akhil Bharatiya Vidyarthi Parishad [ABVP] activists, and local environmentalists successfully fought against an American company namely "Cogentrix Company" which had obtained legal permission from the Karnataka Government to establish a hundred Mega Watt thermal power project at the cost of ₹4000 crores, in Nandikoor village near Mangalore [Karnataka]. The company was

16. ***S.S.T. aeroplanes*** are those that fly at speeds exceeding that of sound. S.S.T. is a source of pollution of the upper atmosphere.

legally and physically not allowed to start its construction work. Environmental scientists and the National Environmental Engineering Research Institute [NEERI] had cautioned against the establishment of such a big thermal project in this eco-sensitive coastal area of the Western Ghat.

4. Chipko Movement: A Unique Environmental Movement - 1973

The famous ***'Chipko Movement'*** represents the most sensational environmental movement spearheaded mainly by women and its message echoed and re-echoed in several parts of the world. It began in 1973 in the small hilly town of Gopeshwar in Chamoli District of Uttara Khand with a large participation of women.

The Hindi word *"chipko"* means "to cling to". This clinging to trees was a particular action especially used by women to save the trees which were crucial to their lives, from being felled by forest contractors.

Movement Guided and Led by Sundarlal Bahuguna and Chandi Prasad Bhatta: The movement began in two or three villages of Uttara Khand when the forest department refused permission to the villagers to fell ash trees for making agricultural tools. But the same forest department gave permission to a sports manufacturer to use trees of the same area for commercial purpose. This dubious policy of the forest department enraged the villagers and they protested against this decision of the Government. **Sundarlal Bahuguna** and **Chandiprasad Bhatta** inspired the people to fight against this decision of the government. The movement began. The struggle soon spread across many parts of Uttarakhand region. Larger issues of ecological and economic exploitation of the region were raised. The villagers demanded that no-forest-exploiting contracts be given to the outsiders and local communities should have effective control over natural resources like land, water and forests. They wanted the government to provide low cost materials to small industries and ensure development of the region without disturbing the ecological balance. The movement also took up the issues of landless forest workers and asked for guarantees of minimum wage.

By Hugging the Trees Women Could Save them from being Felled: When women joined the movement, its strength got doubled. When the wood cutters approached the forest, women put up strong resistance. Forest contractors had planned to neutralize men by supplying them alcohol. This did not deter the fighting spirit of women. By clinging or by hugging the trees women were able to save them from being felled at the hands of forest contractors.

Sustained Agitations by Women Fetched the Desired Results: Women held sustained agitations against the habit of alcoholism also and thereby broadened the agenda of the movement to cover other social issues. Local women leaders by name **Gowra Devi, Sudesha Devi** and **Bachadevi** were able to mobilize women in a relatively large number. The Chipko poet **Rathuri**'s eco-related poems were being sung and echoed in the whole of Himalayan region. The movement achieved a victory when the Government issued a ban on felling of trees in the Himalayan regions for 15 years, until the green cover was fully restored. Thus, it was the women of the Chipko movement who brought to public attention the importance of trees and the need to protect the environment. This incident became world famous for it was staged by uneducated and innocent rural women for the cause of environmental protection.

The Chipko Movement which started over a single issue, became a symbol of many such popular movements emerging in different parts of India during the 1970s and later.

Chandi Prasad Bhatt, the main architect of this movement was honoured with **"Roman Magsaysay"** award in 1982 while **Sundarlal Bahuguna**, the main inspiration behind this movement, was bestowed with the **"Right Livelihood"** award in 1987 and **"Padma Vibhushan"** in 2009.

III ROLE OF THE INDIVIDUAL IN THE PREVENTION OF POLLUTION

Protecting the environment and preventing pollution is not merely the task of the Government and the administration. Each and every responsible citizen has an important role to play in this regard. Hence, incorporation of proper pollution prevention measures in our daily life will go a long way in preventing pollution. Following are some of the ways by which every individual can contribute to lessen pollution.

1. Use of public toilets by citizens can prevent pollution.
2. Use of public transport or *carpool* (which means : 4 - 5 persons going to same destination using only one car for transport) definitely will reduce air pollution.
3. Active participation in reforestation programmes such as *Vanamahosthava* - Trees and shrubs reduce noise pollution and prevent soil erosion. Judicious use of artifical fertilizers as and when required only will help to prevent soil pollution.
4. By judicious use of insecticides and pesticides, water pollution and soil pollution can be prevented.
5. Taking proper care while disposing batteries containing lead.
6. Reuse and recycle of paper, glass, plastic & scrap metal
7. Making sincere attempt to use reusable shopping bags made of cloth.
8. Encouraging the use of organic manures which will automatically bring down the use of chemicals and insecticides.
9. In arranging public meetings, marriage programmes, conferences, etc., while travelling in buses and trains; and in making use of offices, public places, playgrounds, parks and public buildings, much care is to be taken to maintain cleanliness and to preserve environmental health.

By changing the way we use our resources, we can prevent pollution. **Mrs. Indira Gandhi,** the late prime minister of India, had told : *"Modern man must re-establish his unbroken link with nature and with life. He must again learn to invoke the energy and to recognise, as did the ancients in India centuries ago, that we can take from the earth and atmosphere only so much as one put back into them."*[17]

B. Some Environmental Issues and Problems

There is a close interaction between society and environment.The quality of our social life depends on the quality of the natural environment, and human actions have a direct impact on the eco-system.According to **L.F. Milbrath**(1989)., *"human actions have brought about more changes to the planet during last two centuries than changes to our planet from all causes over the course of the last billion years. It is estimated that the global economy has expanded more in the last 7 years than in the 10000 years since agriculture began."*[18]

Development with Dangerous Speed Threatening the Safety and Security of the Environment: The human species has prospered tremendously during these decades. Human population has increased on this planet and the technology is reaching new heights year after year.But these advances have come at a high price .Never before in history have human beings placed such high demands on the earth.This disturbing development is very much reflected in technological advance. Milbrath points out at this dangerous development which is threatening the safety and security of the environment in the following words:

17. **Mrs. Indira Gandhi** in her speech at U.N. Conference on Environment at Stockholm [Sweden] on June 14th, 1972 as quoted by **B.K. Sharma** and **H. Kaur** in *"Air Pollution"* [1993-94 Edition]. Goel Publishing House, Meerut. Page - 15.
18. *"Envisioning a Sustainable Society:Learning Our Way Out"*.-1989 as quoted by **M F Abraham** in *"Contemporary Sociology"*-page-256.

"The technology that enabled the unprecedented economic growth of the 20th century has had a dramatic effect on our natural resources. Global consumption of wood has doubled, paper use has increased six times, and the use of fossil fuels is up nearly five fold. Grain consumption has tripled, and fish consumption has increased five-fold. The resulting environmental stress includes shrinking forest and wetlands, eroding soil and coral reefs, pollution of international waters, collapsing fisheries, vanishing plant and animal species, and rising temperatures. Half the world's population lives on coastlines, rivers and estuaries, including rural people who rely on waterways for their livelihoods-fishing, transportation, communication, and irrigation for farmlands. Based on U.N.population predictions, by 2050 one in five people; is likely to live in a country with severe shortage of fresh water serious enough to threaten health and economic well-being[19].

Environmental Pollution : the Curse of Man-made Progress

Severe Shortage of Resources May Haunt the Future Humans: It is clear from the above, that the *necessary evil* of all man-made-progress is environmental pollution. The fragile balance of ecosystem has been disturbed by the commercial exploitation of natural resources for various human activities. Rapid industrialization and urbanization are leading to the degradation of environment. Increasing human population is extracting more and more of natural resources for its sustenance. This is the cause for rapid depletion of the exhaustible resources. If the situation is left unchecked, mankind may face a severe shortage of these resources in the near future.

Degradation of Environment is Proving to be Deadly and Disastrous: *For example,* due to man"s abusive use, an area nearly the size of Western Europe has lost most of its productivity. Another 2.25 billion acres, an area larger than Australia, has degraded requiring restoration .According to **Worldwatch Institute,** the loss of top soil would cause an annual decrease in grain production of 9 million tons. As we deplete precious natural resources and degrade the environment we also destroy its ability to rejuvenate itself. *For example,* scientists predict that the North Sea will be dead within the next few years .For thousands of years, it was able to absorb the filth of Europe's cities, but it also had the capacity to cleanse itself. Now the assault has become overpowering as European nations dump around 7 lakh tons of mercury,nitrogen, phosphorus cadmium, lead,and zinc into this sea every year.'[20]

Acute water shortage is going to haunt the human society very shortly : Industrialization and various human activities require enormous quantity of water. Increased water consumption is depleting the level of ground water very fast, making it unavailable for human consumption. Acute shortage of water is being felt in all major cities of the world. Dams and reservoirs are constructed to store surface and rain water to be used for domestic, industrial purposes and to generate hydroelectrical power. These vast areas of stored water regions are becoming the cause of loss of biodiversity of the areas where these structures are constructed. The resettlement and rehabilitation of people of the affected area is also becoming a major social issue.

All components of environment are polluted : The components of environment namely air, land and water are polluted by the addition of industrial wastes and various other human activities. The air we breathe, the water we drink and the land on which we live have been subjected to severe degradation making it unsuitable to sustain life. For example,every year,the industrialized West produces millions of tons of industrial and toxic waste and often uses the Third World as a convenient dumping ground. The U S A alone produces around 160 million tons of solid waste per year. *"The forests of the Pillipines, Thailand,Canada, and Malaysia are being destroyed to*

---

19. " Views of **Milbrath** [1989] as a quoted by **M.F.Abraham** in "Contemporary Sociology" 2008 page- 256-257.

20. A.F. Abraham - Page - 257.

fulfil Japanese needs...."[21]. Large number of animal and plant species that inhabit this area get eliminated about which scientists are worried.

The world heading towards a great environmental crisis : As a consequence, a grave environmental crisis is looming large at the mankind in the form of environmental pollution and its subsequent consequences such as *climate change, global warming, acid rain, ozone layer depletion, etc.*

If the situation is left unattended, the survival of mankind along with other life forms are at stake and it won't take too long for the life forms to perish from the face of the earth. Man has landed himself in the self-generated menace of environmental pollution. This environmental pollution / crisis is affecting all the individuals irrespective of caste, creed, religion, developed or developing countries. It has affected the entire social structure of the earth.

Every One has a Role and a Responsibility in Overcoming this Crisis: Thus, now tackling of this environmental crisis and conservation of life on earth requires the services of all people irrespective of their educational background. Active participation of all people is needed to overcome the environmental crisis. It has become a social issue and is to be fought by every single individual who aspires to live on this earth.

(B) SOME ENVIRONMENTAL ISSUES OF SERIOUS CONCERN

It is clear from the previous explanation, that our environment is facing some great challenges. It is a big irony that man is compelled to face these challenges which are his own creation. Of the major environmental issues that confront our mother earth, the following are to be noted.

(i) *Global warming or greenhouse effect,*
(ii) *Preserving rain forests,*
(iii) *Loss of or declining biodiversity, and*
(iv) *Water conservation.*
(v) *Depletion of ozone layer*
(vi) *Problem of acid rains*

1. GLOBAL WARMING OR GREENHOUSE EFFECT

Meaning of Global Warming

"Global warming" or *"greenhouse* effect" is one of the major concerns of the world today. According to the ecologists, *'global warming refers to a rise in the earth,'s average temperature to an increasing concentration of carbon dioxide in the atmosphere"*[22]

"Global warming is the phenomenon of a gradual overall increase in the average temperature of the Earth's atmosphere due to the accumulation of certain gases".[23]

The earth's atmosphere is made up of major gases namely; oxygen and nitrogen, and minor constituents such as water vapour and carbon dioxide. These gases play a crucial role in moderating the earth's temperature. This is because these gases are relatively transparent to incoming visible light from the sun, but absorb the heat radiation given of by the ground and other objects exposed to the sun. As a result, they produce a heating of the atmosphere by what is known as *"the gren house effect"*. Without the *"green house gases"* in the atmosphere and the resulting "greenhouse effect", the Earth's average surface temperature would be as low as - 20°c.

21. A.F. Abraham - Page - 258.
22. J.J Macionis in his **'Sociology'**-Page 594.
23. 'Q' series, Title No. 1, 'What' Pub: National Institute of Science Communication [CSIR]-(1996), Page: 43.

In other words, the atmoshpere has a natural supply of *"green house gases"*. These gases capture heat and keep the surface of the earth warm enough for us to live in. Without the greenhouse effect, the planet would be an uninhabitable frozen wasteland. **Joseph Fourier** the scientist who discovered this phenomenon of greenhouse effect, has warned the world about its dangerous consequeces.

The Relevance of the Expression "Greenhouse": Scientists very often use the expression *"greenhouse effect"* to imply *"global warming"*. Why this expression 'greenhouse' is used - is because of the simple comparision of the earth with a green house consisting of full of plant life. In a glasshouse the glas cover helps to preserve the inside heat. In the same manner, greenhouse gases capture heat and preserve it in the Earth surface. As a result, temperature of the Earth goes in increasing. This development is known as *global warming*!

Why This Global Warming? - The Causes

(i) Heavy concentration of carbon dioxide in the atmosphere is one of the strong reasons for this relatively new development of global warming. The quantum of carbon dioxide is mounting because of the decline and destruction of rain forests.

(ii) Destruction of Rain Forests: Rain forests cleanse the atmosphere of carbon dioxide [CO_2]. Due to industrialization, pollutants from factories, automobiles and other sources have risen dramatically. Much of this CO_2 is absorbed by the oceans. But plants take CO_2 and expel oxygen. This is why rain forests are very much needed for maintaining the chemical balance of the atmosphere. Destruction of the rain forests destroy this chemical balance leading to global warming.

(iii) Burning of Rainforests Further Adding to the Quantum of Carbon Dioxide: The problem that is being faced with is that at present production of CO_2 is mounting while the amount of plant life is shrinking. The problem is further aggravated due to the destruction of rain forests. Added to this, rain forests are being destroyed mostly by burning which releases even more carbon dioxide into atmosphere. As per the opinion of experts,the atmospheric concentration of CO_2 is 20 to 30% higher than what it was 150 years ago.

(iv) Abnormal Levels of Green House Gases Causing Problem: It must be noted that *global warming* or *green house effect* is a natural phenonmenon without which earth would not be warm enough for humans to survive. But when the levels of greenhouse gases [that is, carbon dioxide, methane, nitrogen oxides, ozone, chlorofluro carbons, water vapours] increase, the green house effect becomes stronger. As a result,earth's climate will become warmer than what actually is required. This situation is referred to as the problem of *'global warming'*.

1. Effects of Global Warming

1. ***Increase in temperature :*** Over the last century , the temperature has risen about 1.o Fahrenheit[to an average of 58°F]. Scientists have warned that it could rise by 5°F to10°F during this century. [21st century].

2. ***Melting of polar ice caps :*** Global warming has resulted in the melting of polar ice caps and raise in the sea level which would submerge the low lying land around the globe. Particularly, Artic's Polarice Ice cap is said to be declining at the rate of 9% per decade.

It is said that if the melting of the caps were to take place continuously, water would cover all of Bangladesh and much of the coastal United States, including Washington. A government study in America claims that one in four houses within 500 feet of a shoreline is in danger over the next 60 years.[24]

24. **Macionis** in his *"Sociology"* (2006) Page-594.

SOME SPECIFIC AND SERIOUS ENVIRONMENTAL ISSUES AND PROBLEMS

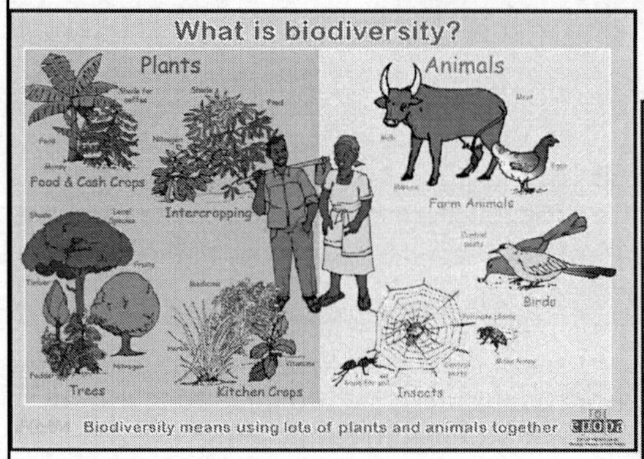

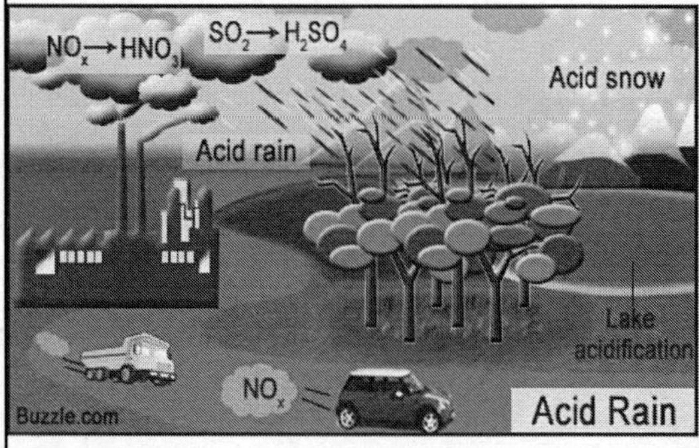

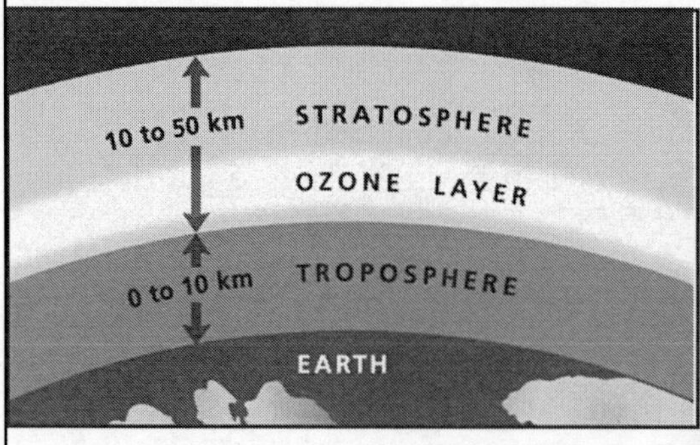

3. ***Disruption of the habitats :*** Warmer earth would cause disruption of habitats such as coral reefs and alphine meadows resulting in the extinction of many plant and animal species.

4. ***Linkage with the depletion of ozone layer :*** Depletion of ozone layer is linked with global warming and this linkage leads to an increase in human skin cancers and disastrous effects on plants and animals. It also leads to re-emergence of diseases such as cholera and viral fevers of the worst type.

5. ***Leads to global climate change :*** Global warming is considered to be a significant cause of global climate change. Human activity is dependent on earth's climate.Any change in the climate pattern is bound to affect human activities and the very sustenance of human life on this earth.

However, not all scientists share this vision of future global warming.Some say that global temperature changes have been taking place throughout history. Although there is some skepticism about the impact of global warming, there is mounting evidence that it is the planet's biggest environmental problem. The U.N. O. too has expressed its concern over this issue. Scientists are at work to find out a permanent and an effective solution for this problem.

2. THE TOUGH TASK OF PRESERVING RAIN FORESTS

Preserving the rain forests is yet another environmental issue. *Rain forests are regions of dense forestation most of which circle the globe close to the equator.*- **J.J Macionis.**

World's largest tropical rain forests are in South America,[notably Brazil], west central Africa and Southeast Asia. The world's rain forests cover an area of some **two billion** acres, roughly **7%** of the earth's total land surface.

Unfortunately, like other global resources, rain forests are falling victims to the needs and appetites of the surging world population. The demand for grazing land,hardwood,and crop land,as well as the construction of huge reservoirs has led to a large scale destruction of forests. *For example,* just to meet the demand for beef, ranchers in Latin America, burn forest areas to increase their supply of grazing land. The forests of the Philippines, Thailand, Canada and Malaysia are being destroyed to fulfil Japan's needs. Almost one billion trees are cut down every year to provide disposable diapers for babies. There are nearly 40,000 huge dams and countless smaller dams around the globe. Though, these dams provide for lot of benefits,they also lead to unmitigated evils.They also mean huge displacement and submergence of vast tracts of land, often precious forest land. We are also losing rain forests to the hardwood trade.

Logging, mining, grazing agriculture,industrialization and urbanization have altered the terrestrial and aquatic habitats affecting very badly the ecosystem. As the demand for food increases, the destruction of forests takes new proportions. "*At the current rate of destruction, the rain forests will disappear by the end of the next century. India has only 2% of the forest and the continuous loss of tree cover and top soil, has led to droughts and floods*"[25]. Indeed, the world's rain forests are now just half of their original size and continue to shrink by 65000 square miles every year. Unless we stop this loss,the rain forests will vanish within a few decades and in such a situation,giving protection for the earth's biodiversity becomes impossible.

3. LOSS OF, OR DECLINING BIODIVERSITY

What is Biodiversity - ?

Living and enjoying life on earth is not the whole and sole contract of man alone. Nor the living world is created for man only. Nature's creation is not only beautiful and wonderful but also diverse. Innumerable animal and plant species, birds, insects, microbes etc. co-exist in it.

---

25. A.F. Abraham - Page - 259.

Thus, *"The sum total of all living plants, animals and microbes is what is called biodiversity".*[26]

- *"The existence of a wide variety of species animals and micro-organisms in a natural community or habitat..."* can be called *biodiversity.*[27]
- ***In simple words,*** *biodiversity refers to diverse forms of life or species such as birds, plants and animals.*

What is Meant by Loss of Biodiversity - ?

Though nature is bountiful in creating millions of living species, many of them are fast disappearing during the recent years. It means the world is witnessing the extinction or destruction of some living species. This development is referred to as the *'loss of biodiversity'*. It has become a serious environment related problem.

Loss of Biodiversity - The Result of Human Activity: With the advent of civilisation, for various reasons this biodiversity which is the gift of nature is fast declining due to human intervention. Declining biodiversity is one of the serious environmental issues or problems which requires immediate attention. Destruction of rain forests also reduces the earth/s biodiversity because rain forests are home to almost half this planet's living species. Man himself is responsible in many of the cases for the reduction of this biodiversity.In his hunt for new articles of fancy, man began to kill birds and beasts, not to improve his living standards but to satisfy his ego and fancy.Some bird species,for example, became almost extinct because they had beautiful feathers with which wealthy women wanted to adorn their hats.

A Problem of Great Environmental Concern: The problem of declining biodiversity is assuming new proportions today because thousands of species of plants and animals are being lost each year due to wars, pests, diseases, climate change ,urbanization, the global marketing of exotic breeding material, and large scale industrial agriculture. On our mother earth, there are as many as 30 million species of animals,plants, and micro-organisms. But several dozen unique species of plants and animals cease to exist every day. A question arises as to why man should bother or worry about the loss of these species when the number of living species is vast. Environmentalists list some important reasons in defence of the need for protecting biodiversity.

Importance of or the Need for Protecting Biodiversity

It is an acknowledged fact that 'biodiversity' is a great gift of nature and hence it has to be protected. In the best interests of the coming generations of humanity, biodiversity is to be preserved and protected. There are genuine reasons for that among which the following ones may be noted.

1. ***Biodiversity provides for vast and varied sources of food :*** Using agricultural high technology,scientists can 'splice' familiar crops with more exotic plant life, making food more bountiful. Biodiversity is needed to feed our planet's rapidly increasing population. Over 10000 varieties of wheat used to be cultivated in China, and the Philippines had thousands of varieties of rice. [Abraham - Page: 260] Even in South India, several varieties of paddy were there a few decades ago. Now there are only a few varieties left. In many countries, the increasing demand for meat,eggs,milk, rice, wheat,etc..has forced producers to abandon many local breeds in favour of an increasingly limited number of high producing livestock and plant variety. In India,a new movement called *Navadhanya movement* has taken birth to respond to the loss of biodiversity by protecting local varieties of wheat rice and other crops.

---

26. Q-Series, Title No.1, What-?, Page: 8.
27. Oxforod Dictionary of Science (2006), Page: 87.

2. ***Biodiversity is highly helpful for medical and pharmaceutical research :*** Biodiversity is a vital genetic resource. Medical researches lead to the invention of hundreds of new compounds each that cures diseases and improves our lives. Scientists are testing tens of thousands of plants for their medical properties.,and many medical and pharmaceutical industries depend on animal and plant diversity in their search for new drugs.

For example, children in the U.S now have a good chance of surviving leukemia,a disease that was almost a sure killer two generations ago. A new compound derived from a tropical flower called the *rosy periwinckle* has proved to be a panacea for leukemia. Similarly, the oral birth control pill is another product of plant research involving Mexican forest yam.

3. ***Loss of biodiversity limits the beauty and the complexity of our natural environment :*** It is a matter of regret that the Chinese Panda, California condor, the spotted owl, a particular variety of ant, are diminished. There are clear warning signs of such loss from many corners of the world. It is said that ¾ of the world's 9000 species of birds are declining in number.The little sparrows, for example, which were very commonly found in almost all towns and cities of India, a few years ago are not to be seen now. T v cables, antennas, mobile towers,have proved to be disastrous for their survival.

Biodiversity is significant for it appears as though it is impossible to think of the world without the Bengal tiger, Chinese panda, Australian kangaroo, the African giraffe or the magnificent African and Indian elephants. Nature would become poor in its beauty if its species start disappearing one after another.[28]

4. ***Extinction of species is irreversible :*** Loss of biodiversity is a permanent loss.Unlike environmental pollution ,the extinction of any species is irreversible and final.An ethical question comes before us. *"Do we, who live today, have the right to impoverish the world for those who live tomorrow ?"*

4. WATER CONSERVATION

Water conservation is yet another environmental issue. Without water life and growth cease .Water is essential for agriculture, industry and domestic purposes. At the global level, agriculture uses about 65% of all water removed from rivers, lakes natural tanks and wells for human activities compared with 25% for industries, and 10% for households and municipalities. It is assessed that 1000 tonnes of water is needed to produce a single tonne of harvested grain.

Shortage of water due to population growth : The worldwide consumption of water estimated at about 5 billion cubic feet per year, has tripled since 1950. Further, it is expanding faster than the world's population. At the present rate of population growth, about 3 billion people, or roughly about 40% of world population, will experience the pinch of shortage of water supply by 2015.

Unmitigated Pollution of Water Resources : Due to heavy population growth, fresh water resources would become the target of exploitation everywhere.This kind of unlimited exploitation leads to immeasureable effects. Ground water mining may lead to variety of evil effects. In coastal areas, overpumping can cause salt water to invade fresh water resources by contaminating the supplies. This has occurred in Gujarath. Ground water depletion can also reduce the earth's natural capacity to store water. Some cities in India dump untreated sewage and partially cremated bodies into the rivers. Industrial wastes, pesticides and herbicides enter the water ways through dumping. Such pollution sometimes causes massive fish kills.

28. *Wide variety of fresh water species are on the verge of extinction today: "About 12% of animal species, including 41% of all recognised fish species, live in 1% of the earth's surface, that is, fresh water. According to experts, at least 1/5 of all fresh water fish species have become extinct, threatened, or endangered in recent years, and entire fresh water faunas have disappeared."* - **A.F. Abraham** in *'Contemporary Sociology'*, Page - 260.

Two Important Issues : It is clear from the above, that two issues are relative to water : 1) *conservation of water* and 2) *cleansing of water ways.*

(i) Conservation of Water

The need for conservation has arisen due to over exploitation of surface water and rapid decline of ground water. This situation necesitates the need to renew the water conservation methods followed by our ancestors and to invent new innovative methods to conserve water.

- The purpose of water conservation is *to recharge the depleting ground water and to collect and use rain water for various purposes.*

Two Methods of Conservation : There are two important methods of water conservation. They are -*1) rain water harvesting; and 2) watershed management.*

- **Rain water harvesting** is the conservation technique of collection and storage of rain water in the rainy season for use during dry period.This could be done in two ways :
  (i) Collection and storage of water in tanks and reserviors for direct use; and
  (ii) Storage of rain water in sub surface rocks so as to recharge the ground water.

• **Watershed Management** *can be defined as an area of land from which rain-water drains out to a common point.* It can occur in all shapes and sizes. The watershed that drains into rivers measures thousands of hectares whereas the watershed that drains into a pond or pool measure only a few hectares.

(ii) The second issue relates to cleaning up of the waterways

As per the requirements of this issue, measures are needed to prevent further pollution of the source of water. Intentional dumping of chemicals, pesticides, industrial wastes etc. must be stopped, proper action plan is required to clean up the river and restore water quality. *The Ganga Action Plan* launched in 1985 is an example in this regard. Indian Prime Minister Narendra Modi [2014] is taking special interest in cleaning the Ganga river and he has set up a separate Ministry for this purpose which has already started its work.

5. OZONE HOLE OR OZONE LAYER DEPLETION

Appearance of *ozone hole* or *depletion of ozone* layer is relatively a recent development of great environmental concern. It is one of the problems associated with environmental pollution.

What is Ozone Layer?

Ozone layer is a deep layer in the *stratosphere*[29] encircling earth at the height of 10km – 50km. It has a large amount of ozone in it. The layer shields the entire Earth from much of the harmful ultraviolet (UV) radiation that comes from the sun. The presence of this layer protects the living organisms, including humans, by absorbing the high energy ultraviolet radiation of the sun.

In the 1980s, the thinning of this layer was first observed over Antarctica by the scientist **Farman**. He also observed a hole in it. This was referred to as the **"ozone hole"**. A similar hole also appeared over the North Pole.

How this Hole is formed?

The hole is formed by destruction of ozone molecules by certain man-made substances. Ozone which is a form of oxygen can be destroyed easily by certain man-made chemicals.

29. **Meaning of Stratosphere :** Above the surface of the earth, there is atmosphere. This atmosphere is divided into different regions. In the lowest region of atmosphere, there is what is known as ***'troposphere'***. Cloud formation, thunder, lightning and thunder storm formation take place in this region. Next to the troposphere there is ***stratosphere***. Clouds are absent in this region and ozone formation occurs here. Temperature increases upto 900° centigrade due to ozone formation.

Causes of Ozone Layer Depletion

(1) Thinning of ozone shield which has led to a hole is caused by a number of pollutants such as chlorofluorocarbons [CFC]. The CFC is commonly used as refrigerants and as propellant in spray cans.

(2) Other pollutants such as nitrogen oxides, halogen, carbon tetrachloride, methyl chloroform also contribute to the depletion of ozone layer.

(3) A large number of rockets fired into space are emitting chlorine which leads to the way for the depletion of ozone layer. *It is known that a single chlorine atom is sufficient to convert or destroy about one lakh molecules of ozone.*

(4) Nitrogen oxide released by the jet into the stratosphere also reacts with ozone to form oxygen. This chemical reaction destroys the ozone layer.

Effects of Ozone Layer Depletion

1. Thinning of ozone layer or a hole in it allows harmful ultraviolet (UV) rays emited by the sun to reach parts of the earth. As a result, skin cancer is caused.
2. Over exposure to UV radiation *suppresses the bodily immune system.* This increases susceptibility to *herpes* and high incidence of *cataract.*

Regarding the Protection of Ozone Layer

1. To create awareness about the adverse effects of ozone layer depletion in general public, the **'World Ozone Day'** is observed on the **16**th of **Sept**ember every year.
2. An international agreement called the **'Montreal Protocol'** was signed by over 30 nations to limit the production and use of ozone depleting substances.[30]

6. ACID RAIN

What is Acid Rain?

Acid rain is one of the issues associated with environmental pollution. It is a phenomenon caused by industrial pollution. *Acid rain is rain that has been made acidic by certain pollutants in the air.*

- *The precipitation of water in the form of rain, snow, and dew having a pH of less than about 5.0 is called acid rain.*
- *Acid rain is rain that is usually acidic. In other words, it is rain that has high levels of Hydrogen ions [low pH].*[31]

The Process of Causation of Acid Rain

In a simple way, it could be said that acid rain is caused when gaseous compounds of ammonium, carbon, nitrogen and sulphur are released into the atmosphere. The wind carries the gases high into the sky. There the compounds react with water in the atmosphere and acids are made.

Causes of Acid Rain

Large scale burning of coal or oil in industries, power plants and vehicles produce large amounts of gases such as sulphur dioxide, nitrogen oxides etc which are released into the

---

30. ***Ozone Hole is Filled in-?:*** Newspapers flashed the news in June 2014, that the Ozone hole is filled in by the nature itself on its own, and there is nothing to worry about it for the time being. However, scientists are yet to confirm this news - **Author**.

31. Meaning of pH : pH refers to the expression of acidity level of a solution measured as per the pH scale. **Source :** *Oxford Dictionary of Science*. Page: 602.

atmosphere. These gases under favourable conditions react with water vapour and oxygen in the atmosphere to produce sulphuric and nitric acids which eventually come down with rain, snow or fog. *This we call acid rain.*

People started producing acid rain gases when they started establishing factories and power stations. These units burn coal or oil and this causes acid rain gases. Automobiles which release nitrogen oxides into the atmosphere also add to the acid rain gases.

Adverse Effects of Acid Rains

(a) Effects on Vegetation

- Studies have shown that acid rains cause considerable damage to vegetation, trees and marine life.
- Increase in the acidity of the soil results in the leaching of essential nutrients. Hence, plant growth is adversely affected for it is deprived of the needed nutrients.

(b) Effects on Aquatic Life

- Acid rains poison rivers and lakes. Fish and other aquatic animals cannot live in acid water
- Acid pollution of the soil also leads to acidification of water draining from the soil into lakes and rivers. This damages the fish life very badly.

(c) Effects on Buildings and Monuments

- Acid rain corrodes metals, marble, stone, slate, painted surface, jewellery, etc
- Many of the world's oldest and most famous historic buildings, monuments and statues have been spoiled due to corrosion caused by acid rain. This phenomenon is often called *'stone cancer'* or *'stone leprosy'*.

Acid Rain – A Problem of International Concern also !: As the gases responsible for acid rains are often produced in one country and acid rains fall in another country damaging its flora and marine life, it has become a cause of concern to all countries.[32]

TOWARDS A SUSTAINABLE DEVELOPMENT

Increasing human population and human activities such as industries, agriculture, etc., are putting enormous stress on the ecosystems. The natural resources are depleting at a faster rate to satisfy increasing human needs. The natural process of formation and replenishment of resources is becoming insufficient to meet the rate at which it is being removed. Besides this, addition of pollutants into the environment is leading to the environmental degradation. Human health is getting affected by the environmental degradation and as a result, economic productivity is decreasing. Unless this pattern of unsustainable development is not checked, fine balance between ecosystems will be destroyed and human survival on the face of the Earth appears bleak.

These aspects have led the mankind to think of a particular type of develoment known as *"sustainable development"*.

Meaning of Sustainable Development

- **M.F. Abraham** : *"Sustainable development is the process which effectively balances the needs of development with concerns for the health of the environment"*.[33]

---

32. **Source of Matter :** *Internet, Oxford Dictionary of Science, "What?" - Q. Series, Title No-1. one of the books in the question series published by 'National Institute of Science Communications CSIR' – 1996.*
33. **M.F.Abraham** in *"Contemporary Sociology"*, Page: 261.

- **J.J. Macionis :** *Sustainable development denotes ecologically sustainable culture. Ecologically sustainable culture refers to a way of life that meets the needs of the present generation without threatening the environmental legacy of future generations'.*[34]

Characteristics of Sustainable Development

Some essential features of sustainable development [S.D.] as pointed out by **M. F. Abraham**[35] may be noted here

1. Sustainable development is characterised by economic and social growth that does not exhaust the natural resource of the host country.
2. It respects and safeguards the economic, the cultural, and natural environment.
3. It involves grass roots participation and builds indigenous institutions.
4. It is nurtured by eco-friendly policies and programmes.
5 Development becomes sustainable only when it permanently enhances the capacity of a society to improve its quality of life.
6. Sustainable developement requires greater attention to develop human potential in areas such as education, health and food security so as to achieve total wellbeing of the population.

The U.N.O's Insistence on Sustainable Development

The U.N.O which is very much concerned about the necessity of sustainable development [S.D.] sponsored two world summits to draw the attention of its member nations towards the pressing environmental issues. These summits are......

(i) *The Rio-Conference on Environment and Development-1992*

(ii) *The Johansburg World Summit On Sustainable Development-2002*

In these summits, the U .N .O encouraged the governments to become partners with N.G.Os and private industry to make a courageous commitment to apply S.D principles wherever it is possible.

"The Times" Expresses its Concern Over the Issue

The concern expressed by the *'Times'* paper in the special issue[Aug-2002] is worth mentioning here: *"With 6.1 billion people relying on the resources of the same small planet, we are coming to realize that we are drawing from a finite account. The amount of crops, animals and other biomatter we extract from the earth each year exceeds what the planet can replace by an estimated 20 percent, meaning it takes 14.4 months to replenish what we use in 12-- deficit spending of the worst kind. Sustainable development works to reverse that, to expand the resource base and adjust how we use it so we are living off biological interest without ever touching principal.*- **Time** special issue(Aug. 2002)[36]

Strategies of Sustainable Development

Successful implementation of the principles of S.D depends on some strategies among which the following may be noted[37].

34. **J.J.Macionis** in **"Sociology"**-595.
35. **M F Abraham**-page-261.
36. **M.F. Abraham**, page- 261.
37. **J J Macionis** in his **Sociology'** page -595 to 596.

1. Population Control : The world needs to bring population growth under control. The present population of more than 6 billion is already a big burden to the natural environment. Of these 6 billion people, two billion people lack dependable access to safe and nutritious food. About 800 million of them, including 300 million children, are deplorably malnourished. This situation implies clearly,the higher the world's population climbs the more difficult environmental problems will become. At the present rate of growth, the world will have 8 billon people by 2050. Most of the analysts argue that somehow or the other we must hold the line at about 7 billion. Some others argue that we must decrease population in the coming years to enjoy the benefits of S.D.

2. Conservation of Finite Resources : The second important strategy is conservation of finite resources. This stresses the need to look wih a responsible eye towards the future by using resources efficiently.This also encourages nations to seek alternative sources of energy, and in some cases,learning to live with less quantity of resources. *Example,* it is now predicted that nearly 2/3 of the world will face acute water shortage by 2025. Further, agriculture accounts for almost 2/3 of the fresh water consumed. It is in this context,the U.N has called for a *'more crop per drop'* approach based on efficient irrigation techniques. Rain water conservation and watershed management seem to be two important water protecting techniques as per S.D principles.

3. Reducing Waste : Preservation and conservation principle demands lesser use and minimum or optimum exploitation of resources.Whenever possible,simply using less is the best solution. Recycling programmes too can be a part of this effort. Dangerous effects of deforestation are very well known. *For example,* at present, 36 million acres of forest are destroyed annually and more than 10000 species of plants and animals are threatened with extinction.Minimising the use of wood and developing new forests could be the solution in this regard.

4. Search for Alternative Resources : Resources that are traditionally and continuously being tapped, are fast decreasing in quantity. Hence, there is the need for searching alternative resources which is possible in some fields. *For example,* the global demands for energy are met by burning fossil fuels such as oil, coal, and gas which release more carbon dioxide and other green house gases. The principle of S.D demands the use of cheaper,cleaner and renewable sources. *Wind and solar power ,for example, can be harnessed very efficiently. At the same time, small communities may be encouraged to set up micro-hydro- electric plants from streams and rivers.*

Conculsion

In the end, it may be noted that strategies alone cannot work for themselves. Making all these strategies work, depends on a more basic change in the way we think about ourselves and our world. *Our ego-centic outlook has to be transformed into eco-centric outlook.* Such an outlook helps us to see how the present is tied to the future and why every one must work together.

It is a fact that most nations in the southern half of the world are *underdeveloped* for they are unable to meet the basic needs of the people. At the same time, most countries in the northern half of the world are *overdeveloped,* using more resources than the earth can sustain over time. The changes that are needed to create a sustainable eco-system will not come easily, nor automatically, and they will be costly. But if such changes are not brought about, the humanity will be forced to pay a much greater price later.

Whatever be the discussion in this regard, "*The programme of sustainable development includes the following: use of indigenous technology, grass roots participation in development, eco-friendly agriculture with organic manure and crop diversity, rain water conservation, recycling waste materials, use of renewable source of energy such as solar and wind power, saving rain forests, minimizing all types of pollution, and preservation of biodiversity*"[38].

38. M.F.Abraham in "*Contemporary Sociology*", Page-262.

In conclusion, we may say that environment and development are not antithetical. Those who profess and advocate the idea of protecting the environment and yet scorn and mock at the goal of developcnt, only undermine both the causes. Both are equally necessary.' *But development that takes little account of sustainability is ultimately self-defeating. Prosperity built on the despoliation of the natural environment is no prosperity at all, only a temporary repreive from future disaster. The issue is not environment vs.development, or ecology vs.economy; the two can be integrated. Nor is this a question of rich vs.poor, both have an interest in sustainable development.* **"Time"** – magazine in its August 2002:19 issue.- as quoted by **M.F. Abraham,** in *"Contemporary Sociology"*, Page 262.

●●●

Chapter 25

ILLITERACY

Literacy and Education - How to Define Literacy ? - The Problem and the Magnitude of Illiteracy in India - Causes for the Widespread Illiteracy - Measures for the Eradication of Illiteracy : National Adult Education Programme - Rural Functional Literacy Programme - National Literacy Mission - Total Literacy Campaign - Literacy Position in India - 2001 Census Highlights - National Policy on Education [NPE]: 1985-86 - Issues Related to Primary Education - Directive Principles of State Policy and Primary Education - Importance of Primary Education - Problems of Universalisation of Primary Education - New Strategies and Schemes for popularising Elementary Eduction-Educational Problems of the Disadvantaged Groups : Educational Problems of Women - Causes for the Low Educational Status of Women - Strategies to Improve Women's Participation in Education - Educational Problems of the OBCs, SCs, and STs - Measures Adopted to Increase and Extend Educational Opportunities for them - Progress of Education in India : A Brief Mention of Educational Institutions of India.

LITERACY AND EDUCATION

The 1948 United Nations *Declaration of Human Rights* stated that everyone has a right to education. Yet, even today, this right is being denied to millions of children. Education is a crucial element in economic and social development. Without education, development can neither be broad based nor sustained. The benefits that accrue to a country by having a literate population are multidimensional. *Spread of literacy is generally associated with modernisation, urbanisation, industrialisation, communication and commerce.* It forms an important input in the overall development of individuals enabling them to comprehend their social, political and cultural environment better, and respond to it appropriately. Higher levels of education and literacy lead to greater awareness and also contribute to improvement of economic conditions and is a prerequisite for acquiring various skills and better use of health care facilities.

How to Define Literacy ?

How is literacy defined ? Who is literate and who is illiterate ? Generally, a person who can read and write, is regarded as *"literate"*. But the *Census Commission of India, 1991* made the definition of literacy specific. It was decided in 1991 Census to use the term literacy rate for the population relating to seven years of age and above. ***A person is deemed as literate if he or she can read and write with understanding in any language.*** A person who can merely read but cannot write is not considered literate. Further, formal education in a school is not necessary for a person to be considered *"literate."* The same concept has been continued in census 2001 and also 2011.

The significant milestone reached in the census 2001 is that the total number of illiterates has come down from 403.29 million in 1991 to 355.54 million in 2001. Thus, for the first time since independence, there is a decline in the absolute number of illiterates in the country. This is a major step forward in improving the literacy status of India. The trend continued in the decade 2001-2011 further reducing the number of illiterates to 314.12 million in 2011. ***Table*** **- 1** shows the literacy rates from 1951 to 2011.

When the first census was conducted in the year 1951, that is, after independence, only **18%** of the people were found to be literate and this figure has increased to **74%** in 2011. In the time span of 60 years [From 1951 to 2011], the percentage of male literacy has increased from 27 to 82.1; while the percentage in the case of females has increased from 10 to 65.5. In 1951, only one woman out of 10 was literate, but in 2011, 2/3 of the total number of women in India are found to be literate. [See Table-4] This increase in literacy is really substantial one, though not revolutionary.

Table - 1

Literacy Rates in India – 1951 - 2011

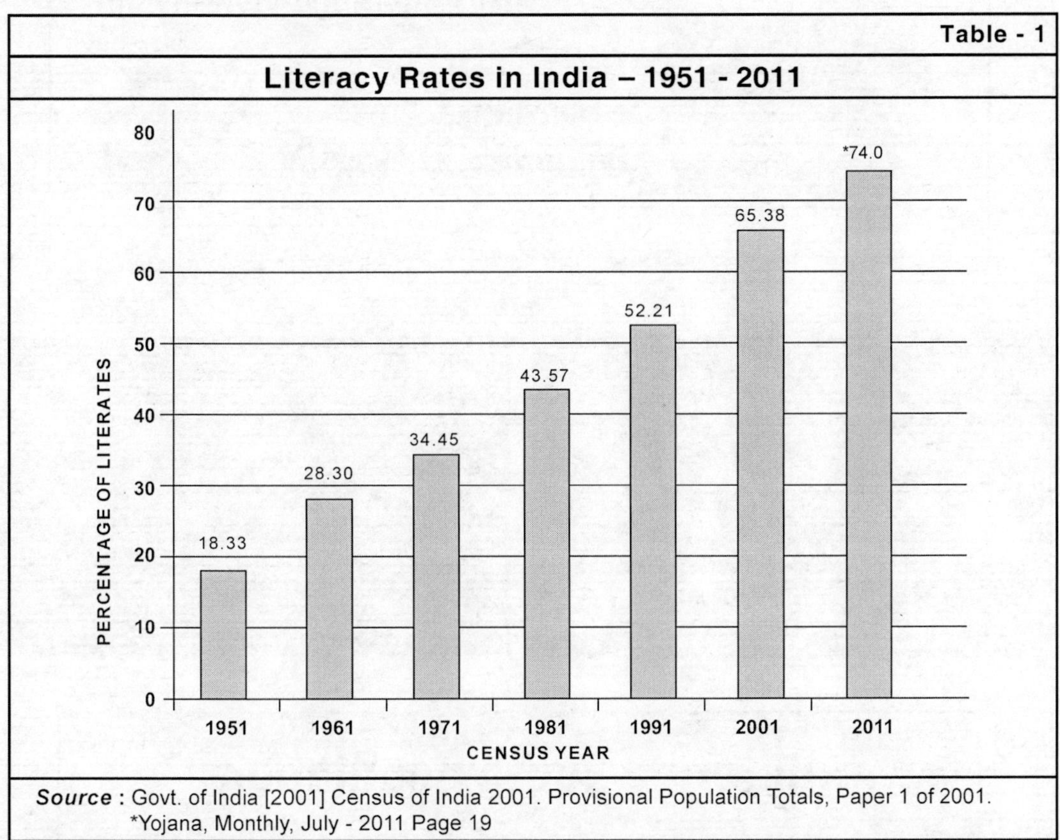

Source : Govt. of India [2001] Census of India 2001. Provisional Population Totals, Paper 1 of 2001. *Yojana, Monthly, July - 2011 Page 19

But the national average of literacy rate is misleading as wide variations exist between the states. ***Table*** **- 3** shows the literacy rates in different major states in India. The literacy rate has improved radically since 1991 census but there is a clear difference between literacy rates among males and females. The national percentage of literates in 2011 in the Indian population above 7 years of age is about 74%, with literate males about 82.1% and females lagging behind with about 65.5%.

Kerala continues to occupy the top rank in the country with about 93.91% literates. Mizoram [91.58%] and Lakshadweep [92.28%] closely follow Kerala. At the other end, is Bihar with 63.82% and Jharkhand with literacy rate of 67.63%. The states which have literacy rates below the national average are Arunachal Pradesh, Andhra Pradesh, Bihar, Jammu & Kashmir, Punjab, Chhattisgarh, Uttar Pradesh, Rajasthan, M.P. Orissa and Jharkhand.

MASSIVE ILLITERACY - A MOCKERY OF OUR PROGRESS

INDIA has the highest number of illiterate adults

That is **39%** of all illiterate adults worldwide.

= four times the population of FRANCE

Illiterate youth population

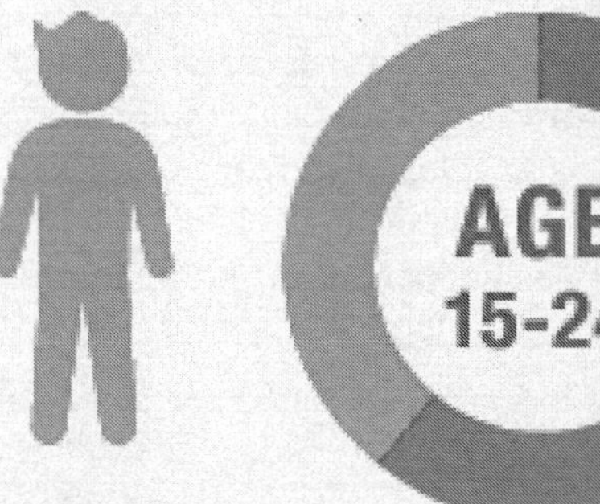

39% are boys

61% are girls

Table No. : 2

The Position of Literacy and Illiteracy in India from 1951 to 2011								
Year	Total Population in Millions	No of Literates in Millions	No of Illiterates in Millions	% of Literates	% of Illiterates	% of Literate Men	% of Literate Women	Decadal Difference in No of Illiterates in Millions
1951	361.1	66.19	294.91	18.33	81.67	27.16	8.86	-
1961	439.2	124.3	314.90	28.30	71.7	40.40	15.34	+19.99
1971	548.2	188.66	359.54	34.45	65.55	45.95	21.97	+44.64
1981	683.3	297.72	385.58	43.57	56.43	53.45	28.46	+26.04
1991	843.9	440.61	403.29	52.21	47.79	64.13	39.29	+17.71
2001	1027.0	671.46	355.54	65.38	34.62	75.00	54.00	-47.75
2011	1210.02	895.9	314.12	74.04	25.96	82.14	65.46	-41.42

Source : Collection of Statistics from Different Sources.

PROBLEM AND THE MAGNITUDE OF ILLITERACY IN INDIA

In the whole world largest number of illiterates are found in India. Even up to 1991, there were as many as 403.29 million illiterate people in the country and the total percentage of literacy for the whole nation stood at 52.1%. Though by 2001 the number of illiterates in the country came down to 355.54 million, it is not a small number. It is however, further reduced in 2011. Out of the total population of 1210.02 million in 2011, about 895.9 million people are literates, and the remaining **0314.12 million** people still continue to be illiterates. Long before independence, illiteracy in India has been regarded as one of the greatest obstacles for development. It is a fact known to everyone that India cannot achieve expected progress without eradicating or at least reducing substantially the extent of illiteracy. No nation in the world has attained high level of advancement in science and technology or in agriculture, industry, trade or commerce without achieving substantial rate of literacy. Hence, education in general, and the spread of literacy in particular, will have to be given high priority in the development process of our country.

CAUSES FOR THE WIDESPREAD ILLITERACY

Various factors contributed for the widespread illiteracy in India among which the following may be noted.

1. Foreign Conquests **:** Incessant foreign conquests of India particularly by the Muslims and later by the British gave a fatal blow to the educational system of India. The British Government wanted an army of clerks to run their bureaucracy. Their interest in educating Indians was mostly limited to produce that army of clerks. They were not interested in enlightening the masses through education. Hence the educational policies pursued by these colonial rulers were highly non-conducive for the spread of literacy in India.

2. Exploited State of Affairs of the People **:** Due to the total exploitation of the resources of India by the British during their rule, Indians had become poor. In the absence of material prosperity, and in the condition of their exploited lot, they could not pursue their educational endeavour. Thus, illiteracy started spreading its tentacles everywhere in India.

3. Neglect of Education **:** India was overwhelmed by the extremes of poverty at the time of its independence and hence educational sector failed to become a priority issue. Spread of literacy was neglected for several years, particularly during the first seven plan periods. Money that was earmarked for education was negligible. For example, the Government spent on the much publicised adult education programme, from the First Plan to the Seventh Plan, ₹ 5 crores,

Table - 3

Percentage of Literacy Rates in Major States of India – 2011

State	*Male Literacy Rate*	*Female Literacy Rate*	*Total Literacy Rate*
Uttar Pradesh & Uttaranchal	71	44	58
Bihar & Jharkhand	62	35	49
Rajasthan	76	44	61
Madhya Pradesh & Chhattisgarh	77	51	64
Haryana	79	56	69
Assam	72	56	64
Gujarat	80	59	70
Orissa	76	51	64
Maharashtra	86	68	77
Punjab	76	64	70
West Bengal	78	60	69
Karnataka	76	56	67
Andhra Pradesh	71	51	61
Tamil Nadu	82	65	73
Kerala	94	88	91
India	**76**	**54**	**65.38**

Source : Govt. of India [2011] Census of India 2011. Provisional Population Totals, Paper 1 of 2011.

Table - 4

Percentage of Literacy Rates Among Males and Females in India : 1951 - 2011

Year	Persons	Males	Females
1951[1]	18.33	27.16	8.86
1961[2]	28.31	40.40	15.34
1971	34.45	45.95	21.97
1981[3]	43.56	56.37	29.75
	(41.42)	(53.45)	(28.46)
1991[4]	52.21	64.13	39.29
2001[5]	65.38	75.00	54.00
*2011	74.04	82.4	65.46

Source : ***Manorama Year Book*** -2010, and Yojana, July 2011.

1 Excluding the population of J & K, Pondicherry and NEFA, D.N. Haveli and G.D. and Diu.

2 Excluding Goa, Daman & Diu, NEFA.

3 Excluding Assam.

4 Excluding J & K.

5 *Yojana July - 2011

Not A Single Literate Person in 10% of the Families in India - 2011

- **Total No. of families in the country:** **24.88 crore**
- Families having **Not a Single** literate person: 2.42 crore
- Families having **Only One** literate person: 3.09 crore
- Families having **Two** literate persons: 5.14 crore
- Families having **Three** literate persons: 4.65 crore
- Families having **Four** literate persons: 9.56 crore

Urban Literacy: 84% Rural Literacy: 68%

Source : Census of India 2011. As published in 'Udayavani' Kannda Newspaper Date: 24/11/2014.

6 crores, 8 crores, 18 crores, 128 crores and 160 crores respectively. This was very meagre for a vast country like India wherein crores of illiterate adults were there.

4. Lack of Educational Awareness Among People : Indians lacked very badly an awareness regarding the value of education. Hence, millions of people remained illiterate throughout their lives. Only recently, that is, after 1990s, educational awareness has been slowly spreading among the people.

5. High Rate of Population Growth: The population of India has been continuously increasing since decades. Independent Indian Government did not take proper steps to spread literacy among the growing population. As a result, in addition to the already existing adult illiterates, millions of newly born individuals also had to join the army of illiterates. Since there was no great thurst on education, our primary schools proved to be ineffective in enrolling children and in retaining those who had joined schools.

6. *Prevalence of Child Labour and the Provision of Poor Educational Facilities* : A large number of children [11.28 millions, according to 1991 census] are still working as child labourers. As per the statement of Central Labour Minister in the Rajya Sabha on March 20th 1995, their number was 17 million [9.5ml boys and 7.5ml girls]. Uneducated rural people consider education as a luxury item, an unproductive venture. They prefer to send their children as labourers for earning a few rupees than to learn at school as students. Heightened poverty on the one hand and widespread unemployment on the other, deterred many parents from sending their children for schools. Being in a state of economic misery, they could hardly realise that education of their children could deliver them economic prosperity in future. Though this tendency is slowly changing today, it maintained its grip for over 50 years.

Facilities given to children at schools are also disappointing. Schools without trained teachers, proper buildings, drinking water and toilet facility, play ground, blackboard, furniture, etc. present only a horrible picture. School environment failed to attract children towards education.

7. ***Indifference of the Government Servants and Lack of Community Spirit on the Part of the People*** have also added to the widespread illiteracy found in India.

MEASURES ADOPTED FOR ERADICATING ILLITERACY

Education is not only an instrument of enhancing efficiency but also an effective tool of augmenting and widening democratic participation in the country. It is also a means of upgrading the overall quality of the individuals and society. Before 1976, education was the exclusive responsibility of the states. The Constitutional Amendment Act of 1976 included education in the Concurrent List. Now education is a joint responsibility of the Centre and the State. While the role and responsibilities of the states in education remained the same, the Union Govt accepted a larger responsibility of reinforcing the national character of education maintaining its quality and standard. It is also observing and studying the educational requirements of the country.

• ***Huge Increase in the Budget Allottment for Education:*** As per its commitment of augmenting resources for education, the Central Govt has been increasing its budget allottment for education. The plan outlay on education during the First Five Year Plan was only ₹ 150 crore. It increased to ₹ 269,873 crore in the 11th plan [2007-2012]. Out of this allocation, ₹ 84943 crores, is for the Dept. of Higher Education, and ₹ 184,930/- crores is for the Dept of School Education and literacy. In the approved Annual Plan outlay for the year 2009-10, ₹ 9600 crores is for Higher Education and ₹ 26,800/- crore is for the Department of School Education and Literacy.

The spread of literacy is of vital importance for achieving progress in all the spheres of life. Hence, appropriate steps are to be taken up for the eradication of illiteracy. As far as the Government of India is concerned, it has adopted over the years, three important measures in this direction, namely; (i) *National Adult Education Programme;* (ii) *Rural Literacy Programme;* and (iii) *National Literacy Mission [NLM].*

(i) National Adult Education [NAE] Programme - 1978

This programme represents a joint and collaborative effort of the Central and State Governments, UT administrations, voluntary agencies, universities, colleges, and youth centres. Having the main aim of providing education and promoting literacy among all illiterate persons, particularly in the age group of 15-35 years, the programme was launched on October 2, 1978. The programme laid special emphasis on the education of women, SCs, STs, and other weaker sections in India.

***International Literacy Year* [I.L.Y.] - 1990 :** In order to generate public awareness about the need for the relevance of literacy, the UNESCO declared the year **1990** as the *International Literacy Year.* In India also, the Prime Minister launched the I LY at Delhi on 22 Jan. 1990 in which he gave a call to the student and non-student volunteers to plunge themselves to the task of spreading the message of literacy throughout the nation.

(ii) Rural Functional Literacy [RFL] Programme - 1986

The RFL programmc was launched as a sub-programme of the *Adult Education Programme* in May 1986. The programme which was fully funded by the Central Government, was implemented by the States and UTs. The programme was designed to involve the NSS and other student volunteers in colleges and universities on the principle of *"Each One Teach One"*. Its broad objectives are : (i) *to develop abilities in the learners to read and write,* and (ii) *to create awareness among learners about their rights and duties and the benefits that they can obtain from various schemes of socio-economic development which the Government launches from time to time.*

The RFL programme which was launched in 1986 included in the beginning 2 lakh volunteers and the number went up to 4.50 lakhs in 1990 covering over 4.10 lakh learners. Under this Programme, the Government undertook another venture in 1987 to involve both students and teachers of schools and colleges to spread literacy among the illiterates keeping in view the needs and languages of the learners. To begin with, the Government selected only 50 districts to improve the quality of adult education. Only after considering its impact, the Government intended to extend it to other areas to spread literacy in the minimum possible time.

(iii) National Literacy Mission [NLM] - 1988

The NLM was launched by the then Prime Minister in May 1988 to achieve the goal of imparting *"functional literacy"* to 80 million illiterates in the 15-35 age group. It intended to make 30 million literates by 1990 and an additional 50 million by 1995. This was also designed to involve the youth and voluntary agencies in the programme. In 1990, there were 513 projects in operation in various States and Union Territories.

Eradication of illiteracy plans and programmes launched by the Government did not yield much results. But things started improving especially after 1991. The number of illiterates came down considerably.

Total Literacy Campaign [TLC] - 1988-89 - First in Kerala

Illiteracy eradication programmes launched by the Government did not yield any satisfactory results even up to 1991. On the contrary, the number of illiterates went on increasing from one census to another. At the beginning of the year 1991, there were as many as 328.10 million illiterates in the country. The NLM launched in the year 1988 did not achieve its targets. This made the Government to formulate a new strategy for the spread of literacy. The spread of literacy campaign now came to be known as ***"Total Literacy Campaign."*** It consisted of the following :

(i) Closure of Adult Education Centres [AEC]

(ii) To introduce radical changes in the scheme of financial assistance to voluntary agencies for adult education

(iii) To organise "Total Literacy Campaign" in selected places

(iv) To make the district collectors as the personnel in charge of the TLC.

The State of Kerala was selected for starting this campaign to achieve total literacy. The trial began in 1988-89 with the help of the NSS [National Social Service] units of the Mahatma Gandhi University in **Kottayam Municipality** area. Within 100 days the city was declared as the first total literacy city of India. Due to the initiative taken by the *Kerala State Sahitya Parishad* [KSSP] another similar campaign was organised in Ernakulam district. The District Collector who was the Chairman of this campaign sanctioned the sum of ₹80 lakhs and the campaign was also a success. As a result, in 1990, Ernakulam was regarded as the first Total Literacy District in India. The example of Kerala inspired South Kanara [Dakshina Kannada] in Karnataka, Burdwan in West Bengal, Union Territory of Pondichery, Sindhudurg in Wardha in Maharashtra which in due course achieved [almost near] total literacy.

Total Literacy Campaign now covers about 401 districts in the country. Now the concentration is on the Hindi-speaking States of U.P., M.P., Rajasthan and Bihar where millions of illiterates are found. The campaign covers around 163 districts out of a total of 200 districts in these states. Though the main aim is to achieve 80-85% literacy in these areas, the report of the achievement is not that encouraging. In the absence of a well equipped adult education project of a permanent nature with proper infrastructure at the local level, the campaign may not fetch the desired result in the fixed time limits. That was the experience of the TLC.

Literacy Position in India : 2001 Census Highlights

After a very long time after independence an impressive rise in the literacy rate has taken place, that is, from 52.21% in 1991 to 65.38% in 2001. The salient features of the increase in the rate of literacy in 2001 can be noted below.[1]

1. As per 2001 census, 75% of males [that is, 339,969,489 males] and 54% of females [that is, 226,745,947 females] are found to be literate in India. This brings down the gap between male-female literacy rates from 28.84% in 1991 to 21.70% in 2001.
2. Kerala has maintained its lead in the literacy level. But its annual growth rate dropped to 0.90 in this decade [1991-2001].
3. Tamil Nadu registered an annual growth rate of 1.06% and Andhra Pradesh 1.30%.
4. Highest rate of literacy is found in Kerala, that is, 90.92% whereas Bihar recorded the lowest literacy rate of 47.53%.
5. At the national level, more than 203 million people including 95.6 million females turned literate in the decade 1991-2001 and the total number of illiterates in the country came down to a little over 296 million [which includes 190 million females].

1 ***Source :*** *Manorama Year Book* - 2002. Pages : 74 - 75.

6. There are 56.67 crore literates in India which include 33.99 crore males and 22.67 crore females.
7. Of the four major Hindi-speaking states of U.P., M.P., Bihar and Rajasthan, significant improvement in male literacy is reported from Rajasthan followed by M.P. In female literacy, Chhattisgarh occupies the first place, with an increase of 24.87% during the decade ending 2001, followed by Rajasthan.
8. A very interesting finding in the field of literacy is increase in female literacy at a faster rate than male literacy rates in all States and Union Territories except Dadra and Nagar Haveli.
9. Of the various states, U.P. has the highest number of illiterates [57.8 million] followed by Bihar [34.9 million] and Andhra Pradesh [25 million]. Bihar, probably is the only state where we find an increase in the number of illiterates, both male and female, during the decade 1991-2001.
10. Of the southern states, Andhra Pradesh has the least literacy rate, that is, 61.11% which is below the national average. Almost one-third of its population is illiterate. Kerala has the literacy rate of 90.92% followed by Tamil Nadu 73.47% and Karnataka 67.04%.
11. *For the first time after independence, the absolute number of illiterates has shown a decline. The decline is as large as 31.96 million during 1991-2001 which includes 21.45 million males and 10.51 million females.*

National Policy on Education [NPE] - 1985-86

In 1980s the Central Government showed great interest in bringing about some important changes in the system of education. Hence, it expressed its eagerness to formulate a *New Educational Policy* for the country. The **119** page document namely *New Educational Policy* [NEP], prepared by the *Ministry of Human Resources Development* was presented to the Parliament in Aug. 1985. The NPE was however, announced in 1986. This Policy laid much emphasis on matters such as the following : (i) *reorganising the educational system,* (ii) *improving the quality of education,* (iii) *promoting national integration,* (iv) *inculcation of moral values,* (v) *stressing the importance of science and technology,* and (vi) *to develop good citizenship qualities in the younger generation.*

The NPE - 1986 contained many proposals among which the following may be noted:

1. Introducing throughout India one common form of educational structure consisting of 10+2+3 years of study.
2. Implementing adult education programme and also vocational education.
3. Imparting value education.
4. Increasing teachers' responsibility and accountability.
5. Delinking degrees from jobs.
6. Bringing about reforms in examination system.
7. Giving importance to sports, games and physical education.
8. Extending equal educational opportunities for women, SCs, STs and OBCs.
9. Redesigning of the higher education courses to suit to the needs of the society.
10. Launching of open university system.
11. Encouraging technical and management education and introducing agriculture-related courses.
12. Promoting technological research.
13. Providing more resources to implement effectively universalisation of elementary education and adult literacy.

14. Making provision for access to education to all the students irrespective of caste, class, religion, or sex.

Critically commenting on this NPE-1986, **Dr. N. Jayaram**[2] writes : *"As far as education is concerned, we are already on the threshold of the 21st century. We educate now to reap the benefit 20 years hence. Any measure to change the educational system should therefore be in tune with the vision of a society that we would like to create. This vision must essentially be a politico-ethical one, and not just a demographic or technical one. Among other things, this vision has to take into account such issues as appropriate technology, developmental priorities and strategies, national income and wage policy, and a definition of a minimum standard of life. We now have an opportunity to debate on "the desirable society" and work out strategies for realising it. If we let this opportunity pass, we may well be faced with a similar situation in the year 2001 discussing another document prepared by another set of bureaucrats."*

ISSUES RELATED TO PRIMARY EDUCATION

Directive Principles of the State Policy and Primary Education

It is increasingly being recognised that education is one of the pre-requisites of social change and social development. All the modern countries have placed high premium on education. India, soon after its independence took great interest in education. The Constitution makers had foreseen the importance of education and accordingly through the 45th Article of the Constitution insisted that India should introduce free and compulsory education before 1960. Independent Indian Government had also shown great enthusiasm to provide compulsory and free education for all boys and girls between the ages 6 and 14.

Insistence on the Compulsory Primary Education by the Directive Principles of the State Policy of the Constitution **:** The Directive Principles of the Constitution of independent India [Article 45] emphatically stated in 1950 : *"The state shall endeavour to provide, within a period of 10 years from the commencement of the Constitution, for free and compulsory education for all children until they complete the age of 14 years."* **The Kothari Commission** in its report [1964-66] had also insisted that free and compulsory education should be provided as a matter of state policy for all the children below 14 years. **The National Education Policy - 1968** in its resolution had also laid down that universalisation of primary education was the need of the hour. It also laid down the time limit [1988] for the introduction of such a policy. The 7th Five Year Plan extended this time limit to 1990.

Emphasis Laid on Compulsory Primary Education by the National Policy on Education 1986: The National Policy on Education - 1986 which highlighted the importance of universalisation of primary education reiterated its resolve that *"by 1995 all children would be provided free and compulsory education up to 14 years of age."*

IMPORTANCE OF PRIMARY EDUCATION

The Government of India by resolving and repeatedly reiterating its resolve to provide elementary education to all the children below 14 years free of cost, has implicitly recognised the *"public good"* of the nature of primary education. All educationists, social reformers, statesmen with farsightedness have stressed upon the importance of primary education especially in the underdeveloped and the developing countries. It is in this context *the importance of primary education may be briefly examined here* :

2 **Dr. N. Jayaram** in his book *"Sociology of Education in India"* writes in the concluding paragraph under the title *"New Educational Policy : A Critique"* [Pages : 225 - 226].

(i) The contribution of primary education to all the spheres of development – social, economic, industrial, agricultural, commercial, scientific, etc. – is significant. In fact, *it provides the general basis for the overall development of the society.*

(ii) *Primary education has its own intrinsic value,* it enhances human capabilities to enjoy life, instils better habits in the individual, and develops in him a new approach to life so that he can improve the quality of his life.

(iii) Primary education is a significant component of human capital. *It is an essential instrument of economic development at personal level* for it enhances the productivity of labour force in the labour market. Studies have revealed that labour force with primary education, more than doubles its earnings in comparison with the illiterates. It has also been estimated that primary education enhances individual earnings at least by 20%.

(iv) *Primary education has also several non-monetary benefits.* It changes the habits of the people, makes them ready for changes, prepares them to accept challenges, and equips them to adopt new methods of farm / industrial practices of production.

(v) The World Bank in its 1993 report stated that *"On the national economic front, primary education is found to contribute to miracles in transforming nations from poor underdeveloped societies to rapidly developing or industrialised tigers."*

(vi) *In the developing countries, primary school education is enabling the whole population to do things they would never have been able to do before.* Literacy helps them to read labels on cans, bottles, tins, to read signboards, newspapers, birth control leaflets, small booklets containing information about new crops, new ways of cultivation, etc., and also to move around the strange town or city independently. These events though look very simple, definitely lead to changes.

(vii) *Primary education is also found to contribute towards the improvement of health.* People are able to understand the need for maintaining good health and seek modern medical advice whenever the health is upset. The awareness of health has led to an improvement in the rates of child survival and life expectancy.

(viii) *Primary education is a big boon for women.* It has elevated their status and made them to play a responsible role at home. They have realised the importance of family planning measures and hence insist on their menfolk to have small family.

(ix) *Primary education contributes to reduction of fertility rates* by indirectly increasing the rate of participation of women in labour force. It has created awareness among men and women regarding the minimum age for marriage. It makes them to adopt better approaches to family planning and development and thereby reduces population growth.

(x) Primary education *is of tremendous importance in the process of socialisation of young children.* It helps the parents to resort to modern approaches to bring up the children.

(xi) Universal primary education is of great importance in yet another manner. *Universal access to education can reduce class, caste and social status barriers to individual advancement.* It can help to equalise earned incomes by educating people and leading to the mobility of people from one status to another, and from one area to another.

(xii) *Primary education creates political awareness among people and helps them to take a greater participation in the political process.* This helps wider distribution of power and enables people to develop greater tolerance towards others.

(xiii) Primary education in general, *helps people in their effective participation in social, cultural, political and economic spheres of development.*

PROBLEMS OF UNIVERSALISATION OF PRIMARY EDUCATION

To attain 100% literacy, it becomes mandatory for any nation to introduce the policy of universalisation in a strict manner. This is not an easy task for the underdeveloped and the poor countries. The experience of the developing nations like India, is also not very much different from it. In spite of Governmental insistence on the compulsory introduction of elementary education, it has not been successful in its efforts. In 1970-71, there were as many as **4.8 lakh** primary schools in the country in which around 57 million students [76.4%] were admitted. The number of schools increased to **5.7 lakhs** in 1991, and the number of students admitted in them also increased to **108.2 million**. Still it was not 100%. The percentage of enrolment at the primary stage had gone up to 92.14% in 1998-99 and around **31.80 lakh teachers** were teaching in primary and upper-primary schools.[3]

Various problems come in the way of effectively implementing the policy of universalisation of primary education. The main problems are : (i) *shortage of budgetary allotment,* (ii) *shortage of essential facilities in schools,* (iii) *problem of admission of students,* (iv) *problem of drop-outs.*

1. Shortage of Budgetary Allotment

In an over-populated country like India, providing for educational facilities for the children of educable age, is a very expensive task. It requires huge fund, judged purely from the economic point of view, money that is spent on education, is unproductive for it yields no immediate results. Only in the long-run it fetches immense wealth. The Government which was more interested in immediate returns, naturally showed its indifference towards education. This is reflected in the poor budgetary allotment it made towards education. In comparison with other countries, for example, India spent just 3.6% of its total annual budget on education in the year 1981, whereas during the same year America spent 19.9%, Japan 19.6%, France 17.8%, Canada 17.3%, Russia 11.2% of their respective annual budgets. More details are given in ***Table* - 5.**

Table - 5

Percentage of Budget Spent on Education [1981] in Some Selected Countries

	Country	*Budget Spent on Education*	*Literacy*
1.	U.S.S.R.	11.2	98.5
2.	U.S.A.	19.9	99.5
3.	Japan	19.6	99.0
4.	England	13.9	99.0
5.	France	17.8	97.0
6.	Australia	14.8	98.5
7.	Canada	17.3	99.0
8.	Germany	10.1	99.0
9.	**India**	**3.6**	**36.2**
10.	Pakistan	2.1	20.7
11.	Bangla Desh	2.1	25.8
12.	Sri Lanka	3.5	86.5
13.	Burma	1.6	65.9
14.	Nepal	3.0	23.3
15.	Bhutan	1.9	18.0
16.	Singapore	N.A.	84.2
17.	Egypt	5.5	68.6

Source* : Myron Weiner** [1991], *The Child and the State in India,* Princeton University Press, p. 159, and ***Frontline, April 27 - May 10, 1991, p. 55.

3 ***Source* :** *Manorama Year Book 2000.*

It is clear from the above, that the attainment of the goal of universal elementary education seems to be very difficult with this meagre fund being spent on education.

Change in the Attitude of the Govt Since the Year 2000 : The Central Govt. however, has started giving more importance to education especially after the year 2000 which is even reflected in its budgetary allottment. *For example,* the Govt. had allotted ₹ 1,52,847 crores for education for the year 2004-05 and it was virtually doubled [₹ 3,72,813 crores] in 2009-10, that is, within five years. The Govt has reserved nearly 45% of its total educational budget to primary school education.

The Govt also doubled its budgetary allottment to **"Sarva Shiksha Abhiyan" [S.S.A.]**, that is, for example, from ₹ 7156 crores in the year 2005-06 to ₹ 15,000 crores in the year 2010-11. It is a matter of pity that many states have failed to make use of this central aid given to them for promoting primary education. *For example*, Bihar could make use of only 51% of the grants released by the Centre in the year 2009-10 for this purpose. Chattisgarh and Uttarkhand have miserably failed in this regard. States like Rajasthan [89%] and West Bengal [74%] have taken the maximum advantage of this grant. The Central Govt is ready to increase the quantum of its financial help if a particular state [like Bihar] is poor and seeks more fund for this purpose. It is an irony that states are not properly equipped to make use of this fund.

Relatively Highter Allotment in 2012-13 Central Budget : In the Central Budget introduced in the Parliament on 16th March 2012, the Govt had earmarked 21% higher grants over the previous year for promoting compulsory education. Similarly, it allotted ₹ 25,555 crores for the S.S.A., and proposed to provide primary education to 19.2 crore children. It also decided to reserve ₹ 11000 crore to provide mid-day meal to the children in the school.Govt's concern regarding elementary education seems to be increasing now a days.

2. Shortage of Essential Facilities in Schools

The population in India is increasing at a fast rate and we have not been able to provide for the educational facilities for all the people newly born. Thousands of villages in India do not have schools. The existing schools do not have good buildings, proper blackboards, chalk-pieces, furniture, toilet facility, playground, library, drinking water facility, etc. Only a few schools have permanent buildings. Many do not have any permanent structure. Hence classes are held in temporary tents, open fields, under the shades of trees, in huts, in the corridors of some temples, etc. As the NEP document [1985] itself pointed out *"Forty percent [of the schools] have no pucca buildings, 39.72% have no blackboards, and 59.30% have no drinking water. 35% schools have a single teacher to teach three or four different classes."* [Page - 35][4] However, things have comparatively changed since them.

Example of Karnataka **:** ***"Dr. M. Nanjundappa Commission"*** in its survey report [2002-2003], has stated that out of 983 *Primary Schools* [1st to 5th standards], which it surveyed on a random basis, 817 schools [83%] do not have electricity supply; 857 schools [87%] do not have toilet facility; 692 schools [70%] do not possess even drinking water facility and 622 schools [63%] do not provide playground facility for their children. Same story repeats in the case of *Higher Primary Schools.* Of the 1510 schools surveyed, 651 schools [43%] do not have electricity; 741 schools [49%] do not possess drinking water facility; 935 [62%] do not have toilet; and 666 schools do not have sufficient space for their students to sit comfortably in the class-rooms.

4. **NEP document** as quoted by **N. Jayaram.** Page - 217.

Educational surveys conducted in various States have also revealed that in most of the States there is a great dearth of school teachers. There are schools in which there are no teachers. There are a number of single-teacher schools in which one person is forced to handle four / five classes in spite of the relatively good strength of the students. Many teachers are not ready to go to rural areas for service. Even if they are forced to go and serve them, they do not go to the schools and take classes regularly. Lack of service-mindedness and commitment to the cause of teaching on the part of the teachers has also added to the indifference of the children towards joining schools for education.

3. Problem of Admission of Students

It is true that over the years education is becoming more and more popular. *For example,* the number of pre-primary schools has gone up during the period from 1961 to 1998 by about 21 times [from 1909 to 40553]. During the same period, the strength of primary schools has almost doubled [from 3.3 lakhs to 6.107 lakhs]; of the middle / senior schools, it increased by 3.5 times [from 49663 to 1.85 lakhs]; of higher secondary schools by about **6** times [from 17,257 to 107,200 and so on].

This increase in the number of the student strength does not assure that all the children of the school-going age are going to schools. Children belonging to SCs, STs and poor sections, especially in the rural areas are not going to schools in an expected number. In rural areas of the States such as Assam, M.P., Orissa, Bihar, Rajasthan, and U.P., the rate of admission of children of school-going age was less than 80% in 1982-83. On an average, in 1984-85 at the all-India level, the admission of male children to school was around 90% and the percentage of female children was 66.2. The atmosphere of admitting children compulsorily to schools as soon as they attain the age of eligibility [that is, 5 year 10 months], is not there in many States. Attempts to motivate the parents to send their children to schools have not been completely successful in many places and in many States.

4. The Problem of Drop-out of Children

In many States, the number of schools and the number of students, both have increased tremendously. At the same time, our attempts to make the children studying without discontinuing or dropping out, have not been successful. A very high number of students drop-out of the schools in the middle of their studies for reasons of their own. Available statistics show that the percentage of such drop-outs was as high as 38% to 41% in 1996. According to the *Human Resources Development Ministry,* in 1997-98, around 38.23% of the boys and 41.34% of girls left the school system before reaching the 5th standard. By the time, the remaining children reach the stage of 8th Standard, more than half [54.14%] drop out. Of these drop-outs, 50.72% are boys and 58.61% are girls.[5] Different States have designed different schemes to reduce considerably the number of school drop-outs. ***For example,*** Karnataka Government is giving textbooks, uniforms, umbrella, etc. free of cost to the needy students. In Government Schools and Government aided Schools, children were also given freely 5-to-6 KGs of rice every month as incentive if they maintained the required minimum attendance at school. The Government now [from 2003] started providing mid-day meal to all the children in the Government schools. In spite of such attractive schemes on the part of the States, 100% success has not been attained.

5. Other Problems

(i) Negligence of Primary Education : Financial constraint is not the sole justification for poor performance though this is often highlighted for poor literacy performance. Many countries

5. As quoted by **Ram Ahuja** in *"Society in India."* Page - 222.

such as Burma, China, Sri Lanka, Indonesia have achieved better literacy and primary education levels with lower percentage of GNP spent on education. The difference is that these countries spared large portions of their education budgets on primary education while in India it is primary education that is neglected and higher education is given prominence. Only during the recent years, say after 1990s, much attention is being paid towards primary education.

(ii) Prevalence of Child Labour **:** In spite of the legislations [*The Child Labour (Prohibition and Prevention) Act 1986*] against the practice of child labour, it still persists. According to 1991 census, the total number of working children in the country is **11.28** million.[6] [As per Central Labour Minister's statement in the Parliament this number is 17 million in 1995.] Prevalence of child labour is found to be one of the strong causes of either non-admission to schools, or school drop-outs. According to one estimate, about 25% of the children in the age group 6-11, and around 70% of the children in the age group 12-14; are not either enrolled in the schools or drop out of them, for they are compelled to work for improving the economic position of the family. Various survey reports too have revealed that more than 50% of the boys and around 40% of the girls drop out of schools due to the economic pressures and the domestic drudgeries.

(iii) Lack of Active Participation of the Community **:** Universalisation of primary education necessarily demands the active participation of the whole community in it. Local people, voluntary organisations, government servants, school teachers all must work with a community spirit to see that all children of school-going age get admitted to school and continue their education without dropping it in the middle. Unfortunately, such a community spirit is lacking in India.

NEW STRATEGIES AND SCHEMES FOR POPULARISING ELEMENTARY EDUCATION

The Central Govt which realised the importance of primary education resolved to resort to some new strategies and schemes to popularise it among which the following may be noted.

Sarva Shiksha Abhiyan [SSA] - 2001

The Sarva Shiksha Abhiyan (SSA) launched in 2001 is one of the major, flagship programmes for universalisation of elementary education. The SSA is implemented in partnership with the State Govts and reaches out to 19.4 crore children in 1203 lakh inhabitations across the country.

The SSA Goals are :-

(i) Enrolment of all children in school, *Education Guarantee Centres, Alternative School, Back-to-School Camp* by 2005.

(ii) Retention of all children in school (with out drop-outs) till the upper primary stage by 2010.

(iii) Bridging of gender and social category gaps in enrolment, retention and learning at schools, and

(iv) Ensuring the basic learning achievement levels on the part of children at primary and upper primary stage.

Achievements of the SSA

- Since inception, SSA has provided support for opening 3,02,872 new schools.
- Construction of 2,42,608 school buildings.
- Construction of 10,77,729 additional class rooms in the existing schools;

6 *Ref* : *India Book of the Year 2002, Encyclopaedia Britannica and The Hindu.* Page - 307.

- Provision of drinking water facilities in 1,92,486 schools,
- Provision of toilets in 3, 19,607 schools,
- Appointment of 10.30 lakh teachers in schools,
- Textbook support for approximately 10 crore children annually;
- Teacher training support for approximately 35 lakh teachers;
- Establishing 2573 K.GBVs *[Kasturba Gandhi Balika Vidyalaya]* in which 2,38,600 girls are enrolled with priority to girls from SC, ST Muslim and BPL groups.

SSA had an annual outlay of ₹ 15000 crore for the year 2010-11. Through these massive efforts India has been able to improve educational access to most of the children in the country, if not all.

Educational Guarantee Scheme (EGS) and Alternative and Innovative Education [AIE]

The **EGS** and **AIE** are an important component of the SSA to bring *"out-of-school"* children into the fold of elementary education. The scheme envisages that child-wise planning is undertaken for each *"out-of-school child"*. Under EGS, educational facilities are set up in habitations that do not have a primary school within a distance of one kilometer. Whereas the AIE makes special effort to provide elementary education to specific categories of deprived children such as - child labourers, street children, migrating children, working children, children living in difficult circumstances, etc. Even children in the 9 - age-group, especially adolescents, are also being supported under this EGS and AIE.

Kasturba Gandhi Balika Vidyalaya Scheme [KGBV Scheme]

The KGBV scheme provides for setting up of residential upper primary schools for girls of SC, ST, OBC and Muslim communities. This scheme targets areas of scattered habitations where schools are at a distance.

The scheme provides for a minimum reservation of 75% seats for girls from SC/ST/OBC and minorities communities.

Mid-day Meals Scheme

With a view to enhance enrollment and school attendance and improve nutritional levels among children, the Central Govt launched the ***"National Programme of Nutritional Support to Primary Eduction [NP-NSPE]"*** scheme on 15th Aug 1995 initially in 2408 blocks in the country. The Central Assistance under the scheme consisted of free supply of food grains at the rate of 100 grams per child per school a day inclusive of subsidy for transportation of food grains.

- By the year 1997-98, the NP-NSPE was introduced in all the blocks of the country.
- In 2002, it was further extended to cover not only children in class I to V of the Govt, but also govt-aided and local body schools, and children studying in EGS and AIE centres.

In Sept 2004, the Scheme was revised to provide cooked mid-day meal with 300 calories and 8 to 12 grams of protein to all children studying in classes from I to Vth std, in Govt and aided schools and EGS/AIE centres. The Central Assistance was inclusive of cooking cost, free supply of food grains and management, monitoring and evaluation costs.

In July 2006, the Scheme was further revised to enhance the cooking cost to ₹ 1.80 per child/school a day for states in the North Eastern Region and for other states and UTs ₹ 1.50 per child/school a day. The corresponding states were expected to contribute ₹ 0.20

and ₹ 0.50 per day/school a day respectively. The Govt also revised the national norm from the existing 300 calories and 8-12 grams of protein to 500 calories and 12 grams of protein.

In Sept 2007, the Scheme name was changed into ***"National Programme of Mid Day Meal in Schools"*** and the scheme was extended to cover children of upper primary classes, that is, class VI to VIII studying in 3479 educationally backward blocks. The calorific value of the Mid-Day Meal for the children of this stage was fixed at 700 calories and 20 grams of protein.

In April 2008, the scheme was further revised to cover all upper primary schools of the country including the recognised Madrassas. The scheme was again revised in Nov 2009.

The Major Objectives of the Mid-Day Meal Scheme

The scheme is designed to address two pressing problems of majority of children in India, namely, hunger and education by -

(i) *improving the nutritional status of children in classes I to VIII in all Govt, Govt-aided and other schools.*

(ii) *encouraging poor children, belonging to disadvantaged sections, to attend school more regularly and help them to concentrate on classroom activities.*

It is observed that the *Mid-Day Meal Scheme* has been able to attract students in a relatively large number of children especially in the rural areas. There is considerable progress in the enrolment of children. It is, indeed, a major step in the direction of achieving 100% literacy in the country at the elementary level.

Table - 6

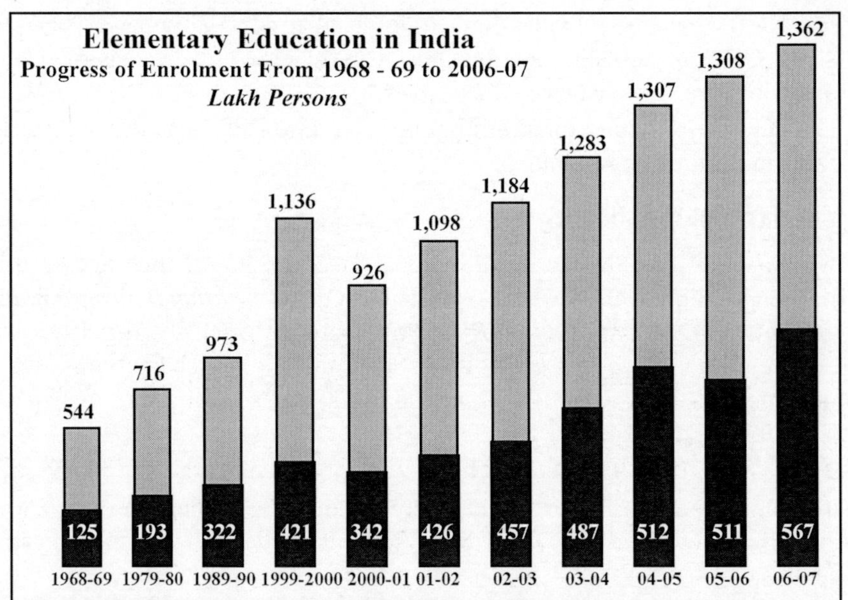

Right To Education Act (RTE - 2009)

April 1st, 2010 is a historic day for the people of India as from this day the *Right to Education* will be accorded the same legal status as the *Right to Life* as provided by Article 21 A.

The Constitution (86th Amendment) Act, 2002, inserted Article 21 A in the constitution which provides for free and compulsory education for all children in the age group of 6 to 14 years. To give effect to this Article 21 A, *the Right of Children to Free and Compulsory Education (RTE) Act, 2009,* was passed in the parliament and it came into force with effect from 1st April 2010.

The RTE Act provides children in the 6 to 14 age group the legal entitlement to free and compulsory education. It has considerable implications for the implementation strategies of S.S.A.

Implications of the Act: As per this Act, no child shall be denied admission for want of document ; no child shall be turned away if the admission cycle in the school is over and no child shall be asked to take an admission test. Children with disabilities will also be educated in the mainstream school. Even the private schools are also obliged to follow the mandate failing which they will be levied a heavy fine. Private schools are given 3 years time to cope with the provisions of this Act. Steps have been taken by the State Govts to harmonise the vision, strategy and norms under SSA with the RTE mandate.

EDUCATIONAL PROBLEMS OF THE DISADVANTAGED GROUPS

Though independent Indian Government has made it a policy to extend educational opportunities to all the citizens of India without making any discrimination on the ground of sex, class, caste, colour, religion, region, and so on. It does not mean all the groups and all the sections have been able to avail of this facility equally. Some sections have gone too far educationally while others are very much lagging behind. *Education of women and Scheduled Caste / Tribe people has been neglected in India since a long time.* In fact, these two groups [women and SC and ST people] can be regarded as educationally disadvantaged groups.

A. EDUCATIONAL PROBLEMS OF WOMEN

1. Poor Literacy Level of Women **:** The literacy level of women is comparatively very low. In 1901, their literacy level was just 0.6%, it increased to 10% in 1951, 29.75% in 1981, 39.29% in 1991 to 54% 2001, and to 65.5% in 2011. In states like Bihar, M.P., U.P. and Rajasthan female literacy rate is found to be very low even in 2011. The literacy rate of females among the SCs in India was 23.76%, and that of the females of the STs was 18.19% in 1999.

2. Increasing Drop-out of Female Children **:** Increasing drop-out of children from schools is another problem. Though female children are getting admitted to primary, middle and high schools in a substantial number, many of them drop out of the school in the middle without completing the course. *For example,* as per the data furnished by the Ministry of Education [New Delhi], in 1984-85 the number of female children enrolled at primary school crossed the figure of 34.2 millions, and at middle school level the enrolment crossed 9.2 millions. More than 74% of these female children, between the age-groups of 6 and 14 years, quit schools and lapsed into ignorance.

3. Admission to School **:** Even in the matter of admitting children to school at elementary level, female children are discriminated against male children. *For example,* in 1984-85, the admission of male children to school was around 90%, the percentage of female children was only 66.2. It means complete awareness is not there among people regarding female education.

4. Majority of Employed Women are Also Illiterate **:** It was found that in 1991, of every 100 women employed, 52.59% of them were illiterate and 28.56% of them had studied only up to elementary level. Of every 100 women working in the rural areas, 88.11% were illiterate. These illiterate women in the unorganised sector were totally exploited by their employers.

Women working in factories, mining industries, building construction process, in dams, bridges and road repair or construction work were not only paid less but also made to work in unhealthy surroundings.

- **Causes For the Low Educational Status of Women**

1. Neglect of Female Education Due to Gender Inequality **:** Ever since the days of Medieval Period, female education has been totally neglected in India. Foreign rulers never took any interest in female education. Even after independence, things did not improve immediately. "Girls are neglected since their birth or even before due to our patriarchal society that prefers sons. *"Girls are withdrawn from education once they attain puberty due to the conservative cultural values of the parents and society. Girls' education is cut short by early marriage."*

2. Imposition of Domestic Responsibilities on Girls **:** Unlike the boys, girls are made to assume domestic responsibility from an early age. They are expected to do domestic work in order to make free their mothers to go out of home for undertaking economically rewarding activities. At home, *"Girls not only sweep, wash, collect water, fuel, fodder, mend younger siblings and animals, but also work in the fields and help their mothers in beedi-rolling, gem-polishing, or any other home-based piece rate work they may be engaged in." Girls belonging to poor class are also made to work in the houses of the well-to-do people as "domestic servants."*

3. Lack of Educational Facilities Especially in the Rural Areas **:** For a very long time we were not able to provide educational services to the remote places in the village areas. Parents of female children were reluctant to send their children to far away places for educational purposes. Acute shortage of women teachers working in rural areas also prevented parents from sending their daughters to the schools where there were no female teachers. Though things have improved much, even today female children in the rural areas have greater problems than the male-children. *For example,* they have hesitation to go to co-education schools. Hostel facilities for girls are not available in the rural areas. Schools exclusively meant for girls are very meagre in the rural areas and so on.

4. Historical and Traditional Factors **:** For centuries together female education in this land was neglected and hence *tradition-bound people came to believe that the education of women is unworthy of any serious consideration.* Since most of the mothers themselves were uneducated they never felt the need for getting education to their female children. In the beginning of the 20th century, that is, in 1901 hardly 6 women out of 1000 were literate. As per 2011 figures, more than 34.54% [25.22 crores] of women remain illiterate in India. It is not easy to inspire them to take up the responsibility of giving education to their children, particularly, female children.

- **Strategies, Measures and Schemes to Improve Girls' / Women's Participation in Education**

Of late, educationists and administrators are very much concerned about improving the educational status of women. Hence, various strategies have been suggested to overcome the problem of low educational status of girls, particularly in the rural areas. Specific steps taken in this direction may be mentioned below.

1. The Government launched the ***"Operation Blackboard"*** scheme in 1987-88 under which it intended to create **one lakh** posts of primary school teachers mainly to be filled by women. By 1992, 75000 posts were filled in, out of which 45000 [60%] posts were filled in by women teachers.
2. Under *the rural literacy programmes,* illiterate adult women were enrolled in a large number. Their enrolment was about 55% in 1995.
3. Special attention is given to *enrolment of women in adult education centres.*

4. In ***Navodaya Vidyalaya*** also a minimum of 28% admission of girls is ensured.
5. A new attempt was made to mobilise rural women for education through the *"Mahila Sanghas."* This project called ***"Education for Women's Equality"*** [*"Mahila Samaikhya"*] was launched in 1989 and the entire expenses of this project were to be borne by the Government of Netherlands. States such as U.P., Gujarat and Karnataka have availed of the assistance for this project.
6. Various incentives and special concessions such as freeships, scholarships, free boarding and lodging facilities have also been provided for the girl students who are in absolute need of them.
7. *Other Measures and Strategies :*

Various economic measures are also undertaken to reduce poverty and generate employment opportunities so that for economic reasons girls' education is not neglected. Attention is also paid to provide more primary and secondary schools in remote areas; recruit a larger number of female teachers for schools in rural areas; to make school-timings more flexible so as to enable rural girls to attend schools without neglecting their domestic responsibilities. Direct incentives such as scholarships, stipends, freeships, free supply of library books, mid-day meal, etc., are also offered to make it more attractive for the parents to send girls to schools.

B. EDUCATIONAL PROBLEMS OF THE BACKWARD CLASSES [OBCS], THE SCHEDULED CASTES [SCs] AND THE SCHEDULED TRIBES [STs]

It is well known that the poor and the under-privileged sections of the Indian society including the OBCs, SCs and STs are lagging behind in education. It is reflected in the literacy level achieved by these sections. *For example,* the average literacy rate for the general population in India, according to 1991 census, was 52.21% whereas it was 37.41% [that is, 15% less than the average] in the case of SCs and only 29.60% [that is, 23% less than the average] in the case of the STs. The state-wise position of the literacy level of the SCs is the highest in Kerala [79.66%, that is, very much above the national average] and lowest in Bihar, that is, 19.49%. In the case of the STs also, highest literacy rate is found in Kerala, that is, 57.22%, whereas the lowest rate is observed in Andhra, that is, 17.16%.[7]

- **Measures Recommended to Improve the Educational Status of SCs and STs**

Even during the British rule under the leadership of Gandhiji a programme for social, educational and economic improvement of the SCs, STs and backward classes had been taken up as early as in 1937 when the popular ministries came to be established in the provinces in British India. Independent Indian Government took up various measures to continue the programme by adding to it several other dimensions as an attempt to pursue and put into practice some of the relevant provisions of the Constitution.

The Central Advisory Board of Education [CABE] as early as in 1976 recommended certain measures to improve the educational status of the SCs, STs and OBCs. Some of them are as follows :

1. Special care should be taken *to implement the programme of universalisation of elementary education in some selected areas* where the level of literacy of SCs, STs and OBCs, has been found to be very poor.
2. *Different types of programmes are necessary to popularise literacy improvement activities* for the SCs, STs and OBCs since they do not represent one single homogeneous community.

---

7. ***Ref*** **:** *India Book of the Year 2002 Encyclopaedia Britannica and The Hindu.* Page - 307.

3. Wherever educational institutions are not found, especially in tribal areas, *a network of educational institutions in the form of Ashrama Schools or residential schools, single-teacher schools, free hostels,* etc. are to be established.

- **Measures Adopted to Extend Opportunities for the Educational Development of SCs and STs**

Due attention is paid to extend the educational opportunities of SCs and STs and hence special provisions have been made in this regard. Providing free education, free distribution of books, stationery, uniform, etc.; giving scholarships, bank loan facilities, providing mid-day meal, arranging for free boarding and lodging facilities, reserving seats for SCs and STs in all the government and government aided institutions, etc., are some of the concrete steps which the Government has taken in this regard.

In addition to the above, there are some centrally sponsored schemes also for the educational benefit of both SCs and STs. The Central Government sponsored the following schemes to facilitate the educational improvement of SCs and STs :– (i) *Free coaching and training for these candidates to appear for the competitive examinations*; (ii) *book-bank scheme*; (iii) *post-matric scholarships for providing financial assistance for higher education*; (iv) *construction of hostels*; (v) *financial assistance to do research work*; (vi) *supply of textbooks free of cost*; and (vi) *national overseas scholarships and passage grants for higher education.* [***Note*** **:** *For more details please refer to Chapter on "Problems of Scheduled Castes".*]

- **Recommendations of National Policy on Education [NEP], 1986**

The NEP - 1986 recommended certain measures to be undertaken to improve the educational status of the SCs and STs. Some of them are mentioned below :

(i) Giving special incentives to SC families to send their children to the schools at least up to 14th year;

(ii) Maintaining a proper record relating to the enrolment of SC and ST children, and their attendance in schools and their performance in the examinations;

(iii) Pre-matric scholarship scheme for children of families engaged in low occupations such as scavenging, sweeping, curing hides, tanning, oil-grinding, shoe making, etc.;

(iv) Appointing teachers from the category of SCs and STs;

(v) Providing for as many hostel facilities as possible;

(vi) Encouraging educated tribals to take up teaching in tribal areas;

(vii) Establishing educational institutions in the remote places like hilly areas, mountainous forest areas;

(viii) Designing instructional materials in tribal languages at least at the initial stages.

Deficiencies Involved in These Educational Programmes

In spite of the special measures undertaken to improve the educational position of the SCs, STs and OBCs, expected results have not come. Because, the measures themselves are not free from defects. Some such deficiencies can be listed here : (i) reservation rules and their implementation are defective; (ii) scholarships, stipends, hostel facilities that are given are inadequate; (iii) the rate of drop-out of children of these three communities is still very high; (iv) teachers appointed in the remote areas are not attending to their duties regularly and in a responsible manner; (v) cultural gap in the case of the tribal children is not yet effectively bridged; (vi) medium of instruction, that is, regional language often creates problems for the tribal children; (vii) proper awareness is not created among the SCs and STs regarding the importance of education.

PROGRESS OF EDUCATION IN INDIA

Education system in India has a prolonged history of its own. As it has already been referred to, education was given very high importance during the ancient period. Even during the medieval period elementary education was very popular, for the community itself had taken up the cause of education. But at the end of the medieval period and in the beginning of the British period, education reached its lowest ebb. The British with their own imperialistic motives introduced some educational measures mainly to produce an army of English knowing clerks to run the British bureaucracy in India.

Though not in tune with the actual demand, education has been given some importance after independence. The Directive Principles of the State Policy of the Constitution of India strongly recommended universalisation of primary education. In the Five Year Plans also some serious interest was shown towards the progress of education. The progress of education in India started with a low profile almost up to 1970s, and afterwards it took a little greater speed. By the end of the year 2011, the literacy rate in India went up considerably [74.04%] and the number of educational institutions increased substantially catering to the educational needs of millions of students.

A Brief Mention of Educational Institutions in India

India's education system which is as old as almost 150 years has made a tremendous headway nowadays. In 1857, there were only 3 Universities – Calcutta, Madras and Bombay – under the British rule. At present, the number of schools, colleges, universities, technical and research institutes has increased considerably. The following statistics gives us an idea of the tremendous increase in the number of educational institutions in India.[8]

Progress of Primary Eduction:

As it has already been noted the **SSA (Sarva Shiksha Abhiyan)** launched in Nov 2000 in partnership with the States, has given a good encouragement to primary education. The achievements of the SSA have been very impressive. (opening of 302872 new schools, construction of 242,608 school buildings, construction of 10,77,729 additional class rooms, 1,92,486 drinking water facilities, construction of 319607 toilets, supply of free textbooks to approximately 10 crore children and in-service training for 35 lakh teachers.)

In India, in 2003-04, there were **7.52 lakh** primary schools and **2.62 lakh** upper primary schools. The enrolment rate of girls at the elementary level was higher than that of the boys during the years 2001 and 2004. Participation of girls at all levels of school education has improved considerably even though vast disparities do exist amongst the States.

Decline in the Rate of Drop-out **:** The drop out rate at elementary level has declined from 78.3 % in 1960-61 to 52.32 % in 2003-04. Ever since 2003, the number of out-of-school children, too has declined. *For example,* it came down to 1.35 crore in Nov. 2005; and the states and UTs have reported in March 2010, that it has further reduced to 95 lakhs only.

As far as *Pupil Teacher Ratio (PTR)* is concerned, it remained almost same at **43 : 1** during 2001 - 02. At the upper - primary level, it was **34 : 1**.

Secondary Education

The number of secondary schools in India increased from 7416 in 1950 - 51 to 1,68,900 in 2006 - 07. Total enrolment in secondary and higher secondary schools also has increased correspondingly from 1.5 million in 1950 - 51 to 39.44 million in 2006-07.

8. ***Source of Statistics and Information*** **:** *Manorama Year Book* 2012.

College and University Level Education

There has been an increase in the number of students studying at higher level, that is, at the level of college and university. This is reflected in an increase in the number of educational institutions catering to the needs of higher learning . See the ***Table No.-7*** Given below.

Table No. 7

List of University Level Educational Institutions (as on 31-12-2010)

No.	Insitutional Category	No. of Institutions
1.	Central Universities	42
2.	Institutions Deemed to be Universities	130
3.	State Univerities	261
4.	Private Universities	73
5.	Institutions of National Importance	33
6.	Institutions Established under State Legislature Acts	5
•	**Total Number of University Level Institutions**	**544**
7.	Number of Colleges	31,324
	recognized under Section 2(f) of the UGC Act 1956	7,678 (24.5%)
	recognized under Section 12 (B) of the UGC Act 1956 V	6,257 (20.0%)
8.	Women's Colleges	3,432
9.	Enrollment (at the beginning of academic year 2010-11 in the formal system	146.25 lakh
	* in University Departments	19.19 lakh (13.1%)
	* in Affliated Colleges	127.06 lakh (86.9%)
	* women enrolment	60.80 lakh (41.6%)
	* women enrolment in Professional Courses	18.45%
10.	* Faculty Strength in Universities (at the beginning of the academic year 2010-11)	6.99 lakh
	* in universities	1.0 lakh (41%)

Source : Manorama Year Book - 2012 Page - 640

List of University Level Educational Institutions as on 31-12-2010

Technical Education

Technical education is important in human resources development of the country. It creates skilled man power, enhances industrial productivity and improves the quality of life. Technical education covers courses and programmes in engineering technology, management, architecture, town planning, pharmacy, applied arts and crafts, hotel management and catering technology.

Institutions that come under technical education can be grouped into three categories:

(i) Centrally funded institutions.

(ii) State Government / funded institutions, and

(iii) Self - financial institutions.

In 2010 - 11, there were 81 centrally funded institutions in the country especially for promoting technical and science education. The list of such institutions is given below. ***[See Table No.-8]***

University and Higher Education

Especially after 2001, there has been an impressive growth in the field of university and higher education. It has been made mandatory for all colleges and universities to undergo accreditation.

- 544 university level institutions including 42 Central Universities.
- 261 State Universities
- 5 institutions established under State Legislature Act
- 130 deemed Universities
- 33 institutes of national importance.
- 31324 colleges including 3432 Womens Colleges in the country.
- 15 + 2 Indian Institutes of Technology (IITs)
- 13 Indian Institutes of Management (IIMS)
- 3419 Engineerings Colleges (Govt - 184, Private - 3235)
- 278 Medical Colleges (Govt - 123, Private - 153)
- 228 Dental Colleges (Govt - 31, Private - 197)
- 2849 MBA Colleges (Govt - 139, Private - 2512)

Table No . 8

Centrally Funded Institutions	Number of Institutions
Indian Institutes of Technology (IITs)	15
Indian Institutes of Management (IIMs)	13
Indian Institutes of Science (IISc)	1
Indian Institutes of Science Education & Research (IISERs)	5
National Institutes of Technology (NITs)	30
Indian Institutes of InformationTechnology (IITs)	4
National Institutes of Technical Teachers Training & Research (NITTTRs)	4
Others	9
School of Planning & Architecture (SPAs)-3, Indian School of Mines (ISM), North-East Regional Institute of Science & Technology (NERIST), National Institute of Industrial Engineering (NITIE), National Insitute of Foundry & Forge Technology (NIFFT), Sant Longowal Institute of Engineering & Technology (SLIET), Central Institute of Technology (CIT)	
Total	**81**

A list of such functioning institutions as of 2010 is given below.

In India, at present, there are : -

Prestigious IITs

There are 15 + 2 IITs that is Indian Institutes of Technology in India at present. IITs at Kharagpur, Mumbai, Madras, Kanpur, Delhi, Guwahati and Roorkee - have been the older ones. Six new IITs one each in Patna (Bihar), Hyderabad (Andhra Pradesh), Jodhpur (Rajasthan), Bhuwaneshwar (Orissa), Gandhinagar (Gujarat), and Ropar (Punjab) have been set up during 2008 - 2009. Two more IITs have been established in 2009-10 one at Mandi (Himachal Pradesh) and the other at Indore (Madhya Pradesh).

IIMS (Institutes of Management)

With an objective of providing management education and to assist the industry through research consulting services, higher centres of learning such as Indian Institutes of Management (IIMS) were established. These IIMS award diplomas and not degrees. There are at present, 13 IIMS in India. They are at different places such as Calcutta (West Bengal), Ahmedabad (Gujarath), Bangalore (Karnataka), Lucknow (U.P.) Kozhikode [Kerala], Indore (M.P.), Shillong (Meghalaya), Ranchi (Jharkhand) Rohtak (Haryana), Raipur (Chattisgarh), Tiruchanapalli (Tamil Nadu), Udaipur (Rajasthan), and Kashipur (Uttarakhand).

Adult Education

The *National Literacy Mission* was launched on May 5, 1988 to impart functional literacy to non literates in the country in the age group of 15 - 35 years. The Mission objective is to attain a sustainable threshold literacy rate of 75 % by 2007.

Since the inception of the Mission in 1988, 556 districts have been covered and 57.96 million people have been made literate under the adult education scheme. Around 60% of the learners under this scheme are found to be women, over 22% are SCs and over 13 % STs.

•••

Chapter 26

COMMERCIALISATION OF HIGHER EDUCATION IN INDIA

Heightened Commercialisation at Higher Level of Education - The Magnitude of Commercialisation - Increase in the Number of Engineering, Medical and MBA Colleges - Medical College Fee Structure: A Comparision - The Higgling Business of Seat - Sharing - Some Unfair Practices of Corporate Institutions - Consequences of Commercialisation of Education - Solutions Suggested for the Prevention and Elimination of Commercialisation of Professional Education in India.

It is heartening to note that the importance of education is getting widely recognized today by the general public of India. For the first time in the history of independent India, a large number of people have started realizing that education is a gate way for achieving economic progress and attaining social status. Even in the educationally backward states like Bihar, Jharkhand, Rajasthan, Andhra Pradesh and U.P., there is a general awakening towards education. Governmental efforts to achieve 100% literacy through *"Sarva Shiksha Abhiyan [SSA]* launched in Nov-2000 in partnership with the States have started yielding comparatively good results. The governmental programme aims at improving the performance of the school system through a community – owned approach and to impart quality elementary education to all children in the age-group of 6-to-14, by 2010.

The Central Govt even took a bold step to introduce ***"The Right of Children to Free and Compulsory Education Act"*** which came into force from ***1st April 2010***. As per this Act, every child in the age group of 6-to-14 years will be provided 8 years of elementary education. Now it is the responsibility of the state to get the child the basic education at its own expenses. No child of the appropriate age be denied educational opportunity on any ground.

These efforts of the Government are laudable even though it is a long way to achieve 100% literacy. The governmental efforts on the one hand and the changing socio-economic scenario which is highly favourable to education, on the other, have changed the traditional approach and attitudes of the people towards education. Thus, education has assumed primacy. Increasing demand for quality education has given a fillip for private entrepreneurs to develop commercial interest in it and convert it into a tradable commodity. The opening up of large scale employment opportunities due to the onslaught of the processes of globalization, liberalization and privatization, has further widened the scope for education.

What is important here is that the private entrepreneurs with their commercial agenda have shown greater interest in higher education rather than in elementary education. They have sensed that investment in higher educational institutions is more profitable for there is an increasing demand for it especially due to IT boom [IT : Information Technology]. The freedom given by the governments for these entrepreneurs to start an era of private educational institutions virtually converted education into an industry. *Educational activity is now a commercial activity and the process that is going on now is a process of commercialization of education.*

In the present era of commercialization of education, education is a part of the globalization process. In fact, education is listed among the **161** types of tradable services defined by GATS and the WTO. [**GATS** : *General Agreement On Trade and Tariffs* and **WTO** : *World Trade Organisation*]. Hence, educational services are now viewed purely from a commercial viewpoint. Even the traditional vocabulary relevant to educational field has changed. *Thus, in the modern context, student is a customer, teacher and colleges are service providers. Education is not a public good, but a private good. It is not a charitable activity but a business, a profit gaining activity. This commercial jargon and market thinking has lasting effects on education.*

Educational institutions on regular basis, hike the fees. As a result, cost per student goes on increasing year after year affecting poor and middle class students for access to education. Profit motive will try to cut the expenditure on infrastructure, equipments and qualified teachers on the one hand and increasing fees on the other. Hence, many institutes offer courses of dubious quality and function as *"degree mills"*. Exploitation of students and teachers continues unabated.

1. HEIGHTENED COMMERCIALISATION AT HIGHER LEVEL OF EDUCATION

The processes of globalization, privatization and liberalization have made education a powerful instrument for reaping economic benefits. These processes have laid greater emphasis on higher education. Assured job opportunities in the home economy and also abroad for higher educated Indians, gave further encouragement for establishing a large number of institutes of higher learning. As a result, *India's higher education system is now the third largest in the world.* Private sector has taken a keen interest in this and hence higher education through private institutions has become the most glaring feature of Indian higher education. Though this is a desirable development, it is often viewed with suspicion. Two factors seem to be responsible for it :

(i) *Exploitative behaviour of some private players of the educational system;* and

(ii) *Absence of clear policy formation regarding higher education on the part of the government, and the frequent intervention of the judiciary to resolve the inconsistencies in the existing legislation. which has been further complicating the higher educational sector.*

(i) Exploitative Activities of the Private Managements

During 1980s itself private professional colleges began to be established in a large number, but there was no effective control over their functioning, nor there was any systematic admission procedure. Some admissions were treated as *"management quota"*. In contrast to the merit based admissions, these seats under *"management quota"* were generally filled through the collection of heavy capitation fees. Several state governments enacted laws to regulate admission and prohibit capitation fees in private professional colleges. These laws were challenged in courts by these private managements and with this they initiated an era of judicial interventions which continues even now. The issue of capitation fees routinely comes up before the Supreme Court also.

(ii) Absence of Common Policy and Intervention of the Judiciary

In 1993, for example, the Supreme Court laid down the framework to regulate admissions on priority of merit with differential fees structure which remained in operation till 2002.

IS HIGHER EDUCATION FOR SALE - ?

In 2002, the Constitution Bench of the Supreme Court gave a ruling that fees could be determined in a manner of generating a reasonable surplus fund for the purpose of institutional development and expansion. This verdict of the Supreme Court was interpreted by the private institutions in their own way stating that the court had given them full power to admit any one by charging any amount of fees that they decide.

In 2003, yet another Bench of the Supreme Court was set up to prevent the misuse of its 2002 verdict. This Bench in its judgment stipulated that fees had to be determined again in all states. It allowed private institutions to retain a management quota. It also stated that students be admitted to the institutions on the basis of merit but merit in such cases could be determined through institutional admission tests.

Absence of Clear-cut Policy has led to Legal Loopholes : As it has been the case previously, the 2003 verdict of the Court was abused by the private institutions which conducted their own admission tests in their own styles and collection of capitation fees too has become a part of their common unofficial practice. These developments clearly reveal that the so called policy of admissions and tuition fees been driven more by judicial interventions than by proactive public policy. This has given enough scope for the private institutions to find out legal loopholes to fulfil their interests.

Miserable Failure of the Govt Appointed Committees : To prevent the private professional colleges from collecting heavy capitation fees from the students in an illegal manner, the Govt thought of appointing Committees which are supposed to supervise fee fixation, admission of students and such other related issues. Many state governments have formed committees for this purpose and most of these have been rendered toothless. In many instances, either the committees somehow have not shown any genuine interest in reporting to the government the teething issues and in resolving them, or, the reports and recommendations submitted to the governments are kept in cold storage without being implemented.

In some instances, even though the committees have stipulated fees for each college, the concerned colleges have collected huge amount of capitation fees much against the Capitation Act, and in opposition to these recommendations. Majority of the colleges never bothered to follow the recommendations of the committees. Some of the committees have even complained against the deliberate non-co-operation on the part of the officials in the implementation of the recommendations. *The overall result is, the financial exploitation of students and their parents.*

THE MAGNITUDE OF COMMERCIALISATION

The above explanations make it clear that neither the political decisions of the government nor the judicial intervention of the courts has been helpful in preventing the private managements from swindling the student public in the process of running educational institutions of higher learning.

Private managements have undoubtedly converted education into an industry. They have made higher educational institutions especially the professional colleges, the high profit-yielding pursuits. Commitment to the cause of education, providing education to the people as a self-less service, running educational institutions on *"no-loss and no-profit"* basis etc..., have become the things of the past. 'Education is included in the present service sector, as a high-yielding concern. Private interests in education are concentrated on higher learning that is, especially in running professional colleges such as engineering, medical, dental, and MBA colleges where the profit margins are very high.

The Factors of Commercialisation of Education

Two factors mentioned below are associated with the developments that are taking place in the realm of higher education in India. These developments have let loose an era of commercialisation of education. These factors are ...

a) *Increase in the number of private engineering, medical and MBA colleges as against the number of government colleges;* and

b) *Abnormal increase in the tuition fee and capitation fee in the private managements.*

(a) Increase in Engineering / Medical / MBA Colleges

There has been an abnormal increase of private Engineering, Medical/MBA colleges during 2001-2010. These *"educational shops"* have mushroomed indiscriminately in many states of India. There is neither any logic nor any scientific explanation for their immediate growth. Increase in private colleges is not in consonance with the proportionate increase in government colleges nor with an increase in the population or any other demographic factors. This is definitely not due to a suddenly developed selfless love towards higher education.

Quite interestingly, in some states, the number of Govt. Engineering and Medical/MBA colleges, has remained more or less unchanged, while in some other states, the number has increased very slightly. There are also states in which Govt colleges have decreased in number slightly over a decade.

(i) Enormous Increase in Private Engineering Colleges

Establishing engineering colleges has become a fashion today in many of the states especially after the year 2000. In states like Andhra Pradesh, Tamil Nadu, Maharashtra and U.P: hundreds of engineering colleges have come-up between "2001-2010". In Andhra Pradesh alone the number of engineering colleges increased from 26 to 634 between "2001-2010". Whereas, in the same state, the Govt Engineering colleges have increased just by 3 or 4 more colleges.[1] Barring a few states like Bihar, Assam, Jammu and Kashmir [J and K], Jharkhand etc., in almost all the other states the private engineering colleges have increased by leaps and bounds. ***[See Table No.1].***

(ii) Sizeable Increase in the Number of Medical Colleges

In comparison with the increase in the number of private engineering colleges, the increase in the number of private medical colleges is quite less. ***[See Table - 2]*** But the extent of commercialization in these colleges has reached new proportions. It also points out at some other features. *For example:*

- Over a period of 10 years [2001-2011], the number of government medical colleges in many states has decreased. *Example:* Bihar, M.P, J and K, Western U.P
- Barring a few states, majority of the states have added one or two more govt medical colleges to their total tally.
- There is a steady growth in the number of private medical colleges and not a single private medical college was closed in between 2001-and-2010.
- Even though All India Medical Association and Medical Universities of the respective States- have identified and recognized some private / Govt medical colleges in some states as institutions of poor standard on the basis of poor infrastructure, absence of quality teaching faculty, lack of proper hospital facilities etc., not a single private medical college has been closed up till now.

---

1. **Source :** Information and statistics given in this chapter including the Tables provided in the succeeding pages, are taken from the booklet *"Eduction is For Sale"* (15-8-2011) a report on commercialisation of education in India, based on a national level survey conducted by ABVP a national level student organisation in 2010-11 and edited by **N. Ravi Kumar.**

Table No – 1

Sudden Increase in the No. of Engineering Colleges								
	2010				2001			
State	Govt.	Aided	Pvt.	% of Pvt.	Govt.	Aided	Pvt.	% of Pvt.
Karnataka	12	8	168	89%	6	11	65	79%
Kerala	11	3	82	85%	10	5	16	52%
Andhra Pradesh	23	3	634	96%	12	124	24	15%
Tamilnadu	7	4	443	98%	7	3	174	95%
Maharastra	7	13	304	94%	8	0	77	91%
Gujarath	18	1	62	77%	5	3	11	58%
Bihar	7	0	2	22%	3	0	0	0%
Punjab	13	0	69	84%	6	5	8	42%
Rajasthan	5	9	80	85%	5	0	16	76%
Delhi	15	0	66	81%	2	0	0	0%
Madhya Bharat	0	0	0	0%	9	24	2	6%
J.K.	1	0	2	67%	2	0	2	50%
Western UP	0	0	235	100%	10	0	48	83%
Estern UP	4	0	41	91%	0	0	0	0%
Jharkhand	5	0	12	71%	3	0	0	0%
Chattisrgh	4	45	0	0%	0	6	4	40%
Mahakoshal	3	0	25	89%	1	0	2	67%
Orissa	6	0	81	93%	6	0	23	79%
West Bengal	25	0	101	80%	9	30	0	0%
Uttaranchal	4	2	26	81%	2	0	2	50%
Assam	3	0	7	70%	3	0	0	0%
Total	**173**	**88**	**2440**		**109**	**211**	**474**	

Table No – 2

Increase in the No. of Medical [MBBS] Colleges								
	2010				2001			
State	Govt.	Aided	Pvt.	% of Pvt.	Govt.	Aided	Pvt.	% of Pvt.
Karnataka	10	0	22	69%	4	8	11	48%
Kerala	5	0	16	76%	5	1	0	0%
Andhra Pradesh	13	0	20	61%	9	4	1	7%
Tamilnadu	15	0	11	42%	11	4	0	0%
Maharastra	16	2	25	58%	10	0	11	52%
Gujarath	6	0	7	54%	6	4	1	9%
Bihar	6	0	3	33%	8	0	0	0%
Punjab	3	1	5	56%	3	1	2	33%
Rajasthan	6	1	3	30%	6	0	1	14%
Delhi	6	0	1	14%	5	0	0	10%
Madhya Bharat	0	0	0	0%	3	1	0	0%
J.K.	1	0	1	50%	3	0	1	25%
Western UP	5	1	7	54%	7	2	1	10%
Estezn UP	34	0	0	0%	0	0	0	0%
Jharkhand	3	0	1	25%	3	0	0	1%
Chattisghar	3	0	0	0%	0	0	1	100%
Mehakoshal	3	0	0	0%	1	0	0	0%
Orissa	3	0	4	57%	3	0	0	0%
West Bengal	9	0	1	10%	8	0	0	0%
Uttaranchal	2	0	2	50%	0	0	1	100%
Assam	2	0	0	0%	3	0	0	0%
Total	**151**	**5**	**129**		**96**	**21**	**31**	

- There are still many private medical colleges which do not have their own hospitals and send their students to different hospitals for practice and clinicals.
- The same story is repeated in the case of dental colleges. ***[See Table No 3.]***

Table No – 3

Increase in the No. of BDS [Dental] Colleges								
	2010				2001			
State	**Govt.**	**Aided**	**Pvt.**	**% of Pvt.**	**Govt.**	**Aided**	**Pvt.**	**% of Pvt.**
Karnataka	2	0	37	95%	1	6	31	82%
Kerala	3	0	18	86%	2	0	0	0%
Andhra Pradesh	3	0	18	86%	3	0	0	0%
Tamilnadu	1	0	24	96%	1	0	10	91%
Maharastra	2	0	30	94%	3	0	6	67%
Gujarath	2	0	9	82%	3	1	0	0%
Bihar	1	0	0	0%	4	0	0	0%
Punjab	4	0	10	71%	2	1	8	73%
Rajasthan	4	0	10	91%	1	0	2	67%
Delhi	3	0	1	25%	1	2	0	0%
Madhya Bharat	0	0	0	0%	1	2	0	0%
J.K.	1	0	1	50%	0	0	0	0%
Western UP	5	1	14	70%	1	0	5	83%
Estezn UP	1	0	2	67%	0	0	0	0%
Jharkhand	0	0	1	100%	1	0	0	0%
Chattisghar	1	5	0	0%	0	0	0	0%
Mehakoshal	0	0	1	100%	0	0	0	0%
Orissa	1	0	4	80%	0	0	1	100%
West Bengal	2	0	1	33%	1	0	0	0%
Uttaranchal	0	0	3	100%	0	0	0	0%
Assam	1	0	0	0%	0	0	0	0%
Total	**37**	**6**	**184**		**25**	**10**	**63**	

(b) Abnormal Increase in Fees in Medical / Engineering Colleges.

The most exploitative character of higher education is to be seen in the enormously and unreasonably high fee structure of the engineering / medical / MBA Colleges. High fee structure and capitation are the two most ugly faces of professional education which have become nightmares to the poor and the meritorious students. These two things have thrown up the morals and the ethos of Indian education and have corrupted the entire professional education system in the country.

The fee structure is related to the policy of seat sharing between the Govt and the private institutions. The bone of contention between the Govts and the private managements is to tilt favorably the seat-sharing ratio this side or that side in order to fix up the Govt fee and the management fee. Once the management fees are fixed, capitation comes into picture which perhaps is the biggest menace to the professional education of the country.

Engineering College Fee Structure : A Comparison

As far as the fee structure in the engineering colleges is concerned, most of the states in India, with the exception of Delhi, M.P and Western U.P, had for a very long time, a reasonable fee structure in comparison with the present fee scenario. More than half of the number of states did not have a single private engineering college. Hence, there was no scope for the exploitation of the students and the quality of education was also relatively high. In 2001, wherever there were private engineering colleges, the management fees ranged between ₹ 35000 to ₹ 1,75,000. It could also be said that on an average, the management fee was around ₹ 40,000. Though there was the problem of capitation fee in 2001 and a few years before it, it was not as pronounced as it is now. *By 2010, capitation fee increased to such an extent, that it converted education into a commodity meant for sale.*

Table No-4. given here provides a glimpse of the vast difference in fees of engineering colleges between 2001 and 2010.

- The Govt fee for the BE course in 2010 was as low as ₹2000/- in J and K and ₹2500/- in Gujarath and as high as Rs:74000/- in Delhi and ₹ 82000/- in Punjab.
- The lowest slab of the management fee was ₹ 35000/- in J and K and ₹ 47000/- in Rajasthan and the highest slab of fee was ₹ 3,00,000/- in Delhi and ₹1,80,000/- in Bihar.
- In the private engineering colleges, the minimum capitation fee [or donation] is around, **2** lakhs and it ranges upto ₹ **15** lakhs. Depending on the demand and the so called *"market forces"* the amount of capitation eventually varies in each academic year.

Medical College Fee Structure : A Comparision

As far as medical education is concerned, many states did not have Govt Medical Colleges during 2001, and in the existing colleges the lowest possible fee on an average was around ₹ 15000/-. West Bengal Govt had fixed a paltry sum of ₹ 20/- per seat whereas Punjab Govt had fixed a relatively high, that is, ₹ 65000/-. The management fee ranged from ₹ 15000/- in Himachalpradesh to Rs 2,50,000/- in Rajashthan. This picture of the fee structure has totally changed and it has reached an incredibly high mark in 2010. ***[See Table No -5]***

- In 2010, the average Govt fee for a medical college was around ₹ 25000/- even though it varied between ₹ 2600/- [In Delhi] to ₹ 85000/- [in Hariyana].
- As it is shown in the Table, management fee has reached its height in 2010. It ranges between an exceptionally low fee of Rs 40000/- [in J.K.] and relatively high fee of ₹ 10,00000/- [in Haryana]. This high amount of fee one has to pay each year for a period of 5 years along with one time payment of capitation which ranges between 5 lakhs to 50 lakhs.
- Post graduate medical education [such as M.D. and M.S.] in a private medical college with a management seat has become the costliest of all the educational courses in India with its fee ranging between 50 lakhs to 1.25 crore ₹ depending on the specialization.
- The story of high fees for medical education repeats in the case of B.D.S. [Bachelor of Dental Surgery]. ***[See Table No -6]***
- The Govt fee for dental course in 2001 was around ₹ 5000/- on an average. During 2010, the Govt fee itself ranged from ₹ 2000/- to ₹ 65,000/-.
- The management fee for BDS in 2010 ranged from ₹ 60,000/- to 2,70,000/- ₹ Along with the course fee, capitation or donation also ranged between ₹ 1,00,000/- to ₹ 8,00,000/-

Table No – 4

Engineering College [BE] Fee Structure					
	For the year 2010			For the year 2001	
State	Govt Fee In ₹	Mgmt. fee In ₹	Donation In ₹	Govt. Fee In ₹	Mgntfee In ₹
Andra Pradesh	15,500	97,200	700,000	0	43000
Assam	7,000	90,000	0	0	0
Bihar	48,000	180,000	90,000	10576	0
Chattisgharh	19635	48300	200000	16500	0
Delhi	74000	300000	400000	22500	65500
Estern UP	25000	75000	3000000	0	0
Gujarath	2500	60000	2500000	500	40000
Haryana	15700	60000	300000	8000	52000
Himachala Pradesh	40000	66000		8536	0
Jaharkhand	7500	80000	0	0	0
Jammu & Kashmir	2000	35000	1000000	2485	0
Karnataka	18590	125000	1000000	6000	44000
Kerala	6200	75000	500000	1000	50000
Madhya Bharath	23435	64000	500000	25500	0
Mahakoshal	36300	55000	0	28500	0
Maharashtra	36000	110000	100000	0	48000
Orissa	40000	70000	0	7500	0
Panjab	82000	82000	600000	0	0
Rajasthan	28000	47000	5000000	9000	60000
TamilNadu	8000	95000	700000	4195	59050
UP	19000	76000	200000-300000	0	0
Uttaranchal	32000	90000	500000	9000	0
West Bengal	9000	175000	0	20	0
Western UP	19000	76000	700000	24000	5110

Table No . 4(A)

MBA Fee structure – 2001 & 10		
State	2001 In ₹	2010 In ₹
Andhra Pradesh	17860	78600
Assam	0	90000
Bihar	0	84000
Chattisghath	0	43400
Delhi	0	1200000
Estern UP	0	75000
Gujarath	12000	57000
Haryana	49600	300000
Himachala Pradesh	2000	100000
Jharkhand	0	150000
Jammu & Kashmir	0	40000
Karnataka	55000	500000
Kerala	0	300000
Madhya Pradesh	0	65000
Mhakoshal	65000	10000
Maharashtra	8000	140000
Orissa	24000	90000
Panjab	0	70000
Rajasthan	0	40000
TamilNadu	0	150000
Uttaranchal	82000	55000
Vidarbha	18000	
West Bengal	5300	185000
Western UP	60000	96000

Medical College [MBBS] Fee structure -						Table No –5
	2010			2001		
State	Govt Fee	Mngmt fee	Donation	Govt Fee	Mngmt fee	Donation
Andhra Pradesh	21,300	400,000	4,000,000	13,000	75,000	
Assam	18,000	Nil	0	0	0	
Bihar	38,000	150,000	200,000	7,760	0	
Chhattisgarh	39,000	375,000	0	13,000	0	
Delhi	2,600	120,000	0	0	0	
Estem UP	18,300	3,32,000	2,500,000	0	0	
Gujarath	6,000	400,000	20,00,000	1,000	120,000	
Haryana	85,000	10,00,000	30,00,000	0	0	
Himachala Pradesh	20,000	0	0	12,000	15,000	
Jaharkhand	6,350	0	0	0	0	
Jammu & Kashmir	2,000	40,000	2,000,000	1,400	0	
Karnataka	16,700	3,25,000	20,00,000	13,000	105,000	
Kerala	25,000	113,000	3,000,000	1,375	50,000	
Madhya Bharath	45,000	278,000	25,00,000	15,000	0	
Mahakoshal	50,000	0	0	0	0	
Maharashtra	33,000	625,000	1,000,000	6,000	105,000	
Orissa	16,000	375,000	0	10,500	0	
Panjab	22,000	162,000	4,000,000	0	0	
Rajasthan	10,000	165,000	25,00,000	2,800	250,000	
Tamil Nadu	15,000	150,000	20,00,000	0	0	
Uttaranchal	15,000	375,000	4,000,000	172,000	0	
Vidarbha	0	0		12,000	126,000	
West Bengal	9,000	375,000	0	20	0	
UP	35,000	75,000	420,000	1,000	110,000	

Dental College [BDS] Fee Structure					Table No –6
	2010			2001	
State	Govt Fee	Mngmt fee	Donation	Govt Fee	Mngmt fee
Andhra Pradesh	18,300	200,000	0	0	0
Assam	68,000	0	0	0	0
Bihar	32,000	60,000	2,000,000	0	0
Chhattisgarh	20,500	190,000	2,000,000	0	0
Delhi	2,400	0	0	0	0
Estern UP	18,300	75,000	800,000	0	0
Gujarath	4,000	244,000	2,000,000	100	0
Haryana	60,600	2,00,000	5,00,000	0	0
Himachala Pradesh	20,000	50,000		12,000	11,000
Jaharkhand	0	20,000	286,200	0	0
Jammu &Kashmir	2,000	40,000	3,00,000	0	0
Karnataka	14,400	2,25,000	5,00,000	0	0
Kerala	23,000	110,000	0	1,375	0
Madhya Bharath	45,000	178,000	10,00,000	0	0
Mahakoshal	0	176,400	550,000	0	0
Maharashtra	12,000	252,000	500,000	4,000	52,500
Orissa	Nil	210,000	0	0	0
Panjab	22,000	80,000	0	0	0
Rajasthan	10,000	120,000	5,00,000	2,800	86,000
TamilNadu	0	0	0	11,000	75,000
Uttaranchal	0	180,000	300,000	0	0
West Bengal	7,500	200,000	0	20	0
UP	15,000	25,000	5,50,000	4,500	75,000

Rising "Price" of MBA Education

MBA [*Master of Business Administration*] is a post graduate degree for which there is a good demand due to widened employment opportunities. Heavy rush of students towards obtaining this degree provided one more opportunity for the private managements to make money. Thus capitation fee in MBA education has started rising like anything. Donation for MBA seat in some of the states has reached a high mark of ₹ 1,20,000/-. ***[See Table – No. 7].*** With such a heavy fee and huge donation, MBA education has become the choice for the rich and the upper middle class.

Along with MBA, many other courses in higher education like MCA [*Master of Computer Applications*] and some post graduate courses in Life Sciences have become only dreams for the poor class. They remain as the choices of the privileged class.

MBA Fee Structure **Table No –7**

	2010			2010	
State	**Govt Fee**	**Mngmt fee**	**Donation**	**Govt Fee**	**Mngmt fee**
Andhra Pradesh	15,500	78,600	500,000	9650	17860
Assam	60,000	90,000	1,00,000	3285	0
Bihar	36,500	84,000	2,00,000	0	0
Chhattisgarh	15,000	43,400	0	0	0
Delhi	50,000	12,00,000	10,00,000	0	0
Estern UP	19,000	75,000	100,000	0	0
Gujarath	2,500	57,000	0	7000	12000
Haryana	7,000	300,000	25000-300000	4200	49600
Himachala Pradesh	4,500	60000-100000	200,000	2240	2000
Jaharkhand	54,000	150,000	100,000	0	0
Jammu &Kashmir	40,000	40,000	500,000	2915	0
Karnataka	60,000	2,50,000	1,500,000	20500	55000
Kerala	75,000	3,00,000	400,000	595	0
Madhya Bharath	32,000	65,000	3,00,000	0	0
Mahakoshal	7,500	10,000	0	15575	65000
Maharashtra	22,000	140,000	700,000	0	8000
Orissa	40,000	90,000	0	0	24000
Panjab	70,000	70,000	400,000	40000	0
Rajasthan	20,000	40,000	500,000	20000	0
TamilNadu	24,000	150,000	0	0	0
Uttaranchal	32,000	90,000	110,000	28000	82000
Vidarbha				9800	18000
West Bengal	0	185,000	0	1324	5300
UP	25,000	96,000	300,000	36000	60,000

The Higgling Business of Seat – Sharing: Reveals Commercialisation of Education

The seat-sharing between the Govt and the private managements has become a system which clearly reveals how higher education is getting more and more commercialized.

Seat sharing is a system which decides the ratio of students to be admitted to the Govt BE/ MBBS/ BDS/ MBA as well as private colleges as per Govt rules and regulations. This ratio fixes the quota of the seats of the private managements for which students could be admitted at abnormally very high fees. Private institutions always bring pressure on the Govts to increase the management quota so that they could get huge source of income through management fee and donation or capitation. This process of seat-sharing between the Govt and the private colleges most of the times leads to a major lobby for increasing management quota.

Incidentally, seat-sharing is an area where different states differ from one another in fixing the so called management quota. ***Table No -8*** clearly indicates to what extent the seat-sharing process differs between different states.

In case of engineering education, the lowest percentage of Govt seats [only 20%] is in Mahakosal and there are states, for example, Madhya Pradesh [85%], West Bengala [96%], and Rajasthan [85%] with highest percentage of Govt seats.

In medical education, Karnataka has the lowest Govt quota, that is 40%, and the private quota that is, 60% while the states like Jharkhand [0%], M.P [15%], Assam [0%], West Bengal [4%] have the least percentage of management seats. As the ***Table -8*** reveals, the southern states such as Karnataka [Govt quota - only 45%], Tamilnadu [50%], Uttaranchal [50%] Kerala [50%] are the states where the seat-sharing process has been tilted in favour of the private managements. Hence, these managements have made professional education the most lucrative sector to invest.

Percentage of Seat-Sharing in Different States (2009-10) **Table No–8**

	BE		MBBS		BDS		BAMS		MBA	
STATE	**Govt.**	**Pvt.**	**Govt.**	**Pvt.**	**Govt.**	**Pvt.**	**Govt.**	**Pvt.**	**Govt.**	**Pvt.**
Karnataka	45	55	40	60	35	65	20	80	70	30
Tamilnadu	50	50	50	50	50	50	50	50	50	50
Maharashtra	85	15	85	15	85	15	85	15	85	15
Andhra Pradesh	70	30	73	27	70	30	0	100	70	30
Gujarath	75	25	75	25	75	25	75	25	75	25
Bihar	85	15	80	20	100	0	100	0	80	20
Punjab	65	35	65	35	65	35	65	35	65	35
Rajasthan	85	15	85	15	85	15	80	20	80	20
Madhya Pradesh	85	15	85	15	85	15	85	15	85	15
Delhi	85	15	85	15	85	15	85	15	85	15
J.K	80	20	80	20	80	20	80	20	80	20
Western UP	75	25	75	25	75	25	75	25	75	25
Eastern UP	85	15	85	15	85	15	85	15	85	15
Uttaranchal	50	50	50	50	50	50	50	50	50	50
Chhattisgarh	85	15	85	15	85	15	85	15	85	15
Jharkhand	0	0	0	0	0	0		100	98	2
Mahakoshal	20	80	100	0	0	100	100	0	0	100
Orissa	70	30	70	30	70	30	70	30	70	30
West Bengal	96	4	96	4	96	4	96	4	95	5
Assam	50	50	0	0	100	0	0	0	0	0

DIFFERENT DIMENSIONS OF COMMERCIALISATION OF HIGHER EDUCATION

The lucrative nature of higher education has attracted wealthy individuals, rich minority groups, religious institutions, private lobbies towards running professional education institutions. A few decades ago, establishing new industries or business firms was considered to be economically and commercially attractive and profitable. But, today higher education, that too professional education, is the centre of attraction for investment.

1) Minority Institutions for Money Making ?

The lucrative business of higher education has lured the minority groups [linguistic and religious minority groups] to enter the field. A large number of minority institutions have come up during the recent years and they too started higgling with the governments to grab a greater part in the seat sharing. In States like Karnataka [58%], Tamilnadu [65%] and Maharastra [71%] they have been successful in getting a greater chunk in the seat sharing ***[See Table No -9].***

2) Private Universities Commercialising Education

When *"Private Universities Bill"* was introduced in Parliament in 1995, many opposed the Bill stating that it would lower the standard and commercialize education. Unfortunately, the same thing has happened in many states and the worst examples are those of Chhattisgarh and Himachal Pradesh.

When **Ajith Jogi** was the Chief Minister of Chhattisgarh during 2001-03, higher education virtually became a mockery when he decided to implement an executive order to start as many as 134 private universities all on a sudden. But fortunately, these were closed down a little later due to widespread public and student protest, and today there are only 6 new private universities in the state.

Table - 9

MINORITY INSTITUTIONS 2010-11
Seats to Govt & Pvt Management

STATE	GOVT.	PVT.
Karnataka	42	58
Kerala	50	50
Tamilnadu	35	65
Maharashtra	29	71
Andra Pradesh	70	30
Bihar	65	35
Punjab	50	50
UP	50	50
Uttaranchal	50	50

3) Mushrooming of Private Universities in Himachal Pradesh

Presently, in Himachal Pradesh [H.P], there are 13 universities which have already started functioning and 7 more private universities are on the offing. It appears that politicians, bureaucrats, business and industrial houses and capitalists – all have combined together to start these private universities with the sole intention of making money. None of these universities has past experience of imparting higher education. It is a wonder that 8 out of 13 private universities have been opened in one district of H.P. called Solan where there are only 3 Govt colleges. The fee structure of these universities is very high. Excepting the J.P. University, in all other universities the quality of teaching faculty is said to be miserable. There are allegations that reservation system for socially backward and SC/ST students is not being followed. Quality of education in these universities is criticised as exceptionally poor. For some time, there was no regulatory Govt body to control the functioning of these universities. [Only after a lot of protest the Govt has announced to form a regulatory body].

4) Deemed Universities and Doomed Students

During the recent years, even deemed universities [those not established by legislation and instead deemed to be universities by the UGC] have become yet another instrument of making money in the name of educational service. A large number of colleges were suddenly granted *"Deemed University"* status during the recent years. *"Prof. Yashpal Committee"* [constituted by the UGC itself] has stated that since 2005, the number of private deemed universities has increased to 108. In Tamil Nadu alone, the number of private deemed universities has increased from 18 in 2007 to 35 in 2008 and many more are in the queue. Some of the private educational institutions have evinced greater interest in getting *"deemed university status"* only to make money and not to improve the quality of education.

Some of the institutions which have managed to obtain the deemed university status, have already started making money setting aside the established rules.[2] Students have lots of complaints about many of these deemed universities particularly regarding the manner in which they are managed. Fee structure of some of these universities also reveal that they are being run for commercial purposes. ***[See Table No -10]***

Fee Structure in Deemed Universities –A Sample (2009-10) **Table - 10**

- Engineering Seat in Tamil Nadu
  - 1.5 lakhs in Amruthananda Mai Institute of Technology.
  - 95,000 in Vellore Institute of Technology.
  - 75,000 in Wells Engineering College.
- MBA Fees - 2, 23,000 in Vellore Institute of Technology.
- MBBS - 5 lakhs 5, 80,000 per annum. Capitation fee 25 to 45 lakhs.
- B.Sc. - 43,000 in Hindustan College.
- B. Com fee in Mahaveer Jain University, Karnataka is ₹ 70,000 per annum.

5) Exposes the Government's Bankruptcy in Educational Planning

The extent of commercialisation of higher education witnessed today in India clearly exposes the dismal failure of both the central and state governments in framing a proper policy of higher education. Institutions of higher education are improperly distributed among the states and the Govts do not have any control over them. *For example,* as per 2010 report, there are around 700 private engineering colleges in Andhra Pradesh, 600 in Tamil Nadu, 400 in Maharastra, and 170 in Karnataka, whereas states like Bihar [9], Assam [7], J and K [3], Jharkhand [17] have only a few colleges. One wonders as to how could the AICTE [All India Council of Technical Education, the Central Government established regulative body of engineering colleges] give permission to start these innumerable private colleges only in some states while a few other states are denied such a permission? Its control over these private institutions is also questionable. The Govt's failure in this regard has further added to the momentum of commercialisation of higher education.

6) Corporatisation of Education in Andhra Pradesh

Privatisation of education has lead to commercialization in many states. But commercialization of education in Andhra Pradesh has gone a step ahead towards a new culture called *"corporatisation"*. *For example,* **"Narayana"** and **"Chaitanya"** are not mere pre-degree or junior colleges [+2 colleges] in the state of Andhra, but are popular brand names of two managements which run around 350 junior colleges in the entire state. They are the trend setters of *"corporate system"* in the field of education.

In this corporate system, the same management administers all the colleges. Excellence of any one college is attributed to all the colleges and with wide publicity being given in the electronic and print media, people are misled and given an impression that all other 200 branches of the *"brand name institution"* are performing in the same scale. Though the quality of education is not of the same standard in all the branches / junior colleges, people are often misled with the brand image of *'Narayana'* or *'Chaitanya'* or any other such institute. Thus, admissions are made in all the branches of the institute by collecting more or less the same exorbitant fee.

2. *For example,* One deemed university is reported to have refused to respond to an RTI [Right to Information] query. In another case, instead of having two separate infrastructures, the same was actually shared by 2 adjacent deemed universities but owned by the single powerful person. This is nothing but manipulating the system and cheating the authorities.

7) Some Unfair Practices of Corporate Institutions

These corporate institutions spend huge amount of money on publicity. Any one rank secured by any one student in any one branch is projected as the prestigious rank of the entire group of institutions. Colleges are run in multistoreyed shopping complexes and no playgrounds are maintained. Sports, NCC, NSS and other non-academic activities are not cared for. In many branches, no practical classes are held for science students. These institutes appoint public relations officers [PRO] who go door to door just before admissions and offer packages and get admissions. They collect ₹ 80,000 to one lakh as fees per student for per year.

- **From Corporate Managements to Educational Mafia**

Yet another development which is witnessed is that, nowadays these corporate managements have turned into a kind of *"Educational mafia"*. The activities of these college level corporate giants are now extended to schools also. They have started opening hundreds of schools by applying pressure tactics and forcing small private schools to close down. Many government schools are also on the verge of closing down. By giving attractive labels like *'e-techno'* etc, they are running hundreds of schools in the state.

Corporate system has now entered professional education. These corporate college managements maintain 20-to-30 engineering colleges. This can be observed in Andhhra Pradesh.

CONSEQUENCES OF COMMERCIALISATION OF EDUCATION

1) Higher Education Becomes a Costly Affair: The immediate effect of commercialization of education is that higher education, especially professional education, becomes extremely costly and persons of average income find it difficult to have access to it.

2) Educational Institutions Become Business Industries: Commercialization of education converts education into an industry, a business wherein only calculative, contractual, artificial, commercial, impersonal, non-intimate and superficial relationship prevails between the *'service-providers and their customers'*. The teacher-and-the-taught relationship also becomes business – oriented. It bids farewell to the once prevailed intimate, personal, inclusive, friendly, and selfless relationship between the pupil and the teacher in India.

3) Widens the Gap Between the Rich and Poor: Commercialisation of education represents a direct attack on our much cherished concept of social equality. It widens the gap between the rich and the poor, the learned and the unlearned. The "haves" or the wealthy who have greater access to the costlier higher education will naturally get into high level jobs with handsome salary. Whereas, those who have the least access to higher education will have to be contented with ordinary jobs with poor salary.

4) Services Become Costlier: In the modern technological and computer-based world, service sector is the main income generating sector. Since individuals who have spent huge amount of money on their higher education get into this sector, they get tempted and even compelled to [recover the money which they have spent on their education] start levying very heavy charges for their services.

Thus, present day doctors, software engineers, advocates, auditors, technical experts, counsellors, company secretaries, corporate advisers and such other people charge exorbitant rates for their services. This situation increases the cost of living and leads to further exploitation of the ordinary people.

5) Leads to the Neglect of Agriculture: The present day commercial education is city-oriented education. Its contribution to boost agriculture and to revolutionize its process is virtually nothing. Animal husbandry, horticulture, and veterinary service closely associated with agriculture, also have not received any impetus at the hands of the *"educational industrialists"*. This is a big setback to crores of village families which depend on agriculture. Present day educated youths have lost their interest in agriculture for they have realized that agriculture can never be a match to the flourishing IT [Information Technology] industry. They have started deserting their villages and moving towards the cities.

6) Commercialisation of Education Invariably Augments the Rate of Speed of Urbanisation: Commercial education caters to the needs of the city and not of the village. Those who have spent lakhs of rupees on their education will not get any opportunity to recover their expenses if they decide to settle in rural areas. Hence, almost all the higher educated individuals decide to work and settle in urban areas even though quite a large number of them are originally from the rural areas. This tendency naturally adds to the speed of the process of urbanization.

SOLUTIONS SUGGESTED FOR THE PREVENTION AND ELIMINATION OF COMMERCIALISATION OF HIGHER EDUCATION IN INDIA

The above explanation gives us a brief glimpse of the process of commercialization of higher education and particularly of professional education that is going on in India. It throws light on some of the corrupt practices of the private educational institutions, their ulterior motives and vested interest in making money. Professional education system as it appears to us today is a sector which needs a careful observation and an in-depth study. Only then, one comes to know about different dimensions of professional education and the manner in which it is abused for money making.

The problem of commercialization of professional education has to be tackled as early as possible for it has already caused a big damage to our cherished goal of social justice and social equality. In order to provide sufficient opportunities for the lower middle class and lower class people to reap the benefits of higher education, the government has to take immediate action to prevent the process of commercialization. Government has to make a comprehensive legislation to contain and curb the growth of the tentacles of greedy private institutions. Since legal loopholes are the very root of this problem, legal expertise is required to frame the legislation. Such a legislation must necessarily include the following.

(i) Legislations must be enacted at the central and at the state level to curb the process of commercialization of education;

(ii) Government should ensure [through appropriate procedures] transparency in every act of private aided / government professional colleges so as to avoid all types of malpractices and exploitations.

(iii) A regulatory body must be constituted to look into the matters like admission, fee structure, seat-sharing, quality control, infrastructure, etc.

(iv) Single window admissions should be followed and a state level common entrance test must be formed in every state.

(v) Central as well as state governments must make honest efforts to establish sufficient number of medical, engineering, dental, management and other professional colleges based on the man power survey.

(vi) Government must take up the full responsibility to see that all private/aided institutions follow strictly rules and regulations relating to reservation policy.

(vii) Private institutions with sub-standard infrastructure and poor quality education must be derecognised or taken over by the Govt.

(viii) The state government shall-levy the service tax under the regular taxes as imposed on any other occupation.

(ix) The govt must be vigilant enough to ensure that no malpractice or abuse of rights takes place in minority institutions under the pretext of *"minority rights"*.

Other Suggestions

- Students seeking admissions in the private professional educational institutions should not get themselves trapped by the money-minting private institutions. On the contrary, as educated people they must stick on to the established rules of admission and should not compromise with policies and principles. Parents also should give encouragement to their law-abiding children and should show courage to fight for justice. This awareness among the students will act as a deterrent force on the private managements which seek to abuse rules and regulations.
- Media should also play an important role in exposing the malpractices of the private managements.
- Private managements which violate triple principles of – *fairness, transparency and non-exploitation*- should be derecognized and their permission be cancelled.
- Highly qualified professors and lecturers working in the private institutions must realize that as intellectuals they have a responsibility towards the cause of education and society and give all the possible help to the relevant public authorities in exposing the dishonest tactics and the malpractices of their own managements.

•••

Chapter 27

PROBLEM OF BONDED LABOUR

Problem of Bonded Labour - Bonded Labour As an Age-old System - Definition of Bonded Labour - Different Names of Bonded Labourers - Main Features of Bonded Labour - Extent of Bonded Labour - Causes of Bonded Labour - Misery and sufferings of the Bonded Labourers - Measures to Eradicate Bonded Labour : Measures taken after Independence to Remove Bonded Labour - State Level Legislations Against this Practice - Abolition of Bonded Labour: - Bonded Labour - Abolition Act by the Central Government - Implications of the Act - Rehabilitation of the Bonded Labouers: Four Stages Involved in the Rehabilitation Work - Government's Role and Assistance in the Rehabilitation Programme - Deficiencies or Lacunae Involved in the Rehabilitation Programme.

"Problem of bonded labour" which is haunting the Indian society is one of the problems of great socio-economic importance. Bonded labour has existed in India for centuries. In fact, *the practice of one man keeping another man in perpetual bondage for his selfish and personal whims and fancies* – seems to be a global phenomenon. It has been in existence for thousands of years, right from the Biblical days to the present era. The system of bonded labour as prevalent in India, appears as a relic of feudal hierarchical society. Social workers, social scientists and the governments have evinced a great interest in this phenomenon during the recent years to know more about it. The magnitude of the problem of bonded labour is also highly distressing for the lakhs of people including men, women and children are condemned to servitude under its yoke. The problem is further aggravated for it is carried on surreptiously in many of the cases.

Bonded Labour As an Age Old System

Bonded labour as a system of practice existed in India during the ancient period. In the classical treatises of *Shasthrakaras* like Manu, Kautilya and others we find vast references to the existence of "*dasa system*" that resembles the present day practice of bonded labour. This itself is a clear proof of its existence in the olden days. Though bonded labour is somewhat different from that of the "*dasa system*", or '*slavery*', we find striking resemblances between the two. In the erstwhile Varna system, the Shudra Varna which had the responsibility of serving the other three varnas, in course of time got transformed into an exploited Varna. The status of the members of this Shudra Varna was reduced to the state of slavery and even today majority of the bonded labourers belong to this Shudra Varna castes, particularly, the '*Scheduled Castes*'.

Definition of Bonded Labour

1. ***The National Commission on Labour*** defines the term *"bonded labour"* as *"labour which remains in bondage for a specific period for the debt incurred."*
2. ***The Commission for Scheduled Castes and Scheduled Tribes*** defines the term *"bonded labour"* in the 24th report of the Commission as – *"persons who are forced to work for the creditors for the loan incurred either without wage or on nominal wages."*
3. ***The Bonded Labour Abolition Act, 1976*** defines bonded labour as – *"the system of forced labour under which a debtor enters into an agreement with the creditor that he would render service to him either by himself or through any member of his family or any person dependent on him, for a specified or unspecified period, either without wages or for nominal wages, in consideration of loan or any other economic consideration obtained by him or any of his ascendants, or in pursuance of any social obligation, or in pursuance of any obligation devolving on him by succession."*

Different Names of Bonded Labourers

Bonded labourers are known by various names in various parts of the country. For example, they are known as *"Jeethadalu"* in Karnataka, *"Jeethams"* in Andhra Pradesh, *"Pandiyals"* in Tamil Nadu, *"Adiyas", "Paniyas"* and *"Kattunaikens"* in Kerala, *"Koltas", "Sevaks"* and *"Haris"* in Uttar Pradesh, *"Halis"* in Gujarat, *"Harwahas"* and *"Halis"* in Madhya Pradesh, *"Kamias"* or *"Kamiantis"* in Bihar, *"Gothees"* in Orissa, and so on.

MAIN FEATURES OF BONDED LABOUR

Main features that are associated with bonded labour are mentioned below:

1. Indebtedness: The poor economic conditions of some rural people especially those belonging to the lowest castes, force them to borrow money from the landlords or other money lenders. The inability to pay back the borrowed money compel them to bind themselves to work for their landlords or moneylenders for a certain number of years at fixed or unfixed wages in order to repay the money borrowed.

2. Forced Labour: As the *Bonded Labour Abolition Act* [1976] says, bonded labour is actually enforced labour. Here, the labour is dedicated to the money - lender or creditor only and not to others. As long as the debt continues so long the forced labour continues. Neither the bonded labourer can work on his own nor can he work for other employers.

Sometimes, bonded labourers are forced to work throughout their lives or even for generations. Forced labour can hereditarily descend from father to son or be passed on for generations together. What is important here is, during the period of bondage the debtor or the bonded labourer cannot seek employment with any other person. Speaking in economic terms, this means that he cannot *"sell his labour in the market at market value."*

• ***Areas of Forced Labour:*** The bonded labour system as we understand it, is mostly found among agricultural labourers in villages. However, it is often extended to labourers working in various other fields such as beedi factories, glass factories, brick kilns, stone quarries, detergent, slate, carpet and other factories.

3. It is Very Much Prolonged and May Even go on For Generations: If the amount borrowed as loan is very heavy and there is no other way of repaying it, then forced labour may go on for a very long time. It may even hereditarily descend from father to son or be passed on for generations together. For the loan borrowed by the father, the son is also compelled to work as bonded labour, sometimes throughout his life.

4. Continuous Labouring for the Loans Taken With Documents or Without Documents: For the loans taken from the money-lender, the labourer may have some written documents or may not have any documental evidence at all. Sometimes, there will be only oral agreement between the lender and the borrower, and yet it becomes morally binding on the borrower to settle it through his personal labour.

5. Bonded Labour Characterised by Poverty and Ignorance: Most of the bonded labourers are found to be extremely poor and do not have any asset or property worth mentioning. Also, most of them are totally innocent and ignorant regarding the financial transactions.

6. People of the Lower Strata are the Main Victims: Surveys and studies have revealed that majority of the bonded labourers belong to the lowest strata of the society. It is observed that majority of the bonded labourers belong to scheduled castes and tribes.

7. No Legal Protection to the Bonded Labourer: Bonded labourer is not protected by any legal rules; leave or even leisure. Such labourers must be ready to work throughout the year and all the 365 days. They do not have any selection as far as different types of works are concerned. They are expected to do whatever they are asked to do. Modern labour laws are not applicable for them.

8. Exploitation of the Family of the Bonded Labourers: Even though the bonded labourer has borrowed money on his personal basis, the money-lender makes the entire family of the labourer a party to the money transaction and keeps his control over it. In some instances, even the family members including women, children and old people are made to work along with the borrower for a very meagre remuneration. Female members of the family are often sexually exploited. Sometimes, the bonded labourer pledges his entire family to the service of the money-lender particularly when he feels that he alone cannot repay the borrowed money by his individual efforts.

9. Mostly Found in Rural Areas: Bonded labour with its associated characteristics as detailed above, is largely found in the rural areas and is almost absent in the cities and in the industrial sector.

10. Slavery and Bonded Labour are not One and the Same: Slavery is normally imposed on the individuals from outside whereas bonded labour comes into being because of the individuals self-committed blunder. In the strict sense of the term, a slave does not have any freedom; he has no salvation, no self-will, and is like a marketable product. Whereas, this extreme and cruel position is not there with the bonded labourers. It is possible for a bonded labourer to come out of the bondage if he makes proper plans in that direction. Slavery as an institution is not there today, but the system of bonded labour continues to exist in spite of the legislation being implemented against its practice.

Bonded Labour and Contract Labour

Bonded labour is often mistaken to be '*contract labour*'. Bonded labour is different from '*contract labour*' employed in industries, mines, plantations and docks, etc. The contract labourers in India are covered by *The Plantations Labour Act 1951, The Factory Act 1948, Mines Act 1952, Dock Workers Act 1948,* so as to give them some benefits under the legislations. The contract labourers are not directly employed by the establishment, their names do not appear in the pay-rolls, and they are not paid wages directly by the employers.

But the so called "*advantages*" [from the point of view of the money-lenders or employers] of bonded labour, and contract labour, are more or less the same:

(i) labour is obtained at the lowest cost,

(ii) the employers need not have to extend the fringe benefits to the workers, and

(iii) The employers are not under any obligation to provide labour welfare and security benefits to the workers as stipulated in the Labour Acts.

The system of "*contract labour*" in the country however, came to an end by the implementation of *The Contract Labour (Regulation and Abolition) Act, 1970.*

Extent of Bonded Labour in India

There are no reliable statistics relating to the extent of bonded labour in India eventhough the system has been in existence for centuries. However, **Gandhi Peace Foundation** [GPF] and **National Labour Institute** [NLI] conducted a survey of bonded labour for ten major states of India for the year 1978-79. The major findings of the survey of these two institutes can be mentioned below :[1]

1. The total number of bonded labourers in the ten states surveyed was estimated to be 26.17 lakhs.
2. For India as a whole, 5.7% of the total agricultural labourers constituted bonded labourers.
3. Uttar Pradesh had the highest number of bonded labourers, that is 5.5 lakhs, followed by Madhya Pradesh [5.0 lakhs], Orissa [3.5 lakhs], and Andhra Pradesh [3.25 lakhs]. These four states accounted for 17.25 lakhs of bonded labourers, that is, about 66% of the total bonded labourers in the country.
4. The most significant aspect of the survey is that about 87% of the bonded labourers belonged to Scheduled Castes and Scheduled Tribes.

● Another estimate of the bonded labourers for 12 states was conducted in March 1990 by the State Governments and the total number of bonded labourers was estimated at 2.45 lakhs.]

● The **International Labour Organisation** [I.L.O.] also has given an estimate. According to its estimation, there are about 150 lakh bonded labourers in our country out of which 50 lakhs are children.

CAUSES OF BONDED LABOUR

Various causes have contributed to the system of bonded labour. These can be grouped into three : (i) *Economic Causes,* (ii) *Social Causes,* and (iii) *Religious Causes.*

(i) Economic Causes: The economic factors are the main causes of bonded labour. They include various factors such as extreme poverty of people, heightened unemployment, poor material resources to fall back upon in times of economic crises, lack of alternative small scale loans for the rural and urban poor, extremes of natural calamities such as famines and floods, destruction of men and animals, drying away of wells, soaring prices and inflation, government's inability to rehabilitate the poor whenever they are afflicted with problems, and so on.

(ii) Social Causes: Social practices, customs and beliefs of the people also contribute to the problem of bonded labour. The social factors include casteism, caste based discrimination, high expenses on occasions like marriage, religious programmes, feasts, birth of a child, death ceremonies, etc. leading to heavy debts, lack of comprehensive social security measures against all kinds of hazards, non-compulsory and unequal educational system, corruption in governmental machinery, irresponsibility and indifferent attitude of the bureaucrats, and so on.

(iii) Religious Causes: Religious factors are also adding to the problem of bonded labour. The illiterate, ignorant and religious minded lower caste people are often made to believe that they have the religious obligation to serve people of high castes. Lack of knowledge, poor living

1. *Ref.*: *"Indian Economy"* [2001] by **Ruddardatt** and **K.P.M. Sundharam.** Page - 607.

conditions and fear of oppression at the hands of higher caste people make the ignorant people to accept their depressed lot.

It is clear from the above discription that the problem of bonded labour originates mainly from the economic constraints, social pressures and religious commitments.

Misery and Sufferings of the Bonded Labourers

Bonded labourers have been existing in India for the past several centuries. It is a peculiar phenomenon of our agricultural economy. The system grew out of extreme poverty and helplessness of the unprivileged sections of the Indian rural populace such as the Scheduled Castes, Scheduled Tribes and semi-tribal people, who depended upon wage income which they received only for a part of the year. When they needed foodgrains or when they needed money for any kind of an emergency they had to borrow the same at the hands of landlords or moneylenders. Since they had no security to offer in the form of land, jewellery or any other property, they pledged themselves.

The moneylenders and the high caste landlords took advantage of their helplessness and ignorance and entered into repressive contracts. The wages were so low and the rate of interest so high - often 25% to 50% - that the total loan got accumulated with the passage of time. The total burden of the loan became so huge that it could not be repaid even with the labour of many generations of the debtors family. Once a landless labourer borrowed money, he and his descendants were doomed to perpetual slavery.

It has been observed that majority of the bonded labourers work as agricultural labourers in villages and belong to the outcastes or tribal communities. Of the total labour force in the rural areas, about 33% are engaged in non-agricultural activities, 42% work as cultivators, and 25% as agricultural labourers. Of those who work as agricultural labourers, 48% belong to SCs and 33% to STs. These labourers are unskilled and unorganised and are forced to sell their personal labour for their livelihood. The bonded agricultural labourers occupy the lowest rung of the rural social ladder. Bonded labourers live in pitiable and miserable conditions. They are socially exploited and made to work sometimes 12 to 14 hours a day, and forced to live with cows and buffaloes in shed. If they fall ill, they may be given medicine collected from the local quacks depending upon the mercy of the employer. In all the possible ways, they are cheated by their employers and maximum labour is extracted from them for minimum remuneration.

MEASURES TO ERADICATE BONDED LABOUR

Bonded labour is not a practice of sudden appearance. It was there prior to independence. Even during the British period also some attempts were made to put an end to it. **For example**, *The Bihar Kamianti Act* was passed in 1920, *The Madras Agency Debt Bondage Regulation in 1940, The Hyderabad Bhagela Agreement Regulation Act in 1943, Kabadi System Regulation Act in Bastar in Madhya Pradesh in 1943*, etc. represent some of the legislative measures which the British Government took to prevent and to control the practice of bonded labour. Despite these efforts the practice continued unabated during and after the independence.

Measures Taken After Independence to Remove Bonded Labour

Independent Indian Government which recognised the evil practice of bonded labour decided to put an end to it at the earliest possible.

- **Article 23 of the Constitution** of India also considers the practice of bonded labour as illegal, for it upholds individual freedom and abolishes forced labour of any type.

- **Indian Penal Code** [IPC - Section-374] is also against any kind of forced labour.
- **The Forced Labour [Abolition] Convention** adopted by the International Labour Organisation [ILO] in 1919 was ratified by India in Nov. 1954. As per this ratification also bonded labour is considered illegal and punishable.
- **Committee headed by D.N. Dhebar** which was constituted by the Government of India to study the practice of bonded labour also recommended the abolition of this practice in its 1961 Report.

State Level Legislations Against this Practice

States such as Bihar, Madras, Madhya Pradesh, Hyderabad, etc. had undertaken legislations prior to independence abolishing the practice of bonded labour.

After Independence, States such as Orissa [1948], Rajasthan [1961], Kerala [1975], Karnataka [1976] had passed legislations abolishing the practice of bonded labour.

Examples of These Legislations

1. *Orissa Debt Bonded Abolition Regulation Act, 1948.*
2. *Rajasthan Sagri System Abolition Act, 1961.*
3. *Bonded Labour System [Abolition] Act, Kerala 1975.*
4. *Karnataka Bonded Labour Abolition Act, 1976.*

ABOLITION OF BONDED LABOUR

Bonded Labour Abolition Act by the Central Government:

Bonded Labour System (Abolition) Act, 1976

A single national level legislation against the practice of bonded labour came into being only in 1976. In fact, it was only after the announcement of the "*20-point programme*" on July 1st, 1975 that the legislative exercise at the national level began with some amount of seriousness and urgency. An ordinance was promulgated on 25th October 1975 and it was later replaced by the Act, namely; **The Bonded Labour System [Abolition] Act, 1976**. All state laws became inoperative after the enactment of this Act by the Union Government in 1976. For the first time, the government took swift action against money - lenders, building contractors, quarry-owners and others who have been found practising some form of bonded and / or contract labour. The government also took some measures to rehabilitate bonded labourers thus freed.

The Implication of the Act, 1976

The Bonded Labour System [Abolition] Act, 1976, consists of the following implications :-

(i) the Act leads to the identification of bonded labourers,

(ii) it leads to immediate release of bonded labourers

(iii) it involves action against the offenders, that is creditors/money-lenders who had forced illegal agreement upon the debtor;

(iv) it makes provision for the holding of regular meetings of the vigilance committees at the district and thaluk level;

(v) it recommends the maintenance of the prescribed registers,

(vi) it offers judicial powers to the executive magistrates to take appropriate action, and

(vii) it also makes provision for the rehabilitation of the bonded labourers who are freed from their creditors/money-lenders.

Amendment to the Act in 1985

The Act was amended in 1985. It was then clarified that the contract workers and interstate migrant workers would be considered as bonded labourers if they fulfil the conditions laid down in the *Bonded Labour System [Abolition] Act, 1976.*

Those who violate this Act and those who directly or indirectly support this practice could be arrested and kept in jails for a period of **3** years and fined to the tune of ₹ 2000/-

REHABILITATION OF THE BONDED LABOURERS

Mere passing of legislations and forcefully liberating the bonded labourers is not going to solve their problem. What is more important is their rehabilitation, that is, providing them reasonable and somewhat dignified means of livelihood. Unless this is done, the position of the bonded labourers becomes still more precarious and miserable.

Four Stages Involved in the Rehabilitation Work

Rehabilitation of the bonded labourers cannot be done at a stretch. On the contrary, it has to be done in a phased manner. In fact, it involves four important stages or phases.

(i) ***Identification of the Bonded Labourers:*** Since the bonded labourers have entered into bondage in a helpless manner, they do not have any courage to speak against their creditors. Hence, those in charge of the implementation of the legislation, must cleverly find out and properly identify the bonded labourers. They should infuse confidence in them and assure all kinds of legal and physical protection to them and release them out of their bondage.

(ii) ***Providing Means of Livelihood:*** Bonded labourers must be provided with immediate physical subsistence soon after their release.

(iii) ***Short-term Measures to Begin a New Life:*** Short-term measures must be thought of to help the freed workers to start a new life. *Example* : Such workers may be allotted a house site, given due assistance to construct the house, allotted a plot of agricultural land and provided a pair of bullocks, and agricultural implements etc. Or, they may also be shown the ways of or guided for, securing gainful employment.

(iv) ***Long-Term Measures Aiming at Permanent Rehabilitation:*** Long-term measures should help such labourers to lead an independent and economically, self-reliant life. Hence, measures must be taken to provide them some credit to start some business on an independent basis; given the needed skills to start a new job and provided with remunerative prices for their produces and so on. If the bonded labourers are immatured children, efforts must be made to provide them formal education so that they will be able to lead an independent life later.

In general, the rehabilitative measures should be such that the freed bonded labourers must be able to identify themselves with the mainstream of a civilised human society and realise the dignity worthy of human existence.

Government's Role and Assistance in the Rehabilitation Programme

The Central Govt. took interest and initiative in providing due financial assistance to rehabilitate bonded labourers at the State level. Accordingly, during the Sixth Plan [1980-85], the maximum cost of rehabilitating a bonded labourer was limited to ₹4,000/= out of which the state governments were given 50% matching grants. The assistance was given to the freed bonded labourers to help themselves to eke out their livelihood.

As per information available with the **Ministry of Labour** from the State Governments, as many as 2,51,424 bonded labourers were identified and released upto 30th March 1995. Of those freed bonded labourers, 2,27,404 were fully rehabilitated. It implies that nearly 90% of the bonded labourers identified, were rehabilitated. This appears to be encouraging. The government further raised the financial assistance to ₹10,000/= per bonded labourer with effect from August 1994. It is now known that the total number of bonded labourers released between May 1978 and September 2001 is 2,82,135.[2]

However, it is highly exaggerative on the part of the *Ministry of Labour* to stake that there are only 5,700 bonded labourers who need to be rehabilitated. A general observation of the Indian rural set up gives us an impression that the exact number of the bonded labourers cannot easily be traced out. There is need to have periodic surveys of bonded labour in collaboration with non-governmental organisations such as the *Gandhi Peace Foundation.* Since the bonded labourers have not been organised as a pressure group they are not able to assert themselves.

Deficiences and Lacunae Involved in the Effective Rehabilitation of Bonded Labourers

The ***Bonded Labour System [Abolition] Act*** has not been practically effective in all the places particularly because of the lack of enforcement machinery. Enactment of any legislation requires dedication and committment. Mere enactment of legislation becomes only a political activity. But its enforcement requires strong will and determination. But this factor has been unfortunately lacking in our country. That is why the system of bonded labour still continues to survive. Some deficiencies are involved in the effective implementation of the legislation and also in the rehabilitation of the bonded labourers.

1. Lack of Co-ordination Between Different Departments and Ministries: The rehabilitation programme has been dealt with separately. This has often led to its failure. Instead of that it should become a part of rural development programme and there should be a proper co-ordination between the rehabilitation programmes and other programmes. *For example,* in the various concerned ministries and departments like those of agriculture, animal husbandry, irrigation, forest ,fisheries child and women welfare, etc., there has to be proper co-ordination regarding the national programme of rehabilitation of bonded labourers.

2. Overburdened Development Departments: The development departments are overburdened with various schemes like IRDP, JRY, TRYSEM, etc. and hence they do not find sufficient time and efforts to spare for the rehabilitation programmes. As a result, they do not also bother to take into account the needs, aptitudes and preferences of the beneficiaries. There is thus, the need to design programmes in such a manner that they serve as *'target-group oriented'* rather than mere *target-oriented.*

3. Failures of the Personnel In-charge of the Implementation of the Rehabilitative Measures: Due to lack of qualified and committed staff and resources, poor infrastructure, the beneficiaries are not provided proper protective covers on a long term basis. As a result, the productive assets turn into liabilities.

4. Continued Interference of the Middlemen: Middlemen are still operating like the parasites and take away the fruits and benefits of the rehabilitation to their advantage. Hence, rehabilitation programmes are to be carefully and rationally formulated so as to avoid the interference of the middlemen.

5. Freedom is Not Given to Exercise the Choice of a Particular Scheme of Rehabilitation: The freed bonded labourers who come from the lowest strata of the society are not given freedom

2. *"India Book of the Year* 2002 – *Encyclopaedia Britannica and The Hindu."* Page - 306.

to select a scheme of rehabilitation but are forced to accept a particular scheme assigned to them by the bureaucrats. It is necessary that the freedom of choice of particular scheme must be provided to these people.

6. The Unchanged Attitude of the Previous Bonded Labour Keepers, Officials of the Govt Departments, and the General Public: Finally, the attitude of the former bonded labour keepers and employers has not completely changed towards the bonded labourers. They take every chance to suppress the efforts of the freed bonded labourers to move towards progress. Hence, it is the need of the hour that the landlords and other employers change their attitude towards the bonded labourers in view of the changed socio-economic conditions.

Concluding Remarks

It is unfair, immoral and also unconstitutional to keep alive the practice of bonded labour. It has to go at the earliest. Mere freeing these labourers is also of not much use. In fact, if the freed bonded labourers are not rehabilitated, they will suffer more. The state governments were assigned the responsibility of rehabilitating them. But the state government officials lack initiative, or remain indifferent to identification and rehabilitation programmes. The social workers working for private non-government organisations are also facing many handicaps in their way. From 1983 onwards, the Central Govt has been sponsoring schemes through the Ministry of Labour for the rehabilitation of the bonded labourers. What is needed is an effective concern from all sides that is, government, public, judiciary, social scientists, social workers and people's representatives to tackle the problem humanistically. Everyone in this context must realise that *"wiping out this system is basic and crucial to human dignity and conformity to constitutional values"*.

•••

Chapter 28

PROBLEMS OF BLACK MONEY

Black Money - Meaning of Black Money - Legal and Illegal Sources of Black Money - Magnitude of the Prevalence of Black Money: Some Estimates of Black Money in India - Estimates of Indian Black Money in Foreign Banks - Different Estimates of Indians' Black Money Deposited in Foreign Banks - Causes of Black Money - Effects of Black Money - Measures to Control Black Money - Present Policy of the NDA Government Regarding the Black Money Deposited Abroad - German Banks Ready to Disclose Names - Some Economic, Administrative and Social Measures to Control Black Money.

'Black Money' which is often referred to as *"parallel economy" or "unrecognised economy"* or *"unofficial economy"* - is both an economic and a social problem. It has both social and economic consequences upon society. Black money is a social problem with a difference. If the problem of poverty affects those who are poor, and if the problem of unemployment affects directly those who are unemployed, the problem of black money does not affect those who have ample of black money, but it affects the common man and the society at large. Hence, all the nations are concerned about checking or controlling the growth of black money.

Meaning of Black Money

- *Black money is that, which is earned or received in contravention of the prevailing Government Acts and regulations, or money that has been retained without the payment of taxes, which are due to the Government.*

Black money accrues everyday and everywhere and ranges from a few rupees to a few lakhs or crores of rupees. **Example :** (i) It is black money when a minister or a parliament member or an official takes payment for giving a licence or a permit. (ii) It is black money when a cement or steel manufacturer or trader, sells the commodity at a price above the controlled rate without the money appearing in the official records. (iii) When a professor goes to another university to conduct an examination and travels in II class train while claiming I class fare, he also acquires money which is not white, but black. These examples could be multiplied. Thus, black money and corruption go together.

Legal and Illegal Sources to Black Money

In simple words, it can be said that *black money is tax-evaded money.* This kind of money can be earned through either legal or illegal means or sources.

(i) ***Its legitimate source*** is that those who earn income through various ways do not reveal their entire income for tax purposes. **Examples :** (i) Teachers earning money through private tuition and book royalty not including it in their income tax returns. (ii) Music

artists earning huge amount of money by giving programmes on contract basis but including only a part of it in their income tax returns and retaining with themselves a major portion of their earnings without paying tax, and so on.

(ii) ***Its illegitimate sources*** are many. **Examples :** Bribes, black marketing, smuggling, selling commodities at prices higher than the controlled prices, and so on.

Magnitude of the Prevalence of Black Money

Black Money or tax-evaded money is not a phenomenon peculiar to India only. Almost all the countries of the world, both developed and developing are facing the problem of tackling or controlling black money. It is not an easy task to deal with it, because the very task of calculating or estimating the magnitude of black money is a highly challenging one. Economists not only in India, even in the highly advanced countries like America, Canada, Japan, France, Germany, etc., find it extremely difficult to make an estimation of that. Different countries have adopted different methods to measure it, but no where the economists have been successful in giving an exact estimate of that. Black money which is regarded as a world-wide phenomenon is playing its role in international trade affecting and influencing various economies of the world.

BLACK MONEY BLOCKING THE PROGRESS OF NATION

Some Estimates of Black Money in India

Attempts have been made ever since 1950s itself to estimate the extent of black money in India.

- *In 1953-54,* **Prof. Kaldor** estimated the amount of unaccounted wealth in India at about ₹ 600 crores.
- **The Wanchoo Committee** estimated it in the year 1965-66 at ₹ 1000/- crore, and ₹ 1400/- crore in ***1969-70***.
- **Chopra** estimated black money [in "*Economic and Political Weekly*", May 1, 1982] at ₹ 916/- crore in the year ***1960-61***, which increased to 8098 crore in ***1976-77***.
- ***In 1985***, *The National Institute of Public Finance and Policy* estimated the magnitude of black money in the economy at around ₹ 1,00,000 crore, or about 20% of the national income.
- As the *'Hindusthan Times'* reported in ***2nd Aug. 1991***, the Planning Commission itself estimated black money in the range of ₹ 70,000 crore and it is generated at the rate of ₹ 50,000 crore per, year.
- ***In 1997***, Jan. 20th, '*The Hindusthan Times*' again reported that the nation's black money was believed to be more than ₹ 40,00,000 crore.

Scholars have given a comparison of the extent of black money between USA and India. According to them, in India about one-fourth [26%] of our income is virtually tax evaded income. In America, this percentage is estimated at 8% of its Gross National Product [GNP]. What is worse about India is that the black money is accrued through mostly illegal sources in India, while in the USA, it is amassed through [about 75%] legal sources.

Estimate of Indian Black Money in Foreign Banks

The issue of black money has become economically and politically one of the most sensational issues today in the Indian polity. In fact, it was made one of the most important issues in the 16th Lok Sabha Elections which were concluded in May 2014. The Bharateeya Janata Party [BJP], one of the main contestants in the Elections went on promising the people that it would bring to India huge amount of black money that is worth lakhs of crores of Indian Rupees, deposited illegally by Indians in the foreign banks, that is, mainly in the Swiss Banks. In the May 2014 Elections, the BJP came to power at the Centre and the nation is anxiously waiting as to what course of action that the newly elected NDA Government would take to contain black money and to bring it back to India from foreign banks.

Different Estimates of Indians' Black Money Deposited in Foreign Banks

As it is in the case of the black money amassed in India, in general, we do not have any authentic and reliable estimate of Indians black money kept abroad. It is only through the print media, we have some information about the quantum of black money kept abroad. **M.V. Kamath,** one of the senior most journalists of India, has given some information about black money in his recent article published in the leading Kannada daily "*Udayavani*", Dated 16th Aug 2014. Information which he has published in his article, is stated below.

- As M.V. Kamath has stated, "*The Hindu*" paper in its recent report has published that the Indians black money kept in foreign banks, amounts to not less than ₹ 14,000 crores. It has also stressed that in the year 2013 itself this amount was increased by nearly 40%.
- As per the statistics released by the Switzerland Central Banking Authority, Indian nationals have kept in the Swiss National Bank, black money amounting to ₹ **13650** crores.

• "*The Nans India*", yet another source puts the figure at ₹ **69228** crores. It has also stated that if the Government is able to bring it back to India, the Central Government will be able to run the administration without imposing a single paisa as tax for about 20 years.

• "*The Indian Express*", yet another leading English Daily, has reported in 2008 itself that the Indian politicians and corrupt officials have deposited around 125 billion dollars in the Swiss Banks in between 2000 and 2008. It has also added that all this money is amassed through corrupt means in India only and later on taken abroad and kept in Swiss Banks.

• "*The Hindusthan Times*" has quoted the report of "*Global Financial Integrity*" according to which the Indians have deposited as much as 28 lakh crores of Rupees in foreign banks in between 1948 and 2008.

• The BJP sources have stated that the amount of Indian black money deposited in foreign banks ranges between 30 lakh crores to 84 lakh crore of ₹. When we compare this with 3 lakh crore rupees which India has been investing in developmental activities every year, this amount is really very huge.

• Some economists have estimated that the quantum of black money in India amounts to almost one-third of its Gross National Product.

• **Ramjeth Malani,** one of the legal luminaries of India, while writing in a paper called "*Indian Prajna*" has quoted a German paper which says that a large number of Indian politicians, corporate giants, and *benami* account holders have deposited as much as 1500 billion dollars [or 750 lakh crores of Rupees] in Swiss Banks about which clear proofs are available. If it is really so, Ramajeth Malalni writes, that *"it is an act of treason"*.

CAUSES OF BLACK MONEY

According to **Prof. Ram Ahuja**, several factors are responsible for black money. He lists the following factors as important ones.[1]

1. High Rate of Tax : An unrealistic and disproportionate increase in taxes and duties compel some people to evade tax and accumulate black money. Even upto 2002-03, the tax free income limit was fixed at ₹50,000/=. It is a known fact that no man belonging to even the lower middle-class group could run his family smoothly and comfortably in this age of inflation within this income limit of ₹50,000/=. A mason or a carpenter or a plumber or a painter earns about ₹300/= to ₹350/= per day in a city. The yearly income of these people definitely exceed ₹50,000/=. But they rarely file their income tax returns and pay their taxes. Similarly, doctors, advocates, chartered accountants, who earn a few lakhs of rupees normally hide their real income to escape paying income tax between 50% to 70% of the total income. There is an argument that if income tax is reduced there is less likelihood of hiding the income and paying more tax. Only recntly, the tax free income limit was increased to ₹ 2 lakh per year, and the present NDA Government under the Prime Ministership of Narendra Modi, further increased it to ₹ 2.5 lakh in May 2014.

2. Different Rates of Excise Duty : The Government has fixed different rates of excise duty. On the basis of the quality, the products [such as paints, pipes, textiles, electric wires, etc.] are classified into different grades and tax duties are levied on the basis of the classification made by the manufacturer. Manufacturers, sometimes downgrade a product to pay lower rates of excise, which will help generate black money.

3. Price-control Policy of the Government : The Government often regulates the prices of some commodities [such as petrol, sugar, cement, steel, paper, vanaspathi, automobile,

1 **Prof. Ram Ahuja** in *"Social Problems in India"* - Page : 384 - 387.

tyres, fertilizers, etc.] by following what is known as *"price-control policy"*. Since this policy is comparatively rigid it does not take into account the ups and downs in the market due to the interplay of demand and supply. The private manufacturers and merchants take the undue advantage of this policy and resort to hoarding, fraud, artificial scarcity, etc., which will result in black money.

4. Inflation : Inflationary situation is said to be one of the causes of black money. In this situation, the prices of certain commodities [like petrol] go up and moneyed people start spending their unaccounted money, they may also divert resources from production to speculation. This will cause inflation.

5. Quota System and Scarcity : The Government has fixed quota for import, export and foreign exchange. This quota system is misused to make black money.

When there arises a **scarcity** of essential goods, people are compelled to pay more for them than the controlled prices. This gives scope for black money. *For example,* people are paying now more money than what is fixed as its price for kerosene oil due to its scarcity. The extra payment made by the customer will add to the black money.

6. Elections in a Democratic System : Elections are a part of the democratic process. Electioneering has become a costly affair today. Hence the candidates contesting for elections are bound to spend more than what is legally permissible for them. These elections are generally financed by the black money holders. There is an unholy alliance between the political parties and the business tycoons. These business oriented black money holders expect political patronage and economic concessions. They obtain such concessions from the political leaders by paying them heavy donations through black money. The concessions will help them to generate more and more black money.

7. Real Estate Transactions : People amass black money through real estate transactions. Purchasing a house and / or land at a cheaper rate and selling it at a higher rate by manipulating to pay very less stamp duty has become a profitable business in all major towns and cities. This is also an important source of black money.

8. Unhohy Alliance Between Politicians and Businessmen: In the Indian context, many politicians are either themselves businessmen or have partnership with businessmen. Hence, while undertaking economic policies they bring heavy pressure on the government to protect their business interests and divert govenment's attention towards the public and to impose tax on it. This gives them scope to generate black money.

THE EFFECTS OF BLACK MONEY

The Adverse Effects of Black Money are Several

(i) Black Money Hampers Economic Development: Generation of black money in society will have adverse economic as well as social consequences. Black money damages the economic development of the nation by hampering developmental programmes and plans. Due to tax evasion the exchequer loses huge amount of money which could have been used for developmental activities. It adds to inflation and the government loses its control over the economy. It contributes to economic instability.

(ii) Damages the Moral Fabric of the Society: Black money holders in society always escape from paying tax while the honest and law-abiding people always bears the brunt of paying tax. This situation damages people's faith in conformity. As a result, they either lose faith in the system or establishment, or they themselves try to find out ways and means of evading tax. In both the ways, the moral fabric of the society gets damaged.

(iii) Leads to Adverse Social Consequences: The social consequences of black money are also severe. It increases social inequality, creates frustrations among honest people, increases crimes like smuggling, bribery, etc. The government may not get enough revenue to undertake social service programmes for the uplift of the poor and downtrodden.

(iv) Widens the Gap Between the Rich and the Poor: Black Money leads to shifts in income and wealth. It is assumed that black money is mostly transferred from low income groups to the relatively large income groups. It appears that there would be a net loss of money to the poorer sections through black money. Needless to say, it contributes to unemployment and poverty.

(v) May Lead to Socio-Economic Conflicts and Social Upheavals: Black money damages social harmony and spreads discontentment everywhere. In some extreme cases, widespread discontentment among people may lead to internal conflicts, social upheavals and even politice - economic revolutions.

MEASURES TO CONTROL BLACK MONEY

The problem of *'black money'* has to be tackled in a realistic and at the same time intelligent manner. Since it is not a problem with the poor but with the well to do people, it should be handled carefully. The problem of black money has been there right from the beginning of the independence days. No Government that ruled India so far has paid any serious attention to curb it, and to control it. This problem has started taking a new dimension when a large number of business tycoons, politicians and other highly rich people started depositing their black money in foreign banks. As per the media reports, lakhs of crores of rupees have been deposited in this manner. Political and public pressure started mounting on the Government to bring back that money to India and spend it for developmental programmes.

Present Policy of the NDA Government Regarding the Black Money Deposited Abroad

Debates and discussions have been going on at political level about the black money and no honest attempts have been made by any Government to bring back this money to India so far. There was no commitment in this regard for any Govt.

For the first time, the NDA Government under the Prime Ministership of **Sri Narendra Modi** has formed a higher level "*Special Search Team*" [SST] to probe into this matter. The Team has Justice **M.B. Shaw** [Retired judge of the Supreme Court] as its President or Chief, and another retired judge, **Justice Arijith Pasasyat** as its Vice-president. The other stalwarts of the Team consist of Central Revenue Secretary, RBI Deputy Governor, Director of Intelligence Bureau, Director of Enforcement Directorate, Director of CBI, Chief of Research and Analysis Wing and a few other top officials.

The present Indian Government has already written letters to the related Swiss officials requesting them to send the names of Indians who have kept their black money in the Swiss Banks. The Swiss officials have not disclosed the names so far. However, the SST has also been asked to provide all the information regarding the developments that take place in this regard to the Supreme Court of India. The SST has been asked to act according to the directions of the Supreme Court. Experts of the internationally reputed organisation "*Tax Justice Network*" have commented that SST has to function within its limits. According to one of its advisors, the SST's actions become effective only if it is able to collect strong evidences regarding the tax evaders. The advisor has also commented that it is not easy to nab the tax evaders or even to collect proper information about their activities, for they are politically and economically highly influential persons.

German Banks Ready to Disclose Names !

Many Indians have kept their black money in some of the German Banks also. As early as in February 2008, German officials have collected information about the black money deposited in the "**Lichenstein Bank**" by the citizens of different countries. The German Finance Minister has also announced that his Ministry would be ready to provide information regarding the owners of foreign money deposited in German Banks, if any of the Governments were to make such a request. As per the media report, as many as 250 names of Indians are there in the list of the Lichenstein Bank.

Whatever may be the facts, some questions still remain to be answered. Whether the present NDA Government will be able to bring back this black money? Will the Swiss Banks co-operate with the Indian Government in this regard? What is the modality of dealing with such money? As per the "*Frontline*" paper report, the Swiss officials are still in favour of the tax evaders only. If it is so, the Govt may have to find out other ways and possibilities of getting the things done. The earlier it becomes possible, the better it will be, for the development of the nation.

Some Economic, Administrative and Social Measures to Control Black Money

The following measures will be of some help in controlling, if not eliminating this problem.

1. More than any other thing, the standards of public morality must be raised. In this regard, politicians, ministers, senior civil servants, intellectuals and the media people must play an important role. They must set up an example for others to emulate by paying taxes properly.
2. Public expenditure must come down and there must be stringent monitoring of expenditure, especially of public sector projects.
3. There must be much more effective supervision of private sector investment expenditures, particularly where there is greater reliance of development on finance institutions and banks.
4. Tax system must be realistic. Unduly high rates of tax are counter-productive. It would lead to tax evasion - whether it is income tax, wealth tax, capital gains tax or transfer tax on real estate - and at a later stage creating black money.
5. Price controls should be done away with. Exchange rates should be realistic reflecting our comparative prices and competitive position in the world economy.
6. Tax collection machinery must be made more efficient than what it is now. Honest officials in this department must be profusely rewarded.
7. Attractive incentives must be given for voluntary disclosures of income [VDS].
8. A thorough overhauling of the economic intelligence unit must be made. Trusted officials must be recruited for this department.
9. Administrative corruption at different levels must be stopped.
10. Exempting tax on money spent on house construction may help mostly middle class salaried people who are normally made to pay taxes without fail.

With regard to this problem the harsh truth is that the government policies are the biggest sources of black money generation. Hence, the government must take extra precaution in framing its policies to give no scope for black money.

•••

BIBLIOGRAPHY

1. Abraham M.F. - "Contemporary Sociology" [2008]
2. Agarwal A.N. - Indian Economy - Problems of Development & Planning
3. Allan G. Johnson - The Blackwell Dictionary of Sociology
4. Amrik Singh & Philip G. Altabach - *The Higher Learning in India,* 'Vikas Publishers'
5. Andersen and Taylor - Understanding Sociology
6. Anjana Maitra Sinha - Women in a Changing Society - [1993]
7. Ashwini Mahajan - Globalisation & Small Scale Industries
8. Avasthi A.P. - Indian Government & Politics
9. Bipin Chandra - Modern India - A History Text Book for Class XII
10. Bipin Chandra - "Communalism in Modern India"
11. Bishwavath Ghosh - Contemporary Social Problems of India
12. Chingamani M.A. - Sociology of Indian Society
13. Coleman J.C. & W.E. Broen - *Abnormal Psychology*
14. David Jary and July Jary - Collins Dictionary of Sociology
15. Desai A.R. - Rural Sociology in India
16. Devaki Jain - Indian Women [National Book Trust of India]
17. Doshi S.L. & Jain P.C. - Rural Sociology
18. Dr. S. Krishna Murthy - *The Dowry Problem*
19. Dube S.C. - Encyclopaedia of Social Work in India - Vol.III
20. Dube S.C. - Indian Society
21. Elliott and Merrill - *Social Disorganisation*
22. Fr. Thomas Pazhayampallil SDB - Pastoral Guide : Moral - Canonical - Liturgical - Vol.II [Sacraments Christian Life & Sexuality]
23. Ghurye G.S. - Caste & Class in India
24. Horton and Hunt - *Sociology*
25. Hunter D.E. and P. Written - "Encyclopaedia of Anthropology"
26. Ian Robertson - Sociology
27. Jayaram N. - "Sociology of Education in India"
28. Kachroo J.L.& Kachroo Vijay - Society in India
29. Kapadia K.M. - Marriage & Family in India
30. Kar P.K. - Indian Society
31. Ketkar S.V. - History of Caste in India
32. Kuppuswamy B. - Social Change in India
33. M.H. Haralambos - Sociology Themes and Perspective
34. M.N. Srinivas - *Caste in Modern India and Other Essays*
35. M.N. Srinivas - *Changing Position of Indian Women*
36. Macionis J.J. - "Sociology" [2007]
37. Madan G.R. - *Indian Social Problems* - Vol. 1, Allied Publishers Pvt. Ltd. - 1966
38. Majumdar D.N. - Races and Cultures of India
39. Mamoria C.B. - Social Problems and Social Disorganisation
40. Mandelbaum David G. - Society in India Vol. I and II
41. Marshall B. Clinard - Sociology of Deviant Behaviour
42. Mathur S.S. - A Sociological Approach to Indian Education
43. Misra S.K. & Puri V.K - Indian Economy

44. Neera Desai & Usha Thakkar - Women in Indian Society - NBT, New Delhi
45. Neera Desai & Vibhuti Patel - Indian Women, Change and Challenge in the Decade - 1975-85
46. Nikki Van der Gaag - Women's Rights, Rawat Publications.
47. Pandey S. - *Naxal Violence - A Socio-Politico Study*
48. Parvathi Appaiah - Hindutva Ideology and Politics
49. Parvathy A.A. - Secularism & Hinduism - A Discursive Study
50. Pothen S. - Divorce - Its Causes and Consequences in Hindu Society [1996]
51. Prabhu P.H. - Hindu Social Organisation
52. Prasad D.N. - "The Myth of Caste System"
53. R.N. Sharma - *Social Disorganisation and Social Problems*
54. Ram Ahuja - Indian Social System
55. Ram Ahuja - Social Problems in India
56. Ram Ahuja - Society in India
57. Ram Ahuja - Violence Against Women
58. Richard T. Schaffer - Sociology - International Edition
59. Ruddar Dutt & K.P.M. Sundharam - Indian Economy - 2010
60. Samuel Koenig - *Sociology - An Introduction to the Science of Soceity*
61. Scarpitti F.R. & Anderson M.L. - Social Problems
62. Shamim Aleem - Women's Development Problems and Prospects - [1996]
63. Shankar Rao C.N. - A Study of Contemporary Indian Society [2002]
64. Shankar Rao C.N. - Study of Indian Society [1996]
65. Shankar Rao C.N. - Sociology of Indian Society (2012)- S Chand
66. Sharma B.K & Kaur H - Air Pollution
67. Sharma K.L. - India Social Structure and Change
68. Sheshagiri N. - Pollution
69. Singh K. - Indian Social System
70. Srinivas M.N. - Caste in Modern India & Other Essays
71. Srinivas M.N. - India's Villages
72. Srinivas M.N. - Social Change in Modern India
73. Srinivas M.N. [Ed.] - "Caste - Its 20th Century Avatar"
74. Swami Vivekananda - India & Her Problems
75. Th. H. Van de Velde - *Ideal Marriage Its Physiology and Technique*
76. Thomas P. - Indian Women Through the Ages
77. Valvalkar P.A. - Hindu Social Institutions
78. Verma S.B., Editor - Status of Women in Modern India
79. Wallace & Wallace - Sociology
80. William P. Scott - Dictionary of Sociology
81. Yogendra Singh - Modernisation of Indian Tradition

OTHER SOURCES

1. Andre Beteille - Article on S.C. Dube in *Economic & Political Weekly,* 20th Mar. 1996
2. Andre Beteille - Article on M.N. Srinivas in *Economic & Political Weekly,* 8th Jan. 2000
3. Antony P. Palatty - Reservation & Its Implementation [*Samaja Shodhana* Vol.I, No.2, Oct. 1992]
4. Apte V.S. - Sanskrit - Hindi Dictionary
5. Chandrashekar Bhat - Article on M.S.A. Rao in *Sociology of Development & Change*

6. Gopala Sarana - Article on D.N. Majumdar *The Eastern Anthropologist,* Vol. XIV, No.2, May April 1961.

7. Jayaram N. - Article on "Caste & Hinduism : Changing Protean Relationships" in the book *Caste : Its 20th Century Avatar* [*Ed.* M.N. Srinivas]

8. Jeevan Kumar Dr. D. - Article *Understanding Globalisation* in Karnataka Journal of Politics

9. Kranti Kumar Reddy - Article *Globalisation & Environment - A Third World Perspective* in Journal *Third Concept* [Oct. 2001]

10. Leela Dube - Caste and Women [Article in *Caste : Its 20th Century Avatar* (*Ed.* M.N. Srinivas)]

11. Madan T.N. - Article on D.P. Mukerji in *Sociological Bulletin* 43(2), Sept. 1994.

12 Rao M.S.A. - Article on K.M. Kapadia in *Sociological Bulletin* Vol. XVII, Mar. 1968, No.1.

13. Ravindranath Rao - Tribal Social Transformation [Article in *Samaja Shodhana* Vol.I, No.2, Oct. 1992]

14. Romila Thapar - Article *Looking Back in History* in *Indian Women*

15. Sadananda Bhatkal - Article on G.S. Ghurye for Birth Centenary Celebration Committee

16. Saxena R.N. - Article on R.K. Mukherji in *Sociological Bulletin* Vol XVII No.2, Sept. 1968.

17. Srinivas M.N. - Social Structure [Article in Gazetteer of India - Vol.I - 1965]

18. Encyclopaedia of Social Work in India - Vol. III

19. India Year Book - 1999, 2000, 2001, 2012

20. Indian Book of the Year - 2002 - Encyclopaedia Britannica and The Hindu

21. Manorama Year Book - 1995, 2000, 2001, 2002, 2004, 2005, 2010, 2012, 2013, 2014

22. Manpower Profile, India - 1998

23. Statistical Outline of India - 1999

24. Students' Britannica [India] Vol. - 1 to 5

25. The Gazetteer of India [Vol. 1] - Publications Division, Govt. of India, 1965

26. The New Encyclopaedia Britannica - Vol. 22 and Vol. 27

27. Times of India - Editorial - June 1982

28. *Hosadigantha* and *Udayavani* Kannada dailies

29. NEP Document

30. Channabassappa .K - Hindulidavaru Yaru ? [Kannada]

31. Indira R. - Mahile, Samaja Mattu Samskriti - [2004] [Kannada]

32. Indira R. - Bharateeya Kutumba

33. Shankar Rao C.N. - Bharatadalli Samajika Samasyegalu Mattu Samajika Vighatane [Kannada]

34. Shankar Rao C.N. - Bharateeya Samaja [Kannada] [1991]

35. Shankar Rao C.N. - Samajashastrada Kiru Vishwakosha [Kannada] [2001]

WEB SITES

1. abenews.go.uk
2. abi-shameena.blogspot.com
3. archive.indianexpress.com
4. article.wn.com
5. blog.sikshasamruddhi.com
6. brainz.org
7. centreright.in
8. emakulam.gov.in
9. en.wikipedia.org
10. english.alarabiya.net
11. epa.ohio.gov
12. evidencebasedivinghuman.cornell.edu
13. fedina.org
14. filfercon.wordpress.com
15. forbesindia.com
16. graceology.org
17. indianexpress.com
18. indiansinsydney.com.au
19. lebbeuswoods.wordpress.com
20. maypalo.com
21. medarlu.blogspot.com
22. missinefrommarx.wordpress.com

23. newslok.com
24. oinionator.blogs.nytimes.com
25. pakarniedforces.com
26. post.jagran.com
27. pseudomonaz.wordpress.com
28. reflectiveindian.wordpress.com
29. socialissues.sagrahjunction.com
30. spreadthewordilliteracy.wordpress.com
31. thermalpollutionerikahundy.weebly.com
32. topics.nytimes.com
33. travel.wikinut.com
34. viewpatna.blogsport.com
35. www.anti-caste.org
36. www.attantadivorcelawyer.co
37. www.bbc.co.uk
38. www.birdsnestsociety.nl
39. www.businessbcause.com
40. www.buzzle.com
41. www.cyberinfocity.com
42. www.desmogblog.com
43. www.dwde
44. www.earthtimes.org
45. www.fedupusa.org
46. www.freechoudhary.com
47. www.frontline.in
48. www.fsifmily.org
49. www.ghanaiahreactoronline.com
50. www.google.com
51. www.gujaratsamachar.com
52. www.hinduismglance.wordpress.com
53. www.huffingtonspot.com
54. www.ibtimes.co.uk
55. www.indg.in
56. www.Indiatvnews.com
57. www.indileat.com
58. www.justforests.org
59. www.kashmirobserver.net
60. www.managementparadise.com
61. www.nasaindia.org
62. www.nc-climate.ncsa.edu
63. www.noisecontrol.com
64. www.patrika.com
65. www.prathamasa.org
66. www.psmag.com
67. www.pvhromani.wordpress.com
68. www.rediff.com
69. www.saharasamay.com
70. www.samwoolte.com
71. www.shahamaasi.com
72. www.siliconindia.com
73. www.soschildrensvillages.org.uk
74. www.splashcreations.net
75. www.thehealthsites.com
76. www.thehindu.com
77. www.topnews.in
78. www.visualdata.in
79. www.voco.com
80. www.walkthroughindia.com
81. www.youthvoices.net
82. www.zawaj.com

BY THE SAME AUTHOR

'SOCIOLOGY OF INDIAN SOCIETY' [Revised Edition 2013] : This is an all-comprehensive sociological treatise on Indian Society. The book with 22 chapters and 766 pages serves as a basic reference book for all the degree classes of all the universities of India and Competitive Examinations. It covers the Syllabi of I.A.S. [Especially for I.A.S. [Main] Paper No. 2], K.A.S. Examinations, and also of MBA, Law, Nursing and other Professional Courses. The Chapters which the book includes are given below.

Publisher : M/s S.Chand & Co. Ltd. New Delhi. Book Code No. : 18051A.

BY THE SAME AUTHOR

"SOCIOLOGY - PRINCIPLES OF SOCIOLOGY"

[27th Reprint and 7th Revised Edition 2014]

This is an all-comprehensive treatise on the fundamentals or basic principles of sociology . The book with 60 chapters and 915 pages serves as a basic reference book for all the degree classes of all the universities of India and Competitive Examinations. It covers the Syllabi of I.A.S. [Especially for I.A.S. [Main] Paper No. 1] and K.A.S. Examinations, and also of MBA, Law, Nursing and other Professional Courses. The Chapters which the book includes are given below.

Publisher : M/s S.Chand & Co. Ltd. New Delhi. Book Code No. : 18044R.

PART - I

INTRODUCING SOCIOLOGY

PART - II

BASIC SOCIOLGOICAL TERMS

PART - III

INDIVIDUAL - CULTURE AND SOCIETY

PART - IV

SOCIAL INEQUALITY

PART - V

SOCIAL INSTITUTIONS

●●●